# New Learning Sol...

Teacher Wraparound Edition

Glencoe

## The Developing Child

Building Brighter Futures

## New Rigor with Academic Integration

- National Academic Standards
- Academic Vocabulary
- Reading Guides
- Writing Tips and Activities
- Math and Science in Action Activities
- Standardized Test Practice

## Relevance with Real-World Connections

- The Developing Brain
- Careers with Childen
- Respond to Special Needs
- Culture Matters

## Build Relationships with Project-Based Learning

- Interpersonal and Collaborative Skills Support FCCLA
- Learning Through Play
- Safe Child, Healthy Child
- Unit Thematic Projects

## Technology Resources

- TeacherWorks™ Plus CD
- ExamView® Assessment Suite CD
- Presentation Plus!™ PowerPoint® Presentations CD
- Early Childhood Observations CD

### Online Learning Center

- *Observation* Guidebook
- *The Developing Brain* Guide and e-Transparencies
- Online Student Edition
- Graphic Organizers
- Evaluation Rubrics
- English Glossary/Spanish Glosario

 Log on to *The Developing Child* Online Learning Center at **glencoe.com**

Teacher Wraparound Edition

# The Developing Child

Glencoe

# The Developing Child

Building Brighter Futures

**Holly E. Brisbane**

Glencoe

## About the Author

**Holly Brisbane** graduated Magna Cum Laude from Minnesota State University Mankato with a Bachelor of Arts degree in English and Home Economics. She then went on to obtain her Master of Arts degree in English. She taught courses in Family & Consumer Sciences and English. She is also an author and editor who has published numerous articles on teaching and motivation, in addition to textbooks in the field of Family and Consumer Sciences. Holly has appeared in Who's Who in America Among Authors and Writers for her top-selling textbooks, including The Developing Child. Holly was also awarded an Outstanding Alumna Award from Minnesota State University Mankato. She is a current member and past president of American Association of University Women (AAUW), whose mission is to advance the equity for women and girls through advocacy, education, and research.

**Glencoe**

The *McGraw·Hill* Companies

Send all inquiries to:
Glencoe/McGraw-Hill
8787 Orion Place
Columbus, OH 43240-4027

ISBN: 978-0-07-888360-6        (Student Edition)
MHID: 0-07-888360-1        (Student Edition)
ISBN: 978-0-07-888432-0        (Teacher Wraparound Edition)
MHID: 0-07-888432-2        (Teacher Wraparound Edition)

2 3 4 5 6 7 8 9   RJE/LEH   15 14 13 12 11 10 09

# Reviewers

## Teacher Reviewers

**Mary Kay Anderson MEd**
Family and Consumer Sciences Teacher
Shorewood High Schools
Shorewood, Wisconsin

**Linda Brown**
Family and Consumer Sciences Teacher
Sanderson High School
Raleigh, North Carolina

**Nancy Campbell**
Family and Consumer Sciences Teacher
Walker Career Center
Warren Central High School
Indianapolis, Indiana

**Mary Elizabeth Carver**
Family and Consumer Sciences Teacher
Canadian Valley Technology Center
Chickasha, Oklahoma

**Kathryn A. Cox**
Family and Consumer Sciences Teacher
William G. Enloe Magnet High School
Raleigh, North Carolina

**Tangela Frost**
Family and Consumer Sciences Teacher
Southern Alamance High School
Graham, North Carolina

**Christine Bunte Halweg**
Family and Consumer Sciences Teacher
Peotone High School
Peotone, Illinois

**Janet Hartline**
Family and Consumer Sciences Teacher
Fort Payne High School
Fort Payne, Alabama

**Vikki Jackson**
Family and Consumer Sciences Teacher
Kathleen Middle School
Lakeland, Florida

**Tammy L. Lamparter**
Family and Consumer Sciences Teacher
Smyrna High School
Smyrna, Tennessee

**Georgia Lash**
Family and Consumer Sciences Teacher
Hillcrest High School
Simpsonville, South Carolina

**Phoebe E. McGuire**
Family and Consumer Sciences Teacher
James Monroe High School
Lindside, West Virginia

**Stephanie M. Meinke**
Vocational Coordinator
Family and Consumer Sciences Teacher
Farmington Public Schools
Farmington, Minnesota

**Valerie Morgan**
Family and Consumer Sciences Teacher
Water Valley High School
Water Valley, Mississippi

**Nancy Plowman**
Family and Consumer Sciences Teacher
Davis County High School
Bloomfield, Iowa

**Karin C. Ohr Pyskaty**
Department Chair
Family and Consumer Sciences
Lyman Hall High School
Wallingford, Connecticut

**Pamela S. Pruett**
Family and Consumer Sciences Teacher
Blytheville High School
Blytheville, Arkansas

**Shirley Rauh**
Department Chair, Family and
   Consumer Sciences
Mehlville High School
St. Louis, Missouri

**Becky F. Roseberry**
Family and Consumer Sciences Teacher
Pulaski County High School
Dublin, Virginia

**Wendy Whatley**
Family and Consumer Sciences Teacher
Randleman High School
Randleman, North Carolina

**Camille Williams**
Family and Consumer Sciences Teacher
Provo High School
Provo, Utah

**Kristina Yarborough**
Family and Consumer Sciences Teacher
Gray's Creek High School
Hope Mills, North Carolina

## Technical Reviewers

**Dr. Scott Bledsoe, PsyD**
Director, Child and Family
   Development Center
Azusa Pacific University
Azusa, California

**Dr. Gayle Mindes, EdD**
Department Chair
DePaul University
Chicago, Illinois

**Gina Montefusco**
Pediatric Nurse
Children's Hospital, Los Angeles
Los Angeles, California

**Victoria Tennent, MEd**
Educational Consultant
Olympia, Washington

**Philip A. Verhoef, PhD, MD**
Departments of Internal Medicine and Pediatrics
University of California, Los Angeles
Los Angeles, California

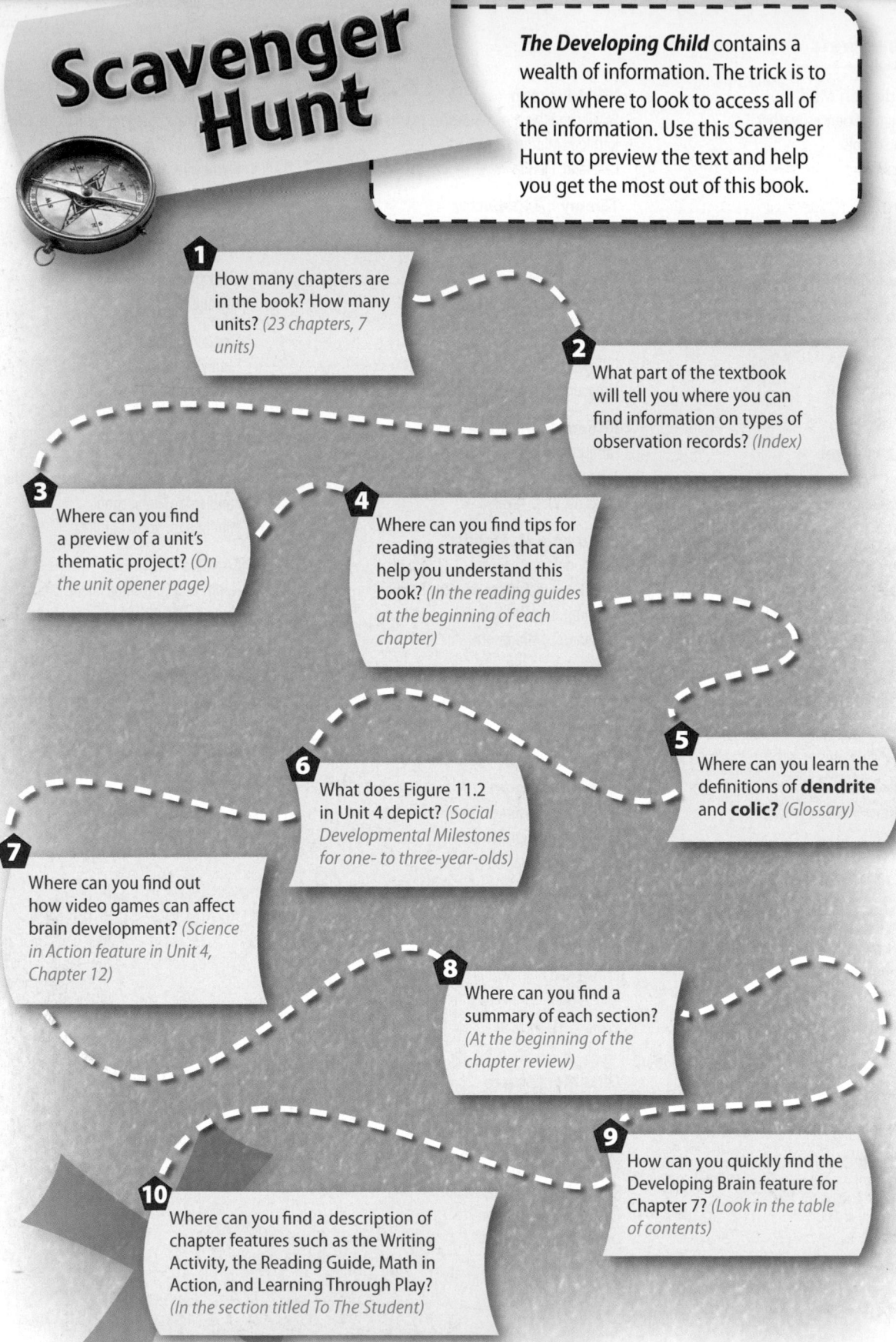

## Scavenger Hunt

*The Developing Child* contains a wealth of information. The trick is to know where to look to access all of the information. Use this Scavenger Hunt to preview the text and help you get the most out of this book.

**1** How many chapters are in the book? How many units? *(23 chapters, 7 units)*

**2** What part of the textbook will tell you where you can find information on types of observation records? *(Index)*

**3** Where can you find a preview of a unit's thematic project? *(On the unit opener page)*

**4** Where can you find tips for reading strategies that can help you understand this book? *(In the reading guides at the beginning of each chapter)*

**5** Where can you learn the definitions of **dendrite** and **colic?** *(Glossary)*

**6** What does Figure 11.2 in Unit 4 depict? *(Social Developmental Milestones for one- to three-year-olds)*

**7** Where can you find out how video games can affect brain development? *(Science in Action feature in Unit 4, Chapter 12)*

**8** Where can you find a summary of each section? *(At the beginning of the chapter review)*

**9** How can you quickly find the Developing Brain feature for Chapter 7? *(Look in the table of contents)*

**10** Where can you find a description of chapter features such as the Writing Activity, the Reading Guide, Math in Action, and Learning Through Play? *(In the section titled To The Student)*

# Teaching & Learning Resources

## Academic Integration Correlated to Standards-Based Instruction

*The Developing Child* provides academic rigor by:

- Providing activities correlated to national standards.
- Integrating learning resources throughout each unit at point-of-use.
- Including projects and activities that create a relevant framework for student learning.

**Unit Thematic Project Preview**
At the end of the unit, students will be assigned a thematic project. This preview allows them to think about how the information they are learning in the unit will apply to the project.

### Unit 3

### The Baby's First Year

**Chapter 7** Physical Development of Infants

**Chapter 8** Emotional and Social Development of Infants

**Chapter 9** Intellectual Development of Infants

**Unit Thematic Project Preview**

**Raise a Healthy Baby**
In this unit, you will learn how infants grow and develop during their first twelve months. You will also learn about the important role of parents and caregivers in a baby's physical and mental health. In your unit thematic project, you will explore how caregivers can support a baby's healthy growth and development.

 **My Journal**

**Healthy Development** Write a journal entry about one of the topics below. This will help you prepare for the project at the end of this unit.
- How can a parent or caregiver help a baby grow up physically healthy?
- How can a parent or caregiver help a baby develop trusting relationships with adults and siblings?
- How can a parent or caregiver help a baby develop language skills?

191

**↑ Explore the Photo**
Parents play a large role in ensuring their baby's health and well-being. *How might a child's early relationships influence his relationships later in life?*

190

**Explore the Photo**
By examining the photo at the beginning of the unit, students will begin to think about the topics covered in the unit. It visually guides the student with an engaging question to help interpret the meaning.

**My Journal**
Journal activities help students with their writing skills. Students are asked to keep a personal journal. The suggested topics will help prepare your students for the project at the end of the unit.

# Integrated at Point-of-Use

## Step-by-Step Projects for All Learners

Each thematic project integrates child development and academic skills at point-of-use. Step-by-step directions allow all learners to gain independence by completing the project at their own pace. All activities include a self-evaluation rubric that students can use to plan their projects.

**Project Checklist**
This at-a-glance checklist allows students to effectively manage their time and resources when planning and implementing their project.

**Project Assignment**
This summarizes the steps students need to take to develop and complete the thematic project.

**Step-by-Step Instructions**
There are five steps in each thematic project. Each step explains how to successfully complete a phase of the project.

---

### Unit Thematic Project

#### Raise a Healthy Baby

In this unit, you have learned that a child's first year is a time of great change. Parents and caregivers play a very important role in helping the child grow and develop. In this project, you will research a specific area of infant growth and development and explore what parents and caregivers can do to support a baby in this area.

**My Journal**

If you completed the journal entry from page 193, refer to it to see if your thoughts have changed after reading the unit.

**Project Assignment**

In this project, you will:
- Choose a feature of infant growth and development that interests you.
- Conduct research about the topic you have chosen.
- Interview a parent or child care professional about your topic.
- Prepare a presentation to share what you have learned with your class.

**Child Development Skills Behind the Project**

- Evaluate parenting roles and responsibilities.
- Identify a child's physical, emotional, and intellectual needs.
- Describe the growth and development of infants.

**Academic Skills**

**English Language Arts Standards**

**NCTE 4** Use written language to communicate effectively.

**NCTE 7** Conduct research and gather, evaluate, and synthesize data to communicate discoveries.

286   Unit 3   The Baby's First Year

---

**Step 1   Choose and Research Your Topic**

The topics below are examples of areas in which infants grow and develop over their first year. Choose one of these topics, or select another topic approved by your teacher. Research its importance to healthy growth and development.
- Language skills
- Motor skills
- Development of emotions
- Vision
- Eating and sleeping
- Attachment to caregivers
- Relating to strangers
- Relating to other children

Write a summary of your research to:
**Describe** milestones of infant growth or development in the chosen area.
**Explain** how parents or caregivers can foster an infant's health in this area.
**Identify** possible problems or disorders that can occur and how caregivers can identify and respond to them.

---

**Step 2   Plan Your Interview**

Use the results of your research to write a list of interview questions about your chosen topic to ask a parent or child care professional in your community.

**Writing Skills**
★ Use complete sentences.
★ Use correct spelling and grammar.
★ Organize your interview questions in the order you want to ask them.

**Step 3   Connect with Your Community**

Identify a child care professional or parent of a young child in your community who works with infants and toddlers. Conduct your interview using the questions you prepared in Step 2. Take notes during the interview and write a summary of the interview.

**Interviewing Skills**
★ Record interview responses and take notes.
★ Listen attentively.
★ Write in complete sentences and use correct spelling and grammar when you transcribe your notes.

**Step 4   Share What You Have Learned**

Use the Unit Thematic Project Checklist to plan and give an oral report to share what you have learned with your classmates.

**Speaking Skills**
★ Speak clearly and concisely.
★ Be sensitive to the needs of your audience.
★ Use standard English to communicate.

**Step 5   Evaluate Your Child Development Skills and Academic Skills**

Your project will be evaluated based on:
- Content and organization of your information.
- Proper use of standard English.
- Mechanics—presentation and neatness.
- Speaking and listening skills.

**Evaluation Rubric** Go to this book's Online Learning Center at **glencoe.com** for a rubric you can use to evaluate your final project.

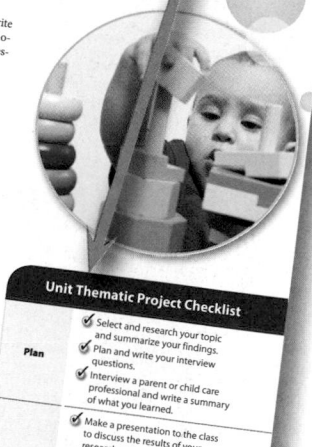

---

### Unit Thematic Project Checklist

| | |
|---|---|
| **Plan** | ✓ Select and research your topic and summarize your findings.<br>✓ Plan and write your interview questions.<br>✓ Interview a parent or child care professional and write a summary of what you learned. |
| **Present** | ✓ Make a presentation to the class to discuss the results of your research and your interview.<br>✓ Invite students to ask any questions. Answer these questions.<br>✓ When students ask you questions, demonstrate in your answers that you respect their perspectives.<br>✓ Turn in the summary of your research, your interview questions, and the summary of the interview to your teacher. |
| **Academic Skills** | ✓ Communicate effectively.<br>✓ Be sensitive to the needs of different audiences.<br>✓ Adapt and modify language to suit different purposes. |

Unit 3   The Baby's First Year   287

---

**Child Development and Academic Skills**
The standards tell students how the information and skills they will learn in the project apply to Child Development and English Language Arts.

**Self Evaluation**
Have students go to *The Developing Child* Online Learning Center through **glencoe.com** to download a rubric they can use to evaluate their final projects.

# Chapters Build Study Skills

*The Developing Child* includes correlated activities:
- Reading guides and reading checks help promote comprehension.
- Writing activities help students preview and focus on chapter content.
- Standards are clearly identified.

**Chapter Objectives**
Read this list to your class to preview the content your students will learn.

Section **8.1** Understanding Emotional Development of Infants

Section **8.2** Understanding Social Development of Infants

Chapter **8** Emotional and Social Development of Infants

**Chapter Objectives**
After completing this chapter, you will be able to:
- **List** six basic emotions that babies experience.
- **Explain** the role of attachment in a baby's emotional development.
- **Describe** how temperament affects a baby's social development.
- **Explain** how the emotional climate of the home can affect a baby's development.
- **Explain** how a baby learns social behavior.
- **Identify** how play and exploration help a baby develop socially.

**Writing Activity** Freewriting

**Building Relationships** From the first moment she is born, a baby begins to develop relationships with her parents or caregivers. Use freewriting to describe your idea of a positive, healthy relationship.

**Writing Tips** To jumpstart your writing, it can be helpful to write out ideas freely. This is called freewriting. Use these tips to start freewriting:
1. Write everything that comes to mind, in any order. You can go back and revise later.
2. Do not worry about having an introduction or conclusion.
3. Focus on ideas. Correct your grammar and spelling after you are done writing.

**Explore the Photo**
This baby's healthy bond with his caregiver can help him form healthy relationships later in life. Why do you think a baby's early experiences can affect his self-esteem later in life?

232

233

**Writing Activity**
The writing activity presents real-life writing assignments relevant to the chapter's main topics.

**Explore the Photo**
By examining the photo at the beginning of the chapter, students will begin to think about the main topics covered in the chapter.

# Chapter Review and Applications: Apply, Assess, Reteach, and Enrich

Questions throughout the review are correlated to national academic standards. Observational skills measure students understanding of Child Development.

**Chapter Summary**
A brief summary of each section tells students the most important concepts and ideas that they should have learned. They can use the summaries to help them assess whether or not they fully comprehended the chapter.

**Review**
Students can demonstrate an understanding of the most important vocabulary and key concepts from the chapter.

**Critical Thinking**
If students can respond to the critical thinking tasks, then you will know that they gleaned the most important ideas in the chapter.

**Academic Skills**
Completing these activities will give students the chance to combine what they have learned with their mathematics, language arts, and science knowledge.

**Observation Skills**
Help students learn the importance of good observation skills by completing these activities related to the chapter content.

**Real-World Relevance**
Help students apply what they have learned in the chapter to situations they might encounter in daily life.

**Standardized Test Practice**
Students can answer a sample standardized test question related to the chapter's content. Also gives students test-taking tips to help them succeed on standardized tests.

---

**Chapter 8 Review and Applications**

## Chapter Summary

Emotional development is the process of learning to recognize and express feelings and to establish a personal identity. Caregivers can help shape babies' emotional development by providing consistent, responsive, and loving care. Babies' unique temperaments and the emotional climate of the home also influence their emotional development. Social development is the process of learning how to interact and express oneself with others. Babies learn social behavior by watching and interacting with others. One normal sign of social development is stranger anxiety. Babies learn about the world by playing and exploring.

## Vocabulary Review

1. Use each of these content and academic vocabulary words in a sentence.

**Content Vocabulary**
◊ emotional development (p. 235)
◊ emotion (p. 235)
◊ colic (p. 238)
◊ reflux (p. 238)
◊ attachment (p. 239)
◊ failure to thrive (p. 240)
◊ temperament (p. 240)
◊ social development (p. 245)
◊ cause and effect (p. 245)
◊ model (p. 245)
◊ stranger anxiety (p. 247)
◊ play environment (p. 249)

**Academic Vocabulary**
■ crucial (p. 239)
■ hinder (p. 243)
■ lead (p. 248)
■ motivate (p. 250)

## Review Key Concepts

2. **List** six basic emotions that babies experience.
3. **Explain** the role of attachment in a baby's emotional development.
4. **Describe** how temperament affects a baby's social development.
5. **Explain** how the emotional climate of the home can affect a baby's development.
6. **Explain** how a baby learns social behavior.
7. **Identify** how play and exploration help a baby develop socially.

## Critical Thinking

8. **Analyze** A baby builds attachment through touch, consistent care, and communication. Do you think a baby could still bond with a parent if one of these elements were missing? Explain your opinion.
9. **Synthesize** Stranger anxiety and attachment to a caregiver develop at around the same time. How might these two developments be related?
10. **Predict** What combination of temperament traits might help a baby cope with a stressful family environment? What combination might make a baby less able to cope with...

---

**Chapter 8 Review and Applications**

## Family & Community Connection

11. **Interview a Single Parent** Interview a single parent about how he or she copes with negative emotions, such as stress, frustration, anger, and fear. What strategies does he or she have for resolving negative emotions? Who does he or she rely on for emotional support? How does he or she try to create a positive emotional climate in the home? Take notes during your interview, and share what you learned with the class.

### Health Skills

12. **Research Infant Massage** Go online to research massage techniques for babies. What is infant massage? What are the benefits? How is it performed? Are there any times when massage should not be used on babies? Write a summary of what you learned and state whether you would be interested in trying infant massage.

## Real-World Skills

| Problem-Solving Skills | 14. **Generate Solutions** What would you do to care for a crying baby? Explain in a report how you would identify the cause of the crying and what strategies you would use to comfort the baby. Also explain what you would do if you were unable to comfort the baby. |
|---|---|
| Technology Skills | 15. **Create a Table** Research three developmental disabilities that may affect a baby's social and emotional development. Use word-processing software to create a table that defines each disability and explains how it is diagnosed and treated. |
| Financial Literacy Skills | 16. **Shop for a Safe Play Environment** Imagine that you have $150 to create a safe play environment for your three-month-old baby. You will need two baby gates, a play mat, and age-appropriate toys. Conduct research to comparison shop for the best quality and prices. How many toys can you buy and stay within your budget? Create a list of the products you would buy, identifying the source or place of purchase and the prices. |

◊ **Additional Activities** For additional activities, go to this book's Online Learning Center at glencoe.com.

## Observation Skills

13. **Observe Babies at Play** Work with your teacher to arrange to observe a baby in a home or at a child care center. Note that an infant six months or older will probably be much more active than a baby five months or younger.

**Procedure** Pay attention to how the baby explores objects in the environment as well as how the baby interacts with the caregivers during playtime.

**Analysis** Write a report to describe your observations. Include an analysis of the physical, social, and emotional skills you think the baby was learning through play.

**NSES1** Develop an understanding of science unifying concepts and processes; evidence, models, and explanations.

---

## Academic Skills

### English Language Arts

17. **Reflect on Your Skills** Parents need many emotional and social skills, such as self-control, empathy, patience, responsibility, caring, and kindness. List and describe the skills that a parent should have in order to care for a baby's emotional and social needs. Which of these skills do you have? Which could you develop further? Summarize your thoughts in a one-page essay.

**NCTE 4** Use written language to communicate effectively.

### Mathematics

18. **Calculate Food Costs** According to the United States Department of Agriculture, the average married couple will spend about $200,000 to raise a child to the age of 17. If food is about 18% of this total, how much does the average couple spend on food for a child through age 17?

**Math Concept** **Multiply Decimals by Whole Numbers** A percent is a ratio that compares a number to 100.

**Starting Hint** Rewrite the percent (18%) as a fraction with a denominator of 100. Convert the fraction to a decimal. Multiply this decimal by the total amount ($200,000).

◊ For math help, go to the Math Appendix at the back of the book.

**NCTM Number and Operations** Understand numbers, ways of representing numbers, relationships among numbers, and number systems.

### Science

19. **Design an Experiment** The scientific method is a way to answer questions. You must collect information, form a hypothesis, study the results, and draw conclusions that other scientists can test. One hypothesis might read: Two-month-old babies can identify the emotions they see on their mothers' faces.

**Procedure** Describe an experiment that would test this hypothesis.

**Analysis** Write a speech to explain how your experiment would prove whether this hypothesis is correct or incorrect.

**NSES A** Develop abilities necessary to do scientific inquiry; understanding about scientific inquiry.

---

## Standardized Test Practice

**READING COMPREHENSION**

Read the passage, then answer the question.

A baby is playing at home when a stranger walks by the window and waves. Confused, the baby looks at his mother, who seems delighted. She waves back at the passerby and smiles. The baby has just demonstrated social referencing, the process of assessing other people's facial expressions to help decide how to react to a new situation.

20. According to the passage, social referencing:
   a. only occurs in babies.
   b. involves facial expressions.
   c. is a self-comforting technique.
   d. usually happens when strangers are present.

**Test-Taking Tip** Read the passage carefully, noting key statements as you go. Answer the questions based only on what you just read in the passage, not based on your previous knowledge.

---

# Reading Guides Enable Successful Learning

To strengthen students' reading success, each section of *The Developing Child* begins with a Reading Guide to preview section content.

**Vocabulary**
Students can check the Content and Academic Vocabulary lists for words they are not familiar with and look them up in the glossary in the back of the book.

**Before You Read**
A pre-reading study tip will help your students be better prepared to learn the section's content.

**Read to Learn**
By reading the Key Concepts and Main Idea, students will know what they can expect to learn in that section.

**Academic Standards**
Students can see which academic standards are integrated into the content of each section.

**Graphic Organizer**
A visual tool will help students organize and remember new content. You and your students can download printable graphic organizers from the *The Developing Child* Online Learning Center at **glencoe.com**.

---

## Section 8.1 — Understanding Emotional Development of Infants

### Reading Guide

**Before You Read**

**Preview** Look at each photo in this section and read the photo captions. Write one or two sentences explaining what you think the section will be about.

**Read to Learn**

**Key Concepts**
- **List** six basic emotions that babies experience.
- **Explain** the role of attachment in a baby's emotional development.
- **Describe** how temperament affects a baby's social development.
- **Explain** how the emotional climate of the home can affect a baby's development.

**Main Idea**
Caregivers play a large role in babies' emotional development, helping them learn to express feelings and develop a personal identity.

**Content Vocabulary**
◇ emotional development
◇ emotion
◇ colic
◇ reflux
◇ attachment
◇ failure to thrive
◇ temperament

**Academic Vocabulary**
You will find these words in your reading and on your tests. Use the glossary to look up their definitions if necessary.
■ crucial
■ hinder

**Graphic Organizer**
As you read, list things a caregiver can do to promote a baby's healthy emotional development. Use a chart like the one shown to help organize your information.

| Healthy Emotional Development |
|---|
| 1. |
| 2. |
| 3. |
| 4. |

**Graphic Organizer** Go to this book's Online Learning Center at **glencoe.com** to print out this graphic organizer.

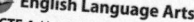

**Academic Standards** ⋅⋅⋅⋅⋅⋅⋅⋅⋅⋅⋅⋅⋅⋅⋅⋅⋅⋅⋅⋅⋅⋅⋅⋅⋅

**English Language Arts**
**NCTE 4** Use written language to communicate effectively.

**Social Studies**
**NCSS I C Culture** Apply an understanding of culture as an integrated whole that explains the functions and interactions of behavior patterns.

**NCSS IV C Individual Development and Identity** Describe influences that contribute to the development of a sense of self.

**NCTE** *National Council of Teachers of English*
**NCTM** *National Council of Teachers of Mathematics*

**NSES** *National Science Education Standards*
**NCSS** *National Council for the Social Studies*

**234** Chapter 8 Emotional and Social Development of Infants

---

# Section Reviews Check Comprehension

After You Read features at the end of each section allow you to test the student's understanding of the content before you get to the end of the chapter. The Key Concept questions are directly related to the main topics of the section.

## Emotional Climate of the Home

Babies are very sensitive to the feelings of people around them. Long before they know the meanings of words, they are influenced by adults' emotions, tone of voice, gestures, and facial expressions. Worried or angry caregivers are likely to be tense in handling their babies. Babies sense these feelings and can become irritable and anxious.

Every family has ups and downs, and a baby adapts to them. It is normal for caregivers to feel occasional frustration and anger toward a beloved child. However, a baby needs to feel that affection and caring are the basis of the

family's interactions. Feelings of bitterness, mistrust, and anger can hinder, or delay, an infant's emotional development.

Handling unwanted feelings, such as anger, frustration, and sadness, is a challenge for every parent and caregiver. It can be an even greater challenge for single parents. Single parents have no other adult to share the work or the worries, and they may feel alone and overwhelmed.

It is important for all parents to find ways of releasing negative feelings away from their children. Dealing with challenging feelings can help parents find the patience to create a caring environment. Every parent needs someone who can give them emotional support.

## Section 8.1  After You Read

### Review Key Concepts
1. **List** the most important influences on a child's emotional development.
2. **Explain** ways to build attachment to support a baby's emotional development.
3. **Describe** ways to resolve temperament conflicts.
4. **Explain** why it is important for parents to *not* express negative feelings around their children.

### Practice Academic Skills

**English Language Arts**

5. Describe your temperament using the nine temperament traits described in the section. Now imagine that you are caring for a child whose temperament is very different from yours. Write a letter to a friend describing how this could be challenging and what strategies you might use to handle the challenge.

> **NCTE 4** Use written language to communicate effectively.

**Social Studies**

6. Temperament, family, culture, and institutions such as schools and churches are important influences on your identity. You are also influenced by your *peers*, or people your same age. Write a report describing the people, places, and things that you think have influenced your identity since you were a baby, and why.

> **NCSS IV C** Describe influences that contribute to the development of a sense of self.

**Check Your Answers** Check your answers at this book's Online Learning Center at **glencoe.com**.

**243**

Section 8.1   Understanding Emotional Development of Infants

---

**Review**
Students can organize and process their understanding of the key concepts found in the section.

**Practice**
Connect the section's content to academic skills with these cross-curricular activities.

**Check Your Answers**
Students can go online and check their answers to ensure comprehension.

# Visuals and Reading Strategies for All Learners

Reading strategies are offered before, during, and after the section content to help enrich your students' reading skills. In addition to the Reading Guide and After You Read, we have a variety of strategies located throughout each section to ensure successful learning.

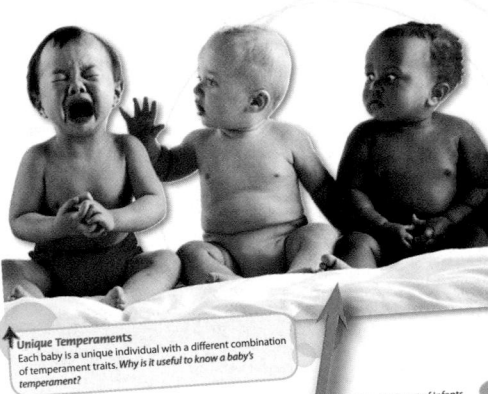

How can you tell a baby's temperament? Observe her in different situations. Is she relaxed or bursting with energy? Does she love or hate surprises? Is she cautious or the first to try something new? You can also note her eating and sleeping patterns, and her general mood.

By recognizing a baby's temperament, you can learn to work with the baby to ensure a happy and healthy emotional development. Parents and caregivers should always keep in mind that every baby is unique. There are many definitions of normal infant behavior. Parents need to accept and nurture their baby's individual style to develop the best relationship possible.

### Resolving Temperament Conflicts

Parents should remember that temperament traits cannot be changed. Rather, parents should learn to adapt their reactions to a child's specific traits. A child should not be punished for a temperament trait. If a child is shy, try holding him when you introduce him to someone new. Give him time to warm up to the new person, instead of handing him to the new person right away.

Caregivers have their own temperaments, too. One of a caregiver's responsibilities is to adapt to the temperament of the child, even if they are different. Look for positive ways to adapt to these differences. Suppose that you have a low energy level, but your infant is constantly on the move. You should provide safe opportunities for energetic play. Enjoy a trip to the park or dancing to music. Avoid activities that require the child to sit a lot. Can you think of other strategies you might try?

✓ **Reading Check** **Analyze** Why is it important to understand a baby's temperament?

**Unique Temperaments**
Each baby is a unique individual with a different combination of temperament traits. *Why is it useful to know a baby's temperament?*

Section 8.1 Understanding Emotional Development of Infants **241**

**Reading Checks**
Students can make a quick comprehension self-check.

**Vocabulary**
Students can easily identify highlighted vocabulary terms and check the definitions in the glossary before and during reading.

## Emotions and Emotional Development

Emotional and social development begin at birth and continue throughout life. They are as important as physical development to becoming a healthy and happy adult.

**Emotional development** is the process of learning to recognize and express feelings and to establish a personal identity. A personal identity is a sense of being a unique individual. A child who experiences healthy emotional development will be self-confident. He or she will be able to handle stress and will have empathy for others.

The most important influences on a child's emotional development are the bond between the caregiver and the child, the temperament of the child, and the atmosphere of the home.

### Emotions in Infancy

We are all born with the ability to experience emotions. An **emotion** is a feeling response to the world around us. Even newborns can feel basic emotions such as contentment and distress. Emotions grow more complex with age. **Figure 8.1** on page 6 shows the development of some basic emotions during a child's first year.

### Learning Emotions Through Interaction

Parents and caregivers play a large role in shaping a baby's emotions. Parents can encourage positive emotions. Parents can also help infants cope with negative emotions. Returning a baby's smile, for example, encourages his joyful expression. Rocking a frightened baby teaches her to become calm again after a scary experience.

Babies also learn from their caregivers to learn how to react to situations. A baby whose caregiver is often joyful may learn to approach life with happiness and interest. A baby whose caregiver is often anxious may learn to approach life with fear.

### Emotions and Crying

Infants do not have words so they show many of their needs and emotions through crying. At around two months of age, babies start to vary their cries to express different feelings.

**Visuals**
Figures and photos add additional information to the text and pose questions designed to actively engage the student and connect the content to the students' lives.

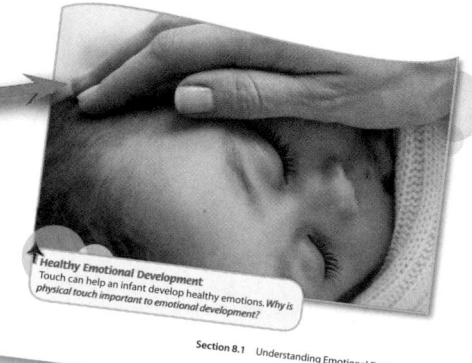

**Healthy Emotional Development**
Touch can help an infant develop healthy emotions. *Why is physical touch important to emotional development?*

Section 8.1 Understanding Emotional Development of Infants **235**

# Point-of-Use Enrichment Activities Through Features

Each chapter contains several academic features that connect the chapter content to students' mathematics and science learning. There are also features designed to help students see the relevance between the classroom and their daily lives.

**Science in Action**
Help students understand how science affects their daily lives.

**Math in Action**
Help students connect the information in the chapter with mathematical concepts they have learned or are learning. The math concept is described for them.

## Science in Action

### Technology and the Family

In today's society, we have many technological inventions available for work, home, and entertainment. This includes newer inventions such as cell phones, MP3 players, and video games. Technology also includes older technology such as television and computers. How might these inventions affect a family?

**Procedure**
Create a survey that lists five technological inventions and asks how much time people feel they spend using these inventions. Ask if they think using these technologies takes away from or adds to their family time. Distribute the survey to at least ten people of various ages.

**Analysis**
Find the average amount of time each invention is used. Then find the overall average. Chart your findings in a bar graph. Write a summary of your research that explains the results and describes people's opinions about whether these technologies are taking away from family time.

**NSES F** Develop understanding of science and technology in local, national, and global challenges.

## Math in Action

### Salary Requirements

Susan earns $8.50 per hour and works 40 hours a week. She is planning for her and Robert's newborn by calculating expected expenses. Her research results in an approximate expense list for one month:

Diapers: $80
Formula: $75
Clothes: $75
Day Care: $400

How much per month does Susan make? What is the total monthly expense of the newborn? What percentage of Susan's salary will go towards the baby?

**Math Concept** **Rates and Percents** A rate is a ratio of two measurements having different kinds of units, such as dollars per hour. A percent is a ratio that compares a number to 100.

**Starting Hint** To find Susan's monthly salary, first multiply the rate (8.50) by the hours (40), then by the weeks in a month (4). To find the percentage, divide the total baby expenses by Susan's monthly salary. Multiply the result by 100.

**Math** For math help, go to the Math Appendix at the back of the book.

**NCTM Number and Operations** Understand numbers, ways of representing numbers, relationships among numbers, and number systems.

**Culture Matters**
Address and teach cultural diversity and cultural sensitivities within child care settings.

## CULTURE MATTERS

### Holding a Baby Close

Carrying babies close to the body is the norm in many cultures. In Somalia, women tie their babies to their backs with long scarves. In Nepal, mothers carry their babies in a garment that also holds money and tools. The Inuit people of the Canadian Arctic can snuggle their babies in the furry linings of their parkas. Baby slings are now growing more popular in North America and Europe. Carrying a baby close provides the baby with a sense of security and lets him feel, see, and smell the parent. It also lets the baby see the world from a different vantage point.

**Build Connections** What are the advantages of sharing space? What are the disadvantages?

**NCSS I C Culture** Apply an understanding of culture as an integrated whole that explains the functions and interactions of behavior patterns.

**Math Handboook**
Students can visit the Math Handbook at the end of the book for more detailed explanations of math concepts.

**Academic Standards**
Mathematics, Science, and Social Studies standards are included in these skills that relate the content to other academic subjects.

# Extend and Enrich
# Child Development Skills

**What Would You Do?**
Ask your students to complete or solve these partial real-life scenarios using the knowledge they gain from the text.

## What Would You Do?

### A Healthy Environment

Anne is a pediatric nurse. She has two nine-year-old patients, Ian and Seth, who have asthma. Aside from their age and diagnosis, their situations are different. "Seth has been to the hospital only once for an asthma attack," Anne says. "His mom also has asthma, so they have learned together how to manage their symptoms. They keep emergency medication on hand and clean their house often to reduce dust. Ian, on the other hand, spends a lot of time in the hospital for asthma attacks." Anne continues, "Two conditions in his home can make his asthma worse: his family has a cat and one of his parents smokes." Ian's parents asked how to help reduce his number of attacks.

**Write About It** How might Ian's parents change his environment to reduce the number of his asthma attacks? Write a brief article for the Health section of your local newspaper to offer ideas for Ian's parents.

**Parenting Skills**
Students can use these features to learn how to be a positive influence on children's lives.

## Parenting Skills

### Helping a Baby Develop a Sense of Trust

Meeting a baby's physical and emotional needs helps a baby build a sense of trust. Try these strategies to help a baby develop trust.
- **Follow a predictable routine.** Routine care helps a baby learn to trust a parent or caregiver. Establish regular times for feeding, baths, and naps.
- **Get to know the baby.** Appreciate the baby's uniqueness. Learn about the baby's likes and dislikes. Learn the baby's signs for hunger, tiredness, and boredom.
- **Bond with the baby.** Spend time nurturing and holding the baby. Talk to the baby in a soft, positive tone. Smile and establish eye contact. Enjoy physical closeness.
- **Meet the baby's needs.** Strive to meet a baby's physical, social, and emotional needs. Provide loving care and affection.

**Take Charge** If you were a caregiver, how could you learn what a baby's different cries mean? Write a one-page journal entry sharing your thoughts.

## Learning Through PLAY

### From Solo to Social

A child's play changes as she grows and develops. Young babies enjoy play that involves touching, grasping, and using their five senses. Older babies are ready for more challenging forms of object play, such stacking blocks. By age one, babies enjoy parallel play. This means that they play next to each other, but not with each other. They watch and copy one another, and they start to learn how to share. Parallel play helps babies understand that other babies have wants and feelings too. By kindergarten age, children enjoy make-believe play full of complex stories. All these kinds of play help children develop social skills such as feeling comfortable in the world, identifying and expressing feelings, cooperating, and taking turns.

**Think About It** You are caring for two young toddlers, Maya and Delon, who are playing next to each other. Maya grabs the ball from Delon, and Delon screams. What could you say and do next to help both babies understand how to share?

**Learning Through Play**
Teach your students how various forms of play promote learning at each stage of development.

## THE DEVELOPING BRAIN

### Neural Connections

Babies learn alot in the first three years of life. Newborn babies' brains contain about 100 billion nerve cells, called neurons. Those neurons have about 50 trillion connections. These connections increase rapidly, and by the age of three, a child has twice as many connections as an adult. As a child matures, unused pathways are removed. This means that babies who live in an environment where they learn more will keep more connections.

**Science Inquiry** A stimulating environment is important for babies' brains to develop to their fullest potential. How would a stimulating environment lead to an increased number of neurological connections?

**The Developing Brain**
These short excerpts on brain development provide additional information to the students at the point of use.

**Careers with Children**
Give your students a picture of the rewards, responsibilities, and requirements of a career dealing with or related to children.

**Safe Child, Healthy Child**
These short features include health and safety information relating to children at specific ages and stages.

## Careers With Children — Storyteller

**B**efore societies had written records, they had storytellers. Storytellers described battles and adventures and told tales of monsters and kings. Today's storytellers educate and entertain as they practice this ancient art. Many traditions are preserved with storytelling.

### What Does a Storyteller Do?

Storytellers captivate their audiences with words. Storytellers use their voices the way musicians use instruments. They write and memorize many stories and tell each one with enthusiasm and creativity. Many storytellers add songs and music to their stories, too. Some storytellers focus on certain traditions, such as African folk tales.

### Where Do Storytellers Work?

Storytellers perform in many different places, such as schools, libraries, museums, festivals, children's parties, senior centers, prisons, and hospitals. Some storytellers might perform on the radio or on television. Some sell recordings of their performances.

### Preparation and Skills

**Education and Training**
Many storytellers study literature, folklore, music, and drama. Public speaking is also good preparation for storytelling. Look for a Storytellers Guild, or association, in your area to find a mentor or receive tips on developing this career. Some of these groups can help you find jobs to get started.

**Aptitudes, Abilities, and Skills**
Successful storytellers have imagination, self-motivation, a good memory, acting talent, and communication skills. Storytellers work hard, so they should be motivated and dedicated to their craft.

**Academic Skills Required**
English Language Arts are used by storytellers in reading and researching stories and ideas, and in writing stories to tell.

**Explore Careers**
Research other careers that involve performing with children or engaging them through play. Choose one career and write a paragraph describing it. Tell if the career interests you, and why.

**Careers Online** For more information on careers, visit the Occupational Outlook Handbook Web site through the link on this book's Online Learning Center at **glencoe.com**.

## SAFE CHILD HEALTHY CHILD

### Exploring Through Taste

Babies' mouths are more sensitive than their hands, so it is no wonder that babies use their mouths to explore tastes, textures, and shapes. *Mouthing* is normal, but it can be dangerous. A baby can choke on small objects or be poisoned by chemicals. Make sure that all toys are too large to fit all the way into a baby's mouth. Keep soaps, medicines, and chemicals out of reach. You can satisfy a baby's need to explore by choosing toys and foods with interesting shapes and textures.

**Be Prepared** Use the library or the Internet to conduct research on child safety. Make a safety checklist of 20 common choking hazards for babies, including toys and toy parts, household objects, and foods. Share your checklist with the class.

...nal Development in Infants

## Expert Advice...

"For infants and toddlers, learning and living are the same thing. If they feel secure, treasured, loved, their own energy and curiosity will bring them new understanding and new skills."

— Amy Laura Dombro and Leah Wallach, early childhood authors, *The Ordinary Is Extraordinary*.

## RESPOND TO SPECIAL NEEDS — Autism

Autism is a brain development disorder that affects the way people relate to others. People with severe autism have an impaired ability to interact and communicate with others. Signs of autism usually appear before a child turns three. Autistic children tend to avoid eye contact and cuddling. They often have restricted interests and repetitive behaviors. They do not like changes in routine and they may be very sensitive to lights and sounds. They may not respond to their own names, and they may start talking late. Early diagnosis is important. A child with autism needs a special treatment program.

Therapy and special education help children with autism lead fuller lives. Special diets may also help. Parents can help by showing love and understanding, setting up routines, and praising successes.

**Critical Thinking** Research the causes of autism. Describe the major theories and explain why some theories are controversial. Summarize your findings in a one-page essay. Cite your sources.

**Expert Advice**
Use these quotes from child development experts to reinforce and validate the information learned in the text.

**Respond to Special Needs**
Teach students how special needs can affect child development and child care.

# *Choose* Proven Teaching Solutions

## Unit Resources Help with Lesson Planning

Write effective lesson plans by previewing resources for each unit.

**Overview**
Chapter Titles and Chapter Objectives give you a preview of unit content.

**Resources**
A key is provided for coded teaching strategies, leveled instruction, and print and digital resources.

**Key to Letters**
These strategies and activities are identified throughout the Teacher Wraparound Edition and directly tied to student content.

**Differentiated Learning**
Activities in the wraparound are coded as **L1**, **L2**, or **L3** to make leveled instruction easy to include in your lesson plans. Also look for **ELL** to find activities especially suited for English Language Learners.

### Unit 3 The Baby's First Year

| Title | Objectives |
|---|---|
| **CHAPTER 7** Physical Development of Infants | • **Identify** the four major influences on an infant's growth and development. • **Summarize** how a baby typically grows in the first year. • **Explain** how to safely hold a baby. • **Identify** how to meet a baby's nutritional needs. • **Describe** the best type of clothing suitable for a baby. • **Describe** how to bathe a baby. • **Explain** why checkups and immunizations are important for babies. |
| **CHAPTER 8** Emotional and Social Development of Infants | • **List** six basic emotions that babies experience. • **Explain** the role of attachment in a baby's emotional development. • **Describe** how temperament affects a baby's social development. • **Explain** how the emotional climate of the home can affect a baby's development. • **Explain** how a baby learns social behavior. • **Identify** how play and exploration help a baby develop socially. |
| **CHAPTER 9** Intellectual Development of Infants | • **Describe** how a baby's experiences increase brain function. • **Explain** how the brain becomes organized. • **List** four abilities that show intellectual growth in infants. • **Identify** specific abilities that babies show during Piaget's first period of learning. • **Name** five ways caregivers can encourage learning. • **Describe** how to choose toys appropriate for babies of different ages. |
| Unit (Thematic Project) **Raising a Healthy Baby** | • **Write** a My Journal entry on Healthy Development. • **Choose** an area of infant growth and development. • **Interview** a parent or child care professional. • **Prepare** an oral report to share what they learned. |

190A

### Unit Overview and Resources

#### Understanding Brackets, Letters, and Ability Levels in the Teacher Wraparound Edition

**Brackets** Brackets on the reduced student edition page correspond to teaching strategies and activities in the Teacher Wraparound Edition. As you teach the lesson, the brackets show you exactly where to use the teaching strategies and activities.

**Letters** The letters on the reduced student edition page identify the type of strategy or activity. See the key below to learn about the different types of strategies and activities.

**Ability Levels** Teaching Strategies that appear throughout the chapters have been identified by one of three codes to give you an idea of their suitability for students of varying learning styles and abilities.

**Resources** Key program resources are listed in each chapter. Icons indicate the format of resources.

#### KEY TO LETTERS

**D** **Develop Concepts** activities help teachers gauge and plan for students' concept development.

**R** **Reading Strategy** activities help you teach reading skills and vocabulary.

**S** **Skill Practice** provides leveled instruction for meeting individual needs and learning styles.

**W** **Writing Support** activities provide writing opportunities to help students comprehend the text.

**C** **Critical Thinking** strategies help students apply and extend what they have learned.

**U** **Universal Access** activities provide differentiated instruction for English language learners, and suggestions for teaching various types of learners.

**NCLB** **No Child Left Behind** activities help students practice and improve their abilities in academic subjects.

#### KEY TO ABILITY LEVELS

**L1** Strategies should be within the ability range of all students. Often full class participation is required.

**L2** Strategies are for average to above-average students or for small groups. Some teacher direction is necessary.

**L3** Strategies are designed for students able and willing to work independently. Minimal teacher direction is necessary.

**ELL** Strategies are especially accessible to English Language Learners.

#### KEY TO RESOURCE ICONS

📖 Print Material
💿 CD or DVD Resources
🖥 Online Learning Center (OLC)

#### TeacherWorks
All-in-One Planner and Resource Center

**Teacher Wraparound Edition**
**Unit Resources:**
Unit Thematic Project Student Rubrics
Unit Family and Community Involvement Activities
**Chapter Resources:**
Lesson Plans
Chapter Summaries, Content and Academic Vocabulary
Graphic Organizers

**Textbook Resources:**
Student Activity Workbook with Academic Integration
Additional Activities
Enrichment Activities
Link to the *The Developing Child* Online Learning Center at glencoe.com.

190B

**TeacherWorks Resources**
A list of the print resources offered on the TeacherWorks software is included.

**Additional Activities** are on this book's Online Learning Center at **glencoe.com**.

# for Professional Success

## Teacher Resources Integrated at Point-of-Use Throughout Unit

- Provides a wealth of teacher-directed activities to choose from.
- Seamlessly integrates activities into your lesson plans.
- FCCLA and SkillsUSA features offer opportunities for students to gain real-life experience and prepare for competitive events.

**Discussion Starter**
Use this activity to activate your students' prior knowledge of the topic to be discussed in the unit.

**Unit Overview**
Introduce the unit with chapter summaries.

**Out of Time?**
Adjust your lesson plan to fit the time available in your class schedule.

**Explore the Photo**
Provides an answer to the question posed in the Student Edition, as well as providing prompts for discussion.

**Unit Thematic Project Preview**
Introduce the topic of the project to your students and prompt them to think more deeply about the project.

**FCCLA & SkillsUSA**
Use these features to promote personal growth and offer students opportunities to participate in a number of individual and chapter programs that strengthen life skills.

# Project-Based Learning Promotes Independence

Step-by-step instructions break down each project so students can complete it independently. All activities are correlated to academic standards. A list of child development skills informs students which skills they will apply to the project.

**Focus**
This project features a four-step teaching plan with teaching strategies for each step of the project.

**Assess and Close**
Students are directed to evaluate their projects. A culminating activity is also provided.

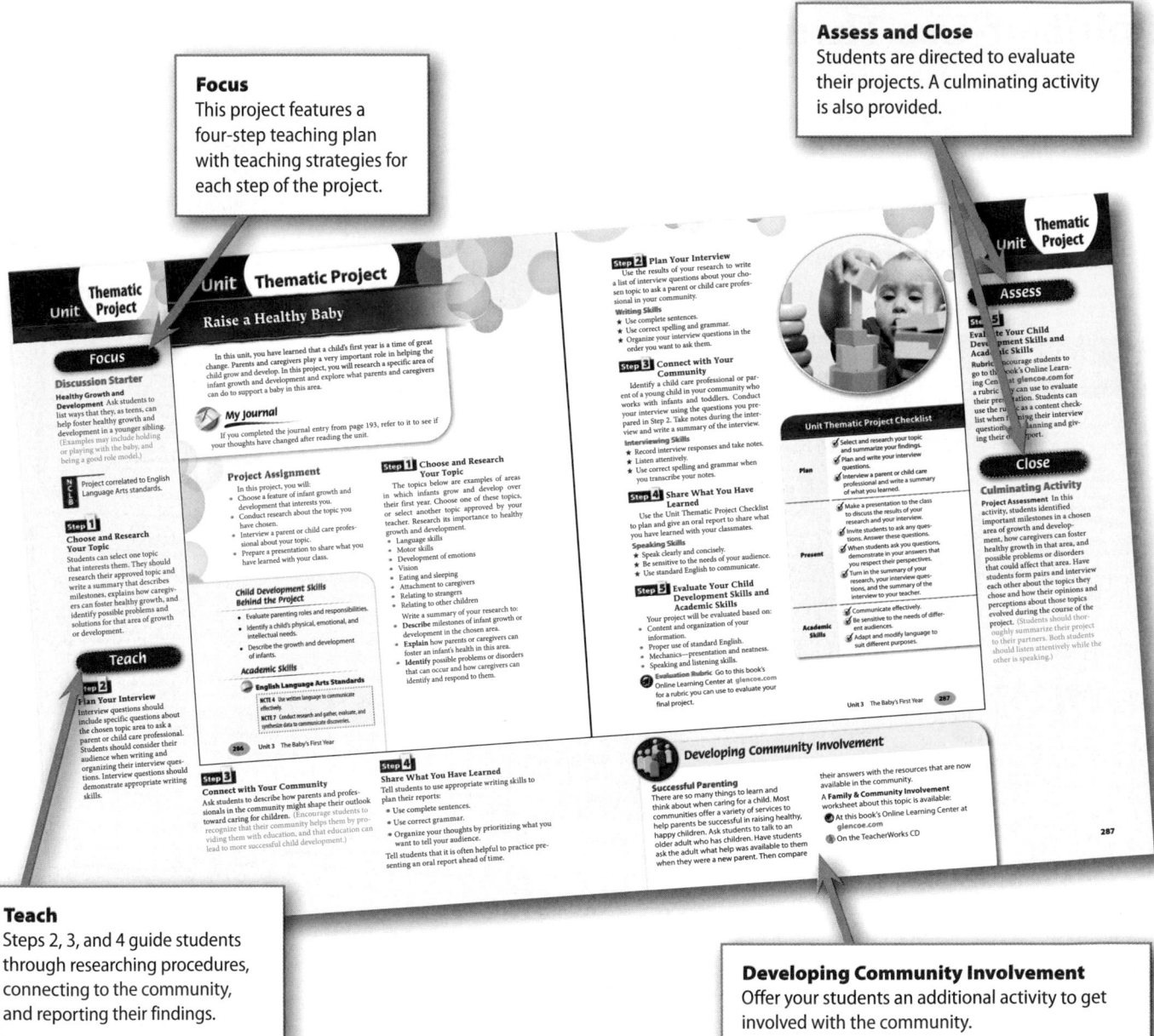

**Teach**
Steps 2, 3, and 4 guide students through researching procedures, connecting to the community, and reporting their findings.

**Developing Community Involvement**
Offer your students an additional activity to get involved with the community.

# Correlations and Planning Guides Introduce Chapters

Important features throughout the chapter are highlighted in the planning guides. An outline helps to organize your lesson plans.

**National Standards Correlations**
You can quickly see where national standards are met within the chapter.

**Professional Development**
Targeted Professional Development clips are correlated throughout *The Developing Child*.

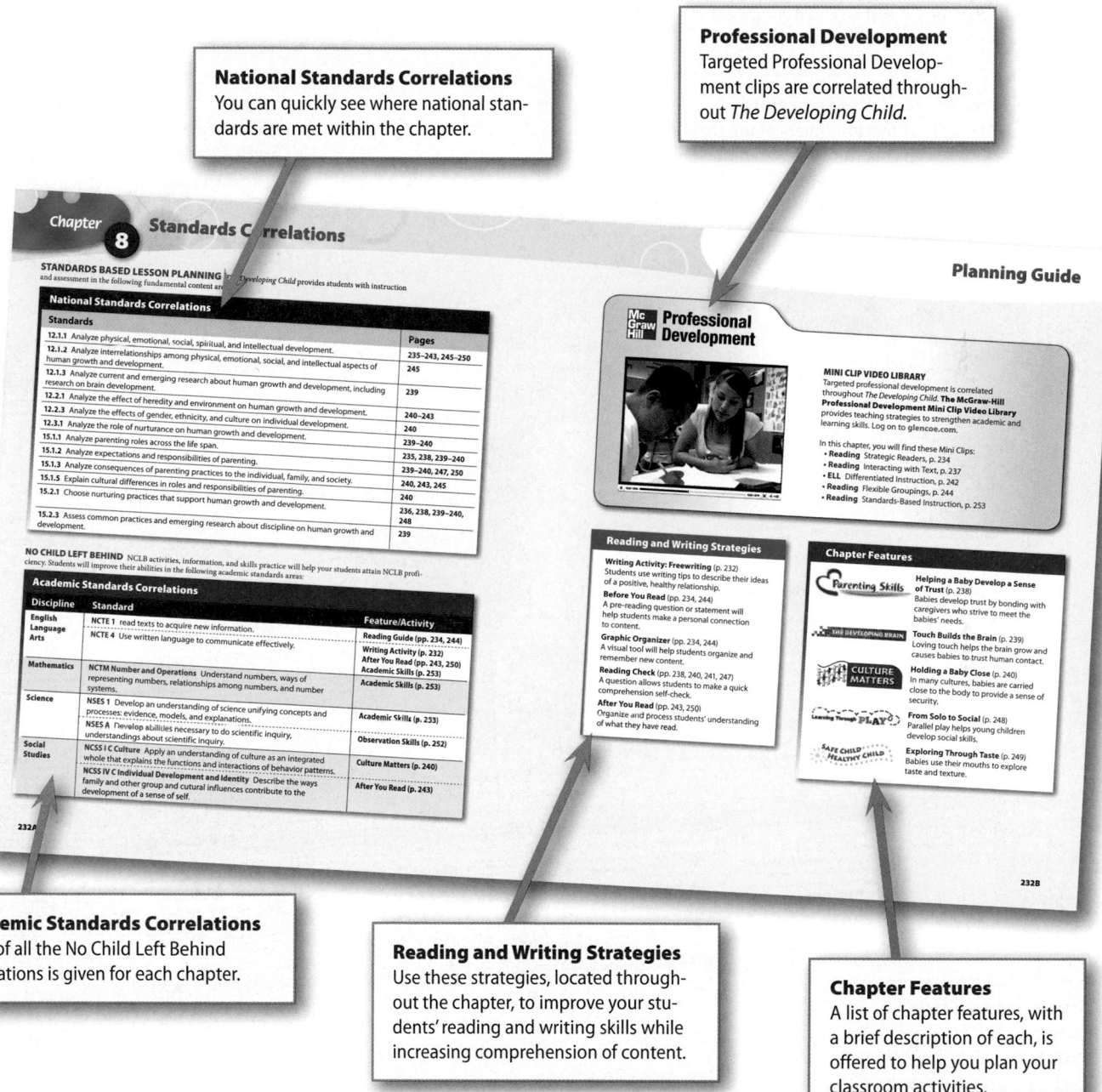

**Academic Standards Correlations**
A list of all the No Child Left Behind correlations is given for each chapter.

**Reading and Writing Strategies**
Use these strategies, located throughout the chapter, to improve your students' reading and writing skills while increasing comprehension of content.

**Chapter Features**
A list of chapter features, with a brief description of each, is offered to help you plan your classroom activities.

# Solutions to Start and End Chapters with Success

Beginning with the Writing Activity, students will gain an understanding of chapter content. Throughout the chapter, students will gain knowledge of child development by focused features and activities. Features throughout *The Developing Child* are correlated to academic standards.

**Chapter Overview**
A short summary of the chapter content is given. The Build Background text offers suggestions for you to access the students' prior knowledge of the chapter topic.

**Review the Sections**
A short summary of the content of each section is given.

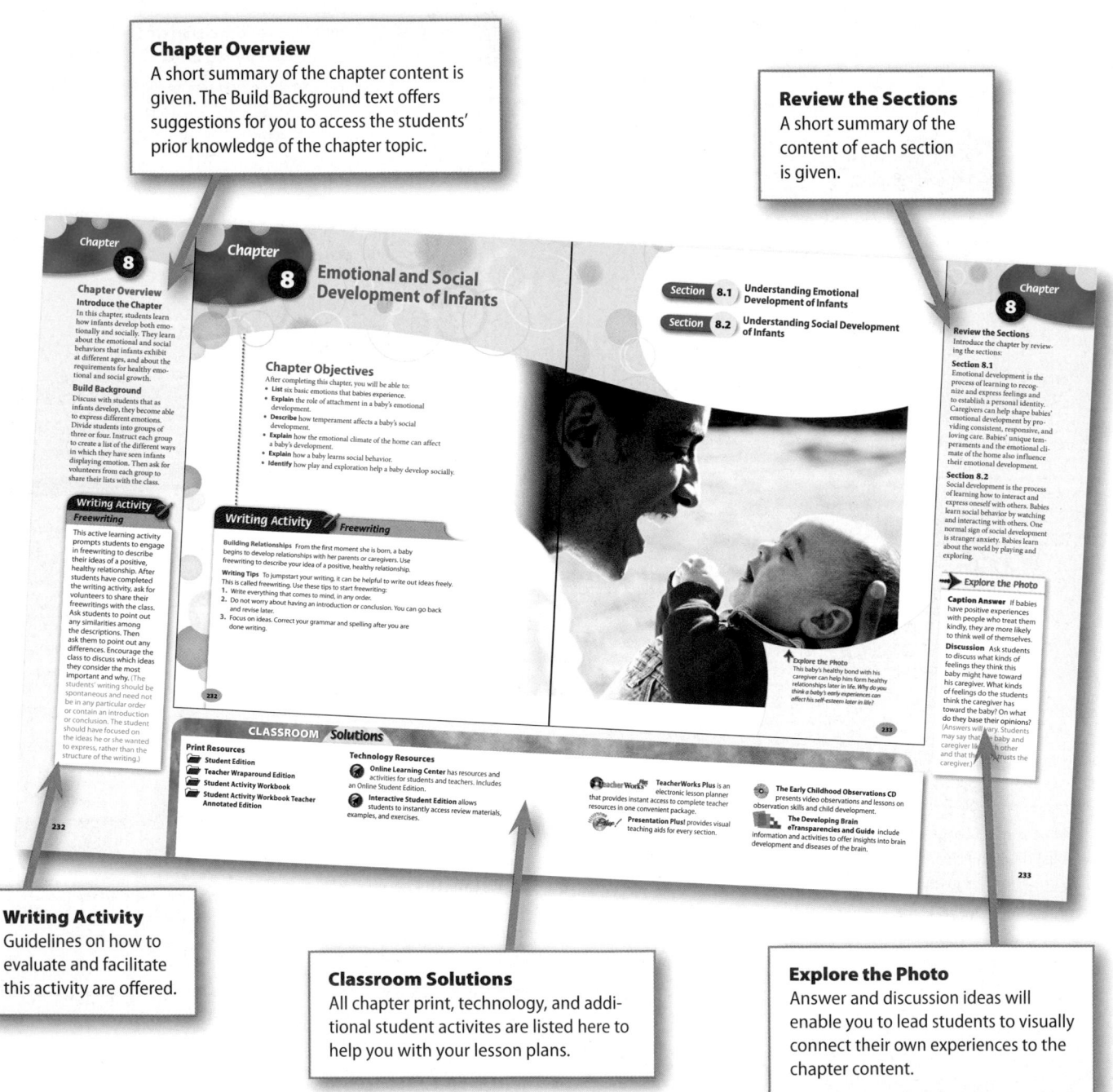

**Writing Activity**
Guidelines on how to evaluate and facilitate this activity are offered.

**Classroom Solutions**
All chapter print, technology, and additional student activites are listed here to help you with your lesson plans.

**Explore the Photo**
Answer and discussion ideas will enable you to lead students to visually connect their own experiences to the chapter content.

# Teacher Wraparound Edition Preview

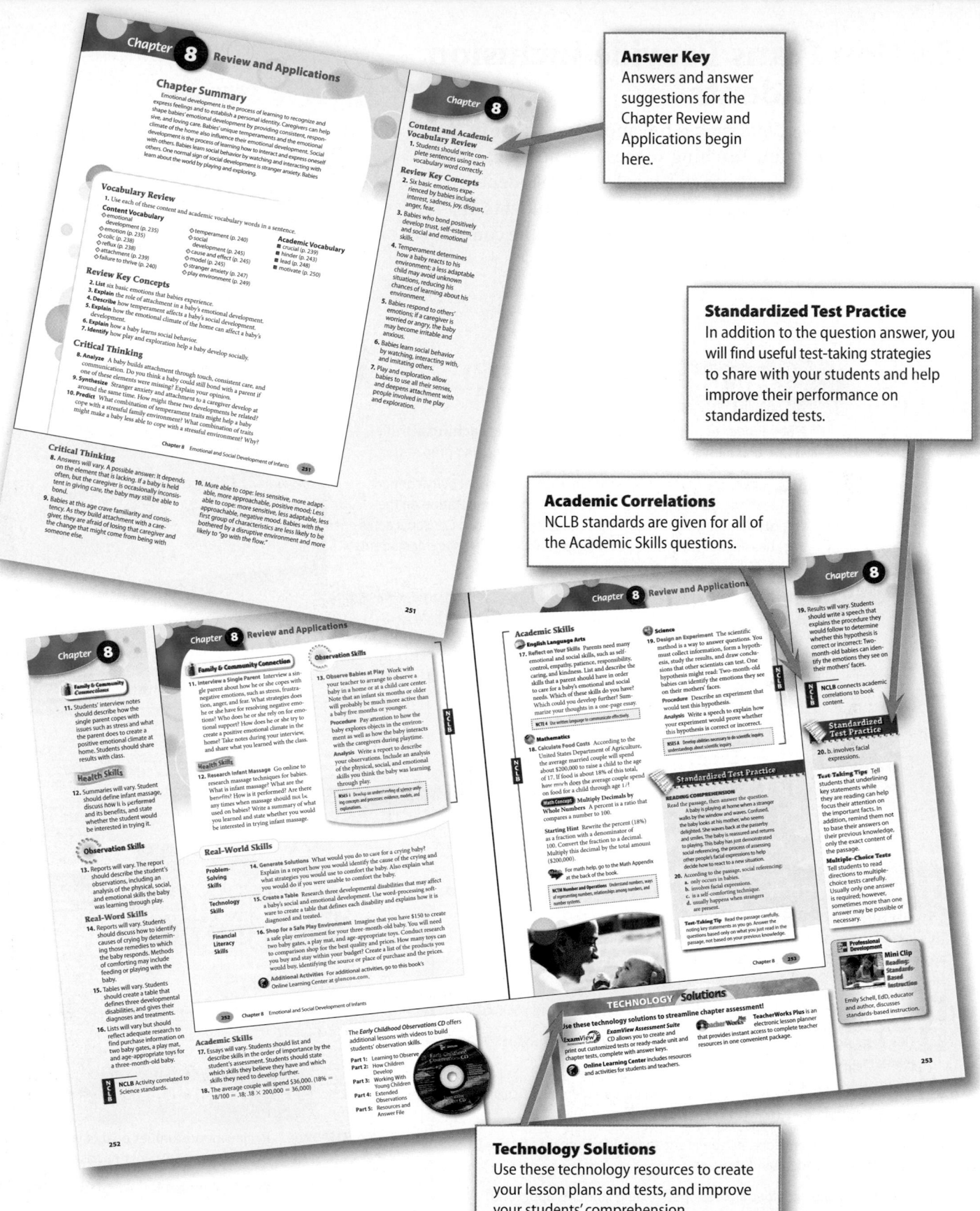

**Answer Key**
Answers and answer suggestions for the Chapter Review and Applications begin here.

**Standardized Test Practice**
In addition to the question answer, you will find useful test-taking strategies to share with your students and help improve their performance on standardized tests.

**Academic Correlations**
NCLB standards are given for all of the Academic Skills questions.

**Technology Solutions**
Use these technology resources to create your lesson plans and tests, and improve your students' comprehension.

# Section Plans Provide Inclusion for All Students

*The Developing Child* makes full and effective use of the six-step teaching plan. Teaching suggestions and ideas are offered to help you motivate and involve your students. These suggestions can assist you in reaching students of all levels of ability and backgrounds, and make the course more rewarding for both you and your students.

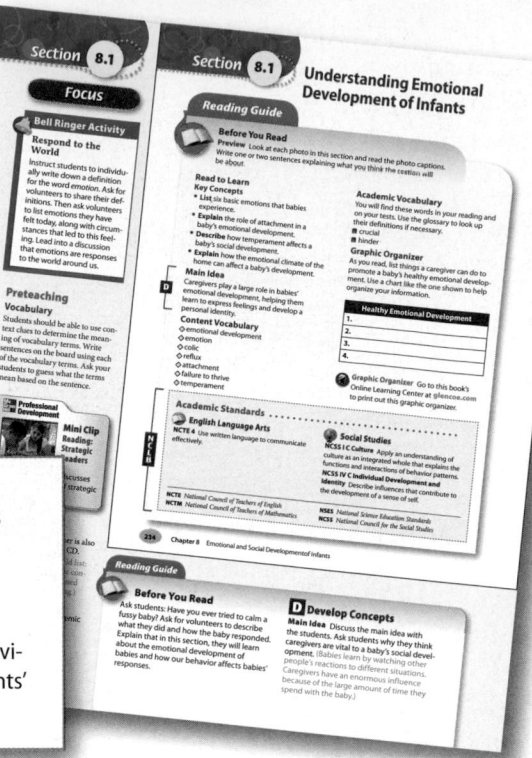

## Focus

A Bell-Ringer Activity begins the lesson, then **Preteaching** activities assure that all students have the same background and preparation.

**D** Coded strategies such as the Develop Concepts activity connect learning activities to content. The bracketed annotation on the student page shows you the related text. Develop Concepts activities use various strategies to help you gauge and plan for students' concept development.

## Teach

This part of the lesson provides suggestions for discussion, reading activities, answers to questions on each page, guided skills practice, and resource suggestions.

**R** Reading Strategy activities help you teach reading skills and vocabulary.

**U** Universal Access activities provide strategies to reach all types of learners in the classroom.

**S** Skill Practice activities provide guided and independent practice and leveled instruction to reach students at all ability levels.

**W** Writing Support provides independent and guided writing practice to help students understand the text.

**C** Critical Thinking activities are designed to help students apply and extend what they learned.

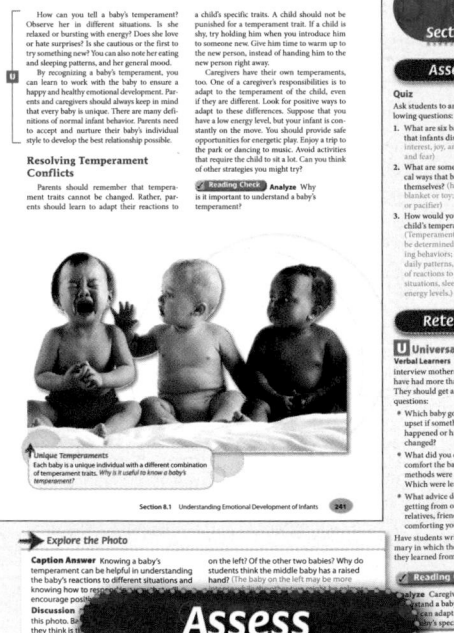

## Assess

Review opportunities enable you to evaluate your students' needs.

# Using the Six-Step Teaching Plan

*The Developing Child* makes full and effective use of a mastery approach in six steps: Focus, Teach, Assess, Reteach, Assess, and Close. This widely accepted instructional method provides you with a consistent framework that makes it easy for you to teach the material.

## Reteach

Different activities are provided to reinforce lesson content. The variety of activities provided in Reteach allows your students to assimilate knowledge using their varied learning styles. Questions are designed to help students apply and extend what they learned.

## Assess

Re-evaluate student comprehension with varied assignments. Answers for the After You Read section review are provided.

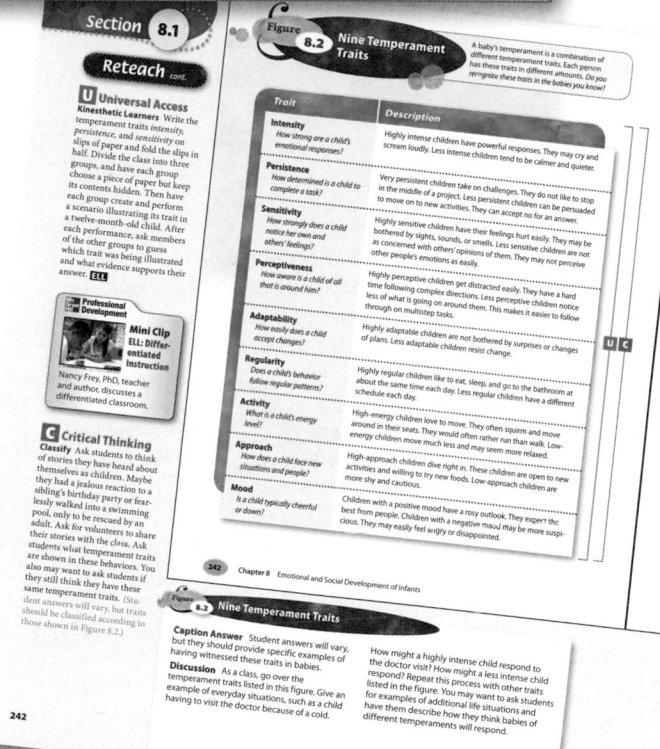

## Close

Provides a Culminating Activity designed to use new knowledge in an independent assignment. The Close activity helps students make the connection between what they read and its meaning and application to the real world.

# *Utilize* Time-Saving

## Help Students Succeed with the Student Activity Workbook

The *Student Activity Workbook* with Academic Integration includes a variety of worksheets and activities, correlated to each chapter in the text:

- Note Taking
- Academics
  - English Language Arts
  - Mathematics
  - Science
  - Social Studies
- Study Skills
- Test Preparation
- Content Vocabulary
- Academic Vocabulary

The Teacher Annotated Edition of the *Student Activity Workbook* includes cyan annotated answers to all of the student activities.

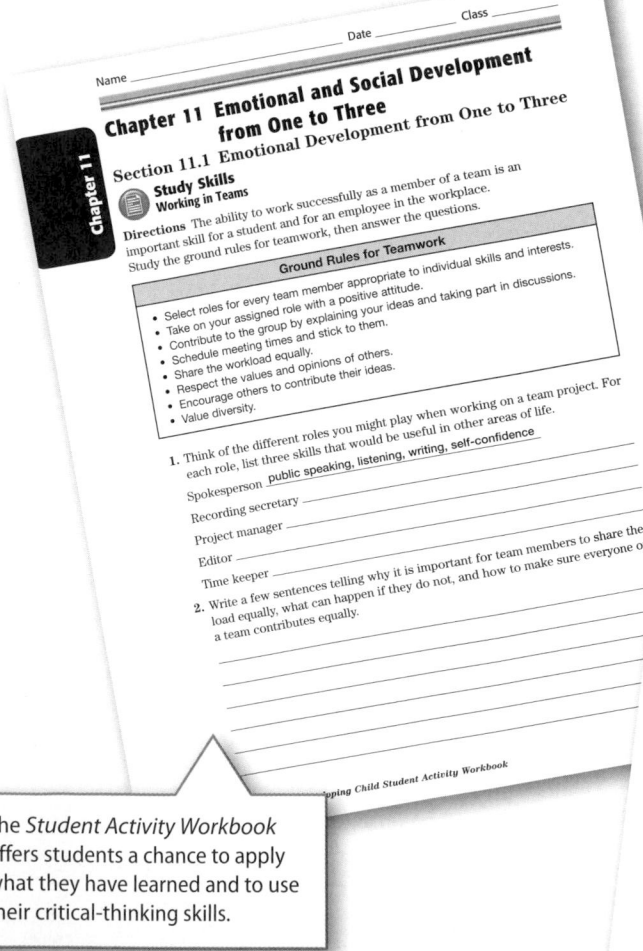

The *Student Activity Workbook* offers students a chance to apply what they have learned and to use their critical-thinking skills.

# Print and Technology Resources

 TeacherWorks™ *Plus* CD-ROM

## Plan Your Lessons in a Few Simple Clicks

*TeacherWorks Plus* gives you instant access to a variety of useful program resources in one easy-to-use CD. The software provides a calendar format that allows you to plan lessons, manage daily activities, access textbook materials, and use Internet resources.

**Customize** your lesson plans to meet your individual classroom needs.

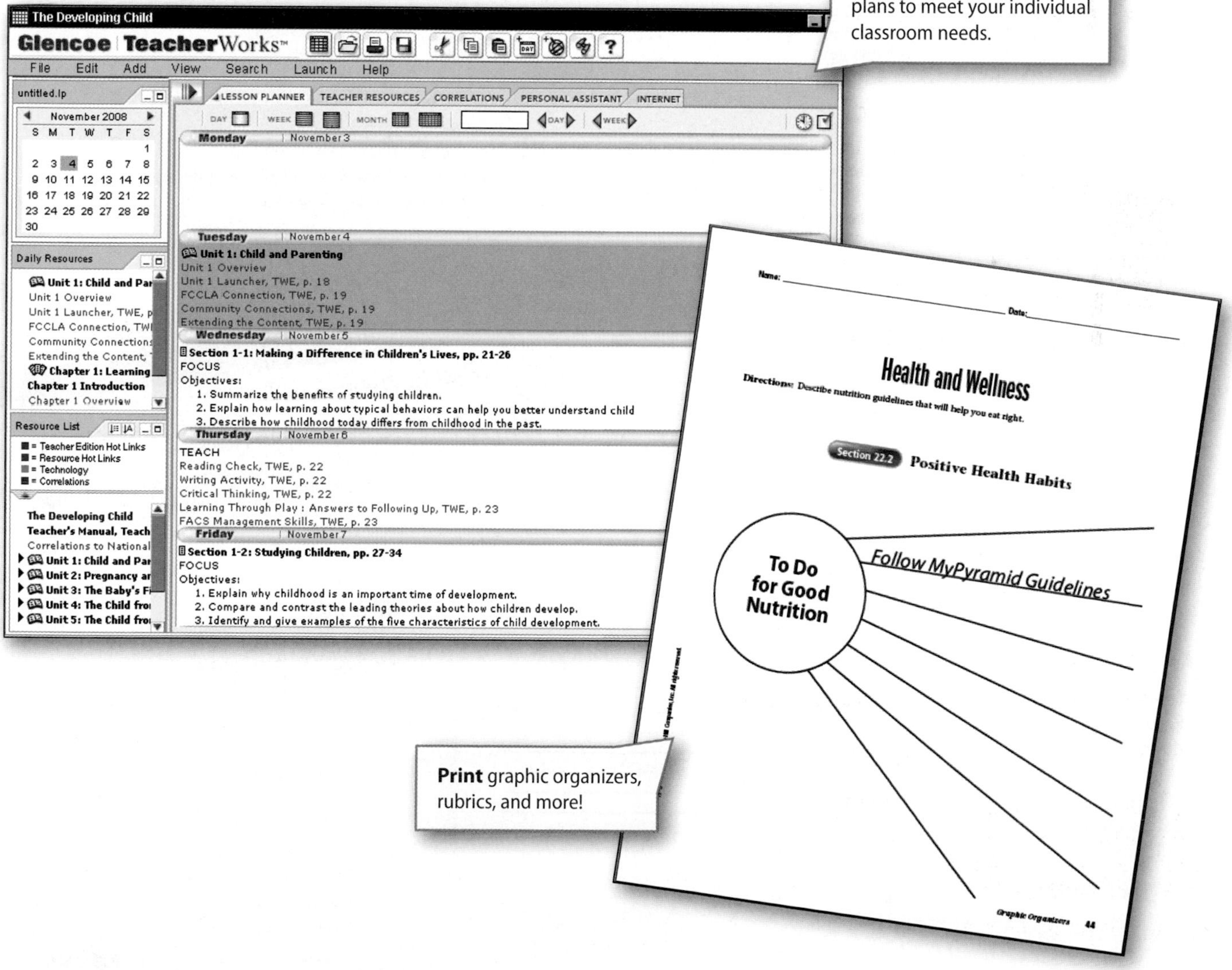

**Print** graphic organizers, rubrics, and more!

 **CD-ROM**

## Customize Assessment

Streamline assessment from start to finish with the *Exam-View® Assessment Suite* CD. This easy-to-use software allows teachers to customize and create unique tests to conduct quizzes, chapter tests, unit tests, mid-term exams, or final exams.

**Answer Keys**
- Develop tests using national standards.
- Automatically score a paper test using a scanner.
- Prepare a variety of useful class and student reports.

**Create Tests**
- Create a paper test in minutes.
- Print multiple versions of the same test.
- Create your own questions.

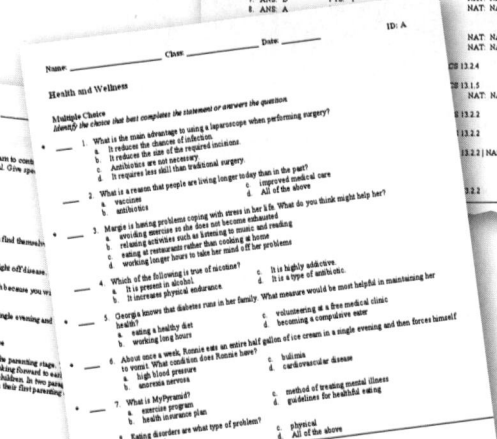

**CD-ROM**

## Reinforce Learning

*The Developing Child* Presentation Plus! PowerPoint CD provides visually motivating presentations that are helpful to both students and teachers. The presentations target key concepts by high-lighting important text, providing graphic organizers, and utilizing visuals from the textbook.

**Printable Outlines**
- Print classroom notes for students.
- Review difficult concepts.
- Use as study guides.

**Presentations**
- Preview key concepts.
- Provide differentiated instruction for visual learners.
- Edit slides to meet the needs of individual learners.
- Review before each test.

# *Early Childhood Observations* CD-ROM

## Develop Observation Skills

Observation skills are best learned through actual practice. It is not always easy though to find real-life situations to practice these skills. Our exclusive CD presents video clips of real children in child care settings, followed by interactive questions. The CD is divided into five areas:

- Learning to Observe
- How Children Develop
- Working with Young Children
- Extended Observations
- Resources and Answer File

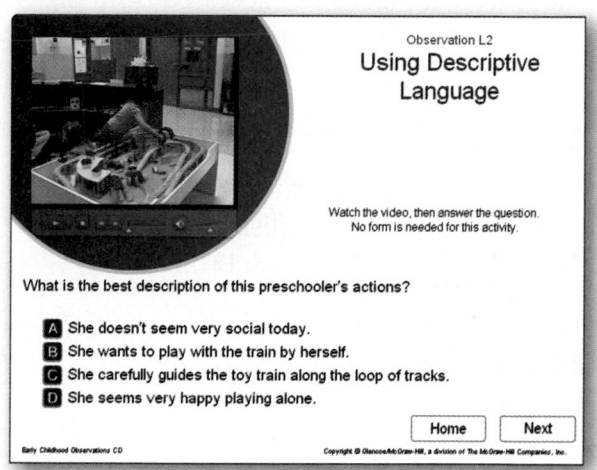

# Online Learning Center Web Site

## Extend and Enrich Learning

*The Developing Child* Online Learning Center provides resources to enrich and enhance learning. There is both a student and teacher Online Learning Center.

### Observation Guidebook

Observation skills are important in all areas of life, but especially so in understanding child development. This printable guidebook includes:

- Building Observation Skills
- Physical Development Observations
- Emotional & Social Development Observations
- Intellectual Development Observations
- Early Childhood Education Observations

## *The Developing Brain* Guide and e-Transparencies

This printable booklet and full-color e-Transparencies expand on the information found in the textbook about brain research and brain development.

- Download the *Developing Brain* activities to further understanding.
- The 48 color e-Transparencies complement the booklet by showing actual brain scans at different stages of development and diseases.

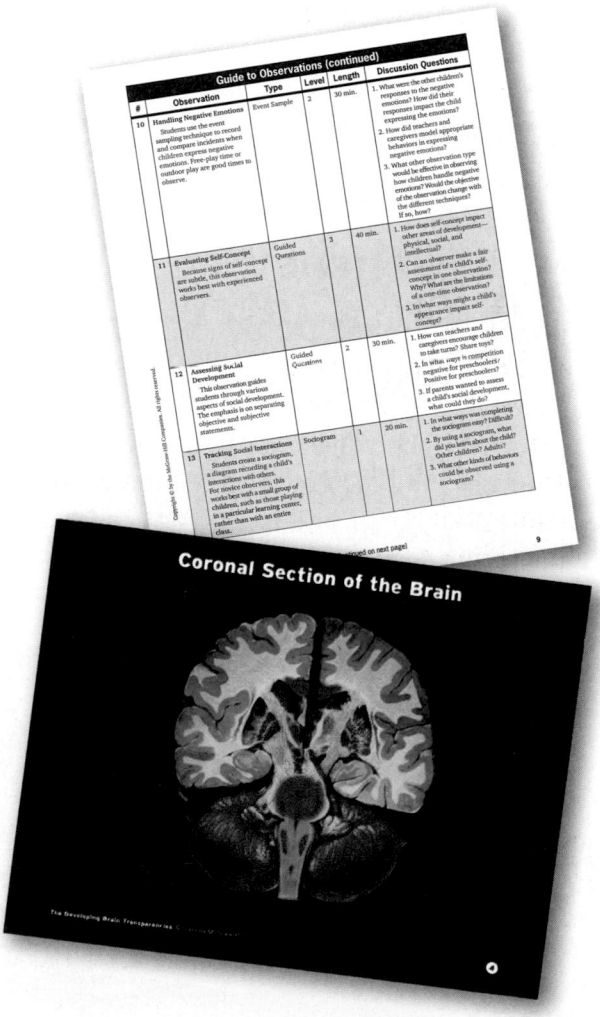

## Online Student Edition

The Online Student Edition is an interactive version of the textbook that can be accessed from the Online Learning Center. This version of the textbook is as easy to read and search.

## Interactive Activities

- Interactive Games
- eFlashcards in English and Spanish
- Printable Activities & Projects
- Study-to-Go

## Printable Activities & Projects

Additional classroom resources are available online:

- Observation Guidebook
- The Developing Brain Guide
- The Developing Brain e-Transparancies
- Learning Through Play
- Additional Activities
- Enrichment Activities
- Graphic Organizers

## Glencoe *FACS Classroom Solutions*™ e-Newsletter

Subscribe to Glencoe's free e-newsletter for educators and receive the latest information about strategies, trends, and technology in family and consumer sciences.

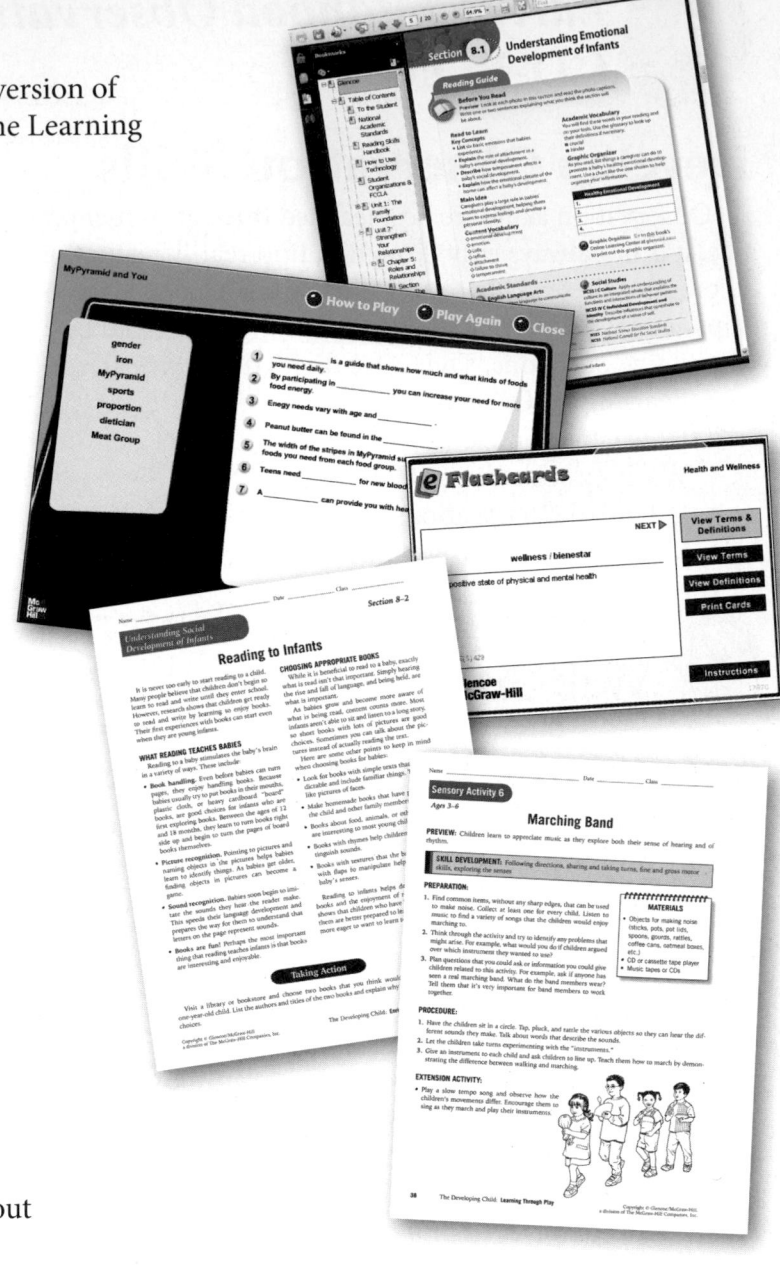

# How to Access the Online Learning Center

The Online Learning Center provides access to a wide variety of teacher resources. Follow these steps to access the textbook resources at *The Developing Child* Online Learning Center.

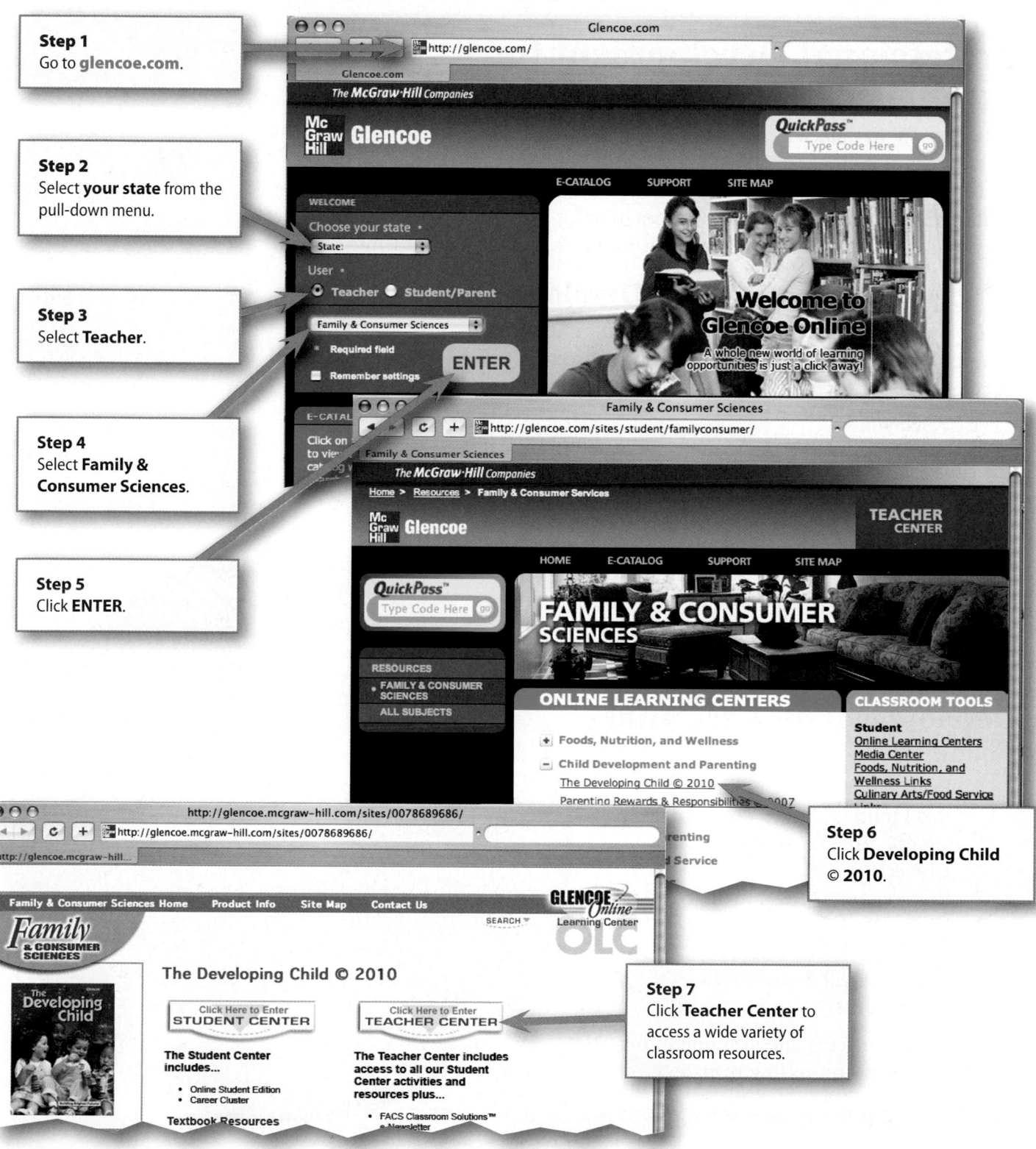

**Step 1**
Go to **glencoe.com**.

**Step 2**
Select **your state** from the pull-down menu.

**Step 3**
Select **Teacher**.

**Step 4**
Select **Family & Consumer Sciences**.

**Step 5**
Click **ENTER**.

**Step 6**
Click **Developing Child © 2010**.

**Step 7**
Click **Teacher Center** to access a wide variety of classroom resources.

# *Online* Professional Development

## Professional Development for Excellence in Teaching

Perkins IV has placed more emphasis than ever on providing a quality professional development for Career and Technology educators. The legislation mandates that the focus of professional development be the integration and reinforcement of academic competencies in order to improve student achievement. Specifically, Perkins requires measurements of students' academic success.

## Glencoe and Professional Development

To support educators in their efforts to meet new professional development requirements, Glencoe now offers a new resource, Glencoe's Online Professional Development for Integrating Academics. This program offers a suite of online products designed to help teachers become more effective in teaching in reinforcing academic skills. The focus of this program is on instructional strategies that can help educators integrate challenging academic content seamlessly into their technical curriculum. These teaching strategies zero in on:

- Math
- Reading
- English Language Arts
- Differentiated instruction
- English Language Learners instruction

## Glencoe's Online Professional Development for Integrating Academics

1. Professional Development Accredited Online Courses (Academic Credit available through Adams University)
2. Professional Development Web Site
3. Video Workshops
4. Mini-Clip Video Library
5. McGraw-Hill Experienced Consultants

For further pricing and ordering information, visit **mcgraw-hill-pd-online.com**.

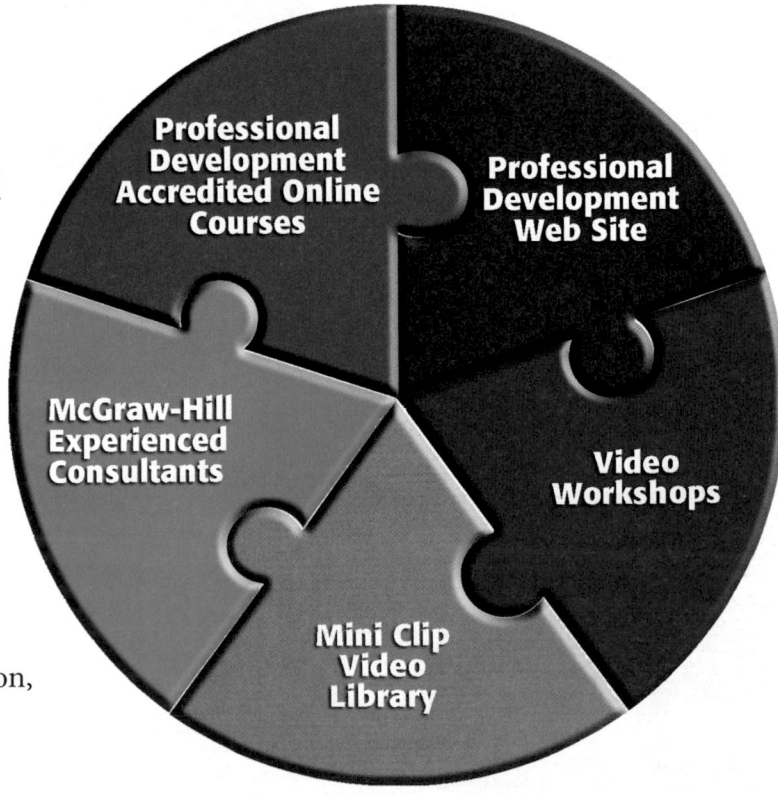

# for Academic Integration

## Professional Development for Academic Integration in the Glencoe 6-Step Teaching Plan

Selected online mini-clips have been integrated into this Teacher Edition's 6-step teaching plan in order to support academic instruction. These mini-clips are free and accessible online at this book's Online Learning Center at **glencoe.com**.

**MINI CLIP VIDEO LIBRARY**
Targeted professional development is correlated throughout *The Developing Child*. **The McGraw-Hill Professional Development Mini Clip Video Library** provides teaching strategies to strengthen academic and learning skills. Log on to **glencoe.com**.

In this chapter, you will find these Mini Clips:
• **ELL** Elaborating on Student Responses, p. 7
• **ELL** Understanding Proficiency, p. 10
• **Reading** Prereading Strategies, p. 12
• **Reading** Strategic Readers, p. 20
• **Reading** During and After Reading, p. 24
• **Reading** Assessment in Standards-Based Instruction, p. 29

**The Professional Development Mini Clip Video Library** offers you instructional support for reading, English Language Learners, and math.

**Integrate teaching strategies in your lesson plans.** Mini-clip videos have been selected and matched to chapter content to help you integrate academics into your planning.

## Mini Clip
## Reading: Building Vocabulary

A teacher introduces and plays two vocabulary building games with her students.

# Child Development Skills and

## Academic Scope and Sequence

These charts provide an overview of the academic standards covered in *The Developing Child*.

| National Council of Teachers of English Standards for English Language Arts | |
|---|---|
| **NCTE 1** Students read a wide range of print and nonprint texts to build an understanding of texts, of themselves, and of the cultures of the United States and the world; to acquire new information; to respond to the needs and demands of society and the workplace; and for personal fulfillment. Among these texts are fiction and nonfiction, classic and contemporary works. | 6, 12, 19, 32, 42, 56, 68, 92, 105, 114, 128, 143, 153, 164, 174, 179, 194, 208, 221, 234, 244, 256, 265, 273, 292, 301, 320, 334, 352, 363, 382, 388, 404, 413, 426, 433, 452, 458, 472, 481, 496, 504, 520, 527, 539, 550, 557, 572, 581, 590, 602, 613, 630, 638 |
| **NCTE 2** Students read a wide range of literature from many periods in many genres to build an understanding of the many dimensions (e.g., philosophical, ethical, aesthetic) of human experience. | 85, 157, 285, 333, 412, 589, 599 |
| **NCTE 3** Students apply a wide range of strategies to comprehend, interpret, evaluate, and appreciate texts. They draw on their prior experience, their interactions with other readers and writers, their knowledge of word meaning and of other texts, their word identification strategies, and their understanding of textual features (e.g., sound-letter correspondence, sentence structure, context, graphics). | 349, 503, 556, 566, 637 |
| **NCTE 4** Students adjust their use of spoken, written, and visual language (e.g., conventions, style, vocabulary) to communicate effectively with a variety of audiences and for different purposes. | 4, 11, 25, 30, 53, 54, 67, 86, 126, 161, 162, 184, 192, 207, 227, 231, 232, 243, 250, 253, 286, 290, 300, 314, 318, 345, 375, 380, 401, 402, 423, 424, 432, 445, 446, 513, 514, 543, 548, 570, 612, 654 |
| **NCTE 5** Students employ a wide range of strategies as they write and use different writing process elements appropriately to communicate with different audiences for a variety of purposes. | 50, 90, 122, 178, 254, 272, 362, 376, 387, 450, 457, 470, 493, 494, 510, 547, 569, 580, 595, 653 |
| **NCTE 6** Students apply knowledge of language structure, language conventions (e.g., spelling and punctuation), media techniques, figurative language, and genre to create, critique, and discuss print and nonprint texts. | 86–87, 188–189, 286–287, 376–377, 446–447, 514–515, 654–655 |
| **NCTE 7** Students conduct research on issues and interests by generating ideas and questions, and by posing problems. They gather, evaluate, and synthesize data from a variety of sources (e.g., print and nonprint texts, artifacts, people) to communicate their discoveries in ways that suit their purpose and audience. | 104, 124, 152, 160, 186, 188, 230, 284, 286, 397, 446, 466, 468, 469, 627 |
| **NCTE 8** Students use a variety of technological and informational resources (e.g., libraries, databases, computer networks, video) to gather and synthesize information and to create and communicate knowledge. | 113, 142, 220, 264, 444, 514 |
| **NCTE 9** Students develop an understanding of and respect for diversity in language use, patterns, and dialects across cultures, ethnic groups, geographic regions, and social roles. | 39, 96, 131, 170, 242, 299, 369, 411, 441, 461, 487, 502, 559, 618, 632 |
| **NCTE 10** Students whose first language is not English make use of their first language to develop competency in the English language arts and to develop understanding of content across the curriculum. | All English Language Learner activities in the Teacher Wraparound Edition |
| **NCTE 11** Students participate as knowledgeable, reflective, creative, and critical members of a variety of literacy communities. | 86–87, 188–189, 286–287, 376–377, 420, 446–447, 514–515, 654–655 |
| **NCTE 12** Students use spoken, written, and visual language to accomplish their own purposes (e.g., for learning, enjoyment, persuasion, and the exchange of information). | 3, 4, 18, 29, 30, 41, 54, 81, 86, 89, 90, 125, 126, 162, 173, 187, 188, 190, 192, 234, 254, 281, 286, 288, 290, 317, 318,350, 372, 376, 378, 380, 402, 424, 446, 448, 450, 470, 480, 489, 494, 514, 516, 518, 526, 538, 548, 570, 600, 624, 628 649, 654 |

# *Academics* at the Same Time

| National Council of Teachers of Mathematics Standards for Grades 9–12 | | |
|---|---|---|
| **Number and Operations** | Understand numbers, ways of representing numbers, relationships among numbers, and number systems. | 29, 36, 53, 85, 150, 187, 231, 253, 457, 485, 547, 569, 599, 612, 649, 653 |
| | Compute fluently and make reasonable estimates. | 383, 401, 423, 445, 526, 627 |
| **Algebra** | Understand patterns, relations, and functions. | 285 |
| | Represent and analyze mathematical situations and structures using algebraic symbols. | 125, 349 |
| | Use mathematical models to represent and understand quantitative relationships. | 317, 469 |
| **Geometry** | Analyze characteristics of two- and three-dimensional geometric shapes and develop mathematical arguments about geometric relationships. | 277 |
| | Use visualization, spatial reasoning, and geometric modeling to solve problems. | 432, 513 |
| **Measurement** | Understand measurable attributes of objects and the units, systems, and processes of measurement. | 306, 375 |
| | Apply appropriate techniques, tools, and formulas to determine measurements. | 493 |
| **Data Analysis and Probability** | Select and use appropriate statistical methods to analyze data. | 161, 362, 503, 608 |

Standards are listed with permission of the National Council of Teachers of Mathematics (NCTM). NCTM *does not endorse the content or validity of these alignments.*

# Academic Scope and Sequence

## National Science Education Standards

| | |
|---|---|
| **Content Standard 1**  Students should develop an understanding of science unifying concepts and processes: systems, order, and organization; evidence, models, and explanation; change, constancy, and measurement; evolution and equilibrium; and form and function. | 28, 252, 355, 400 |
| **Content Standard A**  Students should develop abilities necessary to do scientific inquiry, understandings about scientific inquiry. | 25, 81, 113, 125, 161, 199, 253, 317, 333, 349, 372, 375, 401, 410, 422, 423, 466, 493, 513, 547, 569, 599, 655 |
| **Content Standard B**  Students should develop an understanding of the structure of atoms, structure and properties of matter, chemical reactions, motions and forces, conservation of energy and increase in disorder, and interactions of energy and matter. | 152 |
| **Content Standard C**  Students should develop understanding of the cell; molecular basis of heredity; biological evolution; interdependence of organisms; matter, energy, and organization in living systems; and behavior of organisms. | 53, 97, 207, 285, 300, 387, 445, 456, 561, 627 |
| **Content Standard F**  Students should develop understanding of personal and community health; population growth; natural resources; environmental quality; natural and human-induced hazards; science and technology in local, national, and global challenges. | 29, 66, 85, 122, 142, 184, 187, 231, 264, 397, 469, 556, 568, 624 |

## National Council for the Social Studies Curriculum Standards

| | | |
|---|---|---|
| **I. Culture** | **A**  Analyze and explain the ways groups, societies, and cultures address human needs and concerns. | 39, 52, 67, 96, 131, 157, 170, 173, 220, 227, 272, 314, 345, 369, 374, 618, 632 |
| | **C**  Apply an understanding of culture as an integrated whole that explains the functions and interactions of language, literature, the arts, traditions, beliefs and values, and behavior patterns. | 240, 281, 299, 411 |
| | **D**  Compare and analyze societal patterns for preserving and transmitting culture while adapting to environmental or social change. | 637 |
| **II. Time, Continuity, and Change** | **B**  Apply key concepts such as time, chronology, causality, change, conflict, and complexity to explain, analyze, and show connections among patterns of historical change and continuity. | 104 |

## National Council for the Social Studies Curriculum Standards (continued)

| | | |
|---|---|---|
| **IV. Individual Development and Identity** | **C** Describe the ways family, religion, gender, ethnicity, nationality, socio-economic status, and other group and cultural influences contribute to the development of a sense of self. | 18, 243, 250, 489, 538 |
| | **D** Apply concepts, methods, and theories about the study of human growth and development, such as physical endowment, learning, motivation, behavior, perception, and personality. | 84, 316, 441, 480, 492, 512, 543, 546, 598, 626, 652 |
| | **E** Examine the interaction of ethnic, national, or cultural influences in specific situations or events. | 510 |
| | **F** Analyze the role of perceptions, attitudes, values, and beliefs in the development of personal identity. | 50, 348 |
| | **H** Work independently and cooperatively within groups and institutions to accomplish goals. | 589 |
| | **I** Examine factors that contribute to and damage one's mental health and analyze issues related to mental health and behavioral disorders in contemporary society. | 595 |
| **V. Individuals, Groups, and Institutions** | **A** Apply concepts such as role, status, and social class in describing the connections and interactions of individuals, groups, and institutions in society. | 412 |
| | **B** Analyze group and institutional influences on people, events, and elements of culture in both historical and contemporary settings. | 420 |
| | **F** Evaluate the role of institutions in furthering both continuity and change. | 11, 461, 559 |
| | **G** Analyze the extent to which groups and institutions meet individual needs and promote the common good in contemporary and historical settings. | 566, 580 |
| **VII. Production, Distribution, and Consumption** | **F** Compare how values and beliefs influence economic decisions in different societies. | 41 |
| **VIII. Science, Technology, and Society** | **C** Analyze how science and technology influence the core values, beliefs, and attitudes of society, and how core values, beliefs, and attitudes of society shape scientific and technological change. | 178 |
| **IX. Global Connections** | **A** Explain how language, art, music, belief systems, and other cultural elements can facilitate global understanding or cause misunderstanding. | 498 |

# FACS National Standards Correlation

The following chart shows how *The Developing Child* meets the standards and competencies for the family and interpersonal relationships areas of study as outlined in the Family and Consumer Sciences Education National Standards.

| Human Development | | |
|---|---|---|
| **Comprehensive Standard 12.0:** Analyze factors that influence human growth & development. | | |
| | **Competencies from National Standards** | **Pages in Text** |
| **Content Standard 12.1:** Analyze factors that influence human growth & development. | **12.1.1** Analyze physical, emotional, social, spiritual, and intellectual development. | 14, 69–72, 195–207, 235–243, 245–250, 266–272, 274, 278, 279, 286–287, 293–300, 321–333, 335–345, 353–362, 383–384, 385–387, 389, 401, 405–412, 414–420, 429, 430–432, 434–441, 453–454, 456–457, 473–480, 482–489, 497–498, 508–510, 514–515, 521–523, 528–533, 533–535, 535–538, 542–543 |
| | **12.1.2** Analyze interrelationships among physical, emotional, social, and intellectual aspects of human growth and development. | 58–61, 245, 332–333, 364, 372, 454, 455, 506–507, 537 |
| | **12.1.3** Analyze current and emerging research about human growth and development, including research on brain development. | 14, 15, 137, 176, 182–183, 197, 239, 257–264, 268, 270–272, 276, 296, 353, 355, 358, 368, 387, 409, 428–429, 435, 436, 444, 445, 456, 478, 499–503, 505–506, 525, 529–530, 535–536, 540–541, 542–543, 584, 604 |
| **Content Standard 12.2:** Analyze conditions that influence human growth and development. | **12.2.1** Analyze the effect of heredity and environment on human growth and development. | 14, 16–17, 95–97, 115–122, 177, 195–197, 201, 226, 240–243, 261, 262, 268–269, 293, 295, 418–419, 434–437, 456, 478, 536–537, 552, 627 |
| | **12.2.2** Analyze the impact of social, economic, and technological forces on individual growth and development. | 28, 112–113, 124, 197, 456, 534–535, 551, 559, 627 |
| | **12.2.3** Analyze the effects of gender, ethnicity, and culture on individual development. | 240, 294, 411, 441, 456, 480, 498, 510, 513, 522–523, 526, 528–529, 632 |
| | **12.2.4** Analyze the effects of life events on individuals' physical, intellectual, social, moral, and emotional development. | 38–41, 145, 261, 434–437, 439–441, 522–523 |
| | **12.2.5** Analyze geographic, political, and global influences on human growth and development. | 10–11, 64–67, 272 |
| **Content Standard 12.3:** Analyze strategies that promote growth and development across the life span. | **12.3.1** Analyze the role of communication on human growth and development. | 60–61, 71, 180, 181, 239–240, 327–328, 329–330, 361, 364, 410–411, 462, 554–556, 622 |
| | **12.3.2** Analyze the role of nurturance on human growth and development. | 275–279, 326, 361, 484 |
| | **12.3.3** Analyze the role of family and social services support systems in meeting human growth and development needs. | 26, 59, 220, 490, 512, 524, 579–580, 587–588, 589, 595, 598 |

## Interpersonal Relationships

**Comprehensive Standard 15.0:**
Evaluate the effects of parenting roles and responsibilities on strengthening the well-being of individuals and families.

| | Competencies from National Standards | Pages in Text |
|---|---|---|
| **Content Standard 15.1:** Analyze roles and responsibilities of parenting. | **15.1.1** Analyze parenting roles across the life span. | 38, 73–77, 235, 238, 239–240, 370, 542, 543 |
| | **15.1.2** Analyze expectations and responsibilities of parenting. | 33, 34, 38–41, 86–87, 239–240, 247, 250, 268–269, 275, 277, 279, 300, 302–314, 316, 327, 338, 340, 354, 358–359, 364–367, 368, 390, 395–396, 416–418, 463, 507–508, 521, 532, 551, 573, 582 |
| | **15.1.3** Analyze consequences of parenting practices to the individual, family, and society. | 240, 243, 245, 391–392 |
| | **15.1.4** Analyze societal conditions that influence parenting across the life span. | 396, 463 |
| | **15.1.5** Explain cultural differences in roles and responsibilities of parenting. | 39, 41, 67, 84, 131, 170, 227, 240, 272, 299, 314, 369, 618 |
| **Content Standard 15.2:** Evaluate parenting practices that maximize human growth and development. | **15.2.1** Choose nurturing practices that support human growth and development. | 34, 58–61, 71, 180, 181, 209, 210–211, 222–224, 236, 238, 239–240, 248, 264, 274–275, 302, 312, 313, 329–330, 361, 364, 391, 393–394, 395, 409, 410–411, 412, 435–437, 439–441, 443, 462, 466, 474, 478–479, 487, 508, 551, 554–556, 577, 579, 652 |
| | **15.2.2** Apply communication strategies that promote positive self-esteem in family members. | 275–279, 331, 361, 411–412, 445, 477, 484, 532, 588 |
| | **15.2.3** Assess common practices and emerging research about discipline on human growth and development. | 72–73, 77–81, 137, 197, 239, 257–264, 286–287, 323, 331–332, 340–345, 348, 358, 416–418, 419, 423, 488, 541–542, 622–624 |
| | **15.2.4** Assess the effects of abuse and neglect on children and families and determine methods for prevention. | 211–212, 591–592, 593 |
| | **15.2.5** Apply criteria for selecting care and services for children. | 151, 603–608, 609–612, 625, 652 |
| **Content Standard 15.3:** Evaluate external support systems that provide services for parents. | **15.3.1** Assess community resources and services available to families. | 124, 220, 490, 512, 579–580, 587–588, 589, 594–595, 598, 612 |
| | **15.3.2** Appraise community resources that provide opportunities related to parenting. | 37, 41 |
| | **15.3.3** Summarize current laws and policies related to parenting. | 308, 393, 551, 586–587, 591, 593–594 |
| **Content Standard 15.4:** Analyze physical and emotional factors related to beginning the parenting process. | **15.4.1** Analyze biological processes related to prenatal development, birth, and health of child and mother. | 93, 95–97, 99–104, 106–111, 115–118, 122, 129–133, 134, 165–173, 183–184 |
| | **15.4.2** Analyze the emotional factors of prenatal development and birth in relation to the health of parents and child. | 136–137, 154, 180, 181, 184, 187 |
| | **15.4.3** Analyze implications of alternatives to biological parenthood. | 63, 64, 84 |
| | **15.4.4** Analyze legal and ethical impacts of current and emerging technology on fertility and family planning. | 94, 97–99 |

# Make Your Teaching Flexible

## 90-Day Pacing Guide

| | 18-Week Course | |
| --- | --- | --- |
| | **Traditional Schedule** | **Block Schedule** |
| **Week** | **Student Edition** | **Student Edition** |
| 1 | Ch. 1, 2 | Ch. 1 |
| 2 | Ch. 3 | Ch. 2 |
| 3 | Unit 1 Thematic Project; Ch. 4 | Ch. 3; Unit 1 Thematic Project |
| 4 | Ch. 5 | Ch. 4 |
| 5 | Ch. 6 | Ch. 5 |
| 6 | Unit 2 Thematic Project; Ch. 7 | Ch. 6; Unit 2 Thematic Project |
| 7 | Ch. 8 | Ch. 7 |
| 8 | Ch. 9 | Ch. 8 |
| 9 | Unit 3 Thematic Project; Ch. 10 | Ch. 9; Unit 3 Thematic Project |
| 10 | Ch. 11, 12 | Ch. 10 |
| 11 | Unit 4 Thematic Project; Ch. 13 | Ch. 11, 12 |
| 12 | Ch. 14, 15 | Unit 4 Thematic Project; Ch. 13 |
| 13 | Unit 5 Thematic Project; Ch. 16 | Ch. 14, 15; Unit 5 Thematic Project |
| 14 | Ch. 17, 18 | Ch. 16, 17 |
| 15 | Unit 6 Thematic Project; Ch. 19 | Ch. 18; Unit 6 Thematic Project |
| 16 | Ch. 20 | Ch. 19, 20, 21 |
| 17 | Ch. 21, 22 | Ch. 22, 23 |
| 18 | Ch. 23; Unit 7 Thematic Project | Unit 7 Thematic Project |

Additional activities for each chapter can be found in the *Student Activity Workbook*, Presentation *Plus!* PowerPoint® Presentation CD-ROM, *ExamView® Assessment Suite* CD-ROM, and the Online Learning Center.

# and **Adaptable** to **Any** Schedule

## 180-Day Pacing Guide

| 36-Week Course | | | | | | |
|---|---|---|---|---|---|---|
| | **Traditional Schedule** | **Block Schedule** | | | **Traditional Schedule** | **Block Schedule** |
| **Week** | **Student Edition** | | | **Week** | **Student Edition** | |
| 1 | Ch. 1 (Sect. 1.1) | Ch. 1 (Sect. 1.1) | | 19 | Ch. 11 (Sect 11.2) | Ch. 11 (Sect. 11.1) |
| 2 | Ch. 1 (Sect. 1.2, 1.3) | Ch. 1 (Sect. 1.2) | | 20 | Ch. 12 | Ch. 11 (Sect. 11.2) |
| 3 | Ch. 2 | Ch. 1 (Sect. 1.3), Ch. 2 | | 21 | Unit 4 Thematic Project; Ch. 13 (Sect. 13.1) | Ch. 12 (Sect. 12.1) |
| 4 | Ch. 3; Unit 1 Thematic Project | Ch. 3 (Sect. 3.1) | | 22 | Ch. 13 (Sect. 13.2) | Ch. 12 (Sect. 12.2); Unit 4 Thematic Project |
| 5 | Ch. 4 (Sect. 4.1) | Ch. 3 (Sect. 3.2); Unit 1 Thematic Project | | 23 | Ch. 14 (Sect. 14.1) | Ch. 13 |
| 6 | Ch. 4 (Sect. 4.2, 4.3) | Ch. 4 (Sect. 4.1) | | 24 | Ch. 14 (Sect. 14.2) | Ch. 14 |
| 7 | Ch. 5 (Sect. 5.1) | Ch. 4 (Sect. 4.2, 4.3) | | 25 | Ch. 15 (Sect. 15.1) | Ch. 15 (Sect. 15.1) |
| 8 | Ch. 5 (Sect. 5.2) | Ch. 5 (Sect. 5.1) | | 26 | Ch. 15 (Sect. 15.2); Unit 5 Thematic Project | Ch. 15 (Sect. 15.2); Unit 5 Thematic Project |
| 9 | (Sect. 5.3) | Ch. 5 (Sect. 5.2, 5.3) | | 27 | Ch. 16 | Ch. 16, 17 |
| 10 | Ch. 6; Unit 2 Thematic Project | Ch. 6; Unit 2 Thematic Project | | 28 | Ch. 17 | Ch. 18 (Sect. 18.1) |
| 11 | Ch. 7 (Sect. 7.1) | Ch. 7 (Sect. 7.1) | | 29 | Ch. 18 (Sect. 18.1) | Ch. 18 (Sect. 18.2); Unit 6 Thematic Project |
| 12 | Ch. 7 (Sect. 7.2, 7.3) | Ch. 7 (Sect. 7.2) | | 30 | Ch. 18 (Sect. 18.2); Unit 6 Thematic Project | Ch. 19 (Sect. 19.1) |
| 13 | Ch. 8 | Ch. 7 (Sect. 7.3) | | 31 | Ch. 19 (Sect. 19.1) | Ch. 19 (Sect. 19.2, 19.3) |
| 14 | Ch. 9 (Sect. 9.1) | Ch. 8 | | 32 | Ch. 19 (Sect. 19.2, 19.3) | Ch. 20 |
| 15 | Ch. 9 (Sect. 9.2); Unit 3 Thematic Project | Ch. 9 (Sect. 9.1) | | 33 | Ch. 20, 21 (Sect. 21.1, 21.2) | Ch 21 |
| 16 | Ch. 10 (Sect. 10.1) | Ch. 9 (Sect. 9.2); Unit 3 Thematic Project | | 34 | Ch. 21 (Sect. 21.3) | Ch. 22 |
| 17 | Ch. 10 (Sect. 10.2) | Ch. 10 (Sect. 10.1) | | 35 | Ch. 22, 23 | Ch. 23 |
| 18 | Ch. 11 (Sect 11.1) | Ch. 10 (Sect. 10.2) | | 36 | Unit 7 Thematic Project | Unit 7 Thematic Project |

# Generate High Achievers... and Enhance Student Learning

## Academic Integration

Academic skills are crucial for success both inside and outside the classroom. In addition to traditional academic skills, your students will need communication skills, interpersonal skills, and strong technology skills in order to compete in the workplace. Basic skills will support your students in completing the tasks that their jobs and lives will demand.

## The No Child Left Behind Act

The No Child Left Behind Act of 2001 emphasizes student achievement in basic academic subjects. It introduces strict accountability measures for schools in the form of standardized testing. Traditionally, core academic subjects have been defined as language arts, science, and mathematics. No Child Left Behind names the following academic subjects:

- English
- Reading/Language Arts
- Mathematics
- Science
- World Languages
- Civics and Government
- Economics
- Art
- History
- Geography

## The Importance of Integrating Academics

In a recent survey of high school graduates—many of whom had gone directly to work rather than into postsecondary education—more than half the respondents said their high schools should have placed more emphasis on basic academic skills.

Unfortunately, these students—like so many others—were not able to recognize the relevance of their course work while they were in high school.

By explicitly integrating academic skills into the family and consumer sciences curriculum, you can make students more aware of the connections between schoolwork and the real world.

Integrated learning offers the following additional benefits to students:

- It provides real-world learning and thus establishes patterns of lifelong learning.
- It improves the academic achievement of all students—including those who will begin their careers directly after high school, those who will go on to postsecondary education or training, and those who will obtain four-year college degrees and beyond.
- It helps students make realistic plans for their own careers and education.

## Academics in the Family and Consumer Sciences Curriculum

Integrate academic skills into the classroom as a regular part of your classroom activities. For example, by having students read class assignments and texts, write letters and reports, give presentations, and perform mathematics exercises, you are helping them improve their academic skills. Make expectations clear. For example, if you ask your students to prepare a written report, explain that grammar, spelling, and presentation will be evaluated along with subject content. Stress that clear writing, accuracy, and attention to detail are skills that students will need for success in school and at work.

To integrate academics into your family and consumer sciences course, you must incorporate principles from other subjects in a way that students can understand either on a concrete level or on metaphoric terms. This type of teaching will help those students who learn best when they are exposed to a variety of examples.

 **Efficient Instruction** to *All* **Students**

## Accountability

A consequence of the No Child Left Behind Act, and the reauthorization of the Perkins Act through 2012, is that more states require testing for high-school graduation. Accountability measures new to the Perkins reauthorization bill include:

- Academic proficiency as measured by the state criteria developed under NCLB;
- Graduation rates, also as defined by NCLB;
- Number of students to continue to postsecondary education;
- Number of students to complete state or industry certification or licensure; and
- Student achievement on assignments aligned with industry standards.

## Connection to Relevance

With the mandatory requirements for proven test scores and graduation numbers, how can we assure that our students are learning? Most educators agree it is by connecting the relevance of education to life.

The Association for Career and Technical Education past-president Bob Scarborough says the Perkins reauthorization "ensures we are providing all students with an education that will help them succeed in the workplace and in life." William Daggett writes in *Achieving Academic Excellence through Rigor and Relevance*:

> *What is important is that students enter the global economy with the ability to apply what they learned in school to a variety of ever-changing situations that they may not have been able to foresee before graduating.*

The Rigor/Relevance Framework, developed at the International Center for Leadership in Education, illustrates leveled learning processes that enable students to perform high-level thinking. The learning process defines student performance in four sequential categories: acquisition, application, assimilation and adaptation.

As educators, our goal is to teach students to adapt their acquired knowledge and skills in complex ways to any situations, known and unknown. As educators, we are committed to provide the connectivity between classroom learning and real-world application.

## Applications

Studies show that students understand and retain knowledge when they experience or apply it to relevant situations. The *The Developing Child* program is dedicated to meet the challenge. Every chapter in *The Developing Child* is filled with ways to engage students in experiential learning and applying their knowledge to their lives.

Features designed to help students find the relevance in content include:

- Learning Through Play
- The Developing Brain
- Unit Thematic Project (featuring skills self-assessment, connection to the community, and academic skills correlation)
- Life Skills Checklist
- Careers with Children
- Science in Action and Math in Action
- Safe Child, Healthy Child
- Parenting Skills
- Respond to Special Need
- Culture Matters
- Chapter Review & Applications, including Real-World Skills, Academic Skills, Active Learning, Family and Community Connections, and Net Connection

The content and teaching strategies in *The Developing Child* are designed to help applied learning students acclimate into the real world and to prepare them for relationships throughout their lives.

# Designing Instruction for a Diverse Classroom

## The Diverse Classroom

No two students enter a classroom with identical abilities, backgrounds, experiences, and learning preferences, yet they are all expected to master the curricular objectives. Teachers face the enormous challenge of designing instruction to better meet the diverse learning needs of students.

## Universal Access and Universal Design

Universal access and universal design, as well as differentiated instruction, provide a framework for professional educators to address the challenges and opportunities of a diverse classroom.

## Universal Access

**Universal Access (UA)** means that all people have an equal opportunity to access information, products, and services. Universal access, from an educational perspective, means that all students have an equal opportunity to education.

This means access to high-quality curriculum and instruction regardless of learning diversities. UA may involve the use of specialized technology and environments.

## Universal Design

**Universal Design (UD)** has a foundation in architecture. UD originally focused on accessibility issues for individuals with disabilities. Current UD philosophy focuses on designs that support all individuals, not just individuals with disabilities. From an educational perspective, universal design makes instructional facilities, materials, and activities available so that all learners can achieve success. The key instructional element associated with UD is variety:

- A variety of teaching methods to deliver the content
- A variety of ways for students to interact with teachers and other students
- A variety of ways students can demonstrate their learning
- A variety of ways to assess and evaluate student learning

# Differentiated Instruction

Differentiated Instruction (DI) is a planned, deliberate, sequential, and systematic instructional technique designed to maximize the learning and achievement of all students in the classroom. Because of the diversity in student learning abilities and preferences, instruction needs to be equally diverse. By recognizing and positively responding to diverse student backgrounds, languages, abilities, learning preferences, needs, and interests, teachers are better able to deliver instruction that creates opportunities for improved student learning, achievement, and success within the framework of universal design.

## Five Key Steps for Delivering Differentiated Instruction

### 1. ▶ Know your students' learning profiles

A student's learning profile may include information about learning disabilities, English language ability, learning preferences, customs, needs, interests, and background. Record student inventories, take note of conversations, make observations, and connect with other education specialists to gather student learning profiles. Use the Universal Access activities and suggestions found in *The Developing Child* to craft lessons to suit your students' needs.

### 2. ▶ Use a variety of instructional methods.

Differentiated instruction varies the way that learning expectations are delivered to the students. *The Developing Child* offers suggestions for modifying instructional delivery to include problem-solving activities, writing, models, demonstrations, and graphic organizers.

### 3. ▶ Provide ample opportunities for student/ teacher and student/student interactions.

The varied use of small group, partner, and whole-class instruction provides a differentiated approach that can be used to support many needs, such as language skills, review, enrichment, or acceleration. Modify the independence of the activities in *The Developing Child* using group and partner activity suggestions throughout the book, Interpersonal and Collaborative activities in the chapter reviews, and Guided Practice activities in the Teacher Annotated Edition Lesson Plans.

### 4. ▶ Allow students to demonstrate their learning with a variety of product options.

Students should be given the opportunity to demonstrate their learning in diverse ways. For example, some students who struggle with writing may prefer to demonstrate their learning orally (speech, skit, audio recording), visually (model, exhibit, poster, drawing), or through media applications (video, PowerPoint® presentation, music). Use the Hands-On Labs, Technology Applications, Active Learning activities, and other creative activities throughout *The Developing Child* as models for alternative product options.

### 5. ▶ Use varied methods to assess and evaluate student learning.

Student assessments should be varied and frequent. They should be formal (graded, such as a test or product) and informal (non-graded, such as observations or group questioning for progress monitoring). Self-assessments allow the students to judge their own progress. Assessments should also include a range of low- to high-level thinking and responding skills in both traditional and authentic assessment formats. Use the Self-Evaluation Rubrics, quizzes, critical thinking assignments, and discussion questions in *The Developing Child* to assess and evaluate student learning.

# Delivering Instruction to Reach All Students

## Differentiated Instruction for English Language Learners

Differentiated instruction is important in virtually all classrooms. It is critical in language-diverse classrooms, where many learning activities can be and should be modified and differentiated. Before determining what level of differentiation is needed for your English language learners (ELL), ask yourself two questions:

### 1. Which language proficiency level best describes my English language learners?

Many schools, districts, and/or states typically place their ELL students in one of several language proficiency levels. Each level offers suggested activity verbs that support student learning. The use of verb taxonomies for differentiating both the process and product of learning can be helpful to students. Use the verbs most appropriate for the students' proficiencies, as identified below:

## Language Proficiency Levels

**Beginning/Early Intermediate** These students typically read English at 0–2.5 grade level. They may be able to write short simple paragraphs and identify main ideas and story characters. Activity Verbs: tell, point, circle, underline, name, draw, change, describe, and discuss.

**Intermediate** These students read English at 2.6–3.5 grade level and can often write paragraphs and identify "wh" questions (who, what, when, where, and why). They generally have good oral English skills. Activity Verbs: apply, show, classify, modify, explain, solve, and demonstrate.

**Early Advanced** These students are near proficient. They read at 3.6–5.5 grade level and may be fluent in oral English. They often need help with academic and written English. Activity Verbs: analyze, compare, contrast, criticize, examine, create, predict, design, manage, and prepare.

## 2. Is some degree of activity modification necessary to assure achievement and success?

Some activities may not need modification for ELL students, but many will. There are three common ways to modify an activity:

- **Modify the Language Rigor.**
  Change the activity verb to better align with the student's language proficiency.

- **Modify the Independence Rigor.**
  Change the students' degree of independence to align with his/her needed support. For example, an activity that directs the students to complete a task "independently" could be changed to "with a partner."

- **Provide Product Options.**
  Allow students to demonstrate their learning in multiple ways by asking them to write a report or poem; draw; orally explain; or create a game, poster, commercial, video, presentation, song, or cartoon. Students may also teach a lesson, build a model, construct a diagram, or conduct an experiment.

Prior to any activity modification, confirm that all associated vocabulary is clearly understood by all students. Whenever possible, activity modification should be supported by graphic organizers, such as T-charts, webs, sequence, hierarchical, cluster, vocabulary, and data charts.

### Sample Activity Modified for ELL Students

**W** **Writing Strategy**

**Make a List** Ask students to create a list of questions to ask when evaluating an advertisement. Have them create a worksheet that they can fill out when looking at an advertisement that contains their questions and space to answer them.

#### Modified for Beginner/Early Intermediate Students
**ELL** **Writing Strategy**

As a class, ask students to think of questions to ask when evaluating an advertisement. Write each question on the board. Give the class an advertisement to evaluate. Walk students through each question as a class. Write their answers on the board.

#### Modified for Intermediate Students
**ELL** **Writing Strategy**

In small groups, have students list four questions to ask when evaluating an advertisement. Have students answer each question orally to their group as they evaluate an advertisement.

#### Modified for Early Advanced Students
**ELL** **Writing Strategy**

In pairs, have students list four questions to ask when evaluating an advertisement. Have them create a worksheet listing questions they can answer in writing when looking at an advertisement.

# Empower Your Students with the Reading Skills

## How Can I Motivate My Students to Read?

As a teacher, your role is to help students make personal connections in order to answer the question, "Why do I need to learn this?" Emphasize that reading is not only a necessity for work and for life; it can also bring enjoyment and enlightenment.

### Improving or Fine-Tuning Reading Skills Will Help Your Students:

- ◆ Improve grades
- ◆ Read faster and more efficiently
- ◆ Improve their study skills
- ◆ Remember more information accurately
- ◆ Improve their writing

Ask your students, "What role does reading play in your life?" You can open this discussion by modeling examples: I love historical biographies; I read menus and order meals in Spanish; I read magazines and access the Internet to stay up to date on my favorite sports teams.

## The Reading Process

Good reading skills build on one another, overlap, and spiral in much the same way that a winding staircase goes around and around while leading readers to a higher place. The Reading Skills Handbook is designed to help your students find and use the tools to use before, during, and after reading.

### Reading Strategies

- ◆ Identify, understand, and learn new words
- ◆ Understand why you read
- ◆ Take a quick look at the whole text
- ◆ Try to predict what you are about to read
- ◆ Take breaks during reading and ask questions about the text
- ◆ Take notes
- ◆ Keep thinking about what will come next
- ◆ Summarize

## Vocabulary Development

Word identification and vocabulary skills are the building blocks of reading and writing. By learning to use a variety of strategies to build word skills and vocabulary, your students will become stronger readers.

## Use Context to Determine Meaning

The best way for your students to expand and extend vocabulary is to read widely, listen carefully, and participate in a rich variety of discussions. When reading independently, students can often figure out the meanings of new words by looking at their context, or the other words and sentences that surround them.

## Predict a Possible Meaning

Another way to determine the meaning of a word is to take the word apart. If a reader understands the meaning of the **base,** or **root,** part of a word, and knows the meanings of key syllables added either to the beginning or end of the base word, it becomes easy to figure out what the word means.

# They Will *Use* in the Real World

**Word Origins** Since Latin, Greek, and Anglo-Saxon roots are the basis for much of our English vocabulary, having some background in one of these languages can be a useful vocabulary tool. For example, astronomy comes from the Greek root *astro,* which means relating to the stars. *Stellar* also has a meaning referring to stars, but its origin is Latin. Knowing root words in other languages can help readers determine meanings, derivations, and spellings in English.

**Prefixes and Suffixes** A prefix is a word part that can be added to the beginning of a word. For example, the prefix *semi* means half or partial, so *semicircle* means half a circle. A suffix is a word part that can be added to the end of a word. Adding a suffix often changes a word from one part of speech to another.

**Using Dictionaries** A dictionary provides the meaning or meanings of a word. Look at the sample dictionary entry in the student edition Reading Skills Handbook to see what other information it provides.

**Thesauruses and Specialized Reference Books** A thesaurus provides synonyms and often antonyms. It is a useful tool to use to expand vocabulary. Remind students to check the exact definition of the listed words in a dictionary before using a thesaurus. Specialized dictionaries such as the *Barron's Dictionary of Business Terms* or *Black's Law Dictionary* list terms and expressions not commonly included in a general dictionary.

**Glossaries** Many textbooks and technical works contain condensed dictionaries that provide an alphabetical listing of words used in the text and their specific definitions.

**Recognize Word Meanings Across Subjects** Words often have different meanings when used for different purposes. The word *product* may mean one thing in math and another in science. For example:

**Math** After you multiply the two numbers, explain how you arrived at the **product.**

**Science** One **product** of photosynthesis is oxygen.

**Economics** The Gross National **Product** is the total dollar value of goods and services produced by a nation.

# How Can I Help My Students Understand What They Read?

Reading comprehension means understanding— deriving meaning from—what has been read. Using a variety of strategies can help improve comprehension and make reading more interesting and more fun.

## Read for a Reason

To get the greatest benefit from reading, teach students to **establish a purpose for their reading.** In school, some of the reasons for reading are to:
- learn and understand new information
- find specific information
- review before a test
- complete an assignment
- prepare (research) before you write

As reading skills improve, you will notice that your students apply different strategies to fit the different purposes for reading. For example, a person reading for entertainment may read quickly, but reading to gather information or follow directions might require reading more slowly, taking notes, constructing a graphic organizer, or rereading sections of text.

## Draw on Personal Background

Drawing on personal background, or activating prior knowledge, helps students connect their culture and experiences to their reading. Before introducing a new topic, you may want to encourage students to ask:

- What have I heard or read about this topic?
- Do I have any personal experience relating to this topic?

You can also set common background knowledge with discussion before reading. For example, to prepare students to read the novel *A Farewell to Arms,* you might lead a discussion about these common background themes:

- World War I
- Italy (You might ask a student to show Italy on a map.)
- Other Ernest Hemingway titles
- The Nobel Prize in literature

Having this historical background will help to set the scene for students as they read.

***Using a KWL Chart*** A KWL chart is a good device for organizing information gathered before, during, and after reading. In the first column, students list what they already know, then list what they want to know in the middle column. They use the third column to review and assess what they learned. You or your students can add more columns to record places where they found information and places where they can look for more information.

| K (What I already know) | W (What I want to know) | L (What I have learned) |
|---|---|---|
|  |  |  |
|  |  |  |
|  |  |  |

***Adjust Your Reading Speed*** Reading speed is a key factor in how well students understand what they read. Reading speed can vary depending on the purpose for reading.

**Scanning** means running one's eyes quickly over the material to look for words or phrases. Readers scan to find a specific piece of information.

**Skimming** means reading a passage quickly to find its main idea or get an overview. Skim a passage as a preview to determine what the material is about.

**Reading for detail** involves careful reading while paying attention to text structure and monitoring understanding. Readers read for detail to learn concepts, follow complicated directions, or prepare to analyze a text.

# Techniques to Help Students Understand and Remember What They Read

## Preview

Previewing strategies help students begin at a visual level, then drill down to evaluate, predict, draw conclusions, and use contextual clues about what they will read.

### Previewing Strategies

- ◆ Read the title, headings, and subheadings of the selection.
- ◆ Look at the illustrations and notice how the text is organized.
- ◆ Skim the selection. Take a glance at the whole thing.
- ◆ Decide what the main idea might be.
- ◆ Predict what a selection will be about.

## Predict

As students read, they take educated guesses about story events and outcomes. They make predictions before and during reading. This helps them focus their attention on the text and that focus improves understanding.

## Determine the Main Idea

When students look for the main idea, they are looking for the most important statement in a text. Depending on what kind of text they read, the main idea can be located at the very beginning (news stories in newspaper or a magazine) or at the end (scientific research document).

Encourage students to ask these questions to determine the main idea:

- What is each sentence about?
- Is there one sentence that is more important than all the others?
- What idea do the details support or point out?

***Keep track of the text's structure*** (see below). Looking at headers and content structure will give students important clues about the main idea.

## Taking Notes

***Cornell Note-Taking System:*** There are many methods for note taking. The **Cornell Note-Taking System** is a well-known method that can help students organize what they read. Below is a note-taking activity based on the Cornell Note-Taking System.

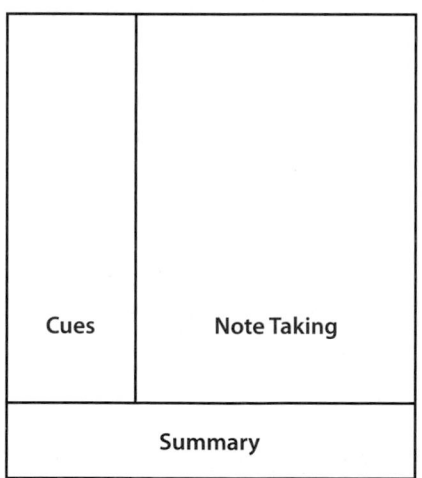

| Cues | Note Taking |
| --- | --- |
| | |
| Summary | |

***Graphic Organizers:*** Using a graphic organizer to retell content in a visual representation will help students remember and retain content. Encourage students to make charts or diagrams to organize what they have read. Some good examples are:

**Venn Diagrams:** A Venn diagram is a good way to organize information in a compare-and-contrast text structure. The outer portions of the circles show how two characters, ideas, or items contrast, or are different, and the overlapping part compares two things, or shows how they are similar.

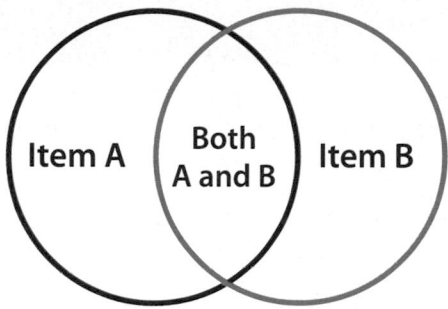

**Flow Charts:** Students can track a sequence of events or cause and effect on a flow chart. Demonstrate how to arrange ideas or events in their logical, sequential order. Then, draw arrows between ideas to indicate how one idea or event flows into another.

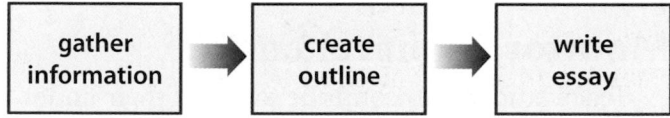

Go to **glencoe.com** for more information about note taking and additional study tools.

## Visualize

Encourage students to try to form a mental picture of scenes, characters, and events as they read. This technique helps them to use the details and descriptions the author gives readers. If students can **visualize** what they read, they will become more interested and will remember the information better.

## Question

Tell students to ask questions about the text while they read. Encourage them to ask about the importance of the sentences they read, how the sentences relate to one another, whether they understand what they just read, and what they think is going to come next.

## Clarify

Encourage students to try these techniques when they don't understand meaning (through questioning):

**What to Do When You Do Not Understand**

- ◆ Reread confusing parts of the text.
- ◆ Diagram (chart) relationships between chunks of text, ideas, and sentences.
- ◆ Look up unfamiliar words.
- ◆ Talk through the text as if explaining it to someone else.
- ◆ Read the passage once more.

## Review

Make sure students take time to stop and review what they have read. Use note-taking outlines or other graphic organizers, charts, or visual aids.

## Monitor Comprehension

Teach students to continue to check their understanding using the following two strategies:

*Summarize* Pause and state the main ideas of the text and the key supporting details. Try to answer the following questions: Who? What? When? Where? Why? How?

*Paraphrase* Pause, close the book, and try to retell what they have just read using their own words. It helps students to retell, or paraphrase reading into their own words.

# Understanding Text Structure

Good writers do not just put together sentences and paragraphs, they organize their writing with a specific purpose in mind. That organization is called text structure. When students understand and follow the structure of a text, it is easier to remember the information they read. There are many ways text may be structured. Each type of structure usually makes use of some specific words. Teach students to watch for these **signal words.** They will help them follow the text's organization (remind them to use these techniques as they write).

## Comparison and Contrast

This structure shows similarities and differences between people, things, and ideas. This is often used to demonstrate that things that seem alike are really different, or vice versa.

**Signal words:** similarly, more, less, on the one hand/on the other hand, in contrast, but, however

## Cause and Effect

Writers use the cause-and-effect structure to explore the reasons for something happening and to examine the results or consequences of events.

**Signal words:** so, because, as a result, therefore, for the following reasons

## Problem and Solution

When writers organize text around the question how, they state a problem and suggest solutions.

**Signal words:** how, help, problem, obstruction, overcome, difficulty, need, attempt, have to, must

## Sequence

Sequencing tells readers in which order to consider thoughts or facts. Examples of sequencing are:

*Chronological order* refers to the order in which events take place.

**Signal words:** first, next, then, finally

*Spatial order* describes the organization of things in space (to describe the placement of objects in a room, for example).

**Signal words:** above, below, behind, next to

*Order of importance* lists things or thoughts from the most important to the least important (or the other way around).

**Signal words:** principal, central, main, important, fundamental

# Thinking about Reading

It is important for students to think about what they are reading to get the most information from a text, to understand the consequences of what the text says, to remember the content, and to form their own opinions about what they read.

## Interpret

Interpreting involves asking, "What is the writer really saying?" and then using what students already know to answer the question.

## Infer

Writers do not always state exactly everything they want readers to understand. They sometimes imply certain information by providing clues and details. To infer involves using reasoning and experience to develop the idea, based on what an author implies, or suggests. What is most important when drawing inferences is to be sure that readers have accurately based their guesses on supporting details from the text. If students cannot point to a place in the selection to help back up an inference, encourage them to rethink that guess.

## Draw Conclusions

A conclusion is a general statement a reader can make and explain using reasoning or supporting details from a text.

## Analyze

To understand persuasive nonfiction (a text that lists facts and opinions to arrive at a conclusion), readers must analyze statements and examples to see if they support the main idea. To understand an informational text, students need to keep track of how the ideas are organized to find the main points.

**Hint:** Have students use graphic organizers and note-taking charts.

# Distinguish Between Facts and Opinions

This is one of the most important reading skills students can learn. A fact is a statement that can be proven. An opinion is what the writer believes. A writer may support opinions with facts, but an opinion cannot be proven. For example:

**Fact:** California produces fruit and other agricultural products.

**Opinion:** California produces the best fruit and agricultural products.

## Evaluate

Remind students that to rely on accurate information, they will need to consider who wrote it and why. Where did the writer get information? Is the information one-sided? Can readers verify the information?

# Reading for Research

To guide students in reading actively to research a topic, encourage them to follow these directions:

- Generate an interesting, relevant, and researchable question.
- Categorize that information.
- Evaluate the information.
- Organize information in a new way for a specific audience.
- Draw conclusions about the original research question.

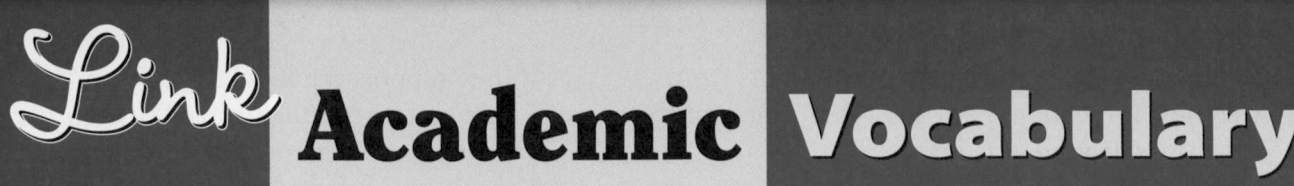

*Link* **Academic** **Vocabulary**

# What Is Academic English?

**by Robin Scarcella, Ph.D.**

Academic English is the language commonly used in business and education. It is the language used in academics, business, and courts of law. It is the type of English used in professional books, including textbooks, and it contains specific linguistic features that are associated with all disciplines. Proficiency in reading and using academic English is strongly related to long-term success in all parts of life.

## What Is an Academic Vocabulary?

By the time they complete elementary school, students should acquire the knowledge they will need to understand academic vocabulary. For example, in academic texts, a full 8% of the words are academic words. A basic 2,000-word vocabulary of high-frequency words makes up 87% of the words. Three percent are technical words that vary depending on the discipline. The remaining 2% are low-frequency words.

## Why Should Students Learn Academic Vocabulary?

English language learners who have mastered a basic 2,000-word vocabulary are ready to acquire the majority of general words found in their texts and on standardized tests.

Knowledge of academic words, combined with continued acquisition of general words, can significantly boost an English learner's comprehension level of academic texts. English learners who learn and practice these words before they graduate from high school are likely to master academic material with more confidence and speed. They waste less time and effort in guessing words than those students who know only the basic 2,000 words that characterize general conversation.

## Academic Vocabulary and Academic English in the Family and Consumer Sciences Classroom

Teachers can provide their students with rich samples of academic vocabulary and help students understand the academic English of their text. To develop academic English, students must have already acquired a large amount of basic proficiency in the grammar of everyday English.

Academic English should be taught within contexts that make sense. Academic English arises not only from a knowledge of linguistic code and cognition but also from social practices in which academic English is used to accomplish communicative goals. The acquisition of academic vocabulary and grammar is necessary to advance the development of academic English.

**Tips for Teaching Academic Vocabulary:**

- **Expose Students to Academic Vocabulary**—Students learn academic vocabulary through use and in reading content. You do not need to call attention to all academic words students are learning because they will acquire them subconsciously.

# to Career & Real-World Content

- **Do Not Correct Students' Mistakes When Using Academic Vocabulary**—All vocabulary understanding and spelling errors are developmental and will disappear once the student reads more.
- **Help Students Decode the Words Themselves**—Once students learn the alphabet, they should be able to decode words. Decoding each word they do not recognize will help them more than trying to focus on sentence structure. Once they can recognize words, they can read authentic texts.
- **Do Not Ignore the English Learner in This Process**—These students can learn academic vocabulary before they are completely fluent in spoken English.
- **Helping Students Build Academic Vocabulary Leads to Broader Learning**—Students who have mastered the basic academic vocabulary are ready to continue acquiring words from the rest of the vocabulary groups. Use the Internet to find lists of appropriate vocabulary words.

## Guidelines for Teaching Academic Vocabulary

There are a number of guidelines that teachers can follow when teaching academic English and vocabulary:

1. Use direct and planned instruction.
2. Employ models that have increasingly difficult language.
3. Focus attention on form by pointing out linguistic features of words.
4. Provide practice opportunities.
5. Motivate student interest and self-confidence.
6. Provide instructional feedback.
7. Use assessment tools on a regular basis.

# Generate the Best Performance

## Assessment

In response to the growing demand for accountability in the classroom, educators must use multiple assessment measures to accurately gauge student performance. In addition to quizzes, tests, essay exams, and standardized tests, assessment today incorporates a variety of performance-based measurements and portfolio opportunities.

Performance assessment activities provide hands-on approaches to learning concepts. Through activities, students are able to actually experience these concepts rather than just reading and listening about them. These types of activities also help students become aware of diverse audiences for their work. Performance assessment tasks are based on what is most essential in the curriculum and what is interesting to the student.

## Performance-Based Assessments

One good way to present a performance assessment is in the form of an open-ended question.
- Journals—Students write from their own perspective on topics that affect their lives.
- Letters—Students write a letter from themselves to friends and family, or another audience.
- Position Paper or Editorial—Students explain a controversial issue and present their own opinions and recommendations, supported with strong evidence and convincing reasons.
- Newspaper—Students write stories from the perspective of a reporter. This could also involve the writing of editorials or letters to the editor.
- Biographies and Autobiographies—Students write about leaders, either from the third person point of view (biography) or from the first person (autobiography).

- Creative Stories—Students integrate family and consumer sciences topics into a piece of fiction.
- Poems and Songs—Students follow the conventions of a particular type of song or poem as they tell about a topic or event.
- Research Reports—Students synthesize information from a variety of sources into a well-developed research report.

## Oral Presentations

Oral presentations allow students to demonstrate their academic and topical literacy in front of an audience. Oral presentations are often group efforts, although this need not be the case.
- Simulations—Students hold simulations of actual events, such as a role play in a scenario.
- Debates—Students debate two or more sides of a policy or issue.
- Interview—Students conduct a mock journalism interview or job interview.
- Oral Reports—Students present the results of research efforts in a lively oral report. This report may be accompanied by visual aids.
- Skits and Plays—Students use specific events or topics as the basis for a play or skit.

## Visual Presentations

Visual presentations allow students to demonstrate their understanding in a variety of visual formats. Visual presentations can be either group or individual projects.
- Museum Exhibit—Students create a rich display of materials around a topic. Typical displays might include models, illustrations, photographs, videos, writings, and presentation software.
- Model—Students make a model to demonstrate or represent a particular process.

# from *Your* Students

- Graph or Chart—Students analyze and represent data in a line graph, bar graph, table, or other chart format.
- Drawing—Students represent an event or period through illustration, including cartoons.
- Posters and Murals—Posters and murals may include maps, time lines, diagrams, illustrations, photographs, and written explanations that reflect students' understanding of the information.
- Videotapes—Students film a video to show a simulation of an event.
- Multimedia Presentation—Students create a computer-generated presentation or slide show containing information and analysis.

## How Are Performance Assessments Scored?

There are a variety of means used to evaluate performance tasks. Some or all of the following methods may be used:

- Scoring Rubrics—A scoring rubric is a set of guidelines for assessing the quality of a process and/or product. It sets out criteria used to distinguish acceptable responses from unacceptable ones, generally on a scale from excellent to poor. Rubrics may be used as guidelines as the students prepare their products. They are also commonly used for peer-to-peer assessment and self-assessment.
- Models of Excellent Work—Teacher-selected models of excellent work concretely illustrate expectations and help students set goals for their own projects.

- Student Self-Assessment—Common methods of self-assessment include ranking work in relation to the model, using a scoring rubric, and writing goals and then evaluating how well the goals have been met. Regardless of which method or methods students use, they should be encouraged to evaluate their behaviors and processes, as well as the finished product.
- Peer or Audience Assessment—Many of the performance tasks target an audience other than the classroom teacher. If possible, the audience of peers should give feedback. Have the class create rubrics for specific projects together.
- Observation—As students carry out their performance tasks, you may want to formally observe them at work. Start by developing a checklist, identifying all the specific behaviors and understandings you expect students to demonstrate. Then observe students as they carry out performance tasks and check off behaviors as you observe them.
- Interviews—As a form of ongoing assessment, you may want to conduct interviews with students, asking them to analyze, explain, and assess their participation in performance tasks. When projects take place over an extended period of time, you can hold periodic interviews as well as exit interviews. In this way, the interview process allows you to gauge the status of the project and to guide the students' efforts along the way.

# Prepare Your Students Well

## Test-Prep Strategies

Students can follow the steps below to prepare for the standardized assessments they are required to take.

- Read About the Test—Students can familiarize themselves with the format, the types of questions, and the amount of time they will have to complete the test. Emphasize that it is very important for students to budget their time during test-taking.

- Review the Content—Consistent study will help students build knowledge and understanding. If there are specific objectives or standards that are tested on the exam, help students review facts or skills.

- Practice—Provide practice, ideally with real tests, to build students' familiarity with the content, format, and timing of the real exam. Students should practice all the types of questions they will encounter on the test.

- Pace—Students should pace themselves differently depending on how the test is administered. As students practice, they should try to increase the number of questions they can answer correctly. If students have trouble with an item, they should mark it and come back to it later.

# and You'll Improve Their Performance

- Analyze Practice Results—Help students improve test-taking performance by analyzing their test-taking strengths and weaknesses. Help students identify what kinds of questions they found most difficult. Look for patterns in errors and tailor instruction to review the appropriate test-taking skills or content.

## Test-Taking Strategies

It's not enough for students to learn facts and concepts. They must be able to show what they know in a variety of test-taking situations.

## Objective Tests

Apply the following strategies to help students do their best on objective tests.

### Multiple-Choice Questions

- Students should read the directions carefully to learn what answer the test requires—the best answer or the right answer. This is especially important when answer choices include "all of the above" or "none of the above."
- Advise students to watch for negative words in the questions, such as not, except, unless, and never.
- Students should try to mentally answer the question before reading the answer choices.
- Students should read all the answer choices and eliminate those that are obviously wrong.

### True/False Questions

- It is important that students read the entire question before answering. For an answer to be true, the entire statement must be true. If one part of a statement is false, the answer should be marked false.
- Remind students to watch for words such as all, never, every, and always. Statements containing these words are often false.

### Matching Questions

- Students should read through both lists before they mark any answers.
- Unless an answer can be used more than once, students should cross out each choice as they use it.
- Using what they know about grammar can help students find the right answer. For instance, when matching a word with its definition, the definition is often the same part of speech (noun, verb, adjective, or adverb) as the word.

## Essay Tests

Essay tests require students to provide thorough and well-organized written responses, in addition to telling what they know. Help students use these strategies on essay tests.

### Read the Question

The key to writing successful essay responses lies in reading and interpreting questions correctly. Teach students to identify and underline key words. This will guide them in understanding what the question asks.

## Plan and Write the Essay

Students should follow the writing process to develop their answer. Encourage students to follow these steps to plan and write their essays.

1. Map out an answer. Make lists, webs, or an outline to plan the response.
2. Decide on an order in which to present the main points.
3. Write an opening statement that directly responds to the essay question.
4. Write the essay. Expand on the opening statement. Support key points with specific facts, details, and reasons.
5. Write a closing statement that brings the main points together.
6. Proofread to check for spelling, grammar, and punctuation.

The table below defines purposes for different writing strategies.

| Writing Strategies | |
|---|---|
| **Analyze** | To analyze means to systematically and critically examine all parts of an issue or event. |
| **Classify or Categorize** | To classify or categorize means to put people, things, or ideas into groups, based on a common set of characteristics. |
| **Compare and Contrast** | To compare is to show how things are similar, or alike. To contrast is to show how things are different. |
| **Describe** | To describe means to present a sketch or impression. Rich details, especially details that appeal to the senses, flesh out a description. |
| **Discuss** | To discuss means to systematically write about all sides of an issue or event. |
| **Evaluate** | To evaluate means to make a judgment and support it with evidence. |
| **Explain** | To explain means to clarify or make plain. |
| **Illustrate** | To illustrate means to provide examples or to show with a picture or other graphic. |
| **Infer** | To infer means to read between the lines or to use knowledge and experience to draw conclusions, make a generalization, or form a prediction. |
| **Justify** | To justify means to prove or to support a position with specific facts and reasons. |
| **Predict** | To predict means to tell what will happen in the future, based on an understanding of prior events and behaviors. |
| **State** | To state means to briefly and concisely present information. |
| **Summarize** | To summarize means to give a brief overview of the main points of an issue or event. |
| **Trace** | To trace means to present the steps or stages in a process or event in sequential or chronological order. |

# Base Your Teaching on Best Practices

## Critical Thinking

One of the factors that determines students' success is their ability to deal with the varied demands of day-to-day life. This requires insightful and ethical decision making, creative problem solving, and collaborating with diverse groups. Thus, teaching critical thinking equips your students with the skills necessary to achieve success.

## The Value of Critical Thinking

Critical thinking is the process of reasonably or logically deciding what to do or believe. It involves the ability to:

- Compare and contrast
- Solve problems
- Make decisions
- Analyze and evaluate
- Synthesize and transfer knowledge
- Engage in metacognition

Critical thinking skills are important for these reasons:

- They help students investigate their own problem-solving mechanisms.
- They help students find creative resolutions.
- They lead students to compare and contrast what they know with unknowns.
- They allow students to make decisions about their own learning while making them aware of their learning processes.

## Cognitive Development

All learning requires thinking. Benjamin Bloom's Taxonomy of the Cognitive Domain is probably the most widely recognized schema of levels of thinking. Each of Bloom's six cognitive categories lists various thinking skills and indicates the types of behavior students are expected to perform to fulfill specific learning goals. See the chart below.

| CATEGORY | GOAL | EXPECTED STUDENT RESPONSE | APPROPRIATE QUESTIONS/PROMPTS |
|---|---|---|---|
| **Knowledge** | Identify and recall information | Define, recognize, recall, identify, label, show, collect, understand, examine | Who...? What...? When...? Where...? How...? Describe.... |
| **Comprehension** | Organize and select facts and ideas | Translate, interpret, explain, describe, summarize, extrapolate | Retell in your own words.... What is the main idea of...? |
| **Application** | Use facts, rules, and principles | Apply, solve, show, experiment, predict | How is...an example of...? How is...related to...? |
| **Analysis** | Separate a whole into component parts | Connect, relate, differentiate, classify, arrange, check, group, distinguish, organize, categorize, detect, compare, infer | Classify...according to.... How does... compare/contrast with...? |
| **Synthesis** | Combine ideas to form a new whole | Produce, propose, design, construct, combine, formulate, compose, plan, hypothesize | What would you predict/infer from...? What might happen if you combined...with...? |
| **Evaluation** | Develop opinions, judgments, or decisions | Appraise, judge, criticize, decide | What do you think about...? Prioritize.... |

## Cooperative Learning

Studies show that students learn faster and retain more information when they are actively involved in the learning process. Cooperative learning is one method that gets students actively involved in learning and at the same time allows for peer teaching.

## Using Cooperative Learning

Your family and consumer sciences course provides many opportunities for students to learn and apply the skills necessary for positive interpersonal relationships. Through the use of cooperative learning, you can offer a structured method of teaching team-building, collaborative social skills, and team decision making while teaching basic concepts—essential skills for understanding families.

## Cooperative Learning in This Text

In *The Developing Child,* students and teachers have a variety of materials to assist with cooperative learning activities. Many of the features and section and chapter assessment activities can be completed in a cooperative learning environment.

## The Benefits of Cooperative Learning

- Cooperative learning emphasizes working toward group goals rather than the traditional emphasis on individual competition and achievement.
- Students discover that not only must they learn the material themselves, but they are also responsible for helping everyone in the group learn the material.
- Cooperative learning increases academic achievement and develops essential social skills.
- Students learn valuable problem-solving, team-building, and creativity skills that transfer to real-world environments and situations.
- People who help each other and work together toward a common goal generally begin to feel more positive about themselves and each other.
- Students have the opportunity to perceive other students as colleagues rather than competitors. As a result, they recognize the value of helping others rather than working competitively.

# Building Relationships to the Real-World

This text helps prepare students to succeed in today's constantly changing world by integrating work skills preparation with course content, academics, and 21st Century Skills. This program also encourages students to develop strong relationships through student organizations, career activities, and community projects.

## School-to-Career

School-to-career programs provide students with real-life experiences which help them to discover the relationship between learning in the classroom and the skills needed to be successful in life and the world of work. An effective school-to-career program involves a close relationship between schools, local businesses, as well as student and professional organizations.

## Student Organizations

As an educator, you can enlist the help of student organizations to encourage, motivate, and teach your students. Organizations provide students with an opportunity to compete in activities that help them to apply their academic knowledge to real scenarios. Most student organizations sponsor annual conferences which allow students the opportunity to build relationships with other students, instructors, and professionals around the country.

### FCCLA

Family, Career and Community Leaders of America (FCCLA) is a dynamic and effective national student organization that helps young men and women become leaders and address important personal, family, work, and societal issues through Family and Consumer Sciences Education. Competitive events, such as the annual STAR Events Program (Students Taking Action with Recognition) allow students from all over the country to compete in events that test their abilities to solve real-life problems that professionals encounter in the workforce.

### SkillsUSA

SkillsUSA is a national organization serving teachers and students who are preparing for careers in technical, skilled, and service occupations. More that 285,000 people join SkillsUSA annually. The annual SkillsUSA Championships showcase the best career and technical students in the nation.

## PURPOSES OF SCHOOL-TO-CAREER PROGRAMS

- To facilitate the creation of a universal, high-quality school-to-career transition system to enable students to identify and pursue paths to progressively more rewarding roles in the workplace

- To utilize workplaces as learning environments in the educational process by making employers and educators joint partners in providing opportunities for students to participate in high-quality, work-based learning

- To promote the formation of partnerships dedicated to linking the worlds of school and work among secondary schools and private and public employers, labor organizations, government, community-based organizations, parents, students, state and local educational agencies, and training and human services agencies

- To increase knowledge and improve student skills by integrating academic and occupational learning and building links between secondary and postsecondary educational institutions

- To motivate all students to stay in or return to school and strive to continue their education in postsecondary institutions

- To expose students to a broad array of career opportunities and facilitate the selection of major areas of study, based on individual interests, goals, and abilities

# Technology

Technology affects how all people work, interact, and live. Technology will affect your students in the real world. For example, they may keep records using a computer or apply for a job over the Internet. It will also affect your students as consumers. An increasing number of people market, buy, and sell products on the Web. It is critical that your students become familiar and comfortable with technology now in order to prepare for successful careers.

## Activities

*The Developing Child* helps you integrate technology into your teaching with technology-based activities:

- Features and assessments provide a link to the *The Developing Child* Online Learning Center (OLC) at **glencoe.com** to assist students in finding answers and to further research the topic or find a project.

- The section-opening **Reading Guide** provides a link to the OLC for students to download the printable graphic organizer for each section.
- Each section **After You Read** review sends students to the OLC to check their answers.
- The **Careers With Children** feature sends students to the OLC for helpful links. **Math in Action** and **Science in Action** send the student to the OLC for more math or science practice.
- Each **Real-World Skills** section in the Chapter Review and Applications assessment contains at least one technology application. Each **Net Connection** assessment activity sends students to the OLC for helpful links and an extension activity.
- Students can use assessment rubrics on the OLC to self-evaluate their thematic projects.

## Using the Internet Effectively

Give these tips to your students to help them use the Internet effectively in the classroom:

- Look for sites that are created by the government or universities (their URLs typically end in .gov or .edu). These are reliable sites with factual integrity and stability.
- Find out who created the site. If the purpose and creator of the Web site are unclear, its content may be unreliable.
- Use multiple search engines when looking for information on a topic. This will call up as many of the pertinent sites as possible.
- Combine Internet research with traditional research methods. Have students ask librarians and experts for information and sources. Use books and magazines.

# Ethics

Helping students learn about ethical behavior and how to consider the effects of a decision before it is made are important life skills for your students preparing for the real world.

## The Benefits of Integrating Ethics

The goal of teaching ethical decision-making skills is not to teach values. It is to help students clarify their ethical beliefs and learn how to evaluate ethical situations. Make your classroom a risk-free environment in which students can discuss issues and make ethical decisions. Students need to learn how to evaluate their actions and to ask questions such as, "Will I be proud of myself if I take this action?" and "Would I want others to know about my actions?"

## The Ethical Decision Model

Your students will learn to analyze ethical situations better if they have a model to use in deliberating the issues that helps them to understand how a decision can affect others. Several decision models exist, but the basic steps for an ethical decision model are as follows:

1. Determine the ethical issue.
2. Identify the actions for handling the situation.
3. Identify the people affected by the situation.
4. Analyze how the situation affects the people involved.
5. Decide which of the actions to take.

### Classroom Strategies

*The Developing Child* provides real-world situations that sometimes pose ethical conundrums. These can be catalysts for lively classroom discussion.

In addition, you might lead discussion about topical ethics issues or have students bring in newspaper or magazine articles that suggest ethical dilemmas. Have students analyze the situations in class and, perhaps, write short reports on their analyses and conclusions. Some formats, such as learning groups, role plays, and debates, are particularly well suited to teaching students about ethics.

### Cooperative Learning Groups

Small groups of students are especially well suited to discuss cases and share their ideas about ethical issues. Divide students into groups of four or five. Observe groups and encourage all students to participate. Allow each group to reach its own conclusions, and then ask a member of each group to share the group's ideas with the class.

### Role Plays and Debates

Have your students role play ethical situations, using their own ideas about how to respond to a given situation. Discuss class responses to the role-play, guiding students in using the ethical decision model. Set up debate teams to present different sides of an ethical issue.

# Diversity

*The Developing Child* is designed to help students recognize and discuss issues of cultural diversity. During class activities, you may also find it appropriate to integrate questions related to cultural diversity. For example, you might expand a class discussion by asking:

- Would your response change if a classmate did not speak the same native language as you speak? If so, how?
- Would you speak to your classmate differently if his or her ethnic background were different from yours?
- Would your decision change if your classmate were a male or female? From your own ethnic background? From a different background? Why?

## Integrating Cultural Diversity

Your students will be faced with a diverse world, meeting people of many different cultures. Cultural knowledge may be the difference between success and failure in our global economy. For students to become productive and responsible citizens, they must be open to cultural differences.

As students learn about skills needed to be successful, they should keep in mind the wide diversity of the people they are likely to encounter in every aspect of their working and personal lives. In the classroom and in one-on-one conferences, you can help your students consider the diversity of the U.S. population, not only in terms of ethnicity, but also in terms of customs, attitudes, religious beliefs, language backgrounds, and physical capabilities. High school students need to understand that ability and success are not related to skin color or gender.

# Multicultural Education

Multicultural education incorporates the idea that all students—regardless of their gender and social class, and their ethnic, racial, or cultural characteristics—should have an equal opportunity to learn in school. Learning about other cultures concurrently with their own culture helps students recognize similarities and appreciate differences, without perceiving inferiority or superiority of one or the other. To foster cultural awareness:

- Recognize that all students are unique, having special talents and abilities.
- Promote uniqueness and diversity as positive traits.
- Know, appreciate, and respect the cultural backgrounds of your students.
- Use authentic situations to provide cultural learning and understanding.
- Make sure people of all cultures are represented fairly and accurately.
- Make sure that historical information is accurate and nondiscriminatory.
- Make sure that materials do not include stereotypical roles.
- Make sure there is gender equity.
- Welcome family and community involvement.
- Use current news stories, advertisements, or other forms of media to call students' attention to cultural differences that influence businesses, communities, and families.

# Table of Contents

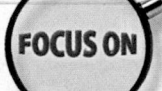 **FOCUS ON** **Reading Strategies**
In each section, look for these reading strategies:

- **Before You Read**
- **Graphic Organizer**
- **As You Read**
- **Reading Check**
- **After You Read**

# Table of Contents

**FOCUS ON** **Academic Success**
To help you succeed in your
classes and on tests, look
for these academic skills:

- Reading Guides
- Writing Tips
- Math Concepts and Hints
- Financial Literacy
- Science in Action

# Table of Contents

**FOCUS ON** Visuals
Images help you learn key ideas. Answer the questions for all:

- **Unit and Chapter Openers**
- **Photos and Captions**
- **Figures and Tables**

# Table of Contents

**FOCUS ON** **Project-Based Learning**
Projects throughout this book can help you use your skills in real-life situations:

- **Real-World Scenarios**
- **Step-by-Step Instructions**
- **Independent and Group Activities**

# Table of Contents

**FOCUS ON** Assessment
Look for review questions and activities to help you remember important topics.

- Reading Checks
- Section Reviews
- Chapter Reviews
- Unit Thematic Projects

# Table of Contents

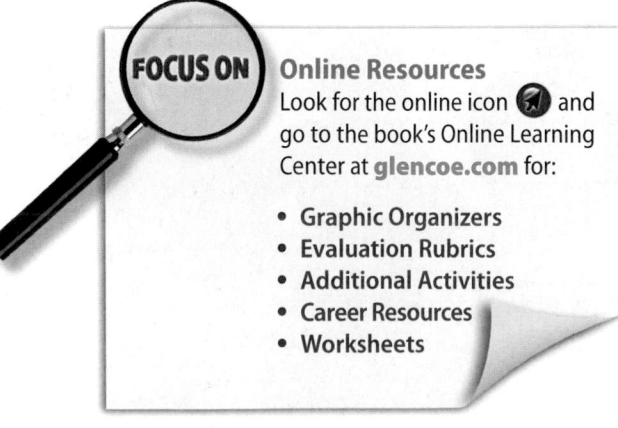

**FOCUS ON**

**Online Resources**
Look for the online icon and go to the book's Online Learning Center at **glencoe.com** for:

- Graphic Organizers
- Evaluation Rubrics
- Additional Activities
- Career Resources
- Worksheets

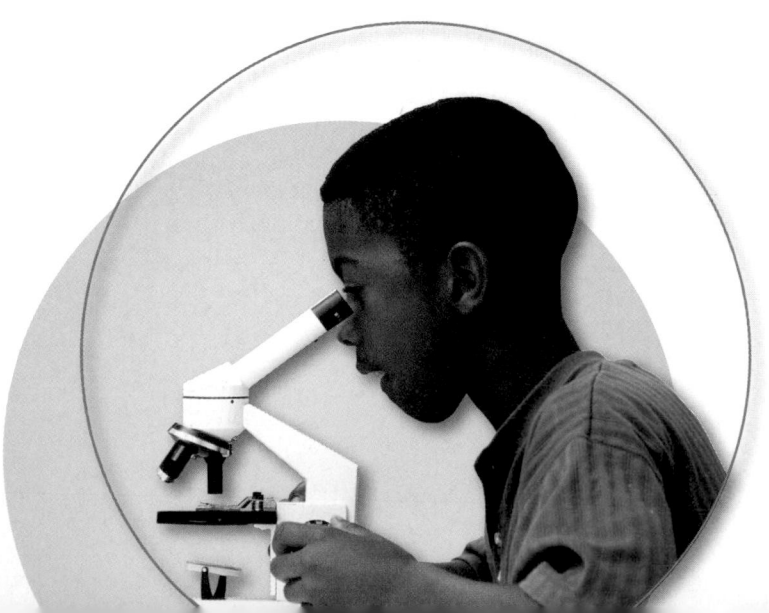

# Table of Contents

# Academic Skills for Life!

How much do you think child care will cost? Do you know why someone has brown hair instead of red hair? How does human contact affect brain development? These academic features will help you succeed in school, on tests, and with life!

## *Math* in Action

## *Science* in Action

## THE DEVELOPING BRAIN

# The Importance of Play

Various forms of play promote learning at each stage of development. It is important to keep children safe while encouraging appropriate play. These features help teach you how!

## Learning Through PLAY

## SAFE CHILD HEALTHY CHILD

## Can You Relate?

Put yourself in someone else's shoes and use what you know to offer advice about real-world problems. Be thoughtful and give your informed opinion.

## What Would You Do?

# Check Out These Skills You Can Use!

Learn basic skills that you can use as a parent, friend, or professional to care for and nurture children. Also learn how special needs can affect child development and child care.

## Parenting Skills

## RESPOND TO SPECIAL NEEDS

# Learn About Children Around the World

Ever wonder how people in other countries are just like you? How are they different? This feature gives you a peek at life in various cultures.

## CULTURE MATTERS

# What Do You Want to Be?

What career options are open to you? What skills will you need to succeed in your career? Learn how to reach your goals to work with children.

**Careers With Children**

# To the Student

# Understand the Development of Children

Successful readers first set a purpose for reading. *The Developing Child* teaches skills you need to understand how children grow and develop, physically, socially, emotionally, and intellectually. Think about why you are reading this book. Use the Unit Opener to help you set a reading purpose and understand what you will learn in each unit. Consider how you might be able to use what you learn in your own life.

**Read the Chapter Titles** to find out what the topics will be.

**Preview the Thematic Project** at the end of the unit. A preview lets you know what is to come. Use the preview to think about how what you are learning applies to the project.

## Unit 3
## The Baby's First Year

**Chapter 7** Physical Development of Infants

**Chapter 8** Emotional and Social Development of Infants

**Chapter 9** Intellectual Development of Infants

### Unit Thematic Project Preview

**Raising a Healthy Baby**

In this unit you will learn how infants grow and develop during their first twelve months. You will also learn about the important role of parents and caregivers in a baby's physical and mental health. In your unit thematic project you will explore how caregivers can support a baby's healthy growth and development.

#### My Journal

**Healthy Development** Write a journal entry about one of the topics below. This will help you prepare for the project at the end of this unit.

- How can a parent or caregiver help a baby grow up physically healthy?
- How can a parent or caregiver help a baby develop trusting relationships with adults and siblings?
- How can a parent or caregiver help a baby develop language skills?

191

**↑ Explore the Photo**
Parents play a large role in ensuring their baby's health and well-being. *How might a child's early relationships influence his relationships later in life?*

190

**Use the Photo** to Predict what the unit will be about. Answer questions to help focus on unit topics.

**Practice Your Writing** in a personal journal. Your writing will help you prepare for the project at the end of the unit.

## Close the Unit

# What Did You Learn About Child Development?

Every unit ends with a Thematic Project that lets you explore an important issue from the unit. To complete each project, you will make decisions, do research, connect to your community, create a visual, and present your project.

**Read the Project Assignment** and numbered steps. The assignment explains what you will need to do.

**Follow the Project Checklist** to make sure that you have done everything you need to complete your thematic project.

---

### Unit Thematic Project

## Raise a Healthy Baby

In this unit, you have learned that a child's first year is a time of great change. Parents and caregivers play a very important role in helping the child grow and develop. In this project, you will research a specific area of infant growth and development and explore what parents and caregivers can do to support a baby in this area.

### My Journal

If you completed the journal entry from page 193, refer to it to see if your thoughts have changed after reading the unit.

#### Project Assignment

In this project, you will:
- Choose a feature of infant growth and development that interests you.
- Conduct research about the topic you have chosen.
- Interview a parent or child care professional about your topic.
- Prepare a presentation to share what you have learned with your class.

#### Child Development Skills Behind the Project

- Evaluate parenting roles and responsibilities.
- Identify a child's physical, emotional, and intellectual needs.
- Describe the growth and development of infants.

#### Academic Skills

**English Language Arts Standards**

NCTE 4 Use written language to communicate effectively.

NCTE 7 Conduct research and gather, evaluate, and synthesize data to communicate discoveries.

286 Unit 3 The Baby's First Year

#### Step 1 Choose and Research Your Topic

The topics below are examples of areas in which infants grow and develop over their first year. Choose one of these topics, or select another topic approved by your teacher. Research its importance to healthy growth and development.
- Language skills
- Motor skills
- Development of emotions
- Vision
- Eating and sleeping
- Attachment to caregivers
- Relating to strangers
- Relating to other children

Write a summary of your research to:
- **Describe** milestones of infant growth or development in the chosen area.
- **Explain** how parents or caregivers can foster an infant's health in this area.
- **Identify** possible problems or disorders that can occur and how caregivers can identify and respond to them.

#### Step 2 Plan Your Interview

Use the results of your research to write a list of interview questions about your chosen topic to ask a parent or child care professional in your community.

**Writing Skills**
★ Use complete sentences.
★ Use correct spelling and grammar.
★ Organize your interview questions in the order you want to ask them.

#### Step 3 Connect with Your Community

Identify a child care professional or parent of a young child in your community who works with infants and toddlers. Conduct your interview using the questions you prepared in Step 2. Take notes during the interview and write a summary of the interview.

**Interviewing Skills**
★ Record interview responses and take notes.
★ Listen attentively.
★ Write in complete sentences and use correct spelling and grammar when you transcribe your notes.

#### Step 4 Share What You Have Learned

Use the Unit Thematic Project Checklist to plan and give an oral report to share what you have learned with your classmates.

**Speaking Skills**
★ Speak clearly and concisely.
★ Be sensitive to the needs of your audience.
★ Use standard English to communicate.

#### Step 5 Evaluate Your Child Development Skills and Academic Skills

Your project will be evaluated based on:
- Content and organization of your information.
- Proper use of standard English.
- Mechanics—presentation and neatness.
- Speaking and listening skills.

 **Evaluation Rubric** Go to this book's Online Learning Center at glencoe.com for a rubric.

#### Unit Thematic Project Checklist

| | |
|---|---|
| **Plan** | ✓ Select and research your topic and summarize your findings. <br> ✓ Plan and write your interview questions. <br> ✓ Interview a parent or child care professional and write a summary of what you learned. |
| **Present** | ✓ Make a presentation to the class to discuss the results of your research and your interview. <br> ✓ Invite students to ask any questions. Answer these questions. <br> ✓ When students ask you questions, demonstrate in your answers that you respect their perspectives. <br> ✓ Turn in the summary of your research, your interview questions, and the summary of the interview to your teacher. |
| **Academic Skills** | ✓ Communicate effectively. <br> ✓ Be sensitive to the needs of different audiences. <br> ✓ Adapt and modify language to suit different purposes. |

Unit 3 The Baby's First Year 287

---

**Evaluate Your Work** A rubric is a scoring tool that lists the project criteria. You can find the Evaluation Rubric at the book's Online Learning Center at **glencoe.com**.

**Apply Skills** that are behind the project. See what child development and academic skills you will use.

## Begin the Chapter

# What Is the Chapter All About?

Use the activities in the opener to help you connect what you already know to chapter topics. Think about the people, places, and events in your own life. Are there any similarities with those in your textbook?

**Read the Chapter Objectives** to preview the key ideas you will learn. Keep these in mind as you read the chapter.

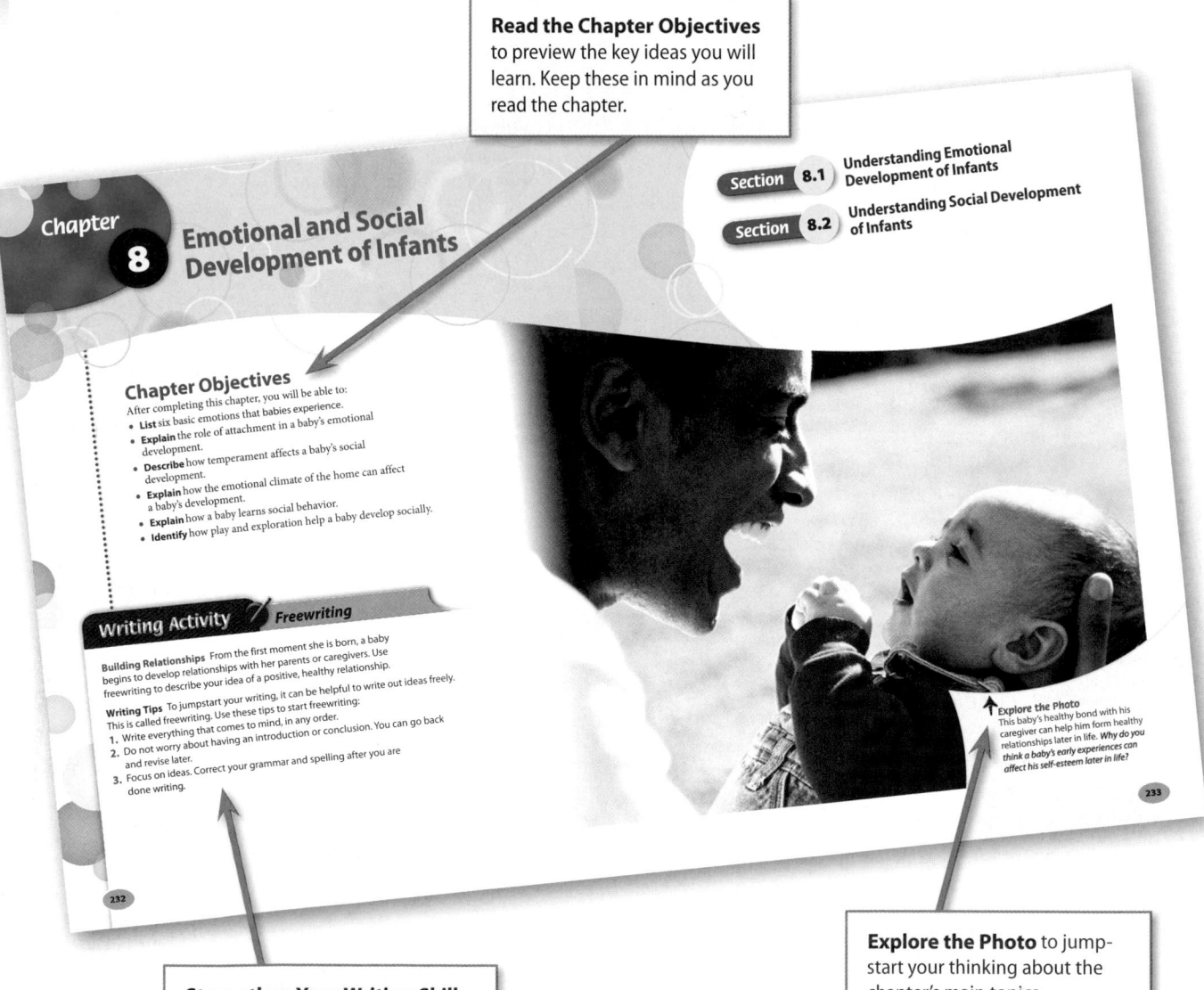

**Section 8.1** Understanding Emotional Development of Infants

**Section 8.2** Understanding Social Development of Infants

**Chapter 8** Emotional and Social Development of Infants

### Chapter Objectives

After completing this chapter, you will be able to:

- **List** six basic emotions that babies experience.
- **Explain** the role of attachment in a baby's emotional development.
- **Describe** how temperament affects a baby's social development.
- **Explain** how the emotional climate of the home can affect a baby's development.
- **Explain** how a baby learns social behavior.
- **Identify** how play and exploration help a baby develop socially.

### Writing Activity — Freewriting

**Building Relationships** From the first moment she is born, a baby begins to develop relationships with her parents or caregivers. Use freewriting to describe your idea of a positive, healthy relationship.

**Writing Tips** To jumpstart your writing, it can be helpful to write out ideas freely. This is called freewriting. Use these tips to start freewriting:

1. Write everything that comes to mind, in any order.
2. Do not worry about having an introduction or conclusion. You can go back and revise later.
3. Focus on ideas. Correct your grammar and spelling after you are done writing.

**Explore the Photo** This baby's healthy bond with his caregiver can help him form healthy relationships later in life. *Why do you think a baby's early experiences can affect his self-esteem later in life?*

232

233

**Strengthen Your Writing Skills** Use the writing tips to continue to develop your writing.

**Explore the Photo** to jump-start your thinking about the chapter's main topics.

## Review the Chapter

# Make Sure You Know and Understand the Concepts

Review what you learned in the chapter and see how this learning applies to your other subjects and other real-world situations.

**Read the Chapter Summary** to review the most important ideas that you should have learned in this chapter.

**Review Vocabulary and Key Concepts** to check your recall of important ideas.

**Critical Thinking** takes your knowledge of the chapter further. If you have difficulty answering these questions, go back and reread the related parts of the chapter.

**Practice Academic Skills** and connect what you learned to your knowledge of language arts, math, science, and social studies.

**Practice Your Observation Skills** by completing these activities in real-life scenarios.

**Apply Real-World Skills** to situations that you might find in your day-to-day life.

**Find More Activities Online** at this book's Online Learning Center at **glencoe.com**.

**Succeed on Tests** with test-taking tips and practice questions.

---

### Chapter 8 — Review and Applications

## Chapter Summary

Emotional development is the process of learning to recognize and express feelings and to establish a personal identity. Caregivers can help shape babies' emotional development by providing consistent, responsive, and loving care. Babies' unique temperaments and the emotional climate of the home also influence their emotional development. Social development is the process of learning how to interact and express oneself with others. Babies learn social behavior by watching and interacting with others. One normal sign of social development is stranger anxiety. Babies learn about the world by playing and exploring.

### Vocabulary Review

1. Use each of these content and academic vocabulary words in a sentence.

**Content Vocabulary**
◇ emotional development (p. 235)
◇ emotion (p. 235)
◇ colic (p. 238)
◇ reflux (p. 238)
◇ attachment (p. 239)
◇ failure to thrive (p. 240)
◇ temperament (p. 240)
◇ social development (p. 245)
◇ cause and effect (p. 245)
◇ model (p. 245)
◇ stranger anxiety (p. 247)
◇ play environment (p. 249)

**Academic Vocabulary**
■ crucial (p. 239)
■ hinder (p. 243)
■ lead (p. 248)
■ motivate (p. 250)

### Review Key Concepts

2. **List** six basic emotions that babies experience.
3. **Explain** the role of attachment in a baby's emotional development.
4. **Describe** how temperament affects a baby's social development.
5. **Explain** how the emotional climate of the home can affect a baby's development.
6. **Explain** how a baby learns social behavior.
7. **Identify** how play and exploration help a baby develop socially.

### Critical Thinking

8. **Analyze** A baby builds attachment through touch, consistent care, and communication. Do you think a baby could still bond with a parent if one of these elements were missing? Explain your opinion.
9. **Synthesize** Stranger anxiety and attachment to a caregiver develop at around the same time. How might these two developments be related?
10. **Predict** What combination of temperament traits might help a baby cope with a stressful family environment? What combination of traits might make a baby less able to cope with a stressful —

---

### Chapter 8 — Review and Applications

#### Family & Community Connection

11. **Interview a Single Parent** Interview a single parent about how he or she copes with negative emotions, such as stress, frustration, anger, and fear. What strategies does he or she have for resolving negative emotions? Who does he or she rely on for emotional support? How does he or she try to create a positive emotional climate in the home? Take notes during your interview, and share what you learned with the class.

#### Health Skills

12. **Research Infant Massage** Go online to research massage techniques for babies. What is infant massage? What are the benefits? How is it performed? Are there any times when massage should not be used on babies? Write a summary of what you learned and state whether you would be interested in trying infant massage.

#### Real-World Skills

| | |
|---|---|
| **Problem-Solving Skills** | 14. **Generate Solutions** What would you do to care for a crying baby? Explain in a report how you would identify the cause of the crying and what strategies you would use to comfort the baby. Also explain what you would do if you were unable to comfort the baby. |
| **Technology Skills** | 15. **Create a Table** Research three developmental disabilities that may affect a baby's social and emotional development. Use word-processing software to create a table that defines each disability and explains how it is diagnosed and treated. |
| **Financial Literacy Skills** | 16. **Shop for a Safe Play Environment** Imagine that you have $150 to create a safe play environment for your three-month-old baby. You will need two baby gates, a play mat, and age-appropriate toys. Conduct research to comparison shop for the best quality and prices. How many toys can you buy and stay within your budget? Create a list of the products you would buy, identifying the source or place of purchase and the prices. |

#### Observation Skills

13. **Observe Babies at Play** Work with your teacher to arrange to observe a baby in a home or at a child care center. Note that an infant six months or older will probably be much more active than a baby five months or younger.

**Procedure** Pay attention to how the baby explores objects in the environment as well as how the baby interacts with the caregivers during playtime.

**Analysis** Write a report to describe your observations. Include an analysis of the physical, social, and emotional skills you think the baby was learning through play.

*NSES 1 Develop an understanding of science unifying concepts and processes: evidence, models, and explanations.*

#### Academic Skills

**English Language Arts**

17. **Reflect on Your Skills** Parents need many emotional and social skills, such as self-control, empathy, patience, responsibility, caring, and kindness. List and describe the skills that a parent should have in order to care for a baby's emotional and social needs. Which of these skills do you have? Which could you develop further? Summarize your thoughts in a one-page essay.

*NCTE 4 Use written language to communicate effectively.*

**Mathematics**

18. **Calculate Food Costs** According to the United States Department of Agriculture, the average married couple will spend about $200,000 to raise a child to the age of 17. If food is about 18% of this total, how much does the average couple spend on food for a child through age 17?

**Math Concept** *Multiply Decimals by Whole Numbers* A percent is a ratio that compares a number to 100.

**Starting Hint** Rewrite the percent (18%) as a fraction with a denominator of 100. Convert the fraction to a decimal. Multiply this decimal by the total amount ($200,000).

For math help, go to the Math Appendix at the back of the book.

*NCTM Number and Operations Understand numbers, ways of representing numbers, relationships among numbers, and number systems.*

**Science**

19. **Design an Experiment** The scientific method is a way to answer questions. You must collect information, form a hypothesis, study the results, and draw conclusions that other scientists can test. One hypothesis might read: Two-month-old babies can identify the emotions they see on their mothers' faces.

**Procedure** Describe an experiment that would test this hypothesis.

**Analysis** Write a speech to explain how your experiment would prove whether this hypothesis is correct or incorrect.

*NSES A Develop abilities necessary to do scientific inquiry, understandings about scientific inquiry.*

#### Standardized Test Practice

**READING COMPREHENSION**

Read the passage, then answer the question.

A baby is playing at home when a stranger walks by the window and waves. Confused, the baby looks at his mother, who seems delighted. She waves back at the passerby and smiles. The baby is reassured and returns to playing. This baby has just demonstrated social referencing, the process of assessing other people's facial expressions to help decide how to react to a new situation.

20. According to the passage, social referencing:
a. only occurs in babies.
b. involves facial expressions.
c. is a self-comforting technique.
d. usually happens when strangers are present.

**Test-Taking Tip** Read the passage carefully, noting key statements as you go. Answer the questions based only on what you just read in the passage, not based on your previous knowledge.

**Additional Activities** For additional activities, go to this book's Online Learning Center at glencoe.com.

252 Chapter 8 Emotional and Social Development of Infants

## Begin the Section

# Prepare with Reading Guides and Study Tools

Use the reading guide at the beginning of each section to preview what you will learn in the section. See if you can predict events or outcomes by using clues and information that you already know.

**Check Vocabulary** lists for words you do not know. You can look them up in the glossary before you read the section.

## Section 8.1 Understanding Emotional Development of Infants

### Reading Guide

**Before You Read**

**Preview** Look at each photo in this section and read the photo captions. Write one or two sentences explaining what you think the section will be about.

**Use Before You Read Tips** to help you understand the section content.

#### Read to Learn
**Key Concepts**
- **List** six basic emotions that babies experience.
- **Explain** the role of attachment in a baby's emotional development.
- **Describe** how temperament affects a baby's social development.
- **Explain** how the emotional climate of the home can affect a baby's development.

**Main Idea**
Caregivers play a large role in babies' emotional development, helping them learn to express feelings and develop a personal identity.

**Content Vocabulary**
◇ emotional development
◇ emotion
◇ colic
◇ reflux
◇ attachment
◇ failure to thrive
◇ temperament

**Academic Vocabulary**
You will find these words in your reading and on your tests. Use the glossary to look up their definitions if necessary.
■ crucial
■ hinder

**Graphic Organizer**
As you read, list things a caregiver can do to promote a baby's healthy emotional development. Use a chart like the one shown to help organize your information.

| Healthy Emotional Development |
|---|
| 1. |
| 2. |
| 3. |
| 4. |

**Graphic Organizer** Go to this book's Online Learning Center at **glencoe.com** to print out this graphic organizer.

**Look for Academic Standards** throughout the text. You can apply what you learn to other subjects.

**Academic Standards** . . . . . . . . . . . . . . . . . .

**English Language Arts**
**NCTE 4** Use written language to communicate effectively.

**Social Studies**
**NCSS I C Culture** Apply an understanding of culture as an integrated whole that explains the functions and interactions of behavior patterns.

**NCSS IV C Individual Development and Identity** Describe influences that contribute to the development of a sense of self.

**NCTE** National Council of Teachers of English
**NCTM** National Council of Teachers of Mathematics

**NSES** National Science Education Standards
**NCSS** National Council for the Social Studies

234  Chapter 8  Emotional and Social Development of Infants

**Take Notes and Study** with graphic organizers. These help you find and identify relationships in the information you read.

## Review the Section

# Check Your Comprehension with Self-Assessments

After you read, use the section closer to check your understanding. Make sure that you can answer the questions in your own words before moving on in the text.

### Emotional Climate of the Home

Babies are very sensitive to the feelings of people around them. Long before they know the meanings of words, they are influenced by adults' emotions, tone of voice, gestures, and facial expressions. Worried or angry caregivers are likely to be tense in handling their babies. Babies sense these feelings and can become irritable and anxious.

Every family has ups and downs, and a baby adapts to them. It is normal for caregivers to feel occasional frustration and anger toward a beloved child. However, a baby needs to feel that affection and caring are the basis of the family's interactions. Feelings of bitterness, mistrust, and anger can **hinder**, or delay, an infant's emotional development.

Handling unwanted feelings, such as anger, frustration, and sadness, is a challenge for every parent and caregiver. It can be an even greater challenge for single parents. Single parents have no other adult to share the work or the worries, and they may feel alone and overwhelmed.

It is important for all parents to find ways of releasing negative feelings away from their children. Dealing with challenging feelings can help parents find the patience to create a caring environment. Every parent needs someone who can give them emotional support.

### Section 8.1 — After You Read

**Review Key Concepts**

1. **List** the most important influences on a child's emotional development.
2. **Explain** ways to build attachment to support a baby's emotional development.
3. **Describe** ways to resolve temperament conflicts.
4. **Explain** why it is important for parents to *not* express negative feelings around their children.

**Practice Academic Skills**

**English Language Arts**

5. Describe your temperament using the nine temperament traits described in the section. Now imagine that you are caring for a child whose temperament is very different from yours. Write a letter to a friend describing how this could be challenging and what strategies you might use to handle the challenge.

> **NCTE 4** Use written language to communicate effectively.

**Social Studies**

6. Temperament, family, culture, and institutions such as schools and churches are important influences on your identity. You are also influenced by your *peers*, or people your same age. Write a report describing the people, places, and things that you think have influenced your identity since you were a baby, and why.

> **NCSS IV C** Describe influences that contribute to the development of a sense of self.

**Check Your Answers** Check your answers at this book's Online Learning Center at **glencoe.com**.

243

Section 8.1 Understanding Emotional Development of Infants

---

**Verify Your Understanding** of key concepts in the section.

**Practice Academic Skills** with these cross-curricular activities.

**Check Your Answers** online at this book's Online Learning Center at **glencoe.com**.

# As You Read | Use Reading Strategies and Visuals to Study Effectively

In addition to the reading guide at the beginning of each section, there are lots of reading strategies to help you comprehend the text.

**Skim the Headings** to help identify the main idea and supporting details.

## Emotions and Emotional Development

Emotional and social development begin at birth and continue throughout life. They are as important as physical development to becoming a healthy and happy adult.

**Emotional development** is the process of learning to recognize and express feelings and to establish a personal identity. A personal identity is a sense of being a unique individual. A child who experiences healthy emotional development will be self-confident. He or she will be able to handle stress and will have empathy for others.

The most important influences on a child's emotional development are the bond between the caregiver and the child, the temperament of the child, and the atmosphere of the home.

### Emotions in Infancy

We are all born with the ability to experience emotions. An **emotion** is a feeling response to the world around us. Even newborns can basic emotions such as contentment and

distress. Emotions grow more complex with age. **Figure 8.1** on page 6 shows the development of some basic emotions during a child's first year.

### Learning Emotions Through Interaction

Parents and caregivers play a large role in shaping a baby's emotions. Parents can encourage positive emotions. Parents can also help infants cope with negative emotions. Returning a baby's smile, for example, encourages his joyful expression. Rocking a frightened baby teaches her to become calm again after a scary experience.

Babies also learn from their caregivers to learn how to react to situations. A baby whose caregiver is often joyful may learn to approach life with happiness and interest. A baby whose caregiver is often anxious may learn to approach life with fear.

### Emotions and Crying

Infants do not have words so they show many of their needs and emotions through crying. At around two months of age, babies start to vary their cries to express different feelings.

**Keep a Vocabulary Journal** Write down vocabulary words then find definitions in the text and in the glossary at the back of the book.

**Healthy Emotional Development**
Touch can help an infant develop healthy emotions. Why is physical touch important to emotional development?

Section 8.1   Understanding Emotional Development of Infants   **235**

**Reading Checks** let you pause to respond to what you have read.

a child's specific traits. A child should not be punished for a temperament trait. If a child is shy, try holding him when you introduce him to someone new. Give him time to warm up to the new person, instead of handing him to the new person right away.

Caregivers have their own temperaments, too. One of a caregiver's responsibilities is to adapt to the temperament of the child, even if they are different. Look for positive ways to adapt to these differences. Suppose that you have a low energy level, but your infant is constantly on the move. You should provide safe opportunities for energetic play. Enjoy a trip to the park or dancing to music. Avoid activities that require the child to sit a lot. Can you think of other strategies you might try?

**Reading Check   Analyze** Why is it important to understand a baby's temperament?

**Examine Visuals** to reinforce content. Answer the questions so you can better discuss topics in the section.

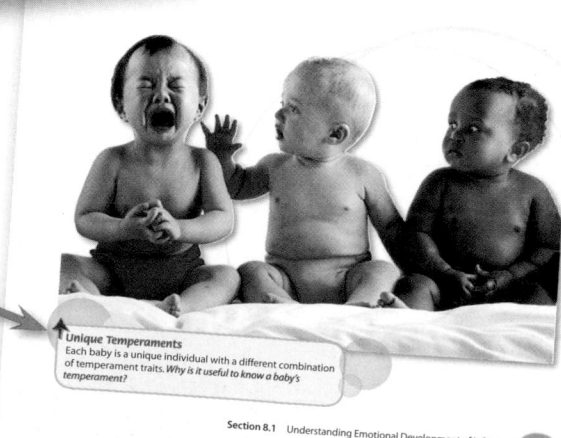

**Unique Temperaments**
Each baby is a unique individual with a different combination of temperament traits. Why is it useful to know a baby's temperament?

Section 8.1   Understanding Emotional Development of Infants   **241**

## Study with Features

# Skills You Can Really Use at School and in Life!

As you read, look for feature boxes throughout each chapter. These features build skills that relate to other academic subjects and prepare you for life on your own.

**Make Math Simple**
You use math every day—even if it is just counting money to buy a snack. Use starting hints to break down math problems and solve them step by step.

**Unlock Mysteries of Brain Development** These short excerpts on brain development provide additional information at the point of use.

### Science in Action

**Technology and the Family**
In today's society, we have many technological inventions available for work, home, and entertainment. This includes newer inventions such as cell phones, MP3 players, and video games. Technology also includes older technology such as television and computers. How might these inventions affect a family?

**Procedure**
Create a survey that lists five technological inventions and asks how much time people feel they spend using these inventions. Ask if they think using these technologies takes away from their family time. Distribute the survey to at least ten people of various ages.

**Analysis**
Find the average amount of time each invention is used. Then find the overall average. Chart your findings in a bar graph. Write a summary of your research that explains the results and describes people's opinions about whether these technologies are taking away from family time.

**NSES Content Standard F** Develop understanding of science and technology in local, national, and global challenges.

### Math in Action

**Salary Requirements**
Susan earns $8.50 per hour and works 40 hours a week. She is planning for her and Robert's newborn by calculating expected expenses. Her research results in an approximate expense list for one month:

Diapers: $80
Formula: $75
Clothes: $75
Day Care: $400

How much per month does Susan make? What is the total monthly expense of the newborn? What percentage of Susan's salary will go towards the baby?

**Math Concept** **Rates and Percents** A rate is a ratio of two measurements having different kinds of units, such as dollars per hour. A percent is a ratio that compares a number to 100.

**Starting Hint** To find Susan's monthly salary, first multiply the rate (8.50) by the hours (40), then by the weeks in a month (4). To find the percentage, divide the total baby expenses by Susan's monthly salary. Multiply the result by 100.

**Math** For math help, go to the Math Appendix at the back of the book.

**NCTM Number and Operations**
Understand numbers, ways of representing numbers, relationships among numbers, and number systems.

**Learn the Secrets of Science**
The secret is that it can be easy! You can use scientific principles and concepts in your everyday activities. Investigate and analyze the world around you with these basic skills.

### THE DEVELOPING BRAIN

**Neural Connections**
Babies learn alot in the first three years of life. Newborn babies' brains contain about 100 billion nerve cells, called *neurons*. Those neurons have about 50 trillion connections. These connections increase rapidly, and by the age of three, a child has twice as many connections as an adult. As a child matures, unused pathways are removed. This means that babies who live in an environment where they learn more will keep more connections.

**Science Inquiry** A stimulating environment is important for babies' brains to develop to their fullest potential. How would a stimulating environment lead to an increased number of neurological connections?

### { Expert Advice... }

"For infants and toddlers, learning and living are the same thing. If they feel secure, treasured, loved, their own energy and curiosity will bring them new understanding and new skills."

— Amy Laura Dombro and Leah Wallach, early childhood authors, *The Ordinary Is Extraordinary*.

**Learn from Professionals**
See what child development professionals think about the section's topic.

## Study with Features (continued)

### Learning Through PLAY

**From Solo to Social**

A child's play changes as she grows and develops. Young babies enjoy play that involves touching, grasping, and using their five senses. Older babies are ready for more challenging forms of object play, such stacking blocks. By age one, babies enjoy parallel play. This means that they play next to each other, but not with each other. They watch and copy one another, and they start to learn how to share. Parallel play helps babies understand that babies have wants and feelings too. By age, children enjoy make-believe

play full of complex stories. All these kinds of play help children develop social skills such as feeling comfortable in the world, identifying and expressing feelings, cooperating, and taking turns.

**Think About It** You are caring for two young toddlers, Maya and Delon, who are playing next to each other. Maya grabs the ball from Delon, and Delon screams. What could you say and do next to help both babies understand how to share?

**Play Matters** See how to help promote child development with different forms of play for each age and stage.

### Parenting Skills

**Helping a Baby Develop a Sense of Trust**

Meeting a baby's physical and emotional needs helps a baby build a sense of trust. Try these strategies to help a baby develop trust.

- **Follow a predictable routine.** Routine care helps a baby learn to trust a parent or caregiver. Establish regular times for feeding, baths, and naps.
- **Get to know the baby.** Appreciate the baby's uniqueness. Learn about the baby's likes and dislikes. Learn the baby's signs for hunger, tiredness, and boredom.
- **Bond with the baby.** Spend time nurturing and holding the baby. Talk to the baby in a soft, positive tone. Smile and establish eye contact. Enjoy physical closeness.
- **Meet the baby's needs.** Strive to meet a baby's physical, social, and emotional needs. Provide loving care and affection.

**Take Charge** If you were a caregiver, how could you learn what a baby's different cries mean? Write a one-page journal entry sharing your thoughts.

**Be a Positive Influence** Learn how to have a positive influence on any children in your life with the tips on encouragement, leadership, and guidance skills.

**Happy Children** Learn how to keep children safe and healthy while encouraging growth and exploration.

### RESPOND TO SPECIAL NEEDS — Autism

Autism is a disability that affects the way people relate to others. People with severe autism have a hard time interacting and communicating with others. Signs of autism usually appear before a child turns three. Autistic children tend to avoid eye contact and cuddling. They do not like changes in routine and they may be very sensitive to lights and sounds. They may not respond to their own names, and they may start talking late. Early diagnosis is important. A child with autism needs a special treatment program. Therapy and special education help children with autism

lead fuller lives. Medications and special diets may also help. Parents can help by showing love and understanding, setting up routines, praising successes, and helping their children learn to play and make friends.

**Critical Thinking** Research the causes of autism. Describe the major theories and explain why some of these theories are controversial. Summarize your findings in a one-page essay. Cite your sources.

**Respond to All Children** Learn how special needs can affect child development and child care.

### SAFE CHILD HEALTHY CHILD

**Exploring Through Taste**

Babies' mouths are more sensitive than their hands, so it is no wonder that babies use their mouths to explore tastes, textures, and shapes. *Mouthing* is normal, but it can be dangerous. A baby can choke on small objects or be poisoned by chemicals. Make sure that all toys are too large to fit all the way into a baby's mouth. Keep soaps, medicines, and chemicals out of reach. You can satisfy a baby's need to explore by choosing toys and foods with interesting shapes and textures.

**Be Prepared** Use the library or the Internet to conduct research on child safety. Make a safety checklist of 20 common choking hazards for babies, including toys and toy parts, household objects, and foods. Share your checklist with the class.

# Study with Features (continued)

**Think About Your Future**
Learn about career options related to children and see what skills you would need to have a similar career.

## What Would You Do?

### A Healthy Environment

Anne is a pediatric nurse. She has two nine-year-old patients, Ian and Seth, who have asthma. Aside from their age and diagnosis, their situations are different. "Seth has been to the hospital only once for an asthma attack," Anne says. "His mom also has asthma, so they have learned together how to manage their symptoms. They keep emergency medication on hand and clean their house often to reduce dust. Ian, on the other hand, spends a lot of time in the hospital for asthma attacks." Anne continues, "Two conditions in his home can make his asthma worse: his family has a cat and one of his parents smokes." Ian's parents asked how to help reduce his number of attacks.

✎ **Write About It** How might Ian's parents change his environment to reduce the number of his asthma attacks? Write a brief article for the Health section of your local newspaper to offer ideas for Ian's parents.

### Careers With Children — Storyteller

**B**efore societies had written records, they had storytellers. Storytellers described battles and adventures and told tales of monsters and kings. Today's storytellers educate and entertain as they practice this ancient art. Many traditions are preserved with storytelling.

#### ✻ What Does a Storyteller Do?

Storytellers captivate their audiences with words. Storytellers use their voices the way musicians use instruments. They write and memorize many stories and tell each one with enthusiasm and creativity. Many storytellers add songs and music to their stories, too. Some storytellers focus on certain traditions, such as African folk tales.

#### ✻ Where Do Storytellers Work?

Storytellers perform in many different places, such as schools, libraries, museums, festivals, children's parties, senior centers, prisons, and hospitals. Some storytellers might perform on the radio or on television. Some sell recordings of their performances.

#### Preparation and Skills

**Education and Training**
Many storytellers study literature, folklore, music, and drama. Public speaking is also good preparation for storytelling. Look for a Storytellers Guild, or association, in your area to find a mentor or receive tips on developing this career. Some of these groups can help you find jobs to get started.

**Aptitudes, Abilities, and Skills**
Successful storytellers have imagination, self-motivation, a good memory, acting talent, and communication skills. Storytellers work hard, so they should be motivated and dedicated to their craft.

**Academic Skills Required**
English Language Arts are used by storytellers in reading and researching stories and ideas, and in writing stories to tell.

**Solve Real-World Problems**
You will encounter disagreements or challenges in your life. Read about real problems and tell how you would resolve the issues.

**Explore Careers**
Research other careers that involve performing with children or engaging them through play. Choose one career and ___ paragraph describing it. Tell if the career interests you ___

🖈 **Careers Online** For more information on care ___ Occupational Outlook Handbook Web site thro ___ on this book's Online Learning Center at **glen** ___

**Find Out More** about careers at this book's Online Learning Center at **glencoe.com**.

### CULTURE MATTERS
#### Holding a Baby Close

Carrying babies close to the body is the norm in many cultures. In Somalia, women tie their babies to their backs with long scarves. In Nepal, mothers carry their babies in a garment that also holds money and tools. The Inuit people of the Canadian Arctic can snuggle their babies in the furry linings of their parkas. Baby slings are now growing more popular in North America and Europe. Carrying a baby close provides the baby with a sense of security and lets him feel, see, and smell the parent. It also lets the baby see the world from a different vantage point.

👤 **Build Connections** What are the advantages of sharing space? What are the disadvantages?

**NCSS I C Culture** Apply an understanding of culture as an integrated whole that explains the functions and interactions of behavior patterns.

**Cultural Diversity**
See how cultures around the world address child development needs.

# Online Learning Center

# Use the Internet to Extend Your Learning

Follow these steps to access the textbook resources at *The Developing Child* Online Learning Center.

**Online Learning Center Icon** Look for this icon throughout the text that directs you to the book's Online Learning Center for more activities and information.

**Graphic Organizer** Go to this book's Online Learning Center at **glencoe.com** to print out this graphic organizer.

**Step 1**
Go to **glencoe.com**.

**Step 2**
Select **your state** from the pull-down menu.

**Step 3**
Select **Student/Parent**.

**Step 4**
Select **Family & Consumer Sciences**.

**Step 5**
Select **ENTER**.

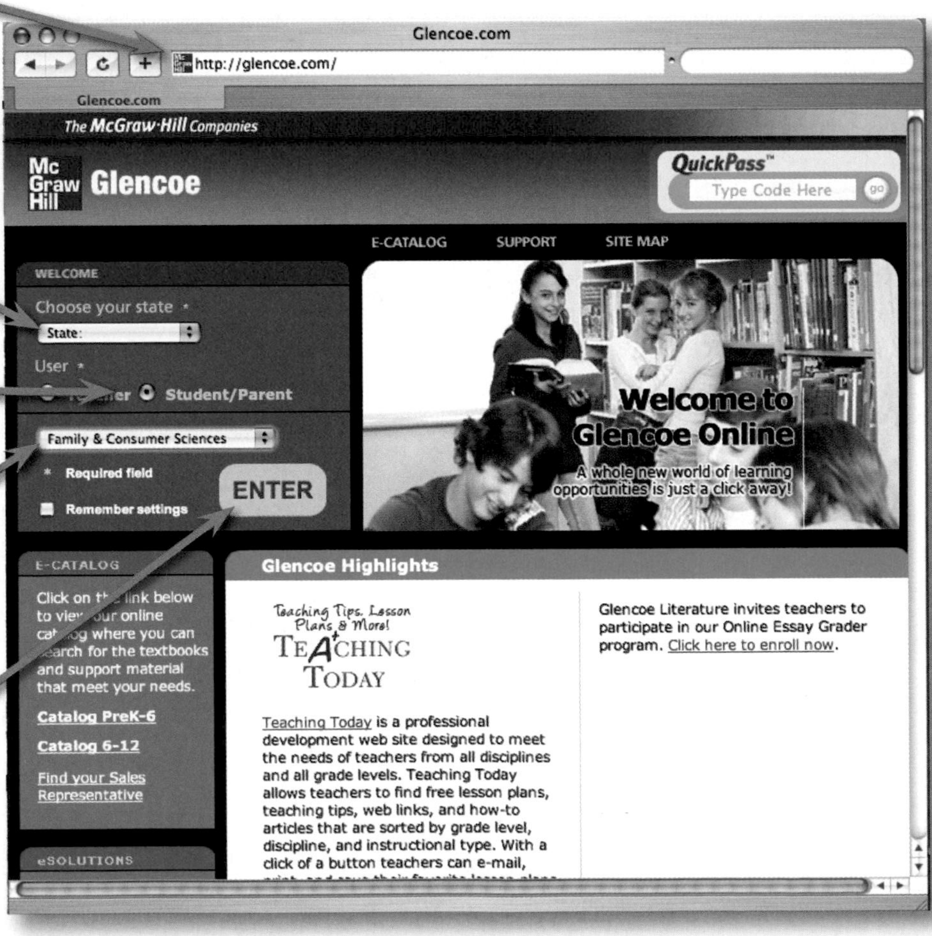

Glencoe.com

http://glencoe.com/

Glencoe.com

*The McGraw·Hill Companies*

**Mc Graw Hill** **Glencoe**

QuickPass™
Type Code Here

E-CATALOG    SUPPORT    SITE MAP

WELCOME

Choose your state *
State:

User *
Teacher    Student/Parent

Family & Consumer Sciences

* Required field
Remember settings

**ENTER**

**Welcome to Glencoe Online**
A whole new world of learning opportunities is just a click away!

E-CATALOG

Click on the link below to view our online catalog where you can search for the textbooks and support material that meet your needs.

**Catalog PreK-6**

**Catalog 6-12**

Find your Sales Representative

eSOLUTIONS

**Glencoe Highlights**

Teaching Tips, Lesson Plans & More!
TEACHING TODAY

Teaching Today is a professional development web site designed to meet the needs of teachers from all disciplines and all grade levels. Teaching Today allows teachers to find free lesson plans, teaching tips, web links, and how-to articles that are sorted by grade level, discipline, and instructional type. With a click of a button teachers can e-mail, print, and save their favorite lesson plans

Glencoe Literature invites teachers to participate in our Online Essay Grader program. Click here to enroll now.

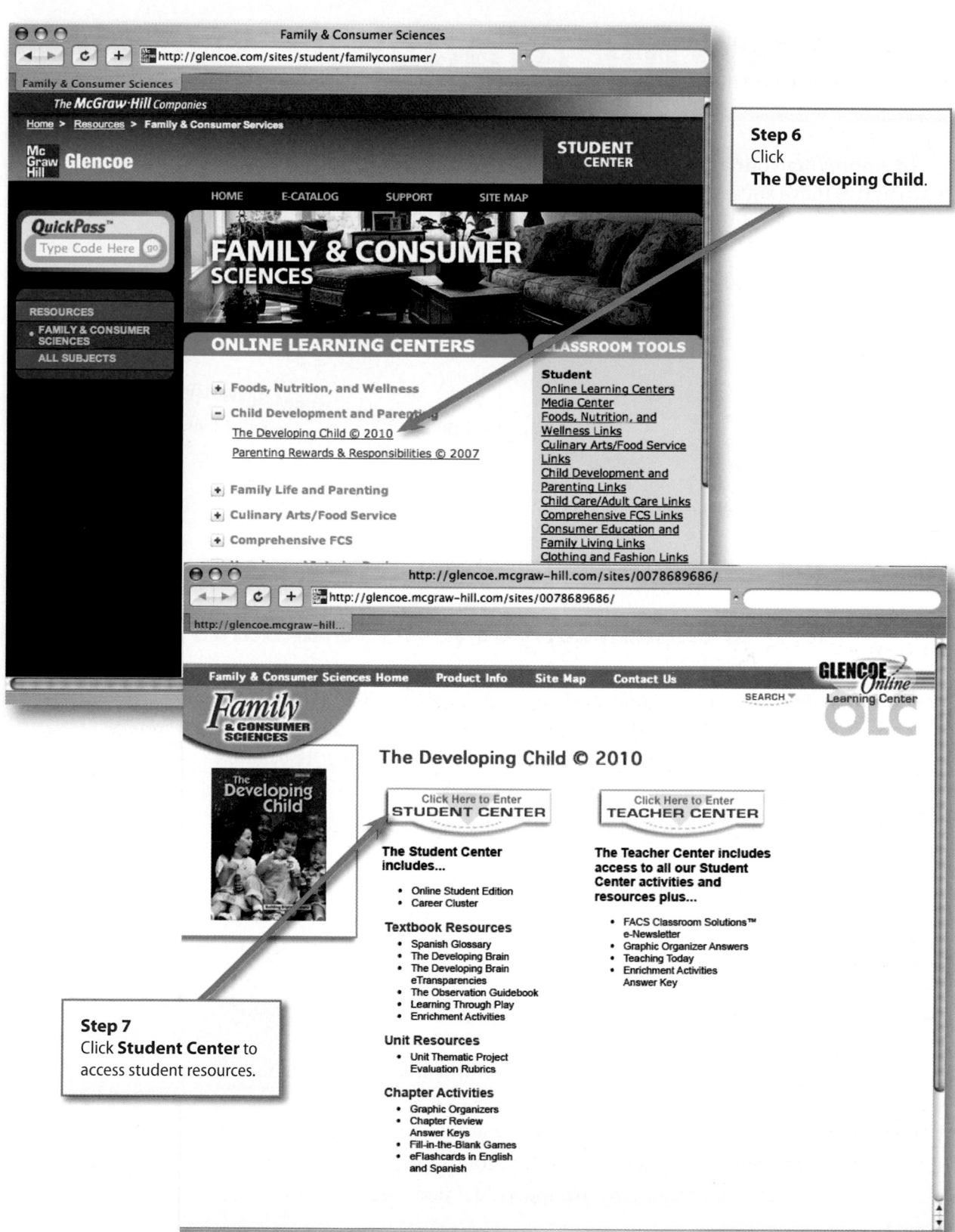

**Step 6**
Click
**The Developing Child**.

**Step 7**
Click **Student Center** to access student resources.

# Prepare for Academic Success!

By improving your academic skills, you improve your ability to learn and achieve success now and in the future. It also improves your chances of landing a high-skill, high-wage job. The features and assessments in *The Developing Child* provide many opportunities for you to strengthen your academic skills.

**Academic Standards** Look for this box throughout the text to know what academic skills you are learning.

**NCTM Number and Operations** Understand numbers, ways of representing numbers, relationships among numbers, and number systems.

## National English Language Arts Standards

To help incorporate literacy skills (reading, writing, listening, and speaking) into *The Developing Child,* each section contains a listing of the language arts skills covered. These skills have been developed into standards by the *National Council of Teachers of English and International Reading Association.*

- Read texts to acquire new information.
- Read literature to build an understanding of the human experience.
- Apply strategies to interpret texts.
- Use written language to communicate effectively.
- Use different writing process elements to communicate effectively.
- Conduct research and gather, evaluate, and synthesize data to communicate discoveries.
- Use information resources to gather information and create and communicate knowledge.
- Develop an understanding of diversity in language use across cultures.
- Participate as members of literacy communities.
- Use language to accomplish individual purposes.

## National Math Standards

You also have opportunities to practice math skills indicated by standards developed by the *National Council of Teachers of Mathematics.**

- Algebra
- Data Analysis and Probability
- Geometry
- Measurement
- Number and Operations
- Problem Solving

**Standards are listed with permission of the* National Council of Teachers of Mathematics (NCTM). NCTM *does not endorse the content or validity of these alignments.*

## National Science Standards

The *National Science Education Standards* outline these science skills that you can practice in this text.

- Science as Inquiry
- Physical Science
- Life Science
- Earth and Space Science
- Science and Technology
- Science in Personal and Social Perspectives
- History and Nature of Science

## National Social Studies Standards

The *National Council for the Social Studies* is another organization that provides standards to help guide your studies. Activities in this text relate to these standards.

- Culture
- Time, Continuity, and Change
- People, Places, and Environments
- Individual Development and Identity
- Individuals, Groups, and Institutions
- Power, Authority, and Governance
- Production, Distribution, and Consumption
- Science, Technology, and Society
- Global Connections
- Civic Ideals and Practices

# Reading Skills Handbook

## ▶ Reading: What's in It for You?

What role does reading play in your life? The possibilities are countless. Are you on a sports team? Perhaps you like to read about the latest news and statistics in sports or find out about new training techniques. Are you looking for a part-time job? You might be looking for advice about résumé writing, interview techniques, or information about a company. Are you enrolled in an English class, an algebra class, or a business class? Then your assignments require a lot of reading.

**Improving or Fine-Tuning Your Reading Skills Will:**

- ◆ Improve your grades.
- ◆ Allow you to read faster and more efficiently.
- ◆ Improve your study skills.
- ◆ Help you remember more information accurately.
- ◆ Improve your writing.

## ▶ The Reading Process

Good reading skills build on one another, overlap, and spiral around in much the same way that a winding staircase goes around and around while leading you to a higher place. This handbook is designed to help you find and use the tools you will need **before, during,** and **after** reading.

**Strategies You Can Use**

- ◆ Identify, understand, and learn new words.
- ◆ Understand why you read.
- ◆ Take a quick look at the whole text.
- ◆ Try to predict what you are about to read.

- ◆ Take breaks while you read and ask yourself questions about the text.
- ◆ Take notes.
- ◆ Keep thinking about what will come next.
- ◆ Summarize.

## ▶ Vocabulary Development

Word identification and vocabulary skills are the building blocks of the reading and the writing process. By learning to use a variety of strategies to build your word skills and vocabulary, you will become a stronger reader.

### Use Context to Determine Meaning

The best way to expand and extend your vocabulary is to read widely, listen carefully, and participate in a rich variety of discussions. When reading on your own, though, you can often figure out the meanings of new words by looking at their **context,** the other words and sentences that surround them.

> ### Tips for Using Context
>
> **Look for clues like these:**
>
> ◆ A synonym or an explanation of the unknown word in the sentence:
> *Elise's shop specialized in millinery, or hats for women.*
> ◆ A reference to what the word is or is not like:
> *An archaeologist, like a historian, deals with the past.*
> ◆ A general topic associated with the word:
> *The cooking teacher discussed the best way to braise meat.*
> ◆ A description or action associated with the word:
> *He used the shovel to dig up the garden.*

## Predict a Possible Meaning

Another way to determine the meaning of a word is to take the word apart. If you understand the meaning of the **base,** or **root,** part of a word, and also know the meanings of key syllables added either to the beginning or end of the base word, you can usually figure out what the word means.

***Word Origins*** Since Latin, Greek, and Anglo-Saxon roots are the basis for much of our English vocabulary, having some background in languages can be a useful vocabulary tool. For example, *astronomy* comes from the Greek root *astro,* which means "relating to the stars." *Stellar* also has a meaning referring to stars, but its origin is Latin. Knowing root words in other languages can help you determine meanings, derivations, and spellings in English.

***Prefixes and Suffixes*** A prefix is a word part that can be added to the beginning of a word. For example, the prefix *semi* means "half" or "partial," so *semicircle* means "half a circle." A suffix is a word part that can be added to the end of a word. Adding a suffix often changes a word from one part of speech to another.

***Using Dictionaries*** A dictionary provides the meaning or meanings of a word. Look at the sample dictionary entry on the next page to see what other information it provides.

***Thesauruses and Specialized Reference Books*** A thesaurus provides synonyms and often antonyms. It is a useful tool to expand your vocabulary. Remember to check the exact definition of the listed words in a dictionary before you use a thesaurus. Specialized dictionaries such as *Barron's Dictionary of Business Terms* or *Black's Law Dictionary* list terms and expressions that are not commonly included in a general dictionary. You can also use online dictionaries.

***Glossaries*** Many textbooks and technical works contain condensed dictionaries that provide an alphabetical listing of words used in the text and their specific definitions.

**Dictionary Entry**

**Forms of the word**

**Part of speech**

**Numbered definitions**

**Example of use**

**Usage label**

**help** (help) **helped** or *(archaic)* **holp**, **helped** or *(archaic)* **hol-pen**, **help-ing**. *v.t.* **1.** to provide with support, as in the performance of a task; be of service to: *He helped his brother paint the room.* ▲ also used elliptically with a pre-position or adverb: *He helped the old woman up the stairs.* **2.** to enable (someone or something) to accomplish a goal or achieve a desired effect: *The coach's advice helped the team to win.* **3.** to provide with sustenance or relief, as in time of need or distress; Succor: *The Red Cross helped the flood victims.* **4.** to promote or contribute to; further. *The medication helped his recovery.* **5.** to be useful or profit-able to; be of advantage to: *It might help you if you read the book.* **6.** to improve or remedy: *Nothing really helped his sinus condition.* **7.** to prevent; stop: *I can't help his rudeness.* **8.** to refrain from; avoid: *I couldn't help smiling when I heard the story.* **9.** to wait on or serve (often with to): *The clerk helped us. The hostess helped him to the dessert.* **10. cannot help but.** *Informal* cannot but. **11. so help me (God).** oath of affirmation. **12. to help oneself to.** to take or appropriate: *the thief helped himself to all the jewels.—v.i.* to provide support, as in the performance of a task; be of service.—*n.* **1.** act of providing support, service, or suste-nance. **2.** source of support, service, or sustenance. **3.** person or group of persons hired to work for another or others. **4.** means of improving, remedying, or preventing [Old English *helpan,* to aid, succor, benefit.] **Syn.** *v.t.* **1. Help, aid, assist** mean to support in a useful way. Help is the most common word and means to give support in response to a known or expressed need or for a definite purpose: *Everyone helped to make the school fair a success.* **Aid** means to give relief in times or distress or difficulty: *It is the duty of rich nations to aid the poor.* **Assist** means to serve another person in the performance of his task in a secondary capacity: *The secretary assists the officer by taking care of his corresponding.*

**Idioms**

**Origin (etymology)**

**Synonyms**

***Recognize Word Meanings Across Subjects*** Have you learned a new word in one class and then noticed it in your reading for other subjects? The word might not mean exactly the same thing in each class, but you can use the meaning you already know to help you understand what it means in another subject area. For example:

**Math** Each digit represents a different place **value**.

**Health** Your **values** can guide you in making healthful decisions.

**Economics** The **value** of a product is measured in its cost.

## ► Understanding What You Read

Reading comprehension means understanding—deriving meaning from—what you have read. Using a variety of strategies can help you improve your comprehension and make reading more interesting and more fun.

### Read for a Reason

To get the greatest benefit from your reading, **establish a purpose for reading.** In school, you have many reasons for reading, such as:

- to learn and understand new information.
- to find specific information.
- to review before a test.
- to complete an assignment.
- to prepare (research) before you write.

As your reading skills improve, you will notice that you apply different strategies to fit the different purposes for reading. For example, if you are reading for entertainment, you might read quickly, but if you read to gather information or follow directions, you might read more slowly, take notes, construct a graphic organizer, or reread sections of text.

### Draw on Personal Background

Drawing on personal background may also be called activating prior knowledge. Before you start reading a text, ask yourself questions like these:

- What have I heard or read about this topic?
- Do I have any personal experience relating to this topic?

***Using a K-W-L Chart*** A K-W-L chart is a good device for organizing information you gather before, during, and after reading. In the first column, list what you already **know,** then list what you **want** to know in the middle column. Use the third column when you review and assess what you **learned.** You can also add more columns to record places where you found information and places where you can look for more information.

| K (What I already know) | W (What I want to know) | L (What I have learned) |
|---|---|---|
|  |  |  |
|  |  |  |

***Adjust Your Reading Speed*** Your reading speed is a key factor in how well you understand what you are reading. You will need to adjust your speed depending on your reading purpose.

**Scanning** means running your eyes quickly over the material to look for words or phrases. Scan when you need a specific piece of information.

**Skimming** means reading a passage quickly to find its main idea or to get an overview. Skim a text when you preview to determine what the material is about.

**Reading for detail** involves careful reading while paying attention to text structure and monitoring your understanding. Read for detail when you are learning concepts, following complicated directions, or preparing to analyze a text.

# ▶ Techniques to Understand and Remember What You Read

## Preview

Before beginning a selection, it is helpful to **preview** what you are about to read.

> ### Previewing Strategies
>
> ◆ Read the title, headings, and subheadings of the selection.
> ◆ Look at the illustrations and notice how the text is organized.
> ◆ Skim the selection: Take a glance at the whole thing.
> ◆ Decide what the main idea might be.
> ◆ Predict what a selection will be about.

## Predict

Have you ever read a mystery, decided who committed the crime, and then changed your mind as more clues were revealed? You were adjusting your predictions. Did you smile when you found out that you guessed who committed the crime? You were verifying your predictions.

As you read, take educated guesses about story events and outcomes; that is, **make predictions** before and during reading. This will help you focus your attention on the text and it will improve your understanding.

## Determine the Main Idea

When you look for the **main idea**, you are looking for the most important statement in a text. Depending on what kind of text you are reading, the main idea can be located at the very beginning (news stories in a newspaper or a magazine) or at the end (scientific research document). Ask yourself the following questions:

- What is each sentence about?
- Is there one sentence that is more important than all the others?
- What idea do details support or point out?

## Taking Notes

***Cornell Note-Taking System*** There are many methods for note taking. The **Cornell Note-Taking System** is a well-known method that can help you organize what you read. To the right is a note-taking activity based on the Cornell Note-Taking System.

***Graphic Organizers*** Using a graphic organizer to retell content in a visual representation will help you remember and retain content. You might make a **chart** or **diagram,** organizing what you have read. Here are some examples of graphic organizers:

**Venn diagrams** When mapping out a compare-and-contrast text structure, you can use a Venn diagram. The outer portions of the circles will show how two characters, ideas, or items contrast, or are different, and the overlapping part will compare two things, or show how they are similar.

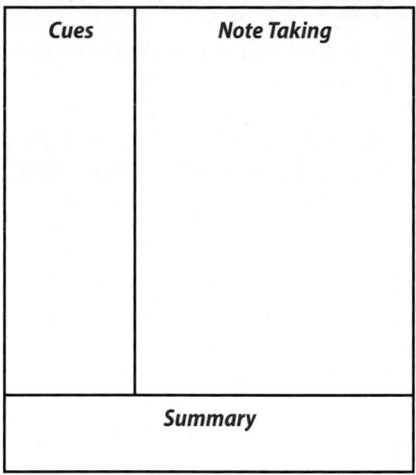

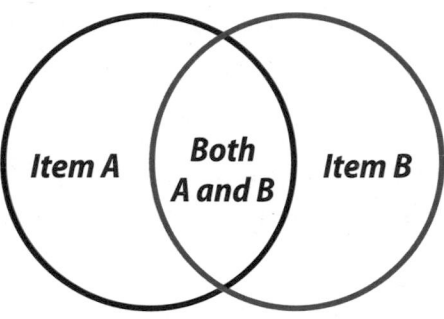

**Flow charts** To help you track the sequence of events, or cause and effect, use a flow chart. Arrange ideas or events in their logical, sequential order. Then, draw arrows between your ideas to indicate how one idea or event flows into another.

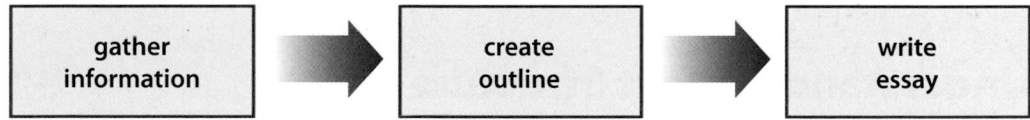

## Visualize

Try to form a mental picture of scenes, characters, and events as you read. Use the details and descriptions the author gives you. If you can **visualize** what you read, it will be more interesting and you will remember it better.

## Question

Ask yourself questions about the text while you read. Ask yourself about the importance of the sentences, how they relate to one another, if you understand what you just read, and what you think is going to come next.

## Clarify

If you feel you do not understand meaning (through questioning), try these techniques:

> **What to Do When You Do Not Understand**
>
> ◆ Reread confusing parts of the text.
> ◆ Diagram (chart) relationships between chunks of text, ideas, and sentences.
> ◆ Look up unfamiliar words.
> ◆ Talk out the text to yourself.
> ◆ Read the passage once more.

## Review

Take time to stop and review what you have read. Use your note-taking tools (graphic organizers or Cornell notes charts). Also, review and consider your K-W-L chart.

## Monitor Your Comprehension

Continue to check your understanding by using the following two strategies:

***Summarize*** Pause and tell yourself the main ideas of the text and the key supporting details. Try to answer the following questions: Who? What? When? Where? Why? How?

***Paraphrase*** Pause, close the book, and try to retell what you have just read in your own words. It might help to pretend you are explaining the text to someone who has not read it and does not know the material.

## ▶ Understanding Text Structure

Good writers do not just put together sentences and paragraphs, they organize their writing with a specific purpose in mind. That organization is called text structure. When you understand and follow the structure of a text, it is easier to remember the information you are reading. There are many ways text may be structured. Watch for **signal words**. They will help you follow the text's organization (also, remember to use these techniques when you write).

## Compare and Contrast

This structure shows similarities and differences between people, things, and ideas. This is often used to demonstrate that things that seem alike are really different, or vice versa.

**Signal words:** similarly, more, less, on the one hand / on the other hand, in contrast, but, however

## Cause and Effect

Writers use the cause-and-effect structure to explore the reasons for something happening and to examine the results or consequences of events.

**Signal words:** so, because, as a result, therefore, for the following reasons

## Problem and Solution

When they organize text around the question "how?" writers state a problem and suggest solutions.

**Signal words:** how, help, problem, obstruction, overcome, difficulty, need, attempt, have to, must

## Sequence

Sequencing tells you in which order to consider thoughts or facts. Examples of sequencing are:

***Chronological order*** refers to the order in which events take place.

**Signal words:** first, next, then, finally

***Spatial order*** describes the organization of things in space (to describe a room, for example).

**Signal words:** above, below, behind, next to

***Order of importance*** lists things or thoughts from the most important to the least important (or the other way around).

**Signal words:** principal, central, main, important, fundamental

# ▶ Reading for Meaning

It is important to think about what you are reading to get the most information out of a text, to understand the consequences of what the text says, to remember the content, and to form your own opinion about what the content means.

## Interpret

Interpreting is asking yourself, "What is the writer really saying?" and then using what you already know to answer that question.

## Infer

Writers do not always state exactly everything they want you to understand. By providing clues and details, they sometimes imply certain information. An **inference** involves using your reason and experience to develop the idea on your own, based on what an author implies or suggests. What is most important when drawing inferences is to be sure that you have accurately based your guesses on supporting details from the text. If you cannot point to a place in the selection to help back up your inference, you may need to rethink your guess.

## Draw Conclusions

A conclusion is a general statement you can make and explain with reasoning, or with supporting details from a text. If you read a story describing a sport where five players bounce a ball and throw it through a high hoop, you may conclude that the sport is basketball.

## Analyze

To understand persuasive nonfiction (a text that discusses facts and opinions to arrive at a conclusion), you need to analyze statements and examples to see if they support the main idea. To understand an informational text (a text, such as a textbook, that gives you information, not opinions), you need to keep track of how the ideas are organized to find the main points.

**Hint:** Use your graphic organizers and notes charts.

## Distinguish Facts from Opinions

This is one of the most important reading skills you can learn. A fact is a statement that can be proven. An opinion is what the writer believes. A writer may support opinions with facts, but an opinion cannot be proven. For example:

**Fact:** California produces fruit and other agricultural products.

**Opinion:** California produces the best fruit and other agricultural products.

## Evaluate

Would you take seriously an article on nuclear fission if you knew it was written by a comedic actor? If you need to rely on accurate information, you need to find out who wrote what you are reading and why. Where did the writer get information? Is the information one-sided? Can you verify the information?

## ▶ Reading for Research

You will need to **read actively** in order to research a topic. You might also need to generate an interesting, relevant, and researchable **question** on your own and locate appropriate print and nonprint information from a wide variety of sources. Then you will need to **categorize** that information, evaluate it, and **organize** it in a new way in order to produce a research project for a specific audience. Finally, **draw conclusions** about your original research question. These conclusions may lead you to other areas for further inquiry.

## Locate Appropriate Print and Nonprint Information

In your research, try to use a variety of sources. Because different sources present information in different ways, your research project will be more interesting and balanced when you read a variety of sources.

***Literature and Textbooks*** These texts include any book used as a basis for instruction or a source of information.

***Book Indices*** A book index, or a bibliography, is an alphabetical listing of books. Some book indices list books on specific subjects; others are more general. Other indices list a variety of topics or resources.

***Periodicals*** Magazines and journals are issued at regular intervals, such as weekly or monthly. One way to locate information in magazines is to use the *Readers' Guide to Periodical Literature.* This guide is available in print form in most libraries.

***Technical Manuals*** A manual is a guide or handbook intended to give instruction on how to perform a task or operate something. A vehicle owner's manual might give information on how to operate and service a car.

***Reference Books*** Reference books include encyclopedias and almanacs, and are used to locate specific pieces of information.

***Electronic Encyclopedias, Databases, and the Internet*** There are many ways to locate extensive information using your computer. Infotrac, for instance, acts as an online reader's guide. CD encyclopedias can provide easy access to all subjects.

## Organize and Convert Information

As you gather information from different sources, taking careful notes, you will need to think about how to **synthesize** the information, that is, convert it into a unified whole, as well as how to change it into a form your audience will easily understand and that will meet your assignment guidelines.

**1.** First, ask yourself what you want your audience to know.
**2.** Then, think about a pattern of organization, a structure that will best show your main ideas. You might ask yourself the following questions:
   - When comparing items or ideas, what graphic aids can I use?
   - When showing the reasons something happened and the effects of certain actions, what text structure would be best?
   - How can I briefly and clearly show important information to my audience?
   - Would an illustration or even a cartoon help to make a certain point?

# How to Use Technology

## Introduction

Technology affects your life in almost every way, both at home and at work. Computers can do wonderful things. They are a path to the libraries of the world. They enhance and enrich your life. You can find the answers to many of your questions on the Internet, often as quickly as the click of your mouse. However, they can also be misused. Knowing some simple guidelines will help you use technology in a safe and secure way.

## Practice Safe Surfing!

The Internet can also be a dangerous place. Although there are many Web sites you can freely and safely visit, many others are ones you want to avoid. Before you sign on to any site or visit a chat room, there are several things to consider:

✧ **Know to whom you are giving the information.** Check that the URL in your browser matches the domain you intended to visit and that you have not been redirected to another site.

✧ **Never give personal information of any sort** to someone you meet on a Web site or in a chat room, including your name, gender, age, or contact information.

✧ **Think about why you are giving the information.** For example, if a parent orders something online to be delivered, he or she will need to give an address. But you should never give out your social security number, your birth date, or your mother's maiden name without adult consent.

✧ **Check with a parent or other trusted adult** if you are still unsure whether it is safe to give the information.

## Tips for Using the Internet for Research

The Internet is probably the single most important tool for research since the public library. There is so much information to access on the Internet that it can be difficult to know where to begin.

A good place to start is with a search engine, such as Google. Google is an automated piece of software that "crawls" the Web looking for information. By typing your topic into the search bar, the search engine looks for sites that contain the words you type. You may get many more sites than you are looking for. Here are some ways to get better results:

> To get the best results when conducting a search online, be sure to spell all your search words correctly.

⬧ **Place quotes around your topic,** for example, "sports medicine." This will allow you to find the sites where that exact phrase appears.

⬧ **Use NEAR.** Typing "sports NEAR medicine" will return sites that contain both words and have the two words close to each other.

⬧ **Exclude unwanted results.** Simply use a minus sign to indicate the words you do not want, for example, "sports medicine" –baseball.

⬧ **Watch out for advertisements.** If you are using Google, know that the links on the right-hand side of the page, or sometimes at the top in color, are paid links. They may or may not be worth exploring.

⬧ **Check for relevance.** Google displays a few lines of text from each page and shows your search phrase in bold. Check to see if it is appropriate for your work.

⬧ **Look for news.** After you have entered your search phrase and have looked at the results, click on a *News* link on the page. This will show you recent stories about your topic.

⬧ **Try again!** If you have made an extensive search and not found what you want, start a new search with a different set of words.

⬧ **Check other sources.** Combine your Internet search with traditional research methods, such as books and magazines.

## How to Evaluate Web Sites

Even though there is a ton of information available online, much of this information can be deceptive and misleading and often incorrect. The books in your library and classroom have been evaluated by scholars and experts. There is no such oversight on the Web. Learning to evaluate Web sites will make you a more savvy surfer and enable you to gather the information you need quickly and easily. When you are trying to decide whether a Web site provides trustworthy information, consider the following:

◇ **First, ask, "Who is the author?"** Once you have the name of the author, do a quick Web search to see what else the author has written. Search online for books he or she has written. This information will help you consider whether the person is credible.

◇ **Look at the group offering the information.** Be wary if they are trying to sell a product or service. Look for impartial organizations to provide unbiased information.

◇ **Look for Web sites that provide sources for each of their facts,** just as you do when you write a term paper. Also, look for clues that the information was written by someone knowledgeable. Spelling and grammatical errors are warning signs that the information may not be accurate.

◇ **Check for the date the article was written and when it was last updated.** The more recent the article, the more likely it will be accurate.

◇ **Finally, when using information from a Web site, treat it as you would treat print information.** Anyone can post information on a Web site. Never use information that you cannot verify with another source.

## Plagiarism

Using your computer in an ethical manner is simple if you follow certain guidelines. Plagiarism is the act of taking someone else's ideas and passing them off as your own. It does not matter if it is just one or two phrases or an entire paper. Be on guard against falling into the trap of cutting and pasting. This makes plagiarism all too easy.

It is acceptable to quote sources in your work, but you must make sure to identify those sources and give them proper credit. Also, some Web sites do not allow you to quote from them. Be sure to check each site or resource you are quoting to make sure you are allowed to use the material. Remember to cite your sources properly.

## Copyright

A copyright protects someone who creates an original work. This can be a single sentence, a book, a play, a piece of music. If you create it, you are the owner. Copyright protection is provided by the Copyright Act of 1976, a federal statute.

If you want to use a portion of a copyrighted work in your own work, you need to obtain permission from the copyright holder. That might be a publisher of a book, an author, or an organization or an estate. Most publishers are willing to grant permission to individuals for educational purposes. If you want to reproduce information you found on the Web, contact the Webmaster or author of the article to request permission.

Once a work's copyright has expired, it is considered to be in the public domain and anyone can reprint it as he or she pleases. Remember the following tips:

◇ **What is copyrighted?** All forms of original expression published in the United States since 1923.

◇ **Can I copy from the Internet?** Copying information from the Internet is a serious breach of copyright. Check the site's *Terms of Use* to see what you can and cannot do.

◇ **Can I edit copyrighted work?** You cannot change copyrighted material, that is, make "derivative works" based on existing material, without permission of the copyright holder.

# Student Organizations

## What Is a Student Organization?

A student organization is a group or association of students that is formed around activities, such as:

- Family and Consumer Sciences
- Student government
- Community service
- Social clubs
- Honor societies
- Multicultural alliances
- Technology education
- Artists and performers
- Politics
- Sports teams
- Professional career development

A student organization is usually required to follow a set of rules and regulations that apply equally to all student organizations at a particular school.

## Why Should You Get Involved?

Being an active part of a student organization opens a variety of experiences to you. Many student clubs are part of a national network of students and professionals, which provides the chance to connect to a wider variety of students and opportunities.

## What's in It for You?

Participation in student organizations can contribute to a more enriching learning experience. Here are some ways you can benefit:

- Gain leadership qualities and skills that make you more marketable to employers and universities.
- Demonstrate the ability to appreciate someone else's point of view.
- Interact with professionals to learn about their different industries.
- Explore your creative interests, share ideas, and collaborate with others.
- Take risks, build confidence, and grow creatively.
- Learn valuable skills while speaking or performing in front of an audience.
- Make a difference in your life and the lives of those around you.
- Learn the importance of civic responsibility and involvement.
- Build relationships with instructors, advisors, students, and other members of the community who share similar backgrounds/world views.

## Find and Join a Student Organization!

Take a close look at the organizations offered at your school or within your community. Are there any organizations that interest you? Talk to your teachers, guidance counselors, or a parent or guardian. Usually posters or flyers for a variety of clubs and groups can be found on your school's Message Board or Web site. Try to locate more information about the organizations that meet your needs. Then think about how these organizations can help you gain valuable skills you can use at school, at work, and in your community.

# What Is FCCLA?

Family, Career and Community Leaders of America is a nonprofit national career and technical student organization for young men and women in Family and Consumer Sciences education in public and private school through grade 12. Everyone is part of a family, and FCCLA is the only national Career and Technical Student Organization with the family as its central focus. Since 1945, FCCLA members have been making a difference in their families, careers, and communities by addressing important personal, work, and societal issues through family and consumer sciences education.

Today over 220,000 members in nearly 7,000 chapters are active in a network of associations in 50 states as well as in the District of Columbia, the Virgin Islands, and Puerto Rico. Chapter projects focus on a variety of youth concerns, including teen pregnancy, parenting, family relationships, substance abuse, peer pressure, environment, nutrition and fitness, teen violence, and career exploration. Involvement in FCCLA offers members the opportunity to expand their leadership potential and develop skills for life—planning, goal setting, problem solving, decision making, and interpersonal communication—necessary in the home and workplace.

# STAR Events Program

STAR Events (Students Taking Action with Recognition) are competitive events in which members are recognized for proficiency and achievement in chapter and individual projects, leadership skills, and occupational preparation. FCCLA provides opportunities for you to participate at local, state, and national levels.

# What Is SkillsUSA?

SkillsUSA is a national organization serving teachers and high school and college students, who are preparing for careers in technical, skilled, and service occupations. More than 300,000 students and instructors join SkillsUSA annually.

One of the most visible programs of SkillsUSA is the annual SkillsUSA Championships. This competition showcases some of the best career and technical students in the nation. It allows students to compete in First Aid/CPR scenarios that will test their abilities to save a child's life. These contests begin locally and continue through state and national levels.

| Title | Objectives |
|---|---|
| **CHAPTER 1**<br>**Learn About Children** | • **Explain** the best way to learn about children.<br>• **Identify** three areas of childhood that researchers have studied.<br>• **Summarize** how children learn and develop important skills.<br>• **List** the stages of development after childhood.<br>• **Determine** why observation is important in the study of child development.<br>• **Compare and contrast** different methods of observation and interpretation. |
| **CHAPTER 2**<br>**Responsibilities of Parenting** | • **Explain** who can benefit from knowing about child development and parenting.<br>• **Describe** the five areas of responsibilities for parents.<br>• **Identify** pressures involved in sexual development.<br>• **Summarize** the benefits of abstinence.<br>• **Describe** the possible consequences of sexual activity.<br>• **Compare and contrast** the options available to a teen parent.<br>• **Explain** what it means to be sexually responsible. |
| **CHAPTER 3**<br>**Building Strong Families** | • **Summarize** the qualities that contribute to building a strong family.<br>• **Describe** the different family structures.<br>• **Discuss** the trends affecting families.<br>• **List** the basic categories of children's needs.<br>• **Identify** the three parenting styles.<br>• **Summarize** effective ways to guide children's behavior. |
| **Unit Thematic Project**<br><br>**Learn Parenting Skills** | • **Write** a My Journal entry on Parenting.<br>• **Choose** a parent role model.<br>• **Interview** the parent role model.<br>• **Create** a parenting handbook. |

## Understanding Brackets, Letters, and Ability Levels in the Teacher Wraparound Edition

**Brackets** Brackets on the reduced student edition page correspond to teaching strategies and activities in the Teacher Wraparound Edition. As you teach the lesson, the brackets show you exactly where to use the teaching strategies and activities.

**Letters** The letters on the reduced student edition page identify the type of strategy or activity. See the key below to learn about the different types of strategies and activities.

**Ability Levels** Teaching Strategies that appear throughout the chapters have been identified by one of three codes to give you an idea of their suitability for students of varying learning styles and abilities.

**Resources** Key program resources are listed in each chapter. Icons indicate the format of resources.

### KEY TO LETTERS

**D** **Develop Concepts** activities help teachers gauge and plan for students' concept development.

**R** **Reading Strategy** activities help you teach reading skills and vocabulary.

**S** **Skill Practice** provides leveled instruction for meeting individual needs and learning styles.

**W** **Writing Support** activities provide writing opportunities to help students comprehend the text.

**C** **Critical Thinking** strategies help students apply and extend what they have learned.

**U** **Universal Access** activities provide differentiated instruction for English language learners, and suggestions for teaching various types of learners.

**NCLB** **No Child Left Behind** activities help students practice and improve their abilities in academic subjects.

### KEY TO ABILITY LEVELS

**L1** Strategies should be within the ability range of all students. Often full class participation is required.

**L2** Strategies are for average to above-average students or for small groups. Some teacher direction is necessary.

**L3** Strategies are designed for students able and willing to work independently. Minimal teacher direction is necessary.

**ELL** Strategies are especially accessible to English Language Learners.

### KEY TO RESOURCE ICONS

📁 Print Material

💿 CD or DVD Resources

🧭 Online Learning Center (OLC)

**TeacherWorks™**
All-In-One Planner and Resource Center

**Teacher Wraparound Edition**

**Unit Resources:**
Unit Thematic Project Student Rubrics
Unit Family and Community Involvement Activities

**Chapter Resources:**
Lesson Plans
Chapter Summaries, Key Terms, and Academic Vocabulary
Graphic Organizers

**Textbook Resources:**
Student Activity Workbook with Academic Integration
Additional Activities
Enrichment Activities

🧭 Link to the *The Developing Child* **Online Learning Center** at **glencoe.com**.

## Unit Overview

### Introduce the Unit
Introduce the unit by describing the main concepts of each chapter in the unit.

### Unit 1
In this opening unit, students will begin their study of children. Students will learn how to make a difference in children's lives and how to study and observe them. Students will also learn many of the challenges of parenting and some of the skills and planning necessary to build strong families.

**Chapter 1** Chapter 1 teaches students how to learn about children. Students will learn that studying children will help them understand why they do what they do. They will also learn that, because of research, attitudes and practices toward the study of children have changed.

**Chapter 2** In this chapter students will learn many of the challenges, responsibilities, and rewards of parenting. They will also learn that parenthood is most successful when it is planned and when both parents are ready for it.

**Chapter 3** Students are introduced to the challenges of building strong families. Some of the topics discussed include common family structures, support systems available for families, parenting styles, and dealing with children's inappropriate behavior.

### OUT OF TIME?

If class time is too short to cover all of the chapters in this unit, have students:
- Write down the vocabulary terms and their definitions.
- Read the chapter summaries at the beginning of each chapter review.
- Go to *The Developing Child* Online Learning Center at **glencoe.com** to download Study-to-Go content.

# Children and Parenting

**↑ Explore the Photo**
Families that spend time together often build strong relationships. *Why would spending time together help to build strong relationships?*

## ►►► Explore the Photo

**Caption Answer** Answers will vary. Families that spend time together get to know one another's likes, dislikes, hopes, and fears. Spending time together can help you better understand the members of your family. Knowing more about and understanding others can lead to strong relationships.

**Discussion** Ask students to think about how things might be different if one of the parents in the photo was missing because of work. (Students might suggest that the parent would have to work harder to find time to spend with children and spouse, and building strong relationships would be more difficult.) Ask students if their families plan activities to do together.

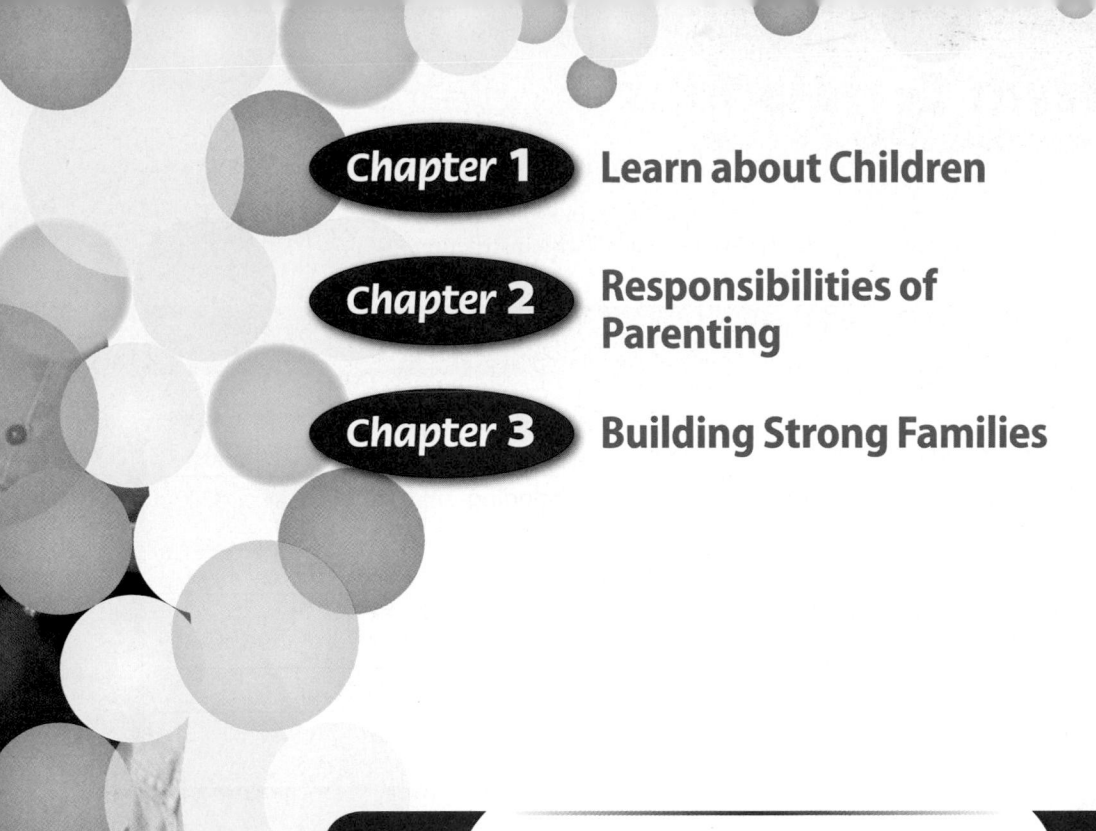

**Discussion Starter**

**Group Interaction**
Have students work together in groups of four or five to develop a list of dos and a list of don'ts related to parenting. After groups have completed their lists, compile class lists and incorporate all of the groups' ideas into a T-chart on the board. Choose a few of the dos and don'ts and ask students why these were included in the list. After completing the unit, revisit the lists and ask if students would make any changes. If so, what would they change? Why?

**Career Investigation**

Using the Career Investigation STAR Event, have students prepare a portfolio and oral presentation on a career related to children. Have the students research a child-related career and report on the qualifications needed, job duties, entry-level positions and advancement opportunities, and salary ranges.

SkillsUSA.

Some first aid or child care competitions may focus on preventing accidents. As children become more independent, they also become more likely to find dangerous situations. For example, infants need safety gates and cabinet latches. For older children, cleaning products should be out of reach and flammable objects should not be near the stove. Is there an emergency fire route for the house? Have students work in groups to create a checklist to use to evaluate the safety of their home for children. Each group should focus on a different age group of children.

## Unit  Thematic Project Preview

### Learn Parenting Skills

By completing this unit, you will learn that using positive parenting skills can help strengthen family relationships. In your unit thematic project, you can show how these skills help to build strong families.

 **My Journal**

**Parenting 101**  Write a journal entry about one of the topics below. This will help you prepare for the unit project at the end of the unit.
- Identify what kind of parent you think you would be someday.
- Determine what you would need to know about children before becoming a parent.
- List resources you could use to learn more about parenting.

## Unit  Thematic Project Preview

### Learn Parenting Skills
Tell students that as part of this unit, they will learn the importance of readiness for parenthood. They will also learn how positive parenting skills can help build strong families. Students will consider how learning about children now could help them if they choose to become parents later.

 **My Journal**

**Parenting 101**  Students should select one topic to write a journal entry about. The journal entry relates to the subject of the thematic project: Learn Parenting Skills. The purpose of the journal entry is to prepare students for the project at the end of the unit. (Journal entries will vary depending on the topic selected and students' personal opinions.)

**STANDARDS BASED LESSON PLANNING** *The Developing Child* provides students with instruction and assessment in the following fundamental content areas:

## National Standards Correlations

| Standards | Pages |
|---|---|
| **12.1.1** Analyze physical, emotional, social, spiritual, and intellectual development. | 14 |
| **12.1.3** Analyze current and emerging research about human growth and development, including research on brain development. | 14, 15 |
| **12.2.1** Analyze the effect of heredity and environment on human growth and development. | 14, 16–17 |
| **12.2.2** Analyze the impact of social, economic, and technological forces on individual growth and development. | 28 |
| **12.2.5** Analyze geographic, political, and global influences on human growth and development. | 10–11 |
| **12.3.3** Analyze the role of family and social services support systems in meeting human growth and development needs. | 26 |

**NO CHILD LEFT BEHIND** NCLB activities, information, and skills practice will help your students attain NCLB proficiency. Students will improve their abilities in the following academic standards areas:

## Academic Standards Correlations

| Discipline | Standard | Feature/Activity |
|---|---|---|
| English Language Arts | **NCTE 1** Read texts to acquire new information. | **Reading Guide (pp. 6, 12, 19)** |
| | **NCTE 4** Use written language to communicate effectively. | **Writing Activity (p. 4)** **After You Read (pp. 11, 25)** |
| | **NCTE 12** Use language to accomplish individual purposes. | **After You Read (p. 18)** **Academic Skills (p. 29)** |
| Mathematics | **NCTM Number and Operations** Understand numbers, ways of representing numbers, relationships among numbers, and number systems. | **Academic Skills (p. 29)** |
| Science | **NSES 1** Develop an understanding of science unifying concepts and processes: evidence, models, and explanations. | **Observation Skills (p. 28)** |
| | **NSES A** Develop abilities necessary to do scientific inquiry, understandings about scientific inquiry. | **After You Read (p. 25)** |
| | **NSES F** Develop understanding of personal and community health. | **Academic Skills (p. 29)** |
| Social Studies | **NCSS IV C Individual Development and Identity** Describe the ways family and cultural influences contribute to the development of a sense of self. | **After You Read (p. 18)** |
| | **NCSS V F Individuals, Groups, and Institutions** Evaluate the role of institutions in furthering both continuity and change. | **After You Read (p. 11)** |

 **Professional Development**

**MINI CLIP VIDEO LIBRARY**

Targeted professional development is correlated throughout *The Developing Child*. **The McGraw-Hill Professional Development Mini Clip Video Library** provides teaching strategies to strengthen academic and learning skills. Log on to **glencoe.com**.

In this chapter, you will find these Mini Clips:
- **ELL** Elaborating on Student Responses, p. 7
- **ELL** Understanding Proficiency, p. 10
- **Reading** Prereading Strategies, p. 12
- **Reading** Strategic Readers, p. 20
- **Reading** During and After Reading, p. 24
- **Reading** Assessment in Standards-Based Instruction, p. 29

## Reading and Writing Strategies

**Writing Activity: Freewriting** (p. 4)
Students use writing tips to generate ways to show caring to a one-year-old child.

**Before You Read** (pp. 6, 12, 19)
A pre-reading question or statement will help students make a personal connection to content.

**Graphic Organizer** (pp. 6, 12, 19)
A visual tool will help students organize and remember new content.

**Reading Check** (pp. 9, 17, 20)
A question allows students to make a quick comprehension self-check.

**After You Read** (pp. 11, 18, 25)
Organize and process students' understanding of what they have read.

## Chapter Features

 **Playing with Babies** (p. 8)
Playing helps babies develop mental, physical, and social skills.

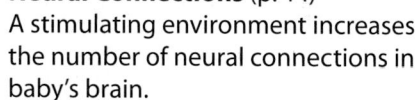 **Neural Connections** (p. 14)
A stimulating environment increases the number of neural connections in a baby's brain.

 **A Healthy Environment** (p. 16)
Asthma attacks often can be reduced by changing the environment.

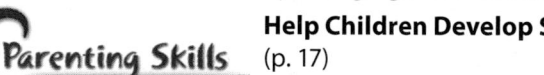 **Help Children Develop Self-Esteem** (p. 17)
Parents and caregivers can use simple techniques to build a child's self-esteem.

**An Observer's Role** (p. 24)
If an observer thinks a child is in danger, they should immediately get help.

 **Parent Educator** (p. 26)
Students learn the career skills needed to succeed as a Parent Educator.

## Chapter Overview

### Introduce the Chapter
In this chapter, students learn the importance of studying child development. They learn about some of the researchers who have had major influences on the study of child development and the different methods used to observe young children.

### Build Background
Discuss with students the steps that a child typically goes through before she is able to walk. For example, she may first sit up, then crawl, pull herself up and stand.) Explain that a child's social, emotional, and intellectual development must go through a specific sequence of stages.

# Learn About Children

## Chapter Objectives
After completing this chapter, you will be able to:
- **Explain** the best way to learn about children.
- **Identify** three areas of childhood that researchers have studied.
- **Summarize** how children learn and develop important skills.
- **List** the stages of development after childhood.
- **Determine** why observation is important in the study of child development.
- **Compare and contrast** different methods of observation and interpretation.

## Writing Activity
### *Freewriting*

This learning activity prompts the students to freely write ideas for how they would show caring to a one-year-old child. After students have completed their writing activity, encourage them to share some of their responses, if they feel comfortable doing so. Student responses can be used to prompt classroom discussions. (Paragraphs should show creative ideas for caring for a one-year-old child. Ideas may include playing with the child, reading to the child, or keeping the child from harm.)

## Writing Activity  *Freewriting*

**Caring** Children of all ages need to be cared for. However, as they get older they need less care. Use freewriting to generate ways to show caring to a one-year-old child you are babysitting.

**Writing Tips** To jumpstart your writing, it can be helpful to write out ideas freely. This is called freewriting. Use these tips to start freewriting:
1. Write everything that comes to mind, in any order.
2. Do not worry about having an introduction or conclusion. You can go back and revise later.
3. Focus on ideas. Correct your grammar and spelling after you are done writing.

**4**

## CLASSROOM  *Solutions*

### Print Resources
 **Student Edition**
 **Teacher Wraparound Edition**
 **Student Activity Workbook**
 **Student Activity Workbook Teacher Annotated Edition**

### Technology Resources
 **Online Learning Center** has resources and activities for students and teachers. Includes an Online Student Edition.

 **Interactive Student Edition** allows students to instantly access review materials, examples, and exercises.

**Review the Sections**
Introduce the chapter by reviewing the sections:

**Section 1.1**
Learning about child development will teach students how to help children grow physically, intellectually, emotionally, and socially. Students will learn more about themselves and become self-confident when interacting with children. Society's understanding of child development has increased enormously over the years.

**Section 1.2**
Because children's brains grow in direct response to stimulation, it is vital that they are exposed to a variety of activities. Many theories involving how children learn have been developed over the years. Development is similar for all children, but proceeds at an individual rate.

**Section 1.3**
Observation is a skill that can help caregivers gain insight into the personalities and development of children. Types of observation records include running records, anecdotal records, frequency counts, and developmental checklists.

↑ **Explore the Photo**
Interacting with children through play can help children learn. *How can playing with children help you learn about the children?*

**Explore the Photo**

**Caption Answer** Playing with children can help you learn about the child's development. This can help you provide appropriate activities to stimulate, but not frustrate, the child.

**Discussion** Ask students to think of a time when an adult asked them to perform an activity that was beyond their capability. Ask: How did this make you feel? Why is it important to provide children with activities that stimulate their interests, but are not beyond their capabilities?

**TeacherWorks Plus** is an electronic lesson planner that provides instant access to complete teacher resources in one convenient package.

**Presentation Plus!** provides visual teaching aids for every section.

**The Early Childhood Observations CD** presents video observations and lessons on observation skills and child development.

**The Developing Brain eTransparencies and Guide** include information and activities to offer insights into brain development and diseases of the brain.

# Make a Difference in Children's Lives

## Focus

### 🔔 Bell Ringer Activity

#### Why Learn About Child Development?

Instruct students to work with partners to create a list of three reasons they want to learn about child development. Ask for volunteers to share their lists with the class. Discuss that not only will they learn about child development in this class, they also will gain a greater understanding of themselves.

## Preteaching
### Vocabulary

Point out that words often can act as different parts of speech. For example, *impact* is used as a noun in this section but can also be used as a verb. Tell students that as a verb, impact means to press together, or to strike forcefully.

### Graphic Organizer

💿 The Graphic Organizer is also on the TeacherWorks CD.

(Graphic organizers should include: Health: Past—disease, Present—many diseases controlled; Education: Past—single classroom, Present—students grouped; Love: Past/Present—unchanged; Work: Past—children worked, Present—children get education; Play: Past—few toys, Present—endless toys; Dress: Past—formal, Present—casual)

**N C L B** NCLB connects academic correlations to book content.

## 📖 Reading Guide

### Before You Read

**Preview** Read the Key Concepts listed below. For each Key Concept, write a short paragraph that explains what you think you will learn in this section.

### Read to Learn
#### Key Concepts
- **Explain** the best way to learn about children.
- **Identify** three areas of childhood that researchers have studied.

#### Main Idea
Caregivers use their skills and knowledge to interact with children. Caregivers can make a positive difference in a child's life. Childhood is viewed differently today than in past years.

#### Content Vocabulary
◇ typical behavior
◇ caregiver

#### Academic Vocabulary
You will find these words in your reading and on your tests. Use the glossary to look up their definitions if necessary.
■ impact
■ moral

 **Graphic Organizer** Go to this book's Online Learning Center at **glencoe.com** to print out this graphic organizer.

### Graphic Organizer

As you read, compare childhood in the past with childhood in the present. Use a chart like the one shown to list the differences.

| Childhood Past and Present | | |
|---|---|---|
| | **Past** | **Present** |
| **Health** | | |
| **Education** | | |
| **Love** | | |
| **Work** | | |
| **Play** | | |
| **Dress** | | |

### Academic Standards ● ● ● ● ● ● ● ● ● ● ● ● ● ● ● ● ● ● ● ● ● ● ● ● ● ● ● ● ● ●

📖 **English Language Arts**
**NCTE 4** Use written language to communicate effectively.

 **Social Studies**
**NCSS V F Individuals, Groups, and Institutions** Evaluate the role of institutions in furthering both continuity and change.

**NCTE** *National Council of Teachers of English*
**NCTM** *National Council of Teachers of Mathematics*

**NSES** *National Science Education Standards*
**NCSS** *National Council for the Social Studies*

**N C L B**

## 📖 Reading Guide

### Before You Read

Ask students: Have you ever wondered why so much time and energy is spent on studying how children learn and develop? Why is this such an important task? Tell students that this section will present some of the reasons.

### D Develop Concepts

**Main Idea** Read aloud the main idea. Ask: How do you hope what you learn in this class might make a difference in children's lives? (Possible answer: They will have a better understanding of how children learn, and therefore will be better teachers or parents.)

## Benefits of Studying Children

Why do babies like to chew on books? Why do toddlers throw their toys again after you have just picked them up? What should you do if a three-year-old lies? Children's behavior can be both fascinating and frustrating, especially when you do not understand it. As you study child development, you will find answers to questions such as these. You will also learn that taking care of children is one of the most important responsibilities you can have.

## Understanding Children and Yourself

Have you ever really thought about the process by which children grow up and become independent adults? You might never have realized that you have an **impact**, or significant effect, on children's lives. People and events help shape who children become. When you live with children, you influence them every day.

If your contact with children is less frequent, what you say and how you act still matter. Even if you do not interact with children regularly, younger children still watch you and pay attention to how you behave. This is true whether the children are relatives, friends of your family, or even strangers that you pass in a store. Do you think that you are a good role model? Studying child development will help you learn how you can make a positive difference in a child's life.

Learning more about how children grow and develop will help you understand children better. It will also improve your understanding of yourself.

Many experts have written about how children learn and how best to care for them. No two children are alike, however, and no expert can explain every aspect of a child's behavior. The best way to learn about children is through your active involvement with them.

By interacting with children and studying their behaviors, you will:

- **Learn why children feel, think, and act the way they do.** It is not always easy to understand children's behavior, especially before they learn to talk. However, there are some typical behaviors. A **typical behavior** is a way of acting or responding that is common at each stage of childhood. Understanding these behaviors can help you respond to children more appropriately. For example, Carrie was puzzled by the actions of her brother Brett and their neighbor Curtis, both two-year-olds.

**Learn by Doing**
Interacting with children is the best way to learn about them. *What can this teen learn about toddlers by playing ball with them?*

Section 1.1    Make a Difference in Children's Lives    **7**

## Teach *cont.*

### S Skill Practice

**Independent Practice**

**Write a Thank You Letter** Have students think of a caregiver they had as a young child who had a positive effect on their lives. Instruct them to write a letter to this person thanking them for being a part of their lives. In the letter, they should give specific examples of how the person had a positive impact on them. **L1**

**Create a Brochure** Tell students they are going to be teaching a seminar in child development to college students. The focus of the seminar will be the positive impact a caregiver can have on a child's life. Students should create a brochure to encourage enrollment in the class. The brochure should emphasize what students will gain by taking the class. Encourage students to illustrate their brochures. (Students should create a brochure that explains the positive effect caregivers can have on a child's development.) **L2**

**Analyze a Game** Think of a game you or another child you know played with a caregiver when you were young. Write an essay describing how this game had a positive impact on your life by meeting your physical and social needs. (Students should write an essay discussing how a particular game they played when young met their physical and social needs.) **L3**

**8**

---

# Learning Through PLAY

## Playing with Babies

As babies grow and develop they learn new mental, physical, and social skills. As they learn more, their play changes. Very young babies learn physical skills by grasping toys such as rattles or stuffed animals. They interact and learn social skills when adults or older children talk to and play with them. Older babies learn social skills by playing games such as peek-a-boo. They might learn physical skills by clapping and moving in time to music. Their toys can be as simple as a bucket and some blocks. They can put the blocks into the bucket. Then they might turn the bucket upside down and dump out the blocks, and start over. Toys that make noise and change colors or have blinking lights can help babies learn to distinguish sounds and colors. For babies, play is their school. Through play, they continue to develop mentally, physically, and socially.

> **Think About It** You are reading to your nine-month-old niece, Rihanna, who is very alert and playful. How is this helping her develop mental, physical, and social skills?

They never interacted when they played. Brett and Curtis usually sat near each other, but they played with different toys. In a child development class, Carrie learned that two-year-olds typically play *alongside* each other but not *with* each other. Carrie understood that her brother's style of play was typical for his age.

- **Discover caregivers' importance.** A person who takes care of a child is called a **caregiver**. Parents and others can be caregivers. As you learn more about how children develop, you will see why they are dependent upon others for many years. Caregivers provide more than food and clothes. They give the affection children need to grow emotionally. They help children learn, and teach children how to get along with others and how to know right from wrong.
- **Enjoy children more.** Learning about children can help you discover what a joy they can be. Spending time with them will give you chances to experience their honesty, humor, energy, and curiosity. Caring for children can be very rewarding.
- **Learn about career opportunities.** Throughout this book, you will be introduced to many jobs related to children. You may find one that interests you.

## Apply What You Learn

You are in an excellent position to study child development. You are close enough to adulthood to think critically, but still young enough to remember what being a child feels like. As you learn about children, some of your views about childhood and child rearing may be reinforced, and you may rethink other views. Interacting and working with children and child care professionals can help you answer questions.

### Gain New Skills

As you learn about children and ways to meet their needs, try to find opportunities to apply your knowledge. You might spend your summers working at a local park or pool, or looking after a younger sibling or a neighbor's child. Knowing how to bathe a baby, prepare a healthy meal for a toddler, or encourage a four-year-old to settle down for a nap can give you confidence. This confidence can help make the children you care for feel more secure with you.

### Understand Yourself

As you gain a better understanding of children, you will also come to know yourself better. You may begin to see your own childhood differently. Think of your childhood.

**8** **Chapter 1** Learn About Children

---

# Learning Through PLAY

## Playing with Babies

Divide the class into four or five groups. Present each group with a toy appropriate for babies from eight to twelve months. Have each group determine how the toy could help a baby develop mental, physical, and social skills. Each group should then share their ideas with the class.

> **Think About It** She is developing mentally by hearing the language and matching words to pictures. She is developing physically by learning to turn the pages or hold the book. She is developing socially by interacting with you.

Try to recall major events in your childhood. Think about how they revealed different parts of your personality, or how they influenced whom you have become.

If you want to work with children, many career paths, such as teacher, children's librarian, or pediatric nurse, are open to you. You may not intend to work with children as an occupation, but you or someone close to you may be a parent someday.

**✓ Reading Check** **Define** What is a typical behavior?

## Views of Childhood

Childhood means different things to different people. The way you think about childhood can depend in part on what your own childhood was like. If your childhood was fairly easy and comfortable, you may think of it as a carefree time of security. If your parents struggled to provide for you, you may think of childhood as a time of hardship. For everyone, childhood is a period of rapid development, dependence on caregivers, and preparation for adult life.

Researchers have made a special study of childhood and its phases. They have looked at how children develop, what their needs are, and how those needs can best be met. One of their most important findings is that childhood has a profound influence on later life.

Childhood has not always been considered a separate, important stage of life. In fact, childhood as it is now known is a fairly recent viewpoint.

{ **Expert Advice...** }

*"Children need people in order to become human . . . It is primarily through observing, playing, and working with others older and younger than himself that a child discovers both what he can do and who he can become."*

—Urie Bronfenbrenner, psychologist and family advocate

**C**

▶ **Explore Careers**
Summer jobs can be a great way to explore career options. *How can this teen's job help him prepare for a career?*

## Assess

**Quiz**
Ask students to answer the following questions:

1. Why is it important that young children have caregivers who understand child development? (It is important so that they can help children learn and develop properly and teach skills appropriate for their ages)

2. Why are teens in a good position to study child development? (They are close enough to adulthood to think critically, but young enough to remember what it feels like to be a child.)

3. What are three areas of childhood in which researchers have made a special study? (how children develop, what their needs are, and how those needs are met)

## Reteach

**C** **Critical Thinking**

**Analyze** Read aloud the quote from Urie Bronfenbrenner on this page. Ask students: What does Bronfenbrenner mean when he states that it is by observing, playing, and working with others that a child discovers "who he can become"? (Answers will vary. Children can only imagine their own potential by seeing the enormous variety of achievements of others.)

**✓ Reading Check**

**Define** A typical behavior is a way of acting or responding that is common at each stage of childhood.

---

▶ **Explore the Photo**

**Caption Answer** Teaching children a skill, such as diving, can help him learn about the responsibilities involved in working with children, how children learn, and how best to relate to and interact with children.

**Discussion** Ask students: What skill is this teen teaching the child? How many other things might the child be learning? (The child is being taught to dive. Other ideas might include: he is learning to follow directions, to be responsible, and the satisfaction of learning a new skill.)

## Compare Childhood Past and Present

Until the twentieth century, some people believed that there was nothing special or important about the early years of life. Some adults believed children were meant to be "seen and not heard." Little was known about the emotional and intellectual needs of children. Changing attitudes, social changes, and advances in technology and medicine have changed views about childhood.

### Health

Before the twentieth century, diseases caused deaths in almost every family, particularly among children. Today, many deadly diseases can be controlled, and better nutrition has helped children to grow and thrive as never before. However, not all children eat well. Some do not have enough food. Others eat too many high-fat, high-sugar foods. Also, lack of regular exercise is increasingly common. The rate of childhood obesity and related problems has increased.

### Education

Public education for all children did not become common in the United States until the early 1800s. Schools were small, and often children of different ages and abilities were in the same classroom. In today's schools, students are grouped according to age and sometimes learning levels. Technology has enhanced learning options. Schools work to meet the special needs of individual students.

### Love

One thing that has not changed through the years is children's need for love. Most parents and other caregivers work hard to build a good life for their children and to raise them as **moral**, or ethical, people who are also responsible and independent.

**Changing Times**
Toys children play with have changed dramatically over time. *Do you think children learn more by playing with today's toys? Explain your answer.*

## Explore the Photo

**Caption Answer** Answers will vary. Some might think children today learn more because toys are more stimulating and many use guided learning. Others may think toys in previous times encouraged more creativity.

**Discussion** Ask students: If you were a parent, which of the toys in the photo would you prefer your child play with? Which toy do you think children would prefer? Why? (Answers will vary. Some parents might prefer the plane, because it probably would encourage more creativity and be less expensive. Most children prefer electronic toys because they find them more fun and stimulating.)

## Work

For settlers in America, a primary concern was survival. Children helped greatly with chores, gathering wood, sewing, and even plowing. Up until the twentieth century, children were expected to work at an early age. Then laws were enacted banning children from working in factories or other adult workplaces. Today, most young children are only expected to work at growing, learning, and playing. Teens may hold jobs, but laws specify the minimum working age and number of hours worked, and most dangerous jobs are banned. Most children are expected to help out at home by cleaning their rooms, feeding pets, helping with yard work, or helping care for siblings.

## Play

Play has always been important to children. It is how they learn. How much children play and what they play with have changed. In the past, children had far fewer toys, and they were simple. Parents often showed their love for their children by making them toys out of materials at hand. A child might have had a doll made of cloth or an animal carved from wood. Toys encouraged children to use their imagination.

Sports like baseball and basketball were not developed until the 1800s. Video and computer games first became available in the 1970s. Today, the variety of toys seems endless. Many toys are electronic and do not involve as much use of the imagination. However, children still enjoy books and other traditional toys. Children today spend much of their time playing.

## Dress

If you look at old pictures, you will quickly notice that children dressed more formally in the past. Infants and toddlers of both genders often wore long gowns. Older boys wore suits, while girls wore dresses. Today, casual clothes for boys and girls are often similar in style. It is not uncommon for infants to wear onesies or t-shirts. They are washable, comfortable, and loose enough to allow freedom of movement.

---

## Section 1.1 — After You Read

### Review Key Concepts

1. **Describe** two ways learning about children can benefit you.
2. **List** six areas in which views about children have changed over the years.

### Practice Academic Skills

#### English Language Arts

3. Use your personal experience and any observations you have made over the years to explain what is meant by the phrase, "Children are dependent upon others for many years." Write your explanation in a paragraph.

> **NCTE 4** Use written language to communicate effectively.

#### Social Studies

4. Children have better health today due to advances in medical technology. Many diseases that were responsible for childhood deaths in the past are treatable today. Conduct research and write a list of four ways medical advances affect our society today.

> **NCSS V F** Evaluate the role of institutions in furthering both continuity and change.

 **Check Your Answers** Check your answers at this book's Online Learning Center at **glencoe.com**.

**N C L B**

---

**Study Tools**

Have students go to the Online Learning Center at **glencoe.com**:

- Take the **Practice Test**.
- Download **Study-to-Go** content.

Use the **Student Activity Workbook** for additional practice.

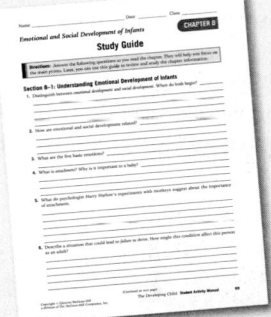

### Close

**Culminating Activity**

**Changing Childhood** Have students select one difference between childhood today and childhood in the past that is discussed in the text. Students should select the difference that surprised them the most. Ask for volunteers to share their choice and explain why it surprised them. Discuss the effects these changes have had on society.

**N C L B** **NCLB** connects academic correlations to book content.

---

## Section 1.1 — After You Read

### Review Key Concepts

1. By learning about children students can gain new skills, such as how to care for children; and they can learn more about themselves and how their childhood affected who they are today.
2. The six areas include health, education, love, work, play, and dress.

### Practice Academic Skills

3. Students' answer will vary, but might include: As babies, children are dependent for all of their needs; as they grow children become more independent. However, complete independence usually is not achieved until the late teen years. It is not until this time, or later, that children are able to completely provide for themselves.

4. Answers will vary, but may include: There are more children in our society because fewer of them die from disease; there are more children with special needs who likely would have died without today's medical technology; there is a need for more caregivers for children; children with special needs are able to function in society.

## Focus

### Bell Ringer Activity

#### Influences on Child Development

Write the words "Heredity" and "Environment" on the board. Ask students to define each word. Encourage them to discuss which they think has the greater influence on a child's development. Then discuss that researchers disagree about the roles of these two factors.

**Professional Development**

**Mini Clip Reading: Prereading Strategies**

A teacher assesses her students prior knowledge about a text selection they are about to read.

## Preteaching

### Vocabulary

The meaning of compound words can often be derived by looking at the meanings of the individual words. For example, self-esteem is the esteem (or value) placed on one's self. Ask students to guess the meaning of the human life cycle and then compare their answers to the definition in this section.

### Graphic Organizer

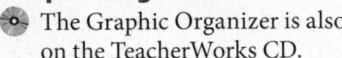 The Graphic Organizer is also on the TeacherWorks CD.

(Graphic organizers should list poor school performance, truancy, and criminal behavior.)

 **NCLB** connects academic correlations to book content.

---

### Reading Guide

#### Before You Read

**Cause and Effect**  A cause is an action or event that makes something happen. An effect is the result of the cause. As you read, look for causes and effects to better understand how the material is related.

#### Read to Learn
**Key Concepts**
- **Summarize** how children learn and develop important skills.
- **List** the stages of development after childhood.

#### Main Idea
Childhood is an important time of physical, mental, and emotional development. A child's heredity and environment affect development. Development continues throughout the life cycle.

#### Content Vocabulary
◇ stimulation
◇ heredity
◇ environment
◇ self-esteem
◇ human life cycle
◇ developmental task

#### Academic Vocabulary
You will find these words in your reading and on your tests. Use the glossary to look up their definitions if necessary.
■ theory
■ sequence

#### Graphic Organizer
As you read, note three effects of low self-esteem on a developing child. Use a chart like the one shown to help organize your information.

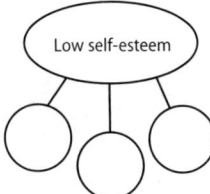

 **Graphic Organizer**  Go to this book's Online Learning Center at **glencoe.com** to print out this graphic organizer.

---

#### Academic Standards . . . . . . . . . . . . . . . . . . . . . . . .

 **English Language Arts**
**NCTE 12**  Use language to accomplish individual purposes.

 **Social Studies**
**NCSS IV C Individual Development and Identity**  Describe the ways family and cultural influences contribute to the development of a sense of self.

**NCTE** *National Council of Teachers of English*
**NCTM** *National Council of Teachers of Mathematics*

**NSES** *National Science Education Standards*
**NCSS** *National Council for the Social Studies*

---

---

### Reading Guide

#### Before You Read

Ask students to think of changes that have occurred in their lives during the last year. Perhaps they learned a new skill or read a book that altered their views on certain people or events. In this section they will learn about how children's development is affected by many factors.

#### D **Develop Concepts**

**Main Idea**  Discuss the main idea with the students. Ask students: If development continues throughout a person's life, why is child development studied more than later development? (Development during childhood occurs much more rapidly and has a much greater effect on later life.)

## Importance of Childhood Development

Imagine spending your whole career researching child development. By the time you retired, do you think you could solve all its mysteries? Many researchers have devoted their careers to the study of children, yet there are still many unanswered questions.

What has been learned, however, has dramatically changed how parents raise children, how educators teach them, and how we think of development today. Today we know development is a lifelong process.

Childhood prepares us for adulthood. Research has shown that early childhood may be the most important life stage for brain development. A child's brain is not yet fully developed at birth. The brain is the least developed of the organs. A baby's brain is about one-fourth the size of an adult's. By age three, it has made trillions of connections among the brain cells.

Scientists have found that a baby's brain develops in direct response to stimulation. **Stimulation** is any activity that arouses a baby's sense of sight, sound, touch, taste, and smell. Such activities can improve a baby's curiosity, attention span, memory, and nervous system development. Babies who receive stimulation develop more quickly and have a more secure self-image.

By the time babies are three to four months old, they are beginning to connect what they see with what they smell, feel, and taste. By the time toddlers start walking, the brain is sending messages faster and more clearly. Repetition of actions, such as throwing a ball, reinforces pathways in the brain. This makes it easier to perform the same action the next time.

## What Researchers Have Found

Child development theorists have provided valuable information about how children learn and develop skills. Some perform experiments involving children to test a **theory**, or belief. For example, children's perception of volume can be tested using the same amount of water in containers of various shapes. Other theories cannot be tested, such as Erik Erikson's belief that each stage of development includes a personal crisis.

Not everyone agrees on how parents, caregivers, and educators should apply theories and research findings. **Figure 1.1** on page 15 summarizes the study and research findings of some of the major child development theorists.

Although they do not always agree, scientific researchers have given us insight about how best to nurture and educate children. They have also laid the foundations upon which future researchers can build. There are five basic areas of child development: physical, emotional, social, intellectual, and moral.

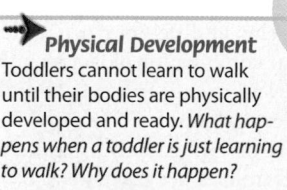

**Physical Development**
Toddlers cannot learn to walk until their bodies are physically developed and ready. *What happens when a toddler is just learning to walk? Why does it happen?*

Section 1.2    Studying Children    **13**

---

> **Explore the Photo**

**Caption Answer** Toddlers fall a lot when learning to walk because their bodies are learning a new skill, which takes time and effort to learn.

**Discussion** Ask students: What do you think would happen if children's parents did not encourage them to learn to walk? Do you think they would still learn this skill? (Responses will vary; children would probably still learn the skill because they would see others walking, but it may take longer.)

---

### Teach

**Discussion Starter**

**Researching Child Development**
Ask students: What do you think are the goals of scientists who research child development? Why do you think they believe their research is important? (Student answers will vary. Possible answer: by understanding how and why children develop in certain ways, we can be in a better position to help them grow up to be happy, successful adults.)

**R Reading Strategy**

**Cause and Effect** Tell students that one way to improve their reading comprehension is to watch for cause and effect. Read aloud the first two paragraphs under Importance of Childhood Development. Ask: What change has taken place? What are the causes of this change? What are the effects? (People started studying child development. They learned how children developed, resulting in changes in how children are raised and taught and how we think of child development today.)

**U Universal Access**

**Visual Learners** Have students watch the movie *The Miracle Worker,* which presents the life of Helen Keller, who was blind and deaf. Tell students to pay particular attention to how Keller's teacher, Annie Sullivan, aids enormously in Keller's development. When students are done, ask them to discuss how Sullivan helped Keller develop intellectually, emotionally, and socially by stimulating her remaining senses, such as her sense of touch. **ELL**

## Teach *cont.*

### C Critical Thinking

**Decide** Read this scenario: A mother has a toddler who delights in running about. The parent is afraid the child will get hurt so she holds him by the hand wherever they go. Is her action good for the child's development? Why or why not? (While the concern for the child's safety is valid, she is reducing the stimulation the child receives.)

### U Universal Access

**English Language Learners** Tell students that during infancy, synaptic connections between neurons are created at up to 3 billion per second. Because of the huge number of connections being formed, the first three years of life are an optimal time for learning. Have students work in groups to think of different ways infants can receive mental stimulation. Then have them collect pictures to create a collage showing infants receiving stimulation. **ELL**

### THE DEVELOPING BRAIN

**Neural Connections**
**Science Inquiry** Babies learn more in a stimulating environment; more learning leads to an increased number of neural connections.

For more information and activities, see *The Developing Brain* guide and eTransparencies.

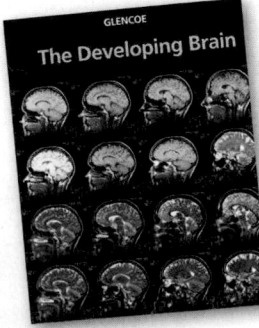

GLENCOE
The Developing Brain

**Different but Same**
No matter where a child lives, research has shown that all children develop skills in about the same order. *What skills might this infant have already mastered?*

### Characteristics of Development

Researchers have found that child development follows five general rules:

- **Development is similar for each individual.** Children go through the same stages in about the same order. All babies lift their heads before they lift their bodies.
- **Development builds upon earlier learning.** Development follows a **sequence**, or an order of steps. The skills learned at one stage build on those mastered earlier.

### THE DEVELOPING BRAIN

**Neural Connections**

Babies learn alot in the first three years of life. Newborn babies' brains contain about 100 billion nerve cells, called neurons. Those neurons have about 50 trillion connections. These connections increase rapidly, and by the age of three, a child has twice as many connections as an adult. As a child matures, unused pathways are removed. This means that babies who live in an environment where they learn more will keep more connections.

**Science Inquiry** A stimulating environment is important for babies' brains to develop to their fullest potential. How would a stimulating environment lead to an increased number of neurological connections?

- **Development proceeds at an individual rate.** While all children pass through the same stages of development, each child goes through these stages at his or her own pace.
- **The different areas of development are interrelated.** Though research tends to focus on one area at a time, changes occur in many areas at the same time.
- **Development is continuous throughout life.** The rate of development varies. No matter what the pace is, development does not stop.

### Influences on Development

If you traveled the world visiting families in various countries, you would see that babies are cared for in different ways in different cultures. However, all infants follow a predictable sequence of development at about the same ages. Babies must learn to lift their heads before they can sit or crawl, stand, and walk.

Children develop at different rates because each has a unique combination of factors influencing their development. These factors fall into one of two categories:

- **Heredity** is the biological transfer of certain characteristics from earlier generations. Blood type, eye color, and hair color are just a few of the characteristics determined by heredity.
- **Environment** is the people, places, and things that surround and influence a person, including family, home, school, and community.

**14** Chapter 1 Learn About Children

### Explore the Photo

**Caption Answer** This infant has already learned to support his head and to push himself up with his arms.

**Discussion** Tell students that jumping is a developmental milestone that toddlers can reach. Ask: what skills do you think a toddler must master before being able to jump? (Answers will vary but might include standing, balancing, or walking.)

Figure
1.1
Child Development Theorists

These are some of the researchers who have made a major contribution to the study of child development. *Which theorist said that each stage of development includes a psychological crisis? Why is this important?*

| Theorist | Findings or Ideas | Significance |
|---|---|---|
| Sigmund Freud (1856–1939) *Father of Psychology* | Believed that personality develops through a series of stages. Experiences in childhood profoundly affect adult life. | Childhood is much more important than previously thought, and its effects are longer lasting. |
| Jean Piaget (1896–1980) | The first to study children scientifically. Focused on how children learned. Believed that children go through four stages of learning. | Children must be given learning tasks appropriate to their level of development. |
| Lev Vygotsky (1896–1934) | Wrote that biological development and cultural experience influence children's ability to learn. Social contact is essential to intellectual development. | Children should be given the opportunity for frequent social interaction. |
| Erik Erikson (1902–1994) | Like Freud, said that personality develops in stages. Thought that each stage includes a unique psychological crisis. If that crisis is met in a positive way, the individual develops normally. | Parents and other caregivers must be aware of, and sensitive to, children's needs at each stage of development and support them through crises. |
| B. F. Skinner (1904–1990) | Argued that when a child's actions have positive results, they will be repeated. Negative results will make the actions stop. | Parents and other caregivers can affect a child's behavior through the use of negative and positive feedback. |
| Urie Bronfenbrenner (1917–2005) | Outlined layers of environment that affect a child's development, such as the child's own biology, family/community environment, and society. | Child's primary relationship with a caregiver needs to be stable, loving, and lasting. |
| Albert Bandura (b. 1925) | Said that children learn by imitating others. Disagreed with Skinner. Pointed out that although the environment shapes behavior, behavior also affects environment. | Caregivers must provide good examples for children to follow. |

**S**

Section 1.2   Studying Children   **15**

---

## Teach cont.

### S Skill Practice
#### Guided Practice

**Create a Time Line** Have students create time lines containing the seven theorists in Figure 1.1. Under each theorist's name, students should use their own words to create a brief summary of that person's findings or ideas. (Students should create a time line containing the names of the theorists in Figure 1.1 along with a summary of each one's findings or ideas.) **L1**

**Apply Feedback** Tell students that Marta takes care of her younger brother, Ramon, for two hours each day after school. Ramon leaves his toys strewn around the family room when he is done playing. Organize students into pairs. Have them create a skit illustrating how Marta could use B. F. Skinner's ideas to get her brother to put away his toys. (Students should create a skit showing how positive or negative reinforcement could be used.) **L2 ELL**

**Analyze Theories** Ask students which of the theorists in the chart were involved with intellectual development and social development. Point out that some of the theorists were involved in more than one area. Have students select a theorist that dealt with multiple areas of development and write a report describing how those areas of activity overlapped. (Answers will vary depending on the theorist chosen. For example, Vygotsky felt that social development was essential to intellectual development because cultural experiences influence the ability to learn.) **L3**

---

## Child Development Theorists

**Caption Answer** Erik Erikson; he stated that if the crisis is met in a positive way, the individual develops normally. Conversely, if it is not, the individual may develop abnormal tendencies.

**Discussion** Have students think of a crisis that might severely affect a two-year-old's development, such as the death of a parent. How do they think the child's development might be altered? (Students should list specific ways, such as the child may have trouble trusting adults.)

### Assess

**Quiz**

Ask students to answer the following questions:

1. At about what age do babies begin to connect what they see with what they feel, taste, and smell? (They begin making the connection at about three to four months of age.)

2. Give an example of how a child's emotional and social development might be interrelated. (Answers will vary. As the child becomes more emotionally mature, he may be better able to develop friendships because he can more easily see the world from others' points of view.)

3. What did Lev Vygotsky state regarding intellectual development? (He stated social contact is necessary for intellectual development.)

### Reteach

**W Writing Support**

**Freewriting**

**Heredity** Instruct students to spend a minute using freewriting to write about how they think heredity has affected their lives. You might want to offer some suggestions, such as do they think their height has affected the kinds of sports they enjoy. Ask for volunteers to share their writings. (Refer to page 4 for tips on freewriting. Students should use freewriting to express ideas concerning how heredity has affected their lives.)

## What Would You Do?

**A Healthy Environment**

Anne is a pediatric nurse. She has two nine-year-old patients, Ian and Seth, who have asthma. Aside from their age and diagnosis, their situations are different. "Seth has been to the hospital only once for an asthma attack," Anne says. "His mom also has asthma, so they have learned together how to manage their symptoms. They keep emergency medication on hand and clean their house often to reduce dust. Ian, on the other hand, spends a lot of time in the hospital for asthma attacks." Anne continues, "Two conditions in his home can make his asthma worse: his family has a cat and one of his parents smokes." Ian's parents asked how to help reduce his number of attacks.

**Write About It** How might Ian's parents change his environment to reduce the number of his asthma attacks? Write a brief article for the Health section of your local newspaper to offer ideas for Ian's parents.

Heredity is often referred to as *nature*. For example, if someone says, "Dylan is musically talented—it's in his nature," they mean that he was born with this gift. *Nurture* is used to refer to influences and conditions in a child's environment. Dylan may play the piano well because he practices each day. For years, scientists and philosophers have debated whether nature or nurture has more influence. Most agree, however, that they work together.

**W**

Children inherit certain physical characteristics from their parents and ancestors. For example, Alejandra has brown hair and brown eyes, as do her parents. Children learn attitudes and beliefs from their environment. Samira's parents take helping family and friends very seriously, and so does she.

Children are also greatly influenced by the world around them. What they read, the music they listen to, the movies and television shows they watch, the type of community in which they grow up, and many other influences play a part in who they become. If you spend time around children, you can count yourself as one of these influences.

**Heredity Affects Development**
Heredity plays a major role in physical characteristics and development. *What are some ways environment might affect development?*

16    **Chapter 1**    Learn About Children

## What Would You Do?

**Write About It** Students' articles will vary. They should indicate that Ian's parents should keep the cat away from Ian and they should eliminate Ian's exposure to smoke.

**▶ Explore the Photo**

**Caption Answer** Answers will vary but may include what they read, the type of community in which they grow up, or their caregivers.

**Discussion** A child who excels at school has parents who did well in school. Discuss whether students think this is an effect of heredity or environment and why. (Answers will vary, but students should provide reasons for their answers.)

Of course, children do not always copy the attitudes and actions of others, and no two children are exactly alike. They react to outside influences in their own ways. That is one reason that brothers and sisters who grow up in the same home may experience life differently. This is also why they may become very different people.

No two children have exactly the same environment. Even children who grow up in the same home have different environments. Their choice of friends, food, and activities will differ, and so will they. They might belong to different clubs. They will be exposed to different classmates. All of these things make up their environment.

During infancy and early childhood, environment plays a particularly important role in development. That is why working with young children is such an important responsibility and such a challenging opportunity.

## The Role of Self-Esteem in Development

**Self-esteem**, or self-worth, is the value people place on themselves. Self-esteem plays a role in people's ability to face and overcome the challenges of each developmental stage, including those of young childhood.

People with low self-esteem often feel that they are failing or constantly disappointing others. Researchers have found a link between low self-esteem and poor school performance, truancy, and criminal behavior.

A sense of self-worth is critical to children's development. Children who feel good about themselves are more likely to show enthusiasm for learning, form friendships, and make healthy choices. Having a sense of self-worth can help children deal with life's frustrations and disappointments, as well as its successes.

✓ **Reading Check** **Identify** Explain what is meant by *nature versus nurture*.

## ♥ Parenting Skills

### Help Children Develop Self-Esteem

Parents and other caregivers play a major role in developing a child's sense of self-esteem. Here are a few ways to have a positive effect.

- **Give praise.** Praise children for their accomplishments or real effort.
- **Do not be overly critical.** When children do not do things quite right, try to find the good in what they have done and discuss how they can do better the next time.
- **Set realistic goals.** Help children set goals that they can reach. Reaching realistic goals makes children feel good about their accomplishments.
- **Encourage new activities.** Help children learn to enjoy trying new things.
- **Model self-esteem.** Children learn by example. If the adults in their lives say negative things about themselves, children will imitate this negative behavior.
- **Be honest about mistakes.** Children need to see that adults have faults and make mistakes, too.

**Take Charge** Write a journal entry that describes a time when someone's criticism lowered your self-esteem. Explain how that person might have encouraged you instead.

Section 1.2 Studying Children **17**

## ♥ Parenting Skills

### Help Children Develop Self-Esteem

Read aloud the list of methods for helping children develop self-esteem. Have students write on a piece of paper which method they think is most helpful. Instruct students to get together with others who chose the same method. Each group should present the reasons for their choice. Encourage students to debate one another.

**Take Charge**
Students' answers will vary depending on the personal situation they choose to write about. They should include a suggestion for how they might have been encouraged through praise, constructive criticism, or a teaching/learning experience.

## Reteach cont.

**R** **Reading Strategy**

**Drawing Conclusions** Explain that good writing draws clear conclusions. Have students individually read the text under the heading "The Role of Self-Esteem in Development." Then instruct them to write one sentence stating the conclusions the author draws. Ask for volunteers to share their sentences. (Sentences will vary, but may be something similar to: Children with positive self-esteem are able to face and overcome life's challenges, whereas those with low self-esteem have difficulties.)

**C** **Critical Thinking**

**Predict** Some people think it is possible for parents to overly praise their children. Ask students what might happen to a child if her parent says, "Good job!" for every minor task the child completes. (A child who is constantly praised over everyday tasks may become overly dependent on the praise. Alternatively, she may begin to think the praise is meaningless so when she has a real achievement, the praise has no effect on her.)

**U** **Universal Access**

**Kinesthetic Learners** Organize students into pairs. Have one play the parent and the other play a fourteen-year-old. Have students imagine that the parent is always critical of the teen. No matter what the teen accomplishes, it is never good enough. Have students prepare skits in which the teens respectfully present their feelings and the two discuss the problem. (Skits will vary. The teens should honestly discuss their feelings and the pair should then discuss the issue with solutions.) **ELL**

✓ **Reading Check**

**Identify** *Nature versus nurture* refers to the effects that heredity has on development as compared to environment.

## Assess

### Study Tools

Have students go to the Online Learning Center at **glencoe.com**:

- Take the **Practice Test**.
- Download **Study-to-Go** content.

Use the **Student Activity Workbook** for additional practice.

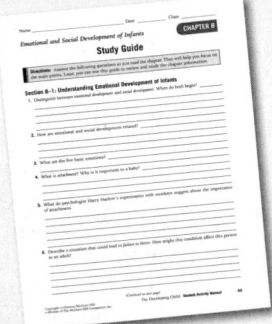

## Close

### Culminating Activity

**Summarize Characteristics of Development** As a class, summarize the five general rules that child development follows. Ask students which rules are related to one another, and why. (See p. 14 for the rules. Students should offer reasons for their decisions.)

**NCLB** connects academic correlations to book content.

---

# Stages of Life After Childhood

Development does not end when childhood does. It continues from birth to death in the human life cycle. The **human life cycle** is a set of stages of human development that each present different challenges to be met or skills to be acquired. The challenge to be met or skill to be acquired in each stage is known as a **developmental task**. These tasks can be such things as creating an identity or starting a career. Individuals differ in how they approach the challenges. Mastering the tasks of one stage helps prepare a person for the next stage.

- **Adolescence** This is the stage of life between childhood and adulthood. Teens work on three developmental tasks: creating an identity, becoming independent, and pursuing education and careers.
- **Young Adulthood** This stage refers to people in their twenties, when many young adults finish their education and begin working. Many marry in this period.

- **The Thirties** This stage presents the challenges of establishing roots, reevaluating life choices made earlier, and finding stability in career and relationships.
- **Middle Age** This stage lasts from about ages 40–55. Parents adjust as their children become more independent. Adults in this stage may make life changes, such as starting a new career.
- **Late Adulthood** At some point during this stage (ages 55–75), many adults retire. They may become more politically or socially active, travel, take classes, or enjoy hobbies they did not have time for before. Some take on a part-time job. Others enjoy having more time with their grandchildren. Health issues may arise.
- **Very Late Adulthood** It is in this stage (beyond age 75) when health problems become more common. However, many older adults are still active, and they contribute their knowledge and experience to society. Those in fragile health often need more assistance or care.

---

## Section **1.2**   After You Read

### Review Key Concepts

1. **Explain** why early childhood is considered the most important period for brain development.
2. **Identify** common characteristics of late adulthood.

### Practice Academic Skills

**English Language Arts**

3. Imagine that you will participate in a panel discussion on *Nature versus Nurture*. Create notes to use that explain how heredity and the environment can work together to shape a child.

> **NCTE 12** Use language to accomplish individual purposes.

**Social Studies**

4. Having a sense of self-worth helps children deal with life's successes and challenges. Research someone who has overcome obstacles in his or her life. Write a paragraph explaining how you think having a sense of self-worth helped them to succeed in life.

> **NCSS IV C** Describe the ways family and cultural influences contribute to the development of a sense of self.

**Check Your Answers** Check your answers at this book's Online Learning Center at **glencoe.com**.

---

## Section **1.2**   After You Read

### Review Key Concepts

1. Children's brains are not yet fully developed at birth. By age three, it has made trillions of connections among the brain cells.
2. At some point during this stage (ages 55–75), most adults retire. They may become more politically or socially active, travel, take classes, or enjoy other activities they didn't have time for before. Others enjoy having more time with their grandchildren. Health issues may arise.

### Practice Academic Skills

3. Notes will vary, but may include: Children inherit certain traits from their parents and ancestors. Children also learn attitudes and beliefs from their environment.

4. Paragraphs will vary depending on the person chosen. Students' should clearly show how the person's self-esteem helped them overcome specific obstacles. For example, Lance Armstrong's strong self-worth gave him strength to fight cancer and compete again.

## Reading Guide

### Before You Read

**Vocabulary** Read the Content and Academic Vocabulary. Choose a term that you are not familiar with and when you see it in the text, write down the definition.

### Read to Learn
**Key Concepts**
- **Determine** why observation is important in the study of child development.
- **Compare and contrast** different methods of observation and interpretation.

**D**

### Main Idea
An important component in learning and understanding child development is observation. Observation allows caregivers to better understand individual children and their particular needs.

### Content Vocabulary
◇ subjective
◇ objective
◇ running record
◇ anecdotal record
◇ frequency count
◇ baseline
◇ developmental checklist
◇ interpretation
◇ confidentiality

### Academic Vocabulary
You will find these words in your reading and on your tests. Use the glossary to look up their definitions if necessary.
■ assumption
■ judgment

### Graphic Organizer
As you read, note the four methods of recording observations described in the text. Use a chart like the one shown to help organize your information.

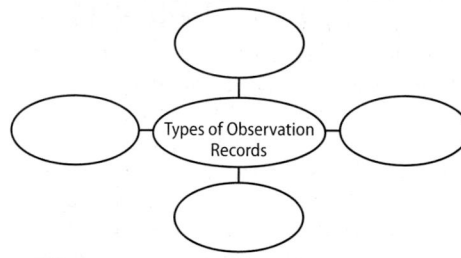

Types of Observation Records

**Graphic Organizer** Go to this book's Online Learning Center at **glencoe.com** to print out this graphic organizer.

**NCLB**

### Academic Standards · · · · · · · · · · · · · · · · · · · · · ·

**English Language Arts**

**NCTE 4** Use written language to communicate effectively.

**Science**

**NSES A** Develop abilities necessary to do scientific inquiry, understandings about scientific inquiry.

**NCTE** *National Council of Teachers of English*
**NCTM** *National Council of Teachers of Mathematics*

**NSES** *National Science Education Standards*
**NCSS** *National Council for the Social Studies*

## Focus

### Bell Ringer Activity

#### Observing Behavior
After students have settled in their seats, spend a few minutes doing three or four random tasks. For example, you might take a pen out of your pocket and scribble a note, gather papers out of a drawer, and close the door. Then ask students to describe your behaviors. Explain that a great deal can be learned by observing another's actions and observing is a skill that can be learned. This section will teach the skills needed to observe children.

### Preteaching
#### Vocabulary
Tell students that suffixes have their own meaning. When added to the end of a word, a new word with a new meaning is created. The suffix *–ive* means tending to. A word that ends in *–ive* is always an adjective.

#### Graphic Organizer
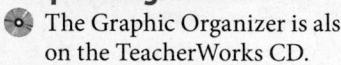 The Graphic Organizer is also on the TeacherWorks CD.

(Graphic organizers should include: running record, anecdotal record, frequency count, and developmental checklist.)

**NCLB** NCLB connects academic correlations to book content.

## Reading Guide

### Before You Read
Ask students: What do you think you can tell by simply observing someone? Do you think you can tell how intelligent they are? Can you tell if they are happy? Tell students that when studying children, observations are very important. In this section, they will learn why and how adults observe children.

### **D** Develop Concepts

**Main Idea** Discuss the main idea with the students. Ask students: How is observing children different from reading about child development? What are some advantages of each? (Answers will vary. Observing provides direct information, but reading allows you to learn from experts.)

### Teach

## Discussion Starter

**Importance of Being a Good Observer** Ask students: What does the word *observe* mean to you? Is it different from the word *watch*? (Observe means to watch carefully.) Ask students why good observation skills are necessary for child care workers and teachers. (Observation skills are vital for these workers because they must keep children safe and they must understand the children in their care well enough to meet their individual needs.)

 **Reading Strategy**

**Predict** Tell students to predict what they will learn in the text under the heading "Why Observe Children?" Have them write down their predictions. After they are done reading, instruct them to re-read their predictions and modify them, if necessary. (Students' predictions and modifications will vary.)

**Professional Development**

**Mini Clip Reading: Strategic Readers**

Author Scott Paris discusses the characteristics of strategic readers.

### ✓ Reading Check

**Recall** Getting to know a child helps you determine the child's personality and learning style so that you can adjust your interactions and teaching methods to be most effective.

↑ **Learning by Observation**
Observation can help you learn traits and personalities of individual children. *What have you learned by observing children?*

## Why Observe Children?

While you can learn a great deal from reading about children, observing them is even more helpful. Observing offers you the chance to see children as individuals. You see them meeting the challenges of development in their own ways and in their own time. Child development comes to life when you observe children in action. Learning how to observe children is an important skill for teachers, parents, and other caregivers.

Observing young children and interpreting their behavior are skills that take time to learn. You will see how one stage leads to the next, for example, as an infant learns to sit up, then pull up, then stand alone, and finally walk. Caregivers who are familiar with the various stages of development can help and encourage children as they progress.

Observing a child will let you see his or her unique personality. If you get to know a child, you will be able to adapt activities to that child's needs. Parents and caregivers who are careful observers often can identify children who may have disabilities or require extra care.

Children developing slowly can be evaluated and treated. Researchers have found that children whose special needs are spotted and treated early do better over the long term.

Finally, observing children provides caregivers with useful feedback. Watch how children respond to your attempts at guiding their behavior, and you will see how successful your methods are. If you stick to what works, you will be more effective at earning children's cooperation and trust.

### ✓ Reading Check    Recall  Why is it useful to get to know a child?

## How to Observe Young Children

Knowing how to record what you observe and analyze it later will give you insight into children's development. Observing means more than just watching. It means following certain steps so that your observations will be useful. You must have a written record of your observation to refer to for analysis.

**20**    **Chapter 1**    Learn About Children

▶ **Explore the Photo**

**Caption Answer** Students' answers will vary depending on their personal experiences, but may include such things as two-year-olds can't throw or catch a ball well and young children have problems sharing.

**Discussion** Ask students to look at the photo and write an objective description of the child on the left. (Answers will vary, but may include that the girl is standing up straight on a merry-go-round with three other children. The girl is smiling and firmly holding onto the bars.)

## Objective Versus Subjective Observations

When observing, you must learn to separate fact from opinion. Compare the two observations of the same event in **Figure 1.2.**

Observation A is subjective. **Subjective** means to rely on personal opinions and feelings, rather than facts, to judge an event. From reading the observation, it is hard to tell what really happened between Ethan and Cody. The observer in this example recorded an opinion about how Ethan felt.

Observation B is objective. **Objective** means something is factual, and leaves aside personal feelings and prejudices. The observer describes only what was actually seen and heard. You know exactly what actions Ethan and Cody performed. Analyzing the observation later will help determine why those actions occurred.

Subjective observations are based on the false assumption that the observer knows what is going on in the child's mind. An **assumption** is a fact that is taken for granted. Subjective observations can be misleading. Ethan might not have been acting selfishly. He might have had an earlier agreement with Cody about taking turns. He might be angry because Cody is not holding up his end of the deal.

Subjective observations do not record facts, so they are hard for others to use. A teacher who knew that Ethan was generally shy at school would probably prefer to hear the objective facts presented in Observation B. The teacher might interpret Ethan's behavior as a sign of growing self-assertion. Ethan might not be behaving appropriately, but the teacher might be pleased that he is sticking up for himself. The teacher might also realize that Cody needs more practice at sharing.

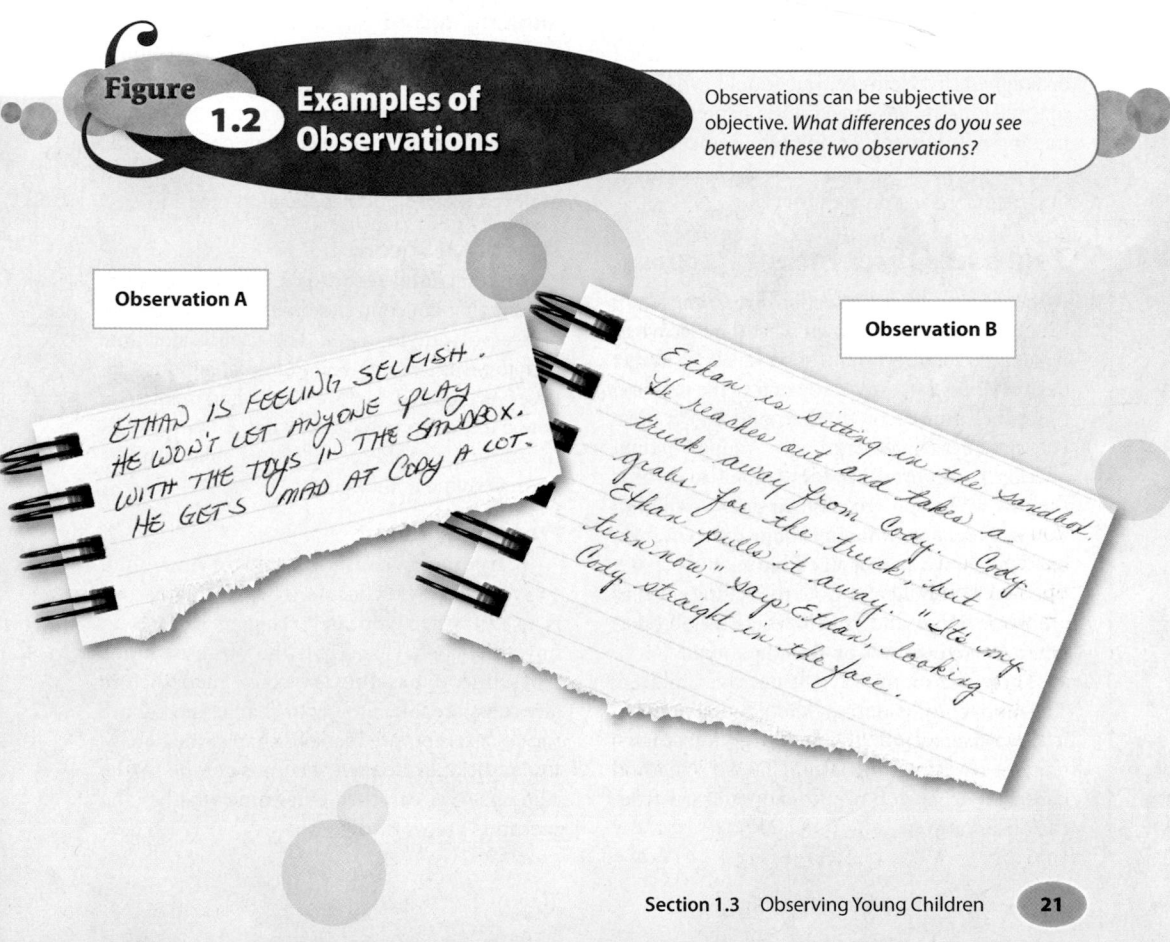

**Figure 1.2 Examples of Observations**

Observations can be subjective or objective. *What differences do you see between these two observations?*

**Observation A**

ETHAN IS FEELING SELFISH. HE WON'T LET ANYONE PLAY WITH THE TOYS IN THE SANDBOX. HE GETS MAD AT CODY A LOT.

**Observation B**

Ethan is sitting in the sandbox. He reaches out and takes a truck away from Cody. Cody grabs for the truck, but Ethan pulls it away. "It's my turn now," says Ethan, looking Cody straight in the face.

## Teach *cont.*

### S Skill Practice
### Guided Practice

**Observations Based on Photographs** Have students bring in a recent photo of themselves performing some activity. They should write an objective observation based on the photo. They should then use the same photo to write a subjective observation. Ask students: Do you think your subjective observation reflects what you actually felt at the time? (Students should have written both an objective and a subjective observation and evaluate their subjective observation.) **L1**

**Interviewing a Teacher** Instruct students to conduct an interview with a preschool or elementary school teacher. They should ask the teachers how they use observations in their work. What are the purposes of observations? Students should prepare short presentations on what they learn. (Students should have prepared presentations on what they learned about how teachers use observations in their work.) **L2**

**Comparing Observations** Show students a short video of some young children at play. Assign half the group to write a subjective observation of the video and the other half to write an objective observation. Instruct students to write a paragraph comparing the two observations. (Students' paragraphs will vary, but should discuss that the objective observations attempt to just present the facts, whereas the subjective ones provide interpretations of the facts.) **L3**

**Figure 1.2 Examples of Observations**

**Caption Answer** Observation A is subjective; the observer's interpretation is included in the observation. Observation B is objective; the observer states the facts as they occur and does not offer an interpretation.

**Discussion** As a class, create a list of words students associate with objective observations. Then create a list of words they associate with subjective observations. (Words associated with objective observations might include action verbs such as talk and play. Words associated with subjective observations might include feel, happy, or jealous.)

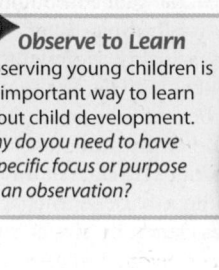

**R** **Reading Strategy**

**Summarize** Instruct students to read the material under Types of Observation Records, and then take a minute to summarize its content. Tell them to pretend they are explaining the material to a classmate. They should start with the major point and then fill in the details. (Summaries might state that students should create objective records of what they observe. Details might include the types of records used: running, anecdotal, frequency, and developmental checklist.) **ELL**

**U₁** **Universal Access**

**Logical Learners** Explain to students that most research on young children is either longitudinal or cross-sectional. Instruct students to work in pairs to conduct research to learn more about these. Students should then come up with two ideas: one for a longitudinal study and one for a cross-sectional study. Each pair should write a summary of the proposed studies. (Summaries will vary but should show an understanding of cross-sectional studies taking place at a single point in time and longitudinal studies involving a series of measurements taken over a period of time.)

**C** **Critical Thinking**

**Analyze** Jeremiah observed a child in a kindergarten class. He created a running record for 15 minutes. On the day he observed, the class had a substitute teacher. Do you think this might have affected what Jeremiah saw? Why? (Any change in daily routine would be likely to affect students' behavior, and having a substitute teacher is a major change. Jeremiah should make a note of the substitute in his observation record and try to do another observation with the normal teacher.)

**Observe to Learn** Observing young children is an important way to learn about child development. *Why do you need to have a specific focus or purpose for an observation?*

Writing objective observations takes practice. An observer can note that a child smiled or laughed, for example, but should avoid saying that this means the child is happy. That is making a **judgment**, or opinion. Remember to record only what you see and hear. Do not make judgments when you are observing.

## Types of Observation Records

When making observations, it is important for observers to write down what they see when it happens. If they wait, observers may forget details. Begin each record by noting the date and time, the number of children and adults present, and their names and ages. Young children develop so quickly that it is helpful to include months when you record their ages. A child of two years and one month is quite different from one who is two years and eleven months of age. The record should also note the setting, such as school or home, and exactly where the observation occurred, such as on the jungle gym.

There are many ways to observe children. The above information should be included in any observation. The following four methods are particularly useful. Choose a method based on what you are hoping to learn from the observation.

### Running Record

A **running record** is a record of everything observed for a set period, such as 15 minutes. This method is useful for observers who are just getting to know the child or children. It is also good when concentrating on a certain area of development, such as social interaction.

### Anecdotal Record

An **anecdotal record** is a report of a child's actions that concentrates on a specific behavior or area of development. The time is not limited for this record. For example, suppose an observer wanted to focus on adjustment to a new child care center. Every day for two weeks the observer could record how a child behaves upon arriving at the center.

### Frequency Count

A **frequency count** is a tally of how often a certain behavior occurs. This kind of record is useful when you are trying to change an unwanted behavior. First, the observer finds a baseline. A **baseline** is a count made before any steps are taken to try to change the behavior. As attempts are made to change the behavior, additional frequency counts can be made. The observer can then determine whether the methods are working.

 **22** **Chapter 1** Learn About Children

---

**▶ Explore the Photo**

**Caption Answer** It is important to have a focus or purpose so that you can choose the most appropriate method of recording the observation and can have direction.

**Discussion** A caregiver wants to observe the development of a friendship between two children. Ask students what type of observation record would be most appropriate and why. (An anecdotal record would be most appropriate because time is not limited and the observer could focus strictly on the children's relationship.)

## Developmental Checklist

A list of skills children should master, or behaviors they should exhibit at a certain age, is called a **developmental checklist**. Observers can use this checklist and simply check off the skills or behaviors they see.

## How to Act While Observing

There are two different ways you can observe young children: formally and informally. A formal observation might be something you set up with a child care center or a family. An informal observation is one where you do not make yourself so obvious. This could be sitting at a mall or airport watching children. When you make informal observations, you will have to estimate the ages of the children you observe. Avoid making quick judgments about children, since you are only getting glimpses of their abilities and behavior.

Whether you observe children formally or informally, you do not want to be noticed. When you observe children, it is generally important to try to blend into the environment as much as possible. Avoid calling attention to yourself. If your presence affects the children's behavior, it may not be possible to gather objective information. Sit or stand slightly outside the area where the children are, and be ready to take notes. Make sure you clearly understand your observation assignment before you begin. Also make sure you have noted the basic information. When you are observing children, things happen very quickly. You need to be prepared. **Figure 1.3** offers more tips on how to take notes that will be useful for later analysis.

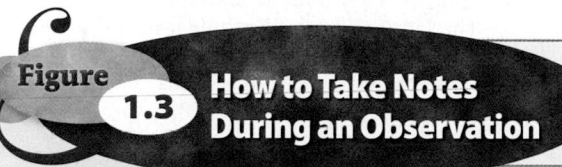

**Figure 1.3 How to Take Notes During an Observation**

Preparing ahead of time will help ensure a successful observation. *How might you prepare your paper to help you complete all the aspects of your observation?*

| Action | Explanation |
|---|---|
| **Know your purpose.** | Before you do your observation, define the purpose of your observation. Ask yourself what you are supposed to observe. |
| **Identify the when, where, who, and what.** | Take note of the physical features of the setting. Who is there? What activities are going on? Make a record of the time and place. |
| **Be descriptive.** | You can use words and phrases to capture the moment. Think of it as giving a picture of what you see. |
| **Make comparisons.** | Look for similarities and differences. If you are watching groups of children, evaluate what each group is doing. If you are focusing your observation on one child, how do his or her skills compare to those of another child of the same age? |
| **Uncover the data.** | Record as much factual information as you can, focusing on the evidence at hand. |
| **Review and clarify.** | At the end, read through your comments, make clarifications or corrections, and add any additional notes. |

Section 1.3  Observing Young Children  **23**

**Figure 1.3  How to Take Notes During an Observation**

**Caption Answer**  Answers will vary, however students should indicate that writing heads such as When, Where, Who, and What will help them remember, and quickly fill in, the necessary information to record.

**Discussion**  What is the purpose of making comparisons when you are observing? (Making comparisons helps you judge how a specific child is doing relative to other children of the same age and at similar levels of development.)

### Assess

**Quiz**

Ask students to answer the following questions:

1. Imagine a friend says, "You don't need to observe children. You were one yourself—didn't that teach you what you need to know?" How might you respond? (Answers may vary. Understanding child development requires learning about the results of years of research. Also, each child is unique.)

2. You are observing a preschooler. Give an example of a situation in which you might need to quit being an observer and interact with the child. (Answers will vary, but might include protecting the child's safety or determining whether the child has a specific skill.)

3. When might you use a developmental checklist to assess a kindergartener's behavior? (This is used when the observer wants to determine which skills a child has mastered.)

### Reteach

**U₂ Universal Access**

**Interpersonal Learners**  Instruct students to go to a public place, such as a park or mall, and observe a preschooler for about 10 minutes. Have them create a running record during this time. Then have them trade their records with a classmate. The classmate should offer suggestions for improving the record. Remind students to watch out for subjective language. **ELL**

## Reteach cont.

### W Writing Support

**Freewriting**

**Being Respectful** Discuss with students that this section explains the importance of being respectful of the children you observe. Showing respect for other people and their privacy is an important trait for everyone to have. Instruct students to spend one minute freewriting about the importance of respect. (Refer to p. 4 for tips on freewriting. Student responses will vary, but should revolve around the importance of being respectful of others.)

### R Reading Strategy

**Topic Sentence** Tell students that identifying a paragraph's topic sentence can help in determining the author's purpose. Ask: What is the topic sentence of the second paragraph on this page? How do the remaining sentences support this topic sentence? (The topic sentence is the first sentence in this paragraph. The subsequent sentences suggest how students might respond to the situation brought up in the topic sentence.) **ELL**

**Professional Development**

**Mini Clip Reading: During and After Reading**

A teacher models for her students and then has them practice what a good reader thinks about.

---

## SAFE CHILD HEALTHY CHILD

### An Observer's Role

Children often do not have the judgment or skills to realize that they are in danger. While observing, if you see a child in a dangerous situation, you must intervene and get help from a teacher or caregiver. For example, imagine you are observing children at a child care center and you notice a young toddler put a small puzzle piece in his mouth. You should get help from a child care worker immediately. Getting help quickly often prevents harm from coming to children.

☀ **Be Prepared** Think of a dangerous situation in which you would intervene immediately. Decide what you would do in the situation. Develop a step-by-step procedure that you would follow in the situation and create a poster with the steps. Hang the poster in the classroom.

Always be respectful of others. If you are doing a formal observation, arrive on time. Be sure to follow any sign-in procedures or other rules a center might have.

Children are naturally curious, and they will want to find out who you are and what you are doing. Answer questions honestly but briefly. You can also just smile and say you are working. Avoid asking questions, which will encourage conversation. If the children need to be persuaded to return to their activities, you might say, "I am writing a story about how children play. If you go back to playing, I can write about you in my story."

There are some situations when you may need to interact with a child. For example, if you are updating a developmental checklist you might need to know how well a child can catch and throw a ball. You could pull the child aside for a few minutes and test for these skills. The Safe Child, Healthy Child feature describes other reasons you might need to step in.

**W**

**R**

↑ **Time to Understand**
It takes time to develop good observation skills and to be able to interpret observations accurately. *Why should you discuss questions about what you observe with your teacher rather than your friends?*

**24** **Chapter 1** Learn About Children

---

## SAFE CHILD HEALTHY CHILD

### An Observer's Role

**Explain** Why must young children be carefully watched to protect their safety? (They do not have the judgment or skills to realize when they are in danger.)

☀ **Be Prepared** Posters will vary depending on the situation chosen. Posters should show a well-thought-out, step-by-step process that addresses the situation.

---

### ▶ Explore the Photo

**Caption Answer** It is way of showing respect for those you are observing and their parents, and to protect their confidentiality.

**Discussion** Why should you avoid starting conversations with the children you are observing? (You are there to study the child's behavior and how he interacts with other children and his caregivers, not how he interacts with you.)

## How To Interpret Observations

Before you use your observations, you will need to finalize your paperwork. In many cases, you will want to transfer your notes to another sheet, or use your notes to write a longer observation record. Some observations are kept in a child's file for future reference, so make sure that your final report appears neat and professional. You might want to type your report using word-processing software. This will allow you to save an electronic file for reference and print a copy for the child's file.

Simply having a half-hour's running record of a child's behavior is of little use unless you analyze it. The analysis an observer forms and expresses about what was observed is called an **interpretation**. In recording the information, it was your job to remain objective. Now it is time to form and express ideas about what you saw. Your study of child development will help you do so.

Anyone who observes children and interprets information about them must maintain confidentiality. **Confidentiality** (ˌkän-fə-ˌden(t)-shē-ˈa-lə-tē) is the protection of another person's privacy by limiting access to personal information. You may share your information only with the child's parents or your child development teacher. It is not ethical to discuss children outside of class.

Remember that most observations are short in length. For this reason, your interpretation may not be accurate. You are just developing your observation skills, so your interpretation may not match that of a professional. These are further reasons that you must avoid discussing the child's behavior with your friends. Comments such as "Lauren is spoiled" or "Caleb is a slow learner" might lead to gossip that could hurt the child or the family. If you have questions or concerns about a child you observed, discuss them only with your child development teacher.

## Assess

### Study Tools

Have students go to the Online Learning Center at **glencoe.com**:

- Take the **Practice Test**.
- Download **Study-to-Go** content.

Use the **Student Activity Workbook** for additional practice.

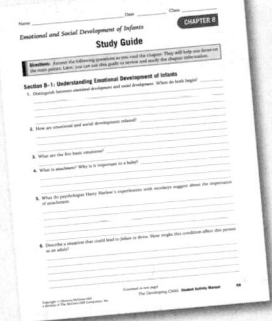

## Close

### Culminating Activity

**Reviewing Observation Records** Have students review the different types of observation records by giving examples of situations in which each would be useful. (Students examples will vary, but should be appropriate to the purpose of the observation.)

 **NCLB** connects academic correlations to book content.

---

## Section 1.3 — After You Read

### Review Key Concepts

1. **List** two reasons why observing children is helpful in your study of child development.
2. **Identify** four basic facts an observation record should include.

### Practice Academic Skills

 **English Language Arts**

3. Imagine that you have just completed your observation of a kindergarten-age boy. Write a paragraph to discuss how you would go about interpreting his behavior. List the steps you would take after recording your information.

> **NCTE 4** Use written language to communicate effectively.

 **Science**

4. With a partner, observe one child for at least ten minutes. One of you will write a running record of all the behaviors observed. The other will write an anecdotal record, focusing on one aspect of behavior, such as attitude toward learning. How are your records similar or different? .

> **NSES A** Develop abilities necessary to do scientific inquiry, understandings about scientific inquiry.

**Check Your Answers** Check your answers at this book's Online Learning Center at **glencoe.com**.

**Section 1.3** Observing Young Children **25**

---

**Section 1.3** After You Read

### Review Key Concepts

1. Any two of the following: offers the chance to see children as individuals; to see how one stage leads to the next; to be able to tailor activities to the child's needs; to identify children who may require extra care.
2. The date and time, the number of children and adults present, names and ages of those present, and the location.

### Practice Academic Skills

3. Student answers will vary, but should include: finalize the paperwork, transfer notes to another sheet or use notes to write a longer observation record; form and express ideas about what was observed; share information only with the child's parents or your child development teacher; discuss any questions with child development teacher.

4. Answers will vary; however, students should show an understanding of running records and anecdotal records and the similarities and differences between them. Differences may include: running records are for a specific amount of time, anecdotal records do not limit the time of the observation.

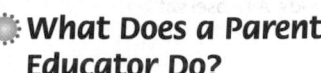

## Careers With Children — Parent Educator

**S**ometimes parents want to do more for their children outside of the home and classroom. Parent educators are trained in child development. They use their training to help educate parents about parenting skills.

### ☀ What Does a Parent Educator Do?

Parent educators provide assistance, instruction, and materials in a variety of areas. These can include academic areas as well as nutrition, parenting styles, and behavioral management. Parent educators can demonstrate techniques to enhance parent-child growth. One primary responsibility of these educators is to teach parents about the resources available to them. They provide referral information for books, Web sites, and workshops.

### ☀ Where Does a Parent Educator Work?

Depending on the area in which they specialize, parent educators have the flexibility of working in schools, community centers, and hospitals. Some parent educators visit the homes of the people they work with.

### Preparation and Skills

**Education and Training**
Most parent educators have bachelor's degrees with an emphasis in early childhood education or psychology. Some hold master's degrees in social work or developmental psychology.

**Aptitudes, Abilities, and Skills**
Parent educators must be proficient in communication and language skills. They should possess a knowledge of early childhood behavior, characteristics, and development. Effective parenting skills, mentoring abilities, and record-keeping abilities are also needed.

**Academic Skills**
Parent educators use English language arts, such as speaking and listening, when they talk to parents or groups of parents. They also use mathematics, science, and social studies skills in the research and skills they teach to parents.

**NCLB**

**Explore Careers**
Research a career related to parent educator, such as teacher or family counselor. Write a paragraph describing the career. Explain why you would or would not pursue that career.

**Careers Online** For more information on careers, visit the Occupational Outlook Handbook Web site through the link on this book's Online Learning Center at **glencoe.com**.

---

## Sidebar (left and right teaching notes)

### Focus

**Discussion Starter**
**Parenting** Discuss with students that our society requires people to take courses or have training before they can perform many jobs. Encourage students to debate whether there should be similar requirements to become a parent.

### Teach

**C** **Critical Thinking**
**Make Judgments** Ask students what kind of parents they think would benefit most from the help of a parent educator. Encourage students to be specific in describing these parents. (Student answers will vary. Parents who are young would probably benefit because they lack life experience. People who did not learn good parenting skills from their own parents and those who had not been around children much also would probably benefit.)

### Assess

**Make Connections**
Ask students to list specific correlations between academic subjects and the skills a good parent educator needs. (Students should show an understanding of how academic skills relate to this job. For example, parent educators should have studied child development so they can tell parents what to expect at different ages.)

**NCLB** This relates academic skills to specific tasks that are performed for this job.

### Close

**Culminating Activity**
**Encouraging a New Parent** Tell students to imagine that they have a twenty-year-old cousin who is pregnant and afraid that she will not have the skills needed to raise a happy, well-adjusted child. What might you suggest to her? (Students might suggest she try to find a parenting class taught by a parent educator. They might suggest that she check hospitals and community centers for such a class.)

**Explore Careers**
Paragraphs will vary depending on the careers chosen. Students should explain why they would or would not choose to pursue the career they researched.

# Chapter Summary

By studying children, you can learn why they act the way they do, discover why caregivers are an important influence, and enjoy children more. As more has been learned about children through research, attitudes and practices have changed. Experiences in the first years of life promote rapid brain development. Heredity and environment both impact development. Self-esteem influences a person's ability to face life's challenges.

You can learn things by observing children that you cannot learn from a book. There are several types of observation methods. All observations should be conducted carefully and kept confidential.

## Vocabulary Review

**1.** Use each of these content and academic vocabulary words in a sentence.

**Content Vocabulary**
◇ typical behavior (p. 7)
◇ caregiver (p. 8)
◇ stimulation (p. 13)
◇ heredity (p. 14)
◇ environment (p. 14)
◇ self-esteem (p. 17)
◇ human life cycle (p. 18)
◇ developmental task (p. 18)
◇ subjective (p. 21)

◇ objective (p. 21)
◇ running record (p. 22)
◇ anecdotal record (p. 22)
◇ frequency count (p. 22)
◇ baseline (p. 22)
◇ developmental checklist (p. 23)
◇ interpretation (p. 25)
◇ confidentiality (p. 25)

**Academic Vocabulary**
■ impact (p. 7)
■ moral (p. 10)
■ theory (p. 13)
■ sequence (p. 14)
■ assumption (p. 21)
■ judgment (p. 22)

## Review Key Concepts

**2. Explain** the best way to learn about children.
**3. Identify** three areas of childhood that researchers have studied.
**4. Summarize** how children learn and develop important skills.
**5. List** the stages of development after childhood.
**6. Determine** why observation is important in the study of child development.
**7. Compare and contrast** different methods of observation and interpretation.

## Critical Thinking

**8. Examine** How might studying the different aspects of child development better help you understand yourself?
**9. Conclude** What are two reasons adults might have less responsibility as they settle into middle age?
**10. Infer** Why might the conclusions of scientific studies, such as those in child development, later be viewed as invalid?

**Chapter 1** Learn About Children **27**

## Content and Academic Vocabulary Review

**1.** Students should write complete sentences using each vocabulary word correctly.

## Review Key Concepts

**2.** The best way to learn about children is to observe them and work with them.
**3.** Three areas of childhood that have been studied are how children develop, what their needs are, and how those needs can best be met.
**4.** Children go through stages in about the same order; development builds upon earlier learning; and development follows a sequence but proceeds at an individual rate.
**5.** The stages are adolescence, young adulthood, the thirties, middle age, late adulthood, and very late adulthood.
**6.** Observation offers the chance to see children as individuals, meeting the challenges of development in their own way and in their own time.
**7.** All are based on watching children. A running record involves writing down everything observed for a set period. Anecdotal records concentrate on a specific area of development. A frequency count tallies how many times a specific behavior occurs. When keeping a developmental checklist, observers check off the skills or behaviors they see.

## Critical Thinking

**8.** Answers will vary, but should include something similar to: As you learn more about children, it will help you understand different things about your own childhood and how you react in specific situations today.
**9.** Answers may vary but should include: Parents have fewer responsibilities as their children become more independent; they may be more settled in their careers.

**10.** Answers will vary. As new studies are conducted, they may invalidate the conclusions of older studies, particularly those studies that were conducted before researchers and educators had a thorough understanding of child development.

**Family & Community Connections**

**11.** Student answers will vary. They should note the specific techniques used to stimulate learning in the children.

## Health Skills

**12.** Answers will vary depending on the vaccines researched. For example, Measles, mumps, and rubella vaccine (MMR)—administer the first dose at age 12–15 months, second dose at age 4–6 years. Side effects can include fever, rash, swelling, and seizures.

## Observation Skills

**13.** Answers will vary but should show that students recognize behavior that is indicative of a lack of interpersonal skills.

## Real-World Skills

**14.** Answers will vary. Students might suggest conducting a frequency count to see how often the behavior occurs and at what times during the day. Suggestions for helping the child learn to take turns might include standing in line with the child.

**15.** Answers will vary depending on the researcher chosen. Report should show that student has a good understanding of the researcher's contributions to the field of child development.

**16.** Answers will vary but should include the name of a computer game that teaches map skills to ten year olds, the cost, and reasons for the choice.

**NCLB** Activity correlated to Science standards.

---

 **Family & Community Connection**

**11. Shadow a Teacher** Work with your teacher to set up a time when you can shadow, or observe, a preschool or kindergarten teacher. Notice how the teacher interacts with the children. Take notes on the techniques used to stimulate learning. Prepare an oral presentation to share your observations with your class.

## Health Skills

**12. Research Childhood Vaccinations** One of the main reasons for the decline in childhood deaths from disease is the development of vaccines. Select and research two vaccines. Find out at what ages they are given to children. Research what diseases they will protect against. How do the vaccines work? Do the vaccines have any side effects? Record your findings in a chart.

## Observation Skills

**13 Observe Child Interaction** Obtain permission to observe elementary school–age children in a class setting. Choose an age in which you have a particular interest. Be sure the class has both boys and girls in it.

**Procedure** Pay close attention to the children's interactions with one another. Do they all get along well? Is there one who does not seem to fit in?

**Analysis** Take notes during your observation. After the observation, rewrite your notes into a short report. Be sure to note any behaviors that show an inability to interact positively with others.

> **NSES 1** Develop an understanding of science unifying concepts and processes; evidence, models, and explanations.

## Real-World Skills

**Problem-Solving Skills**

**14. Making Conclusions** A three-year-old child consistently tries to get in the front of the line for the playground slide. Answer the following questions in a short report: What conclusions can you make about the child's behavior? What are some ways that might help this child learn to take turns?

**Technology Skills**

**15. Research a Theorist** Conduct research about one of the child development theorists mentioned in this chapter. How does this theory help caregivers, parents, and teachers understand children? Use presentation software to create a presentation about your selected theorist and include your answers to the questions. Share your presentation with the class.

**Financial Literacy Skills**

**16. Compare Video Games** Imagine that your brother is celebrating his 10th birthday. You want to buy him an educational computer game that teaches map skills. Do research to find the best game at the best price. Record the name of each game researched, the cost of each game, and its strengths and weaknesses. Which game would you buy? Why?

**Additional Activities** For additional activities, go to this book's Online Learning Center at **glencoe.com**.

## Academic Skills

**17.** Letters will vary but should show an understanding of child development as the main argument for longer recess times. Letters should be written in correct format and should not contain grammatical or spelling errors.

**18.** 29.4% (2.5 ÷ 8.5 = .294; 0.294 × 100 = 29.4%)

The *Early Childhood Observations CD* offers additional lessons with videos to build students' observation skills.

**Part 1:** Learning to Observe
**Part 2:** How Children Develop
**Part 3:** Working With Young Children
**Part 4:** Extended Observations
**Part 5:** Resources and Answer File

## Academic Skills

 **English Language Arts**

**17. Campaign for Change** Imagine that you are campaigning to promote longer recess times in elementary schools. Write a letter to the editor of a local newspaper stating why you feel children this age need more play time. Use the information you have learned about child development to support your arguments.

> **NCTE 12** Use language to accomplish individual purposes.

 **Mathematics**

**18. Respiratory Diseases** Young children spend most of their time at home, where they are exposed to a wide range of hazards. These exposures affect 8.5 million children below the age of 15 every year. 2.5 million of those children have respiratory diseases. What percentage of children exposed to environmental hazards contracted respiratory diseases?

> **Math Concept** **Percentages** A percent is a ratio that compares a number to 100.
>
> **Starting Hint** Divide the number of children with respiratory diseases by the total number of affected children. Multiply by 100 to convert the answer to a percent.

 **Math** For math help, go to the Math Appendix at the back of the book.

> **NCTM Number and Operations** Understand numbers, ways of representing numbers, relationships among numbers, and number systems.

 **Science**

**19. Graph Communicable Diseases** Public health services track communicable diseases that may affect public health. They keep statistics that help them determine when they might have a health disaster and how to avoid it. They also offer prevention services.

**Procedure** Contact your local public health agency to obtain statistics related to communicable childhood diseases in your area during the past ten years.

**Analysis** Create a bar graph to show the incidences of childhood diseases in your area for the past ten years.

> **NSES F** Develop understanding of personal and community health.

### Standardized Test Practice

**MULTIPLE CHOICE**

Read the passage, then answer the question.

Whether you observe children formally or informally, you do not want to be noticed. When you observe children, it is important to try to blend into the environment as much as possible. If your presence affects the children's behavior, it may not be possible to get objective information. Stay slightly outside the area where the children are.

**20.** In this passage, the phrase *blend into the environment* means:
   **a.** wear camouflage clothing.
   **b.** ignore the children if they talk to you.
   **c.** stay slightly outside the area where the children are.
   **d.** participate in the children's activities.

> **Test-Taking Tip** In a multiple-choice test, read the question first, then read all the answer choices. Eliminate answers that you know are incorrect.

---

 **NCLB**

**19.** Answers will vary but should clearly present in a bar graph the incidences of childhood communicable diseases in your area over the past ten years.

**NCLB** connects academic correlations to book content.

 **Professional Development**

**Mini Clip Reading: Assessment in Standards-Based Instruction**
Lois Moseley, author and educator, discusses the role of assessment in standards-based instruction.

### Standardized Test Practice

**20.** c. stay slightly outside the area where the children are.

**Test-Taking Tips** Some people find it helpful to place a small check to the left of those answer choices that they know are incorrect. This makes it easier to focus on the remaining ones.

**Multiple-Choice Tests** If you must choose a single answer, and there are two answers that you believe are correct, always choose the answer that you think is the *best*.

---

## TECHNOLOGY Solutions

**Use these technology solutions to streamline chapter assessment!**

 *ExamView Assessment Suite* CD allows you to create and print out customized tests or ready-made unit and chapter tests, complete with answer keys.

 **TeacherWorks Plus** is an electronic lesson planner that provides instant access to complete teacher resources in one convenient package.

 **Online Learning Center** includes resources and activities for students and teachers.

**STANDARDS BASED LESSON PLANNING** *The Developing Child* provides students with instruction and assessment in the following fundamental content areas:

## National Standards Correlations

| Standards | Pages |
|---|---|
| **12.2.4** Analyze the effects of life events on individuals' physical, intellectual, social, moral, and emotional development. | 38–41 |
| **15.1.1** Analyze parenting roles across the life span. | 38 |
| **15.1.2** Analyze expectations and responsibilities of parenting. | 33, 34, 38–41 |
| **15.1.5** Explain cultural differences in roles and responsibilities of parenting. | 39, 41 |
| **15.2.1** Choose nurturing practices that support human growth and development. | 34 |
| **15.3.2** Appraise community resources that provide opportunities related to parenting. | 37, 41 |

**NO CHILD LEFT BEHIND** NCLB activities, information, and skills practice will help your students attain NCLB proficiency. Students will improve their abilities in the following academic standards areas:

## Academic Standards Correlations

| Discipline | Standard | Feature/Activity |
|---|---|---|
| **English Language Arts** | **NCTE 1** Read texts to acquire new information. | **Reading Guide (pp. 32, 42)** |
| | **NCTE 4** Use written language to communicate effectively. | **Writing Activity (p. 30)** **Academic Skills (p. 53)** |
| | **NCTE 5** Use different writing process elements to communicate effectively. | **After You Read (p. 50)** |
| | **NCTE 12** Use language to accomplish individual purposes. | **After You Read (p. 41)** |
| **Mathematics** | **NCTM Number and Operations** Understand numbers, ways of representing numbers, relationships among numbers, and number systems. | **Math in Action (p. 36)** **Academic Skills (p. 53)** |
| **Science** | **NSES C** Develop understanding of the interdependence of organisms; matter, energy, and organization in living systems; and behavior of organisms. | **Academic Skills (p. 53)** |
| **Social Studies** | **NCSS I A Culture** Analyze and explain the ways groups, societies, and cultures address human needs and concerns. | **Culture Matters (p. 39)** **Observation Skills (p. 52)** |
| | **NCSS IV F Individual Development and Identity** Analyze the role of perceptions, attitudes, values, and beliefs in the development of personal identity. | **After You Read (p. 50)** |
| | **NCSS VII F Production, Distribution, and Consumption** Compare how values and beliefs influence economic decisions in different societies. | **After You Read (p. 41)** |

## Professional Development

**MINI CLIP VIDEO LIBRARY**

Targeted professional development is correlated throughout *The Developing Child*. **The McGraw-Hill Professional Development Mini Clip Video Library** provides teaching strategies to strengthen academic and learning skills. Log on to **glencoe.com**.

In this chapter, you will find these Mini Clips:
- **ELL** Scaffolding Questions, p. 33
- **Math** Real-Life Ratios, p. 36
- **Reading** Flexible Groupings, p. 46
- **ELL** Reading Aloud, p. 48
- **Reading** Planning for Future Instruction, p. 49
- **ELL** Collaborative Work, p. 52

## Reading and Writing Strategies

**Writing Activity: Prewriting** (p. 30)
Students use writing tips to explain what they think it means to be a responsible parent.

**Before You Read** (pp. 32, 42)
A prereading question or statement will help students make a personal connection to content.

**Graphic Organizer** (pp. 32, 42)
A visual tool will help students organize and remember new content.

**Reading Check** (pp. 38, 44, 45, 48, 50)
A question allows students to make a quick comprehension self-check.

**After You Read** (pp. 41, 50)
Organize and process students' understanding of what they have read.

## Chapter Features

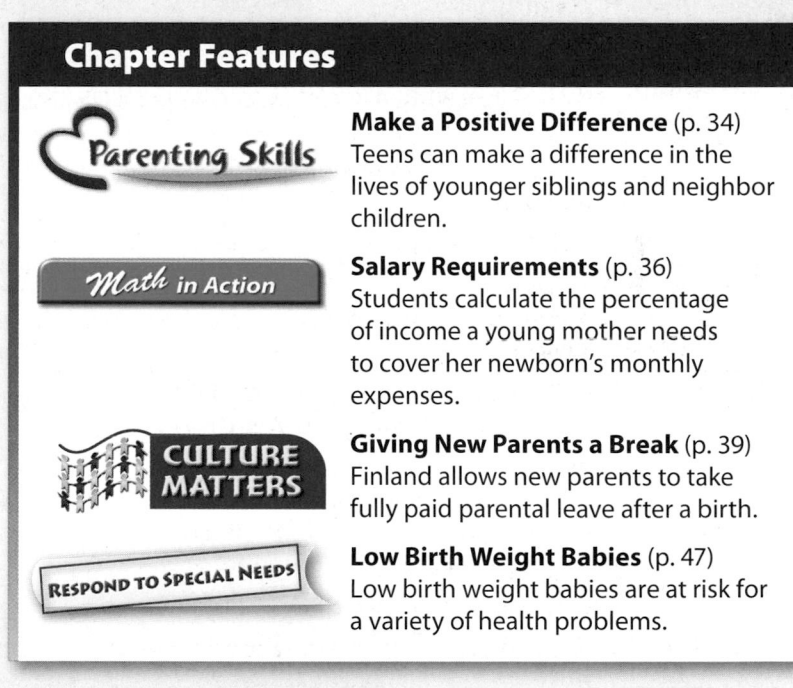

**Make a Positive Difference** (p. 34)
Teens can make a difference in the lives of younger siblings and neighbor children.

**Salary Requirements** (p. 36)
Students calculate the percentage of income a young mother needs to cover her newborn's monthly expenses.

**Giving New Parents a Break** (p. 39)
Finland allows new parents to take fully paid parental leave after a birth.

**Low Birth Weight Babies** (p. 47)
Low birth weight babies are at risk for a variety of health problems.

## Chapter Overview

### Introduce the Chapter

In this chapter, students learn about the responsibilities of being a good parent. They learn that having a baby changes the parents' lifestyle and requires emotional maturity. They also learn about the specific challenges of teen parenthood and the risks involved in teen sexual activity.

### Build Background

Instruct students to imagine a young couple in their early twenties. They have led a fun lifestyle, eating out often and going to friends' parties. Now they have a newborn. Ask students to list the positive effects this baby might have on the couple's relationship. Then ask them to list possible negative effects.

### Writing Activity
#### Prewriting

This writing activity prompts students to organize their ideas in preparation for a future essay about the responsibilities of parenting. After students have finished prewriting, encourage them to share some of their ideas in class, if they feel comfortable doing so. Students' ideas can be used to prompt classroom discussions. (Ideas will vary but should relate to one another and show that the students have put some thought into their writing and have talked with some parents.)

---

# Responsibilities of Parenting

## Chapter Objectives

After completing this chapter, you will be able to:

- **Explain** who can benefit from knowing about child development and parenting.
- **Describe** the five areas of responsibilities for parents.
- **Identify** pressures involved in sexual development.
- **Summarize** the benefits of abstinence.
- **Describe** the possible consequences of sexual activity.
- **Compare and contrast** the options available to a teen parent.
- **Explain** what it means to be sexually responsible.

### Writing Activity 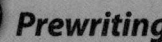 Prewriting

**Responsible Parenting** Until you become a parent, it is impossible to understand all of the responsibilities of parenting. Imagine that you need to write a one-page essay about the responsibilities of parenting. Before you can write the essay, you should do a prewriting activity. This will help your essay be more organized. Talk to some parents about their experiences as new parents. Include their responses in your writing.

**Writing Tips** Use these tips to effectively prewrite:
1. Freewrite or collect ideas from other sources.
2. List ideas and see how they relate to each other.
3. Ask questions to explore and clarify ideas.

**30**

---

## CLASSROOM Solutions

### Print Resources

 **Student Edition**

 **Teacher Wraparound Edition**

 **Student Activity Workbook**

**Student Activity Workbook Teacher Annotated Edition**

### Technology Resources

 **Online Learning Center** has resources and activities for students and teachers. Includes an Online Student Edition.

 **Interactive Student Edition** allows students to instantly access review materials, examples, and exercises.

## Section 2.1 Parenting and Families

## Section 2.2 Teen Parenthood

**Explore the Photo**
No matter your age, you will always be your parents' child. *At what age do you think parents should stop being responsible for their children?*

31

**Review the Sections**
Introduce the chapter by reviewing the sections:

**Section 2.1**
Good parenting is complicated, but it is a skill that can be learned. Before deciding to have a baby, couples should determine whether they are emotionally mature enough to take on the challenge. Parents must be able to manage resources such as money, time, and energy.

**Section 2.2**
The teen years bring sexual maturity. Teens must develop their own beliefs and values concerning their sexuality as they become exposed to pressure to become sexually active. Abstinence offers the advantages of avoiding STIs and pregnancy. It also can help teens avoid behavior for which they are not emotionally ready.

▶ **Explore the Photo**

**Caption Answer** Students' answers will vary. Some may feel that a parent's responsibility ends when a child turns 18 or 21. Some may feel a parent's responsibility never ends.

**Discussion** Ask students: What kinds of responsibilities (if any) do you think parents have toward their adult children? How are these responsibilities different from when the children were younger? How might parents and adult children see these responsibilities differently?

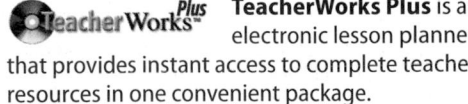

**TeacherWorks Plus** is an electronic lesson planner that provides instant access to complete teacher resources in one convenient package.

**Presentation Plus!** provides visual teaching aids for every section.

**The Early Childhood Observations CD** presents video observations and lessons on observation skills and child development.

**The Developing Brain eTransparencies and Guide** include information and activities to offer insights into brain development and diseases of the brain.

## Section 2.1 — Parenting and Families

## FOCUS

### Bell Ringer Activity

**Parenting on Television**

Tell students to individually choose a television show in which they think the adults exhibit good parenting skills. Have each student create a list of the skills displayed by these television parents. Ask for volunteers to share their lists. Encourage students to discuss similarities among the different lists. End by explaining that parents who are good at their jobs often have similar strengths.

## Preteaching

### Vocabulary

Synonyms are words with similar meanings. In this section, *pride* is defined by the synonym pleasure. Ask students to think of other synonyms for the word *pride*. Point out how different synonyms can convey different meanings, such as *pleasure* and *conceit*.

### Graphic Organizer

 The Graphic Organizer is also on the TeacherWorks CD.

(Graphic organizer should list: emotional maturity, health considerations, financial concerns, resource management skills, and parenting skills.)

**NCLB** connects academic correlations to book content.

---

# Section 2.1 — Parenting and Families

## Reading Guide

 **Before You Read**

**Predict** Look at the photos in this section and read their captions. Write one or two sentences predicting what the section will be about.

### Read to Learn
#### Key Concepts
- **Explain** who can benefit from knowing about child development and parenting.
- **Describe** the five areas of responsibilities for parents.

#### Main Idea
Parenting is a learning process with many demands and rewards. There are many decisions that must be made before and during parenthood.

#### Content Vocabulary
◇ parenting
◇ emotional maturity

#### Academic Vocabulary
You will find these words in your reading and on your tests. Use the glossary to look up their definitions if necessary.
- pride
- prospective

### Graphic Organizer

As you read, list five elements necessary to prepare for parenting. Use a chart like the one shown to organize your information.

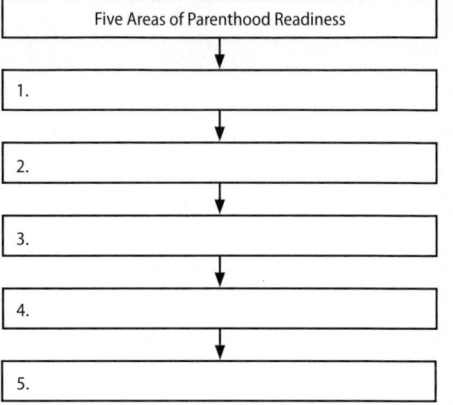

Five Areas of Parenthood Readiness

1.
2.
3.
4.
5.

 **Graphic Organizer** Go to this book's Online Learning Center at **glencoe.com** to print out this graphic organizer.

---

### Academic Standards

 **English Language Arts**

**NCTE 12** Use language to accomplish individual purposes.

 **Social Studies**

**NCSS I A Culture** Analyze and explain the ways groups, societies, and cultures address human needs and concerns.

**NCSS VII F Production, Distribution, and Consumption** Compare how values and beliefs influence economic decisions in different societies.

**NCTE** *National Council of Teachers of English*
**NCTM** *National Council of Teachers of Mathematics*

**NSES** *National Science Education Standards*
**NCSS** *National Council for the Social Studies*

---

**32** Chapter 2 Responsibilities of Parenting

---

## Reading Guide

 **Before You Read**

Encourage students to remember the first time they tried to play a game, such as tennis. They probably were not very good. Likewise, many people feel awkard the first time they care for a child. However, as discussed in this section, parenting is a skill that can be improved over time.

### **D** Develop Concepts

**Main Idea** Discuss the main idea with the students. Ask: Why do you think parenting is described as a learning process? (Answers may include that parents must continually adjust based on a particular child's needs, temperament, or age.)

## Preparation for Parenthood

Being a parent is a job unlike any other. Parents work hard but are not paid. They are on call 24 hours a day, seven days a week. Fortunately, being a parent can bring unique rewards. Parents cherish those times when the family seems especially close or has fun together. They watch with **pride**, or pleasure, as their children become adults, ready to start independent lives of their own. For most parents, the joys outweigh the challenges.

Parenting is complicated. **Parenting** is the process of caring for children and helping them grow and develop. It impacts individuals, families, and societies. Parenting requires knowing and understanding a child's needs and then meeting those needs. It also requires good judgment.

- Parents need to know when to help and when to let children try a task on their own. Sometimes this means the children will fail. Children should learn how to bounce back after setbacks and try again.

- Parents must decide when to encourage children to try different activities. It is important to allow children the freedom to explore their own likes and dislikes. Parents need to avoid pushing children into activities they are not yet ready for. However, parents need to encourage children to engage in enjoyable activities.

- The skills needed by parents will change as the children get older. Parents must adapt their parenting skills to each stage of their children's development.

Being a parent is one of the most important roles a person has in life. It is also a role for which few people are educated and trained. People rarely learn about children and the skills needed for parenting before having children.

It is not just parents who need parenting skills. Anyone who lives or works with children can benefit from knowing about child development and parenting. This includes adult caregivers, older siblings, or other family members. By learning about parenting skills, people who interact with children can have a positive influence on them.

➤ **Normal Behavior**
Knowing how children develop helps caregivers have reasonable expectations about what a child can do. *How can this help prevent some parenting frustrations?*

➤➤ **Explore the Photo**

**Caption Answer** Understanding that children grow out of phases as they mature can help parents endure. Children tend to cry frequently when they are younger and outgrow the phase as they mature.

**Discussion** If a seven-year-old exhibited the same behavior as this toddler, do you think the parent would respond in the same way as she would to the toddler? Why or why not? (No, because the parent would expect the seven-year-old to behave more maturely and have better control over his behavior.)

## Teach

### Discussion Starter

**Twenty-Four/Seven** Ask students: Can you imagine having a job where you worked 24 hours a day? Where even when you went on vacation, you had to work? How might you feel after six weeks of this job? After a year? Conclude by pointing out that this is an important characteristic of being a good parent—to always be available. (Possible answer: they might feel trapped and exhausted. They also might feel that they are being treated unfairly.)

**Professional Development**

**Mini Clip**
ELL: Scaffolding Questions

A teacher uses a series of questions to lead a student to an appropriate verbal response.

### R Reading Strategy

**Analyze Structure** Point out the bulleted list under "Preparation for Parenthood." Ask students: Why do you think the author chose to make this a bulleted list rather than explain these three points in paragraph form? (to make the individual points easier to identify) Have students rewrite the bulleted points in their own words. Ask for volunteers to share what they have written. (Students' bulleted lists will vary, but should restate the points in their own words.)

## Teach cont.

### C₁ Critical Thinking

**Predict** Ask students how they think a four-year-old is likely respond when a parent says to her, "Act your age!" How do students think such a statement might make the child feel? (Student answers will vary. Young children are likely to act even more childish and become rebellious when criticized in this way. They are likely to feel they are being belittled.)

### R Reading Strategy

**Predict** Have students brainstorm a list of traits that they think all people should have before they become parents. Then have the class vote to narrow the list down to the top ten most important traits for parents. As students read more about the areas of parenthood readiness, have them organize each of the top ten traits into one of the five areas discussed. **ELL**

### U₁ Universal Access

**Visual Learners** Have students work in groups to create a collage of photographs showing teens helping young children. Encourage students to bring in their own photos, if possible. They also may want to obtain photos from newspapers, magazines, or the Internet. Instruct them to give the collage an appropriate title. Hang the finished collages where everyone can view them. **ELL**

### Having Reasonable Expectations

"Act your age." "How old are you, anyway?" "Would you grow up?" Do any of these sound familiar? Many parents have made remarks like these to their children. What adults often do not realize is that children usually do act their age. It is adults who do not always know what to expect from children at different ages. That is why understanding child development is so important.

Having reasonable expectations for children is the first step in effective parenting. For example, Kristin grew increasingly frustrated when two-year-old Adam said no to everything. Then her mother told her that children usually go through a negative stage at that age. Relieved that Adam would outgrow the behavior, Kristin was better able to cope with it.

Just knowing what children are like at different ages is not enough. It is important for parents and caregivers to remember that each child is an individual. Some children learn to walk earlier than others. Some need extra encouragement to make friends. Some children immediately respond when given directions. Others may need gentle reminders and more time to complete tasks. It is important to accept and respect the differences among children.

### Parenthood Readiness

People considering parenthood should take a close look at what parenting involves. This includes looking at their own emotional maturity as well as health considerations, financial concerns, and how skilled they are at managing personal resources. Making a careful decision to have a child benefits both you and your child. People should learn about the myths and realities of parenting. Children deserve to be born to parents who are ready for parenthood.

## ♥ Parenting Skills

### Make a Positive Difference

You are probably aware that younger siblings pick up cues on how they should act by watching your behavior. Make sure you are sending appropriate, positive cues!

➤ **Treat others with kindness and consideration.** Make time in your day for younger siblings. Ask about school, friends, and activities they enjoy.

➤ **Some neighborhood children can benefit from having a teen friend.** You might be able to help a struggling reader by listening to him or her practice reading. You might work on a craft project with a group of neighborhood children.

➤ **Volunteer and paid jobs also provide opportunities to work with children.** Volunteer jobs might include tutoring or helping with a sports program. Possible paid jobs include babysitter, swim or dance teacher, and camp counselor. Whatever the job, the interaction with children enriches your own life as much as it does the children's lives.

**Take Charge** Write a paragraph that describes a time when you were a positive influence for a child. How might working with children now prepare you for parenthood later?

## ♥ Parenting Skills

### Make a Positive Difference

Ask students: As you were growing up, were there teens who made a positive difference in your life? If so, what did they say or do? What were your feelings towards them? (Student responses will vary. If there were specific teens, students should explain the ways they made a difference and how they felt about these teens' influence on their lives.)

**Take Charge**
Paragraphs will vary but should show that students have thought through their answers. Students should recognize that any involvement they have with children will help them learn how children grow, think, and act; and this will help them as parents.

**Consider Health Issues**
Being in good health before pregnancy can help lead to a safe pregnancy and a healthy baby. *Why should both of the prospective parents have a medical checkup?*

**U₂ Universal Access**

**English Language Learners**
Have students review the meaning of "emotional maturity." Then organize students into pairs and instruct each pair to come up with a list of the characteristics of an emotionally mature person. Where possible, pair an English language learner with a more proficient speaker. Ask for volunteers to share their lists with the class. (Lists will vary. Pairs should create a list of characteristics of emotional mature people, such as being able to control their temper and placing others' needs before their own.) **ELL**

**C₂ Critical Thinking**

**Evaluate** Explain that sometimes individuals with low self-esteem hope that having a baby will make them feel better about themselves. Ask students why they think people might feel this way. Be sure to point out that becoming a parent does not improve self-esteem. Parenting is hard work and might have the opposite effect. (Student answers will vary. These people might think the baby will cause others to pay more attention to them and think more highly of them.)

### Emotional Maturity

To handle the changes and demands that parenthood brings, a person needs emotional maturity. **Emotional maturity** means being responsible enough to consistently put someone else's needs before your own needs. People with emotional maturity are secure enough to devote their attention to a child without expecting anything in return. They can control their temper when an infant cries for hours on end or a child breaks a favorite possession. They are able to handle being constantly on call.

**Prospective**, or likely, parents should take an inventory of their own emotional maturity. Are they truly equipped to handle the challenges of parenthood? If there are doubts, it is best to put aside the desire for a child until they are convinced they have the maturity it takes to raise one.

Some prospective parents hope that having a child will help them solve some personal problems, such as low self-esteem or marriage difficulties. It will not. These are some of the reasons for wanting children that do not show emotional maturity or a real readiness for parenthood.

### Health Considerations

Before pregnancy, it is best for both prospective parents to have a medical checkup. Some medical problems can affect the health of a baby or the parent's ability to care for a child. The age of the prospective mother is another consideration. If she is under 17 or over 35, pregnancy is riskier for both her and the baby.

Pregnant teens, for example, are less likely than older expectant mothers to get proper nutrition, gain adequate weight, and seek good

 **Explore the Photo**

**Caption Answer** Some medical problems of the mother or father may affect the baby and may also affect the parent's ability to help care for the baby.

**Discussion** Ask students what some of the questions might be that this physician would ask this woman. (Answers will vary but might include whether or not she smokes, drinks alcohol, or has any serious illnesses such as diabetes.)

**Teach** *cont.*

## S Skill Practice

### Guided Practice

**Draw a Flowchart** Instruct students to create a flowchart containing the five steps listed under the Resource Management Skills heading. Students should rewrite each step using their own words. (Flowcharts should contain the five steps, each stated in the student's own words.) **L1** **ELL**

**Create a Matching Game** Instruct students to work individually to create a matching game. Draw a line to divide a sheet of paper in two. On one side, they should list the five key steps in resource management. On the other side, there should be a list of ten different items. Each item should be an example of one of the five steps. For example, one item might state: "Save $500 for piano lessons by fall." This item would match "Set goals." Students should trade and play one another's games. (Games should contain a list of the five key steps along with ten items that match the steps.) **L2**

**Apply Resource Management Skills** Discuss that resource management skills are not only useful for parents. Have students choose one of these resources: money, time, or energy. Students should then create a chart explaining how they could apply the five steps for resource management to this resource in their own lives. (Charts will vary, but should show how students would apply resource management skills to a resource in their own lives.) **L3**

**NCLB** Activity correlated to Mathematics standards.

---

### *Math* in Action

#### Salary Requirements

Susan earns $8.50 per hour and works 40 hours a week. She is planning for her and Robert's newborn by calculating expected expenses. Her research results in an approximate expense list for one month:

Diapers: $80
Formula: $75
Clothes: $75
Day Care: $400

How much per month does Susan make? What is the total monthly expense of the newborn? What percentage of Susan's salary will go towards the baby?

**Math Concept** **Rates and Percents** A rate is a ratio of two measurements having different kinds of units, such as dollars per hour. A percent is a ratio that compares a number to 100.

**Starting Hint** To find Susan's monthly salary, first multiply the rate (8.50) by the hours (40), then by the weeks in a month (4). To find the percentage, divide the total baby expenses by Susan's monthly salary. Multiply the result by 100.

**Math** For math help, go to the Math Appendix at the back of the book.

> **NCTM Number and Operations**
> Understand numbers, ways of representing numbers, relationships among numbers, and number systems.

---

the first year and in the years ahead. It is not unusual for couples to have to change their way of life in order to meet these expenses.

If both prospective parents work, they need to think about what they will do after the baby arrives. Will one parent stop working to care for the baby? If so, how will they cope with the drop in family income? If both parents continue working, they must arrange for reliable child care. How will they pay for it?

### Resource Management Skills

Parents need to wisely use the resources they have available to provide for their families. Money is just one resource. Time, skills, and energy are others. Because most resources are limited, applying a process for managing them can help parents do their best for all family members. There are five key steps to good resource management:

1. **Set goals.** Decide what is important and then turn those things into personal goals. For example, Sara considered preschool an important learning opportunity for her two-year-old son, Eli. Although the family budget was tight, her goal was to send him to preschool when he was four years old.

2. **Identify resources.** Make a list of the resources needed to achieve the goal. Sara checked into the cost of a local preschool program. She had some savings that could pay for part of the tuition. She would need to work part time to earn the rest.

3. **Make a plan.** Decide how to use the identified resources to achieve the desired goal. Sara realized she needed more money to afford Eli's preschool. Because that was two years away, she figured out how much she would need to save each month to have the tuition when Eli turned four. To achieve her goal, she also started looking for a job she could do at home.

4. **Put the plan into action.** Start working toward the goals using the steps outlined in the plan. Sara started watching her neighbor's kindergartener after school. Instead of spending the money, she put it into her savings account. She was actively working toward her goal of saving enough money.

**S**

---

prenatal care. These issues can be harmful to the teen's health as well as her baby's. Women over 35 are at a greater risk for developing diabetes and a potentially dangerous type of high blood pressure during pregnancy. There are also higher rates of birth defects among children born to older mothers.

### Financial Concerns

Raising a child is expensive. It requires the financial resources to pay for clothes, health care, food, equipment, and other expenses. Before deciding on parenthood, couples should consider the costs of having a child during

---

### *Math* in Action

#### Salary Requirements

Susan makes $1,360 per month [(8.50 × 40) × 4 = 1,360]. The total monthly expense of the newborn is $630 [80 + 75 + 75 + 400]. The percent of Susan's salary spent on the baby is 46%. [(630 ÷ 1,360) × 100 = 46%]

---

**Mc Graw Hill Professional Development**

### Mini Clip
**Math: Real-Life Ratios**

A teacher discusses real-life applications of ratios.

**5. Re-evaluate from time to time.** Step back and take stock of progress. Are more or different resources needed? Was the goal achieved? What are some new goals to work toward? That August after Eli's fourth birthday, Sara was pleased to be able to take him to preschool. And, she had already decided on a new savings goal. She would save for a family vacation.

### Parenting Skills

Can parenting be learned? Absolutely! There are many different ways to gain these skills. Classes in child development and parenting are good sources for information and support. Hospitals, schools, community groups, and private instructors offer courses or workshops on parenting skills. Some courses are targeted to age-related issues of children. Others may focus on certain behavioral or health challenges.

Still other courses may focus on helping a parent cope with difficult personal issues that can affect family life, such as financial stress or relationship problems.

There are other ways to build parenting skills too:

- Read reliable books, magazine articles, and online information about parenting.
- Gain experience working with or caring for children, informally or as a job.
- Ask the advice of family and friends who have parenting experience.
- Observe parents and children whenever and wherever possible.

Take advantage of as many learning opportunities as possible. Because each child is different, techniques that work with some do not work with every child. By learning different strategies, you are more likely to find one to match a particular child and situation.

**Manage Financial Resources**
Parents must learn to handle money wisely. *What are some expenses that must be considered when planning to meet a child's needs?*

## Teach *cont.*

 **Universal Access**

**Verbal Learners** Tell students to imagine that they host a 15-minute weekly radio show about their local public library. This week, the topic is on books and magazines to help new parents. Students should visit the public library to learn about the parenting materials it offers. Then they should write a script for the radio show that discusses these materials and how they might be useful to parents. (Scripts will vary but should show that the students have researched the materials available at the library and that they understand how the materials will be useful for new parents.)

### R Reading Strategy

**Determine Cause and Effect** Remind students that identifying cause and effect helps readers understand the point an author is making. Have students read the last paragraph on this page. Ask students: What is the cause of common challenges faced by parents? What is the effect? (The cause of the challenges is that some techniques will work on one child, but not another. The effect is that parents must develop different strategies.)

### Explore the Photo

**Caption Answer** Answers will vary, but might include food, clothing, medical expenses, or child care expenses.

**Discussion** Ask students: How might this couple change its spending habits after the birth of a child? (Answers will vary, but might include eating out less, spending less money on clothing and entertainment, or taking fewer vacations.)

**Quiz**

Ask students to answer the following questions:

1. Why do parents need to allow children to fail some of the time? (Allowing children to try and then fail helps children learn to bounce back after setbacks and keep on trying.)

2. What are some of the health issues associated with pregnant teens? (Teens are less likely to get proper nutrition, gain adequate weight, and get good prenatal care.)

3. Why is it important to periodically re-evaluate a resource management plan? (You need to evaluate progress toward the goal and make any adjustments that may be necessary.)

## Reteach

**W Writing Support**

**Prewriting**

**The Image-Making Stage** Tell students they have been assigned the job of writing a persuasive essay on the importance of the image-making stage of parenthood. Students should use prewriting to prepare for writing the essay. In their prewriting, they should list all major points they plan to make in their essays. (Refer to p. 30 to review the characteristics of prewriting. Students' prewriting will vary, but should list the major points they want to make.)

**✓ Reading Check**

**Explain** It is important for adults to understand child development so they can be good role models and have reasonable expectations for children's behavior.

## Stages of Parenthood

In her book, *Between Generations: The Six Stages of Parenthood,* psychologist Ellen Galinsky describes how parents typically develop through their interactions with their children. Her findings were based on interviews with parents. **Figure 2.1** summarizes Galinsky's six stages.

The stages of parenthood that Galinsky identified are important because they describe how parents develop and change as their children do. When parents are aware of these stages, they can be more prepared for parenthood. By being prepared, they are more likely to be effective parents and lead happier, more satisfied lives.

**✓ Reading Check** **Explain** Why is it important for adults to understand child development?

## Parenting Responsibilities and Rewards

When a new child joins the family, parents feel great joy. This is true whether the child joins by birth, remarriage, or adoption. Some parents also feel that a great burden has been placed on their shoulders. The decision to become a parent is a serious one. Being a parent radically changes a person's life and creates new long-term responsibilities.

When Dominique and Ross adopted baby Tanya from Russia, they were thrilled. The waiting was finally over. Everything felt right. Dominique's parents stayed with them for a week to help with the baby's care. Life with Tanya seemed relatively easy. However, after the baby's grandparents left, the challenges and responsibility of raising a child began to feel overwhelming.

**Figure 2.1 Galinsky's Stages of Parenthood**

The role of the parents changes as the child grows and matures. *During which stage does Galinsky feel parents rethink their role as parents?*

| Stage | Time Period | Parents' Tasks |
|---|---|---|
| **Image-Making** | Pregnancy | ❖ Begin to imagine themselves as parents |
| **Nurturing** | Birth to Age 2 | ❖ Become emotionally attached to the child <br> ❖ May question relative worth of other priorities |
| **Authority** | Age 2 to Ages 4–5 | ❖ Determine rules <br> ❖ Clarify role as authority figure |
| **Interpretive** | Ages 4–5 to Age 13 | ❖ Rethink their role as parents <br> ❖ Decide what knowledge, skills, and values the child needs |
| **Interdependent** | Adolescence | ❖ Establish boundaries <br> ❖ Find disciplinary methods appropriate for teens |
| **Departure** | Child Leaves Home | ❖ Evaluate their parenting |

**38** Chapter 2 Responsibilities of Parenting

**Figure 2.1 Galinsky's Stages of Parenthood**

**Caption Answer** Parents typically rethink their role during the interpretive stage.

**Discussion** Ask students: What does the word *interdependent* mean? (It refers to two people or groups being dependent on one another.) Why do you think Galinsky called the adolescence time period the Interdependent stage? (Possible answer: adolescents are dependent on parents for guidance, and parents must look to the child to determine how to meet his need.)

## CULTURE MATTERS

### Giving New Parents a Break

New parents need all the help they can get from family, community, and society. In Finland, one parent (mother or father) has the right to ten months' fully paid leave from work after the birth of a child. Or couples can split the time. Even a prime minister took two weeks off from work after the birth of his child. The idea behind maternal, paternal, and parental leave is to protect the health of both the mother and child. It also allows parents the chance to take care of their child during the first few months of its life.

⭐ **Build Connections** *Parents in the United States do not get as much parental leave as those in Finland. What effect do you think this may have on the health of the mother and child?*

**NCSS I A Culture** Analyze and explain the ways groups, societies, and cultures address human needs and concerns.

---

Tanya hardly slept at night, so Dominique and Ross did not get much sleep either. Ross went to work each day feeling exhausted. Meanwhile, Dominique was left with the baby. She felt alone and uncertain. They both wondered how so many people managed to raise families. It was clearly not as easy as it seemed.

### New Responsibilities

Many new parents say that having children changes everything. Becoming a parent does present many challenges. However, as the newness of parenthood passes, many parents adjust to the changes and find that their lives are enriched by the presence of a child.

Once people become parents, they can no longer think of only their own needs. They have much less time for themselves. They must always consider their child's needs first. Children need physical care, financial support, love, and guidance.

First-time parents can feel overwhelmed by so many new responsibilities. Family and friends can help in many ways. They can offer to watch the baby while the parent goes shopping, just listen, or help solve a problem.

Communities have many resources too, including religious organizations, government agencies, and support groups.

### Lifestyle Changes

New parents have to adjust to major changes in their daily lives. Caring for a child takes a huge amount of time and energy. This is especially true for a newborn. A newborn needs to be fed every few hours, day and night. Babies also must be diapered, played with, comforted, and supervised for safety.

With children of any age, parents have limits placed on their personal freedom. They have less time to spend with friends. Instead of unwinding after work, they must spend time with their children, feed them, bathe them, and put them to bed. While it can be disappointing, sometimes plans have to be changed. Dennis and Shawna had looked forward to his brother's party for weeks, but had to cancel at the last minute. Their toddler was sick, and they did not feel right leaving him with a babysitter.

Parents are better able to adjust to these changes if they prepare for them. Taking classes and caring for a friend's child can help give an idea of what it is really like to live with a child.

---

**C** **Critical Thinking**

**Draw Conclusions** Tell students that some people think one way to prevent teen pregnancies is to have teens be in charge of caring for a baby for several days. Ask students whether they think this experience would reduce teen pregnancies. Ask students to share any personal experiences they may have had with being responsible for a baby. (Student responses will vary, but they should specify whether they think caring for a baby would discourage teen pregnancies.)

**R** **Reading Strategy**

**Predict Content** Instruct students to write a paragraph predicting what material will be covered under the heading Lifestyle Changes. They should then read the material. After they are done, they should write a paragraph discussing how their predictions compared to the actual content. In particular, they should state any material not covered in their predictions. (Students should write a brief prediction prior to reading the material. They then should write a paragraph comparing their predictions to the actual content.)

**NCLB** Activity correlated to Social Studies standards.

---

## CULTURE MATTERS

### Giving New Parents a Break

**Discussion** Guide students in a discussion of the morning routine of a working parent. Each morning this parent takes her four-month-old to a child care center before going to work at 8:30 A.M. Ask students to speculate what her schedule might be like from 6:00 A.M. to 8:30 A.M. Write the schedule on the board. (Schedules will vary, but should meet the basic needs of the parent and the child.)

**Building Connections** *Students' answers will vary. They may mention that if there are complications or problems of any kind, the health of the mother or child may be adversely affected by a shorter period of leave. Students may also mention that a shorter leave could cause emotional health problems for the mother.*

## Reteach *cont.*

### C Critical Thinking

**Predict** As a class, read through the bulleted list of emotions under the heading Emotional Adjustments. Ask students: If you were a parent, which of these emotions do you think you would be most likely to have? How might you deal with this emotion? (Student answers will vary, but students should provide reasons for their responses.) **ELL**

### U Universal Access

**Kinsethetic Learners** Organize students into pairs. Tell one student to suppose he or she is a new parent. The other student should play the role of the new grandparent. The new parent is feeling overwhelmed with all of his or her new responsibilities. He or she wants to ask for advice from the grandparent, but still wants to appear capable to the grandparent. Students should present a skit based on this scenario. The grandparent should show how he or she would support the new parent and offer empathy as well as advice or help. (Skits will vary but should show an understanding of how a person's relationship might change with his or her own parents after he or she becomes a parent. The new parent might mention the frustrations with taking care of the child as well as the changing relationship with his or her spouse.) **ELL**

**Challenging and Rewarding**
Raising a baby takes patience and dedication. It also brings rewards. *What kinds of rewards do you think parenting might bring?*

There is no substitute for the experience of parenting. Making an effort, though, to learn about child development and parenthood can make the demands of the job less surprising and unsettling.

### Emotional Adjustments

Parenthood requires many emotional adjustments. Going through so many changes is stressful in itself. On top of that, many parents feel conflicting, and sometimes difficult, emotions, such as:

- Fear of not being a good parent.
- Frustration at the loss of personal freedom and the addition of new responsibilities.
- Worry over money matters.
- Jealousy of the baby and the attention he or she gets from the other parent, friends, and relatives.
- Depression due to exhaustion and the physical changes of pregnancy and birth.

Parents can feel confused and troubled by these negative emotions. In time, most parents get over these rough spots. They learn that these emotions are common among new parents. They learn how to handle them. If these feelings persist, however, it is important to talk to a doctor. The doctor can help determine what assistance is needed. A new mother might need medication, or she might need counseling or just sleep and exercise.

### Relationship Changes

When people become parents, they are likely to notice changes in how they interact with each other and with other family members. This is especially true for first-time parents.

The birth of a baby is an exciting time. Sometimes, though, parents may feel overwhelmed by concerns, negative emotions, and lack of sleep. They may argue with one another. Having patience and trying to be understanding can reduce the danger of frustration turning into anger. One key to getting past such trouble spots is for the couple to communicate effectively.

A new baby changes the relationship between the new parents and their own parents. Most grandparents feel love and joy of their own and want to spend time with their grandchild. Some may offer to help with child care or household chores. Some freely share advice based on their own parenting experience. Sometimes, however, offers of help or advice cause friction. New parents may resent advice that they feel is criticism. At the same time, the grandparents may feel hurt if their suggestions or offers of help are rejected.

On the other hand, new parents often find that having a baby brings them closer to their own parents. Understanding the sacrifices and work involved in parenting, they can now appreciate their own parents more.

**40** Chapter 2 Responsibilities of Parenting

### ⏵ Explore the Photo

**Caption Answer** Answers will vary but may include a baby's first smile, first step, or first word; or a baby's unconditional love.

**Discussion** Discuss that new parents are often pressed for time, particularly if both parents work outside the home. Ask the class for suggestions to help a couple better enjoy the rewards of parenting. (Answers will vary. Students might suggest they set aside time each day to play with the baby together.)

## Employment Adjustments

Having children can have an impact on careers. Some parents stop working or cut back on their hours to care for their children. People who work overtime and weekends, or travel for their jobs, may be less willing to do so once they become parents. Some parents will decide to change their careers. They might look for a career path that requires less travel or that is simply less stressful.

Some employers have policies to help working parents. They may offer flexible hours, part-time work, or work-at-home options. Others have child care facilities at or near the workplace. Couples planning to become parents should find out what benefits or programs their employers offer to help parents.

## Legal Responsibilities

Parents, both mothers and fathers, are legally responsible to provide food, shelter, clothing, medical care, an education, and legal help for their children. Physically, fathers can walk away from parenthood more easily than mothers, but the law holds them equally responsible. A father is legally bound to support his child until the child turns 18. This is regardless of the father's age or whether he is married to the child's mother. It does not matter if he ever sees his child. Fathers as young as 14 have been sued for child support.

## Rewards of Parenthood

While parenthood is a lot of work and responsibility, it brings many joys as well. There is nothing quite like a baby's first smile or hearing a toddler say, "I love you, Daddy." Parents feel happiness, pride, and love that they have never felt before.

By helping children discover the world, parents often see it with new eyes themselves. Having children can also enrich an already strong marriage. Finally, raising children can give parents a great sense of accomplishment.

---

## Section 2.1 — After You Read

### Review Key Concepts
1. **Identify** three ways to build parenting skills.
2. **Describe** the types of conflicting emotions new parents often experience.

### Practice Academic Skills

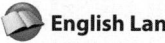 **English Language Arts**
3. Think of a time when you experienced something for the first time. Create a list of the steps you had to take to accomplish the task. Write a paragraph describing some of the challenges you faced and some of the rewards you received by completing the task.

> **NCTE 12** Use language to accomplish individual purposes.

 **Social Studies**
4. What sorts of changes in buying habits do you think parents should make to be able to provide for their family? Research how parents in a different culture would prepare for a new child. Write a one-page essay that compares the culture you researched with the changes you predicted for parents in your culture.

> **NCSS VII F** Compare how values and beliefs influence economic decisions in different societies.

 **Check Your Answers** Check your answers at this book's Online Learning Center at **glencoe.com**.

**NCLB**

Section 2.1  Parenting and Families  **41**

## Section 2.1 — After You Read

### Review Key Concepts
1. Three ways to build parenting skills include reading reliable information about parenting; gaining experience by working with or caring for children; and asking the advice of family and friends who have parenting experience.
2. New parents often experience fear of not being a good parent; frustration at the loss of personal freedom and the addition of new responsibilities; worry over money matters; jealousy of the baby and the attention he or she gets from the other parent, friends, and relatives; and depression due to exhaustion or to the physical changes of pregnancy and birth.

### Practice Academic Skills
3. Students' lists will vary but should clearly show how a task was accomplished for the first time.
4. Answers will vary but may include such comparisons as American parents will buy a crib to prepare for a new baby while many Japanese or Korean parents do not. They plan for the baby to sleep in the parent's bed for the first few years.

## Assess

### Study Tools

Have students go to the Online Learning Center at **glencoe.com**:

- Take the **Practice Test**.
- Download **Study-to-Go** content.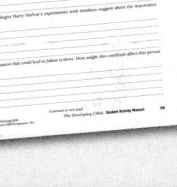

Use the **Student Activity Workbook** for additional practice.

## Close

### Culminating Activity

**Good Parenting** Hold up a picture of a couple with an infant. Ask: What have you learned about the skills these parents will need? (Possible answers: They will need good resource management skills and they will need to adjust their roles as the child grows.)

**NCLB** connects academic correlations to book content.

## Focus

### Bell Ringer Activity

#### Impact of Advertising

Hold up a magazine advertisement that has a sexual component. Ask: What impact does this advertisement have on you? What does it say about sexuality and sexual activity? Why do you think the advertiser emphasizes sexuality? Conclude by explaining that we are constantly bombarded by ads implying that we should live for the moment. However, the fact is that sexual activity is much more complex than shown in this advertisement.

## Preteaching

### Vocabulary

Before discussing the Content Vocabulary, ask students if they can define any of them based on what they have read previously or from their own real-world experience.

### Graphic Organizer

🔅 The Graphic Organizer is also on the TeacherWorks CD.

(Graphic organizer should include health risks, education challenges, financial issues, and emotional and social stress.)

**NCLB** connects academic correlations to book content.

## Reading Guide

### Before You Read

**Be Organized**  A messy environment can be distracting. To lessen distractions, organize an area where you can read comfortably.

### Read to Learn
#### Key Concepts
- **Identify** pressures involved in sexual development.
- **Summarize** the benefits of abstinence.
- **Describe** the possible consequences of sexual activity.
- **Compare and contrast** the options available to a teen parent.
- **Explain** what it means to be sexually responsible.

**D**

### Main Idea
Choosing abstinence from sexual activity allows you to take responsibility for your well-being.

### Content Vocabulary
◇ sexuality
◇ hormone
◇ abstinence
◇ sexually transmitted infection (STI)
◇ paternity
◇ confidential adoption
◇ open adoption
◇ fidelity

### Academic Vocabulary
You will find these words in your reading and on your tests. Use the glossary to look up their definitions if necessary.
- intimacy
- essential

### Graphic Organizer
As you read, list the consequences associated with teen pregnancy. Use a chart like the one shown to help organize your information.

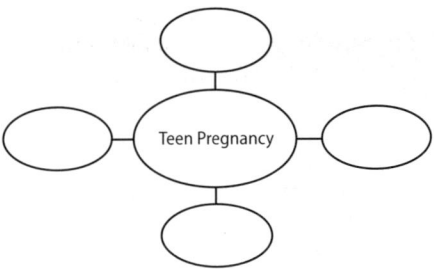

 **Graphic Organizer**  Go to this book's Online Learning Center at **glencoe.com** to print out this graphic organizer.

### Academic Standards · · · · · · · · · · · · · · · · · · ·

**NCLB**

 **English Language Arts**
**NCTE 5**  Use different writing process elements to communicate effectively.

 **Social Studies**
**NCSS IV F Individual Development and Identity**  Analyze the role of perceptions, attitudes, values, and beliefs in the development of personal identity.

**NCTE** *National Council of Teachers of English*
**NCTM** *National Council of Teachers of Mathematics*

**NSES** *National Science Education Standards*
**NCSS** *National Council for the Social Studies*

**42**  Chapter 2  Responsibilities of Parenting

## Reading Guide

### Before You Read

Discuss with students that while this section deals with teen parenthood, it also presents the various challenges that teens face as they mature sexually. While there is a great deal of controversy in our society surrounding this subject, this section will look primarily at the consequences of teen sexual activity.

### D Develop Concepts

**Main Idea**  Discuss the main idea with the students. Ask students: What do you think the word *abstinence* means? Talk about different kinds of abstinence, such as not drinking alcohol. Then discuss the meaning of the term *sexual abstinence*. (It means to refrain from sexual activity, in particular sexual intercourse.)

## Sexual Development

The teen years bring on many physical changes. These changes are the start of adult sexual development. Sexual traits develop. Teens become physically able to reproduce. Interest in the opposite gender increases. Sexual interest is common. The decisions you make about sexual behavior will have a great impact on your life. Choosing to make responsible decisions about sexual behavior is part of becoming mature.

## Sexuality

Sexuality and sexual activity are not the same thing. **Sexuality** is your beliefs and values about sexual behavior. It involves more than physical maturity or the ability to be sexually active. Sexuality includes how people feel about themselves and their sense of responsibility for and understanding of other people and their feelings. Thus, sexuality has physical, intellectual, emotional, and social aspects. Individuals show their sexuality in their attitudes and the way they walk, talk, move, and dress. It affects your behavior and your relationships.

Adolescence is a time when boys and girls begin to develop a sense of their own sexuality. A **hormone** is a chemical in the body that controls the changes that occur as teens become sexually mature. These changes have an emotional and physical impact. They can cause mood swings and emotional ups and downs.

### Sexual Pressures

Social development also shifts into high gear during puberty. Children will have attractions to new friends. Relationships with family members often change as teens become more independent. They want to spend more time with friends. They sometimes question parental authority.

In the midst of these changes, messages about sexual activity seem to be everywhere. Music, television, radio, movies, and advertising often send the messages that sexual activity is a necessary part of sexuality. Peer pressure, the influence of friends and other teens, may come with the mind-set of "Everyone's doing it. Why aren't you?"

With all these pressures, it is easy to lose sight of what is important. Dating can be fun without becoming sexually active. Teens can date as couples or in groups. Dating helps teens discover which qualities and characteristics they find desirable in another person. Teens can learn more about building relationships through dating.

Sexual activity is not the same as intimacy. **Intimacy** is a closeness between two people. You can develop intimacy and express affection by holding hands or hugging. Sharing thoughts, feelings, and dreams also helps build intimacy. A lasting and loving relationship is not based on sexual activity. Sexual activity does not make you an adult. It cannot save a poor relationship either.

**Attraction**
During the teen years, interest in the opposite gender increases. *How might a responsible person deal with these feelings?*

Section 2.2   Teen Parenthood   **43**

## Teach

### Discussion Starter

**Baggage** Ask students what they think the word *baggage* means. Encourage students to discuss how the word is used in its psychological sense—to refer to attitudes, worries, or duties that weigh us down, just like a heavy suitcase might. Ask: What kind of baggage can sexual activity add to a teen's life? (Responses might include: it can make relationships more complex and volatile, and it can lead to STIs and pregnancy.)

### U Universal Access

**Visual Learners** Encourage students to discuss the kinds of advertisements they see every day that send a sexual message. Perhaps a magazine ad shows a young man staring at an attractive woman in a swimming suit. Or a television commercial shows two people kissing. Instruct students to keep track of all the ads they see in a single day which appear to be sending a sexual message. Guide the class in discussing their findings. ELL

### R Reading Strategy

**Compare Terminology** Have students fold a sheet of paper down the center. Instruct them to label the left side Sexual Activity and the right side Intimacy. Students should then work individually to write a list of characteristics of each. Ask for volunteers to share their lists with the class. (Lists will vary, but should be appropriate for the heading.)

## Explore the Photo

**Caption Answer** Answers will vary but may include using self-discipline and control, knowing they are in charge of their actions, or not putting themselves in situations that could be dangerous.

**Discussion** Ask students: How do you let someone know you are attracted to him or her? How do you judge the person's response? (Answers will vary, but may include paying attention to the person or saying flattering things. An interested person typically responds in a similar fashion.)

### Teach *cont.*

**U₁ Universal Access**

**Intrapersonal Learners** Have students work individually to create a list of values their families have taught them. From this list, students should choose one value they believe to be particularly important. Students should then write an essay explaining how this value has influenced the way they live their lives. (Student essays will vary, but they should explain how the chosen value has influenced their lives.)

**W Writing Support**

**Prewriting**

**Speaking Up for Abstinence** Tell students to imagine that they are planning to write a letter to their school newspaper or another local newspaper encouraging sexual abstinence. Instruct students to engage in prewriting to determine the structure of the letter and the advantages of abstinence to be covered. (Refer to p. 30 to review the characteristics of prewriting. Students' prewriting will vary, but should contain the basic structure of the letter and a list of the major points to be made.)

**✓ Reading Check**

**Describe** Values commonly passed on by families include trust, self-respect, respect for others, commitment, and loyalty.

**Group Dates**
Dating does not have to include sexual activity. It can be just getting to know someone. *What can people learn about one another by going on dates?*

Physical and emotional changes often create a desire to act on sexual feelings. Even teens who reject the outside pressures to become sexually active have to be strong about resisting their own sexual feelings. Sexual feelings are natural, and they can be powerful. The best defense is to plan ahead and avoid situations where you may be tempted to engage in sexual activity.

Decisions related to sexuality are too important to be made casually. They deserve careful consideration, because they can have serious lifelong consequences. It can be helpful to discuss decisions about sexuality with other people. While teens often turn to friends for advice, most teens can benefit from talking to a responsible adult. Trusted adults can be valuable resources. A trusted adult might be a parent, an older family member, a religious leader, a school counselor, or a doctor.

### Family Values

One role of families is to pass on the family's and society's values. These are the principles they consider important and the rules they use to guide their lives. Values are based on ideas about what is right, good and desirable. They include trust, self-respect, respect for others, commitment, and loyalty.

Family can help answer questions about sexuality based on values. For example, "How should I treat people of the opposite sex?" "How can I balance old friendships and new relationships with someone of the other sex?" Values help shape each person's response to these questions.

By drawing on their values, teens can choose to build a sense of their own sexuality without becoming sexually active.

**✓ Reading Check** **Describe** What are some values commonly passed on by families?

## Abstinence

Choosing abstinence from sexual activity allows you to take responsibility for your well-being. **Abstinence** is a deliberate decision to avoid high-risk behaviors, including sexual activity and the use of tobacco, alcohol, and other drugs. You show your values and beliefs when you choose abstinence. Abstinence is not always easy. Use these tips to stay firm in your decision.

- **Talk about your feelings before you get in an intimate situation.** Make sure your partner understands your point of view.
- **Say no to any situation that does not feel right.** Refusing to participate in something you believe is wrong is your responsibility to yourself. Choose dating locations and activities that avoid the pressure for sexual activity. This might include a group date or a party with adults present.
- **Show affection in nonsexual ways.** There are nonsexual ways of showing love that can be satisfying, such as holding hands, hugging, or kissing. Talking and sharing dreams and interests can also create a sense of intimacy and closeness. Small sacrifices can express caring more than sexual behavior does.

**44** Chapter 2 Responsibilities of Parenting

---

**Explore the Photo**

**Caption Answer** Answers will vary but may include learning what kinds of foods, music, or movies the other person likes or dislikes; thoughts and dreams about the future; and religious beliefs.

**Discussion** Encourage students to share their experiences with group dating. Ask them to discuss its advantages and disadvantages. (Answers will vary. Advantages might include that it may reduce the chances of sexual intimacy. Disadvantages might include that it could be more difficult to get to know the other person.)

"It can't happen to me." Countless teens have thought that. They were wrong. The threat of sexually transmitted infections is very real, as is the threat of pregnancy. Abstaining from sexual activity is the only guaranteed way of avoiding these problems.

This is a decision that each individual needs to take time to think about thoroughly before encountering a sexual situation. It is much more difficult to reach the decision to abstain in a moment of passion. Once a person has decided to abstain, it is important to stick to the decision. It can help to remember why the decision was made in the first place.

**✓ Reading Check** **Identify** What are three things teens can do to help themselves remain abstinent?

## Consequences of Sexual Activity

Saying yes to sexual pressures as a teen has serious consequences. Those who engage in sexual activity too soon may have major problems. Some of these are emotional, such as trust issues, difficulty committing in future relationships, and a loss of self-respect. Problems can also include physical consequences, such as sexually transmitted infections or pregnancy.

## Sexually Transmitted Infections

A **sexually transmitted infection (STI)** is a disease that is spread from one person to another by sexual contact. These are sometimes called sexually transmitted diseases (STDs). It is estimated that one in five people in the United States has an STI, and 25 percent of new cases of STIs are infected teens. All STIs are preventable. The only way to completely prevent STIs is through abstinence.

Some STIs can be treated. Others last a person's entire life. **Figure 2.2** on page 46 describes some common STIs. Some of the symptoms for an STI may also indicate other diseases or conditions. Anyone who has symptoms should see a doctor for diagnosis and treatment.

### HIV/AIDS

One STI with deadly results is acquired immune deficiency syndrome (AIDS). AIDS is caused by the human immunodeficiency virus (HIV). HIV can stay in a person's blood for many years before it develops into AIDS. AIDS does not directly kill its victims, but it allows other diseases to invade the body. One or more of these diseases usually causes the person's death. There is no known cure for AIDS at this time, although research is continuing.

**Abstinence Takes Courage**
The decision to abstain can be a difficult one. *What are the benefits that make abstinence worth the effort?*

Section 2.2   Teen Parenthood   45

**Teach** cont.

**C Critical Thinking**
**Make Inferences** Studies have shown that the percentage of teens in grades 9 through 10 having sexual intercourse has declined in recent years. Ask students why they think this might be. (Student answers will vary. Many teens are becoming more aware of the dangers of STIs. Others realize that their lives are already complicated enough without becoming involved in sexual activity, which may lead to situations they are not ready to handle.)

**U₂ Universal Access**
**Verbal Learners** Discuss with the class that the decision to be sexually active affects more than just the teen couple involved. Ask students to write a one-paragraph monologue on the subject from each of the following points of view: each of the teens, one of the teens' parents, and a younger sibling of one of the teens. Each teen should write a total of four paragraphs. Ask for volunteers to share their monologues with the class. (Paragraphs will vary but should show thoughtful contemplation about how each of the four people involved might feel about or respond to the situation.)

**✓ Reading Check**

**Identify** Three things teens can do to remain abstinent include talking about feelings before getting in an intimate situation, saying no to any situation that does not feel right, and showing affection in nonsexual ways.

**►►►► Explore the Photo**

**Caption Answer** Answers will vary but may include avoiding sexually transmitted infections including HIV/AIDS, social and emotional stress, and loss of self-respect.

**Discussion** Encourage students to discuss how they might introduce the subject of responsible sexual behavior with someone they care about. When might be a good time to bring up the subject? (Responses will vary. It is best to talk about sexual behavior before the individuals are in a tempting situation.)

## Teach cont.

### S Skill Practice

**Guided Practice**

**Make a Public Service Announcement** Organize students into small groups. Have each group create a two-minute public service announcement (PSA) about STIs. The announcements should include information about the diseases themselves and their effects on teens. Have each group present its PSA to the class. (PSAs should provide information about STIs and their effects on teens.) **L1** **ELL**

**Create a Graph** Have students work in pairs to conduct research about how common each of the STIs listed in Figure 2.2 is in the United States. Student pairs should create a graph showing the number of individuals having each disease. (Graphs should show the number of people in the U.S. having each of the STIs listed in Figure 2.2) **L2** **ELL**

**Finding a Cure** Have students choose one of the STIs for which there currently is no cure. They then should conduct research to learn about scientific studies being done on this STI. They also should investigate whether scientists think they are close to finding a cure. Have students write a report summarizing their findings. (Reports should explain current research being done on one of the STIs presented here.) **L3**

### Mc Graw Hill Professional Development

**Mini Clip**
Reading:
Flexible
Groupings

Teachers use flexible groupings and partner sharing to promote student discussions.

---

**Figure 2.2 Sexually Transmitted Infections**

Anyone who experiences any of these symptoms should be tested so that his or her exact condition can be determined and treatment begun. *Which STIs have no cure?*

| STI | Symptoms | Effects | Treatment |
|-----|----------|---------|-----------|
| **Chlamydia** (klə-ˈmi-dē-ə) | Pain when urinating. Women may feel abdominal pain, nausea, and low fever. Some people show no symptoms. | Can cause *sterility*, the inability to have children. | Can be cured with antibiotics. |
| **Genital herpes** | Open sores on sex organs, which go away in a few weeks. Painful urination, fever. | Can cause brain damage or death if passed to a baby during childbirth. | There is no cure. Symptoms can be treated. |
| **Genital warts** | Small growths on the sex organs, which cause discomfort and itching. | If left alone, they may become cancerous. | There is no cure, but a doctor can remove them. A vaccine is available to prevent the disease. |
| **Hepatitis B** (ˌhe-pə-ˈtī-təs) | Causes flu-like symptoms. | Can lead to liver disease or cancer. | There is no cure. A vaccine is available to prevent the disease. |
| **Gonorrhea** (ˌgä-nə-ˈrē-ə) | Burning, itching, and the discharge of liquids from infected areas. | Can cause sterility in females. A baby born to an infected mother can suffer eye damage. | Can be treated with antibiotics. |
| **Syphilis** (ˈsi-f(ə-)ləs) | In early stages, sores on the sex organs, fever, rash, and hair loss. | Can cause insanity and death. | Can be cured with antibiotics. |
| **HIV/AIDS** | No visible symptoms in first stage of infection. Later stages include fever, headache, sore throat, rashes, diarrhea, swollen glands, body aches, diminished appetite, and weight loss. | AIDS lessens immunity to other illnesses, which can cause death. | There is no cure. Some medicines can delay the development of AIDS. |

---

**Figure 2.2 Sexually Transmitted Infections**

**Caption Answer** There is no cure for genital herpes, genital warts, hepatitis B, or AIDS.

**Discussion** As a class, go over the STIs listed in this figure. Emphasize that some of them, such as genital herpes, have no known cure. Ask students: How do you think having an STI for which there is no cure (such as genital herpes) might affect your life? (Responses will vary. You might be fearful that you could spread the disease to anyone with whom you had sexual activity.)

## Pregnancy

Another possible consequence of sexual activity is pregnancy. Pregnancy causes many problems. These problems affect both the teen mother and father. When Tracy became pregnant, she and Parker married. Parker took a job, planning to finish high school after a year. Before that could happen, their car broke down and he needed to work overtime to pay for the repairs. Soon after, Tracy became pregnant again. By the time their second child was a year old, Parker had been out of high school almost three years. He did not feel like going back, even though he knew he could earn more with a diploma or a GED.

Teen pregnancy creates four basic types of problems. These include health risks, education challenges, financial issues, and emotional and social stress. These problems also affect the teens' families and society.

### Health Risks

Pregnancy presents special health risks for both a teen mother and her baby. A teen is not yet physically or emotionally mature and may not be ready for the extra demands of pregnancy. Teens are also at greater risk than adult women for experiencing serious medical complications from a pregnancy. One such complication is significant iron deficiency, which can deprive the baby and mother of oxygen. A teen is also at greater risk for a dangerous condition called *toxemia*, which can lead to the premature delivery of the baby.

*blood poisoning from bacteria*

A female teen has high nutritional needs. If she becomes pregnant and there is no extra emphasis on nutrition, her body may not be able to provide the nutrients that she and her growing baby both need. In addition, a critical period of development occurs before most mothers are even aware they are pregnant. Babies of teen mothers are more likely to be born early and have low birth weights. These conditions are linked to other problems, including learning difficulties.

### Education Challenges

It is important for pregnant teens to complete their schooling, at least through high school. Unfortunately, many drop out of school. Nearly half of the teen mothers who leave school never finish their education. This is true even for those who plan to return. Without a high school diploma, it is hard to find a job, especially one with a salary to support a small family. This puts a greater strain on society to help support the family.

**C**

---

### RESPOND TO SPECIAL NEEDS — Low Birth Weight Babies

Low birth weight babies are born weighing less than five pounds, eight ounces. These babies are at risk for serious health problems and death. Low birth weight babies may have disabilities such as vision and hearing loss, learning difficulties, mental retardation, and cerebral palsy. These babies need specialized care both as babies and as they grow older.

There are many factors that can cause babies to be born with a low birth weight. These include illness in the mother or fetus, premature birth, the baby is a twin or other multiple, the mother smoked while pregnant, the mother used alcohol or illegal drugs while pregnant, and the age of the mother. Women under the age of 17 and over the age of 35 have an increased risk of delivering a low birth weight baby.

**Critical Thinking** Research steps a woman can take to reduce her risk of delivering a low birth weight baby. Create a poster that includes a list of the steps you find.

---

## Assess

**Quiz**

Ask students to answer the following questions:

1. How do hormones affect teens, both physically and emotionally? (Hormones result in teens' bodies becoming sexually mature and frequently cause mood swings.)

2. Which STI can lead to insanity and death if left untreated? (If left untreated, syphilis can lead to insanity and death.)

3. If a teen wants to avoid sexual activity, what kinds of dating locations might he or she choose? (Locations might include public spots, like the movies, or other teens' homes with their parents present.)

## Reteach

**C** **Critical Thinking**

**Make Judgments** Ask students: What should be a school's responsibility in helping a teen parent stay in school? For example, should the school offer flexible class times so the parent can hold down a job while going to school? Should the school offer free child care? What are some advantages and disadvantages to these options? (Student answers will vary, but should address the school's role in encouraging teen parents to remain in school. Some students may feel that it is not the school's responsibility.)

---

### RESPOND TO SPECIAL NEEDS — Low Birth Weight Babies

**Discussion** Instruct students to imagine they are the doctor of a pregnant woman who smokes. Ask what they might do to help this woman quit smoking. (Responses will vary. After explaining the risks, they might encourage her to join a support group.)

**Critical Thinking** Posters will vary but may include: receive preconception and prenatal medical care, do not smoke, take vitamin supplements on the advice of health care provider, and do not use alcohol or illicit drugs.

### R Reading Strategy

**Contrast** Read aloud the second paragraph under Financial Issues. Ask students: Why did the author use the term "legally responsible," rather than simply "responsible"? How is being legally responsible different from being morally responsible? (Students should explain that while people are morally responsible for caring for any children they may have, they are also breaking the law if they do not provide for their children.) **ELL**

**Professional Development**

**Mini Clip**
**ELL: Reading Aloud**

A teacher reads aloud, modeling fluency, pronunciation, expression, and comprehension strategies.

### U₁ Universal Access

**Verbal Learners** Discuss that some people have proposed that the government offer incentives to reduce the number of young people having children. For example, the government might offer free tuition at a university. Divide the class in half and have the two sides debate whether or not they believe offering incentives would reduce teen pregnancy rates. Before the debate, each group's members should agree on the major points they plan to make. **ELL**

### ✓ Reading Check

**Recall** The only way to completely prevent sexually transmitted infections is through abstinence.

---

Pregnant and parenting teens can work with school counselors and social service agencies to find solutions to such problems. These resources can help find ways to provide care for the babies while their parents take classes. Graduating should be a high-priority goal for young mothers and fathers.

### Financial Issues

Most teen parents experience financial problems. Teen mothers need good medical care. That care costs money, as does childbirth. Teen parents who keep their child must provide food, clothing, housing, and health care. This continues for at least 18 years.

Even when teen parents do not marry, both are legally responsible for providing for their child. If the father chooses not to stay involved with the child, it is especially important to establish paternity. **Paternity** is the legal identification of a man as the biological father of a child. Paternity will legally ensure the father's responsibilities toward the child. A medical test can prove paternity.

For many teen couples, the burden of child care expenses becomes overwhelming. In order to meet financial needs, a young couple's goals and plans for the future must be changed. This tension can lead to arguments. The stress from financial issues can affect other family members and even the baby. Sometimes society must help care for the child through government and welfare programs.

### Emotional and Social Stress

Adjusting to new relationships can cause great stress. Changes to old relationships can also cause stress. Teen parents may miss their old friends, but find they no longer have much in common with them. Teens who enjoyed sports or other after-school activities may have to give them up or cut back. Teen parents quickly realize that their lives have changed in profound ways.

✓ **Reading Check** **Recall** What is the only way to completely prevent sexually transmitted infections?

## Teen Parenting Options

Teens can and do get pregnant. Many, though, have trouble believing and acknowledging the symptoms when it happens. A girl who fears she might be pregnant may try to ignore the possibility. However, for her health and the baby's health, it is **essential**, or necessary, that she confirm the pregnancy and get good care as soon as possible.

A teen who suspects she is pregnant should discuss her concerns with someone close. This could be her boyfriend, a parent or other family member, a trusted friend, or a teacher or counselor. She should also see a doctor as soon as possible to confirm the pregnancy.

Once her pregnancy has been confirmed, a teen can begin to make plans. Her partner

➡ **Parenting and Education**
The birth of a child prompts many teens to drop out of school. *Why is it so important to stay in school?*

---

⬤➤ **Explore the Photo**

**Caption Answer** Without a high school diploma, it is hard to find a job, particularly one with a salary that will support a family.

**Discussion** Ask students: What do you think are the main reasons that many teens drop out of school after having a child? (Reasons will vary, but answers might include child care difficulties and the need to work long hours to pay for the child's needs.)

should be involved, too. After all, the father has rights and responsibilities. The pregnancy will have a long-lasting effect on the lives of both parents. In order to make responsible plans, both teens will have to carefully consider the options and their consequences. Family can be a good resource for support and guidance at this time.

When faced with pregnancy, teens have several options. Each one must be considered seriously. There are several factors that must be considered for each option.

## Marriage

Marriage has many benefits for both the teen parents and their child. At any age, however, marriage is not easy. It takes a special commitment, responsibility, and work.

Married teens face a special set of problems. As the initial excitement of marriage wears off, the strains of responsibility and the new social situation set in. Teens who marry because of a pregnancy face an additional problem. They have to adjust to parenthood at the same time they are adjusting to being married.

Married teens who are able to meet these challenges can find themselves with a strong and rewarding relationship. Having two people share the child care lessens the work of each. With hard work and commitment, married teens can build a caring home for a child.

## Single Parenthood

Having a tiny baby to cuddle and love can seem very appealing. Indeed, it can be rewarding to care for someone who is so small, helpless, and dependent. However, caring for a newborn is a huge responsibility, and becoming a parent is a lifelong commitment.

All these responsibilities can be draining for an adult. They can be even harder for a teen. Not surprisingly, many teen parents suffer from burnout or depression. They need to find support.

Teens considering single parenthood need to be realistic and ask a lot of questions. How much emotional and financial help can one teen parent expect from the other? From his or her own parents and other family members? A

teen considering single parenthood must guard against romanticizing the situation. For example, a teen who is not interested in marriage during the pregnancy is unlikely to change his or her mind after the birth. Parents, counselors, and other adults can help teens develop realistic expectations for their own situations as single parents.

## Adoption

Adoption is another option for pregnant teens. In adoption, the birth mother and father legally give up their rights and responsibilities for raising the child to another family.

The decision to place a baby for adoption is not easy. Teens considering adoption need to think it through carefully, because it is a permanent decision. Many teens choose adoption because they feel they are giving their child an opportunity for more care, guidance, and love than they are able to provide at this stage of their lives. Placing a baby for adoption for these reasons is an act of love. However, even when the decision is made with careful thought and consideration, it is an emotional decision.

There are two different types of adoption. A **confidential adoption** is an adoption in which the birth parents do not know the names of the adoptive parents. There is no exchange of information after the adoption. The access to information about the birth parents is limited by law in a confidential adoption.

## Study Tools

Have students go to the Online Learning Center at **glencoe.com**:

- Take the **Practice Test**.
- Download **Study-to-Go** content.

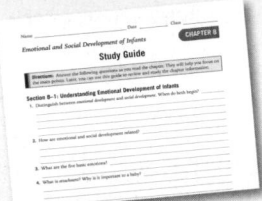

Use the **Student Activity Workbook** for additional practice.

**Close**

## Culminating Activity

**Summarize** Have the class work together to make a chart listing some of the reasons that teens might choose to avoid sexual activity. (Reasons might include to avoid pregnancy, STIs, or emotional turmoil.)

✓ **Reading Check**

**Define** Adoption is when the birth parents legally give up their rights and responsibilities for raising the child.

**NCLB** connects academic correlations to book content.

---

An **open adoption** is an adoption in which the birth parents and adoptive parents know something about each other. There are different levels of open adoption based on how much information is shared with both sets of parents. The parents may or may not meet each other.

✓ **Reading Check** **Define** What is adoption?

## Take Responsibility

What does it mean to be sexually responsible? It means knowing the facts about sexuality. It means thinking about the outcome of your decisions and actions. It means knowing your values and living by them.

Most people want sexual activity to be special. They want their strong feelings of desire to go along with a strong bond to one beloved person. Many people are willing to wait. They want a sexual relationship based on fidelity. **Fidelity** is faithfulness to an obligation, duty, or trust. Saving sexual activity for the committed framework of marriage provides a way to show your responsibility. It also shows respect for yourself and others.

Remember that you and your partner or date both deserve to be treated with consideration and respect. You should be able to communicate your thoughts and feelings honestly with one another. Talk with a trusted adult, such as a parent or guardian, to help you manage your feelings and make informed choices.

Parenthood is a challenging and rewarding time of life, but it can be especially challenging for teens. When people wait to have children until they are physically, emotionally, and financially prepared, it helps assure a bright future for both the children and the parents.

---

**Section 2.2** **After You Read**

### Review Key Concepts

1. **Explain** the difference between sexuality and sexual activity.
2. **Define** abstinence.
3. **Analyze** two risks a teen pregnancy has on the baby.
4. **Distinguish** between confidential and open adoption.
5. **Explain** why people should wait to have children until they are physically, emotionally, and financially prepared.

### Practice Academic Skills

**English Language Arts**

6. Imagine that you write an advice column for a local newspaper. A seventeen-year-old unmarried teen has written to you saying that she thinks she is pregnant. How would you respond? Write an advice column to the teen.

**Social Studies**

7. A decision to abstain from sexual activity is strongly influenced by personal values. Write a paragraph in which you explain how values influence a person's decision to abstain.

🔍 **Check Your Answers** Check your answers at this book's Online Learning Center at **glencoe.com**.

**NCLB**

> **NCTE 5** Use different writing process elements to communicate effectively.

> **NCSS IV F** Analyze the role of perceptions, attitudes, values, and beliefs in the development of personal identity.

---

### Review Key Concepts

1. Sexuality refers to a person's view of himself or herself as a male or female. Sexual activity is when people engage in sexual behavior.
2. Abstinence is a deliberate decision to avoid high-risk behaviors, including sexual activity and the use of tobacco, alcohol, and other drugs.
3. Teens are at greater risk of iron deficiency, which can deprive the baby of oxygen, and of toxemia, which can lead to the premature delivery of the baby.
4. confidential: the birth parents do not know the names of the adoptive parents; open: birth and adoptive parents know each other
5. to help assure a bright future for both the children and the parents

### Practice Academic Skills

6. Advice columns will vary. Students should suggest that the teen talk to an adult she can trust and that she see a doctor for confirmation of the pregnancy.
7. Answers will vary but may include that values such as trust, self-respect, and respect for others help shape each person's sense of his or her own sexuality.

## Chapter Summary

Parenting is a learning process, and offers many challenges and rewards. Before deciding to become parents, it is important to seriously consider one's readiness for parenthood. People who are ready for parenthood have considered their own emotional maturity, health issues, financial concerns, resource management skills, and parenting skills.

Decisions related to sexuality cannot be made casually. Abstinence is the only guaranteed way to prevent pregnancy and sexually transmitted infections. There are several options for teens who are pregnant.

## Vocabulary Review

1. Create a multiple-choice test question for each content and academic vocabulary term.

**Content Vocabulary**
◇ parenting (p. 33)
◇ emotional maturity (p. 35)
◇ sexuality (p. 43)
◇ hormone (p. 43)
◇ abstinence (p. 44)
◇ sexually transmitted infection (STI) (p. 45)

◇ paternity (p. 48)
◇ confidential adoption (p. 49)
◇ open adoption (p. 49)
◇ fidelity (p. 50)

**Academic Vocabulary**
■ pride (p. 33)
■ prospective (p. 35)
■ intimacy (p. 43)
■ essential (p. 48)

## Review Key Concepts

2. **Explain** who can benefit from knowing about child development and parenting.
3. **Describe** the five areas of responsibilities for parents.
4. **Identify** pressures involved in sexual development.
5. **Summarize** the benefits of abstinence.
6. **Describe** the possible consequences of sexual activity.
7. **Compare and contrast** the options available to a teen parent.
8. **Explain** what it means to be sexually responsible.

## Critical Thinking

9. **Summarize** How can people who care for one another show intimacy without sexual activity?
10. **Apply** What should a teen do if she suspects she is pregnant?

Chapter 2 Responsibilities of Parenting **51**

### Content and Academic Vocabulary Review

1. Students should write multiple-choice questions with possible answers for each term.

### Review Key Concepts

2. anyone who lives or works with children

3. lifestyle changes, emotional adjustments, relationship changes, employment adjustments, and legal responsibilities

4. Music, television, movies, and advertising often convey the messages that sexual activity is a necessary part of sexuality. Peer pressure may come with the mind-set of "Everyone's doing it?—why aren't you?"

5. Choosing abstinence allows you to take responsibility for your well-being. You show your values and beliefs, and avoid pregnancy and STIs.

6. pregnancy, sexually transmitted infections, emotional and social stress, and a loss of self-respect

7. Marriage—sharing child care can lessen the work. Single parenthood—many teen parents suffer from burnout or depression and require support. Adoption—many teens feel adoption gives their child an opportunity for more love and guidance. It is very emotional to give up your baby, though.

8. knowing the facts about sexuality, thinking about the outcome of your decisions and actions, and knowing your values and living by them

## Critical Thinking

9. People can show intimacy by holding hands, hugging, or kissing; by talking and sharing dreams and interests; and by making small sacrifices for one another.

10. A teen who suspects she is pregnant should have the pregnancy confirmed, obtain prenatal care, and begin making plans with input from the father and a trusted adult.

## Family & Community Connections

**11.** Bar graphs will vary but should present several different reasons why people surveyed chose to become parents.

### Health Skills

**12.** Brochures will vary but steps may include getting prenatal medical care, exercising, eating healthful foods, not smoking, or getting plenty of rest.

### Observation Skills

**13.** Student's reports will vary but should include the care provided to the newborn, the number of times care was given, the length of the observation, and the average number of times per hour the baby was cared for.

### Real-World Skills

**14.** Self-assessments will vary but should include questions based on the information presented under the Parenthood Readiness subhead of Section 2.1. A scoring system should also be included.

**Professional Development**

### Mini Clip
**ELL: Collaborative Work**

Students work in groups to complete a science lab.

**15.** Students' play scenes will vary but should show good communication skills. Scenes should be free of spelling and grammar errors and should include good formatting.

## Family & Community Connection

**11.** **Conduct a Survey** Create a brief survey in which you ask people why they chose to become a parent. Distribute the survey to at least 10 family members or friends who are parents. Be sure the surveys are anonymous. Make a list of the responses and compile your results in a bar graph. Compare your results graph with your classmates' results.

### Health Skills

**12.** **Research Healthy Babies** Use the online or print resources to find out more about the health concerns related to teen pregnancy. What can teens do to make sure that they will stay healthy? What can they do to ensure they will deliver a healthy baby? Use what you learn in your research to create a brochure. The brochure should include a list of steps teens can take to remain healthy during pregnancy.

## Observation Skills

**13.** **Observe Newborn Caregivers** Caregivers of newborns spend much of their time caring for the baby. Work with your teacher to arrange to observe caregivers of newborn babies at your local hospital.

**Procedure** Choose one baby to observe and take notes on the care provided such as feeding, changing, cleaning, and comforting. Also note the length of your observation.

**Analysis** Use your notes to write a half-page report in which you list the care provided to the newborn, the number of times the baby was cared for, and the length of your observation. Determine the average number of times per hour the baby was cared for.

> **NCSS I A Culture** Analyze and explain the ways groups, societies, and cultures address human needs and concerns.

**NCLB**

## Real-World Skills

| | |
|---|---|
| **Interpersonal and Collaborative Skills** | **14.** **Work in Teams** Work in groups determined by your teacher to develop questions for a self-assessment test for potential parents. Include at least 25 questions and a scoring system. Use information from Section 2.1 of this chapter to help you write the questions. |
| **Technology Skills** | **15.** **Create a Document** Use word-processing software to write a scene for a play in which a young couple discusses whether to start a family. You can end the scene with either decision, but be sure both characters show good communication skills as they talk about the issue. |
| **Financial Literacy** | **16.** **Calculate Diaper Costs** Research diapers that would fit a nine-pound baby and record the price of a box and the quantity in the box. If a baby uses seven of these diapers a day, how much would it cost per day to diaper the baby? How much per week? Per year? |

 **Additional Activities** For additional activities, go to this book's Online Learning Center at **glencoe.com**.

**16.** Answers will vary depending on the cost of diapers. If a box of 92 diapers costs $24.99, the cost per diaper is 27¢. The cost per day is $.27 \times 7 = \$1.89$; per week is $1.89 \times 7 = \$13.23$; and per year is $13.23 \times 52 = \$687.96$.

**NCLB** Activity correlated to Social Studies standards.

The *Early Childhood Observations CD* offers additional lessons with videos to build students' observation skills.

**Part 1:** Learning to Observe
**Part 2:** How Children Develop
**Part 3:** Working With Young Children
**Part 4:** Extended Observations
**Part 5:** Resources and Answer File

**Early Childhood Observations CD**

**Interactive Student CD**

# Academic Skills

 **English Language Arts**

**17. Think About Your Future** Parenting requires a lot of time and effort. Think about what kind of parent you want to be. What will be more important to you: spending time with your family or making lots of money? With this in mind, how might you approach a career path? Why? Write a one-page essay of your thoughts.

> **NCTE 4** Use written language to communicate effectively.

 **Mathematics**

**18. Savings Account for a Newborn** Micah wants to open a savings account for his newborn son. Eastern Bank offers simple interest of 1.5 percent per year. If Micah has $100 to open a savings account, how much money would be in the savings account after 16 years?

**Math Concept** **Multiply Percentages** A percent is a ratio that compares a number to 100. To multiply by a percent, first convert the percent to a decimal.

**Starting Hint** Rewrite the percent (1.5%) as a fraction with a denominator of 100. Convert the fraction to a decimal. Multiply this decimal by the number ($100), and then multiply it by 16. Add your result to the original amount ($100).

 For math help, go to the Math Appendix at the back of the book.

> **NCTM Number and Operations** Understand numbers, ways of representing numbers, relationships among numbers, and number systems.

 **Science**

**19. Investigate a Research Claim** Research reveals that some pregnant teens do not receive adequate care throughout pregnancy. One reason for this is that medical care can be expensive, and teens have no way to pay for that care.

**Procedure** Conduct your own research with print or online resources to learn how this research finding can be useful to parents and other caregivers.

**Analysis** Use the information from your research to write a one-page report.

> **NSES C** Develop understanding of the interdependence of organisms; matter, energy, and organization in living systems; and behavior of organisms.

 **Standardized Test Practice**

**TRUE/FALSE**

Read the passage, then answer the question.

> Many teen mothers are unable to continue attending high school once they have a baby to care for. Statistics show that the dropout rate is higher for teen mothers than for other female teens. Identify programs that help teen mothers stay in school while they raise their child.

**20.** According to the passage, teen mothers never finish high school.

   **a.** True

   **b.** False

> **Test-Taking Tip** Statements that contain extreme words, such as all, none, never, or always, or that have unsupported opinions, are often false.

# Academic Skills

**17.** Students' essays will vary but should include a possible career path based on whether spending time with family or making more money is a priority. Some students might say they do not want to be a parent and making money is their priority; they might describe a career that involves a lot of travel or long hours. Other students might describe a career path that allows them to spend more time with a family.

**18.** After 16 years, an account at Eastern Bank would yield $124. ($1.5\% = .015$; $.015 \times 100 = 1.5$; $1.5 \times 16 = 24$; $100 + 24 = \$124$.)

**19.** Answers will vary but should note that parents or other caregivers of teens may need to seek prenatal care for pregnant teens or offer financial assistance.

**NCLB** connects academic correlations to book content.

**Standardized Test Practice**

**20.** b. False

**Test-Taking Tips**
Carefully restate the question in your own words. This can often help you see it more objectively.

**True/False Tests**
Questions that contain words such as *often*, *frequently*, and *typically* are more often true than false.

---

## TECHNOLOGY Solutions

### Use these technology solutions to streamline chapter assessment!

 ***ExamView Assessment Suite*** CD allows you to create and print out customized tests or ready-made unit and chapter tests, complete with answer keys.

 **TeacherWorks Plus** is an electronic lesson planner that provides instant access to complete teacher resources in one convenient package.

 **Online Learning Center** includes resources and activities for students and teachers.

**STANDARDS BASED LESSON PLANNING** *The Developing Child* provides students with instruction and assessment in the following fundamental content areas:

## National Standards Correlations

| Standards | Pages |
|---|---|
| **12.1.1** Analyze physical, emotional, social, spiritual, and intellectual development. | **69–72** |
| **12.1.2** Analyze interrelationships among physical, emotional, social, and intellectual aspects of human growth and development. | **58–61** |
| **12.2.5** Analyze geographic, political, and global influences on human growth and development. | **64–67** |
| **12.3.1** Analyze the role of nurturance on human growth and development. | **60–61, 71** |
| **12.3.3** Analyze the role of family and social services support systems in meeting human growth and development needs. | **59** |
| **15.1.1** Analyze parenting roles across the life span. | **73–77** |
| **15.1.5** Explain cultural differences in roles and responsibilities of parenting. | **67, 84** |
| **15.2.1** Choose nurturing practices that support human growth and development. | **58–61, 71** |
| **15.2.3** Assess common practices and emerging research about discipline on human growth and development. | **72–73, 77–81** |
| **15.4.3** Analyze implications of alternatives to biological parenthood. | **63, 64, 84** |

**NO CHILD LEFT BEHIND** NCLB activities, information, and skills practice will help your students attain NCLB proficiency. Students will improve their abilities in the following academic standards areas:

## Academic Standards Correlations

| Discipline | Standard | Feature/Activity |
|---|---|---|
| **English Language Arts** | **NCTE 1** read texts to acquire new information. | **Reading Guide (pp. 56, 68)** |
| | **NCTE 2** Read literature to build an understanding of the human experience. | **Academic Skills (p. 85)** |
| | **NCTE 4** Use written language to communicate effectively. | **Writing Activity (p. 54)** **After You Read (p. 67)** |
| | **NCTE 12** Use language to accomplish individual purposes. | **After You Read (p. 81)** |
| **Mathematics** | **NCTM Number and Operations** Understand numbers, ways of representing numbers, relationships among numbers, and number systems. | **Academic Skills (p. 85)** |
| **Science** | **NSES A** Develop abilities necessary to do scientific inquiry, understandings about scientific inquiry. | **After You Read (p. 81)** |
| | **NSES F** Develop understanding of personal and community health; natural resources; environmental quality; science and technology in local, national, and global challenges. | **Science in Action (p. 66)** **Academic Skills (p. 85)** |
| **Social Studies** | **NCSS I A Culture** Analyze and explain the ways groups, societies, and cultures address human needs and concerns. | **After You Read (p. 67)** |
| | **NCSS IV D Individual Development and Identity** Apply concepts, methods, and theories about the study of human growth and development. | **Observation Skills (p. 84)** |

## Professional Development

**MINI CLIP VIDEO LIBRARY**

Targeted professional development is correlated throughout *The Developing Child*. **The McGraw-Hill Professional Development Mini Clip Video Library** provides teaching strategies to strengthen academic and learning skills. Log on to **glencoe.com**.

In this chapter, you will find these Mini Clips:
- **Reading**  Preparing to Read, p. 58
- **ELL**  Words in Action, p. 60
- **Reading**  Interacting with Text, p. 65
- **Reading**  Connecting the Pieces, p. 71
- **ELL**  Level 1 Proficiency, p. 74
- **Reading**  Building Vocabulary, p. 77

## Reading and Writing Strategies

**Writing Activity: Journal Entry** (p. 54)
Students use writing tips to write about a time they worked together with one or more family members.

**Before You Read** (pp. 56, 68)
A pre-reading question or statement will help students make a personal connection to content.

**Graphic Organizer** (pp. 56, 68)
A visual tool will help students organize and remember new content.

**Reading Check** (pp. 62, 64, 72, 73, 77)
A question allows students to make a quick comprehension self-check.

**After You Read** (pp. 67, 81)
Organize and process students' understanding of what they have read.

## Chapter Features

**Learning Through PLAY**

**Families Play Together** (p. 58)
Playing together enriches the lives of both parents and children.

**What Would You Do?**

**Finding a Family** (p. 63)
Being adopted as an older child can have both pluses and minuses.

**Science in Action**

**Technology and the Family** (p. 66)
Students conduct a survey to determine how time spent with technological devices affects family time.

**RESPOND TO SPECIAL NEEDS**

**Autism** (p. 71)
Children with autism need to get into special treatment programs at an early age.

**SAFE CHILD HEALTHY CHILD**

**Spanking as Discipline** (p. 80)
Child development experts disagree on the effectiveness of spanking as discipline.

**Careers With Children**

**Family Court Judge** (p. 82)
Students learn the career skills needed to succeed as a Family Court Judge.

## Chapter Overview

### Introduce the Chapter

In this chapter, students learn about the importance of families and the qualities exhibited by strong families. Various parenting styles are discussed and students learn how parents meet children's varying needs, including providing appropriate guidance and discipline.

### Build Background

Have students spend a minute thinking about their family. Were they born into it, or did they become a family member in another way? Do they have brothers or sisters? Perhaps they are in a foster family. Emphasize that while each family is different, the family is the most important group to which we belong.

### Writing Activity

#### Journal Entry

This active learning activity prompts students to write a journal entry to describe a time when they worked with other family members. After students have completed the writing activity, ask for volunteers to share their entries with the class. Encourage the class to discuss how the activities described helped build a strong family. (Use the following criteria to evaluate students' journal entries: Does one idea lead to another? Does it convey personal reactions? Does it contain possible writing ideas? You might have students keep a list of writing ideas to use for future assignments.)

## Chapter Objectives

After completing this chapter, you will be able to:

- **Summarize** the qualities that contribute to building a strong family.
- **Describe** the different family structures.
- **Discuss** the trends affecting families.
- **List** the basic categories of children's needs.
- **Identify** the three parenting styles.
- **Summarize** effective ways to guide children's behavior.

### Writing Activity  Journal Entry

**Working Together** When families work together to complete household tasks or take care of younger family members, it helps build a strong family. Write a journal entry about a time when you worked together with one or more of your family members.

**Writing Tips** A journal is a record of experiences, ideas, and reflections. To write an effective journal entry, follow these tips:

1. Date your entry.
2. Let one idea lead to another.
3. Write about experiences, reactions, and observations.

## CLASSROOM Solutions

### Print Resources

 **Student Edition**

 **Teacher Wraparound Edition**

 **Student Activity Workbook**

**Student Activity Workbook Teacher Annotated Edition**

### Technology Resources

 **Online Learning Center** has resources and activities for students and teachers. Includes an Online Student Edition.

 **Interactive Student Edition** allows students to instantly access review materials, examples, and exercises.

Section **3.1** **Family Characteristics**

Section **3.2** **Parenting Skills**

**Review the Sections**
Introduce the chapter by reviewing the sections:

**Section 3.1**
Families exist in all societies. Strong families provide a sense of belonging, emotional support, and security. They also prepare children to live on their own. Types of family structures include nuclear, single-parent, and blended. Many current societal trends affect families, including increasing mobility, changes in the economy, and technological changes.

**Section 3.2**
Healthy families meet the physical, emotional, social, and intellectual needs of children. Parenting styles vary; the three main types are authoritarian, assertive-democratic, and permissive. A major responsibility of parenting is to guide children by being a good role model and using both positive and negative reinforcement.

 **Explore the Photo**

**Caption Answer** Student answers will vary but might include eating meals, watching movies, playing games, or traveling.

**Discussion** Do you think it is important for families to have fun together? Explain your answer. (Students should say yes, because these families build good memories. They can draw strength from them if they later face tough times. In addition, their children are more likely to have fun with their own children when they become adults.)

↑ **Explore the Photo**
Families can enjoy many types of activities together. *What activities does your family enjoy doing together?*

55

 **TeacherWorks Plus** is an electronic lesson planner that provides instant access to complete teacher resources in one convenient package.

**Presentation Plus!** provides visual teaching aids for every section.

**The Early Childhood Observations CD** presents video observations and lessons on observation skills and child development.

**The Developing Brain eTransparencies and Guide** include information and activities to offer insights into brain development and diseases of the brain.

# Section 3.1 Family Characteristics

## Focus

### Bell Ringer Activity

**Making a Commitment**

Tell students that one of your neighbors has "family pizza night" every Thursday. Ask students why pizza night might be important to this family. Discuss that creating a strong family is something every member must be devoted to. Even something as seemingly minor as promising to be home for dinner on Thursdays can be important. Ask students to suggest other ways that family members can show commitment to one another.

## Preteaching

### Vocabulary

The definition of words often evolves over time. The word *nuclear* dates back to 1846, and means "relating to the nucleus of a cell." Around 1912, nuclear was first used to mean "central." Using this definition, anthropologist G.P. Murdock coined the term *nuclear family* in 1949.

### Graphic Organizer

 The Graphic Organizer is also on the TeacherWorks CD.

(Graphic organizers should include: celebrations, family traditions, and patterned family interactions.)

 **NCLB** connects academic correlations to book content.

---

## Reading Guide

### Before You Read

**Preview** Write a list of what you want to know about qualities that contribute to a strong family, family structures, and trends that affect families.

### Read to Learn

**Key Concepts**
- **Summarize** the qualities that contribute to building a strong family.
- **Describe** the different family structures.
- **Discuss** the trends affecting families.

**D** ### Main Idea

There are many different family structures. Family members must work together to overcome challenges and to build a strong foundation for the family.

### Content Vocabulary

- ◇ nuclear family
- ◇ single-parent family
- ◇ custodial parent
- ◇ blended family
- ◇ extended family
- ◇ legal guardian
- ◇ foster child
- ◇ intergenerational

 **Graphic Organizer** Go to this book's Online Learning Center at **glencoe.com** to print out this graphic organizer.

### Academic Vocabulary

You will find these words in your reading and on your tests. Use the glossary to look up their definitions if necessary.
- ■ vital
- ■ venture

### Graphic Organizer

As you read, list the three types of family traditions described in the text. Use a chart like the one shown to record your answers.

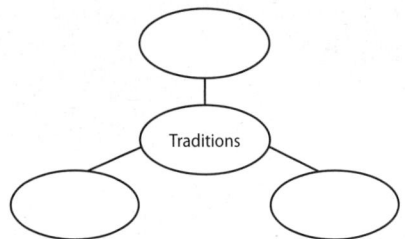

Traditions

---

**N C L B** ### Academic Standards · · · · · · · · · · · · · · · · · · · · ·

 **English Language Arts**

**NCTE 4** Use written language to communicate effectively.

**Science**

**NSES F** Develop understanding of science and technology in local, national, and global challenges.

**Social Studies**

**NCSS I A Culture** Analyze and explain the ways groups, societies, and cultures address human needs and concerns.

**NCTE** *National Council of Teachers of English*
**NCTM** *National Council of Teachers of Mathematics*

**NSES** *National Science Education Standards*
**NCSS** *National Council for the Social Studies*

---

## Reading Guide

### Before You Read

Ask students: How does your family help meet your needs? Write the list of ideas on the board. Encourage students to list not only physical needs, but also emotional, social, and intellectual needs. Explain that in this section they will learn more about how family members help one another.

### **D** Develop Concepts

**Main Idea** Discuss the main idea with the students. Ask: What happens if a building does not have a solid foundation? (It collapses.) Likewise, families must have a firm foundation if they are to stand up to everything that happens over the years.

## Qualities of Strong Families

Within every culture, there are families. A family can be different from group to group. In some cultures, family includes only parents and children. In others, aunts, uncles, grandmothers, and grandfathers are important parts of the family. Families are the foundation on which every human culture is built.

Families are not just a group of individuals who happen to be related. They are a group where all members can feel accepted and safe. In families, adults and children can learn and grow together. Families provide children with a sense of belonging, emotional support, nurturing, protection, and security. As families spend more time together, they form stronger bonds and traditions. Families also give children their first lessons in values and acceptable social behavior. These are lessons they will carry with them throughout their lives.

Developing family relationships is not an easy task. This is especially true when families are spread out. However, just living together under one roof does not guarantee smooth relationships. When individuals need to work together as a group, there are going to be differences of opinion, problems, and conflict. Each family member can help make a family stronger. Strong families can act as a buffer against many of life's problems.

Strong families have a variety of characteristics. Family members work together to provide for the needs of the family and prepare the children to live in our society. They spend time together, share responsibilities, and work together to resolve differences. They listen to each other with an open mind and allow each person to express opinions and share feelings. Families share goals and values and also show appreciation for each other. These are **vital**, or necessary, lessons for life.

▲ **Living in the Community**
Many families participate in activities that help build strong communities. *What family-friendly activities are available in your community?*

 **Explore the Photo**

**Caption Answer** Answers will vary depending on what activities are available in your community.

**Discussion** Tell students that the Sanchez family volunteers to fix lunch at their community's free-lunch program once a month. Encourage the class to discuss what the family might gain from this. (Responses will vary but might include that the family gets the satisfaction of helping others and the family is strengthened by working together.)

## Teach

### Discussion Starter

**Families that Work** Ask students: What do you enjoy most about your family? Ask for volunteers to share their answers. Explain that every family has its strengths and weaknesses, but ultimately all members must help one another to make the family work. (Students responses will vary, but might include things such as they share housework, or they go to one another's sporting events.)

### U₁ Universal Access

**Visual Learners** Explain to students that the way in which family members are related can be shown by creating a family tree. Draw a simple family tree on the board. Label each circle with both the individual's name and that person's relationship to other members. Explain that the names of married couples are placed side-by-side, with their children's names beneath them. Have students work individually to create their own family trees. **ELL**

### U₂ Universal Access

**Musical Learners** There are many preschool songs that talk about families. Instruct students to conduct research to learn about four of these songs. They should then prepare an oral presentation in which they discuss the significance of these songs to young children. Encourage students to either sing or read the lyrics in their presentations. (Students should prepare an oral presentation on four preschool songs about families, such as Hush Little Baby or To Grandma's House. The presentations should analyze why these songs are important to preschoolers.)

## Teach cont.

### R Reading Strategy

**Cooperative Learning** Discuss that one way to make yourself pay attention to what you are reading is by writing questions about the material. Instruct students to work individually to write five true/false questions about the material under Functions of the Family. Then have them trade questions with a partner and take the quiz. (Students should write five true/false questions. They should then answer another student's true/false questions.) **ELL**

### C Critical Thinking

**Government Programs** Government programs often come under attack. Some individuals think it is not helpful to provide services such as food stamps to people because they discourage self-reliance. Others think that these services provide support for people during difficult times. Instruct students to write a persuasive essay in which they argue either for or against these programs. (Essays will vary. Students should write a persuasive essay in which they argue either for or against government programs that provide assistance. Essays should be organized and thought provoking.)

**Professional Development**

**Mini Clip**
**Reading: Preparing to Read**

A teacher uses multiple instructional strategies to prepare her students for reading a persuasive essay.

---

## Learning Through PLAY

### Families Playing Together

One of the many rewards of parenthood is being able to play again! Play is more than just a time for fun. It is also a great learning experience for children. Play teaches children about trust, honesty, cooperation, taking turns, following rules, counting, colors, and having fun. With so much to learn, children need lots of opportunities for play. Parents should set aside time for play and have a variety of toys and games available. Some ideas for engaging in family play include singing nursery rhymes together; using puppets, dolls, or action figures for pretend play; or doing puzzles and playing games together. Activities should be appropriate for the child's age. What a parent and child play is not important. What matters is that families spend time together playing, learning, and enjoying each other.

**Think About It** Your family is traveling by car to visit relatives in a different city. Your 10-year-old brother is bored and beginning to annoy you. What activities can you suggest your family do to help entertain your brother?

## Functions of the Family

Each day after band practice, Marisa picks up her little brother from the after-care program at his school. When they arrive home, they share a snack. Then they read, do homework, or watch television together. While this may sound routine, Marisa's actions show the importance of family. Family members help meet each other's basic needs.

### Meet Basic Needs

Everyone needs food, clothing, and shelter. Families need to make sure that these basic needs, as well as health and safety needs, are met. Family members care for one another when they are sick and teach children basic rules about safety.

Strong families meet emotional and social needs, too. Family members have the chance to love and be loved, to care and be cared for, to help others and receive help. Living in a family teaches sharing and teamwork.

Strong families meet their members' intellectual needs as well. The family is a child's first teacher. The family teaches concepts such as language, numbers, and colors. The family's expectations, support, and involvement in learning can affect success in school.

### Prepare Children to Live in Society

Author Robert Fulghum wrote a book called *All I Really Need to Know I Learned in Kindergarten*. His point was that children learn the basic rules of life in kindergarten, such as "share everything," "play fair," and "don't hit people." Fulghum could have said the same thing about family. By learning how to live with others in the family, children are prepared to live with others in society.

Adults teach children what is important to people in their society. They pass on these values in three ways:

- **Through Example** When adults treat children and each other with respect, they show children how to behave.
- **Through Communication** Parents who explain to toddlers why hitting is wrong, or talk to teens about respecting others' individuality, are passing on values through communication.
- **Through Religious Training** In houses of worship, of any faith, children learn the principles of what is right and what is wrong as taught by people of that faith.

Each society has its own way of life revealed through its art and music, its cooking and clothing styles, and its views of work and play.

---

## Learning Through PLAY

### Families Playing Together

**Discussion** Have students think of a popular board game. Discuss what skills children might learn from this game. Also discuss what a family might gain by playing this game together. (Skills will vary based on the game chosen but might include taking turns and performing math. Families learn to have fun together.)

**Think About It** Answers will vary, but may include suggesting that everyone sing a song of your brother's choosing; try to be the first to locate cars with out-of-state license plates; play twenty questions; or play I-spy.

Families introduce children to their society's way of life. Society can include neighborhoods, cities, states, countries, or nations.

Adults teach children about the traditions of their society, such as holidays. Adults also explain and demonstrate acceptable behavior. What kind of language is appropriate? How should children speak to adults? These and similar questions are first answered in families.

## Provide Support

Family members support each other. However, with all the demands and stresses put on families, parents need to have a support system. This will help them get through rough spots and sometimes just everyday life. Talking to a friend, relative, or coworker can help. These same people may be willing to watch the children so a parent can have a short break.

When stress causes health or relationship problems, it is helpful to consult a professional such as a family doctor, counselor, social worker, or religious advisor. Seeking additional sources of support can help a parent get through the more difficult times.

Some families may feel as though they do not have a support system, but there are people and services ready to help. Besides communicating with friends, neighbors, coworkers, and relatives, a parent can talk to caregivers, teachers, religious leaders, or counselors. A local hospital or place of worship may provide lists of support groups. Local family service agencies are also available for support. By using these sources, parents can help strengthen family relationships and relieve some of their stress.

## Form Traditions

Spending time together is the foundation to building a strong family. This includes doing special activities, such as a family vacation, as well as following everyday routines, such as eating dinner together. These activities and the ways that families do things are what become  family traditions. A *tradition* is a custom that is followed over time. It can be simple or elaborate. Families that form many traditions form strong ties with each other. Friends will come and go through a lifetime, but your family is always there.

**Seeking Help**
It is important for parents to find help when they need it. Sometimes just having someone to listen to you or give another point of view helps a parent get through a difficult time. *When might a parent seek help?*

Section 3.1    Family Characteristics    **59**

 **Explore the Photo**

**Caption Answer** Answers will vary but may include: when they need a caretaker for their child, when they have lost their job and need someone to talk to, or when they are home alone with a child and need an adult to talk to.

**Discussion** Tell students to think of a time they had a personal problem and talked it over with a parent. What kind of response did they want from their parent? (Answers will vary. Often people do not want others to offer solutions; they just want them to listen and show concern.)

## Teach *cont.*

### S Skill Practice
### Guided Practice

**Create a Mural** Organize students into small groups. Provide each group with a large sheet of paper and water colors, felt markers, etc. Each group member should then create an illustration of his or her favorite family tradition for the mural. (Each group member should have created a colorful illustration of their favorite family tradition.) **L1** **ELL**

**Research a Cultural Tradition** Tell students to choose a specific culture they want to know more about. Students should research the traditions of that culture. How do the traditions support cultural values? Have students prepare a brief oral presentation to share what they learn. (Presentations will vary but should describe a specific cultural tradition and explain what values it supports. For example, brides generally wear red in China. This is because red represents good fortune and luck in the Chinese culture.) **L2**

**Evaluate a Television Show** Provide students with a video tape or DVD of a television situation comedy. The episode should show family members participating in one or more traditions. After watching the show, students should write a summary describing the traditions. They then should evaluate whether they think this show accurately reflects their own family's traditions and values. (Students should provide a summary of a family situation comedy and then evaluate whether they believe this show reflects their own family's traditions and values. Traditions may include daily routines or special events.) **L3**

**W Writing Support**

**Journal Entry**

**Examine a Tradition** Tell students to think of a family tradition that they enjoy. Maybe it involves a special dish they always have on their birthday or a favorite camping spot their family visits every Memorial Day. Instruct students to write a journal entry discussing what this tradition means to them. (Refer to p. 54 to review tips for writing a journal entry. Students' entries should discuss a special family tradition and what it means to them.)

**U₁ Universal Access**

**Verbal Learners** Have students work in groups to locate a folk tale that teaches a value. Encourage them to look for folk tales with which they may not be familiar, such as those from South America or Africa. They should carefully read the folk tale, then act out the folk tale for the class. At the end of the role-play, the group should discuss how the value is taught. (Skits will vary but should show that the group has read and understood the folk tale and the value being taught. Discussions should offer explanations for how the group feels the value is taught.) **ELL**

**Professional Development**

**Mini Clip**
**ELL: Words in Action**

Students act out or mime the words they are trying to learn.

**→ Forming Traditions**
Celebrations often turn into family traditions. *What traditions take place in your family?*

Traditions provide a sense of continuity, understanding, and appreciation that brings a family together. They are also opportunities for families to have fun times and establish good memories that will carry them through tough times. Traditions provide a family with time together to communicate, heal from a loss, adapt to new events, affirm family values, celebrate, and connect to the past.

Traditions will vary from family to family and from generation to generation. However, there are three types of traditions that families form:

- **Celebration Traditions** These are activities or events formed around special occasions, such as holidays and birthdays.

- **Family Traditions** These include events and special activities created to fit a family's lifestyle, such as vacations or family meetings.
- **Patterned Family Interactions** These are actions that are centered on daily routines in life, such as dinner time and bedtime.

Traditions are the threads of life that create a sense of togetherness and appreciation in families. It is the little things done together that not only create strong family ties, but also memories to last a lifetime. Quinn enjoyed his families' weekly game nights so much as a child that he plans to build the same tradition with his family someday.

### Share Values

Values are the beliefs held by an individual, family, community, or society. They include feelings about the importance of acceptable behavior in terms of honesty, respect, responsibility, friendliness, kindness, and tolerance. The values that parents pass on to their children are largely shaped by the values that were passed on to them as children, their own life experiences, and their religious beliefs. Society also helps shape a family's values. Society relies on values, such as honesty, to keep order and to function well.

{ **Expert Advice...** }

*"The family is the corner stone of our society. More than any other force it shapes the attitude, the hopes, the ambitions, and the values of the child."*

—Lyndon Baines Johnson, former U.S. president

**····▶ Explore the Photo**

**Caption Answer** Answers will vary but might include such traditions as going out to dinner for a family member's birthday or breakfast in bed for Mother's Day.

**Discussion** Describe a situation in which an extended family got together one summer five years ago and had so much fun that they have continued to have this get-together every summer. Ask students: What do you think causes some events to become family traditions? (Student answers will vary but may include the enjoyment the family has bonding during the event.)

In a strong family, everyone is committed to one another. Family members respect one another and see that each person is different. The family is built on a foundation of shared values. For example, when parents and other caregivers teach children the value of honesty, they foster that trait in their children. When a problem or conflict arises, their children have learned to be honest and that the family will not judge or criticize them. Their children then communicate more openly, and, as a family, they work together to solve the problem.

With a strong foundation of shared values, children feel more at ease. People who learn trust in the family tend to see theworld as a safe place. They experience more success when they **venture**, or proceed, away from the family to meet new people, take on challenges, and become valuable members of society.

## Handle Family Conflict

There is no way around it: Families argue. Sometimes they bicker over seemingly minor issues such as what show to watch or whose turn it is to take out the trash. Other times the conflicts are more serious. Many families have conflicts about money or curfews, for example.

Whether the issue is big or small, families need to know how to resolve their differences. Parents and children need to try to understand each other's viewpoints and feelings. Strong families figure out ways to approach and solve their problems together.

When families resolve their conflicts successfully, the whole family is stronger. Here are some tips for handling conflicts effectively:

- **Keep cool.** When people are angry, they say and do things they do not really mean. It is always a good idea to calm down before trying to resolve a conflict. This lets you use reason and empathy to solve the issue. Physical conflict, such as hitting, should never be a part of teen or adult relationships. If a discussion gets heated, it is wise to call a time out.
- **Be an active listener.** Even in the middle of a conflict it is important to listen carefully to each other's concerns without immediately judging them. Repeat back what you heard to help avoid confusion about feelings and attitudes. Often people are so concerned about what they will say next that they fail to really listen. Active listening encourages problem solving and better communication.

**Interacting with Grandparents**
Grandparents can help teach children family values. *What are some other benefits of having an involved grandparent?*

## Teach *cont.*

### C Critical Thinking

**Analyze** Have students imagine what it would be like to be a nine-year-old girl who could not trust her parents. For example, the parents might stay out late at night and not leave any food prepared for the child's dinner. What kind of adult do you think this child would grow up to be? (Student answers will vary. The child might grow up to be untrusting and suspicious of other people and find it difficult to love anyone.)

### U₂ Universal Access

**Verbal Learners** Organize students into groups of three. Have one person role play a parent, the second a teen. The third should be an observer. Assign each group a common family conflict, such as a disagreement over family chores. Have the parent and teen work out the conflict while the observer watches. Remind students to use active listening skills and positive body language during the discussions. At the end, the observer should offer suggestions for improvements. If time permits, have the students switch roles and do a second role play so that each observer has the chance to participate in the role play.

---

**Explore the Photo**

**Caption Answer** Answers will vary but may include: Children can learn from their grandparents; grandparents can help with parenting responsibilities; grandparents feel like they are contributing to their family.

**Discussion** Ask students what they think might be the advantages of having grandparents live with their grandchildren. What might be some disadvantages? (Advantages might include that grandparents often have more time for the children than parents. Disadvantages might include that the grandparents might require extra care because of health problems.)

## Assess

### Quiz
Ask students to answer the following questions:

1. What are three ways that parents can pass on their values to their children? (They can set an example of proper behavior, explain to children what is acceptable and unacceptable behavior, and teach their children their religious beliefs.)

2. What are the three types of traditions that families form? (Traditions include celebration traditions, family traditions, or patterned family interactions.)

3. List three ways to handle family conflicts. (Handle conflict by keeping cool, being an active listener, and using positive body language.)

## Reteach

### R Reading Strategy
**Connecting Terms** Tell students that sometimes words are taken from other fields of study and used for new purposes. Have someone look up the scientific meaning of "nuclear" and read it aloud (pertaining to the center, such as the nucleus of an atom). Ask students why they think the term *nuclear family* is used to refer to a family unit composed of parents and their children. (The nuclear family is at the center of our social structure.)

### ✓ Reading Check

**Shaping Values** The values that parents pass on to their children are largely shaped by the values that their parents passed on to them as children, their own life experiences, and their religious beliefs.

- **Use positive body language.** People who make eye contact and sit up straight send the message that they are truly listening and do care about the other person. When appropriate, a pat on the back or a hug can do wonders to help break the tension and make the other person feel loved and more at ease.

How would you rate your family's conflict resolution skills? Which technique could you use to improve your own?

**✓ Reading Check** **Shaping Values** What three things shape the values that parents pass on to their children?

## Family Structure

While each family has individual characteristics, most can be categorized as nuclear, single-parent, or blended families.

### Nuclear Families

**R** A **nuclear family** is a family that includes a mother and father and at least one child. In a nuclear family there are two parents to help raise the children. The families may differ depending on how many children there are, whether the parents work outside the home, and other characteristics.

### Single-Parent Families

A **single-parent family** is one that includes either a mother or a father and at least one child. The absent parent might have died or left after a divorce, or the parents may never have married. While single parenting presents special challenges, it can still be effective.

Raising a child alone is a demanding job. A single parent typically has little free time, since there is no one with whom to share the work or to help solve problems related to parenthood. Single-parent families usually have less income than two-parent families. The added cost of child care can increase the challenges for a working single parent.

Many single parents receive help from friends or relatives. They may provide child care while the parent works. They may help simply by giving the parent someone to talk to about frustrations, problems, or challenges, as well as rewards and successes. In the case of a divorce, many children make scheduled visits to the parent who does not live with them. These visits give the custodial parent a needed break from the challenges of single parenthood. A **custodial parent** is the parent with whom the child resides. It also preserves the relationship between the other parent and child.

**A Real Family** Adoption pairs children who need parents with those who want to build a family. *What rights do adopted children have?*

**Explore the Photo**

**Caption Answer** Adopted children have the same rights as biological children.

**Discussion** Ask students: Do you think it would be more challenging for a family to adopt an infant or a ten-year-old? Why? (Student answers will vary; infants require a great deal of care, but an older child may already have values and expectations that are different from the family's.)

**Blended Families**
Trying to blend two unique families into one strong family can create some challenges. *When parents remarry, what can they do to make the transition easier for their children?*

## Blended Families

A **blended family** is formed when a single parent marries another person, who may or may not have children. To a child, the parent's new spouse becomes a stepparent. To the couple, each child of the new spouse is a stepchild. If both spouses have children when they marry, these children become stepbrothers or stepsisters to each other.

Becoming a strong family unit can be a challenge for a blended family. Parents and children need time to adjust to one another. Everyone has to learn about and adapt to each other's habits, likes, and dislikes. Even topics such as how to celebrate holidays can cause conflict. Patience, tolerance for different opinions and habits, and a sense of humor can help families overcome the challenges they face.

## Extended Families

An **extended family** is a family that includes a parent or parents, at least one child, and other relatives who live with them. For example, a grandparent may live with a nuclear family or an aunt may live with a single-parent family. Sometimes extended family is used to refer to family members who do not live with the family but still play important roles in the child's life.

### What Would You Do?

**Finding a Family**
Bree is a typical nine-year-old girl. She lives with Mr. and Mrs. Mason, her foster parents. When Bree was seven, her biological mother and father were not able to care for her, so they gave her up for adoption. For two years, Bree moved from family to family. Going from home to home was hard for her. Sometimes she had to change schools. Each time meant she had to make new friends and leave her old friends. Bree has lived with the Masons for a year now. They would like to formally adopt her. Bree is happy and likes the Masons. She is not sure she wants to become part of their family, though. The Masons have other adopted children who are not always kind to Bree.

🖉 **Write About It** Bree has sent a letter to the local newspaper's advice column asking for help with her problem. Based on your knowledge of families, write a column in response to Bree's letter. Be sure to address Bree's concern that the other children in the family are not always kind to her, and give suggestions for how she might handle it.

Section 3.1 Family Characteristics **63**

### C Critical Thinking

**Predict** Describe a scenario in which two adults are getting married. One has a six-year-old child. The other has a thirteen-year-old and a nineteen year-old, who is away at college. Ask: Which of these three children do you think is going to have the most challenges in becoming part of the blended family? Why? (Student answers will vary; they might choose the thirteen-year-old because this individual is already going through numerous changes, such as puberty.)

### Explore the Photo

**Caption Answer** Answers will vary, but may include listening carefully to children's concerns and adapting existing family traditions.

**Discussion** Social worker Peggy L. Barta states that blended families "are born of loss." Ask students what they think this statement means. Encourage them to discuss how being born of loss can affect the new family. (Answers will vary but might include that it means the families are a result of a relationship that ended, whether by divorce or death.)

### What Would You Do?

**Write About It** Student's answers will vary but should include specific suggestions for how Bree might handle her problem. Suggestions might include to talk with Mr. and Mrs. Mason about the way she is treated by the other children. Students might also suggest that Bree consider whether she wants to continue moving from home to home as a foster child.

## W₁ Writing Support

### Journal Entry

**Adoption** Some adoptive parents choose not to tell their children that they are adopted. Others decide to wait until the children are older. Have students imagine how they might feel if their parents revealed to them today that they were adopted. Have students write a journal entry describing their thoughts and feelings in this situation. (Refer to p. 54 to review the tips for writing a journal entry. Students' writing will vary, but should focus on how they would react in the given situation. Students may feel that this is the only family they have known and that the adoption does not matter. They may be curious about why they were given up for adoption.)

## C Critical Thinking

**Compare and Contrast** Ask students: How do you think your family is the same as or different from the families that your parents grew up in? Have students write an essay describing the differences and similarities between the families. (Answers will vary, but should compare and contrast students' families with the families of their parents.)

## R Reading Strategy

**Create a Table** Instruct students to create a table listing the six stages in the family life cycle. The left column should list the name of each stage. The right column should contain a short summary of each stage in the student's own words. (Tables should list each stage along with a short summary of that stage.)

### ✓ Reading Check

**Family Structure** a blended family

## Joining a Family

A child can join a family in many ways. In the majority of cases, a child is born into a family. This is a *biological child*. In other cases, a child joins a family through a legal process. A **legal guardian** is a person who is designated by a legal process to assume responsibility for raising a child.

Adoption is a legal process in which children enter a family they were not born into. The adopted child has the same rights as any biological children those parents have.

Some children join a family as foster children. A **foster child** is a child that comes from a troubled family or difficult circumstances and is placed in the temporary care of another person or family. Foster parents care for foster children, giving them a home while their parents solve their problems, or sometimes until a permanent adoptive home can be found. Adults apply to the state government to become licensed foster parents. They receive payment to help with the expense of caring for the child.

### ✓ Reading Check Family Structure

Which type of family is formed when two people with children marry?

## Trends Affecting Families

All families are affected by trends in the society around them. These trends may support families or put additional pressure on them. Some current trends include mobility, an aging population, changes in the economy, workplace changes, and the impact of technology. Which of these trends do you think has had an effect on your family?

**Figure 3.1 The Family Life Cycle**

The six stages of family development provide a pattern that most families follow. Families will spend different amounts of time in the same stage. *Do you think moving from one stage to the next is an easy process?*

**Stage 1**

**Couple Stage** Couples grow closer as they share activities. They work together to establish a home and marriage relationship.

**Stage 3**

**Developing Stage** As children grow, parents work to meet children's changing needs. The focus of the family is the socialization and developing independence of children.

**Stage 2**

**Expanding Stage** The arrival of a child signals the beginning of parenthood. The couple prepares for and adjusts to parenthood.

**Figure 3.1 The Family Life Cycle**

**Caption Answer** Answers will vary. Some students may think it is an easy, natural progression from one stage to the next. Others may think each change poses unique challenges.

**Discussion** Ask students: During which of these stages do you think most parents have to work hardest at earning a living? Have students discuss how this might affect their families. (Student answers will vary, but most adults work hardest when they are young. If a parent of young children spends long hours at work, building a close family can be difficult.)

## Mobility

Today many adults move from the community where they were raised. As a result, many families lack close, supportive connections with extended family. Grandparents, aunts, uncles, and cousins may be spread out across the globe. In this situation, families must rely on themselves, neighbors, and close friends for support and assistance.

When extended family members are far away, it takes time and effort to remain close. Many families value a strong family connection and find it worth the extra effort. Such connections help build traditions and reinforce the importance of family history.

This increased mobility also places added stress on children when a family moves to a new home or neighborhood. Children must make new friends and find ways to stay in touch with old friends.

## Aging Population

There are a larger number of older people today than in the past. People are living longer than they used to. Advances in medicine and nutrition have contributed to the longer average lifespan. As a result, more people find themselves caring not only for children, but also helping and caring for aging parents. This can create stress as well as opportunities for intergenerational interaction. **Intergenerational** means occuring between older and younger age groups.

A related trend is that more grandparents are helping to raise their grandchildren because their children are not able to parent on their own. Some grandparents live with the core family, while others just help with babysitting. Having a grandparent involved in raising a child means that the child will learn values and traditions from the grandparent. It also helps teach the child the importance of a strong family.

**W₂ Writing Support**

**Descriptive Paragraph**

**A New Beginning** Have students remember a time when they faced a major change. Perhaps their families moved to a new community or their parents divorced. Instruct students to write a descriptive paragraph expressing how this change made them feel and how it affected their lives. (Students should express their feelings about a change they faced and how this change affected their lives. Paragraphs should use interesting adjectives and adverbs to help paint a picture in the reader's mind. Encourage students to use a thesaurus if necessary.)

**U Universal Access**

**Interpersonal Learners** Explain that more adults are choosing to have children when they are older. In addition, these people's parents are living longer. Many of them are busy raising small children while caring for aging parents. Instruct students to work in pairs to research the challenges that face someone who has children living at home and also has aging parents who require their help. If possible, encourage students to interview someone in this situation. Students should ask the person to discuss the challenges they face. Students should then write a report presenting what they learned.

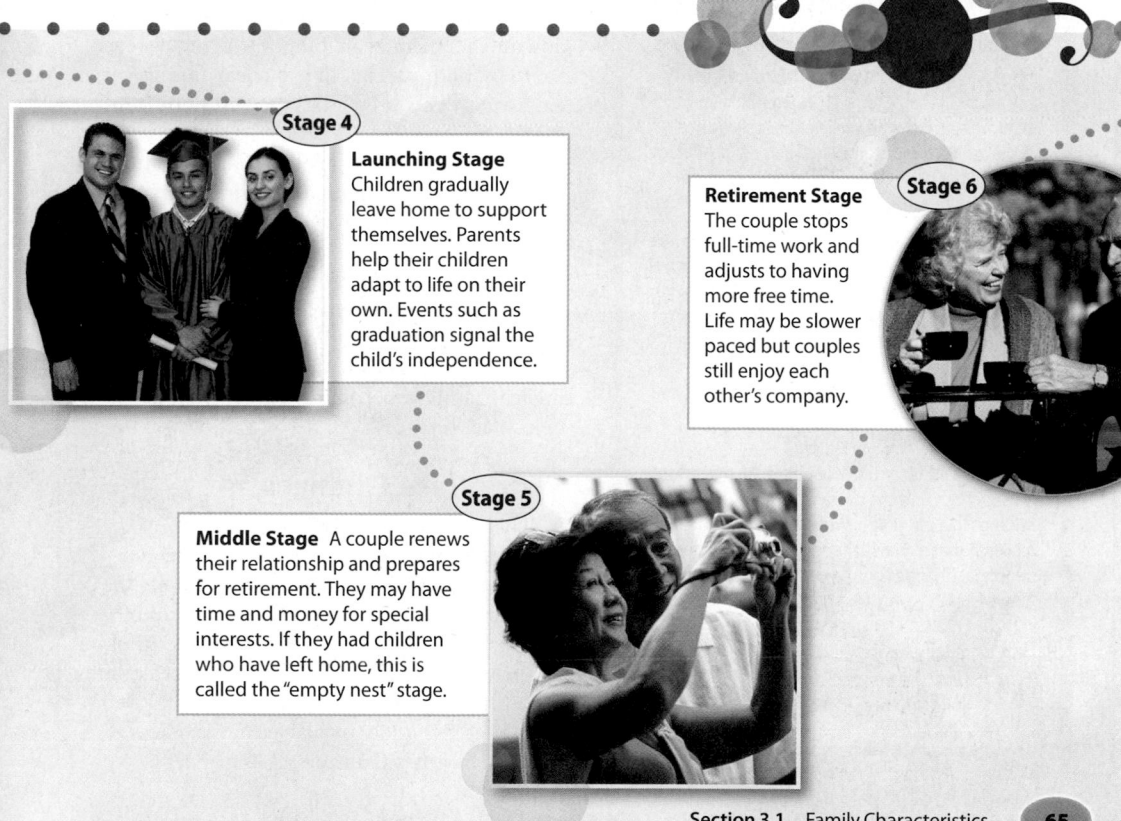

**Stage 4**

**Launching Stage** Children gradually leave home to support themselves. Parents help their children adapt to life on their own. Events such as graduation signal the child's independence.

**Stage 6**

**Retirement Stage** The couple stops full-time work and adjusts to having more free time. Life may be slower paced but couples still enjoy each other's company.

**Stage 5**

**Middle Stage** A couple renews their relationship and prepares for retirement. They may have time and money for special interests. If they had children who have left home, this is called the "empty nest" stage.

**Professional Development**

**Mini Clip**
**Reading: Interacting with Text**

Students work in small groups to make connections and ask higher order questions about a photo they have been given.

### U Universal Access

**Gifted Learners** Organize students into teams. Each team represents a family. As a family, they must create a budget that meets their needs. Give each an annual income and a list of fixed costs, such as food and mortgage payments. The students should then create a budget. Remind students that they must set aside money for unexpected expenses, such as car repairs. (Budgets will vary. Each team should have created a budget based on income, fixed expenses, and estimated unexpected expenses.)

### C Critical Thinking

**Make Judgments** Discuss that many families face tough times when a parent loses his or her job. Describe a scenario in which a father loses his job. The only other job he can find is four hundred miles away and does not pay as well. Ask: As a teen, which do you think would be more difficult—having to move to a new community or having to cut back on spending? (Student responses will vary. Some students may feel that moving away and making new friends is harder.)

### *Science* in Action

**Technology and the Family**

Students should have conducted a survey on how much time people spend using five different technological inventions. They then should have calculated the averages and displayed this information in a bar graph.

**NCLB** Activity correlated to Science standards.

**Establish Limits**
Families must set limits to manage the technology that they use. *What effect can video games have on a family?*

---

### *Science* in Action

**Technology and the Family**

In today's society, we have many technological inventions available for work, home, and entertainment. This includes newer inventions such as cell phones, MP3 players, and video games. Technology also includes older technology such as television and computers. How might these inventions affect a family?

**Procedure**

Create a survey that lists five technological inventions and asks how much time people feel they spend using these inventions. Ask if they think using these technologies takes away from or adds to their family time. Distribute the survey to at least ten people of various ages.

**Analysis**

Find the average amount of time each invention is used. Then find the overall average. Chart your findings in a bar graph. Write a summary of your research that explains the results and describes people's opinions about whether these technologies are taking away from family time.

> **NSES F** Develop understanding of science and technology in local, national, and global challenges.

---

### Economic Changes

Many families struggle to make ends meet. This is particularly true in times of economic downturn. Finances are often the primary reason why both parents in a nuclear family are employed. This trend has had a significant impact on families.

Many families are smaller than they used to be, and some couples are having their first child later in life. The rise in two-income families has also added to the demand for child care, including before- and after-school care for school-age children. Some families count on extra income or child care services from teens or extended family members. Some nuclear families become extended families to help share finances.

### Workplace Changes

The working world is changing rapidly. Many companies employ fewer workers. The types of available jobs are shifting. For example, the number of manufacturing jobs in this country has declined, while jobs in health and technology have expanded. Such changes affect families. After a layoff, a parent may be unemployed for a time. New jobs available may pay less or may not have health insurance as a benefit.

---

### ▶ Explore the Photo

**Caption Answer** Answers will vary but may include that families can play together and make the family stronger or that video games take time away from the family and weaken the family structure.

**Discussion** Have students imagine that they are having an afterschool snack with a friend who talks on his or her cell phone the entire time. Ask: How would this make you feel? What does this say about technology? (Student answers will vary. The student may feel ignored. Technology can be useful; however, we must be careful that it does not keep us from interacting with others.)

In a changing work environment, there is a continuing need to learn new skills. Many workers invest time and money in additional education. When Marianna's mother needed to learn more advanced computer skills, she decided to take a night course. Marianna was happy for her mother, but she also missed having her at home.

Another trend is the growing number of people who work outside of the home. This has both benefits and drawbacks for families. It may increase the family's income and fill a need for socialization. It also means that child care arrangements may be needed for small children and the family will have less time to spend together. Some families may be able to rely on extended family to help with child care.

## Technology

Advances in technology continue to make family life both easier and more complicated. Technology can increase efficiency at home and at work. For example, the Internet allows people to find information in minutes, rather than searching books and archives.

There is a growing need to be sure children use technology safely and within reasonable limits. Critics claim that these new devices isolate people from one another. Linda felt that way when she took her niece on a shopping trip. Thirteen-year-old Ashley passed the time in the car by text-messaging her friends and playing games. Linda had hoped they would spend the day talking to each other.

Even older technology like televisions and video games need to be used within reasonable limits. Parents should monitor children to ensure that enough time is spent on other activities for physical development and social skills.

Strong families find ways to use technology to strengthen their bonds. They make choices based on their values. They manage their resources so that technology is a tool to bring the family together.

### Study Tools

Have students go to the Online Learning Center at **glencoe.com**:

- Take the **Practice Test**.
- Download **Study-to-Go** content.

Use the **Student Activity Workbook** for additional practice.

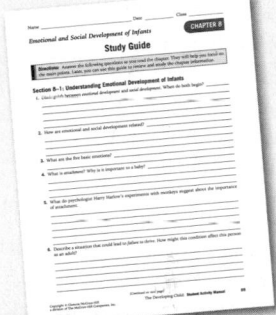

## Close

### Culminating Activity

**Family Similarities and Differences** Show students photos of several different types of families. Encourage them to use what they have learned to discuss the similarities and differences between these families. (While each has its own structure, all work to meet their members' needs.)

 **NCLB** connects academic correlations to book content.

---

## Section 3.1 After You Read

### Review Key Concepts

1. **List** two functions of families.
2. **Analyze** the similarities and differences among the four family structures described.
3. **Identify** three trends that affect families.

### Practice Academic Skills

 **English Language Arts**

4. Determine which family structure fits your family—nuclear, single-parent, blended, or extended. Now choose one of the other family structures. Write a one-page story about how your life would be different if you lived in the other family structure.

> **NCTE 4** Use written language to communicate effectively.

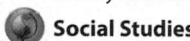 **Social Studies**

5. Choose a country other than the United States and study their family structures. Write a one-page report in which you answer these questions: What are the family structures? How are they similar to and different from the family structures in the United States?

> **NCSS I A** Analyze and explain the ways groups, societies, and cultures address human needs and concerns.

**Check Your Answers** Check your answers at this book's Online Learning Center at **glencoe.com**.

Section 3.1 Family Characteristics **67**

---

**Section 3.1 After You Read**

### Review Key Concepts

1. meeting basic needs of members and preparing children to live in society.
2. Similarities: all include at least one parent and one child; each has support systems; a single-parent family and an extended family may both have only one parent; a nuclear family and a blended family have two parental caregivers. Differences: in a divorced single-parent home, the child may live with a custodial parent but stay with the other parent during scheduled visits; single-parent families rely on outside help; extended family members often help one another.
3. any three: mobility, aging population, economic changes, workplace changes, and technology.

### Practice Academic Skills

4. Answers will vary but may include: I would have to share a bedroom with stepbrothers or sisters.
5. Answers will vary. Students should find that family structures are similar in all countries. Extended families play a more important role in some countries than in the United States.

# Section 3.2  Parenting Skills

## Reading Guide

### Before You Read

**Preview** Choose a Key Concept that is new to you and write it down. When you find the concept in the text, write one or two sentences to explain it.

### Read to Learn
**Key Concepts**
- **List** the basic categories of children's needs.
- **Identify** the three parenting styles.
- **Summarize** effective ways to guide children's behavior.

 **D**

### Main Idea
Parents use a variety of parenting styles to raise children and deal with the responsibilities of being a parent.

### Content Vocabulary
◇ deprivation
◇ parenting style
◇ guidance
◇ self-discipline
◇ conscience
◇ positive reinforcement
◇ negative reinforcement
◇ time-out

 **Graphic Organizer** Go to this book's Online Learning Center at **glencoe.com** to print out this graphic organizer.

### Academic Vocabulary
You will find these words in your reading and on your tests. Use the glossary to look up their definitions if necessary.
■ dispute
■ consistent

### Graphic Organizer
As you read, list the four types of negative reinforcement discussed in the text and write a brief description of each one. Use a chart like the one shown to record your answers.

| Negative Reinforcement | Description |
|---|---|
| | |
| | |
| | |
| | |

---

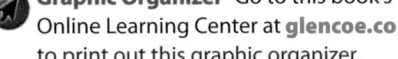

**NCLB**

### Academic Standards . . . . . . . . . . . . . . . . . . . . .

**English Language Arts**
**NCTE 12** Use language to accomplish individual purposes.

**Science**
**NSES A** Develop abilities necessary to do scientific inquiry, understandings about scientific inquiry.

**NCTE** *National Council of Teachers of English*
**NCTM** *National Council of Teachers of Mathematics*

**NSES** *National Science Education Standards*
**NCSS** *National Council for the Social Studies*

---

## Bell Ringer Activity

### Skills for Parenting
Instruct students to work individually to create a list of the skills they think a good parent should have. Ask for volunteers to share their lists and create a master list on the board. Encourage students to discuss whether these skills vary depending on the child's age. Lead into a discussion that the parent must constantly adjust to the child's needs and behavior, always working toward helping the child grow into a happy, productive adult.

## Preteaching

### Vocabulary
Before discussing the Content Vocabulary, ask students if they can define any of the terms based on what they have read previously or from their own real-world experience.

### Graphic Organizer
 The Graphic Organizer is also on the TeacherWorks CD.

(Graphic organizers should include: Natural consequences—child suffers from action's result; Logical consequences—consequences have connection to misbehavior; Loss of privileges—parent removes a privilege; Time-out—child sits apart for a specific amount of time.)

**NCLB** connects academic correlations to book content.

---

## Reading Guide

### Before You Read
Ask students: What do you think is the most important responsibility of being a parent? Discuss that parents first must be able to meet their children's basic needs. Then parents must guide children to become responsible, productive adults. This section will discuss ways in which both of these responsibilities can be met.

### **D** Develop Concepts

**Main Idea** Discuss the main idea with the students. Mention that some parents have a strict parenting style while others are more easy-going. Ask students why they think parenting styles vary. (Student answers will vary; many people follow their parents' style.)

## Children's Needs

Having a child makes a person a parent. It does not make a person an effective parent though. Parenting skills do not always come naturally or easily. Parenting is a learning process that occurs each day. Parents must work to develop the skills required to meet their children's needs, guide their children's behavior, and help their children develop positive relationships. It takes time to figure out what works for each parent, child, and family. Sometimes effective parenting means learning from mistakes and trying to do better each day.

Maria wakes up to Ryan's cries at 4:30 in the morning. She changes his diaper and feeds him. Although she is ready to go back to sleep, Ryan is wide awake and wants to play. She puts him in his bouncy seat on the floor and talks to him about his colorful toys. After an hour, Ryan seems sleepy, so Maria rocks him a bit and returns him to his crib. Just as she is ready to go back to bed, Maria hears, "Mommy?" Two-year-old Karenna is awake and ready for a fresh diaper. Unfortunately, Maria will not be going back to sleep. She goes to the kitchen instead to make breakfast and start the day.

Parents often must put their own needs aside to take care of their children. The list of parenting tasks can seem to be endless. In addition, all children are different, with unique characteristics and needs. Ask a group of parents what it takes to raise happy, healthy, well-adjusted children, and you will hear many different answers.

Children's needs can be grouped into three categories:

- **Physical Needs** These include food, clothing, and shelter.
- **Emotional and Social Needs** Meeting these needs means making sure that children feel safe, loved, and cared for. This allows the children to learn how to make friends and work with other people.
- **Intellectual Needs** All children need stimulation and the opportunity to learn about the world and become educated. By fulfilling this need, parents and caregivers help prepare children for life as independent adults.

**➤ Healthy Physical Development**
Meeting children's physical needs includes providing nutritious food that will fuel their growing bodies. *Why should small children not eat a lot of junk food?*

## Teach

### Discussion Starter

**Comparing Needs** Ask students: Do you think some needs are more important than others? For example, is it more important that a child receive her vaccinations than that she learns to read well? Encourage students to compare the importance of different needs. (Answers will vary. Without proper nutrition and medical care, children can die, or at least not thrive. However, skills such as reading are vital to being productive and able to support oneself.)

### R Reading Strategy

**Determining the Author's Purpose** Explain that being able to determine an author's purpose can help you understand the point the author is trying to make. Have a volunteer read aloud the second paragraph under Children's Needs. Then ask: Why did the author insert this paragraph here? (Answers will vary but may include that describing a specific situation can help the reader more clearly understand the points the author is making.)

### ➤ Explore the Photo

**Caption Answer** Answers may vary but should indicate that junk food does not supply the nutrients a growing body needs to stay strong and healthy.

**Discussion** Hold up several advertisements for fast food restaurants. Ask: How do you think these ads affect a parent's ability to help a child eat a nutritious diet? (Fast food ads encourage children to request these foods and can make them less likely to want healthful foods.)

70

# Teach *cont.*

## S Skill Practice

### Guided Practice

**List** Have students create a three-column chart. Label the columns Physical Needs, Emotional Needs, and Intellectual Needs. In each column, have the students list examples of how parents can meet the needs of their children. (Lists will vary but may include providing food and shelter, comforting fears, or reading to their children.) **L1 ELL**

**Perform a Skit** Organize students into three groups. Assign each group one of these three categories of needs: physical, emotional and social, and intellectual. Have each group perform a skit demonstrating how parents can meet the assigned need. (Skits will vary but should show parents meeting the assigned type of need. For example, the parent might be feeding or reading to a child.) **L2 ELL**

**Analyze Animal Parents** Discuss with students that animals typically work hard to meet the needs of their offspring. Instruct students to choose a mammal, such as a giraffe or a chimpanzee. Students should then conduct research to learn how these parents meet the different needs of their offspring. Students should then prepare a presentation sharing what they have learned. (Students should create a presentation explaining how a particular mammal meets the needs of its offspring. For example, chimpanzees nurse their offspring for several years.) **L3**

**Developing Social Skills**
Children need plenty of opportunities to play. *How does play help children develop social skills?*

Unfortunately, some parents cannot or do not meet all of their children's physical, emotional, social, or intellectual needs. These children tend to lag behind other children in their overall development.

They suffer from deprivation. **Deprivation** is a lack of the critical needs and encouraging environment that are essential for physical, emotional, and intellectual well-being. Some people believe that deprivation and poverty are the same things. This is not true. Deprived children can come from families that are rich or poor, or anywhere in between. Money is not the only factor. Children can be deprived of time, nutrients, stimulation, or love. What matters most is whether a child's basic needs are being met.

## Physical Needs

The most important and obvious task of parenthood is meeting children's basic physical needs. Parents are responsible for providing nourishing meals for their children. Children do not need the latest or most expensive styles of clothes, but their clothes do need to be clean, dry, and comfortable. In addition, children should have a safe, clean place to call home.

Parents are also responsible for the health and safety of their children. Parents schedule regular checkups and provide care when children are sick or hurt. Ensuring children's safety includes using a car seat and seat belt while in a vehicle. It also means making sure toys are safe and appropriate for the child's age, and eliminating hazards in the home so that children can safely explore their environment. Parents should always make an effort to know where their children are, whom they are with, and what they are doing.

## Emotional and Social Needs

A major goal of parents is to raise children who will become happy, independent adults who can support themselves. They may even go on to raise their own children. To become independent, children need to learn how to function in the world and get along with others. For example, children need to learn to show respect for figures of authority. They should show concern for people who are hurt. Children learn these lessons through relationships with people who nurture them. By showing concern for the child, a parent teaches the child how to care for others.

70 **Chapter 3** Building Strong Families

---

## ▶ Explore the Photo

**Caption Answer** Answers may vary but should include: Play helps children learn to get along with others. They learn to share, follow rules, and not to hit others.

**Discussion** Ask: How do you think the social needs of the child on the right are different than those of the other child? (Answers will vary. Toddlers need the stimulation of being around other children, but generally engage in parallel play whereas older children need the give-and-take of interactive play.)

### Nurture Children

Nurturing children means giving them plenty of love, support, concern, and opportunities for enrichment. These factors help meet children's emotional and social needs and help prepare them for their adult lives. Parents aid children's emotional and social development by helping them explore the world on their own, while still keeping them safe. For a preschooler, this might mean letting her play in the sandbox without worrying about whether her clothes will get dirty. With reassurance and freedom to explore, a child develops a healthy emotional well-being.

Parents can show children love and support in many different ways such as a hug, a kiss, or a smile. Unfortunately, some parents find it hard to show affection for their child. They may be embarrassed or feel that affection will make their child too "soft." When parents fail to recognize a child's accomplishments, the child may feel insecure or worthless. He may have a difficult time forming healthy relationships later because he did not learn how to give and receive love.

Communicating with a child shows love and support. Giving time and attention also shows that you care about a child. Actively listening shows children that they are important.

### Show Restraint

Some parents become overprotective, over-attentive, or both. They give a child too much attention, too many toys, and too many treats. They may try to shield the child from all unpleasant experiences. This can harm children, too. Children learn from trial and error. They need to make mistakes so they can learn from them. They must also learn to cope with the ups and downs of life.

## Intellectual Needs

Children begin learning at birth. Parents are a child's first teacher. Researchers have found that with stimulation, the brain undergoes tremendous growth during a child's first years. In the past, it was thought that a baby could not learn much in the first few months of life. Researchers now know that infancy can be a time of constant learning if a baby is given opportunities to learn.

### Learning Through the Senses

Early on, children's lessons come through touching, tasting, hearing, and looking at the objects around them. Parents can nurture this early learning by playing with their children. The child's environment should be filled with interesting sounds, smells, sights, and textures.

---

## RESPOND TO SPECIAL NEEDS — Autism

Autism is a brain development disorder that affects the way people relate to others. People with severe autism have an impaired ability to interact and communicate with others. Signs of autism usually appear before a child turns three. Autistic children tend to avoid eye contact and cuddling. They often have restricted interests and repetitive behaviors. They do not like changes in routine and they may be very sensitive to lights and sounds. They may not respond to their own names, and they may start talking late. Early diagnosis is important. A child with autism needs a special treatment program.

Therapy and special education help children with autism lead fuller lives. Special diets may also help. Parents can help by showing love and understanding, setting up routines, and praising successes.

> **Critical Thinking** Research the causes of autism. Describe the major theories and explain why some theories are controversial. Summarize your findings in a one-page essay. Cite your sources.

---

## Teach *cont.*

### C Critical Thinking

**Predicting** Describe a scenario in which a child is raised in a home where his parents took care of him, but they never showed him any physical affection. They never hugged him or told him they loved him. Ask students: When this child becomes an adult, how do you think he will behave toward his children? (Answers will vary. He may be unable to express affection for his own children because he did not learn to do so as a child.)

**McGraw Hill** **Professional Development**

**Mini Clip** Reading: Connecting the Pieces

A teacher helps students develop predictions and inferences about characters in a story.

### U Universal Access

**Intrapersonal Learners** Instruct students to work individually to write a poem that describes how their parents or caregivers work to meet their physical, emotional, social, and intellectual needs. Some students may wish to set their poems to music. Ask for volunteers to read or perform their poems for the class. Remind students that poems do not have to rhyme, but they should have rhythm.

---

## RESPOND TO SPECIAL NEEDS — Autism

**Discussion** Ask students why it is vital that children with autism be identified at an early age. (Educators have learned many ways to help these children reach their full potential. For example, children who do not talk can be given computers to aid in communication. The earlier children are exposed to these teaching methods, the more likely the methods are to be successful.)

> **Critical Thinking** Students should write a one-page essay describing the major theories on autism and why some of these theories are controversial. Students should cite their sources.

## Teach cont.

### C Critical Thinking

**Problem Solving** Discuss with the class that many parents are very busy. However, most parents want to provide intellectual stimulation for their children. Have the class pick three chores parents often perform and discuss how they might teach the child while they are working on these chores. Create a chart of the ideas on the board. (Ideas will vary. For example, when gardening, parents can teach children the names of different plants and explain how plants grow.) **ELL**

### U Universal Access

**Kinesthetic Learners** Choose three pairs of students. Give each pair a slip of paper with one of the parenting styles discussed here written on it (authoritarian, assertive-democratic, or permissive). Describe a situation in which a teen and a parent are having a conflict. Then have each pair act out the situation using the parenting style assigned to them. The rest of the class should guess which parenting style is being used in each case. **ELL**

### ✓ Reading Check

**Define** Deprivation is a lack of the critical needs and encouraging environment that are essential for physical, emotional, and intellectual well-being.

---

When parents stimulate young children in these ways, they help encourage brain development and a lifetime love of learning.

As children grow older, their intellectual needs expand. They want to play games and explore more of their environment. Parents and caregivers meet these intellectual needs by continuing to provide opportunities for play and learning. These opportunities can be as simple as playing ball in the park or visiting the zoo.

### Learning Through Reading

Children can also help choose books to borrow from the library. Learning to read and enjoying books are keys to intellectual development. Sharing books together can begin at birth. Infants simply enjoy the sound of the reader's voice. As they grow a bit older, they enjoy the pictures and story. They soon learn that the words on the page have meaning. Sharing books with children helps foster a love of books and a joy for reading. It also helps them learn about the world around them.

### Learning Through Exploring

It is a myth that children need a lot of expensive toys. Everyday objects and experiences with nurturing adults can provide great opportunities for learning. The best way to get children ready and excited about learning is to allow them to explore in a safe environment. When intellectual needs are met at an early age, children are better prepared for school.

**✓ Reading Check** **Define** What is deprivation?

## Parenting Styles

A **parenting style** is how parents and other caregivers care for and discipline children. Effective parents use a style they feel comfortable with. This style matches their personality and values. For this reason, no *one* parenting style is considered right. No *one* style works best with all children. Parents also often change their parenting style as children grow and change.

There are three main styles of parenting:

- **Authoritarian** An authoritarian parent believes children should obey their parents without question. The parent tells a child what to do, and the child's responsibility is to do it. When rules are broken, the authoritarian parent typically responds quickly and firmly.

**Meet Intellectual Needs**
Reading together helps children develop a love of reading. Older children can practice reading with a parent. *How can reading help stimulate intellectual growth?*

72    Chapter 3    Building Strong Families

---

**Explore the Photo**

**Caption Answer** Answers may vary but should indicate that reading helps children learn about the world around them.

**Discussion** Remind students that reading together not only helps children develop

needed skills, but also can meet parents' needs. Encourage students to discuss how spending time together can help this father. (Student answers will vary, but may include that he gets to enjoy his son and watch him learn new skills.)

*authoritative*

- **Assertive-Democratic** In this style, children have more input into the rules and limits of the home. Learning to take responsibility is important, so children are given a certain amount of independence and freedom of choice within the rules. When rules are broken, the assertive-democratic parent believes children learn best from accepting the results of their actions or by problem solving together to find an acceptable punishment.

- **Permissive** In the permissive style, parents give children a wide range of freedom. Children of permissive parents may set their own rules. They are encouraged to think for themselves and not follow trends. Permissive parents typically ignore rule breaking.

Few parents follow just one style at all times. A parent may use a more authoritarian style on issues such as health or safety. The same parent may be more assertive-democratic about clothing or hairstyles. Parents may feel that before children become teens, they need firm rules, but that as teens they should be allowed the freedom to make more of their own choices.

✓ **Reading Check** **Determine** Which parenting style allows the child to provide input into the rules?

## Guide Children's Behavior

Amy was frustrated because Grace, age four, never put her toys away. She tried reminding Grace, scolding her, and even banning television until the toys were picked up. Nothing seemed to work. Amy did not know what to do.

Acceptable behavior does not come naturally to children. This is true whether it is putting toys away, getting along with a sibling, or saying please and thank you. Children need to be taught what is acceptable, what is *not* acceptable, and what is expected of them. As children grow, their minds develop and they test their limits. Doing so helps them to learn about the world and their place in it.

Guiding children's behavior can be both the hardest and the most rewarding task of parenting. For years, Ella felt as though she was always reminding her children to get along with each

➤ **Teach by Example**
Children tend to adopt the behavior they see. *What positive behaviors have been modeled in your family?*

other and showing them effective ways to settle a **dispute**, or quarrel. Nothing worked. Finally, one day her message seemed to click, and the two managed to settle a disagreement on their own before it became a shouting match. The children became increasingly more effective at avoiding disputes and finding better ways to resolve their differences. Ella's guidance and patience had paid off. All three of them were able to benefit from it.

### Understand Guidance

**Guidance** means using firmness and understanding to help children learn how to behave. Children learn self-discipline with effective guidance. **Self-discipline** is the ability to control one's own behavior. They also learn how to get along with others and how to handle their feelings in acceptable ways. Guidance promotes security and positive self-esteem. It also helps children learn the difference between what is right and wrong. Very young children understand right from wrong only in terms of being praised or

Section 3.2 Parenting Skills **73**

## Assess

**Quiz**
Ask students to answer the following questions:

1. What typically happens to children whose parents meet only some of their needs? (They suffer from deprivation and their development generally lags behind that of other children.)

2. Why is it important to provide children a safe environment to explore? (With reassurance and freedom to explore, children develop into healthy, well-adjusted individuals.)

3. Is it appropriate for parents to change their parenting style? Why or why not? (Yes, it is appropriate. Parents frequently change their parenting styles as children mature. In addition, different children in the same family may require different parenting styles.)

## Reteach

**W** **Writing Support**
**Step-by-Step Explanation**
**Giving Directions** Read this scenario: A four-year-old is playing with finger paints. You need her to finish painting and clean up, but you do not want her to get paint on herself or the furniture. Have students write out step-by-step directions for the four-year-old. (Directions may vary but students should use appropriate language for a four-year-old. Remind students that they are teaching the child what is acceptable behavior. For example, washing her hands in the sink is good; wiping the paint on her pants is not.)

✓ **Reading Check**

**Determine** The assertive-democratic style allows the child to provide input.

## ➤ Explore the Photo

**Caption Answer** Answers will vary but may include such things as: healthful eating, good personal hygiene, love for reading, or respect for others.

**Discussion** Arriving home after a long day can be a stressful time. What can parents do to make this time more relaxed for the family? (Answers will vary. Parents can emphasize the importance of working together to make a healthful meal and give children tasks appropriate for their ages. Parents can also set aside time for play.)

Reteach *cont.*

## C1 Critical Thinking

**Analyze** Remind students of the saying, "Do as I say, not as I do." Ask students whether they agree with this statement. Do they think it is a good way to raise children? Why or why not? (Students should recognize that it is not a good way to raise children because children imitate adults, so it is vital that adults are good role models.)

## U1 Universal Access

**Interpersonal Learners** Have students work in pairs to create a brief role play. Have one student play the parent and the other student a child. Assign each pair a scenario that specifies the age of the child and a direction the parent needs to give the child. Using the tips in the text, tell the students to create and perform a role play of their scenario. Then have the class evaluate the role play. (Skits will vary based on scenarios given. Encourage evaluations to note if tips were followed.) **ELL**

**McGraw Hill Professional Development**

**Mini Clip**
**ELL: Level 1 Proficiency**

Jana Echevarria discusses the characteristics of Level 1 proficiency English learners.

---

scolded. Gradually, they develop a conscience. A **conscience** is an inner sense of what is right. As children mature, they use their conscience to decide how to act in new situations.

Parents can successfully guide their children in three basic ways. They can be positive role models. They can set limits and redirect their children's behavior. Finally, they can use positive reinforcement to let children know when their behavior is on the right track.

### Be a Role Model

Children are great imitators. They learn best by being shown what to do, rather than just being told what to do. Parents and other people in a child's life serve as role models. Children constantly watch those around them and then imitate the behaviors they see. The old saying is true: Actions speak louder than words. That is why parents need to demonstrate at all times the behaviors they would like to see in their own children. For instance, parents who want their child to talk politely to others need to speak politely themselves.

**Active Listening**
Listening is a communication skill that can help solve conflicts. *How can you show that you are actively listening to someone?*

---

**{ Expert Advice... }**

*"For a parent, it's hard to recognize the significance of your work when you're immersed in the mundane details. But . . . few jobs in the world of paychecks and promotions compare in significance to the job of parent."*

— Joyce Maynard, author, *A Mother's Day*

The desire to imitate applies to all behaviors, not just the acceptable ones. Five-year-old Mark sees his older brothers yell at each other when they disagree. It is no surprise then that Mark yells at his friends when he is upset with them. Parents and other family members should model respect, honesty, and kindness.

### Give Effective Direction

Parents and other caregivers often need to tell children what to do. Sometimes children do not seem to listen, but often the real problem is lack of understanding. These tips can help children understand and follow directions:

- **Be sure you have the child's attention.** Make eye contact. You may have to stoop down or sit beside a young child to do so.
- **Be polite.** A child will respond better if you speak politely in a normal voice.
- **Use positive statements.** Say, "Please walk," rather than, "Don't run."
- **Use specific words that the child can understand.** Say, "Keep the paint on the paper," not, "Don't be sloppy."
- **Begin with an action verb.** Beginning this way helps keep directions simple. Say, "Pick up your socks" or "Get ready for bed."
- **Give a limited number of directions at a time.** Very young children can only remember one step. You can increase the number as the child's memory improves. Remember, though, that fewer directions are easier to understand, remember, and follow.

**U1**

---

**▶ Explore the Photo**

**Caption Answer** Answers may vary but might include making eye contact, nodding, or asking pertinent questions.

**Discussion** How can you tell that this parent is not pleased with the child's behavior? (Clues include that she looks very intent and appears to be speaking firmly. She is holding the child so that the child must make direct eye contact.)

➤ **Give Directions**
Parents must be sure the child is attentive before giving directions. *How can you tell this child is attentive to the parent?*

U

- **Be clear.** Think in terms of the child's point of view as you decide what to say.
- **Give praise and love.** All people need to hear good things about themselves. This is especially true of young children. Praise encourages cooperation.

### Set Limits

Setting limits is another way to guide children toward appropriate, safe behavior. Limits include physical restrictions, such as preventing a child from crossing the street alone. A rule of behavior can also be a limit. For example, hitting other people or using certain words is not allowed.

Children need limits to grow into responsible adults. Having limits helps them to understand expectations and acceptable behavior, and to develop self-control. Children of any age will test limits, but parents should be consistent in enforcing them. A limit will not mean anything if the child is allowed to break it from time to time.

When setting limits, parents and other caregivers often follow this general guideline: Limits should keep children from hurting themselves, other people, or property. Children will respect and follow guidelines if they are reasonable.

The following questions can help parents determine limits:

- **Does the limit allow the child to learn, explore, and grow?** Too much restriction hinders development.
- **Is the limit fair and appropriate for the child's age?** A toddler might be restricted to a fenced-in yard. A school-age child might be allowed to visit a friend living down the street.
- **Does the limit benefit the child, or is it just for the adult's convenience?** Restrictions should be for the child's good, not because they fit a routine.

C2   U2

Children must be told what is expected of them in ways they can understand. Limits should be stated simply and briefly and in a calm, direct tone of voice. For example, "We don't throw toys," stated calmly is a simple limit that is easily understood. If a young child throws a toy, he or she should be reminded of the rule and then redirected to an acceptable behavior. "We don't throw toys. You can go outside to throw a ball."

Redirection is important because it helps the child to do something else *and* it suggests another, acceptable behavior. However, the redirection must be appropriate for the child's age. Infants, for example, may need to be physically moved to another, acceptable activity.

**Section 3.2** Parenting Skills   **75**

## Section 3.2

### Reteach *cont.*

**U₂ Universal Access**

**English Language Learners or Learners Having Difficulties**
Tell students that they are creating a handbook (or Web site) on parenting. One page is going to be on setting limits for preschoolers. The page should contain at least three bulleted points, each in the students' own words. (Pages will vary. Students should create a list of at least three bulleted points on how to set limits for a preschooler. Encourage students to include appropriate artwork on their page.) **ELL**

**C₂ Critical Thinking**

**Make a Judgment** George has a rule that his five-year-old daughter cannot help him make supper because she slows him down. Also, she sometimes spills things. Do you think this is an appropriate rule? (Students' answers may vary. However, students should realize that this rule is for the convenience of the parent and, in fact, stifles the child's desire to be helpful and learn new tasks. Therefore it is not an appropriate rule.)

**➤ Explore the Photo**

**Caption Answer** Answers will vary but may include that the child is making eye contact with the parent and the child is writing down what is said.

**Discussion** Encourage students to imagine that they are a seven-year-old child. Then discuss what they think will happen if a parent gives them a list of five directions. (They would probably become confused and forget all but the first one or two directions, or possibly all of them.)

## Reteach *cont.*

### C Critical Thinking

**Infer** Describe this scenario: Jason's mother has a long list of rules. They vary from "No playing video games until homework is done," to "Do not talk while clearing the table with your sister." Have students raise their hands if they see any problem with these rules. Ask a volunteer to explain what problem there could be. (Student responses will vary; the rule about talking may be overly strict, making it harder to enforce important rules. Also, the children may need to talk to determine who is doing which part of the clearing.)

### U Universal Access

**Gifted Learners** Many child behavior experts believe that children who abuse animals are often abused by their parents. Have students conduct research to learn more about the connection between children abusing animals and abuse in the home. Students then should write a paper exploring this connection. Instruct students to cite their sources. (Students should write a research paper in which they discuss the relationship between children abusing animals and domestic violence. The paper should include citations. For example, the American Humane Association conducted a study that found that animals were abused in 88 percent of homes where child physical abuse was present.)

**Appropriate Behavior**
Preschoolers are capable of learning appropriate behavior. *How can caregivers encourage that behavior?*

Limits must also be clear. Telling three-year-old Madeline that she can have a little snack is not a clear limit. She might not know what makes a snack little. A better limit suggests a specific snack Madeline can have, such as half an apple.

Limits often have to be repeated each time the situation arises. Children, especially young ones, do not always remember limits from one day to the next. They also may not realize that limits stated one day still apply another day.

With very young children, it is not necessary to explain the reasons for expected behaviors. For a one-year-old, the instruction "Be gentle with the kitty," combined with modeling of gentle handling, is enough. Around age three, however, children begin to understand simple reasoning. Then they can understand limits that include the reason for them: "Don't pull the kitty's tail. It hurts the kitty when you pull his tail. If you want to play with him, you need to be gentle."

Once established and explained, limits should be firmly and consistently enforced. Children can become confused if throwing blocks is ignored one day and punished the next. Parents who are not consistent with limits also teach their children that they do not mean what they say. Children take rules more seriously if they are enforced at all times.

### Provide Positive Reinforcement

"You didn't clean your room *again*." "How many times do I have to tell you to pick up your toys?" All too often, parents remind children of all the things they do wrong without noting what they do right. Constant scolding does not change children's behavior. It makes them feel as though they cannot do anything right. After a while, they may decide to stop trying.

Children, like all people, are more likely to change their behavior when they are praised for the things they do right. Giving children attention when their actions are appropriate is an example of positive reinforcement. **Positive reinforcement** is a response that encourages a particular behavior. When children learn that an action wins attention and approval from adults, they are likely to repeat that action.

Positive reinforcement can be used to help change a problem behavior and to strengthen good behavior. Use these guidelines to encourage appropriate behavior:

- **Be specific.** Clearly comment on the behavior being acknowledged: "That was such a nice letter you wrote to Grandpa."
- **Comment on the behavior as soon as possible.** Recognize the behavior right away to help the child link the action and the praise.

**76** Chapter 3 Building Strong Families

### ▶ Explore the Photo

**Caption Answer** Caregivers can model appropriate behavior and they can provide positive reinforcement, for example by praising the child.

**Discussion** Discuss with students that some people think getting a pet for a young child is a good way to teach empathy and responsibility. Ask: Do you agree or disagree? Why? (Student responses will vary. Young children can learn caring and empathy from pets but they must be closely supervised.)

- **Recognize small steps.** Encourage steps in the right direction. Do not wait for perfect behavior. If a child usually leaves toys all over the floor, acknowledge the effort of putting even some of the toys away. This will encourage him to do it again next time, and he will likely do a little more.
- **Help children take pride in their actions.** Saying "That was hard work to get dressed by yourself, but you did it!" helps a young child feel competent.
- **Tailor the encouragement to the needs of the child.** Praise behaviors that are hard for that child. The child who usually forgets to wash his hands should be rewarded with approval for remembering to do so.
- **Use positive reinforcement wisely.** If children are praised for everything they do, it no longer motivates them. The praise must be genuine and deserved.

✓ **Reading Check** **Recall** How can positive reinforcement be used?

## Deal with Inappropriate Behavior

No matter how hard adults try to encourage appropriate behavior, all children misbehave from time to time. Then adults must deal with the situation appropriately and effectively.

The child's age should shape an adult's response to inappropriate behavior. A one-year-old who bites another child can be told "We don't bite." However, the child cannot be expected to understand the meaning of his or her action. A four-year-old should understand why biting is unacceptable.

Here are some questions to consider when deciding how to respond to misbehavior:
- Is the expected behavior appropriate, given the child's age and development?
- Does the child understand that the behavior was wrong?
- Did the child do the behavior knowingly and deliberately, or was it beyond the child's control?

**Reinforce Positive Behavior**
Children should be praised for positive behavior. *Do you think it is possible for a parent to praise a child too much?*

## Reteach *cont.*

 **R** **Reading Strategy**

**Help from Prefixes** Remind students that prefixes can provide strong clues as to the meaning of words. Point out the word *misbehave* in the first sentence in the right column. Ask: What do you think the prefix *mis-* means? *(wrongly or the opposite of)* Based on this information, ask a volunteer to define *misbehave*. Instruct students to keep a list of other words containing prefixes along with each word's meaning.

**Professional Development**

**Mini Clip Reading: Building Vocabulary**

A teacher introduces and plays two vocabulary building games with her students.

✓ **Reading Check**

**Recall** Positive reinforcement can be used to strengthen appropriate behavior, for example by paying attention to a child who is being helpful.

▶ **Explore the Photo**

**Caption Answer** Answers will vary. Some may not think a child can be praised too much. Others may think too much praise will cause a child to always expect it, which is not realistic in the real world; too much praise will also cease to motivate the child.

**Discussion** Ask students: Why do you think praise is such a strong positive reinforcement for most children? Do you think it works best with younger or older children? (Most children want to please their parents, teachers, and other adults. Answers to the second question will vary. Praise generally works for all age groups.)

**77**

### Reteach *cont.*

**W** Writing Support

**Journal Entry**

**A Bad Day** Think of a time when an adult publicly made fun of you for accidentally making a mistake. Perhaps you spilled your milk at dinner or forgot a relative's birthday. Write a journal entry describing your feelings. (Refer to p. 54 for tips on writing a journal entry. In their entries, students should share their feelings of being publicly belittled.)

**U₁** Universal Access

**Verbal Learners** Provide students with a list of parenting books they can find at the school or local library. Have each student choose a title to read. After they are done reading, divide students into discussion groups. Have students explain the merits of each book and state whether or not they would recommend it to parents and caregivers. (Teacher should walk around and mingle with each discussion group. Answer questions if the students have any. Encourage students to give specific things they like or dislike about the book that they read to support their recommendation.)

### Unintentional Misbehavior

With children of any age, misbehavior is sometimes unintentional. A young child may drop a glass of milk that is too heavy or accidentally break something. Such unintentional actions should not be punished.

Misbehavior is also unintentional if the child had no way of knowing it was wrong. For example, Ana picked a flower in the park and brought it to her father. People should not pick flowers in parks, but Ana had never been told that. Rather than scolding her, Ana's father simply explained that she should not have done it. He told her that flowers in the park are there for everyone's enjoyment. He asked her to draw a picture of a flower instead.

### Effective Punishment

By guiding children's behavior, parents and other caregivers are more likely to teach a child acceptable behavior. Still, when children test the limits and misbehave, punishment can be effective if used thoughtfully and with good judgment.

Punishment can help remind children that correct behavior is important and teach them that there are consequences for poor choices. When using punishment, parents should clearly show that they disapprove of the behavior but that they still love the child. They can do this by avoiding blame and criticism.

The first time a child breaks a rule, parents may choose to give a warning rather than a punishment. Even a child with good self-control makes an occasional mistake. A warning reminds the child of the rule and why it is important. It also gives the child a chance to regain self-control.

After a rule has been broken another time, punishment is appropriate. However, the punishment given should be in proportion to and related to the misbehavior. Forgetting to put dirty clothes in the hamper one day does not call for severe punishment. In this case, a simple reminder would be sufficient. Repeated failure to stop throwing sand in the sandbox calls for more action, such as leaving the park or not visiting the park for a few days.

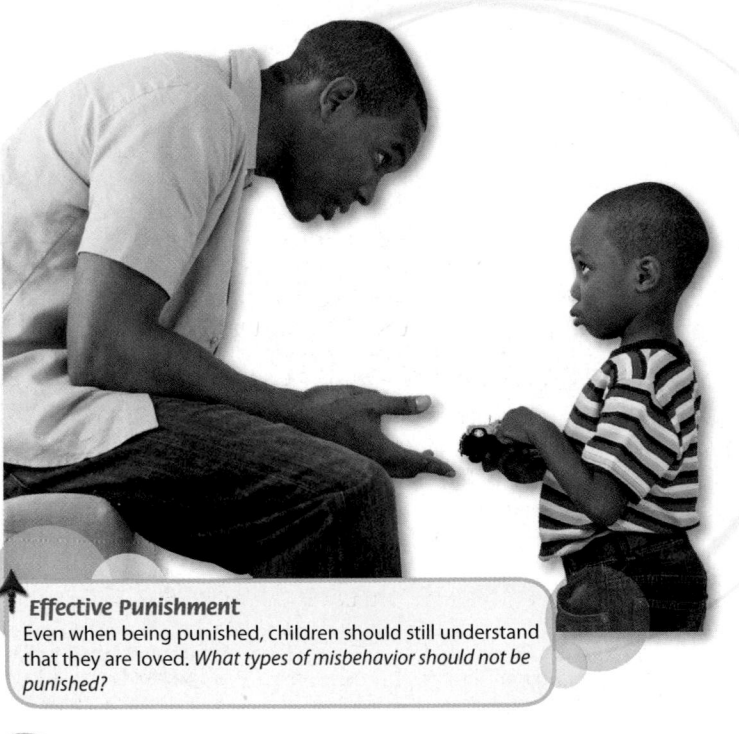

**Effective Punishment**
Even when being punished, children should still understand that they are loved. *What types of misbehavior should not be punished?*

78　　**Chapter 3**　Building Strong Families

### ▶ Explore the Photo

**Caption Answer** Accidents happen and a child should not be punished if he did not know something was wrong.

**Discussion** Describe a scenario in which four-year-old Derrick and his mother visit his aunt's house. The aunt scolds Derrick for touching her knick-knacks. Derrick did not know about this rule. How should his mother respond? (Answers will vary; she could say Derrick did not know the rule and then quietly explain it to Derrick.)

### Negative Reinforcement

**Negative reinforcement** is a response aimed at strengthening desired behavior by removing an unpleasant trigger. Several different methods can be used. These include natural consequences, logical consequences, loss of privileges, and time-out.

When deciding which method of negative reinforcement to use, parents and other caregivers often find that what works for one child may not be effective for another. The same method may not work every time for the same child, or for the same child at different ages.

Parents need to think about which method of negative reinforcement is most appropriate for the child's personality and their own values. For the method to be effective, parents must also be consistent in their use of it. Ideally, punishment should be linked to a child's age and emotional, social, and intellectual development.

**Natural Consequences** With natural consequences, children suffer from the actual result of their action. For example, suppose Kwan loses his new jacket. Using natural consequences, his parents do not replace it and he has to wear his old one.

When a natural consequence occurs, parents should not lecture. For children, it is often difficult enough to have to live with the consequences. Nor should parents attempt to remedy a situation for their children. This defeats the purpose of the consequence. Children who are rescued from their choices will expect to be saved whenever they make poor choices.

**Logical Consequences** Parents may choose to address a child's misbehavior with consequences that have a connection to the misbehavior. Parents often choose logical consequences when natural consequences are inappropriate. For example, when Katy colored on the table with crayons, the natural consequence of a messy table bothered her mother more than it bothered Katy. Instead, her mother told Katy that she was taking the crayons away for the day. This was a logical consequence.

Parents who use logical consequences need to be prepared to follow through. They should think about the logical consequence before giving it and ask themselves "Am I ready to do

**Negative Reinforcement**
A time-out can be a good way for a child to regain self-control. *How long should a time-out be for a four-year-old?*

this?" After all, lack of follow-through shows children that they do not need to take their parents or their limits seriously.

**Loss of Privileges** Sometimes using natural or logical consequences is not appropriate. If a child runs into the street, the natural consequence of being hit by a car is far too dangerous. A parent might take away a privilege instead. This type of punishment is most effective for children ages five and older. It also works best if the privilege taken away is related to the misbehavior. That way, the child is likely to associate the two. In our example, the child might lose the privilege of playing outside to remind him not to run into the street.

**Time-out** Another way to respond to misbehavior is with a time out. A **time-out** is a short period of time in which a child sits away from other people and the center of activity. The purpose of a time-out is to give children a chance to calm down and regain self-control. Time-outs can be especially effective when emotions are running high and the child simply needs a

---

### U₂ Universal Access

**Visual Learners** Have students imagine they are going to conduct a seminar about discipline issues. Sometimes it is difficult to teach a new concept to a group of people without some sort of visual representation. Ask students to create a poster that teaches the ideas of negative reinforcement in a visual way. Students may want to draw a diagram, use pictures from magazines, or illustrate the concepts discussed. (Posters will vary but should accurately and visually show each of the four methods of negative reinforcement discussed in the text.)

### C Critical Thinking

**Make Decisions** Have students consider the following scenario: Connor, who is five, has been slamming doors whenever he gets angry. His mother is getting irritated and wants this behavior to stop. Ask students what method or combination of methods they would suggest to address this problem. (Student answers will vary; they might praise Connor when he closes a door quietly and place him in time-out when he slams a door.)

### Cooperative Learning

**Tic-Tac-Toe** Organize students into pairs. Instruct each pair to create a tic-tac-toe game. The game should contain nine questions based on the material under "Deal with Inappropriate Behavior" on pages 77–81. Each question should be either "true" or "false" ("X" or "O"). After students have completed their games, have them trade with another group and play the game with their partner. **ELL**

---

 **Explore the Photo**

**Caption Answer** The time-out should be four minutes, or one minute for each year of a child's age.

**Discussion** Ask: Do you think a child should be placed in time-out in a room where there is a television turned on? Why or why not? (No, because a time-out should occur in a quiet place where the child can consider why he has been given a time-out.)

## Reteach *cont.*

### U Universal Access

**Logical/Mathematical Learners**
Divide the class into two groups. Explain that one group will be arguing in favor of spanking and the other will argue against it. Have students conduct research to support their views. Encourage them to make their arguments logical, rather than emotional. The two sides should then debate the topic. Afterwards, analyze the debate as a class. Ask students: Did the debate change your mind? Why or why not?

### C Critical Thinking

**Understanding Cause and Effect**
Review the poor disciplinary measures mentioned on pages 80–81 with students. As a class, discuss what could cause parents to use such ineffective methods and what harmful effects they could have on children. (Discussions will vary. For example, students may point out that parents might bribe a child because they are embarrassed by the misbehavior in a public place. Parents may think that they will address the issue later. However, this practice sends the message to the child that misbehaving will ultimately get them what they want. This could lead the child to have trouble developing social skills as they get older and other people do not respond to the behavior in the same way.)

## SAFE CHILD HEALTHY CHILD

### Spanking as Discipline

Few parenting issues are as controversial as spanking. Some parents believe that spanking is an effective way to punish children and teach them how to behave. Other parents feel that certain misbehaviors call for spanking, such as when children push the limits of safety. Most child development experts believe there are more effective ways to get children to behave appropriately. They argue that there are problems with spanking. For example, spanking can physically harm children. Parents who spank serve as models for hitting and other aggressive behaviors. Spanking does not teach lessons about behavior. Children younger than two are unable to make the connection between their behavior and a spanking. Parents must set firm limits and follow through with warnings, redirection, and if necessary, punishment. This helps children make a connection between their actions and the consequences.

**Be Prepared** Choose a country outside of North America. Research the methods used there to guide children's behavior. Be sure to include both positive and negative reinforcement methods. Share your findings with the class in an oral report.

break. One minute of time-out for each year of a child's age is generally a good length of time.

Five-year-old Teresa, for example, took pretzels away from her playmates. She continued to do this, even after her teacher gave her a warning and redirected her to other activities. The third time it happened, her teacher immediately intervened. She explained again why the behavior was inappropriate, and instructed Teresa to sit in the "thinking chair" for five minutes. After five minutes, Teresa had calmed down, and her teacher invited her to do a puzzle.

### Poor Disciplinary Measures

Well-meaning parents and caregivers sometimes use disciplinary methods that are less effective than others and sometimes even harmful. Those who follow the positive discipline techniques already described in this chapter will likely find that they do not need to use the following measures.

- **Bribing** Bribing children so they stop misbehaving can backfire. Instead of learning self-control, children learn to expect rewards for ending inappropriate behavior. Children may even misbehave on purpose, knowing that by stopping they will earn a treat or privilege. Bribing is not the same as rewarding desirable behavior though. Positive reinforcement for acceptable behavior is a more effective way to guide children's behavior.

- **Making Children Promise to Behave** In the process of learning to control their behavior, children will naturally make mistakes. If they made a promise to be good, children may feel forced to lie about misbehavior rather than disappointing someone they love. Children need to know that a parent's love is unconditional.

- **Shouting or Yelling** When children misbehave, parents and caregivers should talk to them in a calm, reasonable voice. A loud, harsh voice can frighten young children. Older children may learn to tune out, or ignore, yelling. Also, adults who yell are not modeling acceptable behavior. If the adult yells, the child might yell back.

- **Shaming or Belittling** Parents and caregivers should not ridicule children's mistakes or make comments such as "If you chew with your mouth open, no one will want to sit with you at the lunch table!" This can make a child feel worthless.

- **Threatening to Withhold Love** Caregivers should never stop loving a child. They should also not threaten to do so. Children take statements very seriously and literally. Statements such as "Treat your brother better or I won't love you anymore" create the fear of being rejected or abandoned. Children should always know that they are loved, even when they

## SAFE CHILD HEALTHY CHILD

### Spanking as Discipline

**Identify** Ask: Why do child development experts say there are problems with spanking? (Children can get hurt, it teaches that hitting is acceptable, and it does not teach lessons about behavior.)

**Be Prepared** Answers will vary depending on the country chosen. Oral reports should include both positive and negative reinforcement methods used. For example, in Thailand, positive reinforcement is largely used to encourage and comfort children. Physical discipline is rare.

misbehave. Children need to understand that the parent is unhappy with the misbehavior, not with the child.

- **Exaggerating Consequences** Parents and caregivers sometimes threaten wildly impractical consequences. When a child refuses to leave a toy aisle in a department store, a tired parent might say "If you don't come now, I'm going to leave you at the store." Such statements frighten children. They also cause a parent to lose credibility. When children see that a parent will not follow through on such exaggerated claims, they may begin to wonder if anything a parent says will actually be done. The child loses trust and respect for the parent.

## Consistency in Guidance

Being **consistent**, or continually the same, is the key to guiding children's behavior. Consistency is a matter of clearly making rules and applying them in the same way whenever the situation occurs. Consistency helps children know what is expected of them. It also lets them know what responses to expect from parents.

Children lose trust and confidence in caregivers who constantly change rules or fail to enforce rules in a consistent way. If parents permit a behavior one day and punish children for the same behavior the next, children will feel confused and insecure. They will pay little attention to the next limit that is set.

Consistency is an especially important issue when more than one person cares for a child. All caregivers need to agree on rules and ways to enforce them. For example, Steve's parents are divorced. When he asked to change his bedtime from eight to nine, his mother first talked to his father to get agreement. If caregivers do not agree, children can use the inconsistency to their advantage, playing one adult against the other.

**Study Tools**

Have students go to the Online Learning Center at **glencoe.com**:

- Take the **Practice Test**.
- Download **Study-to-Go** content.

Use the **Student Activity Workbook** for additional practice.

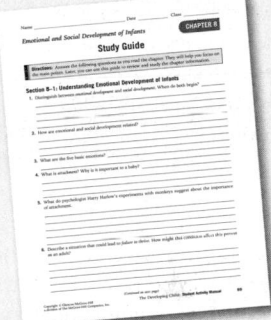

### Section 3.2 After You Read

#### Review Key Concepts

1. **Identify** four factors that are part of nurturing.
2. **Explain** why it is important to set limits.
3. **List** two ways to deal with inappropriate behavior.

#### Practice Academic Skills

**English Language Arts**

4. Think back to your own childhood and the parenting styles used in your home. Which style or styles were used? Do you think they were effective? Why or why not? Would you follow the same parenting style with your children? Write a journal entry explaining your answers.

> **NCTE 12** Use language to accomplish individual purposes.

**Science**

5. On a sheet of paper, list the methods used to guide children's behavior. Get permission to observe supervised children on a playground. Note the methods used by caregivers by putting a checkmark beside the method each time it is used. Create a pie chart to present the information you gather.

> **NSES A** Develop abilities necessary to do scientific inquiry, understandings about scientific inquiry.

**Check Your Answers** Check your answers at this book's Online Learning Center at **glencoe.com**.

### Close

#### Culminating Activity

**Summarize** Have students summarize by comparing positive reinforcement techniques with negative reinforcement techniques. (Positive reinforcement includes giving praise and encouragement. Negative reinforcement includes natural consequences and taking away privileges.)

**NCLB** connects academic correlations to book content.

### Section 3.2 After You Read

#### Review Key Concepts

1. giving children plenty of love, supporting them, showing concern, and providing opportunities for enrichment
2. Setting limits helps keep children from harming themselves, others, or property; and helps them understand expectations and acceptable behavior.
3. any two: giving a warning; natural consequences; logical consequences; loss of privileges; time-out

#### Practice Academic Skills

4. Students' journal entries will vary, but the student should explain the parenting style used in their home and discuss whether they think it was effective and whether they would use the same style. Students should provide reasons for their responses.
5. Students should create a checklist to use during observation and then present findings in a pie chart.

## Focus

### Discussion Starter

**Family Court Judge** Discuss that there are many types of judges. Some preside over traffic infractions while others handle criminal matters. There also are judges who deal strictly with family matters. Ask: Do you think you would like to be a family court judge? Why or why not? (Answers will vary, but students should offer reasons for their preference.)

## Teach

### C Critical Thinking

**Make a Judgment** One decision family court judges must make is determining where children should live following a divorce. Ask students: Do you think the child's preference should be taken into account? Should the child be of a certain age in order for her preference to be considered? Encourage students to explain their responses. (Student responses will vary but should include logical reasons.)

## Assess

### Make Connections

Ask students to list specific correlations between academic subjects and the skills a good family court judge needs. (Answers will vary. Students should understand how academic skills relate to being a family court judge. In addition to a law degree, coursework in sociology and psychology of families and children would be helpful.)

**N C L B** **NCLB** This relates academic skills to specific tasks that are performed for this job.

---

**Careers With Children**     **Family Court Judge**

**F**amily court judges decide who should get custody of children when parents divorce, how much money one spouse should pay to the other, how often parents are allowed to visit their children, and where abused children should live.

### ☀ What Does a Family Court Judge Do?

C

Judges make sure everyone in the courtroom is treated fairly. They decide what evidence may be presented, settle disputes between sides, and interpret laws. Judges are responsible for ensuring rules and procedures are followed.

Family court judges determine guilt or innocence for crimes committed by youth. They often try to arrange for help and treatment, instead of prison time. They try to keep families together whenever possible. Family court judges also decide who can provide foster care or adopt children.

### ☀ Where Do Family Court Judges Work?

Judges most often work in courtrooms and private offices. They must also spend time in law libraries to research past decisions about cases.

### Preparation and Skills

**Education and Training**
A family court judge needs a bachelor's degree and law degree. Judges are usually required to have several years of experience, as well as knowledge of family and child problems.

**Aptitudes, Abilities, and Skills**
Family court judges need listening skills, intelligence, fairness, ability to deal with stress, and an interest in the problems of children and families. They must be able to listen to both sides of a case and make fair, unbiased decisions.

**Academic Skills**
Strong English language arts skills are necessary for family court judges to complete research and to communicate clearly and effectively with each person involved in the court. Social studies skills are useful in understanding people's culture and motivation behind actions.

N C L B

**Explore Careers** Research other careers in the area of family law. Choose one career and write a paragraph describing it. Tell whether or not you think you would be a good candidate for this job.

 **Careers Online** For more information on careers, visit the Occupational Outlook Handbook Web site through the link on this book's Online Learning Center at **glencoe.com**.

**82**     **Chapter 3**    Building Strong Families

---

## Close

### Culminating Activity

Describe a scenario in which two parents are fighting over custody of their child. Both are extremely angry and feel they have been treated unfairly by the legal system. Ask students: If you were their family court judge, what might you do to defuse the situation? (Student responses will vary. The judge should listen attentively and respectfully to what each says.)

**Explore Careers** Students' answers will vary but should include a short description of one job in the area of family law and whether the student would be a good candidate for the job.

## Chapter Summary

Families today serve many functions. Families need to meet children's basic needs and prepare children to live in society. There are three basic family structures. Each structure has unique challenges. Most families follow a series of stages called the family life cycle. Families are affected by trends in society and sometimes need support. Parents use many skills to raise children. Children have physical, emotional, social, and intellectual needs that should be met by a family. Parents must find the parenting style that works best for them and their children. Parents must also learn positive ways to guide children's behavior and deal with misbehavior.

## Vocabulary Review

1. Use at least seven of these content and academic vocabulary terms in an essay about your family.

**Content Vocabulary**
- nuclear family (p. 62)
- single-parent family (p. 62)
- custodial parent (p. 62)
- blended family (p. 63)
- extended family (p. 63)
- legal guardian (p. 64)
- foster child (p. 64)
- intergenerational (p. 65)
- deprivation (p. 70)
- parenting style (p. 72)
- guidance (p. 73)
- self-discipline (p. 73)
- conscience (p. 74)
- positive reinforcement (p. 76)
- negative reinforcement (p. 79)
- time-out (p. 79)

**Academic Vocabulary**
- vital (p. 57)
- venture (p. 61)
- dispute (p. 73)
- consistent (p. 81)

## Review Key Concepts

2. **Summarize** the qualities that contribute to building a strong family.
3. **Describe** the different family structures.
4. **Discuss** the trends affecting families.
5. **List** the basic categories of children's needs.
6. **Identify** the three parenting styles.
7. **Summarize** effective ways to guide children's behavior.

## Critical Thinking

8. **Analyze** This chapter notes that traditions help to strengthen a family. Do you think this is so? Why or why not?
9. **Compare and contrast** How are guidance and punishment similar? How do they differ?
10. **Apply** Nathan lost a library book. His father says Nathan can no longer borrow books from the library. Do you think this is an appropriate punishment? Why or why not?

## Content and Academic Vocabulary Review

1. Students should write an essay about their families using at least seven vocabulary terms.

## Review Key Concepts

2. Qualities include meeting basic needs, preparing children to live in society, providing support, forming traditions, sharing values, and handling family conflict.

3. A nuclear family includes a mother and father and at least one child. A single-parent family includes either a mother or a father and at least one child. A blended family is formed when a single parent marries another person, who may or may not have children. An extended family includes a parent or parents, at least one child, and relatives other than a parent or child who live with them.

4. Trends affecting families include mobility, an aging population, economic changes, workplace changes, and technology.

5. The basic categories of children's needs are physical needs, emotional and social needs, and intellectual needs.

6. The three parenting styles are authoritarian, assertive-democratic, and permissive.

7. Ways to guide behavior include being a role model, giving effective directions, setting limits, providing positive reinforcement, and dealing with inappropriate behavior.

## Critical Thinking

8. Answers may vary but could include: Traditions provide a sense of continuity, understanding, and appreciation that brings a family together. They are opportunities for families to have fun times and establish good memories that will carry them through tough times.

9. Answers may vary but should include: Differences—Guidance uses positive reinforcement, while punishment uses negative reinforcement. Similarities—Both seek to teach children and help them learn self-discipline.

10. Answers will vary. Some students may think the punishment is appropriate because Nathan has not shown that he can be responsible for the books he borrows. Others may feel that it will discourage reading.

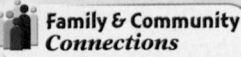

## Family & Community Connections

**11.** Answers will vary. Students should record answers to their interview questions in a table.

## Health Skills

**12.** Answers will vary, but may include suggestions for each family member spending time one-on-one with every other member of the family, or holding family council meetings so members can air grievances and help find solutions.

## Observation Skills

**13.** Students' answers will vary, but should show an understanding of the different parenting styles and whether the techniques used by parents are effective.

## Real-Word Skills

**14.** Dialogues will vary but students should show an understanding of different parenting styles. Dialogues may suggest that parents adopt an assertive-democratic style to deal with the child.

**15.** Answers will vary depending on students' research. Research may include suggestions for the parents to learn about the child's native culture and to find a support group from the child's culture to help teach the child.

**16.** Answers will vary but may include: compare costs of name brand and store brand products, use coupons, compare unit prices, or shop for day-old bakery goods.

**NCLB** Activity correlated to Social Studies standards.

---

## Family & Community Connection

**11. Interview Blended-Family Members** Talk with one or both parents and one or more children in a blended family. Note how many children are in the family. What were the children's ages when the parents married? Create a list of questions to ask each member. You might ask, "How did you deal with the blending process?" "How do you think the family is doing now?" Conduct the interviews. Then, record your answers in a table.

## Health Skills

**12. Research Emotional Balance** The emotional balance in blended families can be fragile. Parents must build effective relationships with each other and with stepchildren. The stepchildren must also build relationships among themselves. Research to identify strategies that can help parents create harmony in blended families. Write an advice column for a newspaper sharing these strategies.

## Observation Skills

**13. Observe a Parent-Child Interaction** Ask family members or friends who have young children if you can observe them interacting with their children. Or go to a public place and observe caregivers interacting with young children.

**Procedure** Watch the interaction between the adult and the child. Take notes during your observation. Write down answers to questions such as: How would you describe the parenting style you observe? Was the parenting style effective? How did the child respond to the parent?

**Analysis** Use your notes to write a report of your observation. Include an analysis of the type of parenting style used and whether you think it was effective.

**NCSS IV D Individual Development and Identity** Apply concepts, methods, and theories about the study of human growth and development, such as behavior, perception, and personality.

**NCLB**

## Real-World Skills

| | |
|---|---|
| **Problem-Solving Skills** | **14. Compromise** Imagine that you see a child in a restaurant who refuses to eat at dinner. One parent has an authoritarian parenting style, and the other has a permissive parenting style. Write a dialogue between the two parents that shows how they might compromise to find a solution. |
| **Technology Skills** | **15. Cultural Presentation** A family adopts an older child from a culture very different from their own. How might the parents help the child maintain his or her culture's traditions? Create an oral report using presentation software or other media to present your answer to the class. |
| **Financial Literacy Skills** | **16. Comparison Shop** Your family has decided that everyone must cut back on spending to help stick to a family budget. You have volunteered to help cut grocery bills by comparison shopping. List the steps you can take to reduce grocery costs. |

 **Additional Activities** For additional activities, go to this book's Online Learning Center at **glencoe.com**.

## Academic Skills

**17.** Students' answers will vary depending on the novel chosen. Analyses should reflect an understanding of the three parenting styles discussed in the text and include answers to the questions posed.

**18.** 7,000 teens do not eat dinner with their family each night. ($100\% - 65\% = 35\%$; $35 \div 100 = .35$; $.35 \times 20,000 = 7,000$)

The *Early Childhood Observations CD* offers additional lessons with videos to build students' observation skills.

**Part 1:** Learning to Observe
**Part 2:** How Children Develop
**Part 3:** Working With Young Children
**Part 4:** Extended Observations
**Part 5:** Resources and Answer File

## Academic Skills

### English Language Arts

**17. Apply Your Knowledge** Think of a book you have read about a family with children. Consider the interaction between the parents and children. Which parenting style was used? Were the parents' actions effective in teaching and training their children? Explain your answers in a one-page analysis of the book.

> **NCTE 2** Read literature to build an understanding of the human experience.

### Mathematics

**18. The Importance of Family** Suppose that out of 20,000 American teenagers, 65 percent said they have dinner with their family each night. What is the total number of those teens that do not eat dinner with their family?

**Math Concept** **Ratios** A ratio is a comparison of two numbers using division.

**Starting Hint** Subtract 65 percent from 100 percent. Then divide that number by 100 and multiply it by the total number of teenagers (20,000).

 For math help, go to the Math Appendix at the back of the book.

> **NCTM Number and Operations** Understand numbers, ways of representing numbers, relationships among numbers, and number systems.

### Science

**19. Environmental Awareness** Making decisions that show respect for the environment is important. There are many ways you and your family can work together to make a positive impact on your local environment. One easy way to help the environment is through recycling.

**Procedure** Research recycling facilities near you. Find out what items can be recycled. Discuss with your family how you might develop a plan to recycle.

**Analysis** Create a poster of your family's recycling plan to place on a wall at home.

> **NSES F** Develop understanding of personal and community health; natural resources; environmental quality in local, national, and global challenges.

## Standardized Test Practice

**ESSAY**
Read and consider the statement about child development. Then read the writing prompt and write your essay.

> Many child development experts believe that the best way to teach children how to behave is by providing positive reinforcement for appropriate behaviors.

**20.** Write a one-page essay in which you identify positive reinforcement techniques. Explain how families can use the techniques effectively. Be sure to proofread your paper and correct any spelling and grammar errors.

> **Test-Taking Tip** Read, re-read, and think about an essay question before you begin writing. Then write a short outline with your main points. Make sure your outline addresses all the questions in the essay writing prompt.

**19.** Answers will vary. However, all students should show a consciousness of environmental issues and develop some ways they and their families might positively impact their environment. Posters should illustrate the family's recycling plan.

> **NCLB** connects academic correlations to book content.

## Standardized Test Practice

**20.** Essays should be one page in length, clearly written with a topic or thesis statement, and should conform to English language rules of grammar and composition.

**Test-Taking Tips**
Encourage students to stay strictly to their outlines to avoid getting side-tracked.

**Test Timing** Essay and short-answer test questions are usually timed. Have your students take one or more timed essay tests or free writing exercises so that they become comfortable with writing for a fixed length of time.

---

## TECHNOLOGY **Solutions**

### Use these technology solutions to streamline chapter assessment!

 **ExamView Assessment Suite** CD allows you to create and print out customized tests or ready-made unit and chapter tests, complete with answer keys.

 **TeacherWorks Plus** is an electronic lesson planner that provides instant access to complete teacher resources in one convenient package.

 **Online Learning Center** includes resources and activities for students and teachers.

## Unit Thematic Project

# Learn Parenting Skills

In this unit, you have learned the importance of being ready to parent. You have also learned that parenting is a full-time job for about 18 years. In this project, you will find a parenting role model. You will create a handbook of things to know before becoming a parent.

## My Journal

If you completed the journal entry from page 3, refer to it to see if your thoughts have changed after reading the unit.

---

## Focus

### Discussion Starter

**Ready to Parent** Ask students whether they feel they are ready to become parents. Have them give reasons for why they feel the way they do. (Students' reasons why they are not ready to become parents will vary. Possible answers may include that they are still in school, have no job, and live with parents.)

**NCLB** Project correlated to English Language Arts standards.

### Step 1

**Choose a Parent Role Model**

Students can select a parent from their community who interests them and who they will be able to question. If students can think of another person not listed, they are welcome to question him or her.

## Teach

### Step 2

**Create a List of Questions About Parenting**

Students' lists will vary but may include the suggestions provided or other traits mentioned in the text such as teaching the values of honesty, tolerance, responsibility, and friendliness to their children. The list of questions about good parenting qualities should be written in complete sentences, with no spelling or grammatical errors.

---

## Project Assignment

In this project, you will:

- Choose a person you know who you believe can teach you good parenting skills.
- Identify four good parenting qualities this person possesses.
- Arrange to meet the parent. Ask prepared questions. Be sure to take a pen and paper to record the answers.
- Use what you learned from the parent to create a parenting handbook.

### Child Development Skills Behind the Project

- Evaluate qualities of a good parent.
- Describe ways to put parenting skills into practice.
- Identify positive parenting qualities in action.

### Academic Skills

 **English Language Arts**

> **NCTE 4** Use written language to communicate effectively.
>
> **NCTE 12** Use language to accomplish individual purposes.

**86** Unit 1 Children and Parenting

---

### Step 1 Choose a Parent Role Model

The parent you choose as a role model can be anyone in your community. A possible parent to talk to might include:

- Friend
- Teacher
- Religious leader
- Neighbor
- Counselor
- Child care worker
- Relative

### Step 2 Create a List of Questions About Parenting

What qualities do you think make a good parent? You might think a good parent treats his or her children with respect, explains what is right or wrong, does not yell or scream, and provides emotional support. Use complete sentences to write a list of four or five questions that can help you learn about parenting with your parenting role model.

**Writing Skills**
- ★ Organize your thoughts.
- ★ Use complete sentences.
- ★ Use correct spelling and grammar.
- ★ Consider your audience.

---

### Step 3

**Connect to Your Community**

Ask students to consider how the interaction with the model parent will affect them both now and in the future. (Possible answers include: It may help them think more about whether parenting is right for them. It may cause them to seek more instruction in parenting skills for use later in life. It may cause them to look at their own parents in a more positive light.)

### Step 4

**Create and Present Your Parenting Handbook**

Give students these tips on creating a handbook and speaking:

- Use graphics software to create and illustrate your handbook. If this is not possible, use hand-drawn or cut-out pictures to illustrate your handbook.
- Develop an outline of your handbook to help organize your presentation.
- Speak concisely (briefly but completely).

## Step 3 Connect to Your Community

Arrange to speak with the parent role model you chose in Step 1. Use the questions you wrote in Step 2 to interview the parent. Questions should focus on the positive parenting qualities you identified in this person. How does the parent use this quality in his or her day-to-day parenting duties? Accurately record the answers to your questions.

### Interpersonal Skills

★ Be polite. Do not interrupt the parent while he or she is talking.
★ Use standard English to communicate.
★ Listen attentively.
★ Ask additional questions to better understand the parent's answers.

## Step 4 Create and Present Your Parenting Handbook

Use the Unit Thematic Project Checklist on the right to plan and create your handbook and make your presentation.

### Handbook Skills

★ Use language appropriate for your audience.
★ Enhance your handbook with illustrations and graphics.
★ Correct all spelling and grammar errors.

## Step 5 Evaluate Your Child Development Skills and Academic Skills

Your project will be evaluated based on:
• Content and organization of your information.
• Mechanics—presentation and neatness.
• Speaking and listening skills.

**Evaluation Rubric** Go to this book's Online Learning Center at **glencoe.com** for a rubric you can use to evaluate your final project.

### Unit Thematic Project Checklist

| | |
|---|---|
| **Handbook** | ✓ Make a handbook that illustrates with words and pictures the parenting skills you learned from your model parent. |
| | ✓ In your handbook, list one skill on each page and include an explanation or example of how the skill might be used. |
| | ✓ Use illustrations throughout the handbook to support your content and to enhance it visually. |
| **Presentation** | ✓ Create a presentation to share your handbook with your class and discuss what you learned. |
| | ✓ Invite the students in your class to ask you any questions they may have. Answer three questions. |
| | ✓ When students ask you questions, demonstrate in your answers that you respect their perspectives. |
| | ✓ Turn in your handbook and the questions and answers from your interview to your teacher. |
| **Academic Skills** | ✓ Be creative in writing and illustrating the content of the handbook. |
| | ✓ Create an outline to organize your presentation. |
| | ✓ Arrange your presentation so the audience can view your handbook as you discuss it. |
| | ✓ Speak clearly and use proper language (not slang). |

## Assess

### Step 5

### Evaluate Your Child Development Skills and Academic Skills

**Rubric** Encourage students to go to this book's Online Learning Center at **glencoe.com** for a rubric they can use to evaluate their questions for the parent, their handbook, and their presentation. Students can use the rubric as a content checklist when completing their project.

## Close

### Culminating Activity

**Project Assessment** In this activity, students identified skills that are important for good parenting. Have students use the skills they have identified to do a self-evaluation of their current parenting skills. Students should make a list of the skills they need to improve. They should describe how they might become proficient in each skill. (Students should provide a list of skills, along with suggestions for improvement.)

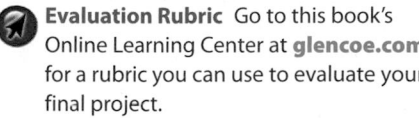

## Developing Community Involvement

### Learning About Parenting

Being ready to be a parent, and learning and practicing good parenting skills, contribute to building a strong family. But even strong families have problems now and then. Have students research resources that are available in your community to help families that are struggling with issues such as lacking the financial resources to pay for food, housing, or medical costs or families that may need child care assistance. Students may think of other issues to research.

A **Family & Community Involvement** worksheet about this topic is available:

⊘ At this book's Online Learning Center at **glencoe.com**
◉ On the TeacherWorks CD

| Title | Objectives |
|---|---|
| **CHAPTER 4**<br>**Prenatal Development** | • **List** the methods of family planning.<br>• **Outline** what occurs during each of the three stages of prenatal development.<br>• **Contrast** miscarriage and stillbirth.<br>• **Identify** how ten major birth defects can be diagnosed.<br>• **Summarize** the hazards that alcohol and other drugs pose to prenatal development.<br>• **Assess** why environmental hazards must be avoided during pregnancy.<br>• **Describe** how a fetus can be affected by certain illnesses the mother may contract. |
| **CHAPTER 5**<br>**Preparing for Birth** | • **Identify** the early signs of pregnancy.<br>• **Explain** the importance of proper nutrition during pregnancy.<br>• **List** six categories of basic baby supplies.<br>• **Describe** why parents need to develop a budget.<br>• **Identify** ways expectant parents can prepare for the birth of a child.<br>• **Compare and contrast** the options for the delivery of a baby. |
| **CHAPTER 6**<br>**The Baby's Arrival** | • **Describe** the progression of labor.<br>• **Explain** what happens during a cesarean birth.<br>• **List** the factors that can contribute to a premature birth.<br>• **Describe** a newborn's appearance immediately after birth.<br>• **Identify** the exams and procedures given to a newborn in the first few days.<br>• **Review** what occurs during the hospital stay after delivery.<br>• **Summarize** the physical and emotional needs of a new mother. |
| **Unit Thematic Project**<br>**Promote Good Health During Pregnancy** | • **Write** a My Journal entry on Keeping Fit and Healthy.<br>• **Choose** a time period related to pregnancy.<br>• **Interview** a health care provider or nutrition specialist.<br>• **Prepare** a menu tailored to the chosen time period. |

## Understanding Brackets, Letters, and Ability Levels in the Teacher Wraparound Edition

**Brackets** Brackets on the reduced student edition page correspond to teaching strategies and activities in the Teacher Wraparound Edition. As you teach the lesson, the brackets show you exactly where to use the teaching strategies and activities.

**Letters** The letters on the reduced student edition page identify the type of strategy or activity. See the key below to learn about the different types of strategies and activities.

**Ability Levels** Teaching Strategies that appear throughout the chapters have been identified by one of three codes to give you an idea of their suitability for students of varying learning styles and abilities.

**Resources** Key program resources are listed in each chapter. Icons indicate the format of resources.

### KEY TO LETTERS

**D** **Develop Concepts** activities help teachers gauge and plan for students' concept development.

**R** **Reading Strategy** activities help you teach reading skills and vocabulary.

**S** **Skill Practice** provides leveled instruction for meeting individual needs and learning styles.

**W** **Writing Support** activities provide writing opportunities to help students comprehend the text.

**C** **Critical Thinking** strategies help students apply and extend what they have learned.

**U** **Universal Access** activities provide differentiated instruction for English language learners, and suggestions for teaching various types of learners.

**NCLB** **No Child Left Behind** activities help students practice and improve their abilities in academic subjects.

### KEY TO ABILITY LEVELS

**L1** Strategies should be within the ability range of all students. Often full class participation is required.

**L2** Strategies are for average to above-average students or for small groups. Some teacher direction is necessary.

**L3** Strategies are designed for students able and willing to work independently. Minimal teacher direction is necessary.

**ELL** Strategies are especially accessible to English Language Learners.

### KEY TO RESOURCE ICONS

📁 Print Material

💿 CD or DVD Resources

🧭 Online Learning Center (OLC)

**TeacherWorks™**
All-In-One Planner and Resource Center

**Teacher Wraparound Edition**

**Unit Resources:**
Unit Thematic Project Student Rubrics
Unit Family and Community Involvement Activities

**Chapter Resources:**
Lesson Plans
Chapter Summaries, Content and Academic Vocabulary
Graphic Organizers

**Textbook Resources:**
Student Activity Workbook with Academic Integration
Additional Activities
Enrichment Activities

 Link to the ***The Developing Child* Online Learning Center** at **glencoe.com**.

## Unit Overview

### Introduce the Unit

Introduce the unit by describing the main concepts of each chapter in the unit.

### Unit 2

This unit discusses issues related to conception, pregnancy, and childbirth.

**Chapter 4** Information presented in this chapter includes the stages of a baby's prenatal development within the uterus; the foundation of conception including the role of genetics, multiple births, and infertility; potential problems in prenatal development; and ways to prevent danger to the baby.

**Chapter 5** Students will learn about physical health, emotional health, and personal care during pregnancy. They will also learn how to prepare for the newborn by making sure the family, home, and budget are ready. Options related to childbirth such as who will deliver the baby and where the baby will be born are discussed.

**Chapter 6** This chapter looks at the stages of labor, cesarean and premature births, examining the newborn, tests for the new baby, bonding with the baby, the hospital stay, care for a premature baby, and postnatal care for the mother.

### OUT OF TIME?

If class time is too short to cover all of the chapters in this unit, have students:
- Write down the vocabulary terms and their definitions.
- Read the chapter summaries at the beginning of each chapter review.
- Go to *The Developing Child* Online Learning Center at **glencoe.com** to download Study-to-Go content.

# Unit 2

# Pregnancy and Childbirth

↑ *Explore the Photo*
Most babies are born healthy. *Do you think parents and doctors can ensure that a baby is born healthy? Explain your answer.*

88

## ▶ Explore the Photo

**Caption Answer** The answer is no. Parents and doctors can do a lot to help ensure a baby is born healthy. They can help the mother maintain good health during pregnancy, making sure she eats healthfully and does not use alcohol, tobacco, or other drugs. But there are things that parents and doctors cannot control such as heredity, certain environmental factors, and chromosome issues.

**Discussion** Have students brainstorm the responsibilities parents face with the birth of a child. Write students' answers on the board. Ask students if they think they could fulfill these responsibilities. (Responsibilities will vary but should include the basics such as providing for food, shelter, medical care, clothing, and so on. Students should realize that they could not yet fulfill all the responsibilities of parenting.)

**Discussion Starter**
**Staying Healthy During Pregnancy and Childbirth**
Ask students to work in groups to develop a list of things they think a pregnant woman should do to help ensure the good health of herself and her unborn baby. After groups have created their lists, have them design fish-bone diagrams that contain the information in their lists. Ask a representative from each group to discuss their group's diagram with the rest of the class. You might want to revisit this exercise after students have completed the unit to see what changes they would make to their diagrams.

**Unit | Thematic Project Preview**

### Promote Good Health During Pregnancy

By completing this unit, you will learn that there are steps a mother can take to help ensure the safety and health of herself and her baby during pregnancy and childbirth. In your unit thematic project, you can examine the importance of the mother's diet during pregnancy.

### My Journal

**Keeping Fit and Healthy** Write a journal entry about one of the topics below. This will help you prepare for the unit project at the end of the unit.
- Why is it important to eat healthfully during all stages of life?
- Why is exercise important to help keep a body fit?
- Where can you learn how to develop an exercise routine that is right for you?

**FCCLA**
Family, Career and Community
Leaders of America
**Make a Difference**

Suggest the FCCLA Chapter sponsor a baby items or clothing drive for a local crisis pregnancy center. Have students collect the items and then deliver them to the center. Students may also want to volunteer their time at the center, helping to organize the items that have been donated.

**Unit | Thematic Project Preview**

**Promote Good Health During Pregnancy**
Tell students that as part of this unit, they will learn what steps a woman can take to help ensure the health of her baby and herself during pregnancy and childbirth. Students will consider how taking steps early in a pregnancy can help prevent problems later.

**My Journal**

**Keeping Fit and Healthy** Students select one topic to write a journal entry about. The journal entry should relate to the subject of the thematic project: Promote Good Health During Pregnancy. The purpose of the journal entry is to prepare students for the project at the end of the unit. (Journal entries will vary based on the topic selected and students' personal opinions.)

**STANDARDS BASED LESSON PLANNING** *The Developing Child* provides students with instruction and assessment in the following fundamental content areas:

## National Standards Correlations

| Standards | Pages |
|---|---|
| **12.2.1** Analyze the effect of heredity and environment on human growth and development. | **95–97, 115–122** |
| **12.2.2** Analyze the impact of social, economic, and technological forces on individual growth and development. | **112–113, 124** |
| **15.3.1** Assess community resources and services available to families. | **124** |
| **15.4.1** Analyze biological processes related to prenatal development, birth, and health of child and mother. | **93, 95–97, 99–104, 106–111, 115–118, 122** |
| **15.4.4** Analyze legal and ethical impacts of current and emerging technology on fertility and family planning. | **94, 97–99** |

**NO CHILD LEFT BEHIND** NCLB activities, information, and skills practice will help your students attain NCLB proficiency. Students will improve their abilities in the following academic standards areas:

## Academic Standards Correlations

| Discipline | Standard | Feature/Activity |
|---|---|---|
| **English Language Arts** | **NCTE 1** Read texts to acquire new information. | **Reading Guide (pp. 92, 105, 114)** |
| | **NCTE 5** Use different writing process elements to communicate effectively. | **After You Read (p. 122) Writing Activity (p. 90)** |
| | **NCTE 7** Conduct research and gather, evaluate, and synthesize data to communicate discoveries. | **After You Read (p. 104) Observation Skills (p. 124)** |
| | **NCTE 8** Use information resources to gather information and create and communicate knowledge. | **After You Read (p. 113)** |
| | **NCTE 12** Use language to accomplish individual purposes. | **Academic Skills (p. 125)** |
| **Mathematics** | **NCTM Algebra** Represent and analyze mathematical situations and structures using algebraic symbols. | **Academic Skills (p. 125)** |
| **Science** | **NSES A** Develop abilities necessary to do scientific inquiry, understanding about scientific inquiry. | **After You Read (p. 113) Academic Skills (p. 125)** |
| | **NSES C** Develop an understanding of the cell; molecular basis of heredity; and biological evolution. | **Science in Action (p. 97)** |
| | **NSES F** Develop understanding of personal and community health; and environmental quality. | **After You Read (p. 122)** |
| **Social Studies** | **NCSS I A Culture** Analyze and explain the ways groups, societies, and cultures address human needs and concerns. | **Culture Matters (p. 96)** |
| | **NCSS II B Time, Continuity, and Change** Apply key concepts such as time and change to analyze and show connections among patterns of historical change and continuity. | **After You Read (p. 104)** |

## Professional Development

**MINI CLIP VIDEO LIBRARY**

Targeted professional development is correlated throughout *The Developing Child*. **The McGraw-Hill Professional Development Mini Clip Video Library** provides teaching strategies to strengthen academic and learning skills. Log on to **glencoe.com**.

In this chapter, you will find these Mini Clips:

- **Reading** Guided Instruction, p. 90
- **ELL** Language Practice, p. 95
- **Math** Simple Events—Probability, p. 97
- **Math** Exponent Rules, p. 99
- **Reading** English Language Success, p. 103
- **Reading** Extending the Big Idea, p. 109
- **ELL** Group Discussions, p. 111
- **Reading** Flexible Groupings, p. 119

## Reading and Writing Strategies

**Writing Activity: Outline** (p. 90)
Students use writing tips to create an outline of Section 4.1.

**Before You Read** (pp. 92, 105, 114)
A pre-reading question or statement will help students make a personal connection to content.

**Graphic Organizer** (pp. 92, 105, 114)
A visual tool will help students organize and remember new content.

**Reading Check** (pp. 99, 106, 118, 120)
A question allows students to make a quick comprehension self-check.

**After You Read** (pp. 104, 113, 122)
Organize and process students' understanding of what they have read.

## Chapter Features

**Isolated Communities and Genetic Diseases** (p. 96)
In isolated communities where marriage to relatives occurs, genetic disease is often widespread.

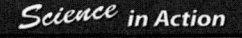

**Understanding Genetic Traits** (p. 97)
Genetic traits are controlled by inherited genes.

**Genetic Birth Defects** (p. 107)
Genetic birth defects should be considered before pregnancy.

**How Does Alcohol Affect a Fetus?** (p. 116)
Alcohol can cause serious problems for an unborn baby.

**Stopping Smoking** (p. 118)
It is important to stop smoking before becoming pregnant.

### Chapter Overview

**Introduce the Chapter**

In this chapter, students learn how pregnancy occurs. They learn how the baby forms during pregnancy and what affects the baby during pregnancy. Students learn that a pregnant woman's consumption of alcohol, tobacco, and other drugs can have devastating affects on the baby.

**Build Background**

Have students list what they know about fetal development during pregnancy. Then have them write a list of things they would like to know. Develop a KWL chart on the board from students' lists. At the end of the chapter, return to the chart and fill in the final column.

---

### Writing Activity ✒

#### *Examining Text Structure*

This active learning activity prompts students to create an outline to identify the main ideas and details of Section 4.1. After students have completed the writing activity, ask for volunteers to share their outlines with the class. Ask students to point out any differences in the outlines. Encourage the class to discuss which points they consider to be main points and why. (Student outlines should follow a standard outline form with letters and numerals.)

---

**Professional Development**

**Mini Clip**
**Reading: Guided Instruction**

A teacher helps students identify major and minor details.

---

## Chapter

**4**  **Prenatal Development**

## Chapter Objectives

After completing this chapter, you will be able to:

- **List** the methods of family planning.
- **Outline** what occurs during each of the three stages of prenatal development.
- **Contrast** miscarriage and stillbirth.
- **Identify** how ten major birth defects can be diagnosed.
- **Summarize** the hazards that alcohol and other drugs pose to prenatal development.
- **Assess** why environmental hazards must be avoided during pregnancy.
- **Describe** how a fetus can be affected by certain illnesses the mother may contract.

---

### Writing Activity ✒  *Outline*

**Examining Text Structure**  Good authors write text that is well structured. They clearly state their main points. Then they add details to these main points as needed. Use the following Writing Tips to create an outline of Section 4.1: The Developing Baby.

**Writing Tips**  Outlining can help you identify an author's main points and understand how these points have been expanded. Use these tips when you are outlining text:

1. Determine the major points or topics.
2. Divide each major point into two or more subpoints.
3. Continue subdividing until you have covered the important details.

---

## CLASSROOM Solutions

### Print Resources

 Student Edition

 Teacher Wraparound Edition

Student Activity Workbook

 Student Activity Workbook Teacher Annotated Edition

### Technology Resources

 **Online Learning Center** has resources and activities for students and teachers. Includes an Online Student Edition.

 **Interactive Student Edition** allows students to instantly access review materials, examples, and exercises.

Section **4.1** The Developing Baby

Section **4.2** Problems in Prenatal Development

Section **4.3** Avoiding Dangers to the Baby

**Review the Sections**
Introduce the chapter by reviewing the sections:

**Section 4.1**
When conception occurs, chromosomes from each parent determine the baby's inherited traits. Prenatal development moves through three stages during the 40 weeks of pregnancy.

**Section 4.2**
Some pregnancies end in miscarriage or stillbirth. Birth defects have a variety of causes. Some causes are factors in the environment, heredity factors, and errors in chromosomes. There are tests such as ultrasound and amniocentesis to help diagnose potential problems.

**Section 4.3**
Everything a pregnant woman eats, drinks, and breathes affects her developing baby. A pregnant woman should avoid alcohol, tobacco, and other drugs. She also should avoid environmental hazards and diseases.

▲ **Explore the Photo**
Regular medical care during pregnancy increases the chances of having a healthy baby. *Why do you think doctors and other medical professionals want pregnant women to come in for regular checkups?*

**91**

▶ **Explore the Photo**

**Caption Answer** Doctors want to monitor the health of the mother and the development of the fetus so that they can immediately deal with any problems that might arise.

**Discussion** Ask students what kinds of emotions they think this mother-to-be might be feeling. Have students discuss what questions they think the mother will ask her doctor. Ask a volunteer to write students' answers on the board.

 **TeacherWorks Plus** is an electronic lesson planner that provides instant access to complete teacher resources in one convenient package.

 **Presentation Plus!** provides visual teaching aids for every section.

 **The Early Childhood Observations CD** presents video observations and lessons on observation skills and child development.

**The Developing Brain eTransparencies and Guide** include information and activities to offer insights into brain development and diseases of the brain.

## Focus

### Bell Ringer Activity

#### Pregnancy 101

Instruct students to individually write down phrases that explain what they know about pregnancy. Then create a class list on the board. Ask students why it is important to be aware of the developmental milestones that occur during pregnancy.

## Preteaching

### Vocabulary

Students should be able to use context clues to determine the meaning of vocabulary terms. Write sentences on the board using each of the vocabulary terms. Ask your students to guess what the terms mean based on the sentence.

### Graphic Organizer

 The Graphic Organizer is also on the TeacherWorks CD.

(Graphic organizers should include: (1) germinal stage, (2) embryonic stage, and (3) fetal stage.)

 **NCLB** connects academic correlations to book content.

---

# Section 4.1 The Developing Baby

### Reading Guide

#### Before You Read

**Compare and Contrast** When a chapter discusses more than one way of performing the same task, try to compare and contrast the different methods.

#### Read to Learn
#### Key Concepts
- **List** the methods of family planning.
- **Outline** what occurs during each of the three stages of prenatal development.

#### Main Idea
A man's sperm fertilizes a woman's egg to begin developing an infant. Many contraception methods are available.

#### Content Vocabulary
- ◇ ovum
- ◇ uterus
- ◇ fallopian tube
- ◇ sperm
- ◇ conception
- ◇ chromosome
- ◇ gene
- ◇ genome
- ◇ DNA
- ◇ infertility
- ◇ surrogate
- ◇ prenatal development
- ◇ zygote
- ◇ embryo
- ◇ amniotic fluid
- ◇ placenta
- ◇ umbilical cord
- ◇ fetus

#### Academic Vocabulary
You will find these words in your reading and on your tests. Use the glossary to look up their definitions if necessary.
- ■ controversial
- ■ spontaneous

#### Graphic Organizer
As you read this section, note each of the three stages of prenatal development. Use a chart like the one shown to help organize your information.

**Three Stages of Prenatal Development**

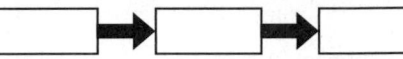

 **Graphic Organizer** Go to this book's Online Learning Center at **glencoe.com** to print out this graphic organizer.

---

#### Academic Standards · · · · · · · · · · · · · · · · · · · · · · · · · · · · · · · · · · · · · ·

**English Language Arts**

**NCTE 7** Conduct research and gather, evaluate, and synthesize data to communicate discoveries.

**Science**

**NSES C** Develop an understanding of the cell; molecular basis of heredity; and biological evolution.

**Social Studies**

**NCSS I A Culture** Analyze and explain the ways groups, societies, and cultures address human needs and concerns.

**NCSS II B Time, Continuity, and Change** Apply key concepts such as time and change to analyze and show connections among patterns of historical change and continuity.

**NCTE** National Council of Teachers of English
**NCTM** National Council of Teachers of Mathematics
**NSES** National Science Education Standards
**NCSS** National Council for the Social Studies

---

---

### Reading Guide

#### Before You Read

Ask students to think of two different methods of birth control of which they have some background knowledge. Have them compare and contrast the two methods. (Comparisons and contrasts will vary depending on the methods of birth control discussed. They might mention abstinence which is guaranteed and the pill which must be taken regularly.)

#### D Develop Concepts

**Main Idea** Discuss the main idea with the students. Ask: What does the term *contraception* mean? Show students that the term can be broken into two parts: *contra*, which means "against" and *conception*, which means "the process of becoming pregnant." (Students should realize that contraception refers to ways to keep conception from occurring.)

## Family Planning

**R** Many families carefully consider whether to have children and when to have them. However, anytime a couple has sexual intercourse, a pregnancy can occur. The only sure way to prevent pregnancy is abstinence, or avoiding sexual activity.

There are other methods of contraception, which can help prevent pregnancy. It is important to understand that most methods of contraception do not prevent sexually transmitted infections (STIs). Abstinence, however, prevents both STIs and pregnancy.

Most family planning methods have possible side effects. These problems develop among some, but not all, users. **Figure 4.1** on page 94 compares different methods of family planning. It also indicates if there are side effects. Families should check with their doctors for complete listings of side effects.

Effectiveness is given as a percentage. A method that is 100 percent effective, such as abstinence, works all the time. If a method is 80 percent effective, there is a one in five chance that a pregnancy could occur when that method is used.

## Conception

About once every 28 days, an ovum ('ō-vəm) is released by one of a woman's two ovaries. An **ovum** is an egg cell. This release is part of a woman's menstrual cycle and is called *ovulation*. At the same time, a woman's body releases specific hormones. These hormones prepare the uterus in the event that the ovum is fertilized. The **uterus** is the organ in a woman's body in which a baby develops during pregnancy. It is a pear-shaped muscle able to expand during pregnancy.

During ovulation, the inner lining of the uterus grows and thickens. If the ovum is not fertilized, the lining breaks down and passes out of the body. This is the bleeding that women experience as a menstrual period.

When an ovum is released from the ovary, it moves through a fallopian tube into the uterus. The **fallopian tube** is a tube that connects the ovary to the uterus. The journey from the ovary to the uterus takes about two or three days.

When the ovum reaches the uterus, it usually breaks up and leaves the body with the menstrual flow. The male cell is known as a **sperm**. When a sperm reaches the fallopian tube, it may penetrate and fertilize the ovum.

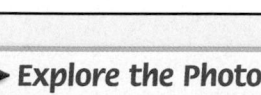
**Pregnancy**
For many couples, looking forward to a new baby is an exciting time. *What kinds of things do you think a couple might talk about during the pregnancy?*

## Teach

### Discussion Starter

**Life Changing Experience** Tell students that the younger people are when they have a baby, the more the baby will change their lives. Ask students what they think this means. Have them give some examples of changes that might occur to a teen with a baby. (Students' answers will vary but should show an understanding that teens often have to give up many of the things they do—such as school and going out with friends—if they have a baby.)

### **R** Reading Strategy

**Fact or Opinion** Have students read the first paragraph under Family Planning. Ask if they think this is a fact or an opinion and why they think the way they do. (Help students understand that this is a fact. They should not think "It can't happen to me" (pregnancy) if they engage in sexual intercourse. Refer students to Figure 4.1 on the next page and review with them the effectiveness percentages for the birth control methods listed.)

---

## Explore the Photo

**Caption Answer** Answers will vary. They might talk about their hopes that the baby will be healthy and happy, what they must do to get ready for the baby, names for the baby, and how their lives will change.

**Discussion** Ask students if they have younger siblings. Ask what changes occurred in their lives and the lives of their parents after the birth of their younger siblings. (Responses will vary; they may have had to give up some of their social lives such as going out with friends so they could help care for the new sibling.)

## Teach cont.

### C Critical Thinking

**Teen Pregnancy Rate** Share the following information with students: Each year in the United States, there are approximately 1 million teen pregnancies. This pregnancy rate is much higher than in many other countries. Ask students why they think the United States has a higher teen pregnancy rate than many other countries. (Students' answers will vary. Some might say it is because it is difficult for teens to obtain effective methods of birth control. Others may feel it is related to cultural values.)

### R₁ Reading Strategy

**Paraphrase** Tell students that paraphrase means to restate text in another form. Paraphrasing is often a good way to confirm understanding of new information. Have students review the information in Figure 4.1. Then have students write a summary to paraphrase what they have learned about the different methods of family planning. (Summaries will vary but should show an understanding of the different family planning methods. Students should use complete sentences and correct grammar.)

### W Writing Support

**Freewriting**

**Understanding Birth Control**
Have students spend a minute using freewriting to describe their feelings about the different types of birth control described in Figure 4.1. (Students' freewriting will vary. Some may not have any knowledge about birth control beyond that discussed in the text. If you choose to read students' papers, make sure the papers are anonymous to protect students' privacy.)

**Figure 4.1** **Methods of Family Planning**

There are many different methods of birth control. Some are more effective than others. *Which of the methods listed here can have the lowest rate of effectiveness?*

C

| Method | Characteristics | Effectiveness |
|---|---|---|
| **Abstinence** | Only method that is 100% effective. | 100% |
| **Hormonal implants** | Capsules placed under skin of upper arm. Possible side effects include hair loss or growth, acne, headaches, and moodiness. | 99% effective, for up to 5 years |
| **Hormonal patch** | Thin patch worn on skin for 3 weeks each month. Possible side effects such as weight gain or moodiness. | 99% |
| **Hormonal injections** | Hormones given by physician monthly or once every 3 months. May cause irregular bleeding. | up to 99% |
| **Intrauterine device (IUD) and Uterine implant** | Device placed inside the uterus to prevent sperm from fertilizing the egg. May cause discomfort and side effects first 3 months of use. | up to 99% |
| **Vaginal implant** | Ring worn internally for 3 weeks each month. Side effects can include vaginal bleeding. | 95–99% |
| **Birth control pills** | Daily pill that contains hormones. Possible side effects such as weight gain or moodiness. | 95–98% |
| **Condom** | Available for females, but more frequently used by males. Helps reduce spread of STDs. | 86% to 97% |
| **Diaphragm** | Covers the cervix to prevent sperm from entering the uterus. Used with spermicide. Increases risk of urinary infections. | 80–94% |
| **Cervical cap** | Small latex thimble that must remain in place eight hours. Increases risk of infection. | 60–91% |
| **Natural family planning** | Known as the rhythm method. Determines when a female can get pregnant based on her menstrual cycle. | 53–80% |
| **Spermicide** | Foams, creams, and gels. May cause allergic reactions. Should be used with condom, diaphragm, and cervical cap. | 72% |

R₁ W

**94** Chapter 4 Prenatal Development

**Figure 4.1** **Methods of Family Planning**

**Caption Answer** Natural family planning is the least effective method of family planning.

**Discussion** Divide the class into small groups. Have each group select one of the methods of birth control listed in the figure and research it more thoroughly. When groups have finished their research, hold a class discussion in which groups share the information they have found.

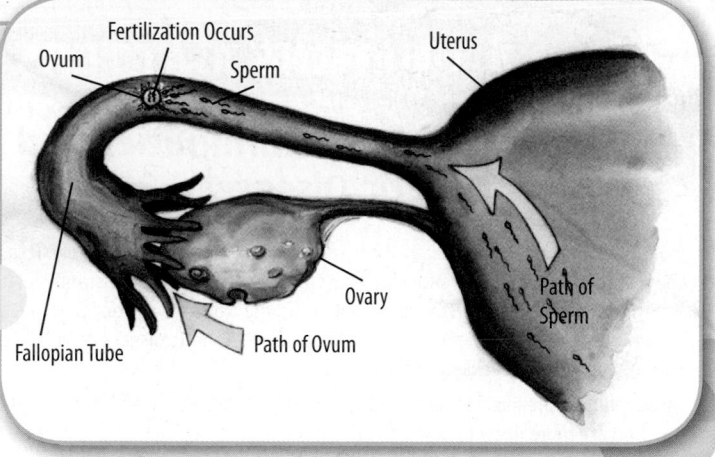

**Conception** For conception to occur, a sperm cell must penetrate an egg cell in the fallopian tube. *What is the fertilized egg called?*

Fertilization Occurs
Ovum
Sperm
Uterus
Ovary
Path of Sperm
Path of Ovum
Fallopian Tube

The process of the sperm fertilizing the ovum is called **conception**. An ovum usually lives 12 to 24 hours, while a sperm is capable of fertilizing an ovum for about 48 to 72 hours. During a woman's menstrual cycle, there are approximately three to four days during which intercourse could lead to conception.

Pregnancy, which lasts about nine months, begins at that time. During this time, a single cell grows and develops into a human being capable of life outside the mother's body.

An *ectopic pregnancy* is one in which the baby starts to grow somewhere other than the uterus, such as the fallopian tube. Ectopic pregnancies are dangerous for the mother. They do not end in a live birth.

**The Role of Genetics**

Why do I have this hair color? Why do I have blue eyes like my mom instead of brown eyes like my dad? Figuring out why people have certain traits can be confusing.

Have you ever compared your relative's looks to your own? Maybe you looked a lot like your father when you were both seven years old. People inherit many physical traits from their parents. These traits may include skin color, hair texture and color, eye color, the size and shape of ears, and more.

Some children are more likely to have certain talents, such as musical or athletic ability, because their parents have those talents. Some medical conditions are also inherited. How

does this happen? Scientists are constantly learning more and more about how heredity, the passing on of characteristics, works.

At the moment of conception, every human baby receives 46 chromosomes. A **chromosome** is a tiny threadlike structure in the nucleus of every cell. These chromosomes come in 23 pairs. The father's sperm and mother's ovum each contribute one chromosome to each pair. Each chromosome has hundreds to thousands of genes. A **gene** is a unit that determines a human's inherited characteristics. The complete blueprint for the creation of a person is called a **genome**. The complex molecules that make up genes are called **DNA** (deoxyribonucleic acid).

---

**{ Expert Advice... }**

*"The development of a baby is quite an intricate journey. From the moment that the egg and sperm meet, a baby is beginning the developmental process. This early part of development lays the foundation for a healthy pregnancy and the birth of a healthy baby."*

— The American Pregnancy Association

---

Section 4.1   The Developing Baby   **95**

**Teach** *cont.*

 **Universal Access**

**English Language Learners** Pair English language learners with students whose primary language is English. Students should study the illustration on this page, and take note of the names of each labeled part. Ask students whose primary language is English to help the English language learners with the pronunciation of the names. Now provide pairs of students with an unlabeled picture and have them work together to label the parts from memory. **ELL**

 **Professional Development**

**Mini Clip**
**ELL: Language Practice**

Students of varying language proficiencies work together to review the content they have just read.

**R₂ Reading Strategy**

**Acronyms** Tell students that acronyms are words formed from the first letter or first few letters of a group of words. Have students scan the chapter to find acronyms. As they find them list them on the board. (Examples include: LSD, STI, AIDS, SIDS, and DNA.) Have students find DNA on page 95 and as a class, write a definition for DNA. (DNA stands for deoxyribonucleic acid, which are the complex molecules that make up genes.)

---

**▶ Explore the Photo**

**Caption Answer** The fertilized egg created after the sperm cell penetrates an egg cell is called a zygote.

**Discussion** Ask a volunteer to read aloud the Expert Advice from The American Pregnancy Association located on this page. Ask students whether they had ever thought that a baby begins the developmental process the moment the egg and sperm combine. Ask for reactions to this statement. (Reactions will vary; some students may not agree that the fertilized egg is actually a life.)

**Teach** cont.

## C₁ Critical Thinking

**Identifying Alternatives** Tell students that DNA can be detected through saliva, hair follicles, bodily fluids, and blood. Ask students: How might DNA be used to aid a person? (Possible answers might include: it can be used to identify a person if, for some reason, they are unable to identify themselves. It can also be used to determine whether a husband and wife have genes that could combine to cause a defect in a child.)

## W₁ Writing Support

**Paragraphs**

**Physical Traits** Be sure students understand that their physical traits come from genes inherited from their parents. Ask students to write one paragraph that explains the physical traits they share with one or both of their parents (for example, blue eyes). Then have them write a second paragraph that explains physical traits they have that neither of their parents have (such as red hair). (Students paragraphs will vary but should show their understanding of physical traits that are passed through genes.)

## U₁ Universal Access

**Visual Learners** Tell students to make a chart showing the generations of their family or a family they know that includes grandparents; parents; and brothers, sisters, or cousins. On the chart, they should show the hair color and eye color of each person. Then have them write a paragraph to describe any patterns shown from the chart. (Charts will vary depending on the family depicted. Paragraphs should point out patterns, such as all generations having brown eyes because they are dominant.)

---

## CULTURE MATTERS

### Isolated Communities and Genetic Diseases

Isolated communities, especially those on islands, often have few people. This means that residents might marry individuals to whom they are at least distantly related. The South Atlantic island of Tristan da Cunha, or simply Tristan to residents, is one such community. All 300 residents of Tristan are cousins. Genetic disease is widespread, and over half of Tristan's residents have asthma.

Close relatives are likely to have similar genetic combinations, which means that their children are more likely to have genetic diseases. These diseases are less likely to appear in places with large numbers of people where parents typically are not related to one another.

⭐ **Build Connections** *Do you think that the residents of Tristan da Cunha should make their genetic information available for scientific research? Explain your answer.*

> **NCSS I A Culture** Analyze and explain the ways groups, societies, and cultures address human needs and concerns.

---

**C₁** A human's 46 chromosomes form that person's unique DNA. No two people, except identical twins, have identical DNA.

**Dominant and Recessive Genes** For each inherited characteristic, a person receives two copies of a gene. One copy comes from the mother and one from the father. When both genes are the same, the child automatically has that characteristic. In many cases, a person receives two different genes. What factors determine the characteristic that person will express? The characteristic is controlled by the dominant gene. A *dominant gene* is a stronger gene. The *recessive gene* is a weaker gene. The recessive gene will not be expressed. The terms *dominant* and *recessive* only refer to the relationship of genes to each other. It does not mean that one characteristic is actually weaker than another.

**W₁** Some people may not look much like their mother or father. They may look a lot like one of their grandparents, though. Some traits may skip a generation when recessive genes are inherited. For example, red hair often skips a generation because the gene for red hair is recessive. A recessive gene is only expressed when it is received from both parents.

Most traits are influenced by multiple genes. Height, weight, personality, and intelligence are examples of these traits. They are determined by a specific combination of genes that are brought together at conception. See the Science in Action feature on page 97 for more information.

**Making a Unique Person** Heredity explains why people in the same family often look alike. You may have a friend who looks a lot like his or her sibling. Heredity also explains why two family members can look quite different.

Each sperm and egg cell contains a different combination of genes. When these genes combine, they make a unique individual. That is why one child in a family can have light brown hair and another can have black or blonde hair. If each child in a family inherited the same genes from both parents, all of the children in the family would look exactly the same.

**W₁**

**U₁**

**96** Chapter 4 Prenatal Development

---

## CULTURE MATTERS

### Isolated Communities and Genetic Diseases

Tell students that Iceland is another isolated population. While it is much larger than the population of Tristan, all of the population is at least distantly related. Ask students whether they think the Icelanders have the same problems with genetic disease, such as asthma, as the people of Tristan. (Answers will vary. Tell students that because the population is larger and extensive genealogical records have been kept, Iceland has not had the problems that have plagued Tristan.)

**Build Connections** *Students' answers will vary. This genetic information might help scientists gain a better understanding of genetic defects, but many people are sensitive about the privacy of medical information.*

The gender of the child is determined at conception. The sex chromosomes come in two types, X and Y. Each ovum in the woman's ovaries carries an X chromosome. Each sperm cell in the man's body carries either an X or a Y chromosome. If the sperm that fertilizes the egg carries an X chromosome, the child receives an X chromosome from each parent. A child with the XX combination is a girl. If the sperm carries a Y chromosome, the child receives an X chromosome from the mother and a Y chromosome from the father. A child with the XY combination is a boy.

## Multiple Births

The number of children a woman will give birth to at one time is determined at conception or soon after. When a woman gives birth to more than one child at a time, it is called a *multiple birth*. The most common instance of multiple births is twins.

There are two types of twins: identical and fraternal. When a sperm fertilizes a woman's ovum, the cell begins to divide right away. As the cells continue to divide, the mass of cells may split in half, creating two separate cell masses. Each cell mass continues to divide and grow into a separate embryo. The result is identical twins. Because only one ovum and sperm were involved in conception, identical twins have very similar physical characteristics and are always the same gender.

Fraternal twins form when two eggs are released from the ovaries at the same time and are fertilized by two different sperm. Because of the different eggs and sperm, fraternal twins may not look alike. They just happen to be in the mother's uterus at the same time. It is common for fraternal twins to be opposite genders.

In a general population, three in 100 births, or about 3 percent, are twins. Identical twins are much less common than fraternal twins. Out of 1,000 births, about 23 will be fraternal twins and about four will be identical twins.

The birth of three or more babies is much more rare than the birth of twins. However, a rise in the use of treatments to help women become pregnant has increased the frequency of multiple births. One potential drawback to some of these treatments is that they can cause

more than one egg to be released at a time, making multiple births more likely. The more children a pregnant woman carries, the more difficult it is for all of them to survive.

## Infertility

Not all couples who want to become parents are able to have a child. These couples are considered infertile. **Infertility** is the inability to conceive a child. There are many causes of infertility in both men and women. About 40 percent of cases are due to female infertility, and about 40 percent are due to male infertility. The other 20 percent have unknown causes or are linked to both partners.

### Science in Action

#### Understanding Genetic Traits

All people have physical traits that are controlled by the genes they inherit. For each trait, one gene comes from the father, and one comes from the mother. Whether a physical trait is related to a dominate or recessive gene determines the chances of a child inheriting it.

#### Procedure

Suppose that two parents each have a dominant gene for brown hair and a recessive gene for red hair. Fill in the following table with the child's four possible gene combinations.

|  | **Mother** | |
|---|---|---|
| **Father** | BROWN | red |
| BROWN | | |
| red | | |

Possible gene combinations of child

#### Analysis

1. What are the chances (in percent) of this child having red hair?
2. What are the chances of brown hair?
3. What are the chances of blonde hair?

> **NSES C** Develop an understanding of the cell; molecular basis of heredity; and biological evolution.

### Science in Action

#### Understanding Genetic Traits

Students should complete the table and use the data to answer the questions:

1. There is a 25% chance that the child will have red hair.
2. There is a 75% chance that the child will have brown hair.
3. There is a 0% chance that the child will have blonde hair.

#### Professional Development

#### Mini Clip
**Math: Simple Events— Probability**

Small groups of students use manipulatives to conduct probability experiments and later discuss results as a whole class.

### Teach *cont.*

#### C₂ Critical Thinking

**Problem Solving** Have students create a two-column chart with the heading Problems on one side and Solutions on the other. Under the Problems heading, students should list all possible problems new parents might face when they are expecting multiple births. In the Solutions column, students should brainstorm ways parents might successfully meet these challenges. (Charts will vary. Possible problem and solution: Parents cannot afford clothing; parents could purchase used clothing.)

#### W₂ Writing Support
**Research**

**Treating Infertility** Have students conduct research to find out the latest developments in treating infertility. Students should answer the following questions in a one-page report: What procedures are new? Are there any side effects involved in these procedures? How costly are these procedures? (Students' answers will vary but may include: clomiphene citrate treatment, which has these common side effects: hot flashes, stomach discomfort and bloating, nausea and vomiting, breast discomfort, visual symptoms, headache, and vaginal bleeding.)

#### U₂ Universal Access

**Kinesthetic Learners** Tell students that before starting a family, a couple should discuss the possibility of infertility. Ask students to role-play what they might say to an infertile partner and what alternatives to traditional conception they might consider. (Students' role-plays will vary but should include what would be said to an infertile partner and what alternatives would be considered, such as adoption.) **ELL**

**NCLB** Activity correlated to Science standards.

## S Skill Practice

### Guided Practice

**Brainstorm Resources** Draw a two-column chart on the blackboard. Label one side Resources and the other side How To Locate. Have the class brainstorm resources that might be available to help infertile couples deal with their emotions and ideas on how to locate those resources. Ask for a volunteer to write the ideas in the chart. (Ideas will vary but may include counselors or support groups. These can be located using the yellow pages of a phonebook.) **L1** **ELL**

**List Local Resources** Have students work in pairs to think of resources that might be available to help infertile couples deal with their emotions. Then have them use the Internet or local yellow pages to create a list of local resources available, and a brief description of the services each resource offers. (Lists will vary depending on local resources available. Possible resources may include support groups, counselors, or doctors.) **L2** **ELL**

**Create a Brochure** Have students work in pairs to create a list of local resources available to help infertile couples cope with their emotions. Resources may be found using local yellow pages or the Internet. Their list should include contact information for the resources as well as services offered. Then have each pair use the information on their list to create an informative and appealing brochure that could be given to infertile couples. (Brochures will vary based on resources available. Encourage students to use colorful fonts and illustrations or photos to make their brochures more appealing. Brochures should clearly give the information on how to contact the resources, as well as a brief description of the services offered by each resource.) **L3**

**↑ Multiple Births**
Twins may be identical or fraternal. *What is the difference between the two types of twins?*

**S** People with infertility problems may feel isolated or abnormal. There are support groups available to help couples in this situation. Also, advances in medicine have helped couples overcome infertility. The treatments used depend on the cause. For example, a doctor can prescribe medication when a woman's ovaries do not release an ovum each month. Some fertility medications, however, can cause uncomfortable or potentially serious side effects, and require the careful supervision of a doctor. As time passes, research is improving the safety and effectiveness of a variety of infertility treatments.

### Options for Infertile Couples

After attempts to treat infertility, some couples still cannot conceive a child. There are several other options they may discuss with each other and with their doctors:

- **Adoption** By adopting a child, a couple legally takes on all responsibilities and rights for raising, loving, and caring for a child in need of a permanent home.
- **Artificial Insemination** In this process, a doctor injects sperm into a woman's uterus. This procedure is timed to take place when a woman's ovary releases an ovum. Often, the sperm is from the woman's husband.

If the spouse has a genetic disorder that prevents his sperm from being used, sperm from a male donor can be used.

- **In Vitro Fertilization** This process is used to treat many causes of infertility, such as when a woman has damaged fallopian tubes. With the help of a microscope, the doctor combines a mature ovum from the woman with sperm from her husband. If the ovum becomes fertilized, the doctor places it in the woman's uterus. Pregnancy occurs if the fertilized egg attaches itself to the uterus.
- **Ovum Transfer** This procedure is similar to in vitro fertilization, except an ovum has been donated by another woman. The ovum is fertilized in a laboratory and placed in the mother's uterus. This procedure is an option for women who lack working ovaries, have poor ovum quality, or who have inherited disorders.
- **Surrogate Mother** A **surrogate** (ˈsər-ə-ˌgāt) is a substitute. A surrogate mother is a woman who becomes pregnant to have a baby for another woman. This option requires legal arrangements be made for everyone involved, including the child. Each state has laws regarding surrogate motherhood.

**98** **Chapter 4** Prenatal Development

### ▶ Explore the Photo

**Caption Answer** With identical twins, a single ovum splits in two, whereas with fraternal twins, two eggs are released and both are fertilized at the same time.

**Discussion** Ask students to think about what some advantages might be to having someone who looked exactly like you. Some disadvantages? (Students' responses will vary. Some might think it would be fun to fool people about your identity. Others might feel they would lack individuality.)

### Questions Raised

Medical specialists can help some infertile couples. Infertility treatments are often very expensive. Medical insurance plans may exclude or limit coverage for these treatments.

As technology and knowledge continue to advance, other options for the treatment of infertility may be discovered. However, personal beliefs may limit a couple's options. Not everyone believes that these alternatives are acceptable. The use of surrogate mothers or sperm and ovum donors is considered **controversial**, or causing opposing views. These practices raise many moral questions. New procedures in the future will raise questions as well.

✓ **Reading Check** **Recall** What is the most common type of multiple birth?

## Three Stages of Pregnancy

The baby's development during a pregnancy is called **prenatal development**. It is often grouped into three stages, called the germinal stage, embryonic stage, and fetal stage. Different developmental milestones are reached during each of the three stages. **Figure 4.2** on pages 102–103 shows month-by-month development of each stage.

### The Germinal Stage

The germinal stage is the first stage in a baby's development. It includes the formation of the zygote. The **zygote** ('zī-ˌgōt) is the fertilized egg. This stage lasts only about two weeks, but includes the key steps in establishing a pregnancy.

### Cell Division

The zygote begins to grow by cell division while it is still in the Fallopian tube. The single cell splits into two cells. Then the two cells rapidly multiply to four, then to eight, and so on. Within a few days, the zygote has grown to about 500 living cells. After about four days of growth and slow movement, the zygote reaches the opening to the uterus.

### Implantation

The lining of the uterus has now thickened enough to provide a place for the zygote to attach itself and continue to grow. The zygote implants in the lining of the uterus and is covered by that lining. Despite the rapid growth of the zygote during the two weeks after fertilization, it is only the size of the head of a pin. Although it is barely big enough to see without a microscope, it is ready to grow into a fully developed human being.

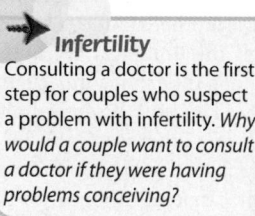

➤ **Infertility**
Consulting a doctor is the first step for couples who suspect a problem with infertility. *Why would a couple want to consult a doctor if they were having problems conceiving?*

---

➤ **Explore the Photo**

**Caption Answer** A couple would want to consult a doctor if they were having problems conceiving because many fertility problems can be overcome with medical treatment.

**Discussion** Have students work together in small groups to create a list of questions a couple who suspects a problem with infertility might ask a doctor. (Questions will vary but likely will include: What are the options? How does it work? What is the cost? Will insurance cover it?)

---

### Assess

**Quiz**
Ask students to answer the following questions:

1. What determines the sex of a child? (Whether the child receives an X or a Y chromosome from the father determines the sex of a child.)
2. Which family planning method is most effective? (Abstinence is the most effective method of family planning.)
3. Which two fertility procedures can use the mother's ovum and the father's sperm? (Artificial insemination and in vitro fertilization can use both the mother's ovum and the father's sperm.)

### Reteach

**C Critical Thinking**
**Cell Division Problems** Review the information about cell division with students. Have students provide answers to the following questions: If a cell divides three times, how many cells would you have? ($2^3$, or eight, cells) How many cells would you have if the cell divides seven times? (You would have 64 cells.) How many cells would you have if it divides 10 times? (You would have 512 cells.)

**Mc Graw Hill Professional Development**

**Mini Clip**
**Math: Exponent Rules**

Algebra teacher Brad Fulton suggests a way to illustrate exponent rules.

✓ **Reading Check**

**Recall** The most common type of multiple births is fraternal twins.

**99**

### W₁ Writing Support

**Paragraph**

**Crucial Stage** Ask students to consider why it is important that expectant mothers understand the early stages of prenatal development even if they do not notice any signs of pregnancy themselves. Have students write a paragraph explaining the risk to the embryo if the mother smokes, drinks, takes drugs, or doesn't eat nutritious foods. (Students' should say that as early as 27 days after conception the developing brain is sensitive to damage from these substances if the mother takes them.)

## Cooperative Learning

**Interpersonal Learners** Divide the class into groups of two or three. Assign each group to research one of the nine months of pregnancy. Then have each group design a segment of a large bulletin board to show fetal development during their assigned month of pregnancy. Encourage students to use charts, pictures, or drawings to illustrate that stage of pregnancy. (Results will vary but should show a completed "time line" of the stages of pregnancy.) **ELL**

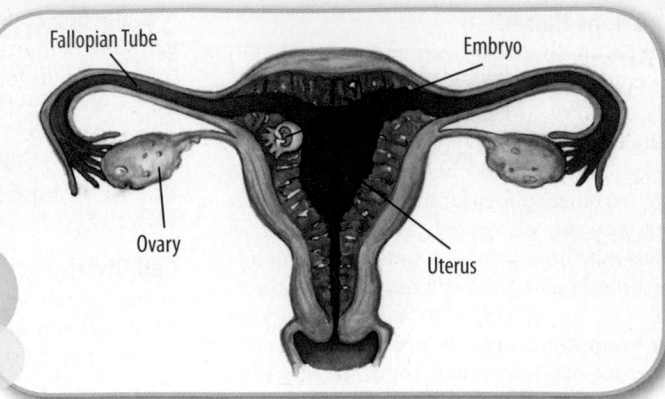

➡️ **Embryo Attaches to Uterus**
The embryo must become implanted in the lining of the uterus in order to grow. *What stage does this occur in?*

Labels: Fallopian Tube, Embryo, Ovary, Uterus

## The Embryonic Stage

The second stage of pregnancy is the embryonic stage. The **embryo** is what the developing baby is called from about the third week of pregnancy through the eighth week. The embryo grows rapidly during this time. It is also during this stage that many important and amazing changes occur. It is during the first eight weeks that the face, eyes, ears, limbs, and bones begin to form.

### Organs and Body Systems

The cells begin to separate and develop into the major systems of the human body. These systems include the heart, lungs, bones, and muscles. However, these internal organs and their systems are not yet ready to function. They will continue to develop throughout the pregnancy.

About 27 days after conception, the neural tube has closed. The neural tube is a tube in the back of the developing baby that will become the brain and spinal cord.

At this point, the brain begins to take control of the various body systems. By about the sixth week after conception, the connections between the brain and the spine allow the first movements of the embryo. The developing brain is sensitive to damage from any drugs or alcohol the mother might take. This is especially true at this crucial stage. It is vital that a pregnant woman avoid these substances throughout her pregnancy.

**W₁**

### Amniotic Sac

A sac filled with liquid forms around the embryo. The liquid that surrounds and protects the developing baby in the uterus is called **amniotic fluid** (ˌam-nē-'ä-tik). The amniotic sac is formed from special layers of cells in the uterus. It cushions the embryo from any bumps or falls that the mother might have. At this point in development, the embryo is still very small (about 1 inch, or 2.5 cm, long). It can float freely in the amniotic fluid.

### Placenta and Umbilical Cord

Also at this stage, the placenta (plə-'sen-tə) develops. The **placenta** is a tissue that connects the developing baby to the uterus. It is formed from special layers of cells in the uterus. The placenta is rich in blood vessels that allow food and oxygen to flow to the baby.

The placenta's job is to absorb oxygen and nourishment from the mother's blood to be sent to the baby through the umbilical cord. The **umbilical cord** is a long tube that connects the baby to the placenta. The umbilical cord also takes carbon dioxide and other waste products away from the baby. These waste products go to the placenta, which releases them into the mother's bloodstream.

The umbilical cord is usually stiff and firm, like a garden hose filled with water. It is generally not flexible enough to loop around the fetus, although this may occur in rare cases. The placenta and umbilical cord provide all of a baby's needs until birth.

**100** **Chapter 4** Prenatal Development

➤ **Explore the Photo**

**Caption Answer** The embryo becomes implanted in the uterus during the germinal stage when the zygote leaves the fallopian tube, about four days after conception.

**Discussion** Have students study the picture and take note of the names of each labeled part. Discuss the names with students and then give them an unlabeled illustration. Have them label the parts from memory. (Students should correctly label the uterus, ovary, embryo, and fallopian tube.)

## The Fetal Stage

The fetal stage is the third and final stage of development. It is also the longest stage. It begins around the eighth or ninth week of pregnancy and lasts until birth. During this stage, the developing baby is called a **fetus** ('fē-təs). The vocal cords develop, and the digestive system and kidneys begin to function. **Spontaneous**, or unplanned, movements are possible by the end of the third month.

### Making Movements

Sometime during the fourth or fifth month, the kicks and other movements of the fetus touch the wall of the uterus. These movements are faint and infrequent at first. These are usually the first fetal movements that the mother can feel. She may feel the movement as a kind of fluttering, like a butterfly. Gradually, these sensations become stronger and more frequent, letting the mother know that she really is carrying a live child within her.

A pregnant woman's doctor usually asks her when she first felt these movements. This information helps the doctor estimate the baby's age and make sure the baby is developing normally. This information can also be used to help project an accurate due date.

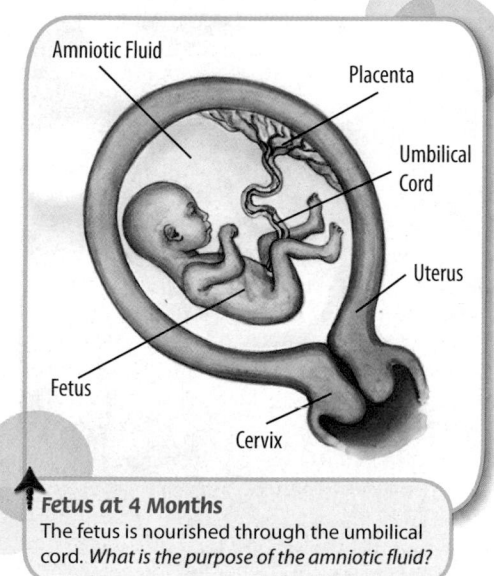

**Fetus at 4 Months**
The fetus is nourished through the umbilical cord. *What is the purpose of the amniotic fluid?*

Sometimes a fetus will roll or stretch just to get more comfortable. A fetus will also move in response to loud noises or familiar voices. Many parents talk, read, or sing to the developing fetus to encourage movement. This also helps the fetus become familiar with the parents' voices. The baby can recognize these voices after birth.

### Completing Development

During the last few months of pregnancy, development continues, preparing the fetus to live independently. By the seventh month, the baby is capable of living outside the uterus, but only with a lot of medical help.

The body's major organs become ready to function without any help from the mother's body. The fetus also gains weight quickly. Fat deposits are formed under the skin. These will help the baby hold body heat after delivery. The fetus goes from thin and wrinkled to the smoother, rounder appearance of a baby. The fetus also stores nutrients and builds immunity to diseases and infections.

By the eighth month of pregnancy, the fetus sleeps about 90 percent of the day. Brain scans have shown rapid eye movement (REM) in some fetuses during this time. That means that fetuses can dream while they sleep!

### Staying Active

The fetus can do a surprising number of things. It uses all five senses. It can suck its thumb, cough, sneeze, yawn, kick, and hiccup. A fetus can even cry. Even though the uterus is crowded, the fetus is still very active and can change positions. Sometimes, around the eighth month, babies will lodge their feet between their mother's ribs. This can be painful for the mother. She can often dislodge the foot with gentle exercises or stretches. Once the baby has moved down, in the ninth month, he usually cannot reach this high anymore.

During the eighth month of pregnancy, the baby should settle into the proper position for delivery. This means the head is angled down to lead the way out of the uterus. The baby will continue to kick and stretch though. By the ninth month, these kicks can be quite powerful, and sometimes painful for the mother.

---

## Reteach *cont.*

### Cooperative Learning

**Verbal Learners** Prepare a list of terms that deal with pregnancy. Make a copy of the list for each student, each copy with a different term highlighted. Tell students to study the highlighted term and prepare to teach its meaning to the class. As each student teaches, the rest of the class should take notes. (See list of Content Vocabulary terms on page 92 for ideas for words to include on the list.) **ELL**

### C Critical Thinking

**Agree or Disagree** Have students conduct research on studies about talking to babies while still in the womb. Students should read a variety of studies and decide whether or not they believe that babies in the womb can recognize voices. Students should write a paragraph explaining why they agree or disagree. (Students' paragraphs will vary but should give the rationale behind their feelings.)

### W₂ Writing Support
**Outline**

**The Five Senses** Tell students that research has shown that during the fetal stage of pregnancy, the fetus uses all five senses: sight, sound, smell, taste, and touch. Have students conduct research to find examples of how each of these senses is used by a fetus. Then, have them create an outline for a report on the topic. (Outlines will vary but students should use proper outline form. For example, they might have a roman numeral for each of the senses, with an A and B under each to list the examples they find.)

---

## ⬤▶ Explore the Photo

**Caption Answer** The purpose of the amniotic fluid is to cushion the baby from any bumps or falls the mother may have.

**Discussion** Ask students what might happen if there were no amniotic fluid in the mother's womb. What might happen to the baby? (Answers will vary but may include that the baby would likely be bumped and bruised with every movement the mother made.)

**Reteach** *cont.*

### C Critical Thinking

**Growth Rates** A fetus quadruples in size between months two and three, and more than doubles in size between months four and five. Have students explain possible reasons for these growth spurts as compared to the more moderate and consistent growth during the later months of pregnancy. (Answers will vary. Students may note that between months two and three the fetus's bones develop and between months four and five the organs are maturing.)

### U Universal Access

**Gifted Learners** Divide the class into small groups, placing a gifted student in each group. Assign the gifted students to be the group's chairperson who makes sure all group members participate. Have each group conduct research and read an article about a different aspect of sensory development in fetuses. Have each group share its discoveries with the class. (Groups should conduct research and develop a presentation for the rest of the class.)

### W₁ Writing Support

**Descriptive Paragraph**

**Fetal Development** A fetus can suck its thumb at four months. Point out other physical development or activities a fetus can do during the second trimester of pregnancy, such as hiccup or form eyelashes. Ask students to use a trusted parenting or medical Web site to research other developments that occur during these first important months and to write a paragraph that describes these developments. (Paragraphs will vary but should describe other physical developments or activities that occur during the fourth through sixth month of pregnancy.)

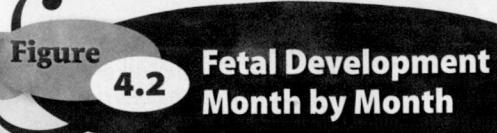

## Figure 4.2 Fetal Development Month by Month

The fetus develops in the uterus for approximately nine months. *When does hair begin to appear?*

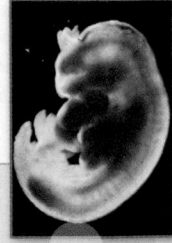

**Month 1**
- ❖ Size: At two weeks, the size of a pin head.
- ❖ Egg attaches to lining of uterus.
- ❖ Critical stage for brain and spinal cord development.
- ❖ Internal organs and circulatory system begin to form.
- ❖ The heart begins to beat.

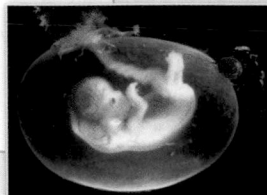

**Month 2**
- ❖ Size: About ¼ inch (6 mm) long as month begins.
- ❖ Face, eyes, ears, and limbs take shape.
- ❖ Bones begin to form.

**Month 3**
- ❖ Size: About 1 inch (25 mm) long as month begins.
- ❖ Nostrils, mouth, lips, and eyelids form.
- ❖ Buds for all 20 baby teeth appear.
- ❖ Fingers and toes almost complete.
- ❖ All organs present but still immature.

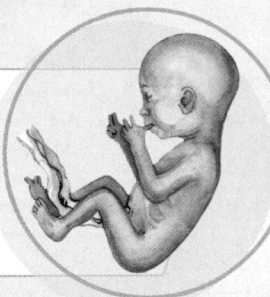

**U**

**Month 4**
- ❖ Size: About 3 inches (7.6 cm) long, weighs 1 ounce (28 g) as month begins.
- ❖ Can suck its thumb, swallow, hiccup, and move around.
- ❖ Facial features become clearer.

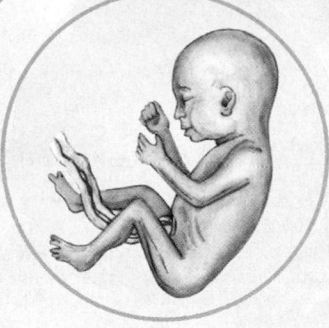

**W₁**

**Month 5**
- ❖ Size: About 6½–7 inches (16–18 cm) long, weighs about 4–5 ounces (113–142 g) as month begins.
- ❖ Hair, eyelashes, and eyebrows appear.
- ❖ Teeth continue to develop.
- ❖ Organs are maturing.
- ❖ Becomes more active.

**C**

## Figure 4.2 Fetal Development Month by Month

**Caption Answer** While in the uterus, hair begins to appear on the fetus at five months.

**Discussion** Ask students to tell when other physical features of the fetus begin to develop. (Answers should include: face, eyes, ears, and limbs at two months; buds for baby teeth appear at three months.)

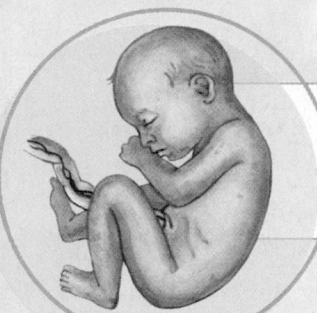

### Month 6
❖ Size: About 8–10 inches (21–25 cm) long, weighs about 8–12 ounces (227–340 g) as month begins.
❖ Fat deposits under skin, but fetus appears wrinkled.
❖ Breathing movements begin.

**W₁**

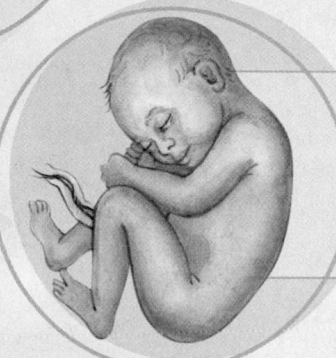

### Month 7
❖ Size: About 10–12 inches (25–31 cm) long, weighs about 1½–2 pounds (680–907 g) as month begins.
❖ Has periods of activity followed by periods of rest and quiet.

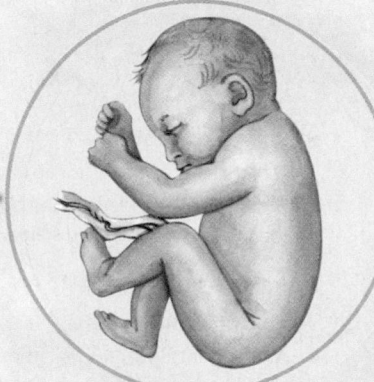

**W₂**

### Month 8
❖ Size: About 14–16 inches (36–41 cm) long, weighs about 2½–3 pounds (1.0–1.4 kg) as month begins.
❖ Rapid weight gain continues.
❖ May react to loud noises with a reflex jerking action.
❖ Moves into a head-down position.

**R**

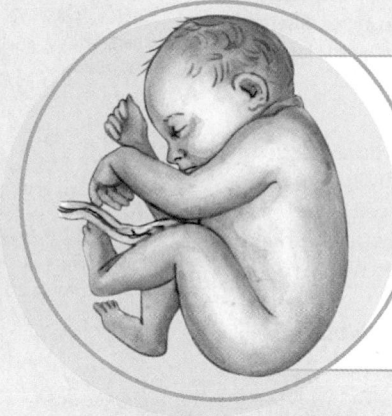

### Month 9
❖ Size: About 17–18 inches (43–46 cm) long, weighs about 5–6 pounds (2.3–2.7 kg) as month begins.
❖ Weight gain continues.
❖ Skin becomes smooth as fat deposits continue.
❖ Movements decrease as the fetus has less room to move around.
❖ Acquires disease-fighting antibodies from the mother's blood.
❖ Descends into pelvis, ready for birth.

**Section 4.1**   The Developing Baby   **103**

## Reteach *cont.*

## W₂ Writing Support
### Interview Notes
**New Mother**  Instruct students to take notes as they interview a woman who is currently pregnant or a new mother. (If both options are available, have them interview the new mother.) In this interview, the student should ask these questions: What is pregnancy like? What different feelings and emotions did you experience? What were your feelings during the last four months of pregnancy? (Answers will vary depending on the woman interviewed. Students should share their interview results with the rest of the class.)

## R Reading Strategy
**Questions**  Have students individually develop a set of questions about the month-by-month development of a fetus. Students should also write answers to the questions. After they have compiled the questions and answers, students should take turns asking a partner the questions. (Questions will vary, but should be based on what students learned from Figure 4.2.)

**Professional Development**

### Mini Clip
**Reading: English Language Success**

Ruben Zepeda, Ed.D., discusses the role of classroom management in the success of English learners.

## Section 4.1

### Assess

**Study Tools**

Have students go to the Online Learning Center at **glencoe.com**:

- Take the **Practice Test**.
- Download **Study-to-Go** content.

Use the **Student Activity Workbook** for additional practice.

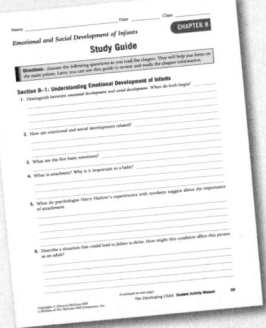

### Close

**Culminating Activity**

**Displaying Different Emotions**
Have students create a chart that shows the major milestones of a pregnancy. Students may add illustrations to the chart. (Charts will vary. At minimum, they should include: conception, the germinal stage, the embryonic stage, and the fetal stage.)

**NCLB** connects academic correlations to book content.

---

### Growing Bigger

As the fetus grows, so does the amount of surrounding amniotic fluid. The uterus also expands, causing the woman's stomach to grow. When the fetus grows large during the last few months of pregnancy, it no longer has room to stretch out. It curls up in what is called the fetal position. This means the baby is curled into a ball. The head is bowed forward and the arms and legs are drawn in.

### Ready for Birth

The common length of pregnancy is about 40 weeks, or 280 days, from the first day of the last menstrual cycle. By the ninth month, the fetus is fully developed and can usually survive outside the mother's body with little medical assistance. Some babies are born either a few weeks early or a few weeks late. This is usually not a problem. Advances in technology allow many babies to survive that are born early.

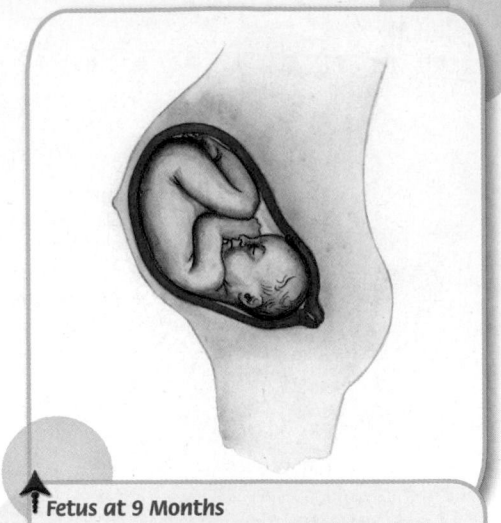

**Fetus at 9 Months**
As the end of pregnancy nears the fetus is folded in the fetal position. *Given its current position in the uterus, how will this baby be positioned when it is born?*

## Section 4.1 — After You Read

### Review Key Concepts

1. **Describe** two options for an infertile couple that wants children.
2. **Explain** how the developing baby receives oxygen and nutrition during the second and third stages of prenatal development?

### Practice Academic Skills

**English Language Arts**

3. Ask students to interview a mother with two or more children. They should ask questions such as: How were the pregnancies different? Did you have any worries about each baby's health? Have students create a chart comparing the mother's experiences.

**Social Studies**

4. Attitudes about pregnancy and pregnant women have changed over the years. Pregnant women were treated differently in the past. Conduct research to find out how pregnancy was viewed in the United States in the 1950s. Include print or online resources, and consider talking to older family members about their memories. Write a paragraph comparing these attitudes to today's attitudes.

**Check Your Answers** Check your answers at this book's Online Learning Center at **glencoe.com**.

**NCTE 7** Conduct research and gather, evaluate, and synthesize data to communicate discoveries.

**NCSS II B** Apply key concepts such as time and change to analyze and show connections among patterns of historical change and continuity.

**104** Chapter 4 Prenatal Development

---

## Section 4.1 After You Read

**Review Key Concepts**

1. Any two of the following: adoption, artificial insemination, in vitro fertilization, ovum transfer, or surrogate mother.
2. The mother's bloodstream carries food and oxygen to the placenta where they are absorbed and transmitted to the baby through the umbilical cord.

**Practice Academic Skills**

3. Charts will vary but should compare the mother's experiences during each of her pregnancies.
4. Answers will vary but may include that pregnant women, especially in the later months, were expected to stay home.

If they worked, they quit their jobs. The pregnant woman was often encouraged to avoid tasks such as housework. Today, pregnancy is seen as a normal part of life and pregnant women routinely work until the baby's birth, continuing most of their previous daily activities.

## Reading Guide

### Before You Read

**Adjust Your Reading Speed** Learning to adjust your reading speed can help you remember information. Reading more slowly can help you to understand more complex concepts.

### Read to Learn
#### Key Concepts
- **Contrast** miscarriage and stillbirth.
- **Identify** how ten major birth defects can be diagnosed.

**D**

### Main Idea
Not all pregnancies end in the birth of a healthy infant. Some end early with the unborn baby's death. Some babies are born with health problems.

### Content Vocabulary
◇ miscarriage
◇ stillbirth
◇ ultrasound
◇ amniocentesis

### Academic Vocabulary
You will find these words in your reading and on your tests. Use the glossary to look up their definitions if necessary.
- predisposition
- serious

### Graphic Organizer
As you read, look for types of prenatal tests that can be used to check for birth defects. Use a chart like the one shown to help organize your information.

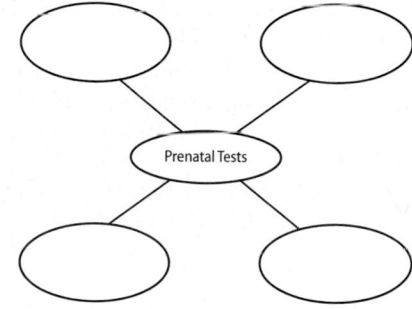

Prenatal Tests

 **Graphic Organizer** Go to this book's Online Learning Center at **glencoe.com** to print out this graphic organizer.

**NCLB**

### Academic Standards . . . . . . . . . . . . . . . . . . . . . . . . . .

 **English Language Arts**

**NCTE 8** Use information resources to gather information and create and communicate knowledge.

 **Science**

**NSES A** Develop abilities necessary to do scientific inquiry, understanding about scientific inquiry.

**NCTE** *National Council of Teachers of English*
**NCTM** *National Council of Teachers of Mathematics*

**NSES** *National Science Education Standards*
**NCSS** *National Council for the Social Studies*

---

### Bell Ringer Activity

#### Birth Defects

Ask students to share their definitions of a birth defect. Ask: What are some of the factors that can cause birth defects? In what ways can birth defects impact the life of the child and the family? Ask students to name specific birth defects and abnormalities.

## Preteaching
### Vocabulary

The term *miscarriage* comes from *miscarry,* which was first used in 1340 to mean "to come to harm, perish;" "to die," or "to be lost or destroyed." Its first known usage meaning "deliver unviable fetus" was recorded in 1527.

### Graphic Organizer

 The Graphic Organizer is also on the TeacherWorks CD.

(Graphic organizers should include: alpha-fetoprotein (AFP), ultrasound, amniocentesis, and chorionic villi sampling.)

 **NCLB** connects academic correlations to book content.

---

## Reading Guide

### Before You Read

Have half the class quickly skim the three paragraphs under Losing a Baby on page 106. Have the other half of the class carefully read the same paragraphs. When students have finished, ask questions that will help students realize that reading slowly and carefully can help them better understand the concepts.

### **D** Develop Concepts

**Main Idea** Discuss the main idea with the students. Ask students if they know anyone whose pregnancy has ended in the death of the baby or with a baby born with health problems. (Students may or may not know anyone who fits these criteria.)

### Teach

## Discussion Starter

**Miscarriage Versus Stillbirth**
Ask students to define the terms *miscarriage* and *stillbirth* without looking at the text. Explain the difference to students and ask how many knew the difference between the two terms. (Students likely will have heard the two terms but may not know that a miscarriage occurs prior to the twentieth week of pregnancy and a stillbirth occurs after the twentieth week.)

## 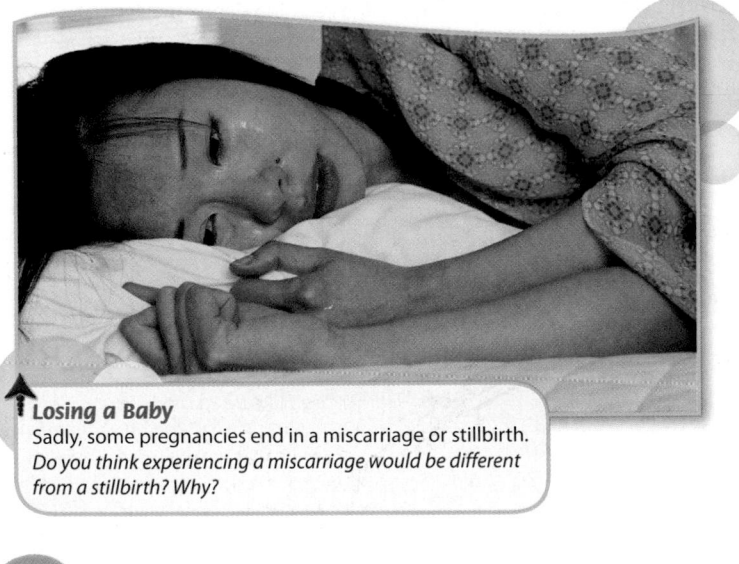U Universal Access

**Intrapersonal Learners** Share with students the following list of emotions and feelings parents might experience at the birth of a special-needs baby. Have them imagine themselves in a hospital, just having received the news that their newborn child has special needs. Ask them to write down ways that they think they might deal with each of these emotions: Denial—Many parents of special-needs children don't believe this can be happening to them; Anger—The anger may be pointed at the medical community or another family member; Fear—Parents fear the unknown or not knowing what may happen to their child; Guilt—Many parents blame themselves for the child's condition; Confusion—Caring for a special-needs child can be much different from regular child care. Many parents experience overload and stress. (Students' ways of dealing will vary but answers should show thoughtfulness.)

## ✓ Reading Check

**Recall** Miscarriage occurs in 15 percent of recognized pregnancies.

## Losing a Baby

Will the baby be healthy? This is a major concern for all expectant parents. Most babies develop normally and are born healthy. However, sometimes the baby does not develop normally. Sometimes the developing baby dies. When the developing baby dies prior to the twentieth week of pregnancy, the event is called a **miscarriage**. If the baby dies after the twentieth week, it is called a **stillbirth**.

Unfortunately, miscarriages are fairly common. About 15 percent of recognized pregnancies end in miscarriage. Medical professionals do not completely understand the causes.

Stillbirth occurs in about 2 percent of pregnancies. The most common causes are problems with the placenta, abnormal chromosomes, poor growth, and infections.

## Dealing with Grief

The loss of a child by miscarriage or stillbirth can be very unexpected and painful for the parents. Most couples look forward to a baby's birth. They feel a great sense of attachment long before the birth. When they lose their baby, they may go through stages of grief similar to those experienced by the loss of a child that was already born. Sometimes these parents feel alone, and may blame themselves for the death. In most cases, however, these deaths are completely beyond the parents' control. Couples may need support to work through their grief. Most couples who suffer a miscarriage or stillbirth are able to have healthy children later.

✓ **Reading Check** **Recall** What percentage of pregnancies end in miscarriage?

## Birth Defects

Some babies survive pregnancy, but are born with serious problems that threaten their health or even their lives. A serious problem that threatens a baby's health, and is present at birth, is called a birth defect. There are hundreds of types of birth defects, each with its own set of symptoms. Some are so mild that no one would ever know the child has a birth defect. Others can result in lifelong disabilities or even death.

Approximately 120,000 babies are born each year in the United States with a birth defect. Scientists and medical professionals are working hard to understand the causes of birth defects. They hope that knowing the causes will help to decrease the number of babies born with birth defects, and improve the lives of children with birth defects.

**U**

**↑ Losing a Baby**
Sadly, some pregnancies end in a miscarriage or stillbirth. *Do you think experiencing a miscarriage would be different from a stillbirth? Why?*

## ▶ Explore the Photo

**Caption Answer** Answers will vary. Both result in the loss of the baby; however, parents might have more difficulty handling a stillbirth because they had more time to experience the coming baby.

**Discussion** Ask students how they think parents who have experienced a miscarriage or stillbirth might deal with the grief and loss they feel. (Answers will vary but should state that parents will likely deal with it as they would deal with any death of someone they cared about.)

For some couples, thinking of having a baby brings up concerns about genetic birth defects. This typically happens when the diseases seem to occur in the family of one or both of the parents. The couple should share their concerns with their family doctor or obstetrician. If there is a family history of one specific disease or symptoms of a genetic disorder, individuals may wish to be tested.

There are different types of genetic testing. Prior to pregnancy, testing can determine whether a person carries the traits for cystic fibrosis, Tay-Sachs disease, or sickle cell. If needed, the doctor can refer the couple to a genetic counselor. The counselor can discuss with the couple the likelihood of their passing on the condition, and the various options.

**Critical Thinking** Research the ethical, legal, and social issues regarding genetic testing. Then write a report in which you analyze how these issues can affect a couple's decision concerning whether to have children.

## Types and Causes of Birth Defects

Some birth defects cause an abnormality in the structure of the body. For example, an affected baby might have a misshapen foot, or an extra or missing finger. Other birth defects cause one or more systems of the body not to function properly. Blindness, deafness, and mental retardation are examples.

Not all birth defects are obvious at birth. Sometimes the abnormality is not discovered until months or years later. **Figure 4.3** on pages 108–109 describes types of birth defects as well as their causes, how to detect them, and treatment for them.

Scientists do not fully understand the causes of most birth defects. However, research continues to be done to find out why the defects occur. Scientists hope this understanding will lead to cures for the defects. So far, they have determined that there are four main causes for birth defects:

- Factors in the environment
- Hereditary factors
- Errors in chromosomes
- A combination of environmental and hereditary factors.

Research is continuing in each area.

### Environmental Causes

In the first few weeks after conception, a baby develops all the bodily systems needed for survival and a healthy, normal life. During this time, the baby depends on the mother's body for nourishment and oxygen.

This early development of the embryo is critical. Many choices the mother makes can affect the lifelong health of her baby. Some of these choices can occur before she even knows she is pregnant.

There may be environmental factors that the mother is unaware of that can affect the development of the baby. Here is a list of some of the environmental causes of birth defects. Which of these factors do you think the mother can control?

- The nutritional balance of the mother's diet.
- Any diseases or infections the mother has during pregnancy.
- Harmful substances the mother consumes, such as alcohol, over-the-counter medications, tobacco, and illegal drugs.
- Some medicines that benefit the mother but hurt the baby.
- Air pollution.
- Exposure to X-rays and high levels of radiation, or to certain chemicals such as solvents and pesticides, especially early in pregnancy.

---

**Genetic Birth Defects** Ask students: Do you think you would undergo genetic testing if you felt there was a possibility of having a baby with a genetic birth defect? (Students' answers will vary but should be thoughtful. Some people want to know early so they can better prepare for the challenge.)

**Critical Thinking** Reports will vary, but should analyze how ethical, legal, and social issues affect couples' decisions whether to bear children. For example, ethics might influence a couple to avoid pregnancy if they were likely to have a child with a birth defect.

---

### C Critical Thinking

**Problem Solving** Read the following scenario to students: Carlos and Tina have recently found out that their son Miguel is deaf. Carlos and Tina do not have any family members who are deaf, and they have never known anyone else with hearing loss. Have students make a list of questions Carlos and Tina might ask a specialist to help them cope with the situation and help Miguel live a full and healthy life. (Students' questions will vary but may include: What might have caused Miguel to be deaf? Can it be corrected through surgery? What services are available to help us learn how to help Miguel? Are there schools where Miguel can learn how to live in a world of hearing people?)

### W Writing Support

**Persuasive Writing**

**Taking Precautions** Discuss with students the list of environmental causes of birth defects. Have students do research to find ways to avoid the causes listed. Then have them write a letter to a prospective mother in which they persuade her to avoid environmental causes of birth defects. (Students' letters will vary but may include suggestions such as: avoid using harsh cleaning supplies, always wash your hands to stop the spread of bacteria that can lead to viruses, make sure to get vaccinated before getting pregnant, make sure physicians and dentists know about the pregnancy so they can avoid prescribing medications or administering tests that could harm the baby.)

## U Universal Access

**Auditory Learners** To meet the needs of verbal/auditory learners, arrange students into pairs. Have students make up questions and verbally quiz each other about birth defects. Students may choose to write true/false, multiple-choice, or short-answer questions. (Questions will vary but should relate to the content. Students can use information from Figure 4.3 to create their questions and answers.) **ELL**

## C Critical Thinking

**Drawing Conclusions** Read the following scenario to students: Three-year-old Rosa is an energetic, intelligent child, but her parents are worried about her health. She has a persistent cough and she is routinely underweight when she goes in for her regular medical checkups. Ask students to use the information in Figure 4.3 to help Rosa's doctor make a diagnosis. What test might the doctor order to determine Rosa's problem? (Students should conclude that Rosa's symptoms fit those of cystic fibrosis. They should indicate that a sweat test can be used to test Rosa.)

## R Reading Strategy

**Take Notes** Have students do research to find out about the life of Chris Burke. They should take notes during their reading and use the notes to write a half-page biography that describes his life as a child and as an adult. (Biographies will vary but should include that Chris Burke was born with Down syndrome and grew to become an actor. He was one of the stars of the television series "Life Goes On.")

**Figure 4.3 Birth Defects**

A birth defect can be a serious threat to a baby's health. *Which of these birth defects can be detected before the baby is born?*

| Birth Defect | Causes | Detections | Treatments |
|---|---|---|---|
| ✓**Cerebral Palsy** *A general term for a variety of problems of the motor system. Symptoms can include lack of coordination, stiffness, difficulty with speech, and paralysis.* | Causes vary but include damage to the brain before, during, or shortly after birth. | Motor skills are typically slow to develop during the first year of life. | Damage caused to the brain is irreversible. Physical therapy, speech therapy, surgery, and medication can often lessen the effects. |
| **Cleft Lip and Cleft Palate** *A gap in the upper lip or palate (the roof of the mouth) that causes problems with eating, swallowing, speech, and appearance.* | May be caused by hereditary, environmental factors, or both. | Conditions are apparent at birth. Often detectable by ultrasound before birth. | Surgery corrects the gap and helps eliminate problems associated with it. |
| ✓**Cystic Fibrosis (CF)** *Affects respiratory and digestive systems. Many with CF die before adulthood, although treatment now allows sufferers to live longer.* | Caused by inheriting defective recessive genes from both parents. Most commonly affects Caucasians. | Blood tests can identify carriers of the gene. Sweat tests can diagnose an affected child. | No known cure. Special diets, lung exercises, therapies, and medication can treat symptoms. |
| **Down Syndrome** *A group of problems that may include mental retardation; heart, blood, and digestive system difficulties; and poor muscle tone.* | The presence of an extra chromosome 21. | Can be detected in a fetus by amniocentesis or chorionic villi sampling, or after birth with a blood test. | No known cure. Treatment includes therapy, special educational assistance, and in some cases corrective surgery. |
| ✓**Muscular Dystrophy** *There are many different types; all involve a progressive weakness and shrinking of the muscles. Most common form begins between the ages of two and six.* | Most types are hereditary. Most common form is transmitted by female carriers of the gene but affects only males. | Recognizable once symptoms appear. Genetic counseling can identify carriers. | No known cure. Physical therapy can minimize the disabilities. |

**Figure 4.3 Birth Defects**

**Caption Answer** Cleft lip and cleft palate, Down syndrome, sickle cell anemia, spina bifida, and Tay-Sachs disease can be detected before the baby is born.

**Discussion** Ask students how knowing their baby has a birth defect before it is born might help parents. (Answers will vary but may include: it will give parents time to deal with their emotions before the birth of the child; it will give them time to learn about the problem and what they can expect; it can help them understand how to help the baby live as normal a life as possible.)

| Birth Defect | Causes | Detections | Treatments |
|---|---|---|---|
| **PKU (phenylketonuria)** *Condition in which the body is unable to process and use a specific protein present in nearly all foods. Brain damage and mental retardation can result.* | Defective recessive genes inherited from both parents. | Newborns are tested for PKU, as required by law in all states. | No known cure. If diagnosed early, a special diet can reduce or prevent brain damage. |
| **Sickle Cell Anemia** *Malformed red blood cells interfere with the supply of oxygen to all parts of the body. Symptoms include tiredness, lack of appetite, and pain. Can lead to early death.* | Defective recessive genes inherited from both parents. Most common in African Americans. | Genetic counseling can identify parents who carry the gene. Amniocentesis or chorionic villi sampling can identify it in a fetus. Blood tests can detect it after birth. | No known cure. Medication can help treat the symptoms. |
| **Spina Bifida and Hydrocephalus** *In spina bifida, an incompletely formed spinal cord may lead to stiff joints, partial paralysis, and problems with the kidneys and urinary tract. Seventy of every 100 children with spina bifida also have hydrocephalus, in which an excess of fluid surrounds the brain.* | Seems to be a combination of hereditary and environmental factors. Taking a folic acid supplement during pregnancy may reduce incidence. | Spina bifida is apparent at birth. Hydrocephalus is indicated by overly rapid growth of the head. Tests of the mother's blood, amniocentesis, and ultrasound can reveal suspected cases in a fetus. | Corrective surgery, physical therapy, and special schooling can minimize disabilities caused by spina bifida. Hydrocephalus can be helped by surgically implanting a shunt that relieves fluid build-up. |
| **Tay-Sachs Disease** *Caused by the lack of a specific chemical in the baby's blood. The body cannot process and use certain fats. This leads to severe brain damage and death, usually by age four.* | Defective recessive genes inherited from both parents. Most common in families of eastern European Jewish descent. | Amniocentesis or chorionic villi sampling can identify it in a fetus. Blood tests can identify carriers and can test for the condition after birth. | No known cure. Treatment involves trying to make the child comfortable. |

**S**

Section 4.2 Problems in Prenatal Development **109**

**Professional Development**

**Mini Clip**
**Reading: Extending the Big Idea**

A teacher assigns group collaborations and consensus building to promote student discussions about a reading selection.

**Teach** *cont.*

## S Skill Practice

### Guided Practice

**Make a Poster of Birth Defects**
Have students work in pairs to create a poster that warns parents or potential parents about birth defects. Posters should include information on a variety of birth defects (students may use information from Figure 4.3, Birth Defects). Posters should indicate what parents can do to help prevent birth defects in their children. (Posters should contain accurate information about a variety of birth defects and include preventative measures parents and potential parents can take.) **L1 ELL**

**Contact the March of Dimes**
The March of Dimes is an international organization whose goal is to prevent birth defects, premature births, and infant mortality. Have students contact a local representative of the March of Dimes and ask them to share what the organization does. Students can also e-mail the organization through their Web site. Students should share with the class what they learn about the March of Dimes. (Students' oral presentations should include basic information about the March of Dimes.) **L2**

**Compare and Contrast Birth Defect Research** Ask students to work in pairs to research medical efforts to prevent birth defects. Organizations students might research include: Centers for Disease Control and Prevention, the National Institutes of Health, and the National Birth Defects Prevention Network. Pairs of students should compile a one-page report of their findings and include a comparison and contrast of the efforts of at least two organizations. (Reports will vary according to which organizations students research. Reports should include a comparison and contrast the research efforts of at least two of the organizations.) **L3**

## Quiz

Ask students to answer the following questions:

1. **What is the definition of a birth defect?** (A birth defect is a serious problem that threatens a baby's health and is present at birth.)
2. **What causes PKU?** (PKU is caused by an inheritance of defective genes from both parents.)
3. **Give examples of some environmental factors that could cause birth defects.** (Birth defects can be caused by poor nutrition, diseases or infections the mother has during pregnancy, mother using harmful substances, use of some medicines, exposure to hazardous materials such as chemicals or radiation.)

## Reteach

### C₁ Critical Thinking

**Identify** Have students identify the concerns of parents who learn that their unborn baby has Down syndrome. Possible prompts: What expectations do parents have when expecting the birth of a child? How would such news affect these expectations? What kind of pressure (financial, social, and emotional) might affect parents under these circumstances? (Student responses will vary. Possible answers include: Parents might expect to play with their baby and take their child to school. The parents might have to lower their expectations for a child with Down syndrome. Medical bills could cause extra pressures on the family. Social pressures might result from not being able to take the child to many places. Emotional pressure might result from having to care for the child around the clock.)

### Hereditary Causes

Every person has approximately 20,000 to 25,000 genes that determine traits, such as eye color and height. These genes also direct the growth and development of all body systems. Half of the genes come from the mother and half from the father. It is normal for children to get five or six imperfect recessive genes passed on to them.

In most cases, a single copy of a faulty recessive gene will have no effect on the baby's development. However, sometimes both parents will pass on the same faulty recessive gene. This causes the baby to have a birth defect. When this happens, it is called *recessive inheritance.* Two conditions caused by recessive inheritance are Tay-Sachs disease and cystic fibrosis.

Sometimes a child will inherit a defective gene that is dominant. It is only necessary for this gene to be passed on by one parent for the child to have the resulting birth defect. This is called *dominant inheritance.* Huntington's disease, a birth defect that does not appear until middle age, is caused by dominant inheritance.

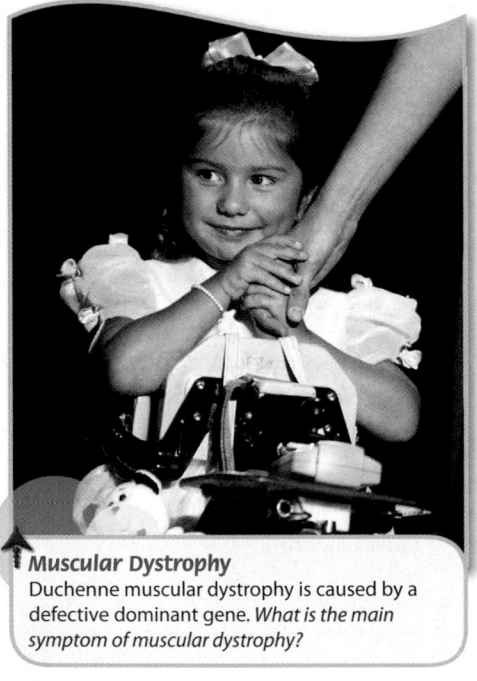

**Muscular Dystrophy**
Duchenne muscular dystrophy is caused by a defective dominant gene. *What is the main symptom of muscular dystrophy?*

Some inherited conditions only affect one gender. Hemophilia is a condition that prevents the blood from clotting. Like color blindness and Duchenne muscular dystrophy, hemophilia usually only affects males.

### Errors in Chromosomes

Several types of birth defects are caused by problems in the number or structure of chromosomes. An error may occur when an egg or sperm cell is developing. This can cause a baby to have too many or too few chromosomes, or to have broken or rearranged chromosomes. These are not hereditary defects because neither parent has the abnormal chromosome.

The most common birth defect of this type is Down syndrome. A child with Down syndrome may have some degree of mental retardation, plus physical problems. One in 800 babies has this condition. Under normal conditions, each sperm and egg cell carries 23 chromosomes. Sometimes an error occurs when an egg or sperm cell is forming, causing an extra copy of chromosome 21. Instead of having two copies of chromosome 21, the child has three. Because each chromosome carries hundreds of genes, the defect can interfere with development in many ways. This includes an increased risk of heart defects and leukemia, poor muscle tone, vision and hearing problems, delayed physical growth and motor development, and distinctive physical characteristics. The risk for having a child with Down syndrome is higher for mothers over the age of 35.

C₁

### Interaction of Heredity and Environment

Some birth defects are caused by a combination of heredity and the environment. For example, a child may inherit a tendency that may later lead to a heart defect. If a factor such as a drug or virus affects the baby during pregnancy, the baby will have the heart defect. If the baby did not inherit the gene for the heart defect *or* did not get exposed to the drug or virus, the heart would be normal. Because both the inherited factor and the environmental factor were present, the baby's heart had a defect.

R

Birth defects such as cleft lip, cleft palate, and spina bifida may be caused by a combination of hereditary and environmental fac-

### ➤ Explore the Photo

**Caption Answer** The main symptom of muscular dystrophy is progressive weakness and shrinking of the muscles. Symptoms often occur between the ages of two and six.

**Discussion** Ask students to explain the treatment for muscular dystrophy. (Treatment includes physical therapy, which can help minimize the disabilities. There is no known cure for muscular dystrophy.)

**Prenatal Testing**
An amniocentesis and other prenatal tests can provide valuable information. *Why are these tests not recommended for all pregnant women?*

tors. See Figure 4.3 on pages 108–109 for more information on these birth defects. Both cleft lip and cleft palate may be caused by a number of inherited genes joined with exposure during pregnancy to certain medications, infections, illnesses, or tobacco or alcohol. A genetic **predisposition**, or tendency, for spina bifida, combined with the use of certain medications during pregnancy, will increase the chance of a child having the defect.

## Prevention and Diagnosis of Birth Defects

It can be challenging for a child born with a **serious**, or severe, birth defect to lead a normal, productive life. Other family members are affected by the emotional and financial strain the defect causes. However, advances in treatment and support groups are helping children and their families cope. Not all causes of birth defects can be anticipated or controlled. There are several things that couples can do, though, to lessen the chances of having a child with birth defects.

Couples who are planning to become parents should get a checkup to evaluate their overall health before trying to conceive. They can discuss lifestyle changes that may improve their chances for a healthy baby. For example, women should stop using tobacco and alcohol prior to pregnancy. Both of these can lead to health problems and birth defects.

Because many women do not know they are pregnant in the early weeks, it is safer to quit smoking and drinking before there is a possibility of pregnancy. Men are also advised to avoid or drink less alcohol, since it has been linked to low sperm count.

Once a woman is pregnant, she should visit her doctor for prenatal care. This care helps ensure a successful pregnancy. The doctor can monitor the mother's health and the baby's growth and development throughout the pregnancy. The mother should continue to avoid substances such as alcohol, drugs, and tobacco. She can talk to her doctor or pharmacist about the effects of any over-the-counter and prescription medications on her baby. A pregnant woman should not take any medication without her doctor's approval.

### Genetic Counseling

Some people seek genetic counseling to assess their risk of having a child with a birth defect that is caused by a defect in the genes.

Section 4.2   Problems in Prenatal Development   **111**

---

**➤ Explore the Photo**

**Caption Answer** Answers will vary; the tests can be expensive and some of them, such as amniocentesis, present risks to the fetus.

**Discussion** Ask students to explain what an ultrasound can test for. (Ultrasounds can check the development of the baby. They can detect certain birth defects and problems with the baby's skeletal, circulatory, or nervous system.)

## Reteach *cont.*

**R Reading Strategy**

**Identifying Facts** Have each student bring in one newspaper, magazine, or Internet article containing information that focuses on the interaction of heredity and environment as a cause of birth defects. Have students work in pairs and read each other's articles. Then ask students to name one interesting fact they learned about birth defects from their reading. Students should share their facts with the rest of the class. (Students' facts will vary. You might ask a volunteer to write the facts on the board.)

**C₂ Critical Thinking**

**Brainstorm** Discuss the following information with students: The man's health can be just as vital as a woman's when trying to conceive a baby. Drinking alcohol, smoking, or using illegal drugs can lead to problems in infertility as well as serious birth defects. Stress and prescription drugs can cause low sperm count. Ask students to brainstorm ways a father can be a responsible parent before conception occurs. Have a volunteer write students' answers on the board. (Students answers will vary. Possible answers include: The father can help make sure the mother takes good care of herself and he can have a good job so he can support the family.) **ELL**

**Mc Graw Hill Professional Development**

**Mini Clip**
**ELL: Group Discussions**

Students discuss academic content they have just read.

## Reteach *cont.*

**Auditory Learners** To help meet the needs of auditory learners, divide the class into groups. Have groups discuss and debate what they might do if they were told by a genetic counselor that there was a possibility that any of their future children could have Tay-Sachs disease. This means that the child would not live past the age of four. (Students' answers will vary. Students should back up their answers with logical reasoning.)

**C** **Critical Thinking**

**Drawing Conclusions** Have students draw conclusions about the purpose of genetic counseling. Ask students if they think learning information about possible birth defects, minor or serious, is worth knowing. (Students' answers will likely vary from those who believe a life is precious whether or not it has physical or mental issues, to those who would not want the responsibility of bringing a life with defects into the world.)

**W** **Writing Support**

**Explanation**

**Doctor's Orders** Read the following questions aloud to the class and then write them on the board: Do you think most doctors recommend the same type of tests for all women? What are the determining factors for each test? Do you think these tests are necessary for every pregnant woman? Have students write a one-page explanation to answer the questions. (Explanations will vary but should be based on the information found in the text. Students should use complete sentences and proper grammar to compose their explanations.)

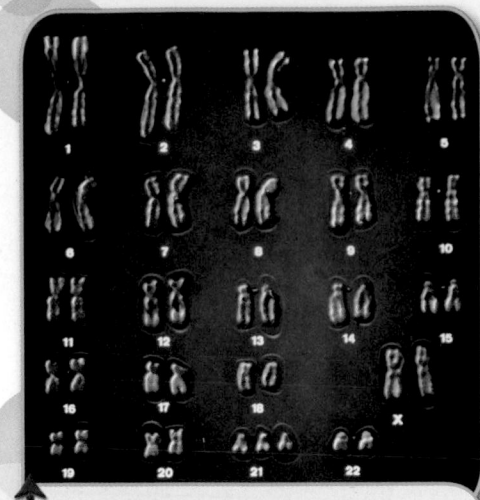

**Down Syndrome**
The fluid obtained from amniocentesis can be used to check chromosomes. *In these chromosomes, Down syndrome is shown by what unusual circumstance?*

There may be a history of birth defects in the family. Some couples may already have a child with a birth defect and want to learn more about the risks for future children. Genetic counselors can explain the options and risks.

Family doctors can perform genetic counseling, but most patients are referred to a genetic counselor. This specialist usually begins by evaluating the family history of both members of the couple. This includes information such as the medical histories, diseases, and causes of death of all known family members.

Along with the family history, a genetic counselor will usually request a physical exam for both parents. If specific birth defects are of concern, some other members of the family may receive physical exams as well. Special lab tests may also be performed. Small samples of blood and body tissue may be analyzed. For example, a blood sample can be tested to determine whether the parents are carriers for the gene that causes cystic fibrosis.

Once all of the testing is complete, the genetic counselor can usually tell the couple what their risks are for having a child with

certain genetic birth defects. It is the couple's decision whether or not to have children. If they do, they will be aware of extra testing that may be needed during pregnancy to closely monitor the development of the baby.

### Prenatal Tests

More than 100 kinds of birth defects can now be detected before a baby is born. There are many tests that are standard for prenatal care in this country. These help a doctor decide whether or not a baby might have a birth defect. These tests can help determine what treatments, if any, are needed for the child before or after birth.

Sometimes prenatal tests are simple blood tests. Other tests involve procedures that carry more risks. The couple must weigh the potential value of the information to be gained against possible risks for the developing baby or the mother. Here are examples of some common prenatal tests.

**Alpha-fetoprotein (AFP)** This blood test is performed on the expectant mother between weeks 15 and 20 of a pregnancy. AFP is a protein produced in the liver of the fetus that is evident in the mother's blood. Abnormal AFP levels can indicate a possible birth defect. Further testing can be done to determine if a birth defect does exist, and what it might be.

**Ultrasound** Ultrasound is a test that uses sound waves to make a video image of an unborn baby. This image is called a *sonogram*. It can help the doctor monitor the development of the baby, pinpoint the baby's age, and detect certain birth defects. Problems with the baby's skeletal, circulatory, or nervous system may be detected during an ultrasound. The sonogram also helps confirm the due date and the presence of more than one fetus.

Many women will have an ultrasound during their pregnancy, usually near the 20th week. Many doctors now do 3D ultrasounds, which give more detailed images and information about the baby's development. Research has shown that an ultrasound poses no threat to the unborn child or the mother. However, it should be performed only when there is a valid medical reason for doing so.

### ▶ Explore the Photo

**Caption Answer** Down syndrome is shown by an extra 21st chromosome. Women age 35 or older run a greater risk of having a child with Down syndrome.

**Discussion** Ask students to explain the treatment for Down syndrome. (Treatment includes therapy, special educational assistance, and in some cases, corrective surgery.)

**Amniocentesis** The process of withdrawing a sample of the amniotic fluid surrounding the unborn baby is called **amniocentesis** (ˌam-nē-ō-(ˌ)sen-ˈtē-səs). The doctor uses the view from an ultrasound to guide a needle through the mother's abdomen into the amniotic sac. Some cells from the fetus are in the amniotic fluid. These cells are then taken to a lab and tested for evidence of birth defects and other health problems.

Amniocentesis is most often used as a test for Down syndrome when the expectant mother is age 35 or older. The test may also be given if uncertain results have been obtained from an ultrasound or AFP blood test. Amniocentesis involves some risk to the fetus and is performed only when there is a strong medical reason to do so. It can be done between the 15th and 20th week of pregnancy.

**Chorionic Villi Sampling** A prenatal test that uses a sample of the tissue from the membrane that encases the fetus to check for specific birth defects is called chorionic villi sampling (ˌkȯr-ē-ˈä-nik ˈvi-ˌlī). Samples of the tissue are cut or suctioned off and analyzed.

Chorionic villi sampling tests for the same disorders as amniocentesis. This test does not detect neural tube defects though. It is used less often because its risks are greater. One advantage is that it can be done much earlier in the pregnancy than amniocentesis. Chorionic villi sampling is usually done between the 10th and 12th week of pregnancy.

**New Prenatal Diagnosis** Several methods of prenatal diagnosis are now in experimental stages. These may someday provide more accurate information earlier in a pregnancy. For example, it is possible to view the fetus directly through a special instrument called a *laparoscope*. Doctors can get samples of fetal blood and tissue, and even do surgery on an unborn child. Currently, these procedures carry a risk. New technology may make these procedures safe for widespread use in the future.

---

**Study Tools**

Have students go to the Online Learning Center at **glencoe.com**:

- Take the **Practice Test**.
- Download **Study-to-Go** content.

Use the **Student Activity Workbook** for additional practice.

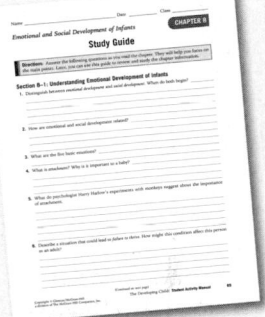

### Close

**Culminating Activity**

**Summarize** Have students summarize what couples planning to become parents can do to help prevent birth defects. (Answers will vary but may include: Couples can evaluate their overall health and make necessary lifestyle changes.)

 **NCLB** connects academic correlations to book content.

---

## Section 4.2 — After You Read

### Review Key Concepts

1. **Summarize** the causes of stillbirth.
2. **List** the four categories of birth defects.

### Practice Academic Skills

 **English Language Arts**

3. Studies show that taking prenatal vitamins with folic acid can help prevent birth defects. Research the amounts of folic acid recommended and how it can help prevent defects. Use the information from your research to create a handout promoting the use of prenatal vitamins. Use art or photos to make your handout visually appealing.

> **NCTE 8** Use information resources to gather information and create and communicate knowledge.

 **Science**

4. Choose one of the birth defects listed in Figure 4.3. Use print or online resources to learn about the current research being done on the causes or treatments of this birth defect. Write a brief report explaining what you learned.

> **NSES A** Develop abilities necessary to do scientific inquiry, understanding about scientific inquiry.

 **Check Your Answers** Check your answers at this book's Online Learning Center at **glencoe.com**.

---

Section 4.2   Problems in Prenatal Development   **113**

---

### Section 4.2 — After You Read

**Review Key Concepts**

1. Stillbirth is caused by problems with the placenta, abnormal chromosomes, poor growth, and infections.
2. Four main areas include environmental causes, hereditary causes, errors in chromosomes, and a combination of heredity and environment.

**Practice Academic Skills**

3. Handouts will vary. Students should offer facts to support the claims and recommendations in their brochures.
4. Reports will vary. Students should discuss current research on either the causes or the treatments of the chosen birth defect.

## Focus

### Bell Ringer Activity

**Unsafe Environments**
Ask students to give examples of situations and environments that a pregnant woman should avoid. Ask: In what ways can alcohol and other drugs impact prenatal development? (Answers will vary but students may say that alcohol and other drugs can cause serious birth defects.)

## Preteaching

### Vocabulary

Tell students that the suffix *-osis* added to a word means an abnormal or diseased condition. Examples include the vocabulary term toxoplasmosis, leukosis (leukemia in animals), and myosclerosis (hardening of the muscle).

### Graphic Organizer

 The Graphic Organizer is also on the TeacherWorks CD.

(Graphic Organizers should include: Drugs—alcohol, prescription drugs, over-the-counter drugs, caffeine, tobacco, illegal drugs; environmental hazards—X-rays, hazardous substances and chemicals; diseases and infections—rubella, toxoplasmosis, chicken pox (varicella), sexually transmitted diseases (STDs))

**NCLB** NCLB connects academic correlations to book content.

---

## Reading Guide

### Before You Read

**Categorize**  Before reading, skim this section to determine whether the dangers to baby can be placed into categories. As you read, categorize each type of danger to help you see the big picture.

### Read to Learn
#### Key Concepts

- **Summarize** the hazards that alcohol and other drugs pose to prenatal development.
- **Assess** why environmental hazards must be avoided during pregnancy.
- **Describe** how a fetus can be affected by certain illnesses the mother may contract.

**D**

### Main Idea

A fetus needs to be protected from many dangers. These include the mother drinking alcohol or taking other drugs, environmental hazards, diseases, and infections.

### Content Vocabulary

◇ fetal alcohol syndrome (FAS)
◇ fetal alcohol effects
◇ SIDS
◇ toxoplasmosis

 **Graphic Organizer**  Go to this book's Online Learning Center at **glencoe.com** to print out this graphic organizer.

### Academic Vocabulary

You will find these words in your reading and on your tests. Use the glossary to look up their definitions if necessary.
- deformity
- congenital

### Graphic Organizer

As you read, list examples of each of the three types of dangers that can affect a baby. Use a chart like the one shown to help organize your information. Add additional boxes as needed.

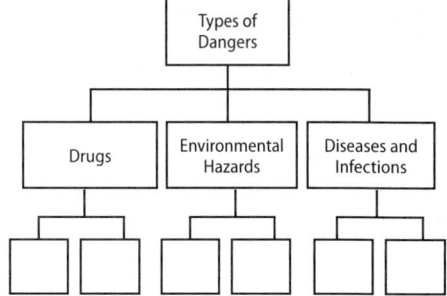

---

**NCLB**

### Academic Standards · · · · · · · · · · · · · · · · · · · · · · · · · · · · · ·

 **English Language Arts**
**NCTE 5**  Use different writing process elements to communicate effectively.

 **Science**
**NSES F**  Develop understanding of personal and community health; and environmental quality.

---

**NCTE** *National Council of Teachers of English*
**NCTM** *National Council of Teachers of Mathematics*

**NSES** *National Science Education Standards*
**NCSS** *National Council for the Social Studies*

---

## Reading Guide

### Before You Read

Point out to students that the title of this section is somewhat negative. Tell students that, while there are many dangers to be aware of, common sense and knowledge of things that might be harmful to the baby will go a long way in keeping baby safe.

### D Develop Concepts

**Main Idea**  Discuss the main idea with the students. Ask students if they think most mothers are aware of things that can be dangerous to a fetus. (Students' answers will vary. Ask students to give reasons for their answers.)

## Effects of Alcohol and Other Drugs on Pregnancy

The mother-to-be has a big responsibility throughout her pregnancy. She must do everything possible to increase the chances of having a healthy baby. She needs to consider the effects of her actions on her unborn child. She must take care of herself physically and emotionally, and avoid potential dangers.

An essential part of good prenatal care is avoiding hazards such as alcohol and other drugs, smoking, X-rays, hazardous chemicals and other substances, and infections. Researchers and doctors believe that drugs consumed during pregnancy are among the major causes of birth defects linked to environmental factors. These drugs include:

- Alcohol, in any form.
- Prescription and over-the-counter medicines.
- Caffeine. This is found in foods such as chocolate, and beverages. The safety of caffeine during pregnancy is controversial. However, until researchers know more about its effects, it is wise to avoid caffeine.

- Nicotine and other toxic chemicals found in cigarettes.
- Illegal drugs such as heroin, LSD, ecstasy, marijuana, and cocaine.
- Inhalants. These are fumes that are inhaled into the lungs.

### Alcohol

Sometimes people forget that alcohol is a drug. It is an especially dangerous one for unborn children. When a pregnant woman drinks alcohol, she puts her baby at great risk. Anything the mother consumes or inhales is passed directly to her child through the placenta. This is true for alcohol too. Even a small amount of alcohol can harm the developing systems of the baby.

Doctors do not know how much alcohol it takes to endanger a developing baby. There is no known safe amount of alcohol that a pregnant woman can drink. For this reason, most doctors recommend that women consume no alcohol when they are trying to become pregnant or during the pregnancy. Abstaining from alcohol will prevent any negative effects on the baby related to alcohol.

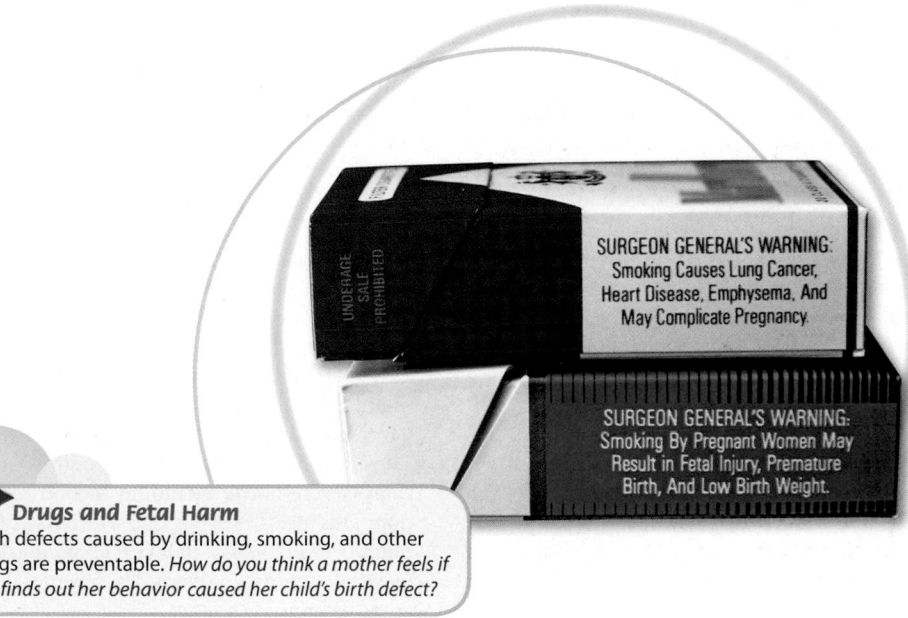

**Drugs and Fetal Harm**
Birth defects caused by drinking, smoking, and other drugs are preventable. *How do you think a mother feels if she finds out her behavior caused her child's birth defect?*

SURGEON GENERAL'S WARNING:
Smoking Causes Lung Cancer, Heart Disease, Emphysema, And May Complicate Pregnancy.

SURGEON GENERAL'S WARNING:
Smoking By Pregnant Women May Result in Fetal Injury, Premature Birth, And Low Birth Weight.

**Section 4.3** Avoiding Dangers to the Baby **115**

**Discussion Starter**

**Awareness** Ask students if they believe the average pregnant woman today understands the risks associated with alcohol consumption more clearly than pregnant women did thirty years ago. What do they think accounts for these changes? (Students' answers will vary. Students may say that better education makes pregnant women today more aware of the risks associated with alcohol consumption.)

**C Critical Thinking**

**Drawing Conclusions** Tell students that many women are pregnant for up to two months or more before they realize it. Ask: How might this impact the development of a healthy fetus? If a woman who does not know she is pregnant drinks alcohol, should the woman be punished for placing her unborn child in danger? (Students' answers will vary but should mention that during the months the woman didn't know she was pregnant, she could have consumed alcohol or other drugs that may harm the fetus. Some students may think a woman should be punished for jeopardizing the health of her fetus, others may say that if she was unaware, she should not be punished.)

### Explore the Photo

**Caption Answer** Answers will vary; she will probably feel guilty because she could have prevented the damage to the baby.

**Discussion** Have a volunteer read the warnings on the packages of cigarettes in the photo. Ask students if they feel that women who smoke during pregnancy and give birth to a baby with complications can honestly deny that they knew smoking could harm their baby. (Responses will vary; most students should acknowledge that the warnings on packages of cigarettes are very clear.)

## S Skill Practice

### Guided Practice

**Create a Flyer** Have students create a flyer to make pregnant women aware of the potential hazards of some prescription and over-the-counter drugs on the developing fetus. The flyers should use symbols as well as text to explain the effects of such medications. (Flyers should contain information about the affects of both prescription and OTC drugs on the developing fetus. Encourage students to illustrate their flyers with symbols or artwork.) **L1**

**Research Supplements** Many people routinely take herbal supplements to promote good health. However, some of these supplements can harm a developing fetus when consumed by a pregnant woman. Have students research an herbal supplement that has been shown to be harmful to a developing fetus. The students should then write a paragraph to describe what supplement they found and what the effects of it might be. Have students share their paragraphs with the class. (Possible answers: senna may cause miscarriage and licorice induces preterm delivery.) **L2**

**Analyze Situations** Read the following scenario to students: Early Sunday morning, a pregnant woman finds that she is experiencing common cold symptoms. She is having trouble sleeping as well. What can she do until she is able to see a doctor? Students should write a one-page essay with their analysis of the situation. Ask volunteers to share their essays with the class. (Essays should indicate that the woman should avoid all cold medicines or medicines of any kind until she speaks to her doctor. She might try drinking warm milk to help her sleep.) **L3**

## SAFE CHILD HEALTHY CHILD

### How Does Alcohol Affect a Fetus?

The dangers of alcohol to an unborn fetus may seem like common sense. Many people are unaware just how dangerous this common drug can be though.

Consuming alcohol during pregnancy can also cause serious health problems for the baby. The alcohol passes directly to the baby through the placenta. It may cause problems in development, especially that of the brain. Even small amounts of alcohol can harm the baby. Greater amounts have been linked to fetal alcohol syndrome (FAS), which causes life-long physical and mental disabilities. Expectant mothers can avoid these risks by completely avoiding alcohol during pregnancy.

**Be Prepared** Imagine that your aunt is pregnant and thinks it is fine to drink occasionally. Conduct research to learn more about how even occasional drinking can affect a fetus. Create a one-page report explaining why any amount of alcohol is unsafe.

**Fetal alcohol syndrome (FAS)** is an incurable condition found in some children of mothers who consumed alcohol during pregnancy. FAS includes a wide range of physical and mental disabilities that last a lifetime.

One in five babies born with FAS does not live to see his or her first birthday. Those who do survive can suffer many problems. These can include delayed physical growth; heart, liver, or kidney defects; hyperactivity; and facial deformity. A **deformity** is a defect in a structure.

Some babies with FAS are mentally retarded. Others have difficulties with learning, attention, memory, or problem solving. Alcohol can interfere with tissue growth and development. Brain tissue is easily injured by alcohol. Other common problems include poor coordination and difficulty controlling behavior.

Some children may suffer from fetal alcohol effects. Like FAS, **fetal alcohol effects** are abnormalities caused by the mother consuming alcohol during pregnancy. These children suffer from many of the same problems as those with FAS, but to a lesser degree.

The extent of damage to the child is often directly related to the amount of alcohol the mother consumed during pregnancy. It may also be affected by the stage of pregnancy when she drank. For example, women who binge drink in the early stages of pregnancy may have an increased risk of having a baby with FAS. Binge drinking means to drink a lot in a short amount of time. The combination of alcohol with other drugs also affects the degree of damage to the child.

## Prescription Drugs and Over-the-Counter Drugs

An expectant mother should check with her doctor every time she considers using any type of medication, vitamin, or herbal supplement. There is no such thing as a completely safe drug for a developing fetus.

An extreme example of an unsafe medication is thalidomide. This drug was prescribed to women in the 1950s to relieve morning sickness. Before its devastating effects were discovered, more than 5,000 babies were born with severe birth defects, such as missing or deformed arms and legs. Had doctors known the effects of this drug, they never would have prescribed it.

More recently, a prescription medicine for acne proved harmful to unborn children. When taken during pregnancy, the drug can cause serious birth defects. Therefore, it is not prescribed for pregnant women or those who may become pregnant.

The first three months of pregnancy are the most critical because the baby's body systems, including the brain, are being formed. The chemicals found in some medications can cause severe harm, including mental retardation. This includes drugs sold without prescriptions, or over-the-counter (OTC) medications. Even something as seemingly harmless as an antacid can harm a fetus.

**S**

## SAFE CHILD HEALTHY CHILD

### How Does Alcohol Affect a Fetus?

**Discussion** According to studies, most people do not read the warning labels on products that contain alcohol. Ask students what they feel the government should do. (Responses will vary. Some students may feel it is not the government's responsibility. Others may think the government needs to make the warnings stronger.)

**Be Prepared** The one-page report should explain that because alcohol passes easily through the placenta to the baby, even occasional drinking can lead to fetal alcohol effects such as developmental abnormalities, learning difficulties, premature birth, and low birth weight.

In the fourth through ninth months of pregnancy, harmful substances may cause slow growth, infections, or bleeding at birth. Drugs taken shortly before delivery will still be in the baby's bloodstream after birth.

Sometimes the expectant mother needs medication for a specific medical condition. For example, some women may need to take medications for epilepsy, diabetes, or high blood pressure. A pregnant woman can take these, as long as her doctor prescribes them and she takes them correctly. Medications that are not absolutely necessary should be avoided.

## Caffeine

Caffeine is in the beverages many people drink each day, such as coffee, tea, cocoa, and most soft drinks. It is also present in some foods and many over-the-counter medications. Because it is consumed so frequently, caffeine is often not considered a drug, but it is.

Caffeine passes easily from a mother to her fetus through the placenta. The fetus may have higher blood levels of caffeine than the mother because of its immature metabolism. Caffeine can increase fetal heart rate and movement.

Small amounts of caffeine, such as two cups of coffee or soft drinks per day, do not appear to pose great pregnancy risks. However, larger quantities have been associated with a variety of prenatal problems. That is why most doctors advise women to avoid caffeine during pregnancy.

When women consume large amounts of caffeine during pregnancy, there is an increased risk of miscarriage, premature birth, and low birth weight. There is also a higher risk of infant death. Birth weight is a critical factor to a baby's survival. Low birth weight is a weight of less than 5 pounds, 8 ounces (2.5 kg) at birth. Babies with low birth weight may have serious health problems as newborns and are at greater risk of long-term problems.

Caffeine can draw fluid and calcium out of the body. It may also interfere with the absorption of iron. These are all vital to the health of the mother and the developing fetus. In addition, drinks with caffeine, such as coffee and tea, can make you feel full. This will spoil your appetite for nutritious foods. Soft drinks may have other chemicals and large amounts of sugar, in addition to the caffeine. The caffeine and sugar can also worsen mood swings and prevent the mother from getting needed rest.

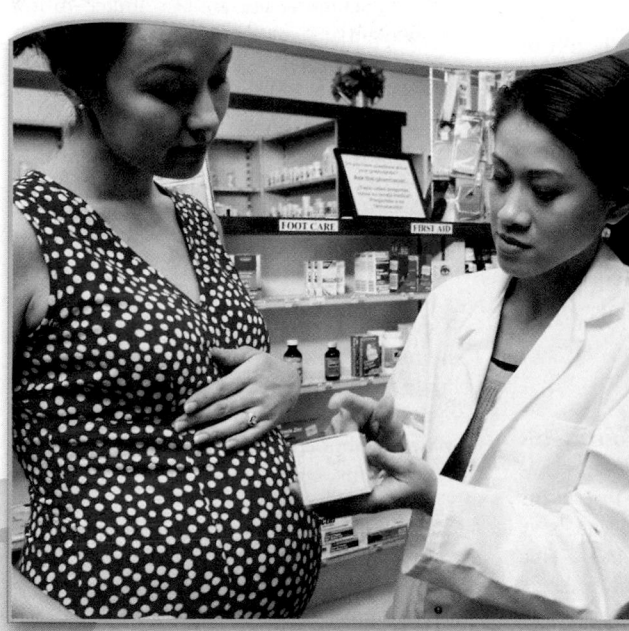

**OTC Drugs and Pregnancy**
Even common medicines that are sold in pharmacies and supermarkets may be unsafe for an unborn baby. *How can a pregnant woman be sure that a medicine is safe?*

## Teach *cont.*

### R Reading Strategy

**Analyze** Have students chart the amount of caffeine found in single serving sizes of ten foods and beverages that they, their family members, or their friends consume regularly. Discuss the level of risk involved to a pregnant woman consuming the foods and beverages students listed in their charts. Ask students if they feel consuming any of the foods while pregnant would be worth the risk. (Students' answers will vary depending on the foods charted. Students might suggest that consuming any amount of caffeine is not worth the risk for a pregnant woman.) **ELL**

### C Critical Thinking

**Drawing Conclusions** Tell students that caffeine is a diuretic, which means it increases the amount of urine passed. If a pregnant woman passes too much urine, she may become dehydrated and this can harm the baby. Experts and studies indicate that moderate consumption of caffeine during pregnancy is acceptable. However, there is disagreement on what is a moderate amount. Ask students what advice they would give a pregnant woman concerning caffeine intake. (Students' answers will vary but may suggest that consuming any amount of caffeine just is not worth the risk of harm it may cause the baby.)

### Explore the Photo

**Caption Answer** To be sure that a medication is safe for a pregnant woman to take, she should ask a health-care professional.

**Discussion** The text states that "There is no such thing as a completely safe drug for a developing fetus." Ask students to state what this means to them. How should pregnant women respond to this knowledge? (Responses will vary; if possible, pregnant women should avoid all drugs during their pregnancy.)

## Assess

### Quiz

Ask students to answer the following questions:

1. **What are some of the characteristics of babies with FAS?** (Babies with FAS may have facial deformity, delayed physical growth, heart defects, hyperactivity, mental retardation, or severe learning problems.)

2. **Why are the first three months of pregnancy a particularly dangerous time to expose the baby to chemicals found in medicines, including those sold over the counter?** (The first three months is when the baby's body systems are forming.)

3. **What could happen to babies whose mothers smoke during pregnancy?** (Babies may have low birth weights, higher risk of premature birth, respiratory infections, and allergies after birth.)

## Reteach

### U Universal Access

**Verbal Learners** Tell students that many communities have banned smoking in restaurants. People who breathe secondhand smoke often experience problems such as a runny nose, irritated eyes, and sneezing. Pregnant women should avoid smoke. Studies have shown decreased oxygen levels and increased carbon monoxide levels in fetuses where the mother has been exposed to secondhand smoke. Have students work in groups to write a letter to their congressman supporting banning smoking in all public places. (Letters will vary. If your area already has a ban on smoking in public areas, students should state their support of the decision in their letters.)

**118**

---

## What Would You Do?

### Stopping Smoking

Lori and her husband want to have a baby, so Lori has been exercising and watching what she eats. Unfortunately, Lori has been a smoker for several years. She knows that she needs to stop smoking before she becomes pregnant. Lori says, "I have tried almost everything to quit: the nicotine patch, other over-the-counter treatments, classes. Nothing worked. I've got to make it work this time. I want to do everything possible to improve my baby's chances for a healthy life. But it's hard when I've failed so many times in the past."

✏ **Write About It** Imagine you are a friend of Lori's. Write a script in which you talk with Lori about specific problems for both her and her baby associated with smoking. Also offer tips that might help her quit. If possible, base your tips on what you have done to break a bad habit.

### Tobacco

U Many studies have shown that the nicotine found in tobacco is harmful to the health of any person. It is especially harmful to a baby's development before birth. Smoking has been shown to cause low birth weights. The more a mother smokes, the smaller her baby is likely to be at birth. Heavy smoking is believed to cause premature birth as well. Finally, smoking during pregnancy is linked to respiratory infections and allergies among children after they are born. Nicotine from secondhand smoke has similar effects.

### Illegal Drugs

Illegal drugs should never be used. This is especially true for women who are pregnant. In addition to the effects on the mother's health, the use of illegal drugs can have devastating effects for an unborn baby. This includes cocaine, marijuana, and other illegal substances.

**118** Chapter 4 Prenatal Development

---

A mother who is addicted to a drug usually passes the addiction on to her baby. All drugs in the mother's bloodstream pass through the placenta to the baby. As a result, addicted newborns may suffer the consequences throughout their lives.

Right after birth, infants with an inherited drug addiction must go through a painful period of withdrawal. This is because the body is no longer receiving the drug upon which it depends. Babies that survive withdrawal have an uncertain future. Many experts believe that the long-term effects of prenatal addiction can be severe. Many of these children have learning and behavioral difficulties.

Cocaine has been proven to increase the risk of miscarriage when used during the early stages of pregnancy. It may also cause stillbirth or premature birth. Cocaine may cause the unborn child to have a stroke. This can result in brain damage, a heart attack, serious birth defects, or even death. Fetuses exposed to cocaine tend to have a low birth weight, smaller heads than other newborns, and a risk of seizures and sudden infant death syndrome. **SIDS**, or sudden infant death syndrome, is the sudden, unexpected death of a baby under one year of age with no clear cause. Marijuana and methamphetamine use are also linked to low birth weight and premature delivery.

Babies exposed to cocaine may also have tremors, exaggerated startle response, sleep and feeding difficulties, irritability, and developmental delay. All of these problems may persist into the school years. Use of marijuana and methamphetamines during pregnancy can cause breathing difficulties, poor attention span, drowsiness, or heart defects in children.

Researchers are still learning about the effects of the drug ecstasy on unborn children. The results are not good. Recent studies have shown that babies of women who take ecstasy are more likely to be born with heart disease or a physical abnormality. This drug is not safe to take any time, but it is especially unsafe during pregnancy.

✓ **Reading Check** **List** What kinds of drugs, other than alcohol, can harm a developing baby?

---

## What Would You Do?

**Write About It** The script should discuss specific problems that can be caused by smoking. Examples include birth defects and low birth weight. Tips for quitting might include thinking about her future with a healthy baby.

✓ **Reading Check**

**List** Both prescription and over-the-counter medicines, caffeine, nicotine, illegal drugs, and inhalants can harm a developing baby.

## Environmental Hazards

Environmental hazards are all around us. However, they may not be obvious. For these reasons, it is vital that pregnant women be aware of them. Two possible hazards to unborn babies are X-rays and chemicals such as pesticides and mercury.

### X-rays

X-rays present a potential danger to the unborn baby. Radiation from X-rays, or from other sources, can cause birth defects. There has been a great deal of debate about the safety of X-rays during pregnancy. If an X-ray is necessary due to an accident, illness, or dental work, the mother should inform the medical staff that she is pregnant. Special precautions can be taken to make sure the fetus is not exposed to much radiation. Patients should always wear abdominal shields during an X-ray to reduce the amount of radiation they are exposed to.

Dental X-rays are generally considered safe, because they are focused very far from the uterus. Many dentists still delay routine X-rays for a patient until after she has given birth.

### Hazardous Substances and Chemicals

A pregnant woman must be careful about hazardous substances in her home and work environment. Some of these substances include:

- Paint. Low-odor latex paint in a well-ventilated area may not pose a problem. A woman should check with her doctor before any exposure.
- Pesticides used to exterminate bugs.
- Lead, in water and paint.
- Carbon monoxide.
- Mercury, found in some fish such as swordfish and shark.
- Solvents, paint thinners, and formaldehyde (used in some workplaces).

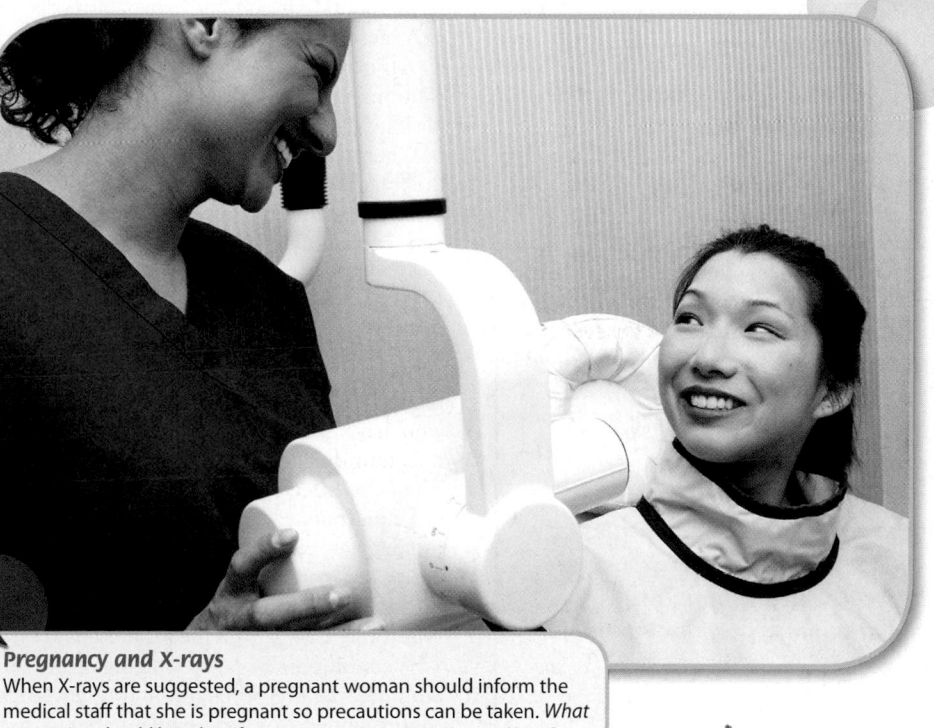

**↑ Pregnancy and X-rays**
When X-rays are suggested, a pregnant woman should inform the medical staff that she is pregnant so precautions can be taken. *What precaution should be taken if a pregnant woman requires an X-ray?*

Section 4.3    Avoiding Dangers to the Baby    **119**

### Reteach *cont.*

### C Critical Thinking

**Drawing Conclusions** Many types of chemicals are harmful if inhaled. Ask students: How does the harmful substance travel from the lungs when inhaled through the body to the fetus? What kind of precautions can a woman take to avoid inhaling these harmful substances? (Students should be aware that inhaled substances can travel through the body to the fetus via the mother's blood stream. Pregnant women can avoid places where harmful chemicals are found and they can avoid using household cleaners.)

### W Writing Support

**Research Report**

**Adverse Effects** Many common chemicals can have adverse effects on a developing fetus. Divide the class into small groups. Have groups research paint, pesticides, lead, mercury, and solvents to determine whether or not any alternatives exist that perform the same functions as these chemical-based products. The groups should create a presentation to deliver the results of their research to the rest of the class. (During their research students should find that there are many environmentally friendly and chemical free paints and cleaners on the market today. Group's presentations should focus on these "green" alternatives to chemical-based products.)

**Professional Development**

**Mini Clip**
**Reading: Flexible Groupings**

Teachers use strategies of flexible groupings and partner sharing to encourage and promote student discussions.

---

### ▶ Explore the Photo

**Caption Answer** A pregnant woman should inform the medical staff that she is pregnant and her abdomen should be shielded during the X-ray.

**Discussion** Even though dental X-rays are generally considered safe, many dentists cover all patients with a shield while X-rays are taken. Ask students why they think dentists do this. (Responses will vary; students should recognize that even a small amount of radiation can be harmful so the dentists are taking precautions.)

**Reteach** *cont.*

## W Writing Support

### Descriptive Paragraph

**Analyzing Infections** Toxoplasmosis is caused by a parasite, chicken pox is caused by a virus, and strep throat can be caused by bacteria or a virus. Have students research the differences between parasites, viruses, and bacteria. Ask students which kinds of infections humans have had the most success curing. Which have been the most difficult to fight? Ask students to write their results in a descriptive paragraph. (Students' paragraphs should indicate that infections caused by bacteria and parasites are more readily cured than infections caused by viruses.)

## C₁ Critical Thinking

**Problem Solving** Read this scenario to students: Adam and Jill have three cats they adopted several years ago from an animal shelter. When Jill discovers she is pregnant, the doctor advises her to avoid cat waste completely throughout her pregnancy, as cats carry the parasite that causes toxoplasmosis. Ask students to identify the problem(s) in this scenario. What are some possible solutions to these problem(s)? (The problem is that if Jill contracts toxoplasmosis from the cats, it could place the unborn child at risk of blindness, hearing loss, learning disabilities, long-term mental disabilities, and possibly, death. They could get rid of the cats, or make the cats stay outdoors, or Adam could do the cleaning of the cat box.)

---

If a pregnant woman must live or work around some of these substances, she should consult her doctor immediately. She should also take extra precautions to minimize her exposure to any of these substances.

✓ **Reading Check** **Explain** Why should a woman tell a dentist when she is pregnant?

## Diseases and Infections

Occasionally, an expectant mother might get an infection during the course of her pregnancy. Some infections pose more of a risk to a fetus than others. The timing of an infection also may have an effect on the level of risk to a fetus. Some infections can be treated without any harm to the unborn baby, if they are found early and treated properly.

### Rubella

If a pregnant woman contracts rubella, also known as German measles, it can have terrible consequences for her unborn baby. The infection can cause severe birth defects, especially in the first three months of pregnancy. These can include blindness, deafness, heart disease, and mental retardation.

---

{ **Expert Advice...** }

*"Each system of the body is most vulnerable to harmful outside influences at the time that it is forming. Since so many body systems are forming in the first weeks and months of pregnancy, this is the time when the risks are greatest of birth defects caused by exposures to certain medications, drugs, radiation, infections, or nutritional problems."*

— Robert Needlman, pediatrician, The Dr. Spock Company

---

---

A vaccine for rubella is available, and millions of children have been vaccinated. The vaccine may be dangerous, however, for women who are pregnant or who become pregnant shortly after receiving it. A woman who is unsure whether she has been vaccinated can check her health records or ask her doctor to test her. Every woman should be sure she is immune to rubella before she considers becoming pregnant.

## Toxoplasmosis

**Toxoplasmosis** (ˌtäk-sə-ˌplaz-ˈmō-səs) is an infection caused by a parasite. This parasite is found all over the world, so the infection is quite common. It is estimated that 60 million people in the United States carry the parasite. Most people have immune systems that are strong enough to keep them from feeling any ill effects. However, developing babies are at risk if their mothers get the disease. Toxoplasmosis can cause blindness, hearing loss, and learning disabilities in babies. Some cases are so severe that a baby dies shortly after birth or has long-term mental disabilities. Toxoplasmosis can also cause miscarriage or stillbirth.

An expectant mother can take several precautions to avoid exposing her baby to toxoplasmosis. She should never clean a cat's litter box, because cats carry the parasite that causes the infection. She should not eat undercooked meat and should wash her hands immediately and thoroughly after touching raw meat.

## Chicken Pox

Varicella is a viral infection that generally occurs in childhood. It is more commonly known as chicken pox. Some women who have not had chicken pox will get the infection during pregnancy. Depending upon when the infection occurs, there can be serious consequences to the fetus. If an expectant mother gets chicken pox during the first half of her pregnancy, her baby has a slight risk of getting a condition called congenital varicella syndrome. **Congenital** means present at birth. This condition can cause scarring of the skin, limb defects, eye problems, and other serious abnormalities. In a very small number of cases, it can cause miscarriage.

---

✓ **Reading Check**

**Explain** X-rays produce radiation which can cause birth defects, so a pregnant woman will require protection if an X-ray is taken.

**Ounce of Prevention**
Washing hands immediately after handling raw meat can help avoid toxoplasmosis. *What other precautions can a pregnant woman take to prevent infections?*

Women who have not had chicken pox should get the vaccine before getting pregnant. They should also avoid contact with people who have chicken pox.

## Sexually Transmitted Infections

As with rubella, sexually transmitted infections (STIs) can do great harm to unborn babies. In some instances, STIs may be passed to the child during the birth process. As you read in Chapter 2, some STIs include syphilis, gonorrhea, hepatitis B, genital herpes, acquired immune deficiency syndrome (AIDS), and chlamydia.

Many of these diseases can be passed on from the pregnant woman to the unborn child. This occurs in the same way that the child receives nutrients from the mother. Some of these diseases can result in serious illnesses, physical disabilities, or even death.

People can get a sexually transmitted infection without realizing it. They may never have any symptoms to indicate a problem. For this reason, special measures are usually taken to protect babies from the effects of STIs. Most

doctors routinely test pregnant women for syphilis and group B streptococcus. Many states require these tests by law. Doctors also usually treat the eyes of newborns with a solution that will kill any gonorrhea germs that could cause blindness.

Medical treatment can cure syphilis and gonorrhea and can relieve the symptoms of herpes in adults. No drug can cure the damage to a newborn that comes from a delay in diagnosis and treatment. Any pregnant woman who thinks she might have been exposed to an STI should discuss this possibility with her doctor as soon as possible.

### Syphilis

The effects of syphilis on an unborn baby can usually be treated if the infection is discovered before the sixteenth week of pregnancy. If left untreated, syphilis can cause a skin rash or lesions, bone or facial deformities, deafness, or brain damage. Many babies infected with syphilis will develop anemia, jaundice, or pneumonia in the first few months of life. About two in five pregnancies with untreated syphilis end in miscarriage, a stillbirth, or a baby who dies soon after birth.

Section 4.3   Avoiding Dangers to the Baby   **121**

---

**Explore the Photo**

**Caption Answer** Answers will vary but could include not changing the cat's litter box, avoiding people with chicken pox, and having vaccinations prior to the pregnancy.

**Discussion** Studies show that the chicken pox vaccination can become ineffective after a certain number of years. Ask students: Does that mean that you will get chicken pox if your vaccination becomes ineffective? (Not necessarily; students should recognize that you will only get chicken pox if exposed to it.)

**U Universal Access**
**Visual Learners** Each year, one in four teens contracts an STI. Many teens don't realize the dangers of STIs until it is too late. Have students design public service announcements aimed at preventing STIs and encouraging teens who might have been exposed to an STI to seek help. (Students' public service announcements will vary but should focus on the dangers of STIs and the necessity of being tested for them.)

**C₂ Critical Thinking**
**Evaluating Changes** Tell students that people are often reluctant to admit, even to their doctors, that they might have been exposed to a sexually transmitted infection (STI) or the AIDS virus. For a pregnant woman, seeking treatment for a possible STI or for AIDS is vital to the normal development of her fetus. Ask students what societal barriers might keep a pregnant woman from discussing such issues with her doctor. Have students compile a list of the kinds of societal changes that might encourage more pregnant women and others to seek help for suspected infections of this kind. (Students' answers will vary but may include the fact that there is a stigma associated with STIs; society often looks down on people with these infections. Public education and understanding about STIs might be one change that would encourage more pregnant women and others to seek help for STIs.)

## Study Tools

Have students go to the Online Learning Center at **glencoe.com**:

- Take the **Practice Test**.
- Download **Study-to-Go** content.

Use the **Student Activity Workbook** for additional practice.

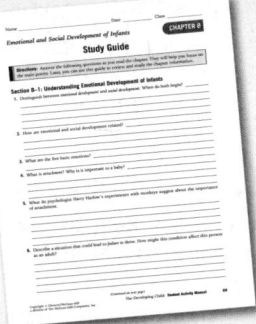

## Culminating Activity

**FAQ Brochure** Have students create a frequently asked questions (FAQs) brochure that provides answers to pregnant women's questions about avoiding dangers to their babies. (Brochures will vary but should include information from the section.)

 **NCLB** connects academic correlations to book content.

### AIDS

When an expectant mother has AIDS, there can be serious consequences for her unborn baby. There is a 35 to 65 percent risk that the virus will be passed on to the baby. AIDS attacks the brain, and infected babies often have seizures and retarded mental development.

Most states now require an AIDS test early in a pregnancy. If a doctor knows that a pregnant woman has AIDS or the virus that causes it, special steps can be taken to reduce the baby's exposure to the disease. For example, the mother can take medication to reduce the chance of the baby being infected with the virus. Also, most babies exposed to the AIDS virus and other STIs are delivered by cesarean section, a surgical procedure. This avoids exposure to the disease that may exist in the birth canal. AIDS testing also helps doctors to prepare for a newborn infected with the HIV virus that causes AIDS.

### Genital Herpes

Managing genital herpes during pregnancy is important to the health of the developing fetus. When the mother develops her first genital herpes infection during pregnancy, the risk to the infant is greater. Herpes simplex can cause the infant to be born with a brain infection or mental retardation. Some newborns will die from a herpes simplex infection.

In most cases, the infection is transmitted to the newborn during the birth process. For this reason, if a doctor knows that the mother is infected, he will often schedule a cesarean birth. You will learn more about this surgical procedure to deliver the baby in Chapter 6. In addition, there are medications that are safe to treat genital herpes during pregnancy. As with any sexually transmitted infection, couples should honestly discuss with their doctor the possibility of either parent having a herpes infection.

## Section 4.3 — After You Read

### Review Key Concepts

1. **Explain** what causes FAS. How can it be avoided?
2. **Identify** three common chemicals a woman should avoid during pregnancy.
3. **Describe** why a woman should be vaccinated against rubella and chicken pox before becoming pregnant.

### Practice Academic Skills

 **English Language Arts**

4. Suppose you are having coffee with a friend when she tells you that she is pregnant. Write a skit in which you urge your friend to avoid caffeine during the pregnancy, explaining the possible effects on her developing baby.

> **NCTE 5** Use different writing process elements to communicate effectively.

 **Science**

5. Health care professionals are concerned about pregnant women eating certain types of fish. Because of environmental pollution, these fish can contain high levels of mercury. Conduct research and create a chart showing the quantities of different types of fish a pregnant woman can safely eat.

> **NSES F** Develop understanding of personal and community health; and environmental quality.

 **Check Your Answers** Check your answers at this book's Online Learning Center at **glencoe.com**.

### Review Key Concepts

1. FAS is caused by a woman consuming alcohol during pregnancy. It can be prevented by the woman abstaining from drinking alcohol while trying to become pregnant as well as during pregnancy.
2. Any three of the following: paint, pesticides, lead, carbon monoxide, mercury, and solvents, paint thinners, and formaldehyde.
3. Rubella can cause severe birth defects, including blindness, deafness, heart disease, and mental retardation. Chicken pox can cause scarring of the skin, limb defects, eye problems, and other serious abnormalities.

### Practice Academic Skills

4. Skits will vary but should show an understanding of the effects caffeine can have on a developing baby, as described in the text on page 117.
5. Charts will vary but should show the quantities of different fish a pregnant woman can safely eat. For example, pregnant women should not eat any shark or swordfish; they can eat up to 12 ounces of salmon or catfish each week.

## Chapter Summary

Any time sexual intercourse takes place, a pregnancy may occur. There are many family planning methods available. Chromosomes from each parent determine the baby's inherited traits. There are three stages in prenatal development. Couples who cannot conceive may seek infertility treatment or adopt a child. Some pregnancies end in miscarriage or stillbirth. Birth defects have a variety of causes. There are tests to help diagnose potential problems. Everything a pregnant woman eats, drinks, and breathes affects her developing baby.

## Vocabulary Review

**1.** Use each of these content and academic vocabulary words in a sentence.

**Content Vocabulary**
◇ ovum (p. 93)
◇ uterus (p. 93)
◇ fallopian tube (p. 93)
◇ sperm (p. 93)
◇ conception (p. 95)
◇ chromosome (p. 95)
◇ gene (p. 95)
◇ genome (p. 95)
◇ DNA (p. 95)
◇ infertility (p. 97)
◇ surrogate (p. 98)

◇ prenatal development (p. 99)
◇ zygote (p. 99)
◇ embryo (p. 100)
◇ amniotic fluid (p. 100)
◇ placenta (p. 100)
◇ umbilical cord (p. 100)
◇ fetus (p. 101)
◇ miscarriage (p. 106)
◇ stillbirth (p. 106)
◇ ultrasound (p. 112)
◇ amniocentesis (p. 113)

◇ fetal alcohol syndrome (FAS) (p. 116)
◇ fetal alcohol effects (p. 116)
◇ SIDS (p. 118)
◇ toxoplasmosis (p. 120)

**Academic Vocabulary**
■ controversial (p. 99)
■ spontaneous (p. 101)
■ predisposition (p. 111)
■ serious (p. 111)
■ deformity (p. 116)
■ congenital (p. 120)

## Review Key Concepts

**2. List** the methods of family planning.
**3. Outline** what occurs during each of the three stages of prenatal development.
**4. Contrast** miscarriage and stillbirth.
**5. Identify** how ten major birth defects can be diagnosed.
**6. Summarize** the hazards that alcohol and other drugs pose to prenatal development.
**7. Assess** why environmental hazards must be avoided during pregnancy.
**8. Describe** how a fetus can be affected by certain illnesses the mother may contract.

## Critical Thinking

**9. Analyze** Why do babies born at full term have a better chance for survival than babies born a few months early?
**10. Predict** What could be the consequences if someone denies that she is pregnant and does not seek any medical care?

## Content and Academic Vocabulary Review

**1.** Students should write complete sentences using each vocabulary word correctly.

## Review Key Concepts

**2.** abstinence, birth control pills, cervical cap, condom, diaphragm, hormonal implant, hormonal injection, hormonal patch, IUD and uterine implant, natural family planning, spermicide, vaginal implant

**3.** germinal: zygote divides; uterine wall thickens; zygote implants in uterus; embryonic: major systems develop; amniotic sac, placenta, and umbilical cord develop; fetal: major organs ready to function outside the mother; fetus gains weight rapidly

**4.** A miscarriage occurs prior to the 20th week of pregnancy; after that the death is a stillbirth.

**5.** Answers will vary. Diagnostic tests include blood test for AFP, ultrasound, amniocentesis, and chorionic villi sampling.

**6.** Drinking alcohol can cause fetal alcohol syndrome. Smoking tobacco can lead to premature birth, low birth weight, and respiratory infections. Other drugs can have a variety of effects.

**7.** They can cause problems such as birth defects.

**8.** Rubella and toxoplasmosis can cause severe birth defects. Chicken pox can lead to congenital varicella syndrome. Some STIs cause serious illnesses, physical disabilities, and even death.

## Critical Thinking

**9.** The organs in the baby's body have become ready to function without the mother's help. Fat deposits have accumulated to help the baby maintain body heat. The baby has stored nutrients necessary for survival. The baby has built immunity to diseases and infections.

**10.** The mother's health could be put at risk and the baby could have serious birth defects that might be detected prior to birth so the baby might not get the treatment it needs. The mother could even have a miscarriage or stillbirth.

### Family & Community Connections

**11.** Reports will vary, but should explain the organization's purpose and the kinds of services it provides.

### Health Skills

**12.** Answers will vary. A major advance is three-dimensional ultrasound, which provides a more detailed image of the fetus, allowing the health care professional to more closely examine it for any anomalies. Birth defects that are frequently diagnosed by ultrasound include organ and other structural abnormalities such as cleft lip and cleft palate, spina bifida, and hydrocephalus. Ultrasound also shows multiple births and the baby's gender.

### Observation Skills

**13.** Students' summaries will vary. Students may mention women wearing pregnancy clothes, having trouble getting in and out of tight places such as cars, and sitting as much as possible.

### Real-World Skills

**14.** Answers will vary, but students should state their decision and what factors they took into account when making it.

**NCLB** Activity correlated to English Language Arts standards.

---

### Family & Community Connection

**11. Local Organizations** There are many organizations that offer support to families with children with birth defects. The March of Dimes and Special Olympics are just two examples. Choose and research one of this type of organization in your community. Find out what the organization's purpose is and what services it provides. Prepare an oral report on what you learn, and, if possible, present it to the class or another group.

### Health Skills

**12. Investigate Ultrasound** Research the latest advances in ultrasound technology. How can these advances help with the diagnosis of birth defects? What specific birth defects can they identify? What else can these new technologies reveal about a developing fetus?

### Real-World Skills

| | |
|---|---|
| **Problem-Solving Skills** | **14. Make Decisions** Follow your teacher's instructions to form groups. Discuss with your group what you might do if a genetic counselor told you any future children might have Tay-Sachs disease. Would you plan to have children? Why or why not? Share your group's response with the class. |
| **Technology Skills** | **15. Research Fetal Development** Conduct research to learn more about fetal development during the last three months of pregnancy. Then use presentation software to prepare a presentation for middle-school students explaining development during this time. Use illustrations and language that is appropriate for this age group. |
| **Financial Literacy** | **16. Family Planning** A couple is planning on having their first baby three years from now. They want to save $10,000 before they have the baby to help with the expenses of the first year. How much money do they need to save each month to have the $10,000 saved in three years? |

 **Additional Activities** For additional activities, go to this book's Online Learning Center at **glencoe.com**.

### Observation Skills

**13. Observe Pregnant Women** Most pregnant women enjoy active lives, despite difficulties such as fatigue. What kinds of changes do you think the average pregnant woman makes in her daily routine? Make a list of your ideas.

**Procedure** Observe pregnant women around you. Write down any accommodations they appear to have made, such as sitting more than usual or wearing different clothes.

**Draw Conclusions** Write a summary describing ways in which pregnant women appear to have changed their lives. Compare your observations to the list of ideas you wrote before you made your observations.

**NCTE 7** Conduct research and gather, evaluate, and synthesize data to communicate discoveries.

**N C L B**

---

**15.** Students should create a multimedia presentation describing fetal development during the third trimester of pregnancy.

**16.** $277.78 (3 years × 12 months = 36 months, $10,000 ÷ 36 = $277.78)

The *Early Childhood Observations CD* offers additional lessons with videos to build students' observation skills.

**Part 1:** Learning to Observe
**Part 2:** How Children Develop
**Part 3:** Working With Young Children
**Part 4:** Extended Observations
**Part 5:** Resources and Answer File

## Academic Skills

###  English Language Arts

**17. Write a Persuasive Letter** Imagine you are a pregnant woman who is exposed to solvents, such as paint thinners, at the factory where you work. Write a persuasive letter to your boss explaining why these solvents present a risk to the baby. Also propose a solution. Conduct research to gather information to strengthen your argument.

> **NCTE 12** Use language to accomplish individual purposes.

###  Mathematics

**18. Prenatal Development** Alcohol consumed during pregnancy increases the risk of alcohol related birth defects. A report from the U.S. Surgeon General states that up to two out of every thousand births show signs of fetal alcohol syndrome. Suppose there are 4.1 million children born in a year. How many of those might have fetal alcohol syndrome?

**Math Concept** **Variables and Expressions** Translate verbal phrases into algebraic expressions by defining a variable.

**Starting Hint** Write your expression as
$$\frac{x}{4.1 \text{ million}} = \frac{2}{1,000}$$

 For math help, go to the Math Appendix at the back of the book.

> **NCTM Algebra** Represent and analyze mathematical situations and structures using algebraic symbols.

###  Science

**19. Pregnancy and Painkillers** Over-the-counter medications such as acetaminophen and ibuprofen are widely used by the public. Pregnant women may be tempted to use these due to the added aches and pains caused by pregnancy. However, scientists and health care professionals are concerned about any effects these painkillers may have on a developing baby.

**Procedure** Choose one type of over-the-counter painkiller. Research to find what is known about its effects on fetuses.

**Analysis** Imagine you are an obstetrician and a pregnant patient has asked you about your chosen painkiller's safety. What would you say? Write a dialogue showing how you would respond to the patient. Be sure to include reasons why she should or should not use that particular painkiller.

> **NSES A** Develop abilities necessary to do scientific inquiry, understand about scientific inquiry.

 **Standardized Test Practice**

### ESSAY QUESTIONS

Answering essay questions can be challenging, especially if time is limited. Before writing a response to an essay question, spend a few moments thinking about the main points you want to make. Think about the structure of your response and how much detail you want to include. Apply these skills to answer this essay question.

**20.** Describe the major changes that occur in a developing baby during the embryonic stage.

> **Test-Taking Tip** When answering essay questions, begin by creating a brief outline. Keep the outline in mind as you write your response.

## Academic Skills

**17.** Letters will vary. Students should use persuasive language to explain that exposure to solvents during pregnancy can lead to birth defects, including deformities. Students should also suggest a solution, such as being moved to a job away from solvents during the pregnancy.

**18.** $x$ / 4.1 million = 2 / 1,000; $1,000x = 8.2$ million; $x = 8.2$ million ÷ 1,000

**19.** Answers will vary. The patient should always obtain doctor's approval, but research has shown acetaminophen to be safe. Ibuprofen is known to cause blood-flow problems during the last trimester; pregnant women generally should avoid taking it.

> **NCLB** NCLB connects academic correlations to book content.

### Standardized Test Practice

**20.** Answers will vary but students should describe the major changes during the embryonic stage.

**Test Taking Tips** Tell students to read the prompt on an essay test carefully to make sure they understand what they are expected to write.

**Pre-Test Study** Remind students that when studying from a textbook, they should begin by re-reading section and chapter introductions and summaries, graphics, and photographs with the purpose of identifying main ideas. Then they should read any end-of-chapter study questions and skim the text to find specific details to answer the questions.

## TECHNOLOGY Solutions

### Use these technology solutions to streamline chapter assessment!

 **ExamView Assessment Suite** CD allows you to create and print out customized tests or ready-made unit and chapter tests, complete with answer keys.

 **TeacherWorks Plus** is an electronic lesson planner that provides instant access to complete teacher resources in one convenient package.

 **Online Learning Center** includes resources and activities for students and teachers.

**STANDARDS BASED LESSON PLANNING** *The Developing Child* provides students with instruction and assessment in the following fundamental content areas:

## National Standards Correlations

| Standards | Pages |
|---|---|
| **12.1.3**  Analyze current and emerging research about human growth and development, including research on brain development. | **137** |
| **12.2.4**  Analyze the effects of life events on individuals' physical, intellectual, social, moral, and emotional development. | **145** |
| **15.1.5**  Explain cultural differences in roles and responsibilities of parenting. | **131** |
| **15.2.3**  Assess common practices and emerging research about discipline on human growth and development. | **137** |
| **15.2.5**  Apply criteria for selecting care and services for children. | **151** |
| **15.4.1**  Analyze biological processes related to prenatal development, birth, and health of child and mother. | **129–133, 134** |
| **15.4.2**  Analyze the emotional factors of prenatal development and birth in relation to the health of parents and child. | **136–137, 154** |

**NO CHILD LEFT BEHIND**  NCLB activities, information, and skills practice will help your students attain NCLB proficiency. Students will improve their abilities in the following academic standards areas:

## Academic Standards Correlations

| Discipline | Standard | Feature/Activity |
|---|---|---|
| **English Language Arts** | **NCTE 1**  Read texts to acquire new information. | **Reading Guide (pp. 128, 143, 153)** |
| | **NCTE 2**  Read literature to build an understanding of the human experience. | **After You Read (p. 157)** |
| | **NCTE 4**  Use written language to communicate effectively. | **Writing Activity (p. 126) Academic Skills (p. 161)** |
| | **NCTE 7**  Conduct research and gather, evaluate, and synthesize data to communicate discoveries. | **After You Read (p. 152) Observation Skills (p. 160)** |
| | **NCTE 8**  Use information resources to gather information and create and communicate knowledge. | **After You Read (p. 142)** |
| **Mathematics** | **NCTM Number and Operations**  Understand numbers, ways of representing numbers, relationships among numbers, and number systems. | **Math in Action (p. 150)** |
| | **NCTM Data Analysis and Probability**  Select and use appropriate statistical methods to analyze data. | **Academic Skills (p. 161)** |
| **Science** | **NSES A**  Develop abilities necessary to do scientific inquiry, understandings about scientific inquiry. | **Academic Skills (p. 161)** |
| | **NSES B**  Develop an understanding of the structure and properties of matter, chemical reactions. | **After You Read (p. 152)** |
| | **NSES F**  Develop understanding of personal and community health. | **After You Read (p. 142)** |
| **Social Studies** | **NCSS I A Culture**  Analyze and explain the ways groups, societies, and cultures address human needs and concerns. | **Culture Matters (p. 131) After You Read (p. 157)** |

## McGraw Hill Professional Development

**MINI CLIP VIDEO LIBRARY**
Targeted professional development is correlated throughout *The Developing Child*. **The McGraw-Hill Professional Development Mini Clip Video Library** provides teaching strategies to strengthen academic and learning skills. Log on to **glencoe.com**.

In this chapter, you will find these Mini Clips:
- **Reading** Prereading Strategies, p. 129
- **ELL** Collaborative Work, p. 133
- **Reading** Connecting the Pieces, p. 139
- **ELL** Vocabulary Activities, p. 143
- **ELL** Accessing Prior Knowledge, p. 154
- **Math** Medians and Quartiles, p. 161

## Reading and Writing Strategies

**Writing Activity: Topic Sentence** (p. 126)
Students use writing tips to write a paragraph with a topic sentence about how a woman can remain healthy during pregnancy.

**Before You Read** (pp. 128, 143, 153)
A pre-reading question or statement will help students make a personal connection to content.

**Graphic Organizer** (pp. 128, 143, 153)
A visual tool will help students organize and remember new content.

**Reading Check** (pp. 137, 150, 154)
A question allows students to make a quick comprehension self-check.

**After You Read** (pp. 142, 152, 157)
Organize and process students' understanding of what they have read.

## Chapter Features

**Korean Taegyo** (p. 131)
Koreans believe in fetal education, for pregnant women.

**Keep On Moving** (p. 133)
Women should exercise while pregnant.

**Nutrition and Fetal Brain Development** (p. 137)
What the mother eats during pregnancy affects the fetus.

**Accepting the New Family Member** (p. 145)
Older siblings may need to be reassured when a new baby is brought home.

**Car Seat Safety** (p. 147)
Proper use of car seats is important to keeping baby safe.

**Health Care Costs** (p. 150)
Prenatal care and delivery costs can be expensive.

**Where to Give Birth** (p. 155)
There are many choices available when deciding where to deliver a baby.

**Toy Designer** (p. 158)
Learn the skills needed to succeed as a Toy Designer.

## Chapter Overview

### Introduce the Chapter

In this chapter, students learn about the early signs of pregnancy and the importance of proper nutrition during pregnancy. Students also learn the many ways parents must prepare for the birth of their child and of the delivery options available.

### Build Background

Tell students that there are many things a pregnant woman can do to help maintain her own health and the health of the unborn child. Have students create lists of the different ways in which they have seen pregnant women taking care of themselves. Then ask for volunteers to share their lists with the class.

### Writing Activity

#### Topic Sentence

This active learning activity prompts students to write a paragraph with a topic sentence about how a pregnant woman can stay healthy. After students have completed the writing activity, ask for volunteers to share their topic sentences with the class. Ask students to point out any similarities or differences among the sentences. Encourage the class to discuss which points they consider to be the most important and why. (Answers will vary but should include a strong topic sentence to begin the paragraph. The topic sentence should state the main idea of the paragraph. Ideas in the topic sentence should be placed in the order in which they will be covered in the paragraph and the topic sentence should not be overly detailed.)

Chapter

**5** Preparing for Birth

## Chapter Objectives

After completing this chapter, you will be able to:

- **Identify** the early signs of pregnancy.
- **Explain** the importance of proper nutrition during pregnancy.
- **List** six categories of basic baby supplies.
- **Describe** why parents need to develop a budget.
- **Identify** ways expectant parents can prepare for the birth of a child.
- **Compare and contrast** the options for the delivery of a baby.

### Writing Activity  Topic Sentence

**A Healthy Pregnancy** Developing a topic sentence is like building a house's frame. If the frame is poorly built, the entire building will collapse. Write a paragraph that includes a topic sentence about how a woman can remain healthy during her pregnancy.

**Writing Tips** A topic sentence provides an overview of a paragraph. Here are some tips for writing a good topic sentence:
1. **State** the main idea of the paragraph.
2. **Place** the ideas in the order in which they will be covered in the paragraph.
3. **Avoid** making the topic sentence overly detailed.

126

## CLASSROOM Solutions

### Print Resources

 **Student Edition**

 **Teacher Wraparound Edition**

**Student Activity Workbook**

 **Student Activity Workbook Teacher Annotated Edition**

### Technology Resources

 **Online Learning Center** has resources and activities for students and teachers. Includes an Online Student Edition.

 **Interactive Student Edition** allows students to instantly access review materials, examples, and exercises.

**Section** **5.1** **A Healthy Pregnancy**

**Section** **5.2** **Preparing for the Baby's Arrival**

**Section** **5.3** **Childbirth Options**

**Explore the Photo**
A pregnancy affects all members of the family, not just the mother. *How do you think each person in this photo is affected by this pregnancy?*

**127**

## Review the Sections
Introduce the chapter by reviewing the sections:

### Section 5.1
A woman should see a doctor when she thinks she is pregnant. She should receive regular prenatal care during her pregnancy. Eating a well-balanced diet with foods from each of the food groups is essential to the health of the developing baby and the mother. Moderate exercise and stress management also are important.

### Section 5.2
Parents-to-be should prepare their home for the birth of the child and have basic baby supplies ready. They should create a budget and decide how they will balance their lives after the baby is born.

### Section 5.3
Prepared childbirth helps expectant parents get ready for labor and delivery. They must choose a health care professional to attend the birth and decide where the birth will occur.

---

**Explore the Photo**

**Caption Answer** Possible answer include: The mother has the excitement of having the baby growing inside her. Both parents will have to adjust to having someone completely dependent on them. They will need to adjust their time and finances to include a child.

**Discussion** Ask students if they think the people in the photo have negative feelings about the birth. (Answers may include: The mother has to deal with a variety of physical changes that may be uncomfortable and may worry about the baby's health.)

**TeacherWorks Plus** is an electronic lesson planner that provides instant access to complete teacher resources in one convenient package.

**Presentation Plus!** provides visual teaching aids for every section.

**The Early Childhood Observations CD** presents video observations and lessons on observation skills and child development.

**The Developing Brain eTransparencies and Guide** include information and activities to offer insights into brain development and diseases of the brain.

## Focus

### Bell Ringer Activity

**Healthy Bodies**

Ask students to make a list of the things they do on a regular basis to stay healthy. (Lists may include: eating nutritious foods, exercising, avoiding alcohol and drugs.) Ask students what they think a pregnant woman should do to remain healthy throughout her pregnancy. (Answers should be similar to the list above.)

## Preteaching

### Vocabulary

Ask students to identify the suffix in the word *obstetrician*. The suffix is *-ician*, which means specialist or practitioner. Ask students if they know other words with this suffix.

### Graphic Organizer

 The Graphic Organizer is also on the TeacherWorks CD.

(Graphic organizer answers may include: Grains: oatmeal, flour; Fruit: apples, peaches; Vegetables: corn, celery; Milk: milk, cheese; Meat and Beans: beef, navy beans; Oils: canola, olive)

**NCLB** connects academic correlations to book content.

## Reading Guide

### Before You Read

**Create a KWL Chart** Create a chart with three columns labeled "What I Know," "What I Want to Know," and "What I Learned." Skim the section and fill in the first two columns. Then fill in the last column after you read.

### Read to Learn
**Key Concepts**
- **Identify** the early signs of pregnancy.
- **Explain** the importance of proper nutrition during pregnancy.

### Main Idea
It is important that pregnant women have regular doctor checkups and practice good nutrition. They also should follow appropriate exercise routines and avoid excess stress.

### Content Vocabulary
◇ obstetrician
◇ anemia
◇ Rh factor
◇ gestational diabetes
◇ preeclampsia
◇ osteoporosis
◇ lactose intolerance
◇ lactase

### Academic Vocabulary
You will find these words in your reading and on your tests. Use the glossary to look up their definitions if necessary.
■ robust
■ alleviate

### Graphic Organizer
As you read, note the food groups pregnant women should eat. List two foods in each group. Use a chart like the one shown to organize your information.

| Food Group | Example 1 | Example 2 |
|---|---|---|
| Grains | | |
| Fruit | | |
| Vegetables | | |
| Milk | | |
| Meat and Beans | | |
| Oils | | |

 **Graphic Organizer** Go to this book's Online Learning Center at **glencoe.com** to print out this graphic organizer.

### Academic Standards

#### English Language Arts
**NCTE 8** Use information resources to gather information and create and communicate knowledge.

#### Science
**NSES F** Develop understanding of personal and community health.

#### Social Studies
**NCSS I A Culture** Analyze and explain the ways groups, societies, and cultures address human needs and concerns.

**NCTE** *National Council of Teachers of English*
**NCTM** *National Council of Teachers of Mathematics*
**NSES** *National Science Education Standards*
**NCSS** *National Council for the Social Studies*

## Reading Guide

### Before You Read

Ask students: What discomforts might a pregnant woman experience? What might she do to help alleviate the discomfort? (Answers will vary. Students may suggest backaches and muscle pains might be eased by gentle stretching and exercise.)

### D Develop Concepts

**Main Idea** Discuss the main idea with the students. Ask: How are the things listed here different from what all people should do? (The things listed are what everyone should do, but it is even more important for pregnant women to do these things.)

## Health During Pregnancy

A pregnant woman's responsibilities grow along with her baby. What happens to a baby during prenatal development can affect both the baby's and parents' lives. Mothers-to-be need to eat a well-balanced diet, exercise moderately, get plenty of sleep, and manage stress. This is important for both the mother's and the baby's health.

## Early Signs of Pregnancy

How do women discover that they are pregnant? Within a few weeks of conception, women usually experience one or more of the following signs of pregnancy:

- A missed menstrual period (often the first indicator)
- A full feeling or mild ache in the lower abdomen
- Tiredness or faintness
- A frequent, urgent need to urinate
- Swollen breasts, causing discomfort or tenderness
- Nausea or vomiting, particularly in the morning

These symptoms are common, but they do not always mean that a woman is pregnant. If a woman believes she is pregnant, she should take a pregnancy test as soon as possible. Doctors can conduct tests to confirm pregnancy. There are also a variety of home pregnancy tests available. They are easy to use and fairly accurate. Early detection of pregnancy is crucial to the health of the expectant mother and her baby.

## Medical Care

Once pregnancy is determined, it is important for a woman to schedule a doctor's visit. Most pregnant women choose an obstetrician for medical care during pregnancy. An **obstetrician** (ˌäb-stə-'tri-shən) is a doctor who specializes in pregnancy and childbirth.

Obstetricians will schedule regular checkups during pregnancy. These checkups will become more frequent as the pregnancy progresses. The doctor also assists during childbirth and examines the newborn. It is important that expectant mothers find a doctor they like, feel comfortable with, and trust.

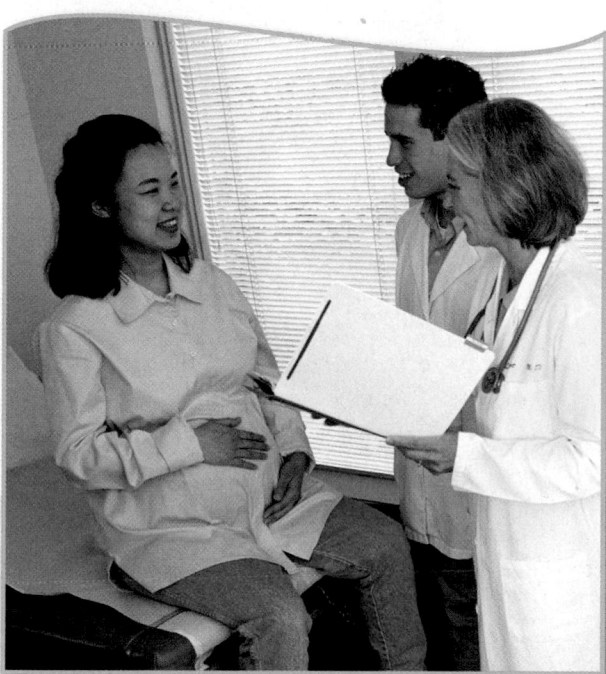

**Meeting with Obstetricians**
A pregnant woman often meets all the doctors in a medical office or clinic. *How can meeting the other doctors help a woman prepare for childbirth?*

Section 5.1    A Healthy Pregnancy    **129**

---

---

### Teach

**Discussion Starter**

**Obstetrician Questions** It is important for pregnant women to find obstetricians that make them feel comfortable. Have students brainstorm a list of questions an expectant mother might ask obstetricians in order to find one that suits her needs. Ask a volunteer to write the questions on the board. (Questions may include: What are your beliefs and philosophies about birth? What are your feelings about pain relief during labor? How will I be included in the decision-making process? What are your feelings about cesarean birth and when would you recommend it?)

**McGraw Hill Professional Development**

**Mini Clip**
**Reading: Prereading Strategies**

A teacher assesses her students' prior knowledge about a text selection they are about to read.

**C Critical Thinking**

**Making Inferences** Ask students to make inferences about why doctors request that pregnant women reveal both their prior and existing medical conditions at the first visit to the doctor. (Students should recognize that all of a woman's medical history is important when she is pregnant. She may have a condition that she thinks is not important, but it may cause complications during the pregnancy or harm to the baby.)

### Teach *cont.*

**R Reading Strategy**

**Skimming** Have students skim the third paragraph on this page. Then read the following scenario to students: Marsha believes she might be pregnant. She missed her last period and tested positive for pregnancy using an over-the-counter test. Marsha is afraid her medical bills will be more than she can afford, so she plans to avoid seeing the doctor until the fourth or fifth month. Ask students to discuss what they would say to Marsha to convince her to visit a doctor. (Skimming the third paragraph should help students realize that nothing is more important to the health of the baby than for the mother to get regular medical care and advice as early as possible in the pregnancy and until after the birth.)

**U Universal Access**

**Students with Learning Disabilities** Pair students with learning disabilities with other students. Have pairs of students rewrite the bulleted list of things included in a woman's first pregnancy exam. Students should rewrite the items for better understanding. Have pairs share their rewritten lists with the rest of the class. (Lists will vary but should include all of the information provided in the bulleted list in the text. Following is one example of how the first bulleted point might be rewritten: The first pregnancy exam will check the woman's blood pressure, pulse, respiration (breathing rate), and weight.)

Many obstetricians work as part of a team with other doctors, taking turns caring for patients at night and on weekends. Although pregnant women usually have a primary doctor, they typically meet all the doctors who work in the office. This is so they know and feel comfortable with all the doctors.

The primary doctor performs most of the woman's checkups. However, if he is not on duty when the woman is ready to deliver, another doctor on the team will deliver the baby. Since no one knows when labor will begin, it could happen on the primary doctor's day off. He also could be ill or on vacation.

Some women believe they will save money by seeing a doctor only when the baby is ready to be born. This is not the case. Most obstetricians set a fee for all the services they provide throughout the pregnancy, from the first exam to the follow-up visits after the baby is born. Nothing is more important to the health of the baby than for the mother to get regular medical care and advice from the beginning to the end of the pregnancy.

**The First Exam**

When pregnancy is confirmed, the woman receives a thorough examination that includes:

- A check of her blood pressure, pulse, respiration, and weight.
- A discussion of her medical history, including existing medical conditions, such as high blood pressure, that may require special treatment or observation during pregnancy.
- A measurement of her pelvis to determine whether it is wide enough to allow a baby of normal size to pass through.
- An analysis of her urine for signs of infection or diabetes, a condition characterized by excessive amounts of urine. Diabetes develops when the body is not able to produce enough insulin to keep blood sugar (glucose) within an acceptable range. This condition affects the body's ability to burn energy.
- Blood tests to rule out anemia. **Anemia** is a condition that results from not having enough red blood cells. Symptoms include fatigue, shortness of breath, rapid heartbeat, and feeling cold and weak.

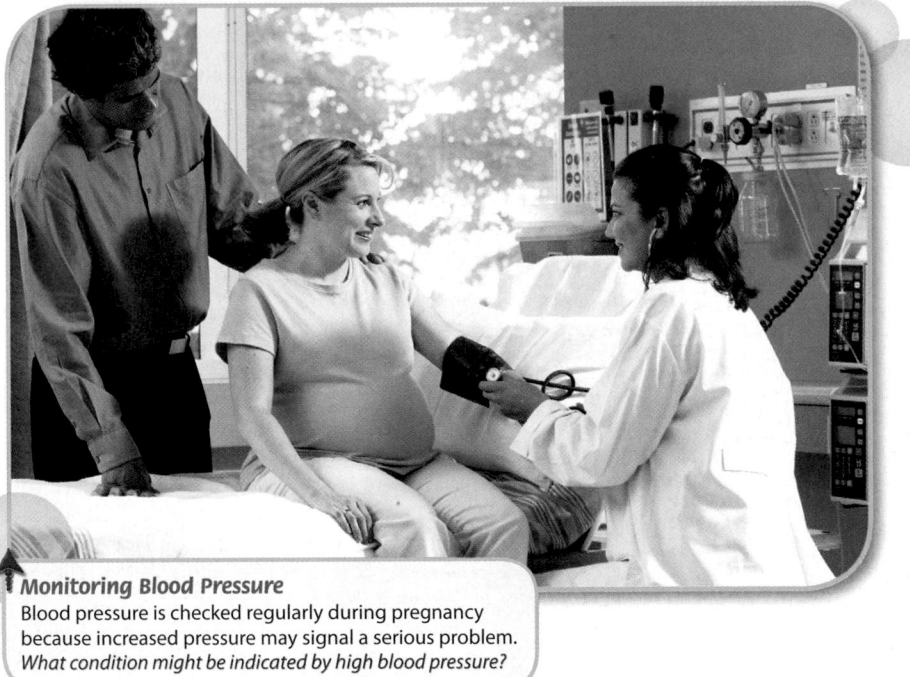

**Monitoring Blood Pressure**
Blood pressure is checked regularly during pregnancy because increased pressure may signal a serious problem. *What condition might be indicated by high blood pressure?*

---

**▶ Explore the Photo**

**Caption Answer** A condition known as preeclampsia might be indicated by high blood pressure. Preeclampsia can prevent the baby from getting enough blood, which provides oxygen and food.

**Discussion** Tell students that when the flow of oxygen is reduced, brain damage and mental retardation may result. Ask students what may result from fetal malnutrition. (As students read in Chapter 4, babies with low birth weight may have serious health problems as newborns and later in life.)

## CULTURE MATTERS

### Korean Taegyo

In Korea, many pregnant women learn a set of practices that have been transmitted to women by word of mouth and through literature for centuries. The word for these practices is taegyo ('tīg-yō). This means fetal education. Koreans believe that fetal education is more important than the first ten years of a child's schooling. Pregnant women are taught to read inspiring books; eat colorful, attractive foods; sit or stand up straight; and listen to beautiful music. They should not deceive anyone or think about anything unpleasant. Koreans believe that the fetus is extremely sensitive to what the mother feels.

⭐ **Build Connections** *Korean women believe that what happens to an unborn baby can affect his or her entire life. Do you think this is true? If yes, in what ways do you think this is true?*

**NCSS I A Culture** Analyze and explain the ways groups, societies, and cultures address human needs and concerns.

---

The blood test also shows whether or not the mother's blood contains a certain protein. This protein is referred to as the **Rh factor**. Knowing about the presence (Rh positive) or absence (Rh negative) of this protein is very important. The Rh factor is determined genetically. If the mother's blood does not have the protein and the fetus's blood does, the mother's blood builds up antibodies that attack the protein in the fetus's blood. This does not affect a first pregnancy, but it can endanger any future pregnancies. Once identified, the mother can receive an injection that will prevent the antibodies from forming, thus protecting any Rh positive fetus.

- A check of the woman's immunity to rubella, also called German measles. If a pregnant woman has not been vaccinated against this disease and has never had it, she must be especially careful to avoid anyone who has it. If she contracts rubella during pregnancy, the fetus could be harmed.

One question every pregnant woman has is "When will my baby be born?" The approximate birth date is easy to calculate. Nine months and one week after the first day of her final period before pregnancy is her baby's due date.

Of course, doctors know that even in a typical pregnancy a variation of up to two weeks before or after that date can be expected.

### Periodic Checkups

Expectant mothers have checkups, or prenatal visits, once a month until about the sixth or seventh month of pregnancy. After that, women see the doctor twice a month. In the final month, checkups occur once a week. During these visits, the doctor monitors the baby's development and the mother's health. Regular checkups allow immediate response should a problem arise.

Between the 24th and 28th weeks of the pregnancy, most women take a glucose tolerance test to check for signs of gestational diabetes. **Gestational diabetes** is a form of diabetes that occurs only during pregnancy. If left untreated, gestational diabetes can cause the baby to be heavier than is normal or healthy.

Some women who do not normally have diabetes develop the condition when they are pregnant. This type of diabetes usually goes away after the baby is born. Gestational diabetes can usually be controlled by a special diet but may require medication.

Section 5.1    A Healthy Pregnancy    **131**

---

## CULTURE MATTERS

### Korean Taegyo

Ask students what they think about the practice of taegyo? (Answers will vary. Some students may realize that the health of the mother—physical, mental, and emotional—affects the unborn baby.) Ask students if they know of any American practices that are similar to taegyo. (Many pregnant women take extra care during pregnancy to eat properly, limit stress, and some play music to enhance the baby's development.)

**Build Connections** *Answers will vary; a mother's choices of healthy foods can increase the chances of having a healthy baby; thinking positive thoughts can lead to a happier, more positive mother, who may pass along this view of the world to her infant.*

---

## Section 5.1

### Teach cont.

**S Skill Practice**

**Guided Practice**

**List** Have students create time lines to show when expectant mothers have checkups, or prenatal visits, with their doctor. (Time lines should show checkups once a month for the first six months, then twice a month until the final month when there is a checkup every week until the baby is born.) **L1**

**Interview** Have students contact an obstetrician or obstetrical nurse and ask what a routine (not the initial exam) prenatal checkup entails. (Routine exams include a urine check for protein, a blood pressure test, a check of the baby's heartbeat, and (after 20 weeks) a measurement of the mother's abdomen to follow the baby's growth.) **L2**

**Compare and Contrast** Most doctors test for gestational diabetes during a pregnancy. Have students research Type 2 diabetes (non-insulin dependent) and compare and contrast it with gestational diabetes. Students should compare the cause, treatment, and duration of the diseases. To present their information, have students create a table with Type 2 diabetes and gestational diabetes at the top and cause, treatment, and duration along the left side. (Tables may vary but should include: Type 2—Cause: insufficient insulin production, Treatment: healthful diet and oral hypoglycemic medications, Duration: life; Gestational—Cause: high blood sugar (glucose) levels during pregnancy, Treatment: nutritional diet and exercise, may require insulin, Duration: usually disappears after birth of baby.) **L3**

**N C L B** **NCLB** Activity correlated to Social Studies standards.

## Teach *cont.*

### R₁ Reading Strategy

**Making Generalizations** Have students scan the page for generalizations. Remind them that generalizations may use words and phrases like *most, some,* or *in general.* Have them make a generalization about the discomforts of pregnancy. (Generalizations on this page include: paragraph 2—sentences 1 and 3, paragraph 3—sentences 1 and 2. Generalizations about the discomforts of pregnancy may include: Many women experience some discomforts during pregnancy.)

### U₁ Universal Access

**English Language Learners** In the United States, there has been a cultural shift toward the presence of fathers during the delivery of their babies. Ask English language learners to share the practices of the father during delivery in their culture. (Answers will vary depending on the cultures represented in your classroom. Some students may not be aware of the practices of fathers during delivery.)

### C Critical Thinking

**Problem Solving** Ask students to determine what pregnant women can do to prevent or treat the following pregnancy-related conditions without medication: constipation (drink lots of water; eat high-fiber food; exercise; drink prune juice), tooth decay (take calcium; see a dentist), hemorrhoids (eat high-fiber food; soak in warm water; exercise), swelling (apply cold compresses; elevate feet; swim), lightheadedness (eat several smaller meals; move more slowly; avoid standing for too long; avoid getting overheated).

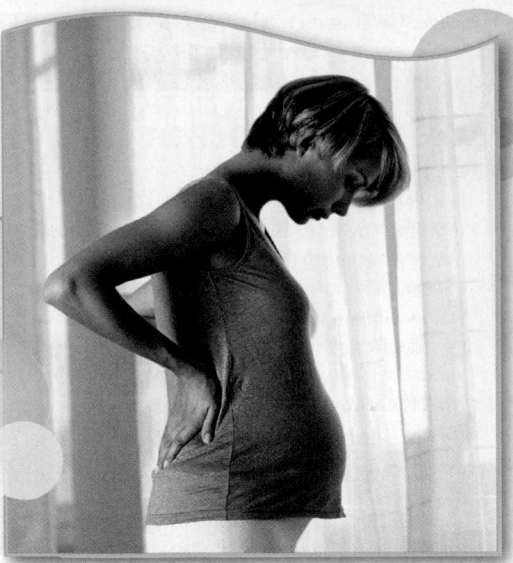

**Aches and Pains**
Many pregnant women experience difficulties such as tiredness and back pain. *Why should pregnant women not take over-the-counter remedies for common problems such as headaches?*

Another serious condition that can occur during the second half of pregnancy is preeclampsia. **Preeclampsia** (ˌprē-i-ˈklam(p)-sē-ə) is a condition characterized by high blood pressure and the presence of protein in the mother's urine. It can prevent the baby from getting enough blood, which provides oxygen and food. Treatment for preeclampsia depends on how far along in the pregnancy a woman is. Treatment might include bed rest or medication. The doctor can recommend the best treatment option.

Most doctors welcome the father or another person who will be attending the birth to accompany the pregnant woman at prenatal visits. This gives the support person a chance to meet the doctor and follow the baby's growth. Also, sometimes it is helpful to have someone else to ask questions and remember important information.

### Discomforts of Pregnancy

Most women experience few problems during pregnancy. In fact, some women say that pregnancy is a time of **robust**, or thriving, health. Many women experience an increase in energy and well-being. Other women feel some discomfort. This usually does not indicate serious problems. However, if a woman experiences one or more of the following symptoms, she should discuss it with her doctor.

- **Nausea or Vomiting** While this is commonly called morning sickness, it can occur at any time of the day. Morning sickness is the most common complaint of pregnant women. It rarely lasts beyond the fourth month of pregnancy. If it is severe or prolonged, however, women should alert their doctors.
- **Sleepiness** Due to hormonal changes, sleepiness is quite common early in pregnancy. Many women feel more energetic in the middle months of pregnancy. For most women, fatigue returns in the final months, since the baby weighs more and takes up more room.
- **Heartburn** This is a burning feeling in the upper abdomen. It has nothing to do with the heart. Women with heartburn should ask their doctors about safe forms of relief.
- **Shortness of Breath** Pressure on the lungs from the baby can cause shortness of breath. This is particularly common late in pregnancy.
- **Varicose Veins** When there is pressure on the blood vessels in the legs, varicose veins can appear. These are swollen veins, or blood vessels, that are close to the skin's

### ▶ Explore the Photo

**Caption Answer** Pregnant women should not take drugs, including over-the-counter medicines, because they can cause problems for both the developing baby and the mother.

**Discussion** Ask students what a pregnant woman might do to avoid having backaches. (Responses will vary; they may say she could wear low-heeled shoes, learn to lift items properly (or not lift at all), she might do exercises to strengthen her back.)

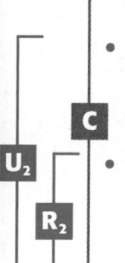

surface. Getting plenty of exercise, resting with the legs elevated, and using support stockings can help relieve the swelling.

- **Muscle Cramps in the Legs** Gentle stretches, rest, and a diet rich in calcium may **alleviate**, or ease, the pain caused by leg cramps.
- **Lower Back Pain** Wearing low-heeled shoes and learning to lift properly, or avoiding lifting altogether, can minimize back problems. Exercises that strengthen the back can also help.

### Possible Serious Complications

A few women experience more serious problems during pregnancy. Any of the following symptoms should be reported to a doctor immediately:

- Vaginal bleeding
- Unusual weight gain or loss
- Excessive thirst
- Diminished need to urinate or pain during urination
- Severe abdominal pain
- Persistent headaches
- Severe vomiting
- Fever
- Increased vaginal mucus
- Swelling of the face, hands, or ankles
- Blurred vision or dizziness
- Prolonged backache

## Physical Changes

The common length of pregnancy is about 40 weeks, or 280 days, from the first day of the last menstrual cycle. See **Figure 5.1** on page 134 for a description of physical changes a woman can expect each month of her pregnancy.

Toward the end of the 40 weeks, the baby's weight seems to shift downward, and most mothers feel more comfortable in their upper abdomen. This shift is called lightening. Sometimes there is a visible change in the shape of the mother's abdomen, giving signs that the baby has dropped into the birth canal. The birth canal is the channel through which the baby passes during birth.

In most births, the fetus is usually upside down at this point, with the head nestled in the mother's pelvis. This is the easiest and safest position for birth. Once the head is out of the mother's body, the rest of the body usually delivers easily.

In some cases, the fetus does not turn to the head-down position in the last few weeks. Instead, the fetus is in a seat-down position in the mother's pelvis. This is called a breech presentation. In many of these instances, a doctor uses a surgical procedure called a cesarean section to deliver the baby. A complete discussion of cesarean birth appears in Chapter 6.

In the last few weeks of pregnancy, the skin of the mother's abdomen appears stretched to capacity. This is when stretch marks will generally appear. The muscles of the uterus and abdomen can be stretched to many times their original size during pregnancy. At the end of pregnancy, the muscles of the uterus contract to push out the baby during delivery. The mother's abdominal and uterine muscles generally return to near-normal sizes approximately six weeks after delivery.

## What Would You Do?

### Keep On Moving

"I guess you'll have to stop working out with me now that you're pregnant," Gwen said to her friend Holly. "I don't know, actually," Holly told Gwen. "I'll ask Dr. Wallace."

From the doctor, Holly learned that a woman *can* and *should* exercise while pregnant. Some aspects of her usual exercise regimen might need to be adjusted to her changing body. Dr. Wallace said, "If you exercised before becoming pregnant, it's okay to continue, with modifications. After the first trimester, do not do any exercises that require you to be on your back and do not do any abdominal work."

**Write About It** Imagine that you are Holly. Write a paragraph describing the exercise routine you are going to follow while pregnant. Also list any activities you would plan to avoid.

## What Would You Do?

**Write About It** Answers will vary; Holly might perform light aerobic activity, such as swimming or walking. She might also do some light weight lifting to help stay toned. She should avoid exercises that put excessive strain on the back or abdomen, such as sit-ups.

 **Universal Access**

**Gifted Learners** Ask gifted learners to interview several mothers about the discomforts of pregnancy and measures that gave them relief. Have students share their findings with the rest of the class. Then have the class work together to compare notes to determine which discomforts were the most common and to summarize the women's coping tips. (Discomforts and tips will vary; class should create a list of the most common discomforts and tips for relief.)

**McGraw Hill Professional Development**

**Mini Clip**
**ELL: Collaborative Work**

Students work in groups to complete a science lab. This requires them to discuss and record their finding using academic vocabulary.

**Reading Strategy**

**Critical Reading** Have students find and read an article on preventing back pain during pregnancy. The article should be from a reliable source. Students should summarize the tips offered in the article. In class, have students demonstrate the tips and compile them into a single checklist. (Tips will vary but may include: sleeping with a pillow under the knees, using massage, doing pelvic tilts, and practicing good posture.)

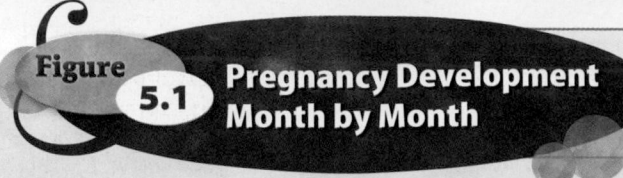

## Teach *cont.*

### Cooperative Learning

**Community Involvement** Hospitals, health clinics, and some health clubs and community centers offer special exercise programs for pregnant females. Have students work in small groups to find out about such programs. Direct each group to select one program to investigate. Ask students to gather the following information: where and when the program is offered, the cost, and the kinds of physical activity and exercise taught. They should also find out if the program is for women in a specific trimester of their pregnancy. Have each group prepare a brief oral presentation to share what it has learned with the class. (Findings will vary based on programs available in your area. Programs may include special swimming courses, yoga or stretch classes, or walking groups.)

### W Writing Support
### Narrative

**Pregnancy Myths** Explain to students that there are many myths about pregnancy that provide inaccurate information. Write the following myths on the board: the shape of a pregnant woman's face can tell you the baby's gender; if the heart rate of a fetus is fast, the gender will be female, if the heart rate is slow, it will be a male; a pregnant woman who has frequent heartburn will give birth to a child with a full head of hair. Have students write a one-page narrative that includes these and other myths about pregnant women they may have heard. Ask students whether they think these myths are harmful to pregnant women. (Narratives will vary depending on myths the student has heard. Some students may think the myths can be harmful if a woman actually believes them. Others may say they are fun but not dangerous.)

**Figure 5.1 Pregnancy Development Month by Month**

Specific changes occur during each month of pregnancy. *During which months is a mother most likely to experience morning sickness?*

| Month | Pregnancy Development |
|---|---|
| Month 1 | ✤ Missed menstrual period.<br>✤ Other signs of pregnancy may not yet be noticeable. |
| Month 2 | ✤ Breasts begin to swell.<br>✤ Pressure on bladder from enlarging uterus results in need to urinate more frequently.<br>✤ Possible nausea (morning sickness) and fatigue. |
| Month 3 | ✤ Breasts become firmer and fuller, may ache.<br>✤ Nausea, fatigue, and frequent urination may continue.<br>✤ Abdomen becomes slightly larger. The uterus is about the size of an orange.<br>✤ Weight gain may total 2–4 pounds (0.9–1.8 kg). |
| Month 4 | ✤ Abdomen continues to grow slowly.<br>✤ Most discomforts of early pregnancy are usually gone.<br>✤ Appetite increases. |
| Month 5 | ✤ Enlarged abdomen becomes apparent.<br>✤ Slight fetal movements felt.<br>✤ Increased size may begin to affect posture. |
| Month 6 | ✤ Fetal movements sensed as strong kicks, thumps, and bumps. Some may be visible.<br>✤ Weight gain by the beginning of this month may total 10–12 pounds (4.5–5.4 kg). |
| Month 7 | ✤ Increased size may affect posture. |
| Month 8 | ✤ Discomfort may result from increased size. Backache, leg cramps, shortness of breath, and fatigue are common.<br>✤ Fetal kicks may disturb the mother's rest.<br>✤ At the beginning of this month, weight gain totals about 18–20 pounds (8.2–9.1 kg). |
| Month 9 | ✤ Lightening is felt as the fetus drops into the pelvis. Breathing becomes easier.<br>✤ Other discomforts may continue.<br>✤ A total weight gain of 25–35 pounds (11.3–15.9 kg) is typical.<br>✤ False labor pains may be experienced. |

**W**

**Figure 5.1 Pregnancy Development Month by Month**

**Caption Answer** A woman is most likely to experience morning sickness during the first through third months. It rarely lasts beyond the fourth month.

**Discussion** Ask students: During which period do you think a pregnant woman has the most discomfort? Explain your answer. (Answers will vary. Some students may think the first trimester is the most uncomfortable and others may think just before giving birth is the most uncomfortable. Students should provide an explanation for their answers.)

### Weight Gain During Pregnancy

Women typically gain between 24 and 30 pounds during a healthy pregnancy. This weight is from the baby itself and from changes to the mother's body. **Figure 5.2** shows how that weight is usually distributed.

Recommended weight gain is about a pound a month during the first three months. In the fourth through ninth months, weight gain should be about three to four pounds per month.

Gaining too little weight can increase the risk of fetal death or premature birth. Gaining too much weight can put added stress on the mother's body and increase the risk of complications. Women who begin a pregnancy underweight or overweight will require special monitoring.

### Maternity Clothes

By around the fourth or fifth month, a pregnant woman needs looser clothing to allow for freedom of movement and circulation as the baby grows. Maternity pants often have a stretch panel in the front. Shirts also are made looser to allow room for the growing baby. When choosing clothing, an expectant mother should consider how garments will fit during her ninth month.

### Daily Routines

Pregnant women can take care of themselves in many ways. While pregnant women can usually follow some of the same daily routines they had before pregnancy, they should also do the following:

- **Eat a healthful diet.** Eat a variety of nutritious meals and snacks to get the nutrients that both mother and baby need.
- **Get plenty of rest.** Taking frequent breaks during the day may provide more energy.
- **Exercise.** Moderate exercise is important to everyone, including pregnant women.

**Figure 5.2 Weight Gain During Pregnancy**

Weight gain during pregnancy is due to many factors besides the actual weight of the baby. *Next to the baby itself, what causes the greatest weight gain during pregnancy?*

| Factor | Pounds |
|---|---|
| Weight of average baby at birth | 7–8 |
| Placenta | 1–2 |
| Amniotic fluid | 1½–2 |
| Increased size of uterus and supporting muscles | 2 |
| Increase in breast tissue | 1 |
| Increase in blood volume | 1½–3 |
| Increase in fat stores | 5 |
| Increase in body fluids | 5–7 |
| **Total** | **24–30** |

**Figure 5.2 Weight Gain During Pregnancy**

**Caption Answer** There are many factors that cause weight gain during pregnancy, however, next to the baby itself, an increase in body fluids causes the greatest weight gain during pregnancy.

**Discussion** As a class, determine the percentage of weight gain contributed by each factor. Use the second (or only) number listed. To find the percentage, divide the factor weight by the total weight (30). (Weight of baby: 27%; placenta: 6%; amniotic fluid: 6%; uterus/muscles: 6%; breast tissue: 3%; blood volume: 10%; fat: 17%; body fluids: 23%.)

## Assess

**Quiz**

Ask students to answer the following questions:

1. What is an obstetrician? (An obstetrician is a doctor who specializes in pregnancy and childbirth.)
2. What is the most important thing for a mother to do to ensure the health of her baby? (A mother should get regular medical care and advice from the beginning to the end of the pregnancy.)
3. What does a thorough prenatal examination include? (Exams include: a check of blood pressure, pulse, respiration, weight, and medical history; measurement of pelvis; urine analysis; and blood tests for anemia and Rh factor.)

## Reteach

### U Universal Access

**Visual Learners** Have students design an attractive maternity outfit. Have them refer to Figure 5.1 on page 134 for the physical developments that occur during a woman's pregnancy. Students should design an outfit for a particular time of pregnancy. Direct students to point out features that make the clothes appropriate for pregnancy. Encourage students to be creative as they illustrate their designs. (Designs will vary. Students should be able to explain why the outfit is appropriate for a pregnant woman.)

## Section 5.1

### Reteach *cont.*

##  Critical Thinking

**Plan a Schedule** Ask students to plan a weekly schedule for a pregnant woman that incorporates these important personal care activities: adequate rest—talk about scheduling bedtime to allow eight hours of sleep and perhaps the need for a nap during the day; exercise—discuss how to plan time to exercise and the appropriateness of various routines; hygiene—stress the importance of bathing daily and washing hands frequently (especially before eating and after toileting) to avoid illness. (Student schedules will vary, but should show time for rest, exercise, and hygiene; and should be logical.)

## U Universal Access

**Verbal Learners** Ask verbal learners to respond to this question: What role does recreation play in helping pregnant women cope with stress? (Recreation can help pregnant women feel more energized. Exercise improves the functioning of the body's systems, makes the pregnant woman feel stronger and more energetic, and reduces her stress levels. It may help pregnant women feel better prepared to give birth.)

## W₁ Writing Support

**Research Report**

**Artificial Foods** Have students research genetically engineered foods, artificial flavors (such as sweeteners), dyes, or colors added to foods. Students should find out if these substances have side effects or if they are dangerous to the pregnant mother or the fetus. Have students write a one-page report of their findings. (Students' research results will vary depending on what they chose to research. Whether or not these substances are safe is typically controversial. Pregnant women, and anyone with concerns about food safety, should avoid them.)

Doctors may recommend walking, yoga, or swimming. Look for exercise classes that are designed for pregnant women.

- **Practice good hygiene.** Keeping the skin clean helps the body maintain a healthy temperature and eliminate waste. A warm bath or shower before bedtime also may help pregnant women relax.

Pregnant women do not need to radically change their activities during pregnancy. Moderation is advised, but most activities can continue as before. Most women are able to continue working throughout their pregnancy.

### Emotional Health During Pregnancy

Pregnancy and birth are major events in a couple's life. They are also times of emotional adjustments. It is vital to talk to each other. Spending time alone together can help. Family and friends can also be sources of information and support.

Pregnancy causes hormonal changes that may lead to mood swings. Most women feel upset and worried at some time during pregnancy. This is why effective stress-reduction techniques are important.

**Depression**

Emotional and physical stress can lead to deep and lasting feelings of sadness. This is known as depression. Expectant mothers who feel overwhelmed need to seek help. There are a number of ways to find support. A woman's doctor may recommend a professional counselor or local support group. Often, women who are going through, or have been through, similar experiences can help the expectant mother. Some books also can help expectant mothers understand their concerns and improve their outlook.

### Stress

If you have experienced stress, you know how it affects you. You may feel moody, anxious, annoyed, or scared. Perhaps you lose your appetite, have nightmares, or feel sweaty and shaky. Pregnancy can be a stressful time.

It is important that pregnant women find ways to ease the stress for themselves and their babies. There are many ways to cope with stress while pregnant.

- **Avoid sugary foods and caffeine.** These can make pregnant women nervous or jumpy.

➤ **Dealing with Stress**
There are many ways to handle the emotional stress that may occur during pregnancy. *What could happen if a woman does not find ways to relieve stress?*

**136** Chapter 5 Preparing for Birth

➤➤➤ **Explore the Photo**

**Caption Answer** A woman who does not find ways to relieve stress may become depressed, moody, anxious, annoyed, or scared. She might lose her appetite, have nightmares, or feel sweaty or shaky.

**Discussion** Discuss with students the many resources available for pregnant women to get help with depression. Ask a volunteer to list resources on the board. (Resources may include: a doctor, professional counselor, local support group, Internet support group.)

- **Exercise.** Gentle exercises, such as stretching, and moderate physical activity, such as walking, can help pregnant women feel lighter and more energetic.

C₂

- **Take a time-out.** Taking time to relax and enjoy a favorite activity or hobby can help relieve stress.
- **Practice relaxation techniques.** Pregnant women can learn breathing or visualization exercises through books or classes.
- **Talk about concerns.** Mothers-to-be can benefit from talking to supportive friends or family members, especially those who have children of their own. They can also talk to their doctors or seek a counselor.
- **Take a class for expectant parents.** The more pregnant women know about the birth process, the greater their sense of control. Feeling prepared can help reduce stress.

**✓ Reading Check** **Explain** Why is it best for pregnant women to avoid sugary foods and caffeine?

# Nutrition During Pregnancy

Good nutrition is the single most important requirement during pregnancy. The baby's growth and development, including crucial brain development, depend on nutrients from the mother. By eating a nutritious, balanced diet, a pregnant woman promotes her baby's development and maintains her own health.

## Five Food Groups Plus Oils

Expecting mothers need a variety of nutrients to keep themselves and their developing babies healthy. The U.S. Department of Agriculture has developed nutritional guidelines for pregnant women. These guidelines are known as MyPyramid for Moms. The guidelines divide foods into five food groups, plus the oils category. (See **Figure 5.3**.)

### Grains

Eating grains is essential to any well-balanced diet. They contain carbohydrates, which provide

---

## THE DEVELOPING BRAIN

### Nutrition and Fetal Brain Development

Some pregnant women do not follow a sensible and balanced diet. Others, wrongly concerned about gaining weight, severely restrict their food intake. Either way, the developing fetus is put in serious danger. One possible outcome of failing to supply adequate nutrition to the fetus is that brain development could be stunted and the baby could be mentally retarded. Alcohol consumption, cigarette smoking, and drug abuse during pregnancy can have similar results.

**◼ Science Inquiry** Dieting during pregnancy can cause problems with fetal brain development. Why do you think a pregnant woman might diet even though she knows this?

---

our body with energy. Grains fortified with folic acid can help prevent defects to the baby's nervous system. The nutrients in grain also reduce the risk of heart disease and keep the digestive system working properly. The grains group includes any food made from wheat, rice, cornmeal, barley, or other grains. Examples include bread, pasta, oatmeal, and tortillas.

Grains are divided into whole grains and refined grains. Whole grains, such as whole-wheat flour and oatmeal, contain the entire grain kernel. Refined grains have been milled, causing parts of the grain to be removed. This gives them a finer texture and slows down the rate at which they spoil. However, refining also removes fiber, iron, and some vitamins. Examples of refined grain products include white bread and white rice. Most refined grains are enriched. This means that some vitamins and iron have been added back into them. However, they are still missing the fiber and some of the vitamins of whole grains.

Because whole grains are generally more nutritious than refined grains, it is recommended that at least half of the grains eaten be whole grains. Look to see that grains such as wheat, rice, oats, or corn are referred to as "whole" in the list of ingredients.

W₂

Section 5.1   A Healthy Pregnancy   **137**

---

## Reteach *cont.*

### C₂ Critical Thinking

**Brainstorm Ideas** Have students brainstorm a list of relaxation practices that can be used during pregnancy. Divide students into small groups and assign each group one of these practices to research. Have each group prepare a demonstration of the relaxation practice, allowing audience participation. (Relaxation practices will vary but may include meditation or breathing exercises. Groups should present an audience participation demonstration for the rest of the class.)

### W₂ Writing Support

**Menu Descriptions**

**Nutritious Meals** Ask students to write menus for an imaginary restaurant featuring nutritious meals for pregnant women. Have students describe each dish, along with its special nutritional value for pregnant women. Menus should include dishes made from whole grains, vegetables, fruits, milk products, and meat and beans. (Menus will vary but should show some creativity on the part of the students. Menus should also show an understanding of the nutritional needs of pregnant women.)

### ✓ Reading Check

**Explain** Sugary foods and caffeine can make a pregnant woman feel jittery and increase feelings of stress.

---

## THE DEVELOPING BRAIN

### Nutrition and Fetal Brain Development

**Science Inquiry** Answers will vary but may include: Many pregnant women diet because they are extremely concerned with gaining more weight than they should during pregnancy, or they might be afraid of making the baby overweight.

For more information and activities, see **The Developing Brain** guide and eTransparencies.

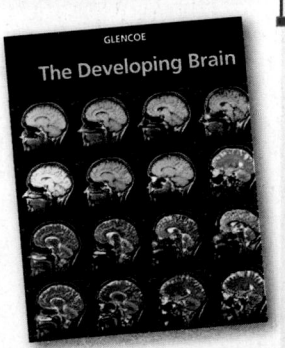

GLENCOE
The Developing Brain

### Reteach *cont.*

## C₁ Critical Thinking

**Analyzing Information** Bring in or have students bring in food labels from vegetables and fruit items. (These can be canned, frozen, or dried.) Ask students to analyze the information on the labels. Which foods would they recommend to a pregnant woman based on the labels? Which would they not recommend? Ask students to explain their answers. (Students' answers will vary but may focus on the high sodium content in some canned foods and the high sugar (fructose) content of some canned fruits.)

## U₁ Universal Access

**Intrapersonal Learners** Ask students to make a list of all the vegetables and fruits they have consumed over the past two days. Ask if they feel they are including enough vegetables and fruits into their diets. If not, what can they do to improve their eating habits? (Students' answers will vary. Encourage students to honestly evaluate their vegetable and fruit intake and to determine whether improvement is necessary. Many people do not consume the recommended five servings of fruits and vegetables per day. Students may suggest adding fruit to their breakfast or having carrot sticks for a snack.)

### Vegetables

Eating vegetables keeps the mother's heart healthy. Vegetables also can reduce her chances of getting diabetes, high blood presure, and some kinds of cancer.

Vegetables are rich in potassium and dietary fiber. Many are rich in folic acids and vitamins A, C, and E. Most are low in fat and calories, and therefore can help to control the mother's weight. Different colored vegetables typically provide different nutrients. They are divided into the following categories:

- Dark green vegetables, such as broccoli and spinach
- Orange vegetables, such as carrots and pumpkin
- Dry beans and peas
- Starchy vegetables, such as potatoes and corn
- Other vegetables, such as celery and onions

### Fruits

Any fruit or 100 percent fruit juice is part of this group. Some common fruits include apples, bananas, tomatoes, avocados, strawberries, and oranges. Fruit juices are high in calories and do not contain fiber. Eat a variety of fruits rather than just fruit juice for most of your fruit choices. Fruits can be fresh, frozen, canned, or dried.

Fruits have many of the same benefits as vegetables. Fruits also help maintain a healthy heart and blood vessels. Fruits can help control body weight. Many fruits are good sources of potassium, dietary fiber, vitamins A and C, and folic acid.

### Milk Products

Foods in the milk group include all varieties of milk, cheese, ice cream, and yogurt.

**Figure 5.3 MyPyramid for Moms**

MyPyramid for Moms divides foods into five basic groups, plus oils. *Which group contains nuts and seeds?*

**Vegetable Group** Vary your veggies. In general, more colorful vegetables, such as broccoli, carrots, and kidney beans, have more vitamins and minerals than lighter colored ones.

**Grains Group** Make half your grains whole. Eat at least three ounces of whole-grains every day. One ounce is about one slice of bread, one cup of breakfast cereal, or ½ cup of cooked rice or pasta.

**Fruit Group** Focus on fruits. In general, two cups of fruit should be eaten each day. For example, have one small banana, one large orange, and ¼ cup of dried apricots or peaches.

**Figure 5.3 MyPyramid for Moms**

**Caption Answer** The Meat and Beans group contains nuts and seeds. It also contains meats, poultry, fish, and beans.

**Discussion** Discuss with students why a pregnant woman should not only consider what she eats but also how the food she eats is prepared. (Pregnant women should be concerned about what they eat—they should avoid sugary foods and caffeine—and they should be concerned about how the food they eat is prepared—they shouldn't eat too many fried foods.)

Nutrients in milk products include calcium, potassium, vitamin D, and protein. Calcium is vital for building healthy bones and teeth. It is important that pregnant women get adequate calcium to prevent osteoporosis. **Osteoporosis** is a condition in which bones become fragile and break easily.

Choosing milk products that are low-fat or fat-free is important. High-fat milk products contain saturated fats and cholesterol that can lead to a greater risk of heart disease. If you cannot consume milk, choose lactose-free milk products and calcium-fortified foods and beverages.

### Meat and Beans

Meat, poultry, fish, dried beans, nuts, and eggs belong to this group. Choose meat and poultry cuts that are low-fat. They provide protein, which is vital to the baby's growth and development of bones and teeth. Protein also helps keep the mother's body healthy. Expectant mothers need more protein than they did before they were pregnant.

### Oils

Oils are fats that are liquid at room temperature. They can come from either plants or fish. Common oils include olive oil, corn oil, and canola oil. Many foods are naturally high in oils, including nuts, olives, and some fish.

Solid fats, such as butter, contain more saturated or trans fats than oils. These kinds of fats can increase your risk for heart disease. Oils have more monounsaturated and polyunsaturated fats, which are healthier. Oils are healthier than solid fats, but they are still high in calories, so their intake should be limited.

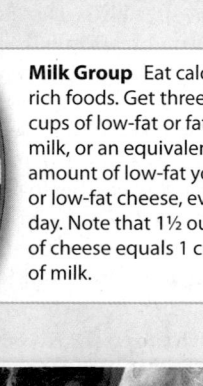

**Milk Group** Eat calcium-rich foods. Get three cups of low-fat or fat-free milk, or an equivalent amount of low-fat yogurt or low-fat cheese, every day. Note that 1½ ounces of cheese equals 1 cup of milk.

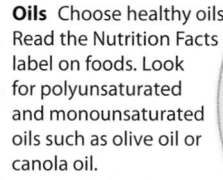

**Oils** Choose healthy oils. Read the Nutrition Facts label on foods. Look for polyunsaturated and monounsaturated oils such as olive oil or canola oil.

**Meat & Beans Group** Go lean with protein. Choose lean meats and poultry. Bake it, broil it, or grill it. And vary your protein choices with more fish, beans, nuts, and seeds.

Section 5.1    A Healthy Pregnancy    **139**

**Professional Development**

**Mini Clip**
**Reading: Connecting the Pieces**
A teacher helps students develop predictions and inferences about characters in a story.

### Reteach *cont.*

### U₂ Universal Access

**Interpersonal Learners** Divide the students into small groups. Ask each group to respond to the following questions: How is it possible for a pregnant woman to meet all of her nutritional needs if she has a limited amount of money to spend on food and vitamins? What suggestions would you give her? Have each group compile a list of suggestions and share them with the rest of the class. (Answers will vary. Students may suggest that the woman purchase store brands or generic brands to save money, use coupons, or get help from a food bank. Pregnant women might also share their problem with their obstetrician and ask for advice. Local social service agencies might be able to provide help. Tell students that government programs such as Women, Infants, and Children (WIC) help ensure that women and children get the proper food products, such as milk, cheese, and cereal.)

### C₂ Critical Thinking

**Evaluate Nutrients** Have students consider all the nutrients a pregnant woman needs. Ask students which nutrient they believe would cause the most harm if it were lacking in a pregnant woman's diet. (Answers may vary. Students should realize that all of the nutrients discussed are important to the health of both the pregnant woman and her baby. Students may suggest that lack of protein might cause the most harm if it were missing from the pregnant woman's diet because it is vital to the growth and development of the baby's bones and teeth. Expectant mothers need more protein than they did before they were pregnant.)

### U Universal Access

**English Language Learners** Pair English language learners with students whose first language is English. Ask a volunteer to read the first paragraph on this page. Ask pairs to find the definition of a *supplement*. (A supplement is a pill, powder, liquid, or the like containing only nutrients, not a food.) Then ask English language learners to explain what a supplement is in their own words. Ask the class why a variety of pills, powders, and liquids are called supplements. (People use them to *supplement*, or add to, the nutrients they get from foods they eat.)

### R₁ Reading Strategy

**Vitamin Deficiency** Write the word *deficiency* on the board. Ask students to define the word in their own terms and to give examples of deficiencies. (A deficiency is too little of a nutrient in the body. Students' examples will vary.) After discussing the definition, ask students what it means to have a vitamin deficiency. (Students should recognize that it means there are not enough vitamins in the body to maintain good health.)

### C₁ Critical Thinking

**Drawing Conclusions** Ask students if they think it is better to eat too many vitamins or too few. (Students' answers will likely vary. Make sure that students understand that eating too many or too few vitamins can both be harmful. Having too much of a vitamin can cause a person to become ill just as a deficiency can. In some cases it can even cause death.)

**Nutrition and Pregnancy**
Eating nutritiously is one of the best gifts a pregnant mother can give her unborn baby. *What can happen if a mother does not eat a balanced diet?*

## Vitamins and Minerals

A variety of vitamins and minerals are vital to both the fetus and the mother. Whenever possible, it is best to get these from a healthy diet, rather than by taking supplements. Pregnant women should take vitamins, minerals, or other supplements only with their doctor's approval.

### { Expert Advice... }

*"Pregnancy is such a demanding time nutritionally on a woman's body. If she can make even one positive change, it can make all the difference in her health, as well as in the health of her developing child."*

— Maggie McHugh, registered dietitian and certified nutritionist

### Vitamins

Vitamins help to maintain a healthy pregnancy. Research has determined some birth defects, such as spina bifida, are linked to vitamin deficiency. Women usually need more vitamins during pregnancy. Here are some of the most important ones.

- Vitamin A ensures proper eye development and helps keep skin healthy.
- The B vitamins assist in general fetal development.
- Vitamin C helps build healthy teeth and gums. It also helps form the connective tissue of skin, bone, and organs.
- Vitamin D aids in the creation of bones and teeth.
- Folic acid is necessary for normal spinal development in the fetus. Lack of folic acid can lead to spina bifida. Pregnant women need twice the normal amount. Even women who are considering becoming pregnant should increase their intake of folic acid.

### Minerals

Pregnant women need iron, a mineral that helps prevent anemia and assists in developing the baby's own blood supply. Extra iron is stored in the baby's liver and is used in the months right after birth. During this time, a baby who lives on breast milk lacks iron in the diet. The mother can get iron from dried beans, raisins, dates, meat, and leafy green vegetables.

Calcium and phosphorous are also important minerals during pregnancy. These nutrients work together to produce strong bones and teeth and ensure regular elimination of waste from the body. Milk and other dairy products are good sources of calcium and phosphorous.

### Food Quantities

All pregnant women should eat a wide variety of healthy foods. However, the exact quantities needed vary depending on the mother's age, weight, and activity level, as well as the stage of pregnancy.

When you visit the MyPyramid for Moms Web site, you can create a specific plan based on these factors. **Figure 5.4** shows a sample nutrition plan made using this Web site. The

---

### ▶ Explore the Photo

**Caption Answer** The baby's development, including brain, bone, and teeth development can be adversely affected. By eating a nutritious, balanced diet, a pregnant woman promotes her baby's development and maintains her own health.

**Discussion** Ask a volunteer to read aloud the Expert Advice on this page. Ask students what one positive change they think might make a difference in a pregnant woman's diet. (Responses will vary. Students might suggest that eating fewer sugary and high-calorie foods would make a difference.)

nutrition plan will show you how much food you need from each food group, during each stage of pregnancy.

Within each food group, pregnant women should choose foods that are rich in the vitamins and minerals needed. For example, carrots, winter squash, and spinach are good choices from the vegetable group for pregnant women.

## Nutrition and Pregnant Teens

Teens' bodies have special nutritional needs because they are still developing. Pregnancy places additional strain on the body. Many teens fill up on high-calorie, low-nutrient foods. Pregnant teens must be especially careful to eat nutritious meals and snacks. It is essential for a teen's own body and for her growing baby to get all the needed nutrients for proper growth and development.

It is especially important for pregnant teens to get enough calcium and iron. Calcium is essential for growing bones. Iron helps the blood carry oxygen to all parts of the body. During pregnancy, a woman has more blood in her body, so iron is even more important to her health. As with any pregnant woman, pregnant teens should discuss their nutritional needs with their doctor.

## Special Diets

Some people are sensitive to certain foods, such as dairy. Some people choose to avoid certain foods for personal reasons, such as vegetarians. A pregnant woman needs to discuss these considerations with her doctor to ensure that her fetus gets the needed nutrients for healthy growth and development.

### Sensitivities to Milk

Milk and other dairy products are a rich source of calcium, protein, and other key nutrients. Expectant mothers who cannot tolerate milk products need special eating strategies. One alternative is to eat larger amounts of other calcium-rich foods, such as broccoli,

### Figure 5.4 — MyPyramid for Moms Sample Nutrition Plan

This nutrition plan Is for a 30-year-old woman who weighs 140 pounds. *Amounts in which groups increase over the course of the pregnancy?*

|  | 1st Trimester | 2nd Trimester | 3rd Trimester |
|---|---|---|---|
|  | Jan - Mar | Apr - Jun | Jul - Oct |
| ▶ Grains | 7 ounces | 9 ounces | 9 ounces |
| ▶ Vegetables | 3 cups | 3½ cups | 3½ cups |
| ▶ Fruits | 2 cups | 2 cups | 2 cups |
| ▶ Milk | 3 cups | 3 cups | 3 cups |
| ▶ Meat & Beans | 6 ounces | 6½ ounces | 6½ ounces |

For more tips and information, visit **MyPyramid.gov**.

### Figure 5.4 — MyPyramid for Moms Sample Nutrition Plan

**Caption Answer** According to the nutrition plan for a 30-year-old woman who weighs 140 pounds, amounts in the Grains, Vegetables, and Meat & Beans groups increase over the course of the pregnancy.

**Discussion** Ask students to explain why, in this nutrition plan, they think the amounts in the fruits and milk groups do not increase over the course of the pregnancy. (Students' answers will vary. Possible answers may include: Fruits have many of the same benefits as vegetables but are typically higher in calories.)

## Reteach cont.

### C2 Critical Thinking

**Applying Knowledge** Have students work together in pairs to develop a nutritionally sound, one-week menu for a pregnant woman. Students should specify for which month of pregnancy the menu is for. Menus should include breakfast, lunch, dinner, and snacks. Students should provide some rationale for why they chose the foods they did. (Menus will vary but should provide adequate nutrition for a pregnant woman as suggested by My Pyramid.)

### R2 Reading Strategy

**Internet Research** Assign each student to read a current article about nutrition for pregnant teens. Refer students to Web sites, such as the March of Dimes, as well as health periodicals, such as the *Journal of the American Dietetic Association*. Have each student create a visual aid that represents the information in the article and share it with the class. (Visual aids will vary but should accurately represent the information found in the articles.)

### W Writing Support

**Explanatory Paragraphs** Ask students to write a paragraph in which they discuss the following question: Why is it particularly important for pregnant teens to get enough calcium and iron? (Answers should include: Calcium is essential for both the growing bones of the pregnant teen and her baby's development; iron helps blood carry oxygen to all parts of the body, and during pregnancy there is more blood moving around in a woman's body.)

## Assess

### Study Tools

Have students go to the Online Learning Center at **glencoe.com**:

- Take the **Practice Test**.
- Download **Study-to-Go** content.

Use the **Student Activity Workbook** for additional practice.

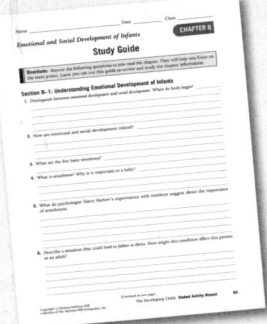

## Close

### Culminating Activity

**Total Recall** Ask students: In addition to eating nutritional food, in what other ways should pregnant women take care of themselves? (Answers may vary but should include: getting adequate rest, getting appropriate exercise, and practicing good hygiene.)

**N C L B** **NCLB** connects academic correlations to book content.

---

tofu, and leafy green vegtables. Protein can come from meat, fish, dried beans, and nuts.

Some people are lactose intolerant. Lactose is a type of sugar found in milk. A person is **lactose intolerant** if milk products cause symptoms such as abdominal pain and gas. Many people who have problems digesting lactose can still eat dairy foods, if they are served in small quantities or eaten with other foods. Fortified soy milk can also provide nutrients for people who are lactose intolerant.

**Lactase** is an enzyme that helps digest lactose. Eating foods with lactase, such as yogurt, helps some people digest milk. Taking lactase in liquid or tablet form can also relieve symptoms. Before taking a lactase supplement, pregnant women should consult their doctors.

### Vegetarians

Vegetarians do not eat meat, which is high in protein. Some vegetarians, called *vegans*, do not eat any animal products at all, including eggs and milk. Vegetarians eat food from plant sources, such as vegetables, fruits, grains, beans, nuts, and seeds. People may choose this diet for religious or cultural reasons, because of their concern for animals, or health reasons. By eating enough tofu and other soybean products, dried beans, nuts, and nut butters such as peanut butter, pregnant vegetarians can still get the protein they need. As with any pregnant woman, pregnant vegetarians should discuss their diet with their doctor. This will help ensure they get the needed nutrients for a healthy baby and a healthy mother.

## Section 5.1    After You Read

### Review Key Concepts

1. **Explain** why it is important for a pregnant woman to receive prenatal care from the beginning through the end of her pregnancy.
2. **List** three vitamins and explain each one's purpose.

### Practice Academic Skills

**English Language Skills**

3. Visit the MyPyramid for Moms Web site and explore the tools for an expectant mother. Use what you have learned to make a poster explaining MyPyramid for Moms. Use simple language and art to emphasize the importance of good nutrition, both for the mother and the developing baby.

> **NCTE 8** Use information resources to gather information and create and communicate knowledge.

**Science**

4. Pregnant women often feel more tired than normal and require extra sleep. However, women often find it difficult to sleep due to the discomforts of pregnancy. Conduct research to find out what pregnant women can do to help them sleep better without medication. Include talking to women with children, or women who are pregnant as part of your research.

> **NSES F** Develop understanding of personal and community health.

**Check Your Answers** Check your answers at this book's Online Learning Center at **glencoe.com**.

**N C L B**

---

**Section 5.1**    After You Read

### Review Key Concepts

1. Regular medical care is vital to the well being of the fetus and the mother, and allows the physician to track the progress of the pregnancy.
2. Any three of the following: Vitamin A ensures proper eye development, helps keep skin healthy; Vitamin B assists in general fetal development; Vitamin C helps build healthy teeth and gums, and helps form the connective tissue of skin, bone, and organs; Vitamin D aids in the creation of bones and teeth; Folic acid is necessary for normal fetal spinal development.

### Practice Academic Skills

3. Posters will vary but should include the basic food groups and emphasize the importance of good nutrition for both the mother and the baby.

4. Student answers will vary. Women can try meditation or gentle stretching to help them relax and ease muscle pain. They should sleep on their side with a pillow between their legs to ease the pressure on their backs. If they have heartburn, they can try sleeping with their head elevated.

# Preparing for the Baby's Arrival

## Reading Guide

### Before You Read

**Self-Checking** As you read, stop when you come to a new heading. Ask yourself questions about what you have just read. If you cannot remember the answers, go back and find them. This is called self-checking.

### Read to Learn
#### Key Concepts
- **List** six categories of basic baby supplies.
- **Describe** why parents need to develop a budget.

### Main Idea

**D**

New babies require items such as clothing, equipment, and a place to sleep. Parents also should create a budget and prepare any siblings for the new baby.

### Content Vocabulary
 formula
 pediatrician
◇ fixed expense
◇ flexible expense
◇ maternity leave
◇ paternity leave

**Graphic Organizer** Go to this book's Online Learning Center at **glencoe.com** to print out this graphic organizer.

### Academic Vocabulary

You will find these words in your reading and on your tests. Use the glossary to look up their definitions if necessary.
- slat
- reimbursement

### Graphic Organizer

As you read this section, note three advantages of breast-feeding and three advantages of bottle-feeding. Use a T-chart like the one shown to organize your information.

| Feeding Decisions | |
|---|---|
| **Breast-Feeding** | **Bottle-Feeding** |
|  |  |
|  |  |
|  |  |

### Academic Standards . . . . . . . . . . . . . . . . . . . . . . . . . . . .

**NCLB**

**English**

**NCTE 7** Conduct research and gather, evaluate, and synthesize data to communicate discoveries.

**Mathematics**

**NCTM Number and Operations** Understand numbers, ways of representing numbers, relationships among numbers, and number systems.

**Science**

**NSES B** Develop an understanding of the structure and properties of matter, chemical reactions.

**NCTE** National Council of Teachers of English
**NCTM** National Council of Teachers of Mathematics
**NSES** National Science Education Standards
**NCSS** National Council for the Social Studies

## Reading Guide

### Before You Read

Ask students what preparations they might make on the weekend to plan for the coming week. (Students might suggest filling in a calendar with their schedule for the week.) Tell them that parents of new babies must make many preparations before the arrival of the baby.

### **D** Develop Concepts

**Main Idea** Discuss the main idea with the students. Ask students if they have younger siblings. Ask how their parents prepared them for the arrival of their younger sibling. (Students' answers will vary but may include that parents sat down and explained things to me.)

---

## Focus

### Bell Ringer Activity

#### Getting Ready

Ask students to brainstorm the essential items new parents will need to take care of the baby so it will grow strong and healthy. (Answers will vary but should focus on items such as food, clothing, shelter, or medical care.)

## Preteaching

### Vocabulary

Tell students that *maternity* and *paternity* come from the Latin terms for mother and father. Synonyms include motherhood and fatherhood.

**Professional Development**

**Mini Clip**
**ELL: Vocabulary Activities**

Students practice vocabulary using synonyms, antonyms, definitions, and words in context.

### Graphic Organizer

 The Graphic Organizer is also on the TeacherWorks CD.

(Graphic organizers should include three for each category: Breast-Feeding: best source of nutrition; immunity against diseases; bond with mother; boost brain development; fewer digestive upsets; Bottle-Feeding: father can participate; flexible schedule for mother; feed less often)

**NCLB** connects academic correlations to book content.

## Teach

### Discussion Starter

**Wanted: Good Parents** Ask the class to brainstorm an advertisement for the job of parent. Advertisements should include hours, qualifications, experience, salary, fringe benefits, and opportunities for advancement. Have a volunteer write out the ad on the board. (Advertisements will vary but may include: hours—24/7 for 18 years; qualifications—patience, time management skills, sense of humor; experience—recommended, but on-the-job training available; salary—lots of love, headaches, disappointments, and happiness; fringe benefits—celebrating children's successes; opportunities for advancement—becoming a grandparent.)

### W₁ Writing Support

**Create a Brochure**

**Time Management Skills** Time management is an important resource for parents preparing for a new baby. Have students create a brochure of time management skills. Students can expand on the suggestions made in the text or do Internet or library research. You might suggest that students illustrate their brochures. (Brochures will vary but may include such time management skills as setting goals and making written plans; prioritizing tasks; avoiding wasting time; limiting time spent watching television, listening to music, reading, and visiting with friends; organizing the home and work spaces; using the right tools for the job; getting help from others when needed.)

**Preparing for the Baby**
New babies require preparation, such as preparing a nursery. *Why is it important to have a nursery set up before the baby arrives?*

## Preparing for Parenthood

Pregnancy is a time of anticipation and preparation. It is also a time for expectant parents to think about what their baby's physical, emotional, and intellectual needs will be and how they are going to meet them. Many expectant parents worry that they may not be up to the demands of raising a child. This is especially true for first-time parents. Parents should discuss their hopes, fears, worries, and other aspects of parenting with each other before the baby's arrival.

How will they handle guidance and discipline? How will parenting tasks be shared? How will they manage the new expenses? Of course, no one can plan for every situation. Parents' ideas often change as they gain parenting experience. Agreeing on certain ground rules, however, can help reduce confusion and conflict in relationships later on.

Parents-to-be must also prepare for their changing responsibilities. They may already be spouses, employees, students, volunteers, sisters or brothers, or daughters or sons. Now they will become parents as well. Some of the existing roles will change due to the time and energy that parenthood demands.

Everyone can benefit from good time-management skills. These skills are especially important for parents. Developing a basic daily schedule helps keep things on track. Routines also help infants and young children know what to expect and when to expect it. This helps them feel secure. Using time wisely can help staying on a schedule easier. For example, combining errands or taking advantage of nap times can help parents feel less overwhelmed.

**W₁**

## ▶ Explore the Photo

**Caption Answer** It is important to have the nursery set up so that the baby will have a safe and comfortable place to sleep, be dressed and changed, and so on.

**Discussion** Ask students what might happen if parents brought home a new baby but had not made preparations for it. (Answers will vary but may include that it might cause extra stress for the parents as they try to prepare things and take care of the new baby.)

## Other Children in the Family

It is not always easy for children to accept a new baby in their lives. Older siblings may not be excited about the new addition to the family. Who can blame them? All of a sudden their world is turned upside down. They have to share their parents' attention, their toys, and their space. It is a big adjustment. Of course, many children are happy to have a sibling. They look forward to helping care for the new baby. They also enjoy showing their sibling how things work.

How children react to a new sister or brother depends on how well prepared they were before the baby's arrival, how they react to change, and their age. Parents should be prepared for a wide range of attitudes, from jealousy and confusion to excitement and love. A two-year-old does not really understand what is happening. Adjusting takes time. Talking about concerns and acceptance of a child's feelings can help foster a positive relationship between siblings.

## Clothes, Equipment, and Space

The list of basic supplies for a baby can be overwhelming for many new parents. Babies need clothes, bedding, bath supplies, and travel equipment such as a stroller. Parents who choose bottle-feeding need bottles, plastic nipples, and lids. **Figure 5.5** describes basic baby supplies. Parents can get specific suggestions from doctors, family, friends, and magazines and books that test products.

### Baby's Room

Newborns may sleep as many as 18 to 22 hours a day. During the first six months, most babies sleep 15 to 18 hours a day. Some parents feel that babies sleep better in their parents' room. This arrangement makes late-night feedings easier. Others think that babies need a quiet space of their own in which to sleep. Of course, many babies share a sibling's room. Comfortable conditions are more important than a large amount of space. If the baby does not have a separate room, curtains or other room dividers can be used to create a quieter, more private space.

## Parenting Skills

### Accepting the New Family Member

Many parents are concerned about how an older child will react to having a new baby brother or sister. Here are some tips parents can use to reassure an older sibling:

- Try not to change the older child's routine any more than necessary.
- If your local hospital offers sibling classes, consider enrolling your child.
- If possible, have the child come to the hospital to see the new baby.
- When relatives and friends visit, make sure the older child feels included.
- Encourage the older child to help with the baby's care. For example, he can bring you a diaper or entertain the baby while you are changing her clothes.
- Set aside time each day to spend with the older child without the baby being around.

**Take Charge** Imagine that a friend recently had a second child. Your friend is worried that visitors will pay attention to the new baby, but ignore the older child. Write an advice column on how your friend might handle this situation.

## Parenting Skills

### Accepting the New Family Member

Ask students to write down what they would do as a parent to make sure their oldest child was prepared for the arrival of a new sibling. How would they make the older child feel important after the baby's arrival? (Students' answers will vary but may include giving the child some responsibilities for the new baby, based on the child's age).

**Take Charge**
Answers will vary. Students might say that the parent could play with the older child while the visitor cares for the new baby, or the parent could ask the older child to help introduce the new baby to the visitor.

## Section 5.2

### Teach cont.

**W₂ Writing Support**
**Freewriting**
**Stranger in the House**  Have students imagine that they are a two-year-old who has suddenly become the older sibling to a new baby. Tell students to quickly write down any emotions they think they would feel. Students should not worry about grammar or spelling at this point, but try to clearly express their feelings. Ask for volunteers to share their freewriting with the class. (Students should let their thoughts go and write whatever comes to mind. They should not worry about grammar and spelling. You might want to set a time limit on this activity. Ask volunteers to share their writing with the rest of the class. Responses will vary, but may include words like frightened, scared, anxious, confused, or lonely.)

**U Universal Access**
**Kinesthetic Learners**  Divide students into two groups. Have each group prepare a skit to perform in front of the class. The first group's skit should show the "don'ts" of telling a child they will have a new sibling. The second group's skit should focus on the "do's" of explaining to a child that he or she will have a new sibling. (Role-plays will vary. Students should understand that parents need to accept a child's feelings whatever they are. Parents should not scold a child for being angry or jealous, but should show empathy and help the child cope with his or her emotions.) **ELL**

## Teach cont.

### S Skill Practice

**Guided Practice**

**Categorize Needed Items** Divide the class into small groups. Have each group categorize the items in Figure 5.5 under the following categories: replace frequently; replace once in a while; can be used throughout infancy; and save for a second child. (Groups' lists may vary somewhat. However, disposable items should be on the replace frequently list and larger, more permanent items such as a crib should be on the save for a second child list. Cars seats might be used throughout infancy. Some items may go in more than one category.) **L1 ELL**

**Determine Needs** Discuss how each of the baby supplies listed is used and why it is needed. Ask why the following are needed: receiving blankets (These are used to keep babies warm indoors since their internal thermostats are not fully developed.); hats (Hats keep babies out of the sun in warm months and warm in cold months.); breast pump (This is used to extract breast milk for times the mother is away.); blunt-tipped nail scissors (These are used because they are safer than pointed scissors.) **L2**

**Making Comparisons** Have students compare the advantages and disadvantages of using cloth versus disposable diapers. Make sure they consider the following: cost, convenience, health, and ecological impact. (Students' answers will vary but may include: disposable diapers are more expensive, and clog landfills; cloth diapers cause more laundry and can be unsanitary.) **L3**

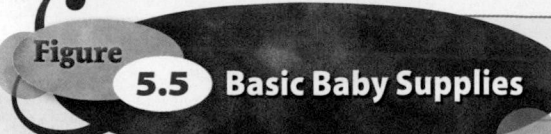

**Figure 5.5 Basic Baby Supplies**

It is important to have baby supplies ready when the infant first arrives home. *Why do you think sun hats or bonnets are important?*

### Needed Baby Items

**Diapering Needs**
- ❖ A changing table, or some surface to use for changing the baby
- ❖ If using disposable diapers, about 70 (a week's supply)
- ❖ If using cloth diapers: 3–4 dozen diapers and diaper pins
- ❖ Covered diaper pail
- ❖ Washcloths or disposable wipes, and diaper rash ointment

**Clothing**
- ❖ 6–8 undershirts; 4–6 one-piece footed sleepers or gowns
- ❖ 6 cotton receiving blankets; 1 warm outer wrapping blanket
- ❖ 1–2 sun hats or bonnets
- ❖ 1 sweater, 1 coat or warm wrap, and warm hat (if weather is cold)

**Feeding Equipment**
- ❖ Breast-feeding: Breast pump and pads; plastic bottles or bags for storing breast milk
- ❖ Bottle-feeding: 6–8 small bottles; nipples and bottle caps; bottle and nipple brush
- ❖ Bibs
- ❖ High chair

**Bedding/Bedroom**
- ❖ Crib and waterproof mattress (if the baby will sleep alone); bumper pad
- ❖ Waterproof mattress cover
- ❖ 4 fitted crib sheets
- ❖ 2–3 lightweight blankets and a heavier crib blanket
- ❖ Storage space, such as chest of drawers

**Bathing and Other Supplies**
- ❖ Baby bathtub
- ❖ Rubbing alcohol and cotton swabs (for umbilical cord)
- ❖ Mild, pure soap; baby shampoo
- ❖ Several washcloths and 2 soft cotton bath towels
- ❖ Cotton balls, baby oil, and baby lotion
- ❖ Blunt-tipped nail scissors
- ❖ Baby comb and brush set
- ❖ Thermometer

**Travel Equipment**
- ❖ Car seat that meets the government safety standards
- ❖ Tote bag for carrying supplies
- ❖ Stroller, carriage, or infant carrier (optional)

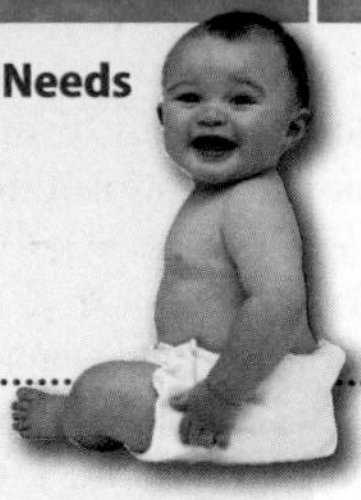

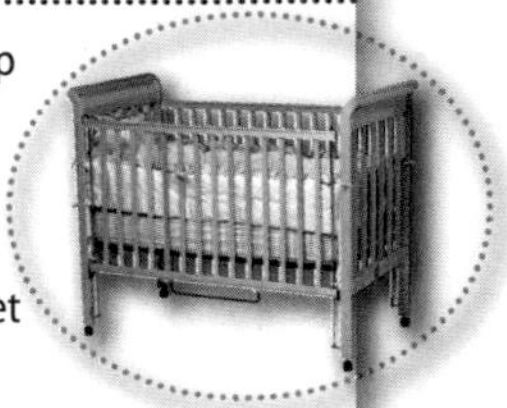

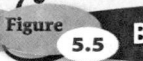

**Figure 5.5 Basic Baby Supplies**

**Caption Answer** Some babies have very little hair to protect their scalps and many babies' skin is fair and delicate and should be protected from the sun.

**Discussion** As a class, go over the baby items listed in this figure. Have students explain whether or not they feel the items are essential and what they are used for. For example, some students might not see the need for 6–8 undershirts. They may not realize how often a baby must be changed.

**The Crib** Babies spend countless hours alone in a crib. That means crib safety should be a high priority. Here are the characteristics of a safe crib:

- **Slats** Slats should be no more than 2⅜ inches apart. A **slat** is the flat, narrow strip of wood on the sides of a crib. If they are farther apart than this, a baby's head could become trapped between them.
- **Paint** If the crib is painted, the paint should not contain lead and should be smooth, with no flaking.
- **Structure** Corner posts should all be the same height. If some corner posts are taller than the sides of the crib, the baby's clothing or bedding could catch on the posts.
- **Sides** When lowered, crib sides should be about 9 inches above the mattress to keep the baby from falling out. When they are raised, they should be at least 26 inches above the mattress.
- **Latch** The latch to raise and lower the sides should lock securely. Never use a crib with a broken latch.
- **Mattress** The mattress should be firm and fit the crib exactly. There should be no space between the crib and the mattress. Infants can get trapped in this space.
- **Safe Bedding** Soft bedding should *not* be placed in a crib. While soft bedding such as pillows and quilts may look cute and comfortable, babies can suffocate on it. Even stuffed toys should be removed when a baby is in the crib. Basic bumper pads around the crib, just above the mattress, can be used to protect the baby from the crib's sides though.
- **End Panels** If the end panels have decorative cutouts, they should be very small, so the baby's head, arms, and legs cannot become caught in them.
- **Age** If the crib was pre-owned, it should be carefully checked to be sure it meets these current safety standards.

Parents may choose to put a baby monitor near the crib. The device picks up sounds from the room and sends them to a speaker in another part of the home. Baby monitors let parents know if the baby needs attention.

## SAFE CHILD HEALTHY CHILD

### Car Seat Safety

Children should be restrained using the appropriate car seats for their size and weight. There are three classes of car seats.

- Infant-only seats fit babies up to 22 pounds. The infant faces to the rear. The seat should be placed in the back seat.
- Convertible seats fit children from birth to about 40 pounds. They are used facing to the rear for the first year, then can be turned around when the baby is at least one year old and weighs at least 20 pounds.
- Children between four and seven years old should use booster seats locked securely in place with adult seat belts.

**Be Prepared** Most parents are careful to properly place their babies in car seats. However, many parents do not place children in the four to seven age group in booster seats. Conduct research to determine the percentage of injuries that could be prevented if all four- to seven-year-olds were placed in booster seats.

**The Diaper-Changing Area** Parents need to set aside a space where the baby can be changed and dressed. They can buy a changing table or use almost any sturdy, flat surface. Whatever surface is used, it should be covered with a cloth or towel that can be washed regularly.

Many changing tables or pads have rails around the sides to help prevent falls. They also come with a restraint strap to help secure the baby. Even young babies can wiggle, roll, or move quickly. That is why a baby should never be left unattended on any elevated surface such as a changing table or a bed, even if restraint straps are used. Even babies who cannot yet roll can still wiggle out of them if not properly supervised. Falls can occur within seconds.

Section 5.2    Preparing for the Baby's Arrival    **147**

## Teach cont.

### C Critical Thinking

**Calculate Costs** Have students calculate the cost of preparing a baby's room. Assign small groups to find costs of cribs, safe bedding, chest of drawers, or diaper-changing tables. Groups should find the average costs for the items. Each group should prepare a presentation of their information for the rest of the class. After each group gives their presentation, have the class total all costs. Mention that parents can reduce costs by shopping at garage sales or secondhand stores and by borrowing from friends or relatives. (Average costs will vary. Students should find prices from up-scale stores, low-cost stores, garage sales, and secondhand stores if possible.)

### U Universal Access

**Visual Learners** Divide the class into small teams. Have each team design a baby's room. Students should keep in mind the placement of the crib and the diaper changing area, as well as any other major pieces of furniture the room might have such as a rocking chair. Suggest that students find or draw pictures of what furnishing and toys they would include and place them on poster board to create an example of what the room would look like when completed. Have teams present their posters to the class as if they were presenting design ideas to expecting parents. (Designs will vary but should include all of the essentials that should be included in a baby's room.)

## SAFE CHILD HEALTHY CHILD

### Car Seat Safety

**Identify** Ask students why they think some parents do not place their four-to-seven-year-old children in booster seats. (Answers will vary. Possible answers include: parents may not be aware of the need to put their child in a booster seat or parents may not be able to afford another car seat.)

**Be Prepared** Studies show that approximately 59 percent of injuries to four- to seven-year-olds received during an automobile accident could be prevented by placing them in booster seats, rather than simply in standard seat belts.

## Teach *cont.*

**C Critical Thinking**

**Compare and Contrast** Refer students to Figure 5.6 and point out that the many advantages of breast-feeding are the reason most doctors advise it. However, note that there may be reasons not to breast-feed. Ask each student to decide how he or she would rank the following factors from most important to least important: convenience, saving money, sharing all aspects of child-rearing, baby's health, mother's health, mother's emotional attachment, time efficiency, ease of preparation. Using their rankings, have students decide which type of feeding would best match their priorities. (Students' rankings and responses will vary. Students should be able to support their decisions.)

**R Reading Strategy**

**Internet Research** Encourage students to find out how other cultures handle babies' sleep, feeding, and health care. For example, in China and Japan, parents and children sleep together. Ask students to research the following areas: where infants usually sleep, how infants are usually fed, what kind of health care infants usually have. Students should present their findings in a one-page report. After students have presented their findings, discuss the differences and similarities among various cultures. (Reports will vary depending on the country chosen by students. Reports should address the three areas mentioned.)

**R** **Figure 5.6** **Breast-Feeding vs. Bottle-Feeding** **C**

Both breast-feeding and bottle-feeding have advantages. *What factor do you think is most important in determining if a mother will breast-feed her baby? Why?*

| | Advantages | Disadvantages |
|---|---|---|
| **Breast-feeding** | ❖ Best source of nutrition for baby. <br> ❖ Gives the baby some immunity against diseases. <br> ❖ Creates a bond through physical closeness with the mother. <br> ❖ May boost brain development. <br> ❖ Reduces baby's risk of allergies. <br> ❖ Causes fewer digestive upsets. <br> ❖ Speeds the return of the mother's uterus to normal size. <br> ❖ Reduces the mother's risk of later having breast or ovarian cancer. <br> ❖ Reduces the risk that the mother will feel depressed. <br> ❖ Is available at all times. <br> ❖ Is free, though a nursing mother needs additional food. | ❖ Baby has to be fed more often. <br> ❖ In rare cases, may be medical reasons that suggest breast-feeding is not desirable or possible. <br> ❖ May be painful for some mothers. <br> ❖ May be difficult because of work schedule. <br><br> 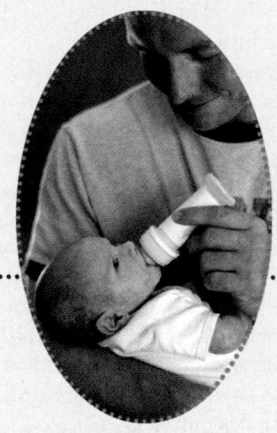 |
| **Bottle-feeding** | ❖ Allows mother to have a more flexible schedule. <br> ❖ Eliminates concern about mother's diet or medications she takes. <br> ❖ Ensures that baby gets essential nutrients. <br> ❖ Babies need feeding less often. <br> ❖ Available in shelf-stable forms for easier storage and portability. | ❖ Can be expensive. <br> ❖ Does not give the baby any natural immunities to disease. <br> ❖ Involves a greater chance of baby developing allergies. <br> ❖ Creates risk that baby may not be given close physical contact during feeding. |

**Figure 5.6** **Breast-Feeding vs. Bottle-Feeding**

**Caption Answer** Answers will vary. Many breast-feeding mothers are mainly concerned with the baby's nutritional needs while mothers who must quickly return to work may find breast-feeding overly difficult.

**Discussion** If you have students from countries other than the United States, ask them to compare breast-feeding vs. bottle-feeding in their country. Is one more prevalent than the other? If so, why do they believe it is so? (Students' answers and comments will vary. They may not know the customs of their birth country or may be uncomfortable sharing them with the class.)

## Decisions About Feeding

All parents must decide whether to breast- or bottle-feed their baby. There are several factors for parents to consider when making that choice. **Figure 5.6** lists many advantages and disadvantages of breast-feeding and bottle-feeding.

Breast milk has many benefits. Health care professionals recommend it whenever possible, even for a short time. There are breast pumps available that allow many mothers to successfully store breast milk. Other caregivers can then feed the baby when the mother is not available. This is an option for mothers who must return to work but want to continue breast-feeding their child.

Using bottles enables the baby's father or other caregivers to enjoy time alone with the baby. Babies who are bottle-fed drink formula. **Formula** is a mixture of milk or milk substitutes, water, and essential nutrients. It comes in either a powdered form, which is mixed with water, or in liquid form.

Whether a baby is bottle-fed or breast-fed, the nurturing and touch that comes with being held and fed is as important as the food itself.

## Choosing a Pediatrician

Before the baby is born, parents should choose a doctor to care for the child. Many parents choose pediatricians. A **pediatrician** is a doctor who specializes in treating children. This doctor may be the child's primary doctor for years.

Some families choose a family doctor or family practice medical group so the whole family can go to one place for medical care. A family doctor may treat people of all ages. The medical group may include a pediatrician to care for children.

Parents can ask their own doctors for recommendations for pediatricians. Parents can also ask friends who have children for suggested doctors. Once they have a few names,

**C**

**Mothers and Work**
If a new mother plans to provide breast milk for her baby, she needs to discuss these plans with her employer ahead of time. *What other work arrangements should be considered?*

Section 5.2  Preparing for the Baby's Arrival  **149**

**Section 5.2**

## Assess

**Quiz**
Ask students to answer the following questions:

1. What factors can affect a child's reaction to a new brother or sister? (How well prepared he or she was before the baby's arrival; how the child typically reacts to change; and age.)
2. Name some considerations when choosing a safe crib. (Soft bedding, pillows, fluffy blankets, and stuffed toys can be suffocation hazards. Slats that are spaced too widely pose potential for baby getting stuck. Paint should not contain lead. Sides should lock securely.)
3. What is a doctor who specializes in treating children called? (pediatrician)

## Reteach

**C** **Critical Thinking**
**Evaluate Pediatricians** Have students consider sensible ways to select a pediatrician. Point out the value of talking with a pediatrician before the birth to ask questions, assess compatibility, and make arrangements. (Suggestions might include: referral from doctors or other parents; if parents want a doctor close to their home, they might check the phone book; they also may need to find a doctor who is part of their insurance plan.)

---

**▶ Explore the Photo**

**Caption Answer** Answers will vary. Possible answer: Both parents may need to look at the hours worked to ensure child care coverage.

**Discussion** In America, many fathers are now taking a more active role in child care. Why might a father give up his job to stay home with children instead of the mother? (Answers will vary but might include that the mother has a better paying career.)

### R₁ Reading Strategy

**Vocabulary Terms** Focus students' attention on the vocabulary terms *fixed expense* and *flexible expense*. To ensure students' understanding of the difference between the two terms, ask students to give examples (other than those provided in the text) for both fixed expense and flexible expense. (Students' examples will vary but should show an understanding of the difference between the two terms. Examples may include: fixed expenses—cable television service, some cell phone services have flat rates, newspaper delivery service; flexible expenses—the price of gasoline, travel expenses.)

### W Writing Support

**Topic Sentence**

**Medical Costs** Locate several articles about the current costs for newborn medical care, such as the cost for delivery and the hospital stay, the cost for the doctor, and any costs that might result if there are complications. Ask students to choose an article and read it. Then have them write an outline stating the main idea of the article, along with major and minor supporting details. The main idea should be expressed as a topic sentence. (Students' answers will vary depending on the article chosen. Outlines should correctly identify the main ideas, along with supporting details.)

### ✓ Reading Check

**Compare** Pediatricians see only children as patients whereas family doctors see people of all ages.

---

## Math in Action

### Health Care Costs

Medicaid covers 92 percent of prenatal care and delivery cost of a newborn for qualified parents. The new parents must pay the remaining expenses out-of-pocket. Suppose delivery cost is $4,577 and prenatal care is $1,962. What are the expected out-of-pocket expenses?

**Math Concept** **Multiply Decimals by Whole Numbers** A percent is a ratio that compares a number to 100. The percent difference (100%-92%) is divided by 100 and multiplied by total expenses (whole number).

**Starting Hint** Add the delivery cost and prenatal care costs to find the total expenses. Subtract 92% from 100%. Convert the resulting percent to a decimal and multiply it by the total expenses.

 For math help, go to the Math Appendix at the back of the book.

**NCTM Number and Operations**
Understand numbers, ways of representing numbers, relationships among numbers, and number systems.

---

parents should interview each doctor to see if they like the doctor and agree with his or her ideas about caring for children. Most pediatricians welcome this opportunity to talk with prospective patients.

When choosing a doctor, some considerations are practical. Where is the doctor's office? What are the office hours? What are the fees for checkups, tests, and vaccinations? Which insurance plans are accepted? Other considerations are emotional. Do you feel comfortable with the doctor and staff?

### ✓ Reading Check **Compare** How is a pediatrician different from a family doctor?

## Making a Budget

Prenatal care is an important expense that can be quite costly. Add these costs to the extra expenses involved with having a baby, and the

amount of money needed to support a baby climbs higher than many new parents expect. Planning can help parents meet these expenses. Creating a budget is one way to plan.

A budget is simply a spending plan that people use to help estimate their present and future income and expenses. A budget allows people to set goals for saving and to develop a spending plan that meets their needs. Budgets are helpful for everyone, but especially for expectant and new parents.

The first step in making a budget is to identify income, such as money from jobs. The next step is to list where that income currently goes. A **fixed expense** is a payment that generally cannot be changed. This can include bills such as a car payment, housing payment and expenses, and taxes. A **flexible expense** is an expense that can be changed, such as food costs, household items, clothes, and entertainment. For example, you could go out to eat less often to reduce food costs if necessary.

## Estimating Health Care Expenses

Health care costs for pregnancy and childbirth can be high. This includes doctors' fees and the cost of staying in the hospital or birthing center. Hospitals charge different fees based on the care provided. Most health insurance plans will cover these expenses, but only if the woman has insurance coverage at the time she becomes pregnant. If a pregnant woman does not have insurance, some hospitals have free or lower-cost clinics to help people who cannot pay the full fees. Some hospitals will make arrangements for payment plans. There are also government programs that offer financial assistance for health care costs.

Many employers offer health insurance to their employees, and these plans often cover their spouses and children, too. Workers should find out what part of the expenses insurance will cover and what they must pay on their own.

If employers do not provide insurance, people can purchase their own health insurance. It is always a good idea to shop around for a health care plan before buying into one. Insurance companies charge different amounts, and

---

## Math in Action

### Health Care Costs

The new parents would be responsible to pay $523.12; [($4,577 + $1,962) × (100% − 92%) = $6,539 × 8% = $6,539 × 0.08 = $523.12].

**NCLB** Activity correlated to Math standards.

**Financial Responsibility**
Making a budget becomes more important when a couple starts a family. *How are fixed expenses different from flexible expenses?*

people can save money by making comparisons. As part of this process, it is important to carefully check the cost of the insurance and know exactly what services it will cover. Some insurance plans pay doctors and hospitals directly. Other plans require the insured persons to pay the bills themselves and then submit a claim for **reimbursement**, or repayment.

## Consider Child Care Options

Once expectant parents have developed their budget, they need to review their options for child care. Parents must consider many factors when deciding how to care for their child. These factors include each other's goals, skills, and time available. Will one parent be able to cut back on working hours or stay at home full-time to care for the child? What other child care options are available, and what are their costs?

Many new parents who work take maternity or paternity leave. **Maternity leave** is time taken off work by a mother after the birth of a baby. **Paternity leave** is when the father takes time off work after a baby's birth. Under a federal law called the Family Medical Leave Act, employers with more than 50 workers must offer 12 weeks of unpaid family or medical

leave to new mothers and fathers. Many workers do not take the entire 12 weeks of leave for financial reasons. Many employers also offer some time off with full or partial pay. Many parents choose to take maternity or paternity leave to help bond with their new child.

Couples sometimes decide that one parent will care for the child and not work outside the home. In the past, this was usually the mother. Today, many fathers are full-time caregivers.

Regardless of who takes primary responsibility for daily caregiving, both parents should share the work of caring for their children. In many families, both parents decide to return to work. In others, there is just one parent to support the family. These single parents need to consider child care options.

## Estimate Other Expenses

In addition to health care expenses, there are other costs that expectant parents must think about. Some of these include:

- Maternity clothes
- The supplies listed in Figure 5.5 on page 146
- Formula, if a baby is bottle-fed, which can cost between $1,200 and $2,200 per year
- Substitute child care, if needed

---

**▶ Explore the Photo**

**Caption Answer** Fixed expenses, such as car payments and rent, typically do not change, whereas flexible expenses, such as food and clothing can vary.

**Discussion** Do you think it is more difficult to plan for fixed or flexible expenses? Why? (Answers may vary. Students will likely say it is more difficult to plan for flexible expenses because you cannot know for certain what they will be.)

---

**Reteach** *cont.*

### U Universal Access

**Verbal Learners** Write the following statement on the board: Mothers should stay at home with their children until they are at least two years old. Have students decide whether or not they agree with this statement. They should be able to support their positions. (Students' positions will vary. Some may feel this bonding is needed. Others may say that income to provide for physical needs is more important. All students should logically support their positions.)

### R₂ Reading Strategy

**Re-reading** Have students re-read the third paragraph in the right column. Discuss with students how roles in families are changing. Point out that families' decisions about the work-family balance are often based on factors such as: income needs, availability of relatives for child care, parent values, and job options. Ask students if they know any families who have made decisions based on any of these factors. (Students may or may not know anyone who has made decisions based on these factors.)

### C Critical Thinking

**Problem Solving** Baby clothes can be expensive. Bring in a catalog or store ads, or ask students to visit a baby-clothing store, to research current prices. Have students brainstorm ways parents can save money when it comes to baby clothing. Students should consider unisex outfits, hand-me-downs, and baby showers as ways parents can save money. (Students might also consider shopping at garage sales or thrift stores for gently-used baby clothing. Many towns also have consignment stores where people sell their used baby clothing and other baby items.)

## Assess

### Study Tools

Have students go to the Online Learning Center at **glencoe.com**:

- Take the **Practice Test**.
- Download **Study-to-Go** content.

Use the **Student Activity Workbook** for additional practice.

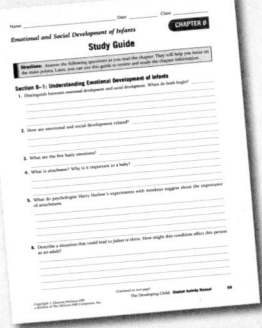

## Close

### Culminating Activity

**Guest Speaker** Invite a new parent to the classroom. Ask students to write questions beforehand on these topics to ask the guest: how the parent adapted to a new schedule; what type of planning was involved; and any ways the parent has been able to reduce expenses.

 **NCLB** connects academic correlations to book content.

## Make a Plan

Once parents have made a list of all the expected expenses, they can compare the expenses to their income and savings. If the couple's monthly income is less than their projected monthly expenses, it may be necessary to cut back on flexible expenses or to explore other sources of income.

If the mother works outside of the home, she should consider whether her income will be disrupted when the baby arrives and she is off work. Parents who have saved money will have an easier time. Even those with no prior savings should include saving a regular amount in their budget. This cushion helps families deal with unexpected expenses and future needs. Parents should use their plan as a guide to control their spending. Adjustments may need to be made periodically as expenses or income changes.

## Reduce Expenses

There are several ways to reduce costs. Shopping for baby clothes at store sales, garage sales, or secondhand stores can save money. Using coupons can help decrease the family's food budget. Borrowing baby equipment and clothes is another way to save money. However, all used or borrowed items should be carefully cleaned. You should also make sure the items meet any current safety standards.

One of the most important duties of a parent is to make sure children are as safe as possible when traveling in a car. Restraining a child properly is the best way to prevent injuries in a crash. Car seats should not be bought used. The seat may have been damaged in some way. Car seats more than five years old should not be used. To avoid injury, never put a child age 12 or under in the front seat of a car that has passenger-side airbags.

## Section 5.2    After You Read

### Review Key Concepts

1. **Identify** some important safety considerations when choosing a crib.
2. **Describe** factors parents must consider when deciding on child care for a new baby.

### Practice Academic Skills

 **English**

3. Disposable diapers have become increasingly popular over the last 40 years. Conduct research to compare the advantages of using cloth or disposable diapers. Pay particular attention to cost and environmental issues. Create a chart comparing the two. Then write a paragraph stating which you believe is the better choice and why.

> **NCTE 7** Conduct research and gather, evaluate, and synthesize data to communicate discoveries.

 **Science**

4. Research has shown that breast-fed babies have fewer allergies than bottle-fed babies. Conduct research using print and online resources to determine why scientists believe this is true. Write a summary explaining what you have learned.

> **NSES B** Develop an understanding of the structure and properties of matter, chemical reactions.

 **Check Your Answers** Check your answers at this book's Online Learning Center at **glencoe.com**.

---

## Section 5.2 After You Read

### Review Key Concepts

1. Slats must be no more than 2⅜ inches apart, paint must be smooth with no flaking, corner posts must all be of same height, latch to raise and lower side must be secure, mattress must be firm and fit the crib exactly.
2. They must consider if one of them can leave their job to stay home with the baby, whether one of them will take

leave to stay home for a while. If they choose substitute child care, they must consider the types available and their costs. They should also discuss how they will divide child care responsibilities.

### Practice Academic Skills

3. Charts will vary, but should include items such as: disposable diapers may keep the baby's skin drier; disposable diapers are typically more convenient;

cloth diapers may be less expensive; disposable diapers fill up landfills. Students should state which they think is the best option and why.

4. The early feedings of colostrum provide the intestines with a barrier against agents that can produce allergens. In addition, breast milk provides the body with antibodies from the mother's body.

## Reading Guide

### Before You Read

**Re-reading** If you do not understand a difficult topic, stop immediately and re-read the section. Continuing on in the text will only make you feel discouraged.

**D**

### Read to Learn
#### Key Concepts
- **Identify** ways expectant parents can prepare for the birth of a child.
- **Compare and contrast** the options for the delivery of a baby.

### Main Idea
Taking childbirth classes can help prepare parents for the birth. Parents must decide who will deliver the baby and where the birth will take place.

### Content Vocabulary
◇ prepared childbirth
◇ labor
◇ delivery
◇ midwife
◇ alternative birth center

 **Graphic Organizer** Go to this book's Online Learning Center at **glencoe.com** to print out this graphic organizer.

### Academic Vocabulary
You will find these words in your reading and on your tests. Use the glossary to look up their definitions if necessary.
■ complication
■ compressed

### Graphic Organizer
As you read, compare and contrast the places women might give birth. Use a Venn diagram like the one shown to organize your information.

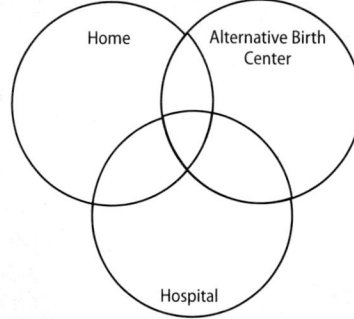

Home

Alternative Birth Center

Hospital

**NCLB**

### Academic Standards . . . . . . . . . . . . . . . . . . . . . . . . . . . . . . .

 **English Language Arts**

**NCTE 2** Read literature to build an understanding of the human experience.

 **Social Studies**

**NCSS I A Culture** Analyze and explain the ways groups, societies, and cultures address human needs and concerns.

**NCTE** *National Council of Teachers of English*
**NCTM** *National Council of Teachers of Mathematics*

**NSES** *National Science Education Standards*
**NCSS** *National Council for the Social Studies*

## Section 5.3

### Focus

 **Bell Ringer Activity**

### Discovering Options
Ask students what options are. (choices) Ask what childbirth-related options students are aware of. (Students' answers will vary. Some may be aware of the home, alternative care center, and hospital options. They may also be aware of the different medical professionals available to assist with childbirth.)

## Preteaching

### Vocabulary
Write *prepared childbirth* on the board. As a class, discuss possible definitions. Record the responses on the board. Read the term in context on page 154. Discuss with students the accuracy of their possible definitions.

### Graphic Organizer
 The Graphic Organizer is also on the TeacherWorks CD.

(Graphic organizers should contain: Similarities: goal is to deliver a healthy baby, make mother comfortable; Differences—Home: familiar; help may not be available; Alternative Birth Center: attended by midwife; natural childbirth; handle low risk pregnancies; home-like; Hospital: physician; high-tech equipment.)

 **NCLB** connects academic correlations to book content.

## Reading Guide

### Before You Read
Ask students to give examples of options they typically face. Ask how they determine the best option. (Students may mention what food to eat or which college to attend. They should have a process to help them make the best choices.) **Tell students that childbirth offers parents many options to choose from.**

### **D** Develop Concepts

**Main Idea** Discuss the main idea with the students. Ask if they were aware of the options parents have to choose from when preparing for the birth of their child. (Students who have a younger sibling may be aware of the options their parents had to choose from.)

## Teach

### Discussion Starter

**Birth Plans** Making decisions while rushing to the hospital in the middle of labor is not what expectant mothers want to do. That is why expectant parents are encouraged to make birth plans. A birth plan usually covers pain relief options, birthing positions, who will accompany the mother, treatment of the baby after birth, and what to do in an emergency. Ask students if they know any expectant parents who have made birth plans. (Answers will vary. If students do know expectant parents who have made birth plans, ask them to share the plans that have been made.)

**Professional Development**

**Mini Clip**
**ELL: Accessing Prior Knowledge**

A teacher helps students connect what they already know and the topic of the upcoming section.

### R Reading Strategy

**Build Connections** Have students read the second paragraph on the page (including the bulleted list). Invite a childbirth education instructor to class to talk with students about what he or she teaches and lead demonstrations of such things as breathing techniques. Afterward, discuss as a class the benefits pregnant women would experience if they were to use some of these methods. (Benefits will vary; some may recognize that the more prepared a woman is for childbirth, the easier it should be. NOTE: You may need to secure administrative and parental permission to do this activity with your class.)

## Prepared Childbirth

**Prepared childbirth** means reducing pain and fear during the birth process through education and the use of breathing and conditioning exercises. Many expectant parents attend childbirth education classes to help them prepare for labor. **Labor** is the process in which the baby gradually moves out of the uterus and into the vagina to be born. This leads to delivery. **Delivery** is the birth of the baby. The father or another designated person can offer support to the mother during labor and delivery.

Childbirth education classes may be offered by hospitals, health care providers, or private teachers. In addition to learning breathing techniques, participants learn so much more, including the following:

- How the baby grows and develops throughout pregnancy
- Tests that may be performed during the pregnancy, such as amniocentesis
- Warning signs that may indicate a serious problem during pregnancy
- What to expect during labor and delivery, including the stages of labor
- The role of the support person
- Breathing and conditioning exercises to make pregnancy, labor, and delivery more comfortable and less painful
- What to expect after the baby is born

Classes offered by hospitals may also include a tour of the facility. Parents-to-be are shown where to go when they arrive and where they will be during labor and delivery, and after delivery. Classes might also review specific rules of the hospital regarding visitors, support persons, and electronics. For example, some hospitals will not allow cameras in the delivery room. Most hospitals have specified areas where cell phones can be used.

Childbirth education classes will also help parents make a plan for the labor and delivery. This is called a birth plan. This tells the medical staff what the couple would like to have happen during the childbirth process, including the possible use of pain medication.

✓ **Reading Check** **List** What are three things parents might learn about in a childbirth education class?

➤ **Preparing for Childbirth**
Many hospitals and health care providers offer childbirth education classes. *How can taking a class help reduce expectant parents' fears?*

✓ **Reading Check**

**List** Answers can include any three of the following: fetal development, warning signs of serious problems, stages of labor, role of the support person, breathing and conditioning exercises, or what to expect after the baby is born.

➤ **Explore the Photo**

**Caption Answer** Parents learn what to expect and how to work together to increase the chances of the birth going smoothly.

**Discussion** Ask students whether they think parents who attend childbirth education classes will make better parents than those who do not attend classes. (Answers will vary but may include no, because there are other ways to learn besides going to classes.)

## Delivery Options

Years ago, most babies were born at home, often with the aid of a midwife. Mothers did not have the option of going to a hospital or the availability of today's lifesaving technology. Today, there are many options for where a baby will be born and the type of health care professional who will attend the birth.

## Health Care Professionals

A health care professional attends most births, regardless of where the birth occurs. There are several types of professionals that can assist with the labor and delivery. The following health care professionals are qualified to deliver babies:

- **Obstetricians** Because these doctors specialize in the care of mothers and babies both before and right after birth, they are qualified to handle any emergencies or problems that might occur.
- **Family Doctors** Some family doctors provide prenatal care and deliver babies. If problems arise, however, they may call in an obstetrician.
- **Licensed Midwives** A **midwife** is a health care professional trained to assist women in childbirth. There are two types of midwives: certified nurse-midwives (CNMs) and certified midwives. CNMs are registered nurses. Both types of midwives have advanced training in normal pregnancy and birth. All midwives must pass a certification exam before they can practice. Midwives will usually call in an obstetrician if a **complication**, or problem, occurs.

The health care professional chosen will generally be involved in the care of the mother and baby throughout the pregnancy. This helps the doctor or midwife be better prepared for possible complications. It is important that the parents feel comfortable with their health care professional.

 Many mothers also choose to have a *doula* present during their labor and delivery. A doula is a woman experienced in childbirth who provides advice and support to a mother during labor and delivery, and after childbirth.

 **What Would You Do?**

### Where to Give Birth

Gabrielle and Antoine are expecting a baby in four months. They are having a hard time deciding where to have the baby. They have read several books about childbirth and listened to advice from friends. Gabrielle wants to have a natural childbirth, but she is worried about the pain. The couple recently toured an alternative birth center that was relaxed and comfortably furnished with a large bed, living area, and even kitchen facilities. There was even a place for Antoine to sleep in the same room with Gabrielle and the baby. However, anesthesia was not readily available. Another hospital a little further away offered tubs for water birth in its birthing center. A nurse told Gabrielle that the warm water relaxes the muscles and takes the weight off the mother's back during birth. The nurse also explained what kinds of anesthesia were available.

**Write About It** Imagine that you are either Gabrielle or Antoine. Write a letter to your doctor explaining your decision. In your letter, give specific reasons for your choice.

Doulas often have suggestions for how to cope with labor pains. They can help keep the mother calm and focused during the delivery. Most hospitals will allow both the father and a doula in the delivery room to support the mother.

## Places to Give Birth

Not all babies are born in a hospital. Parents have a choice of where the birth will occur. Expectant parents should explore the hospitals or birth centers in their area before deciding where to deliver their baby.

Their options may be limited by their health insurance or by which hospital their doctor uses. Many hospitals offer tours and will gladly discuss concerns and special needs. Parents should discuss their options with their doctor before making a final decision.

**Section 5.3** Childbirth Options **155**

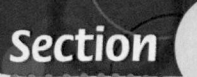
**Teach** *cont.*

**S Skill Practice**
### Guided Practice
**Identifying Responsibilities**
Have students read the last paragraph under Health Care Professionals. Ask students to define doula and list the responsibilities of a doula. (A doula is a woman experienced in childbirth who provides advice and support to a mother during labor and delivery. The responsibilities of a doula include: providing advice and support during labor and delivery, offering suggestions for how to cope with labor pains, and keeping the mother calm and focused during the delivery.) **L1**

**Survey Parents** Have students create a questionnaire for parents to fill out in order to narrow down their options and find the health care professional that meets their needs. (Survey questions might include: Do you believe in natural childbirth? Would you like pain relief available to you if you should need it?) **L2**

**Analyzing Viewpoints** Ask students to analyze why some pregnant women might opt to deliver a baby without medications to ease their pain and why others wouldn't think of not using medication. (Answers will vary but may include: some mothers may not want their baby subjected to the pain medications that are given to the mother. Others may want to enjoy the experience as much as possible with as little pain as possible.) **L3**

 **What Would You Do?**

**Write About It** Students should use the information they have gained from the text and friends or relatives to write a letter stating where they have decided the baby will be born and give specific reasons for their choice.

## Assess

### Quiz

Ask students to answer the following questions:

1. Which health care professional is the most qualified to handle childbirth emergencies or complications? (an obstetrician)
2. How do midwives become licensed? (They must pass a certification exam.)
3. Who often assists at a home birth instead of a doctor? (A midwife or doula often helps with a home birth.)

## Reteach

### C Critical Thinking

**Create a Plan** Have students read the second paragraph under Home. Ask students to create a plan that parents who choose to give birth at home should have ready for dealing with the unexpected. (Students' plans will vary. They might recommend having the phone numbers of the local hospital and ambulance ready. They might suggest notifying the doctor in advance of their intent to give birth at home.)

### W Writing Support

#### Rewriting

**Being Informed** Read and discuss with students the Expert Advice on this page. Once students understand the quote, ask them to rewrite it in their own words. Then have students make a poster of the rewritten quote to place in a childbirth education classroom. (Rewritten quotes will vary but should retain the essence of the original quote. Students might also illustrate their posters.) ELL

➡ **Delivery Options**
There are many factors to be considered when deciding where to give birth. *Why is it helpful to visit different facilities before making your decision?*

### Home

It is only in the last 100 years that most babies have been born in hospitals. Some women still choose a home birth. If a couple is considering a home birth, they should consult their doctor. Together, a decision can be made that will take into account all risk factors.

**C** Unfortunately, it is not possible to know what problems might arise. For example, the umbilical cord might become **compressed**, or flattened. This can threaten the baby's oxygen supply and force the need for a special or early delivery. No one can predict these types of problems. Parents should have a plan for dealing with the unexpected.

Many couples who choose home births have a midwife present to assist with the delivery. A couple should interview many midwives and find one that they are comfortable with prior to the birth. Remember, a midwife can assist with labor and delivery, but does not have the training of a doctor should problems arise. A doula, or a non-medical assistant, may also be used at a home birth, but does not have the training of a midwife.

### Hospital

Depending on health insurance and other issues, new mothers and their babies may spend two to three days in a hospital after a routine delivery, or up to a week in the hospital if there are complications. The government requires insurance companies to cover at least two days in the hospital after delivery for women who have routine, vaginal births.

Hospitals have a full staff of medical professionals to help parents through labor and delivery. They also have staff to assist with the care of both mother and child after the delivery. In addition to doctors and nurses, many hospitals have staff to teach parents how to care for their new baby, including how to change a diaper and feed the child.

The trained personnel, sanitary conditions, and presence of high-tech medical equipment make many parents more comfortable with a hospital birth. Should a complication arise during or after delivery, a hospital has the staff and resources necessary to respond right away. Hospitals also may offer several types of services to meet the needs of expectant parents.

**W** { **Expert Advice...** }

*"Pregnancy and the birth of a child are ranked as one of the most memorable experiences for women, so being well informed of all your options can help ensure a gratifying experience for you and your family."*

— American Pregnancy Association

**156** Chapter 5 Preparing for Birth

➡➡➡ **Explore the Photo**

**Caption Answer** Visiting different facilities gives the expectant parents' the option to choose the facility that best matches their own philosophy of childbirth and that they feel most comfortable in.

**Discussion** Many obstetricians are associated with a particular hospital, so the choice of where to give birth has been made for the parents. Ask students if this would be true by choosing a midwife. (No, a midwife will assist with a birth at home, in some hospitals, or in an alternative birthing center.)

Parents should ask if the hospital offers any of the following:

- Classes that prepare parents for delivery and infant care.
- Programs for siblings and fathers.
- Private rooms that provide soft lighting, music, and comfortable furniture. Mothers and their families can stay in these rooms for labor, delivery, and recovery, unless a complication occurs. Additional medical equipment is kept out of sight but is ready for immediate use.
- The option for mother and baby to room together during their time in the hospital.

### Alternative Birth Center

Some couples choose an alternative birth center for their delivery. These centers may or may not be part of a hospital. An **alternative birth center** is a facility that provides a more homelike environment for labor and delivery. Food and drink is generally offered during labor.

Most hospitals allow the mother to eat only ice chips after admittance, as anything else might interfere with anesthesia. Birth centers emphasize prepared, natural childbirth and so do not offer pain medication during labor.

Alternative birth centers also might offer beds large enough for both the mother and father to rest. Music and friends are generally allowed. Many birth centers have birthing tubs for women who choose a water birth. A water birth means the mother is in water during the birth. This would be discussed and agreed upon prior to the birth, as part of the birth plan.

Midwives generally handle births in these centers. Most accept only mothers with a low risk of complications. A nearby hospital or obstetrician is on call to handle any problems that may develop. These centers typically charge less than hospitals do. Time spent at the facility is usually shorter. Parents and their baby typically leave the center within 24 hours if there are no complications.

---

## Section 5.3 — After You Read

### Review Key Concepts

1. **Explain** what is meant by the term *prepared childbirth*.
2. **Describe** three types of health care professionals who can assist with the birth of babies.

### Practice Academic Skills

**English Language Skills**

3. Locate a novel that contains a description of childbirth. If necessary, ask your teacher, parent, or another appropriate adult for ideas. Read the portion of the novel describing childbirth and write a summary. Was it presented as a pleasant or unpleasant experience?

> **NCTE 2** Read literature to build an understanding of the human experience.

**Social Studies**

4. There are a number of different types of childbirth classes available. Two popular ones are the Lamaze method and the Bradley method. Research these two methods and write a report briefly describing each one. In your report, discuss whether you think the methods might appeal to different kinds of parents and why.

> **NCSS I A** Analyze and explain the ways groups, societies, and cultures address human needs and concerns.

 **Check Your Answers** Check your answers at this book's Online Learning Center at **glencoe.com**.

**NCLB**

Section 5.3 Childbirth Options **157**

---

**Section 5.3 — After You Read**

### Review Key Concepts

1. Prepared childbirth refers to becoming educated about the birthing process with the goals of reducing fear and learning about breathing and conditioning exercises that may make the birth easier and reduce pain.
2. Obstetricians are doctors who specialize in the care of mothers and babies both before and immediately after birth. Family doctors are physicians who specialize in the care of entire families. Licensed midwives are trained to assist women in childbirth. Midwives may be certified nurse-midwives or certified midwives.

### Practice Academic Skills

3. Student answers will vary based on the novel read, but should accurately summarize the event and state whether it was described as being pleasant.

4. The Lamaze method emphasizes pain-reduction methods such as specific breathing techniques. The Bradley method places more emphasis on the active participation of the support person. Bradley emphasizes a natural birth, with avoidance of medications if possible, while Lamaze does not advocate for or against drugs.

---

## Assess

### Study Tools

Have students go to the Online Learning Center at **glencoe.com**:

- Take the **Practice Test**.
- Download **Study-to-Go** content.

Use the **Student Activity Workbook** for additional practice.

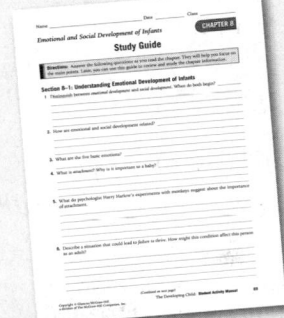

## Close

### Culminating Activity

**Compare Information** Have students talk to a mother about her childbirth experience and compare it to the information presented in this text. Ask who delivered the baby and who was with her during the birth. (Students' comparisons will vary depending on the mother's experience.)

**NCLB** NCLB connects academic correlations to book content.

# Focus

## Discussion Starter

**Designing Toys** Ask students if they have ever thought about who came up with the ideas for the toys they played with as a child. Ask if they ever made themselves a toy. (Answers will vary. Point out that if a student made his or her own toy, they are a toy designer.)

# Teach

## C Critical Thinking

**Analyze** Toy designers need knowledge of child development so they can create toys that children will want to use. Why else might a toy designer need to know child development? (Answers may vary, but students should recognize that knowledge of child development will help a toy designer create the right toys for a particular age group. For example, you would not want to create something too challenging or too easy for an age group.)

# Assess

## Make Connections

Ask students to list specific correlations between academic subjects and the kinds of skills toy designers need. (Answers will vary. Students should show an understanding of how academic skills relate directly to the job of toy designer. For example, toy designers would need to know math to help engineer the toy.)

 **NCLB** This relates academic skills to specific tasks that are performed for this job.

---

**T**oy designers create everything from simple rattles to complex, computer-controlled educational games. They begin with a basic concept. They then go through rigid development guidelines to come up with a final product.

 ## What Does a Toy Designer Do?

Designing toys is challenging work. Toys must be attractive, interesting enough to capture a child's attention, safe, and easy to keep clean. New toys must look original, must function properly, and are often expected to be educational. The toy designer might get ideas from watching children play with existing toys. They might design a new toy based on a make-believe toy that a child thought up.

## Where Do Toy Designers Work?

Most toy designers work for toy manufacturers. There is a lot of competition for jobs, so successful candidates must have skills that make them stand out from the crowd. Some designers start their own companies to create the toys they want to sell.

### Preparation and Skills

**Education and Training**
Recommended courses of study include child psychology, graphic design, children's literature, and fine arts. Most toy designers apply for internships with toy companies.

**Aptitudes, Abilities, and Skills**
Toy designers need the ability to take an idea and turn it into a product. It is also helpful to know how to use computer design programs or how video games work. Knowledge of children's likes and dislikes, and a sense of fun are also needed to be successful as a toy designer.

**Academic Skills**
Design and basic engineering skills are used to determine how a new toy will work and how it will be built. Knowledge of child development allows a designer to create toys that children will want to use.

**Explore Careers**
Some toy designers work independently to develop ideas that they then submit to toy manufacturers. These people are called *entrepreneurs*. Use the Internet to learn more about being an independent toy designer. Write a report presenting what you learn.

 **Careers Online** For more information on careers, visit the Occupational Outlook Handbook Web site through the link on this book's Online Learning Center at **glencoe.com**.

---

# Close

## Culminating Activity

**Creating a Toy** Tell students to imagine they work for a toy manufacturer and must come up with an idea for a new toy. Have them draw the toy or explain it in words and then tell whether they feel they would make a good toy designer. (Students' toys will vary as will their determination as to whether they would make a good toy designer.)

**Explore Careers**
Reports should discuss that independent toy designers have a variety of skills. They are aware of what is in the market and must be able to create new ideas that appeal to toy buyers.

# Chapter Summary

A woman should see a doctor when she thinks she is pregnant. She should receive regular prenatal care during her pregnancy. Eating a well-balanced diet with foods from each of the five food groups is essential to the health of the developing baby and the mother. Moderate exercise and stress management also are important. Parents-to-be should prepare for the birth of the child. They should create a budget and decide how they will balance their lives after the baby is born. Prepared childbirth helps expectant parents get ready for labor and delivery. They must choose a health care professional to attend the birth and decide where the birth will occur.

## Vocabulary Review

1. Use these content and academic vocabulary terms to create a crossword puzzle on graph paper. Use the definitions as clues.

### Content Vocabulary

◇ obstetrician (p. 129)
◇ anemia (p. 130)
◇ Rh factor (p. 131)
◇ gestational diabetes (p. 131)
◇ preeclampsia (p. 132)
◇ osteoporosis (p. 139)
◇ lactose intolerance (p. 142)
◇ lactase (p. 142)

◇ formula (p. 149)
◇ pediatrician (p. 149)
◇ fixed expense (p. 150)
◇ flexible expense (p. 150)
◇ maternity leave (p. 151)
◇ paternity leave (p. 151)
◇ prepared childbirth (p. 154)
◇ labor (p. 154)
◇ delivery (p. 154)

◇ midwife (p. 155)
◇ alternative birth center (p. 156)

### Academic Vocabulary

■ robust (p. 132)
■ alleviate (p. 133)
■ slat (p. 147)
■ reimbursement (p. 151)
■ complication (p. 155)
■ compressed (p. 156)

## Review Key Concepts

2. **Identify** the early signs of pregnancy.
3. **Explain** the importance of proper nutrition during pregnancy.
4. **List** six categories of basic baby supplies.
5. **Describe** why parents need to develop a budget.
6. **Identify** ways expectant parents can prepare for the birth of a child.
7. **Compare and contrast** the options for the delivery of a baby.

## Critical Thinking

8. **Drawing Conclusions** Why do you think some women might suffer more from emotional stress during pregnancy than at other times in their lives?
9. **Apply** If you knew a pregnant couple who had a very limited budget, what suggestions might you offer for preparing for the baby?
10. **Infer** Why might someone choose a midwife instead of a doctor to deliver her baby?

## Content and Academic Vocabulary Review

1. Students should create unique crossword puzzles using all of the vocabulary terms.

## Review Key Concepts

2. Early signs include missed menstrual period; full feeling or mild ache in lower abdomen; feeling tired or faint; a frequent, urgent need to urinate; swollen breasts; and nausea or vomiting.

3. Without proper nutrition, a baby can have birth defects and the mother's health can be damaged.

4. Categories include diapering needs, clothing, feeding equipment, bedding/bedroom, bathing, and travel equipment.

5. Costs for a baby can be high; having a budget allows parents to set goals and develop a spending plan.

6. They can take childbirth classes, choose the physician, and determine where the baby will be born.

7. Options include: (1) Home delivery: most personal, but medical equipment and specialized professionals are not available if needed. (2) Alternative birth center: more personal than a hospital, but not as private as a home delivery, hospital on-call, less expensive than hospital. (3) Hospital: Has high-tech equipment and a variety of trained professionals, safer than home births.

## Critical Thinking

8. Answers will vary. Women may be concerned about the health of the baby, they may be more physically tired, they may worry that they will not be good mothers. Physical changes in their bodies may also cause emotional stress.

9. The student might suggest they ask friends for items they can borrow, go to garage sales, or go to secondhand shops.

10. Answers will vary. The mother might feel she will get more personal attention, or that the midwife might have more time to spend with her and will take a more natural, less medical approach to the birth.

## Family & Community Connections

**11.** Answers will vary; students should discuss where the birth took place and who was present, and compare it with what they learned.

## Health Skills

**12.** Answers will vary by state; oral reports should explain state requirements.

## Observation Skills

**13.** Students' charts will vary, but should summarize the factors that each shopper used.

## Real-World Skills

**14.** Students' scripts should emphasize that children need to be placed in car seats to reduce the chance of injury. Infants under one should be in rear-facing seats, ages one to four in forward-facing seats, and ages four to eight in booster seats.

**15.** The budget worksheet should be divided into fixed expenses and flexible expenses. The spreadsheet should total the fixed expenses and flexible expenses, and then calculate the total of both.

**16.** Students should create a table showing the new and used price for each item and the difference between the prices. *Note:* Tell students that car seats should never be purchased secondhand and buyers should check for recall notices and obvious wear and tear on secondhand products.

**NCLB** Activity correlated to English Language Arts standards.

---

## Family & Community Connection

**11. Interview a Mom** Talk to your mother or another relative or friend about her childbirth experience. Ask the following questions: Where did you give birth? What health care professionals assisted you? Who else was with you during your labor and delivery? Create a chart to compare and contrast the information from your interview with the information you learned in the text.

## Health Skills

**12. Midwife Requirements** Requirements for becoming a licensed midwife vary from state to state. For example, some states require midwives to be registered nurses, and others do not. Use print or online resources, or contact the state medical board, to research your state's requirements. Create an oral report to share what you learn with your class.

## Observation Skills

**13. Shopping for Baby Supplies** Many factors go into making purchases for a new baby. Go to a store that sells baby equipment. Choose one item, such as a crib, stroller, or car seat. Watch at least four different people shopping for the chosen item.

**Procedure** As you watch the shoppers, keep track of their main concerns. For example, do they seem more concerned with the product's features or its appearance?

**Analysis** Create a chart in which you summarize the features of the product that seemed most important to each shopper. List the factors they took into consideration when making purchasing decisions.

> **NCTE 7** Conduct research and gather, evaluate, and synthesize data to communicate discoveries.

## Real-World Skills

| | |
|---|---|
| **Interpersonal and Collaborative Skills** | **14. Write a Radio Announcement** Follow your teacher's instructions to form into groups. Work with your group to create the script for a one-minute public service announcement for the radio. The script should emphasize the importance of car safety seats and discuss the kinds of seats appropriate for different aged children. |
| **Technology Skills** | **15. Create a Spreadsheet** Use a spreadsheet software program to track the monthly budget for a family expecting a baby. Divide the budget into fixed expenses and flexible expenses. The spreadsheet should calculate a fixed expense total, a flexible expense total, and a total of all expenses. |
| **Financial Literacy** | **16. Thrifty Shopping** Choose three items new babies need, such as strollers, cribs, and sleepers. Use the Internet to find average prices for each item. Then check classified ads and secondhand stores to determine their secondhand cost. Create a table showing the difference in prices. |

**Additional Activities** For additional activities, go to this book's Online Learning Center at **glencoe.com**.

## Academic Skills

**17.** Students should write a letter discussing specific changes they made during pregnancy to keep their child safe and healthy. Student should provide the reasons they made these changes.

The *Early Childhood Observations CD* offers additional lessons with videos to build students' observation skills.

**Part 1:** Learning to Observe
**Part 2:** How Children Develop
**Part 3:** Working With Young Children
**Part 4:** Extended Observations
**Part 5:** Resources and Answer File

## Academic Skills

 **English Language Arts**

**17. Letter to Your Child** Imagine you are the father or mother of a new baby. Write a letter to your child to read when he or she is older describing what you did to keep the baby safe and healthy during pregnancy. For example, if you were a new mother, how did you adjust your eating habits? Why did you do this? If you were a new father, how did you support the mother? Did you talk to the baby in the womb?

> **NCTE 4** Use written language to communicate effectively.

 **Mathematics**

**18. Child Care Costs** Many new parents must include the cost of child care in their monthly budgets. According to the National Association of Child Care Resources, day care costs for young babies can be as low as $366 per month and as high as $1,221 per month. What is the range of child care costs?

**Math Concept** **Range** Range is a statistical measure used with a set of numbers. Calculate range by subtracting the lowest value in the set from the highest value.

**Starting Hint** Subtract the minimum ($366) from the maximum ($1,221) costs for monthly day care.

 **Math** For math help, go to the Math Appendix at the back of the book.

> **NCTM Data Analysis and Probability** Select and use appropriate statistical methods to analyze data.

 **Science**

**19. Rate Anesthesia Use** Whether or not to have pain-relieving medication during a birth is an important decision each pregnant woman must make. Many women have local anesthesia. Others choose to have a natural childbirth, without pain-relieving medication.

**Procedure** Speak to several mothers. Ask them if they used local anesthesia. Try to find some women who did use anesthesia and some who did not. Ask each woman to rate her discomfort on a scale of 1 to 10, with 1 being completely comfortable and at ease and 10 being in unbearable pain.

**Analysis** Find the average rating for each group. Write a summary discussing which group appeared to have the least discomfort during childbirth.

> **NSES A** Develop abilities necessary to do scientific inquiry, understandings about scientific inquiry.

## Standardized Test Practice

**TRUE/FALSE QUESTIONS**
Carefully read the statement and determine if it is true or false.

**20.** While following established nutritional guidelines is important for the health of a developing fetus, it matters little to the health of the mother.
 a. True
 b. False

> **Test-Taking Tip** If you have time at the end of a true/false test, check your answers. Did you read the statement carefully? Was there any part of the statement that was false? If so, the entire statement is false.

 **TECHNOLOGY** **Solutions**

**Use these technology solutions to streamline chapter assessment!**

**ExamView** Assessment Suite

**ExamView Assessment Suite** CD allows you to create and print out customized tests or ready-made unit and chapter tests, complete with answer keys.

 **Online Learning Center** includes resources and activities for students and teachers.

**TeacherWorks** *Plus* **TeacherWorks Plus** is an electronic lesson planner that provides instant access to complete teacher resources in one convenient package.

---

**18.** The answer is $855.00; ($1,221 − $366 = $855).

**19.** Students' summaries will vary, but should be based on the results of their research.

**NCLB** **NCLB** connects academic correlations to book content.

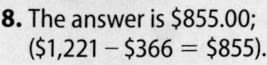  **Professional Development**

**Mini Clip**
**Math:**
**Medians and Quartiles**

Algebra teacher Brad Fulton suggests a strategy for helping students understand the meaning of median and quartile.

## Standardized Test Practice

**20.** False; while the first part is true, the second part is false, making the entire statement false.

**Test-Taking Tips** Tell students that neatness counts on automated tests. Tell them to write neatly and fill in bubbles carefully.

**True/False Tests** Help students develop techniques for evaluating the quality of their own work on standardized tests. Explain that all of us make careless mistakes when we are working against a deadline. For example, we may skip a question or misread a true/false statement. If we are aware that mistakes will inevitably be made, and have a plan for finding those mistakes, we can better control the quality of our work.

**STANDARDS BASED LESSON PLANNING** *The Developing Child* provides students with instruction and assessment in the following fundamental content areas:

## National Standards Correlations

| Standards | Pages |
|---|---|
| **12.1.3** Analyze current and emerging research about human growth and development, including research on brain development. | 176, 182–183 |
| **12.2.1** Analyze the effect of heredity and environment on human growth and development. | 177 |
| **12.3.1** Analyze the role of nurturance on human growth and development. | 180, 181 |
| **15.1.5** Explain cultural differences in roles and responsibilities of parenting. | 170 |
| **15.2.1** Choose nurturing practices that support human growth and development. | 180, 181 |
| **15.4.1** Analyze biological processes related to prenatal development, birth, and health of child and mother. | 165–173, 183–184 |
| **15.4.2** Analyze the emotional factors of prenatal development and birth in relation to the health of parents and child. | 180, 181, 184, 187 |

**NO CHILD LEFT BEHIND** NCLB activities, information, and skills practice will help your students attain NCLB proficiency. Students will improve their abilities in the following academic standards areas:

## Academic Standards Correlations

| Discipline | Standard | Feature/Activity |
|---|---|---|
| **English Language Arts** | **NCTE 1** Read texts to acquire new information. | **Reading Guide (pp. 164, 174, 179)** |
| | **NCTE 4** Use written language to communicate effectively. | **Writing Activity (p. 162)** **After You Read (p. 184)** |
| | **NCTE 5** Use different writing process elements to communicate effectively. | **After You Read (p. 178)** |
| | **NCTE 7** Conduct research and gather, evaluate, and synthesize data to communicate discoveries. | **Observation Skills (p. 186)** |
| | **NCTE 12** Use language to accomplish individual purposes. | **After You Read (p. 173)** **Academic Skills (p. 187)** |
| **Mathematics** | **NCTM Number and Operations** Understand numbers, ways of representing numbers, relationships among numbers, and number systems. | **Academic Skills (p. 187)** |
| **Science** | **NSES F** Develop understanding of personal and community health. | **After You Read (p. 184)** **Academic Skills (p. 187)** |
| **Social Studies** | **NCSS I A Culture** Analyze and explain the ways groups, societies, and cultures address human needs and concerns. | **Culture Matters (p. 170)** **After You Read (p. 173)** |
| | **NCSS VIII C Science, Technology, and Society** Analyze how science influences the core values, beliefs, and attitudes of society, and how core values of society shape scientific change. | **After You Read (p. 178)** |

## Mc Graw Hill Professional Development

**MINI CLIP VIDEO LIBRARY**
Targeted professional development is correlated throughout *The Developing Child*. **The McGraw-Hill Professional Development Mini Clip Video Library** provides teaching strategies to strengthen academic and learning skills. Log on to **glencoe.com**.

In this chapter, you will find these Mini Clips:
- **Reading** Lesson Reflections, p. 165
- **Reading** Another Point of View, p. 166
- **Reading** Interacting with Text, p. 169
- **ELL** Graphic Organizers, p. 172
- **ELL** Vocabulary Activities, p. 174
- **ELL** Group Discussions, p. 175
- **ELL** Reading Aloud, p. 179
- **Reading** Planning and Classroom Management, p. 183
- **Math** Introducing Multi-Step Equations, p. 187

## Reading and Writing Strategies

**Writing Activity: Write Using Details** (p. 162)
Students use writing tips to describe the emotions a five-year-old might have in response to the arrival of a new baby brother.

**Before You Read** (pp. 164, 174, 179)
A pre-reading question or statement will help students make a personal connection to content.

**Graphic Organizer** (pp. 164, 174, 179)
A visual tool will help students organize and remember new content.

**Reading Check** (pp. 171, 172, 177, 183)
A question allows students to make a quick comprehension self-check.

**After You Read** (pp. 173, 178, 184)
Organize and process students' understanding of what they have read.

## Chapter Features

**What's in a Name?** (p. 170)
In many cultures, children are given names to honor relatives or to describe characteristics their parents hope the children will possess.

**Brain Size and Growth** (p. 176)
Proportionally, infants have larger heads than adults.

**Cystic Fibrosis** (p. 177)
Babies can be tested for cystic fibrosis by measuring the amount of chloride in their sweat; the disease currently has no cure, but there are promising treatments.

**Bonding with a Baby** (p. 181)
Ways of bonding including touching and interacting with the baby.

## Chapter Overview

### Introduce the Chapter
In this chapter, students learn about labor and birth. Labor is divided into three distinct stages. After birth, the baby is immediately examined for any signs of abnormalities. Parents immediately begin bonding with the newborn. During the post-natal period, women have special physical and emotional needs.

### Build Background
Ask for volunteers to discuss the birth of a younger sibling. For example, students may share how they felt when they first saw the baby, what their family did to prepare, and so forth. Explain to students that childbirth is one of the most fundamental events shared around the world. The birth of a new life has enormous significance to the child's immediate family and to others around the child.

### Writing Activity
#### Writing Using Details

This active learning activity prompts students to write paragraphs using details to describe the emotions of a five-year-old who has just become an older sibling. After students have completed the writing activity, ask for volunteers to share their paragraphs with the class. Ask students to point out good uses of details. Encourage the class to discuss which details they consider to be the most effective and why. (Students should turn in their outlines along with their paragraphs. Outlines should include two heads with details under each head. Paragraphs should describe the emotions a five-year-old child might go through when a new sibling is brought home.)

---

Chapter

**6** **The Baby's Arrival**

## Chapter Objectives

After completing this chapter, you will be able to:
- **Describe** the progression of labor.
- **Explain** what happens during a cesarean birth.
- **List** the factors that can contribute to a premature birth.
- **Describe** a newborn's appearance immediately after birth.
- **Identify** the exams and procedures given to a newborn in the first few days.
- **Review** what occurs during the hospital stay after delivery.
- **Summarize** the physical and emotional needs of a new mother.

### Writing Activity   *Write Using Details*

**Describe Emotions** Having a new baby in the home is an emotional time for every family member. Imagine that you are five years old and your parents have just brought home your new baby brother. Write two paragraphs using details to describe your emotions.

**Writing Tips** Before you write, create an outline to organize the details you will include in your paragraphs.
1. Create a head for the main idea for each paragraph.
2. List specific details under each head.
3. Follow the outline to write your paragraphs.

---

## CLASSROOM Solutions

### Print Resources
 **Student Edition**

 **Teacher Wraparound Edition**

 **Student Activity Workbook**

**Student Activity Workbook Teacher Annotated Edition**

### Technology Resources
 **Online Learning Center** has resources and activities for students and teachers. Includes an Online Student Edition.

 **Interactive Student Edition** allows students to instantly access review materials, examples, and exercises.

**Chapter 6**

| Section | 6.1 | **Labor and Birth** |
| Section | 6.2 | **The Newborn** |
| Section | 6.3 | **The Postnatal Period** |

## Review the Sections
Introduce the chapter by reviewing the sections:

### Section 6.1
Labor is divided into three stages. In stage 1, contractions open the cervix. The baby is born in stage 2, and the placenta is expelled in stage 3. If complications arise, a cesarean birth may be necessary. A premature birth occurs when a baby is born before 37 weeks.

### Section 6.2
Once a baby is born, its body systems, including the lungs and heart, begin functioning independently. Newborns may have skinny limbs and misshapen skulls. The Apgar scale is used to evaluate the baby's physical condition. Later, other tests, such as hearing screenings, are performed.

### Section 6.3
The first month after birth, or the neonatal period, is a time of recovery and adjustment for the mother and infant. Bonding, which is vital to proper brain development, begins immediately and can be enhanced by touching and talking to the baby. Lactation consultants can help mothers learn to breast feed.

 **Explore the Photo**
After nine months, the parents finally get to meet their new child. *What feelings do you think these parents are experiencing?*

163

### ►►►► Explore the Photo

**Caption Answer** Answers will vary but might include excitement, thankfulness, love, fear, or joy.

**Discussion** Ask students how important they think a mother's and father's first response to their newborn is. Do students think this impression will affect how parents feel about their child in the future? Why or why not? (Responses will vary, but students should provide reasons for their responses.)

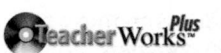 **TeacherWorks Plus** is an electronic lesson planner that provides instant access to complete teacher resources in one convenient package.

 **Presentation Plus!** provides visual teaching aids for every section.

**The Early Childhood Observations CD** presents video observations and lessons on observation skills and child development.

**The Developing Brain eTransparencies and Guide** include information and activities to offer insights into brain development and diseases of the brain.

**Section 6.1**

## Focus

### Bell Ringer Activity

**What Is Labor?**

Ask for a volunteer to read the general definition of the term *labor* from a dictionary. Ask: Why do you think the word labor is used to refer to the process of giving birth? Mention that many people think giving birth is the hardest work a woman will ever perform.

## Preteaching

### Vocabulary

Discuss that there is a common belief that the term *cesarean birth* derives from a story that Julius Caesar was surgically removed from his mother's abdomen. This is generally considered a myth because his mother lived for many more years. At that time, such a procedure would have been performed only on a dead or dying mother.

### Graphic Organizer

 The Graphic Organizer is also on the TeacherWorks CD.

(Graphic organizers should follow a standard outline form with numerals and letters. For example: 1. The Beginning of Labor, a. Early Signs of Labor, b. Premature Labor.)

**NCLB** connects academic correlations to book content.

---

## Reading Guide

### Before You Read

**Predict** Look at the photos in this section and read their captions. Write one or two sentences predicting what you think the section will be about.

### Read to Learn
**Key Concepts**
- **Describe** the progression of labor.
- **Explain** what happens during a cesarean birth.
- **List** the factors that can contribute to a premature birth.

**D** **Main Idea**
Pregnant women go through different stages of labor before delivering a baby. Some women have a cesarean or premature birth.

### Content Vocabulary
◇ cervix
◇ contraction
◇ fetal monitoring
◇ dilate
◇ cord blood
◇ stem cells
◇ cesarean birth
◇ incubator

### Academic Vocabulary
You will find these words in your reading and on your tests. Use the glossary to look up their definitions if necessary.
■ induce
■ anesthesia

### Graphic Organizer
As you read the first part of this section, use the heads to create an outline. Use a structure like the one shown to help build your outline.

| The Progression of Labor |
|---|
| 1. _____ |
| a. _____ |
| b. _____ |
| c. _____ |
| d. _____ |
| 2. _____ |
| a. _____ |
| b. _____ |
| c. _____ |
| d. _____ |

 **Graphic Organizer** Go to this book's Online Learning Center at **glencoe.com** to print out this graphic organizer.

---

**NCLB**

### Academic Standards · · · · · · · · · · · · · · · · · · · · · · · ·

**English Language Arts**

**NCTE 12** Use language to accomplish individual purposes.

**Social Studies**

**NCSS I A Culture** Analyze and explain the ways groups, societies, and cultures address human needs and concerns.

**NCTE** National Council of Teachers of English
**NCTM** National Council of Teachers of Mathematics

**NSES** National Science Education Standards
**NCSS** National Council for the Social Studies

---

---

## Reading Guide

### Before You Read

Ask students: How many of you have ever seen the birth of an animal? Did the birth go as you expected? Did anything about the birth surprise you? Did the newborn(s) look like you expected? Explain that the birth of human babies is surprisingly similar to that of other mammals.

### **D** Develop Concepts

**Main Idea** Discuss the main idea with the students. Ask students: Why do you think labor is divided into distinct stages? How might knowing about the different stages help the mother? (Answers will vary. Identifying each stage helps mothers know what to expect next.)

## The Progression of Labor

Nine months is a long time to wait to hold a new baby. Many expectant mothers have felt like their due date would never come. Finally, though, it does. A nervous, excited woman goes into labor, and her baby arrives.

Giving birth is a powerful physical and emotional experience. It leaves most new mothers feeling both exhausted and exhilarated. Giving birth, or labor, occurs in two basic parts: the beginning of labor and the stages of labor.

## The Beginning of Labor

During the last few weeks of pregnancy, time often seems to slow down for the expectant mother. Many women become anxious for the baby to be born. During this time, they feel what is called lightening. This occurs when the baby settles deep in the pelvis near the time of birth. Because the baby has moved down, the pressure on the woman's upper abdomen is reduced, or lightened. With a first pregnancy, lightening may occur days or weeks before labor. A woman who has already had a baby may experience this change just before labor begins.

### Early Signs of Labor

There are many signs that the baby is on its way. A new mother may experience one or more of these signs. A woman in her first pregnancy may have more trouble recognizing some of the early signs.

One is commonly called the "show" or "bloody show." This refers to the few drops of blood or a pinkish vaginal stain that occurs when the mucus that plugs the uterus during pregnancy dissolves. This plug seals the cervix ('sər-viks) and prevents bacteria from moving into the uterus. This may occur as early as a few days prior to birth. The **cervix** is the lower part of the uterus.

**R**

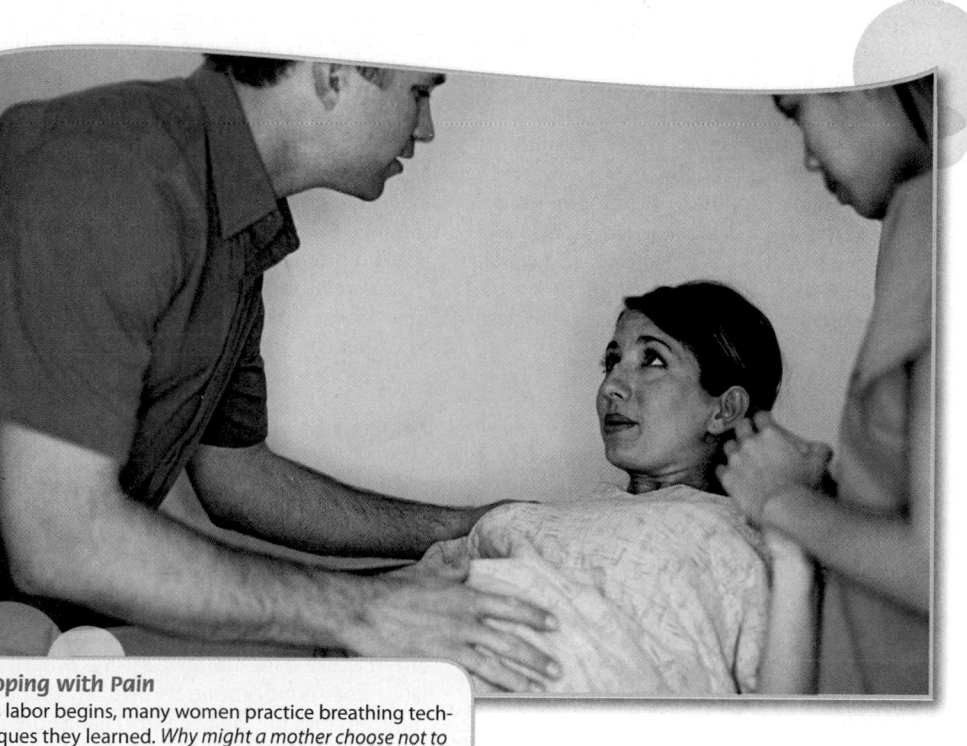

 **Coping with Pain**
As labor begins, many women practice breathing techniques they learned. *Why might a mother choose not to have anesthesia during labor and delivery?*

## Teach

### Discussion Starter

**Thoughts on Childbirth** Have students work individually to create a list of ten words that they associate with childbirth. Ask for volunteers to share their lists with the class. Encourage students to discuss how they have learned about childbirth. Their information might come from their family or friends, or perhaps it comes from movies they have seen or books they have read. Explain to students that this section will present fascinating factual information about childbirth.

### **R** Reading Strategy

**Cause and Effect** Explain that identifying cause and effect can help you understand the author's purpose. Ask for a volunteer to read aloud the last paragraph on this page. Ask: What causes the 'bloody show'? (The mucus plugging the uterus dissolves.) What is the effect of this event? (The cervix is no longer sealed and the baby will now be able to descend into the birth canal.)

 **Professional Development**

 **Mini Clip**
**Reading: Lesson Reflections**

A narrator discusses various instructional strategies suitable for use with English learners.

----

◄◄◄● **Explore the Photo**

**Caption Answer** Answers will vary, but may include that she wants to be conscious and alert during the process, or she does not want the baby to be affected by the drugs.

**Discussion** Ask the class whether they think they would have anesthesia if they were giving birth. Encourage them to discuss the reasons for their choices. Emphasize that because this is an extremely personal decision, the mother's decision should be respected. (Responses will vary, but students should provide reasons for their choices.)

### Teach *cont.*

### U₁ Universal Access

**Logical Learners** Tell students that a specific kind of contractions, called Braxton Hicks contractions, typically occurs before labor, sometimes as early as the second trimester. Instruct students to conduct research on Braxton Hicks contractions and write a paragraph explaining their purpose. (Paragraphs will vary but should explain that Braxton Hicks contractions help the mother get used to the feeling of being in labor. They also may tone the uterus and promote blood flow.)

### R₁ Reading Strategy

**Helpful Poems** Sometimes using rhyme can help people remember information. Have students create a short rhyming poem to help them remember the differences between false labor and true labor. Ask for volunteers to share their poems with the class. (Students should create rhyming poems that explain the differences between false labor and true labor. For example, "walking sends false labor away/but true labor is here to stay.")

Some women realize that they are in labor when they feel a trickle or gush of warm fluid from the vagina. This indicates that the membrane, or amniotic sac, holding the fluid around the baby has broken. Often, the membrane does not rupture until much later in labor. This is what is meant when a woman says that her water has broken.

If the mother experiences this, she should note the time, the amount of fluid, and the color and odor of the fluid. She should call her doctor or midwife and report this information. Once the membrane has broken, delivery should be within 24 to 48 hours to protect the baby from infection.

A **contraction** is the tightening and releasing of the muscles of the uterus. This is also a sign of labor. When the uterus contracts, it shortens and closes, pushing the fetus against the cervix. Then the uterus relaxes before the next contraction. This is why contractions may last a few minutes. Earlier in labor, the period between them is longer. This time gets shorter as labor advances.

Mothers often report that contractions are painful but bearable. There is time between them to rest and recover. After the baby is born and the placenta is also pushed out, contractions end and there is no lingering pain.

As labor and contractions begin, the baby's heart can be monitored. **Fetal monitoring** is the watching of an unborn baby's heart rate for indications of stress. This is usually done during labor and birth. There are different types of fetal monitoring. One of the most common methods is with an ultrasound device. This method provides a beat-to-beat picture of the baby's heart in relationship to the mother's contractions.

### Premature Labor

A full-term pregnancy usually lasts 40 weeks. Giving birth a week or two earlier or later is still considered normal though. Premature, or preterm, labor occurs when the fetus has been developing in the womb for 37 weeks or less. Warning signs of premature labor include having contractions every ten minutes or less; feeling a constant, dull backache; or leaking fluid or blood. Sometimes, doctors can give medication to stop premature labor.

### False Labor

Some women feel what is called false labor hours or even days before their real labor starts. They begin to feel strong contractions and believe that labor may have begun. Doctors look for three signs that indicate false labor:

- Contractions are not regular or rhythmic.
- Contractions do not get stronger over time.
- Contractions end with light exercise, such as walking or stretching.

When contractions follow a regular pattern and grow in intensity, a woman is having real labor. The woman and her labor coach should time the contractions by noting how long they last and how often they occur.

It can be difficult to determine the right time to go to the hospital or birthing center. The doctor or nurses at the obstetrician's office or medical center can provide guidance.

### Inducing Labor

If necessary, the doctor can **induce**, or start, labor by artificial means. This can be done by using medication or puncturing the amniotic sac. Labor is often induced for medical reasons or in emergencies. If the baby has been slow to develop or is still in the womb after 42 weeks, the doctor may decide to induce labor. This is also the case if the amniotic sac has broken and labor does not begin on its own. Having labor induced does not significantly change the process. The labor will probably *not* be longer, more painful, or more difficult than natural labor.

---

### { Expert Advice... }

*"Some mothers start their labor with a bang—suddenly, undoubtedly, powerfully—and progress fast. Others ease into labor slowly, sometimes unconvincingly, and progress gradually, yet efficiently."*

— William and Martha Sears, pediatric medical specialists

**Professional Development**

**Mini Clip**
**Reading: Another Point of View**
Emily M. Schell, EdD, educator and author, discusses standards-based instruction.

## Stages of Labor

Once labor begins, it moves through three basic stages:

- **Stage 1** Contractions open the cervix.
- **Stage 2** The baby is born.
- **Stage 3** The placenta is expelled.

See **Figure 6.1** on pages 168–169 for more details about each stage. During these three stages, the baby makes its way out of the mother's womb and into the world. The amount of time it takes to give birth depends on the mother and baby. It often takes longer if the baby is the woman's first. For a first birth, the first stage may last from six to 18 hours. It may be two to five hours for a later child.

It is often hard to tell exactly when real labor starts. This makes it hard to determine a typical length for the first stage of labor. The second stage is usually one to two hours for a first child. However, it is often only 15 to 30 minutes for a later child. The third stage is the shortest. It can take anywhere from 10 to 30 minutes.

## The First Stage

The first stage of labor officially begins when contractions are coming at regular intervals. The contractions in the uterine muscle pull up on the cervix, slowly softening and thinning it and allowing it to open. Contractions increase in strength, length, and frequency. When this stage begins, contractions usually last for about 30 seconds and occur up to 20 minutes apart. When they last about 60 seconds and occur two to five minutes apart, then the woman is in "active labor". Some hospitals prefer not to admit the mother until she is in active labor.

To cope with the demands of labor, the woman becomes more focused and needs support from her partner. This is when the woman will use the coping techniques that she may have learned, such as breathing exercises or walking. It is during this stage that the mother would receive pain medication if she wanted it. Some medications may affect how long this stage of labor will last.

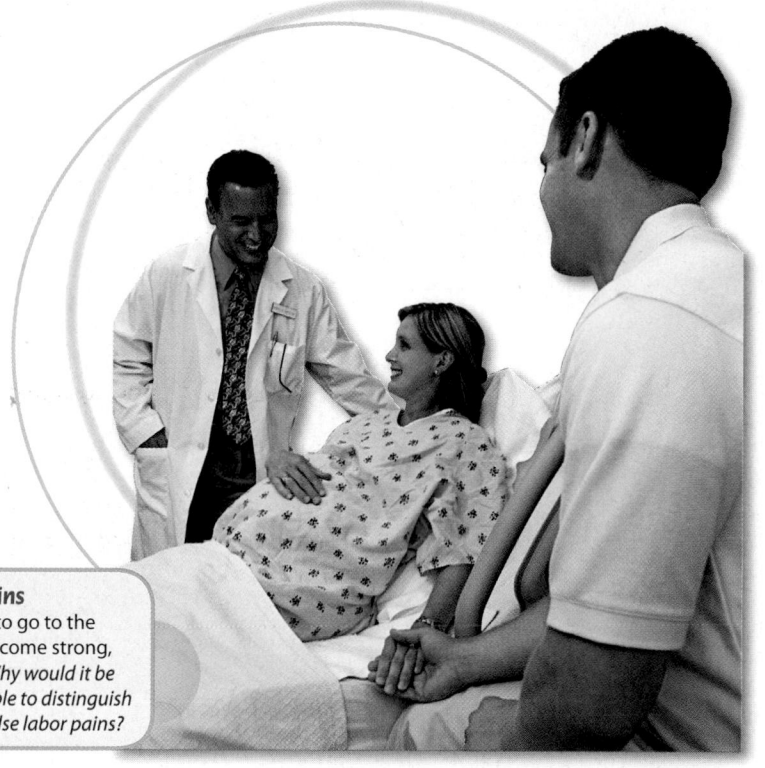

**Recognizing Labor Pains**
Many doctors advise patients to go to the hospital when contractions become strong, regular, and closer together. *Why would it be important for a woman to be able to distinguish between real labor pains and false labor pains?*

---

## Explore the Photo

**Caption Answer** Answers may vary, but might include: so she wouldn't make unnecessary trips to the hospital and so the doctor wouldn't have to make unnecessary trips to the hospital.

**Discussion** Explain that sometimes women will be sent home from the hospital because they are experiencing false labor pains and are not yet ready to give birth. Have students discuss how such a woman might feel. (Answers will vary; this situation can be discouraging. However, remembering that the goal is to have a healthy child can be helpful.)

---

## Teach *cont.*

### R₂ Reading Strategy

**Examine Structure** Point out to students that the stages of labor are listed at the beginning of this page and then are expanded on over the remainder of this section. Ask students: Why do you think the author lists these three stages first and then goes back to add more detail later? (Providing an overview up front gives the reader a framework on which to add the more detailed information that follows.)

### C Critical Thinking

**Hypothesize** Ask students why they think the contractions of true labor are regular and rhythmic whereas those of false labor are typically sporadic. (Answers may vary. An enormous amount of pressure is required to dilate the cervix and push the baby out of the uterus and through the birth canal; this requires the steady push of strong, regular contractions.)

### U₂ Universal Access

**Kinesthetic Learners** Remind students that a doula is a person who is trained to help in preparing and supporting a woman through the childbirth process. Organize students into pairs. Students should conduct research to learn about doulas and then prepare a skit in which a doula explains to a pregnant woman how she can help the woman through childbirth process. (Skits will vary but should show adequate research and preparation. Doulas might mention that they can help teach the woman breathing or focus techniques.)

### U Universal Access

**Gifted Learners** Have students conduct research to learn about the labor and birthing process of another mammal, such as cats or elephants. They then should write a report explaining what they have learned. The report also should contain information such as the gestation period and average number of babies born at a single time. (Students should write a report explaining the labor and birthing process of a mammal of their choosing, including gestation size and average number of babies born at once. For example, a giraffe carries its baby for about 400 days and usually only has one at a time.)

### C Critical Thinking

**Analyze** Tell students that there are three basic ways the baby can be positioned: cephalic, breech, and transverse. Explain that in a breech presentation, the baby is either buttocks-first or feet-first. Ask for a volunteer to read aloud from a dictionary the definition of *cephalic*. Ask: What is a cephalic presentation? Repeat this process with the term *transverse*. Conclude by asking which of these is the normal presentation. (Cephalic (head-first) is the normal presentation. Transverse means the baby is shoulder or back down. This position is rare.)

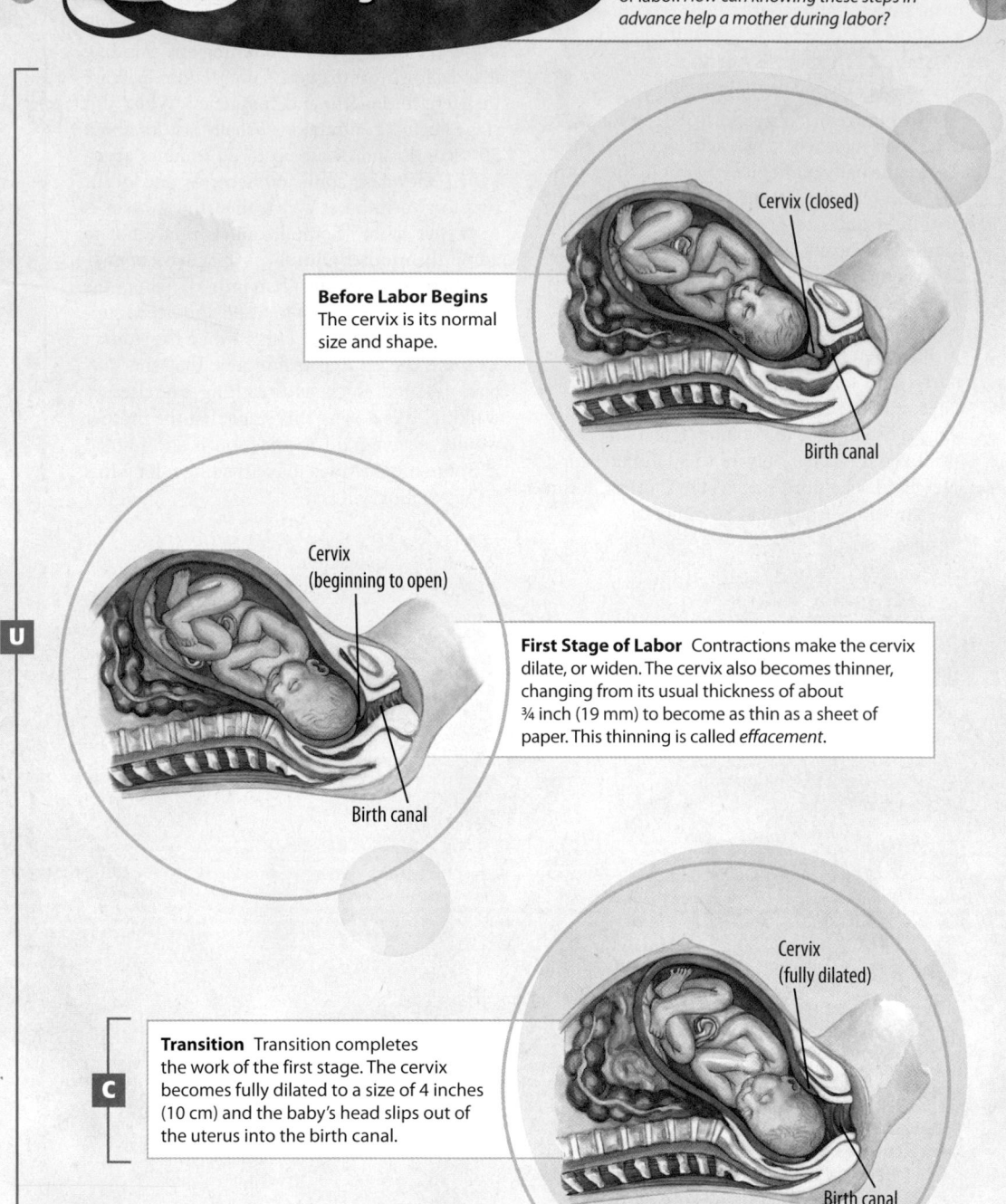

**Figure 6.1 The Stages of Labor**

Women who go through natural childbirth will go through each of these stages of labor. *How can knowing these steps in advance help a mother during labor?*

Cervix (closed)

**Before Labor Begins** The cervix is its normal size and shape.

Birth canal

Cervix (beginning to open)

**First Stage of Labor** Contractions make the cervix dilate, or widen. The cervix also becomes thinner, changing from its usual thickness of about ¾ inch (19 mm) to become as thin as a sheet of paper. This thinning is called *effacement*.

Birth canal

Cervix (fully dilated)

**Transition** Transition completes the work of the first stage. The cervix becomes fully dilated to a size of 4 inches (10 cm) and the baby's head slips out of the uterus into the birth canal.

Birth canal

**168** Chapter 6 The Baby's Arrival

---

**Figure 6.1 The Stages of Labor**

**Caption Answer** Answers may vary but could include that it lets the mother know what to anticipate, and knowledge of the steps helps her ask questions she might not otherwise think of.

**Discussion** Divide students into pairs. Instruct each pair to cover all text in Figure 6.1 (perhaps they can cut small rectangles of paper to place over the text boxes.) Then students should take turns explaining the birth process to their partners, using the illustrations to guide them. Encourage students to make their explanations as detailed as they can.

**Second Stage of Labor: Crowning**
When the top of the head appears at the opening of the birth canal, it is called *crowning*.

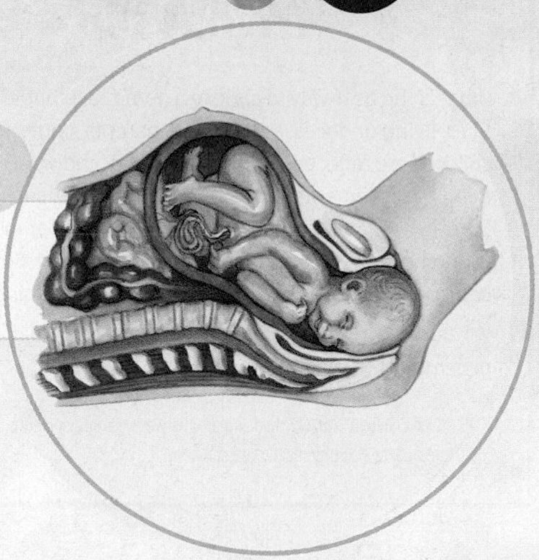

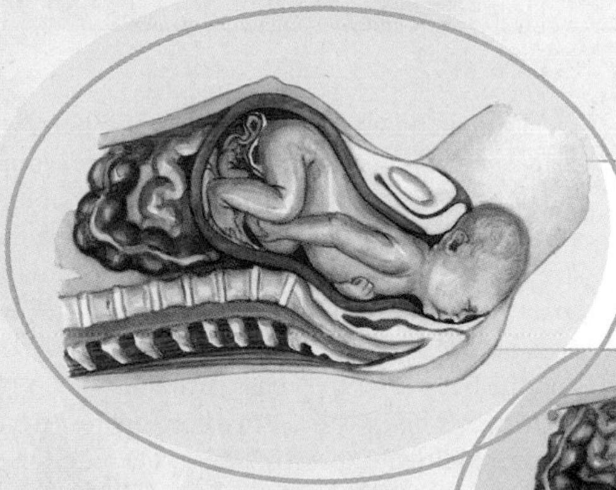

**Second Stage of Labor: Head Emerges** The baby's head emerges first. The head has changed its shape to ease passage through the birth canal. It will later return to normal. After the head, the shoulders follow. Then the rest of the baby slips out easily.

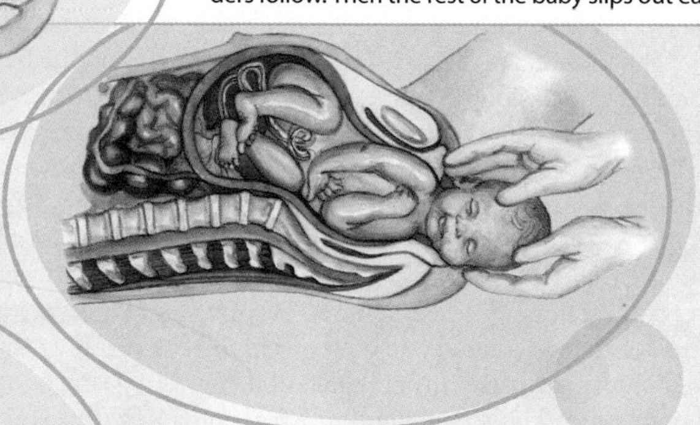

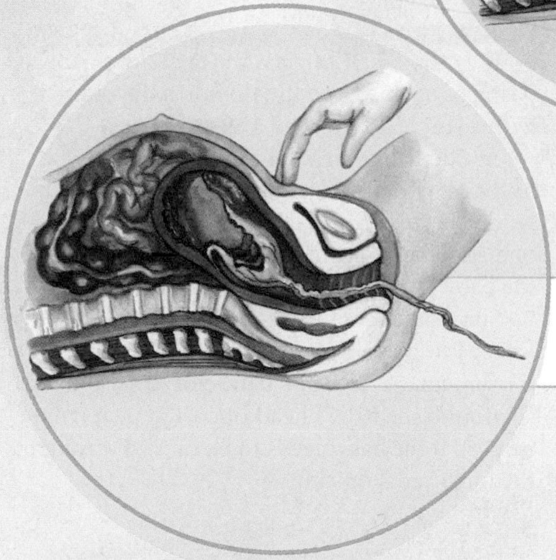

**Third Stage of Labor** The woman gives birth to the placenta, no longer needed by the baby.

Section 6.1  Labor and Birth  **169**

**Mc Graw Hill Professional Development**

**Mini Clip**
**Reading: Interacting with Text**
Students work in small groups to make connections and ask higher order questions about a photo they have been given.

**S** **Skill Practice**
**Guided Practice**

**Create a Time Line** Have students create a time line showing the events that occur during labor. For example, the first event could be "Regular contractions begin." Tell the students that their time lines should be based on the approximate times given in the textbook for a first-time birth. (Students should create a time line that contains the major events of labor in the correct order.) **L1** **ELL**

**Label Illustrations** Point out to students that only a few anatomical components are labeled in Figure 6.1. Have students copy the illustrations and enlarge them. (You may wish to do this step for them.) They then should paste these copies onto a poster board and label them as thoroughly as they can. For example, they might label the mother's spinal column, her navel, the placenta, and umbilical cord. (Students should create a poster showing the stages of labor. They should have thoroughly labeled the illustrations in their posters.) **L2**

**Conduct Research** Have students conduct research to obtain a more thorough understanding of one of the three stages of labor. Students should then create an illustrated poster explaining this stage. Alternately, they may want to create several Web pages or a slide show. Ask for volunteers to share their presentations with the class. (Students should conduct research to learn more about one of the stages of labor and prepare a poster or other presentation on their chosen stage.) **L3**

### Assess

## Quiz

Ask students to answer the following questions:

1. **Why is fetal monitoring important?** (Monitoring is important because an abnormal heart rate can indicate signs of fetal stress.)

2. **What does it mean to induce labor and what are two ways that labor can be induced?** (Inducing labor means starting it by artificial means and can be done by breaking the amniotic sac or by using medication.)

3. **To what does the term *transition* refer? When does transition occur?** (Transition refers to the full dilation of the cervix and occurs at the end of the first stage.)

### Reteach

 **Universal Access**

**Verbal Learners** Instruct students to choose a country other than America, such as Vietnam or Egypt. Students should research how parents in that country name their children and write a paragraph explaining the naming process. They also should create a list of common names given to infants in that country. (Answers will vary. A possible answer is that in Nigeria, couples ask the grandfather or great-grandfather to send a name. There is generally a formal naming on the seventh day after the birth, in which the family elders present the name to the baby's father.)

---

# CULTURE MATTERS

## What's in a Name?

What is the best way to choose a name for a baby? Children are often named after relatives, living or deceased. In China, parents' hopes for a healthy, prosperous life for their children are reflected in the names they choose. Girls' names typically include words relating to elements of beauty or composure, such as *ting* (graceful) or *hua* (flower). Boys' names are designed to honor ancestors or indicate strength, such as *shaozu* (bring honor to our ancestors) and *gang* (steel). Some Chinese names are combinations of elements, such as *po yee*, meaning treasured child.

⭐ **Build Connections** *How can names link children to past generations?*

**NCSS I A Culture** Analyze and explain the ways groups, societies, and cultures address human needs and concerns.

---

As the cervix dilates, the baby moves into the lower pelvis. **Dilate** means to widen or open. Most babies enter the world headfirst. However, some enter the pelvis with their feet or buttocks first. These positions are known as breech presentation. Babies in these positions may have a difficult time moving through the pelvis. The doctor will decide whether a normal delivery is possible.

The first stage ends with a period called transition. A transition is a change. In labor, the change refers to the cervix. Transition is when the cervix becomes fully dilated to a diameter of about 10 centimeters (4 inches). Strong contractions that last up to 90 seconds and are two to three minutes apart occur in this period. This is the more difficult part of labor. A woman needs encouragement and reassurance from her support partner at this time.

### The Second Stage

Contractions during the second stage are more productive, pushing the baby through the pelvis and out of the vagina, or birth canal. During this stage, it is safe for a woman to push. When she pushes, she uses her muscles to expel the baby. Earlier pushing might have resulted in tearing of delicate tissues, or other types of injuries.

How can a baby fit through such a narrow space? Ligaments, or connective tissue, join the bones of the mother's pelvis. During labor, a hormone called relaxin allows this tissue to stretch like rubber bands. This stretching moves apart the pelvic bones. Relaxin also makes it possible for the walls of the vagina to stretch so that the baby can safely pass through.

A baby's body is designed for this journey. A soft skull lets the baby's head become longer and narrower than usual. The skull consists of five separate bones that move together and allow for the baby's head to fit through the pelvis and vagina.

Sometimes the opening in the mother's body is too small to accommodate the baby's passage. In this case, the doctor may widen it with a surgical cut called an episiotomy.

As the baby's head emerges, the doctor or midwife provides gentle support and help guide the baby out. The head is followed by one shoulder, and then the other. The rest of the baby follows quickly.

Sometimes doctors use surgical tongs called forceps to grasp the baby's body and guide its movement. A vacuum extractor that applies suction to the baby's head once it appears may be used if the baby needs to be moved through the birth canal quickly.

**170** Chapter 6 The Baby's Arrival

---

# CULTURE MATTERS

## What's in a Name?

**Discussion** Ask the class: Do you think it is a good idea to give a baby a name that indicates the parents' expectations for the child? For example, do you think having a name that means "warrior," "beautiful," or "gift from God" might affect a child? Why or why not? (Student responses will vary. Some will feel it has no effect. Others may feel it sets an expectation for the child to strive to reach.)

**Build Connections** *Answers may include: when a child carries the name of a family member, the child may want to know more about that person. This creates opportunities for the family to recall its history.*

## The Third Stage

After birth, the mother may be able to rest briefly, and then may feel a few contractions and a desire to push. These contractions usually are not painful. They help the placenta, the organ that develops in the mother and helps supply oxygen to the fetus, separate from the uterine wall.

Once the mother pushes the placenta out of her body, the birth process is complete. The new mother may begin bonding with her child. If needed, the doctor or midwife will stitch up the episiotomy or tears that may have occurred during the birth. The final stage of labor is brief but important.

Scientists have discovered that cord blood contains stem cells. **Cord blood** is the blood left behind in the umbilical cord and placenta following birth. **Stem cells** are cells capable of producing all types of blood cells. The stem cells can be used to treat many serious blood-related illnesses in the baby or other family members. Parents can arrange to have the cord blood stored in case there is a future medical need. It may also be donated for use by others.

### How to Cope with Labor

**W**

Most first-time mothers worry about how much pain is involved in the birth process. The answer is it varies. Some women find it very painful and tiring, while others do not. There are many ways to cope with the pain, including medication.

Mothers and fathers can participate in childbirth classes. These classes teach breathing and relaxation techniques, as well as focusing exercises that may help distract a woman from pain. These classes are often referred to as Lamaze classes. However, Lamaze is just one approach to childbirth education. Some classes teach a form of self-hypnosis that can significantly reduce pain.

When choosing a childbirth class, parents should consider:

- Who is teaching the class? If it is offered by the hospital, it is probably a nurse. Does the teacher's philosophy agree with yours?
- How big is the class? Smaller is better.
- What is the format of the class? Does the class offer time for practicing techniques?

**W**

There are several types of **anesthesia**, or drugs that cause a loss of feeling, used for pain relief during childbirth. Some are injected into veins or muscles, where they act on the entire body. These do not slow labor but may make women and their babies sleepy. Others, called epidural blocks, are injected into the lower back, where they numb the lower half of the body. Epidural blocks still allow women to feel some pressure as the baby's head descends. Sometimes, if the pain is worse than expected, or there are other problems, more medication may be needed.

**U₂**

✓ **Reading Check** **Summarize** What happens during the third stage of labor?

**Learning to Cope**
Many couples take childbirth classes together. *Why is it important for the father to attend childbirth classes?*

Section 6.1  Labor and Birth  **171**

## Section 6.1

### Reteach *cont.*

**W** **Writing Support**

**Write Using Details**

**Coping with Labor** Instruct students to write a paragraph summarizing ways that mothers can cope with labor. The paragraph should begin with an introductory sentence. The remainder of the paragraph should contain at least three specific details on coping with labor. (Refer to p. 162 to review characteristics of writing using details. Paragraphs and details will vary but may include walking, meditation, breathing exercises, or a warm shower.)

**U₂** **Universal Access**

**English Language Learners**

Pain relief options for pregnant women include epidural anesthesia, general anesthesia, local anesthesia, narcotics, pudendal block, and spinal block. Divide students into small groups. Groups should combine English language learners with native English speakers. Assign each group a pain relief option to research. Tell students to document how the medicine works and what possible side effects it may have on the mother or baby. Once the research is complete, have the class compile its findings into one chart to compare the options side-by-side. **ELL**

✓ **Reading Check**

**Summarize** The mother delivers the placenta.

## Explore the Photo

**Caption Answer** Answers will vary but may include: The childbirth classes will help the father better understand what the mother is going through and can show him how to support the mother.

**Discussion** Ask the class: What are the emotional benefits of parents attending a childbirth class as a couple? (Responses will vary; the couple can grow closer by practicing techniques to help the mother. They can also share their hopes and concerns about the welfare and future of their baby.)

### Reteach *cont.*

**R** **Reading Strategy**

**Create a Venn Diagram** Instruct students to create a Venn diagram in which they compare a cesarean birth to a natural birth. (Cesarean: surgical procedure; baby is removed from an incision in abdomen; mother has some kind of anesthetic, possibly general anesthesia; mother typically takes longer to recover; Natural: mother pushes baby out; baby travels through the birth canal; mother may or may not have anesthetic; Similarity: both result in baby being born) **ELL**

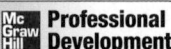

**Professional Development**

**Mini Clip**
**ELL:**
**Graphic Organizers**

Students use graphic organizers to distinguish between major and minor details in a reading selection.

**C** **Critical Thinking**

**Predict** Ask students: How do you think a pregnant mother might react to hearing her baby is in breech presentation and she will need a cesarean birth? Explain your answer. (Answers will vary; while the mother may be relieved that everything is being done to protect the well-being of her child, she may be disappointed in having to miss the experience of natural childbirth.)

### ✓ Reading Check

**List** Reasons include lack of normal progress during labor, discovering that the baby is in distress or turned in the wrong direction, or having multiple births.

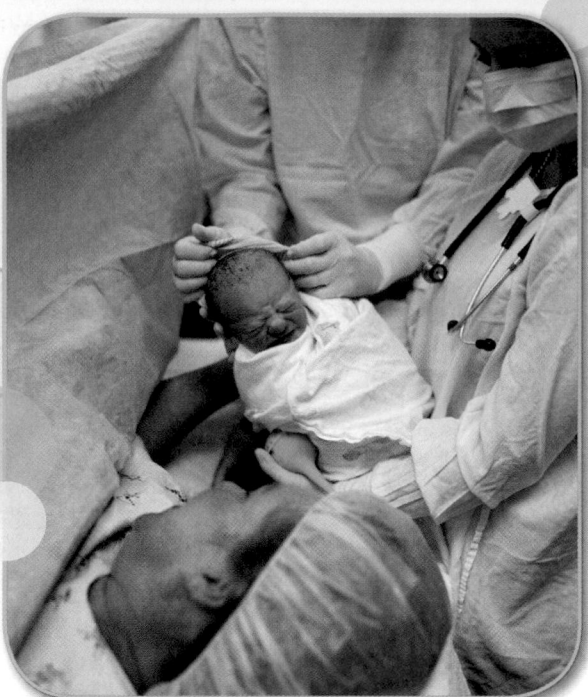

→ **Cesarean Birth**
A cesarean birth may be necessary when complications arise during labor. *How does a cesarean birth differ from natural birth?*

## Cesarean Birth

**R** Not all births progress through the stages of labor. If complications arise during pregnancy or labor, a cesarean birth (si-ˈzer-ē-ən), also known as a cesarean section or c-section, may become necessary. A **cesarean birth** is the delivery of a baby through a surgical incision in the mother's abdomen.

**C** Cesarean delivery might be performed for several reasons. It could be due to lack of normal progress during labor or discovering that the baby is in distress or turned in the wrong direction. Cesarean deliveries are often planned for multiple births. If a cesarean birth is anticipated during pregnancy, special childbirth classes can help parents prepare.

Pain medication is used for cesarean births. With certain types of medication, such as an epidural, women can remain awake during the surgery. In other situations, general anesthesia that puts the mother to sleep is used. With the doctor's permission, the father or other support partner may be present.

Because a cesarean birth is surgery, it carries some risks. However, when necessary, it can relieve stress on the baby and speed up delivery. It also allows the doctor to better control the birth process.

The mother may be able to hold the baby in the delivery room after a cesarean delivery. This will depend on hospital rules as well as the mother's condition. If the mother cannot hold the baby, the father may be able to. In some hospitals, it is standard procedure to take the baby to an intensive care nursery after a cesarean. This is not necessarily cause for alarm.

After a cesarean delivery, mothers are taken to a recovery area where they stay for a few hours. They are encouraged to stand or walk with help as soon as possible to speed the healing process. Women who have had cesarean births may need up to six weeks to fully recover.

### ✓ Reading Check **List** What are three reasons a mother might have a cesarean delivery?

172 **Chapter 6** The Baby's Arrival

→ **Explore the Photo**

**Caption Answer** During a cesarean birth, the baby is delivered through a surgical incision in the mother's abdomen. In a natural birth, the baby is delivered through the birth canal without surgery.

**Discussion** Ask students: Why might a mother prefer to have an epidural during a cesarean birth? Why might she prefer general anesthesia? (With an epidural, the mother is awake and can see the baby immediately; however, she also is aware of the surgical process, which some individuals might find difficult.)

## Premature Birth

Between 5 and 6 percent of all babies are born prematurely. Premature babies are those born before reaching 37 weeks of development and weighing less than five pounds, eight ounces (2.5 kg). The earlier babies are born, the less developed their organs are and the lower their birth weight.

Why are babies born prematurely? No one knows for sure. However, mothers who have had other premature births, are carrying more than one baby, or have other medical problems are more likely to have premature babies. Teen mothers also are more likely to give birth prematurely. Women can reduce their risks by eating well and getting proper prenatal care.

Premature babies, or preemies, require special care. They are not really ready to live outside their mother's body. Their systems for controlling body temperature, breathing, and feeding are not yet mature. These systems are controlled by the brain. A premature baby's brain is not yet ready to control these systems. Doctors are sometimes able to delay an infant's birth. Even a few extra days in the womb can help promote the baby's development.

To help control the undeveloped body systems, a premature baby is usually placed in an incubator. An **incubator** is a special enclosed crib where the oxygen supply, temperature, and humidity can be closely controlled. Some preemies are able to suck and can be breast-fed or fed using a bottle. This allows the mother to begin bonding with her child while still in the hospital.

Some preemies will have long-term health problems, learning problems, or even brain damage. However, advances in medical technology allow many to survive and grow to be healthy. Many premature infants will reach developmental milestones in the first year a little later than the average child. By the time they are toddlers, though, it is often impossible to know if a child was born prematurely.

---

### Section 6.1 — After You Read

#### Review Key Concepts

1. **Identify** two early signs of labor.
2. **List** three reasons for cesarean birth.
3. **Explain** why premature babies require special care.

#### Practice Academic Skills

 **English Language Arts**

4. Think about when you have seen babies being born on television or at the movies. Write a half-page essay in which you compare and contrast what you have seen in the media with what you read in this section.

> **NCTE 12** Use language to accomplish individual purposes.

 **Social Studies**

5. Childbirth in the United States is generally done with the guidance and assistance of a medical professional. This is not always the case in other countries. Select a country other than the United States and learn about its childbirth process. Prepare an oral report to share your findings with the class.

> **NCSS I A** Analyze and explain the ways groups, societies, and cultures address human needs and concerns.

 **Check Your Answers** Check your answers at this book's Online Learning Center at **glencoe.com**.

**N C L B**

Section 6.1   Labor and Birth   **173**

---

### Section 6.1 — Assess

#### Study Tools

Have students go to the Online Learning Center at **glencoe.com**:

- Take the **Practice Test**.
- Download **Study-to-Go** content.

Use the **Student Activity Workbook** for additional practice.

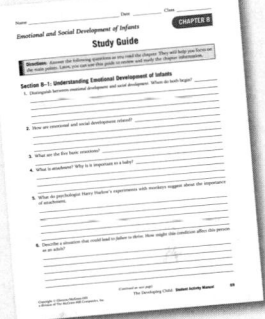

### Close

#### Culminating Activity

**Identify Stages of Labor** State an event that occurs during labor, such as "Effacement begins." or "The head enters the birth canal." Then ask for a volunteer to identify the stage of labor in which this event occurs.

**NCLB** connects academic correlations to book content.

---

### Section 6.1 — After You Read

#### Review Key Concepts

1. any two of the following: The "bloody show" of mucus, fluid from the vagina, contractions
2. lack of normal progress during labor, if the baby is in distress or turned the wrong direction, or having multiple births
3. Premature babies have less developed organs and low birth weight. They are not ready to live outside the mother's body. Their body systems are immature.

#### Practice Academic Skills

4. Answers will vary. Students might note that some movies show women easily and quickly go through labor and delivery without following the stages described, or they might point out that their water broke, signaling labor as described in the text.

5. Answers will vary depending on the country chosen. Newly industrialized or developing countries may not have the same level of medical treatment available as industrialized countries such as the United States.

## Focus

### Bell Ringer Activity

**Newborn Testing**
Explain that this section will discuss tests performed on newborns. One common method of evaluating infants is by using the Apgar scale. Pass around a sample Apgar scale or display an enlarged version for the entire class. Point out that the test gets its name from the first letters of the items being checked: **A**ctivity, **P**ulse, **G**rimace, **A**ppearance, and **R**espiration.

## Preteaching

### Vocabulary
Remind students that a synonym is a word that means the same as another word. Have students search page 175 for synonyms for the following words: windpipe (trachea); existence (survival); uneven (irregular); durable (sturdy).

### McGraw Hill Professional Development

**Mini Clip**
ELL: Vocabulary Activities

Students practice vocabulary using synonyms and words in context.

### Graphic Organizer
The Graphic Organizer is also on the TeacherWorks CD.

(Graphic organizers should list: heart rate, breathing, muscle tone, response to stimulation, and clear skin color.)

**NCLB** connects academic correlations to book content.

## Reading Guide

### Before You Read
**Explain** Read the Key Concepts and Content Vocabulary. Write one or two sentences to explain what you think the section will be about.

### Read to Learn
**Key Concepts**
- **Describe** a newborn's appearance immediately after birth.
- **Identify** the exams and procedures given to a newborn in the first few days.

**D**

### Main Idea
A newborn baby is examined immediately after birth. A newborn also receives numerous tests shortly after birth.

### Content Vocabulary
◇ fontanel
◇ lanugo
◇ vernix
◇ Apgar scale

### Academic Vocabulary
You will find these words in your reading and on your tests. Use the glossary to look up their definitions if necessary.
■ fuse
■ secure

### Graphic Organizer
As you read, find the five factors that are checked during a baby's first exam. Use a fishbone diagram like the one shown to organize your information.

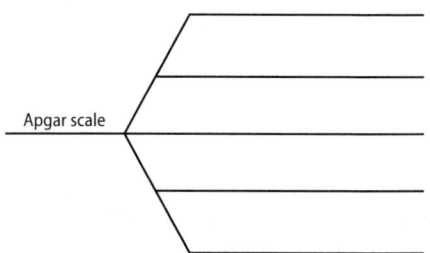

 **Graphic Organizer** Go to this book's Online Learning Center at **glencoe.com** to print out this graphic organizer.

### Academic Standards . . . . . . . . . . . . . . . . . . . . .

**N C L B**

 **English Language Arts**
**NCTE 5** Use different writing process elements to communicate effectively.

**Social Studies**
**NCSS VIII C Science, Technology, and Society** Analyze how science influences the core values, beliefs, and attitudes of society, and how core values of society shape scientific change.

**NCTE** *National Council of Teachers of English*
**NCTM** *National Council of Teachers of Mathematics*

**NSES** *National Science Education Standards*
**NCSS** *National Council for the Social Studies*

## Reading Guide

### Before You Read
Ask students what kinds of tests they receive when they go in for a physical. (Examples might include: the doctor listens to their heart, takes their pulse and temperature, or gives them an eye test.) Explain that newborns also are given specific tests.

### D Develop Concepts

**Main Idea** Discuss the main idea with the students. Ask students what kinds of things they think health care professionals might be checking for when they perform these tests. (Possible answer—they are checking to make certain the baby has no birth defects and that body systems, such as the lungs and heart, appear to be functioning normally.)

## The Baby Arrives

At birth, a newborn goes through many physical changes that are necessary for the baby's survival outside of the mother's body. Before birth, parents often wonder, "What will my baby look like?"

When parents imagine the answers to this question, they usually imagine a sturdy, smiling baby of about six months. Newborns look nothing like that. It will take some time before they are picture perfect.

A newborn baby has a tiny measure of independence. No longer reliant on the mother for oxygen, the baby will take a first breath. During the pregnancy, the baby's lungs are collapsed. Oxygen is delivered through the mother's blood, and the lungs are not used.

During delivery, the lungs fill with the amniotic fluid that was in the baby's trachea. This is the tube that delivers air from the mouth to the lungs. Most of the fluid is squeezed out during the trip through the birth canal.

Whatever remains in the mouth is suctioned out immediately after birth. Newborns usually breathe naturally. If the baby needs help, medical personnel may gently rub or pat the baby's back to encourage breathing.

For the first few months, newborns breathe through their noses. Their breathing may be irregular. They may even pause briefly in their breathing while they sleep. This is perfectly normal. Newborns may sneeze often in order to clear mucus from their noses. A newborn's breathing becomes regular a month or two after birth.

Once the lungs have begun to take in oxygen, the baby's circulatory system changes. Blood now circulates to and from the lungs, rather than bypassing them as before.

The heart changes, too. The heart must pump harder to get more blood to the lungs. Two small openings in the heart begin to close. A new type of hemoglobin develops. Hemoglobin is a part of the red blood cell that delivers oxygen to the body.

**Look Beyond Appearance**
A newborn baby might not be as cute as the parents expect. *Do you think the baby's appearance will affect the parent's feelings toward the baby?*

---

## Explore the Photo

**Caption Answer** Answers will vary. Students might say that appearance shouldn't matter to the parents.

**Discussion** Ask students: Have you ever been introduced to a newborn that you thought was unusual looking? What did you say to the parents about the newborn? (Answers will vary; students may say that they commented on a specific trait such as the eyes or hair.)

 **Professional Development**

**Mini Clip**
**ELL: Group Discussions**

Students discuss academic content they have just read.

---

## Teach

### Discussion Starter

**Modern Diagnostic Techniques and Parents' Expectations** Remind students that it was not that long ago that parents knew little about their unborn child. Today's diagnostic equipment, such as ultrasound, allows parents to know such things as the baby's sex and whether the baby is likely to have any birth defects. Ask students how they think this knowledge might affect parents. (Students' responses will vary. Being reasonably certain their baby will be healthy can be a relief.)

### C Critical Thinking

**Predict** Ask students: Based on what you have learned in this chapter, which baby do you think is more likely to have a misshapen head—one who is born naturally or one who is born by cesarean section? Why? (Because babies who are born naturally must pass through the birth canal, they are more likely to have misshapen heads.)

### R Reading Strategy

**Know When to Slow Down** Tell students that being able to recognize when to slow down their reading speed and read more thoroughly can help in digesting difficult information. For example, the discussion of how the baby's lungs begin functioning may require careful reading. Ask students: How can you quickly identify paragraphs where you may need to read more slowly? (Possible answer: when a paragraph uses unfamiliar terms.)

## S Skill Practice

### Guided Practice

**Make a Collage** Organize students into groups. Have each group create a collage with pictures of newborns. You may wish to supply a variety of photos and illustrations for them. When they are done, encourage the groups to discuss the babies' appearances. **L1 ELL**

**Write an E-mail** Tell students that they have just received an e-mail from an older friend whose wife has given birth to a baby girl. The father is concerned that the baby's face is lopsided, with one eye larger than the other. Tell students to write a response to this new father's concerns. (Students' responses should explain that babies' heads and faces are often distorted by the pressure of passing through the birth canal, but soon return to normal.) **L2**

**Create a Presentation** Tell students that they are teaching a childbirth preparation class. Tonight, they plan to address the appearance of newborns. Instruct them to create an oral presentation. Including several images which thoroughly explain the appearance of a typical newborn. (Presentations should explain the appearance of typical newborns based on information in the text.) **L3**

### Explore the Photo

**Caption Answer** If there is a problem, doctors want to start treatment as soon as possible.

**Discussion** Ask students: Do you think a baby born at home should be given the same tests as one born in a hospital? (Yes, if possible, because it is important to identify health issues early.)

---

## THE DEVELOPING BRAIN

### Brain Size and Growth

At birth, a baby's head is about one-fourth of the baby's total height, which averages about 20 inches (50 centimeters). That is twice the size, compared to the rest of the body, of an adult's head. An infant's head is big because the brain is big. After birth, the head and brain grow much less than the rest of the baby's body.

■ **Science Inquiry** Having a bigger head and brain does not necessarily mean a smarter baby. Why does size not determine intelligence?

---

The umbilical cord once provided the baby with nourishment and oxygen. This cord is no longer needed. Within a few minutes of birth, the cord stops pulsing with the mother's heartbeat and begins to shrink. The cord is clamped and cut off, leaving a small stump at the baby's navel. The father is often allowed to cut the cord. The stump will fall off in the first few weeks. The navel should be kept clean and dry until the cord stump falls off.

## The Newborn's Appearance

Most people think of bright eyes and plump arms and legs when they picture babies. Newborns tend to look a little different though. Their limbs may be skinny, and their features sometimes appear flattened.

The newborn's head is wobbly and looks too large for the body. The baby's skull may appear pointed or lopsided due to the passage through the birth canal. A baby's skull bones are not fully fused. The skull will have soft spots, or fontanels. A **fontanel** is an open space found on the baby's head where the bones are not yet joined. One of these soft spots is just above the baby's forehead. The other is toward the back of the skull. Fontanels allow the bones to move together during birth. As the baby develops during the first year and a half of life, the bones grow together and **fuse**, or combine. The fused bones cover the fontanels. In the meantime, a thick layer of skin covers them and protects the brain.

The face of the newborn may be swollen or puffy after the birth process. Typically, newborns have fat cheeks; short, flat noses; and receding chins. The small features make it easier for the baby to nurse at the mother's breasts. At birth, babies' eyes are nearly adult-size.

**S**

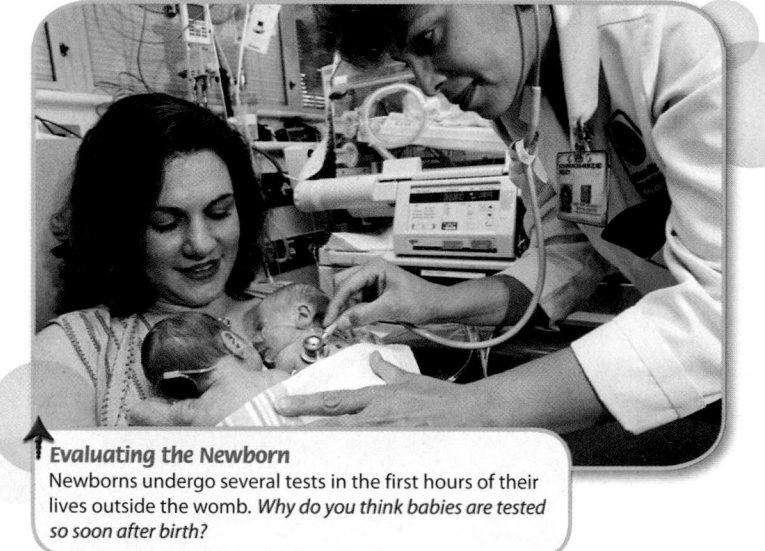

▲ **Evaluating the Newborn**
Newborns undergo several tests in the first hours of their lives outside the womb. *Why do you think babies are tested so soon after birth?*

---

## THE DEVELOPING BRAIN

### Brain Size and Growth

**Science Inquiry** Students should recall from Chapter 1 that there are many influences on child development and intelligence including heredity and environment. If children do not have a stimulating environment, they will not develop to their full potential.

For more information and activities, see *The Developing Brain* guide and eTransparencies.

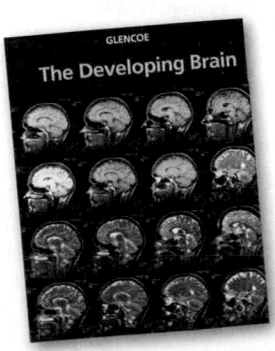

## RESPOND TO SPECIAL NEEDS | Cystic Fibrosis

Colleen's parents had heard the saying, "A baby whose sweat tastes salty will have a miserable life." What they did not know is that very salty sweat is one of the signs of a genetic disease called cystic fibrosis. While it affects all racial groups, the disease is most common in Caucasians, and affects both boys and girls equally. Doctors tested Colleen, a newborn, by taking a few drops of her sweat and measuring the chloride (a body salt) in it. The test was painless, and the results came back the same day. Colleen tested positive for the disease. This did not mean she would have a miserable life. Some people with the disease have breathing problems and trouble digesting food. However, Others show no signs of the disease except very salty sweat. Currently, there is no cure for cystic fibrosis, but there are many promising treatments in use.

**Critical Thinking** Research treatments currently in use for cystic fibrosis. Explain how one treatment works and whether it is for all people with cystic fibrosis. Record your findings in a one-page report. Be sure to cite your sources.

---

Babies of African, Asian, and Hispanic descent often have brown eyes at birth, and they remain this color. Caucasian babies' eyes are usually a dark grayish-blue at birth, but the color may change. The color becomes permanent at three to six months.

Babies' circulatory systems must make adjustments to the changing temperatures of the outside world. Tiny fingers and toes may be slightly cooler than the rest of the body for the first 24 hours. Keeping babies wrapped in blankets makes them feel more **secure**, or safe. A knitted cap keeps their heads warm. Hospitals may put babies under warming lamps immediately after birth.

Some babies, especially preemies, have lanugo (lə-'nü-(ˌ)gō). **Lanugo** is fine, downy hair growing on newborns' foreheads, backs, and shoulders. This hair soon disappears.

While in the uterus, the baby is floating in amniotic fluid, and is covered with vernix. **Vernix** is a thick, white, pasty substance made up of the fetus's old skin cells and the secretions of skin glands. It acts as a protection against constant exposure to the amniotic fluid. Any remaining vernix is washed off during the baby's first bath.

Many babies have tiny, white bumps called milia, or baby acne, on their nose and cheeks. They are plugged oil ducts caused by stimulation from the mother's hormones, which remain in the baby's system for a short time after delivery. The milia disappear in a week or so.

**✓ Reading Check** **Recall** What is the first measure of independence a newborn baby has?

## Examining the Newborn

When babies are born, their condition is usually evaluated using the Apgar scale. The **Apgar scale** is a system of rating the physical condition of a newborn baby. The baby is also given other tests soon after birth. **C**

### First Exam

Using the Apgar scale, five factors are checked when the baby is one minute old. The same factors are checked again five minutes after birth. These factors are heart rate, breathing, muscle tone, response to stimulation, and skin color. Crying is a desired response to stimulation and shows good breathing. Many newborns have a blue tint to their skin tone.

Section 6.2   The Newborn   **177**

---

## RESPOND TO SPECIAL NEEDS | Cystic Fibrosis

**Discussion** Have students imagine they are Colleen's parents. Ask: What kinds of emotional support might you need? How might you get it? (Responses will vary. Family and friends can be a good source of emotional support. The parents might want to talk with parents of children having this condition and possibly join a support group.)

**Critical Thinking** Reports will vary. One treatment is chest physical therapy in which the back and chest are clapped on vigorously to break up the thick mucus in the lungs.

---

## Assess

### Quiz
Ask students to answer the following questions:

1. **How do the baby's lungs change during delivery?** (During pregnancy, the lungs are collapsed. During delivery, the lungs expand and fill with amniotic fluid, which is then squeezed out as the baby travels through the birth canal. After birth, the baby usually breathes naturally.)
2. **What happens to the umbilical cord after birth?** (It quits pulsing and begins to shrink. It is then cut off, leaving a small stump at the baby's navel which will eventually fall off.)
3. **What is the purpose of the fontanels?** (They allow the bones in the baby's skull to move closer together during birth so that the head can more easily move down the birth canal.)

## Reteach

### C Critical Thinking
**Extrapolate** Explain to students that sometimes even normal, healthy babies perform below average on these tests. Ask students to speculate on what might cause a healthy baby to perform poorly. (Possible answers: the baby may be affected by drugs the mother took during delivery, the baby may have had a particularly strenuous birth and be exhausted, or the test may have been improperly administered.)

### ✓ Reading Check

**Recall** He can breathe on his own.

Assess

## Assess

### Study Tools

Have students go to the Online Learning Center at **glencoe.com**:

- Take the **Practice Test**.
- Download **Study-to-Go** content.

Use the **Student Activity Workbook** for additional practice.

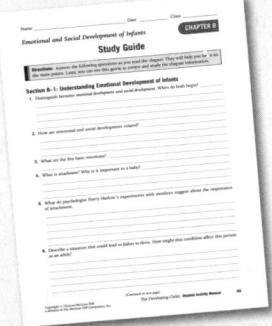

## Close

### Culminating Activity

**Summarize** Have students summarize tests performed on newborns along with each test's purpose. (The Apgar scale measures heart rate, breathing, muscle tone, stimulation response, and skin color. Other tests include hearing screenings and a blood analysis for type and certain diseases.)

**N C L B**
**NCLB** connects academic correlations to book content.

---

The Apgar scale rates each of the five areas from zero to two. A normal total score is in the six-to-ten range. Ten is a perfect score. A lower score indicates that the baby may need some medical assistance.

Nurses also examine the baby for any condition that might require special care. They weigh, measure, and dry the baby. They apply antibiotic to the baby's eyes to prevent infection. The baby often receives an injection of vitamin K to prevent a rare bleeding disorder.

Shortly after birth, certain records are created. The baby's foot is printed in ink for the public record. Plastic bands are fastened to the mother's wrist, to the baby's wrist or ankle, and to the wrist of someone of the mother's choosing. The bands have matching numbers and are checked each time the baby leaves the mother's room. The baby may be moved to the hospital nursery. In most hospitals, only hospital staff members with the appropriate identification are permitted into the hospital nursery.

### Later Tests

Newborns are given several other tests and medical procedures during their first few days of life. Most newborns receive at least one and often two hearing screenings. Blood is taken from the umbilical cord immediately after birth to check the baby's blood type and to screen for certain diseases.

While the baby is still in the hospital, blood will be taken from the heel to test for certain diseases and disorders. Which tests are done currently varies from state to state. Some hospitals will also give the first hepatitis B vaccine before the baby is discharged.

Babies that are born at home should still receive the same tests as those born in a hospital. Parents should plan ahead and discuss the birth with their doctor. If a midwife is present, she may be able to perform some of the initial tests. Parents should schedule visits with a pediatrician for routine shots and tests.

---

## Section 6.2    After You Read

### Review Key Concepts

1. **Explain** why the face of a newborn might be swollen after birth.
2. **List** the five characteristics that are rated on the Apgar scale.

### Practice Academic Skills

**N C L B**

#### English Language Arts

3. Imagine that you have learned that your older cousin is about to give birth for the first time. She is excited and a little nervous. She knows what to expect during the birth process, but is not sure what happens to the baby immediately after birth. Write a letter to your cousin explaining what happens to the newborn immediately after birth.

> **NCTE 5** Use different writing process elements to communicate effectively.

#### Social Studies

4. Stem cells can be used in the treatment and cure of many human diseases and disorders. There is a lot of debate over the ethical use of stem cells for research. Conduct research to find out why stem cell research is controversial. Write a brief essay on your findings.

> **NCSS VIII C** Analyze how science influences the core values, beliefs, and attitudes of society, and how core values of society shape scientific change.

**Check Your Answers** Check your answers at this book's Online Learning Center at **glencoe.com**.

---

### Review Key Concepts

1. The birth process itself may cause the baby's face to swell.
2. heart rate, breathing, muscle tone, response to stimulation, and skin color

### Practice Academic Skills

3. Letters will vary but should explain that, using the Apgar scale, five factors are checked at one minute, and again five minutes after birth. They are heart rate, breathing, muscle tone, response to stimulation, and clear skin color. Nurses also examine the baby, checking especially for any condition that might require special care. They weigh, measure, and dry the baby. They apply antibiotic drops or ointment to the baby's eyes to prevent infection. The baby often receives an injection of vitamin K to prevent a rare bleeding disorder.
4. Answers will vary but students should explain that much research is done with embryonic stem cells. The embryo dies when the stem cells are collected. Many people believe that this is homicide since the embryo could have developed into human life.

## Reading Guide

### Before You Read

**Discover** Choose a Content or Academic Vocabulary term that is new to you. When you find it in the text, write down the definition.

### Read to Learn
**Key Concepts**
- **Review** what occurs during the hospital stay after delivery.
- **Summarize** the physical and emotional needs of a new mother.

### Main Idea
**D** After the baby is born, the parents begin to bond with the baby while still at the hospital. Both mother and baby receive postnatal care.

### Content Vocabulary
◇ neonatal period
◇ jaundice
◇ bilirubin
◇ bonding
◇ colostrum
◇ lactation consultant
◇ rooming-in
◇ postnatal period
◇ postpartum depression

### Academic Vocabulary
You will find these words in your reading and on your tests. Use the glossary to look up their definitions if necessary.
- major
- stable

### Graphic Organizer
As you read, write a one-sentence summary of each physical need of the mother after the baby is born. Use a chart like the one shown to organize your information.

| Postnatal Need | Summary |
|---|---|
| Rest | |
| Exercise | |
| Medical checkups | |

 **Graphic Organizer** Go to this book's Online Learning Center at **glencoe.com** to print out this graphic organizer.

### Academic Standards · · · · · · · · · · · · · · · · · · · · · · · · ·

**NCLB**

 **English Language Arts**
**NCTE 4** Use written language to communicate effectively.

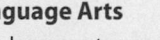 **Science**
**NSES F** Develop understanding of personal and community health.

**NCTE** *National Council of Teachers of English*
**NCTM** *National Council of Teachers of Mathematics*

**NSES** *National Science Education Standards*
**NCSS** *National Council for the Social Studies*

## Reading Guide

### Before You Read
Show students a picture of an animal, such as a mother cat, curled up, with a litter of kittens. Ask: What can humans learn from the way in which animals interact with their babies? (We can learn the importance of warmth, touch, and feeling protected early in life.)

### **D** Develop Concepts
**Main Idea** Discuss the main idea with the students. Ask students how relatives and hospital personnel might encourage bonding. (Answers will vary, but might include showing new parents how to interact with their baby and giving them time alone.)

---

## Focus

### Bell Ringer Activity

#### Developing a Bond
Ask the class if anyone knows what the term *bond* means in chemistry. (It is an attractive force that holds together matter, such as the parts of an atom.) Explain that to develop a healthy relationship, parents must bond with their babies in much the same way that an atom's parts bond.

## Preteaching
### Vocabulary
Some of the words covered in this section are difficult to pronounce. Read aloud each word. Then have the class read the words aloud together.

 **Professional Development**

 **Mini Clip**
**ELL: Reading Aloud**

A teacher reads aloud, modeling fluency, pronunciation, and expression.

## Graphic Organizer
 The Graphic Organizer is also on the TeacherWorks CD.

(Graphic organizers should include: Rest—Mother should rest when baby rests. Exercise—Gentle exercise helps mother regain strength and lose weight. Medical checkups—Mother should have a checkup four to six weeks after birth.)

**NCLB** NCLB connects academic correlations to book content.

### Discussion Starter

**Hospitals and Bonding** Tell students that in the past, many hospitals kept babies in nurseries almost all the time except when they were being fed. Ask students how they think this might have affected the mother and the baby. (It might have affected their ability to form emotional ties.) Health care professionals now know the importance of establishing these ties, a process called bonding. Some hospitals even delay certain tests to allow more time for bonding after birth.

### C Critical Thinking

**Hypothesize** Ask students: What challenges do you think new parents face during the neonatal period? Why might new parents feel helpless? How can parents feel more secure about their parenting skills? Where can they turn for help? (Answers will vary. Students should recognize that parenting is a big responsibility and involves many new skills. Parents can feel more secure by attending education classes prior to the birth and by joining support groups after the birth.)

### R Reading Strategy

**Break Down Compound Words** Discuss that the meaning of a compound word can often be determined by dividing it into components. Explain how this can be done with the word *phototherapy* (*photo*—light; *therapy*—treatment.) Instruct students to locate at least one other example of a compound word on this page. (Possible example: *neonatal* [*neo*—new; *natal*—related to birth])

## After the Birth

Once the baby has arrived, parents quickly begin forming emotional ties with their newborn. This enjoyable process plays an important role in the emotional and physical development of the baby. It also helps the parents. Mothers go through emotional changes, and it is important that they receive needed support.

**C** The neonatal period involves **major**, or significant, adjustments for mother and baby. The **neonatal period** is the first month after the baby is born. Labor and delivery are tiring. Both mother and baby need time to rest and recover. In some facilities, a healthy mother and baby may go home as soon as 12 hours after birth. In hospitals, the average stay following birth is one to two days.

**Jaundice** ('jȯn-dəs) causes the baby's skin and eyes to look slightly yellow. This condition occurs in more than 50 percent of newborns because the liver cannot remove bilirubin (ˌbi-li-'rü-bən). **Bilirubin** is a substance produced by the breakdown of red blood cells. The baby's body may be producing too much of this substance, or the developing liver may not be able to remove it fast enough. If left untreated, jaundice can damage the nervous system.

**R** In the hospital, doctors may prescribe phototherapy to help the liver do its job. Phototherapy is treatment using ultraviolet light. Sometimes the treatment is continued at home.

## Bonding

In recent years, many researchers have given attention to the emotional needs of the newborn. Studies have emphasized bonding. **Bonding** is forming emotional ties between parents and child. Knowing how important bonding is, most hospitals now delay some of the routine procedures after birth, if there are no complications. Parents are allowed to hold the child and begin forming an attachment sooner. When complications do occur and the parents are not able to hold the baby right away, bonding can still occur later.

Immediately after birth, nurses may place the baby on the mother's stomach. This lets the baby feel the warmth of her mother's skin. The baby can also hear the mother's voice and heartbeat that became so familiar in the uterus. At this point, many fathers examine their newborn's tiny toes and fingers. Parents often begin touching and talking to the baby, looking into the baby's eyes and stroking the baby's cheeks. By instinct, the newborn focuses on the human face. This helps the newborn bond.

Bonding also helps brain development. During the first year, a baby's brain cells are making millions of connections. Parents' efforts to bond with their baby help build connections in the brain. Through simple interactions, such as holding or singing to the baby, parents help strengthen the baby's brain development.

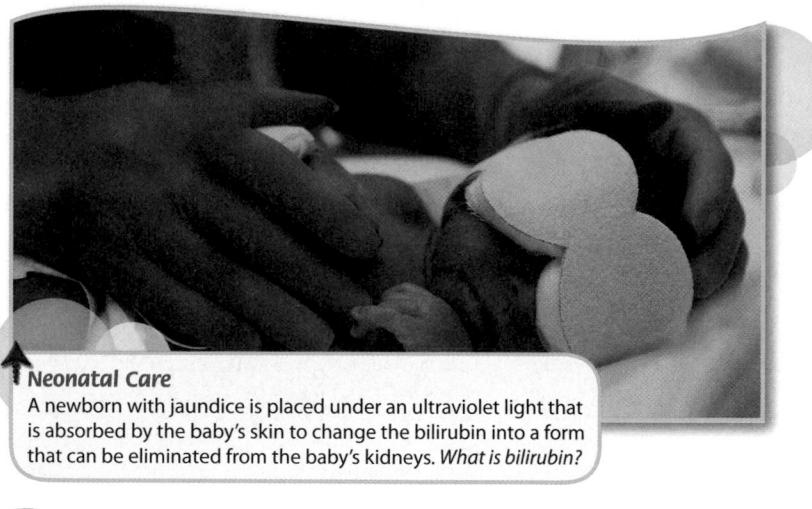

**Neonatal Care**
A newborn with jaundice is placed under an ultraviolet light that is absorbed by the baby's skin to change the bilirubin into a form that can be eliminated from the baby's kidneys. *What is bilirubin?*

## ➤ Explore the Photo

**Caption Answer** Bilirubin is a substance produced by the breakdown of red blood cells.

**Discussion** Ask students: Why is it vital that health care professionals closely watch for conditions such as jaundice? (If these conditions are not treated quickly, they can lead to permanent damage to the newborn. For example, jaundice can damage the nervous system.)

If the baby will be breast-fed, the mother may begin nursing right away. Newborns are born with a strong sucking reflex. They are usually alert right after delivery. Each breast-feeding session tells the mother's body to continue making milk. It also helps the mother's uterus contract after birth, stopping any bleeding.

**Colostrum** (kə-'läs-trəm) is a high-calorie, high-protein early breast milk. It satisfies the baby's appetite and provides protection from illnesses. When the baby becomes too sleepy to nurse, the father or another relative can hold the baby while the mother rests.

### Help with Feeding

All babies lose weight during the first few days of life, but gain it back later. By the fourth day, breast-feeding mothers begin producing more milk. Some mothers have trouble with breast- or bottle-feeding. Parents can get help while they are still in the hospital.

Many hospitals offer lactation consultants. A **lactation consultant** is a professional breast-feeding specialist who shows mothers how to encourage adequate milk production and how to position babies properly so that they can nurse. Nurses can also help. During the first few days of life, some babies are too sleepy to eat. To wake them, mothers can try unwrapping their babies to expose them to the air in the room. A little stimulation, such as a light massage, can also help wake the baby for a feeding.

### Rooming-in

Many hospitals offer the option of full or partial **rooming-in**. Full rooming-in means that the baby remains with the mother in her room during the entire hospital stay. Partial rooming-in means that the baby stays in the nursery part of the time, such as during the night. Mothers can ask that their babies be brought to their rooms for night feedings. Hospitals that offer rooming-in generally allow the father to visit whenever he wishes.

## Parenting Skills

### Bonding with a Baby

Babies crave touch. Close emotional ties help their brains and bodies develop. When parents include the baby in their usual activities, they give the baby varied experiences and strengthen their own relationship. Here are some ideas to promote bonding.

- **Use a baby carrier.** Being comfortably strapped to a parent's body keeps the baby close to the heart. The rhythm of a heartbeat comforts babies.
- **Sing or read to the baby.** It is not necessary to wait until the baby is old enough to understand what is being read. The sound of a familiar voice can be very comforting.
- **Allow dad time with the baby.** Fathers who spend time alone with their babies get to know them better. Giving a late-night bottle or going for walks can enhance the bonding experience.
- **Let the baby handle you.** Babies are interested in different textures, like beards and long hair. But be careful! Babies have a tight grasp and do not like to let go.

**Take Charge** Playing with babies is another way for parents and babies to bond. Can you think of some ways to play with a baby that would promote bonding?

## Parenting Skills

### Bonding with a Baby

Ask students: What factors might keep a parent and infant from bonding? Which of these factors can be controlled by parents? Which cannot? (Factors will vary but might include that either the parent or the child is ill after the birth or the parent sees the baby as a burden. Some issues, such as health, cannot be controlled.)

**Take Charge**
Student answers will vary but may include putting one's face close to the baby and blowing gently on his face, singing or reading to the baby, or playing pat-a-cake.

## Teach *cont.*

### S Skill Practice
#### Guided Practice

**Create a Skit** Organize students into pairs. Give each pair a doll. The doll will represent an infant. Each pair should create a skit that shows as many different ways of bonding with the infant as they can think of. Have students perform their skits for the group. (Skits will vary but should show multiple ways to bond, such as singing or reading to the infant, tickling the infant, or feeding the infant.) **L1** **ELL**

**Categorize Bonding** Have students create a table that contains a column for each of the five senses: vision, hearing, touch, smell, and taste. Under each heading, they should list ways that parents can use that sense to bond with their baby. When done, ask for volunteers to share their bonding ideas with the class. (Charts will vary but should include examples for all five senses. Possible answers: vision—making eye contact; hearing—singing or reading; touch—holding or hugging; smell—using same lotions and soaps so baby will recognize smell; taste—feeding.) **L2**

**Make a Judgment** Discuss how each of the five senses might be used in bonding. Instruct students to choose the sense that they think is most important in an infant bonding with a parent. Students should then write a paragraph defending their choice and giving specific examples of why they think this sense is vital to bonding. (Paragraphs will vary but should offer sound reasons for the students' choice.) **L3**

## Assess

### Quiz

Ask students to answer the following questions:

1. **What causes jaundice and how is it treated?** (It is caused by the inability of the baby's liver to remove bilirubin, a substance produced by the breakdown of red blood cells, and results in a slight yellowing of the skin and eyes. It is treated with phototherapy.)

2. **How does drinking colostrum help a newborn?** (Colostrum satisfies the baby's appetite and provides protection from illnesses.)

3. **Explain the difference between full rooming-in and partial rooming-in.** (In full rooming-in, the baby is in the mother's room all of the time. In partial rooming-in, the baby spends some time in the nursery.)

## Reteach

### U Universal Access

**Intrapersonal Learners** Have students obtain a copy of their birth certificates. (If necessary, photocopy the birth certificates so that students are not using the originals.) Have students paste these copies onto a piece of poster board. They should then create labels identifying the document's components. They also may want to decorate their artwork in other ways. For example, they could print their names across the top in decorative lettering or add pictures of themselves as infants.

Rooming-in programs have advantages for the entire family. Rooming-in babies tend to have only one main caregiver, usually a nurse, attending to their needs. These babies seem to cry less. As a result, a rooming-in mother gets more rest and does not worry about her baby in the nursery. Also, parents start learning how to take care of them right away.

## Legal Documents

A birth certificate is the most important piece of personal identification anyone has. It is required for entrance into school. Getting one is simple. The parents fill out a form provided by the hospital or birthing center. Several weeks later, the parents receive one copy of the birth certificate. Another one is sent to a government office to be filed. Processes for filing a birth certificate for a home birth will vary by state.

The federal government recommends that a baby receive a social security number in the first year. Hospitals provide new parents with the necessary forms. Parents should fill out the forms to obtain a number for their child. They can then claim an exemption on their income taxes, obtain medical coverage for the child, and take part in government programs.

## Caring for Premature Babies

Premature babies are born before 37 weeks of development. Many premature babies spend time in a hospital's neonatal intensive-care unit (NICU). The NICU has special equipment and highly trained nurses. Not all hospitals have these units. In many areas, babies are transferred to a larger hospital that has a NICU.

There are three levels of NICU care. Level I facilities provide routine care for preemies. This includes keeping them warm and nourished. Level II care is for preemies who need to be monitored closely. Some states have only one or two hospitals with Level III facilities. These provide care for very premature (less than 34 weeks) babies or full-term infants who have serious or life-threatening conditions. A baby born far from a Level III facility may be taken there by ambulance or helicopter, depending on the baby's condition.

### Special Needs

Premature babies do not have enough body fat to maintain their temperature, even with blankets. NICUs have incubators and special warmers for preemies. These decrease the chance of infection and surround the baby with warm air.

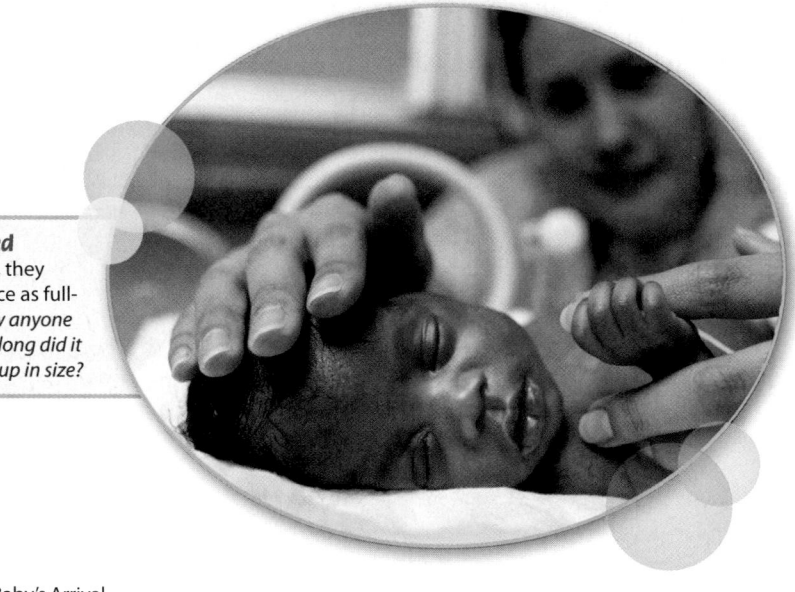

**➤ Extra Care Needed**
As preemies gain weight, they have the same appearance as full-term babies. *Do you know anyone who was a preemie? How long did it take for the baby to catch up in size?*

## ➤ Explore the Photo

**Caption Answer** Answers will vary. Some preemies reach normal size quickly, others remain on the small side.

**Discussion** Have students examine this photo. Ask students: What do you think it would be like to only be able to touch your baby through a hole in an incubator? What concerns might you have? (Possible answer: you might worry about your baby's health and not being able to comfort the baby by holding it.)

Preemies also need special types of nourishment because they grow more quickly than full-term babies. Their digestive systems are immature. Most preemies are fed breast milk through feeding tubes. Breast milk helps protect against infection and disease. Many preemies receive extra vitamins and nutrients. Once they are in a **stable**, or unchanging, condition and show signs of sucking, the doctor determines whether they can breast-feed. Sometimes preemies need special pacifiers to help them learn how to suck properly. Preemies may be fed through a tube in the stomach until they learn to suck and swallow milk.

Babies in the NICU are frequently tested for infections. Their blood cell and blood sugar levels are also checked often. Nurses and doctors will change individual care plans to reflect each baby's needs.

Premature babies stay in the hospital until their organs develop enough to function without help. This may take from a few days to a month, or more. Breathing machines are often used to help babies whose lungs are immature.

### Improved Care

The care for premature babies has improved greatly over the years. They still have an increased risk of medical and developmental problems though. How well a preemie thrives often depends on how close the baby was born to the due date. Premature babies can experience long-term difficulties such as cerebral palsy and developmental delays. The earlier the baby is born, the more risks the baby faces.

As premature babies grow, doctors decide when they can leave incubators and be placed in open cribs. Babies must be able to breathe without a machine, drink, maintain a steady body temperature, and maintain a weight of 5 pounds or more before they can leave the hospital. Other problems may require a longer hospital stay.

Premature babies need constant monitoring, which can interrupt parent-child bonding. Incubators and machines can be scary to parents. If a baby is extremely premature, the parents may touch the baby through special openings in the incubator. As the babies grow, parents can hold, sing, talk to, and bathe them.

As with full-term babies, contact helps them develop faster. Breast-feeding mothers also can provide milk for their babies.

✓ **Reading Check** **List** What four criteria must premature babies meet before they are allowed to go home?

## Mother's Postnatal Care

The **postnatal period** is the time following the baby's birth. During this time, a new mother has special needs. She may be physically exhausted from birth, and she is now responsible for the well-being of a newborn. Nurses will explain how the new mother should care for herself as she meets the needs of her baby. Mothers who give birth by cesarean section have a longer recovery time since they have had major surgery.

## Physical Needs

Recovery from pregnancy and childbirth takes time. The new mother's hormone levels change. Her sleep may be interrupted by the baby's feedings. Breast-feeding mothers experience additional changes related to producing milk. Women who have had a cesarean section require additional care. They are generally required to stay in the hospital longer and will be more fatigued. The physical needs of the new mother include rest, exercise, nutrition, and checkups.

> **{ Expert Advice... }**
>
> *"Babies enter the world with only one power—the power to elicit the emotion of tenderness and a caring response to them from other humans, especially and specifically from their mothers."*
>
> — James Kimmel, author, *Whatever Happened to Mother?*

## Reteach *cont.*

### W Writing Support
**Write Using Details**

**Life of a Preemie** Instruct students to use what they have learned in this section to write a detailed, two-paragraph essay about the kinds of care a preemie receives during his or her stay in a neonatal intensive care unit. Have students begin by creating an outline to help guide their writing. (Refer to p. 162 to review characteristics of writing using details. Student's essays should include details on the NICU and the kinds of care and tests the baby receives.)

### C Critical Thinking

**Problem Solve** Have students imagine that their next-door neighbor has a newborn. They can see that the mother is exhausted and feels that she has no control over her life. Ask students what they might do to help. (Responses will vary. They might volunteer to watch the baby for an hour or two after school so the mother could rest, or possibly clean house or run errands. Just showing they care can be important.)

✓ **Reading Check**

**List** They must be able to breathe without a machine, drink, maintain a steady body temperature, and maintain a weight of five pounds or more.

**Mini Clip**
**Reading: Planning and Classroom Management**
Nancy Frey, PhD, educator and author, discusses the instructional strategies that support a differentiated classroom.

## Assess

### Study Tools

Have students go to the Online Learning Center at **glencoe.com**:

- Take the **Practice Test**.
- Download **Study-to-Go** content.

Use the **Student Activity Workbook** for additional practice.

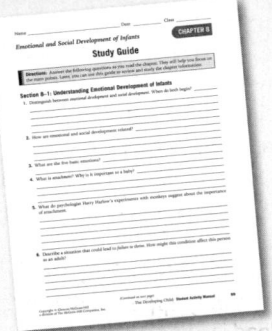

## Close

### Culminating Activity

**Meeting Mothers' Needs** Organize students into small groups. Each group should create a list of a new mother's physical and emotional needs and ways in which each need can be met. Discuss the lists as a class.

 **NCLB** connects academic correlations to book content.

---

- **Rest** During the first few weeks, the new mother may be tired. She should try to sleep whenever the baby does. Relatives and friends can help by preparing meals, doing chores, or watching the baby for a few hours.
- **Exercise** With her doctor's approval, a new mother can usually begin exercising gently. Stretching and walking short distances can help her lose weight and feel more energetic.
- **Good Nutrition** As during pregnancy, eating right is important for new mothers. They should continue to follow the USDA's MyPyramid Plan. Breast-feeding mothers are providing nutrition for their own bodies and for their babies. They need about 300 calories per day more than before pregnancy. They also need plenty of fluids.
- **Medical Checkups** Four to six weeks after birth, a new mother should have a postnatal checkup. Her doctor makes sure her uterus is returning to normal and that there are no other problems.

### Emotional Needs

In addition to physical changes, a new mother goes through emotional changes. Many women feel confused a few days after birth. Some have mood swings. The "baby blues" are very common. The mother may cry for no reason. She may feel irritable, lonely, anxious, or sad. Joining a support group for new mothers or talking with other mothers often helps.

A small percentage of new mothers experience these symptoms to a greater degree. The blues do not go away. Instead, they get worse. **Postpartum depression** is a condition in which new mothers may feel very sad, cry a lot, have little energy, feel overly anxious about the baby or have little interest in the baby, and, in extreme cases, think of harming the baby.

Treatment is available for postpartum depression. It is very important for women who have any of these symptoms to talk with their doctors about treatment. Talking to a therapist can help, as can medication.

## Section 6.3 — After You Read

### Review Key Concepts

1. **Explain** how bonding is promoted between parents and their baby in the hospital.
2. **Describe** four areas of physical needs in a mother's postnatal care.

### Practice Academic Skills

 **English Language Arts**

3. Imagine that your cousin, who is pregnant, has told you that she and her husband have toured the local NICU. She is confused about the purpose of a NICU. Write a letter to your cousin explaining the services NICUs provide.

> **NCTE 4** Use written language to communicate effectively.

 **Science**

4. In many countries, people do not understand the importance of postnatal care for the mother. Write a one-page report in which you summarize the reasons for postnatal care for the mother and what forms that care should take.

> **NSES F** Develop understanding of personal and community health.

 **Check Your Answers** Check your answers at this book's Online Learning Center at **glencoe.com**.

**184** Chapter 6 The Baby's Arrival

---

## Section 6.3 — After You Read

### Review Key Concepts

1. Newborns can immediately be placed on the mother's abdomen to feel her warmth and hear her heartbeat.
2. rest, exercise, nutrition, and checkups

### Practice Academic Skills

3. Answers will vary, but may include that NICUs have incubators and special warmers for preemies. Babies are frequently tested for infections, and blood cell and blood sugar levels. NICUs also provide care for full-term infants who have serious or life-threatening conditions.

4. Reasons for postnatal care for mothers include that recovery from pregnancy and childbirth takes time. The new mother's hormone levels change and her sleep may be interrupted by the baby's feedings. Women who have had a cesarean section are generally required to stay in the hospital longer and will be more fatigued. Postnatal care for mothers should include rest, exercise, good nutrition, and medical checkups.

## Chapter Summary

There are three main stages of labor. A cesarean birth may be necessary if the mother's or baby's health is in danger. A premature baby will require special medical care. Immediately after birth, a newborn's physical condition is evaluated through a variety of tests. Bonding after birth strengthens the emotional connection between parents and their child. A new mother needs postnatal care. New mothers need rest, exercise, good nutrition, and follow-up medical care. They may also have emotional needs.

## Vocabulary Review

**1.** Arrange the vocabulary terms below into groups of related words. Explain why you put the words together.

**Content Vocabulary**
◇ cervix (p. 165)
◇ contraction (p. 166)
◇ fetal monitoring (p. 166)
◇ dilate (p. 170)
◇ cord blood (p. 171)
◇ stem cells (p. 171)
◇ cesarean birth (p. 172)
◇ incubator (p. 173)
◇ fontanel (p. 176)
◇ lanugo (p. 177)
◇ vernix (p. 177)
◇ Apgar scale (p. 177)

◇ neonatal period (p. 180)
◇ jaundice (p. 180)
◇ bilirubin (p. 180)
◇ bonding (p. 180)
◇ colostrum (p. 181)
◇ lactation consultant (p. 181)
◇ rooming-in (p. 181)
◇ postnatal period (p. 183)
◇ postpartum depression (p. 184)

**Academic Vocabulary**
■ induce (p. 166)
■ anesthesia (p. 171)
■ fuse (p. 176)
■ secure (p. 177)
■ major (p. 180)
■ stable (p. 183)

## Review Key Concepts

**2. Describe** the progression of labor.
**3. Explain** what happens during a cesarean birth.
**4. List** the factors that can contribute to a premature birth.
**5. Describe** a newborn's appearance immediately after birth.
**6. Identify** the exams and procedures given to a newborn in the first few days.
**7. Review** what occurs during the hospital stay after delivery.
**8. Summarize** the physical and emotional needs of a new mother.

## Critical Thinking

**9. Draw Conclusions** What are some reasons a woman might choose labor without pain medication?
**10. Infer** What feelings might a new mother have during the postnatal period? Why might she have these feelings?

Chapter 6   The Baby's Arrival   **185**

### Content and Academic Vocabulary Review

**1.** Students should provide logical reasons for how they grouped the vocabulary terms.

### Review Key Concepts

**2.** Progression of labor includes beginning of labor and the three stages of labor. First stage: contractions open the cervix; second stage: baby is born; third stage: placenta is expelled.

**3.** The baby is delivered through a surgical incision in the mother's abdomen.

**4.** Factors include carrying more than one baby, having a medical problem, and teenage pregnancies.

**5.** Limbs may be skinny and features may appear flattened. Head is wobbly and looks overly large. Skull may be misshapen and face swollen.

**6.** Factors checked after birth include heart rate, breathing, muscle tone, response to stimulation, and clear skin color. Baby is weighed, measured, and dried. Antibiotic drops are placed in eyes, hearing screenings are given, and blood is taken from the umbilical cord.

**7.** Bonding begins and parents start learning how to care for the baby.

**8.** Physical needs include rest, exercise, good nutrition, and medical checkups. Emotional needs include support from others and treatment if postpartum depression occurs.

### Critical Thinking

**9.** Answers will vary but may include: Some women dislike taking pain medication for any reason. They might want to experience every aspect of the birth process including the pain. Some parents do not want their child exposed to the medications.

**10.** Answers will vary but may include that mothers should feel joy and pride in their new child. They might also feel irritable, lonely, anxious, sad, or depressed. Reasons might include that they are physically exhausted from the birth process or they are overwhelmed by the responsibility of having a child to care for.

### Family & Community Connections

**11.** Reports will vary, but should include descriptions of a real mother's birth and postnatal experience.

### Health Skills

**12.** Flyers may vary. Heart murmurs are usually mild and harmless. Hypoplastic left heart syndrome, transposition of the great arteries, heart valve abnormalities, and coarctation of the aorta are some serious congenital heart defects. Viruses like rubella during early pregnancy increase the risk of congenital heart defects, as do certain medications.

### Observation Skills

**13.** Reports will vary but should include ratio of babies to health care workers, frequency of touch, and frequency of checking the infants.

### Real-Word Skills

**14.** Answers will vary, but students should recommend that the cousin get plenty of rest, exercise, eat well, and have medical checkups. If symptoms continue, she should seek professional help.

**15.** Students' graphs should illustrate the information stated. As of 2007, Angola had the highest infant mortality rate. Singapore ranked lowest. The United States ranked 180 of 221 countries surveyed.

**16.** Student answers will vary based on people interviewed. Each student should develop a table that contains the data.

**NCLB** Activity correlated to English standards.

### Family & Community Connection

**11. Interview a Mother** Talk to a mother about her experience with the birth of her first child. Questions to ask might include: If you delivered naturally, were you prepared for the reality of labor? Did you use pain medication? What were your concerns after the baby was born? Use your notes to write a one-page report describing the mother's experience.

### Health Skills

**12. Research Congenital Heart Defects** In 8 out of every 1,000 live births, the newborn has some kind of congenital heart defect. Conduct research to answer these questions: Which of these heart defects are mild? Which of them are severe? What are their possible causes and treatments? Use the answers from your research to create a flyer or brochure that raises awareness of these conditions.

### Observation Skills

**13. Observe a Hospital Nursery** Work with your teacher to arrange to observe your local hospital's nursery. Note that you will probably not be allowed into the nursery. Your observation may be through the viewing window.

**Procedure** As you observe, take note of the number of babies in the nursery and the number of health care workers. Note how many times the babies are touched by the workers and how often the infants are checked or tested. Note how long you observed the nursery.

**Analysis** Write a report of your observation. Include the ratio of babies to health care workers. Note the frequency of touch, as well as frequency and nature of checking on the babies.

> **NCTE 7** Conduct research and gather, evaluate, and synthesize data to communicate discoveries.

**NCLB**

### Real-World Skills

| | |
|---|---|
| **Problem-Solving** | **14. Recommend Action** Imagine that your cousin has delivered her first baby and is feeling a little anxious. She thinks something might be wrong because she should be happy, but she is not. Write a letter with tips to ensure her physical and emotional health are provided for. |
| **Technology Skills** | **15. Create a Graph** Use online resources to research information about infant mortality rates in different countries. Search for answers to these questions: Which nation has the highest infant mortality rate? Which has the lowest? Where does the United States rank? Use graph-making software to create a graph that illustrates your findings. |
| **Financial Literacy** | **16. Calculate the Cost of Child-Rearing** Talk to two or more people you know who have children. Ask them to estimate the costs for items such as food, clothing, education, and medical costs for each child for one year. Present your data in a table. |

 **Additional Activities** For additional activities, go to this book's Online Learning Center at **glencoe.com**.

### Academic Skills

**17.** Replies will vary but should show students' understanding that the face of the newborn may be swollen or puffy after birth. Typically, newborns have fat cheeks; short, flat noses; and receding chins. Their features will change in the first few months of life.

The *Early Childhood Observations CD* offers additional lessons with videos to build students' observation skills.

**Part 1:** Learning to Observe
**Part 2:** How Children Develop
**Part 3:** Working With Young Children
**Part 4:** Extended Observations
**Part 5:** Resources and Answer File

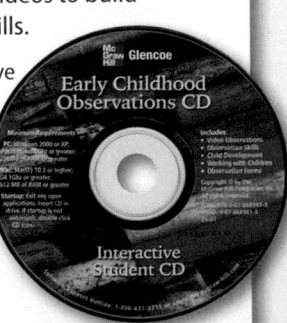

## Academic Skills

 **English Language Arts**

**17. Use Your Knowledge** A new mother is worried because her baby's face is not round and chubby like babies on television. She writes an e-mail to her sister expressing her concern. Use your knowledge of a newborn's appeareance to write a reassuring e-mail reply from the perspective of her sister.

> **NCTE 12** Use language to accomplish individual purposes.

 **Mathematics**

**18. The Baby's Arrival** A magazine published a survey of 2,000 women. It showed that in the first four months of a baby's life, most mothers averaged 5 hours of sleep per night. If adults require 8 hours of sleep, how many hours of sleep are lost per mother over the four-month period? Assume that each of the four months has 30 days.

**Math Concept** **Multi-Step Problems** When solving problems with more than one step, think through the steps before you start.

**Starting Hint** Calculate how many hours are lost in one night. Then, determine how many days are in four months, and multiply that number by the number of hours lost per night.

 **Math** For math help, go to the Math Appendix at the back of the book.

> **NCTM Number and Operations** Understand numbers, ways of representing numbers, relationships among numbers, and number systems.

 **Science**

**19. Research Postpartum Depression** Postpartum depression is a serious complication in 10 to 15 percent of all deliveries. For adolescents who give birth, the incidence is between 26 and 32 percent.

**Procedure** Conduct research to answer these questions: Why is the percentage higher in adolescents? What are some of the warning signs of postpartum depression? Identify treatment alternatives.

**Analysis** Take notes as you do your research. Write a speech based on your notes. Deliver the speech to your class. Include answers to all of the questions in your speech.

> **NSES F** Develop understanding of personal and community health.

### Standardized Test Practice

**READING COMPREHENSION**
Read the passage, then answer the question.

> Mothers often report that contractions are painful but bearable. There is time between them to rest and recover. After the baby is born and the placenta is also pushed out, contractions end. There is no lingering pain.

**20.** In this passage, the word *bearable* means:
  **a.** able to be endured
  **b.** having characteristics of a bear
  **c.** extremely difficult
  **d.** not to be endured

> **Test-Taking Tip** Read the paragraph carefully to make sure you understand what it is about. Read the answer choices. Then read the paragraph again before choosing the answer.

**18.** 360 hours of sleep are lost. ($8 - 5 = 3$ hours per night; 30 days $\times$ 4 months = 120 days; $120 \times 3 = 360$)

 **Professional Development**

**Mini Clip Math: Introducing Multi-Step Equations**
A teacher walks his students through the process of solving multi-step equations.

**19.** Speeches will vary. The higher percentage in adolescents is often due to lower social support and self-esteem. Symptoms may include being overly anxious about the baby, having little interest in the baby, or thinking of harming the baby. Treatment may include talking to a therapist or medication.

 **NCLB** connects academic correlations to book content.

### Standardized Test Practice

**20. a.** able to be endured

**Test-Taking Tips** Remind students to take questions one at a time. All their attention should be focused on correctly answering the current question.

**Multiple-Choice Tests** Tell students that test-takers generally do better if they read the passage before looking at the multiple choice question itself.

## TECHNOLOGY Solutions

**Use these technology solutions to streamline chapter assessment!**

 **ExamView Assessment Suite** CD allows you to create and print out customized tests or ready-made unit and chapter tests, complete with answer keys.

 **TeacherWorks Plus** is an electronic lesson planner that provides instant access to complete teacher resources in one convenient package.

 **Online Learning Center** includes resources and activities for students and teachers.

# Promote Good Health During Pregnancy

## Focus

### Discussion Starter

**Taking Responsibility** Ask students to list things they do to stay healthy. Ask volunteers to explain why they do these things. (Examples may include eating healthful foods, getting regular exercise, getting enough sleep, or dealing with stress in positive ways. Reasons may include that they feel better when they eat right or that exercise helps them control stress.)

 Project correlated to English Language Arts standards.

### Step 1

### Choose Your Topic

Students can select a time period they would like to focus on. Be sure students understand the significance of the mother's health during each time period. If students would like to modify the assignment and include all three time periods, they are welcome to do so. They might also focus on a specific trimester during pregnancy.

## Teach

### Step 2

### Complete Your Research

You may want to suggest that after completing cursory research, students develop an outline to follow for more extensive research. Students' research should yield some fairly comprehensive knowledge of the nutritional requirements of women in the stage being researched. They might include some sample menus in their research.

In this unit, you have learned that there are many things health care professionals and mothers-to-be can do to help ensure the delivery of a healthy baby. In this project, you will research nutrition for the different phases of pregnancy. You will use what you learned to develop menus for women in one of the stages related to pregnancy.

 **My Journal**

If you completed the journal entry from page 89, refer to it to see if your thoughts have changed after reading the unit.

### Project Assignment

In this project, you will:
- Choose a pregnancy-related time period, like pre-conception, pregnancy, or post-natal, you want to know more about.
- Conduct research on recommended nutrition for the time period you have chosen.

> #### Child Development Skills Behind the Project
>
> - Identify actions that can affect the health of an unborn baby.
> - Determine the nutrition needs of an unborn baby.
> - Identify professionals who can offer guidelines to enhance the health of the unborn baby.
>
> #### Academic Skills
>
>  **English Language Arts**
>
> **NCTE 7** Conduct research and gather, evaluate, and synthesize data to communicate discoveries.
>
> **NCTE 12** Use language to accomplish individual purposes.
>

- Identify and interview a health care provider or nutrition specialist in the community who works with women in different stages of pregnancy.
- Arrange the interview and take notes.
- Use what you learned in the interviews to create menus.

### Step 1 Choose Your Topic

The health of the mother before, during, and after pregnancy, is critical to the health of the baby. If the mother does not eat healthful foods or keep her body fit, the chances are greater that the baby will have one or more medical issues. Choose a time period to focus on.
- Before conception
- During pregnancy
- After giving birth

### Step 2 Complete Your Research

Conduct research to determine what you need to know about a woman's nutritional needs during the time period you chose. Write a summary of your research.

**Research Skills**
★ Use reputable Web sites.
★ Use dictionaries and encyclopedias.
★ Cite the sources you use. Give credit to the author of the information.

### Step 3

#### Connect to Your Community

Ask students to describe how professionals in the community will influence their development of menus. (Students should recognize that the health care provider or nutrition specialist will be an excellent resource in the development of menus for a woman in different stages of pregnancy.) Ask students how they might use the information they collect to help others in your community. (Students might suggest sharing the information and menus at community health care clinics.)

### Step 4

#### Create and Present Your Menu

Give students these tips on creating and presenting their menus:

- Use presentation software to create your menu. If this is not available, create your menu using poster board.
- Talk to your audience and encourage them to ask questions.

## Step **3** Connect to Your Community

Discuss your research findings from Step 2 with a health care provider or nutrition specialist in your community. During the discussion, share your research findings. Ask the health care provider or nutrition specialist for their comments or feedback on the material. Take notes of their responses. Ask for advice about nutrition for the stage you researched.

**Discussion Skills**

★ Know the material you will be discussing.
★ State your findings clearly.
★ Ask for feedback or comments.
★ Listen attentively.

## Step **4** Create and Present Your Menu

Use the Unit Thematic Project Checklist on the right to plan and create your menu and make your presentation.

**Presentation Skills**

★ Present your ideas clearly.
★ Engage your audience.
★ Organize your presentation by developing an outline.
★ Speak concisely (briefly but completely).

## Step **5** Evaluate Your Child Development Skills and Academic Skills

Your project will be evaluated based on:
- Content and organization of your information.
- Mechanics—presentation and neatness.
- Speaking and listening skills.

**Evaluation Rubric** Go to this book's Online Learning Center at **glencoe.com** for a rubric you can use to evaluate your final project.

### Unit Thematic Project Checklist

| | |
|---|---|
| **Menus** | ✔ Research the nutritional needs of a woman during the time of pregnancy you have selected and summarize your findings. |
| | ✔ Discuss your findings with a health care provider or nutrition specialist in your community and take notes of your discussion. |
| | ✔ Use presentation software or make a poster of menus based on your research and discussion. |
| | ✔ In your menus, show how the nutritional needs suggested by your research and your discussion are met. |
| | ✔ Make menus for breakfast, lunch, and dinner for two days. |
| **Presentation** | ✔ Make a presentation to your class to share your menus and discuss what you learned. |
| | ✔ Invite the students in your class to ask you any questions they may have. Answer three questions. |
| | ✔ When students ask you questions, demonstrate in your answers that you respect their perspectives. |
| | ✔ Turn in your research summary, the notes from your discussion, and your menus to your teacher. |
| **Academic Skills** | ✔ Create visuals to enhance a presentation. |
| | ✔ Organize a presentation. |
| | ✔ Speak clearly and concisely. |

## Assess

### Step **5**

**Evaluate Your Child Development Skills and Academic Skills**

**Rubric** Encourage students to go to this book's Online Learning Center at **glencoe.com** for a rubric they can use to evaluate their menus and presentation. Students can use the rubric as a content checklist when developing their discussion, creating their menus, and preparing their presentation.

## Close

### Culminating Activity

**Project Assessment** In this activity, students identified the nutritional needs for women prior to, during, or after pregnancy. Have students form small groups. Each of the time periods—prior to, during, and after pregnancy—should be represented in each group. Group members should compare and contrast their menus. Groups should develop a table that shows the similarities and differences of the menus for the three periods. (Tables will vary but should show that students have a good understanding of the nutritional needs for the three different time periods.)

---

## Developing Community Involvement

### Meeting Fitness Needs

In addition to making sure her nutritional needs are met, a woman who is pregnant or recently pregnant must meet specific fitness needs. Have students talk with a certified fitness instructor about the exercises he or she recommends for women in one of the three stages listed above. Students should demonstrate the exercises for the class or take photos of the instructor demonstrating the exercises to share with the class.

A **Family & Community Involvement** worksheet about this topic is available:

At this book's Online Learning Center at **glencoe.com**

On the TeacherWorks CD

| Title | Objectives |
|---|---|
| **CHAPTER 7**<br>**Physical Development of Infants** | • **Identify** the four major influences on an infant's growth and development.<br>• **Summarize** how a baby typically grows in the first year.<br>• **Explain** how to safely hold a baby.<br>• **Identify** how to meet a baby's nutritional needs.<br>• **Describe** the best type of clothing suitable for a baby.<br>• **Describe** how to bathe a baby.<br>• **Explain** why checkups and immunizations are important for babies. |
| **CHAPTER 8**<br>**Emotional and Social Development of Infants** | • **List** six basic emotions that babies experience.<br>• **Explain** the role of attachment in a baby's emotional development.<br>• **Describe** how temperament affects a baby's social development.<br>• **Explain** how the emotional climate of the home can affect a baby's development.<br>• **Explain** how a baby learns social behavior.<br>• **Identify** how play and exploration help a baby develop socially. |
| **CHAPTER 9**<br>**Intellectual Development of Infants** | • **Describe** how a baby's experiences increase brain function.<br>• **Explain** how the brain becomes organized.<br>• **List** four abilities that show intellectual growth in infants.<br>• **Identify** specific abilities that babies learn during Piaget's first period of learning.<br>• **Name** five ways caregivers can encourage learning.<br>• **Describe** how to choose toys appropriate for babies of different ages. |
| **Unit Thematic Project**<br>**Raising a Healthy Baby** | • **Write** a My Journal entry on Healthy Development.<br>• **Choose** an area of infant growth and development.<br>• **Interview** a parent or child care professional.<br>• **Prepare** an oral report to share what they learned. |

## Understanding Brackets, Letters, and Ability Levels in the Teacher Wraparound Edition

**Brackets** Brackets on the reduced student edition page correspond to teaching strategies and activities in the Teacher Wraparound Edition. As you teach the lesson, the brackets show you exactly where to use the teaching strategies and activities.

**Letters** The letters on the reduced student edition page identify the type of strategy or activity. See the key below to learn about the different types of strategies and activities.

**Ability Levels** Teaching Strategies that appear throughout the chapters have been identified by one of three codes to give you an idea of their suitability for students of varying learning styles and abilities.

**Resources** Key program resources are listed in each chapter. Icons indicate the format of resources.

### KEY TO LETTERS

**D** **Develop Concepts** activities help teachers gauge and plan for students' concept development.

**R** **Reading Strategy** activities help you teach reading skills and vocabulary.

**S** **Skill Practice** provides leveled instruction for meeting individual needs and learning styles.

**W** **Writing Support** activities provide writing opportunities to help students comprehend the text.

**C** **Critical Thinking** strategies help students apply and extend what they have learned.

**U** **Universal Access** activities provide differentiated instruction for English language learners, and suggestions for teaching various types of learners.

**NCLB** **No Child Left Behind** activities help students practice and improve their abilities in academic subjects.

### KEY TO ABILITY LEVELS

**L1** Strategies should be within the ability range of all students. Often full class participation is required.

**L2** Strategies are for average to above-average students or for small groups. Some teacher direction is necessary.

**L3** Strategies are designed for students able and willing to work independently. Minimal teacher direction is necessary.

**ELL** Strategies are especially accessible to English Language Learners.

### KEY TO RESOURCE ICONS

📂 Print Material

💿 CD or DVD Resources

🖱 Online Learning Center (OLC)

**TeacherWorks™**
All-In-One Planner and Resource Center

**Teacher Wraparound Edition**

**Unit Resources:**
Unit Thematic Project Student Rubrics
Unit Family and Community Involvement Activities

**Chapter Resources:**
Lesson Plans
Chapter Summaries, Content and Academic Vocabulary
Graphic Organizers

**Textbook Resources:**
Student Activity Workbook with Academic Integration
Additional Activities
Enrichment Activities

 Link to the ***The Developing Child* Online Learning Center** at **glencoe.com**.

## Unit Overview

**Introduce the Unit**

Introduce the unit by describing the main concepts of each chapter in the unit.

**Unit 3**

This unit describes the physical, emotional, social, and intellectual development of infants in their first year of life.

**Chapter 7** Students will learn how an infant grows physically in the first year of life and how to care for an infant to best nurture physical development.

**Chapter 8** Introduce students to an infant's basic emotions and social development. The text will guide students in how to influence and encourage emotional and social development.

**Chapter 9** This chapter examines how an infants' brain grows and develops. An emphasis is placed on how to promote intellectual growth.

### OUT OF TIME?

If class time is too short to cover all of the chapters in this unit, have students:

- Write down the vocabulary terms and their definitions.
- Read the chapter summaries at the beginning of each chapter review.
- Go to *The Developing Child* Online Learning Center at **glencoe.com** to download Study-to-Go content.

# The Baby's First Year

**Explore the Photo**

Parents play a large role in ensuring their baby's health and well-being. *How might a child's early relationships influence his relationships later in life?*

190

---

 **Explore the Photo**

**Caption Answer** Answers will vary but students might say that if children have loving, trusting relationships early in life, they might be more willing to trust others when they are older.

**Discussion** Ask students how the mother in the photo is contributing to the baby's health and well-being. (Students may say that she is playing with the child and showing him love and attention which contributes to his emotional health, or that by playing with the stacking blocks she is helping him learn motor skills and problem-solving skills.)

**Chapter 7** Physical Development of Infants

**Chapter 8** Emotional and Social Development of Infants

**Chapter 9** Intellectual Development of Infants

## Unit | Thematic Project Preview

### Raise a Healthy Baby

In this unit, you will learn how infants grow and develop during their first twelve months. You will also learn about the important role of parents and caregivers in a baby's physical and mental health. In your unit thematic project, you will explore how caregivers can support a baby's healthy growth and development.

### My Journal

**Healthy Development** Write a journal entry about one of the topics below. This will help you prepare for the project at the end of this unit.
- How can a parent or caregiver help a baby grow up physically healthy?
- How can a parent or caregiver help a baby develop trusting relationships with adults and siblings?
- How can a parent or caregiver help a baby develop language skills?

**191**

## Unit | Thematic Project Preview

**Raise a Healthy Baby**
Tell students that as part of this unit, they will learn how parents and caregivers influence and support a baby's physical and mental health. They will learn that a caregiver's attitude toward a child is as important as the food and physical care they give the child. Students will consider the different needs of an infant, and how parents and caregivers can meet those needs.

**My Journal**

**Healthy Development** Students should select one topic to write a journal entry about. The journal entry relates to the subject of the thematic project: Raise a Healthy Baby. The purpose of the journal entry is to prepare students for the project at the end of the unit. (Journal entries will vary depending on the topic selected and the students' personal opinions.)

### Discussion Starter
**KWL Chart**
Have students make a list of what they know about an infant's growth and development. Next, ask them to skim Unit 3 and notice the headers, figures, and photos. Have them list what they now want to know about infant growth and development. Discuss the lists and create a KWL chart with their responses. After completing the unit, revisit the chart and reassess their knowledge by asking them what they learned about growth and development in the first year of a baby's life.

**FCCLA** Children's Health Fair

Suggest the FCCLA Chapter sponsor a children's health fair. Invite local physicians to participate and speak. Offer workshops on infant care, in-home safety, health issues, childhood diseases, and how to find the best child care. Ask area businesses to help sponsor the event by donating door prizes.

**SkillsUSA.**

An important skill to learn for first aid or child care competitions is infant CPR. Arrange to have a representative from the American Red Cross visit the class and teach basic infant CPR. After the demonstration, have students list the key steps of CPR. Then lead a class discussion on how infant CPR differs from adult CPR. Answers can include that you use fingers instead of the palm for chest compressions, and that your mouth covers the baby's nose and mouth for rescue breathing.

**STANDARDS BASED LESSON PLANNING** *The Developing Child* provides students with instruction and assessment in the following fundamental content areas:

## National Standards Correlations

| Standards | Pages |
|---|---|
| **12.1.1** Analyze physical, emotional, social, spiritual, and intellectual development. | 195–207 |
| **12.1.3** Analyze current and emerging research about human growth and development, including research on brain development. | 197 |
| **12.2.1** Analyze the effect of heredity and environment on human growth and development. | 195–197, 201, 226 |
| **12.2.2** Analyze the impact of social, economic, and technological forces on individual growth and development. | 197 |
| **12.3.3** Analyze the role of family and social services support systems in meeting human growth and development needs. | 220 |
| **15.1.5** Explain cultural differences in roles and responsibilities of parenting. | 227 |
| **15.2.1** Choose nurturing practices that support human growth and development. | 209, 210–211, 222–224 |
| **15.2.3** Assess common practices and emerging research about discipline on human growth and development. | 197 |
| **15.2.4** Assess the effects of abuse and neglect on children and families and determine methods for prevention. | 211–212 |
| **15.3.1** Assess community resources and services available to families. | 220 |

**NO CHILD LEFT BEHIND** NCLB activities, information, and skills practice will help your students attain NCLB proficiency. Students will improve their abilities in the following academic standards areas:

## Academic Standards Correlations

| Discipline | Standard | Feature/Activity |
|---|---|---|
| **English Language Arts** | **NCTE 1** Read texts to acquire new information. | **Reading Guide (pp. 194, 208, 221)** |
| | **NCTE 4** Use written language to communicate effectively. | **Writing Activity (p. 192)** **After You Read (pp. 207, 227)** **Academic Skills (p. 231)** |
| | **NCTE 7** Conduct research and gather, evaluate, and synthesize data to communicate discoveries. | **Observation Skills (p. 230)** |
| | **NCTE 8** Use information resources to gather information and create and communicate knowledge. | **After You Read (p. 220)** |
| **Mathematics** | **NCTM Number and Operations** Understand numbers, relationships among numbers, and number systems. | **Academic Skills (p. 231)** |
| **Science** | **NSES A** Develop understandings about scientific inquiry. | **Science in Action (p. 199)** |
| | **NSES C** Develop understanding of molecular basis of heredity; biological evolution. | **After You Read (p. 207)** |
| | **NSES F** Develop understanding of personal and community health. | **Academic Skills (p. 231)** |
| **Social Studies** | **NCSS I A Culture** Analyze and explain the ways groups, societies, and cultures address human needs and concerns. | **After You Read (pp. 220, 227)** |

## McGraw Hill Professional Development

**MINI CLIP VIDEO LIBRARY**
Targeted professional development is correlated throughout *The Developing Child*. **The McGraw-Hill Professional Development Mini Clip Video Library** provides teaching strategies to strengthen academic and learning skills. Log on to **glencoe.com**.

In this chapter, you will find these Mini Clips:

- **Math** Medians and Quartiles, p. 198
- **ELL** Language Practice, p. 200
- **Reading** Interacting with Text, p. 205
- **Reading** Addressing Idioms, p. 208
- **ELL** Using Realia, p. 211
- **Reading** Obstacles to Achievement, p. 217
- **Math** Small Group Work, p. 226

## Reading and Writing Strategies

**Writing Activity: Paragraph** (p. 192)
Students use writing tips to describe what they think makes a healthy, happy baby.

**Before You Read** (pp. 194, 208, 221)
A pre-reading question or statement will help students make a personal connection to content.

**Graphic Organizer** (pp. 194, 208, 221)
A visual tool will help students organize and remember new content.

**Reading Check** (pp. 197, 212, 218, 225)
A question allows students to make a quick comprehension self-check.

**After You Read** (pp. 207, 220, 227)
Organize and process students' understanding of what they have read.

## Chapter Features

**Interactive Play** (p. 196)
Even six-month-old infants enjoy and learn from interactive play.

**Language Development** (p. 197)
Talking to and playing with infants is important for brain development.

**Interpreting Infant Development** (p. 199)
One way doctors monitor infants' growth is by measuring their length.

**Down Syndrome** (p. 201)
This genetic condition affects the development of the body and brain.

**Getting Help** (p. 202)
Parents need to know where to get good parenting advice.

**What Is Sudden Infant Death Syndrome?** (p. 212)
SIDS is the unexpected death of an infant with no obvious cause.

**Food Poisoning** (p. 215)
Parents need to be aware of food poisoning with infants.

**Respiratory Syncytial Virus** (p. 224)
Respiratory syncytial virus affects nearly all babies by the age of two.

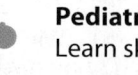
**Pediatrician** (p. 228)
Learn skills needed for this career.

### Chapter Overview

#### Introduce the Chapter

In this chapter, students learn how infants develop physically. They learn the four major influences on an infant's growth and development. They also learn how a baby grows during the first year and how to take care of a baby's needs.

#### Build Background

Discuss an infant's physical development during the first year. They become able to sit up, crawl, and, in many cases, walk. Divide students into small groups. Instruct each group to create a list of the different ways in which infants grow and develop physically during the first year. Ask for volunteers from each group to share their lists.

### Writing Activity
#### *Paragraph*

This active learning activity prompts students to write a paragraph describing what makes a happy, healthy baby. After students have completed the writing activity, ask for volunteers to share their paragraph with the class. Encourage the class to discuss similarities and differences in their paragraphs. (Students' thoughts will vary. Some may think a happy baby's needs are being met. Others may feel a positive home environment helps ensure a baby's happiness. Some may recognize that there is a combination of factors that relate to a baby's happiness.)

## Chapter
**7** Physical Development of Infants

## Chapter Objectives

After completing this chapter, you will be able to:

- **Identify** the four major influences on an infant's growth and development.
- **Summarize** how a baby typically grows in the first year.
- **Explain** how to safely hold a baby.
- **Identify** how to meet a baby's nutritional needs.
- **Describe** the best type of clothing suitable for a baby.
- **Describe** how to bathe a baby.
- **Explain** why checkups and immunizations are important for babies.

### Writing Activity 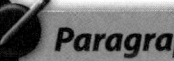 *Paragraph*

**Growing a Happy Baby** During the first year of life, babies grow and develop in many ways. Caregivers have many responsibilities to make sure a baby's needs are met. For example, the caregiver must feed the baby and change the baby's diapers. These are just two of the many physical needs. Infants also have emotional needs that must be met. Write a paragraph in which you describe what you think makes a happy, healthy baby.

**Writing Tips** To write a good paragraph, follow these tips:
1. Make sure the paragraph focuses on one main idea.
2. Use transition words to link ideas. These include words such as then, however, and because.
3. Make sure all the sentences in each paragraph support the main idea.

## CLASSROOM *Solutions*

### Print Resources

 **Student Edition**

 **Teacher Wraparound Edition**

 **Student Activity Workbook**

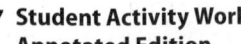 **Student Activity Workbook Teacher Annotated Edition**

### Technology Resources

 **Online Learning Center** has resources and activities for students and teachers. Includes an Online Student Edition.

 **Interactive Student Edition** allows students to instantly access review materials, examples, and exercises.

Section **7.1** Infant Growth and Development

Section **7.2** Caring for an Infant

Section **7.3** Infant Health and Wellness

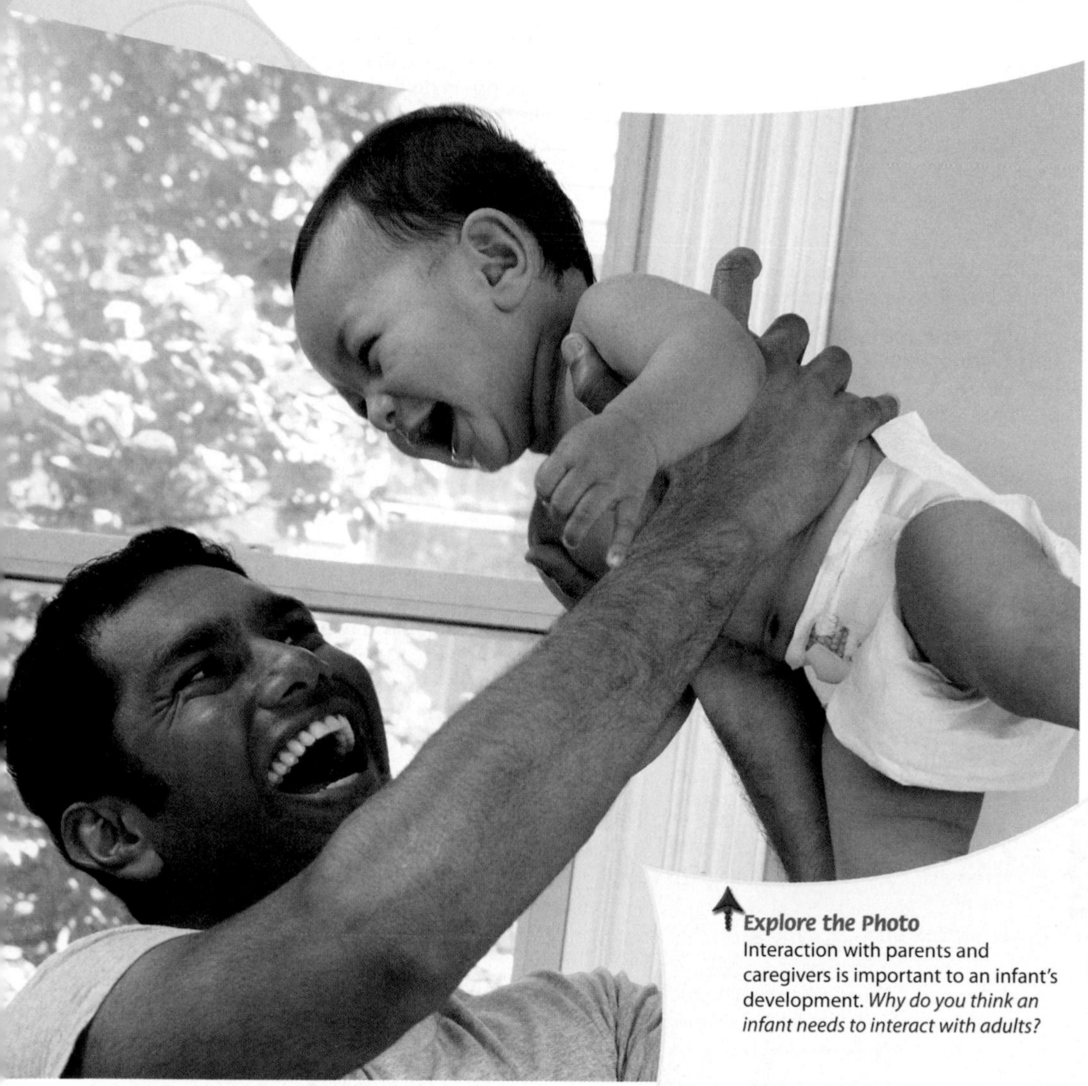

## Review the Sections
Introduce the chapter by reviewing the sections:

### Section 7.1
Heredity, nutrition, health, and environment all play a role in a baby's growth and development. Babies grow rapidly in the first year, usually tripling their birth weight and increasing their length by 50 percent.

### Section 7.2
Babies must be handled carefully and must never be shaken. Feeding babies breast milk or formula meets the nutrition needs for the first six months. Other foods should be introduced gradually. A baby's clothing should be comfortable and easy to put on and take off.

### Section 7.3
Babies should be bathed regularly but never be left alone in the bathtub. Parents should follow a recommended schedule of checkups and immunizations to protect the health of their babies.

▶ **Explore the Photo**

**Caption Answer**
Students' answers will vary. Some might suggest that infants learn through interaction or that their needs are met through interaction with adult caregivers.

**Discussion** Ask students if they have ever seen an infant interacting with an adult. Ask if they agree with the statement "Interaction with parents and caregivers is important to an infant's development." Have students explain their answers.

⬆ **Explore the Photo**
Interaction with parents and caregivers is important to an infant's development. *Why do you think an infant needs to interact with adults?*

193

**TeacherWorks Plus** is an electronic lesson planner that provides instant access to complete teacher resources in one convenient package.

**Presentation Plus!** provides visual teaching aids for every section.

**The Early Childhood Observations CD** presents video observations and lessons on observation skills and child development.

**The Developing Brain eTransparencies and Guide** include information and activities to offer insights into brain development and diseases of the brain.

# Section 7.1 Infant Growth and Development

## Reading Guide

### Before You Read

**Contribute** Share at least one piece of information you expect to learn with your classmates.

### Read to Learn
#### Key Concepts
- **Identify** the four major influences on an infant's growth and development.
- **Summarize** how a baby typically grows in the first year.

**D**

### Main Idea
There are four main influences on a baby's growth and development. An infant's growth and development follow many patterns.

### Content Vocabulary
◇ developmental milestone
◇ stimulating environment
◇ growth chart
◇ proportion
◇ depth perception
◇ reflex
◇ gross motor skill
◇ fine motor skill
◇ hand-eye coordination

### Academic Vocabulary
You will find these words in your reading and on your tests. Use the glossary to look up their definitions if necessary.
■ makeup    ■ accommodate

### Graphic Organizer
As you read, list the six areas an infant develops in his first year of life. Use a diagram like the one shown to help organize your information. The first area has been filled in for you.

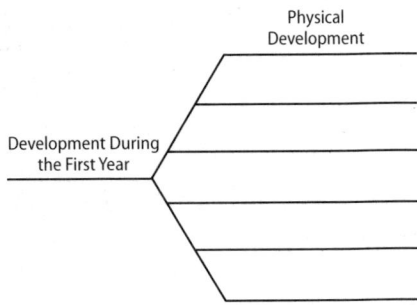

Physical Development

Development During the First Year

**Graphic Organizer** Go to this book's Online Learning Center at **glencoe.com** to print out this graphic organizer.

### Academic Standards . . . . . . . . . . . . . . . . . . . . . . . . . . . . .

**NCLB**

 **English Language Arts**

**NCTE 4** Use written language to communicate effectively.

 **Science**

**NSES C** Develop understanding of molecular basis of heredity; biological evolution; matter, energy, and organization in living systems.

**NSES A** Develop abilities necessary to do scientific inquiry, understandings about scientific inquiry.

**NCTE** *National Council of Teachers of English*
**NCTM** *National Council of Teachers of Mathematics*

**NSES** *National Science Education Standards*
**NCSS** *National Council for the Social Studies*

---

## Bell Ringer Activity

### Growing and Changing
Ask students to share in what ways they think a baby grows and changes in the first year. What are some of the factors that influence a baby's growth and development? (Some students may be aware of the four main influences on a baby's growth and development: heredity, nutrition, health, and environment.)

## Preteaching
### Vocabulary
Write *fine* and *gross* on the board. Have students brainstorm meanings of each of the terms (fine: penalize, very thin, delicate, high quality, small; gross: objectionable, big, an amount of money or sum, 12 dozen, large.) Explain that in the field of child development, the words refer to a kind of motor skill, a term for muscle use.

### Graphic Organizer
The Graphic Organizer is also on the TeacherWorks CD.

(Graphic organizers should list: patterns of physical development, senses, voice, reflexes, motor skills, hand-eye coordination.)

**NCLB** connects academic correlations to book content.

---

## Reading Guide

### Before You Read
Ask students: Have you ever tried to help a baby sit up or walk before it was developmentally ready to do so? You probably weren't very successful. In this section, you will learn the developmental milestones that infants typically reach during their first year.

### **D** Develop Concepts

**Main Idea** Discuss the main idea with the students. Ask: Why do you think an infant's growth and development may follow many patterns? (Answers may include that not all children develop at the same rate; not all children have the same type of influences and interactions.)

# Influences on Growth and Development

Babies experience a tremendous amount of physical growth and development in their first year of life. In just twelve months, babies who begin as helpless newborns learn to stand alone, feed themselves, and even walk. While babies typically follow the same development patterns, they do so at their own rate. Parents have the responsibility to help their baby grow and develop normally.

The terms growth and development are often used interchangeably, but they are not the same things. Growth refers to changes in size, such as weight and length. Development refers to increases and changes in physical, emotional, social, or intellectual skills.

Researchers have found that both heredity and environment play important roles in a baby's growth and development. Heredity is sometimes referred to as nature. It includes the physical **makeup**, or structure, that a baby inherits from his or her parents. Environment is a more complex concept. It includes influences such as nutrition, amount of stimulation, health, and relationships. Environment is also known as nurture. All these factors work together to influence a baby's physical growth and development. However, at various times one or more of these factors can play a larger role than the others in an infant's growth and development.

Development experts have studied the range of ages to determine the average ages at which children acquire certain skills. A key skill used to check a child's progress is called a **developmental milestone**. For example, Jeffrey may inherit a strong, healthy body from his parents. But if Jeffrey becomes sick for an extended period, he may miss out on opportunities for active play that would strengthen the large muscles of his legs. As a result, he may reach some developmental milestones, such as learning to walk or climb steps, later than a healthy baby. Another baby, Aisha, inherits a strong, healthy body and enjoys good health. She therefore has more opportunities for physical play than Jeffrey had and will more likely develop at a normal rate.

## Heredity

As explained in Chapter 4, genes provide a blueprint for the development of the human body and how it functions throughout life. Children inherit a unique combination of genes

**Hereditary Traits**
Children inherit many physical characteristics from their parents. *What other factors influence a baby's growth and development?*

---

## Teach

### Discussion Starter

**Nature vs. Nurture** Divide the class into groups. Each group will conduct their own mini-debates. Half of each group should prepare arguments supporting the idea that nature, or heredity, has more influence on the way an infant will grow and develop, and the other half should do the same with nurture, or environment. After the mini-debates, ask the class to offer their opinions on the subject and to discuss which side was easier to defend and why. (Opinions will vary as will arguments for nature or nurture. Students may suggest that nurture has more influence on how an infant will grow and develop because it is more controllable.)

### W Writing Support
#### Paragraph

**Learning Process** Ask students to think about a time in their own lives when they had to learn something new, starting with the simplest motions or elements and moving to more complex motions or strategies. Have students write a paragraph to describe this memory. (Refer to p. 192 for tips on writing paragraphs. Paragraphs will vary. For example, students may describe learning to multiply first by one digit, then by two, and so on. Paragraphs should include details and examples and contain good grammar and no spelling errors.)

---

## Explore the Photo

**Caption Answer** Environment, which includes nutrition, amount of stimulation, health, and relationships, also influences a baby's growth and development.

**Discussion** Ask students to think of a quality that they inherited and one they think came from their environment. Ask volunteers to share these characteristics. (Responses will vary; students may mention eye or hair color as an inherited trait. They may mention being sociable as an environmental trait caused growing up in a large family.)

### Teach cont.

from their parents. This combination of genes determines traits such as eye and hair color, when the teeth first emerge, whether certain diseases are likely to develop, and much more. The genes also shape or influence larger traits, such as a person's intellectual potential or artistic abilities.

Having certain genes, though, does not mean a person will automatically exhibit those traits. Nature and nurture both play a role in determining how a child grows and develops. For example, a girl's genes may give her the potential to be musically gifted, but if she is never given the opportunity to sing or play an instrument, her talent may never emerge. Think of people you know who seem to have inherited physical characteristics or artistic abilities from their parents.

### Nutrition

The body needs essential nutrients to grow and develop. Eating foods that contain these nutrients is vital to a child's lifelong health. Even newborns who spend most of their time sleeping are growing and developing. Proper nutrition fuels that development. Research has shown that nutrition affects many aspects of a baby's physical growth and development, including bone strength, brain development, and height.

When a baby does not get enough calories or necessary nutrients, he or she is at risk for illness, delayed growth, or even death. You will learn more about proper nutrition for an infant in Section 7.2 of this chapter.

### Health

Staying healthy is closely linked to other factors that influence growth and development. A baby who is healthy is more likely to eat well and have the energy to be active. A healthy baby is more likely to have varied experiences that stimulate the brain and aid in muscle development. An infant with poor health is at risk of falling behind developmentally.

Parents and other caregivers must guard children's health. In addition to providing good nutrition, they must provide a safe environment. Children also need regular medical checkups and care.

### Environment

An infant's experiences are an important part of development. Brain development, which impacts all areas of development, is linked to the quantity and variety of experiences a child has. Infancy is a critical period. Failure to achieve normal brain development at this stage can have lifelong effects.

## Learning Through PLAY

### Interactive Play

Babies may seem too young to play games, but even a six-month-old infant can enjoy simple interactive play. All that is usually needed is an adult, a baby, and some creativity. Peek-a-boo and hide-and-seek with toys are favorites. Babies also enjoy listening to music and clapping hands together. They like to hear an adult sing nursery rhymes or mimic animal sounds. Whatever the activity, it is important to remember that it is not the type of play that matters. It is the benefits that count. Playing with babies is not only fun, it helps promote physical development, brain development, and social interaction. The contact that occurs during play also helps nurture a baby's sense of security and well-being.

**Think About It** Imagine that you are helping care for your seven-month-old niece. She is not hungry or tired, but she is getting fussy. What could you do to help entertain her?

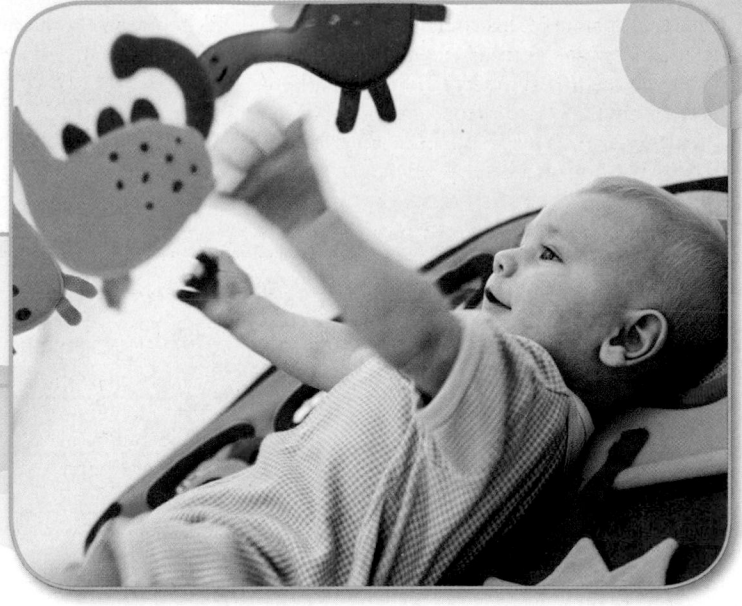

**Stimulating Baby**
Interaction with toys helps stimulate development in a baby. *How can toys help a baby develop?*

**Teach** cont.

A stimulating environment promotes brain development. A **stimulating environment** is an environment in which the baby has a wide variety of things to see, taste, smell, hear, and touch. A world with plenty of ways to use all the senses provides wonderful opportunities for an infant. While investigating their world, all that they experience is stored in the brain. As associations form, such as the high chair means food, more brain connections are made.

An environment lacking in stimulation can result in fewer or weaker connections in the brain and delayed or slow development in other areas. For example, infants are not born with language skills. During the first few months of life, connections form in the part of the brain responsible for language. This eventually allows the child to begin speaking. If the child is not exposed to language and not encouraged to speak during this time, there will be fewer connections in the brain. This can delay normal language development.

Other environmental factors can have a harmful impact on a child's development as well. For example, children who breathe secondhand smoke are more likely to suffer from poor health. It increases the risk of sudden infant death syndrome. Other possible health problems can include respiratory infections, ear infections, bronchitis, and asthma. These conditions can make it more difficult for a child to develop normally. They also increase the chances of lung cancer and heart disease later in life.

✓ **Reading Check** **Explain** What is the difference between nature and nurture?

### THE DEVELOPING BRAIN

**Language Development**

Some people think, "How silly!" when they see adults talking to newborns. Is it a waste of time? How can a baby possibly understand? In fact, talking to and playing with infants are important for brain development and learning. These activities help babies to learn language and to develop social skills.

🔲 **Science Inquiry** Babies need interaction with humans to develop their language and social skills. Would a baby develop language skills if adults did not talk to them?

Section 7.1   Infant Growth and Development   **197**

---

**U** **Universal Access**

**Auditory Learners** Caregivers can provide a stimulating environment through the sounds that an infant hears at home. Have students close their eyes. Play some soothing music, or talk to them using a positive, soothing voice. Ask students to relate what they felt while hearing these sounds. Then have students close their eyes again. This time, make distracting sounds, such as slamming a book down on the floor or blowing a whistle. Have students again comment on the sounds they heard. Discuss how these sounds might affect an infant. (Students will likely say that they felt peaceful when listening to the pleasant sounds and may have been on edge when hearing the negative sounds. They should realize that sounds have similar effects on a baby.)

### THE DEVELOPING BRAIN

**Language Development**
**Science Inquiry** Babies might develop language skills without interaction with adults, but the development would be delayed until they did have interaction. Lack of interaction with adults will also negatively affect development of a baby's social skills.

For more information and activities, see *The Developing Brain* guide and eTransparencies.

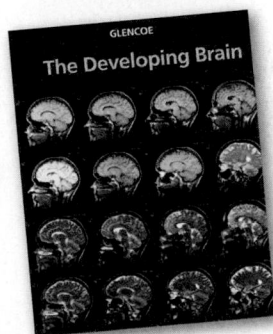

GLENCOE
The Developing Brain

---

**Explore the Photo**

**Caption Answer** Toys can help a baby develop by stimulating the baby's senses.

**Discussion** Ask the class to name different baby toys. Have a volunteer write the answers on the board. Ask students to discuss how each toy would stimulate a baby's senses. (Answers will vary but should include the sense that would be stimulated.)

✓ **Reading Check**

Nature refers to heredity and inherited traits. Nurture refers to a child's environment and experiences.

**Teach** *cont.*

### W Writing Support

**Research Report**

**Growth Rates** Have students research the relationship between the height and weight of infants and their environment. Guide students to investigate studies that show growth rates in highly industrialized countries as well as developing countries. Ask students to answer the following questions in a report: How does a country's economy affect the growth rates of its children? What environmental or societal factors do you think affect growth rates the most? (Students' reports will vary depending on the country studied. Infants in highly industrialized countries are typically bigger than infants in developing countries. Availability of resources such as food is a major factor.)

### U Universal Access

**Mathematical Learners** Review with students how to calculate averages. Remind the class that the numbers used in the text are based on averages calculated after documenting the length and weight of many newborns. Write these numbers on the board: 15, 16, 10, 13, 15, 17, and 12. Explain that these represent the weight measurements of a group of infants at three months. Have students calculate the average measurement (14 pounds). Encourage students to come up with their own problems involving the average length of infants.

**Mc Graw Hill Professional Development**

**Mini Clip**

**Math: Medians and Quartiles**

Algebra teacher Brad Fulton describes the meaning of medians and quartiles.

**Figure 7.1 Average Lengths and Weights**

A baby's length and weight increase rapidly during the first year. *Should a parent be concerned if their child's length or weight does not match the averages on this growth chart?*

| Age | MALES | | FEMALES | |
|---|---|---|---|---|
| | Length/ Inches | Weight/ Pounds | Length/ Inches | Weight/ Pounds |
| **Birth** | 19¾ | 7½ | 19½ | 7½ |
| **3 months** | 24 | 13 | 23½ | 12¼ |
| **6 months** | 26½ | 17½ | 25½ | 15½ |
| **9 months** | 28 | 20½ | 27½ | 18¾ |
| **12 months** | 29 | 22½ | 29 | 21 |

## Growth and Development During the First Year

Babies go through remarkable changes during their first year. They grow faster physically than during any other time of their life. They also grow emotionally, socially, and intellectually.

### Growth During the First Year

From birth to age one, babies typically triple their birth weight. They usually increase their length by about 50 percent. One way doctors can judge whether a baby is growing at a healthy pace is by using growth charts. A **growth chart** shows the average weight and height of girls and boys at various ages. **Figure 7.1** focuses on average heights and weights for boys and girls from birth to age one. Boys and girls are shown separately because their growth rates and patterns differ.

Very few babies match the average measurements on growth charts. That is because children grow at their own rate. Instead of focusing on any one measurement, doctors watch for a steady pattern of growth. Sudden drops in a baby's weight could indicate health concerns. If parents are concerned about their baby's growth, they should talk to the doctor.

### Weight

Weight gain is one of the best signs of good health. Most newborns lose about 10 percent of their birth weight in the first five days of life. After that, they begin to gain weight rapidly. In the first six months, a healthy baby gains about one to two pounds (0.45 to 0.9 kilograms) per month. In the following six months, the average monthly weight gain is about one pound (0.45 kilograms). A baby's birth weight usually doubles in the first few months and triples by the twelfth month. The average weight of a one-year-old is 20 to 22 pounds (9 to 10 kilograms). However, boys tend to weigh slightly more than girls during infancy.

### Length

In the first year, physicians talk about the length of a baby rather than the height. This is because babies are measured while lying down.

**Figure 7.1 Average Lengths and Weights**

**Caption Answer** Parents should not be concerned if their child does not match the averages on the growth chart. Very few babies match the exact measurements on growth charts. They all grow at their own rate.

**Discussion** Point out to students how babies triple their weight and grow by about 50 percent by one year of age. Have students imagine what they would look like if their weight and height increased at that rate during the teen years. (Students will likely say they would be giants.)

Babies steadily grow in length during the first year, in part because bone growth is rapid at that time. For example, the average newborn measures 20 inches (51 cm) long. One year later, the average is about 30 inches (76 cm) long.

Again, not all babies grow at the same rate, and boys tend to be slightly longer than girls. Heredity has a stronger influence on height than weight. A baby with tall parents is more likely to be tall as an adult than a baby with short parents.

### Body Shape

Newborns tend to hold themselves in a tightly curled position with their fists clenched, legs bent, and feet curved inward. The head may have an elongated shape from moving through the birth canal. Arms and legs are skinny, and the abdomen is large. The umbilical cord stump usually dries up and drops off within about three weeks after birth, revealing the navel. Babies will gradually stretch out their arms and legs and uncurl their fingers. Their legs and feet generally straighten out over the first six months.

Babies typically look chubby by three months of age, but they usually lose that look as they grow longer and become more active. After about eight months, when babies begin to practice standing, their typical posture includes a protruding belly and a slight lean forward.

## Science in Action

### Interpreting Infant Development

One way that doctors monitor infants' growth is by measuring their length. By recording this information each month, the doctor can ensure that the baby is continuing to grow and develop.

#### Procedure

Make a bar graph of the following data.

| Infant Development | |
| --- | --- |
| End of Month | Length (inches) |
| 3 | 24 |
| 4 | 25 |
| 5 | 25.5 |
| 6 | 26 |
| 7 | 27 |
| 8 | 27.5 |
| 9 | 28 |

#### Analysis

1. During which month does the greatest increase in length occur?
2. On average, how many inches does the baby grow per month?

**NSES A** Develop abilities necessary to do scientific inquiry, understandings about scientific inquiry.

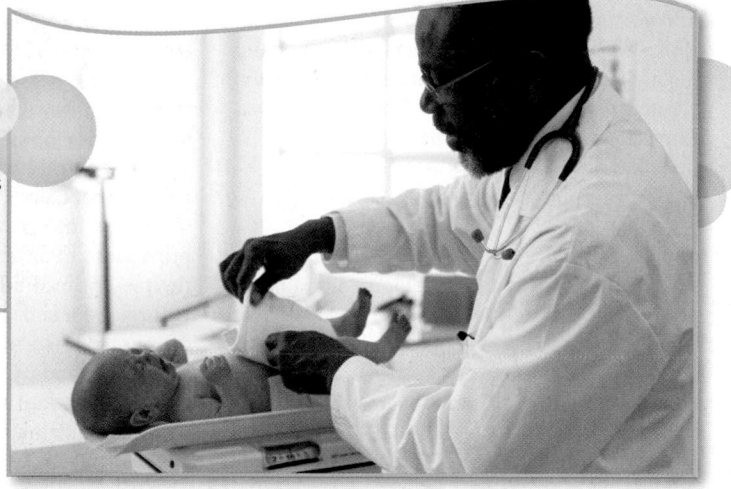

**Measuring Growth**
During the first year, physicians talk about and track an infant's length rather than height. *Why do doctors track a baby's length instead of height?*

#### ⟫ Explore the Photo

**Caption Answer** During the first year, doctors talk about the length of a baby rather than the height because babies are measured while lying down.

**Discussion** Ask students why they think infants are weighed without clothes on but older children and adults are weighed fully clothed. (Answers may vary but students should realize that an infant's weight is so small that they are still weighed in ounces. Clothing could affect that weight.)

## Teach cont.

### C Critical Thinking

**Explain** Discuss with students how a baby's body changes in the first year. Ask students: How can you recognize a newborn? A six-month-old? A one-year-old? (Answers will vary but students should recognize that newborns are curled up and more wrinkled than older infants. A six-month-old will be longer and chubbier. A one-year-old will have a protruding belly and a slight lean forward.)

### R Reading Strategy

**Outlining** Have students read the section Body Shape. After they read, have them create an outline of the main points provided in the text. Outlines should follow basic format—each main point should have at least two supporting details. Ask volunteers to share their outlines with the class. (Outlines may vary. One possibility is: 1. Newborns, a. Tightly curled position, b. Fists clenched, c. Elongated head, d. Skinny arms and legs, e. Large abdomen. 2. Three-month-olds, a. Chubby, b. More active. 3. Eight-month-olds, a. Protruding belly, b. Slight lean forward.)

## Science in Action

### Interpreting Infant Development

1. The greatest increase in length (1 inch) occurs during months 4 and 7.
2. On average the baby grows about 0.67 in. per month.

**NCLB** Activity correlated to Science standards.

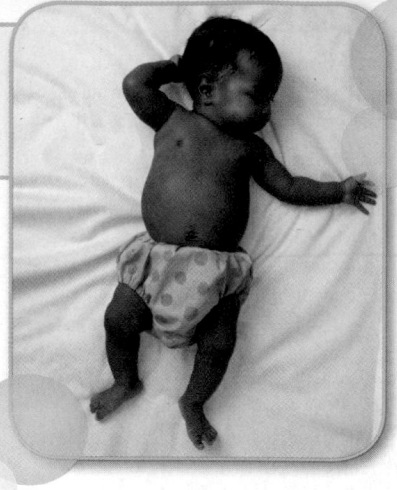
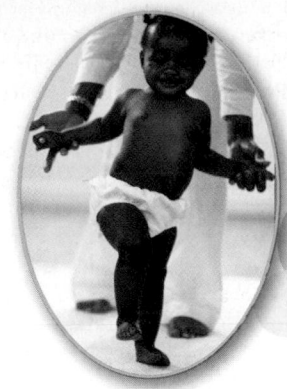

> → **Dramatic Changes**
> The growth and development of a child during the first year of life is dramatic. *What changes are obvious from these two photos?*

### Proportion

In child growth, **proportion** refers to the size relationship between different parts of the body. Compared to the rest of the body, a baby's head and abdomen are large. The legs and arms are short and small. A baby's head grows rapidly during the first year to **accommodate**, or make room for, the swiftly developing brain. More than half the total growth of the head occurs during this time. As you read in Chapter 6, the bones of a newborn's skull have gaps called fontanels, where bones of the skull have not yet joined together. During birth, these gaps allowed the head to change shape to pass through the birth canal. During infancy, they allow the head to grow as the brain develops. They later close up permanently.

### Development During the First Year

A baby's growth and development are both quite rapid during the first year. Each month brings changes and new abilities. Growth and development are not nearly as obvious in older children. There are dramatic changes in appearance and abilities between a one-year-old and a two-year-old. The same is true of a two- and three-year-old. In a group of teens you could probably tell older teens from younger ones, but it would be difficult to guess their exact age. A fifteen-year-old and a sixteen-year-old sister look and act much alike.

### Patterns of Physical Development

An infant's physical development follows three basic patterns. Infants develop from head to foot, from near to far, and from simple to complex. Understanding these patterns can help you understand and follow the sequence of a typical baby's development.

**Head to Foot** This pattern of development begins long before birth. It starts during the prenatal stage, when a baby's head takes the lead in development. This pattern continues after birth and can be seen in the increasing control that babies gain over their body.

Babies first develop some control of head movement. For example, they will support their own head when being held. Then they will raise their head to see an object. Control of muscles then moves down the body to the arms and hands. Control of the baby's legs and feet occurs more slowly. It is not until about the age of one that a baby develops all the skills needed to walk.

---

### ▶ Explore the Photo

**Caption Answer** Answers will vary. Possible answers include that the one-year-old is taller or heavier, he can stand, or has more hair.

**Discussion** Have students look at the photos and estimate the age of each baby. Then have them note similarities and differences between the two infants and write them in a Venn diagram. (Venn diagrams will vary but should note similarities and differences between the younger and older infants.)

**Near to Far** An infant's development also starts close to the body and moves outward. For example, babies will first simply wave their arms when they see an object they want. Later, they develop more precise hand and finger control and can point to an object they want. Later still, they can reach out and grasp for an object with their fingers.

**Simple to Complex** In the developmental pattern of simple to complex, babies first develop their large muscle groups. This includes those in the neck, arms, torso, and legs. The *torso* is the upper body. As babies strengthen and gain control over these muscles, they learn to do increasingly complex tasks. These tasks begin with controlling the head, rolling, reaching, and crawling. They continue through to walking. Even more complex movements that need small muscle development come later. Coloring, for example, requires good control of the fingers to grasp, hold, and direct a crayon.

### Senses

As babies grow and develop during their first year, their senses are also developing. Babies' perception of the world increases through their vision, hearing, touch, smell and taste.

**Vision** A baby's eyesight improves rapidly during the first year. At first, vision is blurry. Within a week or so, a newborn is increasingly aware of the environment and can focus on objects that are seven to ten inches away. Babies' eyes can also follow an object moved slowly past their face. By one month, babies can focus on objects up to three feet away. By six months, their eyesight reaches the clarity and sharpness of the adult level.

At first, a baby sees the world in two-dimensions. This means it is like looking at a picture. Infants begin to demonstrate depth perception in their second month of life. **Depth perception** is the ability to perceive objects that are three-dimensional. This ability has a major impact on a child's interaction with the world. They can track people's movements. They also learn to reach for objects by judging how far away they are.

Patterns and colors are also important to a baby's world. Young babies seem to prefer patterns that show high contrast, such as alternating stripes, bull's-eyes, or simple faces. When shown the same object in different colors, they typically look at red or blue objects most often. Aside from an inability to focus in the early days, some babies appear to have

**S**

## RESPOND TO SPECIAL NEEDS — Down Syndrome

Down syndrome is a genetic condition that affects the development of the body and brain. It is the most common cause of birth defects in humans. Children with Down syndrome have certain physical characteristics. The head may be smaller than normal and abnormally shaped. The inner corner of the eyes may be rounded instead of pointed. They also may have decreased muscle tone at birth, a flattened nose, a single crease in the palm of the hand, small ears, a small mouth, upward slanting eyes, or wide, short hands with short fingers. Physical development in children with Down syndrome is often slower than normal. Most children with

Down syndrome never reach their average adult height. Social and mental development may also be delayed. According to the National Institute of Child Health and Human Development, most people with Down syndrome have mild to moderate mental retardation.

**Critical Thinking** Children with Down syndrome often have one or more medical conditions. Research some of those conditions and write a one-page report of your findings.

## RESPOND TO SPECIAL NEEDS — Down Syndrome

**Discussion** Explain to the class that mild retardation is indicated by an IQ of 69–55 on the Wechsler IQ scale. Moderate retardation is indicated by an IQ of 54–40. People with mild retardation are considered capable of learning. People with moderate retardation are considered capable of learning basic skills.

**Critical Thinking** Reports will vary but may include birth defects involving the heart, eye problems, gastrointestinal blockages, hearing problems, hip dislocation, sleep apnea, or an underactive thyroid (hypothyroidism).

## Teach *cont.*

### S Skill Practice
**Guided Practice**

**View** Provide students with glasses or goggles that simulate different stages of infant vision. The glasses should create some level of blurriness for the students. Have students discuss how accurately they can do things while wearing the blurry glasses. (Students' answers will vary but likely will indicate that they cannot do many things with accuracy while wearing the blurry glasses.) **L1 ELL**

**Compare** Bring in a digital camera and take photos of items or people in the classroom. Print the photos and have students compare the two-dimensional photos with the actual object or person. Ask students to describe the differences between looking at a two-dimensional photo and the real object. (Students' descriptions will vary but should indicate the flatness of the two-dimensional photo as compared to the actual object.) **L2 ELL**

**Examine** Have students examine the stages of visual development in infants and how they affect a baby's responsiveness. Students should write a one-page report summarizing their findings. (Students' reports will vary but should summarize the information presented in the text. Reports should include: Initially, a baby's vision is blurred; within a week a baby is more aware of the environment and can focus on objects seven to ten inches away; by six months the clarity is equal to that of adults; depth perception is two-dimensional at first; by two months, babies can perceive objects that are three-dimensional.) **L3**

**Teach** cont.

### W Writing Support

**Personal Letter**

**Infant Memories** Note that some of the strongest sensory experiences for babies, such as the sound of a mother's voice, will be remembered. Encourage students to write a letter to themselves in which they describe their earliest auditory memories. The letters should be written from the perspective of themselves as an infant. (Student's letters will vary but should include students' thoughts and feelings about their earliest memories of sounds. Letters should include a greeting, body, and closing.)

### C Critical Thinking

**Analyze** Read the following scenario to students: Jerri and Derek are not sure if their baby is paying attention to sounds, and they wonder if he has a hearing problem. Ask students the following questions: How can you recognize lags in a baby's sensory development? (Student answers will vary, but should mention awareness of physical development milestones for infants such as those listed in Figure 7.2.) What should you do if you suspect a problem? (Students should recommend taking the baby to a specialist, such as a pediatrician, to be tested and examined.)

### What Would You Do?

**Write About It** Students' advice columns will vary, but should suggest that Landon's mother discuss the issue with a doctor, such as Landon's pediatrician.

**202**

---

**Exploring the World** For much of the first year, children explore the world through the senses of sight, sound, and taste. After they learn to grasp objects, they begin to explore more of the world through touch. *What kinds of small objects can present hazards for babies?*

#### Getting Help

Three-month-old Landon was a happy baby. He smiled and gurgled when his parents held him and talked to him. He also ate well and had good sleeping habits. Landon's father commented that his son was so easygoing that even the dog's loud bark at the door did not seem to bother him. But his mother was puzzled that Landon was not starting to imitate sounds. When she stood a few feet behind him and clapped, Landon flinched and looked around, but when she gently rustled paper by his right ear, he did not seem to notice. Landon's mother was not sure what to do. Landon's father told her not to worry. He said that Landon was just a calm, quiet child. Landon's mother did not know whether Landon's behavior was normal though. She wanted to believe her husband but was afraid something was wrong.

✏ **Write About It** Suppose Landon's mother wrote a letter to the local paper asking advice. Write an advice column for Landon's mother with suggestions for what she should do.

---

eyes that are slightly crossed, or one eye that seems to wander outward. This condition typically improves by the fourth month as the eye muscles strengthen.

**Hearing** A baby's sense of hearing develops even before birth. Unborn babies often respond to sounds with changes in heart rate or activity level. A young pregnant woman who attended a loud concert found that out firsthand. For an hour after the concert, the baby continued to move to the beat of the music.

At birth, a full-term baby can already tell the general direction that a sound comes from. Newborns respond to the tone of a voice, rather than to the words. A soothing, loving voice calms them, and an angry or loud voice alarms them. By the age of seven months, babies recognize their parents and other caregivers by their voices. Some people believe that the baby will recognize these voices at birth if they heard them enough in the womb.

Language development begins with hearing spoken words first, and then imitating and understanding them. Premature babies and those who have had frequent ear infections tend to have more hearing problems. This can delay language development.

**W**

**C**

---

**⟶ Explore the Photo**

**Caption Answer** Objects that are sharp, dirty, or small enough for the baby to choke on can present hazards and should be kept out of baby's reach.

**Discussion** Ask students: How do many babies explore an object once they pick it up? (Babies typically put things in their mouths.) Help students realize that because of the way babies explore, care must be taken to ensure that toys and other objects are safe for the baby.

**Touch** Newborns lack both sufficient brain development and movement skills to explore their world through the sense of touch. However, they rely on the touch of others to teach them about their environment. Meeting a young baby's needs promptly and with a gentle touch builds trust.

Touch becomes a more important sense for learning as the first year progresses. At first, a baby may begin to notice different textures such as a soft blanket or a father's scratchy chin. As the ability to reach and grab objects develops, a baby uses touch for exploration.

**Smell and Taste** Since babies are surrounded by amniotic fluid until birth, their sense of smell does not have an opportunity to develop until after birth. A study has shown, however, that even newborns have some sense of smell. They respond differently to different scents. The sense of smell develops quickly. Within ten days, they can distinguish their mother from another person by smell.

The sense of taste also develops rapidly in children. Research studies have shown that two-week-old babies can taste the difference between water, sour liquids, sugar solutions, salt solutions, and milk. Even at this early age, babies show a preference for sweet tastes.

Throughout the first year, babies put anything and everything into their mouths. This is one of the main ways babies learn about their world. It is important to be sure that anything a baby grabs is clean, not sharp, and not so small that it could cause choking. Any object that can fit into a paper towel tube is likely too small for a baby to play with. Even food can be harmful for an infant.

### Voice

The newborn's cry is shrill, but it softens as the baby's lungs mature. The change in the voice of the child also results from the physical growth of the throat muscles, tongue, lips, teeth, and vocal cords. The tongue and the inside of the mouth change in shape and proportion during the first months of life. This growth makes speech development possible. Babies prepare for speech by making word-related sounds. They begin babbling vowel sounds, such as *ooh* and *ah* as early as two months of age. By the age of one year, many babies can imitate some speech sounds and understand simple phrases. It is important to talk and sing to babies as much as possible. The more babies hear speech, the more opportunities they have to learn it.

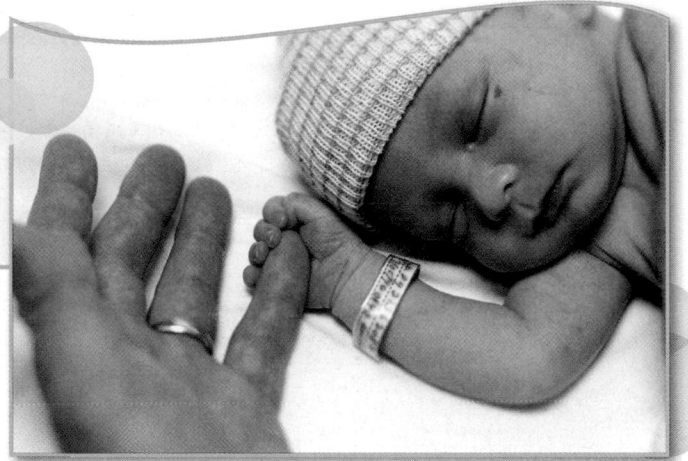

**Automatic Reflexes**
A newborn shows an automatic reflex when grabbing a finger. *What are some other automatic reflexes?*

Section 7.1 Infant Growth and Development **203**

**Quiz**
Ask students to answer the following questions:

1. What two factors play a significant role in a baby's growth and development? (heredity and environment)
2. How can parents and caregivers help strengthen a baby's connections in the brain? (They can make sure the baby has a stimulating environment—give the baby a wide variety of things to see, taste, smell, hear, and touch.)
3. Of the five senses, which one develops before birth? (hearing)

**Reteach**

**U Universal Access**

**Interpersonal Learners** Divide the class into teams, with each team having one English language learner. Have each team brainstorm a list of ways a caregiver or parent could help an infant develop a sense of smell and taste. Provide these questions for students to answer: What items could be used to encourage smelling and tasting? Have teams share their ideas with the class. (Ideas will vary. Students may suggest providing the baby with things to smell, such as flowers, and taste, such as applesauce.) **ELL**

---

**Explore the Photo**

**Caption Answer** Other automatic reflexes include sucking, rooting, shutting eyes under bright lights, stepping motions when feet touch the floor, and throwing arms back with fists clenched when arms are held and suddenly released.

**Discussion** Ask the class: Why do most of the reflexes exhibited by a newborn disappear within a few months? (Students should realize that the reflexes are to help the baby survive during the first few weeks of life and that as babies learn to control their muscles, they no longer need the reflexes.)

## Reteach cont.

### U₁ Universal Access

**Visual Learners** Have students plot the developmental milestones from Figure 7.2 onto a time line. Students may draw pictures or symbols that represent each milestone. Ask students why parents should be aware of these milestones. (Time lines will vary but should accurately show the developmental milestones. Parents should be aware of the milestones so they know where their child should be developmentally. If the child is behind developmentally, they should consult a physician.)

### C Critical Thinking

**Discover** Have students discuss what they were like as children with their parents or other caregivers. Encourage students to find out when they reached certain physical milestones like walking. Ask them to create a list of developmental milestones and the ages at which they reached them. Ask volunteers to share the information with the rest of the class. (Student answers will vary, but lists should reflect when they reached certain developmental milestones. For example, one student may discover that he rolled over at five months, crawled at nine months, and walked at 13 months.)

## Figure 7.2 — Physical Developmental Milestones—1st Year

During the first year babies reach many developmental milestones. *At which age does a baby typically begin to pull herself up?*

| Age | Developmental Milestone |
|---|---|
| 1 Month | ❧ Lifts head and turns it from one side to the other when placed on stomach<br>❧ Focuses on objects from about 10 inches to up to 3 feet away<br>❧ Reacts to parent's voice |
| 2 Months | ❧ Makes sounds such as "ooh" and "aah"<br>❧ Watches objects moved about 6 inches away from face<br>❧ Responds to more sounds and different pitches of voice |
| 3 Months | ❧ Opens and closes hands<br>❧ Holds head steadily when held up<br>❧ Lifts head and chest when on stomach<br>❧ Swipes at objects<br>❧ Brings hands together |
| 4 Months | ❧ Supports upper body on hands when lying on stomach<br>❧ Shows preference for red and blue over yellow<br>❧ May begin to use vowels and consonants in babbling, such as "ah ga"<br>❧ Grasps rattle<br>❧ Puts hands in mouth<br>❧ Rolls from tummy to back |
| 5 Months | ❧ Rocks on stomach while kicking legs and making swimming motions with arms<br>❧ Reaches out and grabs toys<br>❧ Turns head in direction of sound<br>❧ Knows positive speech from unhappy speech |
| 6 Months | ❧ Passes a block from one hand to the other<br>❧ Puts objects to mouth with hand<br>❧ May begin creeping<br>❧ Recognizes basic sounds of native language |

## Figure 7.2 — Physical Developmental Milestones—1st Year

**Caption Answer** A baby typically begins to pull herself up to a standing position at 8 months of age.

**Discussion** Bring in a variety of pictures of babies of all ages. Ask students to put the pictures in chronological order, illustrating the changing sizes of infants as they grow and develop. Have students identify the developmental milestone illustrated by each picture.

| Age | Developmental Milestone |
|-----|------------------------|
| **7 Months** | ❖ Rolls over both ways<br>❖ Sits up steadily<br>❖ Stands with assistance<br>❖ Knows parents and caregivers by their voices and by sight<br>❖ Can follow a path of moving objects with eyes<br>❖ Babbles with strings of vowels and consonants, such as "ba, ba, ba"<br>❖ Grabs for objects with raking motion |
| **8 Months** | ❖ Pulls self up to standing<br>❖ Bangs blocks together<br>❖ Propels self by arms, knees, or squirming motion<br>❖ Looks at objects with sustained attention |
| **9 Months** | ❖ Uses index finger to poke<br>❖ Puts objects in containers<br>❖ Leans forward to pick up toy<br>❖ Notices small objects<br>❖ May start associating sounds with objects |
| **10 Months** | ❖ Crawls well<br>❖ Can put objects in containers<br>❖ Uses index finger to start pointing<br>❖ Imitates new word sounds more frequently |
| **11 Months** | ❖ Walks while holding onto furniture or crib rails for support<br>❖ Uses gestures like shaking head for no<br>❖ Releases objects intentionally<br>❖ Grasps with thumb and forefinger |
| **12 Months** | ❖ May walk a few steps alone<br>❖ Stands alone for short time<br>❖ Picks up small objects using thumb and forefinger<br>❖ Puts objects into and takes them out of containers<br>❖ Holds and drinks from cup |

## U₂ Universal Access

**Kinesthetic Learners** Arrange students into teams. Have each team create a board game based on the developmental milestones of infants. Provide teams with markers, scissors, index cards, poster board, and game pieces (buttons or dried beans work well). Have each team exchange their board game with other teams and play them. Take a class vote to see which board game was the most challenging, the most fun, and the most creative. (Board games will vary but should be based on the developmental milestones of infants.)

## W Writing Support

### Journal Entry

**Curiosity** Ask students to write a journal entry about the curiosity that drives infants to explore everything that comes into their world. Have students reflect on the naturalness of this behavior, and how teens and adults can learn something by remembering what it was like to be so curious. Tell students that to write an effective journal entry they should let one idea lead to another, date the entry, and write about experiences, reactions, or observations. (Journal entries will vary. Use these questions to check journal entries: Does one idea lead to another? Does it convey personal reactions? Does it contain possible writing ideas?)

**Professional Development**

**Mini Clip**

**Reading: Interacting with Text**

Students work in small groups to make connections and ask higher order questions about a photo they have been given.

### C Critical Thinking

**Evaluate** Arrange students into small groups. Assign each group an infant age such as one to two months or three to four months. Each group is responsible for finding out what safety concerns exist because of the infants' motor skills at their particular age. Groups will prepare a Safety First skit that would teach parents and caregivers about the potential safety issues for their infants. Students should explore what parents and caregivers can do to avoid these safety hazards. (Skits will vary but should focus on the safety issues of the infant age assigned to the groups. Possible answers may include: moving things off the floor when a baby begins to crawl or moving things off low pieces of furniture when a baby begins to pull up.)

### R Reading Strategy

**Highlighting** Provide students with copies of an article on infant development. (Appropriate articles are available on the Internet at the March of Dimes site or the Medline Plus site, which is sponsored by the U.S. National Library of Medicine and the National Institutes of Health.) Have students highlight the main point of the article as they read. Afterward, discuss how highlighting main ideas leads a reader to a better understanding of the article. (Highlighting should include the main points of the article.)

### Reflexes

At birth, babies have little control over their muscles. Most movements are due to reflexes. A **reflex** is an instinctive, automatic response, such as grasping or sucking. Newborns begin life with many reflexes to help them survive in the first weeks of life. Most of these reflexes go away within a few months. Babies learn to control their muscles and develop motor skills.

**The Sucking Reflex** This reflex is stimulated when something is put in a baby's mouth. This reflex allows a newborn baby to feed from the mother's breast or a bottle.

**The Rooting Reflex** This happens when the baby's cheek is stroked. The baby turns toward the side of his or her face that was stroked.

**Other Automatic Reflexes** These include shutting the eyes under bright lights, grabbing a finger when it is placed in the hand, or stepping motions when the feet touch the floor. The Moro reflex causes a baby to throw the arms back with fists clenched when the arms are held and suddenly released.

### Motor Skills

Much of a baby's physical development in the first year is in muscle movement, also called motor skills. These skills depend mainly on direct control and use of muscles. For example, the arms and legs must get stronger and become coordinated before a baby can crawl.

There are two basic types of motor skills. A **gross motor skill** is a skill that involves the large muscles of the body such as those of the legs and shoulders. These are sometimes called large motor skills. Gross motor skills have to do with the ability to make large movements, such as jumping and running.

A **fine motor skill** involves the smaller muscles of the body such as those in the fingers. These are also called small motor skills. Fine motor skills require small, precise movements, such as using scissors or writing.

During their first year, babies' gross motor skills develop more rapidly than fine motor skills. **Figure 7.2** on pages 204–205 shows some of the major gross motor and fine motor skill milestones during the first year.

**Gross Motor Skills** The large muscles of the body involved in gross motor skills are primarily in the legs, arms, torso, and neck. Newborns can turn their head, wave their arms, and kick their legs. However, these movements occur as the result of reflexes and not because the baby purposefully controls the muscles.

One of the first motor skills that infants acquire is control of the head. A newborn's head is large and heavy, and the neck muscles are weak. For example, by age one month, when Chen was placed on his stomach he could lift his head slightly. By three months, he was able to prop himself up with his arms and lift his

**Safely Exploring**
The increased development of gross motor skills during the first year gives a child great mobility. *What can a caregiver do to let a child explore without getting hurt?*

## ➤ Explore the Photo

**Caption Answer** Answers will vary. Caregivers can make sure the baby's environment is safe: there are no sharp or dirty objects the baby can reach, there is nothing small enough for the baby to choke on, and so on.

**Discussion** Have students look carefully at the baby in the photo. Ask: How old do you think the baby is? What skills has the baby acquired? How can the parents and caregivers encourage the baby's development of motor skills? (Answers may include: around seven months; can stand and walk with assistance; parents can provide a stimulating environment.)

head and chest. In the next few months, Chen learned to roll over, and keep his head steady when he was held in a sitting position. By his first birthday, he could stand while holding on to something. This sequence of development is typical during a baby's first year.

By about nine months, many babies are crawling. They begin to explore their world. This is an exciting time for babies. They have more independence than ever before. This newfound mobility adds many new opportunities for learning.

**Fine Motor Skills** Fine motor skills involve the smaller muscles of the body, such as those of the fingers. By three months of age, babies' clenched fists have relaxed and they can open and close their hands. This is an important milestone in the development of fine motor skills. It means the child can grab objects by choice. By about five or six months, babies can reach for toys and pass a block from one hand to the other. By about seven months, babies can pick up objects by raking at them with the fingers and hand. Between nine and twelve months, babies fine-tune the ability to self-feed. They also learn to pick up objects with the thumb and forefinger.

### Hand-Eye Coordination

The ability to move the hands and fingers precisely in relation to what is seen is called **hand-eye coordination**. This is an essential skill for many tasks in life. It is what allows people to eat, catch a ball, color pictures, and tie shoes.

Newborns have poor hand-eye coordination. It develops as vision and motor skills improve. Around the age of three or four months, babies begin to reach and grab for objects they see and bring them to their mouths. By the end of their first year, babies can pick up an object and put it in another place.

---

## Section 7.1 — After You Read

### Review Key Concepts

1. **Explain** how growth differs from development.
2. **Describe** the head to foot, near-to-far, and simple to complex patterns of development.

### Practice Academic Skills

 **English Language Arts**

3. Imagine that you have a friend who is pregnant for the first time. How would you explain to her the importance of an infant's health and environment? Write a letter to your friend describing the effect they might have on the baby's growth and development.

> **NCTE 4** Use written language to communicate effectively.

 **Science**

4. Gina's baby weighed 7 pounds when she was born. The baby has been sick and is now a year old and weighs 15 pounds. Gina is concerned that the baby does not weigh enough. Should Gina be concerned? Write a paragraph explaining whether Gina should be concerned and what advice you would offer her.

> **NSES C** Develop understanding of molecular basis of heredity; biological evolution; matter, energy, and organization in living systems.

 **Check Your Answers** Check your answers at this book's Online Learning Center at **glencoe.com**.

**N C L B**

 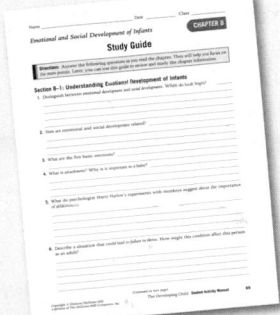
## Close

### Culminating Activity

**Problem-Solving Skills** Have students choose an age from 1 month to 12 months. Then have students review the developmental milestones for that age and design a toy that would be appropriate for a baby of that age.

**N C L B** NCLB connects academic correlations to book content.

---

## Section 7.1 — After You Read

### Review Key Concepts

1. Growth refers to changes in size; development refers to increases or changes in physical, emotional, social, or intellectual skills.
2. Head to foot: babies first develop some control of head movement, control of muscles moves down the body. Near to far: development starts near the trunk of the body and moves outward. Simple to complex: babies first develop the large muscle groups, as they strengthen and gain control over these muscles, they learn to do increasingly complex tasks.

### Practice Academic Skills

3. Answers will vary but should mention that the health and environment can play a big role in his acquisition of new skills as well as the opportunity to express and practice the skills.
4. Answers will vary, but Gina should be concerned. Since babies typically triple their birth weights in the first year, her baby should weight about 21 pounds. Gina should consult a doctor.

## Focus

### Bell Ringer Activity

**Taking Care of Baby**

Ask: What kinds of things need to be kept in mind to handle a baby safely? How can parents prevent their baby from becoming malnourished? (Answers will vary but may include making sure the baby's area is free from harmful objects. Parents can learn the nutritional needs of a baby.)

## Preteaching

### Vocabulary

Write *wean* on the board. Explain that in this text, wean means "to change from drinking from a bottle or breast to a cup." This word can also mean "raised on" as in "The drummer was weaned on rock and roll."

**Professional Development**

**Mini Clip Reading: Addressing Idioms**

A teacher models using and understanding idioms.

### Graphic Organizer

The Graphic Organizer is also on the TeacherWorks CD.

(Graphic organizers should list: Put the baby down and take some deep breaths to calm down. Ask someone to care for the baby for a few hours. Talk about the problem. Use a parenting hotline or crisis nursery.)

**NCLB** connects academic correlations to book content.

## Reading Guide

### Before You Read

**Buddy Up for Success** One advantage to sharing your notes with a buddy is that you can fill in gaps in each other's information. You can also compare notes before you start quizzing each other.

### Read to Learn

**Key Concepts**
- **Explain** how to safely hold a baby.
- **Identify** how to meet a baby's nutritional needs.
- **Describe** the best type of clothing suitable for a baby.

 **D**

### Main Idea

Caregivers need to know the proper ways of handling, feeding, and dressing a baby. This knowledge will help keep a baby healthy.

### Content Vocabulary

◇ shaken baby syndrome
◇ antibody
◇ weaning
◇ malnutrition

### Academic Vocabulary

You will find these words in your reading and on your tests. Use the glossary to look up their definitions if necessary.
- aggravate
- curb

### Graphic Organizer

As you read, look for things a frustrated caregiver might do when they are unable to get a baby to stop crying. Use a chart like the one shown to help organize your information.

| How to Relieve Stress if a Baby Will Not Stop Crying |
|---|
| 1. |
| 2. |
| 3. |
| 4. |

 **Graphic Organizer** Go to this book's Online Learning Center at **glencoe.com** to print out this graphic organizer.

### Academic Standards . . . . . . . . . . . . . . . . . . . . .

**NCLB**

 **English Language Arts**

**NCTE 8** Use information resources to gather information and create and communicate knowledge.

**Social Studies**

**NCSS I A Culture** Analyze and explain the ways groups, societies, and cultures address human needs and concerns.

**NCTE** *National Council of Teachers of English*
**NCTM** *National Council of Teachers of Mathematics*

**NSES** *National Science Education Standards*
**NCSS** *National Council for the Social Studies*

## Reading Guide

### Before You Read

Ask students: Have you ever tried to hold a baby? Encourage students to share their experiences of holding newborns and older infants. Ask students if they felt comfortable while doing so and how they learned to do it. (Answers may include they felt awkward, or they learned from a parent.)

### D Develop Concepts

**Main Idea** Discuss the main idea with the students. Ask: Where do you think most parents learn the proper ways of caring for a baby? (Students' answers may include: by babysitting, by watching parents with their children, or by taking classes.)

## Handling a Baby

A baby requires a huge amount of physical care. Each simple need, from a clean diaper to being comforted, requires someone's help. When caregivers pick up and hold a baby they can strengthen emotional bonds as well.

### Holding the Baby

Babies need to be held for many reasons. They need to be changed, fed, bathed, dressed, cuddled, and hugged. Safety, physical care, and emotional bonding are all involved in picking up and holding a baby.

Newborns and very young babies require the most careful handling. A newborn's neck muscles are not strong enough to support the head. For that reason, anyone picking up and holding a newborn must support the baby's neck and head at all times. **Figure 7.3** on pages 210–211 shows how to safely pick up, hold, and put down a newborn.

By about four months of age, babies can hold up their head without support. Even then, handling babies gently and holding them close gives the babies a sense of security. Whenever picking up or putting down an infant, try to

move smoothly and gently to avoid startling him. A crying baby can often be calmed by being picked up and held. Sometimes rocking the baby and gently patting the back can also be soothing.

### Bedtime Routines

Sleep is essential for growth and development. It also appears to be necessary for the brain to work properly. In babies, children, and teens, sleep allows the release of chemicals in the body that contribute to growth. In addition, the body's cells are hard at work during sleep, building and repairing themselves.

Some infants sleep more than others. Generally, a baby who is active needs more sleep than an inactive baby. Babies also need more sleep on some days than on others. Additional stimulation can cause a baby to sleep more, even if the baby is not more active.

As harmless as sleeping may seem, there are safety precautions to follow when putting babies to sleep. You need to do more than just choose a safe bed. Pillows, fluffy blankets, puffy bumper pads, and stuffed toys need to be removed. They can cause suffocation.

➤ **Bed Time Safety**
While a crib may seem like a safe place for infants to sleep, there are safety hazards to be aware of. *What are some safety precautions when putting a baby to sleep in a crib?*

NO = bumpers

**S Skill Practice**

### Guided Practice

**List** Ask students the following question: What would you do if a baby cries and cries? Have students create a list of solutions. (Lists will vary but may include rocking, walking with the baby, taking the baby for a ride in the stroller, and so on.) **L1**

**Interview** Ask students to interview one or more experienced parents or caregivers. Students should ask the parents or caregivers what they do to calm a crying baby. Students should write a summary of the interview and compare solutions if they have interviewed more than one person. (Solutions will vary but may include: distracting the infant with toys, rubbing the baby's back, singing, or playing music. Summaries should accurately reflect the content of the interview(s).) **L2**

**Research** Call students' attention to the sentence in the text that says, "Experts vary in their advice about what to do if a baby continues to cry." Divide the class into small groups and have each group research a different parenting expert and record the advice he or she gives about what to do if a baby continues to cry. As a class, compare the advice from the experts researched. (Advice will vary based on which experts are researched. There are many Internet sites that offer parenting advice. Students might also consult parenting magazines or research specific experts such as Benjamin Spock, T. Berry Brazelton, or Jesper Juul.) **L3**

Babies should be placed face up when put to bed. This is to help prevent a death from sudden infant death syndrome. Read more about this in the Parenting Skills feature on page 212.

Putting a baby to sleep should be a relaxed and pleasant experience. A consistent bedtime routine is one of the best ways to help a baby calm down and go to sleep. Some common routines include a warm bath, reading a story, and rocking the baby gently. Parents need to find a routine that works for them. Put the baby in the crib, gently pat the baby goodnight, and leave the room. The baby may cry or whimper a bit but usually will fall asleep within a few minutes.

Lupe wants to begin a bedtime routine with her three-month-old son, Miguel. The first night, she gives Miguel a warm bath and puts a fresh diaper and some pajamas on him.

She then rocks Miguel gently as she sings him a lullaby. After a few minutes, Miguel seems drowsy. Lupe gently lays him in his crib and creeps out of his room.

Experts vary in their advice about what to do if a baby continues to cry. Some recommend leaving the baby alone to cry it out. Others say the baby should be held and comforted immediately.

Today, many experts say to go to the baby after a few minutes of crying, offer comfort without picking up the baby, and then leave the room. If the baby cries again, stay away a bit longer than before and repeat the sequence. This process reassures the baby that a parent will always be near. However, any baby who continues to cry for more than 15 minutes should be checked for a wet diaper, sickness, or other problems.

**S**

### Figure 7.3 Handling a Newborn Safely

Newborns must be handled with extreme care. *Why is it important to support a newborn's neck and head when lifting and holding him?*

**Lifting a Newborn** Slide one hand under the baby's bottom and the other under the shoulders and head. Use your forearm to support the neck and head as you raise your hands together to lift the newborn.

**Holding a Newborn in Your Arms** Hold the baby upright, cradled in the curve of your arm. Your arm supports the baby's head and neck. You can easily maintain eye contact with the baby.

### Figure 7.3 Handling a Newborn Safely

**Caption Answer** A newborn's neck and head must be supported to prevent injury; a newborn's muscles are not yet strong enough to support the head.

**Discussion** Bring in dolls to simulate babies at various stages of development. Have students use the dolls to practice holding newborns, as well as babies at various stages of development. Discuss the importance of supporting a newborn's head and neck. After students are comfortable holding a baby, have them practice handing the baby to another person and putting the baby down in a crib.

## Sleep Patterns

The amount of time a baby spends sleeping decreases greatly during the first year. A newborn may sleep a total of 12 to 20 hours a day. By one year, however, a baby often has as few as two or three sleep periods, including naps. **Figure 7.4** on page 213 shows how much sleep babies typically need during the course of the first year.

## Responding to Cries

It is important to respond to a baby's cries. Doctors say that a prompt response to a very young baby does not spoil the baby. As discussed earlier, the only time parents and other caregivers may be advised to let a baby cry is at bedtime, when they are trying to establish good sleep habits. At other times, the reason for crying may be as simple as a wet diaper or feeling cold or hungry. Pain or sickness may also cause crying. Some babies may simply be startled by loud noises. First, make sure a crying baby is comfortable, fed, and dry. Next, try rocking, talking, singing, or other comforting techniques to soothe the baby.

## Shaken Baby Syndrome

No one should ever vigorously shake or jiggle a baby. These actions are extremely dangerous. Every year thousands of babies suffer serious problems due to shaken baby syndrome. **Shaken baby syndrome** is a condition that occurs when someone severely shakes a baby, usually in an effort to make her stop crying. Shaken baby syndrome can lead to brain damage, including mental retardation, cerebral palsy, or blindness. Sometimes the shaking breaks bones or injures the neck and spine. It can even cause death.

**Holding a Newborn Against Your Chest** Hold the baby against your chest, so that the baby faces or peeks over your shoulder. Use your hand to support the baby's neck and head.

**Putting a Newborn Down** Continue to support the neck, head, and body. Bend over and rest the child on a surface that can support the baby's body. Then remove your arms.

Section 7.2    Caring for an Infant    **211**

**Mini Clip**
**ELL: Using Realia**

A teacher uses realia to make lesson concepts more real to students.

## Teach cont.

**C Critical Thinking**

**Problem Solving** Read the following scenario to students: David was distressed because his five-month-old baby, Jacob, was crying in his crib and would not go to sleep. Jacob's crying was waking up the other children in the family. Ask students what David should do. Encourage students to see the value of trying a variety of methods to comfort a baby who needs to sleep. (Students may suggest: The baby may be wet, uncomfortable, overstimulated, overtired, or sick. David could take Jacob to an area of the home as far away as possible from the other children and try changing, feeding, rocking, and other soothing techniques.)

**U Universal Access**

**Auditory Learners** Explain that when a baby is shaken, the brain bumps into the skull, and blood vessels may bleed into the brain. If a clot forms and presses on the brain, it can disturb a function, such as seeing, hearing, or thinking. Bring to class a small cardboard box and a soft object with some weight such as a bean bag. Put the bean bag in the box and have a student shake the box gently and then with more force. Students should be able to hear the bean bag bumping against the sides of the box. Tell students that this demonstration is not unlike what a baby's brain experiences when a baby is shaken. Ask students for their reactions to the demonstration. (Students' reactions will vary; but most should understand how severely damaging it can be to shake a baby.)

## Teach cont.

### R Reading Strategy

**Finding Information** Have students scan your local telephone directory to locate agencies in your area that could be of help to a parent who cannot get the baby to stop crying and is afraid he or she will lose control and injure the baby. Students might look under Abuse/Victims' Services, Children/Youth Services, Community/Social/Human Services, Emergency Assistance/Crisis Intervention, Hot Lines, or Help Lines. (Local agencies will vary depending on what is available in your community.)

### C Critical Thinking

**Determine Importance** Before they have read the section Feeding an Infant, ask students to describe feeding time for an infant. (Descriptions will vary depending on feedings students have seen or participated in.) Then ask what they think is the most important aspect of feeding an infant. (Students will likely say, "Feeding the infant.") Point out to students the sentence that says, "The cuddling, body contact, and encouragement that go along with feeding are almost as important as the food." Ask students if they agree with this statement and to explain why. (Answers will vary. Students should recognize the importance of touch and bonding that occur during feeding. They help the baby feel secure and learn to trust.)

### ✓ Reading Check

**Explain** The reason for crying may be a wet diaper, feeling cold or hungry, feeling pain or sick. Responding to a baby's cries helps him or her feel secure.

---

The baby cries and cries and nothing you do seems to help. You are scared, frustrated, and angry. You are afraid you will lose control and hurt the baby. You may think this could never happen to you, but it might. Even experienced adults sometimes come close to losing control. For new parents and child care providers, the odds are higher. What can you do in such a situation?

- Put the baby down in a safe place, go into another room, and take some deep breaths or look out the window to calm down.
- Ask a friend or relative to care for the baby for a few hours.
- Call someone and talk about the problem.
- Call a parenting hotline or take the baby to a crisis nursery if available in your area. Both can give immediate help and teach you how to handle stress in the future.

Gently rocking or playfully bouncing a baby on the knee is not dangerous. However, shaking or hitting a baby can be deadly. A baby cannot purposely **aggravate**, or anger, a parent. If you or someone you know is ever in this situation, ask for help.

**✓ Reading Check** **Explain** Why is it important to respond to a baby's cries?

## Feeding an Infant

Mealtime provides babies with the nutrients they need to grow and develop. It also gives them much more though. It is an opportunity for babies to interact with others, learn more about their world, and practice skills. The cuddling, body contact, and encouragement that go along with feeding babies are almost as important as the food. Feeding an infant is a great opportunity for parents to bond with their child.

### ♡ Parenting Skills

#### What Is Sudden Infant Death Syndrome?

Sudden infant death syndrome (SIDS) is the unexpected death of an infant with no obvious cause. The baby dies during sleep, with no crying and no evidence of struggle. The vast majority of children who die of SIDS are between two and four months old. However, SIDS can affect infants up to twelve months old. SIDS happens to about 2,500 infants each year in the United States.

The cause of SIDS is unknown, but researchers have identified some groups who are more at risk. Among those groups, the most likely victims are male babies who had a low birth weight. Premature babies, babies who live with a person who smokes, and babies who sleep on their stomachs also have a greater risk of SIDS.

To reduce the risk of SIDS:

➤ Put babies to sleep on their backs.
➤ Avoid smoking both during pregnancy and after the baby is born.
➤ Avoid exposing the baby to smoke from others.

**Take Charge** Research to find out more about the Back to Sleep campaign sponsored by the National Institute of Child Health and Human Development. Create a flyer to explain the 10 ways you can help prevent SIDS.

### ♡ Parenting Skills

#### What is Sudden Infant Death Syndrome?

Ask students what other dangerous effects cigarette smoke can have on babies. (It can stunt growth and development and endanger the baby's overall health.) Ask students why parents who lose a child to SIDS might feel guilty. (Parents might feel that they could have done something to prevent the baby's death.)

**Take Charge**
Flyers will vary but should include the Safe Sleep Top 10 promoted by the Back to Sleep campaign, which can be viewed at the National Institutes of Health Eunice Kennedy Shriver National Institute of Child Health and Human Development Web site.

## Figure 7.4 How Much Do Babies Sleep?

Babies up to a year old sleep more than half the time. *Why do babies need so much sleep?*

| Age | Hours of Sleep | Description |
|---|---|---|
| **Newborn** | 16 | ✤ Takes four or five naps a day, each about 3 to 4 hours.<br>✤ Between each nap is a period of wakefulness that may last a few hours. |
| **3 months** | 14 to 15 | ✤ Total amount of sleep decreases but takes longer naps—about 4 to 5 hours long.<br>✤ Longer sleeping periods at night. |
| **4 months** | 12 to 14 | ✤ Takes naps midmorning and late afternoon.<br>✤ Sleeps at night. |
| **6 months** | 12 to 14 | ✤ Sleeps about six hours at night.<br>✤ Takes two long naps in the day. |
| **1 year** | 12 hours | ✤ Sleeps about 9 to 10 hours at night.<br>✤ May take one or two naps in the day. |

U

## Nutritional Needs

W

In the first year, a baby's basic source of nutrition is breast milk or formula. In fact, for the first six months of life, a healthy baby's nutritional needs can be met solely through breast milk or iron-fortified formula.

At about six months, solid foods can be introduced. Watery rice cereal is offered first, followed by other thin cereals and strained fruits and vegetables. These foods are key sources of the calories, or food energy, needed for growth. After about eight months of age, babies can get about half of their calories from solid food and half from breast milk or formula. The amount of solid food should continue to increase gradually. By the first birthday, most nutrition usually comes from solid foods.

Babies under age one should not be fed cow's milk because it is hard for them to digest. It lacks important nutrients that breast milk and formula provide. Fruit juice seems like a nutritious food for infants. However, fruit juice promotes tooth decay and may **curb**, or limit, a child's appetite for more nutritious foods. It is usually best to wait until the baby is six months old before introducing fruit juice. Then, it should be watered down for the baby. Parents should discuss their baby's eating plan with the baby's doctor.

### Breast Milk

If a mother is capable, nutrition experts recommend breast-feeding. There are many advantages to breast milk:

- It contains all the nutrients a baby needs.
- It also contains antibodies. An **antibody** is a substance produced by the body to fight off germs. Antibodies boost a baby's defenses against infection. Colostrum, or the first breast milk, is especially rich in nutrients and antibodies.



## Section 7.2

### Teach cont.

### U Universal Access

**Mathematical Learners** Have mathematical learners compute the percentage of the day (24 hours) babies sleep based on the averages provided in Figure 7.4. (Newborns sleep an average of 67 percent of the day (16 ÷ 24); three-month-olds sleep an average of 58 percent to 63 percent of the day; four- and six-month olds sleep an average of 50 percent to 58 percent of the day; and one-year-olds sleep an average of 50 percent of the day.)

### W Writing Support

#### Question and Answer

**Feeding Options** Have students poll parents (their own or others) on whether their babies were breast-fed or bottle fed, and why. Students should deliver their findings in a question-and-answer format. They should write out the questions; plan answers that connect to the key words of the questions; and organize their answers with an introduction, a body, and a conclusion. (Questions and answers may vary, but should focus on whether babies were breast-fed or bottle-fed and why. Students' findings should include answers that: relate to key words in the questions; contain a sentence with the main idea; include an introduction, a body, and a conclusion.)

### Figure 7.4 How Much Do Babies Sleep?

**Caption Answer** Sleep is essential for growth and development, necessary for the brain to work properly, coincides with the release of chemicals in the body that contribute to growth, and allows cells to build and repair themselves.

**Discussion** Make sure students understand that the number of hours of sleep identified in Figure 7.4 are averages, and that some babies will sleep more and others will sleep less. Ask students to check with their parents to find out if the student's sleeping patterns were below average, average, or above average when he or she was an infant. Ask volunteers to share what they learn with the class.

## Assess

### Quiz

Ask students to answer the following questions:

1. **Why is it important to support a newborn's head and neck while lifting him?** (to prevent injury; a newborn's muscles are not strong enough to support the head)

2. **What are *antibodies*?** (Antibodies are substances produced by the body to fight off diseases. Breast milk contains antibodies that boost a baby's defenses against infection.)

3. **At what weight is a baby's stomach large enough to allow her to sleep through the night?** (at about 12 pounds)

## Reteach

###  Critical Thinking

**Compare Costs** Have students compare the daily costs for a newborn and a six-month-old for these types of formula: powdered, concentrate, and ready-to-use. Students will need to identify the cost of each and multiply by the amount used daily at both stages of infancy. Students should use the amounts recommended on the formula package. Ask students what conclusions they can draw from their calculations. (Answers will vary depending on the cost of the three types of formula. In general, the cost of feeding a newborn is less than the cost of feeding a six-month-old.)

---

- It is germ-free and easy to digest.
- Breast-fed babies get fewer ear infections, respiratory infections, and allergies than formula-fed babies. They are also less likely to develop asthma.

Breast milk lacks vitamin D, a nutrient important for bone growth. Fortunately, the skin makes this vitamin when it is exposed to sunlight. A young baby in a cold climate might need extra vitamin D in the winter. Parents should check with the baby's doctor.

The World Health Organization encourages mothers to breast-feed for at least one year. This gives babies the best possible nutrition and a good start in life. Refer back to Section 5.2 for more information on breast milk and baby formula.

### Baby Formula

Many babies are fed formula for part or all of their infancy. Not every mother is physically able to breast-feed. Other parents choose to use formula.

Baby formula is specially made to meet babies' nutritional needs. Milk-based formula is used most often. The cow's milk used as an ingredient has been modified to eliminate digestive problems. Soy-based formula is also available. Formula comes in three forms: ready to use, a concentrated liquid that is mixed with water, and a powder that is mixed with water. $C_1$

## Feeding Schedules

A newborn's schedule of eating and sleeping is unpredictable. Pediatricians recommend that newborns be fed as much and as often as they want to eat. A newborn will generally stop eating when he or she is full.

Frequent feedings are necessary because a newborn's stomach can hold only a small amount. In the first few weeks of life, breast-fed babies may want to eat as many as eight to twelve times a day or more. Formula-fed babies may eat every three to four hours for the first few weeks.

➤ **Bonding Through Feeding**
Bottle-feeding, whether with breast milk or formula, gives the father a chance to participate in the closeness of feeding an infant. *What do babies gain at mealtime besides nutrients?*

---

◄••• ➤ **Explore the Photo**

**Caption Answer** In addition to nutrients, at mealtime babies gain an opportunity to interact with others, learn more about their world, and practice motor skills.

**Discussion** Ask the class: How might older siblings get involved with a baby during mealtime? (Young children can learn to feed a baby under close supervision of an adult. Older children might take the responsibility alone. This allows siblings to interact with the baby and the baby to interact with siblings.)

By the second or third month, most babies are eating on a regular schedule. They may wake for a feeding every three or four hours. Eventually babies no longer need a late-night feeding. This is typically when they weigh about 12 pounds (5.4 kg). At this weight, their stomach is usually large enough to allow them to sleep through the night, about six hours.

## Feeding Methods

Most babies under the age of six months eat only breast milk or formula. This means there are only two ways they can be fed: by breast or bottle. With either method, babies should be allowed to eat until they are satisfied. Healthy babies usually eat only the amount they need, so overeating is generally not an issue with young babies.

### Breast-Feeding

Breast-feeding is very natural, but it does not always come naturally. It can take practice. Many hospitals have consultants on staff to offer assistance if needed. They can help new mothers learn how to find the best way to hold the baby and get the baby to eat. They can also give advice on the mother's nutritional needs and how to deal with problems.

### Bottle-Feeding

There are certain guidelines for bottle-feeding. The first deals with preparing the formula. If using a powdered or concentrated formula, mix it with sterile (germ-free) bottled water or water that has been boiled.

Bottles should be washed in a dishwasher or with hot, sudsy water followed by a boiling water rinse. Bottles with disposable liners are a popular alternative. Bottles can be prepared up to 24 hours ahead and stored in the refrigerator.

Most infants prefer their bottles at room temperature or warm. To warm a bottle, place it in a pan of warm water. Heat the formula until it is lukewarm. Special bottle warmers are also now available. Always test the temperature by dripping a small amount of formula onto the inside of your wrist. If it is hot, allow it to cool down before feeding. Formula should never be warmed in a microwave oven. The microwave

can leave pockets of hot liquid that will burn a baby's mouth.

For bottle-feeding, hold the baby close to you in a semi-upright position. The head needs support in the first few months. You should never prop up the baby and bottle and leave the baby to drink alone. It deprives the baby of important physical contact. In addition, babies should not be put to bed with a bottle. The milk can pool around the gums and cause decay in developing teeth. This practice also leads to an increased risk of ear infections.

If a baby does not finish the contents of the entire bottle, the remainder should be thrown away. Disease-causing bacteria can grow quickly in leftover formula and if eaten, could lead to illness.

### Burping the Baby

Babies often swallow air as they drink whether they are bottle- or breast-fed. To feel comfortable, a baby must be burped from time to time to expel the air. Without burping, a

## U Universal Access

**Interpersonal Learners** Demonstrate for students the correct way to burp a baby. Show various positions, such as laying the baby across the knees, holding the baby against the chest, and sitting the baby up. Divide the class into small groups. Provide each group with a life-size baby doll. Have group members take turns using the doll to practice burping a baby. Ask group members to provide tips and positive critiques to help improve students' techniques. (Before allowing students to practice with the doll, review the burping technique provided in the text. Students' techniques should follow that of the text.)

## C₁ Critical Thinking

**Determine** Tell students that sometimes a baby may not burp right away. Ask: Why is it important to continue trying to burp a baby during feeding? (It is important to burp a baby during feeding so air in the baby's stomach does not prevent the baby from finishing the feeding, and so the baby does not develop indigestion.)

## W₁ Writing Support

**Paragraph**

**Starting Solid Foods** Relate this experience to the students: Megan is worried because she was told to feed cereal to the six-month-old baby she is caring for, but the baby is spitting up and drooling more food than she is eating. Ask students to write a paragraph to explain what Megan should do. (Paragraphs will vary but should indicate that Megan should relax. The baby is perfectly normal. Managing and swallowing food is a motor skill babies need to learn, and they learn only with practice. Paragraphs should contain a topic sentence and be free of spelling and grammar errors.)

baby may spit up, become irritable, or have gas. Burping is a technique that anyone who cares for a baby needs to know.

**U**
- Burp a baby at least twice during a feeding. Depending on how much the baby is drinking, try burping at least once during a feeding and once after a feeding.
- Find the most comfortable position to burp a baby. Many caregivers lay the baby across their knees. Others hold the baby across their chests with the baby's head above their shoulders. Some prefer to hold the baby in a sitting position for burping.
- Pat the baby on the back to cause the burp. A gentle tap works as well as a firmer one, so be very gentle.
- Protect your clothing. Put a towel or cloth under the baby's head to catch any liquid that comes up.

**C₁**
- Remember that it is perfectly normal for a baby not to burp each time. Each baby's liquid intake is different. Although a baby may not burp each time, it is important to try.

It is also common for most babies to spit up from time to time. This may occur after the baby has eaten more than his or her stomach can hold. Sometimes a baby will spit up while burping. It is a good idea to protect your clothes with a cloth while holding or burping a baby. Avoid placing the baby in a seated position after eating because this can put pressure on the stomach and cause the baby to spit up. If a baby vomits forcefully, or does not appear to be gaining weight, consult a doctor.

### Introducing Solid Foods

**W₁** Babies are typically given their first solid foods around the age of four to six months. There is no rush to start, however. Once babies have started to eat cereal, other new foods can be introduced. It is not unusual for a baby to have a bad reaction to a certain food. It may cause a skin rash, digestive trouble, or an allergic reaction. By introducing new foods at least four days apart, it is easier to figure out which food is the problem.

**Eating Solid Food**
By six months old, a baby can eat solid foods. *What is the first type of solid food a baby can eat?*

### ▶ Explore the Photo

**Caption Answer** Watery rice cereal is often the first solid food babies eat. This is followed by other thin cereals and strained fruits, vegetables, and cooked meats.

**Discussion** After about eight months of age, about half of a baby's calories should come from solid food. Ask students why this is so. (Answers should indicate that the baby, including the stomach, is growing and the solid food helps satisfy the appetite for longer periods than breast milk or formula.)

## Weaning

Sometime around their first birthday, many babies are ready for weaning. **Weaning** is changing from drinking from the bottle or breast to a cup. Weaning is an important sign of a baby's increasing independence.

There is no absolute time at which a baby should be weaned. Many babies show signs that they are ready. They may show less interest in breast- or bottle-feeding. Typically this occurs between nine and twelve months of age. Other signs that a baby is ready to be weaned may include playing or looking around while feeding, pushing the breast or bottle away, or showing a preference for eating solids.

It is best to approach the weaning gradually. If a mother is breast-feeding, her body can adjust to decreasing demands on milk production. The slower transition also gives children time to get used to drinking formula or milk, depending on their age. Forced weaning may result in other feeding or behavior problems for the child.

Some pediatricians suggest going directly from breast-feeding to a cup if the child is old enough to drink from one. This avoids later transitions from bottles to cups. If an infant moves from breast-feeding to a bottle, the breast milk should slowly be replaced with formula or milk first.

## Self-feeding

When babies can sit up steadily in a high chair, they can start to eat with their fingers and reach for a spoon. This is often at about eight or ten months. Being able to pick up food and self-feed is an important developmental milestone because it signals increased independence. Finger foods are small pieces of food that can easily be picked up with the fingers and eaten. They encourage self-feeding.

When a baby begins to self-feed, it is important to avoid foods that could get stuck in a baby's throat. Some of the foods to avoid include raw vegetables, hot dogs, nuts, peanut butter, whole grapes, candy, chips, pretzels, and popcorn. Any hard, round food can get stuck in a baby's throat. Foods that break up easily in the mouth are best. This might include dry toast, cereal pieces, small pieces of chicken, small pieces of cooked pasta, and chunks of banana.

A baby's first efforts at self-feeding with a spoon will probably be fun for the baby but not very productive. At first, mealtime may consist of the baby trying to self-feed finger foods while the caregiver spoons in extra food whenever possible. Babies may not become expert spoon users until eighteen months of age or later. It takes patience and a sense of humor. You should allow plenty of time for each meal and anticipate some messiness.

## Nutritional Concerns

Just like adults, babies who are eating solid foods should eat nutritious, well-balanced meals that include grains, fruits or vegetables, and protein. They should be able to eat whenever they are hungry, rather than on a rigid schedule. Foods should be soft and easy to gum or chew and swallow. Salty snack foods should be limited because they are likely to be low in nutritional value. Certain other foods may contain substances that are not good for a baby. Babies have very specific nutritional needs. They include the following:

- Enough calories to provide for activity and rapid growth
- Foods that provide key nutrients, such as vitamins and minerals
- Adequate amounts of liquid

Some babies do not receive enough of the right types of food. Others may have a medical condition that prevents them from absorbing enough nutrients after they eat. Malnutrition in infancy can cause lasting physical problems.

---

{ **Expert Advice...** }

*"When you comfort your baby, you are letting her know the world is a safe place and that someone cares about her feelings."*

— Claire Lerner, LCSW; Amy Dombro, MS; and Karen Levine, coauthors, *The Magic of Everyday Moments: 0–4 months*

---

**Mc Graw Hill** Professional Development

**Mini Clip**
**Reading: Obstacles to Achievement**

Teachers work together to determine why their students are struggling with mastery of a particular standard.

## W₂ Writing Support
### Presenting Information

**Analyzing Food** Collect a variety of foods for children including formula, cereal, strained baby foods, and finger foods. Display these foods along with foods children should not eat such as candy, potato chips, popcorn, nuts, grapes, hot dogs, and so on. Have students analyze the foods using the following questions: Which foods are appropriate for newborns and infants? What nutritional value does the food have? Which foods do you think the children would like? Dislike? Which foods could be unsafe for children to eat? Why are they unsafe? (Students' presentation of the answers to these questions will vary. You might suggest that students develop a table or lists in which to present the information. Students should recognize that formula is for babies, cereal and strained baby foods for infants six months or older, and adult foods probably shouldn't be listed for either age group. Students also should recognize the foods that should not be served to babies and infants.)

## C₂ Critical Thinking

**Infer** Tell students that brain growth is strongly affected by an infant's diet. For instance, iron is needed to maintain the production of oxygen-rich red blood cells, which in turn promote brain growth. Have the class brainstorm reasons why specialists recommend iron-fortified foods for infants. Why might infants need fortified foods to get enough iron in their diets? (Answers will vary. Students should recognize that because a baby's brain is developing so rapidly, it needs extra iron. Also, babies cannot yet eat some of the foods, such as meat or leafy vegetables, that are major sources of iron for adults.)

## U₁ Universal Access

**Gifted Learners** Have gifted learners research the areas of the world where malnutrition is widespread. Students should find out what the specific causes of malnutrition are in the area and what governmental and international organizations are doing about those causes. Ask students to share their information with the class. (Research papers will vary depending on the area of the world on which students focus. Information in the papers should be organized under Area, Causes, and Intervention. For example, in Tanzania, malnutrition is caused by lack of safe drinking water and illnesses. A project improving health coverage and access to safe water, as well as growth monitoring and promotion, has produced a drop in malnutrition. Papers should be logically constructed and be free of spelling and grammar errors.)

## C₁ Critical Thinking

**Analyze** Discuss common childhood allergies with students. Have the class share information about their own experiences with allergies. Ask students the following: When was your allergy detected? What were the signs and symptoms that led to the detection? What tests can health care professionals use to detect an allergy? What measures can be taken to avoid allergic reactions? (Personal information about allergies will vary from student to student. Students may mention skin or blood tests for allergies. People can avoid foods or substances that cause an allergic reaction.)

### ✓ Reading Check

**Explain** Lasting physical problems and poor brain development, which can lead to learning difficulties, can result from malnutrition.

**218**

➡ **Learning to Self-Feed**
Older babies can begin to eat solid food. *What are some appropriate solid foods for babies?*

**Malnutrition** is inadequate nutrition. Poor nutrition is also linked to poor brain development, which can lead to learning difficulties.

There are many government and community programs working to eliminate infant and childhood malnutrition. Some of these programs provide food. Others teach parents how to make good nutritional choices for children.

While most babies eat only the amount they need, it is possible to overfeed a baby. This is more common with bottle-fed babies. They may be encouraged to drink all the formula in their bottle, even if they are already full. A chubby baby will not necessarily be an obese adult. Research shows that obesity in adults is linked to heredity. However, poor eating habits in the first year can lead to health problems later in life. Talk to your doctor about the best ways to meet a baby's nutritional needs.

## Allergies

An allergy is an oversensitivity to a particular common substance that is harmless to most people. When a person has an allergy, the body's immune system attacks the substance. Allergy symptoms are the side effects of the attack. People may have an allergic reaction when they eat, breathe in, are injected with, or touch the thing they are allergic to. The reaction may be as mild as puffy, itchy eyes or as severe as anaphylactic shock, a life-threatening condition that makes it difficult to breathe.

It is important to watch for signs of allergies in babies. Parents who have allergies themselves should be especially careful, since the tendency to develop allergies runs in families. Signs of a food allergy in a baby may include excessive crying, vomiting almost all food after a feeding, or eight or more watery stools a day.

Babies should not eat eggs, citrus fruits, honey, peanut butter, corn, or shellfish during their first year of life. All of these foods can cause allergic reactions. Children often outgrow allergies to eggs, milk, and soy, but other food allergies are likely to continue throughout life. The best treatment for a food allergy is to avoid the food. Breast-feeding mothers should also avoid foods to which a baby is allergic.

### ✓ Reading Check **Explain** What can result from malnutrition in babies?

---

➡ **Explore the Photo**

**Caption Answer** Appropriate solid foods include dry toast, cereal pieces, small pieces of chicken, small pieces of cooked pasta, and chunks of banana.

**Discussion** Ask the class: Why is it important to offer finger food that is in small pieces to an infant? (Answers will vary, but students should realize that small chunks help to minimize the possibility of the child choking.)

## Dressing a Baby

Have you ever seen babies who seem over- or under-dressed for the weather? Babies lose body heat more easily than adults do, but they are also sensitive to overheating. As a general rule, doctors recommend dressing babies in one more layer of clothing than an older child or an adult would wear.

A new baby does not need a lot of fancy clothing. Babies do need diapers, undershirts, and simple outer garments. Socks and booties are not always necessary for everyday wear. Many newborns spend their days and nights in a sleeper, a one-piece stretchy garment that has feet or a simple drawstring at the bottom. On hot days, just a diaper and an undershirt will do. It is not unusual to change a newborn's clothes a couple of times during the day. Newborns often spit up or drool on their clothes.

When babies begin to crawl, they need more durable clothes that allow for movement. Some baby clothes have padded knees to add durability. Shoes are not essential until a baby starts to walk outdoors. When babies are learning to walk, going barefoot gives them more flexibility at the ankle and allows them to grip the floor with the toes. Once the baby is ready for shoes, either flexible sneakers or soft leather shoes are good choices. **U₂**

## Choosing Clothing

Many clothes for infants are made of knit fabrics that are comfortable and stretchy, making it easy for the baby to move around.

Clothing size is determined by a baby's weight and age, although weight is typically the more reliable guide. In general, clothes should not be so snug that the baby has trouble moving. Many parents buy clothes a little large so they will last longer and the baby can move around. However, they also should not be so large that they get wrapped around or stuck under the baby. **C₂**

When choosing baby clothes, comfort and ease in dressing are important. Features such as snaps along the inner legs help make changing diapers easy. Shirts that snap rather than go over the head are also easy to use with young babies. To get longer use out of clothes, look for clothes with cuffs or generous hems that can be let down, extra buttons on shoulder straps, and elastic waistbands that allow for growth.

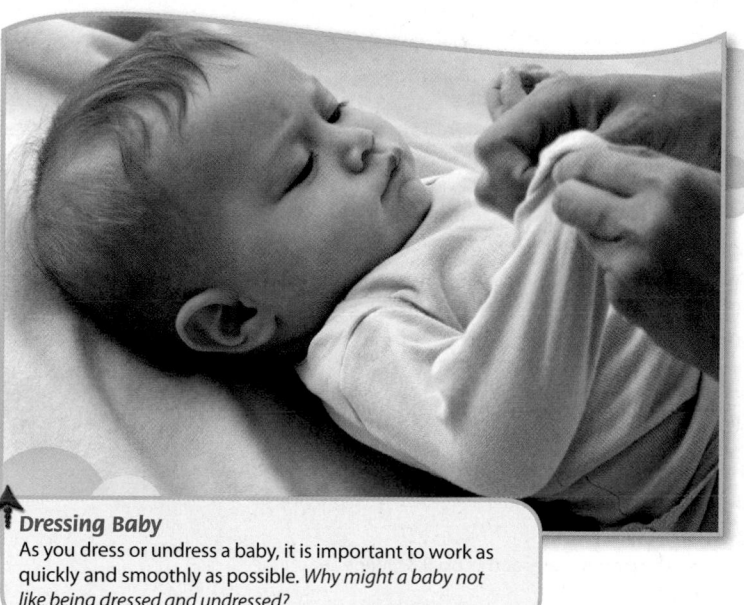

**↑ Dressing Baby**
As you dress or undress a baby, it is important to work as quickly and smoothly as possible. *Why might a baby not like being dressed and undressed?*

Section 7.2   Caring for an Infant   **219**

**▶ Explore the Photo**

**Caption Answer** Babies may not like being dressed and undressed because there is usually an abrupt change in temperature and they are being pushed and pulled through clothes.

**Discussion** Ask the class to imagine what a baby goes through when it is dressed or undressed. Ask volunteers to share a commentary about the experience from the baby's point of view and from the caregiver's point of view. (Commentaries will vary but should show an understanding of the dressing and undressing process.)

## Study Tools

Have students go to the Online Learning Center at **glencoe.com**:

- Take the **Practice Test**.
- Download **Study-to-Go** content.

Use the **Student Activity Workbook** for additional practice.

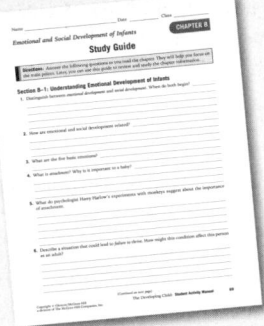

### Close

## Culminating Activity

**Observation** Have students observe young infants as they try to feed themselves. They should note the kinds of foods they are eating and how the caregivers interact with the baby. Students should share an oral report of their experience.

**NCLB** connects academic correlations to book content.

---

# How to Dress a Baby

Dressing and undressing a baby quickly and smoothly takes some practice. It is easy to understand why babies do not really like the process. There is usually an abrupt change in temperature, as well as being pushed and pulled through clothes. Here are some hints for dressing babies in different types of clothing.

## Pullover Garments

These clothes have a stretchable neck opening. If the neck opening is large, put the opening around the baby's face first, and then pull it over the back of the head. If the opening is small, gather the garment into a loop and slip it over the back of the baby's head. Stretch the garment forward, down, and away from the face and ears. Put the baby's fist into the armhole and pull the arm through with the other hand. Repeat with the other arm, and then straighten out the bottom of the garment.

When undressing the child, carefully stretch the garment away from the chin and face as it is lifted off.

## Open-Front Shirt

Set the shirt out, with the front open. Lay the baby down on the shirt, face up. Gently pull the baby's arms through the sleeves. Fasten the front.

## One-Piece Garment with Feet

Putting on this type of garment is easier when the zipper or the snaps go from neck to toes. Lay the baby on the open garment. Start with the bottom part of the garment. If the zipper or snaps go down only one leg, put the baby's leg on the side without the zipper or snaps first. Follow this by putting in the other leg. Then gently pull the sleeves over the baby's arms. Finish by zipping or snapping the garment closed.

---

## Section 7.2 — After You Read

### Review Key Concepts

1. **Describe** a possible routine to use when putting a baby to bed at night.
2. **Identify** signs that a baby has a food allergy.
3. **List** three factors you should consider when choosing a clothing gift for a newborn.

### Practice Academic Skills

 **English Language Arts**

4. Many new parents do not recognize when a young baby is not getting the proper nutrition. Do research to learn the warning signs of malnutrition in a baby. Use the information you learn to create a poster titled Signs of Malnutrition in Babies.

 **Social Studies**

5. Research organizations in your community that help meet the nutritional needs and clothing needs of young children. Combine your findings with those of your classmates and create a directory to provide to parents of young children.

 **Check Your Answers** Check your answers at this book's Online Learning Center at **glencoe.com**.

> **NCTE 8** Use information resources to gather information and create and communicate knowledge.

> **NCSS I A** Analyze and explain the ways groups, societies, and cultures address human needs and concerns.

**N C L B**

---

## Section 7.2  After You Read

### Review Key Concepts

1. Answers may vary. An example is giving a warm bath, reading a story, and gently rocking the baby.
2. Signs of food allergy in a baby may include excessive fussiness, vomiting almost all food after a feeding, or eight or more watery stools a day.
3. any three of the following: whether the garment is comfortable, allows room for growth, is easy to put on and take off, or is durable

### Practice Academic Skills

4. Posters may vary depending on the specific type of malnutrition students focus on. General symptoms include fatigue, dizziness, weight loss, and decreased immune response.
5. Directories will vary depending on the organizations in your community that provide for the nutritional and clothing needs of young children. Students may list organizations such as the Salvation Army or Women, Infants, and Children (WIC).

## Reading Guide

### Before You Read

**Understanding** Write down any questions you have while reading. Many of them will be answered as you continue. If they are not, you will have a list ready for your teacher when you finish.

### Read to Learn
**Key Concepts**
- **Describe** how to bathe a baby.
- **Explain** why checkups and immunizations are important for babies.

**D**

### Main Idea
Keeping a baby healthy involves bathing, diapering, and taking care of baby's teeth. A baby needs regular checkups and scheduled immunizations.

### Content Vocabulary
 cradle cap       immunization
 diaper rash      vaccine
 teething

### Academic Vocabulary
You will find these words in your reading and on your tests. Use the glossary to look up their definitions if necessary.
- designate
- emerge

 **Graphic Organizer** Go to this book's Online Learning Center at **glencoe.com** to print out this graphic organizer.

### Graphic Organizer
As you read, note the steps for changing a baby's diaper. Use a chart like the one shown to record your information.

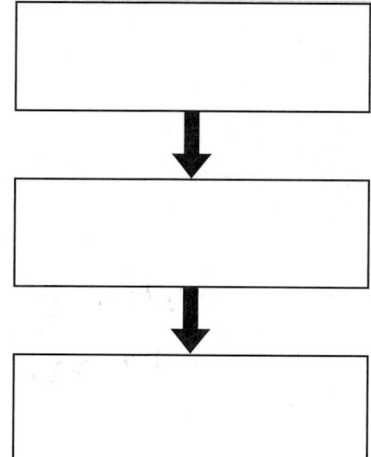

**N C L B**

### Academic Standards · · · · · · · · · · · · · · · · · · · · · · · · ·

 **English Language Arts**
**NCTE 4** Use written language to communicate effectively.

 **Social Studies**
**NCSS I A Culture** Analyze and explain the ways groups, societies, and cultures address human needs and concerns.

**NCTE** *National Council of Teachers of English*
**NCTM** *National Council of Teachers of Mathematics*

**NSES** *National Science Education Standards*
**NCSS** *National Council for the Social Studies*

---

## Focus

### Bell Ringer Activity

#### Keeping Baby Well
Have students read the Key Concepts under Read to Learn. Ask what they think this section is about. (Students should recognize that it is about keeping baby healthy and well.) Ask students what other ways they can think of to help keep baby well. (Answers will vary but may include providing proper food and clothing.)

## Preteaching

### Vocabulary
The terms *immunization* and *vaccine* are often confused. Point out to students that an immunization is a shot of a small amount of a dead or weakened disease-carrying germ. A vaccine is the actual disease-carrying germ that is injected. Immunization is the process, a vaccine is the substance injected.

### Graphic Organizer
The Graphic Organizer is also on the TeacherWorks CD.

(Graphic organizers should include: (1) Remove the diaper and clean the baby. (2) Put on a fresh diaper. (3) Dispose of used supplies.)

**N C L B** NCLB connects academic correlations to book content.

---

## Reading Guide

### Before You Read
Ask students: Why are regular checkups and immunizations important for babies? (Students may know that checkups and immunizations can help prevent sickness.) Tell students that in this section they will learn ways to help keep babies healthy and well.

### **D** Develop Concepts

**Main Idea** Discuss the main idea with the students. Ask: What do bathing, diapering, and taking care of baby's teeth have to do with keeping baby well? (Answers may include: these help keep baby clean and free from bacteria and germs that may cause illness.)

### Teach

### Discussion Starter

**Bonding** Ask students: If you were a caregiver, how do you think that bath time would help you bond with a baby? (Answers may include that bath time can help you bond as a caregiver because you are focusing all of your attention on the baby. In addition, the gentle touching and soothing warmth associated with a bath reinforce bonding. It is also a good time for a caregiver to talk and play with the baby.)

### **U** Universal Access

**Visual and Kinesthetic Learners**
Demonstrate how to give a baby a sponge bath. Explain why sponge baths are easier to manage than a tub bath. (They do not require as much preparation and the baby is not fully wet.) Explain why it is important to collect everything you need before you begin (because you cannot leave the baby unattended once he or she is in the tub), check the temperature of the room and the water, hold the baby firmly, and support the baby's neck (all of these are for the safety of the baby). After the demonstration, have students use a life-size doll to demonstrate bathing a baby. **ELL**

# Keeping Baby Clean

The first year of a baby's life can be very demanding for the parents. Beyond the everyday care of a baby, parents have to maintain their baby's overall wellness. Positive caregiving techniques include everything from bathing the baby to keeping the baby safe.

## Bathing a Baby

Regular baths help keep babies clean and healthy. There are two types of baby baths: a sponge bath and a tub bath. Newborns should have sponge baths until the navel heals. This is usually about two weeks after birth. After that, the baby can be given a tub bath. Many parents use a portable baby bathtub or a sink. It is best to wait until a baby can sit up on his own before using a full-size tub.

A sponge bath can be done any time a baby needs to be cleaned. Use a soft, clean sponge and warm water to gently clean the baby. Avoid the naval area. Your doctor may advise you to clean the naval using rubbing alcohol and a cotton swab. Immediately pat dry the baby and dress her to prevent chills.

Around age two to three months, babies should have baths two or three times a week. By age seven to eight months, when most babies can sit up steadily in the bath, they tend to really enjoy bath time. They love to splash and play in the water with floating toys and plastic cups. Through much of early childhood, the bathtub can be a favorite play place. Bath toys and a child's imagination merge for delightful play.

### How to Bathe a Baby

Bath time can be a lot of fun for babies. Some like to kick and splash in the water or play with bath toys. Caregivers often talk, sing, or play games with a baby. It is important to handle a slippery baby carefully. Follow these guidelines for safely bathing a baby.

- **Prepare for the baby's bath.** Gather everything needed for the baby's bath ahead of time. Set up the baby bathtub, towels, washcloths, shampoo, and other supplies. Put about two inches of warm water in the baby's bathtub. Test the temperature of the water with your arm. When the bath is ready, undress the baby.

- **Put the baby in the tub.** Support a very young baby's head and neck with one hand and arm. Hold the baby's body with the other hand. Lower the baby into the tub feet first. Many baby bathtubs will support the baby in a reclined position until they can sit up on their own. However, you must stay with the baby at all times.

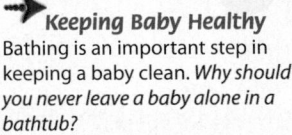

**Keeping Baby Healthy**
Bathing is an important step in keeping a baby clean. *Why should you never leave a baby alone in a bathtub?*

## ▶ Explore the Photo

**Caption Answer** A baby should never be left alone in a bathtub because it could very easily drown or fall off the counter where the tub is located.

**Discussion** Ask students at what age they think children are old enough to take a bath on their own. Why? (Responses will vary; they may say four or five years of age because children at that age can take fairly good care of themselves and know that it's dangerous to put their head under the water.)

- **Wash the baby's face.** Use clear water and a damp, soft washcloth to wash the baby's face. Then gently pat it dry.
- **Wash and rinse the baby's hair.** About twice a week, wash the baby's hair with baby shampoo. Wet the baby's hair. Add a bit of shampoo and rub gently. Rinse by pouring water toward the sides and back of the baby's head.
- **Wash the baby's body.** While supporting the baby's body, use your free hand to wash and rinse the baby.
- **Dry the baby's body.** To prevent chills, wrap the baby in a clean towel immediately. Pat the baby dry. Diaper and dress the baby right away.

Sometimes infants develop cradle cap. **Cradle cap** is a skin condition known for yellowish, crusty patches on the scalp. Most cases disappear after a few weeks or months. Parents can treat it by washing the baby's scalp daily with a mild shampoo. Other treatments, such as baby oil or excessive shampooing, can worsen the scales or dry the skin.

Bath time is also a good time to trim a baby's nails. If needed, use baby nail clippers or nail scissors to trim the nails. You might also want to use a baby file to help smooth the sharp edges. Baby nails are soft but sharp, and they can scratch the baby's face.

## Diapering a Baby

Diapers are the most essential part of a baby's wardrobe. A very young baby may need diaper changes 12 to 15 times each day. A newborn wets several times an hour but in small amounts that do not require changing each time. An older baby probably needs fewer diaper changes each day. The older baby might let you know when a clean diaper is needed. Many babies are uncomfortable in a wet or dirty diaper. They will cry when they need a clean diaper.

A common problem that occurs is diaper rash. **Diaper rash** is a condition that includes patches of rough, red, irritated skin in the diaper area. Sometimes painful raw spots develop. Controlling bacteria in diapers helps prevent this condition.

**Caring for Baby**
Changing diapers is a significant part of a caregiver's responsibility. *Why is changing diapers regularly important?*

## Teach cont.

### S Skill Practice
**Guided Practice**

**List** Divide students into small groups. Have each group create a list of supplies needed for diapering a baby. Once lists are complete, have the class compare their lists. What differences were there? Lead a class discussion about how necessary each of the listed items is. (Lists will vary. Note that some items on the list will depend on whether the group was using cloth or disposable diapers. Also, some students may feel that it is always necessary to use powder or cream, whereas others may feel these are only needed when diaper rash occurs.) **L1 ELL**

**Demonstrate** Use a doll to demonstrate how to diaper a baby with both cloth and disposable diapers. Explain the use of diaper wipes, medicated cream, and plastic refuse bags. If time allows, ask for student volunteers to repeat your demonstration. Have students discuss how diapering a baby would differ from diapering the doll. (Students may say the baby will wiggle and not necessarily be still while the diaper is being changed.) **L2 ELL**

**Compute** Ask students to visit stores to compare various types of diapers and their costs. Then ask students to compute the weekly cost of using disposable diapers, considering that young babies are changed 12 to 15 times a day. Also, have them research the weekly cost of a diaper service and the cost of cloth diapers and detergent. Finally, have students compare the costs using a bar graph. (Costs will vary depending on the area in which you live. Bar graphs should graphically show the comparison of costs to use disposable versus the costs to use cloth diapers.) **L3**

## Explore the Photo

**Caption Answer** Regularly changing diapers helps control bacteria that can cause diaper rash.

**Discussion** Read this scenario to students: When Darnell changes his baby's diaper, he notices the baby has diaper rash. How can Darnell cure the diaper rash? (Answers will vary, but students should say change the diaper frequently, thoroughly clean the baby, or use medicated cream.)

### Teach cont.

## Cooperative Learning

**Parenting Handbook** Divide the class into groups. Ask each group to develop a handbook for new mothers and fathers that focuses on infant routines: feeding, diapering, dressing, bathing, sleeping, crying, and playing. You may also want to assign each group a topic and make one handbook as a class. The handbooks can include drawings, photos, and clipart, as well as text that demonstrate students' comprehension of the text material. Some students may wish to write the handbook in another language as well as English. The finished products might be shared with a nearby child care center, as a parent resource. (Students' handbooks should be creative and organized, and include accurate information on infant routines such as feeding, diapering, dressing, bathing, sleeping, crying, and playing.)

## C Critical Thinking

**Compare and Contrast** Have students use the information provided in the text to construct a compare-and-contrast chart for disposable and cloth diapers. Charts should include the advantages and the disadvantages of each. (Charts may vary but should include: Disposable diapers: Advantages—more convenient, more effective at keeping baby dry, more comfortable, more sanitary; Disadvantages—can cause rash, add to environmental waste. Cloth diapers: Advantages—most economical if washed at home, more environmentally friendly; Disadvantages—cost more if provided and cleaned by a commercial diaper service.)

---

### SAFE CHILD HEALTHY CHILD

**Respiratory Syncytial Virus**

Respiratory syncytial virus (RSV) affects nearly all babies by the age of two. In adults and children, RSV usually causes mild, cold-like symptoms. In premature babies, it can develop into a serious respiratory illness. High-risk children who are infected with RSV often need to be hospitalized. Parents and other caregivers should follow these steps to help a baby stay free of RSV.

- Always wash hands with warm water and soap before touching the baby.
- Keep the baby away from anyone with a runny nose, cold, or fever.
- Avoid taking the baby to crowded areas.
- Keep the baby away from smoke.

**Be Prepared** All babies are at risk for RSV. Many are infected with it. When diagnosed, there are a number of treatments depending on the severity and risk level of the baby. Do research to find common treatments for RSV. Share your information in an oral presentation to your class.

---

Mild cases of diaper rash can be treated by changing the diaper more frequently and being sure to thoroughly clean the baby at each changing. More severe cases need treatment such as a medicated cream. Exposing the area to air and avoiding waterproof pants can also help the rash heal.

### Diaper Options

It is a personal choice whether to use disposable or cloth diapers. Some parents opt to use cloth at home but use disposable when they go out. Each has advantages and disadvantages. Parents will need to consider each option carefully before making the best decision for their child. Doctors and nurses can offer advice if needed when making these decisions. Here are a few things to consider in the decision.

---

- **Disposable Diapers** Many people feel that these are more convenient and more effective at keeping babies dry and comfortable than cloth diapers. Some babies develop a sensitivity to disposables, causing a rash. Infant care centers generally use disposable diapers for convenience and sanitation. Disposable diapers add significantly to environmental waste.
- **Cloth Diapers** These are the most economical choice if they are washed at home. However, they cost more than disposable diapers if they are provided and cleaned by a commercial diaper service. Cloth diapers are more environmentally friendly.

**C**

You should **designate**, or specify, a changing area. This makes it easy to keep diapers and other supplies close at hand. Any flat, clean surface may be used. A changing table is a good choice because it has sides to help keep the baby from rolling off. However, it is never safe to leave a child alone on a raised surface. Diapering supplies may include wet washcloths, disposable wipes, and dry cloths for cleanup.

For outings away from home, a diaper bag can hold diapers and supplies. It is also a good idea to include extra clothes and a plastic bag for diaper disposal.

### How to Change a Diaper

Diaper changes are an opportunity for positive interaction by talking and laughing with the baby while changing the baby's diaper. There are three basic steps to changing a diaper:

1. **Remove the diaper and clean the baby.** Thoroughly clean the diaper area with a damp washcloth or disposable wipe.

2. **Put on a fresh diaper.** Hold the baby's ankles and lift the body to slide the diaper underneath the baby. With disposable diapers, be sure the adhesive tabs are on the back side of the diaper. With cloth diapers, place the folded side in the back for girls and in the front for boys. Then, bring the diaper up between the baby's legs. Fasten a disposable diaper together with the adhesive tabs. Fasten a cloth diaper with diaper

---

### SAFE CHILD HEALTHY CHILD

**Respiratory Syncytial Virus**

**Identify** Ask students: Do you think it is possible to prevent a baby from contracting RSV? (Caregivers can do many things to help prevent RSV, but it may not be possible to prevent it completely.)

**Be Prepared** Presentations will vary but should state that treatment for RSV can include cough and cold medicines, humidifiers, respiratory therapy, and drinking lots of fluids.

pins or diaper tape. When using pins, keep a finger between the pin and the baby's skin. Parents may choose to add plastic or cloth diaper covers over cloth diapers.

3. **Dispose of used supplies.** Throw out all used wipes and disposable diapers, preferably in a trash container with a lid. Disposable diapers clog plumbing, so never flush one down a toilet. Dirty cloth diapers should be rinsed in a clean, flushing toilet and soaked in a covered container that is filled with water, detergent, and bleach. Later, they should be washed in hot water with mild detergent.

✓ **Reading Check** **Explain** What is cradle cap?

## Health Care

Parents and caregivers must be careful to help keep the baby healthy. Cleaning teeth is one part of baby's health care. Regular check-ups and immunizations and watching for illness are also important parts of maintaining a baby's health.

### Teeth

The development of a baby's teeth begins about the sixth week of pregnancy. However, a baby's teeth do not begin to break through the gums until about six months of age or later. The first set of teeth a baby gets are called primary teeth, or baby teeth. The complete set of primary teeth generally comes in by the time a child is twenty months old. The timetable for when each tooth will appear varies somewhat from child to child. Children can start teething as early as four months. Some children do not get the last primary teeth until they are almost three years old.

**Teething** is the process of the teeth pushing their way through the gums. The gums around the new teeth swell and become tender, so it can be a painful experience. During teething, a baby may become cranky, fuss during meals, drool a lot, develop a low-grade fever, and want to chew on something hard. Teething can cause different reactions in different children.

Massaging the gums and allowing the baby to chew on a cold, hard, unbreakable object, such as a refrigerated teething ring, can bring relief to some. Babies will often put anything they can grab into their mouths at this time to chew for relief. Also note that what soothes one child may not work for another child.

Most physicians do not recommend using medications to soothe the pain. Teething medication does not always bring much relief because it washes out of the mouth in minutes. Also, numbing medications can make it difficult for the baby to eat. If a baby develops a higher fever or cannot be comforted, parents should check with a doctor. You should never give an infant any medication without first asking the baby's doctor. This is true even for over-the-counter medications that are labelled for infants.

Once the baby's first teeth **emerge**, or appear, it is a good idea to begin cleaning them regularly. The best way is to wipe them with a soft, damp cloth or gently brush them with a soft baby's toothbrush. Some dentists recommend cleaning the gums even before the first teeth emerge.

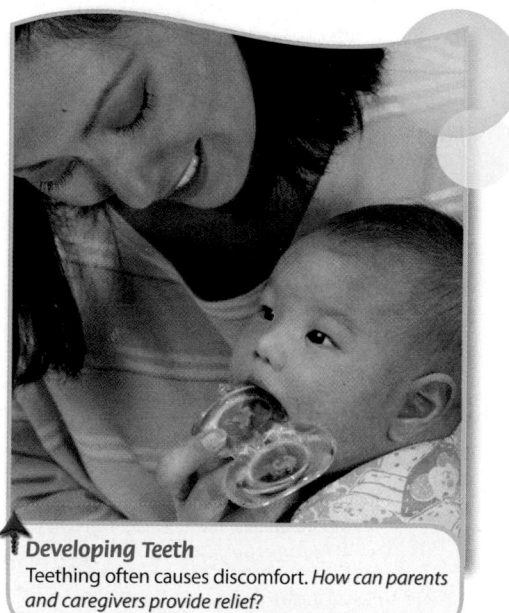

**Developing Teeth**
Teething often causes discomfort. *How can parents and caregivers provide relief?*

Section 7.3 Infant Health and Wellness **225**

### Assess

**Quiz**
Ask students to answer the following questions:

1. What are two types of baby baths? (sponge bath and tub bath)
2. Who needs fewer diaper changes—a newborn or an older baby? (An older baby needs fewer diaper changes.)
3. How can severe cases of diaper rash be treated? (It can be treated by using a medicated cream, exposing the area to air, and avoiding waterproof pants.)

### Reteach

**W** **Writing Support**
**Advertisements** Have students locate and read an article about infant teething. Articles may be found in magazines that focus on parenting. Students may also use the Internet to locate resources. Ask students to create an advertisement for a particular type of teething product based on the information they find in the articles. Ads should target a specific audience, draw attention to the information, and cause action. The ads should appeal to people's feelings, but be truthful. (Use the following questions to evaluate students' advertisements: Does the ad promote the product? Does it provide facts and opinions to persuade the audience? Does it appeal to people who may not be interested?)

### ▶ Explore the Photo

**Caption Answer** Relief may be provided by massaging the gums or allowing the baby to chew on a cold, hard, unbreakable object.

**Discussion** Ask the class: What are some signs that a baby is teething? (Answers should include: The baby may be cranky, fuss during meals, drool a lot, develop a low-grade fever, and want to chew on something hard.)

✓ **Reading Check**

**Explain** Cradle cap is a skin condition known for yellowish, crusty patches on the scalp.

### Reteach cont.

### C Critical Thinking

**Summarizing Information** Ask students to summarize the information about infant safety in a one-page summary, focusing on main ideas. Have students exchange summaries to see if they can shorten each other's summaries without losing any important information. (Students' summaries will vary but should include information on child safety in these areas: choking, suffocation, water, falls, poisoning, burns, sun, animals, and clothing.)

### U Universal Access

**Spatial Learners** Tell students that a doctor checkup is an important time for caregivers to ask questions about a baby's health and care. Emphasize that parents and caregivers should keep notes on questions to ask the doctor. They should also keep notes on the dates of any health conditions and the dates of important developments, such as when a baby rolls over, sits up, and crawls. Such information can help the doctor to understand the baby's overall health and development. Have students work in groups to design a booklet that provides parents a place to keep the information mentioned above. The booklet should allow space for listing questions and for taking notes. Students can also illustrate the booklet. (Booklets will vary but should provide space for parents to write questions for the doctor and to take notes when observing the baby or when listening to the doctor. Students should be creative in their designs.)

It is important for babies to get fluoride after six months of age to build healthy teeth. However, most babies do not need fluoride toothpaste. Usually babies get enough fluoride from their drinking water or water used in formula. If their local drinking water does not contain fluoride, a doctor can determine if a baby needs fluoride supplements.

## Infant Safety Concerns

Keeping children safe is one of a caregiver's greatest responsibilities. Caregivers can help prevent accidents before they happen by learning how to keep infants safe. The following are some safety guidelines for infants:

- **Choking** Keep floors clear of small objects such as buttons, coins, and safety pins. Do not feed infants solid food until the child's doctor says it is safe. Then be sure to follow the doctor's guidelines on what foods are safe to eat. Some foods are choking hazards for children until they are three years old.
- **Suffocation** Soft, flexible objects that can cover an infant's nose and mouth may cause suffocation. Keep all plastic bags away from infants. Do not put stuffed animals or loose blankets in a child's crib.
- **Water** Never leave a baby alone near or in water. This includes water in a bucket, bathtub, or wading pool. A baby can drown in as little as one to two inches of water.

> ### { Expert Advice... }
>
> *"Even healthy infants have days when they don't feel so good. Germs are all around us, and infections such as coughs and colds, stomach upsets and eye problems are not uncommon in young infants."*
>
> — Donald Schiff, MD, and Steven Shelov, MD, co-editors, *The American Academy of Pediatrics Guide to Your Child's Symptoms: The Official, Complete Home Reference, Birth Through Adolescence*

- **Falls** Do not leave a baby alone on *any* raised area, including an adult bed or a changing table.
- **Poisoning** Babies put everything into their mouths. Keep all medicines, household cleaners, paints, and other poisonous substances in locked storage areas.
- **Burns** Never leave children alone around hot liquids, ovens, or irons. Use safety covers on all electrical outlets. Keep the water heater set at no higher than 120°F (49°C).
- **Sun** Infants should wear sunglasses and hats with a brim when outdoors. Avoiding direct sun exposure and dressing babies in lightweight long pants and long-sleeved shirts are the best ways to protect them from sunburn. For infants older than six months of age, sunscreen should be used when adequate clothing and shade are not available.
- **Animals** Babies do not know how to act around animals, even pets. Never leave a child alone with any animal.
- **Clothing** It is very important that a baby's clothing be flame retardant. This is especially true for sleepwear. Check clothing labels for this information.

## Regular Checkups

An infant's first checkup usually occurs within a day of birth. A doctor does a thorough check of the newborn, including all parts of the body, the baby's reflexes, the fontanels, the heart rate and breathing, the skin color, the umbilical stump, the nostrils and mouth, and the eyes. The health care staff will also record the first measurement of the baby's weight, length, and head circumference. These measurements will be tracked over the next year. A blood sample will be drawn to test for a range of disorders and diseases. A follow-up visit often occurs two or three days after a baby is born.

Additional checkups are often scheduled at 1 month, 2 months, 4 months, 6 months, 9 months, and 12 months. During these exams, the doctor will continue to track the baby's growth and development, thoroughly examine and measure the baby, and respond to parents' questions and concerns.

**Mc Graw Hill Professional Development**

### Mini Clip
**Math: Small Group Work**

Students work in cooperative groups to graph an equation.

## The Importance of Immunizations

Some checkups include immunizations. An **immunization** is a shot of a small amount of a dead or weakened disease-carrying germ given so that the body may build resistance to the disease. The most common way to immunize against a disease is with a vaccine. A **vaccine** is the disease-carrying germ that usually is injected in the body.

Immunizations are one of the most important ways caregivers can protect children against certain diseases. After being immunized, the body produces antibodies to fight off the germs for that disease. If the person is later exposed to the disease, he or she already has antibodies that fight it and will be less likely to get the disease or will only get a mild form of it. Only in very rare cases does a child have a bad reaction to a vaccine.

State regulations and schools typically require that children have certain immunizations before being admitted to a school. Many child care centers also require babies and toddlers to have immunizations before they are allowed in the center.

It is up to parents and other caregivers to keep a record of their child's immunizations and to make sure that they receive immunizations on time. To find out what types of vaccines infants need and when they need them, refer to the recommended schedule of immunizations in Chapter 20.

### Watching for Illness

Babies cannot say when they do not feel well. Therefore, it is important to watch for signs of illness. Such signs may include irritability, lack of energy, constipation, nasal congestion, persistent coughing, diarrhea, rashes, vomiting, or fever. Parents and caregivers should never hesitate to call the doctor if a child shows any significant symptoms that are of concern.

Many illnesses do not require medication. In fact, many experts now feel that infants should be allowed to fight off some infections on their own so they can build stronger immune systems. The child's doctor can direct you on the best course of action for your child. For more information on illnesses, see Chapter 20.

---

## Section 7.3  After You Read

### Review Key Concepts

1. **Explain** how a sponge bath is different from a tub bath.
2. **Describe** what happens during a baby's regular checkup.

### Practice Academic Skills

 **English Language Arts**

3. Imagine that you are caring for a six-month-old baby. You have put her down for a nap but she begins to cry. What techniques could you use to get the baby to stop crying? Write a list of suggestions.

> **NCTE 4** Use written language to communicate effectively.

 **Social Studies**

4. Methods for diapering a baby differ from country to country. Choose a country in a different part of the world and research the baby diapering methods used. Write step-by-step directions and demonstrate the method for the class.

> **NCSS I A** Analyze and explain the ways groups, societies, and cultures address human needs and concerns.

 **Check Your Answers** Check your answers at this book's Online Learning Center at **glencoe.com**.

---

## Assess

### Study Tools

Have students go to the Online Learning Center at **glencoe.com**:

- Take the **Practice Test**.
- Download **Study-to-Go** content.

Use the **Student Activity Workbook** for additional practice.

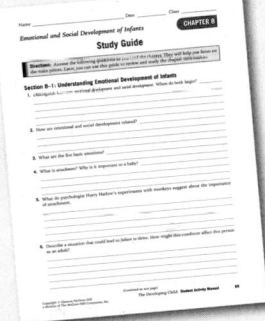

## Close

### Culminating Activity

**Review** Have students review the infant safety concerns listed on page 226. Ask them to picture their own homes and identify situations that may pose a hazard for infants. (Students' answers may include: no covers on electrical outlets, medicines are not locked up, and so on.)

 **NCLB** connects academic correlations to book content.

---

## Section 7.3  After You Read

**Review Key Concepts**

1. A wet sponge is applied to the baby's skin during a sponge bath. A baby sits in water during a tub bath.
2. Growth and development will be tracked, the baby will be thoroughly examined and measured, and the doctor will respond to parents' questions and concerns.

**Practice Academic Skills**

3. Lists will vary, but may include rocking, walking with the baby, using a stroller, distracting with toys, rubbing the baby's back, singing, or playing music.
4. Methods will vary depending on the country chosen. Students should describe the method step-by-step and demonstrate for the class.

## Focus

### Discussion Starter

**Pediatrician** Lead a discussion about the benefits of having a pediatrician rather than a general doctor to treat a young child. (Answers will vary but may include that pediatricians are specially trained in childhood illnesses, that they are more familiar with developmental milestones, and that they are more able to deal with children's temperaments.)

## Teach

### C Critical Thinking

**Application** After reading the feature, divide the class into groups. Have groups create lists of characteristics not mentioned in the feature that pediatricians might need to be able to do their job well. After groups have compiled their lists, create a class list. (Lists will vary, but may include such responses as: sensitivity, friendliness, excellent understanding of health concerns for children, and the ability to make children and their parents comfortable.)

## Assess

### Make Connections

Ask students to list specific correlations between academic subjects and the kinds of skills a pediatrician needs. (Answers will vary but might include that pediatricians must communicate well to ask questions to gain information to help diagnose an illness.)

**NCLB** This relates academic skills to specific tasks that are performed for this job.

**P**ediatricians are doctors who specialize in treating children. Pediatricians work in offices, clinics, hospitals, and pharmaceutical companies. Some specialize in caring for children who have diseases such as cancer or diabetes.

### ☀ What Does a Pediatrician Do?

Pediatricians keep track of children's growth and development. They also vaccinate children against disease. They diagnose and treat injured or sick children. In addition, they show parents how to care for sick children. Many children are afraid of doctors, so pediatricians must be patient and kind.

### ☀ Where Do Pediatricians Work?

Most pediatricians see patients in their offices. Some pediatricians work in a group office or hospital. Others have a private practice. They also visit patients in the hospital. The hours can be long, and some pediatricians remain on duty when they are at home. This means they can be called into the office for emergencies.

### Preparation and Skills

**Education and Training**

Pediatricians earn bachelor's and medical degrees. This is followed by three years of training in pediatric medicine. Pediatricians must pass a state exam to earn their medical license.

**Aptitudes, Abilities, and Skills**

Pediatricians must have strong communication skills and compassion to talk to both sick children and their families. They need keen observation abilities to analyze a child's illness, even though children often cannot explain what is wrong. Respect for patients' privacy is also a must.

**Academic Skills**

English language arts skills are used to talk to parents and medical associates. Pediatricians also need science and math skills to learn and understand anatomy and medical procedures.

**C**

**NCLB**

### Explore Careers

Work with your teacher to set up a time when you can talk with or observe a pediatrician or pediatric nurse. Prepare questions in advance and take notes as you talk. Share the information in an oral report to your class.

 **Careers Online** For more information on careers, visit the Occupational Outlook Handbook Web site through the link on this book's Online Learning Center at **glencoe.com**.

## Close

### Culminating Activity

**Hiring a Pediatrician** Tell students to imagine they are a pediatrician who is applying for a job at a children's hospital. They have graduated from medical school and completed their internship. Have the students write a résumé. (The résumé should reflect an understanding of aptitudes, abilities, and skills needed by pediatricians and should be correctly formatted and phrased.)

### Explore Careers

Reports will vary depending on the interview questions asked and answers received. Reports should be delivered using good grammar and should indicate a good understanding of the profession explored.

## Chapter Summary

Heredity, nutrition, health, and environment all play a role in a baby's growth and development. Babies grow rapidly in the first year. Babies must be handled carefully and must never be shaken. Feeding babies breast milk or formula meets the nutrition needs for the first six months. Other foods should be introduced gradually. A baby's clothing should be comfortable and easy to put on and take off. Babies should be bathed regularly but never be left alone in the bathtub. Parents should follow a recommended schedule of checkups and immunizations.

## Vocabulary Review

1. Create a fill-in-the-blank sentence for each vocabulary term. The sentence should contain enough information to help determine the missing term.

### Content Vocabulary

◇ developmental milestone (p. 195)
◇ stimulating environment (p. 197)
◇ growth chart (p. 198)
◇ proportion (p. 200)
◇ depth perception (p. 201)
◇ reflex (p. 206)
◇ gross motor skill (p. 206)
◇ fine motor skill (p. 206)

◇ hand-eye coordination (p. 207)
◇ shaken baby syndrome (p. 211)
◇ antibody (p. 213)
◇ weaning (p. 217)
◇ malnutrition (p. 218)
◇ cradle cap (p. 223)
◇ diaper rash (p. 223)
◇ teething (p. 225)

◇ immunization (p. 227)
◇ vaccine (p. 227)

### Academic Vocabulary

■ makeup (p. 195)
■ accommodate (p. 200)
■ aggravate (p. 212)
■ curb (p. 213)
■ designate (p. 224)
■ emerge (p. 225)

## Review Key Concepts

2. **Identify** the four major influences on an infant's growth and development.
3. **Summarize** how a baby typically grows in the first year.
4. **Explain** how to safely hold a baby.
5. **Identify** how to meet a baby's nutritional needs.
6. **Describe** the best type of clothing suitable for a baby.
7. **Describe** how to bathe a baby.
8. **Explain** why checkups and immunizations are important for babies.

## Critical Thinking

9. **Compare and Contrast** the role heredity and nutrition play in an infant's growth and development.
10. **Examine** why it is or is not acceptable for an eight-month-old to drink the same milk as the rest of the family.

Chapter 7   Physical Development of Infants   **229**

## Content and Academic Vocabulary Review

1. Students should write fill-in-the-blank sentences that have context clues for the missing terms.

## Review Key Concepts

2. heredity, nutrition, health, and environment

3. Babies typically triple their birth weight, increase their length by about 50 percent, and more than half the total growth of the head occurs.

4. Hold the baby upright, cradled in the curve of your arm, or against your chest with your hand supporting his neck and head.

5. Until six months, a baby's nutritional needs can be met through breast milk or formula. At about six months, parents can introduce solid foods. By one year, most nutrition should come from solid foods.

6. Baby's clothing should be comfortable and stretchy so the baby can move easily.

7. Support a very young baby's head and neck with one hand and arm. Hold the baby's body with the other hand. Lower the baby into the tub feet first. Stay with the baby at all times. Wash and dry the baby.

8. Checkups are important because the doctor tracks the baby's growth and development, thoroughly examines the baby, and responds to parents' questions and concerns. Immunizations help protect against certain diseases.

## Critical Thinking

9. Answers will vary but should include that heredity plays a role in when the first teeth emerge and whether certain diseases are likely to develop. Nutrition affects factors such as bone strength, brain development, and height.

10. It is not acceptable, because it is difficult for a baby to digest cow's milk. Cow's milk also lacks nutrients important for infants.

### Family & Community Connections

**11.** Answers will vary. Reports should show a comparison of the techniques used by the parent or caregiver interviewed with techniques described in this text. Techniques described in this text can be found on pages 222–224.

### Health Skills

**12.** Answers will vary depending on your state's rules for licensed childcare facilities.

### Observation Skills

**13.** Answers will vary depending on the age of the child observed. See Chapter 1 to review observation records. Students' presentations should reflect their observations and answer the questions posed under Procedure.

### Real-World Skills

**14.** Answers will vary. Each group should create a list of tips for dressing and undressing an infant.

**15.** Students' time lines should reflect the information presented in Figure 7.2 on pages 204–205.

**16.** They can save $30. (200 × $0.23 = $46; 200 × $0.08 = $16; $46 − $16 = $30)

### Family & Community Connection

**11. Interview Caregivers** Work with your teacher to set up an interview with a parent or caregiver. Ask the caregiver about the techniques he or she uses to bathe and diaper an infant. Take good notes during the interview. Using your notes, write a report in which you compare and contrast the techniques described in the interview with the techniques described in this text. End your report with a brief summary of any differences noted. Why do you think the caregiver used a different technique?

### Health Skills

**12. Research State Rules** Contact a local licensed childcare facility and ask for an answer to this question: What are the state rules for appropriate sanitation and hygiene for infants, toddlers, children, and staff at a licensed childcare facility? If necessary, conduct additional research to adequately answer the question. Write a brief essay to report your findings.

### Observation Skills

**13. Observe a Baby** Work with your teacher to arrange to observe a baby in a home or childcare center. The baby should be under the age of 12 months. Children this age are developing more physical abilities and independence.

**Procedure** Be sure to note the age of the baby and if there are other children present. As you observe, note how interested the baby is in moving around independently. What signs of such interest do you see?

**Analysis** Complete an observation record to formally record the baby's actions. You can use an anecdotal record or a running record. Share your findings in an oral report to your class. Be sure not to reveal personal information such as the child's name in your report.

> **NCTE 7** Conduct research and gather, evaluate, and synthesize data to communicate discoveries.

### Real-World Skills

| | |
|---|---|
| **Interpersonal and Collaborative Skills** | **14. Work in Teams** Follow your teacher's instructions to form into groups. Work with your group to practice dressing and undressing baby-sized dolls. As team members take turns, offer comments about their techniques. Be sure your comments are constructive and not critical. Then, as a group, create a list of tips for dressing and undressing an infant. |
| **Technology Skills** | **15. Create a Time Line** Use graphics software to create a time line that shows the physical developmental milestones for a baby's first year. Refer to Figure 7.2 for information to include on your time line. |
| **Financial Literacy** | **16. Determine Baby Food Costs** Your friends have been paying $0.23 per ounce for baby food. They can make their own baby food with the same nutritional value for about $0.08 per ounce. How much will they save on 200 ounces of baby food by making their own? |

 **Additional Activities** For additional activities, go to this book's Online Learning Center at **glencoe.com**.

### Academic Skills

**17.** Essays will vary. Students may say pat-a-cake, clapping hands to music, encouraging a baby to reach out and grab by placing toys and food within reach, and physical play are all good for helping babies develop motor skills.

**18.** The baby can roll two times before reaching the side. [(6 ÷ 2) ÷ 1.5 = 3 ÷ 1.5 = 2]

The *Early Childhood Observations CD* offers additional lessons with videos to build students' observation skills.

**Part 1:** Learning to Observe
**Part 2:** How Children Develop
**Part 3:** Working With Young Children
**Part 4:** Extended Observations
**Part 5:** Resources and Answer File

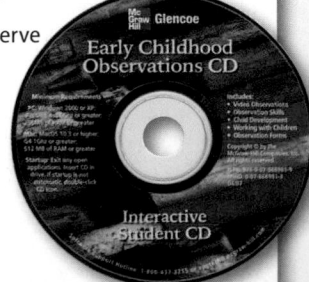

## Academic Skills

 **English Language Arts**

**17. Use Your Knowledge** Research has found that infants who are confined to carriers, strollers, and playpens for extended periods of time will roll over, crawl, and walk later than other children. Write a one-page essay to describe interactive activities that can help children develop gross motor skills.

> **NCTE 4** Use written language to communicate effectively.

 **Mathematics**

**18. Rolling Distance** An infant four to six months of age can roll over. The amount of distance an infant can cover in one turn is 1½ feet. If an infant is placed in the middle of a play yard that is 6 feet wide, how many rolls can the baby make before reaching the side?

**Math Concept** **Dividing with Fractions** To divide a whole number by a fraction, first convert the fraction to a decimal.

**Starting Hint** Since the baby is in the middle of the play yard, divide 6 by 2. to find out how many total feet are between the baby and the side. Then divide your answer by the amount of feet covered in each roll (1½).

**Math** For math help, go to the Math Appendix at the back of the book.

> **NCTM Number and Operations** Understand numbers, ways of representing numbers, relationships among numbers, and number systems.

 **Science**

**19. Motor Skills Development** Research has found that an iron deficiency in infants leads to lower mental functioning and delays in motor skills development. In addition, infants need more iron as their growth accelerates during the second half of the first year.

**Procedure** Use print or online resources to identify good sources of iron for infants. Remember that the sources will probably change as an infant gets older and is able to eat more foods. Explain why this information is important for parents and other caregivers.

**Analysis** Create a brochure for parents and caregivers that states the reasons children need iron as well as good sources of iron for infants.

> **NSES F** Develop understanding of personal and community health.

 **NCLB**

### Standardized Test Practice

**OPEN-ENDED RESPONSE**
Read the passage and follow the directions.

**20.** Cara is caring for her 15-month-old nephew, Jamie. Jamie is asleep and Cara is on the phone with her best friend. Jamie wakes up and begins to cry. He cries for several minutes while Cara continues to talk with her friend. Write a paragraph that describes what Cara should do.

> **Test-Taking Tip** Open-ended test questions are often looking for a specific response rather than an opinion. These may include definitions, comparisons, or examples.

**19.** Brochures will vary but should include the dangers of iron deficiency in infants. Good sources of iron include breast-milk and iron-enriched formula, iron-enriched cereals, greens including spinach, sweet potatoes, minced meat, and poultry.

 **NCLB** connects academic correlations to book content.

### Standardized Test Practice

**20.** Answers will vary but may include that Cara should hang up the phone immediately and check Jamie for a wet diaper, hunger, or other problems. She should change him or feed him, if necessary. She should try to calm him by reading to him, singing to him, or playing with him.

**Test-Taking Tips**
The best practice for short-answer test questions is frequent writing assignments with an emphasis on clarity, concision, and correct grammar and spelling.

**Pre-Test Study** Remind students that when studying from a textbook, they should begin by re-reading section and chapter introductions and summaries, graphics, and photographs with the purpose of identifying main ideas. Then they should read any end-of-chapter study questions and skim the text to find specific details to answer the questions.

 ## TECHNOLOGY Solutions

### Use these technology solutions to streamline chapter assessment!

 **ExamView Assessment Suite** CD allows you to create and print out customized tests or ready-made unit and chapter tests, complete with answer keys.

 **TeacherWorks Plus** is an electronic lesson planner that provides instant access to complete teacher resources in one convenient package.

**Online Learning Center** includes resources and activities for students and teachers.

**STANDARDS BASED LESSON PLANNING** *The Developing Child* provides students with instruction and assessment in the following fundamental content areas:

## National Standards Correlations

| Standards | Pages |
|---|---|
| **12.1.1** Analyze physical, emotional, social, spiritual, and intellectual development. | 235–243, 245–250 |
| **12.1.2** Analyze interrelationships among physical, emotional, social, and intellectual aspects of human growth and development. | 245 |
| **12.1.3** Analyze current and emerging research about human growth and development, including research on brain development. | 239 |
| **12.2.1** Analyze the effect of heredity and environment on human growth and development. | 240–243 |
| **12.2.3** Analyze the effects of gender, ethnicity, and culture on individual development. | 240 |
| **12.3.1** Analyze the role of nurturance on human growth and development. | 239–240 |
| **15.1.1** Analyze parenting roles across the life span. | 235, 238, 239–240 |
| **15.1.2** Analyze expectations and responsibilities of parenting. | 239–240, 247, 250 |
| **15.1.3** Analyze consequences of parenting practices to the individual, family, and society. | 240, 243, 245 |
| **15.1.5** Explain cultural differences in roles and responsibilities of parenting. | 240 |
| **15.2.1** Choose nurturing practices that support human growth and development. | 236, 238, 239–240, 248 |
| **15.2.3** Assess common practices and emerging research about discipline on human growth and development. | 239 |

**NO CHILD LEFT BEHIND** NCLB activities, information, and skills practice will help your students attain NCLB proficiency. Students will improve their abilities in the following academic standards areas:

## Academic Standards Correlations

| Discipline | Standard | Feature/Activity |
|---|---|---|
| **English Language Arts** | **NCTE 1** read texts to acquire new information. | **Reading Guide (pp. 234, 244)** |
| | **NCTE 4** Use written language to communicate effectively. | **Writing Activity (p. 232)** **After You Read (pp. 243, 250)** **Academic Skills (p. 253)** |
| **Mathematics** | **NCTM Number and Operations** Understand numbers, ways of representing numbers, relationships among numbers, and number systems. | **Academic Skills (p. 253)** |
| **Science** | **NSES 1** Develop an understanding of science unifying concepts and processes: evidence, models, and explanations. | **Academic Skills (p. 253)** |
| | **NSES A** Develop abilities necessary to do scientific inquiry, understandings about scientific inquiry. | **Observation Skills (p. 252)** |
| **Social Studies** | **NCSS I C Culture** Apply an understanding of culture as an integrated whole that explains the functions and interactions of behavior patterns. | **Culture Matters (p. 240)** |
| | **NCSS IV C Individual Development and Identity** Describe the ways family and other group and cultural influences contribute to the development of a sense of self. | **After You Read (p. 243)** |

## McGraw Hill Professional Development

**MINI CLIP VIDEO LIBRARY**

Targeted professional development is correlated throughout *The Developing Child*. **The McGraw-Hill Professional Development Mini Clip Video Library** provides teaching strategies to strengthen academic and learning skills. Log on to **glencoe.com**.

In this chapter, you will find these Mini Clips:
- **Reading**  Strategic Readers, p. 234
- **Reading**  Interacting with Text, p. 237
- **ELL**  Differentiated Instruction, p. 242
- **Reading**  Flexible Groupings, p. 244
- **Reading**  Standards-Based Instruction, p. 253

## Reading and Writing Strategies

**Writing Activity: Freewriting** (p. 232)
Students use writing tips to describe their ideas of a positive, healthy relationship.

**Before You Read** (pp. 234, 244)
A pre-reading question or statement will help students make a personal connection to content.

**Graphic Organizer** (pp. 234, 244)
A visual tool will help students organize and remember new content.

**Reading Check** (pp. 238, 240, 241, 247)
A question allows students to make a quick comprehension self-check.

**After You Read** (pp. 243, 250)
Organize and process students' understanding of what they have read.

## Chapter Features

**Helping a Baby Develop a Sense of Trust** (p. 238)
Babies develop trust by bonding with caregivers who strive to meet the babies' needs.

**Touch Builds the Brain** (p. 239)
Loving touch helps the brain grow and causes babies to trust human contact.

**Holding a Baby Close** (p. 240)
In many cultures, babies are carried close to the body to provide a sense of security.

**From Solo to Social** (p. 248)
Parallel play helps young children develop social skills.

**Exploring Through Taste** (p. 249)
Babies use their mouths to explore taste and texture.

## Chapter Overview

### Introduce the Chapter

In this chapter, students learn how infants develop both emotionally and socially. They learn about the emotional and social behaviors that infants exhibit at different ages, and about the requirements for healthy emotional and social growth.

### Build Background

Discuss with students that as infants develop, they become able to express different emotions. Divide students into groups of three or four. Instruct each group to create a list of the different ways in which they have seen infants displaying emotion. Then ask for volunteers from each group to share their lists with the class.

### Writing Activity
#### Freewriting

This active learning activity prompts students to engage in freewriting to describe their ideas of a positive, healthy relationship. After students have completed the writing activity, ask for volunteers to share their freewritings with the class. Ask students to point out any similarities among the descriptions. Then ask them to point out any differences. Encourage the class to discuss which ideas they consider the most important and why. (The students' writing should be spontaneous and need not be in any particular order or contain an introduction or conclusion. The student should have focused on the ideas he or she wanted to express, rather than the structure of the writing.)

---

**Chapter**

**8**

# Emotional and Social Development of Infants

## Chapter Objectives

After completing this chapter, you will be able to:

- **List** six basic emotions that babies experience.
- **Explain** the role of attachment in a baby's emotional development.
- **Describe** how temperament affects a baby's social development.
- **Explain** how the emotional climate of the home can affect a baby's development.
- **Explain** how a baby learns social behavior.
- **Identify** how play and exploration help a baby develop socially.

### Writing Activity
#### Freewriting

**Building Relationships** From the first moment she is born, a baby begins to develop relationships with her parents or caregivers. Use freewriting to describe your idea of a positive, healthy relationship.

**Writing Tips** To jumpstart your writing, it can be helpful to write out ideas freely. This is called freewriting. Use these tips to start freewriting:

1. Write everything that comes to mind, in any order.
2. Do not worry about having an introduction or conclusion. You can go back and revise later.
3. Focus on ideas. Correct your grammar and spelling after you are done writing.

---

## CLASSROOM Solutions

### Print Resources

 **Student Edition**

 **Teacher Wraparound Edition**

 **Student Activity Workbook**

 **Student Activity Workbook Teacher Annotated Edition**

### Technology Resources

 **Online Learning Center** has resources and activities for students and teachers. Includes an Online Student Edition.

 **Interactive Student Edition** allows students to instantly access review materials, examples, and exercises.

Section **8.1** Understanding Emotional Development of Infants

Section **8.2** Understanding Social Development of Infants

**Review the Sections**
Introduce the chapter by reviewing the sections:

**Section 8.1**
Emotional development is the process of learning to recognize and express feelings and to establish a personal identity. Caregivers can help shape babies' emotional development by providing consistent, responsive, and loving care. Babies' unique temperaments and the emotional climate of the home also influence their emotional development.

**Section 8.2**
Social development is the process of learning how to interact and express oneself with others. Babies learn social behavior by watching and interacting with others. One normal sign of social development is stranger anxiety. Babies learn about the world by playing and exploring.

▲ *Explore the Photo*
This baby's healthy bond with his caregiver can help him form healthy relationships later in life. *Why do you think a baby's early experiences can affect his self-esteem later in life?*

**233**

► **Explore the Photo**

**Caption Answer** If babies have positive experiences with people who treat them kindly, they are more likely to think well of themselves.

**Discussion** Ask students to discuss what kinds of feelings they think this baby might have toward his caregiver. What kinds of feelings do the students think the caregiver has toward the baby? On what do they base their opinions? (Answers will vary. Students may say that the baby and caregiver like each other and that the baby trusts the caregiver.)

 **TeacherWorks Plus** is an electronic lesson planner that provides instant access to complete teacher resources in one convenient package.

**Presentation Plus!** provides visual teaching aids for every section.

 **The Early Childhood Observations CD** presents video observations and lessons on observation skills and child development.

**The Developing Brain eTransparencies and Guide** include information and activities to offer insights into brain development and diseases of the brain.

# Focus

## Bell Ringer Activity

### Respond to the World

Instruct students to individually write down a definition for the word *emotion*. Ask for volunteers to share their definitions. Then ask volunteers to list emotions they have felt today, along with circumstances that led to this feeling. Lead into a discussion that emotions are responses to the world around us.

## Preteaching

### Vocabulary

Students should be able to use context clues to determine the meaning of vocabulary terms. Write sentences on the board using each of the vocabulary terms. Ask your students to guess what the terms mean based on the sentence.

**Professional Development**

### Mini Clip
Reading: Strategic Readers

Author Scott Paris discusses the characteristics of strategic readers.

### Graphic Organizer

The Graphic Organizer is also on the TeacherWorks CD.

(Graphic organizers should list: return a baby's smile, offer consistent care, rock a frightened baby, and respond to crying.)

**NCLB** connects academic correlations to book content.

---

## Reading Guide

### Before You Read

**Preview** Look at each photo in this section and read the photo captions. Write one or two sentences explaining what you think the section will be about.

### Read to Learn
**Key Concepts**
- **List** six basic emotions that babies experience.
- **Explain** the role of attachment in a baby's emotional development.
- **Describe** how temperament affects a baby's social development.
- **Explain** how the emotional climate of the home can affect a baby's development.

**D**

### Main Idea
Caregivers play a large role in babies' emotional development, helping them learn to express feelings and develop a personal identity.

### Content Vocabulary
◇ emotional development
◇ emotion
◇ colic
◇ reflux
◇ attachment
◇ failure to thrive
◇ temperament

### Academic Vocabulary
You will find these words in your reading and on your tests. Use the glossary to look up their definitions if necessary.
■ crucial
■ hinder

### Graphic Organizer
As you read, list things a caregiver can do to promote a baby's healthy emotional development. Use a chart like the one shown to help organize your information.

| Healthy Emotional Development |
|---|
| 1. |
| 2. |
| 3. |
| 4. |

 **Graphic Organizer** Go to this book's Online Learning Center at **glencoe.com** to print out this graphic organizer.

**N C L B**

### Academic Standards ·····························

 **English Language Arts**

**NCTE 4** Use written language to communicate effectively.

**Social Studies**

**NCSS I C Culture** Apply an understanding of culture as an integrated whole that explains the functions and interactions of behavior patterns.

**NCSS IV C Individual Development and Identity** Describe influences that contribute to the development of a sense of self.

**NCTE** *National Council of Teachers of English*
**NCTM** *National Council of Teachers of Mathematics*

**NSES** *National Science Education Standards*
**NCSS** *National Council for the Social Studies*

---

## Reading Guide

### Before You Read

Ask students: Have you ever tried to calm a fussy baby? Ask for volunteers to describe what they did and how the baby responded. Explain that in this section, they will learn about the emotional development of babies and how our behavior affects babies' responses.

### D Develop Concepts

**Main Idea** Discuss the main idea with the students. Ask students why they think caregivers are vital to a baby's social development. (Babies learn by watching other people's reactions to different situations. Caregivers have an enormous influence because of the large amount of time they spend with the baby.)

## Emotions and Emotional Development

Emotional and social development begin at birth and continue throughout life. They are as important as physical development to becoming a healthy and happy adult.

**Emotional development** is the process of learning to recognize and express feelings and to establish a personal identity. A personal identity is a sense of being a unique individual. A child who experiences healthy emotional development will be self-confident. He or she will be able to handle stress and will have empathy for others.

The most important influences on a child's emotional development are the bond between the caregiver and the child, the temperament of the child, and the atmosphere of the home.

### Emotions in Infancy

We are all born with the ability to experience emotions. An **emotion** is a feeling response to the world around us. Even newborns can feel basic emotions such as contentment and distress. Emotions grow more complex with age. **Figure 8.1** on page 236 shows the development of some basic emotions during a child's first year.

### Learning Emotions Through Interaction

Parents and caregivers play a large role in shaping a baby's emotions. Parents can encourage positive emotions. Parents can also help infants cope with negative emotions. Returning a baby's smile, for example, encourages his joyful expression. Rocking a frightened baby teaches her to become calm again after a scary experience.

Babies also learn from their caregivers how to react to situations. A baby whose caregiver is often joyful may learn to approach life with happiness and interest. A baby whose caregiver is often anxious may learn to approach life with fear.

### Emotions and Crying

Infants do not have words, so they show many of their needs and emotions through crying. At around two months of age, babies start to vary their cries to express different feelings.

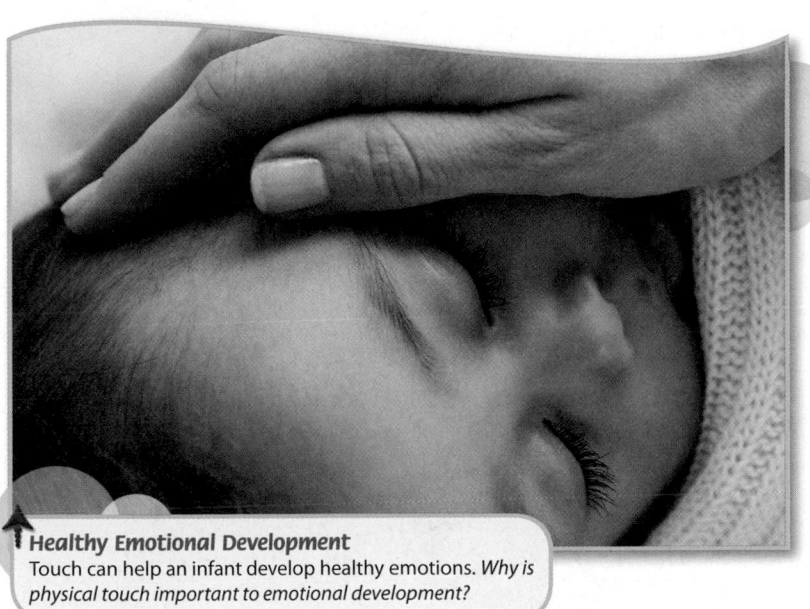

**Healthy Emotional Development**
Touch can help an infant develop healthy emotions. *Why is physical touch important to emotional development?*

Section 8.1   Understanding Emotional Development of Infants   **235**

## Teach

### Discussion Starter

**A Sense of Self** Ask students: What do you think the term *self-confident* means? What are some of the characteristics of a self-confident person? What experiences do you think help babies develop self confidence? (Answers may include that self-confident people see themselves as unique, show empathy toward others, and are better able to handle stressful situations. Babies become self-confident when their caregivers are basically joyful and respond to their needs.)

### R Reading Strategy

**Inferring** Ask students: What does the word *infer* mean? (To derive a conclusion based on other facts or events.) Read aloud the last two sentences in the second paragraph under Emotions and Emotional Development. Ask students what they can infer about children who do not experience healthy emotional development. (They probably will not be self-confident and will have problems handling stress and having empathy for others.) **ELL**

### U Universal Access

**English Language Learners** Organize the class into small groups. Distribute English language learners equally among the groups. Have groups create a list of emotions a baby might express. Then have them create a table and write each of the emotions at the top of one column. Under each emotion, they should place as many synonyms for that word as they are able. If necessary, explain that a synonym is a word that has the same or similar meaning as another word. For example, synonyms for sad might include unhappy, gloomy, and cheerless. **ELL**

---

### Explore the Photo

**Caption Answer** Infants respond strongly to physical touch because they are not capable of meaningful communication through words. Touch becomes an important way in which caregivers can show concern for the infant.

**Discussion** Babies in orphanages, particularly in poorer countries, may experience little human touch. Ask students: What kinds of emotional problems might these babies develop? Do you think these problems can be overcome at a later age? Why or why not? (Responses will vary; they may not be able to trust others and may lack self-confidence. Students should offer reasons for why they believe the problems can or cannot be overcome.)

**Teach** *cont.*

## U Universal Access

**Logical Learners** Discuss with the class some of the basic flow-charting symbols, such as an oval to represent a beginning or ending, and a diamond shape to represent a decision process. Then instruct students to create a flowchart to aid caregivers in determining why a child is crying. For example, the caregiver might first determine if the child needs a diaper change, and then proceed to determine if the child is hungry. If students need more help on creating flowcharts, have them conduct research on the Internet. (Students' flowcharts should show actions caregivers can take to comfort a crying child, in an appropriate order.)

## C Critical Thinking

**Analyze** Explain to the class that mimicking can be helpful in dealing with an upset infant. Researchers have found that if a parent first mimics a child's unhappy expression, then lightens the mood by using a positive voice and smiling at the infant, the child is likely to smile back to. Ask students why they think this might be. (Student answers will vary. Because the parent has shown an understanding of the infant's feelings, the infant may be more willing to respond to the parent's smiles and positive behavior.)

## W Writing Support

**Freewriting**

**Caregivers and Emotional Growth** Have students spend a minute using freewriting to describe ways that a caregiver can respond to an infant that encourage positive emotional growth. (Refer to p. 232 to review the characteristics of freewriting. Students' writing will vary, but should focus on how caregivers' responses can encourage positive emotional growth.)

---

Parents may eventually learn what each cry means. This adds to the baby's comfort and encourages the expression of emotions. It also strengthens the parent-child bond.

Some babies rarely cry and are easy to comfort when they do. Often these babies are labeled as "easy" or "good" babies. Other babies may cry loudly and often. It can be difficult to comfort them.

A baby who is crying needs attention and care. How should you comfort him? First, check for a physical problem. Is the baby hungry? Does he need a diaper change? Is he cold or hot? Did he burp at the last feeding? If none of these is the cause and the baby does not seem ill, he probably needs something else. Perhaps he needs company or cuddling. These are real needs, too. Sometimes, babies just need help to go to sleep.

Getting to know the baby helps you to discover which comforting measures work best. Here are a few time-tested techniques.

- **Cuddle** Cuddle up with the baby in a rocking chair or hold the baby close while walking around. The combination of being held and rocked is soothing.
- **Move the Baby** Move the baby to a new position. The baby may be too young to roll over on her own. Try placing her in an infant seat so she can see what is happening.
- **Sing** Talk softly or sing to the baby. The tone and rhythm of your voice may comfort him.
- **Offer a Toy** Offer a toy to interest the baby. She may be bored and want something to do.
- **Massage** Stroke or gently rub the baby's back. You can also try rubbing baby lotion on his back and legs.

**Figure 8.1 Development of Basic Emotions**

By nine months of age, babies experience and show many basic emotions. *How would you judge whether a baby was angry or sad?*

Parents and caregivers play a large role in shaping babies' emotions. Basic emotions lead to more complex emotions—such as pride, shame, and embarrassment—later in life.

**Sadness** Very young babies express discomfort or unhappiness by crying.

**Interest** Babies watch their mothers very closely. Often, this is the first sign of interest in babies.

**236** Chapter 8 Emotional and Social Development of Infants

---

**Figure 8.1 Development of Basic Emotions**

**Caption Answer** Student answers will vary; angry babies typically have more intense facial expressions than sad babies.

**Discussion** Divide students into pairs. Instruct each pair to examine the photos in Figure 8.1 and discuss together how they think the baby is feeling. For each photo, the pair should write a caption explaining what happened immediately before the photo was taken. Remind students to keep in mind each baby's age. Encourage them to be creative when writing their captions. Ask for volunteers to share their captions with the class.

## Self-Comforting

Babies also find ways to comfort themselves. Many babies soothe themselves with a favorite blanket or stuffed toy. Babies may develop a special attachment to the object and use it for comfort when they are sleepy or anxious. Other babies comfort themselves by twisting their hair or by rocking themselves back and forth. Children usually give up these habits when they are ready.

### Thumb Sucking

The most common self-comforting technique is sucking. A baby will suck on a thumb, a fist, or a pacifier. Sucking is a basic urge in infants. Many babies stop sucking their thumbs on their own at six or seven months of age, when their first teeth appear. Parents should only be concerned about thumb sucking if it starts to change the shape of a child's teeth or mouth. A pediatrician can check to see whether thumb sucking is causing physical problems.

### Pacifiers

Many infants find comfort in sucking on a pacifier. A pacifier can help a baby calm down and fall asleep. Some people fear that pacifiers can cause physical or emotional harm. The American Academy of Pediatrics disagrees. The Academy recommends that, if using a pacifier, caregivers should use one that is the correct size and shape for their baby's age. The pacifier shield should be large enough to prevent the entire pacifier from fitting in the baby's mouth. Caregivers should sanitize a pacifier frequently. They should never tie a pacifier around a baby's neck or hand or use it as a replacement for food.

**Joy** Babies show joy by smiling, perhaps in response to an adult who is making funny faces at them.

**Anger** Babies show anger through crying. Signs of anger may appear as early as three to six months of age.

**Disgust** Babies begin to show their dislikes very clearly.

**Fear** Babies show fear by startling, turning away, and screaming, especially in response to strangers.

237

**Professional Development**

**Mini Clip**
**Reading: Interacting with Text**
Students work in groups to make connections and ask higher order questions about a photo.

**Teach** *cont.*

**S Skill Practice**
### Guided Practice

**List** Have students create time lines to show the order in which babies develop different emotions. Have students create simple drawings to illustrate their time lines. (Time lines should illustrate the stages of emotional development in the correct order.) **L1** **ELL**

**Categorize** Have students gather photos of themselves or other family members as children. (Alternatively, they may obtain photos of children from other sources, such as magazines.) Encourage them to find photos that show a variety of emotions. Help students to make photocopies or scan these photos into the computer, so the originals will not be harmed. Have the students create a collage in which their photos are organized using the categories of emotions shown in Figure 8.1. (Students should create a collage in which photos are correctly categorized by emotion.) **L2** **ELL**

**Observe and Report** Instruct students to visit a child care center that cares for infants, or choose an available home care setting with infants. Tell students to observe for an hour, focusing on two infants of different ages. They should keep records of the emotions each infant expresses. Then have the students write a summary discussing how each infant's emotional behavior compared to what would be expected at that age. (Students should write a summary comparing each infant's behavior to typical emotional development at that age.) **L3**

**Teach** *cont.*

## C Critical Thinking

**Solve Problems** Ask students: What do you think people mean when they say a baby is fussy? Tell students that some babies seem to cry a lot more than others and that this can become a serious problem for the caregiver. For example, parents may not get enough sleep and be irritable if continually awakened during the night. Ask: How might this affect their treatment of the baby? What might they do to reduce these difficulties? (Parents need to remind themselves that they should not feel guilty about the baby's fussiness. Perhaps if there are two parents, they can take turns getting up at night or ask for outside help from a friend or relative.)

## U Universal Access

**Gifted Learners** Tell students that a local health clinic would like a handout to give to new parents who have babies who cry uncontrollably. Instruct students to use appropriate resources, such as a library or the Internet, to conduct research on colic and other causes of excessive crying. Students should then create a handout on this topic, explaining common causes and what parents might do to handle the situation. Have students use word-processing software to add simple graphics or photographs to their handouts.

## ✓ Reading Check

**Summarize** Try to determine whether the baby has a physical need, such as being hungry, needing a diaper change, or being too hot or cold. If there does not seem to be a physical reason, cuddle the baby, move her around, sing, offer a toy, or massage the baby's back.

238

---

## Uncontrollable Crying

**C** It is normal for infants to cry between one and three hours a day. Some healthy babies cry more than this and can be difficult to comfort. Two common causes for excessive crying in infants are colic and reflux.

## Colic

Some babies who cry for long periods may have colic. **Colic** is uncontrollable crying by an otherwise healthy baby. A colicky baby cries for three hours or more each day, for three or more days a week, for three weeks or more. **U** Babies with colic usually cry at the same time each day. The crying is often worst between six o'clock in the evening and midnight. A colicky baby is difficult or impossible to comfort. The symptoms of colic are often the most intense when the baby is about six weeks old. These periods of crying usually end around three or four months of age.

Doctors are not sure why babies get colic. It may be caused by anxiety or allergies. It may be caused by gas in the stomach. Caregivers can try burping the baby more frequently or rubbing the baby's belly. Colic may be caused by sensitivity to certain foods, such as milk or wheat. The solution can sometimes be as simple as eliminating a problem food. Breast-feeding mothers can try avoiding strong foods such as cabbage, onions, and spicy foods.

## Reflux

If an infant cries constantly, she might have a physical problem, such as reflux. **Reflux** is a condition in which partially digested food rises in the throat. Reflux can cause forceful vomiting and intense crying. Parents should talk to their pediatrician if they cannot figure out why their baby is constantly crying. The doctor can advise a course of action to help and can prescribe medication if needed.

**U**

**✓ Reading Check** **Summarize** How should you respond to a crying baby?

## Parenting Skills

### Helping a Baby Develop a Sense of Trust

Meeting a baby's physical and emotional needs helps a baby build a sense of trust. Try these strategies to help a baby develop trust.

❥ **Follow a predictable routine.** Routine care helps a baby learn to trust a parent or caregiver. Establish regular times for feeding, baths, and naps.

❥ **Get to know the baby.** Appreciate the baby's uniqueness. Learn about the baby's likes and dislikes. Learn the baby's signs for hunger, tiredness, and boredom.

❥ **Bond with the baby.** Spend time nurturing and holding the baby. Talk to the baby in a soft, positive tone. Smile and establish eye contact. Enjoy physical closeness.

❥ **Meet the baby's needs.** Strive to meet a baby's physical, social, and emotional needs. Provide loving care and affection.

**Take Charge** If you were a caregiver, how could you learn what a baby's different cries mean? Write a one-page journal entry sharing your thoughts.

---

## Parenting Skills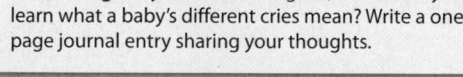

### Helping a Baby Develop a Sense of Trust

Ask students what they think the word *trust* means. Why is it important to raise trusting children? How does having a sense of trust help society as a whole? (People who trust others are more likely to be kind to them and to think of the good of society as a whole, rather than only being concerned with meeting their own personal needs.)

**Take Charge**
Students' answers will vary, but journal entries should discuss that by paying attention to when the baby cries, and what actions then satisfy the baby, the caregiver can learn to recognize the meanings of different cries.

→ **Physical Contact**
Babies need physical contact to grow and develop normally. *How can a caregiver help a child grow up to trust others?*

**Teach** *cont.*

## Attachment and Emotional Development

Attachments are **crucial**, or essential, to the healthy emotional development of an infant. An **attachment** is a baby's bond to his or her main caregiver. A healthy attachment helps a baby develop trust, self-esteem, and social and emotional skills.

Attachment begins to develop in the first few months of life. It is fully formed around age two. A child who has not formed a strong attachment by age two may have difficulty with relationships later in life.

A baby's attachment to a caregiver helps her build healthy, loving relationships later in life. Psychologist Erik Erikson suggested that people learn to trust or mistrust the world during their first year. Love and affection from parents and other caregivers fosters a sense of trust.

### Building Attachment Through Touch

Physical contact helps build attachment. Infants have a basic need for physical contact. They need to be held and cuddled. Touch helps build trust and affection between a baby and a caregiver. Touch is a primary sense for infants. Touch is how babies experience and respond to their environment. Being held or massaged helps to soothe crying babies. This is a natural way for a caregiver to show love or affection to a child. The baby is learning that the parent or caregiver will be there when needed.

### Building Attachment Through Consistent Care

Babies develop trusting relationships when caregivers meet their needs. The world is a strange place for newborns. Depending on a baby's early experiences, it may be a comfortable place or a confusing, difficult place. If the newborn's needs are met and he bonds with adults, he learns that the world is a comfortable place and he develops a sense of security.

### THE DEVELOPING BRAIN

**Touch Builds the Brain**

Touching babies does more than comfort them. It helps their brains grow. Touch causes new pathways, or networks of neurons, to form in a baby's brain. Experiences of loving touch also cause a baby's brain to trust human contact. Lack of contact can also affect brain development. Abused and neglected children who do not receive love, touch, and opportunities for learning can have brains that are 20 to 30 percent smaller than average.

■ **Science Inquiry** Physical touch is especially helpful for the mental and emotional development of deafblind babies. What might explain this?

### R Reading Strategy

**Explain** Have students imagine that a friend has started caring for a two-month-old boy every day after school. The friend says that the infant cries a lot but she ignores him because she does not want to spoil him. Using what they have learned in this section, ask students what they might say to explain that the infant needs his caregiver to respond to his crying? (Infants develop a sense of trust and security by having others respond to their needs.)

### THE DEVELOPING BRAIN

**Touch Builds the Brain**
**Science Inquiry** Babies who are lacking in one or more sense, such as vision, lose the stimulation they would normally get through this sense. Therefore, the remaining senses become more important in their development.

For more information and activities, see *The Developing Brain* guide and eTransparencies.

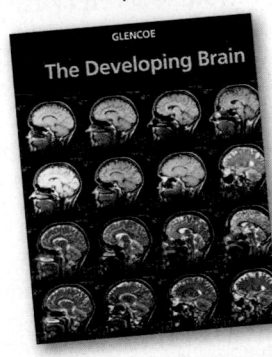

GLENCOE
The Developing Brain

➤ **Explore the Photo**

**Caption Answer** Caregivers can help a baby grow up trusting others by being kind and caring in their treatment of the baby and by responding to the baby's needs.

**Discussion** Ask the class: Do you believe that adults' behavior can be attributed to their treatment as infants? For example, do they think adults' inability to trust other people stems from their treatment by caregivers when they were young? Encourage them to give specific examples. (Answers will vary, but students should provide reasons and examples for why they think an adult's behavior can or cannot be attributed to his or her treatment as an infant.)

## C Critical Thinking

**Compare and Contrast** Tell students that many people place babies in baby seats, in which babies may sit for long periods of time. (Many of these seats are car seats that can be detached and carried independently.) How are these baby seats similar to a baby sling? How are they different? What might be an important disadvantage to using a baby seat rather than a sling? What might be an advantage? (The primary disadvantage is that the baby does not have continuous human contact, and may be easier for the caregiver to ignore. In addition, the baby may not have the same feeling of security. Advantages include that the caregiver can more easily perform tasks such as housekeeping.)

## R Reading Strategy

**Examine a Word's Context** Ask students: Based on the context in which it is used here, what do you think the word *thrive* means? Why do you think this condition is known as *failure to thrive* rather than *failure to develop* or *failure to grow*? (Student answers will vary; thrive means to grow vigorously, which has a stronger meaning than the words develop and grow.)

### ✓ Reading Check

**Identify** Parents can build an attachment through touch, consistent care, and communication.

 **NCLB** Activity correlated to Social Studies standards.

240

### Holding a Baby Close

Carrying babies close to the body is the norm in many cultures. In Somalia, women tie their babies to their backs with long scarves. In Nepal, mothers carry their babies in a garment that also holds money and tools. The Inuit people of the Canadian Arctic can snuggle their babies in the furry linings of their parkas. Baby slings are now growing more popular in North America and Europe. Carrying a baby close provides the baby with a sense of security and lets him feel, see, and smell the parent. It also lets the baby see the world from a different vantage point.

🔖 **Build Connections** *What are the advantages of sharing space? What are the disadvantages?*

**NCSS I C Culture** Apply an understanding of culture as an integrated whole that explains the functions and interactions of behavior patterns.

Caregivers need to try to be consistent in their care and responses toward an infant. If schedules change often, or if caregivers are patient and loving at times and impatient and harsh at other times, babies have difficulty building trust.

### Building Attachment Through Communication

Communication between infants and caregivers is also important in building attachment. Infants respond to a caregiver's voice, facial expressions, and eye contact. Babies gaze into the eyes of those who care for them, track their movements, and cuddle. These are signs of growing attachment. As babies get older, they respond to their caregivers with sounds and hugs. Later, babies crawl or walk to their caregivers.

### Failure to Thrive

Infants enjoy healthy emotional development when their emotional and physical needs are met. Lack of love and attention can cause failure to thrive. **Failure to thrive** is a condition in which babies do not grow and develop properly. They do not respond to people and objects. Their cries weaken and their smiles fade. They become withdrawn. As adults, they may be unable to develop caring relationships with others, even with psychological help.

⚡ Failure to thrive can be caused by neglect, abuse, or another form of stress. Babies can fail to thrive if they are left alone most of the time or do not receive enough physical contact. Children who live in poverty are more likely to fail to thrive than other children.

### ✓ Reading Check **Identify** How can parents build an attachment with their child?

## Understanding Temperament

Temperament is another key factor in a baby's emotional development. **Temperament** is a person's unique emotional makeup. Each person is born with a unique temperament. A baby's temperament helps determine how he reacts to his environment. Understanding a baby's temperament can help you give him exactly the type of care he needs. **Figure 8.2** on page 242 can help you identify a baby's temperament traits.

### Holding a Baby Close

**Discussion** Bring in a baby sling. Place a doll inside the sling and ask a volunteer to wear the sling. Ask the class: What do you think the baby feels, sees, hears, and smells while in the sling? How do you think this might affect the baby's development? (The baby will be stimulated not only by the person wearing the sling, but by seeing the world through the vantage point of the caregiver.)

**Building Connections** *Advantages include that the baby has a sense of security and feels, sees, and smells the parent. Disadvantages include that carrying the baby can interfere with the parent's work and tasks.*

How can you tell a baby's temperament? Observe her in different situations. Is she relaxed or bursting with energy? Does she love or hate surprises? Is she cautious or the first to try something new? You can also note her eating and sleeping patterns, and her general mood.

By recognizing a baby's temperament, you can learn to work with the baby to ensure a happy and healthy emotional development. Parents and caregivers should always keep in mind that every baby is unique. There are many definitions of normal infant behavior. Parents need to accept and nurture their baby's individual style to develop the best relationship possible.

## Resolving Temperament Conflicts

Parents should remember that temperament traits cannot be changed. Rather, parents should learn to adapt their reactions to a child's specific traits. A child should not be punished for a temperament trait. If a child is shy, try holding him when you introduce him to someone new. Give him time to warm up to the new person, instead of handing him to the new person right away.

Caregivers have their own temperaments, too. One of a caregiver's responsibilities is to adapt to the temperament of the child, even if they are different. Look for positive ways to adapt to these differences. Suppose that you have a low energy level, but your infant is constantly on the move. You should provide safe opportunities for energetic play. Enjoy a trip to the park or dancing to music. Avoid activities that require the child to sit a lot. Can you think of other strategies you might try?

✓ **Reading Check** **Analyze** Why is it important to understand a baby's temperament?

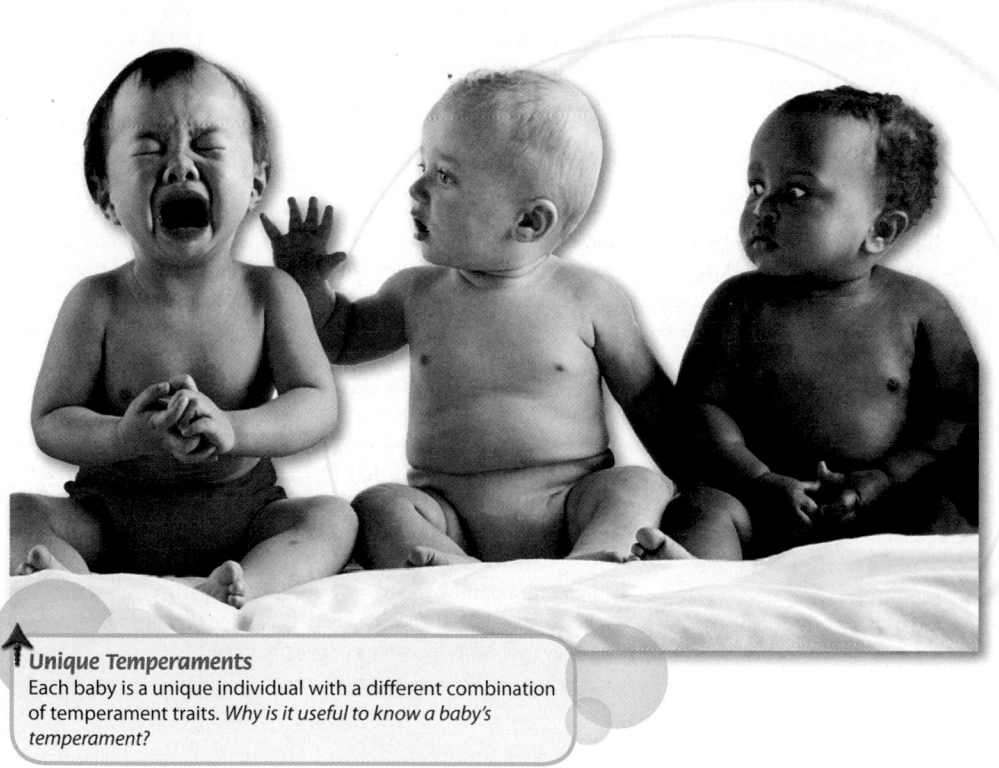

↑ **Unique Temperaments**
Each baby is a unique individual with a different combination of temperament traits. *Why is it useful to know a baby's temperament?*

Section 8.1 Understanding Emotional Development of Infants **241**

**Quiz**
Ask students to answer the following questions:

1. What are six basic emotions that infants display? (sadness, interest, joy, anger, disgust, and fear)
2. What are some of the typical ways that babies comfort themselves? (hold a favorite blanket or toy; suck a thumb or pacifier)
3. How would you determine a child's temperament traits? (Temperament traits can be determined by watching behaviors; monitoring daily patterns, keeping track of reactions to different situations, sleep patterns, and energy levels.)

**Reteach**

**U Universal Access**

**Verbal Learners** Have students interview mothers or fathers who have had more than one baby. They should get answers to these questions:

- Which baby got the most upset if something unexpected happened or his routine was changed?
- What did you do to try to comfort the baby? Which methods were most effective? Which were least effective?
- What advice do you remember getting from others (doctor, relatives, friends) about comforting your babies?

Have students write a brief summary in which they discuss what they learned from the interview.

✓ **Reading Check**

**Analyze** Caregivers need to understand a baby's temperament so they can adapt their reactions to the baby's specific traits.

## ▶ Explore the Photo

**Caption Answer** Knowing a baby's temperament can be helpful in understanding the baby's reactions to different situations and knowing how to respond in a way that will encourage positive emotional development.

**Discussion** Encourage students to analyze this photo. Based on this photo, what might they think is the temperament of the baby on the left? Of the other two babies? Why do students think the middle baby has a raised hand? (The baby on the left may be more intense while the other two might be calmer and quieter. The middle baby might be raising a hand in response to the crying, perhaps in an effort to get the crying to stop.)

## U Universal Access

**Kinesthetic Learners** Write the temperament traits *intensity*, *persistence*, and *sensitivity* on slips of paper and fold the slips in half. Divide the class into three groups, and have each group choose a piece of paper but keep its contents hidden. Then have each group create and perform a scenario illustrating its trait in a twelve-month-old child. After each performance, ask members of the other groups to guess which trait was being illustrated and what evidence supports their answer. **ELL**

**Professional Development**

**Mini Clip**
**ELL: Differentiated Instruction**

Nancy Frey, PhD, teacher and author, discusses a differentiated classroom.

## C Critical Thinking

**Classify** Ask students to think of stories they have heard about themselves as children. Maybe they had a jealous reaction to a sibling's birthday party or fearlessly walked into a swimming pool, only to be rescued by an adult. Ask for volunteers to share their stories with the class. Ask students what temperament traits are shown in these behaviors. You also may want to ask students if they still think they have these same temperament traits. (Student answers will vary, but traits should be classified according to those shown in Figure 8.2.)

**Figure 8.2** **Nine Temperament Traits**

A baby's temperament is a combination of different temperament traits. Each person has these traits in different amounts. *Do you recognize these traits in the babies you know?*

| Trait | Description |
|---|---|
| **Intensity** *How strong are a child's emotional responses?* | Highly intense children have powerful responses. They may cry and scream loudly. Less intense children tend to be calmer and quieter. |
| **Persistence** *How determined is a child to complete a task?* | Very persistent children take on challenges. They do not like to stop in the middle of a project. Less persistent children can be persuaded to move on to new activities. They can accept no for an answer. |
| **Sensitivity** *How strongly does a child notice her own and others' feelings?* | Highly sensitive children have their feelings hurt easily. They may be bothered by sights, sounds, or smells. Less sensitive children are not as concerned with others' opinions of them. They may not perceive other people's emotions as easily. |
| **Perceptiveness** *How aware is a child of all that is around him?* | Highly perceptive children get distracted easily. They have a hard time following complex directions. Less perceptive children notice less of what is going on around them. This makes it easier to follow through on multistep tasks. |
| **Adaptability** *How easily does a child accept changes?* | Highly adaptable children are not bothered by surprises or changes of plans. Less adaptable children resist change. |
| **Regularity** *Does a child's behavior follow regular patterns?* | Highly regular children like to eat, sleep, and go to the bathroom at about the same time each day. Less regular children have a different schedule each day. |
| **Activity** *What is a child's energy level?* | High-energy children love to move. They often squirm and move around in their seats. They would often rather run than walk. Low-energy children move much less and may seem more relaxed. |
| **Approach** *How does a child face new situations and people?* | High-approach children dive right in. These children are open to new activities and willing to try new foods. Low-approach children are more shy and cautious. |
| **Mood** *Is a child typically cheerful or down?* | Children with a positive mood have a rosy outlook. They expect the best from people. Children with a negative mood may be more suspicious. They may easily feel angry or disappointed. |

**U** **C**

**Figure 8.2** **Nine Temperament Traits**

**Caption Answer** Student answers will vary, but they should provide specific examples of having witnessed these traits in babies.

**Discussion** As a class, go over the temperament traits listed in this figure. Give an example of everyday situations, such as a child having to visit the doctor because of a cold.

How might a highly intense child respond to the doctor visit? How might a less intense child respond? Repeat this process with other traits listed in the figure. You may want to ask students for examples of additional life situations and have them describe how they think babies of different temperaments will respond.

## Emotional Climate of the Home

Babies are very sensitive to the feelings of people around them. Long before they know the meanings of words, they are influenced by adults' emotions, tone of voice, gestures, and facial expressions. Worried or angry caregivers are likely to be tense in handling their babies. Babies sense these feelings and can become irritable and anxious.

Every family has ups and downs, and a baby adapts to them. It is normal for caregivers to feel occasional frustration and anger toward a beloved child. However, a baby needs to feel that affection and caring are the basis of the family's interactions. Feelings of bitterness, mistrust, and anger can **hinder**, or delay, an infant's emotional development.

Handling unwanted feelings, such as anger, frustration, and sadness, is a challenge for every parent and caregiver. It can be an even greater challenge for single parents. Single parents have no other adult to share the work or the worries, and they may feel alone and overwhelmed.

It is important for all parents to find ways of releasing negative feelings away from their children. Dealing with challenging feelings can help parents find the patience to create a caring environment. Every parent needs someone who can give them emotional support.

## Section 8.1    After You Read

### Review Key Concepts

1. **List** the most important influences on a child's emotional development.
2. **Explain** ways to build attachment to support a baby's emotional development.
3. **Describe** ways to resolve temperament conflicts.
4. **Explain** why it is important for parents to *not* express negative feelings around their children.

### Practice Academic Skills

 **English Language Arts**

5. Describe your temperament using the nine temperament traits described in the section. Now imagine that you are caring for a child whose temperament is very different from yours. Write a letter to a friend describing how this could be challenging and what strategies you might use to handle the challenge.

> **NCTE 4**  Use written language to communicate effectively.

 **Social Studies**

6. Temperament, family, culture, and institutions such as schools and churches are important influences on your identity. You are also influenced by your *peers*, or people your same age. Write a report describing the people, places, and things that you think have influenced your identity since you were a baby, and why.

> **NCSS IV C**  Describe influences that contribute to the development of a sense of self.

**Check Your Answers**  Check your answers at this book's Online Learning Center at **glencoe.com**.

**NCLB**

---

### Review Key Concepts

1. The bond between the caregiver and the child, the temperament of the child, and the atmosphere of the home.
2. Attachment can be built through touch, consistent care, and communication.
3. Accept and adapt to the baby's temperament; do not punish for a temperament trait.
4. Babies can sense negative feelings and can become irritable and anxious.

### Practice Academic Skills

5. Answers will vary. Students should describe their temperament using the nine temperament traits. Students' letters should accurately explain the challenges of caring for a child with different traits and their strategies for handling these challenges.

6. Answers will vary. Students' reports should clearly describe how they feel their families, other individuals, culture, and institutions have influenced their identity.

---

## Assess

### Study Tools

Have students go to the Online Learning Center at **glencoe.com**:

- Take the **Practice Test**.
- Download **Study-to-Go** content.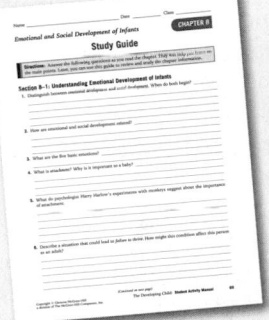

Use the **Student Activity Workbook** for additional practice.

## Close

### Culminating Activity

**Displaying Different Emotions** Have students list the basic emotions developed by infants and give an example of a situation in which each one might be displayed. (Answers will vary, but might include an infant showing disgust when given a type of food she does not like.)

**NCLB** connects academic correlations to book content.

### Bell Ringer Activity

**Play and Social Development**

Hold up a picture of a parent playing with a child. Tell students that play is a vital part of a baby's social development. Ask students if they agree with this saying, and if so, why. Lead a discussion on how playing with a caregiver is different from playing with a toy.

**Professional Development**

**Mini Clip Reading: Flexible Groupings**

Teachers use flexible groupings and partner sharing to promote student discussions.

## Preteaching

### Vocabulary

Tell students that suffixes can often have different meanings. The suffix *–ment* can mean an action or process, as in *development,* or it can mean a concrete result of object, as in *environment.*

### Graphic Organizer

The Graphic Organizer is also on the TeacherWorks CD.

(Graphic organizers should list ways to encourage healthy social development, such as rewarding positive behavior, being consistent, being patient, and sending clear messages.)

**NCLB** connects academic correlations to book content.

---

### Reading Guide

**Before You Read**

**Preview** Look at the headings and key terms in the section. Write one or two sentences explaining what the section will be about.

### Read to Learn

**Key Concepts**
- **Explain** how a baby learns social behavior.
- **Identify** how play and exploration help a baby develop socially.

### Main Idea

**D**

Caregivers play a large role in a baby's social development. They help the infant learn to form relationships and feel comfortable in his or her world.

### Content Vocabulary

◇ social development
◇ cause and effect
◇ model
◇ stranger anxiety
◇ play environment

### Academic Vocabulary

You will find these words in your reading and on your tests. Use the glossary to look up their definitions if necessary.

- lead
- motivate

### Graphic Organizer

As you read, describe actions a caregiver can take to assist in a baby's healthy social development. Use a chart like the one shown to help organize your information. Add more circles as necessary.

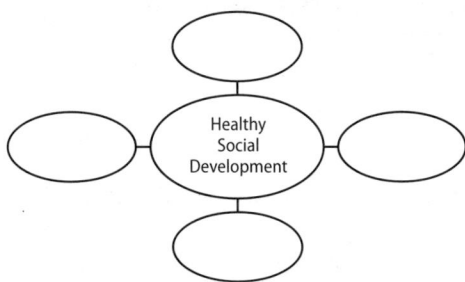

Healthy Social Development

**Graphic Organizer** Go to this book's Online Learning Center at **glencoe.com** to print out this graphic organizer.

---

**Academic Standards** . . . . . . . . . . . . . . . . . . . . . . . . . . . . . . . . . . .

 **English Language Arts**

**NCTE 4** Use written language to communicate effectively.

 **Social Studies**

**NCSS IV C Individual Development and Identity** Describe the ways family, and other group and cultural influences contribute to the development of a sense of self.

**NCTE** *National Council of Teachers of English*
**NCTM** *National Council of Teachers of Mathematics*

**NSES** *National Science Education Standards*
**NCSS** *National Council for the Social Studies*

**244** Chapter 8 Emotional and Social Development of Infants

---

### Reading Guide

**Before You Read**

Ask students to give examples of cause and effect in their lives. Perhaps they studied hard for a biology test and got a good grade. Learning about cause and effect is an important milestone in a baby's social development.

**D** **Develop Concepts**

**Main Idea** Discuss the main idea with the students. Ask students why they think caregivers are vital to a baby's social development. (Babies learn by watching other people's reactions to different situations. Caregivers have an enormous influence because of the large amount of time they spend with the baby.)

## Social Development and Learning

**Social development** is the process of learning how to interact and express oneself with others. A child who experiences healthy social development will be able to communicate well with others, connect with others, and show tolerance for others.

Social development is closely related to emotional development. Children who have good feelings about themselves relate well with others. Children who relate well to others feel good about themselves.

**Figure 8.3** on page 246 shows common steps in an infant's social development. Children grow and develop at their own pace. They may reach these milestones at different times or in a different order.

## Learning Through Cause and Effect

Babies learn by observing cause and effect. **Cause and effect** is a relationship between events in which one event, the effect, is caused by another event. For example, infants learn that they can get their needs met by crying. They learn that letting go of a toy will cause it to fall.

Babies learn that certain behaviors earn a positive response from adults. When babies coo and smile, for example, they are rewarded with laughter, hugs, and praise. Love is important to babies, so they repeat these behaviors. Babies also learn that other behaviors bring frowning or other unwanted behaviors from adults. They are less likely to repeat these behaviors.

## Learning Through Imitation

Babies learn through imitation too. As children grow, they watch the behavior of important adults in their lives and then imitate those actions. Parents and caregivers should model desirable behaviors, such as kindness and patience. To **model** a behavior means to teach it through example.

### Sending Clear Messages

Babies develop better social behaviors if they get many more positive responses than negative responses. Always try to give a baby clear messages. Smiling while expressing love or approval sends a clear message. Smiling while expressing disapproval sends an unclear message. Babies become confused if the same behavior leads to a positive response one time and a negative response another time. Provide consistent responses to help a baby understand what behaviors are desirable.

**→ Model Positive Behaviors**
Treating a baby with patience and kindness helps him learn to feel good about himself and treat others with respect. *What other positive behaviors should a parent model for a child?*

### Discussion Starter

**Parents and Social Development** Ask students to consider the role a parent plays in an infant's social development. Does an infant's behavior reflect the ways a parent reacts to the infant, other people, and the environment? (Answers will vary. Some people believe an infant's social behavior depends primarily on the baby's temperament, whereas others believe it is primarily in response to caregivers and the environment; most believe it is a combination.)

### R Reading Strategy

**Scanning** Give students approximately two minutes to scan this section. Instruct them to pay particular attention to the headings, photographs, and figures. Then have them write down a question to which they think they will learn the answer while reading. As they read, students should write down the answers to their questions when they encounter them. (Questions will vary, but should be based on what students learned as they scanned the section.)

### C Critical Thinking

**Predict** Tell students to suppose that a caregiver ignores a baby whenever he giggles and laughs but pays attention to him when he fusses or cries. How do they think the baby would respond over an extended period of time? (The baby might quit giggling and laughing and spend more time fussing in order to get the caregiver's attention.)

## ➡ Explore the Photo

**Caption Answer** Answers will vary. Positive behaviors might include showing concern for the baby when he falls, and laughing and hugging the baby when he smiles.

**Discussion** Ask students what might happen if, rather than playing with this baby, the parent left him alone for long periods of time. How might the baby's social development be affected? (Answers will vary but may include that the baby might not be able to interact with others positively.)

## Teach cont.

### S Skill Practice

**Guided Practice**

**Describe Developmental Milestones Through Illustrations**
Have students create a poster containing cartoons illustrating different developmental milestones. Depending on the size of the group, you may want them to illustrate the milestones of only one or two developmental age groups. For example, students might illustrate 9–10 months by having a baby waving to a parent while saying "bye-bye." (Posters should illustrate specific developmental milestones.) **L1** **ELL**

**Make a Developmental Chart**
Tell students to imagine that they are teaching a class designed to prepare teenagers to babysit young children. Their job is to create a developmental milestone chart for babysitters to gain a better understanding of the baby. The chart should contain the developmental milestones listed in Figure 8.3, but be rewritten in the student's own words and illustrated with pictures or art. (Chart should list the milestones for each age group, written in student's own words and with appropriate art.) **L2**

**Analyze a Developmental Stage**
Students should pick a developmental age period and use the library, Internet, or other appropriate resource to learn more about this period. Encourage students to learn why babies develop these skills. Instruct students to write a brief report analyzing what needs are met by the developmental milestones of their chosen age period. (Student should have written about the milestones of a particular age period and analyzed how achieving these milestones helps meet the baby's needs at this stage.) **L3**

## Figure 8.3 Social Developmental Milestones

Social development in infants follows a pattern. *When do babies begin to like being around other children?*

| Age | Developmental Milestone |
|-----|-------------------------|
| **1 Month** 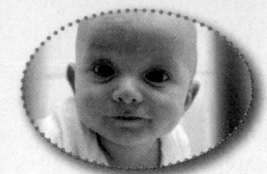 | ✤ Coos and babbles<br>✤ May cry a lot, but quiets down when he sees the caregiver's face, hears the caregiver's voice, or is lifted or touched |
| **2–3 Months** | ✤ Maintains brief eye contact while being fed<br>✤ Makes different crying sounds for different needs<br>✤ Begins to smile and show excitement<br>✤ Eyes can follow moving objects<br>✤ Wants companionship<br>✤ May like being tickled<br>✤ Can tell a smile from a frown |
| **4–6 Months** | ✤ Turns to sound of familiar voices<br>✤ Laughs, squeals, babbles<br>✤ Can tell the difference between family members<br>✤ Reaches out to play<br>✤ May cry when left alone |
| **7–8 Months** | ✤ Tries to imitate sounds made by adults<br>✤ Plays alone and plays longer with other people and toys<br>✤ Enjoys other children<br>✤ Begins to experience stranger anxiety and clings to familiar caregivers |
| **9–10 Months** | ✤ Responds to "no" and own name<br>✤ Says simple words, such as "no," "bye-bye," "dada," and "mama"<br>✤ Objects if a toy is taken away<br>✤ Crawls around to look for parents<br>✤ Enjoys playing peek-a-boo and sound games |
| **11–12 Months** | ✤ Uses the words "Dada" and "Mama" to refer to specific people<br>✤ Uses gestures as well as simple body language<br>✤ Shows stronger likes and dislikes<br>✤ Spends time looking in mirrors |

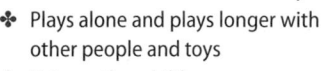

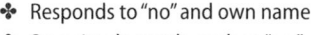
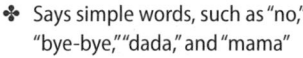

## Figure 8.3 Social Developmental Milestones

**Caption Answer** Babies begin to like being around other children at about 7 to 8 months.

**Discussion** Remind students that the milestones are guidelines and that all children develop at their own pace. Ask students how knowing these developmental milestones can be both positive and negative for a parent. (Positive: parents can use milestones to gauge their child's development. Negative: parents can worry if their child is slow in meeting some of the milestones.)

**Familiar People**
A parent's best friends or relatives are still strangers to a new baby. *What can a parent do to help a baby feel secure when meeting new people?*

**Teach** *cont.*

**R Reading Strategy**
**Cooperative Learning** Organize students into pairs and ask them to read and discuss the three paragraphs under the heading Stranger Anxiety. Ask students to write a quiz question, including the answer, for each of the three paragraphs. (Quiz questions will vary but should relate to the content.) **ELL**

## Stranger Anxiety

Beginning at around eight months of age, many babies show signs of stranger anxiety. **Stranger anxiety** is a fear of unfamiliar people, usually expressed by crying. A baby who used to sit cheerfully on a stranger's lap suddenly screams and bursts into tears when an unfamiliar person approaches. Some babies bury their heads in a parent's shoulder.

Stranger anxiety is a normal part of social development. Most babies simply need time and understanding. A caregiver can help a baby through this fear by providing consistent responses. Act welcoming toward new people. Encourage friends and relatives to quietly let the baby get used to them. Never force a baby to be held by an unfamiliar person. Instead, hold the baby yourself and sit next to the person to introduce them. While still holding the baby in your lap, encourage him to play with the new person. Give the baby time to become comfortable. When the baby seems ready, hand him to the new person. Stay nearby to provide comfort and reassurance.

A baby might feel this same anxiety with a parent if he or she looks different. For example, if a father puts on a hat and then greets the baby, the baby might not recognize him. This is normal. When the baby hears the father's voice, and smells his scent, he will recognize him again.

✓ **Reading Check** **Explain** How can toys help a baby learn cause and effect?

{ **Expert Advice...** }

*"For infants and toddlers, learning and living are the same thing. If they feel secure, treasured, loved, their own energy and curiosity will bring them new understanding and new skills."*

— Amy Laura Dombro and Leah Wallach, early childhood authors, *The Ordinary Is Extraordinary.*

**W Writing Support**
**Freewriting**
**Left with a Stranger** Have students imagine that they are an eight-month-old baby who has suddenly been left in the care of someone they do not know. Tell students to quickly write down any emotions they think they would feel. Students should not worry about grammar or spelling at this point, but try to clearly express their feelings. Ask for volunteers to share their freewriting with the class. (Refer to p. 232 to review the characteristics of freewriting. Responses will vary, but may include words like frightened, scared, anxious, confused, or lonely.)

**U Universal Access**
**Kinesthetic Learners** Divide students into two groups. Have each group prepare a skit to perform in front of the class. The first group's skit should show the "don'ts" of dealing with a child with stranger anxiety. The second group's skit should focus on the "dos" of interacting with the fearful child appropriately. **ELL**

✓ **Reading Check**

**Explain** Babies can see how toys respond to their actions, such as shaking a rattle to make noise.

Section 8.2  Understanding Social Development of Infants  **247**

---

**Explore the Photo**

**Caption Answer** A parent can welcome the new person, encourage the person to quietly let the baby get used to him or her, and hold the baby while sitting near the person, encouraging them to play together.

**Discussion** Ask students how they think a two-month-old infant might react to a stranger holding him. How might this same baby respond when eight months old? Why is there this difference? (An infant will generally react positively to anyone who is kind whereas an eight-month-old baby typically is fearful of unknown people. This is part of the baby's normal developmental process.)

# Learning Through PLAY

### From Solo to Social

A child's play changes as she grows and develops. Young babies enjoy play that involves touching, grasping, and using their five senses. Older babies are ready for more challenging forms of object play, such as stacking blocks. By age one, babies enjoy parallel play. This means that they play next to each other, but not with each other. They watch and copy one another, and they start to learn how to share. Parallel play helps babies understand that other babies have wants and feelings too. By kindergarten age, children enjoy make-believe play full of complex stories. All these kinds of play help children develop social skills such as feeling comfortable in the world, identifying and expressing feelings, cooperating, and taking turns.

**Think About It** You are caring for two young toddlers, Maya and Delon, who are playing next to each other. Maya grabs the ball from Delon, and Delon screams. What could you say and do next to help both babies understand how to share?

## Social Development Through Play

The job of a baby is to play. Babies learn about the world around them through play. Play strengthens all areas of growth and development. Play helps children learn to interact with adults and other children. Caregivers and babies strengthen their attachment through play. Play also helps babies develop motor skills and learn about the world.

## Play from Birth to Six Months

Try these strategies with babies who are in their first six months of life:
- Play games with toys or objects that the baby can grasp.
- Place colorful toys where the baby can learn to recognize and reach them. Name the colors of the toy as the baby chooses one to play with.
- Make noise with a rattle or other toy.
- Gently shake, stretch, and exercise the baby's arms and legs while smiling and talking to the baby.
- Follow the baby's **lead**, or example. Laugh and smile after the baby laughs and smiles.

## Play from Six to Twelve Months

Babies from six to twelve months of age can play somewhat more complicated games and handle more toys. Try these play strategies with older babies:
- Play peek-a-boo with the baby. Hold a blanket up to hide your face and then pull it away. As the baby gets older, let her pull the blanket away to find you.
- Set toys just out of reach so that the baby has to crawl to them. Encourage the baby to crawl to the object and praise his success.
- Read to the baby from simple books that have big pictures. It is never too soon to start introducing a child to books.
- Play silly songs and dance with the baby. Help the baby clap or bounce in rhythm with the music.
- Give babies plastic buckets or other containers that they can fill up with water, sand, or toys and dump out. Talk the baby through the activity, describing what can be done.

After each play activity, reward the baby for success by showing positive responses. Babies love to see their parents clapping hands, smiling, laughing. The parent should also tell the baby what a great job he or she did.

**248** Chapter 8 Emotional and Social Development of Infants

# Learning Through PLAY

### From Solo to Social

**Discussion** Do you think a young toddler is capable of understanding the feelings of another child whose toy she has taken? Why or why not? (Responses will vary. Toddlers typically think of only their own needs and do not understand how their actions affect others or that others also have feelings.)

**Think About It** Student responses will vary. You could give Delon another toy and play with him. Hopefully this would calm Delon and show Maya that she will not get attention if she takes other children's toys

## Create a Safe Play Environment for Infants

**C₂** Parents and other caregivers need to provide a safe play environment for babies to explore. A **play environment** is a comfortable space free of dangers and with toys that are safe and interesting. Many caregivers use safety gates to keep infants away from dangerous areas like stairs.

**R** **W** Infants love toys that are colorful and that move around and make noise. Hanging mobiles, rattles, and stuffed animals are wonderful toys for infants. Babies from six to twelve months of age enjoy more complicated toys, such as those they can push or pull.

### Choose Safe Toys

It is important to choose toys that are safe and appropriate for the age of the baby. Toys should be big enough so that babies cannot put them all the way in their mouths. Choose toys that do not have small parts. Babies can swallow and choke on small parts, or stick them in their nose or ears. Toys should also be sturdy.

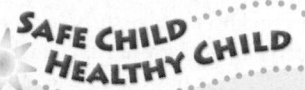

### SAFE CHILD HEALTHY CHILD

#### Exploring Through Taste

Babies' mouths are more sensitive than their hands, so it is no wonder that babies use their mouths to explore tastes, textures, and shapes. *Mouthing* is normal, but it can be dangerous. A baby can choke on small objects or be poisoned by chemicals. Make sure that all toys are too large to fit all the way into a baby's mouth. Keep soaps, medicines, and chemicals out of reach. You can satisfy a baby's need to explore by choosing toys and foods with interesting shapes and textures.

☀ **Be Prepared** Use the library or the Internet to conduct research on child safety. Make a safety checklist of 20 common choking hazards for babies, including toys and toy parts, household objects, and foods. Share your checklist with the class.

**↑ Exploring Through Play**
Babies learn about the world through play. *What kinds of skills do you think this baby is learning?*

---

 **Explore the Photo**

**Caption Answer** Possible answers include ability to focus on an object of interest, cause and effect, motor skills.

**Discussion** Why do you think stuffed animals are such popular toys for young children? (Answers will vary. Stuffed animals are soft and can be cuddled, an activity that babies enjoy.)

### SAFE CHILD HEALTHY CHILD

#### Exploring Through Taste

**Identify** Ask students: What do you think babies learn through exploring objects by putting them in their mouths? (The baby can learn about its size, shape, and texture.)

☀ **Be Prepared** Students should conduct research to develop a safety checklist of 20 common choking hazards for babies.

---

## Reteach *cont.*

**R** **Reading Strategy**

**Main Idea** Ask students to work independently to determine the main idea of the section titled Create a Safe Play Environment for Infants. Students should then write the main idea in a single sentence. Have students share and discuss their sentences with the class. (Sentences will vary, but may be something similar to: Caregivers are responsible for creating a comfortable and safe play environment with a variety of toys appropriate for the child's age.)

**C₂** **Critical Thinking**

**Analyze** Explain to students that some caregivers take children to facilities where they can interact with other children through play. Ask students to discuss how these experiences support healthy social development in children. (Answers may vary. Children may learn how to interact with others, either through parallel or interactive play. They also learn about other children's needs and wants.)

**W** **Writing Support**
**Freewriting**

**Thoughts on a Toy** Show the class four or five toys designed for babies of various ages. Ask students to choose one toy and engage in freewriting about that toy. Questions they might consider: How might the toy attract an infant? What might a baby do with it? What might the baby learn? Encourage students not to worry about grammar and punctuation, but simply to express their thoughts. (Refer to p. 232 for tips on freewriting. Student responses will vary based on the selected toy. Students may discuss the shape of the toy or how it is used, or how babies might respond to the toy and what they might learn from it.)

Assess

## Study Tools

Have students go to the Online Learning Center at **glencoe.com**:

- Take the **Practice Test**.
- Download **Study-to-Go** content.

Use the **Student Activity Workbook** for additional practice.

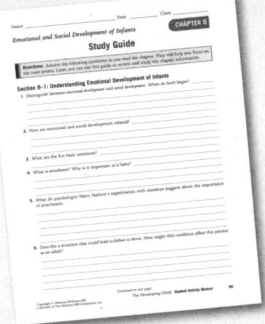

## Close

## Culminating Activity

**Summarize** Have students summarize the play activities that are recommended to support social development in babies. (Play activities vary by age, and may include making noise with a rattle, shaking and stretching baby's arms and legs, playing peek-aboo, reading simple books, playing silly songs, and dancing.)

**NCLB** connects academic correlations to book content.

---

Use a safety checklist to make sure the rooms where a baby plays do not have any hidden dangers. See Chapter 10 for tips on how to child-proof a room. It is also important to keep toys clean. Wash new toys with soap and water. Wash them again each time the baby plays with them.

## Social Development Through Exploration

Babies have a need to explore. They explore with all their senses: touch, vision, hearing, smell, and taste. Babies often put toys, stuffed animals, and other objects into their mouths. Sometimes babies repeatedly throw or drop things just to see what happens.

When babies start rolling, and later crawling and walking, they can explore more of their environment. Many babies will try to pull themselves up to reach objects on furniture. They will often try to take away keys or telephones from their parents. To a baby, these items look like new toys. As infants get older, they will want to explore and learn about everything in their environment.

## Play and Exploration

Play and exploration are related. Babies use play to explore their world. They look at and play with toys to explore colors and textures. Blocks, for example, let babies explore how things stack up and balance. Caregivers can help babies explore by giving them safe and interesting objects to explore. Even basic household items such as plastic spoons or cups and empty boxes that can be filled are interesting to infants. A kitchen pot and wooden spoon make an instant drum set for an infant.

Encouragement and positive responses from adults **motivate**, or provide a reason for, babies to explore and learn. Everything in the world is new to a baby. By participating in explorations with the baby, caregivers can deepen their attachment to their children. For example, a parent could take the baby to a park or garden. The parent can participate in the exploration by showing the baby the different colors and shapes of flowers and trees. The parent can help the baby feel the textures of the leaves and bark.

---

### Section 8.2 — After You Read

#### Review Key Concepts

1. **Describe** how a parent can give a baby clear messages about behavior.
2. **Explain** how parents can help babies to explore and learn.

#### Practice Academic Skills

 **English Language Arts**

3. Imagine that you write an advice column on parenting. A young parent asks for advice on how to handle her nine-month-old son, who cries and acts terrified around friends and neighbors. Write an answer to explain why the baby is behaving this way and give some tips on how to help him feel more comfortable.

> **NCTE 4** Use written language to communicate effectively.

 **Social Studies**

4. Brainstorm actions that a parent or caregiver can take to help a baby's healthy social development. Group your ideas into major topics, such as "play" and "modeling positive behaviors." Create a table of information, devoting three activities to each of your major topics.

> **NCSS IV C** Describe the ways family, and other group and cultural influences contribute to the development of a sense of self.

**Check Your Answers** Check your answers at this book's Online Learning Center at **glencoe.com**.

---

#### Review Key Concepts

1. Parents should be consistent. Always smile when the baby behaves appropriately; never smile when the baby does something of which you do not approve.
2. Provide a comfortable, safe place for exploration and colorful, age-appropriate toys that are safe for the baby.

#### Practice Academic Skills

3. Answers will vary. Students should point out that stranger anxiety is normal for children this age. The parent might try holding the child for reassurance while letting the child see the parent interact with others. This will give the son a chance to become more comfortable with other people at his own pace.

4. Students should create a table listing actions caregivers can take to aid in healthy social development. These actions should be arranged by major topics, with at least three activities listed under each topic.

# Chapter Summary

Emotional development is the process of learning to recognize and express feelings and to establish a personal identity. Caregivers can help shape babies' emotional development by providing consistent, responsive, and loving care. Babies' unique temperaments and the emotional climate of the home also influence their emotional development. Social development is the process of learning how to interact and express oneself with others. Babies learn social behavior by watching and interacting with others. One normal sign of social development is stranger anxiety. Babies learn about the world by playing and exploring.

## Vocabulary Review

**1.** Use each of these content and academic vocabulary words in a sentence.

**Content Vocabulary**

◇ emotional development (p. 235)
◇ emotion (p. 235)
◇ colic (p. 238)
◇ reflux (p. 238)
◇ attachment (p. 239)
◇ failure to thrive (p. 240)
◇ temperament (p. 240)
◇ social development (p. 245)
◇ cause and effect (p. 245)
◇ model (p. 245)
◇ stranger anxiety (p. 247)
◇ play environment (p. 249)

**Academic Vocabulary**

■ crucial (p. 239)
■ hinder (p. 243)
■ lead (p. 248)
■ motivate (p. 250)

## Review Key Concepts

**2. List** six basic emotions that babies experience.
**3. Explain** the role of attachment in a baby's emotional development.
**4. Describe** how temperament affects a baby's social development.
**5. Explain** how the emotional climate of the home can affect a baby's development.
**6. Explain** how a baby learns social behavior.
**7. Identify** how play and exploration help a baby develop socially.

## Critical Thinking

**8. Analyze** A baby builds attachment through touch, consistent care, and communication. Do you think a baby could still bond with a parent if one of these elements were missing? Explain your opinion.
**9. Synthesize** Stranger anxiety and attachment to a caregiver develop at around the same time. How might these two developments be related?
**10. Predict** What combination of temperament traits might help a baby cope with a stressful family environment? What combination of traits might make a baby less able to cope with a stressful environment? Why?

Chapter 8   Emotional and Social Development of Infants   **251**

## Content and Academic Vocabulary Review

**1.** Students should write complete sentences using each vocabulary word correctly.

## Review Key Concepts

**2.** Six basic emotions experienced by babies include interest, sadness, joy, disgust, anger, fear.
**3.** Babies who bond positively develop trust, self-esteem, and social and emotional skills.
**4.** Temperament determines how a baby reacts to his environment; a less adaptable child may avoid unknown situations, reducing his chances of learning about his environment.
**5.** Babies respond to others' emotions; if a caregiver is worried or angry, the baby may become irritable and anxious.
**6.** Babies learn social behavior by watching, interacting with, and imitating others.
**7.** Play and exploration allow babies to use all their senses, and deepens attachment with people involved in the play and exploration.

## Critical Thinking

**8.** Answers will vary. A possible answer: It depends on the element that is lacking. If a baby is held often, but the caregiver is occasionally inconsistent in giving care, the baby may still be able to bond.

**9.** Babies at this age crave familiarity and consistency. As they build attachment with a caregiver, they are afraid of losing that caregiver and the change that might come from being with someone else.

**10.** More able to cope: less sensitive, more adaptable, more approachable, positive mood; Less able to cope: more sensitive, less adaptable, less approachable, negative mood. Babies with the first group of characteristics are less likely to be bothered by a disruptive environment and more likely to "go with the flow."

### Family & Community Connections

**11.** Students' interview notes should describe how the single parent copes with issues such as stress and what the parent does to create a positive emotional climate at home. Students should share results with class.

### Health Skills

**12.** Summaries will vary. Student should define infant massage, discuss how it is performed and its benefits, and state whether the student would be interested in trying it.

### Observation Skills

**13.** Reports will vary. The report should describe the student's observations, including an analysis of the physical, social, and emotional skills the baby was learning through play.

### Real-World Skills

**14.** Reports will vary. Students should discuss how to identify causes of crying by determining those remedies to which the baby responds. Methods of comforting may include feeding or playing with the baby.

**15.** Tables will vary. Students should create a table that defines three developmental disabilities, and gives their diagnoses and treatments.

**16.** Lists will vary but should reflect adequate research to find purchase information on two baby gates, a play mat, and age-appropriate toys for a three-month-old baby.

**NCLB** Activity correlated to Science standards.

---

### Family & Community Connection

**11. Interview a Single Parent** Interview a single parent about how he or she copes with negative emotions, such as stress, frustration, anger, and fear. What strategies does he or she have for resolving negative emotions? Who does he or she rely on for emotional support? How does he or she try to create a positive emotional climate in the home? Take notes during your interview, and share what you learned with the class.

### Health Skills

**12. Research Infant Massage** Go online to research massage techniques for babies. What is infant massage? What are the benefits? How is it performed? Are there any times when massage should not be used on babies? Write a summary of what you learned and state whether you would be interested in trying infant massage.

### Observation Skills

**13. Observe Babies at Play** Work with your teacher to arrange to observe a baby in a home or at a child care center. Note that an infant six months or older will probably be much more active than a baby five months or younger.

**Procedure** Pay attention to how the baby explores objects in the environment as well as how the baby interacts with the caregivers during playtime.

**Analysis** Write a report to describe your observations. Include an analysis of the physical, social, and emotional skills you think the baby was learning through play.

> **NSES 1** Develop an understanding of science unifying concepts and processes: evidence, models, and explanations.

**N C L B**

### Real-World Skills

| Problem-Solving Skills | **14. Generate Solutions** What would you do to care for a crying baby? Explain in a report how you would identify the cause of the crying and what strategies you would use to comfort the baby. Also explain what you would do if you were unable to comfort the baby. |
| --- | --- |
| Technology Skills | **15. Create a Table** Research three developmental disabilities that may affect a baby's social and emotional development. Use word-processing software to create a table that defines each disability and explains how it is diagnosed and treated. |
| Financial Literacy Skills | **16. Shop for a Safe Play Environment** Imagine that you have $150 to create a safe play environment for your three-month-old baby. You will need two baby gates, a play mat, and age-appropriate toys. Conduct research to comparison shop for the best quality and prices. How many toys can you buy and stay within your budget? Create a list of the products you would buy, identifying the source or place of purchase and the prices. |

 **Additional Activities** For additional activities, go to this book's Online Learning Center at **glencoe.com**.

---

### Academic Skills

**17.** Essays will vary. Students should list and describe skills in the order of importance by the student's assessment. Students should state which skills they believe they have and which skills they need to develop further.

**18.** The average couple will spend $36,000. (18% = 18/100 = .18; .18 × 200,000 = 36,000)

---

The *Early Childhood Observations CD* offers additional lessons with videos to build students' observation skills.

**Part 1:** Learning to Observe
**Part 2:** How Children Develop
**Part 3:** Working With Young Children
**Part 4:** Extended Observations
**Part 5:** Resources and Answer File

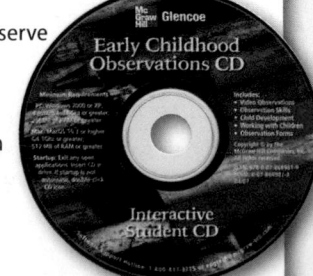

## Academic Skills

###  English Language Arts

**17. Reflect on Your Skills** Parents need many emotional and social skills, such as self-control, empathy, patience, responsibility, caring, and kindness. List and describe the skills that a parent should have in order to care for a baby's emotional and social needs. Which of these skills do you have? Which could you develop further? Summarize your thoughts in a one-page essay.

> **NCTE 4** Use written language to communicate effectively.

###  Mathematics

**18. Calculate Food Costs** According to the United States Department of Agriculture, the average married couple will spend about $200,000 to raise a child to the age of 17. If food is about 18% of this total, how much does the average couple spend on food for a child through age 17?

**Math Concept** **Multiply Decimals by Whole Numbers** A percent is a ratio that compares a number to 100.

**Starting Hint** Rewrite the percent (18%) as a fraction with a denominator of 100. Convert the fraction to a decimal. Multiply this decimal by the total amount ($200,000).

> **Math** For math help, go to the Math Appendix at the back of the book.

> **NCTM Number and Operations** Understand numbers, ways of representing numbers, relationships among numbers, and number systems.

###  Science

**19. Design an Experiment** The scientific method is a way to answer questions. You must collect information, form a hypothesis, study the results, and draw conclusions that other scientists can test. One hypothesis might read: Two-month-old babies can identify the emotions they see on their mothers' faces.

**Procedure** Describe an experiment that would test this hypothesis.

**Analysis** Write a speech to explain how your experiment would prove whether this hypothesis is correct or incorrect.

> **NSES A** Develop abilities necessary to do scientific inquiry, understandings about scientific inquiry.

## Standardized Test Practice

### READING COMPREHENSION

Read the passage, then answer the question.

> A baby is playing at home when a stranger walks by the window and waves. Confused, the baby looks at his mother, who seems delighted. She waves back at the passerby and smiles. The baby is reassured and returns to playing. This baby has just demonstrated social referencing, the process of assessing other people's facial expressions to help decide how to react to a new situation.

**20.** According to the passage, social referencing:
  a. only occurs in babies.
  b. involves facial expressions.
  c. is a self-comforting technique.
  d. usually happens when strangers are present.

> **Test-Taking Tip** Read the passage carefully, noting key statements as you go. Answer the questions based only on what you just read in the passage, not based on your previous knowledge.

**NCLB**

**19.** Results will vary. Students should write a speech that explains the procedure they would follow to determine whether this hypothesis is correct or incorrect: Two-month-old babies can identify the emotions they see on their mothers' faces.

> **NCLB** **NCLB** connects academic correlations to book content.

### 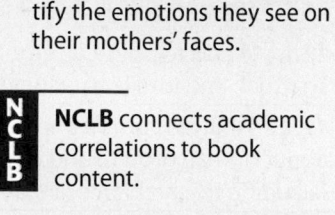 Standardized Test Practice

**20.** b. involves facial expressions.

**Test-Taking Tips** Tell students that underlining key statements while they are reading can help focus their attention on the important facts. In addition, remind them not to base their answers on their previous knowledge, only the exact content of the passage.

**Multiple-Choice Tests** Tell students to read directions to multiple-choice tests carefully. Usually only one answer is required; however, sometimes more than one answer may be possible or necessary.

> **McGraw Hill Professional Development**
>
>
>
> **Mini Clip** Reading: Standards-Based Instruction
>
> Emily Schell, EdD, educator and author, discusses standards-based instruction.

---

## TECHNOLOGY Solutions

**Use these technology solutions to streamline chapter assessment!**

 **ExamView Assessment Suite** CD allows you to create and print out customized tests or ready-made unit and chapter tests, complete with answer keys.

**TeacherWorks Plus** is an electronic lesson planner that provides instant access to complete teacher resources in one convenient package.

 **Online Learning Center** includes resources and activities for students and teachers.

# Standards Correlations

**STANDARDS BASED LESSON PLANNING** *The Developing Child* provides students with instruction and assessment in the following fundamental content areas:

## National Standards Correlations

| Standards | Pages | Standards | Pages |
|---|---|---|---|
| **12.1.1** Analyze physical, emotional, social, spiritual, and intellectual development. | **266–272, 274, 278, 279** | **15.1.2** Analyze expectations and responsibilities of parenting. | **268–269, 275, 277, 279** |
| **12.1.3** Analyze current and emerging research about human growth and development, including research on brain development. | **257–264, 268, 270–272, 276** | **15.1.5** Explain cultural differences in roles and responsibilities of parenting. | **272** |
| **12.2.1** Analyze the effect of heredity and environment on human growth and development. | **261, 262, 268–269** | **15.2.1** Choose nurturing practices that support human growth and development. | **264, 274–275** |
| **12.2.4** Analyze the effects of life events on individuals' physical, intellectual, social, moral, and emotional development. | **261** | **15.2.2** Apply communication strategies that promote positive self-esteem in family members. | **275–279** |
| **12.2.5** Analyze geographic, political, and global influences on human growth and development. | **272** | **15.2.3** Assess common practices and emerging research about discipline on human growth and development. | **257–264** |
| **12.3.2** Analyze the role of communication on human growth and development. | **275–279** | | |

**NO CHILD LEFT BEHIND** NCLB activities, information, and skills practice will help your students attain NCLB proficiency. Students will improve their abilities in the following academic standards areas:

## Academic Standards Correlations

| Discipline | Standard | Feature/Activity |
|---|---|---|
| **English Language Arts** | **NCTE 1** Read texts to acquire new information. | **Reading Guide (pp. 256, 265, 273)** |
| | **NCTE 2** Read literature to build an understanding of the human experience. | **Academic Skills (p. 285)** |
| | **NCTE 5** Use different writing process elements to communicate effectively. | **Writing Activity (p. 254) After You Read (p. 272)** |
| | **NCTE 7** Conduct research and gather, evaluate, and synthesize data to communicate discoveries. | **Observation Skills (p. 284)** |
| | **NCTE 8** Use information resources to gather information and create and communicate knowledge. | **After You Read (p. 264)** |
| | **NCTE 12** Use language to accomplish individual purposes. | **After You Read (p. 281)** |
| **Mathematics** | **NCTM Algebra** Understand patterns, relations, and functions. | **Academic Skills (p. 285)** |
| | **NCTM Geometry** Analyze characteristics and properties of two- and three-dimensional geometric shapes. | **Math in Action (p. 277)** |
| **Science** | **NSES C** Develop understanding of the cell; organization in living systems; and behavior of organisms. | **Academic Skills (p. 285)** |
| | **NSES F** Develop understanding of personal and community health. | **After You Read (p. 264)** |
| **Social Studies** | **NCSS I A Culture** Analyze and explain the ways groups, societies, and cultures address human needs and concerns. | **After You Read (p. 272)** |
| | **NCSS I C Culture** Apply an understanding of culture that explains the functions of tradition, and beliefs and values. | **After You Read (p. 281)** |

## McGraw Hill Professional Development

**MINI CLIP VIDEO LIBRARY**
Targeted professional development is correlated throughout *The Developing Child*. **The McGraw-Hill Professional Development Mini Clip Video Library** provides teaching strategies to strengthen academic and learning skills. Log on to **glencoe.com**.

In this chapter, you will find these Mini Clips:
- **ELL** Words in Action, p. 259
- **ELL** Building the Context, p. 261
- **Reading** Strategic Readers, p. 266
- **Reading** During and After Reading, p. 271
- **Math** Comparing Similar Figures, p. 277
- **ELL** Scaffolding Questions, p. 279

## Reading and Writing Strategies

**Writing Activity: Personal Letter** (p. 254)
Students use writing tips to write a personal letter asking about a friend's new baby.

**Before You Read** (pp. 256, 265, 273)
A pre-reading question or statement will help students make a personal connection to content.

**Graphic Organizer** (pp. 256, 265, 273)
A visual tool will help students organize and remember new content.

**Reading Check** (pp. 260, 269, 279)
A question allows students to make a quick comprehension self-check.

**After You Read** (pp. 264, 272, 281)
Organize and process students' understanding of what they have read.

## Chapter Features

**What Would You Do?**
**Learning Through Music** (p. 261)
Music has been shown to strengthen a baby's neural pathways.

**THE DEVELOPING BRAIN**
**Environment and the Brain** (p. 263)
The number of neural connections in a baby's brains increases with stimulation.

**THE DEVELOPING BRAIN**
**Human Contact Needed** (p. 268)
Babies require human interaction for brain development.

**Learning Through PLAY**
**Sensory Play** (p. 269)
Babies use their senses to explore and learn about the world.

**SAFE CHILD HEALTHY CHILD**
**Safe Learning** (p. 275)
Homes should be childproofed so that babies are free to explore and learn.

**Math in Action**
**Geometric Shapes** (p. 277)
Researchers recommend exposing babies to geometric shapes.

**Careers With Children**
**Storyteller** (p. 282)
Learn the skills needed to succeed as a Storyteller.

## Chapter Overview

### Introduce the Chapter

In this chapter, students learn how babies develop intellectually and the abilities that infants exhibit which demonstrate this development. They learn about the organization of the developing brain and what caregivers can do to stimulate infants' intellectual development.

### Build Background

Hold up an infant's t-shirt with snaps at the side of the neck. Ask students: Why do baby's t-shirts often have these snaps? (because a baby's head is proportionally larger than the rest of its body) Explain that while babies are born with large brains, what happens after birth determines the extent to which their potential will be met.

### Writing Activity

**Personal Letter**

This active learning activity prompts students to write a personal letter to find out about the growth and development of a friend's new baby. After students have completed the writing activity, ask for volunteers to share their letters with the class. Student responses can be used as a basis for classroom discussion. (Use these criteria when evaluating your students' writing: Have students explored personal concerns? Have students used details to make events come alive for the reader? Has grammar and spelling been checked?)

# Intellectual Development of Infants

## Chapter Objectives

After completing this chapter, you will be able to:

- **Describe** how a baby's experiences increase brain function.
- **Explain** how the brain becomes organized.
- **List** four abilities that show intellectual growth in infants.
- **Identify** specific abilities that babies learn during Piaget's first period of learning.
- **Name** five ways caregivers can encourage learning.
- **Discuss** how to choose toys appropriate for babies of different ages.

### Writing Activity

**Personal Letter**

**Understanding Babies** Having a baby can be an exciting adventure for adult couples. You may know someone who has a new baby. Write a personal letter to a real or imaginary friend who has a new baby. Ask your friend questions that will give you a better understanding of the baby's growth and development.

**Writing Tips** Use the following tips to write your personal letter effectively:
1. Express your thoughts and feelings.
2. Ask clear questions that are not too personal.
3. Check your grammar and spelling.

## CLASSROOM Solutions

### Print Resources

 **Student Edition**

 **Teacher Wraparound Edition**

 **Student Activity Workbook**

 **Student Activity Workbook Teacher Annotated Edition**

### Technology Resources

 **Online Learning Center** has resources and activities for students and teachers. Includes an Online Student Edition.

 **Interactive Student Edition** allows students to instantly access review materials, examples, and exercises.

**Review the Sections**

Introduce the chapter by reviewing the sections:

**Section 9.1**
A great deal has been learned about infant brain function in recent years. The infant's brain contains billions of neurons which, in response to stimuli, link together to create neural pathways. Gradually, through a process of branching and pruning, the brain becomes organized.

**Section 9.2**
During their first year, babies show their growing intellect by remembering experiences and understanding concepts such as cause and effect. Psychologist Jean Piaget divided learning into four distinct categories, beginning with sensorimotor learning and ending with formal operations.

**Section 9.3**
Caregivers can encourage intellectual development by providing age-appropriate toys, giving the child their attention, and talking with the child. Sign language is one way of communicating with babies who cannot yet speak. Everyday objects can make excellent toys.

**↑ Explore the Photo**
Play is an important learning experience for babies. *What do you think babies can learn by playing with toys?*

255

**▶ Explore the Photo**

**Caption Answer** Answers will vary. Babies learn sensory information about touch, taste, smell, sight, and sound from toys.

**Discussion** Ask students: As this baby plays, which senses are being stimulated? In what ways are these senses being stimulated? (Answers will vary but may include that the sense of touch is stimulated when he touches the different fabrics, and sight is stimulated by the colors and patterns.)

**TeacherWorks** *Plus* **TeacherWorks Plus** is an electronic lesson planner that provides instant access to complete teacher resources in one convenient package.

**Presentation Plus!** provides visual teaching aids for every section.

 **The Early Childhood Observations CD** presents video observations and lessons on observation skills and child development.

**The Developing Brain eTransparencies and Guide** include information and activities to offer insights into brain development and diseases of the brain.

## Focus

### Bell Ringer Activity

**Expanding Abilities**
Organize students into groups. Each group should create two lists. One should list the abilities of a typical newborn while the other should list the abilities of a typical one year old. Ask for volunteers to share their lists. Emphasize that the increase in abilities over a one-year period is absolutely amazing.

## Preteaching

### Vocabulary
In science, an object's name often tells you something about its shape or structure. For example, the term *dendrite* describes an object that has a branching structure like a tree. In this section, a dendrite is the part of a nerve cell that branches like a tree limb.

### Graphic Organizer
The Graphic Organizer is also on the TeacherWorks CD.

(Graphic organizers should list: Cerebrum—Controls speech, memory, etc. Thalamus—Controls emotional expression. Cerebellum—Controls muscular coordination. Spinal Cord—Transmits information between body and brain. Brain Stem—Controls involuntary activities. Pituitary Gland—Secretes hormones.)

**NCLB** connects academic correlations to book content.

## Reading Guide

### Before You Read
**Examine** As you read the section, write down any questions you have about the material. Then write the answers as you find them.

### Read to Learn
#### Key Concepts
- **Describe** how a baby's experiences increase brain function.
- **Explain** how the brain becomes organized.

#### Main Idea
The information in babies' brains develops as they acquire new skills. This information evolves at a very rapid rate during the first few years of life.

#### Content Vocabulary
◇ neuron  ◇ myelin
◇ neural pathway  ◇ dendrite
◇ cortex  ◇ synapse
◇ axon  ◇ neurotransmitter

#### Academic Vocabulary
You will find these words in your reading and on your tests. Use the glossary to look up their definitions if necessary.
- function
- receptor

### Graphic Organizer
As you read, list six different parts of the brain and give a brief description of each. Use a chart like the one shown to help organize your information.

| Parts of the Brain |
| --- |
| 1. |
| 2. |
| 3. |
| 4. |
| 5. |
| 6. |

**Graphic Organizer** Go to this book's Online Learning Center at **glencoe.com** to print out this graphic organizer.

### Academic Standards . . . . . . . . . . . . . . . . . . . . . . . . . . . . . .

 **English Language Arts**
**NCTE 8** Use information resources to gather information and create and communicate knowledge.

**Science**
**NSES F** Develop understanding of personal and community health.

**NCTE** *National Council of Teachers of English*
**NCTM** *National Council of Teachers of Mathematics*

**NSES** *National Science Education Standards*
**NCSS** *National Council for the Social Studies*

## Reading Guide

### Before You Read
Have students think of someone's house they visit regularly, such as a friend or relative. Then have them think of a place that is about the same distance away, but that they have only been to once. Ask students which route they know better. Likewise, neural pathways become stronger with regular use.

### D Develop Concepts
**Main Idea** Discuss the main idea with the students. Ask: Why do you think babies' brains develop so quickly at such an early age? (Possible answer: they are responding to the enormous quantity of stimuli that are new to them.)

## The Structure of the Brain

Sabrina and Joe had watched six-month-old Abby's every twitch, gulp, burp, gurgle, and coo with rapt attention. They often worried whether Abby was developing as she should. The doctor said she was healthy, but they wanted her to be smart too. Their families and friends offered lots of advice, but some was conflicting. Sometimes they tried to guess what Abby was thinking, or if she was thinking. When they took a parenting class they were amazed to find out how much was already going on in a six-month-old's brain.

One of the most important areas of recent scientific research has been about the development of infant brain function. What scientists have learned has great significance for caregivers. It has long been known that in the first year, babies' intellectual and motor skills grow and change at an amazing rate. Development happens faster in the first year than at any other time of life. This growth is what allows babies to learn to sit, crawl, walk, and talk. Yet recent research has shown that the infant brain's capacities are even greater than scientists suspected.

Research shows that the environment has a major impact on brain development. By providing new activities, parents and other caregivers can stimulate, or awaken, a baby's senses of sight, sound, touch, taste, and smell. Doing so helps the infant's brain develop new abilities. In fact, it now appears that much of a baby's increased brain function is due to the quantity and quality of experiences the baby has.

At birth, the brain has billions of neurons. A **neuron** is a nerve cell. In response to experiences, babies' brains immediately begin to develop links between these neurons. The link between neurons is called a **neural pathway**. These pathways "wire" the brain so that it can control different body functions and thinking processes. Neural pathways are created quickly. For example, babies just four days old have demonstrated that they are able to make fine distinctions in hearing. This means they are able to distinguish between their parents' voices and other people's voices. This ability is the result of links in the brain that the baby has formed in the few days after birth. Such links form continuously during a child's early years. They reach their maximum number at around age ten.

**Providing Brain Stimulation**
One of the first skills a baby gains is the ability to visually track moving objects. *What experiences can help a baby learn this skill?*

Section 9.1   Early Brain Development   **257**

**S Skill Practice**

**Independent Practice**

**Create a Table** Instruct students to create a table. In the left column, they should list the brain components shown in Figure 9.1. In the right column, they should list activities that require the use of that part of the brain. For example, one item next to Brain Stem might be Breathing. (Tables will vary but should list the components of the brain in one column and activities controlled by that component in the second column.) **L1 ELL**

**Make a Game** Have students create a game to test people's knowledge of the functions of the brain's components. First they should choose the type of game (for example, tic-tac-toe or a memory game). They then should write questions that require the player to identify which brain component controls a specific function. (Games will vary but should test the player's knowledge of the functions of different brain components.) **L2**

**Develop a Web Page** Instruct students to create a Web page that explains the functions of the different brain components shown in Figure 9.1. Students may wish to conduct research to add more information to their pages. Web pages should include graphics for visual appeal. Encourage students to add hyperlinks to additional information, where appropriate. (Students should create a Web page explaining the functions of different brain components.) **L3**

How the brain develops in a baby's first year of life has profound effects on the baby's whole life. Before birth, the fetus's world is warm and dark. This changes radically at birth. The newborn child is showered with input to the senses. Eyes closed for so long are exposed to bright lights. There are new sounds and smells. The baby feels a sudden drop in temperature from the familiar 98.6 degrees Fahrenheit. It is no wonder that so many babies cry when they enter the world! However, it is this variety of sensory input that the brain uses to build neural pathways. Babies' brains will make use of every bit of noise and new sensations.

Newborns learn about the world through their senses. The senses include what they see, hear, smell, taste, and touch. A baby's mobile moves when it is touched, and brightly colored objects dance before the baby's eyes. It might play soothing lullabies to calm the baby. The voices of caregivers sound familiar. The smells of parents and caregivers are familiar too. A fist or a finger tastes different from milk. A blanket feels soft and warm.

In general, most of the responses of a newborn are reflexes. As you learned in Chapter 7, a reflex is an instinctive, automatic response. For example, the newborn will instinctively grasp a finger placed in its palm. An overheated baby will kick until a blanket falls off or is removed. These are not planned actions that come from learned responses. They are only reflexes.

By the time the baby is six months old, he or she is aware that blankets and socks can be kicked or pulled off. By the time a child is a year old, he or she has the ability to stack toys, stand up, and maybe even walk. All these skills result from the brain's growing ability to direct the body's actions.

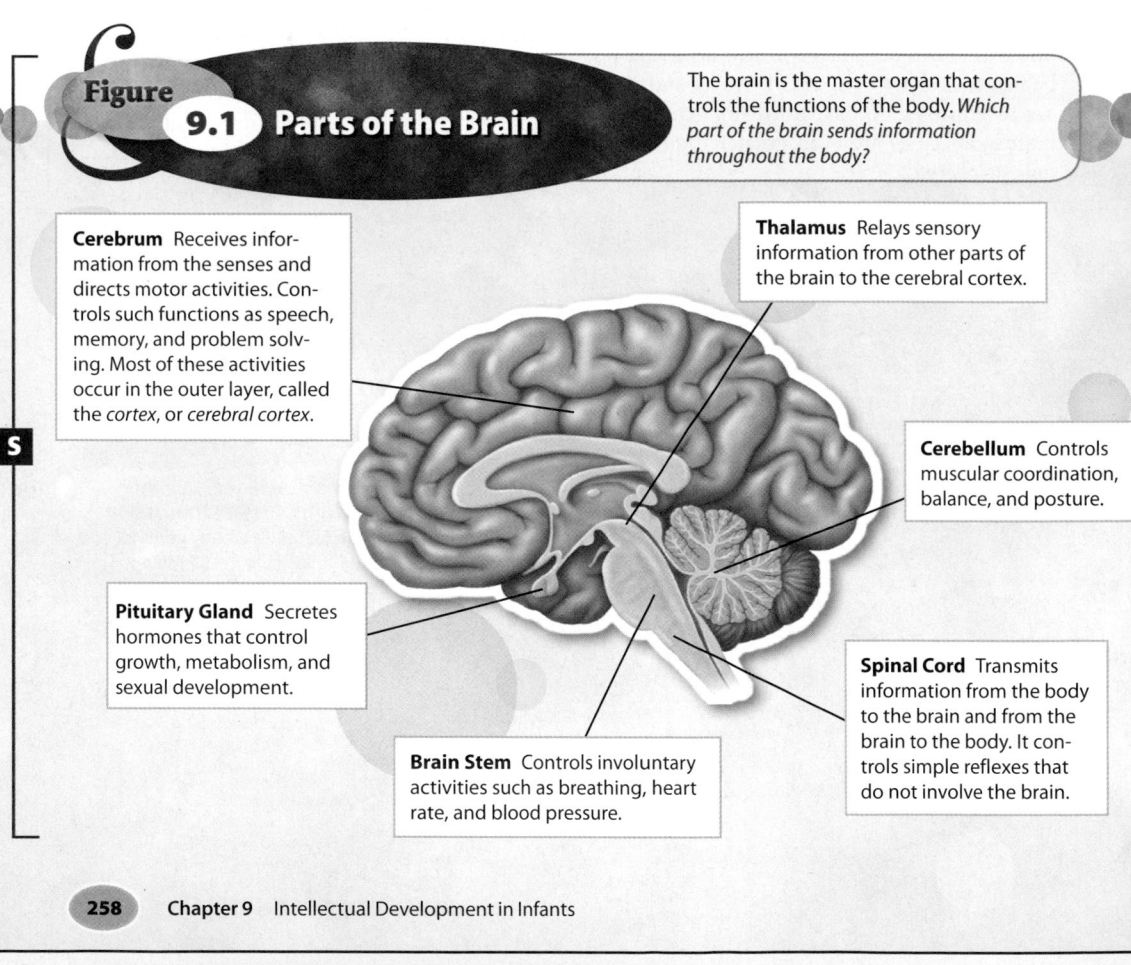

**Figure 9.1 Parts of the Brain**

The brain is the master organ that controls the functions of the body. *Which part of the brain sends information throughout the body?*

**Cerebrum** Receives information from the senses and directs motor activities. Controls such functions as speech, memory, and problem solving. Most of these activities occur in the outer layer, called the *cortex*, or *cerebral cortex*.

**Thalamus** Relays sensory information from other parts of the brain to the cerebral cortex.

**Cerebellum** Controls muscular coordination, balance, and posture.

**Pituitary Gland** Secretes hormones that control growth, metabolism, and sexual development.

**Spinal Cord** Transmits information from the body to the brain and from the brain to the body. It controls simple reflexes that do not involve the brain.

**Brain Stem** Controls involuntary activities such as breathing, heart rate, and blood pressure.

**258** Chapter 9 Intellectual Development in Infants

**Figure 9.1 Parts of the Brain**

**Caption Answer** The spinal cord sends information throughout the body.

**Discussion** Point out to students that the cerebral cortex is where speech, thinking, problem-solving, and other high-level functions occur. Ask students why they think the cortex is covered with "wrinkles." (The cortex has folds (called *gyri*) and grooves (called *sulci*.) (so that it can have more surface area for neural pathways)

## Parts of the Brain

The brain is divided into different sections. Each section controls a specific **function**, or job, of the body. The major sections are shown in **Figure 9.1**, along with a description of the functions they control.

One of the most important parts of the brain is the cortex ('kȯr-,teks). The **cortex** is part of the brain's cerebrum and its growth permits more complex learning. At one year, a baby's cortex is far more developed than it was at birth.

As babies experience more input from the world around them, their brains respond by forming more connections in the brain. It is in this way that the quality of caregiving affects brain growth. As caregivers hold, play with, and talk to an infant, the baby actually uses these experiences to build the brain's capacity.

## How the Brain Works

The brain contains billions of nerve cells called neurons. Neurons are tiny messenger cells that transmit information in the brain and nervous system through an electrical-chemical process.

Neurons are connected by axons ('ak-,säns) and dendrites. An **axon** is the connection between neurons that transmits instructions from the cell body to another neuron. Each axon is coated with myelin ('mī-ə-lən). **Myelin** is a fatty, insulating substance, which helps transmit information from one nerve cell to another. A **dendrite** is a branchlike feature at the end of each axon that receives the electrical messages from other neurons. This process actually begins when the baby is developing in the mother's uterus. After birth, it happens more quickly.

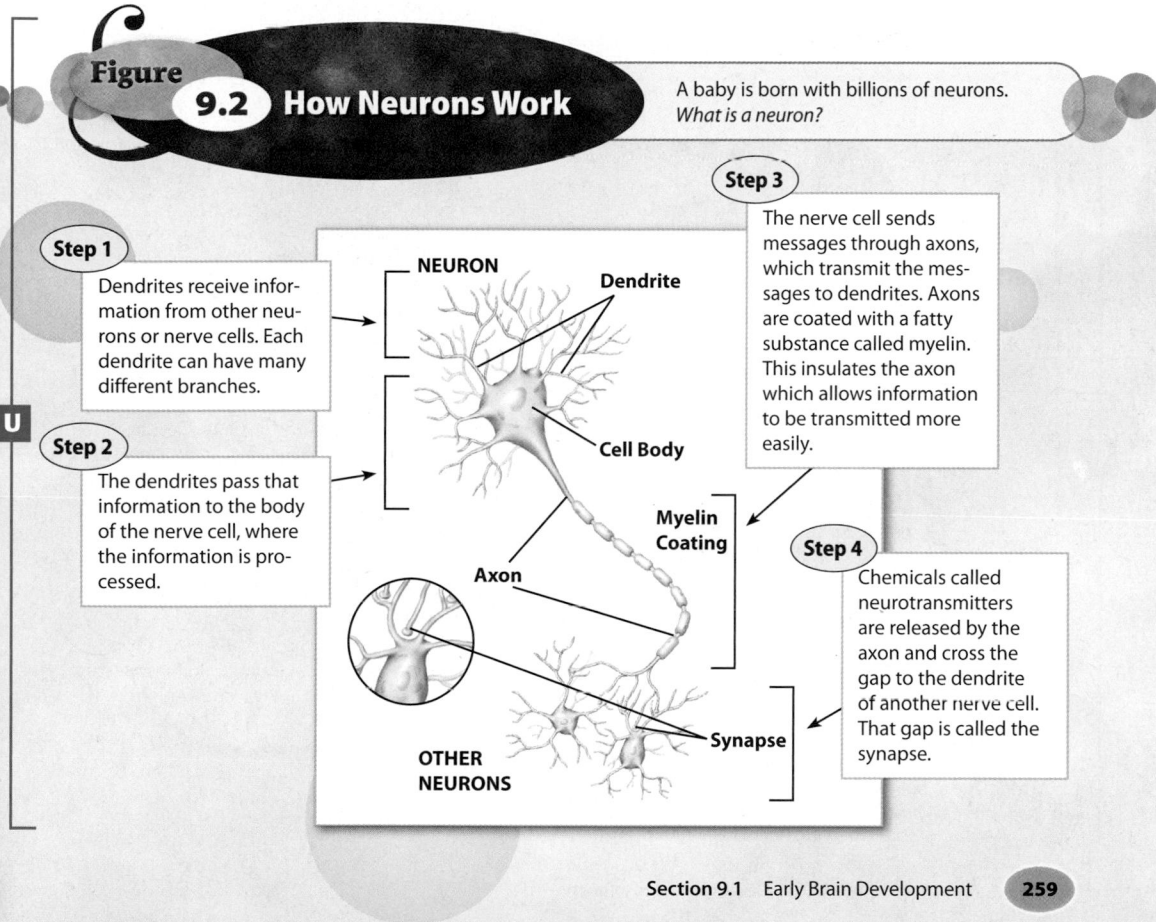

**Figure 9.2 How Neurons Work**

A baby is born with billions of neurons. *What is a neuron?*

**Step 1**
Dendrites receive information from other neurons or nerve cells. Each dendrite can have many different branches.

**Step 2**
The dendrites pass that information to the body of the nerve cell, where the information is processed.

**Step 3**
The nerve cell sends messages through axons, which transmit the messages to dendrites. Axons are coated with a fatty substance called myelin. This insulates the axon which allows information to be transmitted more easily.

**Step 4**
Chemicals called neurotransmitters are released by the axon and cross the gap to the dendrite of another nerve cell. That gap is called the synapse.

NEURON
Dendrite
Cell Body
Myelin Coating
Axon
Synapse
OTHER NEURONS

Section 9.1 Early Brain Development **259**

**Figure 9.2 How Neurons Work**

**Caption Answer** A neuron is a nerve cell.

**Discussion** Ask students: Why is myelin important to brain function? (When axons are coated with myelin, information can be transmitted more easily; this speeds up the learning process and allows individuals to think more quickly and efficiently.)

## Teach *cont.*

**C Critical Thinking**

**Make a Judgment** Tell students that one research study found that 87 percent of parents believe that the more stimulation a baby receives, the better off he or she is. Ask students: Do you think stimulation is always good for a baby? Why or why not? (Answers will vary. Some people think that too much stimulation can lead to restless, and even hyperactive, children who have difficulty performing quiet tasks such as reading.)

**U Universal Access**

**Kinesthetic Learners** Instruct students to act out the process of transmitting messages by having different students play the roles of neurons, dendrites, myelin, axons, synapses, and neurotransmitters. Students should show how the various components function and interact with one another. Have those students who are not involved in performing the actions help direct the others by offering suggestions. (Students should act out the process of transmitting messages from one neuron to another.) **ELL**

**Professional Development**

**Mini Clip**
**ELL: Words in Action**

Students act out or mime the words they are trying to learn.

## Assess

**Quiz**

Ask students to answer the following questions:

1. What is a neural pathway and how are neural pathways created? (It is a link between neurons that is created in response to experiences.)

2. Why is proper functioning of the cerebellum important? (Without a functioning cerebellum, an individual will not have proper muscular coordination, balance, or posture.)

3. What is the purpose of a neurotransmitter and how does it work? (It acts as a messenger, carrying signals from one neuron to another. An axon releases the neurotransmitter, which then attaches to a dendrite with the correct kind of receptor.)

## Reteach

### U Universal Access

**Gifted Learners** Tell students that in 1982, Benoit Mandelbrot wrote a book titled *The Fractal Geometry of Nature*. Explain that fractals are geometric shapes that are "self-similar," and yet each is unique. Snowflakes are an example. Instruct students to conduct research on fractal geometry, then write a paper explaining the basic concepts of fractals and how the brain's neural pathways exhibit fractal behavior. Students should cite their sources. (Students should write papers on the basic concepts of fractal geometry, including how neural pathways exhibit fractal behavior.)

### ✓ Reading Check

**Analyze** Repetition causes axons and dendrites to connect. The more times the same axon and dendrite connect, the stronger the connection becomes.

**260**

---

As **Figure 9.2** shows, dendrites reach out toward the axons of other neurons. The dendrites and axons do not touch, but they come close. A **synapse** ('si-,naps) is the tiny gap between the dendrites where messages are transmitted from one neuron to another.

A **neurotransmitter** (,nür-ō-tran(t)s-'mi-tər) is a chemical released by the axon. The neurotransmitter acts as a messenger between the neurons. This chemical looks for a dendrite to attach to, but they can only attach to those dendrites with the right kind of **receptor**, or receiver. The more times the same axon and dendrite connect, the stronger the connection grows. As a result, they can send and receive messages more quickly.

**✓ Reading Check** **Analyze** Why is it important to provide infants with repeated sensory input?

## Developing the Brain

More dendrites indicate increased learning. The more dendrites that neurons grow and the more links that develop between neurons, the more neural pathways are created in the brain. More pathways give the brain more power. It can do more tasks and control more actions. Think of a road system around a city. The more roads there are, the more places a driver can go, and the quicker he can get there.

The increased number of connections gives the brain more flexibility. Again, this is like a road system. The more roads there are, the more choices a driver has. If one road is shut down, there are alternate routes.

This increase in connections is the direct result of sensory input. The more the baby interacts with the world, the more complex the brain's "wiring" becomes.

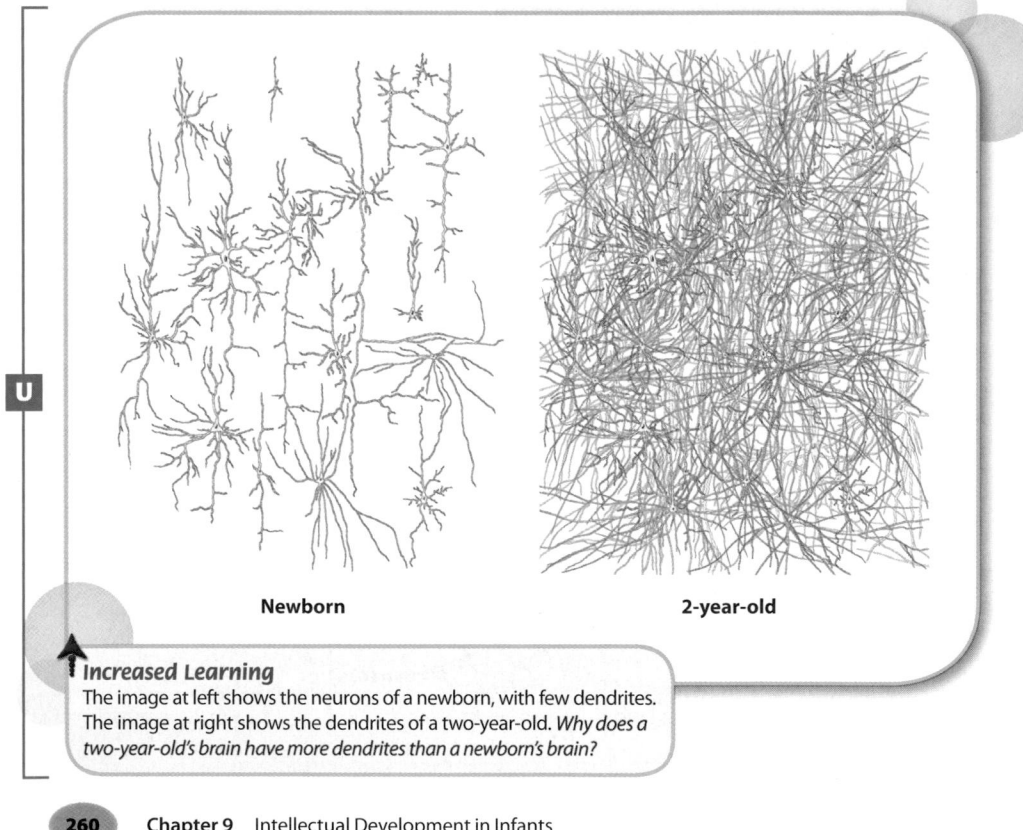

**Newborn**      **2-year-old**

**Increased Learning**
The image at left shows the neurons of a newborn, with few dendrites. The image at right shows the dendrites of a two-year-old. *Why does a two-year-old's brain have more dendrites than a newborn's brain?*

---

## ➤ Explore the Photo

**Caption Answer** The number of dendrites grow as result of stimulation.

**Discussion** Ask students: In what ways do these neural pathways look like a road map? In what ways are they different? (Roads connect different parts of a region and neural pathways connect different parts of the brain. Larger roads typically provide access to smaller local roads. Neural pathways, on the other hand, appear to be random.)

## How the Brain Becomes Organized

Each child's brain becomes organized in a unique way. This is because the organization is based on the particular experiences unique to that child. As connections between dendrites and axons grow stronger, a group of neurons becomes linked together. They become systems of nerve cells that control a certain action or thinking task.

For instance, one group of neurons can work together to control drinking from a cup. Each time a ten-month-old drinks from a cup, this network of synaptic connections fires together, in a particular sequence. At first, the connections take time to move the muscles. Eventually, after many repetitions, the neurons work together so well that it becomes easy for the child to drink from a cup. The child's skills increase as a result of the greater number of neural pathways. The child learns.

These connections affect not only actions but all areas of behavior. Systems of neurons work together to influence how babies see and hear, as well as how they think and remember. This process is how all learning takes place. The system is so flexible that humans continue to learn new behaviors and form new ideas all their lives.

Note that the connections between neurons are not permanent. They can be broken when the behavior or idea is not repeated, and the synaptic pathways fade away if they are not used. This is called pruning. People lose synapses in this way all through their lives. They forget what they have learned.

At the same time that some connections are being lost, however, new ones are being added. This building of new connections is called branching. The new connections become part of the brain as new skills are learned or new experiences are stored as memories.

Indeed, children form so many synaptic connections that they must lose some surplus connections in the process of refining a new skill and becoming proficient at it. This branching and pruning helps the brain focus only on useful connections, and thus acquire more skills.

### Is the Brain Organized Only Once?

The answer is no. There are many circumstances that prove this is not the case. Some children who suffered damage to the brain area that controls language have still learned to speak. Neurons in a specific area of the brain die during a stroke. Older people who suffer strokes can relearn skills by learning to use other areas of the brain.

The brain can be reorganized. In practical terms, that means a child does not have to be exposed to every possible activity in the first year, or even few years, of life. The brain will continue to develop through responses to life's experiences. It is important to give young children a stimulating environment. By doing so, parents and other caregivers help children's responsive brains develop many pathways and connections. See **Figure 9.3** on page 262 for tips on stimulating brain development.

### Learning Through Music

Donna has always loved music, so it was only natural that she share it with her baby, Michael. Donna sings to Michael every night when she puts him to bed. She was pleased to learn that listening to music may have a positive effect on certain thinking skills. Musical stimulation helps strengthen pathways in the brain, increasing the ability to learn. Some researchers believe that musical training creates new pathways in the brain. Now Donna tries to include music in Michael's day in a number of ways. She wants to enroll Michael in a Music for Tots program at the park district. Donna's husband believes Michael is too young to be in a class. He believes babies should learn and grow naturally. He has asked Donna not to take Michael to the music class.

✎ **Write About It** Write a letter from Donna to her husband in which she explains why it is good for Michael to attend music class. What does he learn there? How can it help him? How might it improve his learning in the future? Read your letter to the class.

**Write About It** Letters will vary but should include answers to the questions posed, such as music might create new pathways in the brain, giving Michael the potential to learn more.

## Reteach *cont.*

### R Reading Strategy

**Develop Connections** Ask students to think of how they expand on their existing knowledge when learning something new. Perhaps they learned a little about chemistry in a general science class but are now taking an organic chemistry class. Did they have a solid base on which to build? Did they have to "unlearn" some things that they thought they knew? Tie these experiences into the idea of pruning and branching.

**Professional Development**

**Mini Clip**
**ELL: Building the Context**

A teacher models an activity that will provide students with background information they may need to understand the text they are about to read.

### C Critical Thinking

**Problem Solve** Tell students to suppose that they always take the same route to their grandparents' house, which is five miles from where they live. Suddenly, a road is blocked off. How would they find a new route? How long would it take to get used to this new route? (Answers will vary. Once a task has to be relearned in a new way, the relearning process can take longer than the initial learning.) Encourage students to discuss how this process might be applied to a brain that needs to learn a new way of performing a task after the brain has been damaged.

## Reteach cont.

W

### Writing Support

**Personal Letter**

**Everyday Learning** Tell students that they have a relative who has decided not to work outside the home now that his or her baby is born. Have students write a personal letter to the relative offering suggestions for how he or she can stimulate her baby's intellectual development without spending money. (Refer to p. 254 for tips on writing a personal letter. Students should offer a variety of suggestions, such as cuddling and talking with baby and taking the baby to a nearby park.)

### C Critical Thinking

**Infer** Describe this scenario: Rita and Bill wanted their son Lucas to have a head start in learning. They showed Lucas flash cards of famous people and places every day. When Lucas began recognizing printed words, Rita called her sister, who had a child the same age. Rita discovered her sister's child had also started reading, but without the aid of flash cards. Ask students what they might infer from this. (Answers will vary but students might infer both began reading because they were at the right developmental stage.)

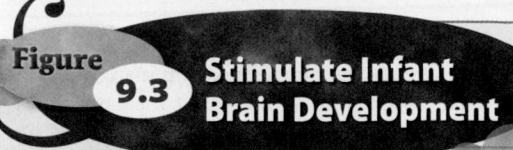

**Figure 9.3 Stimulate Infant Brain Development**

There are many ways to help foster intellectual development in children. *How could you interact with a one-year-old to stimulate her intellectual development?*

**Keep it simple and natural.** Everyday experiences, such as changing a diaper or giving a bath, build the pathways between neurons when combined with cuddling, talking, or singing to the baby. Experts urge parents to give children an environment rich with positive interaction and talking.

**Match experiences to the child's mental abilities.** Babies need physical experiences. That is how they learn. It is important to provide experiences at their level of understanding. For example, a safe interactive toy can help infants learn. However, flashcards are too advanced for a three-month-old.

**Practice makes perfect.** The more repetition, the stronger the connections between neurons become. Establish routines with the baby so the baby learns what to expect. Include reading a bedtime story, even when the baby cannot read. An infant will learn that sitting down with you and a book is important.

**Actively involve the baby.** Provide experiences in which the child takes part. Children of all ages learn best by doing.

**Provide variety, but avoid overload.** Some parents try to expose their baby to as many different experiences as possible to enhance brain development. Babies do benefit from a variety of experiences, but too many can overwhelm them.

**Avoid pushing the child.** Children learn better if they are interested in what they are doing. Look for clues as to whether the child shows interest in the activity. If not, do not pursue it.

**Figure 9.3 Stimulate Infant Brain Development**

**Caption Answer** Answers will vary. Possible answers include playing with blocks or simple toys, singing, moving to music, playing peek-a-boo, reading books, telling stories, or rolling a ball.

**Discussion** Point out that one of the suggestions for brain development is "Practice makes perfect." Ask students: Do you think this is truer for young children than for teens? Why or why not? (Possible answer: everyone performs better with extensive practice. Athletes and musicians are aware of this when they practice skills until they can perform them by rote.)

## Speeding the Brain's Work

R

Myelin, the fatty substance that coats axons, makes it easier for axons to transmit signals. It speeds the neuron's work. When a baby is born, only those nerves that control basic instincts, such as nursing, have this myelin coating.

Other axons get a coating of myelin as the child grows. This process continues until about age twenty. The myelin coating is added in different areas of the brain at different times. Axons in the area of the brain that controls motor skills, vision, and hearing receive the coating the earliest. As a result, those are the areas in which babies first show development. Myelin formation occurs in cycles that coincide with a child's mastery of increasingly complex learning.

The rate at which axons receive this fatty coating may explain why some children have difficulty learning certain tasks. If the nerves

### THE DEVELOPING BRAIN

#### Environment and the Brain

The number of connections in an infant's developing brain can be increased by a stimulating environment. Playing simple games like peek-a-boo stimulates a child to learn. This is proven when the child imitates the actions. The number of connections can also be decreased by a lack of stimulation. If no one talks to an infant, the connections for language will not form properly. The change can be as much as 25 percent in either direction. Babies love visual stimulation, and they have a preference for high-contrast images, such as black and white.

**Science Inquiry** Stimulating all of a baby's senses can dramatically increase the number of connections in a baby's brain. Why is it important to stimulate all of a baby's senses?

U

**Stimulating the Brain**
Touching and talking to a baby will stimulate dendrite growth in the baby's brain. *How do attention and experiences contribute to brain development?*

Section 9.1   Early Brain Development   **263**

### THE DEVELOPING BRAIN

#### Environment and the Brain
**Science Inquiry** Answers will vary but may include that all of a baby's senses should be stimulated so that they all develop equally. Babies learn different things through different senses and will learn better if more than one sense is involved in the learning process.

For more information and activities, see *The Developing Brain* guide and eTransparencies.

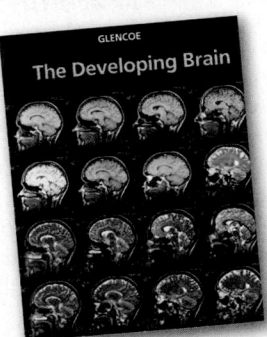

GLENCOE
The Developing Brain

## Section 9.1

### Reteach *cont.*

**R** **Reading Strategy**
**Connect to Real Life**  Discuss that myelin increases the speed of brain function. Ask students for examples of similar substances that people use every day to increase the speed or efficiency of objects. (Possible answers: oil in engines, wax on skis, rosin on the bow of string instruments.)

**U** **Universal Access**
**Interpersonal Learners**  Discuss whether students feel that placing an infant in child care can limit the child's intellectual development. Divide students into two groups and have them debate this topic focusing on the importance of brain stimulation. Have students conduct research to back up their statements with facts. (Students should debate the impact placing an infant in child care has on the child's intellectual development. Pros include that the child gets out of the house and is around other children. Cons include that parents know their children best and are more likely to provide them with a properly stimulating environment.)

### Explore the Photo

**Caption Answer**  The more stimulation a child receives, the more dendrites will grow and the more links will develop. This gives the brain more power for learning.

**Discussion**  Ask students: Based on what you have learned about brain development in babies, what would you look for when choosing child care for a nine-month-old? (Possible answer—staff that is knowledgeable about child development and is interested in providing appropriate stimulation.)

### Assess

**Study Tools**

Have students go to the Online Learning Center at **glencoe.com**:

- Take the **Practice Test**.
- Download **Study-to-Go** content.

Use the **Student Activity Workbook** for additional practice.

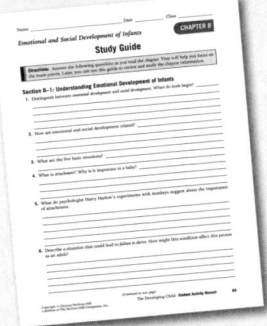

### Close

**Culminating Activity**

**Identify** Draw an unlabeled neuron with neural pathways on the board. Ask for volunteers to add labels and to explain how stimulating experiences cause the pathways to grow. (Students should identify the cell body, dendrite, axon, and synapse and explain how neural pathways grow.)

 **NCLB** connects academic correlations to book content.

---

controlling a certain activity are not yet covered with myelin, it is difficult for a child to learn that activity. The presence of myelin makes learning much easier by speeding up the signal.

Myelin is so crucial to the speed at which nerves function that if this coating is lost, it affects the way the brain and body function. Multiple sclerosis is a disease in which the absence of myelin plays a role. Scientists are working hard to find new treatments for this and other diseases.

**How Caregivers Can Help**

Parents and caregivers can support the brain's work by giving the child a stimulating environment. The child needs opportunities to see, hear, smell, and touch new things. The child might learn the terms *red* and *flower* by looking at a picture. However, the child is more likely to learn the terms quicker if he can see and smell a real flower, and touch its petals.

Another important way to help the brain develop is with repetition. By doing the same task over and over, synaptic connections are strengthened. This improves memory. Caregivers are likely to tire of Itsy Bitsy Spider after singing it once or twice. The child may want to hear it over and over again for several minutes. This repetition is how the child learns.

### { Expert Advice... }

*"Children need lots of practice doing things over and over again to succeed at a new skill. Think of the pride a baby feels when she can finally grasp the rattle and put it into her mouth by herself."*

— Claire Lerner LCSW, and Lynette Ciervo, authors, *Getting Ready for School Begins at Birth: How to help your child learn in the early years*

---

## Section 9.1     After You Read

**Review Key Concepts**

1. **Explain** how dendrites and axons function together in the brain.
2. **Describe** how repeated experiences help organize the brain.

**Practice Academic Skills**

**English Language Arts**

3. Choose a country other than the United States and research the child-rearing practices. What kinds of practices do they typically use to stimulate intellectual growth and understanding in infants? Write your answer in a one-page report. Use illustrations if possible.

> **NCTE 8** Use information resources to gather information and create and communicate knowledge.

**Science**

4. Conduct research on multiple sclerosis. In your report, be sure to provide answers to the following questions: What is multiple sclerosis (MS)? What are the typical symptoms of MS? What causes the symptoms?

> **NSES F** Develop understanding of personal and community health.

**Check Your Answers** Check your answers at this book's Online Learning Center at **glencoe.com**.

---

## Section 9.1     After You Read

**Review Key Concepts**

1. Axons and dendrites, which transmit information, connect neurons. Axons transmit messages to dendrites.
2. Groups of neurons work together, controlling the way muscles work while doing an activity. After many repetitions, the neurons work together so well that it becomes easier to do the activity.

Connections between neurons become part of the brain as new skills are learned or new experiences are stored as memories.

**Practice Academic Skills**

3. Students' answers will vary depending on the country chosen. Reports should answer the question posed and also include illustrations.

4. Multiple sclerosis is a chronic disease of the central nervous system. Symptoms may vary and may include abnormal fatigue, numbness and tingling, loss of balance and muscle coordination, slurred speech, tremors, stiffness, and bladder problems. Symptoms are caused when myelin is destroyed and replaced by scars of hardened tissues.

# Intellectual Development During the First Year

## Reading Guide

### Before You Read

**Use Color** As you read this section, try using different colored pens to take notes. For example, use blue to write main ideas and green to write vocabulary terms. This can help you learn new material and study for tests.

### Read to Learn
#### Key Concepts
- **List** four abilities that show intellectual growth in infants.
- **Identify** specific abilities that babies learn during Piaget's first period of learning.

### Main Idea
During the first year of a baby's life, growth occurs in many areas. These areas include size, intelligence, motor skills, social skills, and personality.

### Content Vocabulary
◇ perception
◇ attention span
◇ concept
◇ sensorimotor period
◇ object permanence
◇ imaginative play
◇ symbolic thinking

### Academic Vocabulary
You will find these words in your reading and on your tests. Use the glossary to look up their definitions if necessary.
■ elicit
■ determined

### Graphic Organizer
As you read, compare the intellectual and sensorimotor development of 1–4 months old babies. Use a chart like the one shown to list the characteristics.

| Developmental Milestones Ages 1–4 Months | |
|---|---|
| **Intellectual** | **Sensorimotor** |
| | |
| | |
| | |

 **Graphic Organizer** Go to this book's Online Learning Center at **glencoe.com** to print out this graphic organizer.

### Academic Standards · · · · · · · · · · · · · · · · · · · · · · · · · · · · ·

**English Language Arts**
**NCTE 5** Use different writing process elements to communicate effectively.

**Social Studies**
**NCSS I A Culture** Analyze and explain the ways groups, societies, and cultures address human needs and concerns.

---

**NCTE** *National Council of Teachers of English*
**NCTM** *National Council of Teachers of Mathematics*

**NSES** *National Science Education Standards*
**NCSS** *National Council for the Social Studies*

## Focus

### Bell Ringer Activity

#### On the Move
Hold up a picture of infant. Then hold up a picture of a one-year-old crawling or walking. Ask students: How do you think the increased mobility of this older child contributes to intellectual development? (The child can explore many more objects and also has the ability to choose what to explore.)

## Preteaching
### Vocabulary
Tell students that most of the vocabulary terms in this section consist of content area words. Words in the previous section, such as neuron and cortex, are used in many areas of science and medicine. However, terms such as sensorimotor period and imaginative play are primarily limited to child development.

### Graphic Organizer
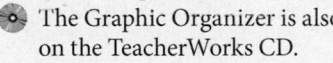 The Graphic Organizer is also on the TeacherWorks CD.

(Graphic organizers should list: Intellectual—gains information through senses, makes eye contact, can distinguish voices, can distinguish faces, can tell a smile from a frown. Sensorimotor—combines two or more reflexes, develops hand-mouth coordination.)

 **NCLB** connects academic correlations to book content.

## Reading Guide

### Before You Read
Ask students: Have you ever had the experience of having a baby stare intently at you? How did it make you feel? Why do you think the baby did this? (Answers will vary; babies study people's faces intently because their brains are trying to make sense of them.)

### D Develop Concepts
**Main Idea** Discuss the main idea with the students. Ask students whether they think these skills are interrelated. For example, are increasing social skills related to increasing intelligence? (Answers will vary; for example, developing social skills, such as playing with someone, requires the intelligence to understand the interaction.)

**265**

## Teach

### Discussion Starter

**Analyzing Perception** Discuss that the scientific meaning of the term *perception* is "the ability to learn from sensory information." Ask students: How does this definition differ from the way in which people frequently use this term? (People often use it to mean that different individuals have different interpretations of the same event.) How is the scientific definition similar to the way the term is frequently used? (People's perceptions will vary because each one's senses provide slightly different input and each person has different experiences.)

### **R** Reading Strategy

**Summarizing** Give students several minutes to read the material under Signs of Intellectual Growth. Instruct students to write a one- or two-sentence summary of what they learned. Ask for volunteers to read their summaries. Offer feedback as appropriate. (Summaries will vary but may be something like, "During their first year, babies begin remembering their experiences, making associations between events, and understanding cause and effect. Their attention spans also increase.")

**Mc Graw Hill Professional Development**

**Mini Clip**
**Reading: Strategic Readers**

Author Scott Paris discusses the characteristics of strategic readers.

## Early Learning Abilities

During the first year of life, children undergo a greater change than they ever will again. In just 12 months, a helpless newborn becomes a whirlwind of energy and activity. Babies go from not being able to move, to crawling or walking. A newborn communicates only by crying. However, as social skills begin to appear, a one-year-old can use gestures or even a few words. By age one, a baby has likes and dislikes, an imagination, and a unique personality.

Babies have many abilities at birth. A newborn can hear, see, taste, smell, and feel. These abilities are the building blocks of learning. The brain is fed by what is experienced through the senses. A babies' perception improves as experiences are repeated. **Perception** is the ability to learn from sensory information. The brain's neurons begin to become organized, increasing the baby's learning and skills. A newborn cannot purposely grasp and lift objects, but a three-month-old can. In time, babies' hand-eye coordination improves further. They develop many skills. **Figure 9.4** on page 267 summarizes the intellectual developmental milestones for a baby's first 12 months.

## Signs of Intellectual Growth

In just the first year of life, babies develop four abilities that show their growing intellectual abilities. They learn to remember experiences, make associations, understand cause and effect, and pay attention.

### Remembering Experiences

In the first few months, babies develop the ability to remember. The information from the senses can be interpreted in light of past experiences. A two- or three-month-old baby may stop crying when someone enters the room because the baby anticipates being picked up.

### Making Associations

When the baby ceases to cry, it also indicates association. The baby associates a parent or other caregiver with receiving comfort.

### Understanding Cause and Effect

Babies also develop an understanding of cause and effect, the idea that one action results in another action or condition. Sucking causes milk to flow. If the baby stops sucking, the milk stops. In short, every time the infant does something, something else happens.

**Increased Attention Span**
During the first year, a baby's attention span becomes much longer. *At what age do babies begin to study objects carefully?*

266    **Chapter 9**    Intellectual Development in Infants

---

**▶ Explore the Photo**

**Caption Answer** Babies begin to study objects carefully at approximately 5–6 months.

**Discussion** Ask students: What kinds of associations might this baby be making while playing with this object? (Possible answers— that as he moves the object, its appearance in his field of vision changes; that if he drops the object, it always falls in the same direction.)

Figure **9.4** **Intellectual Developmental Milestones—1st Year**

Motor skills are essential to intellectual development. *How might you encourage an 11-month-old baby who identifies objects in books?*

| Months | Developmental Milestone |
|---|---|
| **1–2 Months** | ❖ Gains information through senses<br>❖ Makes eye contact<br>❖ Prefers faces to objects<br>❖ Can distinguish between familiar and unfamiliar voices |
| **3–4 Months** | ❖ Can distinguish between familiar and unfamiliar faces<br>❖ Makes vowel-consonant combinations such as "ah-goo"<br>❖ Can tell a smile from a frown |
| **5–6 Months** | ❖ Is alert for longer periods of time, up to two hours<br>❖ Studies objects carefully<br>❖ Recognizes own name<br>❖ Distinguishes between friendly and angry voices<br>❖ Recognizes basic sounds of native language |
| **7–8 Months** | ❖ Imitates the actions of others<br>❖ Begins to understand cause and effect<br>❖ Remembers things that have happened<br>❖ Sorts objects by size<br>❖ Solves simple problems<br>❖ Forms sounds such as *da, ga, ma, ba*<br>❖ Recognizes some words<br>❖ Babbling imitates speech inflections |
| **9–10 Months** | ❖ Looks for dropped objects<br>❖ Responds to some words and phrases, such as "no" and "all gone"<br>❖ Takes objects out of containers and puts them back in<br>❖ May say a few words |
| **11–12 Months** | ❖ Can point to and identify objects in books<br>❖ Fits blocks or boxes inside one another<br>❖ Says "Mama" and "Dada" for parents<br>❖ Understands simple words and phrases like "Come to Mommy"<br>❖ Speaks some words regularly |

**S**

## Teach cont.

### S Skill Practice
**Guided Practice**

**Identify Intellectual Milestones**
Have students fold a sheet of paper into thirds. Label each section with one of these headings: "1–2 months," "3–4 Months," and "5–6 Months." Read aloud a developmental milestone for one of these age groups. Instruct students to write this milestone under the correct heading. Repeat this process for ten or twelve different milestones. (Students should place each milestone under the correct heading.) **L1** **ELL**

**Write Guidelines** Tell students to imagine that they run a child care center for children between five months and one year. Instruct them to write guidelines suggesting activities the center's workers should provide for each of these four age groups: 5–6 months, 7–8 months, 9–10 months, and 11–12 months. Their guidelines should include at least three specific activities for each group. (Students should provide at least three developmentally appropriate activities for each of the four groups.) **L2**

**Evaluate Intellectual Milestones**
Have students make arrangements to visit a child care center. While there, they should study at least two of the age groups listed in Figure 9.4. They should evaluate the intellectual milestones exhibited by each group and compare it to the milestones in the chart. When done, students should write a brief report summarizing their findings. (Reports will vary but should focus on the intellectual milestones exhibited by two different age groups and compare these milestones to those listed in the chart.) **L3**

**Figure 9.4 Intellectual Developmental Milestones—1st Year**

**Caption Answer** Answers will vary. Students may say they would look at more books with the baby or look at photographs of people the baby knows.

**Discussion** Ask students: What is a speech inflection? At what age do children begin imitating adults' speech inflections? Why is this an important skill? (Inflections are changes in the tone or loudness of words that express subtle variations of meaning. Babies begin this imitation at about 7–8 months. It helps them understand the components of language on which they will build.)

### Teach cont.

**C Critical Thinking**

**Draw Conclusions** Ask students: Why do you think a baby with above-average intelligence might have a short attention span while an older child with above-average intelligence typically has a longer attention span than other children his or her age? (Possible answer: The baby responds more intensely to the environment, so therefore builds more pathways; the older child can learn more by paying attention for longer periods of time and intently examining objects and events.)

**U₁ Universal Access**

**Visual Learners** Instruct students to use what they have learned to create a mobile that will stimulate an infant's sense of sight. Have students show their creations to the class and explain how they used what they have learned about infants when creating the toy. (Students should create a mobile that will stimulate an infant's sense of sight. They should explain to the class why they created it in the way they did; for example, they may have used bright colors because they know infants respond to them.) **ELL**

**▶ Explore the Photo**

**Caption Answer** Answers will vary but may include soft, stuffed toys or rattles.

**Discussion** Tell students to suppose that they are taking a ten-month-old on a 400-mile trip. Organize students into groups of three or four. Each group should create a list of ten toys that would be appropriate for the trip. (Lists will vary but should include age-appropriate toys, such as stuffed animals or board books.)

**268**

---

As babies' motor skills develop, cause-and-effect learning changes. By seven or eight months, babies can throw things deliberately. They can pull the cord on a toy and make the toy move. At this age, babies have a better understanding of their own power to make things happen.

**Paying Attention**

As babies grow, their attention span grows too. **Attention span** is the length of time a person can concentrate on a task without getting bored. If the same object is presented over and over again, the baby's response to the object will eventually become less enthusiastic. The baby's diminishing response is a way of saying, "That's old stuff. I've seen it before."

Generally, infants with above-average intelligence have a short attention span. They tend to lose interest sooner than babies of average or below-average intelligence. However, beyond infancy, children with above-average intelligence typically have a longer attention span than others their age.

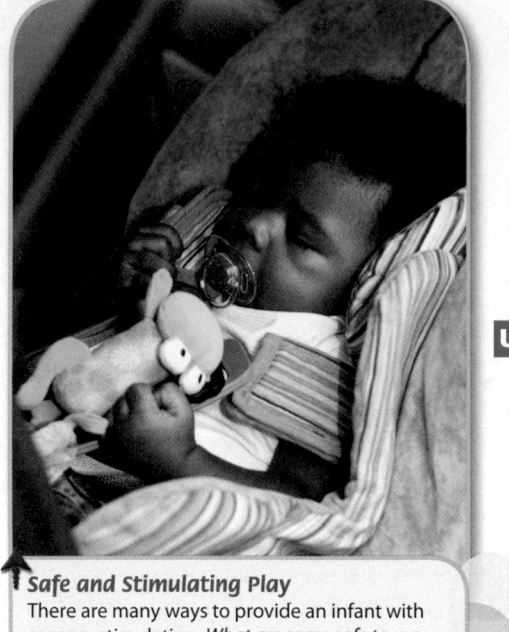

**↑ Safe and Stimulating Play**
There are many ways to provide an infant with sensory stimulation. *What are some safe toys a baby could play with while riding in a car?*

### THE DEVELOPING BRAIN

**Human Contact Needed**

When babies are bored, they will often announce their boredom by letting out a loud wail. Parents can come to the rescue by giving the infant a toy to play with. They might also talk to or play with the baby. Some parents and other caregivers use the television as a substitute. However, television cannot take the place of live interaction. Researchers have found that language not connected to the events around an infant is nothing but noise to the child. Studies show that no new pathways are being created when a child is watching television. Human contact, though, stimulates all of a child's senses.

**▪ Science Inquiry** Human interaction is generally the best interaction for a baby. When might it be appropriate to use the television to entertain a baby?

## Stimulating the Senses

A child's senses can be easily stimulated each and every day. For example, a baby's senses of touch and taste are routinely stimulated as he or she is changed and fed.

Very young infants prefer looking at people, rather than things. They can focus on and follow objects. They can also see shapes and forms. Hanging a mobile in an infant's crib will help stimulate a baby's sense of sight. Mobiles should be hung about 12 inches from the baby's eyes. Infants will respond to brightly colored objects, perhaps soft stuffed dolls with smiling faces and large eyes. Change the baby's position from time to time to vary the view.

Infants are very sensitive to sound. They recognize the voices of family and friends and can be calmed by a loving voice, even from another room. They are increasingly aware of their own voices and will babble back to an adult, mimicking the adult's tone of voice. Talking,

---

### THE DEVELOPING BRAIN

**Human Contact Needed**
**Science Inquiry** Answers will vary. Some students might feel that is it never appropriate. Others might feel it is appropriate for short periods of time or perhaps to lull the baby to sleep. The American Academy of Pediatrics advises that children under two should not watch any television.

For more information and activities, see *The Developing Brain* guide and eTransparencies.

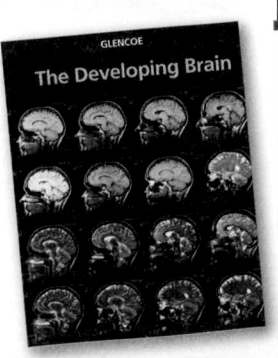

## Learning Through PLAY

### Sensory Play

During the sensorimotor period of development, children learn through their senses and their environment. In the first few months, babies learn about their own bodies. They learn how to move hands and feet at will, and hold bottles and small toys. At about eight months to one year, children learn to crawl and then to walk. This greatly expands the world they can explore. Everything in their path becomes an opportunity for learning. Besides seeing, touching, smelling, and listening, babies put almost everything into their mouths. Feedback from this sensory exploration teaches infants about their world.

By providing everyday objects and toys that will stimulate the child's senses, parents and other caregivers can enhance learning. As the baby grows, new objects and toys that stimulate all of the senses can be introduced.

**Think About It** Imagine you are babysitting your nine-month-old nephew. He spends his time crawling around, picking up things, and putting them in his mouth. You spend your time removing things from his mouth. What can you do so that you are not constantly removing things from his mouth?

---

reading, singing, and humming are wonderful ways to vary and stimulate an infant's hearing. These early stimulations from talking and singing will also help build the foundation for language development.

Touch is one of the most important ways to communicate love to an infant. The infant's sense of security and trust are built through cuddling, rocking, and patting. This also helps the infant gain a sense of his or her own body. This sense is crucial to the development of motor skills. A slowly swaying rocking chair or baby swing is a deeply comforting sensation for a baby, and helps him or her develop an awareness of space. In some areas, infant massage classes are available for learning more formal techniques to stimulate a baby's sense of touch.

### Concept Development

**U₂** As they continue to learn, young children between ages one and three begin to organize the information they receive from their senses. They start to form concepts. A **concept** is a general category of objects and information. Concepts range from categories for objects, such as fruit, to qualities, such as color or shape. Concepts also include abstract ideas, such as time.

Children learn words and concepts by using three principles:

- Children start by thinking that labels are for whole objects, not parts. Suppose Dwayne's father points to an animal and says "dog." How does Dwayne know that the label "dog" applies to the whole animal and not to its nose or its tail?
- Children believe that labels apply to the group to which the individual objects belong, not to the particular object. Any four-legged creature may **elicit**, or bring forth, "doggy!" from Dwayne.
- Young children tend to believe that an object can only have one label. That may be why it takes time for young children to learn to use pronouns. They have to learn to recognize that "mommy" and "she" can mean the same person.

As a child matures, concepts become more accurate. Babies begin with two broad concepts of "the baby" and "not the baby." Later, children make very broad distinctions between people and things.

**U₂**

✓ **Reading Check** **Explain** Why is the sense of touch so important to infants?

Section 9.2 Intellectual Development During the First Year **269**

---

## Learning Through PLAY

### Sensory Play

**Discussion** Ask students: Which senses do you rely on the most? How does this compare to the way in which a four-month-old relies on her senses? (Responses will vary. Babies, like older people, rely heavily on vision. They are probably less dependent on hearing because they do not yet understand speech. Smell and touch are important in examining new objects.)

**Think About It** Students might suggest that they pick up all items small enough to go in the baby's mouth before he arrives. They might keep him entertained by playing with him or reading to him.

## Assess

### Quiz
Ask students to answer the following questions:

1. Give an example of a situation in which a baby has made an association. (Answers will vary; a baby may stand up in her crib when she hears her father's voice because she knows he will lift her out of the crib.)
2. What skills do babies typically learn when they are 3 to 4 months old? (They learn to distinguish between familiar and unfamiliar faces, to make vowel-consonant combinations, and to tell a smile from a frown.)
3. Why is it difficult for young children to learn to use pronouns? (Young children tend to believe that an object can have only one label.)

## Reteach

### U₂ Universal Access

**Interpersonal Learners** Organize students into pairs. Tell them that one will play a well-known expert on child development and the other a host of a radio show devoted to families. The topic for discussion today is "Concept Development." The pair should create a script in which the host questions the expert on what skills are required for children to form concepts. Students should present their radio shows to the class. (Skits will vary but should show an understanding of concept development in children.) **ELL**

✓ **Reading Check**

**Explain** Through touch, love is communicated to an infant. The sense of touch also is crucial to the development of motor skills.

**269**

**C Critical Thinking**

**Create Analogies** Tell students that Piaget's theories recognize that babies see the world differently than adults. In addition, learning must proceed in sequential steps. Ask students to draw an analogy to something else that must occur in sequential steps. (Possible answers—an animal must reach a certain stage in maturity before it can have babies and a plant must create a bud before the bud can open into a flower.)

**R Reading Strategy**

**Analyzing Words** Discuss that readers often use several tools at once when determining the meaning of an unknown word. Ask students: How might you determine the meaning of the term *sensorimotor*? Encourage students to describe several different methods. Discuss how the word can be divided into components and also how context can be used to determine its meaning. (Possible methods include noting the context of the word and analyzing the meanings of the word's parts *sensori* and *motor*.)

**U₁ Universal Access**

**Learners Having Difficulties and English Language Learners** Go over the four periods of learning with the group. Discuss that the names of these periods can be somewhat challenging to remember. Encourage the group to create a memory device to help them remember the four periods. (Possible answer—Students might create a sentence such as "Some people can fret." The first letter of each word stands for the first letter in each of the periods.) **ELL**

## Periods of Learning

Jean Piaget, a psychologist, had a great influence on what is known about how children learn. In an effort to understand how children's intellectual skills developed, Piaget observed infants and children. He then recorded his observations about the growth of their ability to reason, or the increases in the level of their intellectual understanding. He found that intellectual development followed a pattern. His theory identified four major learning stages, or periods, that take place from birth to adulthood.

According to Piaget, these four periods appear in the same order in all children. They are the sensorimotor period, the preoperational period, the concrete operations period, and the formal operations period. Although the ages at which the periods emerge may vary from child to child, researchers have established average ages at which they appear. These periods are described in **Figure 9.5**.

Piaget **determined**, or reasoned, that children must learn to master one thinking skill before they can move on to another. Children cannot be forced to understand a concept or master a skill any faster than the speed at which their abilities mature. He also noted that children who do not get the opportunity to apply new skills during each stage might never reach their full potential. For this reason, it is important for children to have constant learning opportunities.

### The Sensorimotor Period

The **sensorimotor period** is Piaget's first stage of learning and lasts from birth to about age two. During this period, babies learn mainly through their senses and their own actions. This period happens during the time when the neurons in the infant's brain establish pathways that enable learning.

The exact role played by the brain in infant learning was not known when Piaget first developed his theories. Later scientific discoveries about neural pathways confirmed Piaget's observations. Sensory stimulation in the first year of life is vital for fostering a child's intellectual development. The more stimulation a child receives, the more dendrites the child's brain creates.

**Figure 9.5 Piaget's Four Periods of Learning**

Most people go through these periods during the ages indicated. *What might cause a child to go through the periods at a later age than indicated?*

| Period | Characteristics |
|---|---|
| **Sensorimotor** *Birth–2 years* | Children learn through their senses and own actions. |
| **Preoperational** *2–7 years* | Children think in terms of their own activities and what they perceive at the moment. |
| **Concrete Operations** *7–11 years* | Children can think logically but still learn best through experience. |
| **Formal Operations** *11–adult* | People are capable of abstract thinking. |

**Figure 9.5 Piaget's Four Periods of Learning**

**Caption Answer** Answers will vary. Possible answers include: sickness, injury, developmental disability, or lack of stimulation.

**Discussion** Organize students into four groups, one for each learning period. Each group should develop at least three examples of the types of learning that occur during their period. When they are done, have each group share their examples with the class.

Figure 9.6

**Piaget's Sensorimotor Period: Birth to Age Two**

Babies move from stage to stage as their sensorimotor skills develop. *How does a baby feeding itself a cracker demonstrate Stage 2?*

| Stage | Approximate Ages | Characteristics |
|-------|------------------|-----------------|
| Stage 1 | Birth to 1 month | ✤ Practices inborn reflexes<br>✤ Does not understand self as separate person |
| Stage 2 | 1 to 4 months | ✤ Combines two or more reflexes<br>✤ Develops hand-mouth coordination |
| Stage 3 | 4 to 8 months | ✤ Acts intentionally to produce results<br>✤ Improves hand-eye coordination |
| Stage 4 | 8 to 12 months | ✤ Begins to solve problems<br>✤ Finds partially hidden objects<br>✤ Imitates others |
| Stage 5 | 12 to 18 months | ✤ Finds hidden objects<br>✤ Explores and experiments<br>✤ Understands that objects exist independently |
| Stage 6 | 18 to 24 months | ✤ Solves problems by thinking through sequences<br>✤ Can think using symbols<br>✤ Begins imaginative thinking |

Piaget noted that during the sensorimotor period, babies come to understand an important concept. This concept is called object permanence. **Object permanence** is the concept that objects will continue to exist, even when they are out of sight. This usually occurs at about ten months of age. For example, at four months, when Megan drops her rubber ring toy and it rolls behind her, she simply looks for something else to play with. But at eleven months, Megan actively looks for her ball when it rolls out of sight. She has learned the concept of object permanence. This is why babies enjoy playing peek-a-boo. They learn that Mommy is still there, even if they cannot see her face.

### Six Stages

As seen in Figure 9.6, the sensorimotor period can be broken down into six shorter stages. At each stage, a baby has specific intellectual abilities. This can help you better understand how learning occurs.

Note that the child's abilities at each stage after Stage 1 build on the stage before. For example, the inborn grasping reflex in Stage 1 establishes a pattern that permits learning to grasp and hold a desired object. At Stage 2, an infant has learned how to grasp a desired object, such as a piece of food or a teething ring, and bring it to the mouth. Acquiring these abilities lets an infant move on to learn a more complex set of skills at each stage.

Figure 9.6

**Piaget's Sensorimotor Period: Birth to Age Two**

**Caption Answer** During Stage 2, babies develop hand-mouth coordination, which is required to feed oneself.

**Discussion** Have students think back to the earlier discussion of how neurons work and the importance of myelin. Ask: Why does an infant have basic reflexes at Stage 1? (The neurons needed to control these basic instincts are coated with myelin at birth.)

---

## Reteach *cont.*

 **Universal Access**

**Verbal Learners** Assign students to read a biographical sketch on Jean Piaget or an article about Piaget's theories and write a summary on what they learn. Instruct them to discuss why Piaget's studies were revolutionary for their time. (Students should write a summary of their readings. Piaget's studies were revolutionary because he was the first to scientifically analyze infant learning.)

 **Professional Development**

 **Mini Clip Reading: During and After Reading**

A teacher models for her students and then has them practice what a good reader thinks about.

## **W** Writing Support

**Personal Letter**

**New Skills** Tell students to imagine they are parents of a baby girl. When your baby was five months old, you wrote a letter to a friend describing her skills. Now your baby is one year old. Write a letter describing what your baby has learned since the last letter. (Refer to p. 254 for tips on writing a personal letter. Students should write a letter describing appropriate abilities, such as crawling, finding hidden objects, and using simple words.)

### Study Tools

Have students go to the Online Learning Center at **glencoe.com**:

- Take the **Practice Test**.
- Download **Study-to-Go** content.

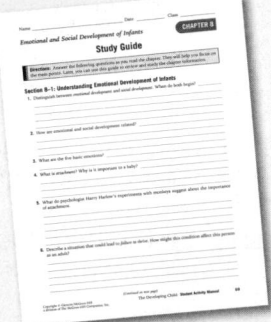

Use the **Student Activity Workbook** for additional practice.

## Close

### Culminating Activity

**Describe** Conclude this section by having students describe the characteristics of Piaget's four periods of learning. (Sensorimotor: learn through senses and own actions; preoperational: think in terms of own activities; concrete operations: think logically; formal operations: think abstractly)

**NCLB** connects academic correlations to book content.

---

At the end of Stage 6, children have used their experiences of the physical world to construct a consistent view of the world they live in. At this point, children can hold an image in their minds of a period beyond the immediate moment. This is especially true if they have been read to regularly. Words such as soon or later now have meaning because the child is able to think of a time in the future.

Imaginative play also becomes possible at Stage 6. **Imaginative play** is pretending. The child can imagine things that might happen but have not happened yet. Children will start pretending by mimicking the actions of those around them. For example, after watching a parent cook a meal, they might pretend to cook. After visiting the doctor, they might go home and want to "listen" to mom's heartbeat or look in dad's throat.

This is also the time when symbolic thinking begins, and the foundations for reading are established. **Symbolic thinking** is the use of words and numbers to stand for ideas. Children can begin to learn pre-reading skills when they are read to on a daily basis. They might begin to understand that print stands for words. Many children will want to read and re-read the same book. They often will memorize the story before they know how to read. This allows them to match the words they know with the words and letters they see on the page. Books with rhyming and alliteration make it easier for the child to remember the story.

Remember that reading is not just for intellectual development though. Reading to a child is also a great way to bond with the child. It also teaches the child that reading is fun.

---

## Section **9.2** After You Read

### Review Key Concepts

1. **Define** *perception* and give an example of how a baby's perception changes during the first year of life.
2. **Identify** what babies use to learn during Piaget's first period of development.

### Practice Academic Skills

 **English Language Arts**

3. When your friend babysits his six-month-old niece, he usually puts her in the crib so he can do homework. Write a convincing letter to your friend explaining how the loving touch of a caregiver helps a baby develop certain senses that are important to the development of motor skills.

> **NCTE 5** Use different writing process elements to communicate effectively.

 **Social Studies**

4. Though cosleeping is a recent trend in America, it has a long tradition in many other countries. *Cosleeping* is when a baby sleeps with one or both parents, rather than in a crib, for up to two years of his or her life. Conduct research on a culture that promotes cosleeping. Write a paragraph to answer the following questions: Why is it considered the most acceptable method of infant care in that society? What benefits does that society feel cosleeping has for a baby?

> **NCSS I A** Analyze and explain the ways groups, societies, and cultures address human needs and concerns.

 **Check Your Answers** Check your answers at this book's Online Learning Center at **glencoe.com**.

---

## Section **9.2** After You Read

### Review Key Concepts

1. Perception is a baby's ability to learn from sensory information. Examples will vary. Possible examples include that a baby gradually learns to hold a bottle while drinking from it, or learns to push a ball.
2. Babies use their senses and their own actions to learn during the first period of development.

### Practice Academic Skills

3. Letters will vary, but should provide a convincing argument that explains how an infant gains security, trust, and a sense of her body through a caregiver's touch. This sense is crucial to the development of motor skills.

4. Paragraphs will vary. Many nonWestern cultures view a baby as an extension of the mother and feel they should spend both waking and nonwaking hours together. Sleeping with a new baby allows the mother to respond more quickly to the baby's needs.

## Reading Guide

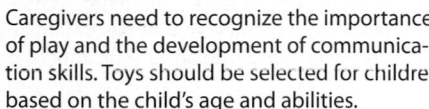

### Before You Read

**Discuss** Read the heads in the section and write a paragraph in which you discuss the meaning of the heads.

### Read to Learn
#### Key Concepts
- **Name** five ways caregivers can encourage learning.
- **Discuss** how to choose toys appropriate for babies of different ages.

### Main Idea
Caregivers need to recognize the importance of play and the development of communication skills. Toys should be selected for children based on the child's age and abilities.

### Content Vocabulary
 age appropriate
 childproof
◇ manipulate

 **Graphic Organizer** Go to this book's Online Learning Center at **glencoe.com** to print out this graphic organizer.

### Academic Vocabulary
You will find these words in your reading and on your tests. Use the glossary to look up their definitions if necessary.
- responsiveness
- hazard

### Graphic Organizer
As you read, list toys appropriate for different ages. Use a spider web chart like the one shown to help organize your information.

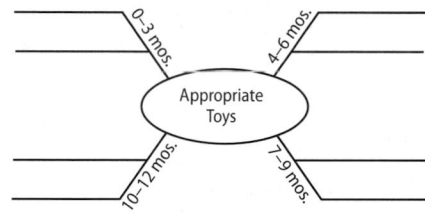

0–3 mos.  4–6 mos.

Appropriate Toys

10–12 mos.  7–9 mos.

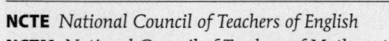

### Academic Standards . . . . . . . . . . . . . . . . . . . . . . . . .

#### English Language Arts
**NCTE 12** Use language to accomplish individual purposes.

#### Mathematics
**NCTM Geometry** Analyze characteristics and properties of two- and three-dimensional geometric shapes and develop mathematical arguments about geometric relationships.

#### Social Studies
**NCSS I C Culture** Apply an understanding of culture as an integrated whole that explains the functions and interactions of traditions, beliefs and values, and behavior patterns.

**NCTE** *National Council of Teachers of English*
**NCTM** *National Council of Teachers of Mathematics*

**NSES** *National Science Education Standards*
**NCSS** *National Council for the Social Studies*

**NCLB**

---

## Focus

### Bell Ringer Activity

#### The Importance of Toys
Ask for volunteers to discuss their favorite childhood toys. Ask: What did this toy mean to you? Why do you think you were so attached to this particular toy? Did you learn anything from the toy? If so, what? Discuss that babies often become very attached to favorite toys, and many of these toys encourage intellectual development.

## Preteaching
### Vocabulary
Ask students "What do you think *childproof* means? (safe from being accessed by children) How does the first part of the word help you determine its meaning? (by telling you that the word relates to children) On the board, create a list of other words that start with *child*.

### Graphic Organizer
 The Graphic Organizer is also on the TeacherWorks CD.

(Graphic organizers should list: 0–3 months: Mobiles, pictures. 4–6 months: teething rings, rattles, squeaky toys. 7–9 months: Books that make noise, blocks, balls, pots and pans. 10–12 months: Push-and-pull toys, picture books.)

**NCLB** NCLB connects academic correlations to book content.

---

## Reading Guide

### Before You Read
Ask students to describe some of the ways in which they communicate with one another. (Examples may include talking, using gestures, e-mailing, and text messaging.) Tell students that this section discusses the ways in which babies communicate and how caregivers can encourage these skills.

### D Develop Concepts

**Main Idea** Discuss the main idea with the students. Teaching babies to communicate their needs is an important responsibility of caregivers. Ask: Why is teaching babies to communicate so important to their development? (Appropriately communicating is vital to being able to function in society and to getting an individual's needs met.)

**273**

## Discussion Starter

**Infants' Responses** Ask students how they think parents' love for their infant affects the parents' responsiveness to the infant. How does this responsiveness affect the infant's learning? How does playing with someone who loves them affect the infant's experience? (Having someone who truly cares about the infant respond to his or her needs lets the infant know that the world is a warm, welcoming place and encourages the infant to respond positively and be more attentive, thereby increasing learning.)

## R Reading Strategy

**Draw Conclusions** Ask for a volunteer to read aloud the second paragraph on this page. Ask students: Based on what you have learned about babies' intellectual development, what conclusion can you draw from the last sentence in this paragraph? (You can infer that babies who do not recognize patterns in events around them will not have the same rate of intellectual development as those who do recognize patterns.)

## C Critical Thinking

**Evaluate** Jason, who is fifteen, loved interlocking building blocks as a child. So when his nephew was born, he immediately took a set of building blocks as a gift. Do you think this was an age-appropriate gift? Why or why not? (No, because the baby would not be able to manipulate the blocks. In addition, they could be a choking hazard.)

# Encouraging Learning

Intellectual development in an infant is closely linked with the **responsiveness**, or reactions, of others in the baby's environment. This means babies learn more and learn faster when caregivers comfort them, smile at them, talk to them, and play with them. A baby treated in this way is likely to develop more skills more quickly than a child who receives less interactive care. Babies' most important teachers are the people who care for them every day.

Even the youngest babies learn about the world from the care they receive. When Tyler's stomach feels uncomfortable, he cries. Then his mother picks him up and nurses him, and he feels better. Everyday events like discomfort, crying, cuddling, and being fed are connected. The child learns to recognize this pattern. If the baby's cries are not answered, the baby sees no relationship between his or her needs and the caregiver's actions. There is no pattern to help the baby form new pathways in the child's brain. No new pathways means no new abilities or associations.

In addition to giving a child basic care, there are things that parents and other caregivers can do to help build and influence their child's learning, or intellectual development. Encouraging learning does not require money or special toys. Rather, it depends on the attention, knowledge, and time that parents and other caregivers can give to the child.

Here are some ways that parents and other caregivers can encourage learning:

- **Learn about child development.** Caregivers should understand how an average child develops. This can help caregivers provide toys and learning experiences that are age appropriate. **Age appropriate** means something is suitable for the age and individual needs of a child. Understanding age-appropriate behavior also helps caregivers have realistic expectations for what their child should be able to do.

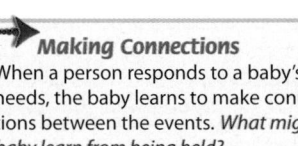

**Making Connections**
When a person responds to a baby's needs, the baby learns to make connections between the events. *What might a baby learn from being held?*

## ►► Explore the Photo

**Caption Answer** Answers will vary, but may include a feeling of love, safety, or security.

**Discussion** Lead the class in a discussion of how this adult is benefiting by her relationship with the baby. (Possible answers—she receives the baby's affection, gets the satisfaction of knowing she is doing a good job of raising the child, and is able to enjoy seeing the child progress every day.)

- **Give the child time and attention.** Caregivers know to give a child attention when he or she cries. However, no baby needs attention every waking moment. A caregiver can help a baby thrive and learn just by talking to and playing simple games with the baby.
- **Provide positive feedback.** When the baby demonstrates a new skill or tries out a new activity, showing pleasure and responding with praise will encourage the baby to keep trying new things. You can show your pleasure to a child with a hug, by clapping your hands, or sometimes just by smiling or laughing.
- **Express love.** Caregivers who use their personal style to show their love for the baby are helping the baby grow in self-confidence. They are also encouraging the baby to try more and to learn more.
- **Read.** A child is never too young for books. Caregivers should make reading part of a daily routine.
- **Talk, talk, talk.** Talking has many benefits. When caregivers talk to infants, they help them learn about their environment and learn language. Current research shows that the more caregivers talk to a baby, the faster the child's brain develops. Talking builds feelings of security, too.

## Developing Communication

One of an infant's major tasks is to learn to communicate with others. This skill depends on development in all areas: physical, emotional, social, and intellectual. There are wide differences in the rate of development from baby to baby. However, healthy babies should show steady improvement in communication skills.

**S**

### Communicating Without Words

Babies communicate long before they can talk. Most children do not have the ability to speak with words until they are about 11-months-old. By the end of the first year, though, they can effectively make most of their needs and wants known without words.

At first, crying is simply an automatic way to communicate discomfort. However, babies quickly learn that crying produces a response.

Someone will come and try to make them feel better. Within a month or so, the crying takes on a pattern. A cry is followed by a pause to listen for reactions. If no response arrives, the baby resumes crying. The baby soon develops different cries for different problems. A cry indicating hunger may be interrupted by wails of frustration as the baby learns to manipulate a bottle. A cry of pain may include groans and whimpers.

Babies also send messages with movements and gestures. An eleven-month-old who pushes away a bowl of a favorite food has had enough to eat. The baby who clings with both arms to a parent's leg is showing a sure sign of anxiety. The use of gestures continues into adulthood, but they are used more to reinforce words than as a substitute for words.

Finally, a baby communicates by making special sounds. Some sounds, such as giggles and cooing, carry obvious messages.

**S**

---

# SAFE CHILD HEALTHY CHILD

### Safe Learning

To encourage learning, allow babies as much freedom of movement at home as possible. In the first few months, the baby should be moved from one room to another to be with the family. A baby who spends time with the family as they go about their daily routine learns more than a baby who is left alone in a crib. Older babies who can crawl or walk should not be restricted to playpens for long periods of time. It is better to childproof the home and monitor the child's activities. To **childproof** means to take steps to protect the child from possible dangers.

☀ **Be Prepared** Research ways to childproof a home for a toddler. Choose three of the safety measures you learn and create a poster to illustrate them. With your teacher's permission, mount your poster in the classroom.

# SAFE CHILD HEALTHY CHILD

### Safe Learning

**Identify** Why is it important that an infant be moved around the home with the family? (Being with the family allows the infant to be stimulated by the activity.)

☀ **Be Prepared** Posters will vary but should illustrate three childproofing safety measures for toddlers.

---

## Teach *cont.*

## **S** Skill Practice

### Guided Practice

**List Ways Infants Communicate**
Instruct students to create a list of the different ways that babies who cannot speak communicate with their caregivers. Remind students to include gestures, facial expressions, cries, and so forth on their lists. Encourage students to illustrate their lists. (Students should create a list of ways in which babies communicate with their caregivers.) **L1 ELL**

**Talk with a Parent** Have students talk with a parent of a child who cannot yet speak. They should ask the parent, "How does your baby communicate with you? Can you tell what your baby needs based on the sound of its cry?" Instruct the students to write a paragraph summarizing the parent's answers. (Students should interview parents concerning how their babies communicate with them and write a summary of what they learn.) **L2**

**Observe Infant Communication**
Instruct students to observe a child who cannot yet speak. Have them watch closely for ways in which the child communicates with caregivers. Students should keep track of the different methods and how effective each method appears to be. Students should write a brief report summarizing the methods of communication and caregivers' responses to them. (Reports will vary but should show an understanding of ways in which the child communicated and how the parent responded to the child. For example, the child might have cried and the parent responded by holding and talking to the child.) **L3**

**275**

## Teach cont.

### C Critical Thinking

**Make a Decision** Tell students to suppose that they are parents of a baby who is too young to speak. Ask them if they think they would teach the baby sign language. What might be an advantage? Can they think of any disadvantages? (Answers will vary. The main advantage might be that it could reduce the frustration felt by parents and children when they have communication problems. While many studies show that signing enhances language development, some professionals are concerned that signing might slow down the process of learning speech. One disadvantage might be that it takes time to learn and the baby typically only uses signs for a short time, until they begin speaking.)

### U₁ Universal Access

**Visual Learners** Organize students into pairs. Instruct students to conduct research on teaching sign language to babies. Then have the students prepare skits in which parents and babies communicate by using sign language. Have students present their skits to the class. Encourage the class to interpret what is being communicated. (Skits will vary but should show a mother and child communicating with sign language. The students may present signs for activities such as eating or drinking, and may show them being used in different settings, such as at home and at a play group. Students should research and use actual signs that babies can be taught.)

**Sign Language** In the United States and Canada, some parents are using sign language to communicate with babies between six and twelve months old. Experts say that babies as young as six months have the memory to recognize and remember signs their parents make, and to respond. Parents teach their babies to use simple hand signals for words such as "no," "eat," "more," "milk," and "dog."

Scientific studies have shown that signing enhances babies' language development by allowing them to learn language before they develop the ability to speak. The physical skills needed for speech include coordinating the movements of the tongue, jaw, and lips. These skills do not develop until babies are between eleven and eighteen months of age.

The motor skills needed to produce hand signals develop much sooner. Signing also helps children learn social skills by allowing them to express themselves. It is a relief to some children to have a way to communicate with their parents.

There are many resources available to help you learn basic signs to teach to your baby. These include books, Web sites, and classes. It is important to be consistent when you teach a baby sign language. The child should see the same signs for the same thing in different settings, and if possible from different people. This will reinforce the connection between the sign and the meaning.

Chase's mom has started using the sign for drink each time she offers Chase a cup. If Chase only sees this sign at home and from his mom, he may associate it with his mom. When his grandpa uses the same sign in a restaurant, Chase begins to understand that the sign goes with the action. Next time Chase is thirsty, he may try to make the sign himself.

It is best to choose three or four signs to teach your baby. Try to use them consistently for several days or weeks. Once your child has mastered them, then you can add a few more to expand his vocabulary.

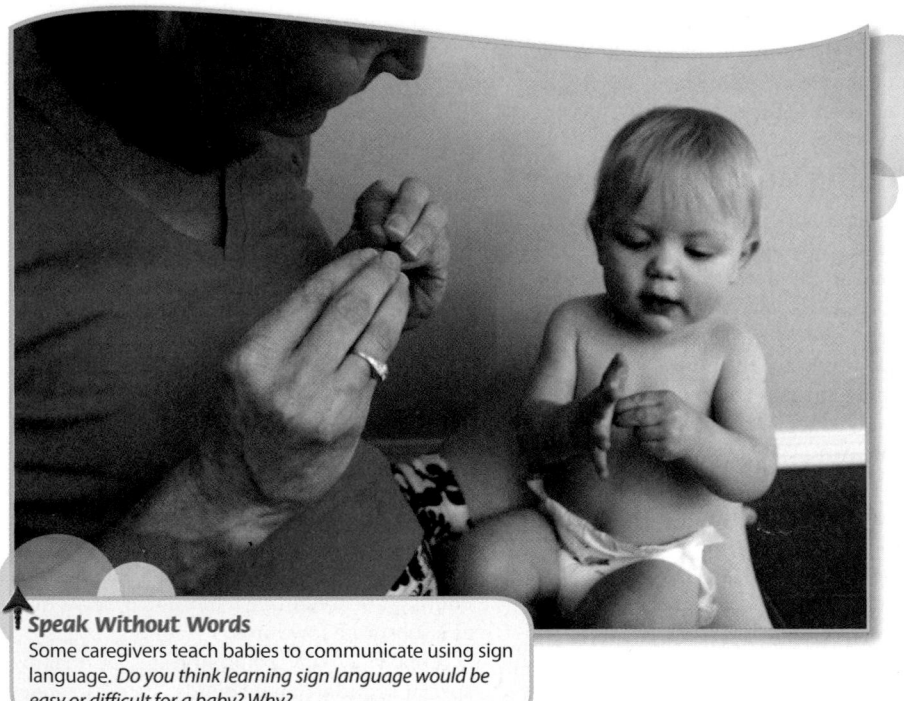

**Speak Without Words**
Some caregivers teach babies to communicate using sign language. *Do you think learning sign language would be easy or difficult for a baby? Why?*

### ▶ Explore the Photo

**Caption Answer** Students' answers will vary. According to the text, babies have motor skills needed to produce hand signals before they have the skills necessary for speech.

**Discussion** Ask students: What do you think would happen if a caregiver constantly ignored the hand gestures of a baby? For example, if the baby signaled he wanted to drink, but the caregiver pretended he did not understand, how do you think the baby would respond? Why? (The baby might become frustrated at first and then finally give up making any gestures.)

## Math in Action

### Geometric Shapes

Researchers recommend adding abstract props to a baby's play area. One such prop is a set of wooden geometric shapes called tangrams. These shapes can be triangles, squares, rectangles, or trapezoids. They fit together to create larger geometric shapes. What geometric shape do two equal-size trapezoids create when their longer bases are placed side by side?

**Math Concept** **Geometric two-dimensional shapes** A trapezoid is a shape with four sides where two of the sides are parallel.

**Starting Hint** Draw two trapezoids that are the same size. Cut them out and place the two long bases together.

**NCTM Geometry** Analyze characteristics and properties of two- and three-dimensional geometric shapes and develop mathematical arguments about geometric relationships.

 **Math** For math help, go to the Math Appendix at the back of the book.

### Learning to Speak

Before learning to talk, a baby must learn to associate meanings with words. This is a gradual process. It depends on caregivers talking to the baby, even when the baby does not appear to respond. For example, when taking the baby for a walk, caregivers can talk about what they see.

When talking to a baby, use simple words, but avoid baby talk. Children are experts at repeating what they hear. If they learn baby talk first, regular speech is more difficult. Caregivers should speak clearly using simple words. In this way, the child will become accustomed to hearing real words. For example, parents should say "Does Susie want a bottle?" instead of "Susie want baba?"

Although babies will not understand much of what caregivers say, they are beginning to establish an important habit. Listening to other people's talk is essential for an infant's language development. This is especially true if the talk is directed to the baby. This interaction also helps build speech centers in the child's brain. Parents and caregivers can increase the amount of speech a baby hears by talking to the baby about everything they do. For instance, they can describe each step of the process as they change a baby's diaper.

**Developmental Milestones** A newborn is physically unable to speak. Over the first year, physical changes take place that allow the baby to make the sounds necessary for speech. Babies get ready for real speech by babbling, or repeating syllables and sounds. You may have heard babies endlessly repeating consonant and vowel sounds such as "babababa" or "gogogogo." Babbling is a baby's preparation for saying recognizable words. To encourage babbling, respond to and imitate the baby's sounds. This encourages the baby to continue practicing.

A child's first real words are usually understandable between the ages of eight and fifteen months. Because the infant typically has been babbling and coming close to real word sounds for some time, it is not always easy to know exactly when a specific word is spoken on purpose. First words are usually common, simple words that have special meaning for the baby, such as "mama," "dada," or "bye-bye." Most children do not have a large vocabulary and cannot combine words into sentences until after their first birthday.

There are predictable stages that children go through as they develop speech. **Figure 9.7** on page 278 outlines some typical speech milestones. Of course, children vary in their development of speech, so these milestones serve only as a guide to normal development. They help doctors and caregivers determine when and if a child may need extra help to develop his or her speech. If parents are concerned about their child's development, they should speak to their pediatrician.

A baby's first words are one of the most exciting milestones parents and other caregivers experience with their child. A parent will love to hear "mama" or "dada" instead of a cry from their child. When a child learns to talk, it opens the door to a whole new world of communication and learning.

### Quiz

Ask students to answer the following questions:

1. Why should a caregiver provide a child with age-appropriate activities? (Possible answer—so that the child will be able to learn from the activities and will not become frustrated.)

2. Why is it vital that caregivers talk to infants? (Talking promotes intellectual development and builds a feeling of security.)

3. Give an example of a way that a baby can communicate, even if the baby is unable to speak. (Answers will vary. A baby may lift his arms up if he wants to be held or throw food on the floor if he does not like its taste.)

### Reteach

### U₂ Universal Access

**Gifted Learners** Discuss that the Math in Action feature explains one way of using geometric shapes in a baby's play area. Have students use their creativity to develop an original toy that uses geometric shapes to help babies develop intellectually. Explain the concept of the term *prototype*. Have students create a prototype of their toy and show it to the class. They should discuss how their toy is intended to aid in intellectual development. (Students should create a toy that uses geometric shapes to encourage intellectual development.)

## Math in Action

### Geometric Shapes

Two trapezoids placed together will create a hexagon.

 **Mc Graw Hill** **Professional Development**

### Mini Clip
**Math: Comparing Similar Figures**

Students use manipulatives and scale factors to create similar figures.

## Reteach *cont.*

### C Critical Thinking

**Analyze** Ask students: At what stage in speech development do children show that they are capable of symbolic thinking? What behaviors let you know they are beginning to think this way? (Children are capable of symbolic thinking when they show that they understand that a word, such as "dada," which has no intrinsic meaning of its own, represents something else, such as a specific person.)

### U Universal Access

**Logical Learners** Tell students that babies learn language by the immersion method—they are completely surrounded by the language every day. Have students conduct research to learn how adults can be taught language using the immersion method. They then should write a report comparing this method to the more formal methods often used in classrooms. (Students should conduct research on the immersion method of teaching language in which the learner is exposed to the language without formal teaching of such things as grammar and vocabulary. Students should compare this method to more formal methods of teaching language.)

**Figure 9.7 Speech Developmental Milestones—Birth–Age 5**

Language development must be encouraged at each age level. *How might you encourage an eight-month-old baby to talk?*

| Months | Developmental Milestone |
|---|---|
| **Birth–3 Months** | ❖ Watches your face when you speak<br>❖ Babbles<br>❖ Cries to express hunger, anger, pain, or discomfort |
| **4–6 Months** | ❖ Babbling sounds more like speech with different sounds such as *p*, *b*, and *m*<br>❖ Voices excitement and displeasure<br>❖ Gurgles |
| **7 Months–1 Year** | ❖ Babbling has long and short groups of sounds<br>❖ Uses speech to get attention<br>❖ Imitates different speech sounds<br>❖ Says one or two words |
| **1–2 Years** | ❖ Adds more words to vocabulary each month<br>❖ Makes animal sounds such as "moo"<br>❖ Begins using pronouns such as "mine"<br>❖ Asks one- to two-word questions, such as "Go bye-bye?"<br>❖ Puts two words together, such as "more milk" |
| **2–3 Years** | ❖ Has a word for almost everything<br>❖ Uses two- to three-word sentences to talk about and ask for things<br>❖ Begins to use plurals such as "shoes" or "socks" |
| **3–4 Years** | ❖ Talks about activities<br>❖ Uses four- or more words sentences |
| **4–5 Years** | ❖ Voice is clear<br>❖ Uses sentences with a lot of details<br>❖ Tells stories<br>❖ Says most sounds correctly |

**Figure 9.7 Speech Developmental Milestones—Birth–Age 5**

**Caption Answer** Answers will vary but should indicate that a baby of that age will imitate sounds, so the baby can be encouraged by talking to and coaxing him or her to respond.

**Discussion** Have students give real-life examples to help understand the differences between these speech developmental milestones. For example, at 4 months, a baby may be able to make a simple "m" sound, at 9 months he may be able to say "mama," and at fourteen months, he may be able to put words together, as in "mama cookie."

**Reading Teaches Speech** Children need to hear speech and learn that sounds have meanings before they can develop language skills of their own. Parents and caregivers can help with this by reading to children.

- The vivid pictures in children's books help infants connect the sounds they are hearing to concrete objects. Rhymes help children remember words.
- Repetition is vital to children's learning. Reading favorite books over and over produces a familiar pattern of sounds. Children recognize these familiar patterns and attempt to repeat them, even if they do not know what the words mean.
- If children read with caregivers, they will start to associate books with attention and care. They will be much better prepared to learn to read when the time comes. They also will likely be more motivated to do so.
- Reading to young children helps to increase their vocabularies and promotes their ability to read aloud.

✓ **Reading Check** **Summarize** How does a baby learn from the care he or she receives?

# The Importance of Play

For children, play is work as well as pleasure. Research has clearly shown that playtime is essential to intellectual development. Toys are the tools for learning.

Play is also a physical necessity through which development takes place. When a baby shakes a rattle, stacks blocks, throws a ball, or chews on a teething toy, it is not just for amusement. These are serious, absorbing tasks that let infants strengthen their muscles, refine their motor skills, and learn about the world.

Babies learn from listening too. The familiar voices of the primary caregivers are the first sounds a baby learns to recognize. Rattles and squeak toys introduce different sounds. Babies enjoy music from a wind-up toy, a CD, or a person singing. They can also enjoy different rhythms. With exciting music, they can dance in the arms of a caring adult. With soothing music, they can cuddle and be rocked.

## Different Toys for Different Ages

Babies mature and change rapidly during the first year. They will need different toys to play with as they develop. A toy that delights a three-month-old may bore a ten-month-old. Also, a fun toy for a twelve-month-old might be dangerous for a two-month-old.

### Birth to Three Months

A baby at this age needs little more than things to look at and listen to. Bright colors, moving objects, and interesting sounds stimulate development of the senses. A mobile hung safely above the crib is interesting for the baby to listen to and watch, and allows him or her to practice following objects with the eyes. Brightly colored wallpaper and pictures can also provide interest.

### Four to Six Months

The sense of touch is important at this age. Babies need things to touch, handle, bang, shake, suck, and chew. Make sure that toys are small enough to handle easily but too large to swallow. All items and pieces should be at least 1½ inches across. A good rule of thumb is that it should be too large to fit into a standard paper towel tube.

Teething rings, cups, rattles, and plastic toys are good choices. Stuffed toys are fun to touch. Toys that squeak or make noise give results that the baby can learn to produce. Providing

---

**{ Expert Advice... }**

*"Other scholars have shown that the most powerful factor influencing reading skills is auditory processing skill—the very skill that is honed as infants listen to parents speak to them in sophisticated, adult language."*

— Clayton M. Christensen, author, *Disrupting Class: How Disruptive Innovation Will Change the Way the World Learns*

---

**R** **Reading Strategy**
**Recognizing Cause and Effect**
Have students create a two-column table. In the left column, they should list reading activities that help children develop language skills. In the right column, students should list the specific effects of each activity. For example, the pictures in children's books help children connect specific sounds with concrete objects. (Possible answers: Rhymes help children remember words; repetition encourages children to repeat patterns; reading aloud teaches children to associate books with attention and care.)

**W** **Writing Support**
**Personal Letter**
**Why Play?** Tell students to imagine that they are the fathers or mothers of an eight-month-old. Write your sister or brother a personal letter describing what you have learned about why play is important in your child's life. (Refer to p. 254 for tips on writing a personal letter. Students should write a letter describing how much their child enjoys play and what he or she learns from playing.)

✓ **Reading Check**

**Summarize** Babies learn that when they express their needs, their caregivers meet their needs. This teaches them about cause and effect, and in turn helps them form new pathways in the brain.

---

**Professional Development**

**Mini Clip**
**ELL: Scaffolding Questions**

A teacher uses a series of questions to lead a student to an appropriate verbal response.

### U Universal Access

**Interpersonal Learners** Organize students into three groups. Explain that each group will be designing a play area for babies between seven and twelve months old. Assign each group one of these senses: vision, hearing, or touch. Each group should create an illustration of what their play area will look like. The play area should contain appropriate activities that will stimulate the sense that has been assigned to that group. Have the groups share their designs with the class. (Each group should have designed, on paper, a play area containing activities that stimulate the sense that was assigned to that group. For example, pots and pans might stimulate hearing. Books can stimulate vision.)

### C Critical Thinking

**Understand Cause and Effect** Discuss toy safety with students. Have students think about the causes and effects related to this issue. Display several toys (or household objects that could be used as toys) that might be hazardous to children who are under a certain age or under certain circumstances. Have students create labels for these toys that take into consideration their safety hazards. (Students should explain the causes and effects of hazardous toys and create appropriate warning labels for several toys or household objects.)

objects with different textures helps the child learn by touch. Babies this age like simple picture books, and love being read to. Choose sturdy, washable books with big, colorful pictures of familiar objects.

### Seven to Nine Months

Babies still need things to handle, throw, pound, bang, and shake. Anything that makes a noise fascinates infants at this age. Look for books that have different textures to feel, or places to press on the page that produce noises. Children of this age enjoy blocks, balls, large plastic beads that pop apart, and toys that can be pushed or kicked. Safe household items are just as interesting as purchased toys. Pots and pans with lids, and plastic containers to stack make great playthings. Be sure to thoroughly wash any used containers before giving them to a child. Make sure there are no sharp edges that could harm the child.

### Ten to Twelve Months

By the end of their first year, babies need things to crawl after. Those who are already walking enjoy toys they can push or pull. Children this age especially enjoy toys that they can manipulate. **Manipulate** means to work with the hands. Baskets, boxes, and other containers are fun. Babies like to put things into them and then dump them out again. Picture books are good for looking at alone or for brief story times during the day or before bed. Vinyl books are now available that can even go in the tub. Floating toys are also great choices.

## Choosing Toys

When choosing playthings for a young child, look for toys that encourage participation and use. Younger children need simpler toys. As a baby's abilities increase, toys can be more complex.

**Alternative Toys**
Even simple household objects can make fun toys for babies. *What other household objects would be appropriate as toys for babies?*

### ➤ Explore the Photo

**Caption Answer** Answers will vary but may include plastic bowls or containers, wooden spoons, or empty boxes.

**Discussion** Ask students: How might you use household objects to teach a child about categorizing? About arranging by size? (Answers will vary. You could teach about categorizing by helping the child sort objects by color. You could teach about arranging by size by giving the child nesting measuring cups.)

## Usefulness

Toys, especially those labeled educational, can be expensive. Sometimes they have limited usefulness. Parents can provide a baby with as much fun and learning by making common household items available. Items such as plastic measuring spoons and cups, a clean plastic bucket, plastic bowls, a metal pan or mixing bowl and a large wooden spoon, or a large cardboard box with a window cut in it all make great toys because young children can use them in many different ways. With any toy, however, supervision is important for safe play.

When buying toys, caregivers should look for ones that will remain interesting and appropriate for a number of years. A set of blocks is a good example. At the age of six months, Reynaldo grasped and inspected his blocks. By his first birthday, he could stack several blocks into a tower. At the age of three, he used the blocks to make roads for his cars. Now, at age six, Reynaldo creates elaborate houses and castles, using every available block.

## Safety

Safety should also be a concern when considering toys for babies. A very tempting and common choking **hazard**, or danger, for babies is an older child's toys. Babies may see an older sibling playing with toys that look very inviting. It only takes a few seconds for a baby to pick up one of those toys and put it in his or her mouth. Make sure that babies are kept away from these toys while the older child is playing with them. Also, be sure to clean up all small pieces right away after playing, and store them out of a baby's reach. Babies are also interested in anything their caregivers use, such as keys, pens, and forks. Caregivers need to keep these out of babies' reach.

### Assess

**Study Tools**

Have students go to the Online Learning Center at **glencoe.com**:

- Take the **Practice Test**.
- Download **Study-to-Go** content.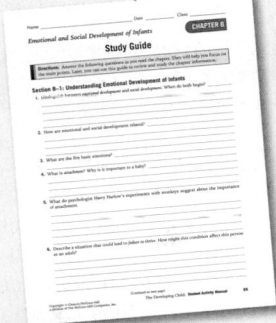

Use the **Student Activity Workbook** for additional practice.

---

## Section 9.3    After You Read

### Review Key Concepts

1. **Discuss** whether or not babies communicate before they learn to talk. Explain your answer.
2. **Explain** why caregivers should choose toys that are age appropriate.

### Practice Academic Skills

 **English Language Arts**

3. Imagine that you write an advice column for your local newspaper. A young couple has written to you because they are worried about their six-month-old daughter. They are concerned because she cannot say any words. Write a column with your advice.

> **NCTE 12** Use language to accomplish individual purposes.

 **Social Studies**

4. Many cultures use toys as part of celebrations and traditions. For example, in Mexico a piñata is a part of a birthday celebration. Kites are a traditional toy used in Japanese New Year celebrations. Choose a foreign culture and research the traditional toys that are still popular today. Write a one-page essay describing the toys and how they are used. Note any similarities the toys have to American toys that you may have played with. Include pictures, if possible.

> **NCSS I C** Apply an understanding of culture as an integrated whole that explains the functions and interactions of traditions, beliefs and values, and behavior patterns.

 **Check Your Answers** Check your answers at this book's Online Learning Center at **glencoe.com**.

**NCLB**

Section 9.3    Helping Infants Learn    **281**

### Close

**Culminating Activity**

**Summarize** Have students work individually to write a paragraph summarizing the importance of play. Ask for volunteers to share their paragraphs with the class. (Possible answer: children learn about cause and effect, to recognize different sounds, and to categorize. They strengthen muscles and refine motor skills.)

**NCLB** connects academic correlations to book content.

---

## Section 9.3    After You Read

### Review Key Concepts

1. Babies communicate long before they can talk. They use movements, gestures, and different tones and patterns of crying.
2. Age appropriate describes things that are suitable for the age and individual needs of the child. Toys that are not age appropriate may not be stimulating and may be dangerous for a child.

### Practice Academic Skills

3. Columns will vary. Students should tell the parents that they need not worry about their daughter. Children from seven months to one year may speak one to two words. A child's first real words are usually understandable between the ages of eight and fifteen months.
4. Answers will vary based on the culture chosen. Students should use vivid adjectives to describe the toys and how they are used.

**Focus**

## Discussion Starter

**Storytelling** Ask students if they have ever listened to a storyteller. What was it like? Why do people enjoy storytellers? What do storytellers offer that we cannot get from television or a movie? (Answers will vary. Storytellers are live and interact with the audience.)

**Teach**

## C Critical Thinking

**Draw Conclusions** A one-year-old child has two caregivers. Both caregivers love stories. The first one reads books in a straight-forward fashion, with little variation in his voice. The second one varies her voice for each character and sometimes acts out the story. How do you think the baby might respond to each caregiver? Why? (The baby might listen to the first caregiver and enjoy the story; the baby is more likely to become stimulated and involved, laughing and moving around, with the second caregiver.)

**Assess**

## Make Connections

Ask students to list specific correlations between academic subjects and the kinds of skills a good storyteller needs. (Answers will vary. Students should show an understanding of how academic skills relate directly to the job of a storyteller. For example, good public speaking and drama skills are needed to perform the stories.)

**NCLB** This relates academic skills to specific tasks that are performed for this job.

**B**efore societies had written records, they had storytellers. Storytellers described battles and adventures and told tales of monsters and kings. Today's storytellers educate and entertain as they practice this ancient art. Many traditions are preserved with storytelling.

### ☼ What Does a Storyteller Do?

**C** Storytellers captivate their audiences with words. Storytellers use their voices the way musicians use instruments. They write and memorize many stories and tell each one with enthusiasm and creativity. Many storytellers add songs and music to their stories, too. Some storytellers focus on certain traditions, such as African folk tales.

### ☼ Where Do Storytellers Work?

Storytellers perform in many different places, such as schools, libraries, museums, festivals, children's parties, senior centers, prisons, and hospitals. Some storytellers might perform on the radio or on television. Some sell recordings of their performances.

### Preparation and Skills

**Education and Training**
Many storytellers study literature, folklore, music, and drama. Public speaking is also good preparation for storytelling. Look for a Storytellers Guild, or association, in your area to find a mentor or receive tips on developing this career. Some of these groups can help you find jobs to get started.

**Aptitudes, Abilities, and Skills**
Successful storytellers have imagination, self-motivation, a good memory, acting talent, and communication skills. Storytellers work hard, so they should be motivated and dedicated to their craft.

**Academic Skills Required**
English Language Arts are used by storytellers in reading and researching stories and ideas, and in writing stories to tell.

**NCLB**

**Explore Careers**
Research other careers that involve performing with children or engaging them through play. Choose one career and write a paragraph describing it. Tell if the career interests you, and why.

 **Careers Online** For more information on careers, visit the Occupational Outlook Handbook Web site through the link on this book's Online Learning Center at **glencoe.com**.

**Close**

## Culminating Activity

**Hiring a Storyteller** Tell students to imagine they work for a library that wants to hire a storyteller to present stories during the library's story hour. Have the students write the job advertisement. The ad should list all of the skills required. (The ad should reflect an understanding of aptitudes, abilities, and skills needed by storytellers and should be correctly formatted and phrased.)

**Explore Careers**
Students' paragraphs will vary depending on the career chosen. For example, children's librarians frequently interact with children by acting out books or plays.

## Chapter Summary

An infant's brain undergoes major changes in response to stimulation. The transmission of information between nerve cells in the brain creates neural pathways that organize the brain. Piaget said that all children go through four periods of learning. During the sensorimotor period (birth–two years), children learn through their senses and own actions. A child learns and practices new skills through play. Appropriate toys can help babies learn. Children communicate before they can talk. Reading to a child promotes vocabulary.

## Vocabulary Review

1. Create a multiple-choice test question for each content and academic vocabulary term.

**Content Vocabulary**

◇ neuron (p. 257)
◇ neural pathway (p. 257)
◇ cortex (p. 259)
◇ axon (p. 259)
◇ myelin (p. 259)
◇ dendrite (p. 259)
◇ synapse (p. 260)
◇ neurotransmitter (p. 260)
◇ perception (p. 266)

◇ attention span (p. 268)
◇ concept (p. 269)
◇ sensorimotor period (p. 271)
◇ object permanence (p. 271)
◇ imaginative play (p. 272)
◇ symbolic thinking (p. 272)
◇ age appropriate (p. 274)

◇ childproof (p. 275)
◇ manipulate (p. 280)

**Academic Vocabulary**

■ function (p. 259)
■ receptor (p. 260)
■ elicit (p. 270)
■ determined (p. 270)
■ responsiveness (p. 274)
■ hazard (p. 281)

## Review Key Concepts

2. **Describe** how a baby's experiences increase brain function.
3. **Explain** how the brain becomes organized.
4. **List** four abilities that show intellectual growth in infants.
5. **Identify** specific abilities that babies learn during Piaget's first period of learning.
6. **Name** five ways caregivers can encourage learning.
7. **Discuss** how to choose toys appropriate for babies of different ages.

## Critical Thinking

8. **Analyze** Why is it important to read and talk to a baby even if the baby does not understand?
9. **Extend** Piaget determined that children must learn to master one thinking skill before they can move on to another. Why is this so?
10. **Compare** How do the speech capabilities of two- to three-year-olds and four- to five-year-olds differ?

Chapter 9 Intellectual Development in Infants **283**

## Content and Academic Vocabulary Review

1. Students should write multiple-choice questions with possible answers for each vocabulary term.

## Review Key Concepts

2. In response to experiences, babies' brains immediately begin to develop links between neurons. The link is called a neural pathway. They wire the brain so that it can control different body functions and thinking processes.
3. As connections between dendrites and axons grow stronger, a group of neurons becomes linked together. They become systems of nerve cells that control a particular action or thinking task.
4. Remembering experiences, making associations, understanding cause and effect, and paying attention.
5. Babies learn to combine two or more reflexes, develop hand-mouth coordination, act intentionally to produce results, improve hand-eye coordination, imitate others, find hidden objects, explore and experiment, understand that objects exist independently, solve problems by thinking through sequences, think using symbols, and begin imaginative thinking.
6. Learn about child development, give the child time and attention, provide positive feedback, show love, and talk.
7. Look for toys that encourage participation, and that will stay interesting for many years.

## Critical Thinking

8. Children need to hear speech and learn that sounds have meanings before they can develop language skills of their own. Listening to other people talk helps build speech centers in the baby's brain.
9. Thinking skills act as building blocks. A child must master more basic concepts before he or she is able to learn more complex concepts.
10. Two- to three-year-olds have a word for almost everything, and use two-to three-word sentences to talk about and ask for things. Four- to five-year-olds speak with clear voice, use sentences with a lot of details, tell stories, and say most sounds correctly.

### Family & Community Connections

**11.** Interviews will vary but answers should be similar to activities suggested in the text, such as talk to the child, provide age-appropriate toys, or read to the child.

### Health Skills

**12.** Answers will vary but might include moving breakable or valuable items out of reach of the child, making sure small items were removed, or using pillows to block sharp corners.

### Observation Skills

**13.** Posters will vary, but should indicate that the toys of younger babies are not as complex as the toys of older babies. Posters should accurately indicate students' findings.

### Real-World Skills

**14.** Answers will vary but should follow the information provided in the text, such as talk to the baby, read to the baby, and provide age-appropriate toys.

**15.** Answers will vary depending on researchers used. Chart should accurately compare the results.

**16.** Lists will vary but should show that students understand what is age-appropriate for a one-year-old.

**NCLB** Activity correlated to English Language Arts standards.

### Family & Community Connection

**11. Interview a Child Care Provider** Interview a person who provides child care for one or more one-year-old infants. This could be in a home or in a child care center. Ask the provider to describe what he or she does to help stimulate the babies. How does he or she encourage the baby to learn? Compile a list of the answers. Does your list match with the information you have learned in this chapter?

### Health Skills

**12. Childproofing a Home** Childproofing a home allows babies more freedom to explore their environment. There are many different ways to childproof a home, such as covering electrical outlets, moving small or fragile items out of a baby's reach, or installing cabinet locks. What steps could you take to temporarily childproof a room in your home for a visiting baby?

### Observation Skills

**13. Observe Babies Playing** Work with your teacher to arrange to observe babies from ages six months to one year at play.

**Procedure** Find out the ages of the babies you observe. Write a list of the toys each baby plays with.

**Analysis** Compare and contrast the toys used by babies of different ages. How did the toys used by younger babies differ from the toys used by older babies? Were the toys used by older babies more complex than those used by younger babies? If so, in what way? Were any of the same toys used by children of varying ages? If so, were they used in different ways? Create a poster to present your findings.

**NCTE 7** Conduct research and gather, evaluate, and synthesize data to communicate discoveries.

**NCLB**

## Real-World Skills

| | | |
|---|---|---|
| **Problem-Solving** | **14. Make Decisions** Imagine you are going to babysit a seven-month-old baby for a couple of hours. How will you keep the baby entertained? What activities or toys will you use? Make a list of how you plan to spend the two hours. | |
| **Technology Skills** | **15. Create a Chart** Choose a researcher who studied intellectual development, such as B. F. Skinner or Albert Bandura, and compare their findings with those of Jean Piaget. How are they similar? How are they different? Use word processing software to create a chart showing your research results. | |
| **Financial Literacy** | **16. Birthday Shopping** Imagine you have $25 to spend on a birthday gift for your neighbor who is turning one. How would you spend the money? Visit a local store and find age-appropriate toys and activities you could purchase. Create a list of your findings. | |

 **Additional Activities** For additional activities, go to this book's Online Learning Center at **glencoe.com**.

### Academic Skills

**17.** Scenes will vary but should show students' understanding of how a caregiver can encourage an infant who is learning a new skill, such as praise or clapping hands.

**18.** The average number of words learned per year is 2,450. (10,000 − 200 = 9,800; 9,800 ÷ 4 = 2,450)

The *Early Childhood Observations CD* offers additional lessons with videos to build students' observation skills.

**Part 1:** Learning to Observe
**Part 2:** How Children Develop
**Part 3:** Working With Young Children
**Part 4:** Extended Observations
**Part 5:** Resources and Answer File

## Academic Skills

 **English Language Arts**

**17. Research Literature** Conduct research to find literature that describes how caregivers can help and encourage infants who are learning new skills. Use the information you find to write a scene that shows a caregiver providing an infant with encouragement while the baby is trying to master a new skill in intellectual development.

> **NCTE 2** Read literature to build an understanding of the human experience.

 **Mathematics**

**18. Semantic Development** Research shows that the average child knows 200 words by age two and 10,000 words by age six. What is the rate of average words per year between the ages of two and six?

**Math Concept Determining Rates** A rate is a ratio of two measurements having different kinds of units. The rate for this problem is words per year.

**Starting Hint** Subtract the the number of words the child already knows at age two (200) from the number of words at age six (10,000). Divide your answer by the number of years spanned (4).

 For math help, go to the Math Appendix at the back of the book.

> **NCTM Algebra** Understand patterns, relations, and functions.

 **Science**

**19. Create a Flow Chart** The nerves in the human body send and receive messages from the brain thousands of times a day. Conduct research using print or online resources to discover how this communication takes place.

**Procedure** List the steps involved when the nerves send and receive information from the brain.

**Analysis** Create a flow chart showing how nerves send information to the brain and send instructions from it.

> **NSES C** Develop understanding of the cell; interdependence of organisms; matter, energy, and organization in living systems; and behavior of organisms.

**N C L B**

### Standardized Test Practice

**SHORT ANSWER**

Read the passage, then answer the question.

> Some people believe that one way for a child's brain to grow intellectually is to expose the child to classical music during infancy. Other people do not agree with this.

**20.** Do you agree or disagree that classical music can help a child grow intellectually? Why? Use your knowledge of how a baby's brain develops to support your answer.

> **Test-Taking Tip** Put as much information into your answer as possible. Use easy-to-read, short sentences that define key words. Also give an example that explains your answer.

  **TECHNOLOGY Solutions**

**Use these technology solutions to streamline chapter assessment!**

**ExamView** Assessment Suite **ExamView Assessment Suite** CD allows you to create and print out customized tests or ready-made unit and chapter tests, complete with answer keys.

**TeacherWorks** Plus **TeacherWorks Plus** is an electronic lesson planner that provides instant access to complete teacher resources in one convenient package.

 **Online Learning Center** includes resources and activities for students and teachers.

**19.** Flow charts will vary but should show neurons connected by axons and dendrites and indicate that axons are coated with myelin, which helps transmit information from one nerve cell to another. The process works when information is being sent to, and is coming from, the brain.

**N C L B** **NCLB** connects academic correlations to book content.

### Standardized Test Practice

**20.** Students' answers will vary. However, they should indicate that since music is a form of stimulation for the child, it could help in the child's intellectual development. Students should also point out that human touch and interaction is most effective in stimulating intellectual growth in infants.

**Test-Taking Tips** Remind students to pay attention to their grammar. While taking a test, students should try to allow time to carefully check spelling and punctuation.

**Short Answer Test** Tell students to create a brief outline before beginning to write their answers. Each item in the outline only needs to be one or two words long. When done writing, review the outline to make certain every point is covered.

# Unit Thematic Project

## Raise a Healthy Baby

### Discussion Starter

**Healthy Growth and Development** Ask students to list ways that they, as teens, can help foster healthy growth and development in a younger sibling. (Examples may include holding or playing with the baby, and being a good role model.)

 Project correlated to English Language Arts standards.

### Step 1

### Choose and Research Your Topic

Students can select one topic that interests them. They should research their approved topic and write a summary that describes milestones, explains how caregivers can foster healthy growth, and identify possible problems and solutions for that area of growth or development.

## Teach

### Step 2

### Plan Your Interview

Interview questions should include specific questions about the chosen topic area to ask a parent or child care professional. Students should consider their audience when writing and organizing their interview questions. Interview questions should demonstrate appropriate writing skills.

In this unit, you have learned that a child's first year is a time of great change. Parents and caregivers play a very important role in helping the child grow and develop. In this project, you will research a specific area of infant growth and development and explore what parents and caregivers can do to support a baby in this area.

 **My Journal**

If you completed the journal entry from page 191, refer to it to see if your thoughts have changed after reading the unit.

### Project Assignment

In this project, you will:
- Choose a feature of infant growth and development that interests you.
- Conduct research about the topic you have chosen.
- Interview a parent or child care professional about your topic.
- Prepare a presentation to share what you have learned with your class.

> ### Child Development Skills Behind the Project
>
> - Evaluate parenting roles and responsibilities.
> - Identify a child's physical, emotional, and intellectual needs.
> - Describe the growth and development of infants.
>
> ### Academic Skills
>
>  **English Language Arts Standards**
>
> **NCTE 4** Use written language to communicate effectively.
>
> **NCTE 7** Conduct research and gather, evaluate, and synthesize data to communicate discoveries.

### Step 1 Choose and Research Your Topic

The topics below are examples of areas in which infants grow and develop over their first year. Choose one of these topics, or select another topic approved by your teacher. Research its importance to healthy growth and development.
- Language skills
- Motor skills
- Development of emotions
- Vision
- Eating and sleeping
- Attachment to caregivers
- Relating to strangers
- Relating to other children

Write a summary of your research to:
- **Describe** milestones of infant growth or development in the chosen area.
- **Explain** how parents or caregivers can foster an infant's health in this area.
- **Identify** possible problems or disorders that can occur and how caregivers can identify and respond to them.

### Step 3

### Connect with Your Community

Ask students to describe how parents and professionals in the community might shape their outlook toward caring for children. (Encourage students to recognize that their community helps them by providing them with education, and that education can lead to more successful child development.)

### Step 4

### Share What You Have Learned

Tell students to use appropriate writing skills to plan their reports:
- Use complete sentences.
- Use correct grammar.
- Organize your thoughts by prioritizing what you want to tell your audience.

Tell students that it is often helpful to practice presenting an oral report ahead of time.

### Step 2 Plan Your Interview

Use the results of your research to write a list of interview questions about your chosen topic to ask a parent or child care professional in your community.

**Writing Skills**

★ Use complete sentences.
★ Use correct spelling and grammar.
★ Organize your interview questions in the order you want to ask them.

### Step 3 Connect with Your Community

Identify a child care professional or parent of a young child in your community who works with infants and toddlers. Conduct your interview using the questions you prepared in Step 2. Take notes during the interview and write a summary of the interview.

**Interviewing Skills**

★ Record interview responses and take notes.
★ Listen attentively.
★ Use correct spelling and grammar when you transcribe your notes.

### Step 4 Share What You Have Learned

Use the Unit Thematic Project Checklist to plan and give an oral report to share what you have learned with your classmates.

**Speaking Skills**

★ Speak clearly and concisely.
★ Be sensitive to the needs of your audience.
★ Use standard English to communicate.

### Step 5 Evaluate Your Child Development Skills and Academic Skills

Your project will be evaluated based on:

- Content and organization of your information.
- Proper use of standard English.
- Mechanics—presentation and neatness.
- Speaking and listening skills.

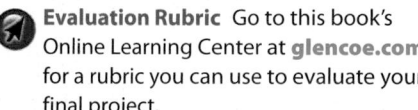 **Evaluation Rubric** Go to this book's Online Learning Center at **glencoe.com** for a rubric you can use to evaluate your final project.

### Unit Thematic Project Checklist

| Plan | ✓ Select and research your topic and summarize your findings. |
| | ✓ Plan and write your interview questions. |
| | ✓ Interview a parent or child care professional and write a summary of what you learned. |
| Present | ✓ Make a presentation to the class to discuss the results of your research and your interview. |
| | ✓ Invite students to ask any questions. Answer these questions. |
| | ✓ When students ask you questions, demonstrate in your answers that you respect their perspectives. |
| | ✓ Turn in the summary of your research, your interview questions, and the summary of the interview to your teacher. |
| Academic Skills | ✓ Communicate effectively. |
| | ✓ Be sensitive to the needs of different audiences. |
| | ✓ Adapt and modify language to suit different purposes. |

### Step 5

**Evaluate Your Child Development Skills and Academic Skills**

**Rubric** Encourage students to go to the book's Online Learning Center at **glencoe.com** for a rubric they can use to evaluate their presentation. Students can use the rubric as a content checklist when forming their interview questions and planning and giving their oral report.

## Close

### Culminating Activity

**Project Assessment** In this activity, students identified important milestones in a chosen area of growth and development, how caregivers can foster healthy growth in that area, and possible problems or disorders that could affect that area. Have students form pairs and interview each other about the topics they chose and how their opinions and perceptions about those topics evolved during the course of the project. (Students should thoroughly summarize their project to their partners. Both students should listen attentively while the other is speaking.)

---

 ## Developing Community Involvement

### Successful Parenting

There are so many things to learn and think about when caring for a child. Most communities offer a variety of services to help parents be successful in raising healthy, happy children. Ask students to talk to an older adult who has children. Have students ask the adult what help was available to them when they were a new parent. Then compare their answers with the resources that are now available in the community.

A **Family & Community Involvement** worksheet about this topic is available:

- At this book's Online Learning Center at **glencoe.com**
- On the TeacherWorks CD

| Title | Objectives |
|-------|------------|
| **CHAPTER 10**<br>**Physical Development from One to Three** | • **Identify** five changes in a child's physical growth from ages one to three.<br>• **Explain** how developmental milestones are used.<br>• **Describe** how a parent should respond to typical changes in a child's sleeping patterns.<br>• **Explain** why it is important to establish good eating habits early in life.<br>• **Identify** why young children are particularly at risk for accidents.<br>• **List** four factors to consider when choosing clothing for young children. |
| **CHAPTER 11**<br>**Emotional and Social Development from One to Three** | • **Identify** the factors that contribute to a child's emotional development.<br>• **Describe** six specific emotions children ages eighteen months to three years show.<br>• **List** the four signs of a healthy relationship between parents and a child.<br>• **Identify** four ways to help children get adequate sleep.<br>• **Compare and contrast** parallel play and cooperative play.<br>• **List** six ways to help children develop social skills.<br>• **Explain** the purpose of guidance. |
| **CHAPTER 12**<br>**Intellectual Development from One to Three** | • **Summarize** how heredity and the environment shape intelligence.<br>• **Describe** the four methods of learning used by young children.<br>• **List** the seven areas of intellectual activity.<br>• **List** 11 ways to help guide a child's learning.<br>• **Identify** four parts of language that children have an inborn ability to decipher.<br>• **Summarize** how to evaluate toys for young children. |
| **Unit Thematic Project**<br>**Help Children Learn** | • **Write** a My Journal entry on Learning and Growing.<br>• **Choose** an area of child development.<br>• **Observe** children in a child care center.<br>• **Develop** an original activity to promote child development.<br>• **Prepare** a demonstration to share what they learned. |

## Understanding Brackets, Letters, and Ability Levels in the Teacher Wraparound Edition

**Brackets** Brackets on the reduced student edition page correspond to teaching strategies and activities in the Teacher Wraparound Edition. As you teach the lesson, the brackets show you exactly where to use the teaching strategies and activities.

**Letters** The letters on the reduced student edition page identify the type of strategy or activity. See the key below to learn about the different types of strategies and activities.

**Ability Levels** Teaching Strategies that appear throughout the chapters have been identified by one of three codes to give you an idea of their suitability for students of varying learning styles and abilities.

**Resources** Key program resources are listed in each chapter. Icons indicate the format of resources.

### KEY TO LETTERS

**D** **Develop Concepts** activities help teachers gauge and plan for students' concept development.

**R** **Reading Strategy** activities help you teach reading skills and vocabulary.

**S** **Skill Practice** provides leveled instruction for meeting individual needs and learning styles.

**W** **Writing Support** activities provide writing opportunities to help students comprehend the text.

**C** **Critical Thinking** strategies help students apply and extend what they have learned.

**U** **Universal Access** activities provide differentiated instruction for English language learners, and suggestions for teaching various types of learners.

**NCLB** **No Child Left Behind** activities help students practice and improve their abilities in academic subjects.

### KEY TO ABILITY LEVELS

**L1** Strategies should be within the ability range of all students. Often full class participation is required.

**L2** Strategies are for average to above-average students or for small groups. Some teacher direction is necessary.

**L3** Strategies are designed for students able and willing to work independently. Minimal teacher direction is necessary.

**ELL** Strategies are especially accessible to English Language Learners.

### KEY TO RESOURCE ICONS

📁 Print Material

💿 CD or DVD Resources

🌐 Online Learning Center (OLC)

### TeacherWorks™
All-In-One Planner and Resource Center

**Teacher Wraparound Edition**

**Unit Resources:**
Unit Thematic Project Student Rubrics
Unit Family and Community Involvement Activities

**Chapter Resources:**
Lesson Plans
Chapter Summaries, Content and Academic Vocabulary
Graphic Organizers

**Textbook Resources:**
Student Activity Workbook with Academic Integration
Additional Activities
Enrichment Activities

🌐 Link to the ***The Developing Child*** Online Learning **Center** at **glencoe.com**.

## Unit Overview

### Introduce the Unit

Introduce the unit by describing the main concepts of each chapter in the unit.

### Unit 4

In this unit, students will learn about the physical, emotional, social, and intellectual growth and development of children ages one to three years.

**Chapter 10** Introduce students to the physical growth and development of children from ages one to three. Teach students how to care for children of this age group, and see how heredity and environment play key roles in child development.

**Chapter 11** Students will learn about the emotional and social development of children between the ages of one and three. Children of this age group go through a series of emotional stages, both positive and negative. Each child develops emotionally in his or her own way.

**Chapter 12** Understanding brain development and supporting learning for one- to three-year-olds are discussed in this chapter. Students will learn that intelligence is determined by heredity and environment; children learn concepts and the words for those concepts in stages; and children use different methods to learn.

### OUT OF TIME?

If class time is too short to cover all of the chapters in this unit, have students:

- Write down the vocabulary terms and their definitions.
- Read the chapter summaries at the beginning of each chapter review.
- Go to *The Developing Child* Online Learning Center at **glencoe.com** to download Study-to-Go content.

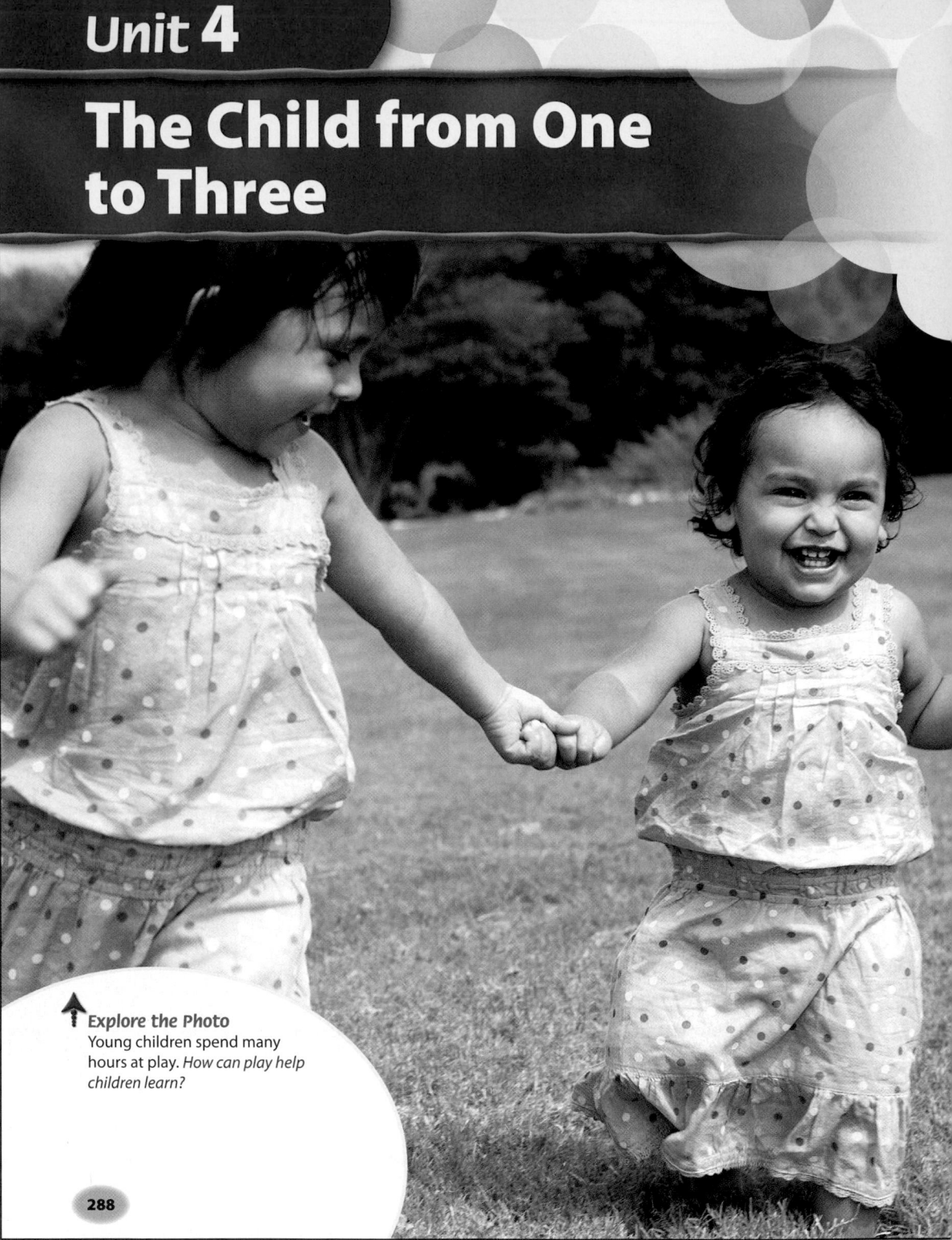

# The Child from One to Three

**Explore the Photo**
Young children spend many hours at play. *How can play help children learn?*

**288**

---

## ➤ Explore the Photo

**Caption Answer** Play can help children learn about their world by imitating adults or others around them. It can also help them learn socialization skills by playing with other children. Play offers children opportunities for physical exercise, which can help them grow stronger; and it offers practice in fine and gross motor skills.

**Discussion** Have students brainstorm toys and activities that would be appropriate for children ages one to three. (Answers will vary but may include toys that will challenge but not frustrate the child such as age-appropriate puzzles, clothes to play dress up, or sorting toys. Activities might include playing house or dress up or playing with a large ball.)

## Discussion Starter

### Web Diagram

Have students make a web diagram that includes the four areas of development of one- to three-year olds that are discussed in this unit—physical, emotional, social, and intellectual. Then have them skim the unit and write down characteristics of each area of development. After completing the unit, revisit the diagram and reassess their knowledge by asking students what they learned about the four areas of development that was not included in their original diagram.

### FCCLA Car and Booster Seat Safety

Using the *Families Acting for Community Traffic Safety (FACTS) Program,* suggest that the FCCLA Chapter cosponsor a Child Car and Booster Seat Inspection Day with the local fire department. Check with the State Department of Transportation for free handouts and information that can be given to those who participate.

## Unit Thematic Project Preview

### Help Children Learn

By completing this unit, you will learn that children ages one to three learn and develop physically, emotionally, socially, and intellectually. In your unit thematic project, you can create an activity to help children learn in one of these areas.

### My Journal

**Learning and Growing** Write a journal entry about one of the topics below. This will help you prepare for the unit project at the end of the unit.

- Identify social activities in which one- to three-year-olds participate.
- Describe activities that will intellectually stimulate a one- to three-year-old.
- Tell about physical activities that are appropriate for one- to three-year-olds.

289

---

## Unit Thematic Project Preview

### Help Children Learn

Tell students that as part of this unit, they will learn how one- to three-year-old children grow and develop physically, emotionally, socially, and intellectually. Students will consider how children in this age group can be stimulated and guided in their growth and development by participation in a variety of learning opportunities.

### My Journal

**Learning and Growing** Students select one topic to write a journal entry about. The journal entry should relate to the subject of the thematic project: Help Children Learn. The purpose of the journal entry is to prepare students for the project at the end of the unit. (Journal entries will vary depending on the topic selected and students' personal opinions.)

**STANDARDS BASED LESSON PLANNING** *The Developing Child* provides students with instruction and assessment in the following fundamental content areas:

## National Standards Correlations

| Standards | Pages |
|---|---|
| **12.1.1** Analyze physical, emotional, social, spiritual, and intellectual development. | 293–300 |
| **12.1.3** Analyze current and emerging research about human growth and development, including research on brain development. | 296 |
| **12.2.1** Analyze the effect of heredity and environment on human growth and development. | 293, 295 |
| **12.2.3** Analyze the effects of gender, ethnicity, and culture on individual development. | 294 |
| **15.1.2** Analyze expectations and responsibilities of parenting. | 300, 302–314, 316 |
| **15.1.5** Explain cultural differences in roles and responsibilities of parenting. | 299, 314 |
| **15.2.1** Choose nurturing practices that support human growth and development. | 302, 312, 313 |
| **15.3.3** Summarize current laws and policies related to parenting. | 308 |

**NO CHILD LEFT BEHIND** NCLB activities, information, and skills practice will help your students attain NCLB proficiency. Students will improve their abilities in the following academic standards areas:

## Academic Standards Correlations

| Discipline | Standard | Feature/Activity |
|---|---|---|
| **English Language Arts** | **NCTE 1** read texts to acquire new information. | **Reading Guide (pp. 292, 301)** |
| | **NCTE 4** Use written language to communicate effectively. | **Writing Activity (p. 290)** <br> **After You Read (p. 300, 314)** |
| | **NCTE 12** Use language to accomplish individual purposes. | **Academic Skills (p. 317)** |
| **Mathematics** | **NCTM Algebra** Use mathematical models to represent and understand quantitative relationships. | **Academic Skills (p. 317)** |
| | **NCTM Measurement** Understand measurable attributes of objects and the units, systems, and processes of measurement. | **Math in Action (p. 306)** |
| **Science** | **NSES A** Develop abilities necessary to do scientific inquiry, understandings about scientific inquiry. | **Academic Skills (p. 317)** |
| | **NSES C** Develop understanding of the biological evolution; and behavior of organisms. | **After You Read (p. 300)** |
| **Social Studies** | **NCSS I A Culture** Analyze and explain the ways groups, societies, and cultures address human needs and concerns. | **After You Read (p. 314)** |
| | **NCSS I C Culture** Apply an understanding of culture as an integrated whole that explains the functions and interactions of the arts, traditions, and behavior patterns. | **Culture Matters (p. 299)** |
| | **NCSS IV D Individual Development and Identity** Apply concepts, methods, and theories about the study of human growth and development, such as learning, motivation, and behavior. | **Observation Skills (p. 316)** |

## McGraw Hill Professional Development

**MINI CLIP VIDEO LIBRARY**

Targeted professional development is correlated throughout *The Developing Child*. **The McGraw-Hill Professional Development Mini Clip Video Library** provides teaching strategies to strengthen academic and learning skills. Log on to **glencoe.com**.

In this chapter, you will find these Mini Clips:
- **Reading** Flexible Groupings, p. 290
- **Reading** Planning and Classroom Management, p. 295
- **Reading** Modeling Reading Strategies, p. 297
- **ELL** Comprehension and English Learners, p. 298
- **ELL** Collaborative Work, p. 305
- **ELL** Graphic Organizers, p. 309
- **Reading** Vocabulary, p. 315

## Reading and Writing Strategies

**Writing Activity: Dialogue** (p. 290)
Students use writing tips to create a dialogue between a caregiver and a five-year-old.

**Before You Read** (pp. 292, 301)
A pre-reading question or statement will help students make a personal connection to content.

**Graphic Organizer** (pp. 292, 301)
A visual tool will help students organize and remember new content.

**Reading Check** (pp. 295, 303, 307, 312)
A question allows students to make a quick comprehension self-check.

**After You Read** (pp. 300, 314)
Organize and process students' understanding of what they have read.

## Chapter Features

**Learning Abilities and Facts** (p. 296)
Different parts of the brain control the learning of different types of activities.

**Changes in Play** (p. 297)
As children grow older, their play becomes more imaginative.

**Dexterity Among the Navajos** (p. 299)
Teaching traditional crafts improves the fine motor skills of Navajo children.

**Getting a New Bed** (p. 303)
Moving a child from a crib to a regular bed requires thought and preparation.

**Child Nutrition** (p. 306)
Parents need to be aware of serving sizes for children.

**Climbing** (p. 310)
Children must be protected from climbing injuries.

**Helping a Child Learn to Brush** (p. 312)
Caregivers must teach children to properly care for their teeth.

## Chapter Overview

### Introduce the Chapter

In this chapter, students learn about the extensive physical changes undergone by children from ages one to three. Motor skills improve dramatically and sensory integration occurs. Caregivers must ensure that children get proper nutrition and medical care, and are kept safe.

### Build Background

Organize students into pairs. Each pair should draw a picture of a typical one-year-old and a second picture of a typical three-year-old. When students are done, place all the drawings where the entire class can see them. Discuss the physical differences that help us distinguish one age group from the other.

**Professional Development**

**Mini Clip Reading: Flexible Groupings**

Teachers use partner sharing to encourage and promote student discussions.

### Writing Activity
#### Dialogue

This active learning activity prompts students to write a dialogue between a caregiver and a five-year-old. After students have completed the writing activity, ask for volunteers to share their dialogues with the class. Student responses can be used as a basis for classroom discussion. (Dialogues will vary. Use these criteria when evaluating your students' writing: Do the details reflect the age, personality, and background of each person? Did the student use quotation marks correctly?)

**290**

---

Chapter

# 10 Physical Development from One to Three

## Chapter Objectives

After completing this chapter, you will be able to:

- **Identify** five changes in a child's physical growth from ages one to three.
- **Explain** how developmental milestones are used.
- **Describe** how a parent should respond to typical changes in a child's sleeping patterns.
- **Explain** why it is important to establish good eating habits early in life.
- **Identify** why young children are particularly at risk for accidents.
- **List** four factors to consider when choosing clothing for young children.

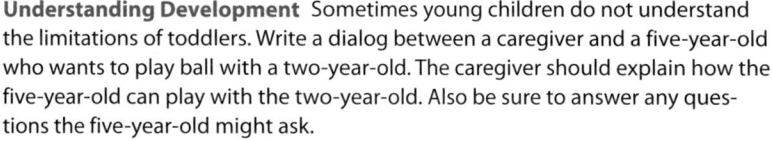

### Writing Activity — Dialogue

**Understanding Development** Sometimes young children do not understand the limitations of toddlers. Write a dialog between a caregiver and a five-year-old who wants to play ball with a two-year-old. The caregiver should explain how the five-year-old can play with the two-year-old. Also be sure to answer any questions the five-year-old might ask.

**Writing Tips** To write an effective dialogue, you should
1. Let the people speak for themselves.
2. Use dialogue for a purpose.
3. Use language that sounds real and appropriate to the people talking.
4. Use quotation marks appropriately.

---

## CLASSROOM Solutions

### Print Resources

 **Student Edition**

 **Teacher Wraparound Edition**

 **Student Activity Workbook**

 **Student Activity Workbook Teacher Annotated Edition**

### Technology Resources

 **Online Learning Center** has resources and activities for students and teachers. Includes an Online Student Edition.

 **Interactive Student Edition** allows students to instantly access review materials, examples, and exercises.

**Section 10.1** Growth and Development from One to Three

**Section 10.2** Caring for Children from One to Three

**Explore the Photo**
One- and two-year-olds, called toddlers, begin to develop independence. *What are some tasks that a toddler can perform on his own?*

291

### Review the Sections
Introduce the chapter by reviewing the sections:

#### Section 10.1
From ages one to three children not only grow in height and weight, but their fine and gross motor skills improve significantly. Their bodies increase in size more quickly than their heads and their posture becomes straighter. Sensory integration occurs as the brain matures.

#### Section 10.2
Caregivers must work to make certain that children in this age group develop good sleeping habits and eat nutritious and well-balanced meals. Regular checkups are vital to determining whether children are progressing normally. Children also must receive the proper immunizations to protect them from a wide variety of diseases.

#### ▶ Explore the Photo

**Caption Answer** Answers will vary. Toddlers are able to perform simple tasks, such as picking something up, climbing stairs, walking, or undressing themselves.

**Discussion** Explain that sometimes toddlers may want to do something for themselves, but parents cannot let them, perhaps for safety reasons or because of lack of time. How should parents react if the toddler then becomes angry? (Possible answer: Parents should use a matter-of-fact tone to explain the situation to the toddler in clear and simple language.)

 **TeacherWorks Plus** **TeacherWorks Plus** is an electronic lesson planner that provides instant access to complete teacher resources in one convenient package.

**Presentation Plus!** provides visual teaching aids for every section.

**The Early Childhood Observations CD** presents video observations and lessons on observation skills and child development.

**The Developing Brain eTransparencies and Guide** include information and activities to offer insights into brain development and diseases of the brain.

**Section 10.1**

# Growth and Development from One to Three

## Focus

### Bell Ringer Activity

#### Controlling Our Muscles

Perform for the class a gross motor skill, such as jumping. Ask: Could a one-year-old perform this task? Then perform a fine motor skill, such as writing your name on the board. Ask: At what age could a child perform this task? Emphasize that learning to control our muscles is an important part of maturing.

## Preteaching

### Vocabulary

Write the term *developmentally appropriate* on the board. Ask students to identify words that are contained within *developmentally* (develop, development). Using this knowledge and their own experiences, have students define the term.

### Graphic Organizer

The Graphic Organizer is also on the TeacherWorks CD.

(Graphic organizers should include: 12–18 months: may walk alone or while holding a hand; sits down without help; slides down stairs backwards. 18–24 months: walks well; jumps in place; climbs up or down one stair; pulls toys with wheels. 24–30 months: walks with more coordination; jumps off the bottom step; pushes self on wheeled toys. 30–36 months: alternates feet going up stairs; runs but may not be able to stop smoothly; throws a ball overhead but inaccurately.)

**NCLB** connects academic correlations to book content.

## Reading Guide

### Before You Read

**Predict** Look at the photos in this section and read their captions. Write one or two sentences predicting what the section will be about.

### Read to Learn

#### Key Concepts

- **Identify** five changes in a child's physical growth from ages one to three.
- **Explain** how developmental milestones are used.

#### Main Idea

**D** Children ages one-year-old to three-years-old grow, change, and develop in many ways. Motor skills improve noticeably.

#### Content Vocabulary

- ◇ toddler
- ◇ preschooler
- ◇ sensory integration
- ◇ developmentally appropriate
- ◇ dexterity

### Academic Vocabulary

You will find these words in your reading and on your tests. Use the glossary to look up their definitions if necessary.

- ■ variation
- ■ proportion

### Graphic Organizer

As you read, write down the gross motor skills for children one- to three-years-old. Use a time line like the one shown to illustrate your information.

| 12 months | 18 months | 24 months | 30 months | 36 months |

 **Graphic Organizer** Go to this book's Online Learning Center at **glencoe.com** to print out this graphic organizer.

 **Academic Standards**

 **English Language Arts**

**NCTE 4** Use written language to communicate effectively.

 **Science**

**NSES C** Develop understanding of the biological evolution; and behavior of organisms.

 **Social Studies**

**NCSS I C Culture** Apply an understanding of culture as an integrated whole that explains the functions and interactions of the arts, traditions, and behavior patterns.

**NCTE** *National Council of Teachers of English*
**NCTM** *National Council of Teachers of Mathematics*

**NSES** *National Science Education Standards*
**NCSS** *National Council for the Social Studies*

## Reading Guide

### Before You Read

Ask students: Have you ever worked to improve a particular type of motor skill? If so, what did you do? Discuss that babies typically develop motor skills after much hard effort. In fact, much of toddlers' time is spent learning tasks such as walking, manipulating toys, and feeding themselves.

### D Develop Concepts

**Main Idea** Discuss the main idea with the students. Ask: What do you think of when you hear the word *toddler*? When you hear *preschooler*? (Possible answer: toddlers have large heads and weak motor skills, whereas preschoolers are older and have longer limbs and better motor skills.)

# Growth from One to Three

The growth and development of a child from infancy to the preschool years is dramatic. A one-year-old still moves with some uncertainty, needs help dressing, and eats messily. A three-year-old can run and jump, get dressed alone, and eat fairly neatly with a fork and spoon.

A number of different influences impact the way children develop. Heredity plays a major role in child development. Physical traits such as body size, eye color, and even risk of disease can be passed on through genes. However, genes are not the only factor for growth and physical development. They act as a basic road map for physical development while other factors fill in the gaps. These other factors include nutrition, health, and life experiences.

Watching a child's growth during the toddler years can be amazing and informative. At this stage, changes in a child's physical growth are evidenced mainly by height, weight, body proportion, posture, and teeth. Motor development and ability progress as a child's physical development progresses.

## Toddlers to Preschoolers

After the fast pace of the first year of life, physical growth slows somewhat. Children's skills improve dramatically between their first and fourth birthdays though. At about the age of one, most children begin to walk a few unsteady steps. The term **toddler** refers to one- and two-year-olds. By age three, children are typically far from toddling. Three-year-olds not only walk steadily but they also hop, skip, and run. Most of their other physical skills have advanced as well. A **preschooler** is a child from age three to about age five, when most children start going to school.

To build their physical skills, young children need plenty of space and room to move around. They need time each day for active play so they can exercise their muscles and use their stored-up energy. Although their attention span is longer than that of infants, they still want to change games and activities often. Each day brings new learning. Young children should have safe opportunities to explore, ask questions, use their imagination, and practice their growing motor skills.

**Parental Influence**
A child could have the same color eyes or hair as a parent. These physical traits are passed on by genes. *What other factors influence a toddler's growth and development?*

---

### Discussion Starter

**Learning to Move** Ask students: What do you think of when you hear the term *motor skills?* Why is developing good motor skills vital to children? Encourage students to provide examples of activities, jobs, and so forth that require different kinds of motor skills. (A motor skill is a skill that requires using muscles to perform deliberate movement. These skills are necessary to interact with the world. Any activity or job that requires movement uses motor skills.)

### U Universal Access

**Learners Having Difficulties and English Language Learners**
Discuss the meaning of the word *heredity.* Have students create a list of those items about themselves that they inherited from their parents. They may wish to illustrate their lists. Ask for volunteers to share their lists with the group. (Appropriate responses might include the color of their skin, hair, and eyes; their height; and the shapes of their facial features. Students also might list special skills, such as the ability to run fast.)

### C Critical Thinking

**Evaluate** Ask students: Do you think toddlers' stocky build is helpful to them when they are learning to walk? Why or why not? (Possible answer: Yes, because their short legs mean that they do not have far to go when they fall. They also are less likely to be injured by falls because of their compactness.)

---

## ▶ Explore the Photo

**Caption Answer** Answers will vary but students should say the environment also plays a role in toddler's growth and development.

**Discussion** Remind students about what they have learned concerning neural pathways. Have them suppose that they know parents whose baby is having problems learning to walk. What might they say to these parents? (They might say that sometimes it simply requires longer for some children to develop the neural pathways needed to perform certain activities. These pathways are strengthened by repetition.)

## Teach cont.

### S Skill Practice

#### Guided Practice

**Create a Table** Have students create a table to which doctors can refer when determining the average height of boys at ages one, two, and three. Students should calculate the average height for boys at each age, then place their results in a labeled table. (Table should contain the following averages: one year: 29.75; two years: 34.375; three years: 37.75.) **L1** **ELL**

**Make a Graph** Instruct students to create a line graph showing the average heights and weights of girls at ages one, two, and three. The line for weight should be a different color than the one for height. The graph should be clearly labeled and easy to understand. (Students should calculate and chart the averages for girls' height and weight. Height should include 29, 33.75, and 37.375. Weight should include 21, 26.5, and 30.75.) **L2**

**Write a Test** Tell students to create a 10-question multiple choice test that will require the test-taker to analyze the data in Figure 10.1. Have students work individually to write the test. They then should take one another's test. Finally, ask for volunteers to read aloud some of their questions. Encourage students to evaluate these questions. Ask questions such as: Are the questions clearly worded? Are the options appropriate? (Students should write and evaluate 10-question multiple choice tests based on the data in Figure 10.1.) **L3**

### Figure 10.1 Average Heights and Weights: Ages 1–3

Growth charts help monitor a child's growth. *Should parents be overly concerned if their child does not fit within these ranges? Why or why not?*

| AGE | BOYS | | GIRLS | |
| --- | --- | --- | --- | --- |
| | Height / Inches | Weight / Pounds | Height / Inches | Weight / Pounds |
| **One year** | 29 to 30½ | 21 to 24½ | 28¼ to 29¾ | 19½ to 22½ |
| **Two years** | 33½ to 35¼ | 26 to 30 | 32¾ to 34¾ | 24½ to 28½ |
| **Three years** | 36¾ to 38¾ | 29¼ to 34 | 36¼ to 38½ | 28¼ to 33¼ |

## Height and Weight

Children from ages one to three gain less than half the average monthly weight they did during the first year of life. Growth in height also slows by about half. **Figure 10.1** shows the average heights and weights for boys and girls from ages one to three.

Heredity and environment influence the rate at which children grow in height and weight. These influences are more noticeable among children ages one to three than among infants. After their first birthdays, children begin to show greater **variation**, or difference, in size. Some are much larger than average, while others are smaller. These size differences often continue through life. A tall two-year-old often grows to be a tall adult.

## Proportion and Posture

Because of changes in physical **proportion**, or size, a child's posture generally improves between the ages one to three. Until age two, the circumference, or measurement around, of a child's head, abdomen, and chest are about the same. Between ages two and three, however, the chest becomes larger around than the head and abdomen. During this time, the arms, legs, and torso get longer. These changes in proportion help improve the child's balance and motor skills.

By the age of two, a child's posture is straighter but the child still does not stand completely erect. The typical toddler still has a protruding abdomen. The head is still bent forward somewhat. The toddler's knees and elbows are also slightly bent. By their third birthday, children stand straighter because their spines are stronger.

## Teeth

A child's teeth emerge at different rates, but there are averages. One-year-olds typically have about eight teeth. During the second year of life, eight more teeth usually come in. For most children, the last four back teeth emerge early in the third year, giving them a complete set of 20 primary, or baby, teeth. These teeth will eventually fall out and be replaced by adult, or permanent, teeth.

There are several factors that influence the health of a child's teeth. These include diet, heredity, and dental care. Healthy teeth are important for eating and for preventing infection and pain.

### Figure 10.1 Average Heights and Weights: Ages 1–3

**Caption Answer** The answer is probably not. These measurements are average. Some children are above or below average height and weight. However, concerned parents should check with their child's medical professional.

**Discussion** Ask students: How do you think the changes in the proportions of children's bodies as they grow affect their motor skills? (As children's posture improves and their arms, legs, and torso get longer, their balance improves. Their gross motor skills, such as running and jumping, improve dramatically.)

## Diet

Diet greatly influences the quality of a child's teeth. Teeth are formed before birth. This means the mother's diet during pregnancy affects the quality of her baby's teeth. The child's diet during the first two years is also important because adult teeth are forming under the primary teeth. Dairy products, which are rich in calcium and phosphorus, are especially important to good dental health. The vitamin D in milk also helps in the development of strong and healthy teeth and bones. Children should drink water that contains fluoride. Most tap water contains fluoride but most bottled waters do not. You can check with your dentist to be sure that a child is getting enough fluoride.

A poor diet can cause tooth decay. To promote good dental health, sweets should be limited in a child's diet. Gum-like candy, raisins, and fruit snacks that stick to the teeth are a particular problem. In addition to regular brushing, children should brush their teeth after eating sugary cereals. If left between the teeth, they can promote dental decay. Do not put a child to bed with a bottle unless it contains only water. When sweet liquids, such as juice or milk, are left in the mouth too long, they can cause tooth decay. In babies, it can lead to a condition called baby bottle decay, which destroys young children's teeth.

## Heredity

Heredity appears to play a role in tooth quality. Dentists have identified a protective mechanism that discourages decay. Some children inherit this trait from their parents.

## Dentist

Most doctors recommend taking children to a dentist at about the age of 18 months. This will help them become comfortable with dental visits from an early age and begin preventive care long before the permanent teeth come in.

Some family dentists will see toddlers. Others may refer you to a pediatric dentist. Toddlers can be challenging for a dentist due to their energy and temperaments. Pediatric dentists, just like pediatric doctors, are specially trained to deal with young children. They

**Dental Development**
During the second year of life, eight teeth usually come in, giving the two-year-old a set of sixteen teeth. *How many total primary teeth will there be?*

often have books and toys in the waiting room to entertain the children. Once in the exam room, many dentists will ask the child to sit on a parents lap for the exam. This gives them an added sense of security.

**✓ Reading Check** **Explain** How does diet influence the quality of a child's teeth?

---

{ **Expert Advice...** }

*"The toddler stage is very important in a child's life. It is the time between infancy and childhood when a child learns and grows in many ways. Everything that happens to the toddler is meaningful. With each stage or skill the child masters, a new stage begins. This growth is unique to each child."*

— Cathy Malley, child development educator, University of Connecticut

---

**Teach** *cont.*

## U Universal Access

**Verbal Learners** Have students conduct research to answer the following questions. Instruct them to use appropriate print or online reference materials, or to interview a pediatric dentist.

- Why do dentists want to exam children at an early age?
- How can parents and caregivers help children enjoy visits to the dentist?
- What is the most important advice dentists have for caregivers of children between ages one and three?

Instruct students to create an oral report to share what they learn.

## R Reading Strategy

**Determine Main Points** Instruct students to close their books. Read aloud the quote in the Expert Advice box. Have students work individually to write down the three main points made in this quote. (Students should identify the three main points: toddlers learn and grow in many ways; upon mastering one stage, toddlers immediately move to the next; and each child's growth is different.) **ELL**

**✓ Reading Check**

**Explain** The mother's diet during pregnancy must be nutritious because the baby's teeth are formed before birth. The child's diet during the first two years is important because adult teeth are forming. Calcium, vitamin D, and phosphorous all contribute to the development of healthy teeth.

---

### ●●●● ▶ Explore the Photo

**Caption Answer** There will be 20 primary teeth.

**Discussion** What are some of the reasons that children should be taken to the dentist at an early age? (It gets them used to going to the dentist regularly, and helps to start preventive care long before permanent teeth arrive.)

 **Mc Graw Hill Professional Development**

**Mini Clip**
**Reading: Planning and Classroom Management**

Nancy Frey, PhD, educator and author, discusses the instructional strategies that support a differentiated classroom.

**Quiz**

Ask students to answer the following questions:

1. How does a child's weight gain from ages one to three compare to weight gain during the first year of life? (Between one and three, children gain weight less than half as fast as they do during the first year.)

2. What are primary teeth and how many primary teeth will a child eventually have? (They are baby teeth that are later replaced by the permanent teeth. Children eventually have 20 primary teeth.)

3. Why should parents avoid giving a baby a bottle of milk or juice when putting him to bed? (If these liquids are left in the mouth too long, they can cause tooth decay.)

### THE DEVELOPING BRAIN

**Learning Abilities and Facts**
**Science Inquiry** Answers will vary. Students may list skills such as eating, writing, riding a bicycle, walking, or jumping.

For more information and activities, see *The Developing Brain* guide and eTransparencies.

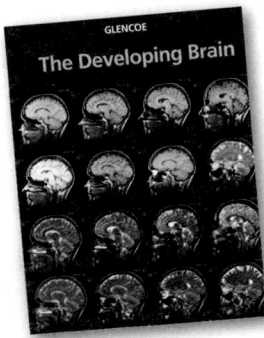

**Developing Through Exercise**
Exercise is necessary for gross motor development. *How does physical activity promote the development of gross motor skills?*

# Development from One to Three

The three general patterns of physical development (from head to foot, from near to far, and from simple to complex) are evident in this age span. When you compare the skills of children at age one with those at the end of their third year, you can see big changes. Hand skills, for instance, show a pattern of development from simple to complex. At thirteen months, a child can bang blocks together or may manage to build a short stack of blocks. By age four, the same child can manipulate the blocks skillfully to create much more complex structures, such as towers, houses, and roads.

## Sensory Integration

As children grow, their senses develop. This gives them greater awareness of their environment. **Sensory integration** is the process by which the brain combines information taken in through the senses to make a whole. This process is how a child knows how wide to open the mouth to eat a bite of orange. It also tells the child the orange dripped when he feels the juice on his chin. Some children are unable to normally process all the information their senses take in. These children are said to have sensory dysfunction. They may react more strongly to some types of stimulation, such as noises or lights, and less strongly to other types. When this happens, a child may have learning and behavioral problems.

### THE DEVELOPING BRAIN

**Learning Abilities and Facts**

Scientists have discovered that the learning of abilities, such as riding a bike, and the learning of facts, such as names and dates, are handled by different parts of the brain. Once a skill is learned, it forms a very durable memory. You never forget how to ride a bike. The same is not true of fact memories. Facts that are not used often slowly fade away until they are forgotten.

■ **Science Inquiry** Skills often become so automatic that you do not have to think about how to do them. What skills do you perform with little or no thought?

**296** Chapter 10 Physical Development from One to Three

### ▶ Explore the Photo

**Caption Answer** As children exercise, they slowly build the strength, confidence, and coordination to perform the gross motor skills.

**Discussion** Organize students into small groups. Instruct each group to come up with a list of skills the child in the photo is learning. Have the class compare their final lists. (Answers might include: to track the ball with his eyes, to keep his body close to the ball, and to maintain his balance.)

## Developmental Milestones

It is not always predictable when children from ages one to three will acquire various physical skills. Although they were born just two weeks apart, Blake and his cousin Damon have not mastered physical skills at the same pace. That is not surprising since some children learn skills earlier or later than average. These variations can be caused by differences in a child's physical size, health and diet, interests, temperament, and opportunities for physical play.

Child development experts have studied the range of ages at which children acquire certain important skills and have determined average ages. These developmental milestones for physical development of one-, two-, and three-year-olds are shown in **Figure 10.2** on page 298 These arc used to compare the average abilities of children of different ages. They also help caregivers plan developmentally appropriate activities. **Developmentally appropriate** describes toys, activities, and tasks that are suitable for a child at a specific age. For example, an 18-month-old can stack two blocks. That means activities that involve large building blocks would be developmentally appropriate for 18-month-olds.

## Motor Skills

During this period, both gross and fine motor skills improve dramatically. Keep in mind that not all children develop physical skills at the same rate.

### Gross Motor Skills

Physical exercise promotes the development of gross motor skills. Gross motor skills involve the use and control of the large muscles of the back, legs, shoulders, and arms. As children exercise, they slowly build the confidence, strength, and coordination that helps them run, jump, and kick a ball.

Walking is a significant gross motor milestone for children. It gives them a feeling of pride and much more mobility for exploration. Most children begin to walk at about one year of age. At first, children walk by holding on to furniture for stability. This is called cruising.

When they first let go of the furniture, they are wobbly and uncertain. Their toes are pointed outward, their feet are spread apart, and their arms are held out for balance. After a few shaky steps, they collapse into a sitting position. This is normal. With practice, children improve in steadiness, balance, and body control.

## Learning Through PLAY

### Changes in Play

How children play changes as they grow and develop. By the time they are one, children begin to discover what objects are used for. A one-year-old understands that a telephone is used for speaking to another person. However, by the time they are three, the role of imagination has begun to play a part in children's play. A telephone may no longer be a phone but could be used as a remote for turning on a pretend television. A two-year-old will play with small plates and silverware. However, by the age of three, the same child might use her imagination to pretend that a piece of paper is a plate and a crayon is a spoon. During this time period, children go from just being curious about objects to using their imagination with objects.

**Think About It** Your neighbor's three-year-old son is sitting in a box "driving" to the store. Your neighbor is concerned because her son has a toy car to play in. How can you assure your neighbor that her son is normal?

## Reteach

### R Reading Strategy

**Examine Context** Read aloud the first sentence under "Motor Skills." Ask students: If you did not know what the word *gross* meant in this context, what might you speculate based on this sentence? (that gross means the opposite of fine) Tell students that *gross* is one of those words that can have many different meanings. In this case, it simply means large. **ELL**

**Mc Graw Hill Professional Development**

**Mini Clip Reading: Modeling Reading Strategies**
A teacher uses a read-aloud to model fluent reading strategies.

### U Universal Access

**Gifted Learners** Have students conduct research using reliable print or online sources about the role of myostatin in the regulation of muscle mass. Have students write a report on what they learn. (Reports may vary. Scientist have determined that myostatin is a gene that works to limit muscle growth. If the gene is defective, the individual can have excessive muscle development. Scientists hope studying this gene will lead to treatments for muscle-related disorders.)

## Learning Through PLAY

### Changes in Play

**Discussion** Organize students into groups. Give each group an everyday object, such as a kitchen timer or an empty wallet. Each group should come up with ideas on how one-, two-, and three-year-olds might play with this item. Have the groups demonstrate their ideas.
(Students should present ideas for how each age group might play with their assigned item.)

**Think About It** Answers will vary but students should point out that the three-year-old is simply exercising his imagination and using one thing (the box) to represent another (a car). They should assure the neighbor that this is normal behavior.

## U₁ Universal Access

**Visual Learners** Organize the class into five groups. Assign each group one of the age classifications listed in Figure 10.2. Each group should create a mural of activities children in their age classification can perform. They should divide the mural into two parts: those activities requiring fine motor skills and those activities requiring gross motor skills. Encourage students to include some activities that are not listed in the figure itself. **ELL**

**McGraw Hill Professional Development**

**Mini Clip**
**ELL: Comprehension and English Learners**
Author Josefina Tinajero discusses comprehension strategies that are appropriate for English learners.

## C₁ Critical Thinking

**Draw Conclusions** Describe the following scenario: Two-year-old Camille loves to climb stairs. Most of the time, the stairs at home are blocked off with a gate. When Camille's family visits the children's museum, she runs right to an out-of-the-way staircase and spends an hour climbing three steps, then turning around and, with her father's help, climbing back down. Ask: What is Camille doing? (She is using this opportunity to practice skills she is not able to practice at home.)

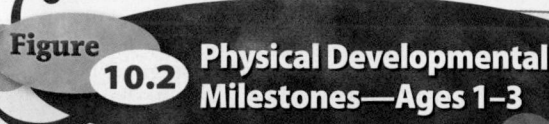

## Figure 10.2 Physical Developmental Milestones—Ages 1–3

Children typically meet one milestone before moving on to the next. At what age will a toddler likely be able to push herself on a wheeled toy?

| Age | Fine Motor Skills | Gross Motor Skills |
|---|---|---|
| 12–18 Months | ❖ Turns several pages of a book at a time<br>❖ Picks up small objects with thumb and forefinger<br>❖ Moves objects from hand to hand | ❖ May walk alone or while holding a caregiver's hand<br>❖ Sits down without help<br>❖ Slides down stairs backwards, one step at a time |
| 18–24 Months | ❖ Stacks from two to four blocks<br>❖ Grasps crayons with a fist and scribbles | ❖ Walks well<br>❖ Jumps in place<br>❖ Climbs up or down one stair<br>❖ Pulls toys with wheels |
| 2–2½ Years | ❖ Stacks six blocks<br>❖ Turns one page of a book at a time<br>❖ Picks up objects from the floor without losing balance | ❖ Walks with more coordination and confidence<br>❖ Jumps off the bottom step<br>❖ Pushes self on wheeled toys |
| 2½–3 Years | ❖ Stacks eight blocks<br>❖ Screws lids on and off containers<br>❖ Draws circles and horizontal and vertical lines | ❖ Alternates feet going up stairs but not going down<br>❖ Runs but may not be able to stop smoothly<br>❖ Throws a ball overhead but inaccurately |
| 3–4 Years | ❖ Stacks nine or ten blocks<br>❖ Cuts with scissors<br>❖ Draws recognizable pictures | ❖ Jumps up and down in place with both feet<br>❖ Catches a ball with arms straight<br>❖ Rides a tricycle |

### Figure 10.2 Physical Developmental Milestones—Ages 1–3

**Caption Answer** At 2–2½ years a toddler will probably be able to push herself on a wheeled toy.

**Discussion** Ask students how the gross motor skills that children develop around age three enable them to play a greater variety of games than they could when they were two. (Because they can better control their bodies, they can begin playing catch, although not with a great deal of accuracy. They also become better at games that involve running and jumping.)

## CULTURE MATTERS

### Dexterity Among the Navajos

At first, researchers were puzzled when they discovered that many Navajo children's fine motor skills were better developed than those of their peers. The Navajo children also displayed above average ability in visual perception. Then the researchers learned that many Navajo children are taught traditional handicrafts, such as painting, weaving, and working with silver, at a young age. The researchers realized that the Navajo children had refined their small motor skills by practicing these traditional crafts, many of which use intricate patterns that are kept in the mind and never written down.

⭐ **Build Connections** *How would you recommend teachers present new information to Navajo children, based on what you have learned about them?*

**NCSS I C Culture** Apply an understanding of culture as an integrated whole that explains the functions and interactions of the arts, traditions, and behavior patterns.

---

Climbing skills follow a similar sequence if the child has stairs to climb. Climbing is not limited to stairs, however. Nothing is safe from the climbing toddler. Furniture, counters, shelves, and even people are conquered like mountains! This motion, of course, makes safety an important concern for caregivers. You will learn more about how to help make areas safer for children's exploration in Section 10.2.

### Fine Motor Skills

One of the major developmental milestones that children reach at about age one is the ability to pick up small objects between their thumb and forefinger. This fine motor skill allows them to better grasp and lift small objects. This also increases the need to watch what they put in their mouth!

Between their first and second birthdays, children use fine motor skills as they learn to feed themselves and to drink from a cup. At first, young children often spill because they have poor hand-eye coordination. With practice, their success and neatness improve.

Toys offer children the chance to practice fine motor skills. One-year-olds usually enjoy playing with blocks, large beads, and stacking games. They might stack two or three blocks, only to knock them down and start over. They also like play phones, toys that roll, and musical toys.

Two-year-olds typically display greater dexterity. **Dexterity** is the skillful use of the hands and fingers. Two-year-olds can turn the pages of a book one at a time. They can turn on a faucet. They enjoy using crayons and typically color with such happy abandon that they leave marks running off the paper and on the table or floor. Another favorite activity of children in this age group is stacking blocks. They build small towers of blocks that usually topple after five or six blocks.

Three-year-olds show more success than younger children at tasks that require fine motor skills. They usually delight in taking things apart and putting them back together. Children this age have enough dexterity to draw circles, lines, and crosses.

---

## CULTURE MATTERS

### Dexterity Among the Navajos

**Discussion** Ask students: Suppose you work in a child care center. What kinds of activities might you use to encourage young children to develop manual dexterity? (Possible answers: stacking blocks, putting together puzzles, simple weaving, drawing, painting, and using modeling clay.)

**Building Connections** *Based on the information in the passage, Navajo children would probably learn best from hands-on lessons and visual materials.*

---

## Reteach *cont.*

### C₂ Critical Thinking

**Analyze** Tell students that the Iroquois, a group of Native Americans in the Northeastern United States, have a long tradition of working on building the iron structures of skyscrapers. Workers from this group have built many New York City high-rise buildings. Ask students what kinds of skills this work would require. Why do they think Iroquois might excel at this work? (Student answers will vary; the work requires an excellent sense of balance and a willingness to do work that many people find too dangerous.)

### U₂ Universal Access

**Learners Having Difficulties** Draw a Venn diagram on the board. Ask students to list the similarities and differences between fine motor skills and gross motor skills. Fill in the diagram with students' responses. (Similarities: both require control of muscles, both improve with practice; Fine motor skills: use small muscles, used for more intricate tasks such as using silverware; Gross motor skills: use large muscles, used for tasks such as walking and jumping.) **ELL**

### W Writing Support
**Dialogue**

**Messy Eating** Your relative is complaining that his two-year-old makes a mess when eating. Food ends up in the toddler's hair and covers the floor. Write a dialogue in which you help your relative understand this situation. (Refer to p. 290 for tips on writing a dialogue. Students should emphasize that it is important to see the messiness as a step to the toddler improving her fine motor skills so she can feed herself neatly.)

## Study Tools

Have students go to the Online Learning Center at **glencoe.com**:

- Take the **Practice Test**.
- Download **Study-to-Go** content.

Use the **Student Activity Workbook** for additional practice.

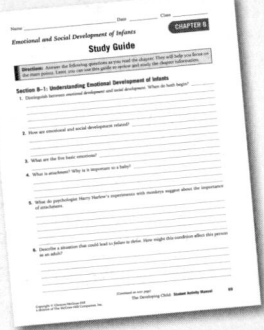

### Close

## Culminating Activity

**Compare** Have students compare the motor skills of a one-year-old to those of a four-year-old. (One-year-olds can pick up small objects, walk, and slide down stairs; four-year-olds have much more physical dexterity and can cut with scissors, draw recognizable pictures, and ride a tricycle.)

**NCLB** connects academic correlations to book content.

---

Before the age of two, it is difficult to determine whether a child will be left-handed or right-handed. They generally use both hands equally as they continue to develop motor skills and build muscles and coordination. In fact, if a one-year-old seems to prefer one hand most of the time, it might indicate a physical problem with the other hand or arm. Parents should check with their physician if they feel there might be a problem.

Around age two or three, some children make their preference clear by favoring one hand over the other. This means they will consistently use the same hand to hold crayons, spoons, or toys. Other children, however, may continue switching between hands well into their preschool years. Physicians say that such switching back and forth is not a problem as long as it does not inhibit a child's ability to complete developmentally appropriate tasks.

## Hand-Eye Coordination

Hand-eye coordination continues to improve among children in this age group, giving them the ability to zero in on small objects and pick them up for examination. Shortly after their first birthday, children start picking up very small objects between their thumb and forefinger. At first, this is difficult. With practice, however, their skill improves. By about eighteen months of age, children have mastered it.

This milestone in hand-eye coordination and fine motor skills gives children greater ability in using objects, poking fingers in holes, opening boxes, and playing with balls. It also aids them in building structures, sorting beads, and coloring with crayons. By their second birthday, children's coordination and strength has increased so much that they can turn doorknobs and pick up small objects on the ground without losing their balance.

---

## Section 10.1 — After You Read

### Review Key Concepts

1. **Explain** the difference in growth between the ages of one and three and growth during the first year of life.
2. **Identify** what developmentally appropriate means.

### Practice Academic Skills

**English Language Arts**

3. Imagine that a parent said, "I can give my child whatever she wants to eat while she's little. Her baby teeth are going to fall out anyway." Write a short essay in which you explain what is wrong with this reasoning, as it pertains to teeth.

> **NCTE 4** Use written language to communicate effectively.

**Science**

4. Three-year-old Tammy's mom has given her sorting beads, writing utensils, and dolls with removable clothing because she believes girls develop fine motor skills more quickly than boys. Write Tammy's mom a letter explaining why her viewpoint might be dangerous. Include suggestions on more age-appropriate toys.

> **NSES C** Develop understanding of the biological evolution; and behavior of organisms.

**Check Your Answers** Check your answers at this book's Online Learning Center at **glencoe.com**.

---

## Section 10.1 After You Read

### Review Key Concepts

1. A child grows faster during his first year than between the ages of one and three. Children from ages one to three gain less than half the average monthly weight they did during the first year of life. Growth in height also slows by about half.

2. Developmentally appropriate means that the activity is suited to the child's physical and mental ability level.

### Practice Academic Skills

3. Essays will vary but should state that a child's diet during the first two years is important because adult teeth are forming under the primary teeth.

4. Students' letters will vary. They should point out that most three-year-olds (whether girls or boys) are not developmentally ready for these types of fine motor skills. Tammy could become frustrated and angry if her mother pushes her to do things she's not developmentally ready to do.

## Reading Guide

### Before You Read

**Discover** Choose a Content or Academic Vocabulary term that is new to you. When you find it in the text, write down the definition.

### Read to Learn
**Key Concepts**
- **Describe** how a parent should respond to typical changes in a child's sleeping patterns.
- **Explain** why it is important to establish good eating habits early in life.
- **Identify** why young children are particularly at risk for accidents.
- **List** four factors to consider when choosing clothing for young children.

### Main Idea
One- to three-year-olds experience many changes in sleep patterns, nutritional needs, eating, hygiene, dressing, health, illness, and safety.

### Content Vocabulary

◇ night terrors
◇ hygiene
◇ sphincter muscles
◇ synthetic fibers
◇ flame-resistant

### Academic Vocabulary
You will find these words in your reading and on your tests. Use the glossary to look up their definitions if necessary.
■ incident
■ pollutant

### Graphic Organizer
As you read, list five things a caregiver can focus on to make meals appealing to a young child. Use a chart like the one shown to help organize your information.

| Promoting Nutritious Foods |
|---|
| 1. |
| 2. |
| 3. |
| 4. |
| 5. |

 **Graphic Organizer** Go to this book's Online Learning Center at **glencoe.com** to print out this graphic organizer.

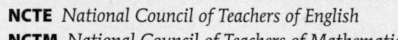

### Academic Standards . . . . . . . . . . . . . . . . . . . . . .

 **English Language Arts**
**NCTE 4** Use written language to communicate effectively.

**Mathematics**
**NCTM Measurement** Understand measurable attributes of objects and the units, systems, and processes of measurement.

**Social Studies**
**NCSS I A Culture** Analyze and explain the ways groups, societies, and cultures address human needs and concerns.

**NCTE** *National Council of Teachers of English*
**NCTM** *National Council of Teachers of Mathematics*

**NSES** *National Science Education Standards*
**NCSS** *National Council for the Social Studies*

---

## Focus

### Bell Ringer Activity

#### The Importance of Good Habits
Tell students about a habit you have. Perhaps you never drink anything during your meals or you must have a fan on while sleeping. Encourage students to discuss similar habits they have. Explain that when good habits are developed at any early age, they can make a profound impact on a person's entire life. Encouraging such habits is a vital part of being a parent.

## Preteaching
### Vocabulary
Discuss that being aware of a word's origins can be helpful in knowing how to spell it. Words that use a "y" to create an "i" sound, such as "hygiene" and "synthetic," typically have Greek origins. Have students look up the Greek words from which these words originate. **ELL**

### Graphic Organizer
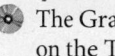 The Graphic Organizer is also on the TeacherWorks CD.

(Graphic organizers should list: color, texture, shape, temperature, and ease of eating.)

 **NCLB** connects academic correlations to book content.

---

## Reading Guide

### Before You Read
Ask students if they ever had nightmares when they were younger. Do they still have them now? Do they think parents can do anything to help children when they have scary dreams? Explain that this section discusses sleep disturbances and how parents can appropriately respond to them.

### D Develop Concepts

**Main Idea** Discuss the main idea with the students. Ask students which of these habits has the greatest influence on long-term health: Good sleeping patterns, good eating habits, or good hygiene. (Reponses will vary; possible answer: good eating habits are essential for remaining healthy and active.)

## Teach

### Discussion Starter

Tell students to imagine that they are parents of a two-year-old. Your spouse refuses to eat all vegetables except for potatoes. How do you think you would handle this situation? (If one parent is vocal about not liking vegetables, the child is likely to follow. It would be very important for you to eat vegetables regularly and state how much you enjoy them. You also might ask your spouse to not say anything negative about vegetables.)

### **W₁** Writing Support
#### Dialogue

**Not Enough Sleep** Suppose you work at a child care center. A three-year-old seems exhausted all the time. Write a dialogue in which you talk with the parent about your concerns. Be sure to discuss the importance of sleep for young children. (Refer to p. 290 for tips on writing a dialogue. Students should write a dialogue in which they discuss with the parent their concerns and explain that young children cannot develop properly without 10 to 14 hours of sleep.)

### **U₁** Universal Access

**Musical Learners** Instruct students to write a song with lyrics that tell about a child getting ready for bed. For example, the song might tell about taking a bath, putting on pajamas, brushing teeth, and so forth. Encourage students to be creative in their lyrics. Ask for volunteers to perform their songs for the class. (Students may ask friends to join them in their performances. Students should write songs about a child's bedtime activities.)

## Sleeping

Changes in sleeping needs and patterns are common for children ages one to three. Sleeping habits often change around a child's second birthday. Children usually require less sleep than before, and they may not fall asleep as easily. It is important for parents to make sure their children still get enough rest.

### Sleep Patterns

Most one-year-olds continue the pattern of sleeping eight or more hours at night. They typically take naps of several hours during the day. As they get older, daytime naps become shorter. The length of time they sleep at night slowly increases. By the age of two, most children no longer take a morning nap. Afternoon naps may continue for several years. In total, two-and three-year-olds sleep about 10 to 14 hours a day.

Fears or anxiety about separation from parents can make falling asleep difficult for toddlers and preschoolers. Some may call parents back into their room again and again, asking for a drink of water, another story, or one more trip to the bathroom. What they usually want, however, is just comfort and reassurance.

Children feel more comfortable when their lives are predictable. A nightly routine such as brushing teeth, reading stories, singing, and choosing a soft toy to take to bed can help prepare children for sleep. When the routine is broken because of a late bedtime or a lost toy, it is more difficult for a child to fall asleep. It is common for children to use self-comforting techniques at bedtime, such as thumb sucking or cuddling a favorite blanket.

### Sleep Disturbances

Sometimes the quantity or quality of a child's sleep is upset. When this happens, the child may be tired and irritable the next day.

It is not unusual for toddlers to wake up briefly when sleeping. Some fall back to sleep. Others may begin to cry or try to get a caregiver's attention. The best response depends on the problem. For example, a trip to the bathroom may be needed.

**Getting Ready for Bed**
Most children do not like to be rushed from one activity to the next. Reading can be a part of a child's bedtime routine to help transition from the day. *Why is it important to establish a bedtime routine?*

## ▶ Explore the Photo

**Caption Answer** Answers may vary. Children are more comfortable when their lives are predictable. Also, a bedtime routine can help a child calm down from an active day and be ready to rest.

**Discussion** Ask students: What kind of bedtime routine did you have as a young child? Do you think this routine helped you get ready for the night? Why or why not? (Possible answers might include putting dolls and stuffed animals to bed and talking about the day's activities.)

Fear of the dark is common at ages two and three and may prevent a child from falling asleep. A nightlight or calmly discussing fears may help. Never tease a child about fears.

Nightmares and night terrors sometimes disturb children's sleep. **Night terrors** are a type of sleep disturbance that occurs during the first few hours of sleep, when children are sleeping deeply. Children who are not fully awake may sit up with their eyes open and scream. Such children are often very upset but unable to explain what is wrong. By morning, the child usually does not remember anything about the **incident**, or action. In general, night terrors are not a cause for alarm. Children who experience them need reassurance.

Nightmares are frightening dreams that often seem real. Some children have difficulty separating dreams from reality. Experts recommend responding right away with words of comfort to a child who has had a nightmare.

Nightmares may occur because of stress or major changes in a child's life, such as starting preschool. Sometimes reassurance and reduction of pressure can help relieve a child's anxiety. Avoiding exposure to frightening images on television may also help.

**✓ Reading Check** **Recall** What seems to be the best way for caregivers to deal with a child's fear of the dark, night terrors, and nightmares?

# Nutritional Needs and Eating

The habits and attitudes toward food that children learn at this stage will influence their eating habits throughout life. That is why it is vital to establish good eating habits early in life. Teaching good habits means helping children learn to enjoy nutritious foods and to eat correct portions of food.

Meals sometimes become a battle of wills between parents and young children. Experts suggest offering children a variety of healthy foods at mealtime and letting them choose what to eat. Like adults, children develop likes and dislikes. Children accept and try new

foods more easily if they are not pressured to try them. Adults can encourage children to try new foods and develop good habits by modeling those behaviors. Young children often mimic their parents. So if mom or dad likes a food, the child is more likely to try it.

Children this age like consistency at mealtimes. They may insist that a sandwich be cut just the right way. They may become upset if they do not get lunch on a certain plate or a drink in a favorite cup.

## Self-Feeding

Children at this stage will want to feed themselves. This is a natural part of their growing independence. Self-feeding depends on a child's fine motor skills, and it also helps refine them.

## What Would You Do?

### Getting a New Bed

Jamie, age two and one-half, kept climbing out of his crib, even when he was tired. His parents were concerned that he could hurt himself. They decided that it was time to get Jamie a toddler bed.

On an afternoon visit to his grandmother's, Jamie took a nap in a bed for the first time. His grandmother let him choose a blanket to use and bring his favorite stuffed animal. She read a story to him, and Jamie fell asleep.

Back at home, Jamie's parents asked him about his visit to Grandma's house. He proudly talked about sleeping in the big bed. Jamie's mother said she wanted to get him a big bed too. Jamie looked a little uncertain. His mother said she would need his help picking out sheets and a blanket to go with the bed. Then Jamie looked excited.

✏ *Write About It* Jamie's new bed had a rail on one side so he would not fall out. Besides getting a special toddler bed with a rail, how might you keep a child from getting hurt by falling out of bed? Create a list of your suggestions.

**Write About It** Lists will vary but may include pushing the bed next to a wall and putting a mattress or cushion on the floor next to the bed, or tucking pillows in with the toddler so she cannot roll over them.

**✓ Reading Check**

**Recall** Parents and caregivers should use reassurance, soothing gestures, and words of comfort.

**Teach** *cont.*

## **C** Critical Thinking

**Contrast** Ask students: How are night terrors different from nightmares? Create a chart on the board listing the differences. (A night terror is a sleep disturbance that occurs during deep sleep. Children may have their eyes open and scream. They may have no memory of the incident by morning. Nightmares are frightening dreams that many children think are real. They sometimes occur because of stress.)

## **W₂** Writing Support
### Dialogue

**A Frightening Event** Describe a scenario in which two-year-old Amanda wakes up screaming after having a nightmare. Instruct students to write a dialogue in which Amanda's parent talks with her about her all-too-lifelike dream. Students should use what they have learned here to write the parent's response. (Refer to p. 290 for tips on writing a dialogue. Students should write a dialogue in which they describe Amanda's fears and the parent's responses, such as reassurances that the parent will not let anything bad happen.)

## **U₂** Universal Access

**Interpersonal Learners** Divide the class into groups. One group will play parents and the other will play three-year-olds. The three-year-olds express reluctance to try new foods during a family dinner. The students acting as the three-year-olds will determine what the problem foods are and why, and secretly write down these reasons. Parents should use communication skills to discover the reasons for the reluctance. Three-year-olds will tell the group when a parent has discovered the reason for their reluctance and has constructively addressed it. **ELL**

## Teach *cont.*

### S Skill Practice

#### Guided Practice

**Draw a Picture** Instruct students to draw a picture of a well-balanced meal for a two- or three-year-old. Encourage students to choose colorful foods that will appeal to young children. The picture should also indicate the amount of each food the child should be served. (Pictures should illustrate a well-balanced meal for a two- or three-year-old, along with correct portion sizes.) **L1** **ELL**

**Create a Skit** Organize students into pairs. One person should role play an expert on children's nutrition and the other a parent of a two-year-old. The children's nutritionist should explain the types and quantities of food needed by the child. The parent should ask appropriate questions which the nutritionist then answers. Have students perform their skits for the class. (Students should perform a skit in which a nutritionist explains to a parent the types and quantities of food needed by a two-year-old.) **L2** **ELL**

**Analyze a Kid's Meal** Have students choose a children's meal from a fast-food restaurant. They should determine how many of the categories of foods in Figure 10.3 are contained in the meal. Students also should analyze each item's portion size. They then should write a paragraph summarizing what they discovered. (Students should write a paragraph summarizing the portion sizes and kinds of foods contained in a children's meal from a fast-food restaurant.) **L3**

### One-Year-Olds

Children at this age eat a variety of foods. Finger foods, such as slices of banana, are popular. They should avoid hard foods like raw carrots that can cause choking. Using a spoon to eat usually begins before the age of one. There is still a lot of spilling though.

When children first start drinking from a cup, a training cup is a good choice. These are also called sippy cups. These cups' handles, lid, and spout or straw reduce spills.

### Two-Year-Olds

Children in this age group can usually feed themselves and learn to use a fork, but they often take a long time to eat. They are still improving their fine motor skills, as well as getting nutrition. Most children drink from a cup fairly well by age two. At this age, a child should eat with the rest of the family.

### Three-Year-Olds

By age three, most children are quite skillful using a spoon and fork. Three-year-olds have a full set of primary teeth, so chewing foods is not a problem. Three-year-olds generally eat meals with the family. They also eat the same food as the rest of the family. Meats and other tough foods should be cut into small pieces for them.

## Nutritional Needs

Since they are growing less rapidly than in their first year of life, children ages one to three do not eat as much. Because their stomachs are still small, most need food every three or four hours. However, the amount that children eat may vary greatly from day to day, depending on appetite and level of activity. Nutritious snacks, such as fresh fruit, can help keep them full between meals.

**Figure 10.3 Serving Sizes for Children Two and Three** Parents and caregivers need to know appropriate serving sizes for toddlers. *Why is it important to know the correct serving size for small children?*

Toddlers need smaller serving sizes of food but they still need to eat a variety of food from all five food groups.

**Milk Group**
Milk, yogurt—½ cup
Frozen yogurt, pudding—¼ to ½ cup
Cheese—½ to 1 oz.

**Grain Group**
Whole-grain bread—¼ to ½ slice
Ready-to-eat cereal—¼ to ⅓ cup
Spaghetti, rice, macaroni—¼ to ⅓ cup
Crackers—2 to 3
Hamburger bun—¼ to ½

304    Chapter 10    Physical Development from One to Three

**Figure 10.3 Serving Sizes for Children Two and Three**

**Caption Answer** Toddlers have small stomachs and it is easy to overfeed them. Overfeeding could cause obesity and poor health.

**Discussion** Tell students that a parent has taken a young child to a fast-food restaurant. The parent has placed an entire hamburger in front of the child. Ask: What thoughts might be going through the child's mind? (Possible response: The child might feel overwhelmed by the hamburger's size and may be thinking she cannot hold it in her small hands.)

## Nutritious Foods

Children should be provided with a variety of beneficial foods to establish good health. Offer nutritious foods at both mealtimes and snack times. Avoid foods high in sugar, salt, and fat. Sticky foods such as raisins may cause tooth decay. Read the nutrition labels and ingredient lists on frozen, canned, and dried foods for help in making nutritious choices.

MyPyramid is a food guidance system from the U.S. Department of Agriculture (USDA). It was developed as a guide for healthful eating and active living for people ages two and older. Learn more about MyPyramid in Chapter 16.

Because their stomachs are smaller, young children need smaller servings, or portions, when they eat. **Figure 10.3** gives examples of a child-size serving for two- and three-year-olds in each food group. Children four and older need larger servings.

## Teaching Children Good Nutrition

Parents and other caregivers are role models for children when it comes to food choices and eating habits. Sharing nutritious meals with children, trying new foods together, and letting children help in the kitchen all promote good eating habits. Parents should keep nutritious snacks, such as fruit, on hand. They should also let their child see them making good choices.

In addition to modeling good behavior, parents and other caregivers can encourage children to eat only when hungry and to eat slowly. Caregivers should not use food as a reward for good behavior. Likewise, they should not withhold food as a punishment. Children can also be encouraged to drink water when thirsty rather than milk or sugary drinks. If parents have nutritional concerns, they should consult their physician.

**Meat and Beans Group**
Egg—1
Chicken, hamburger,
 fish—1 to 2 oz.
Baked beans—¼ cup
Peanut butter—1 to 2 Tbsp.

**Vegetable Group**
Carrots—¼ to ½
Corn, green beans,
 peas—¼ cup

**Fruit Group**
Apple, banana—¼ to ½
Fruit juice—⅓ cup
Grapes, strawberries,
 peaches—¼ cup

Section 10.2    Caring for Children from One to Three    **305**

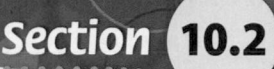
**Teach** *cont.*

### U Universal Access

**Interpersonal Learners** Organize students into small groups. Have each group conduct research to learn what child development professionals say about introducing new foods. Each group should then create an illustrated poster showing the appropriate steps in introducing new foods. (Posters might contain steps such as: present the new food repeatedly; encourage the child to take a small bite; tell the child you expect them to at least try the food. In addition, the poster should show parents eating the food themselves.) **ELL**

### C Critical Thinking

**Analyze** Ask students: If you were a parent, would you use treats, such as ice cream cones or a candy bars, as rewards? Why or why not? (Answers will vary. Students should recognize that providing treats as rewards can teach children to reward themselves with non-nutritional food. This can lead to individuals overeating these kinds of foods.)

**McGraw Hill** | **Professional Development**

**Mini Clip**
**ELL: Collaborative Work**

Students work in groups to complete a science lab.

### Teach cont.

**R** **Reading Strategy**

**Think in Pictures** Explain that visual images can make a group of facts easier to remember. To remember the first three bulleted items under "Meal Appeal," tell students to think of a piece of broccoli. (It is colorful and has an interesting texture and shape.) Then ask: How might you build on this image to include the last two bulleted items? (Possible answer: They might envision that the broccoli is warm and a child is holding it by its stalk.)

**C₁** **Critical Thinking**

**Compare** Hold up several different types of cups for the class to see. For example, you might show a light-weight disposable cup, a cup with one handle, and a sippy cup with two handles. Ask: Which of these do you think a toddler would find easiest to drink from? Why? (Probably the sippy cup because the liquid only comes out of one hole, similar to a bottle. It might also have two handles, making it easy to grasp, and liquid will not splash everywhere if the cup is dropped.) **ELL**

### Math in Action

**Overweight Children**

Approximately 18 percent, from the West Coast region, is the highest percent overweight for that age group.

**N C L B** **NCLB** Activity correlated to Mathematics standards.

---

**NCLB**

## Math in Action

### Overweight Children

What is the highest percent overweight reported in the graph below of a child 1–3 years of age?

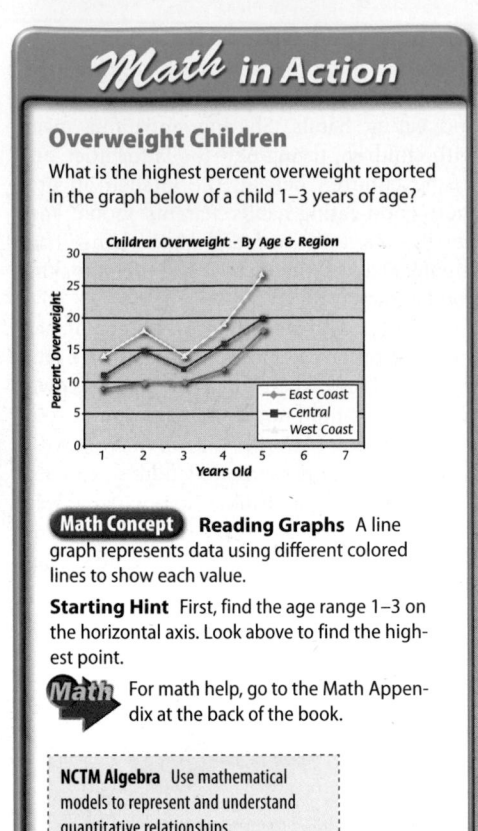

**Math Concept** **Reading Graphs** A line graph represents data using different colored lines to show each value.

**Starting Hint** First, find the age range 1–3 on the horizontal axis. Look above to find the highest point.

**Math** For math help, go to the Math Appendix at the back of the book.

**NCTM Algebra** Use mathematical models to represent and understand quantitative relationships.

---

### Meal Appeal

One way to promote interest in nutritious foods is to try to make meals appealing for children. Think about the following elements as you plan their meals.

- **Color** Think about how dull a meal of fish, applesauce, milk, and vanilla pudding looks. Varying foods can add more color. Fresh fruits and vegetables are brightly colored and nutritious.
- **Texture** Foods with different textures add variety to a meal. Try adding crackers, cheese, or cut-up, juicy grapes to a child's plate to provide different textures.
- **Shape** Foods with a variety of shapes also add appeal. Your goal does not have to be to make a child's plate look like a circus, but you might cut sandwiches into rectangles or triangles or use large cookie cutters. Consider adding cucumber slices, zucchini sticks, or orange wedges to a plate. Help children identify the shapes.
- **Temperature** Try serving both hot and cold foods at a meal. Always check the temperature of any hot foods before serving them. If a food has been cooked or warmed in the microwave, stir it thoroughly to even out the temperature. Hot spots from foods warmed in a microwave can burn a child's mouth.

**R**

**Gaining Independence** It may be messy at first, but a child shows growing independence by using a spoon or drinking from a cup. *What beverages are appropriate for a child this age?*

**C₁**

---

▶ **Explore the Photo**

**Caption Answer** Water, milk, and 100% fruit juices are best for children this age. Note that juices should be diluted with water.

**Discussion** Ask students what the chart in the feature says about the importance of milk in a child's diet. (The daily serving size for milk is larger than for any other food category.) Encourage students to discuss ways to incorporate dairy products into a two-year-old's diet. (In addition to milk, they might serve frozen yogurt, cheese, or cottage cheese.)

- **Ease of Eating** Certain foods are easier than others for young children to eat. Ground beef, for example, is easier to chew and swallow than a pork chop. Many children like spaghetti, but they can handle it more easily when the strands are cut into short pieces.

✓ **Reading Check** **Explain** Why is it important for parents and caregivers to share nutritious meals with children and try new foods together?

## Physical Health and Wellness

Keeping a child healthy and safe is a top priority for parents and other caregivers. Doing so requires knowing both how to prevent problems and how to deal with them when they occur. Children ages one to three are especially at risk for accidents. They are old enough to be mobile, but they are too young to understand the many hazards. They are also still unsteady as they are building their motor skills. Children at this age are also ready to begin learning personal hygiene.

### Checkups

Most children have a checkup at 12 months. The physician checks the child's growth and development. The doctor may ask about the child's language ability, interest in learning and practicing new skills, and behavior. Additional checkups are often scheduled at 15, 18, and 24 months. These checkups will include growth measurements, immunizations, and routine examinations of the eyes, ears, teeth, genitals, and other body parts.

### Immunizations

Immunizations protect children from a specific disease, usually by giving a child a vaccine. When a child is given a vaccine, a small amount of disease-carrying germs is introduced to the body on purpose so that the body can build resistance to that disease. Vaccines boost the immune system so that if a child is exposed to a certain disease, he or she can

**Staying Healthy**
Regular checkups are important for the lifelong health of a child. *At what ages should children have checkups?*

more easily fight infection. Children at this age are more likely to get diseases since they spread easily in child care centers and preschools. For a complete list of childhood immunizations, see Chapter 20.

Many parents feel that keeping children at home when they are young helps prevent illness. Being in a child care center does tend to expose children to more germs. However, some studies have shown that children exposed to more germs through child care centers and older siblings had lower rates of asthma. This is probably because getting sick early in life stimulated their immune responses. No parent wants to see their child get sick. However, for common illnesses like a cold or the chicken pox, it is often better for a child to have them early in life. This allows their body to fight the illness and build resistance against future outbreaks, similar to an immunization.

**U Universal Access**

**Verbal Learners** Tell students that most county health departments provide well-child clinics where children can obtain developmental checkups and immunizations. Instruct students to conduct research to learn about any services provided by their county. They then should write an illustrated brochure promoting these services. (Brochures will vary depending on services offered by your county health department. Students should explain the services offered and add illustrations for visual appeal.)

**C₂ Critical Thinking**

**State an Opinion** Tell students to suppose that their county health department is planning to reduce the number of well-child clinics it provides. This means that not all parents who wish to take their children to the clinic will be able to. Write a letter to your local newspaper explaining why this clinic is vital to the community. (Students should write a letter to the local newspaper explaining that maintaining children's health and immunizations provides a more positive future for everyone.)

✓ **Reading Check**

**Explain** Parents and caregivers serve as role models for children, sharing nutritious meals and trying new foods together helps promote healthful eating habits.

**▶ Explore the Photo**

**Caption Answer** Children usually have checkups at 12, 15, 18, and 24 months.

**Discussion** Ask: What do you think this doctor will be looking for during the checkup? (He will be checking the child's basic health, growth, and overall development. The doctor may also check his language skills, interest in learning, and general behavior.)

Some people are concerned about the safety of vaccines, but severe complications from vaccines are *very* rare. State law requires that children receive certain vaccinations before entering school, and physicians recommend that children receive most of their immunizations by age two. Children are also required to have certain vaccinations to attend child care centers. To find out what types of vaccines children need and when they need them, refer to the recommended schedule of immunizations in Chapter 20.

### Illnesses

It is not uncommon for children between the ages of one and three to get sick. Some common illnesses are respiratory and ear infections. These illnesses are often mild and usually require no medical intervention, although chronic ear infections do require attention. Other illnesses, such as the flu, can cause more severe problems. They are preventable with vaccinations.

#### Environmental Influences on Health

Pollutants can be found both in the home and outside it. A **pollutant** is something that makes the environment dirty. One of the chief indoor pollutants is environmental tobacco smoke (ETS), also known as second-hand smoke. This smoke comes from burning cigarettes. Researchers have shown that environmental tobacco smoke puts children at increased risk for respiratory infections, middle ear infections, and problems with asthma. Adults can avoid these increased risks for health problems by keeping children away from smokers and smoky areas.

Lead is another harmful substance that is found both inside and outside older homes, especially in paint. Caregivers must prevent children from putting bits of dried paint in their mouths. Children under the age of six are vulnerable to high levels of lead because their brain and central nervous system are still forming. Exposure to lead affects children in many ways, from delayed growth and hearing loss to irritability and hyperactivity.

### Safety

Children ages one to three are interested in exploring their environment. They open drawers and cabinets, turn knobs, and put objects in their mouth. As they try to learn about their world, their curiosity can often put them in danger's path. Rather than trying to curb a child's curious nature, it is better to childproof the home and make it as safe as possible for the child.

➤ **Protective Measures**
Young children are usually not aware of dangerous situations. *How can parents and caregivers make an environment safe for young children?*

➤➤➤ ► **Explore the Photo**

**Caption Answer** Answers will vary, but should include some of the ideas presented in the sections Childproof the Home and Environmental Concerns.

**Discussion** Ask students: Why do you think electrical cords and phone cords might be dangerous to children? (They can get tangled in them, pull them around their necks, or bite on them.) **How might you solve this problem?** (You can avoid using them when possible, use cord covers, or tape them to the wall or floor.)

## Childproof the Home

Young children love to explore the world around them. The average home contains a variety of conditions that can be hazardous. To ensure a child's safety while they explore, caregivers must childproof their homes.

To prevent falls, check to see that the floors and stairs are clear of clutter. Make sure floors are dry. Use safety gates on stairways until children learn to go up and down stairs safely. Remove furniture that might tip.

Check that open windows have screens with secure locks. Install window safety latches. Use window blinds with safety features. Keep blind cords away from children.

To prevent burns, teach children not to touch a range. Consider buying a stove guard. Use back burners when possible. Turn pot handles toward the range's center. Check the temperature of water from the faucet. Lower the water heater setting if it exceeds 120 degrees Fahrenheit (49 degrees Celsius). Place safety caps on unused electrical outlets. Keep toasters, irons, and other small appliances unplugged.

Store cleaning supplies, paints, insecticides, and medicines in locked containers. Keep knives, razors, scissors, and matches away from children. Inspect toys and other play equipment regularly for broken parts or sharp edges. It is usually best to throw away broken toys for young children rather than trying to fix them. Glueing toys together makes them easier to break again and exposes the child to harmful chemicals.

## Environmental Concerns

There are hazards in a baby's environment, both inside and outside the home. The following tips are ways a caregiver can help provide a safer environment for children:

- **Choking Hazards** To help prevent choking, make sure that children stay seated while eating. Parents and other caregivers should encourage children to take small bites of food during meals, to chew all food thoroughly, and to swallow before taking another bite.
- **Toys** Take time to select toys that are age appropriate. Small toys or toys with small, removable parts are choking hazards.

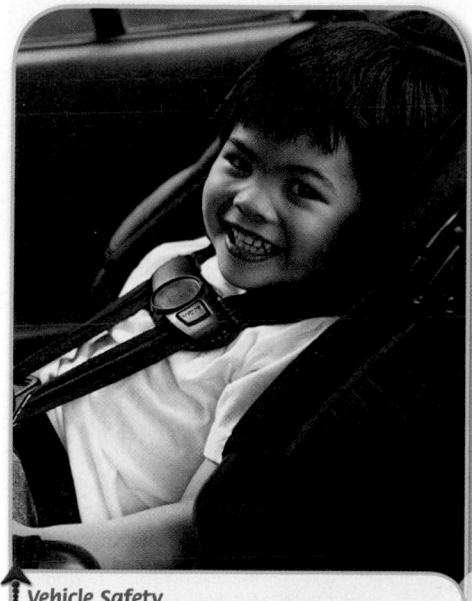

**Vehicle Safety**
Children should always be safely buckled up in car seats when on the road. *What could happen to a child not secured in a car seat during an accident?*

- **Poisons in the Home** Avoid using strong household cleaning products. Keep all poisonous substances and medications locked up. Learn what to do in case a child ingests a poisonous substance. Keep the phone numbers of the poison control center and your local hospital handy. See the chart in Chapter 20 for a list of common household poisons.
- **Fire and Burns** Keep children away from candles, fireplaces, matches, and lighters. Teach children the stop, drop, and roll technique for extinguishing fire on their clothes or in their hair. If a burn looks more serious than a slight reddening of the skin, consult a doctor immediately.
- **Motor Vehicles** Children must ride in a car seat that is secured with seatbelts in the back seat of a vehicle. Children over 12 months of age and weighing 20 pounds or more may ride in a car seat that is facing forward. Always be sure children are wearing seatbelts while the vehicle is in motion.

## Reteach cont.

### U Universal Access

**Logical Learners** Tell students to pretend that a two-year-old is coming to visit their home for several days. Students should check their home for child safety and make a list of items that need to be changed. On their lists, they should include suggestions for childproofing or modifying each hazardous item. (Students should create a list of hazards, along with suggested changes. For example, they may suggest putting safety gates on stairs and safety caps on unused electrical outlets.)

### R Reading Strategy

**Create a Diagram** Have students create a web diagram on a sheet of paper. In the center of the sheet, they should draw an oval containing the words Environmental Concerns. As they read this section, they should complete the diagram by drawing an oval for each hazard listed under this heading. (Students should draw a graphic organizer with Environmental Concerns at the center surrounded by ovals with the following topics: Choking Hazards, Toys, Poisons in the Home, Fire and Burns, Motor Vehicles, Sunburn, Pets, and Drowning.) **ELL**

**Professional Development**

**Mini Clip**
**ELL: Graphic Organizers**

Students use graphic organizers to distinguish between major and minor details in a reading selection.

---

## Explore the Photo

**Caption Answer** A child not secured could be seriously injured or killed during an accident.

**Discussion** Mention that many young children dislike being confined in car seats. Ask for suggestions concerning what parents might do to alleviate this difficulty. (Responses might include providing appropriate toys, playing DVDs that the parent and child can sing along with, or telling stories.)

## Reteach *cont.*

### R Reading Strategy

**Connection** Have students ask their parents if they were climbers as children. They should ask for specific examples. They also should ask whether they ever injured themselves or frightened their parents. Ask for volunteers to share what they learned with the class. (Students should share with the class what they discovered concerning their climbing habits as a young child, and any consequences of their behavior.)

### U₁ Universal Access

**Learners Having Difficulties**
Have students create posters illustrating the environmental hazards discussed on pages 309 and 310. Encourage students to make their posters multimedia by pasting small objects or fabrics on to them. (Posters will vary. Students should create posters illustrating environmental hazards that young children may encounter. For example, students might draw a sun to represent the hazard of sunburn; or they might paste small objects such as marbles on the poster to represent choking hazards.) **ELL**

---

### SAFE CHILD HEALTHY CHILD

#### Climbing

Climbing is an important safety concern for children ages one to three. Toddlers love to explore their environment by climbing stairs, furniture, and play equipment. Use safety gates near stairs so that children cannot go up or down without adult supervision. Bolt heavy bookcases to the wall to avoid tipping if a child tries to climb them. Teach children to sit instead of stand on furniture.

☀ **Be Prepared** Imagine that you are a caregiver and you have a pool surrounded by a fence. What other precautions should you take at the pool to ensure the children you care for do not climb over the fence and go into the water unsupervised?

---

- **Sunburn** Have children wear protective hats and sunglasses. Apply sunscreen to their skin. Reapply sunscreen every few hours, or more frequently.

- **Pets** Young children should not be left alone with a dog or a cat because they are not mature enough to know how to behave with animals. Teach children to wash their hands after handling an animal.

- **Drowning** Water safety is crucial at any age, but it is especially important for children ages one to three. Drowning is one of the leading causes of death for toddlers. Drowning can happen very quickly, in shallow water, bathtubs, swimming pools, backyard ponds, hot tubs, and even buckets and sinks with water. Toddlers ages one to three are at the highest risk because they are curious about their surroundings and do not understand the danger of water.

  To reduce a child's risk of drowning, never leave a child unattended in a bathtub or swimming pool. Empty bath water immediately. A child should always wear an approved flotation device when in or

---

around water other than a bathtub. If you have a pool, install fencing at least five feet high on all sides of the pool, as well as a self-closing or self-latching gate. Do not leave anything close to the fence that would allow the child to climb over it. Teach children who are old enough how to swim.

Above all, always keep a watchful eye on young children. Accidents can occur in a matter of seconds.

## Hygiene

Children in this age span need to learn the basics of good hygiene. **Hygiene** is personal care and cleanliness. These range from using a tissue for a runny nose to bathing and effective hand washing. Also, most children learn to use the toilet during this time.

### Washing and Bathing

A daily bath helps children develop good hygiene skills. For most families, evening baths are the most practical. They can become an enjoyable part of the bedtime routine. Between the ages of one and three, many children enjoy splashing in the tub. Bath toys can add to the fun. Even simple plastic containers and measuring cups can become playthings in the bath.

Children often assert their independence at bath time. One-year-olds often want to wash themselves. At first, this means merely rubbing the washcloth over the face and stomach. By age two, however, most children can wash, rinse, and dry themselves fairly well, except for hard-to-reach places like the back. By age three, children can wash by themselves, with supervision.

Bathtub safety is very important. A child can drown in as little as 1 inch of water. Never leave a young child alone in the bath—not even for a minute! To help prevent falls, use no-slip stickers or a rubber mat on the bottom of the tub.

### Caring for Teeth

Experts urge teaching good dental hygiene practices early. At age one, most children have eight teeth. These need to be brushed with a small, soft toothbrush daily. By age two, children can begin practicing brushing their own teeth.

---

### SAFE CHILD HEALTHY CHILD

#### Climbing

**Identify** Ask students: Why can objects such as bookcases, TV stands, and tall chests of drawers be serious hazards to children? (This type of furniture can be top-heavy and tip over on the child, causing serious injury.)

☀ **Be Prepared** Make sure there is nothing close to the fence that would allow the child to climb over it and gain access to the pool.

← **Bath Time Precautions**
Bath time offers a child entertainment as well as an opportunity to get clean. *What should you do if the phone rings while you are bathing a child?*

Their first attempts to brush will not be very successful. They will improve, though, with encouragement and practice. For the most effective results, caregivers need to do most of the brushing for a toddler. Even three-year-olds may need adult help with this task.

Children should brush their teeth twice a day to fight cavities. Most small children do not need fluoride toothpaste. Check with your dentist on what toothpaste is best for your child. Regular checkups are an important part of good dental care. Many dentists suggest that 18 months is a good age for the first checkup. Preschoolers should visit the dentist every six months.

### Toilet Training

Most children begin to learn to use the toilet sometime between their second and third birthdays. Some parents begin a training program before the age of two. Some experts say that when parents teach toileting too early, the process takes longer.

**Readiness** To successfully learn toileting, a child must be both physically and emotionally ready. Physical readiness means that children are able to control their bladder and bowel functions. They must also be able to remove their clothes easily.

Bowel control involves the use of the sphincter ('sfiŋ(k)-tər) muscles. **Sphincter muscles** are the muscles that help regulate elimination from the bowels. Typically, children reach this level of maturity at about eighteen months of age. To control the bladder and bowel, a child must also be able to recognize the signals that elimination is necessary.

Emotional readiness means the child shows an interest in wanting to use the toilet. There are books and videos to help prepare the child. Training during a calm period in family life increases the chance that it will go smoothly.

**Toilet Training Basics** Caregivers' attitudes toward toilet training are very important. Calm encouragement is more effective than rules and punishment, and it helps build self-esteem. Remember that the child who is physically and emotionally ready for toilet training genuinely wants to succeed. Even after a child is toilet trained, some accidents should be expected.

When children begin to use the toilet, they may prefer to use a child seat on the toilet or a potty chair. Using a child seat on the toilet eliminates the need for adjustments later. On the other hand, using a potty chair allows the young child more independence than the seat that fits the toilet.

**Section 10.2** Caring for Children from One to Three **311**

**U₂ Universal Access**

**Visual Learners** Have students locate a video tape or DVD that is designed to encourage young children in toilet training. (Many public libraries have these items.) Students should watch the video and write a review of it. In the review, they should discuss whether or not they think it would be helpful in toilet training a toddler. (Reviews will vary. Students should watch a toilet-training video and evaluate it. They should offer logical reasons for why they feel it would or would not be helpful in toilet training a toddler. For example, some videos only offer tips for the parents, while other videos have motivational cartoons for the toddler. Students might feel that the video would encourage toddlers to want to try using the toilet.)

**C Critical Thinking**

**Solve Problems** Discuss with students that toilet training can become an area of conflict between children and parents. Ask students to suggest reasons that this might be true. Then encourage students to brainstorm solutions to these challenges. (Answers will vary. Possible response: Other adults may be telling the parent that the child is at an age where the child should be using the toilet, even if the child is not yet ready. The parent needs to remember that each child is different.)

 **Explore the Photo**

**Caption Answer** Let it ring. Never leave a child in the bathtub unattended—not even for a minute!

**Discussion** What kinds of bath toys might a one-year-old enjoy? How about a three-year-old? (One-year-olds might enjoy large, brightly colored toys that they could push in the water. Three-year-olds might enjoy more intricate toys with parts, such as boats containing people or games such as throwing a ball through a hoop.)

**R** **Reading Strategy**

**Summarize** Tell students that summarizing an author's main points makes it easier to remember them. Have students create a bulleted list summarizing the points made in these two paragraphs. (Lists might include: Bowel training usually comes first; Watch for facial expressions that suggest the child needs to use the toilet; Always be available and encouraging; Consider using training pants.)

**W** **Writing Support**

**Dialogue**

**Big-Kids Pants** Read this scenario to the class: You believe your three-year-old is ready for toilet training. Write a dialogue between you and the child in which you explain the importance of changing from diapers to training pants. (Refer to p. 290 for tips on writing a dialogue. Students might begin by explaining how grown-up the child is becoming and that wearing "big-kid" pants is a sign the child is old enough to use the toilet. They also might emphasize how easy it is to pull down the pants to use the toilet.)

**C₁** **Critical Thinking**

**Evaluate** Ask students: What message is a parent sending to a child if he gives the child a toothbrush and then immediately leaves the room? How about if he places the child on a potty chair and then goes elsewhere? What might be an appropriate way for the parent to change his behavior? (The parent is telling the child that this activity is not important to the parent. The parent should remain to supervise and support the child.)

✓ **Reading Check**

**Review** The child shows an interest in wanting to be grown up and use the toilet.

Flushing toilets frighten some children. It may be better to flush the toilet after the child has left the bathroom.

Bowel training usually comes before bladder training, although some children learn at the same time. Most children are ready when they show awareness that a bowel movement is about to happen. When caregivers see this awareness in the child's facial expressions or gestures, they should suggest that the child sit on the toilet seat or potty chair. They should be encouraging. If caregivers are too demanding, toilet learning will become more difficult.

Many young children are encouraged in toileting when they are given cloth or disposable training pants in place of diapers. Training pants are heavy, absorbent underpants. Wearing training pants, instead of diapers, makes it possible for a young child to use a toilet or potty chair on their own. Most children also see wearing underpants instead of diapers as a sign of maturity.

✓ **Reading Check** **Review** How can you tell when a child is ready for toilet teaching?

## Clothing

Parents and caregivers need to be aware of the types of clothing that are appropriate for young children. Appropriate clothing is important so that a child can learn to dress and undress himself. It is also important for comfort, durability, and economy.

### Self-Dressing

Young children are eager to learn how to dress and undress themselves. Being able to put on her own clothes makes a child feel independent. It is important to encourage self-dressing whenever a child begins to show interest. Dressing involves a number of gross and fine motor skills that must be learned one step at a time. These skills require frequent practice. Caregivers need to be patient and encouraging. Be sure to allow plenty of time to get dressed so the child does not feel rushed.

Undressing is easier than dressing. Most children will start undressing themselves around thirteen or fourteen months of age. They generally will first pull off shoes, socks, or pants. They will then work up to removing loose t-shirts. Parents can make the process easier by buying clothes without buttons or fasteners.

## Parenting Skills

### Helping a Child Learn to Brush

Tooth decay occurs faster in children than in adults. It is important to clean a child's teeth in the first few years of life. Young children do not have the ability to brush teeth effectively, but they need to learn. The key to getting a child to brush is to make it fun.

Use only a pea-sized amount of mild-flavored toothpaste on the toothbrush. Brush gently and for at least one minute. Make sure the child spits out the toothpaste when finished instead of swallowing it. Swallowing toothpaste can lead to a condition called fluorosis, in which spots appear on the teeth. Helping a child learn to brush well and regularly can preserve a smile for a lifetime.

**Take Charge** How could you help make brushing fun for a child? Create a poster with at least three ideas for making brushing fun.

## Parenting Skills

### Helping a Child Learn to Brush

Some parents are concerned that their toddlers cannot do a good job of brushing their teeth. These parents often insist on doing the job for the child. Ask students: Do you have any suggestions for these parents? (Toddlers need to learn this task. Parents might let the child brush his or her teeth and then perform additional brushing while "checking" them.)

**Take Charge**
Students' posters will vary. Ideas may include: make up a song to sing during brushing, brush along with the child, reward the child after brushing is finished.

**Learning to Self-Dress**
Young children enjoy trying to dress themselves. *What should parents and caregivers look for when buying clothing for young children?*

**C₂ Critical Thinking**

**Problem Solve** Your toddler has been good so you want to reward him. You decide to take him to the store and let him choose his clothes. However, it turns into a disaster because he keeps changing his mind and never reaches a decision. Why did this happen? What might you do the next time? (The child became overwhelmed by the enormous number of options. Next time, you might select three or four items and let him choose from those.)

**U Universal Access**

**Interpersonal Learners** Tell students that it is chilly outside, but two-and-a-half-year-old Lucy wants to go to the park wearing ballet shoes, tights, a leotard, and a tutu. Divide the class in half and instruct the students to conduct a debate. Half the students will argue Lucy's side and the other half the parent's side. Students should back up their arguments with specific points. (Debates will vary. Students should conduct a debate in which one side argues that Lucy should be able to wear what she wants to the park and the other side argues that there are reasons she should not be allowed to wear what she wants. Arguments on Lucy's side might include that by letting her go out in her leotard and tutu, you will avoid an argument and she will come back in or ask for a jacket if she is cold. The side of the parent may include such points as Lucy might get sick if she is not dressed properly and children don't always know what is best.) **ELL**

About the same time, they might start helping to dress themselves by holding out an arm for the sleeve of a shirt. Next, they may learn to push an arm through a sleeve. By two years of age, the child can pull up pants, but putting on shirts is still difficult. Children may put their clothes on inside out or backwards. By age three, children can dress themselves but need help with fasteners like buttons and shoelaces. They may still put shoes on the wrong feet.

With self-dressing, a child learns independence and responsibility. This helps boost self-esteem. Caregivers can encourage self-dressing by choosing clothes that are easy to put on and take off. Shirts with loose necks and pants with elastic waists are easiest for young children to handle.

## Choosing Clothes

When you shop for clothing, choose clothes that allow for growth. Look for deep hems or cuffs that can be let down. Check that the straps on overalls or jumpers are long enough to allow the buttons to be moved.

Consider buying pants that are a size larger but will fit when you roll up the pant legs. A child with a long torso will get more wear out of pants and a shirt than overalls or onesies.

Whenever possible, let children help choose their own clothes. They usually love bright colors and tend to choose their clothes more by color than for any other reason. Children also enjoy clothes printed with pictures of animals, toys, or familiar story characters. When choosing clothes for young children, there are several factors to consider.

**C₂ U**

### Comfort

Look for clothes that allow a child to move freely. Knits that stretch as a child moves are good choices. Soft and sturdy fabrics are comfortable. Stiff or scratchy fabrics can bother children's skin. Size is an important factor in comfort. Clothes that are too small restrict movement, and clothes that are too large can get in the way. Look for clothes that are large enough to allow the child to move comfortably. All clothes labeled with the same size may not fit the same way.

 **Explore the Photo**

**Caption Answer** They should look for features that make the clothing easy to get on and off, durability, comfort, and economy.

**Discussion** Have the class create a list of reasons that learning to dress oneself is an important skill. (Reasons might include: It improves motor skills, gives the child a sense of accomplishment and independence, and eventually will free the parent from the task.)

## Assess

### Study Tools

Have students go to the Online Learning Center at **glencoe.com**:

- Take the **Practice Test**.
- Download **Study-to-Go** content.

Use the **Student Activity Workbook** for additional practice.

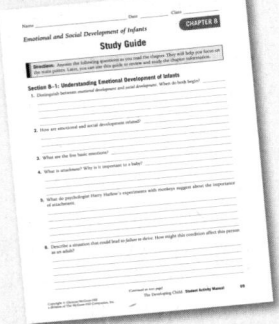

## Close

### Culminating Activity

**Create a List** Have each student create a list of the parental responsibilities discussed here. Discuss the lists as a class. (Lists might include: teaching good nutritional and hygiene habits, ensuring children have medical checkups and immunizations, and protecting children from environmental hazards.)

 **NCLB** connects academic correlations to book content.

## Fabric

Cotton is a comfortable natural fiber often used in children's clothing. It absorbs moisture, wears well, and washes well. It may shrink though. **Synthetic fibers** are fabrics made from chemicals, rather than natural sources. Clothes made from synthetic fibers such as polyester and acrylic are durable, wrinkle resistant, and quick-drying.

Unlike cotton, most synthetic fibers do not absorb moisture well and hold heat and perspiration against the body. This characteristic makes them a good choice for clothes that will be worn in cool weather.

Often natural and synthetic fibers are blended to take advantage of the benefits of each. By law, all clothing must have a label that identifies the fibers used. Clothing labels also state how to care for each garment.

Federal law requires that the fabric used in children's sleepwear be flame-resistant. **Flame-resistant** means that the fabric can still catch on fire, but will not burn as quickly as other fabrics.

## Durability

Children's clothes must withstand hard wear and repeated washings. Their *durability*, or ability to last, is influenced by the quality of the fabric and the construction of the clothing. When you check the construction of clothes, look for close, even stitching with strong thread. The stitching should be reinforced at points of strain.

All fasteners and trims should be firmly attached. Some pants have the knees reinforced with extra fabric which also helps improve durability.

---

## Section 10.2 — After You Read

### Review Key Concepts

1. **Compare** the sleep needs of one-year-olds and three-year-olds.
2. **Describe** the most important consideration in preparing meals and snacks for young children.
3. **List** three ways children can develop good hygiene skills.
4. **Explain** why it is best to let a child help with dressing at an early age.

### Practice Academic Skills

 **English Language Arts**

5. Oftentimes, children do not want to take a bath or brush their teeth. Imagine that you are a caregiver for young children. How can you encourage good hygiene with the children you care for? Write your ideas in a short essay.

> **NCTE 4** Use written language to communicate effectively.

**NCLB**

 **Social Studies**

6. Many cultures take a different approach to toilet training. In some countries, toilet training begins when a child is only one month old. Research to find more information on toilet training in another culture. Create a chart to compare the practices in your chosen culture with the methods discussed in this chapter.

> **NCSS I A** Analyze and explain the ways groups, societies, and cultures address human needs and concerns.

**Check Your Answers** Check your answers at this book's Online Learning Center at **glencoe.com**.

---

## Section 10.2 — After You Read

### Review Key Concepts

1. Most one-year-olds sleep eight or more hours at night and take naps of several hours a day. By the age of three, children sleep for about 10 to 14 hours a day.
2. Offer nutritious foods at mealtimes and snack times, and avoid foods that contain a great deal of sugar, salt, and fat.
3. Answers will vary, but may include take daily baths, brush their teeth every day, and regularly wash their hands.
4. Dressing uses gross and fine motor skills, teaches independence and responsibility, and boosts self-esteem.

### Practice Academic Skills

5. Essays will vary, but could include praising children for using a tissue when blowing a runny nose, or making bath time fun by adding toys to the tub.
6. Charts will vary depending on the country chosen. Students may cite that many parents in China use open-crotch pants instead of diapers and begin toilet training at one month.

# Chapter Summary

Heredity and environment play key roles in child development, affecting body size, eye color, and disease risk. A poor diet can cause tooth decay. As children grow, their senses develop, giving them greater awareness of their environment. Gross and fine motor skills improve as children get older. Some toddlers experience sleep disturbances. Children should be given nutritious foods and encouraged to feed themselves. Homes should be childproofed to help keep children safe. Toilet training should not be attempted before a child is ready. Parents should provide comfortable clothes and teach good hygiene.

## Vocabulary Review

**1.** Label each of these content and academic vocabulary terms as a noun, verb, or adjective.

**Content Vocabulary**
◇ toddler (p. 293)
◇ preschooler (p. 293)
◇ sensory integration (p. 296)
◇ developmentally appropriate (p. 297)
◇ dexterity (p. 299)
◇ night terrors (p. 303)
◇ hygiene (p. 310)
◇ sphincter muscles (p. 311)
◇ synthetic fibers (p. 314)
◇ flame-resistant (p. 314)

**Academic Vocabulary**
■ variation (p. 294)
■ proportion (p. 294)
■ incident (p. 303)
■ pollutant (p. 308)

## Review Key Concepts

**2. Identify** five changes in a child's physical growth from ages one to three.
**3. Explain** how developmental milestones are used.
**4. Describe** how a parent should respond to typical changes in a child's sleeping patterns.
**5. Explain** why it is important to establish good eating habits early in life.
**6. Identify** why young children are particularly at risk for accidents.
**7. List** four factors to consider when choosing clothing for young children.

## Critical Thinking

**8. Compare** Toddlers' fine motor skills develop rapidly. How does self-feeding differ for a one-year-old and a three-year-old?
**9. Differentiate** Many young children experience night terrors and nightmares. What is the difference between night terrors and nightmares?
**10. Examine** Young children must be physically and emotionally ready for toilet training. How do physical and emotional factors play a role in toileting readiness?

## Content and Academic Vocabulary Review

**1.** Students should correctly identify the part of speech for each vocabulary term.

**Mc Graw Hill Professional Development**

**Mini Clip**
Reading: Vocabulary

Author Josefina Tinajero describes the importance of academic language.

## Review Key Concepts

**2.** From ages one to three changes in a child's physical growth are evidenced mainly by height, weight, body proportion, posture, and teeth.
**3.** Developmental milestones help caregivers plan developmentally appropriate activities.
**4.** Parents should provide the child with comfort, reassurance, and a bedtime routine.
**5.** The habits and attitudes toward food learned early in life will influence eating habits throughout life.
**6.** Children from one to three are interested in exploring their environment. They often put objects in their mouth. As they try to learn about their world, their curiosity can often put them in danger's path.
**7.** Comfort, fabric, durability, and economy should be considered when choosing clothing for young children.

## Critical Thinking

**8.** One-year-olds can use a spoon, but often spill. They should use a training cup. Three-year-olds are often skillful using spoons and forks, and chew foods fairly easily.

**9.** Night terrors occur during the first few hours of sleep, when children are sleeping deeply. Children generally do not realize why they have awakened so upset, and they do not remember what happened in the morning. Nightmares are frightening dreams that may seem real. They may be remembered in the morning.

**10.** Physical readiness means that children can remove their clothing easily and can control their sphincter muscles. Emotional readiness means that the child shows interest in wanting to be grown up and in using the toilet.

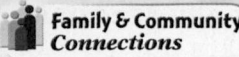

## Family & Community Connections

**11.** Answers will vary. Students' Q&A should accurately reflect the interview and should focus on age-appropriate activities for preschoolers.

## Health Skills

**12.** Posters will vary but should contain dos and don'ts to promote good dental health for preschoolers. Possible dos include: Make brushing fun. Provide a positive example of good dental hygiene. Possible don'ts include: Avoid making brushing a chore. Do not be inconsistent.

## Observation Skills

**13.** Charts and answers will vary. Sample answer: one-year-old cannot hold crayon, two-year-old can hold crayon but cannot color within lines, three-year-old holds crayon and stays within lines sometimes.

## Real-Word Skills

**14.** Answers will vary but may include: Hazard: cleaners are stored in cabinet under sink; Solution: put a child-proof lock on cabinet door or move cleaning supplies out of reach of child.

**15.** Possible answers: Four-year-old—fine motor skills: dresses and undresses self, cuts on a line with scissors, copies a circle and a cross. Gross motor skills: hops on one foot, throws ball overhand, alternates feet walking up and down stairs, walks backward easily. Five-year-old—fine motor skills: draws a person with head, body, arms, and legs; prints some letters; buttons clothing; copies a triangle and a square; uses spoon and fork to eat. Gross motor skills: turns somersaults, skips

## Family & Community Connection

**11. Interview a Preschool Teacher** With your teacher's help, contact a local preschool teacher and set up a time for an interview. Prior to the interview, write questions to ask. Questions should focus on age-appropriate activities for preschoolers. For example, "What are some age-appropriate activities?" "How do you find or create these activities?" "Do any of the activities differ for the older preschoolers and the younger ones?" After the interview, write up your findings in a question-and-answer format.

## Health Skills

**12. Research Dental Hygiene** Conduct online research to find dos and don'ts for parents and caregivers to use in promoting good dental health for children. Create and illustrate two posters with your findings. One poster should contain dos, the second poster should contain don'ts.

## Observation Skills

**13. Observe Preschoolers** Work with your teacher to arrange to observe a group of children in a child care setting. The children should range in age from one to three years. You may need the help of the child care staff to identify children of different ages.

**Procedure** As you observe a one-year-old, a two-year-old, and a three-year-old, look for evidence of the fine and gross motor skill level of each child. This would be a good opportunity to use a developomental checklist.

**Analysis** Create a chart in which you record the fine and gross motor skills observed for the one-year-old, two-year-old, and three-year-old children.

**NCSS IV D Individual Development and Identity** Apply concepts, methods, and theories about the study of human growth and development, such as learning, motivation, and behavior.

**NCLB**

## Real-World Skills

| Problem-Solving | **14. Provide Solutions** How might you make a bathroom safe for a two-year-old child? Look around a bathroom in your home and make a list of potential hazards for a two-year-old. Then generate a list of possible solutions to the hazards. |
| --- | --- |
| Technology Skills | **15. Create a Table** Research the average fine and gross motor skills developed in children ages four and five. Use word-processing software to create a table that shows the age and the fine and gross motor skills typical for that age. |
| Financial Literacy | **16. Calculate Clothing Costs** Conduct research to find out what clothes a two-year-old needs. Use a catalog or go to a store to estimate their cost. Write a report summarizing your findings. End your report with tips on how parents could save money on toddler clothes. |

 **Additional Activities** For additional activities, go to this book's Online Learning Center at **glencoe.com**.

with alternating feet, balances on each foot for short period.

**16.** Answers will vary. Students' answers should be realistic. Ways parents could save money on toddler clothes include: exchanging clothing with other families or shopping at yard sales, second-hand stores, and thrift stores.

 **NCLB Activity** correlated to Social Studies standards.

The *Early Childhood Observations CD* offers additional lessons with videos to build students' observation skills.

**Part 1:** Learning to Observe
**Part 2:** How Children Develop
**Part 3:** Working With Young Children
**Part 4:** Extended Observations
**Part 5:** Resources and Answer File

## Academic Skills

 **English Language Arts**

**17. Analyze the Text** A child's fine motor skills typically improve as the child gets older. The chapter notes that self-feeding both depends on and helps improve children's fine motor skills. Write a half-page report to explain why this is true.

> **NCTE 12** Use language to accomplish individual purposes.

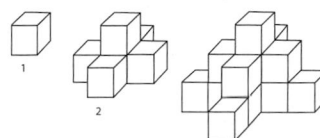 **Mathematics**

**18. Building Blocks** Children ages 1 to 3 like to stack blocks. In the series shown below, how many blocks would a child need to build the fourth tower?

**Math Concept** **Multi-Step Problem** When solving problems with more than one step, think through each step before you start.

**Starting Hint** Remember the tower in the middle that you cannot see! Count how many blocks are in the first and second towers. Then subtract these amounts to find the amount of increase. Repeat this for the second and third in the series. Apply the pattern of increasing amounts to the third tower to predict the fourth.

 For math help, go to the Math Appendix at the back of the book.

> **NCTM Algebra** Use mathematical models to represent and understand quantitative relationships.

 **Science**

**19. Test a Hypothesis** A hypothesis is an assumption that is made to test the validity of a theory or idea. Use the data in Figure 10.2 on page 298 to choose a gross motor skill listed for a specific age group.

**Procedure** Use the chosen motor skill and age to form a hypothesis. For example: All two-year-olds can push themselves on wheeled toys. Describe an experiment you would conduct to test your hypothesis.

**Analysis** Create a step-by-step presentation that describes the experiment and explains how the experiment would test your hypothesis.

> **NSES A** Develop abilities necessary to do scientific inquiry, understandings about scientific inquiry.

**NCLB**

## Standardized Test Practice

**TIMED WRITING**

Read the prompt and respond in a one-page essay.

**20.** Three-year-old Trina loves to build towers out of blocks. Her eighteen-month-old brother, James, loves to knock them down. Trina has begun to push James when she sees him approaching her play area. What are some specific ways that Trina and James's caregiver can address the problem?

> **Test-Taking Tip** Use the essay prompt as a basis for your thesis statement to help you focus your essay and ensure that you address the prompt in the time given. For example, you might say, "The children's caregiver can address the problem by . . ."

## TECHNOLOGY **Solutions**

**Use these technology solutions to streamline chapter assessment!**

 **ExamView** Assessment Suite

**ExamView Assessment Suite** CD allows you to create and print out customized tests or ready-made unit and chapter tests, complete with answer keys.

**TeacherWorks** Plus **TeacherWorks Plus** is an electronic lesson planner that provides instant access to complete teacher resources in one convenient package.

**Online Learning Center** includes resources and activities for students and teachers.

---

## Academic Skills

**17.** Reports will vary, but may include that a child cannot feed herself if she doesn't have the basic fine motor skills to allow her to do this. As she practices feeding herself, she will refine and improve her fine motor skills.

**18.** The fourth tower would require 28 blocks.

**19.** Answers will vary. Presentations should show the step-by-step process students would use to test their hypothesis.

**NCLB** **NCLB** connects academic correlations to book content.

## Standardized Test Practice

**20.** Answers will vary. Students might suggest that the caregivers need to make sure Trina does not hurt James and that she has time to herself to play and build towers without fearing that James will come and knock them down. Essays should provide specific ways to address the problem.

**Test-Taking Tips** When writing an essay, make certain each paragraph has a topic sentence. Work at making a paragraph's sentences flow and build on one another.

**Timed Writing** Tell students that the term *thesis* means "the act of laying down." As they write, students are laying down the foundation that supports their thesis. Only those arguments that are needed to build this solid foundation should be used.

# Standards Correlations

**STANDARDS BASED LESSON PLANNING** *The Developing Child* provides students with instruction and assessment in the following fundamental content areas:

## National Standards Correlations

| Standards | Pages |
|---|---|
| **12.1.1** Analyze physical, emotional, social, spiritual, and intellectual development. | 321–333, 335–345 |
| **12.1.2** Analyze interrelationships among physical, emotional, social, and intellectual aspects of human growth and development. | 332–333 |
| **12.3.1** Analyze the role of nurturance on human growth and development. | 327–328, 329–330 |
| **12.3.2** Analyze the role of communication on human growth and development. | 326 |
| **15.1.2** Analyze expectations and responsibilities of parenting. | 327, 338, 340 |
| **15.2.1** Choose nurturing practices that support human growth and development. | 329–330 |
| **15.2.2** Apply communication strategies that promote positive self-esteem in family members. | 331 |
| **15.2.3** Assess common practices and emerging research about discipline on human growth and development. | 323, 331–332, 340–345, 348 |

**NO CHILD LEFT BEHIND** NCLB activities, information, and skills practice will help your students attain NCLB proficiency. Students will improve their abilities in the following academic standards areas:

## Academic Standards Correlations

| Discipline | Standard | Feature/Activity |
|---|---|---|
| **English Language Arts** | **NCTE 1** Read texts to acquire new information. | **Reading Guide (pp. 320, 334)** |
| | **NCTE 2** Read literature to build an understanding of the human experience. | **After You Read (p. 333)** |
| | **NCTE 3** Apply strategies to interpret texts. | **Academic Skills (p. 349)** |
| | **NCTE 4** Use written language to communicate effectively. | **Writing Activity (p. 318)** **After You Read (p. 345)** |
| **Mathematics** | **NCTM Algebra** Represent and analyze mathematical situations and structures using algebraic symbols. | **Academic Skills (p. 349)** |
| **Science** | **NSES A** Develop abilities necessary to do scientific inquiry, understandings about scientific inquiry. | **After You Read (p. 333)** **Academic Skills (p. 349)** |
| **Social Studies** | **NCSS I A Culture** Analyze and explain the ways groups, societies, and cultures address human needs and concerns. | **After You Read (p. 345)** |
| | **NCSS IV F Individual Development and Identity** Analyze the role of perceptions, attitudes, values, and beliefs in the development of personal identity. | **Observation Skills (p. 348)** |

## McGraw Hill Professional Development

### MINI CLIP VIDEO LIBRARY

Targeted professional development is correlated throughout *The Developing Child*. **The McGraw-Hill Professional Development Mini Clip Video Library** provides teaching strategies to strengthen academic and learning skills. Log on to **glencoe.com**.

In this chapter, you will find these Mini Clips:
- **Reading**  Differentiated Instruction, p. 323
- **ELL**  Modeling Reading Strategies, p. 324
- **Reading**  Extending the Big Idea, p. 336
- **Reading**  On Workshops, p. 338
- **Reading**  Fluency Development, p. 341
- **Math**  The Meaning of Variable, p. 349

## Reading and Writing Strategies

**Writing Activity: Poem** (p. 318)
Students use writing tips to create a poem about a toddler having a temper tantrum.

**Before You Read** (pp. 320, 334)
A pre-reading question or statement will help students make a personal connection to content.

**Graphic Organizer** (pp. 320, 334)
A visual tool will help students organize and remember new content.

**Reading Check** (pp. 325, 330, 332, 337, 339)
A question allows students to make a quick comprehension self-check.

**After You Read** (pp. 333, 345)
Organize and process students' understanding of what they have read.

## Chapter Features

**Managing Changes in a Child's Routine** (p. 327)
Parents can help young children handle changes to their routines.

**Not Enough Sleep** (p. 332)
Parents must search for the causes of children's sleep disturbances.

**Antisocial Personality Disorder** (p. 339)
Children who do not develop empathy and ignore the rights of others may have antisocial personality disorder.

**Sharing** (p. 341)
Parents must teach children to share appropriately for their age.

**Handling Tantrums** (p. 343)
There are a number of ways to deal with tantrums.

**Speech-Language Pathologist** (p. 346)
Learn the skills needed to succeed in this career.

### Chapter Overview

**Introduce the Chapter**

In this chapter, students learn about emotional and social development from age one to three and how parents and caregivers can encourage healthy development. At the beginning of this period, children openly express their emotions. By the end, they are learning to express emotions in more socially acceptable ways.

### Build Background

Remind students of the emotional and social milestones achieved by infants that were covered in Chapter 8. Ask students to list some of these milestones and write them on the board. Discuss that maturation is a gradual process and in this chapter students will learn about how young children build on their previous achievements.

### Writing Activity

#### Poem

This active learning activity prompts students to write a poem describing the emotions of a toddler during a tantrum. After students have completed the writing activity, ask for volunteers to share their poems with the class. Student responses can be used as a basis for classroom discussion. (Student should create a poem that describes a child having a temper tantrum. The poem should use words to create interesting images and to convey strong emotions, and it should have a tempo.)

# Emotional and Social Development from One to Three

## Chapter Objectives

After completing this chapter, you will be able to:

- **Identify** the factors that contribute to a child's emotional development.
- **Describe** six specific emotions children ages eighteen months to three years show.
- **List** the four signs of a healthy relationship between parents and a child.
- **Identify** four ways to help children get adequate sleep.
- **Compare and contrast** parallel play and cooperative play.
- **List** six ways to help children develop social skills.
- **Explain** the purpose of guidance.

### Writing Activity  Poem

**Temper Tantrum** Imagine that a toddler is having a temper tantrum. She is frustrated that she cannot have her way. Write a poem about the tantrum. Make your poem funny or serious, but be sure it expresses emotion.

**Writing Tips** Remember that not all poems rhyme. Here are some tips to help you get started:

1. Use language that creates interesting images.
2. Use emotion-packed words.
3. Your poem should have a tempo or rhythm. Try setting your poem to music!

**318**

## CLASSROOM Solutions

### Print Resources

 **Student Edition**

 **Teacher Wraparound Edition**

 **Student Activity Workbook**

 **Student Activity Workbook Teacher Annotated Edition**

### Technology Resources

 **Online Learning Center** has resources and activities for students and teachers. Includes an Online Student Edition.

 **Interactive Student Edition** allows students to instantly access review materials, examples, and exercises.

**Section 11.1** Emotional Development from One to Three

**Section 11.2** Social Development from One to Three

**Review the Sections**
Introduce the chapter by reviewing the sections:

**Section 11.1**
Emotional development is controlled by a child's individual temperament and experiences. As children develop, they become less self-centered; however, their growing desire for independence can lead to conflicts with parents and caregivers. Emotions such as anger, jealousy, and fear are common. Emotionally healthy children also learn to express love and empathy.

**Section 11.2**
Between their first and fourth birthdays, children develop social skills that will stay with them throughout their lives. Their experiences—especially with their families—help them learn self-discipline and skills such as sharing and taking turns, which help them get along with others.

➤ **Explore the Photo**
Even toddlers enjoy playing around other children. *What do you think these children are learning from each other?*

**319**

---

**•➤ Explore the Photo**

**Caption Answer** Answers will vary. They are learning how other children play and how they respond to others. They also may teach one another motor skills.

**Discussion** Ask students: What do you think might happen if the boy on the left suddenly grabbed this toy away from the boy on the right? (Answers will vary. The two boys might get into a struggle over the toy, or the boy on the right might simply go off and play with another toy.)

---

 **TeacherWorks Plus** is an electronic lesson planner that provides instant access to complete teacher resources in one convenient package.

 **Presentation Plus!** provides visual teaching aids for every section.

 **The Early Childhood Observations CD** presents video observations and lessons on observation skills and child development.

**The Developing Brain eTransparencies and Guide** include information and activities to offer insights into brain development and diseases of the brain.

# Emotional Development from One to Three

## Focus

### Bell Ringer Activity

Describe for students a scenario in which a parent has promised to take a three-year-old to a water park, but the family car has suddenly developed mechanical problems. Ask: How do you think the child will respond? Discuss with the class that children's responses to specific situations can typically be predicted by their age.

## Preteaching

### Vocabulary

Explain that *phobia* is Latin, from the Greek word *phobos*, meaning "fear." Ask students for other words containing this root and write them on the board.

### Graphic Organizer

 The Graphic Organizer is also on the TeacherWorks CD.

(Graphic organizers should include: give choices, redirect the child, and encourage talking)

**NCLB** connects academic correlations to book content.

## Reading Guide

### Before You Read

**Get Your Rest** The better rested you are when you study, the more likely you will be to remember the information later. Studying in the same state of mind as when you take a test helps ensure your best performance.

### Read to Learn
#### Key Concepts

- **Identify** the factors that contribute to a child's emotional development.
- **Describe** six specific emotions children ages eighteen months to three years show.
- **List** the four signs of a healthy relationship between parents and a child.
- **Identify** four ways to help children get adequate sleep.

**D**

### Main Idea

Children go through a series of emotional stages. Each child develops differently based on his or her experiences and temperament. Adequate sleep is vital to good emotional development.

### Content Vocabulary

◇ self-centered
◇ negativism
◇ temper tantrum
◇ phobia
◇ separation anxiety
◇ sibling rivalry
◇ empathy
◇ self-concept
◇ sleep-deprived
◇ REM sleep
◇ NREM sleep

### Academic Vocabulary

You will find these words in your reading and on your tests. Use the glossary to look up their definitions if necessary.
- perceptive
- adequate

### Graphic Organizer

As you read, look for the three types of positive guidance to use with a negative child. Use a chart like the one shown to help organize your information.

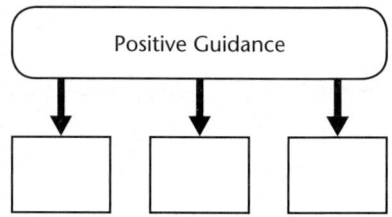

Positive Guidance

**Graphic Organizer** Go to this book's Online Learning Center at **glencoe.com** to print out this graphic organizer.

### Academic Standards · · · · · · · · · · · · · · · · · · · · · · · · · · · · · · · ·

**NCLB**

 **English Language Arts**

**NCTE 2** Read literature to build an understanding of the human experience.

**Science**

**NSES A** Develop abilities necessary to do scientific inquiry, understanding about scientific inquiry.

**NCTE** *National Council of Teachers of English*
**NCTM** *National Council of Teachers of Mathematics*

**NSES** *National Science Education Standards*
**NCSS** *National Council for the Social Studies*

## Reading Guide

### Before You Read

Ask students: Have you ever seen a two-year-old be fun and loving one minute and then suddenly be furious and screaming? How do you explain this? (Answers will vary. Two-year-olds are undergoing enormous changes and do not have good control of their emotions.)

### D Develop Concepts

**Main Idea** Discuss the main idea with the students. Ask students to suggest ways in which parents can help children develop emotionally. (Possible answers: by listening to their concerns and helping them express emotions, such as anger, in acceptable ways.)

## Emotional Patterns

Emotional development tends to go in cycles throughout childhood. The cycles are especially pronounced in children ages one to three years old. They develop new emotions, such as jealousy, that they had not felt before. They have periods of frustration and rebellion, but they also have periods of happiness, calmness, and stability. Negative periods tend to alternate with positive periods, and they are generally related to the age of the child.

Of course, each child is an individual. Claire may go through a negative period at eighteen months, while Jamal may not experience this until age two. Matthew may not seem to go through it at all. Generally, though, children can be expected to go through certain distinct emotional phases at certain ages, as shown in **Figure 11.1** on pages 322–323.

Emotional development depends primarily on two factors: the child's experiences and the child's temperament. Understanding these factors can help in dealing with such issues as negativism, tantrums, or sibling rivalry. It also helps you guide a child to desirable behavior.

## Individual Differences

There are general patterns to how children develop emotionally. However, each child is unique and will develop in a special way. Individual differences can be very noticeable between the first and fourth birthdays. The differences are partly due to the different experiences that each child has. An only child, for example, will have different experiences from a child who is one of five children. The experiences of twins or triplets will be different from the experiences of other children.

Individual differences in emotional development also result from the child's temperament. Temperament is the way the child naturally responds to other people and events. An intense child may become more frustrated than an adaptable child. A more **perceptive**, or observant, child may show more empathy than one who is less perceptive.

It is important to keep in mind these differences in temperament when teaching children how to control their emotions. Connor, for example, is very perceptive. He is aware of his environment. He can also be easily distracted.

**Family Members**
Each member of a family is an individual. *What are some ways that the emotional needs of a parent are different from those of a two-year-old?*

### ➤➤ Explore the Photo

**Caption Answer** Answers will vary. Students may say that parents need to feel they can care for their children properly and that their children love and respect them. Children need to feel safe and know that their parents will meet their needs.

**Discussion** Ask students: How might these children help meet the emotional needs of their parents? (Answers will vary but might include that children provide love and affection to the parents and raising happy, healthy children fulfills the parent's sense of responsibility.)

### Teach

## Discussion Starter

**Expectations** Describe a scenario in which a two-year-old throws herself on the floor and screams because her father will not buy a toy. Then describe the same situation, but with an eight-year-old. Ask: How would you view these two situations? (While the behavior is not unusual for a two-year-old, most people would not expect an eight-year-old to behave this way.) Conclude by discussing that children follow a normal pattern of emotional development. Because of this, we expect children of certain ages to behave in certain ways.

## C Critical Thinking

**Predict** Describe a scenario in which a two-year-old is allergic to a common food, such as wheat. The parent is not aware that this food gives the toddler stomach cramps. Because of this, the child is often cranky. Ask students: How might this affect the toddler's emotional development? (Possible answers: The child may not see the world as a happy, welcoming place and therefore might not reach out to others as much as other children.)

## R Reading Strategy

**Building on Previous Knowledge** Discuss with students that as they read, they should always look for material that builds on information they have previously learned. Have a volunteer read aloud the second paragraph under Individual Differences. Ask: What have you previously learned that helps you understand this material? (Chapter 8 emphasized individual differences in emotional development and discussed that each infant has his or her own temperament.)

**C** **Critical Thinking**

**Identify Cause and Effect** Have students identify the cause of a child's behavior and then state the likely effect. Remind students of the importance of a child's age when determining how he is likely to respond to a specific event. For example, an eighteen-month-old may drop his cup because of lack of motor control and then may become angry. (Answers will vary. Students should identify causes and effects of different behaviors at different ages.)

**U** **Universal Access**

**Kinesthetic Learners** Organize students into pairs. One student should role play a stubborn toddler who has just learned to say "No," while the other portrays a caregiver. Students should prepare a skit showing how the caregiver appropriately handles the child's negativism. Encourage students to use props. Have students present their skits to the class. (Skits will vary but should show a caregiver appropriately responding to a toddler's negativism.) **ELL**

**W** **Writing Support**

**Poem**

**I Want to Be Free** Tell students to put themselves inside the mind of an eighteen-month-old who wants to do everything for himself. Instruct students to write a humorous poem describing their drive for independence. Ask for volunteers to read their poems to the class. (Refer to p. 318 to review tips on writing poetry. Students' poems should take a humorous look at an eighteen-month-old's desire for independence.)

When Connor begins a temper tantrum, his mother tries to turn his attention to something new. She might point out a squirrel playing outside the window. Such a technique may not work on Nala, who adapts to change slowly. She dislikes surprises—even pleasant ones. Her parents have to give her plenty of warning and time to adjust before any change in her routine. This could include visitors arriving or even a new food for dinner.

### Eighteen Months

By the age of eighteen months, children have become self-centered. The term **self-centered** refers to thinking about one's own needs and wants and not those of others. This is not surprising. During infancy caregivers promptly meet the child's needs and desires. This is appropriate for infants. By eighteen months, though, caregivers begin to teach the child that some desires will not be met right away. Some requests will never be met. This is a difficult lesson for the eighteen-month-old to begin learning.

Spoken instructions are not always successful with children of this age. The young toddler is likely to do the opposite of what is asked. At this age, the child's favorite response to everything is "no." Saying "no" allows the child to feel some control over his or her world.

It is important to realize that negativism is normal for a young toddler. **Negativism** means doing the opposite of what others want. It has a number of causes:

- **The Desire for Independence** Saying "no" is a child's way of saying, "Let me decide for myself." The child may even say "no" to things that he or she would really like to do. Children just want the chance to make the decision.

**Figure 11.1 An Emotional Roller Coaster**

Most young children go through predictable stages in their emotional development. *How do children typically change between eighteen months and two years of age?*

**Two Years** The two-year-old is affectionate and may often be in the caregiver's way.

**Eighteen Months** The eighteen-month-old is defiant, trying to establish some control over her life.

**Figure 11.1 An Emotional Roller Coaster**

**Caption Answer** They typically become less defiant and more affectionate.

**Discussion** Ask for a volunteer to define the word *analogy* (an inference that two things agree with one another in some respect). Ask students: Do you think a roller coaster is a good analogy for a young child's emotional development? Why or why not? Encourage students to list other appropriate analogies to a young child's emotional development.

- **Frustration** Toddlers want to do more than their bodies are able to do. They do not have the language skills yet to express all their feelings. The frustration that results is often expressed in a simple and emphatic "No!"
- **The Realization of Being a Separate Person** This idea is both exciting and frightening. The child welcomes the power and independence of being a separate person. At times, though, he or she still wants a tight bond with a primary caregiver.

Negativism can produce a battle of wills between child and parent. There are strategies to help prevent conflicts. One is to eliminate as many restrictions as possible. For example, put fragile objects away instead of asking an eighteen-month-old not to touch them. As the child gets older, they can be put back in place.

Positive guidance can also help deal with a child who is negative. Use these tips:

- **Give Choices** Instead of saying "Pick up your books and toys," ask, "Which will you pick up first—the books or the toys?" Having choices allows the child to have control. Limit choices to two options, however. Toddlers cannot think about three or four things at a time.
- **Redirect the Child** If possible, distract the child from the issue that is causing the negative response. You may be able to go back to the issue later, when the child is calmer. For example, Julia was having trouble stacking her blocks. So her mother suggested instead that they read a book.
- **Encourage Talking** You can help children learn to use words to communicate how they feel. Being able to talk will help both you and the child understand and deal with those feelings. Asking "What's wrong, Susie?" or "Don't you like that?" encourages children to share what they are feeling.

**Three Years** The three-year-old is generally a happy child who is eager to help.

**Two and One-Half Years** At two and one-half, the child may feel overwhelmed. Frustration then becomes anger.

**Three and One-Half Years** At three and one-half years, a child is often bothered by fears.

**Professional Development**

**Mini Clip**
**Reading: Differentiated Instruction**

Nancy Frey, PhD, educator and author, discusses elements of a differentiated classroom.

**Teach** *cont.*

**S Skill Practice**
**Guided Practice**

**Roller Coaster** Have students create a time line that looks like a roller coaster. The time line should describe a child's emotional development from ages eighteen months to three and one-half years. Those time periods when a child is typically happier should be placed on the roller coaster's hills whereas those times when the child faces more challenges should be in its valleys. (Time lines should be shaped like a roller coaster and list various stages of emotional development.) **L1 ELL**

**Perform a Skit** Have the class think of a typical scenario, such as a child eating breakfast on a busy morning. Organize students into pairs and assign each pair a specific age from eighteen months to three and one-half years. Each pair should create a skit around the chosen scenario. The skit should illustrate the child's emotional development at the assigned age. (Students should create a skit that demonstrates a child's emotional development at a specific age.) **L2 ELL**

**Prepare a Presentation** Instruct students to choose one of the ages shown in Figure 11.1 and conduct additional research on emotional development at this age. Encourage students to look at specific research that has been done on children of this age. Students then should create an oral report covering what they learn. If possible, encourage students to use presentation software to present their information to the class. (Students should create a presentation on emotional development at a specific age.) **L3**

## Teach cont.

### C₁ Critical Thinking

**Analyze** State that temper tantrums often result in "battles of the will." Ask students: What does this phrase mean to you? Then ask: Why do you think toddlers win these battles so often? (Answers will vary. Possible answers: Toddlers can be extremely stubborn and parents are often tired after a day at work or are embarrassed if their children throw a tantrum in a public place.)

### C₂ Critical Thinking

**Generalize** The emotional development stage at age two is often referred to as "the terrible twos." Have students think of a more positive nickname for this stage. Tell students to consider what a child is going through emotionally at this time. Write students' suggestions on the board and take a vote on which one the class believes is the most suitable. (Suggestions will vary but could focus on the affection that a two-year-old feels or their desire for independence.) **ELL**

### U₁ Universal Access

**English Language Learners**
Organize students into pairs. One student should be an English language learner and the other a student who is fluent in English. Read aloud the Expert Advice box at the bottom of page 324. Have the partners work together to rewrite this quote in their own words. Make certain that they simplify the language. Ask for volunteers to read aloud the results. (Students should work in pairs to rewrite this quote in simpler language.) **ELL**

---

Around eighteen months, a child may start to have temper tantrums. A **temper tantrum** is when children release anger or frustration by screaming, crying, kicking, pounding, and sometimes holding their breath. These tantrums may occur until age three or four. Even seemingly minor frustrations can cause temper tantrums. Try to help the child find calmer ways of expressing these feelings. For ways to calm a toddler who is having a temper tantrum, see the Parenting Skills feature on page 343.

### Two Years

Emotionally, two-year-olds are less at odds with the world than eighteen-month-olds. The speech and motor skills of a two-year-old have improved. This eases some frustration. Christy can now say she wants milk instead of juice. A two-year-old also understands more and is able to wait longer for various needs to be met.

At age two, a child expresses love and affection freely and seeks approval and praise. Though the child still has some emotional outbursts, they are fewer and less intense. Two-year-olds are easier to reason with. They usually get along better with parents and other children. They tend to be more outgoing and friendly, and less self-centered.

### Two and One-Half Years

Just as parents and caregivers begin to adjust to a smoother, less intense toddler, the child enters another difficult stage. This period may seem even more difficult for caregivers than the eighteen-month-old stage. At two and one-half, toddlers are not as easily distracted as they were at eighteen months.

Children this age are learning so much that they often feel overwhelmed. Their desires and their ability to understand tasks exceed their physical ability to perform. For example, they may want their blocks stacked up in a certain way. However, they might accidentally knock the blocks over before they finish the structure. They may know what they want to say but cannot always say it clearly. These situations produce frustrations that may boil over.

At two and one-half, children struggle with immaturity and a powerful need for independence. Their drive for independence causes children to resist pressures to conform. They are sensitive about being bossed, shown, helped, or directed during this stage. They can be stubborn, demanding, and domineering. However, their moods change rapidly, and within a short time they can become lovable and completely charming.

Children at this age have a need for consistency. They want the same routines, carried out the same way, every day. Following a routine is their way of coping with a confusing world. A routine helps children build confidence and a feeling of security.

At two and one-half, children feel both independent and dependent. Sometimes they seek help. Other times, they want to do things by themselves. They require love and patience, especially when their behavior is neither lovable nor patient. They need flexible limits rather than hard-and-fast rules.

### Three Years

Three-year-olds generally have a happier nature than two-year-olds. They are more cooperative and are learning to be considerate. They are more physically capable and, therefore, less frustrated than two-year-olds.

Three-year-olds become more willing to take directions from others. They will modify their behavior to win the praise and affection they crave. In general, three-year-olds have fewer temper tantrums than younger children.

---

### U₁

{ **Expert Advice...** }

*"Emotional well-being and social competence provide a strong foundation for emerging cognitive abilities, and together they are the bricks and mortar that comprise the foundation of human development."*

— *The Science of Early Childhood Development,* National Scientific Council on the Developing Child

---

**Mc Graw Hill Professional Development**

### Mini Clip
**ELL: Modeling Reading Strategies**

A teacher uses a read-aloud to model fluent reading strategies.

**Temper Tantrums**
Toddlers go through negative periods as well as positive ones. *What are some causes of negativism?*

At three, children like to talk and are much better at it. They talk to their toys, their playmates, themselves, and even to their imaginary friends. They often want to tell their parents all about their day. They also respond when others talk to them, and they can be reasoned with and controlled by words.

### Three and One-Half Years

The self-confident three-year-old suddenly becomes very insecure at age three and one-half. Parents may feel that the child is going backward rather than forward emotionally.

Fears are common at this age. The child may be afraid of the dark, imaginary monsters, strangers, or loud noises. Emotional tension and insecurity often show up in physical ways too. Some children may start habits, such as thumb sucking or nail biting, to provide self-soothing. Others stumble or stutter.

At three and one-half, children try to ensure their own security by controlling their environment. They may issue insistent demands, such as "I want to sit on the floor to eat lunch!" or "Talk to me!"

**✓ Reading Check** **Identify** What are three ways a parent can help a child who is being negative?

### Specific Emotions

Even young babies have specific emotions. How children express emotions changes as they get older. Children express their emotions openly until the age of two or three. They begin to learn socially acceptable ways of displaying feelings after the age of three. For example, eighteen-month-old Marta shows anger by kicking and screaming. Jonathan, at age three and one-half, expresses anger through words. The specific emotions children between the ages of eighteen months and three years generally show include anger, fear, jealousy, love, affection, and empathy.

### Anger

Anger is often the child's way of reacting to frustration. How children show that anger changes over the years. By the time children are three years old, they are less violent and explosive. They are less likely to hit or kick. Physical attacks give way to name-calling, pouting, or scolding.

The target of a child's anger changes in these years as well. An eighteen-month-old who has a tantrum usually does not direct the anger toward a specific person or thing. Beginning around ages two to three, children are more

---

**U₂ Universal Access**

**Auditory Learners** Bring in a recording of young children speaking to one another or speaking to adults. Have students listen to the recording and take notes about what they hear. Discuss with students the probable ages of the children on the recording and what information they might use to estimate ages. Discuss how factors such as clarity of speech, correctness of grammar, and the way in which they express themselves and their feelings are helpful in estimating a child's age. **ELL**

**R Reading Strategy**

**Connect Concepts** Have students write the word "anger" vertically on a piece of paper. Next to each letter of the word, have them write a word or phrase starting with that specific letter that indicates how a young child might express anger. For example, next to "A," they might write "act out." (Students should write a word or phrase next to each letter in "anger" that indicates how a young child might express anger.)

**✓ Reading Check**

**Identify** The parent can give choices, redirect the child, and encourage the child to talk.

---

#### ➤ Explore the Photo

**Caption Answer** Negativism can be caused by an inability to be understood or the desire to exert control.

**Discussion** Tell students that this mother is having a difficult time controlling her anger toward the child. What might they say to her to help her cope with this situation? (Possible answer: That this is a stage that virtually all children go through as they mature.)

### Teach cont.

### C₁ Critical Thinking

**Evaluate** Ask for a volunteer to read aloud the tips for helping children learn acceptable ways of handling anger. Ask: Do you think these tips would work well with children of all ages? Why or why not? Based on your personal experience, do you have any additional tips? (Responses will vary. The first tip, in particular, is aimed at children who are fairly verbal and may not work with young children whose vocabulary is limited. All three tips would probably work well with older children. Answers to the last question will vary.)

### U Universal Access

**Intrapersonal Learners** Have students reflect on a moment when they were afraid of something in their childhood. In a narrative essay, ask students to describe the fear in detail and the ways they overcame the fear. They might want to include whether caregivers and parents helped them conquer their fears or if they did so alone. (Essays will vary but should describe a childhood fear and how the students overcame that fear. For example, a student may say he was afraid of the dark and he overcame it by using a nightlight, or by learning what made each shadow in his room when the lights were out.)

likely to aim their anger at the object or person they hold responsible for their frustration.

Many common causes of anger are temporary. Most children experience this kind of anger from time to time. If a child is sick, tired, uncomfortable, or hungry, frustration is more likely to turn into anger. Children also often feel angry when they do not get their way. Caregivers should not make the child feel guilty about his or her anger. It is a normal emotion.

Sometimes anger is expressed as aggression. Toddlers can become aggressive over toys. They may not want to share. By hitting and otherwise acting aggressively, toddlers are trying out ways of getting along. They have not yet learned how to play with others or control strong feelings like anger. Children can learn more acceptable ways of handling anger. Use these tips:

- **Use words.** Rather than hitting or lashing out, children and adults should try to express feelings with words.
- **Speak calmly.** Even when angry, people should speak calmly instead of screaming or yelling.
- **Take deep breaths.** Have a child try to take a few deep breaths to calm down.

It may help to have an angry child rest for a while. Discuss the misbehavior and any punishment after the child has calmed down. Then help the child see why the action was misbehavior. Explain what the child should have done. Be sure to use a calm and loving voice when talking to the child.

Certain factors can cause a child to be angry more often than normal. Angry outbursts are more frequent in anxious, insecure children. Children whose parents are overly critical or inconsistent may become frustrated easily and show anger. A child who has not learned self-control tends to have more frequent outbursts. It is important that the demands placed on children be limited and reasonable. Adults need to respond to a child's anger in a controlled way. Reacting to anger with anger will only make the situation worse and set a poor example.

## Fear

Children have specific fears at different ages. While a one-year-old may be frightened of strangers, a three-year-old might be afraid of the dark. Some fears are actually useful since they keep the child from dangerous situations.

**Dealing with Misbehavior**
Discussing misbehavior and punishment is easier once a child has calmed down. *What are three acceptable ways of handling anger?*

### Explore the Photo

**Caption Answer** Acceptable ways of handling anger include using words rather than hitting, speaking calmly, and taking deep breaths.

**Discussion** Ask: What do you think is this parent's primary goal in dealing with his child's misbehavior? (Answers will vary. Possible answer: to guide her in the hope that she will learn correct behavior and not misbehave in the same way in the future.)

Other fears must be overcome in order for the child to develop in a healthy way. An unexplainable and illogical fear is called a **phobia**. Two of the most common phobias include a fear of heights or public speaking. Phobias are more likely to develop in children who are shy and withdrawn. Parents who think a child might be developing a phobia should talk to their pediatrician.

Adults sometimes pass their own fears to children. Even if the fear is never discussed, a parent who runs away or crosses the street whenever a dog comes near may cause a child to be afraid of dogs. Do you have any of the same fears as your parents?

One common fear is separation anxiety. **Separation anxiety** is the fear of being away from parents, familiar caregivers, or the normal environment. Babies can show signs of separation anxiety as early as six or seven months, but the crisis age for most children is between twelve and eighteen months. Most commonly, separation anxiety strikes when parents leave a child to go to work or run an errand. Children can also experience separation anxiety at night when they are safely tucked in their own cribs with their mom and dad in the next room.

Separation anxiety can upset parents and other caregivers. They may feel guilty about a child's tears and clinging when they try to leave the child with a babysitter or at a child care center. The parents need to remember that they have chosen a safe, secure caregiver for the child. Separation anxiety is simply a stage that children will go through. It shows that the child is attached to his parents. Parents can help by spending special time with the child at home.

They can also be specific about when they will return. Telling the child, "I'll be back after you've had your nap," gives the child a better sense of what to expect than "I'll be back at three o'clock." Sometimes a parent gives the child something special, such as a stuffed animal or blanket, for safe keeping or comfort until the parent returns.

## Parenting Skills

### Managing Changes in a Child's Routine

Toddlers and preschoolers find a sense of security in a predictable routine. When their routine is changed, some become anxious. Transitions from one activity to the next are also difficult for some children this age. The following tips can be helpful:

- **Make time for transitions.** Warn children ahead of time of changes in activities. For example, you might let a child know it will be time to leave for the store in five minutes. Such advance notice helps give children a sense of control and security.
- **Familiarize children with the unfamiliar.** Give them time to check out new places and people. For example, if a child is going to a new preschool, take time to visit the school before the child's first day.
- **Be as clear and consistent as possible.** Children will find security in the predictability of adults' reactions when the rules are clear and caregivers respond to them consistently.

**Take Charge** Providing children with predictable routines is an important parenting skill. Write a paragraph explaining how you would provide a child with a predictable bedtime routine.

## Assess

**Quiz**
Ask students to answer the following questions:

1. **What does it mean when we say that eighteen-month-old children are self-centered?** (They think about their own needs and wants, rather than those of others.)
2. **How can a parent teach a young child to express his feelings through words?** (The parent can ask questions concerning the child's feelings, such as "Can you tell me what you are feeling?" The parent then can listen carefully to the child's response.)
3. **Why might two-and-one-half-year-olds feel overwhelmed, frustrated, and angry?** (They are learning so much that their comprehension exceeds their physical ability to perform, and immaturity clashes with a desire for independence.)

## Reteach

**C₂ Critical Thinking**

**Make Judgments** In a national poll, researchers found that half of all parents believe that the more caregivers a child has before age three, the better that child will be at adapting to change. Ask students: Do you think this is true? Why or why not? (Answers will vary, but students should provide reasons for their answers. Possible answer: No, because young children gain a sense of security when their lives are predictable.)

## Parenting Skills

### Managing Changes in a Child's Routine

Describe a situation in which a child must get up two hours early on a Saturday to visit his grandparents. What might his parents do to help the child deal with this change? (Parents might explain that they will be getting up earlier than usual and why. They might remind the child of how much fun they had during their last visit to his grandparents.)

**Take Charge**
Answers will vary. The parent might tell the child when bedtime is approaching, have the child use the bathroom and brush her teeth, read a book while the child is in bed, and perform a tucking-in routine.

**W Writing Support**

**Poem**

**All Alone** Instruct students to write a poem expressing the fears a child feels when left alone in his or her bedroom at night. Encourage students to express the specific emotions of the child and why the child feels this way. Students may wish to set their poems to music. Ask for volunteers to present their poems to the class. (Refer to p. 318 to review tips on writing poetry. Students' poems should clearly express the fears of a child left alone at night.)

**C₁ Critical Thinking**

**Propose a Solution** Tell students to suppose that a cousin is concerned at the changes in his three-year-old son's behavior since his sister was born. In the last few months the situation seems to be growing worse. Now his son wants a pacifier when he is tired, something he had given up at eighteen months. How might you suggest that your cousin respond to his son's behavior? (Answers may vary. Students should recognize that the child needs his father's support. You might suggest he spend more time alone with the child and praise him for any "grown-up" behavior he exhibits.)

**Toddlers and Jealousy**
A new baby sometimes causes jealousy in a toddler. *What are some ways parents can help prevent sibling rivalry?*

**W** Many children who feel separation anxiety have trouble going to sleep at night. A bedtime routine and a reminder that a parent is nearby can help lessen these fears. Here are some other ways to help toddlers deal with their fears:

- Offer support and understanding. Never make children feel ashamed of their fears.
- Encourage children to talk about their fears. Be sure to listen intently. Often talking about fears can diminish their impact.
- Sometimes, it is best to accept the fear and avoid trying to force the child to confront it. Often, it will go away on its own. Lily became suddenly afraid of lizards when she was two. By the time Lily was three, though, she enjoyed looking for the lizards. She was not afraid anymore.
- Read books together about a child who experiences fear. Talking about the book may help relieve the child's fears.
- Make unfamiliar situations more secure. Discuss new experiences and events in advance to help the child know what to expect. If possible, go with the child to new places.
- Teach the child how to control frightening situations. Getting in a swimming pool terrified Jacob, so his aunt showed him how to sit on the side and dangle his feet in the water.

### Jealousy

Jealousy is an emotion that usually crops up some time during a child's second year. A twelve-month-old does not show any jealousy. By the age of eighteen months, though, jealousy becomes very pronounced. It reaches its peak when a child is about three. Then it becomes less intense as outside relationships begin to loosen a child's ties to home and parents. Sometimes parents become the target of a child's jealousy. For example, a toddler may resent any show of affection between parents because the child cannot yet understand that parents have enough love for everyone.

**Sibling rivalry** is the competition between brothers or sisters for parents' affection and attention. It is a common cause of jealousy. Children sometimes become jealous when a new baby is born. For example, a toddler finds that the attention he once received is now focused on a new baby. Some young children react to a new baby by trying to get more attention. They may show off or act in inappropriate ways. Sometimes they revert, or go back, to baby-like behaviors, such as wetting the bed or using baby talk. Some may behave aggressively towards the younger sibling.

**C₁**

---

### ⮞ Explore the Photo

**Caption Answer** Answers will vary but might include letting the older child help take care of the newborn or scheduling time for the older child to spend alone with a parent.

**Discussion** Explain to students that young children often do not know positive ways of getting attention, so they resort to sibling rivalry. Ask: How is this mother helping her daughter learn about positive ways of obtaining the attention she needs? (She is providing her with attention for behaving in a caring way toward the baby.)

Parents should understand that fear of losing the parent's love caused the negative behavior. The child needs more affection and reassurance, not punishment. Because of sibling rivalry, many experts say it is never safe to leave a baby alone with a toddler.

Sibling rivalry does not occur only when there is a newborn. One day Glen came home from work to find himself overwhelmed by hugs from both his four-year-old, Becky, and his three-year-old, Curt. The children soon began pushing and shoving, trying to block the other child from getting near their father.

There are steps a parent can take to help cut down on sibling rivalry:
- Make sure that each child feels love and appreciation.
- Set aside one-on-one time with each child.
- Avoid making comments that compare one child to another.
- Let the children take turns in choosing activities, such as a game the family plays together or a movie to watch.
- Make it clear that you will not accept one child tattling to get another one in trouble.
- Talk to children about their jealousy, how hard it can be to have siblings, and how lucky they are to have each other.

## Love and Affection

The relationships that children have with others between the ages of one and three form the basis of their capacity for love and affection in later life. Young children must learn to love.

Babies first love those who satisfy their physical needs. Gradually, as children grow older, their affection expands to include siblings, pets, and people outside the home.

Loving relationships between parents or other caregivers and children need to be strong but not smothering. A child who depends entirely on caregivers for love has difficulty forming other relationships.

## Empathy

For years, people believed that infants and toddlers were so self-centered they could not feel anything toward someone who was unhappy. Research shows that view to be false.

**Showing Affection**
Young children gradually learn to show love and affection for others. *Have you seen a young child try to comfort someone who seemed unhappy?*

Section 11.1 Emotional Development from One to Three **329**

### C2 Critical Thinking

**Predict** Review the different temperament traits exhibited by children. (They are listed in Figure 8.2.) List each trait and then ask students how they think a preschooler with this trait would respond to a new family member. Ask: Which type of child would be most likely to express sibling rivalry? Why? (Answers will vary. Students should explain how children with different temperament traits are likely to respond to a new sibling. For example, an intense child is likely to have more difficulty adjusting than an adaptive child.)

### U Universal Access

**Verbal Learners** Instruct students to go to a library and examine three books aimed at helping preschoolers adjust to the birth of a sibling. Students should write a short review of each book and then choose the book that they thought did the best job. You might want to consider allowing students to read their chosen books aloud to the class and having the class discuss them. (Students should review three books aimed at helping young children adjust to a new baby and select the book they believe did the best job. They should offer reasons for their choice.)

## Explore the Photo

**Caption Answer** Responses will vary. Very young children are not capable of empathy but older toddlers or preschoolers might try to offer comfort to an upset parent, peer, or sibling.

**Discussion** Ask students: Do you think empathy is related to love? Why or why not? (Answers will vary. Understanding other people's needs and views of the world can help us to feel a bond with them and therefore have affection toward them.)

### C₁ Critical Thinking

**Relate** Have students suppose that they are parents of a two-year-old and a newborn. When the newborn begins crying, the older child kisses the baby and shakes a rattle to distract her. This is the first time the older child has shown concern for the baby. Ask students: How do you think you, as the parent, would feel? (The parent probably is happy and grateful that the child is able to express concern for the welfare of others, particularly a sibling.)

### U Universal Access

**Visual Learners** Have students spend an hour or so in a location where they can observe parents with their young children, such as a mall or playground. Tell students to keep track of how many times they see signs of a healthy parent-child relationship. In each case, they should keep notes on what happened. For example, they may see a child looking for a parent's praise after going down a slide or running to a parent after scraping a knee. After students have completed their observations, have them discuss the results as a group. (Students should watch parents and children interacting and take notes on the signs of healthy parent-child relationships that they observe.) **ELL**

### ✓ Reading Check

**Describe** Those who are anxious and insecure, or whose parents are inconsistent or overly critical, are more likely to feel angry.

**Individual Traits**
Every child develops in a unique way because of his or her individual traits. *How can caregivers help children develop empathy for other people?*

It is true that a toddler is mainly self-focused. However, the self is not their only focus. Children this age are becoming more aware of people around them. They may be exposed to more children through child care or play groups.

Between twelve and eighteen months of age, children begin to understand that their actions can hurt others. This is the first step toward developing empathy. **Empathy** is the ability to understand how another person feels. Children as young as one year old may pat and talk to another child who is unhappy. By age two, a child can show empathy. For example, when two-year-old Antonio saw that Avery was upset, he offered Avery his favorite stuffed animal as a way to cheer him up.

Caregivers can help teach children to show empathy. If a child in your care does something to hurt someone's feelings, such as grabbing a toy, have the child give back the toy and apologize. Then ask the child to take an active step toward making the wronged child feel better, such as sharing another toy.

### ✓ Reading Check  Describe What types of children are more likely to feel angry?

## Emotional Adjustment

How can parents tell whether a child's emotional development is on the right track? Between their first and fourth birthdays, the most important clue is the relationship of children with their parents or other primary caregivers. The early pattern established between the familiar adults and the child will shape the child's relationships later in life as a friend, coworker, and spouse.

These are signs that a child has a healthy relationship with his or her parents:

- Seeks approval and praise
- Turns to parents and caregivers for comfort and help
- Tells caregivers about significant events so they can share in the joy and sorrow
- Accepts limits and discipline without too much resistance

Another indicator of emotional adjustment is a child's relationship with siblings. Some quarreling with brothers and sisters is bound to occur. However, the child who is continuously and bitterly at odds with brothers and sisters, in spite of parents' efforts to ease the friction,

330    Chapter 11   Emotional and Social Development from One to Three

---

### ▶ Explore the Photo

**Caption Answer** Answers will vary but might include: Encourage children to apologize when they have hurt another child and have them take a positive step to making the wronged child feel better.

**Discussion** How can playing together in a sandbox help children develop emotionally? (In order to get along, these children must be considerate of one another's feelings. For example, if they want others to respect their area of the box and not destroy what they are building, they must show the same consideration of others.)

may need counseling. If emotional problems are dealt with early, it can make a difference for a lifetime.

## Promote Positive Self-Concept

As they grow, children become more aware of their individual differences. The individual traits that make them special become part of their self-concept. **Self-concept** is how people see themselves. Self-concepts can be positive or negative. Children who see themselves as good and capable have a positive self-concept. Children who see themselves as bad or unable to do tasks have a negative self-concept.

Self-concept is different from self-esteem. Self-concept is what you think you are like as a person. Self-esteem is how highly you value yourself.

Children form their self-concept in response to the actions, attitudes, and comments of others. The years from one to three are crucial in a child's development of self-concept. Parents or primary caregivers usually spend the most time with the young child during this time. Therefore, they have the strongest influence on the child's self-concept.

Young children believe what others say about them. The opinions of others influence how children behave. Often, when children hear adults say that they are good, they try to act the part. If they constantly hear that they are bad or stupid, they will believe it and live up to that image.

Even young toddlers who cannot yet understand words are tuned in to the body language and tone of voice of adults. Adults' words and actions continue to have a strong influence on children until they are old enough to judge their own actions. By that time, however, their self-concept can be firmly established.

Another factor in building a positive self-concept is mastery of skills. For this reason, it is important to give infants and toddlers the chance to explore their world. Through exploration, children have the opportunity to master skills. Being able to learn skills such as finding toys and stacking blocks gives a sense of confidence. Self-confidence helps lead to a positive self-concept.

## Discourage Negative Behavior

Some parents worry that correcting misbehavior will damage their child's self-concept. However, a positive self-concept is based on actual achievement. By teaching and praising young children for appropriate behaviors, self-esteem is enhanced. Here are some effective ways to discourage negative behaviors.

**Giving Praise**
It is important that young children have a good relationship with parents and other caregivers. *Why is it important that young children receive love from parents and caregivers?*

Section 11.1   Emotional Development from One to Three   **331**

### Reteach *cont.*

**R** **Reading Strategy**

**Create a Venn Diagram** Discuss that knowing the similarities and differences between two terms can help you understand each term's meaning. Draw on the board a Venn diagram that explains the similarities and differences between the terms self-concept and self-esteem. (Both are terms that refer to ourselves as individuals. Self-concept refers to how we view ourselves, such as whether or not we are fast runners. Self-esteem refers to our feelings of worth and self-respect.) **ELL**

**C₂** **Critical Thinking**

**Solve Problems** Describe the following scenario: During a game of hide-and-seek, three-year-old Adam punches Sam. Ask students how a caregiver can help Adam understand the seriousness of his actions and make him understand that he hurt Sam. You might want to have students act out this discussion between Adam and the caregiver. (Students should discuss that the caregiver should clearly state that hitting other children is not allowed and that what Adam did hurt Sam. If Adam is angry at Sam, he should use words to express his feelings.)

---

## ▶ Explore the Photo

**Caption Answer** It sets the foundation for them being able to develop loving relationships later in life.

**Discussion** Describe a scenario in which parents do not encourage a child to learn new skills, such as running, or to expand her vocabulary. While they do not discourage her from learning new skills, they also do not praise her. How might this child's emotional development be affected? (Responses will vary. The child may feel that the parents do not care about her and rarely try anything new.)

## Reteach cont.

### U Universal Access

**Interpersonal Learners** Divide the class into small groups. Assign each group one of these common bedtime problems: fear of the dark, fear of being alone, insistence on sleeping in the parents' room, separation anxiety, nightmares, getting out of bed, and crying at bedtime. Each group should develop a brief skit showing how a parent might handle the assigned problem. (Skits will vary. Many of them may emphasize the comfort of a bedtime routine. For example, if the skit is about the fear of being alone, the students may show the parents rocking the child and reading a bedtime story before putting the child to bed. This routine would let the child know that the parent would be leaving. The parent could then offer a favorite stuffed animal to "stay" with the child so he is not alone.)

### C Critical Thinking

**Generalize** Ask students: How do you think a lack of sleep affects your emotional behavior? Do you think the same would be true of a two-year-old? Encourage students to discuss their responses. (Students' responses will vary. Possible answer: People of all ages are more tense and react more negatively when things do not go their way when they do not have adequate sleep.)

### ✓ Reading Check

**Summarize** Parents discourage negative behavior when they explore the child's feelings and discuss ways of handling problems, acknowledge feelings, and offer the child simple choices.

---

## What Would You Do?

**Not Enough Sleep**

Jenny, the mother of two-year-old Amber, was baffled that her daughter fought going to bed every night. Amber would cry and beg to stay up. Amber would usually throw a temper tantrum when Jenny carried her into the bedroom.

Getting Amber up in the morning was just as hard. Jenny took Amber to child care at 7:00 A.M. every day. The child care workers said that Amber had become aggressive. She would grab toys from other children and even hit them sometimes. On the way home, Amber always fell asleep. The bedtime battle would be repeated later that night.

✐ **Write About It** Imagine you are Amber's mother. Write a paragraph explaining what you would do to help Amber get adequate sleep so that she would be able to get up in morning and be happier during the day.

- **Explore feelings.** Read stories to a child or watch children's videos together. Then discuss ways that the characters handled their feelings or problems. This shows the child that others have the same feelings. It also helps the child cope with the feelings.
- **Acknowledge feelings.** When a playmate takes a toddler's toy, grabbing or hitting may be a natural reaction. Caregivers should explain why this response is not acceptable and give an alternative. They might say, "Everyone gets angry at times, but it's not okay to hurt people. Ask your friend for the toy back or choose another one."
- **Give choices.** Offer simple choices to empower children. Choosing what shirt to wear or what book to read makes a child feel important. Making a choice also gives them a sense of control.

**✓ Reading Check** **Summarize** What are three ways that a parent can discourage negative behavior?

---

# Sleep and Emotional Behavior

A scream woke Joshua's parents in the middle of the night. It was not the first time that their three-year-old son had awakened terrified from a bad dream. Every time that Joshua woke up screaming, his parents rushed into his room and comforted him. Sometimes he was so scared that a parent had to stay with him so that he could go back to sleep.

Most sleep problems in children are normal. In fact, they are one of the most common problems that children experience. Parents can help ease sleep problems by understanding what causes them. Fears are a frequent cause of sleep problems. A bedtime routine and a reminder that a parent is nearby can help lessen these fears. Separation anxiety can also cause nightmares that wake the child. Asking the child to describe the nightmare can help calm him or her. Also, by hearing about a dream, the parent may gain insight into the cause of the nightmare.

Some children find it hard to fall back asleep after waking in the night. Children may associate a certain routine, such as being rocked or hearing a lullaby, with sleeping. Parents may need to repeat bedtime routines in the middle of the night to restore sleep.

Sleep problems also can be caused by something as simple as pajamas that are too tight. Or there could be a more serious cause such as an ear infection or other illness. Parents concerned about the cause of a child's sleep problem should talk to their pediatrician.

## The Importance of Adequate Sleep

**Adequate**, or sufficient, sleep is as essential to good physical and emotional health as adequate nutrition. Without enough sleep, children can become sleep deprived. **Sleep deprived** means lacking adequate sleep. Being sleep deprived can affect a child's temperament and ability to do even simple tasks during the day. Children may be less alert, inattentive, and even hyperactive. To develop and function properly, one- to three-year-olds need twelve to fourteen hours of sleep each night.

---

## What Would You Do?

**Write About It** Paragraphs will vary but should explain the steps to take. Steps might include setting up a strict bedtime routine, getting Amber up at the same time every day; preventing her from sleeping on the way home, by talking or singing; and talking to her about how her aggressive behavior at child care affects others.

## Sleep Cycles

Children, like adults, go through cycles of sleep each night. **REM sleep** is a sleep cycle characterized by rapid eye movement. This is a light sleep during which dreams occur. **NREM sleep** is a cycle of sleep in which rapid eye movement does not occur. NREM sleep is a deep sleep. Children are more likely to wake up during the REM sleep cycle.

Newborns have short sleep cycles and can go through an entire cycle of REM and NREM in about an hour. By about four months of age, babies can sleep six to eight hours at a time. This increases to ten to twelve hours by six months of age.

## Prevent Sleep Deprivation

What are signs of sleep deprivation? Children who do not get enough sleep must be awakened each morning and tend to be tired all day. They have trouble thinking and are at risk of hurting themselves while playing. They can also be fussy and hard to get along with. Sleep deprivation is more apparent when a child has to get up on a regular schedule. Here are some ways to help ensure that children get adequate sleep:

- **Determine a child's best bedtime.** People need different amounts of sleep. When does a child usually begin to get tired? Use that as a guide. Children who stay up past this normal bedtime may get a second wind and have trouble falling asleep.
- **Limit toys in the bed.** Toys might signal playtime rather than sleep time. A favorite stuffed animal is okay.
- **Establish a bedtime routine.** Every night, follow the same pattern such as a bath, brushing teeth, and a bedtime story.
- **Keep bedtime pleasant.** Talk and cuddle with the child. You might also try giving a soothing backrub.

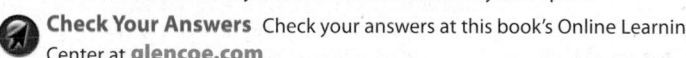

## Section 11.1 After You Read

### Review Key Concepts

1. **Describe** the changes in emotions that occur in children between ages three and three and one-half years.
2. **Explain** the difference between self-concept and self-esteem.
3. **Identify** what separation anxiety is and at what age it typically becomes the strongest.
4. **Summarize** what parents can do to minimize sibling rivalry.

### Practice Academic Skills

 **English Language Skills**

5. Locate a book for young children that deals with emotional issues such as a fear of the dark or a new baby in the family. Write a paragraph evaluating the book. Do you think it would help a young child?

> **NCTE 2** Read literature to build an understanding of the human experience.

**Science**

6. Conduct research to learn more about sleep cycles and the differences between REM and NREM sleep. Write a report describing what you have learned. You may wish to include charts in your report.

> **NSES A** Develop abilities necessary to do scientific inquiry, understanding about scientific inquiry.

 **Check Your Answers** Check your answers at this book's Online Learning Center at **glencoe.com**.

**NCLB**

Section 11.1 Emotional Development from One to Three **333**

## Study Tools

Have students go to the Online Learning Center at **glencoe.com**:

- Take the **Practice Test**.
- Download **Study-to-Go** content.

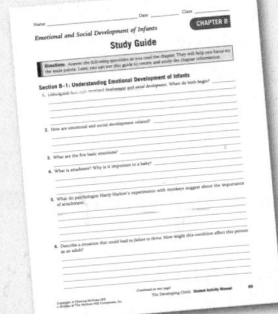

Use the **Student Activity Workbook** for additional practice.

## Close

### Culminating Activity

**Encourage Emotional Growth**
Have students give examples of how parents can encourage emotional growth. Write the examples on the board and encourage other students to expand on them.

**NCLB** connects academic correlations to book content.

---

## Section 11.1 After You Read

### Review Key Concepts

1. Three-and-one-half-year-olds become less secure, make insistent demands, and they may become afraid of things that did not bother them before.
2. Self-concept is what you think you are like as a person. Self-esteem is how highly you value yourself.
3. Separation anxiety, the fear of being away from familiar caregivers, or the normal environment, becomes strongest between 12 and 18 months.
4. make sure that each child feels loved and appreciated, set aside one-on-one time with each child, not compare children to one another, let children take turns in choosing family activities, not let children tattle on one another, and talk with children about their jealousies

### Practice Academic Skills

5. Answers will vary depending on the book chosen. Paragraphs should evaluate the emotional issue and tell how the book might be helpful.
6. Reports will vary, but should discuss the differences between REM and NREM sleep.

## Focus

### Bell Ringer Activity

**Being Fair**

Ask five students to perform a brief skit for the class, in which, they decide who will go first when playing a game by "counting out." For example, they may recite the rhyme "eeny, meeny, miney, mo . . ." Ask the class: Why are games like this important to a child's social development? (They are built around the ideas of fairness and taking turns.)

## Preteaching

### Vocabulary

Ask students: What does the word *parallel* mean in mathematics? How might this meaning help you determine the definition of parallel play? (In mathematics, parallel means "not intersecting," and in parallel play, children do not interact with one another.)

### Graphic Organizer

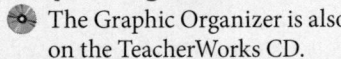 The Graphic Organizer is also on the TeacherWorks CD.

(Graphic organizers should include: Set limits by explaining the limit, acknowledging the child's feelings, and giving alternatives. Encourage independence by letting the child feed himself, and help dress and bathe himself. Promote sharing by engaging children in activities that require sharing. Deal with aggression by determining the cause and making it clear that the behavior is unacceptable.)

 **NCLB** connects academic correlations to book content.

## Reading Guide

### Before You Read

**Prefixes** Prefixes can help you determine a word's meaning. The prefix *co-* provides a clue to the meaning of *cooperation*. As you read, look for words with prefixes and check their meanings in a dictionary.

### Read to Learn
#### Key Concepts
- **Compare and contrast** parallel play and cooperative play.
- **List** six ways to help children develop social skills.
- **Explain** the purpose of guidance.

#### Main Idea
Children learn to get along with others through a process called *socialization*. They begin to make friends and deal with conflict. With adult guidance, they gradually achieve self-discipline.

#### Content Vocabulary
◇ socialization
◇ parallel play
◇ cooperative play
◇ self-discipline
◇ autonomy
◇ time-out

 **Graphic Organizer** Go to this book's Online Learning Center at **glencoe.com** to print out this graphic organizer.

### Academic Vocabulary
You will find these words in your reading and on your tests. Use the glossary to look up their definitions if necessary.
■ gauge
■ distraction

### Graphic Organizer
As you read, look for ways to guide behavior. Note a brief description of each approach. Use a chart like the one shown to help organize your information. Add additional circles as needed.

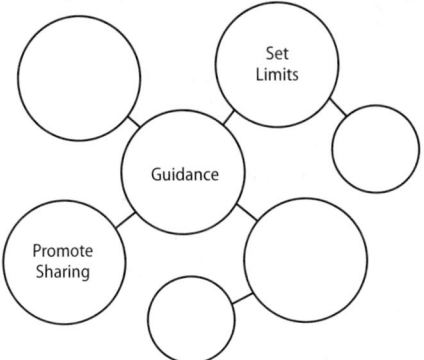

## Academic Standards

 **English Language Arts**
**NCTE 4** Use written language to communicate effectively.

 **Social Studies**
**NCSS I A Culture** Analyze and explain the ways groups, societies, and cultures address human needs and concerns.

**NCTE** *National Council of Teachers of English*
**NCTM** *National Council of Teachers of Mathematics*

**NSES** *National Science Education Standards*
**NCSS** *National Council for the Social Studies*

## Reading Guide

### Before You Read
Ask students: Who was your first friend? Why were you friends? What activities and games did you play together? Discuss that developing friendships with peers is an important part of socialization.

###  Develop Concepts

**Main Idea** Discuss the main idea with the students. Ask students: Why is it important to always keep children's ages in mind when determining how they should act in specific social situations?

## General Social Patterns

Young children gradually learn how to get along with other people. They first learn how to get along with members of their own families, and then with people in other groups. The process of learning to get along with others is called **socialization**. These social skills will stay with them throughout their lives. Through socialization, children can be expected to learn various social skills by certain ages, as seen in **Figure 11.2** on page 337. Of course, as with other areas of development, individual differences may influence when, and in what order, social skills are learned. If parents are concerned about a child's development, they should talk to their pediatrician.

## Eighteen Months

Children usually begin developing some independence from the family unit by eighteen months of age. For most children, the closest relationships continue to be those with their families. However, toddlers need to learn about the outside world. This may mean trips to the playground or other opportunities to be with children and adults who are not part of the family, such as at child care centers.

Children at this age do not really interact with one another much, even when they are playing in the same area. Instead, children engage in parallel play. **Parallel play** is when children play near, but not actually with, other children. Each child plays independently. Two or more children may reach for the same toy, but the children are not really interacting with one another.

At eighteen months, toddlers often seem to treat other people more as objects than as human beings. At this stage, the toddler is intent on satisfying strong desires without regard for the person who interferes. There may be conflicts over toys that result in screaming, hitting, biting, or hair pulling. Suppose Billy really wants a certain truck, but Keith is playing with it. Billy might hit Keith to try and get the truck.

Children of this age can understand that their actions have consequences for others. However, this understanding is limited to actions that have direct, immediate, and physical results. For

**Toddlers at Play**
At eighteen months, toddlers will play in the same area, but they will not play together. *What kind of play is this called?*

## Teach

### Discussion Starter

**Encouraging Social Development** Write on the board "Do to others as you would have them do to you." Ask for volunteers to rephrase this statement, for example as "treat others as you want to be treated." Discuss that this philosophy is common around the world in many different cultures. Ask students to describe ways in which parents can promote this kind of thinking in a two- or three-year-old. (Responses will vary, but may include learning to take turns, sharing, and always treating others with kindness.)

### C Critical Thinking

**Make Judgments** Ask Students: Do you think socialization is more important in a democracy or in a society that has an authoritarian form of government? Why? (Student answers will vary, but students should provide reasons for their answers. Possible answer: In a democracy, because everyone is expected to be involved in creating the government and in working toward acceptable compromises.)

### R Reading Strategy

**Take Notes** Ask students what the word *succinct* means (to the point). Instruct students to take succinct notes as they read the text under the Eighteen Months heading. When done, have them compare notes with a partner and determine whose notes were more succinct.

## ➤ Explore the Photo

**Caption Answer** It is called parallel play.

**Discussion** Have students discuss what this girl might be learning from this boy even though she is not directly interacting with him. Emphasize that even though children may not be directly interacting, they are still watching one another. (She might be learning how he manipulates the truck and what kinds of tasks he performs with it, such as loading sand and then dumping it back out.)

## W Writing Support

### Persuasive Paragraph

**Child Care Centers** Have half of the class work individually to write persuasive paragraphs about how experiences at a child care center help two-year-olds develop social skills. Ask the other half of the class to write persuasive paragraphs that say children should be with a parent or primary caregiver until they are at least three years old. Ask for volunteers to share their viewpoints with the class. As an alternative, have the students use their paragraphs to stage a debate. (Paragraphs will vary. Students should offer logical, persuasive arguments for their viewpoints.)

**Professional Development**

### Mini Clip
Reading: Extending the Big Idea

A teacher assigns group collaborations and consensus building to promote student discussions about a reading selection.

## C₁ Critical Thinking

**Make Decisions** Describe the following scenario: Your sister has asked your two-and-one-half-year-old to be flower girl at her wedding. Unfortunately, your child is going through a period of negativism. Write a letter to your sister responding to her offer. (Letters will vary. Possible response: You might explain to your sister that while you are flattered by the offer, you feel that your child is not socially mature enough to handle the situation, and might cause difficulties during the ceremony.)

→ **Cooperative Play**
By the age of three, children engage in cooperative play. *What type of strategies do children use to resolve conflicts when playing together?*

example, eighteen-month-old Jill hits Rachel. Rachel cries. Jill can see the immediate result her action caused.

## Two Years

By age two, children have begun to develop an impressive list of social skills. Two-year-olds are especially good at understanding and interacting with their main caregivers. Children can read their caregiver's moods and **gauge**, or judge, what kind of behavior the caregiver is likely to accept. As their speech abilities develop, toddlers are increasingly able to communicate with others.

Two-year-olds have fun playing with someone else, though they usually continue to engage in parallel play. At two, they start to understand the idea of sharing or taking turns. Children this age like to please other people. Occasionally, they are willing to put the wishes of someone else (usually an adult) above their own wishes.

## Two and One-Half Years

The negativism that characterizes the emotional development of the child at age two and one-half carries over into the child's social relationships. During this stage, a child may refuse

to do anything at all for one person, while happily doing almost anything another person asks. This can be especially frustrating if the child refuses to listen to a parent or caregiver.

At this age, children are beginning to learn about the rights of others. They begin responding to the idea of fairness, although at first they are more concerned with what is fair to them. Social play is still parallel and works best with only two children. There are frequent, but brief, squabbles during play. Children generally forget them quickly though.

## Three Years

People become important to children of this age. A three-year-old will share, help, or do things another person's way just to please someone.

Three-year-olds begin to engage in cooperative play. **Cooperative play** is a type of play in which children play and interact with one another. They build sand castles together, push toy tractors down the same roads, and park their toy cars side by side in the same area. They also can work together in small groups to build with blocks, act out events for doll families, and fit puzzles together.

Parents or other main caregivers are still very important to three-year-olds, but they are no longer all-powerful in the children's social

⟩ **Explore the Photo**

**Caption Answer** They may learn to share or they may ignore one another.

**Discussion** Ask students how learning to play cooperatively might help these preschoolers when they later reach high school. Encourage students to give specific examples. (Examples might include they will be better prepared to play team sports and to work on team projects for classes.)

lives. Most toddlers of this age seek friends on their own. They also may prefer some children over others as friends.

## Three and One-Half Years

By age three and one-half, children's play becomes more complex and includes more conversation. Disagreements with playmates occur less often. Because children this age enjoy the company of others, they realize they must share toys and accept some things they do not like in order to get along with friends.

At three and one-half, children can use several different strategies to resolve conflicts. Esteban tried to take a block that was behind Ramon, who was also playing with blocks. When Ramon said, "That's my block," Esteban replied, "Oh, okay," and put it down. Kelly and Rosa were playing with cars. When Kelly reached for Rosa's yellow car, Rosa objected and then said "You can have it if you give me that red one of yours."

Children this age show an increasing ability to evaluate friendships. For example, a child may say, "I don't like to have Kevin come here. He doesn't play nice." Children who are closer friends begin to exclude others. A child may become jealous and not want to "share" a friend with other children.

At this age, children also take more notice of what others are like. They become more likely to compare themselves to other children. The comparison is not always to their own advantage. One day, Allison asked her mother, "Why does Libby always win when we race?" Her mother agreed that Libby was faster but also pointed out things that Allison did well. In this way, she acknowledged that Allison was not as skilled as Libby in one area but had other skills of her own.

**✓ Reading Check** **Compare** Describe the social development of a child who just turned two. How does it differ from that of a child six months older?

**Figure 11.2** **Social Developmental Milestones—Ages 1–3**

Children begin engaging in cooperative play and sharing when they are about three years old. *How do you think a child's social development reflects the child's emotional development?*

| Age | Developmental Milestones |
|---|---|
| 1 Year | ❖ Plays alone but often near others<br>❖ Dislikes sharing toys<br>❖ Desires approval<br>❖ Fears some strangers |
| 2 Years | ❖ Engages in parallel play<br>❖ Plays simple games with others<br>❖ Bosses other children<br>❖ Says "please" if prompted |
| 3 Years | ❖ Engages in some cooperative play<br>❖ Takes turns<br>❖ Likes to help<br>❖ Shows affection |

Section 11.2 Social Development from One to Three **337**

**Figure 11.2** **Social Developmental Milestones—Ages 1–3**

**Caption Answer** The more emotionally secure and empathic the child is, the more the child will be able to reach out to others socially, for example by sharing.

**Discussion** Ask students: Why do you think children are not capable of engaging in cooperative play until they are about three years old? What emotional skills are needed for cooperative play? (The child must have the ability to see the world from others' points of view and a sense of fairness in order to engage in the give-and-take of cooperative play.)

## Teach cont.

### U Universal Access

**Kinesthetic Learners** Ask students if they remember any rhymes they recited as youngsters that involve performing hand movements with a partner. A popular example is "Peas Porridge Hot." Have students demonstrate several games with which they are familiar. Encourage any students from other cultures to share their rhymes. Ask: What do children gain from these activities? (Possible answers: They develop motor skills, a sense of rhythm, and learn to work cooperatively.) **ELL**

### C₂ Critical Thinking

**Extrapolate** Ask students to share examples of situations in which they felt they were treated unfairly. Ask: How did this treatment make you feel? Do you think being treated fairly is as important to young children as it is to you? (Answers will vary. Young children are very sensitive to unfair treatment and can become extremely upset if they feel another child has taken their toy or not let them have their turn.)

**✓ Reading Check**

**Compare** Two-year-olds can understand and interact with caregivers and are beginning to communicate with others. They begin to understand the idea of sharing, like to please others, and usually engage in parallel play. Two-and-one-half-year-olds begin to develop negativism and may be less cooperative than a younger child. While they begin to understand fairness, they often apply it only to themselves.

### S Skill Practice

**Guided Practice**

**Give Examples** Organize students into small groups. Assign each group one of the bulleted points under Social Skills. Students should then create a skit illustrating the social skill they were assigned. Have students present their skits to the class. (Skits will vary but should illustrate the social skill assigned to the group.) **L1 ELL**

**Make a Picture Book** Have students write an illustrated book aimed at helping preschoolers learn social skills. Encourage students to create colorful drawings that will attract the attention of young children. Each book should cover at least three of the items listed under Social Skills. (Students should create illustrated books explaining at least three of the social skills.) **L2 ELL**

**Produce a Television Show** Organize students into groups of five or six. Each group should have a moderator, a child development expert, and a group of parents of young children. They should suppose they are producing a television show with the topic, "Helping Preschoolers Develop Social Skills." The parents should ask questions of the child development expert, who then appropriately answers each question. Have each group present its television show to the class. (Students should present a television show that answers questions on how to help preschoolers develop social skills.) **L3 ELL**

---

{ **Expert Advice...** }

*"Your preschool child is positively asking you to tell him what does and does not earn approval, so he is ready to learn any social refinement of being human which you will teach him . . . He knows now that he wants your love and he has learned how to ask for it."*

— Penelope Leach, child development specialist and author, *Your Baby and Child*

## Making Friends

The ability to make friends is important to normal social development. A child who is comfortable and friendly with others and who has at least one friend is usually developing normally. However, if a child is unable or unwilling to make friends, it is important to discover the cause and take steps to help. For example, a shy child sometimes needs coaching on what to say or how to act so that he or she can join others in play.

Even very young children need contact with other people. This is how they learn the give-and-take of socializing. Children who begin to play with others at the age of one or two are less likely to be afraid in these early social situations. They learn to cope with the occasional punches and toy snatching of other one- and two-year-olds.

When young children spend almost all of their time with adults, they may have difficulty interacting with others their own age. Adults are more polite and considerate than children. Children need to learn to enjoy the rough-and-tumble friendship of other children. If this learning is delayed until school age, the adjustment is more difficult. A five- or six-year-old's feelings are more easily hurt.

All children sometimes have disagreements and arguments. Whether or not a caregiver should step in depends on the situation.

If two children are relatively evenly matched and there is no physical or emotional harm being done, the caregiver can simply observe the situation. Children need to learn how to solve social problems on their own. If it looks as though someone might get hurt, the caregiver needs to help the children solve the problem. It is best for the children if the caregiver does not impose a solution but instead guides the children to find one for themselves.

## Social Skills

Knowing how to get along with others is key to success and happiness. This ability depends upon social skills. Here are some ways to help children develop social skills:

- **Establish a basic set of rules to guide social behavior.** The rules will probably center on teaching respect for self, for others, and for things. For example, "No throwing toys." "Don't hit people."
- **Model good social skills.** Children are great imitators. They learn best by being shown what to do rather than by just being told. For instance, parents who talk politely to others are more likely to get their children to do so.
- **Help children understand and respect others' feelings.** You might show a child pictures of people's faces with a variety of expressions. Ask the child to guess how the person in the picture might be feeling, such as sad or angry. Talking about what these feelings mean can help the child develop empathy. Also, talk to the child about how you are feeling.
- **Show respect for other people's belongings.** Tell a child, for example, not to touch grandma's flower vase, because it might get broken. This would make grandma very sad.
- **Show children how to use words rather than physically striking out.** Explain how using appropriate words when they are angry is better than hitting or shoving.
- **Help children learn specific social skills.** Demonstrate how to share a toy, wait for a turn, and be kind to one another.

**S**

**Mc Graw Hill Professional Development**

**Mini Clip**
**Reading: On Workshops**

Doug Fisher, PhD, author and educator, discusses the Workshop Approach to teaching.

### RESPOND TO SPECIAL NEEDS
### Antisocial Personality Disorder

### RESPOND TO SPECIAL NEEDS
### Antisocial Personality Disorder

Many children do things such as biting and kicking other children that catch their parents and caregivers off guard. Occasionally, these behaviors go beyond what is considered normal. Some children never develop empathy. They consistently ignore the feelings and rights of others.

When this behavior is extreme, the child may be diagnosed with antisocial personality disorder. This is a serious psychiatric condition. Because individuals typically start showing signs of antisocial personality disorder in childhood, here are some signs caregivers should watch for:

- Is cruel to animals
- Sets fires
- Fights with other children much more frequently than others of that age
- Shows no concern when others are sad or hurt

Children with these symptoms need to be evaluated by a mental health professional. If they are diagnosed with antisocial personality disorder, treatment should begin as early as possible. Both medication and psychotherapy may be used to aid the child's social and emotional development.

> **Critical Thinking** Conduct research to find out what mental health professionals believe causes antisocial personality disorder. Create an oral presentation discussing what you learned. Conclude by explaining what you think can be done to reduce its occurrence.

## Imaginary Friends

Many toddlers begin to have imaginary friends. Some keep the same imaginary friend for a long time. It can last from several months to a year. Others have several different imaginary friends. Some toddlers have imaginary animals as friends. Some even have dragons or other imaginary creatures as friends. All of these are normal.

Imaginary friends may appear in a toddler's imagination as early as age two. These friends are even more common when a child is between ages three and four. This is when children have rich imaginations and are interested in fantasy.

Some parents worry that their child invents imaginary friends because he or she is unable to make real friends. They are concerned that an imaginary friend is a sign of unhappiness or problems coping with life. In fact, an imaginary friend helps a child experiment with different feelings. Some children use an imaginary friend as a way of working through their negative feelings. For others, the friend mirrors everything the child does or experiences. The child may then talk to the family about how the imaginary friend felt about these experiences. In this way, children can examine their own thoughts and feelings.

Imaginary friends usually fade away. Crystal simply stopped talking about her imaginary friend when she started school. Paul had an imaginary friend when he was three, but the friend was gone by the time Paul turned four. There is no cause for concern unless the child continues to talk to an imaginary friend after about age six. If a parent is concerned, a pediatrician or counselor may be able to help.

> ✓ **Reading Check** **Infer** What may happen to the social development of children who spend most of their time with adults?

## Teach cont.

### U Universal Access

**Musical Learners** Organize students into groups of two or three. Instruct each group to create a song about an imaginary friend. The song might talk about what the friend looks like or what games they play with the friend. Students may wish to set the song to a familiar childhood melody or write their own original music. Students may also develop hand gestures to accompany the song. Encourage volunteers to perform their song for the class. (Songs will vary. Students should be creative in their lyrics.) **ELL**

### C Critical Thinking

**Infer** Tell students that research has shown that children who regularly engage in imaginative play are likely to be better problem solvers than those who do not. Ask students why they think this might be. (Possible answer: Students who engage in imaginative play may look at problems in more creative ways and therefore may be more resourceful in coming up with possible solutions.)

### ✓ Reading Check

**Infer** They may have difficulty interacting with children their own age. Because adults tend to be more polite and giving, children will not learn how to stand up for themselves.

### RESPOND TO SPECIAL NEEDS
### Antisocial Personality Disorder

**Discussion** Ask students: What would you do if you were a preschool teacher and were concerned that a child in your class was being deliberately cruel to animals? (Possible answer: The teacher should suggest that the child be evaluated by a mental health professional. The teacher should emphasize to the child, and any other children who may have heard the child talking, that this behavior is wrong.)

> **Critical Thinking** Presentations will vary but should explain that the condition is more common in neglectful or abusive homes. Students may suggest that these children be placed in special facilities to receive more individual attention.

## Assess

### Quiz

Ask students to answer the following questions:

1. How does negativism affect the social relationships of two-and-one-half-year-olds? (They may refuse to do things for one person, but happily do them for another person.)

2. Why do disagreements with playmates become less common when a child reaches three and one-half? (Children learn that they must share and be cooperative if they want to get along with others who are their age.)

3. What is an important reason that children may have imaginary friends? (The imaginary friend may allow the child to experiment with different feelings and help the child work through negative feelings.)

## Reteach

### U₁ Universal Access

**Gifted Learners** Explain to students that American psychologist Lawrence Kohlberg divided the development of moral standards in children into three distinct stages. Have students conduct research to learn more about Kohlberg's research on moral development. Students then should write a research paper on what they learn. (Students should write a paper discussing Kohlberg's research on development of moral standards in children. Kohlberg divided moral development into preconventional, conventional, and post-conventional [or principled] stages.)

# Guiding Behavior

Guiding children's behavior does not simply mean making children behave and punishing them when they do something wrong. Punishment is only a small part of guidance. Guidance means using firmness and understanding to help children learn self-discipline. **Self-discipline** is the ability of children to control their own behavior. Effective guidance helps children learn to get along with others and to handle their own feelings. It promotes security and a positive feeling about self.

Guidance also helps children with moral development. Very young children understand right from wrong only in terms of being praised or scolded. Gradually, children develop a conscience, or an inner sense of what is right. As children mature, they use their conscience to act morally when facing new situations.

## Approaches by Age

Effective guidance depends upon a child's age as well as emotional and social development. There is no one best approach to guidance.

Caregivers need to consider the unique personality of each child, as well as each child's age, stage of development, and ability to understand. Different approaches may be more or less effective at various ages. Parents may also need to use different approaches with each sibling.

Being consistent is a major factor in guiding children's behavior. Make clear rules and apply them in the same way in all situations. Consistency helps children know what is expected of them and what responses they can expect from caregivers. Consistency is especially important when more than one person cares for a child. Parents and other caregivers need to agree on rules and ways to enforce them.

### One Year to Fifteen Months

Distracting children and physically removing them from forbidden activities or places works best for this age. This is because they cannot yet understand adult reasoning. For example, Kareem tried to follow the lawn mower around the yard when his brother was cutting the grass. His older sister picked Kareem up and took him into the house, saying, "Let's see if we can find the book about the bear."

**Offer Guidance**
Preschoolers begin to understand adult reasoning and more readily accept guidance. *What is a major goal in guiding a child's behavior?*

## ▶ Explore the Photo

**Caption Answer** Teaching self-discipline is the main goal in guiding a child's behavior.

**Discussion** Ask: How is guiding an eighteen-month-old's behavior different from guiding a three-year-old's behavior? (An eighteen-month-old only reacts to whether he or she is being praised or scolded, whereas a three-year-old can begin learning to have an inner sense of right and wrong.)

### What Would You Do?

#### Sharing

Madison and Morgan are sisters and love to play together. Madison is two and Morgan is three. Because they are so close in age, they share everything, from a bedroom to clothes to toys. Madison gets clothes and toys that her sister has outgrown, which is fine with her. She is delighted when she can finally call a toy her own. This can create a problem, however. Sometimes if Madison is playing with a toy that once belonged to Morgan, Morgan wants it back. She tries to snatch it away from her little sister. While both girls have difficulty sharing, Morgan is better able to understand the concept of taking turns. But for two-year-old Madison, if someone else is playing with her toy, she cries until it is returned to her. Morgan, however, has learned about sharing at preschool, where she must share things with eleven other children.

*Write About It* Imagine that you are these two girls' parent. Write a paragraph describing a situation where Morgan has grabbed a toy that used to belong to her. What might you say to Morgan to help her understand Madison's point of view?

#### Fifteen Months to Two Years

Children this age require spoken restrictions as well as a **distraction**, or diversion. Lee began playing with toy cars on the driveway. His father took him by the hand and said, "Let's take your cars into the backyard. You'll have more room there. The driveway isn't a safe place to play." His father removed him from the dangerous place, but also told him why. Lee may have to be reminded of the restriction a few times, but will eventually understand it.

#### Two to Three Years

By the age of two, children are usually able to understand spoken commands and simple explanations. Two-year-olds can begin to grasp the reasoning of adults. Caregivers who explain their reasons to children over age two get better results than those who only issue commands. When Kerri's mother saw that the two-and-one-half-year-old was still not dressed, she said, "Kerri, you need to get dressed now because Grandma will be here soon to go shopping with us. We can't go unless we are ready. Do you need any help?"

#### Three Years

Three-year-olds accept reasonable, loving guidance more readily than children of other ages. They like to please, and they may be quick to remind a parent that they are obedient. Marcus came inside on a rainy day and said, "I remembered to wear my boots today. See my clean shoes? I'm a good boy, right?"

### Set Limits

Parents can help children learn self-regulation and self-discipline by setting and enforcing limits. Setting limits is another way of guiding children toward appropriate, safe behavior. When parents and caregivers set limits, it helps children begin to set limits for themselves.

Make sure you state limits clearly. Telling three-year-old Kyle that he can have a small snack does not set a clear limit. Kyle is not old enough to decide what makes a snack big or small. A better way to state the limit would be, "You can have either an apple or a banana." Speak in a calm, direct tone of voice to indicate that the limit is real and should be respected.

Setting limits includes four steps. Here is how a caregiver might set limits about where a toddler can draw pictures:

1. **Show an understanding of the child's desire.** "I know you think it's fun to draw on the wall."
2. **Set the limit and explain it.** "But you may not draw on the wall because it's hard to clean crayon marks off the wall."
3. **Acknowledge the child's feelings.** "I know you like drawing on the wall, but walls are not for drawing."
4. **Give alternatives.** If possible, give the child a chance to continue the same activity in an acceptable way. "If you want to draw, you may draw on this paper. Or you can play with your blocks. Which do you want to do?"

#### U₂ Universal Access

**Verbal Learners** Have students locate a television show in which an adult attempts to guide the behavior of a young child. (Alternatively, you may wish to supply a video.) After students have watched the show, have them write a paragraph evaluating how well they think the adult handled the situation. Instruct them to discuss whether they might have handled the situation differently. (Paragraphs will vary but should evaluate how well the adult guided the child's behavior.)

#### R Reading Strategy

**Use Your Own Words** Discuss that one of the best ways to determine whether you understand a statement or idea is to rephrase it in your own words. Have students work independently to rewrite, in their own words, each of the four items listed under Set Limits. For example, number 4 might be rewritten as "Give the child an idea of a similar activity they can do." (Students should rewrite in their own words each of the four items listed under Set Limits.)

**Mc Graw Hill Professional Development**

**Mini Clip Reading: Fluency Development**

A teacher uses three different instructional strategies to help develop her students' reading fluency.

### What Would You Do?

**Write About It** Paragraphs will vary but should offer an appropriate response by the parent. The parent might tell Morgan that she understands Morgan's feelings, but now Morgan has toys for older children and it is Madison's turn to have the toys that are for younger children.

**R Reading Strategy**

**Examples** Discuss that authors often expand on their main ideas by providing specific examples. Have students work individually to determine the main idea of the section titled Encourage Independence. They then should create a list of the examples the author provides that relate to this main idea. When done, ask for volunteers to read their lists to the class. (The main idea is: "Caregivers can help young children in their strive for independence." Details include: Caregivers can help by supplying appropriate eating utensils, teaching children to dress themselves, providing appropriate grooming supplies, and teaching children to perform simple household tasks.)

**C1 Critical Thinking**

**Contrast** Have students work independently to write a description of how autonomy for a two-year-old differs from autonomy for a sixteen-year-old. Discuss the various descriptions as a class. (Students' descriptions should indicate that sixteen-year-olds are capable of performing much more complex tasks and are given much more freedom than a two-year-old. Autonomy for a two-year-old might involve going up and down stairs and feeding herself, whereas for a sixteen-year-old it might include having a part-time job and driving a car.)

It is important to firmly and consistently enforce limits once they are set. If children beg to go beyond the limits and parents give in, the parents teach the children that they do not mean what they say. Parents who enforce limits strictly at some times and not at all at other times send an inconsistent message. Children are more likely to take rules seriously if the rules remain in force at all times.

## Encourage Independence

"Me do it! Me do it!" insisted two-year-old Justine when her mother tried to pull socks over Justine's feet. Children ages one through three want more autonomy. **Autonomy** means independence. They want to be able to do things for themselves, including bathing, dressing, and eating. Caregivers can help young children achieve some independence. The caregiver still bears the main responsibility of meeting a young child's basic needs though.

It is important to have realistic expectations of what a child can do at a certain age. When a child begins learning to self-feed, the process will be messy. Using unbreakable dishes, a child-size spoon and fork, and a cup with a spill-proof lid will minimize the mess. Give the child small servings of food that are cut into bite-size pieces and are easy to handle.

When teaching toddlers how to dress themselves, choose clothes that are easy to put on and take off. Look for pants, skirts, and shorts with elastic waistbands and roomy tops that fasten in the front. Fasteners can cause problems for little fingers. Hook-and-loop fasteners, large buttons, and zippers are easiest for toddlers to manage. Learning to get dressed requires a whole set of skills. Let the child begin by helping with pulling up a zipper or slipping a foot into a shoe.

Providing toddlers with their own towel, washcloth, brush or comb, and toothbrush can encourage independence in staying clean and neat. These items should be within the child's reach. A step stool can help a child cope with an adult-size bathroom. Then set up and follow daily routines that include bathing, brushing teeth, combing hair, and washing hands before eating.

During this age span children can begin to help with simple household tasks. Putting toys away can start as a picking-up game. Also, let toddlers and preschoolers help you with simple chores, such as sweeping, sorting and folding laundry, and setting the table. Devon felt like a big boy because he could match all the socks when his dad did the laundry. Three-year-old Laura enjoyed wiping off the table after mealtime.

Remember to be patient. Encourage but do not force a young toddler to do too much. A child's efforts will always be slower and less efficient than your own. Jelly may get smeared on the table, shorts put on backwards, and tops fastened wrong. Learning self-help skills increases confidence and independence. However, skills cannot be learned without lots of practice.

**↑ Meal Time**
Toddlers learning to feed themselves are apt to be messy eaters at first. *What steps can a caregiver take to make the process less messy?*

## ► Explore the Photo

**Caption Answer** Cut food into small pieces and use unbreakable dishes, a child-size spoon and fork, and a training cup to make mealtime less messy.

**Discussion** Tell students to suppose that they are taking their eighteen-month-old to his great-grandmother's house for dinner. What might they do to make the experience more pleasant? (Possible answers: Take appropriate dishes and a bib. Parents also might consider taking a portable high chair and a piece of plastic to place under the chair.)

## Promote Sharing

How to share is one of the first social skills that toddlers should learn. Here are some ways to help them develop this skill:

- Engage children in activities that require them to share, such as playing on a see-saw.
- Place them in situations where they must take turns, such as going down a slide.
- Limit the materials available for an activity so that children have to share or take turns. For example, when making paper crafts, provide only one pair of scissors and one glue stick so the children will have to share.
- Have children take turns handing out snacks. Parents can let siblings take turns choosing a game or movie for family night.
- Make clear what behavior you are trying to encourage. Call it sharing or taking turns.
- Recognize and praise a child when they share or take turns. "Thank you for letting Joy have some of your crackers. That was very nice."

Not all sharing experiences are equal for a child. For example, a child may have a strong emotional attachment to a stuffed animal or be very happy with a new birthday toy. It can be much more difficult for the child to share these things than to take turns using scissors. If there is a reason not to share something, it is best to put it away when other children are around.

Parents of an only child should be sure to give their child opportunities to learn sharing. An only child who attends child care or play groups will quickly gain experience sharing and taking turns. It is also important for the adults and older siblings in children's lives to demonstrate and model sharing behavior.

## Deal with Aggressive Behavior

Children at times behave in ways that are far different from their normal behavior. An easy-going child may become aggressive. The child might start kicking, biting, or hitting other children. Behavioral problems among children ages one to three are quite common. There is almost always a reason for the disruptive behavior.

## Parenting Skills

### Handling Tantrums

Toddlers may have tantrums when they are tired or frustrated. Giving in to tantrums teaches toddlers how to get their way. It also makes children more likely to have tantrums. Here are some ways to deal with tantrums:

- If a tantrum is about to begin, try to avoid it. Distract the child with a toy or by pointing out an activity going on elsewhere.
- If a child has a tantrum at home, try ignoring it.
- If a child has a tantrum in public, take the child to a quiet spot to cool down.
- Always remain calm and speak quietly yet firmly.
- Acknowledge the child's feelings and restate why the child's demands cannot be met.
- Adhere to set limits.
- Keep toddlers from hurting themselves or others.
- Once the tantrum is over, praise the child for calming down.

**Take Charge** Along with a partner, create a skit about how you would handle a two-year-old having a temper tantrum at the mall.

## Reteach *cont.*

### W Writing Support
**Poem**

**Sharing** Explain that a haiku is a traditional form of Japanese poetry containing unrhymed lines of five, seven, and five syllables. Instruct students to write a haiku on the importance of sharing. Ask for volunteers to read their haiku to the class. (Refer to p. 318 to review tips on writing poetry. Students should write a haiku on the importance of sharing.)

### C₂ Critical Thinking

**Plan** Read this scenario and have students discuss ways to address the problem: Two-and-one-half-year-old Elijah, an only child, has a play date coming up at his house with two other children. His mother knows he is possessive about his toys. What can she do ahead of time to avoid conflict between Elijah and the other children? (Possible answer: She can discuss with Elijah the importance of sharing. She then can ask if there are any special toys he wants to put in a closet so that the other children will not be able to play with them.)

## Parenting Skills

### Handling Tantrums

Ask for volunteers to answer the question: What do you think is the worst way that a parent can respond to a temper tantrum? Why? (Responses will vary. Some people think that the worst response is to give in to the child because this will encourage the child to behave in the same way in the future.)

**Take Charge**
Students should write a skit with dialogue describing how they would respond to the child. Students might calmly and firmly state that they understand that the child wants to get his way, but cannot. Students may want to try distracting the child. If that does not work, they should leave the mall.

## C Critical Thinking

**Appraise** Describe a scenario in which a caregiver turns around to see three-year-old James kicking Juanita in the leg. Ask: What should be the first thing that the caregiver does? Why? (Answers will vary. The first step should be to try to determine why James kicked Juanita. Perhaps James has had a difficult morning or is not feeling well. Or perhaps Juanita pushed James when the caregiver was not looking. Attempting to determine the cause of aggressive behavior can help the caregiver in determining how to handle the situation.)

## U Universal Access

**Gifted Learners** Tell students that after the huge spurt in synapse development of infancy, a two-year-old has a cerebral cortex with at least a hundred trillion synapses. However, the center of the brain that controls impulses develops later than those parts that control sensory functions such as vision. Instruct students to conduct research to learn more about the development of impulse control in young children. Have students prepare an oral presentation on what they learn. Encourage them to prepare illustrations to accompany the presentation. (Students should conduct research on how impulse control develops in young children and prepare an oral presentation on this topic.)

**↑ Share with Others**
Caregivers can help children learn social skills to help them be happy and successful. *What are some ways that caregivers can teach children to share?*

Behavior is a form of communication. Inappropriate or aggressive behavior says that a child is upset or that some need is not being met. Young children can have a hard time using words to explain their feelings. Two-year-old Austin was jealous of his sister getting new toys for her birthday. Since Austin could not express his feelings with words, he started throwing toys. His parents realized why Austin was acting this way and calmly explained that he would have a birthday soon and get new toys too. On the other hand, sometimes children misbehave just because they enjoy the sensation. For example, Alex might repeatedly kick a table leg.

Caregivers need to look for and understand the problem behind aggressive or otherwise inappropriate behavior. Finding the cause of the behavioral problems can go a long way toward changing the behavior.

### Biting

Marguerite was shocked when her two-year-old son ran up and bit her on the arm. He bit hard enough to leave a bruise.

It is not uncommon for young children to bite, and they bite for different reasons at different ages. Infants may bite because they fail to see any difference between chewing on a toy and chewing on a big brother or sister. One-year-olds may bite just to discover what happens when they do. Two- and three-year-olds may bite to get their way with other children or just to get attention. They may also bite when they are angry or frustrated.

Caregivers need to determine what is causing a child to bite. They can then take steps to guide the child toward more appropriate behavior. A teething baby, for example, can be given a teething ring or a soft cloth to bite on to relieve the discomfort of cutting teeth. A one-year-old needs to know biting is not okay and will not make his or her parents smile.

Wilson discovered his two-year-old daughter biting her brother in a fight over a toy wagon. He set her on his knee, looked directly into her eyes, and calmly but firmly told her, "Do not bite. Biting hurts your brother. It makes him cry."

---

## ••◗ Explore the Photo

**Caption Answer** A caregiver can try to engage children in activities that require sharing, limit materials for an activity so that children have to take turns, and make clear what behavior is appropriate.

**Discussion** Ask students: How do you think the girl in this photo is feeling? Why? (Responses will vary. She may be pleased with herself that she is making the boy happy by giving him something he wants.)

## Hitting, Kicking, and Shoving

Have you seen an adult react to a young child's aggressive behavior with anger? Unfortunately, this sends the message that anger and aggression are appropriate solutions to a problem.

Two- and three-year-olds have trouble controlling these impulses, or aggressive reactions to emotions and situations. At these ages, the part of the child's brain that controls impulses is not well developed. In addition, children are still very self-centered and concerned mainly with their own needs and desires. When something stops them from getting their needs met, they become angry or frustrated.

Hitting, kicking, and shoving are aggressive behaviors often seen in toddlers. Emma wanted a ball that Juan was playing with. Juan refused to let go, so Emma began hitting him.

Their preschool teacher intervened when Emma began to hit Juan. "I know that you want to play with the ball. I can see that it makes you angry when Juan will not give it up, but you must not hit people. Use words to tell Juan you are angry." The teacher then guided Emma toward some choices. "You can wait your turn to play with the ball, or you can color a picture. Which would you like to do?" At this age, it is still useful and sometimes necessary to offer a distraction. By suggesting Emma color a picture, the teacher gave Emma something besides the ball to focus on.

Many child development experts believe that time-outs are an effective way to help children understand that certain behaviors are not acceptable. A **time-out** is when a child is removed from the group, perhaps by being required to sit in a special chair for a short period of time. A time-out is another way of saying, "You cannot do that." A time-out can give a toddler time to calm down when they are upset.

---

## Assess

### Study Tools

Have students go to the Online Learning Center at **glencoe.com**:

- Take the **Practice Test**.
- Download **Study-to-Go** content.

Use the **Student Activity Workbook** for additional practice.

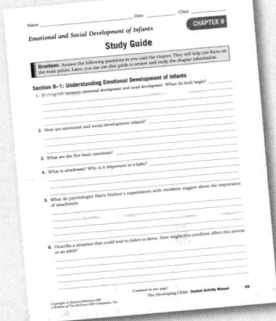

---

# Section 11.2    After You Read

### Review Key Concepts

1. **Explain** why it is important to give young children opportunities to play with friends.

2. **Compare and contrast** shoes with laces and shoes with Velcro fasteners. Which ones would you choose for a three-year-old? Why?

3. **Identify** two ways that parents can communicate to their children that they respect them.

### Practice Academic Skills

 **English Language Skills**

4. Write six negative statements that someone might say to a three-year-old child. Exchange papers with a partner. Turn each statement on the list into a more positive one that conveys the same message. Share your revised statements with the class.

> **NCTE 4** Use written language to communicate effectively.

 **Social Studies**

5. The Montessori method of early childhood education was developed in the early 1900s by educator Maria Montessori. Conduct research to learn how the Montessori method encourages positive socialization among children. Create an oral presentation on what you learn.

> **NCSS I A** Analyze and explain the ways groups, societies, and cultures address human needs and concerns.

**Check Your Answers** Check your answers at this book's Online Learning Center at **glencoe.com**.

**Section 11.2** Social Development from One to Three    **345**

---

## Close

### Culminating Activity

**Summarize** Ask students to describe the social skills of each age group discussed in this section. Write the skills on the board as a pyramid. At the bottom should be the most basic skills, with the more advanced ones near the top. Emphasize that these skills build on one another.

**NCLB** connects academic correlations to book content.

---

# Section 11.2    After You Read

### Review Key Concepts

1. Young children learn socialization skills, such as sharing and taking turns, showing affection, and handling disagreements when playing with friends.

2. The ones with Velcro fasteners would support the need for independence, because a three-year-old could fasten them himself.

3. Parents can listen to their children and tell them they understand how they feel.

### Practice Academic Skills

4. Each student should have written six negative statements. After switching papers, students should have rewritten each statement so that it expresses the same meaning, but in a positive way.

5. Presentations will vary. The Montessori method emphasizes the importance of recognizing individual initiative and differences, and encourages the performance of group tasks such as performing housekeeping chores. It stresses the importance of kindness and peacefulness.

# Speech-Language Pathologist

## Focus

### Discussion Starter

**Speech-Language Pathologist** Read this scenario: Matt was a second-grader who had a minor speech problem; he could not properly pronounce some words containing "T"s. For example, he said "lil" instead of "little." The speech-language pathologist worked with Matt twice a week. After five months, Matt's problem was corrected. Encourage students to share any similar experiences they may have had.

## Teach

### R Reading Strategy

**Determining a Word's Meaning** Ask students what they think the word *pathologist* means. Ask for a volunteer to read its definition from a dictionary. (a person who studies and diagnoses diseases) A speech-language pathologist determines what type of speech problem an individual has. It is vital to be able to understand the exact problem before work can begin on correcting it.

## Assess

### Make Connections

Ask students to list specific correlations between academic subjects and the skills a good speech-language pathologist needs. (Answers will vary. Students should show an understanding of how academic skills relate to a speech-language pathologist's job. For example, he or she must have an understanding of the therapies required for various speech problems.)

**NCLB** This relates academic skills to tasks that are performed for this job.

---

**R** **S**peech-language pathologists help people overcome difficulties in communicating. For example, some children have problems making certain sounds. Others struggle with speech rhythm difficulties, such as stuttering. Speech-language pathologists can help these children communicate more effectively.

### ☼ What Does a Speech-Language Pathologist Do?

Speech-language pathologists who work with children use special tests to find out each child's speech problem. Then they create a plan for working with that child. They teach sign language to children who cannot speak and help other children make sounds more clearly. They also advise parents on how to help their children practice speaking correctly.

### ☼ Where Do Speech-Language Pathologists Work?

Many speech-language pathologists work in elementary schools. Others have jobs in hospitals, private clinics, or nursing homes.

### Preparation and Skills

**Education and Training**

Speech-language pathologists must earn a master's degree and pass a national licensing exam. Then they must work a certain number of hours to become licensed. Specific requirements vary by state.

**Aptitudes, Abilities, and Skills**

Patience, optimism, excellent communication skills, and teaching ability are needed to excel in this career. Speech-language pathologists must also show a commitment to their client's care.

**Academic Skills**

A basic understanding of childhood development, an understanding of the physical aspects of speech, and knowledge of the appropriate therapies for different speech problems are required. Required courses cover anatomy and physiology, as well as psychological aspects of communication.

**NCLB**

**Explore Careers**
Research the work speech-language pathologists do in schools. How do they find out which students need help? What kinds of therapy are provided? Write a summary of what you learn.

**Careers Online** For more information on careers, visit the Occupational Outlook Handbook Web site through the link on this book's Online Learning Center at **glencoe.com**.

## Close

### Culminating Activity

**Stuttering** One common speech difficulty seen in children is stuttering. Have students research how a speech-language pathologist might help a child who faces this challenge, and then write a brief summary of the kinds of techniques used in treating it. (Students should write a brief summary of techniques used to help children who stutter.)

**Explore Careers**
They often receive references from others, such as classroom teachers and then conduct tests to determine each child's communication problems. They then create a detail plan of treatment for each child. Treatment will vary depending on the specific problem.

## Chapter Summary

Children go through a series of emotional stages. Each child develops emotionally in his or her own way, based on temperament and past experiences. With help, children learn to show empathy for others and to handle emotions such as anger and jealousy. Adequate sleep is critical to many areas of a child's development. The socialization process involves gradually developing social skills and learning to get along with others. Behavior needs to be guided by caregivers. With the caregivers' guidance, children begin to develop a conscience.

## Vocabulary Review

**1.** Arrange the vocabulary terms below into groups of related words. Explain why you put the words together.

### Content Vocabulary

◇ self-centered (p. 322)
◇ negativism (p. 322)
◇ temper tantrum (p. 324)
◇ phobia (p. 327)
◇ separation anxiety (p. 327)
◇ sibling rivalry (p. 328)
◇ empathy (p. 330)
◇ self-concept (p. 331)

◇ sleep-deprived (p. 332)
◇ REM sleep (p. 333)
◇ NREM sleep (p. 333)
◇ socialization (p. 335)
◇ parallel play (p. 335)
◇ cooperative play (p. 336)
◇ self-discipline (p. 340)

◇ autonomy (p. 342)
◇ time-out (p. 345)

### Academic Vocabulary

■ perceptive (p. 321)
■ adequate (p. 332)
■ gauge (p. 336)
■ distraction (p. 341)

## Review Key Concepts

**2. Identify** the factors that contribute to a child's emotional development.
**3. Describe** six specific emotions children ages eighteen months to three years show.
**4. List** the four signs of a healthy relationship between parents and a child.
**5. Identify** four ways to help children get adequate sleep.
**6. Compare and contrast** parallel play and cooperative play.
**7. List** six ways to help children develop social skills.
**8. Explain** the purpose of guidance.

## Critical Thinking

**9. Apply** What are two common behavioral problems? How would you deal with them in a three-year-old?
**10. Make Judgments** Eric is the father of two boys, ages three and four. To reduce fighting, he avoids situations in which the children must share. For example, if they are drawing, each child will have his own box of crayons. What do you think about Eric's plan for avoiding conflict?

**Chapter 11** Emotional and Social Development from One to Three **347**

## Content and Academic Vocabulary Review

**1.** Students should provide logical reasons for how they group the vocabulary terms.

## Review Key Concepts

**2.** Emotional development depends on the child's past experiences and individual differences in temperament.

**3.** Children this age feel anger, fear, jealousy, love, affection, and empathy.

**4.** child seeks parents' approval and praise; child turns to parents for comfort and help; child tells parents about significant events; and child accepts limits and discipline without too much resistance

**5.** Determine a child's best bedtime; limit toys in the bed; establish a bedtime routine; and keep bedtime pleasant.

**6.** Parallel play is when children play near one another, but do not interact. Cooperative play is when children interact with one another while playing.

**7.** Establish a basic set of rules to guide social behavior; model good social skills; help children understand and respect others' feelings; show respect for others' belongings; show children how to use words rather than physically striking out; and help children learn specific social skills.

**8.** The main purpose of guidance is to teach self-discipline.

## Critical Thinking

**9.** Answers will vary. With aggressive behavior, such as kicking, biting, or hitting, try to determine the cause and deal with it. Clearly state that the behavior is unacceptable. If a child refuses to obey limits, state that you understand the child's desires, but that they cannot always be met. Try to offer alternatives.

**10.** Answers will vary. Students may say that by avoiding putting the children in situations where they must share, he is keeping them from learning an important social skill.

## Family & Community Connections

**11.** Students should write a brief summary of the parent's opinions on violence in cartoons, and state whether the parent allows the child to watch these cartoons.

## Health Skills

**12.** Ads will vary. A person must have general nursing skills. In addition, he or she must be familiar with the social and emotional development of children and be able to spot any unusual or abnormal behaviors.

## Observation Skills

**13.** Answers will vary but the student should attempt to describe the child's feelings. For example, the child may have been tired or angry because the parent would not buy a specific toy.

## Real-Word Skills

**14.** Answers will vary. The student might begin by asking if the parents have noticed any changes in the child recently or if there have been any problems at home. Then the student might tell what they observed and suggest that the parents talk with an appropriate professional about it.

**15.** Presentations will vary, but should include the different stages of emotional development and explain the characteristics of each one.

**16.** Answers will vary. Typically, day care centers are more expensive than in-home day care.

**N C L B** Activity correlated to Social Studies standards.

## Family & Community Connection

**11. Cartoon Violence** Interview the parent of a young child concerning violence in cartoons. Ask specific questions, such as "Do you think the make-believe violence in some cartoons increases children's aggressive behavior towards others?" "Do you restrict your child's viewing of such cartoons?" Write a summary of the parent's responses.

## Health Skills

**12. Child Care Center Nurse** Imagine that a local child care center is looking for a nurse. Research the requirements to be a nurse at a child care center. What education is needed? What kinds of skills must the nurse have? How are these skills different from other nurses? Use what you learn to create a newspaper advertisement for the position.

## Observation Skills

**13. Analyzing Causes of Misbehavior** Young children often misbehave, even to the extent of having temper tantrums. But these tantrums happen for a reason. Examining the situation from the child's point of view can be helpful in identifying the causes.

**Procedure** Go to a public place where you can observe parents and children. Watch for children having temper tantrums. Record what you observe during one of these tantrums.

**Analysis** Based on your record, write a paragraph describing what you think might have led to the tantrum. How do you think the child was feeling? Be specific.

> **NCSS IV F Individual Development and Identity**
> Analyze the role of perceptions, attitudes, values, and beliefs in the development of personal identity.

**N C L B**

## Real-World Skills

| | |
|---|---|
| **Problem-Solving** | **14. Antisocial Behavior** A preschooler has begun to exhibit troubling behavior. She fights constantly with others and has no friends. She told a story about mistreating her puppy. What might you say to this child's parents? |
| **Technology Skills** | **15. Emotional Development** Suppose a parenting class teacher has asked you to create a presentation explaining the emotional stages of children ages one to three. Use software to create your presentation. Use illustrations where appropriate. Be sure your presentation looks good so it catches the attention of your audience. |
| **Financial Literacy** | **16. Child Care Costs** When choosing child care, parents must decide how to best meet their child's emotional and social needs. Most parents also must consider financial costs. Conduct research to learn about the cost of in-home child care as compared to child care centers. Create a chart comparing the costs. |

 **Additional Activities** For additional activities, go to this book's Online Learning Center at **glencoe.com**.

## Academic Skills

**17.** Summaries will vary. Erikson said that during this stage, children begin mastering skills such as talking and feeding themselves. They have the chance to build self-esteem and achieve greater autonomy as they learn to control their bodies. They also begin learning right from wrong.

The *Early Childhood Observations CD* offers additional lessons with videos to build students' observation skills.

**Part 1:** Learning to Observe
**Part 2:** How Children Develop
**Part 3:** Working With Young Children
**Part 4:** Extended Observations
**Part 5:** Resources and Answer File

# Academic Skills

### English Language Arts

**17. Eight Stages** Erik Erikson was a psycho-analyst who theorized that there are eight stages in a person's emotional and social development. The second stage involves children eighteen months to three years of age. Research the second stage of Erikson's theory and write a brief summary.

> **NCTE 3** Apply strategies to interpret texts.

### Mathematics

**18. Temper Tantrums** Children ages one to three tend to have temper tantrums because they cannot put their needs into words. Translate the following verbal statement about tantrums into an algebraic expression: Cathy and Robert's baby has twice as many temper tantrums per day than Scott and Betsy's baby.

> **Math Concept** **Algebraic Expressions** Algebraic expressions use variables as placeholders for changing value.

**Starting Hint** Assign a variable for Cathy and Robert's baby (x) and one for Scott and Betsy's baby (y).

**Math** For math help, go to the Math Appendix at the back of the book.

> **NCTM Algebra** Represent and analyze mathematical situations and structures using algebraic symbols.

### Science

**19. Young Children and Play** As you have learned in this chapter, parallel play is more common in young toddlers, while older children increasingly engage in cooperative play. Develop a hypothesis based on this fact. A sample hypothesis might be: two-and-one-half-year-olds engage in cooperative play more often than eighteen-month-olds.

**Procedure** Work with your teacher to arrange to observe a group of children at play. You will need to find out the ages of the children you are observing. Keep track of how children in different age groups play.

**Analysis** Calculate your results. Create a table that explains these results. State whether or not your hypothesis was true.

> **NSES A** Develop abilities necessary to do scientific inquiry, understandings about scientific inquiry.

## Standardized Test Practice

**SHORT ANSWER**

Short answer questions are not the same as essay questions. These questions call for brief, to-the-point responses. Write a response to this short answer question:

**20.** At about eighteen months, many children begin to exhibit negativism. List three ways to deal with a toddler who is being negative.

> **Test-Taking Tip** Keep your language simple and direct in short answer questions. Avoid overly elaborate answers. Bulleted or numbered lists can help clarify your response.

Chapter 11 **349**

---

**18.** $x = 2y$

**Mc Graw Hill** **Professional Development**

**Mini Clip**
**Math: The Meaning of Variable**

Students and teacher discuss the meaning of variable.

**19.** Students should create a table that explains the results of their experiment and states whether their hypotheses are true.

**NCLB** NCLB connects academic correlations to book content.

## Standardized Test Practice

**20.** Ways of dealing with a toddler who is being negative include offering choices, redirecting the child, and encouraging the child to talk.

**Test-Taking Tips** Tell students: When studying for a test with a partner, take turns asking one another questions similar to those that are likely to be on the test.

**Short Answer Test** Tell students that as they study for a short answer test, they should ask themselves, "What questions might be asked about this material?" Then practice writing out the answers to these questions.

---

## TECHNOLOGY Solutions

### Use these technology solutions to streamline chapter assessment!

**ExamView Assessment Suite** CD allows you to create and print out customized tests or ready-made unit and chapter tests, complete with answer keys.

**TeacherWorks Plus** is an electronic lesson planner that provides instant access to complete teacher resources in one convenient package.

**Online Learning Center** includes resources and activities for students and teachers.

**STANDARDS BASED LESSON PLANNING** *The Developing Child* provides students with instruction and assessment in the following fundamental content areas:

## National Standards Correlations

| Standards | Pages |
|---|---|
| **12.1.1** Analyze physical, emotional, social, spiritual, and intellectual development. | **353–362** |
| **12.1.2** Analyze interrelationships among physical, emotional, social, and intellectual aspects of human growth and development. | **364, 372** |
| **12.1.3** Analyze current and emerging research about human growth and development, including research on brain development. | **353, 355, 358, 368** |
| **12.3.1** Analyze the role of nurturance on human growth and development. | **361, 364** |
| **12.3.2** Analyze the role of communication on human growth and development. | **361** |
| **15.1.1** Analyze parenting roles across the life span. | **370** |
| **15.1.2** Analyze expectations and responsibilities of parenting. | **354, 358–359, 364–367, 368** |
| **15.1.5** Explain cultural differences in roles and responsibilities of parenting. | **369** |
| **15.2.1** Choose nurturing practices that support human growth and development. | **361, 364** |
| **15.2.2** Apply communication strategies that promote positive self-esteem in family members. | **361** |
| **15.2.3** Assess common practices and emerging research about discipline on human growth and development. | **358** |

**NO CHILD LEFT BEHIND** NCLB activities, information, and skills practice will help your students attain NCLB proficiency. Students will improve their abilities in the following academic standards areas:

## Academic Standards Correlations

| Discipline | Standard | Feature/Activity |
|---|---|---|
| **English Language Arts** | **NCTE 1** Read texts to acquire new information. | **Reading Guide (pp. 352, 363)** |
| | **NCTE 4** Use written language to communicate effectively. | **Academic Skills (p. 375)** |
| | **NCTE 5** Use different writing process elements to communicate effectively. | **After You Read (p. 362)** |
| | **NCTE 12** Use language to accomplish individual purposes. | **Writing Activity (p. 350)** **After You Read (p. 372)** |
| **Mathematics** | **NCTM Data Analysis and Probability** Select and use appropriate statistical methods to analyze data. | **After You Read (p. 362)** |
| | **NCTM Measurement** Understand measurable attributes of objects and the units, systems, and processes of measurement. | **Academic Skills (p. 375)** |
| **Science** | **NSES A** Develop abilities necessary to do scientific inquiry, understandings about scientific inquiry. | **After You Read (p. 372)** **Academic Skills (p. 375)** |
| | **NSES 1** Develop an understanding of science unifying concepts and processes. | **Science in Action (p. 355)** |
| **Social Studies** | **NCSS I A Culture** Analyze and explain the ways groups, societies, and cultures address human needs and concerns. | **Culture Matters (p. 369)** **Observation Skills (p. 374)** |

## McGraw Hill Professional Development

**MINI CLIP VIDEO LIBRARY**
Targeted professional development is correlated throughout *The Developing Child*. **The McGraw-Hill Professional Development Mini Clip Video Library** provides teaching strategies to strengthen academic and learning skills. Log on to **glencoe.com**.

In this chapter, you will find these Mini Clips:
- **Reading**  Options for Learning, p. 356
- **ELL**  Scaffolding Questions, p. 361
- **Math**  Real-Life Connections—Proportions, p. 366
- **Reading**  Focus Lesson, p. 370
- **Math**  Surface Area and Volume, p. 375

## Reading and Writing Strategies

**Writing Activity: Explanation** (p. 350)
Students use writing tips to explain why reading to children is essential.

**Before You Read** (pp. 352, 363)
A pre-reading question or statement will help students make a personal connection to content.

**Graphic Organizer** (pp. 352, 363)
A visual tool will help students organize and remember new content.

**Reading Check** (pp. 355, 356, 367, 370)
A question allows students to make a quick comprehension self-check.

**After You Read** (pp. 362, 372)
Organize and process students' understanding of what they have read.

## Chapter Features

**Video Games and Brain Development** (p. 355)
Research suggests that playing video games may damage developing brains.

**Long-Term Memory** (p. 358)
Children do not develop long-term memory until at least 17 months.

**Memory Games** (p. 358)
As a toddler's intellectual abilities grow, so do the possibilities for play.

**Learning About Differences** (p. 360)
Children are curious about other people.

**Encourage Imagination and Creativity** (p. 361)
All children need creative play.

**Learning by Helping** (p. 366)
Young children can learn by helping with everyday activities.

**Preschool in France** (p. 369)
Preschools in France bring together children from various communities.

**Basic Toy Safety** (p. 370)
Parents should be sure toys are safe.

## Chapter Overview

### Introduce the Chapter

In this chapter, students learn how heredity and environment shape intelligence; the four methods of learning used by young children; seven areas of intellectual activity; four parts of language that children have an inborn ability to decipher; and how to evaluate toys for young children.

### Build Background

Discuss with students that from ages one to three, children gain an incredible amount of knowledge. Ask students if they have been around children in that age range. If so, ask what kinds of intellectual development and learning they have observed.

### Writing Activity
#### Explanations

This active learning activity prompts students to write an explanation of why reading to children is essential. After students have completed the writing activity, ask for volunteers to share their paragraphs with the class. Student responses can be used as a basis for classroom discussion. (Paragraphs will vary. Possible answers include: Reading to children is important because it familiarizes them with the way that books work, it helps them associate printed words with spoken words, and it provides an opportunity to bond with the child. Use these criteria when evaluating your students' writing: Does it explain why reading to children is essential? Would a person understand the explanation?)

# Intellectual Development from One to Three

## Chapter Objectives

After completing this chapter, you will be able to:

- **Summarize** how heredity and the environment shape intelligence.
- **Describe** the four methods of learning used by young children.
- **List** the seven areas of intellectual activity.
- **List** 11 ways to help guide a child's learning.
- **Identify** four parts of language that children have an inborn ability to decipher.
- **Summarize** how to evaluate toys for young children.

### Writing Activity  Explanation

**Reading to a Child** One of the most important things parents can do for their children is to read to them. Write a paragraph explaining why reading to children is essential.

**Writing Tips** People often write to explain, whether it is to defend a political view or to provide instructions on assembling a bike. When writing an explanation, keep these tips in mind:

1. Write clearly and avoid vague language.
2. Be specific in your explanation.
3. Keep your audience in mind.

## CLASSROOM Solutions

### Print Resources

 **Student Edition**

 **Teacher Wraparound Edition**

 **Student Activity Workbook**

 **Student Activity Workbook Teacher Annotated Edition**

### Technology Resources

 **Online Learning Center** has resources and activities for students and teachers. Includes an Online Student Edition.

 **Interactive Student Edition** allows students to instantly access review materials, examples, and exercises.

**Section 12.1** Brain Development from One to Three

**Section 12.2** Encouraging Learning from One to Three

**Explore the Photo**
Imagination and creativity play an important role in a toddler's brain development. *What do you think this child is learning while doing this activity?*

351

### Review the Sections
Introduce the chapter by reviewing the sections:

#### Section 12.1
Intelligence is determined by both heredity and environment. Children learn concepts and the words for those concepts in stages. Learning methods include incidental, trial-and-error, imitation, and directed learning. The seven areas of intellectual activity include: attention, memory, perception, reasoning, imagination, creativity, and curiosity.

#### Section 12.2
Children's learning can be guided by adults. Caregivers can encourage reading and math readiness during play and everyday activities. Toys should be safe, appealing, and appropriate to a child's age. Speech difficulties include problems with articulation and stuttering. Toys and play are important parts of a child's development.

#### ▶ Explore the Photo

**Caption Answer**
Responses will vary, but might include that she is improving her motor skills and using her imagination. She is also learning social skills, even though she might be playing with imaginary friends.

**Discussion** Ask students to discuss how a child who is playing can be learning. Ask for examples of a time when students were playing but learning, too. (Students might say that children at play are learning rules of the game or how to draw. Students might learn while they play a new video game, for example.)

 **TeacherWorks Plus** is an electronic lesson planner that provides instant access to complete teacher resources in one convenient package.

**Presentation Plus!** provides visual teaching aids for every section.

**The Early Childhood Observations CD** presents video observations and lessons on observation skills and child development.

**The Developing Brain eTransparencies and Guide** include information and activities to offer insights into brain development and diseases of the brain.

## Section 12.1

# Brain Development from One to Three

**Bell Ringer Activity**

### Brain Development

Ask students whether they think imagination and creativity play an important role in the brain development of one- to three-year olds. Then ask them to explain their answers. (Students' answers will vary. Most should recognize the connection between imagination and creativity to brain development.)

## Preteaching

### Vocabulary

Explain that the prefix *neuro* is Greek for "nerve." Neuroscience is the study of the brain, which controls our nerves. Ask students if they know other words that include neuro.

### Graphic Organizer

The Graphic Organizer is also on the TeacherWorks CD.

(Graphic organizers should list two from each category. **1 Year:** puts two words together; names common objects; understands "no;" finds hidden objects; **2 Years:** uses two- to three-word sentences; knows about 500 words; follows simple directions; identifies colors; **3 Years:** uses longer sentences; knows about 900 words; follows two-part directions; sorts by color and shape.)

**NCLB** NCLB connects academic correlations to book content.

## Reading Guide

### Before You Read

**Restating Definitions** Knowing the meanings of vocabulary words is vital to understanding what you are reading. Locate the content vocabulary words in this section. Read each word's definition. Then restate the definition using your own words.

### Read to Learn
**Key Concepts**
- **Summarize** how heredity and the environment shape intelligence.
- **Describe** the four methods of learning used by young children.
- **List** the seven areas of intellectual activity.

**D**

### Main Idea
Both heredity and environment play major roles in the development of a child's intelligence. Intellectual activity becomes increasingly complex.

### Content Vocabulary
◇ neuroscience
◇ intelligence
◇ incidental learning
◇ trial-and-error learning
◇ imitation
◇ directed learning
◇ creativity

 **Graphic Organizer** Go to this book's Online Learning Center at **glencoe.com** to print out this graphic organizer.

### Academic Vocabulary
You will find these words in your reading and on your tests. Use the glossary to look up their definitions if necessary.
- elicit
- stifle

### Graphic Organizer
As you read, look for two milestones of intellectual development for 1-, 2-, and 3-year-old children. Use a web diagram like the one shown to help organize your information. Add additional circles as needed.

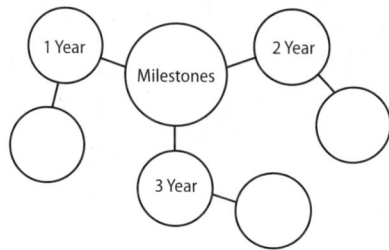

**NCLB**

### Academic Standards . . . . . . . . . . . . . . . . . . . .

 **English Language Arts**
**NCTE 5** Use different writing process elements to communicate effectively.

**Mathematics**
**NCTM Data Analysis and Probability** Select and use appropriate statistical methods to analyze data.

**Science**
**NSES 1** Develop an understanding of science unifying concepts and processes: systems, order, and organization; and evidence, models, and explanation.

**NCTE** *National Council of Teachers of English*
**NCTM** *National Council of Teachers of Mathematics*

**NSES** *National Science Education Standards*
**NCSS** *National Council for the Social Studies*

## Reading Guide

### Before You Read

Ask students: What were your favorite creative and imaginative games or activities when you were a young child? Did these activities help you learn? (Students' answers will vary. Some may mention drawing or playing dress up. Students may not recognize the connection between creative and imaginative play and learning.)

### D Develop Concepts

**Main Idea** Discuss the main idea with the students. Ask: What is heredity? (Students should recall that heredity is the biological transfer of certain inherited characteristics.) What is environment? (Environment is the people, places, and things that surround and influence a person.)

## Brain Development

Lisa, age two and one-half, examined her doll with a toy stethoscope after returning from a visit to the pediatrician. This simple act of play revealed the growing power of her mind. A one-year-old is still much like a baby, just learning to make sense of the world. However, Lisa has learned so much by two and one-half that she can engage in imaginative play. She is using her imagination when she imitates the actions of her doctor or a character in her favorite book. In doing so, she develops her own ideas and extends her investigation of the world.

Most researchers agree that the brain plays a major part in directing behavior and determining intelligence. However, the exact functions of the brain were unknown until recent years. For a long time, people could do little but observe human behavior and guess about exactly how the brain controlled human actions and abilities.

Cells from the nervous system, called neurons, were observed to have fibers radiating from them, called axons and dendrites. As you learned in Chapter 9, these fibers were found to conduct information to and from other neurons in the brain. Later, scientists discovered that connections between axons and dendrites formed pathways in the brain that controlled particular actions or thinking tasks.

Since then, neuroscience has provided further important discoveries and insights about the functions of the human brain. **Neuroscience** is the modern study of the brain. These discoveries have greatly expanded the knowledge of how a child's brain develops. This knowledge has had an impact on recommendations for care of children.

People used to think that providing a child with food, clothing, and shelter in a loving, healthy, and safe environment was all a child needed for the development. Neuroscience has shown that a child's experiences can help determine the physical structure of the brain and the

**↑ Brain Development and Coordination**
Connections in the brain control actions and thinking tasks. *Why can a three-year-old perform more tasks than a one-year-old?*

### Teach

**Discussion Starter**

**A Toddler's Brain** Tell students that at the age of two, a toddler's cortex has more than half of the synapses that it will have later in life. While these unused synapses disappear, the toddler's mind starts to process information more rapidly than before. Insulating the pathways with myelin also occurs at this time, but at a slower rate than in infancy. This process helps in the areas of language, memory, and attention. Ask students who know a two-year-old to share some of their observations about the learning that is occurring in the child. (Students may say that the child uses his imagination a lot or likes to pretend.)

**R Reading Strategy**

**Generalizing** Have students read the first two paragraphs in the right column. After students have read the paragraphs, re-read to them the last sentence, "This knowledge has had an impact on recommendations for care of children." Ask students to think about how this knowledge might have impacted or changed how people care for children. Ask volunteers to share their thoughts. (Students' answers will vary. Some might recall that in the past children were thought of as small adults and there was little or no understanding about how children learn and what they are capable of doing. Today, with continuing studies, researchers learn more about how children learn and teachers, and parents use that information to help children learn in the best ways possible.)

---

**▶ Explore the Photo**

**Caption Answer** The brain of a one-year-old is not developed enough to be able to perform the fine motor skills of a three-year-old.

**Discussion** Show video clips of a one-year-old and a three-year-old. Ask students to describe the differences in the ability levels of the children. (Responses will vary. Students may note that a one-year-old, if walking, is wobbly while a three-year-old is steady on his feet.)

**Teach** cont.

**C** Critical Thinking

**Compare and Contrast** Have students imagine a young child who lives in a poverty stricken country and compare that child's environment with that of an average young child in the United States. Ask: How might the environments be similar? How might they differ? Which environment would best stimulate a child's learning? Why? (Student answers will vary. They may recognize that there are few similarities and many differences. An average young child in the United States will typically have a very stimulating environment at home and perhaps at preschool, with many toys and games. Students may note that children in poverty stricken countries typically do not have as many toys to help stimulate learning, but students may say this encourages the children to use their imagination and their natural surroundings to play and interact.)

**U₁** Universal Access

**Interpersonal Learners** Have students imagine that they are in a public place, such as a shopping mall or park. Ask students to jot down noises, smells, feelings, and sights they might experience in that environment. Then ask students to imagine what a one- to three-year-old might feel in such a place where their senses are overloaded. Discuss how they would approach giving directions to a one- to three-year-old in the middle of so much stimulation. (Students' answers will vary. Possible answers may include: having the child look directly at them when they are speaking to the child.)

extent to which a child reaches his or her potential. A parent can help ensure a child reaches his or her potential by offering a stimulating environment.

### The Role of Intelligence

**Intelligence** is the ability to interpret and understand everyday situations and to use prior experiences when faced with new situations or problems. Intelligence is also the capacity to learn. Both heredity and environment shape intelligence. Everyone is born with certain limits of possible intellectual development. However, the extent to which a person's potential is actually developed is greatly influenced by that person's environment.

It is crucial for young children to have an environment that promotes learning and stimulates the senses. Such an environment includes interactions with caregivers and other children, a variety of appropriate toys, and plenty of encouragement. An enriched learning environment provides the best opportunity for learning. In fact, recent studies of brain development show that connections are made and the brain grows in complexity based partly on the opportunities for learning available to a child. A stimulating environment boosts learning. Children need bright colors and fun activities to learn.

Toddlers and preschoolers form attitudes about learning that can last a lifetime. If they are given many opportunities for learning, they are likely to develop a positive attitude toward learning.

### Concept Development

Concepts are general categories of objects and information. Children learn concepts and the words for those concepts in stages. It takes time for misconceptions that result from a toddler's broad generalizations to be sorted out. Young children often over-apply labels. For example, toddlers may think that any round fruit is an orange. Young children gradually

**Object Classification**
By age three, many children can classify items by size, shape, or color. *What is an example of a misconception a toddler might have?*

---

**► Explore the Photo**

**Caption Answer** Answers will vary. Young toddlers might think that all animals are dogs or that all round objects are balls.

**Discussion** Ask students to suggest ways they might help a toddler distinguish between a dog and a cat. (Suggestions will vary. Students might say they would focus on the different sounds—barking and mewing—that dogs and cats make.)

learn to categorize objects by shape, color, and size. Balls are round, and so are cookies and plates. Grass and leaves are both green. Size distinctions come in two steps. The relationship between two items as big and little may be recognized as early as eighteen months. Not until age three, however, can children pick out the middle-sized ball from three possibilities.

Concepts concerning what is alive and what is not alive are not learned until later. A young child believes that anything that moves or works is alive. This includes clouds, toys, cartoon characters, and the washing machine!

Concepts of time improve during the second and third years. Two-year-olds may show more patience because they know what *soon* means and can wait a short time. They know the difference between before and after. However, a child may not understand today, tomorrow, and yesterday until kindergarten.

✓ **Reading Check** **Recall** What are concepts?

## Methods of Learning

Children learn much from everyday experiences and play. There are four methods that children use for learning. These include incidental, trial-and-error, imitation, and directed learning.

Recall that Jean Piaget divided learning into four distinct periods, as shown in **Figure 12.1** on page 356. Between the ages of one and three years, toddlers progress from the sensorimotor period to the preoperational period. As you read about the four methods of learning, think about how they might fit into Piaget's periods of learning.

### Incidental Learning

**Incidental learning** is unplanned learning. For example, five-month-old Evan pushes a button on a musical toy and discovers that this action causes music to play. After this happens a few times, Evan learns a cause-and-effect situation. Then he pushes the button on purpose to hear the music.

### Trial-and-Error Learning

**Trial-and-error learning** is learning that takes place when a child tries several solutions to find one that works. At about twelve to eighteen months, this means experimenting. Trial-and-error learning may be more advanced for a three-year-old.

For example, three-year-old Krista wants to play with her younger brother's toy robot. First, Krista grabs the robot from her brother. He screams, and their mother makes her give it back. Next, Krista tells her brother to go play in the sandbox, but he does not want to. Finally, Krista offers to let her brother play with her stuffed horse if she can play with his toy. He agrees to the trade, and Krista gets what she wants. She has learned the best way to get what she wants from her brother by trying ways that did not work.

**Teach** cont.

**U₂ Universal Access**

**Verbal Learners** Ask students to recall their earliest learning memories. Discuss what the students were learning and how they went about it. Ask students to explain with details: where they were during the learning experience; who was present; what toys, games, and so on were involved; and what was the outcome of the learning experience. (Students recollections will vary. Students should describe the learning experience in as much detail as possible.)

**W Writing Support**

**Descriptive Paragraph**

**Learning Event** Have students write a paragraph in which they describe an incidental learning event. This can be something that happened to themselves, someone else, or it can be fictitious. Students should: decide what mood they want to create in the paragraph; write a strong topic sentence; orient the reader by presenting details in a logical order; and select precise transition words. (Paragraphs will vary but should describe an incidental learning event. Use the following questions to evaluate students' paragraphs: Does the paragraph include a strong topic sentence? Does the paragraph convey a mood that is supported by all of the details? Does the paragraph present details in a logical order? Does the paragraph include precise transition words?)

✓ **Reading Check**

**Recall** Concepts are general categories of objects and information.

**Science** in Action

**Video Games and Brain Development**

Students' reports and conclusions will vary, but the student should thoroughly analyze the research and provide reasons for whether or not they support its results.

**NCLB** Activity correlated to Science standards.

### W Writing Support

**Explanation**

**Offering Help** Sometimes a teacher, parent, or caregiver must recognize when to offer help and when to step back and let the child work things out on her own. Ask students to write an explanation about a situation in which a parent, caregiver, or teacher might refrain from interfering rather than trying to help. Ask students to answer the question: In what kinds of learning situations should teachers or caregivers of children between one and three years old remain in the role of observer? (Refer to p. 350 for tips on writing explanations. Students' explanations will vary but should include a situation in which a parent, caregiver, or teacher had not interfered and should answer the question posed above. Use the following criteria to evaluate students' essays: Is the thesis statement clear? Does the essay explain the student's point of view? Are the verbs vivid?)

**Professional Development**

**Mini Clip**
**Reading: Options for Learning**

Two teachers explain to their students multiple ways to read and respond to the assigned text.

### ✓ Reading Check

**Compare** Directed learning involves actual teaching. Imitation learning is when a child simply observes and copies, rather than being formally taught.

## Imitation

**Imitation** is learning by watching and copying others. Older children are often annoyed when a younger sibling copies everything they do or say. The younger child uses the older as a model for behavior of all kinds. Both skills and attitudes can be learned by imitation. Toddlers also carefully watch and mimic the actions and attitudes of their parents and caregivers. Have you ever seen a toddler talking on a toy phone? He is imitating the action of the adults around him. The best way to teach children to eat their vegetables or say please and thank you is to do these things yourself!

## Directed Learning

Learning that results from being taught, often by parents, other caregivers, teachers, or older siblings, is **directed learning**. Directed learning occurs in school or other places that offer formal instruction, as well as at home. Unlike incidental learning or trial-and-error learning, directed learning involves an older person purposely teaching a specific skill, fact, or attitude to the child. Joel's kindergarten teacher helps him learn the letters of the alphabet by showing pictures of items that begin with each letter. At home, his sister demonstrates how to play Go Fish with playing cards. Joel learns how to play soccer from his coach. Directed learning begins in the early years and continues throughout life.

### ✓ Reading Check  **Compare** How is directed learning different from imitation?

## Intellectual Activity Areas

Intellectual activity can be broken down into seven areas. These are attention, memory, perception, reasoning, imagination, creativity, and curiosity. These areas develop throughout life, but their development from ages one to three is especially remarkable. As you read more about each area, try to think of ways that caregivers can encourage development in that area. Some basic intellectual milestones for these ages are described in **Figure 12.2** on page 359.

**Figure 12.1 Piaget's Four Periods of Learning**

Piaget's four periods of learning begin at birth and continue to adulthood. *At what age does a child begin thinking in terms of what they perceive at the moment?*

| Period | Characteristics |
|---|---|
| **Sensorimotor** *Birth-2 years* | Children learn through their senses and own actions. |
| **Preoperational** *2–7 years* | Children think in terms of their own activities and what they perceive at the moment. |
| **Concrete Operations** *7–11 years* | Children can think logically but still learn best through experience. |
| **Formal Operations** *11-Adult* | People are capable of abstract thinking. |

**Figure 12.1 Piaget's Four Periods of Learning**

**Caption Answer** Children begin to think in terms of perception, or what they perceive at the moment, during the preoperational period, at age 2.

**Discussion** According to Piaget's periods of learning, children in the sensorimotor and preoperational stages of development learn through their own senses and perceptions. Ask students in what ways caregivers can use directed learning methods during these stages to help the intellectual development of children. (Specific answers may include: teaching children how to dress themselves or put away toys.)

## Attention

At any given moment, the five senses are bombarded with information. Right now, for instance, you see the words on the page. You are aware of the size, shape, and color of the book and the amount of light in the room. You hear pages being turned, and perhaps you see other students jotting down notes. You feel the paper of the book. It is smooth and cool. If you were unable to screen out all of the extra information you take in, you would not be able to read.

In order to function, adults must be able to focus their attention on the task at hand. This means blocking out much of the sensory information they receive. Infants and young children are unable to do this. Their attention goes from one bit of sensory information to another as they try to make sense of it all. This is why toddlers are so easily distracted.

A caregiver may be struggling to dress a toddler. She may find that while she turned to get the shirt, the child wandered away to see what was going on outside the window. It is important for caregivers to understand how difficult it is for a child to pay attention to one thing at a time.

As children mature, they gradually build the ability to ignore most sensory information and to concentrate on one item of interest. Their learning becomes more focused on one topic or activity at a time. One- to three-year-olds tend to have very short attention spans. However, a three-year-old can focus on one activity for much longer than a one-year-old. The more children are able to block out distractions, the more they can learn. Caregivers may notice this as children spend more time interested in a story.

## Memory

Without memory, there would be no learning. Experiences that are forgotten cannot affect later actions or thoughts.

Older children and adults have both short- and long-term memory. Short-term memory is brief and allows people to accomplish many everyday tasks without making the brain store

**Pay Attention to Memories**
Toddlers use memories to remember a favorite book. *How do you think an increasing attention span can help build memories?*

unimportant information indefinitely. People use short-term memory when they look up a number in the phone book. They remember the number just long enough to place their call. They will look up the same number the next time they need to call it. Long-term memory is for more important data. First, this information must enter the short-term memory and be judged important enough to remember. Then it is stored in the long-term memory.

Babies begin to demonstrate memory early. They quickly learn to recognize the faces of their primary caregivers, for example. Much of babies' memory abilities have to do with faces and foods. Between six months and a year, babies develop recall memory. This is the ability to remember more information for longer periods of time. This is especially true for things that had a strong emotional impact. For example, by this time Kylee can remember that she did not like cats because one scratched her.

---

### Teach *cont.*

### S Skill Practice
#### Guided Practice

**Describe** Have students think of useful memory devices that parents and caregivers could introduce to children in the toddler age group. Students should write a description of each memory device. (Memory devices will vary. Examples may include: using their fingers when learning to count or creating rhymes.) **L1**

**Construct** Have students work in pairs to develop a memory game for toddlers. Have them create a rubric for evaluating the game, including such aspects as durability, safety, and appeal to children. Ask students to include design drawings, along with references to any materials adapted from published examples. Students should present the game to the class as their peers use the rubric to evaluate the game. (Games will vary. Rubrics should evaluate durability, safety, appeal to children, and so on.) **L2** **ELL**

**Diagram** Have students investigate the way the brain stores information. Have them learn about the process of taking in stimuli through the nervous system—how the information finds its way to the brain, recalling past information based on familiar sights, smells, tastes, and feelings—and how short-term memory works. Ask students to draw a diagram that demonstrates these mental processes. (Students' diagrams will vary but should show the process of taking in stimuli through the nervous system.) **L3**

---

#### ➤ Explore the Photo

**Caption Answer** An increased attention span allows children to learn more. The more they learn, the more memories they will build.

**Discussion** Have students think about how they remember important information. Do they use memory devices, like mnemonics, to study for tests? Have they ever pictured a map or landmark in their mind while trying to get somewhere? (Answers will vary, but students should describe memory devices they use.)

## Assess

### Quiz

Ask students to answer the following questions:

1. How does an enriched learning environment affect a child' learning? (It stimulates the senses; is related to the formation of connections and complexity in brain growth.)
2. Describe four different methods of learning. (Incidental, trial-and-error, imitation, and directed learning.)
3. How can adults help two- and three-year olds improve their perceptions? (By talking about what they are doing; using descriptive observations; and answering the children's questions)

### THE DEVELOPING BRAIN

**Long-Term Memory**

**Science Inquiry** There must be neural connections between the two brain areas called the frontal lobe and the hippocampus. Interactions with adults aid in brain development.

For more information and activities, see *The Developing Brain* guide and eTransparencies.

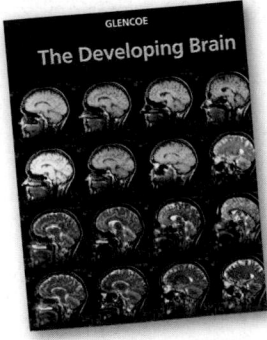

---

### THE DEVELOPING BRAIN

**Long-Term Memory**

Long-term memory is the ability to remember an event in one's life for a long time. It depends on connections between neurons in two brain areas called the frontal lobe and the hippocampus. Research has shown that these parts of the brain are not able to form long-term memories until a baby is 17 to 21 months old. Even if a baby is too young to remember a story or a song, interactions with adults keep the child alert and interested. These interactions also aid brain development.

■ **Science Inquiry** Children do not have long-term memory until at least 17 months. What must take place in the brain before long-term memory can occur?

As children develop, they become able to react to a situation by remembering similar experiences in the past. A one-year-old who was frightened by a dog may be afraid of all animals for a time. A three-year-old can remember the specific dog and compare it with others. A three-year-old also can recall a celebration and look forward to the next one.

Children develop more long-term memories at age three. This is when they can retain facts such as "the girl next door is named Keisha." They can remember observations such as "I love to go to the park." They can also recall their own personal history such as "I got a new puppy last year."

### Perception

A newborn learns about the world through perceptions. Perception is the information received through the senses. This sensory information reinforces established connections in the brain. It also sparks new connections. Although a newborn's brain is developing these neural connections and pathways at a rapid rate, the infant is just starting to interpret the information. Gradually, the brain organizes itself to handle increasingly complex learning as a child grows. This allows sensory information to be used more effectively.

If you care for young children, you can play a key role in the development of perception. By talking about what you and the children are doing, you encourage children's perception. Use descriptive observations that children can understand and expand on. For example, when playing with blocks, you might say, "Look at the

---

## Learning Through PLAY

### Memory Games

As a toddler's intellectual abilities grow, so do the possibilities for play. A three-year-old is able to use his or her memory to play games. Do you remember playing card games where the object was to place cards face down, turn over one card, and then turn over another to find its match? Three-year-olds are able to successfully play such a memory game for two reasons. They are able to keep an idea in mind for longer periods of time than when they were younger. They also can complete a task without being easily distracted. Simple

puzzles can be good for developing memory as well. Increasing a child's memory can help with later development of skills such as reading and writing.

**Think About It** Imagine you are babysitting a three-year-old. You bring along a memory game. The game involves matching 20 pairs of different animals. The child is having problems matching the cards. What might you do to make the game more appropriate for her age?

---

## Learning Through PLAY

### Memory Games

**Discussion** Ask the class: What do you think are good memory games for a one-year-old child? (Answers will vary but some examples are: ask a one-year-old to identify familiar people, parts of the body, or how to put certain shaped blocks into their appropriate shaped holes.)

**Think About It** You might try reducing the number of cards being used to four or five pairs. You can then increase the level of difficulty, if necessary, by adding more cards.

## Figure 12.2 Intellectual Developmental Milestones—Ages 1–3

Toddlers reach certain milestones every year. *What change occurs in the ability to follow directions between ages 2 and 3?*

| Age | Developmental Milestone |
|---|---|
| 1 Year | ✤ Begins to put two words together<br>✤ Names common objects and people<br>✤ Understands "no," but ignores it<br>✤ Finds hidden objects |
| 2 Years | ✤ Uses two- to three-word sentences<br>✤ Knows about 500 words<br>✤ Follows simple directions<br>✤ Identifies colors |
| 3 Years | ✤ Uses longer sentences<br>✤ Knows about 900 words<br>✤ Follows two-part directions<br>✤ Sorts by color and shape |

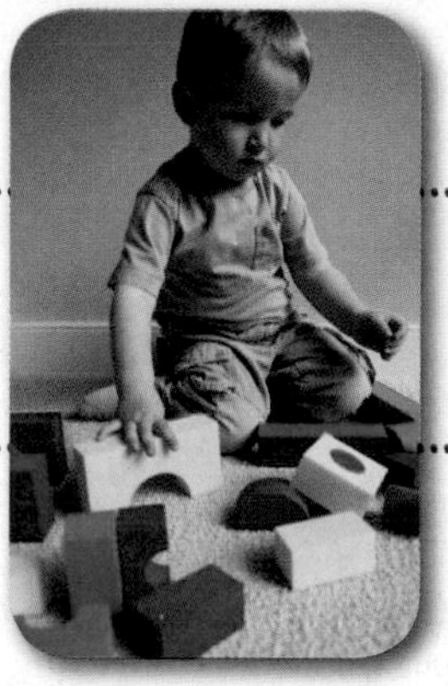

C

blue block. Your shirt is blue, too. Let's build a tower using only blue blocks."

Two- and three-year-olds seem to ask questions constantly. "Why?" "What's that?" "How does it work?" Responding to these questions helps improve a child's perception. It can be hard for caregivers to answer these endless questions. However, when questions are ignored or dismissed a child loses opportunities for learning. If the response is often an absent-minded "Uh-huh" or "Don't bother me right now; I'm busy," the child may stop asking questions.

### Reasoning

Reasoning is necessary to solve problems and make decisions. It is also important in recognizing relationships and forming concepts.

Babies show the signs of simple problem-solving skills at about four to six months of age. One-, two-, and three-year-olds gradually learn more sophisticated reasoning skills. At fourteen months, Jason solves problems by trying out all possible solutions. When playing with a shape sorter box, he tries to fit each piece into each hole until one works. By his third birthday, Jason's problem solving is less physical and more mental. He can think through possible solutions and eliminate those that will not work without actually acting out each one. He can see that the square shape will fit in the square hole, and not the round one.

Making decisions involves choosing from different alternatives. Children learn to make good decisions through practice. This is why it is important to give young children plenty of opportunities to make real decisions. At first, these decisions should be choosing between two options in which neither choice could cause any harm. For example, an eighteen-month-old can choose between two books to read at bedtime. A two-year-old child can choose between two different shirts.

W



## Section 12.1

### Reteach

#### C Critical Thinking

**Develop Alternatives** Have students discuss ways to avoid using the word "no" excessively with toddlers. Challenge students to think of ten ways to tell a child without saying "no" that he cannot have ice cream for breakfast, ride his tricycle in the house, or climb up on the roof of the garage. (Answers will vary. Possible answers include: We have cereal for breakfast and ice cream in the afternoon. You may ride your tricycle in the yard. You might hurt yourself if you climb on the roof of the garage.)

#### W Writing Support

**Observation Notes**

**Studying Behavior** Ask students to visit local child care centers to observe the behavior of one-, two-, and three-year-old children. Students' observations should focus on what kinds of decisions children of different ages are allowed and encouraged to make in a child care setting. Students should take notes during the observation and turn them in. Notes should include enough information to allow the reader to understand what occurred at the observation. Notes should be neat and legible with no grammar or spelling errors. (Student's notes should contain facts about decision making for one-, two-, and three-year-olds gathered at the observation site. For example, the children may be allowed to decide if they want apple juice or orange juice with their snack. Notes should be clearly legible and not contain grammar or spelling errors.)

### Figure 12.2 Intellectual Developmental Milestones—Ages 1–3

**Caption Answer** Three-year-olds usually can follow directions with two parts, whereas two-year-olds typically can only follow one-part directions.

**Discussion** Have students look at the chart. Ask students how old they think the boy in the photo appears to be. (around two-years-old) What does he appear to be doing? (playing with blocks) If you tried to stop his play to have lunch, how do you think he would react? (He may become upset.) If he said "no," what would you do? (Answers will vary.)

### Reteach *cont.*

### C₁ Critical Thinking

**Problem Solving** Read this scenario to students: When two-year-old Stephanie's parents arrive at the child care center at the end of the day, Stephanie runs past them into the large indoor play area where she plays on the slide. Her parents wait quietly, looking embarrassed and calling occasionally to their daughter. Sometimes they wait twenty or thirty minutes before Stephanie allows them to put on her jacket and carry her out to the waiting car. Ask students: What advice would you offer Stephanie's parents about choices and decision making during this daily transition time? (Student answers will vary. Possible answers may include asking Stephanie: Do you want help putting on your jacket, or would you like to put it on yourself? Do you want to play on the slide or the swing for five more minutes?)

### What Would You Do?

**Write About It** Scenarios will vary. Students could explain to their child that some people have bodies that do not work quite right. Luckily, this child has a hearing aid to help his ears work better. Emphasize that the child's feelings are hurt when others tease him, and that teasing is wrong. Encourage their child to be kind to the child with the hearing aid. Students also should talk to the child care workers about what their child says is happening.

### What Would You Do?

**Learning About Differences**

Three-year-old Zack was curious about his surroundings, especially about other people. He was not at all shy, and his mother was happy that he so often smiled and greeted people. One day, Zack and his mother went grocery shopping. "What's wrong with her?" Zack asked loudly. "Why is she walking like that?" Zack's mother drew him into a nearby aisle, and after a quick review of the use of inside and outside voices, she assured him that there was nothing wrong with the person he had seen. She was using crutches to help her walk because her legs might not work the way that Zack's do. On their way home, she reminded Zack that all people are different. She told Zack that it might hurt people's feelings when he asks personal questions too loudly.

**Write About It** Suppose your child tells you that some children at the child care center are teasing a child who must wear a hearing aid. Write a scenario in which you describe how you would respond to this situation. In your scenario, state exactly what you would say to your child.

Parents of newly independent two-year-olds know that this approach has the added advantage of avoiding questions that may **elicit**, or bring about, a negative response. For example, a child could easily say no to the question, "Would you like to have fish for dinner?" A better question is, "Do you want beans or corn with your fish?" What kinds of decision-making opportunities might be appropriate to offer to a three-year-old?

## Imagination

Imagination becomes very apparent at about two years of age. An active imagination improves learning because it allows the child to try new things. The child also can act out a variety of roles. Laundry baskets become airplanes, boxes are buildings, and closets are caves. The child becomes a ferocious lion or a busy airline pilot.

Children use their imagination to connect what they see and hear with themselves. For example, Yvonne may see an airplane. Then she imagines that she *is* an airplane, and zooms around the backyard with her arms outstretched. Imagination can also help children cope with anxiety and frightening new concepts. For instance, some children may pretend

**Imagination**
Children often use their imaginations to try out new ideas and roles. *Why should you not tell a toddler he is lying when he uses his imagination?*

### ► Explore the Photo

**Caption Answer** Young children use their imaginations to connect what they see and hear with themselves and to relieve anxiety, making them feel more comfortable with events around them. A toddler is not yet capable of lying.

**Discussion** All humans seem to possess the capacity to imagine and create. Ask students to discuss the possible purposes of imagination and creativity in human life. What role do artists and inventors play in society? (Answers may include: imagination and creativity add enjoyment to life. Artists and inventors help improve people's lives.)

C₂ to throw a scary monster out the bedroom window as a way of managing their fear. Using a toy doctor's kit and pretending to be a doctor can help calm fears about an upcoming medical procedure.

It is important to respect a child's imagination and respond carefully. When three-year-old Kim makes up a story, she is not lying. She is using her imagination. However, suppose Kim's mother says, "Don't be silly. You know that didn't really happen." Kim might be discouraged from using her imagination again. In fact, until about the age of five, children are not always sure where reality ends and imagination begins.

## { Expert Advice... }

*"As the child gathers more and more experience, eventually she is forced to give up her old theories, and create new ones. This process drives the child from one stage in cognitive development to the next."*

— Benjamin Spock, pediatrician and author, *The Common Sense Book of Baby and Child Care*

## Creativity

U An ability that is related to imagination is creativity. **Creativity** is a mental ability that involves using the imagination to produce original ideas. These ideas are often displayed through an object that others can see, such as a drawing or finger painting. The creative product is not always an object, though. It might be daydreams, dramatic play, or silly stories. Creativity is most readily developed in early childhood and is an asset throughout life. Creativity helps promote self-esteem and confidence. U

## ♡ Parenting Skills

### Encourage Imagination and Creativity

While some children may naturally be more imaginative than others, all children need opportunities for creative play. Here are some ways to support a child's creativity:

- **Encourage exploration.** Promote activities that depend on exploration and imagination. Examples include drawing, dressing up in grown-up clothes, and telling stories.
- **Provide multipurpose toys.** Children need toys that can be used in more than one way. Wooden blocks can become cars, doll beds, or castle walls.
- **Allow for unstructured time.** Children need uninterrupted time to themselves. The less television they watch, the more their imaginations will grow.
- **Resist the inner critic.** Remember that the process of creating is more important than the product. There is more than one right way to paint or mold things from clay.
- **Reward the young creator.** Praise the child's efforts with both deeds and words. Display the child's pictures. Talk with others about what the child has made.

**Take Charge** Many caregivers worry about the mess resulting from creative play. Write a paragraph explaining what you might do to reduce the mess.

## ♡ Parenting Skills

### Encourage Imagination and Creativity

Ask students to offer additional examples of how parents, teachers, and caregivers can encourage imagination and creativity in young children. (Possible answers include: making up the beginning of a story and having children finish it; or providing empty boxes, which can become fire trucks, houses, or doll beds.)

### Take Charge

Possible answers include: Try to use supplies that create less mess. For example, use felt-tip markers rather than watercolors. Teach children to use materials with care. Involve children in the clean-up process and have a place for everything.

## Reteach *cont.*

### C₂ Critical Thinking

**Communicate Advice** Have students offer specific, practical advice to parents on how to use a younger child's natural capacity for imagination and creativity to address each of these fears: the image of a monster in a children's book has upset a two-year-old; a three-year-old is worried about attending a new child care center; a young child is afraid to go into the basement; a child is nervous about being the ring-bearer at his aunt's wedding. (Student answers will vary, but should be specific, practical, and logical solutions or suggestions for the fears listed. For example, to ease a child's fear of the basement, you might have the child imagine what could be in the basement and act out how he could respond.)

### U Universal Access

**Visual Learners** Have students plan an art or craft project that would be engaging and appropriate for a three-year-old. What materials do they need to consider? How will they instruct the child? Ask students to demonstrate the project in front of the class. You might have the student audience participate in the project. Afterward, ask the class to vote on the most creative, fun, and practical projects.

**Professional Development**

**Mini Clip**
ELL: Scaffolding Questions

A teacher uses a series of questions to lead a student to an appropriate verbal response.

**Study Tools**

Have students go to the Online Learning Center at **glencoe.com**:

- Take the **Practice Test**.
- Download **Study-to-Go** content.

Use the **Student Activity Workbook** for additional practice.

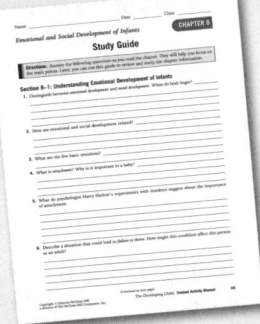

### Close

**Culminating Activity**

**Stimulating Environments** Have students imagine a toddler is going to spend an hour in their classroom. What activities could they do to encourage the child's interest in learning? (Answers will vary, but might include using pencils and paper to stimulate creative drawing.)

 **NCLB** connects academic correlations to book content.

---

There are many ways that parents can encourage creativity. One of the most important and simple ways is just to allow the child free time, or unstructured play. Many people think of toys when they think of play. However, in previous years, children were more likely to play at make-believe. Whether indoors or outside, children can make up their own rules and games. This is a great, inexpensive way to build creativity.

## Curiosity

Children are curious about the world around them, and that curiosity helps brain development and learning. It is curiosity that makes children wonder why and how about things. Curiosity makes children try new activities. However, parents may sometimes **stifle**, or suppress, that curiosity by overprotecting a child. Although children need a safe environment, they also need the freedom to explore the world around them.

Most young children seem to get into everything. They peek into every corner and closet. They touch and examine everything within reach. They like to climb just to see what is out of sight. It is often impossible to anticipate what a one-, two-, or three-year-old may do next. A doll may end up covered in bandages because "she fell down."

Toddlers are especially curious about the activities of their parents and caregivers. They might take the phone away from their dad to find out why he is talking to an object instead of to them. Remember that a toddler is still very self-centered. Anything that takes your attention away from them will raise their curiosity to find out why.

Parents should encourage a child's curiosity whenever possible. A child should not be allowed to do something that will harm him, like climb a bookshelf. However, if the child wants to stop during a walk to watch a snail, it is stimulating his brain development.

## Section 12.1    After You Read

### Review Key Concepts

1. **Explain** why it is vital that young children have a stimulating learning environment.
2. **Describe** how trial-and-error learning supports Piaget's description of the sensorimotor period.
3. **Identify** why curiosity is important.

### Practice Academic Skills

 **English Language Arts**

4. Write four test questions describing situations in which a child is learning something. In each question, ask the person taking the test to identify the learning method (incidental, trial-and-error, imitation, or directed). Switch questions with classmates and take their tests.

 **Mathematics**

5. Interview 20 of your classmates. Ask: What is your earliest memory as a child? How old were you when this event occurred? Calculate the average age of all the students at the time of their earliest memory.

 **Check Your Answers** Check your answers at this book's Online Learning Center at **glencoe.com**.

> **NCTE 5** Use different writing process elements to communicate effectively.

> **NCTM Data Analysis and Probability** Select and use appropriate statistical methods to analyze data.

**362    Chapter 12** Intellectual Development from One to Three

---

## Section 12.1    After You Read

**Review Key Concepts**

1. A stimulating learning environment increases the child's intellectual ability by helping the brain grow in complexity and increase neural connections between different parts of the brain. It also forms positive attitudes about learning that last a lifetime.

2. Children learn through their own actions in the sensorimotor period. Trial-and-error learning is when a child tries different actions to discover what happens or what will give the desired result.

3. Curiosity helps brain development and learning. It causes children to wonder *why* and *how,* and to try new things.

**Practice Academic Skills**

4. Students should write four questions that describe specific learning methods. Have students take each other's tests to help study.

5. Students should calculate the average age of at least 20 students when they reported their earliest first memory.

# Section 12.2  Encouraging Learning from One to Three

## Reading Guide

### Before You Read

**Predict** Predicting what you will learn can help focus your attention. Write down what you think might be covered under "Reading Readiness" in this section. Then read the section. Was your prediction accurate?

### Read to Learn

**Key Concepts**

- **List** 11 ways to help guide a child's learning.
- **Identify** four parts of language that children have an inborn ability to decipher.
- **Summarize** how to evaluate toys for young children.

**D**

### Main Idea

Children need to have certain skills before they are ready to read or learn basic math concepts. During this time, their language skills grow rapidly. Toys play an important developmental role.

### Content Vocabulary

 reading readiness
 math readiness
◇ articulation
◇ stuttering

### Academic Vocabulary

You will find these words in your reading and on your tests. Use the glossary to look up their definitions if necessary.

■ unstructured
■ decipher

### Graphic Organizer

As you read, look for ways in which reading aloud to children prepares them to be ready to learn to read. Use a chart like the one shown to help organize your information.

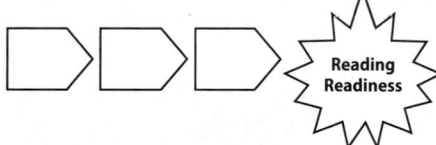

Reading Readiness

 **Graphic Organizer** Go to this book's Online Learning Center at **glencoe.com** to print out this graphic organizer.

**NCLB**

### Academic Standards · · · · · · · · · · · · · · · · · · · · · · · · · · ·

 **English Language Arts**

**NCTE 12** Use language to accomplish individual purposes.

**Science**

**NSES A** Develop abilities necessary to do scientific inquiry, understandings about scientific inquiry.

 **Social Studies**

**NCSS I A Culture** Analyze and explain the ways groups, societies, and cultures address human needs and concerns.

**NCTE** *National Council of Teachers of English*
**NCTM** *National Council of Teachers of Mathematics*

**NSES** *National Science Education Standards*
**NCSS** *National Council for the Social Studies*

---

## Focus

### Bell Ringer Activity

#### Learning Opportunities

Ask students to brainstorm some routine activities they do that might be interesting learning opportunities for a young child. Ask a volunteer to write the ideas on the board. (Ideas will vary and could range from brushing teeth to putting on shoes.)

### Preteaching

#### Vocabulary

Tell students that the suffix *-ness* means "state, condition, quality, or degree." Ask students to use this knowledge to define *reading readiness* and *math readiness.*

#### Graphic Organizer

 The Graphic Organizer is also on the TeacherWorks CD.

(Graphic organizers should include: teaches them to handle books and turn pages; helps them associate the written word with the spoken word; and gives them a sense of accomplishment.)

**NCLB** NCLB connects academic correlations to book content.

---

## Reading Guide

### Before You Read

To provide students with a better understanding of the concept of readiness, ask students to give examples of being ready to learn something new in their own lives. (Examples will vary but may include learning to add before learning to multiply, learning to ride a tricycle before learning to ride a bicycle.)

### D Develop Concepts

**Main Idea** Discuss the main idea with the students. Ask students to determine what kinds of skills children would need. (Children will need to know the alphabet and the sounds the letters make, and they will need to have basic number sense.)

### Discussion Starter

**Ready or Not** Have students think about a time in their young childhood when they were not ready to do something, but they tried anyway. What happened? Why did they attempt the task when they were not ready for it? What role did parents or caregivers take in the situation? Ask volunteers to share their experiences. (Experiences will vary. Students may mention such experiences as falling down when trying to ride a bicycle.)

### R Reading Strategy

**Scanning** Give students approximately two minutes to scan the section Readiness for Learning. Instruct them to pay particular attention to the headings, photographs, and figures. Then have them write down a question to which they think they will learn the answer while reading. As they read, students should write down the answers to their questions when they encounter them. (Questions will vary, but should be based on what students learned as they scanned the section.)

### C Critical Thinking

**Categorizing Information** Have students make a list of intellectual skills and activities that a three-year-old is ready for but a two-year-old is not. Have students refer to Figure 12.2 on page 359 for ideas. Discuss the reasons behind the students' decisions. (Students lists will vary, but may include: three-year-olds have a longer attention span than two-year-olds so are better able to sit quietly and "read" or "write.")

## Readiness for Learning

Learning begins very early in life. However, children can learn a new skill only when they are physically and intellectually ready. For example, it would be a waste of time trying to teach a six-month-old to put on a coat. The baby has neither the physical nor intellectual maturity that the skill requires. Most two-year-olds lack the fine motor skills and conceptual development necessary to learn to write letters and words.

**R** Sometimes adults push children to learn things they are not ready for. When children are not able to succeed, they may feel frustrated or feel they are a failure. These feelings may become stumbling blocks for learning. It is important to remember that children learn and grow at different rates. Therefore, worries such as "Brad is not talking as early as Mackenzie" should be minimized.

**C** On the other hand, children should be taught skills they are ready to learn. For example, two-year-old Ben struggled with dressing himself. His mother helped by dressing him every day. She found out later that her helping was causing problems. When Ben was well past the age when he should be able to dress himself, he continued to ask for help. He had not developed enough confidence to complete the task on his own.

Most importantly, children need plenty of time for undirected play and safe exploration. As children explore their environment and everything in it, they will naturally make many discoveries.

## Reading Readiness

**R** A child's readiness to read depends in large part on the environment caregivers create. Enjoying books is vital for learning to read. The act of being read to should be a well-established, daily routine and a special time together. Even very brief sessions of reading to infants can be helpful in developing a joy of reading.

Interact with young children while reading to them. Let the children point at the pages and comment. Ask them to predict what will happen next. The more enthusiastic the reader is, the more enthusiastic children will become about story time.

**↑ Learn New Skills**
Children are ready to learn different skills at different times. *What skills do children usually learn before they walk?*

### ➤ Explore the Photo

**Caption Answer** Before walking, children usually crawl and scoot around. In addition, they stand by hanging on to furniture or an adult's hands.

**Discussion** Tell students that in this section they will learn about reading readiness and math readiness. Ask them to explain what *walking readiness* might be. (Answers will vary. Young children must have both leg strength and balance before being able to walk.)

**Reading Readiness**
Reading to a young child can help them develop reading readiness skills. *How is reading to the child helpful?*

### S Skill Practice
### Guided Practice

**Read Aloud** Divide the class into teams. Have each member of the team bring to class a children's book appropriate for children ages two or three. Have students take turns reading their book to their team, pretending the team members are two- and three-year-olds. Write these questions on the board to remind students what they should keep in mind during their readings: How can I get the children to interact with the story? What types of questions can I ask? What tone of voice should I use to engage the listeners? Ask teams to evaluate the readings. (Evaluations will vary. Students may feel that they need more practice.) **L1** **ELL**

**Explain Readiness** Ask students to explain why a three-year-old is more ready to read than a two-year-old. (Three-year-olds use longer sentences and have a much larger vocabulary than two-year-olds.) **L2**

**Analyze Reading Activities** Ask students to plan reading readiness activities for toddlers. When plans are complete, assign students to small groups. Ask the groups to analyze the plans and determine whether each is appropriate. In a follow-up, review the characteristics of activities that facilitate reading growth in young children. Discuss how some activities that seem fun may not be the most effective. (Students' plans should show a level of understanding of what is appropriate for the age level.) **L3**

**Reading readiness** means learning the skills necessary for reading, including letter recognition and the understanding that letters of the alphabet combine to form words on a page. Before age three, reading readiness focuses on children's excitement about reading. The bedtime story accomplishes more than many parents realize.

- Children learn how to handle books and turn pages.
- They begin to associate written words that appear on the page with words being read aloud.
- Finishing a book creates a sense of accomplishment, especially when the child can choose what to read next.

The next stage of reading readiness involves letter recognition. This includes the understanding that letters of the alphabet combine to form words. Some children are ready to recognize letters at age three. During reading time, you can encourage the child to say the letters they see on the page. You might respond,

"You're right! That's a B. Your name begins with a B. B for Brianna!"

Children's readiness to read on their own may vary widely. Do not expect a strict timetable for gaining the preliminary skills needed for reading. It is more important that children learn to enjoy the process.

**S**

### { Expert Advice... }

*"The kind of care a child receives plays a big role in how the brain chooses to wire itself. Parents who talk and read to their babies are helping them develop important language connections."*

— Dr. Diane Bales, at-risk children, youth, and families coordinator, University of Georgia

**Section 12.2**  Encouraging Learning from One to Three  **365**

### ► Explore the Photo

**Caption Answer** Children begin to associate written words on the page with words being read aloud and they learn how to handle books and turn pages.

**Discussion** Read the Expert Advice aloud to the class. Ask students if they agree or disagree with the quote. Ask them to explain their answers. (Students may agree or disagree but should recognize that this quote is in agreement with the content of this text book.)

**W** **Writing Support**

### Write a Description

**Math in Nature** Nature is full of numbers, shapes, and patterns that can be used to help develop a child's math readiness. Take students on a walk in a park or other natural area and ask them to notice aspects of nature that might encourage counting, shape identification, or pattern recognition. In the classroom, have students write a descriptive paragraph in which they share their observations and reflect on how such a walk might encourage a three-year-old's math readiness. (Paragraphs will vary. Students might say they counted the types of trees or noticed that pine trees look like triangles while oak trees look more like circles. Use the following criteria to evaluate the paragraphs: Does the paragraph include a strong topic sentence? Does the paragraph convey a mood that is supported by all of the details? Does the paragraph present details in a logical order? Does the paragraph include precise transition words?)

**U₁** **Universal Access**

**Mathematical Learners** Have mathematical learners think of ways parents and caregivers can teach the following concepts during a typical day: more/less; more/fewer; big/small; and counting objects. (Suggestions will vary. Examples may include: asking which glass has more milk in it and which has less milk; asking which plate has more grapes on it and which has fewer grapes; asking which teddy bear is bigger and which is smaller; or asking how many apples are in the bowl.)

## What Would You Do?

### Learning by Helping

Three-year-old Molly was excited when she woke up. Liz was taking care of her today! When Liz arrived that morning, Molly asked to have pancakes for breakfast. "I'll help you," said Molly confidently. While Liz got out the pancake mix, Molly watched. "How many cups of mix do we use, Molly?" asked Liz. "Two!" said Molly, "You put it in a bowl."

"That's right. Let's use the big blue bowl today." Molly got out the bowl and handed it to Liz. "Thank you," said Liz. "Now I'll measure the mix." Liz filled a measuring cup and let Molly level the cup with a spatula and put the mix in the blue bowl. Liz asked, "How many eggs?" "One!" "Right again!" Liz smiled at her helper. Liz measured the milk and Molly stirred it into the mix herself. Molly liked to count the pancakes in the pan as Liz cooked them. Molly also commented that the pancakes were the same color as the kitchen floor—brown!

**Write About It** Think of a task you perform frequently, such as making your bed or feeding a pet. Write a scenario in which you and a three-year-old perform the task together. Include what you would say and do to help the child learn during this activity.

## Math Readiness

Math is a part of everyday life. People may count out a dozen apples, measure ingredients from a recipe, or count out coins. People use math so often and so unconsciously, they may miss experiences they could share with young children. **Math readiness** is the level of knowledge of basic math concepts, such as number recognition, needed for learning math. It also involves an interest in learning basic math concepts. As with reading, math can become a welcome and pleasant part of everyday experiences. Children can explore sizes, shapes, amounts, and proportions long before they ever enter a classroom.

To teach numbers, you can talk to children as they go about their daily routine. "Are there two bananas left this morning, or only one?" "How many plates are set out for dinner?" Counting and number recognition can be taught by making a game of finding numbers. How quickly can a child find a "3" on the signs in the grocery store?

Blocks and puzzles can teach shape recognition. They also help in learning the shape names. Sorting is a good mathematics skill. You can work with children to sort blocks and other items by shape, color, and size.

## Guiding Learning

There are many ways to help guide children's learning. As you read the suggestions, try to remember a time when someone helped improve your learning in this way.

- **Give your time and attention.** Children learn best when a caring person pays attention to them and encourages them.
- **Allow time for thinking.** Solving problems and making decisions are new experiences for young children. They need time to consider choices and make decisions.
- **Give only as much help as the child needs.** If a toddler is struggling to put on a shirt, do not take over. Just help slip the shirt over the child's head before it gets caught. Children feel a sense of accomplishment when they do things on their own. Try to let children do the final step in any task they are struggling with.
- **Encourage children to draw their own conclusions.** "Let's find out" is better than an explanation. Seeing and doing helps reinforce learning and allows for discoveries that prompt further curiosity.
- **Demonstrate how to solve problems.** When a toddler's tower of blocks keeps falling down, demonstrate that stacking one block directly on top of another provides the balance. Then leave building the tower to the toddler.
- **Model problem solving.** Talk out loud as you solve everyday problems. This allows children to hear how you think your way to a solution.

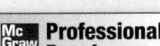 **Professional Development**

### Mini Clip
**Math: Real-Life Connections—Proportions**

A teacher introduces and models scale factors and similar figures using real-life examples.

## What Would You Do?

**Write About It** The scenario should include explanation and dialogue of what the student would say and do to encourage learning while they are performing the task.

- **Maintain a positive attitude.** Express confidence in the child's abilities. One way is to praise the child's efforts. "Thank you for helping me plant the daisies. You did a great job!" You can also point out improvements in a specific action, such as coloring.

- **Keep explanations simple and on the child's level.** Too much information can cause a young child to stop listening. When a child asks about why fish live in water, an appropriate explanation might be, "Fish breathe in water. People need air to breathe."

- **Allow children to explore and discover.** Exploration is often a messy business. It is important to give children opportunities to roll in the grass, splash in puddles, and squeeze mud through their fingers and toes. Safety is important, but constantly saying "Don't do this" and "Don't touch that" limits the sensory and motor experiences that promote learning.

- **Help children understand the world and how it works.** Take young children along, even on routine errands. On trips to the library, the supermarket, and the gas station, you could talk about what is happening and why it is happening. Helping out at home also boosts learning. While raking leaves together, for example, you might call attention to the different colors and the crackling sounds of the dried leaves.

- **Take frequent breaks.** Children need stimulation. They also need opportunities for unstructured play. **Unstructured** means lacking formal organization. Watch for clear signals that a child has had enough of an activity. Fussing, wiggling in a chair, or looking distracted suggest that it is time to move on.

✓ **Reading Check** **Analyze** Why is it important that children be allowed to explore and discover on their own?

**↑ Exploration and Discovery**
Children learn by being able to explore on their own. *What might a child learn by playing in the mud?*

## ➤ Explore the Photo

**Caption Answer** He might learn how water flows and splashes. He might also learn that he will get wet if he splashes the water.

**Discussion** The text states that "Exploration is often a messy business." Ask students to suggest ways children might be allowed to explore and keep messiness to a minimum. (Suggestions may include such things as putting smocks or large shirts on children when they paint or work with clay.)

## Teach *cont.*

### C Critical Thinking

**Solving Problems** Read this scenario to students: Abby loves to draw with crayons, but this morning she is becoming increasingly frustrated while trying to draw a perfect circle for a sun. She crumples up her paper and throws it on the floor, then scribbles hard on another sheet of paper. Have students think of different ways to address Abby's frustration. Prompt students to create solutions that maintain a positive attitude and model problem-solving skills. (Students' solutions will vary. They may suggest picking up the crumpled paper and admiring how carefully Abby drew the circle. They might assure her that it is very difficult, even for adults, to draw a perfect circle.)

### U₂ Universal Access

**Logical Learners** Ask logical learners to think of simple, straightforward, and logical answers to the following questions. (Answers should be appropriate for two- or three-year-olds.) Why do people live in houses? Why do birds fly? Discuss what parents and caregivers should do if they do not know the answers to a child's question. (Students' answers will vary. They might suggest: People live in houses so they won't be cold or so they have a place to put their things. Birds fly so they can catch bugs in the air or so they can move quickly from place to place. Students may say they would look up an unknown answer or ask someone else.)

✓ **Reading Check**

**Analyze** Exploring and discovering provides sensory and motor experiences that promote learning.

### Quiz

Ask students to answer the following questions:

1. Why should caregivers give only as much help as a child needs? (When children can do things on their own or with little help, they feel a sense of accomplishment, which encourages learning.)

2. Why is it important to provide simple explanations about concepts? (Too much information can cause a young child to stop listening.)

3. Why are frequent breaks in structured play important for children? (They need time for unstructured play and a rest from stimulation.)

## Reteach

### W₁ Writing Support

**Report**

**Language Development** Ask students to spend an hour playing with a child between the ages of one and three. This could be a younger sibling, niece, nephew, cousin, or neighbor. Students should pay attention to the level of language development, taking notes to record specific sounds, words, and sentences. Have students write a report addressing these questions: Does the child pronounce letter sounds correctly? What sounds does he or she have trouble with? Does the child speak in sentences? Is the child easy to understand? (Students' reports should answer the questions posed. Reports should be written in a logical order and should be written in paragraph form. Paragraphs should contain a topic sentence and sentences with details that support the topic sentence. Reports should contain no grammar or spelling errors.)

# Language Abilities

In the toddler and preschool years, language abilities grow at a very rapid pace. As with other areas of development, children's speech varies greatly. Brain development research has brought new insights into how children learn to use language. Children have an inborn ability to **decipher**, or interpret, sounds, words, sentences, and grammar from the language they hear. Most children develop language skills in the first three years of life.

## Speech Development

Infants learn to recognize the speech of their parents and other caregivers early in life. Soon after, infants begin practicing the sounds of speech by babbling. Beginning at around twelve months of age, babbling gradually transforms into a child's first words.

**W₁** Between their first and second birthdays, children work at learning new words. They like to learn the names of everything. They also enjoy listening to the sounds the words make. At this point, rhyming books that tell stories are ideal. At twelve months of age, a child may speak two to eight words, but by age two, that jumps to about 50 words. During this period, most children use one or two words rather than a whole sentence to express a thought. For example, Chloe points to a jar on the counter and says "cookie" to mean "I want a cookie."

Encourage language development by talking to young children about their lives. Speak clearly about children's everyday experiences. For example, take the time to describe whatever they are seeing or doing. "Look at the big bite you've taken out of that yellow banana. Does it taste sweet and yummy?"

**W₁** At about age two, children usually start combining a few words to make short sentences, such as "Doggie bark" or "Jimmy fall down." Between ages one and two, a child typically calls himself or herself by name. At about two years of age, children begin to use pronouns, such as I, we, you, and they.

At about two and a half, children begin to learn some basic grammar rules. They learn by listening to other people talk, rather than by any formal teaching. For example, a child begins to add an *s* to words to make them plural. The child then applies this rule to all words. Foots and tooths make as much sense to them as hands and eyes.

Language skills continue to develop, but at varying rates. Most three-year-olds can:
- Say their name and age.
- Make all the vowel sounds and say the consonants P, B, M, W, H, D, T, and N.

**Model Language**
Children's language development is influenced by how adults around them speak. *Why is it important to use good grammar when speaking to a child?*

## Explore the Photo

**Caption Answer** Children learn speech by imitating adults, so they will use the kind of grammar that they hear. If they hear good grammar, they will use it.

**Discussion** Ask students to consider what might happen to the language development of a child who was not exposed to language before three years of age. (Answers will vary, but students should recognize that the child would be delayed in learning speech.)

## CULTURE MATTERS

### Preschool in France

In France, nearly every child attends preschool, which is free of charge. It costs the French government about $3,300 per child per year. These schools bring together children from a variety of communities and encourage social development. They also prepare children for further education.

French preschools are staffed with highly trained teachers. The French government pays for teachers' education, and the government inspects each school every year. Preschool teachers in France earn salaries equal to those of elementary school teachers. In comparison, preschool teachers in the United States usually earn about two-thirds as much as elementary school teachers.

★ **Build Connections** *What do the relative salaries of teachers in France and in the United States tell you about preschool education in these two countries?*

**NCSS I A Culture** Analyze and explain the ways groups, societies, and cultures address human needs and concerns.

---

- Speak without repeating a word or syllable.
- Use sentences of at least four words.
- **C** Usually be understood by others, even by strangers.
- Answer what and where questions.
- Understand what is meant by words such as *on, in,* and *under.*
- **U** Follow a command with several parts.

## Speech Difficulties

Parents become concerned when they believe their child is a late talker. Some make the mistake of pressuring the child. This pressure just makes the child aware of the problem, and possibly makes it worse.

A child who does not seem to understand what is said, does not speak at all, or speaks very little should have a thorough examination. Local public school districts often provide free screenings by a speech-language pathologist. A speech-language pathologist is a specialist who is trained to detect and help correct speech problems. Speech difficulties can often be treated

beginning at age three or earlier. It is important to identify any physical problem that may be interfering with a child's language development as early as possible. Hearing problems, learning disabilities, and mood disorders may all hinder a child's speech development.

Children with speech difficulties need to be lovingly encouraged, but not pressured. Such an attitude can help the child cope with, and perhaps even overcome, the problem. Teasing or constant corrections only make the problem worse. Children need to know they are loved, regardless of any learning difficulties.

### Articulation

The term **articulation** refers to the ability to use clear, distinct speech. It is normal for children to have trouble with articulation until at least age three or four. Some children skip syllables or leave off the endings of words. These problems usually correct themselves over time. A speech-language pathologist can determine whether a problem is likely to go away on its own or if speech therapy is needed. **W₂**

Section 12.2 Encouraging Learning from One to Three **369**

---

## CULTURE MATTERS

### Preschool in France

**Discussion** Ask students if they agree with the following statement: Some people think high-quality preschool should be available to all children, regardless of their family's income. (Students may agree or disagree. They may feel that high-quality preschool should be a right not a privilege, and that it benefits everyone in society. Some may say that education will never be equal and point out the university system.)

**Build Connections** *Answers will vary but students might conclude that people in France value preschool education more than those in the United States. They might also suggest that preschool in France is valued as much as elementary school.*

## Reteach *cont.*

**C** **Critical Thinking**
**Analyze** The text states that most three-year-olds can usually be understood by others, even strangers. Ask students why it is important that a child be understood by strangers as well as by parents and caregivers. (Answers will vary. Children need to be able to speak clearly in case they become lost or a parent or caregiver becomes incapacitated.)

**U** **Universal Access**
**Verbal Learners** Ask verbal learners to discuss the following: Most three-year-olds can follow a command with several parts. What does a child's ability to follow a multiple-step command say about his or her memory? (Students answers will vary but may include: When a child is able to follow a multiple-step command, it means the child's memory has developed the ability to keep more than one idea in mind until a task is completed. It also means that the child has developed the ability to focus without being distracted from a task.)

**W₂** **Writing Support**
**Explanation**
**Articulation** Read this scenario to students: Two-year-old Sean is very articulate for his age, but he consistently uses "him" when he means "he," as in "Him took the book from me." Discuss with students how Sean's parents and caregivers could address the problem. Then have students write an explanation of the most effective method for handling the problem. (See p. 350 for tips on writing an explanation. Students explanations should include how the method works and how it can be implemented in Sean's case.)

### R Reading Strategy

**Main Idea** Ask students to work independently to determine the main idea of the section titled Stimulating Play Activities. Students should then write the main idea in a single sentence. Have students share and discuss their sentences with the class. (Sentences will vary, but may be something similar to: It is important for parents and caregivers to spend time playing with young children.)

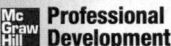

**Mini Clip**
**Reading: Focus Lesson**

A teacher models how to find the main idea or theme of a selection by identifying the major and minor details.

### C₁ Critical Thinking

**Make a Deduction** The text states that some adults do not like to get on the floor and play with children. Ask students to deduce why playing on the floor with a young child is important. (Answers will vary. Playing on the floor with a young child is important because the parent or caregiver can respond instantly and individually to the child and can use the time to learn about the child's interests and talents.)

### ✓ Reading Check

**Recall** Hearing problems, learning disabilities, and mood disorders may all hinder a child's speech development.

---

## SAFE CHILD HEALTHY CHILD

### Basic Toy Safety

Everyone involved in a child's life should make sure all toys are safe. Here are some safe toy guidelines:

- Any fabric should be labeled flame resistant or flame retardant.
- Paint must be lead-free.
- Crayons, paints, and other art materials should be labeled nontoxic.
- Toys should not be able to break into sharp pieces.

For younger children:

- Toys should not have long cords or strings that could wrap around a child's neck.
- Toys and rattles should not be able to get lodged in a child's mouth.
- Objects should be over 1.75 inches in diameter to avoid choking hazards.

**Be Prepared** Spend about a half hour examining the toys of a child under age four. If you need help finding a child, ask your parent or teacher for help. Check each toy for safety. Write a summary of what you find. Tell the child's parents if you find any toys you feel are unsafe.

---

Instead of constantly correcting a child's pronunciation of words, it is important for adults to set a good example with their own speech. Suppose a toddler says "ba" and reaches for a bottle. The caregiver can give the bottle to the child and say, "Here's your bottle."

### Stuttering

Stuttering is a more serious speech difficulty for young children. **Stuttering** is when a person speaks with sporadic repetition or prolonged sounds. However, many adults mistake normal speech hesitations for stuttering. A child may repeat whole words or phrases: "Johnny . . . Johnny . . . Johnny. He . . . he . . .

---

he hit Zoe!" This is not true stuttering. In this case, the child's speaking and thinking abilities are still immature. It is difficult to get the words out quickly and smoothly.

True stuttering can be identified by the rhythm, pitch, and speed of speech. It is rapid, forced, short, and sharp in sound. Usually, the child repeats only the beginning sound of a word: "I c—c—c—can't g—g—g—go outside." The child often also shows tension in some way, such as gasping, sputtering, or rapid blinking.

The cause or causes of stuttering are still not completely understood. Some children overcome the problem with speech therapy. However, most children who stutter outgrow it. Experts advise against finishing words for a child. Children who stutter need time to say the words on their own.

### ✓ Reading Check

**Recall** What are three things that might interfere with a child's speech development?

## Play Activities and Toys

Toys are an important part of play. They help children explore, imagine, and try out different roles. They encourage the development of motor skills and help children learn to share and cooperate with others, making further learning easier and more fun.

### Stimulating Play Activities

Often a child's favorite toy is really a caregiver. A caregiver can respond instantly and individually to the child's efforts at play and imagination. A toy cannot respond in the same way. Some adults do not like to get on the floor and play with children. However, such interaction can expand the child's learning. At the same time, the parent or caregiver can learn more about the child's interests and talents.

**R**

**C₁**

### Evaluating Toys

With thousands of toys to choose from, knowing what to buy is important. Parents should ask themselves these questions:

- **Is the toy safe?** This is the single most important consideration. Make sure there are no small parts that could be swallowed

---

## SAFE CHILD HEALTHY CHILD

### Basic Toy Safety

**Identify** Ask students to identify how parents and other caregivers can best choose safe, appropriate toys for young children. (They should check all aspects of the toy and follow the guidelines presented in the text.)

**Be Prepared** Summaries will vary, but they should indicate whether students found any unsafe toys. If so, they should explain why they thought the toys were unsafe.

or sharp edges that could cut. Be aware that a toy that is safe for a three-year-old may not be safe for a one-year-old. Also make sure the toy is not flammable and indicates nontoxic when appropriate. The federal government's Consumer Products Safety Commission alerts the public about unsafe toys.

- **Is it well-made and durable?** There is nothing more discouraging for a child or an adult than having a toy break the first time it is played with. Can the toy withstand the rough treatment it will receive?

- **Will it be easy to care for?** A well-loved stuffed animal needs to be washable. Similarly, books with hard pages and wipe-clean covers are the most practical choice for toddlers.

- **Does it encourage the use of a child's imagination?** Some toys do everything for the child. With no need to pretend, the child's imagination develops more slowly. Look for simple toys that can be used in a variety of ways. A talking doll may say ten phrases, but a child can make an ordinary doll say anything!

- **Is it colorful?** Young children respond more readily to colorful objects. These toys also encourage children to learn the names of colors.

- **Will it be easy for the child to handle?** Think about the size of the toy and its level of difficulty. The excitement of receiving a motorized car is quickly lost if the child is too young to use it on her own.

- **Is it something the child will enjoy?** A toy that a child finds engaging is much better than a toy forced upon him by a well-intentioned parent or relative.

## Age-Appropriate Toys

Toys should be appropriate for a child's age. Infant toys are usually not challenging enough for three-year-olds. An older child's toys are not able to hold the attention of most fourteen-month-olds. Children at different ages enjoy and learn from different kinds of toys. The following are some suggestions for age-appropriate toys.

**Appropriate Toys**
Toys should be safe, age-appropriate, and enjoyable for a child. *How would you rate the toy in the photo based on the questions in this section?*

### Reteach *cont.*

**U Universal Access**

**Kinesthetic and Visual Learners**
Have students review the bulleted item: Does it encourage the use of a child's imagination? Be sure students understand the concepts presented. Have students select a toy that encourages the child to use his or her imagination and create an advertisement for that toy. The ad should be written for parents and caregivers. It should draw attention, arouse interest, create desire, and cause action on the part of the parent or caregiver. Students should illustrate their ads. (Ads will vary depending on the toy chosen. Use these criteria when evaluating your students' writing: Does the ad promote? Does it provide facts and opinions to persuade the audience? Does it appeal to people who may not be interested?)

**C₂ Critical Thinking**

**Evaluate** Show students various advertisements for toys and have them decide if each toy is most appropriate for a one-, two-, or three-year-old child. Ask students to explain their decisions. (Students' answers will vary depending on the toys shown in the advertisements. The rationale behind their explanations should show an understanding of the physical and intellectual abilities of one-, two-, and three-year-old children.)

## ➤ Explore the Photo

**Caption Answer** Students' answers will vary, but should be based on what they have learned. Students may rate it as good because it is colorful, easy to handle, and engaging for the child.

**Discussion** Ask students how parents might handle a situation in which their child was given a puzzle that was developmentally inappropriate. What might they say to the child? (Answers might include: This is a wonderful puzzle. We can work on it together now and you can work on it alone when you're older.)

# Section 12.2

## Assess

### Study Tools

Have students go to the Online Learning Center at **glencoe.com**:

- Take the **Practice Test**.
- Download **Study-to-Go** content.

Use the **Student Activity Workbook** for additional practice.

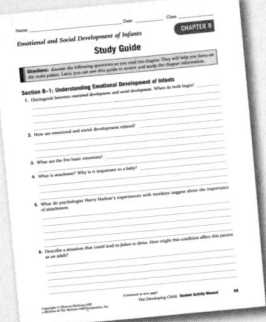

## Close

### Culminating Activity

**Summarize** Have students summarize ways that parents can encourage language development in young children. (Parents can talk to children about their lives; speak clearly; take time to describe events, actions, and things; guide children in talking about what they are seeing or doing.)

**NCLB** connects academic correlations to book content.

---

### One to Two Years

At this age, a child practices motor control and learns through exploration. Some favorite toys are household items, such as metal pans, wooden spoons, and plastic storage bins. Pull toys, floating bath toys, toys that make music, and sorting toys are also popular.

Most toys that allow the child to use large muscles are also good choices. These toys may include swings, riding toys, balls, and cardboard boxes. One-year-olds also enjoy stuffed animals, sturdy books, simple puzzles, and toy cars. Avoid toys with parts that are small enough to fit into the cardboard tube from a roll of toilet paper.

### Two to Three Years

Coordination and understanding improve greatly during this year. In addition, the child wants to do what adults are doing. The desire to imitate and role play provides ideas for many toys. Good choices are a child-size vacuum cleaner or lawn mower, telephone, plastic or wooden tools, play dishes, and empty food containers. Crayons, play dough, books, and large blocks are popular. A sandbox with a toy bucket and shovel can provide hours of enjoyment.

### Three to Four Years

Preschoolers' improved motor skills and increased imagination bring interest in more complex toys. These often use fine motor skills. Dolls to dress, construction sets, and similar toys are popular. Three-year-olds love to mold play dough, color, cut with blunt scissors, and paint. Three-year-olds also spend longer periods with books than younger children. They enjoy listening to music. They like to do puzzles and use swings and slides. Many three-year-olds love to ride a tricycle.

## Section 12.2 — After You Read

### Review Key Concepts

1. **Describe** one of the principles for guiding a child's learning and give an example of a caregiver putting it into practice.
2. **Identify** two kinds of speech difficulties that might indicate that speech therapy is needed.
3. **List** at least four toys that are appropriate and fun for toddlers between the ages of one and two.

### Practice Academic Skills

 **English Language Arts**

4. Suppose you are applying for a summer job at a local preschool. You have heard that this preschool emphasizes reading readiness. Write a letter to the school's director explaining ways in which you would encourage reading readiness in young children.

> **NCTE 12** Use language to accomplish individual purposes.

 **Science**

5. Most researchers believe that genetic, neurological, and social factors all play a role in stuttering. Conduct research to learn more about how these factors are related to stuttering. Write a one-page report to share what you learn.

> **NSES A** Develop abilities necessary to do scientific inquiry, understandings about scientific inquiry.

 **Check Your Answers** Check your answers at this book's Online Learning Center at **glencoe.com**.

---

### Review Key Concepts

1. Possible answer: Give only as much help as the child needs. If a child can put on his own shoes, but does not know left from right, mark one of them. If the child is left-handed, mark the left shoe. Then say, "Which hand do you hold your spoon in?"
2. Examples of speech difficulties include problems with articulation and stuttering.
3. Possible answers include household items such as metal pans, pull toys, floating bath toys, toys that make music, and sorting toys.

### Practice Academic Skills

4. Letters will vary but students should explain that they would read dynamically and with enthusiasm, encourage children to recognize the relationship between written and spoken words, and practice associating specific sounds with written letters.
5. Reports will vary but should list the research done with the goal of determining genetic, neurological, and social factors involved in stuttering.

## Chapter Summary

Intelligence is determined by both heredity and environment. Children learn concepts and the words for those concepts in stages. Learning methods include incidental, trial-and-error, imitation, and directed learning. There are seven areas of intellectual activity. Children's learning can be guided by adults. Caregivers should encourage reading and math readiness during play and everyday activities. Toys should be safe, appealing, and appropriate to a child's age. Speech difficulties include problems with articulation and stuttering.

## Vocabulary Review

1. Write each of the vocabulary terms on an index card, and the definitions on separate cards. Work in pairs or small groups to match each term to its definition.

**Content Vocabulary**
- neuroscience (p. 353)
- intelligence (p. 354)
- incidental learning (p. 355)
- trial-and-error learning (p. 355)
- imitation (p. 356)
- directed learning (p. 356)
- creativity (p. 361)
- reading readiness (p. 365)
- math readiness (p. 366)
- articulation (p. 369)
- stuttering (p. 370)

**Academic Vocabulary**
- elicit (p. 360)
- stifle (p. 362)
- unstructured (p. 367)
- decipher (p. 368)

## Review Key Concepts

2. **Summarize** how heredity and the environment shape intelligence.
3. **Describe** the four methods of learning used by young children.
4. **List** the seven areas of intellectual activity.
5. **List** 11 ways to help guide a child's learning.
6. **Identify** four parts of language that children have an inborn ability to decipher.
7. **Summarize** how to evaluate toys for young children.

## Critical Thinking

8. **Evaluate** Recall a toy you enjoyed playing with as a child. Evaluate the benefits of that toy for young children.
9. **Apply** Suppose you are visiting a mother. Her toddler is feeding himself spaghetti. The mother gets upset at the mess. What might you say?
10. **Judge** Some people argue that in order to create an equal society, preschool must be free to all children. Do you agree? Explain your answer.

## Content and Academic Vocabulary Review

1. Students should create vocabulary flash cards and practice in pairs or groups.

## Review Key Concepts

2. Intelligence capacity is inherited. Stimulation of the environment and encouragement of caregivers help children realize their potential.

3. Incidental—unplanned learning. Trial-and-error—child tries several solutions before finding one that works. Imitation—child watches and copies others. Directed—results from being taught.

4. attention, memory, perception, reasoning, imagination, creativity, and curiosity

5. Give time and attention, allow time for thinking, give as much help as the child needs, encourage children to draw conclusions, demonstrate problem solving, model problem solving, maintain a positive attitude, keep explanations on the child's level, allow children to explore and discover, help children understand the world and how it works, and take frequent breaks.

6. sounds, words, sentences, and grammar

7. Points to consider: Is it safe, well-made, durable, colorful, and easy to care for? Will it encourage children to use their imagination? Will it be easy for the child to handle and be enjoyable?

## Critical Thinking

8. Student answers will vary depending on the toy. Possible benefits might include bright colors or multiple uses.

9. Responses will vary. Even though the mess creates more work for the parent, this is an important stage for children who need to feel independent and learn new skills. Student might suggest putting a mat under the child's chair, making sure the child is wearing old clothes, or having the toddler help with clean-up.

10. Students' answers will vary; students should give specific reasons for their answers.

### Family & Community Connections

**11.** Student presentations will vary. Typically, when the reader is more animated and the child is encouraged to become involved, the child will enjoy the story more.

### Health Skills

**12.** Letters will vary. Students should clearly state their opinion and use appropriate research to support their opinion. Students may say that children need more free playtime to help develop their imaginations.

### Observation Skills

**13.** The student should create a chart listing the 11 ways adults can guide children's learning. They should have kept track of the number of times they observed each method. In their summary, they should discuss which methods appeared to be most effective.

### Real-World Skills

**14.** Ads will vary but should list the skills that could be learned from the toy.

**15.** Books will vary but should teach how to categorize objects.

**NCLB** Activity correlated to Social Studies standards.

### Family & Community Connection

**11. Make Reading Time Fun** Read a book to a child. Act out the story and involve the child by asking questions. Then read the same book to another child. This time, though, simply read the words with no emotion. Compare and contrast the two situations. Prepare a short oral presentation on what you observe.

### Health Skills

**12. Unstructured Time** Many parents today are enrolling young children in more academic classes and structured activities. This means children have less unstructured time for play. Conduct research on the benefits of free, unstructured playtime. Write a letter to the editor of a local newspaper stating whether you believe young children need more unstructured time. Use the information from your research to support your opinion.

### Observation Skills

**13. Guided Learning** A child develops best when adults guide his learning in appropriate ways. Guided learning builds on a child's natural desire to understand more about his world. This chapter discusses 11 ways to guide learning.

**Procedure** Create a chart listing the 11 ways adults can guide a child's learning. Then visit a child care center, park, or other place where adults and young children interact. Use the chart to keep track of how many of the 11 ways you observe being used.

**Analysis** Analyze your chart. Write a summary stating how many of the guidance methods you observed. Discuss which ways you feel were most effective.

> **NCSS I A Culture** Analyze and explain the ways groups, societies, and cultures address human needs and concerns.

**N C L B**

### Real-World Skills

| | | |
|---|---|---|
| **Interpersonal and Collaborative Skills** | **14. Work in Teams** Follow your teacher's direction to form into teams. As a team, think of an idea for a new toy. Then create an advertisement with a drawing of your toy and a list of the skills it teaches. Class members will vote on which toy they think will best teach the listed skills. | |
| **Technology Skills** | **15. Write a Children's Book** Use a desktop publishing or word processing application to write a children's book. The book should teach children how to categorize objects. For example, you might say, "Point to all the round things on this page." Either create original drawings or use clip art. Make the book colorful and fun so it will appeal to toddlers. | |
| **Financial Literacy** | **16. Buying Toys** Imagine that you are offering child care in your home. You will have 8 three- and four-year-olds. You have $400 to spend on toys. Create a list of appropriate toys. Research the Internet or go to local stores to get ideas for toys and to determine the toys' prices. | |

 **Additional Activities** For additional activities, go to this book's Online Learning Center at **glencoe.com**.

**16.** Lists will vary. There should be age-appropriate toys for eight children. The total should not be more than $400.

### Academic Skills

**17.** Paragraphs will vary. For example, by encouraging the toddlers to finger paint, students are teaching about color, shapes, and texture. Students should also include necessary supplies.

The *Early Childhood Observations CD* offers additional lessons with videos to build students' observation skills.

**Part 1:** Learning to Observe
**Part 2:** How Children Develop
**Part 3:** Working With Young Children
**Part 4:** Extended Observations
**Part 5:** Resources and Answer File

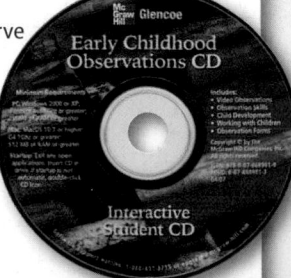

## Academic Skills

 **English Language Arts**

**17. Promote Learning** Suppose you are a teacher of three-year-olds in a child care center. Choose one kind of activity related to art, music, or language, such as painting. Write a paragraph to describe how you would use this activity to promote learning. In addition, describe any toys or supplies you would use.

> **NCTE 4** Use written language to communicate effectively.

 **Mathematics**

**18. Childproofing** To childproof her kitchen, a mother wants to move all cleaning products to a cabinet that is out of reach for her three-year-old. She needs to make sure the new cabinet is large enough. The cabinet under the sink has dimensions of 1'6" x 2' x 16". What is the volume of this cabinet in cubic inches?

**Math Concept** **Compute Volume**
Volume is the measure of space occupied by a solid region. The volume of a rectangular solid equals its length times its width times its height.

**Starting Hint** Convert all three dimensions to inches. Then multiply them together to find the total volume.

**Math** For math help, go to the Math Appendix at the back of the book.

> **NCTM Measurement** Understand measurable attributes of objects and the units, systems, and processes of measurement.

**Science**

**19. What's So Funny?** The ability to understand jokes often requires abstract thinking and a level of language skills that young children do not have. The type of abstract thinking needed to understand many jokes does not develop until about age 11.

**Procedure** Find a joke that requires abstract thinking. Tell it to three 4-year-olds. Then tell it to three 12-year-olds. Keep track of their reactions.

**Analysis** Write a paragraph in which you compare the responses of the two groups. Draw a conclusion based on these responses.

> **NSES A** Develop abilities necessary to do scientific inquiry, understandings about scientific inquiry

 **Standardized Test Practice**

### ANALOGY

Some objective tests contain questions that test your ability to recognize analogies. These are problem-solving questions. You determine the relationship between two or more words and then apply that relationship to another set of words. Read the Test-Taking Tip. Then answer the multiple choice question.

**20.** *Toy* is to *play* as *book* is to ____.
   a. paper
   b. draw
   c. read
   d. word

> **Test-Taking Tip** To solve an analogy, begin by determining the relationship between the first two terms. Then choose the term that has the same relationship to complete the second pair. Review your choice. Ask yourself: Is it logical?

Chapter 12 **375**

**18.** The volume is 6,912 cu. in. (1'6" = 18", 2' = 24"; 18 × 24 × 16 = 6,912)

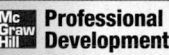 **Professional Development**

 **Mini Clip** Math: **Surface Area and Volume**

A teacher reviews how the formula for the volume of a cube can be extended to the formula for the volume of a rectangular prism.

**19.** Students should write a summary of their findings, as well as a discussion of whether or not the responses were what would be expected. Generally, 12-year-olds can understand jokes requiring abstract thinking, but 4-year-olds cannot.

**NCLB** connects academic correlations to book content.

 **Standardized Test Practice**

**20.** c. read

**Test-Taking Tips** Tell students to study for tests over a few days or weeks, and continually review class material. Suggest that they vary their approach and sometimes work with a study partner.

**Analogies** Tell students to pay careful attention to a word's position in an analogy. They can create a simple sentence that states the relationship between the first pair of words, and then try each of the answer choices in a similar sentence as part of the second word pair.

## TECHNOLOGY Solutions

**Use these technology solutions to streamline chapter assessment!**

 **ExamView Assessment Suite** CD allows you to create and print out customized tests or ready-made unit and chapter tests, complete with answer keys.

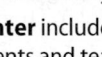 **TeacherWorks Plus** is an electronic lesson planner that provides instant access to complete teacher resources in one convenient package.

**Online Learning Center** includes resources and activities for students and teachers.

# Unit Thematic Project

## Help Children Learn

In this unit you have learned that one- to three-year-olds grow and develop physically, emotionally, socially, and intellectually. You have also learned that children often develop at different rates and in their own way. In this project, you will observe a group of one- to three-year-olds. You will use what you learned to create an activity that will help one- to three-year-olds learn a physical, emotional, social, or intellectual skill.

 **My Journal**

If you completed the journal entry from page 289, refer to it to see if your thoughts have changed after reading the unit.

### Project Assignment

In this project, you will:
- Choose an area of child development.
- Create an observation checklist.
- Arrange to observe one- to three-year-olds in a child care setting.
- Take notes during your observation.

### Child Development Skills Behind the Project

- Evaluate the skill levels of one- to three-year-olds.
- Identify age-appropriate learning activities for one- to three-year-olds.
- Determine activities that would be enjoyed by one- to three-year-olds.

### Academic Skills

 **English Language Arts**

> **NCTE 5** Use different writing process elements to communicate effectively.
>
> **NCTE 12** Use language to accomplish individual purposes.

**376** Unit 4 The Child from One to Three

- Ask a child care center worker to clarify any activities or procedures that you did not understand.
- Write an age-appropriate learning activity for one- to three-year olds in one of the four areas of child development.
- Present and demonstrate the learning activity to your class.

### Step 1 Choose an Area of Child Development that Interests You

The topics below are four areas of development that can be observed in children. As you consider your area of interest, think about the types of activities that would help children develop skills in that area.
- Physical development
- Emotional development
- Social development
- Intellectual development

### Step 2 Prepare for Your Observation

Make a checklist that will help you take notes during your observation. It may include such things as: name of the activity, number of children involved, materials needed, and behaviors observed.

---

### Step 3

**Connect to Your Community**

Ask students what they might learn from observing child care professionals conducting learning activities. (Students may say that they will learn how to organize an activity, how to give directions to young children, how to keep the children on task.) Ask students if they think the observation might help them in other ways. (Possible answers include that it might provide ideas to use while babysitting or for future use with their own children.)

### Step 4

**Write and Demonstrate Your Activity**

Give students these tips on writing and demonstrating their activity:

- Write the activity in step-by-step format.
- List all materials and equipment needed.
- Ask for volunteers from the class to help you demonstrate the activity.

---

## Focus

### Discussion Starter

**Teaching Children** Ask students to list things they have done that have helped a young child learn a new skill. (Students may suggest such things as playing games with a younger sibling, or helping a child to dress.)

 Project correlated to English Language Arts standards.

### Step 1

**Choose an Area of Child Development that Interests You**

Students should select an area of child development that interests them. As students begin work on their learning activities later in the project, they may discover that they can use one activity to teach skills in more than one developmental area. Students may choose multiple areas if this occurs.

## Teach

### Step 2

**Prepare for Your Observation**

Observation checklists should allow students to take minimal notes and allow them more time to observe. Students should be able to call on their own experiences to develop the checklist. Suggest that students think about activities in their own classes. What kinds of things would they need to know besides the number of participants and the materials needed?

**Writing Skills**

★ Organize the information on the checklist in a logical order. Keep like items together.

★ Leave enough space to fill in information about the observations.

★ Check your spelling.

## Step 3 Connect to Your Community

Work with your teacher to arrange an observation at a child care center in your community. During your observation, note how the staff conduct activities with the children. Fill in your observation checklist.

**Observation Skills**

★ Sit or stand quietly outside of the activity area.

★ Do not engage the children in conversation.

★ Take careful notes.

★ After the activity, ask the child care workers for clarification if there is anything you do not understand.

## Step 4 Write and Demonstrate Your Activity

Use the Unit Thematic Project Checklist on the right to plan, write, and demonstrate your activity.

**Presentation Skills**

★ Organize and distill information.

★ Write creatively.

★ Speak clearly and concisely.

## Step 5 Evaluate Your Child Development Skills and Academic Skills

Your project will be evaluated based on:

• Content and organization of your information.

• Mechanics—presentation and neatness.

• Speaking and listening skills.

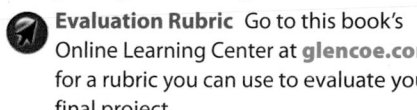 **Evaluation Rubric** Go to this book's Online Learning Center at **glencoe.com** for a rubric you can use to evaluate your final project.

### Unit Thematic Project Checklist

| | |
|---|---|
| **Activity** | ✓ Develop an observation checklist to aid you in taking notes during your observation at a child care center. |
| | ✓ Write an original activity to promote physical, emotional, social, or intellectual growth for one- to three-year-olds. |
| | ✓ Label the parts of your activity: Goal (what you want the children to learn), Preparation (what must be done before the activity), Materials (all supplies needed for the activity), Step-by-Step Directions (how the activity is completed), Conclusion (how the activity will end such as asking the children questions or cleaning up). |
| **Presentation** | ✓ Make a presentation to your class to demonstrate your new activity and discuss what you learned. Explain how the activity is promoting growth in your chosen area of development. |
| | ✓ Ask for class volunteers to participate in your demonstration. |
| | ✓ Invite the students to ask questions. Answer three questions. |
| | ✓ Demonstrate in your answers that you respect their perspectives. |
| | ✓ Turn in your observation checklist and the directions for completing your activity. |
| **Academic Skills** | ✓ Communicate effectively. |
| | ✓ Organize your presentation so the audience can follow along easily. |
| | ✓ Thoughtfully express your ideas. |

## Assess

### Step 5

**Evaluate Your Child Development Skills and Academic Skills**

**Rubric** Encourage students to go to this book's Online Learning Center at **glencoe.com** for a rubric they can use to evaluate their activity and presentation. Students can use the rubric as a content checklist when developing observation checklists, writing activities, and preparing demonstrations.

## Close

### Culminating Activity

**Project Assessment** In this activity, students created a learning activity to stimulate physical, emotional, social, or intellectual growth in one- to three-year-olds. Have students form pairs and exchange activities. Students should read their partner's activity and offer suggestions for how to add to or extend the activity to make it more challenging, while still keeping it age appropriate. (Be sure students understand that they are not evaluating or critiquing their partner's activity; they are only making suggestions to extend the activity.)

## Developing Community Involvement

### Learning about Children

There are many things to learn about the physical, emotional, social, and intellectual development of children. Ask students to contact a child care facility and ask about volunteer opportunities. Students may want to volunteer an hour or two a week to learn more about working with young children. Explain that the skills they would learn will be helpful

now if they babysit or in the future if they have children of their own or decide to work with children.

A **Family & Community Involvement** worksheet about this topic is available:

📎 At this book's Online Learning Center at **glencoe.com**

💿 On the TeacherWorks CD

| Title | Objectives |
|---|---|
| **CHAPTER 13**<br>**Physical Development from Four to Six** | • **Summarize** how an average child's posture and body shape change from ages four to six.<br>• **Compare and contrast** average motor skills development for four-, five-, and six-year-olds.<br>• **Explain** why good nutrition is essential for children ages four to six.<br>• **Identify** three ways that four- to six-year-olds are able to care for themselves.<br>• **Describe** three steps that can help minimize toileting accidents.<br>• **List** three areas of outdoor safety to discuss with four- to six-year-old children. |
| **CHAPTER 14**<br>**Emotional and Social Development from Four to Six** | • **Identify** a single characteristic that marks the emotional development of four- to six-year-olds.<br>• **List** five ways to help children reduce worry and tension.<br>• **Describe** how to help children develop self-confidence.<br>• **List** three social skills children must learn as they begin school.<br>• **Identify** seven guidelines for encouraging moral development in children.<br>• **Describe** three ways to encourage conflict resolution and cooperation in children. |
| **CHAPTER 15**<br>**Intellectual Development from Four to Six** | • **List** eight types of intelligences.<br>• **Identify** the common element of all theories of intellectual development.<br>• **Identify** three ways to encourage children's interest in learning.<br>• **Describe** the link between speech development and physical development.<br>• **Explain** how parents can help their children adjust to kindergarten. |
| **Unit Thematic Project**<br>**Teach New Skills** | • **Write** a My Journal entry on Growth and Development.<br>• **Interview** a child growth and development expert.<br>• **Create** a brochure to share what you learn. |

## Understanding Brackets, Letters, and Ability Levels in the Teacher Wraparound Edition

**Brackets** Brackets on the reduced student edition page correspond to teaching strategies and activities in the Teacher Wraparound Edition. As you teach the lesson, the brackets show you exactly where to use the teaching strategies and activities.

**Letters** The letters on the reduced student edition page identify the type of strategy or activity. See the key below to learn about the different types of strategies and activities.

**Ability Levels** Teaching Strategies that appear throughout the chapters have been identified by one of three codes to give you an idea of their suitability for students of varying learning styles and abilities.

**Resources** Key program resources are listed in each chapter. Icons indicate the format of resources.

### KEY TO LETTERS

**D** **Develop Concepts** activities help teachers gauge and plan for students' concept development.

**R** **Reading Strategy** activities help you teach reading skills and vocabulary.

**S** **Skill Practice** provides leveled instruction for meeting individual needs and learning styles.

**W** **Writing Support** activities provide writing opportunities to help students comprehend the text.

**C** **Critical Thinking** strategies help students apply and extend what they have learned.

**U** **Universal Access** activities provide differentiated instruction for English language learners, and suggestions for teaching various types of learners.

**NCLB** **No Child Left Behind** activities help students practice and improve their abilities in academic subjects.

### KEY TO ABILITY LEVELS

**L1** Strategies should be within the ability range of all students. Often full class participation is required.

**L2** Strategies are for average to above-average students or for small groups. Some teacher direction is necessary.

**L3** Strategies are designed for students able and willing to work independently. Minimal teacher direction is necessary.

**ELL** Strategies are especially accessible to English Language Learners.

### KEY TO RESOURCE ICONS

Print Material

CD or DVD Resources

Online Learning Center (OLC)

**TeacherWorks™**
All-In-One Planner and Resource Center

### Teacher Wraparound Edition

**Unit Resources:**
Unit Thematic Project Student Rubrics
Unit Family and Community Involvement Activities

**Chapter Resources:**
Lesson Plans
Chapter Summaries, Content and Academic Vocabulary
Graphic Organizers

**Textbook Resources:**
Student Activity Workbook with Academic Integration
Additional Activities
Enrichment Activities

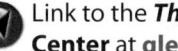 Link to the **The Developing Child Online Learning Center** at **glencoe.com**.

## Unit Overview

### Introduce the Unit

Introduce the unit by describing the main concepts of each chapter in the unit.

### Unit 5

This unit discusses the physical, emotional, social, and intellectual growth and development of children from four to six years old.

**Chapter 13** The discussion in this chapter focuses on the physical growth and development of four- to six-year-olds. Topics of discussion include steady growth, changes in body shape, growth of permanent teeth, refining of gross and fine motor skills, and establishing eating habits.

**Chapter 14** This chapter teaches students how children develop increased independence, curiosity, and boldness; how they express anger and resolve conflicts as they mature; how their imaginations grow and develop; and how preschool and kindergarten can expand their world.

**Chapter 15** Students will learn about the intellectual development of four- to six-year-olds in this chapter. Traditional intelligence tests; Howard Gardner's eight intelligences; the theories of Piaget, Vygotsky, and Montessori; everyday opportunities for learning; development of language skills; and children in school are topics of discussion.

# Unit 5

# The Child from Four to Six

**Explore the Photo**
Four- to six-year-olds enjoy being active. *What kinds of activities might appeal to this age group?*

378

## Explore the Photo

**Caption Answer** Students' answers will vary but may include ideas such as playing tag, running, throwing or bouncing a ball, jumping, painting, putting together puzzles, building with blocks, drawing, coloring, playing house, playing soccer, jumping rope, playing on swings and slides, or climbing on playground equipment.

**Discussion** Ask students whether they think the children in the photo look happy and healthy. Ask them to explain what would contribute to a child being happy and healthy. (Answers will vary but may include that the children are well taken care of, they eat healthful foods, get plenty of exercise, or live in nurturing environments.)

**Chapter 13** Physical Development from Four to Six

**Chapter 14** Emotional and Social Development from Four to Six

**Chapter 15** Intellectual Development from Four to Six

## Unit | Thematic Project Preview

**Teach New Skills**

After completing this unit, you will learn that four- to six-year-olds are constantly learning new physical, emotional, social, and intellectual skills. In your unit thematic project you can identify activities that will help promote the development of these skills.

### My Journal

**Growth and Development** Write a journal entry about one of the topics below. This will help you prepare for the unit project at the end of the unit.

- Identify how four- to six-year-olds differ physically from one- to three-year-olds.
- Describe intellectual activities a four- to six-year-old could do that a one- to three-year-old could not do.
- Discuss the difference in social skills between one- to three-year-olds and four- to six-year-olds.

**379**

**Discussion Starter**
**Activity Table**
Create a four-column table on the board. Label the columns Physical, Emotional, Social, and Intellectual. Have the class brainstorm activities for each of these categories that would be appropriate for four- to six-year-olds. After you have created the lists, go over each activity and ask students to evaluate whether it truly meets the criteria. If it does not meet the criteria, have students explain why. Some activities may be appropriate for more than one column.

**FCCLA Assessing Children's Media**

Have students create a list of children's media that teaches important skills or values to young children. Watch the various videos and DVDs and have students write a summary for each. Ask the local library to include the list and written summaries for parents to review prior to showing the media to their children.

## Unit | Thematic Project Preview

**Teach New Skills**
Tell students that as part of this unit, they will learn how four- to six-year-olds grow and develop physically, emotionally, socially, and intellectually. Students will consider how understanding the growth and development experienced by four- to six-year-olds can help parents and caregivers provide better care and learning experiences for children.

### My Journal

**Growth and Development** Students select one topic to write a journal entry about. The journal entry should relate to the subject of the thematic project: Teach New Skills. The purpose of the journal entry is to prepare students for the project at the end of the unit. (Journal entries will vary depending on the topic selected and students' personal opinions.)

**STANDARDS BASED LESSON PLANNING** *The Developing Child* provides students with instruction and assessment in the following fundamental content areas:

## National Standards Correlations

| Standards | Pages |
|---|---|
| **12.1.1** Analyze physical, emotional, social, spiritual, and intellectual development. | 383–384, 385–387, 389, 401 |
| **12.1.3** Analyze current and emerging research about human growth and development, including research on brain development. | 387 |
| **15.1.2** Analyze expectations and responsibilities of parenting. | 390, 395–396 |
| **15.1.3** Analyze consequences of parenting practices to the individual, family, and society. | 391–392 |
| **15.1.4** Analyze societal conditions that influence parenting across the life span. | 396 |
| **15.2.1** Choose nurturing practices that support human growth and development. | 391, 393–394, 395 |
| **15.3.3** Summarize current laws and policies related to parenting. | 393 |

**NO CHILD LEFT BEHIND** NCLB activities, information, and skills practice will help your students attain NCLB proficiency. Students will improve their abilities in the following academic standards areas:

## Academic Standards Correlations

| Discipline | Standard | Feature/Activity |
|---|---|---|
| **English Language Arts** | **NCTE 1** Read texts to acquire new information. | **Reading Guide (pp. 382, 388)** |
| | **NCTE 4** Use written language to communicate effectively. | **Writing Activity (p. 380)** **Academic Skills (p. 401)** |
| | **NCTE 5** Use different writing process elements to communicate effectively. | **After You Read (p. 387)** |
| | **NCTE 7** Conduct research and gather, evaluate, and synthesize data to communicate discoveries. | **After You Read (p. 397)** |
| **Mathematics** | **NCTM Number and Operations** Compute fluently and make reasonable estimates. | **Math in Action (p. 383)** **Academic Skills (p. 401)** |
| **Science** | **NSES 1** Develop an understanding of science unifying concepts and processes: systems, order, and organization; evidence, models, and explanations. | **Observation Skills (p. 400)** |
| | **NSES A** Develop understandings about scientific inquiry. | **Academic Skills (p. 401)** |
| | **NSES C** Develop understanding of matter, energy, and organization in living systems; and behavior of organisms. | **After You Read (p. 387)** |
| | **NSES F** Develop understanding of personal and community heath. | **After You Read (p. 397)** |

## Professional Development

**MINI CLIP VIDEO LIBRARY**
Targeted professional development is correlated throughout *The Developing Child*. **The McGraw-Hill Professional Development Mini Clip Video Library** provides teaching strategies to strengthen academic and learning skills. Log on to **glencoe.com**.

In this chapter, you will find these Mini Clips:
- **ELL** Level 2 Proficiency, p. 386
- **ELL** Using Manipulatives, p. 389
- **Reading** During and After Reading, p. 393
- **Reading** Obstacles to Achievement, p. 395
- **Reading** Standards-Based Instruction, p. 401

## Reading and Writing Strategies

**Writing Activity: Question and Answer** (p. 380)
Students use writing tips to pose a question concerning caring for a four- to six-year-old and write a detailed essay in response.

**Before You Read** (pp. 382, 388)
A pre-reading question or statement will help students make a personal connection to content.

**Graphic Organizer** (pp. 382, 388)
A visual tool will help students organize and remember new content.

**Reading Check** (pp. 384, 393, 394, 396)
A question allows students to make a quick comprehension self-check.

**After You Read** (pp. 387, 397)
Organize and process students' understanding of what they have read.

## Chapter Features

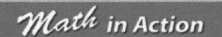
**Physical Education** (p. 383)
Children need physical education each week.

**Cerebral Palsy** (p. 385)
Cerebral palsy affects body movement and muscle coordination.

**Encourage Physical Activity** (p. 391)
Adults can encourage children to be physically active.

**Taking on Roles** (p. 393)
Children express their creativity and explore the world by taking on the roles of adults around them.

**What Is the Best Way to Handle Bedwetting?** (p. 395)
Children often continue wetting the bed even after they are toilet trained.

**Keep Children Safe from Strangers** (p. 396)
Children should be taught to avoid contact with adults they do not know.

**Children's Activity Director** (p. 398)
Learn the skills needed to succeed as a Children's Activity Director.

## Chapter Overview

### Introduce the Chapter

In this chapter, students learn how children physically develop from ages four to six. Their body shapes change as their limbs become longer and their posture becomes straighter. Both fine and gross motor skills improve. Parents and caregivers must teach children how to care for their bodies, including developing good eating habits.

### Build Background

Hold up a cell phone. Ask students: Do you think you could teach a two-year-old to use this phone? How about a four-year-old? Discuss that in this chapter students will see how the rapidly improving motor skills of children from four to six greatly expands their potential for learning different types of skills.

## Writing Activity

### Question and Answer

This active learning activity prompts students to write a question and answer about the concerns a caregiver might have for a four- to six-year-old child. After students have completed the writing activity, ask for volunteers to share their writing with the class. Student responses can be used as a basis for classroom discussion. (When evaluating students' questions and answers, determine whether the question can be answered using generally known facts; the answer responds to key words in the question; the answer contains a statement identifying the main idea; and the answer includes an introduction, a body with specific details, and a conclusion.)

# Chapter

## 13 Physical Development from Four to Six

## Chapter Objectives

After completing this chapter, you will be able to:

- **Summarize** how an average child's posture and body shape change from ages four to six.
- **Compare and contrast** average motor skills development for four-, five-, and six-year-olds.
- **Explain** why good nutrition is essential for children ages four to six.
- **Identify** three ways that four- to six-year-olds are able to care for themselves.
- **Describe** three steps that can help minimize toileting accidents.
- **List** three areas of outdoor safety to discuss with four- to six-year-old children.

## Writing Activity  Question and Answer

**Caring for Four- to Six-Year-Olds** There are many challenges associated with caring for four- to six-year-olds. Children this age are becoming more independent but still need a lot of care and guidance from their parents. Use your knowledge of children in this age range to write a question and answer. The question should focus on the concerns a caregiver might have. Answer the question in a detailed essay.

**Writing Tips** Use these tips to write an effective question and answer:
1. Develop a question that is challenging but realistic.
2. Plan an answer that connects to the key words of the question.
3. Organize your answer with an introduction, a body, and a conclusion.

380

## CLASSROOM Solutions

### Print Resources

 **Student Edition**

 **Teacher Wraparound Edition**

 **Student Activity Workbook**

 **Student Activity Workbook Teacher Annotated Edition**

### Technology Resources

 **Online Learning Center** has resources and activities for students and teachers. Includes an Online Student Edition.

 **Interactive Student Edition** allows students to instantly access review materials, examples, and exercises.

**Section** **13.1** Growth and Development from Four to Six

**Section** **13.2** Caring for Children from Four to Six

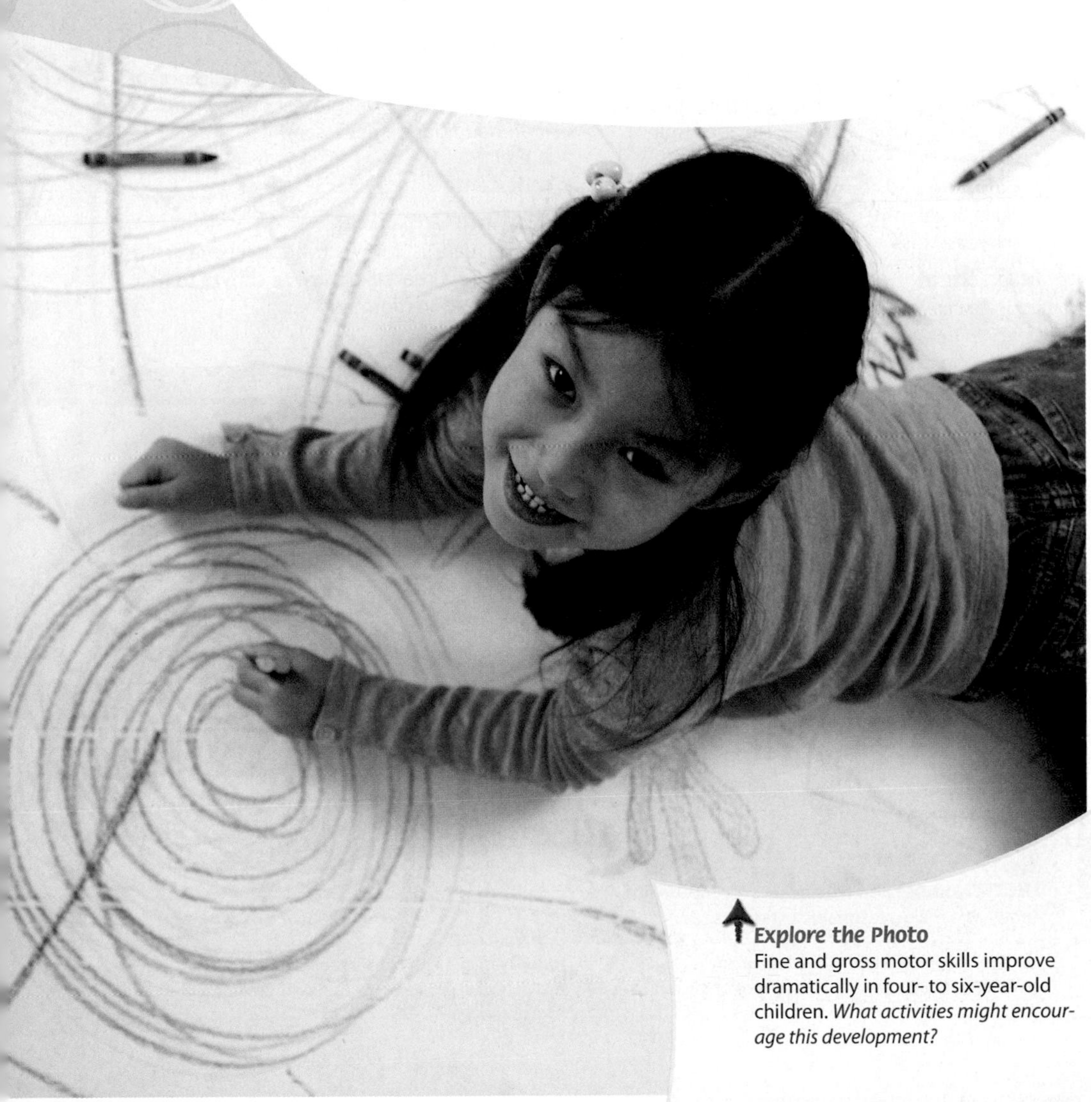

## Review the Sections

Introduce the chapter by reviewing the sections:

### Section 13.1

From ages four to six, children's growth slows down slightly, but their bodies become straighter and slimmer. Their permanent teeth begin to come in. As gross motor skills improve, they become adept at running and jumping. Improved fine motor skills allow them to learn to print, draw, and fasten buttons.

### Section 13.2

Parents and caregivers should use the USDA's MyPyramid Plan as a guide to make certain that children are getting appropriate nutrition based on their ages and activity levels. Children's ability to care for themselves grows as they mature, so they should be taught skills such as dressing themselves, properly brushing their teeth, and outdoor safety.

### ▶ Explore the Photo

**Caption Answer**
Students' answers will vary, but should include activities appropriate for the age level. Answers might include coloring, building with blocks, running, jumping, or playing hopscotch.

**Discussion** Ask students: Why is art an excellent way to help young children develop their fine motor skill? (Many art projects, such as working with clay, painting, and cutting out pictures for collages, require the use of small muscles. In addition, most children enjoy being creative.)

↑ **Explore the Photo**
Fine and gross motor skills improve dramatically in four- to six-year-old children. *What activities might encourage this development?*

**381**

 **TeacherWorks Plus** is an electronic lesson planner that provides instant access to complete teacher resources in one convenient package.

**Presentation Plus!** provides visual teaching aids for every section.

 **The Early Childhood Observations CD** presents video observations and lessons on observation skills and child development.

**The Developing Brain eTransparencies and Guide** include information and activities to offer insights into brain development and diseases of the brain.

## Focus

### Bell Ringer Activity

**Developing Fine Motor Skills**

Display a collection of objects that children must learn to manipulate by using their fine motor skills. Objects might include scissors, a pencil, a paint brush, a shoe with a shoelace, or silverware. Explain that learning these skills gives children a sense of accomplishment and independence. However, the learning process also takes time and determination.

## Preteaching

### Vocabulary

Write the word *ambidextrous* on the board, underlining the separate parts: *ambi* and *dextrous*. Explain that *ambi* is Latin for "both" and *dexter* is Latin for "hand." Discuss other words that contain these components such as *ambiguous* and *dexterity*.

### Graphic Organizer

The Graphic Organizer is also on the TeacherWorks CD.

(Graphic organizer should include any four of the following: primary teeth are lost, permanent teeth appear, first molars are first permanent teeth to appear, there are four first molars, primary teeth are lost in the same order they came in.)

**NCLB** connects academic correlations to book content.

---

### Reading Guide

#### Before You Read

**Stay Engaged** One way to stay engaged when reading is to turn each of the headings into a question. Then read the section to find the answer.

#### Read to Learn
**Key Concepts**
- **Summarize** how an average child's posture and body shape change from ages four to six.
- **Compare and contrast** average motor skills development for four-, five-, and six-year-olds.

 **Main Idea**
Four- to six-year-old children grow and develop in many areas. These include height, weight, posture, body shape, teeth, motor skills, and hand preference.

#### Content Vocabulary
 permanent teeth
 ambidextrous

 **Graphic Organizer** Go to this book's Online Learning Center at **glencoe.com** to print out this graphic organizer.

#### Academic Vocabulary
You will find these words in your reading and on your tests. Use the glossary to look up their definitions if necessary.
- erect
- dexterity

#### Graphic Organizer
As you read, list four facts about six-year-olds' teeth. Use a chart like the one shown to help organize your information.

| Six-Year-Olds' Teeth |
|---|
| 1. |
| 2. |
| 3. |
| 4. |

### Academic Standards · · · · · · · · · · · · · · · · · · ·

**NCLB**

 **English Language Arts**
NCTE 4 Use written language to communicate effectively.

**Mathematics**
NCTM Number and Operations Compute fluently and make reasonable estimates.

**Science**
NSES C Develop understanding of matter, energy, and organization in living systems; and behavior of organisms.

**NCTE** National Council of Teachers of English
**NCTM** National Council of Teachers of Mathematics

**NSES** National Science Education Standards
**NCSS** National Council for the Social Studies

---

### Reading Guide

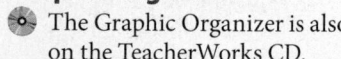

#### Before You Read

Have students think of a sport that they are good at. Then ask for a volunteer to discuss how he or she became skilled at this sport. Perhaps they practiced their hook shot every night or took swimming lessons each summer. In the same way, young children become proficient at physical activities because they are constantly practicing.

####  Develop Concepts

**Main Idea** Discuss the main idea with the students. Ask: How do you think a child's change in body shape during this time might be related to his improved gross motor skills? (As a child grows slimmer and straighter, he is better able to perform activities such as running and jumping.)

## Growth from Four to Six

If you have ever been around four-, five-, or six-year-old children, you know how active they are at this time of life. Instead of sitting still, they wiggle. Rather than walk, they run. It is sometimes hard to get them to stay in one place long enough to put on their clothes or to eat. So what is the purpose behind all this activity? The answer is simple: Practice makes perfect. Children this age are constantly improving their physical skills.

## Height and Weight

The rate of physical growth in children between the ages of four and six is only slightly slower than in children ages one to three. The average increase in height during these years is about 2½ to 3 inches (6.4 to 7.6 cm) per year. Most children gain about 4 to 5 pounds (1.8 to 2.3 kg) each year as well. These are just average gains among children, so larger or smaller gains are common, too. Boys tend to be slightly taller and heavier than girls during this period. See **Figure 13.1** on page 384 for the average heights and weights for boys and girls during each year of this age range.

### *Math* in Action

#### Physical Education

An elementary school wants to improve its physical education program. An ideal physical education program in elementary school will offer three periods a week of approximately 45 minutes duration. If the school follows this recommendation, how many hours per month will each student spend in physical education?

**Math Concept** **Multi-Step Problem** When solving problems with more than one step, think through each of the steps before you start.

**Starting Hint** First, calculate how many minutes are spent in physical education class each week (3 periods × 45 minutes). Then multiply your answer by the number of weeks in a month (4). Convert your final answer to hours (60 min = 1 hour).

 **Math** For math help, go to the Math Appendix at the back of the book.

**NCTM Number and Operations** Compute fluently and make reasonable estimates.

**Growing and Changing**
Four- to six-year-olds walk and run with their arms close to their bodies. *Why do four- to six-year-olds no longer hold their arms away from their bodies when they walk or run?*

---

➤ **Explore the Photo**

**Caption Answer** Toddlers hold their arms away from their body to help them balance. Four- to six-year-olds have better balance and can hold their arms closer to their bodies.

**Discussion** Ask students: What are some games that a six-year-old can play that a three-year-old is not capable of playing? (Responses will vary. Possible answers: jump rope, kickball, tag.)

---

## Section 13.1

## Teach

### Discussion Starter

**Get Moving** Show a photo of a two-year-old walking with arms out for balance. Then show a photo of a five- or six-year-old running. Ask: How old do you think the first child is? How about the second? What do these two photos tell you about development between these two ages? (They tell you that children become much more adept at gross motor skills as they become older.)

### C Critical Thinking

**Analyze** Ask students: Why is physical education important in elementary school? How do you think it might affect a child's learning in the classroom? (Children need encouragement in developing motor skills, which physical education can provide. They also need to run off excess energy so that they are better able to focus in the classroom.)

### R Reading Strategy

**Slow Down** Explain that solving math problems requires a careful reading of the instructions. The Math in Action feature is an example of this type of problem. Tell students to carefully write down and label each value they will need in solving this problem. They may need to re-read the problem several times before they can calculate the answer.

### *Math* in Action

**Physical Education**
Answer: There will be 9 hours of physical education per month (3 × 45 = 135; 135 × 4 = 540; 540 ÷ 60 = 9).

**NCLB** Activity correlated to Mathematics standards.

## S Skill Practice

### Guided Practice

**Create a Diagram** Have students work in pairs to create a diagram showing the 32 permanent teeth that most children will eventually have. Instruct students to conduct research to learn the names of the teeth and label their diagrams appropriately. (Diagrams should show the 32 permanent teeth with appropriate labels.) **L1 ELL**

**Label a Diagram** Have students conduct research to learn the names of the 32 permanent teeth. In addition, they should determine the approximate age at which each tooth comes in. They then should create a diagram with each tooth's name and the age at which it typically erupts. (Students should create a diagram of the 32 permanent teeth, including each tooth's name and the approximate age at which that tooth erupts.) **L2**

**Conduct a Survey** Organize students into small groups. Instruct each group to interview children and teens from ages six through eighteen. They should attempt to interview at least four individuals in each age group. Students should determine how many permanent teeth each individual has. They then should create a graph showing the average number of teeth for each age group. (Students should create a graph showing the average number of permanent teeth for each age group in the range from six through eighteen.) **L3**

### ✓ Reading Check

**Recall** They are constantly working to improve their physical skills.

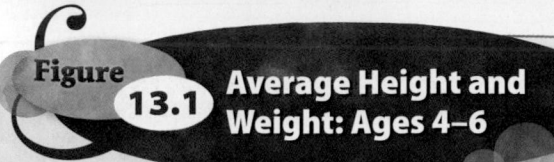

**Figure 13.1 Average Height and Weight: Ages 4–6**

As children grow older, they experience significant differences in height and weight. *What is the average weight gain for a girl from age four to age six?*

| Age | BOYS Height / Inches | Weight / Pounds | GIRLS Height / Inches | Weight / Pounds |
|---|---|---|---|---|
| Four years | 40½ | 36 | 39½ | 35½ |
| Five years | 43 | 40½ | 42½ | 39¾ |
| Six years | 45½ | 46 | 45¼ | 44½ |

## Posture and Body Shape

Children's posture changes noticeably between their fourth and seventh birthdays. Their bodies become straighter and slimmer, and the protruding tummy from babyhood flattens. Children this age hold their shoulders back and their upper bodies more **erect**, or straight. The chest, which had previously been rounded, broadens and flattens with improved abdominal strength. The legs also lengthen rapidly, growing straighter and firmer. Even the neck becomes longer.

Balance and coordination show improvement in these years as well. Four- to six-year-olds hold their arms nearer to their body when they walk or run.

## Teeth

It is common for school pictures of a six-year-old to show a gaping hole in the child's smile. Children this age are losing their primary teeth. The larger permanent teeth generally begin to appear at about this time. **Permanent teeth** are teeth that will not be naturally replaced by another set. They replace the primary teeth that the child has lost. Children will eventually have a total of 32 teeth in the permanent set, to replace the 20 primary teeth.

The six-year-old molars are also called the first molars. These are the first permanent teeth to appear. These are new teeth, not replacements for primary teeth. There are four first molars. There are two upper ones and two lower ones. They are positioned behind the primary teeth. These molars act as an anchor. They keep all the teeth in front of them in place. The primary teeth are lost in the same order as they came in. This is generally the two lower front teeth first, then the two upper front teeth.

### Thumb Sucking

Some four-, five-, and six-year-olds continue to suck their thumbs. This is a way to comfort themselves or handle stress. Adults may worry about this habit, but in most cases, it is best ignored. Trying to force a child to quit can cause more problems than the habit itself. Generally, children stop sucking their thumbs on their own.

If thumb sucking seems excessive, check with a dentist. After the child's fifth birthday, thumb sucking may cause changes in the shape of the roof of the mouth or in the way the teeth line up.

### ✓ Reading Check

**Recall** Why are four-, five-, and six-year-old children so active?

**Figure 13.1 Average Height and Weight: Ages 4–6**

**Caption Answer** The average weight gain for a girl from age four to age six is nine pounds.

**Discussion** Ask students: At what age are boys and girls weights most different? (age 6) At what age are their heights most different? (age 4)

## Development from Four to Six

Children ages four to six change in many ways. They change in height and weight, and in posture and body shape. They also change in motor skills. Both gross and fine motor skills are improved. Children also usually develop a hand preference during this time period.

### Motor Skills

Between the ages of four and six, most basic gross and fine motor skills improve significantly in children. Many motor skills, such as throwing a ball, must be taught. Children require guidance and practice. The timetable for the development of these skills varies. Just as in the earlier years, some children master one skill but are not as proficient at another.

For example, five-year-old Cheryl may have the skills to put together complex puzzles but not yet be able to jump rope. Her friend Gail may be comfortable with easier puzzles but may excel at jumping rope. Ishaan may be able to tie his shoes before he can write words. The chart in **Figure 13.2** on page 386 summarizes typical motor skills at each age.

### Gross Motor Skills

Recall that gross motor skills are also called large motor skills. This is because they use the large muscle groups, such as those in the arms, legs, abdomen, and back. Four-, five-, and six-year-olds are very energetic. Their favorite activities are usually physical actions such as running, jumping, climbing, or turning somersaults. After age four, children are learning how to throw and catch both large and small balls. Five-year-olds show improved speed and coordination in all their activities. The movements of six-year-olds are even more smoothly coordinated. Six-year-olds enjoy balancing activities, such as walking on a curb or learning to ride a bicycle. Also, activities that involve rhythm appeal to them. This includes such activities as dancing to music and jumping rope to chanted songs.

Children need plenty of opportunities to develop their motor skills. Giving them time and space to run, jump, and climb on play structures helps them develop their large motor skills. As with any skill, motor skills take practice. If Michelle never plays with balls, then she will not develop the skills of throwing or catching a ball. Gabriel is not allowed to ride his bicycle because his mom is afraid

---

## RESPOND TO SPECIAL NEEDS — Cerebral Palsy

The term *cerebral palsy* refers to a number of neurological disorders that appear in infancy or early childhood and permanently affect body movement and muscle coordination. These disorders do not worsen over time. The majority of children with cerebral palsy are born with it. However, it may not be detected until months or years later. The most common signs are a lack of muscle coordination when performing voluntary movements, stiff or tight muscles and exaggerated reflexes, and muscle tone that is either too stiff or too floppy.

Cerebral palsy cannot be cured. Treatment will often improve a child's capabilities, though. Treatment may include physical and occupational therapy; speech therapy; drugs to control seizures, relax muscle spasms, and alleviate pain; surgery; braces and other orthotic devices; wheelchairs and walkers; and communication aids such as computers with attached voice synthesizers.

**Critical Thinking** Research the causes of cerebral palsy. Summarize your findings in a one-page report and be ready to share your findings with the rest of the class.

---

## Assess

### Quiz

Ask students to answer the following questions:

1. What is the average gain in height for a boy from age four to age six? (The average gain in height is five inches.)
2. What are the first teeth that children get that are not replacements for their baby teeth? (They are the six-year-old molars, or first molars.)
3. Why can it become a problem if a child continues to suck a thumb after his or her fifth birthday? (It can cause changes in the shape of the roof of the mouth or in the way the teeth line up.)

## Reteach

### C Critical Thinking

**Solve Problems** Tell students that five-year-old Joe is frustrated because all of his friends can ride a two-wheel bike and he cannot. Recognizing that this motor skill develops sooner for some children than others, how might Joe's parents help him? (The parents can explain that it is just taking him longer to learn this skill and they can help him practice. They also can engage him in other activities to develop his gross motor skills and sense of balance, such as walking on a line on the floor, or playing ball. Joe's parents could also point out some of the skills that he is already good at, such as drawing or running.)

---

## RESPOND TO SPECIAL NEEDS — Cerebral Palsy

**Discussion** Ask the class: How might caregivers encourage a child with cerebral palsy to develop gross motor skills? (Possible answer: by modifying activities in ways that allows the child to perform them, for example, by providing a bar to hang onto while jumping.)

**Critical Thinking** Reports will vary but should include that cerebral palsy is caused by abnormalities in parts of the brain that control muscle movements. A small number of children have cerebral palsy as the result of brain damage early in life.

**Reteach** *cont.*

### U Universal Access

**Kinesthetic Learners** For this activity, students will need access to some type of video recording equipment. Organize students into pairs or small groups. Each group should choose a fine motor skill that they will teach a four-year-old. Examples might include brushing teeth or properly using scissors. They then should create a video demonstrating how to properly perform this skill. Instruct students to remember the age of their audience and to keep the instructions as simple as possible. (Students should create a video aimed at four-year-olds that demonstrates how to perform a specific fine motor skill.) **ELL**

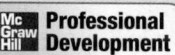

**McGraw Hill Professional Development**

**Mini Clip ELL: Level 2 Proficiency**

Author Jana Echevarria discusses the characteristics of Level 2 proficiency English learners.

### W Writing Support

**Question and Answer**

**Motor Skill Development** Tell students to use their understanding of the difference between gross motor skills and fine motor skills to write a question related to the development of these skills in children between ages four and six. They then should write a thorough answer to their question. (Refer to p. 380 for tips on writing questions and the corresponding answers. Students' questions will vary but should be related to the difference between the two types of motor skills.)

---

**Figure 13.2 Physical Developmental Milestones—Ages 4–6**

A four-year-old can cut on a line with scissors. *What fine motor skills does a six-year-old have?*

| Age | Fine Motor Skills | Gross Motor Skills |
|---|---|---|
| **4 Years** | ❖ Dresses and undresses self<br>❖ Cuts on line with scissors<br>❖ Copies a circle and a cross | ❖ Hops on one foot<br>❖ Throws ball overhand<br>❖ Alternates feet walking up and down stairs<br>❖ Walks backward easily |
| **5 Years** | ❖ Draws a person with head, body, arms, and legs<br>❖ Prints some letters<br>❖ Buttons clothing<br>❖ Copies a triangle and a square<br>❖ Uses spoon and fork to eat, but still uses fingers for some foods | ❖ Turns somersaults<br>❖ Skips with alternating feet<br>❖ Balances on each foot for short period |
| **6 Years** | ❖ Cuts, pastes, and colors skillfully<br>❖ Writes entire words<br>❖ Ties shoelaces | ❖ Can ride a two-wheel bicycle with training wheels<br>❖ Jumps rope<br>❖ Throws and catches a ball with more ease and accuracy (also requires fine motor skills and good hand-eye coordination) |

he will fall and get hurt. However, he can only learn with practice. Gabriel's mother can help him develop the skills and still keep him safe by ensuring that he wears a bicycle helmet and safety pads.

### Fine Motor Skills

Fine motor skills are also called small motor skills. This is because they involve coordination of small muscle groups such as those in the fingers, wrists, and ankles. Four- and five-year-olds show improved dexterity. Dexterity is ease and skill in physical activity. So improved dexterity means physical activity comes more easily. Children can use their hands and fingers skill-fully. Most four-year-olds can learn to lace their shoes. However, most children cannot tie their shoelaces until they are five or six. While most four-year-olds can dress themselves, they may not be able to fasten buttons until they are five.

Five-year-olds' hand-eye coordination has improved to the point that they can pour liquids from a pitcher into a glass, as long as the pitcher is not too heavy or too full. They enjoy cutting, pasting, and using glue. They also can print some letters but might have trouble printing words. Six-year-olds show even greater fine motor skills and hand-eye coordination. Most children this age are able to draw detailed pictures, use scissors, and write their own names.

---

**Figure 13.2 Physical Developmental Milestones—Ages 4–6**

**Caption Answer** A six-year-old can cut, paste, and color skillfully; write entire words; and tie shoes.

**Discussion** Ask for volunteers to state a specific motor skill and then have the class categorize it as either a gross or fine motor skill. (Gross motor skills might include jumping rope, playing hop-scotch, batting a ball, or swinging on a swing. Fine motor skills might include tying shoelaces, writing words, pouring juice, or brushing teeth.)

Hand-eye coordination also improves some skills children already had. For example, Mia enjoyed playing catch with her dad. When she was four, she usually had to chase the ball across the yard. By the time she was six, Mia could catch the ball most of the time.

Activities such as making cards, painting pictures, drawing, tracing outlines, cutting, and playing games help improve fine motor skills. Many child care centers will encourage children this age to do crafts, such as making animal masks from paper plates or making cards for Mother's Day. Children with well-developed fine motor skills may be more successful at learning to print.

## Hand Preference

As mentioned in Chapter 10, some children express a preference for using one hand more than the other after the age of two. Others may continue to switch off during the preschool years. By about the second half of the fifth year, most children consistently use either their right or left hand for most activities, such as holding crayons or feeding themselves. Naturally, whichever hand they choose becomes the stronger, more skillful one. About 85 percent of all children prefer to use their right hand for most activities. Only a few people are ambidextrous. **Ambidextrous** means being able to use both hands with equal skill.

Research continues on how a preference for one hand develops. Some people believe that heredity is probably the source of right- or left-handedness. Others think it depends on which hand parents usually put objects in during the child's early years. Some research links hand preference to the areas of the brain controlling motor skills or language. Whatever the cause, professionals now agree that there is no reason to influence a child toward using one hand over the other.

**Study Tools**

Have students go to the Online Learning Center at **glencoe.com**:

- Take the **Practice Test**.
- Download **Study-to-Go** content.

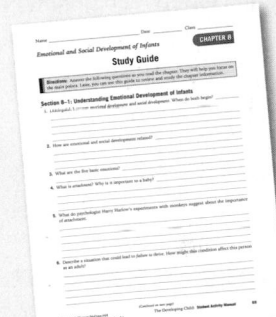

Use the **Student Activity Workbook** for additional practice.

---

## Section 13.1   After You Read

### Review Key Concepts

1. **Explain** the best way to generally deal with a five-year-old who sucks his or her thumb.

2. **List** three motor skills that an average six-year-old has mastered that most three-year-olds would not be able to do.

### Practice Academic Skills

 **English Language Arts**

3. Brainstorm activities that can help children this age refine their fine motor skills. Suggest activities that are not mentioned in the chapter. Be sure to include activities that use different tools and implements. Create a poster that shows at least three ideas.

> **NCTE 5** Use different writing process elements to communicate effectively.

 **Science**

4. Research teeth in the human body. Find out when teeth typically come in and in what order. Do this for both the primary and permanent teeth. Do primary and permanent teeth come in the same order? What makes primary teeth fall out? Write a one-page report with your findings.

> **NSES C** Develop understanding of matter, energy, and organization in living systems; and behavior of organisms.

 **Check Your Answers** Check your answers at this book's Online Learning Center at **glencoe.com**.

**NCLB**

### Close

## Culminating Activity

**Displaying Different Emotions** Have students work in groups to create a poster illustrating the motor skills of a typical six-year-old. The illustrations should be divided into two categories: fine motor skills and gross motor skills. Have the groups share their posters with the class.

**NCLB** NCLB connects academic correlations to book content.

---

## Section 13.1   After You Read

### Review Key Concepts

1. It is generally best to ignore thumb-sucking in a five-year-old.

2. Most three-year-olds would not be able to ride a two-wheeled bicycle with training wheels, jump rope, or catch a ball.

### Practice Academic Skills

3. Posters will vary but may include activities such as tracing, preparing a sandwich, or playing with marbles.

4. Reports will vary. Babies typically begin getting teeth when they are 6 to 12 months old. Most children have the entire set of 20 primary teeth by the time they are 3 years old. At age 5 or 6, the primary teeth begin to come out and by age 12 or 13, most children have all of their permanent teeth. There are 20 primary teeth and 28 permanent teeth. Four additional teeth, called wisdom teeth, usually grow in the back of the mouth giving a complete set of 32 teeth.

## Focus

### Bell Ringer Activity

#### Providing Guidance

Have students work individually to create a definition of the word *guidance*. When they are done, ask for volunteers to share their definitions. Ask: What is the difference between guiding a child's actions and directing a child's actions? (Giving direction involves simply telling a child what to do whereas guidance involves encouraging the child to make the best decision with the aid of the parent.)

## Preteaching

### Vocabulary

Ask students: What part of speech is *identification*? (noun) What verb does it come from? (identify) Discuss that many verbs can be changed into nouns by using the suffix *-tion*. Some examples include *protect*, *define*, and *inform*.

### Graphic Organizer

The Graphic Organizer is also on the TeacherWorks CD.

(Graphic organizers should list: caregivers not being aware of the need for good nutrition; not understanding the basics of good nutrition; relying too heavily on convenience foods; relying on fast foods; setting a poor example of good eating habits; and allowing children to choose their own food without guidance.)

**NCLB** connects academic correlations to book content.

## Reading Guide

### Before You Read

**Understanding** Write down questions while reading. Many of them will be answered as you read. If they are not, share the list with your teacher.

### Read to Learn
#### Key Concepts
- **Explain** why good nutrition is essential for children ages four to six.
- **Identify** three ways that four- to six-year-olds are able to care for themselves.
- **Describe** three steps that can help minimize toileting accidents.
- **List** three areas of outdoor safety to discuss with four- to six-year-old children.

#### Main Idea
Caregivers must provide for children's nutritional needs, teach them about good nutrition, and teach them self-care. School-age children need to be taught about outdoor safety.

#### Content Vocabulary
◇ group identification
◇ fluoride
◇ enamel

### Academic Vocabulary
You will find these words in your reading and on your tests. Use the glossary to look up their definitions if necessary.
- persuade
- undermine

### Graphic Organizer
As you read, look for six reasons children may have poor nutrition. Use a diagram like the one shown to help organize your information.

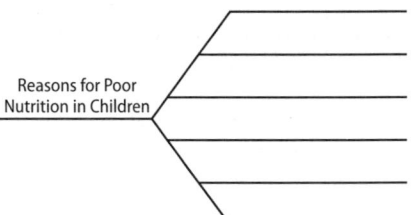

Reasons for Poor Nutrition in Children

 **Graphic Organizer** Go to this book's Online Learning Center at **glencoe.com** to print out this graphic organizer.

### Academic Standards . . . . . . . . . . . . . . . . . . . . . . .

#### English Language Arts
**NCTE 7** Conduct research and gather, evaluate, and synthesize data to communicate discoveries.

#### Science
**NSES F** Develop understanding of personal and community health.

**NCTE** National Council of Teachers of English
**NCTM** National Council of Teachers of Mathematics
**NSES** National Science Education Standards
**NCSS** National Council for the Social Studies

## Reading Guide

### Before You Read

Ask students: What kinds of food did you love as a child? What did you hate? Do you still have the same food preferences today? Discuss that young children can have very distinct food preferences and that sometimes these preferences can make it a challenge to see that they eat healthfully.

### D Develop Concepts

**Main Idea** Discuss the main idea with the students. Ask students how important they think it is for parents to model the behaviors they are teaching. (Possible answer: It is absolutely vital. For example, if a parent eats poorly, the child probably will too, regardless of what the parent teaches the child.)

## Health and Wellness

A steady and varied supply of nutritious foods is the best fuel for children's physical and intellectual development. The recommendations in MyPyramid can help parents choose foods for good nutrition. The amount of food children need varies depending on their weight and level of physical activity.

For example, Stephanie spends hours kicking a soccer ball, running with her dog, and riding her bike. She needs more food energy than her cousin, who prefers coloring and building with blocks. Older or very active children need more food daily. Younger or less active children require less food each day. The USDA's MyPyramid Plan gives guidance. You will learn more about MyPyramid in Chapter 16.

Research has shown that four- to six-year-old children do better when they eat five or six small, nutritious meals and snacks a day instead of three large ones. Small meals and snacks are better suited to their small stomach size and provide a more constant level of energy. Snacks should be nutritious, appealing foods rather than convenience foods that are high in salt, sugar, or fat. Apple slices, grapes,

cheese, yogurt, and raisins are nutritious and popular with this age group.

Parents and other caregivers can encourage good eating habits by making food appealing and by modeling good food habits. Researchers have found that forcing a child to eat, making an issue of eating certain foods, or using foods as a reward may lead to poor eating habits and weight issues.

**Growing Independence**
Four-, five-, and six-year-olds are more independent and need less physical care than younger children do. *What are children this age able to do for themselves?*

---

**Explore the Photo**

**Caption Answer** Answers will vary but may include dressing themselves, brushing teeth, cleaning up toys, or feeding themselves.

**Discussion** Why do you think these children are smiling? (Possible answers: They are smiling because they enjoy being physically active and are pleased with their abilities to move and interact with one another.)

---

**Discussion Starter**

**Parents and Nutritional Guidance** Hold up an advertisement for a fast food restaurant. Ask students: At what age do you think most children begin to be influenced by this type of ad? What can parents do to reduce the influence of these ads? (Possible answers: Children may be influenced by these as young as three or four years old. Parents can make healthy food choices available, set an example of nutritious eating, and emphasize the importance of developing a strong, healthy body.)

**McGraw Hill Professional Development**

**Mini Clip**
**ELL: Using Manipulatives**

A teacher uses concrete objects to illustrate lesson concepts.

**C Critical Thinking**

**Infer** Have a volunteer read aloud the quote in the Expert Advice box. Ask: What can you infer from this statement? What message is Naomi Aldort sending to parents? (Answers may vary. Aldort is telling parents to not pressure their children into trying to perform skills for which they are not ready as this can only lead to difficulties. Instead, parents should model appropriate behavior and follow the child's lead.)

**Teach** cont.

**C Critical Thinking**

**Apply** Tell students that four-year-old Kendra fills up on sugary snacks and then will not eat at mealtime. When Kendra's Aunt Janice takes care of her, Kendra continually begs for candy and cookies. Ask students: Based on what you have learned in this section, what might Janice do to encourage Kendra to eat more nutritious foods? (Possible answers: Janice might find out what nutritious foods Kendra will eat and purchase those foods. She might engage Kendra in preparing nutritious foods; for example Kendra might help spread peanut butter on celery sticks.)

**U Universal Access**

**Students with Learning Disabilities** As a class, discuss the importance of preschools providing nutritious snacks for children. Create a list of nutritious snacks. Instruct students to include foods from each of the following groups: vegetables, fruits, milk, meat and nuts, and grains. (Students should create a list of nutritious snacks for preschoolers, such as carrot and celery sticks, pear slices, dried fruit, yogurt, toasted nuts, and whole wheat crackers with cheese slices or peanut butter.) **ELL**

➤ **Eager to Help**
Children ages four to six like to help around the kitchen. *What are some tasks parents can ask them to perform?*

## Teaching Children About Nutrition

Nutrition lessons learned early in life can lay the foundation for a lifetime of better health and prepare children to make wise food choices at home and at school.

It is also important that parents limit how much time children spend in front of the television. Children may watch television instead of participating in physical activity. In addition, TV commercials try to **persuade**, or convince, kids to choose high-fat snacks and high-sugar drinks and cereals. Parents should make children aware of these pressures. Children are more likely to make better choices when they understand the pressures.

### At Home

Parents can take advantage of children's natural curiosity at this stage and use food as a rich source for learning. Involving children in the ways food is obtained and prepared can increase their interest in it. For example, children who visit or help tend a garden are often more willing to try new vegetables.

Children this age can help prepare meals. They can tear lettuce for salads, stir orange juice concentrate, or mix batter. They enjoy cutting shapes out of bread using cookie cutters. They can make mini pizzas by flattening pizza dough, pouring on tomato sauce, and sprinkling on cheese or other toppings. They can add premeasured ingredients to a bowl. They like to help decorate cookies or cupcakes.

Teaching children about food in this way offers other advantages as well. Children feel proud of the contributions they have made to family meals. Activities like these also help children improve their fine motor skills. Spending time in the kitchen together adds to the amount of positive time that parents and children spend working together, which rewards both adults and children.

### At School

Schools also use food as a learning tool, especially with younger children. Teachers might ask children questions about the texture, quantity, appearance, or nutrition of food. Consider a preschool snack of peanut butter, celery, and raisins. For preschoolers, spreading peanut butter on a celery stick and sprinkling raisins on the top provides a variety of lessons, as well as practice with fine motor skills.

Children can learn that these ingredients are good for them and help them grow. They learn that the foods come from different food groups. They can answer questions about the different textures of these foods. A teacher also might have them count the number of raisins they used to practice everyday math skills.

➤ **Explore the Photo**

**Caption Answer** Some tasks children this age can perform are tearing lettuce for salad, stirring orange juice concentrate, mixing batter, cutting shapes out of bread, and making mini pizzas. Encourage students to think of other tasks appropriate for this age group.

**Discussion** Besides getting help with this task, what other benefits is this father obtaining when he and his son work together? (Possible answers: He is getting the satisfaction of knowing that he is teaching his son important skills and is raising a responsible child. He also is getting to spend time with his son.)

For many children, school lunch will be the first time they will make an independent choice about what to eat. Children who are in school all day usually eat the lunch offered at school or bring lunch from home. However, what children are given to eat and what they actually eat may be quite different. They often trade food or throw food away.

Classmates or school lunch programs may introduce children to foods they never receive at home. Some of these foods may be high in sugar, fats, or salt. It is a good idea for parents to review which foods are more healthful than others. For example, an apple is better than a candy bar, or pretzels are a better choice than french fries. In addition, children who bring their lunches will be less likely to trade foods if they already have tasty, appealing foods of their own.

## Nutritional Concerns

There are two basic signs that children are meeting their nutritional needs for normal growth and development. These are gaining weight at an appropriate rate and eating a variety of nutritious foods. Even picky eaters can stay healthy and grow if their choices result in a well-balanced diet.

### Poor Nutrition

Lack of money to buy healthful foods is *not* the most common cause of poor nutrition. Some parents and caregivers are simply not aware of the need for good nutrition, or they may not understand the basics of good nutrition. They may rely too heavily on convenience foods or foods from fast-food restaurants to save time. Although some of these foods may be nutritious, they are often very high in calories, salt, and fats.

## Parenting Skills

### Encourage Physical Activity

Teaching young children to enjoy regular physical activity can bring lifelong health benefits. Here are some ways to help get children up and moving:

- **Involve children in daily activities.** Children gain exercise and a sense of accomplishment when they help out at home.
- **Enjoy fun activities together.** Activities such as biking, swimming, and walking, can involve the whole family.
- **Focus on age-appropriate activities.** Choose activities that are developmentally appropriate for the child.
- **Model active behavior in everyday activities.** Be a role model. Ride a bicycle or walk to get places. Limit such sedentary activities as television and computer games.
- **Find a sport that the child enjoys.** If a child enjoys a sport, support that interest by playing the sport with the child or finding a team for the child to join.
- **Find friends to join the fun.** Bring along friends on a trip to the park.

**Take Charge** Some parents struggle to find time to play with their children and encourage physical activity. What would you recommend parents do to encourage physical activity in their child?

Section 13.2   Caring for Children from Four to Six   **391**

## Parenting Skills

### Encourage Physical Activity

Describe a scenario in which a father frequently plays softball and tennis with friends, but rarely participates in physical activities with his five-year-old son. The father claims to be too busy. Ask students: What might you say to this father? (The father needs to spend time being physically active with the child in order to establish this important habit.)

**Take Charge**
Answers will vary but may include: make time for family activities on weekends, walk or bike instead of driving places, find a neighborhood play buddy, or have the child help with household chores.

**Teach** cont.

**S** **Skill Practice**
**Independent Practice**
**Describe a Fun Day** Have students create posters illustrating a fun day that they might have with their families or friends. The day should include at least three different physical activities. Encourage students to include activities that everyone would enjoy. (Posters should illustrate at least three different physical activities that could be enjoyed by a family or a group of friends.) **L1** **ELL**

**Investigate Options** Instruct students to research one place in their community where friends and families can go to be physically active. For example, they might choose a local park or a public recreation center. Students should write a description of the place, where it is located, and the kinds of activities available there. (Descriptions will vary based on location researched, but should include examples of types of activities possible.) **L2**

**Plan Activities** Tell students to suppose that their families are planning a "family fun fest" for an upcoming weekend. Students should learn about local places, such as recreational facilities or hiking and biking trails, where families can go to be physically active. They then should create a schedule of activities for the weekend. They also should create a map showing where each place is located. (Students should create a schedule of physical activities for a family weekend. The activities should be built around local recreational facilities or parks. Students should include a map showing each activity's location.) **L3**

**Teach** *cont.*

## U₁ **Universal Access**

**Interpersonal Learners** Organize students into two groups. Explain that some people think that fast food businesses should not be allowed to air television commercials aimed at young children because they are overly vulnerable to this type of advertising. Other people think that advertisers should not be prevented from airing these ads and it is up to parents to make certain their children eat properly. Assign one group to be in favor of such ads and the other group to oppose them. Have the two groups debate one another. Encourage students to conduct research ahead of time so that they can present strong, well-reasoned arguments. (Students should debate whether advertisements for fast food should be allowed to target young children. Debates will vary but students should provide sound arguments for their viewpoints.) **ELL**

## C **Critical Thinking**

**Hypothesize** Ask students: Why do you think the number of overweight children in this age group has been increasing? Encourage students to provide specific reasons. (Possible answers: Less exercise than in the past with fewer children walking to school and playing outdoors, the ready availability of fast food, the extensive advertising of fast food and convenience foods, and increasingly tight schedules for both parents and children.)

➤ **Family Fun Time**
Doing physical activities as a family instills good lifetime habits in children. *What physical activities can families do together?*

**U₁** Some adults set a poor example by frequently snacking on high-calorie foods. Some allow young children to choose their own food without guidance. It is the responsibility of parents and caregivers to provide children with healthful food and help them to learn to make appropriate choices.

Poor nutrition will **undermine**, or weaken, the health of children. Children who lack essential nutrition have less resistance to illness. They also may not grow adequately and may have learning difficulties.

### Weight Problems

Children from four to six vary in their body type. They may look chunky or slim and still be healthy. When there are concerns about a child's weight, parents should consult the child's doctor. The doctor can accurately decide if the child is overweight or underweight.

If the doctor detects an issue with weight, there are many ways to help the child. Parents and caregivers might record the child's physical activity and what he or she eats for one week. Often, this record alone will help the doctor identify needed changes.

MyPyramid is always a good place to start in planning healthful meals and snacks. Other resources are available when the child has a more severe weight problem though. A dietitian or nutritionist can help parents and caregivers design a program to promote changes in diet or activity level.

When a child eats more calories than the body uses through physical activity, the body stores the extra calories as fat. If this happens consistently over time, the child is at risk for being overweight. The opposite is also true. A child who consistently eats fewer calories than his or her body needs may become underweight. Neither of these conditions typically occurs suddenly. Instead, both result from poor eating habits over time. If a child has a sudden weight gain or loss, a pediatrician should be consulted. This could indicate a medical problem.

The number of overweight children has been rising. Overweight children are at increased risk of being overweight or obese as adults. They also have a greater chance of developing life-threatening diseases, such as diabetes and heart disease. Good nutrition is the first step in preventing a child from becoming overweight. **C**

 **Explore the Photo**

**Caption Answer** Answers will vary but may include that families can play physical games together, go for walks, ride bikes, do yard work, or clean house.

**Discussion** Ask students if any of them have family members with physical disabilities. Ask for suggestions on how family activities might be modified so that individuals with disabilities can participate in activities with the rest of the family. (Suggestions will vary. Possible answer: Families can hike on less hilly ground in order to accompany members who cannot negotiate uneven terrain.)

## Checkups and Immunizations

Most children will begin kindergarten at age five or six. Before they can attend school, they are typically required to receive a medical checkup and certain immunizations. Most schools require immunizations against hepatitis B, diphtheria, tetanus, pertussis (whooping cough), polio, measles, mumps, and rubella (German measles). More and more schools also require immunization against chicken pox. Parents should check with the school to find out the specific requirements.

✓ **Reading Check** **Explain** What happens when a child eats more calories than his body uses through physical exercise?

## Self-Care Skills

As the physical strength and motor skills of four- to six-year-olds improve, they become increasingly able to care for themselves. They can wash and dress themselves, brush their own teeth, and begin to care for their clothes. Parents and caregivers should encourage this increasing independence. They should also remember, though, that the child is still learning and will need help to do things correctly.

## Clothing

Despite their increased level of independence, four- to six-year-olds still need guidance in developing self-care skills. Choosing clothes, dressing, and caring for clothes are areas where children in this age group continue to learn and develop.

### Dressing and Choosing Clothes

Four-, five-, and six-year-olds are usually able to dress themselves. Some may need help with certain fasteners such as shoelaces or buttons down the back.

Many children have difficulty figuring out which clothes match. Parents can help a child learn about matching colors and clothes. Help the child select coordinating outfits ahead of time and store them together.

Comfort, durability, and economy are still the main guidelines for choosing clothes. However, as children start school, two other factors become important in clothes selection.

First, children this age have definite likes and dislikes. Some become attached to a favorite garment, as they might have in the past to a specific toy. Second, group identification becomes important at this age. Children may have a desire to wear clothes like those of classmates.

# Learning Through PLAY

## Taking on Roles

Children of all ages frequently take on roles of other people when they play. Using dress-up clothes and other props, children love to pretend to be other people. Very young children choose roles in play that are close to their own experience. Children will frequently pretend to be a parent or teacher. However, as children learn more about the world, other characters become a part of their play. Some of these characters include firefighters, police officers, nurses, or doctors. Children may begin to pretend by suggesting a plan, such as "Let's drive to the store and get something to eat." Playing different roles is a way for children to express their creativity and to explore a world outside of their own.

**Think About It** Suppose you are baby-sitting three-year-old, Sam, and his six-year-old sister, Olivia. Olivia is trying to get Sam to play school with her, but Sam just takes the pencil and scribbles on the paper. Olivia is getting upset. What can you do?

# Learning Through PLAY

## Taking on Roles

**Discussion** What types of props and clothing might a preschool provide to encourage children to take on roles of others? (The school might provide costumes such as police, firefighter, or paramedic uniforms and props such as dishes and kitchen appliances for playing house.)

**Think About It** Students' answers will vary but should suggest explaining to Olivia that Sam is too young to understand how to play school. Olivia might pretend to be a preschool teacher and create activities that Sam would like.

## Teach cont.

### U₂ Universal Access

**Logical Learners** Assign students the task of choosing three appropriate outfits for a five-year-old boy or girl. Give them a specific budget. Instruct students to peruse catalogs or Web sites to select clothing that meets the guidelines discussed here. (Students should select three outfits for a five-year-old that meet the guidelines given in this section and stay within the specified budget.)

### R Reading Strategy

**Predict** Explain to students that predicting what an author is going to say about a particular subject is one way of preparing to read. Ask: What do you think the author will say about children taking on roles while they play? Have students offer suggestions. Then read aloud the Learning Through Play feature. Have the class compare this text to their predictions.

**McGraw Hill Professional Development**

**Mini Clip Reading: During and After Reading** A teacher models for her students and then has them practice what a good reader thinks about.

✓ **Reading Check**

**Explain** The body stores the extra calories as fat and the child gains weight.

## Assess

### Quiz

Ask students to answer the following questions:

1. How can parents and caregivers encourage good eating habits? (They can prepare healthful food that is also appealing and they can model good food habits.)
2. What future problems can children have as a result of being overweight? (They have a greater chance of being overweight or obese adults and a greater risk of developing diseases such as diabetes and heart disease.)
3. What are some guidelines to follow when choosing clothing for children from ages four to six? (Guidelines include choosing clothing that is comfortable, durable, and economical. The child's likes and dislikes also should be considered, along with the desire to wear clothes similar to those of classmates.)

## Reteach

### C₁ Critical Thinking

**Solve Problems** Explain that some children appear to be truly afraid of having a toothbrush placed in their mouth. Ask students for ideas on how they might handle a four-year-old who has a strong aversion to having his teeth brushed. (Responses will vary. One solution might be to try to get the child to place the brush into his mouth for a short period of time, perhaps only ten or fifteen seconds, and then gradually increase this time each day. Providing praise for even minor improvements might prove helpful.)

### ✓ Reading Check

**Summarize** Children in this age group want to feel the security of belonging.

**394**

---

Group identification is a feeling of belonging with others. Collin was excited to be starting first grade. When his mother took him shopping for clothes, he wanted only those with his favorite cartoon character on them.

Parents can help satisfy a child's desire to wear certain clothes by allowing him to select some of his own clothes. Children this age might enjoy shopping for their clothes. Collin's mom told him he could pick out two of his shirts by himself, but that she got to help choose the rest. Collin's mom was able to stay within their family's budget. And Collin was able to practice his independence by making his own choices.

### Caring for Clothes

Once children begin to care about what they wear, they can learn basic clothing care. To start, they can put dirty items in the appropriate place. When it is laundry time, children can help sort their clothes. Then they can help fold and hang up clean clothes. Putting clothes away is easier if the child has storage within reach. Hooks at eye level, low rods, and handy shelves and drawers are helpful.

Good habits for taking care of clothes will not develop overnight. They will require consistent but gentle reminders. To many parents, it just seems easier to continue doing such tasks for their children. However, this is the stage of development when children need to increase their independence and sense of responsibility. Parents who continue to pick up and put away clothes for their children run the risk of having teens who expect the same service.

### Washing and Bathing

Although bath time continues to be fun for some children, many this age are less interested in washing and bathing regularly than they were when they were younger. Some children just do not like to stop playing to bathe.

Praising children for taking a bath or shower is much more effective than nagging them to do so. Parents should set up and maintain hygiene routines. This helps children accept these tasks as expected behavior.

**Learning to Brush** Regular tooth brushing helps children prevent tooth decay. *Why is tooth decay of greater concern at this age than for younger children?*

### Caring for Teeth

Regular tooth brushing and flossing is another essential routine that parents can teach their children. Until a child handles a toothbrush well, at about the age of five, dentists recommend that parents help with brushing and flossing, especially at night.

Tooth decay is a special concern at this age because permanent teeth are coming in. Regular dental checkups and cleanings are important. Sometimes dentists apply a coating of fluoride to children's teeth. **Fluoride** is a substance that strengthens the enamel of teeth to help prevent decay. **Enamel** is the hard, outer coating of teeth. Fluoride is often added to drinking water and most toothpastes.

### ✓ Reading Check

**Summarize** Why is group identification important for children in this age group?

---

### ▶ Explore the Photo

**Caption Answer** Tooth decay is a special concern because permanent teeth are coming in.

**Discussion** Discuss with students that techniques for trying to get children to brush properly are endless. Examples include toothbrushes that play music and special rinses that check for adequate brushing. Ask students:

Do you think these items encourage children to brush their teeth? Why or why not? (Answers will vary, but students should provide reasons for their answers. Some children like the rinses that change color if brushing is inadequate because they provide visual feedback.)

## Sleeping and Toileting

For most four- to six-year-olds, their need for sleep, especially naps, decreases while their independence in toileting increases. In spite of this, parents and caregivers must continue to monitor these two important areas of children's development.

### Sleeping

By the age of four, many children no longer take an afternoon nap. Some continue taking a daily nap until they begin a full day of school, depending on their needs. Without an afternoon nap, nighttime sleep becomes even more important. Most children this age need ten to twelve hours of sleep each night.

In order to ensure this amount of sleep, parents and caregivers need to decide on an appropriate bedtime. If the child has to wake up early for school or child care, an early bedtime is best. This can often be hard on parents who work all day and do not have much time to spend with their children. However, it is important to keep in mind that a well-rested child will be healthier and happier than a tired and irritable one.

Children this age are generally more cooperative about going to bed. Some use delaying tactics, but many will ask to go to bed. After saying goodnight and perhaps looking at a book or listening to soft music for a few minutes, most go to sleep easily. Some children may need conversation, companionship, or the comfort of a stuffed toy or favorite blanket to sleep. Reading bedtime stories continues to be a way that parents can nurture children and encourage an interest in books and reading. Ongoing bedtime rituals remain comforting to many young children.

### Toileting

By their fourth birthday, most children have few toileting accidents, either at night or during the day. When accidents do occur, it is often because the child is concentrating on an activity and forgets to go to the bathroom. Sometimes a child is in a new place and feels uncomfortable asking where the bathroom is.

## Parenting Skills

### What Is the Best Way to Handle Bedwetting?

It is not unusual for children who have learned to use the toilet to occasionally wet the bed at night. Either the child's bladder is not large enough to hold urine during the night, or the child is not awakened by the feeling of a full bladder. Sometimes the cause is an infection in the urinary tract. Here are some tips for dealing with bedwetting:

- Treat bedwetting accidents casually. Shaming or scolding a child does not help.
- Make sure the child understands that bedwetting is not his or her fault and that it will eventually stop.
- Reduce the amount of fluid the child drinks before bed.
- A small percentage of children continue to wet the bed as they get older, but almost all stop by the time they are teens. Children need continued support and reassurance that they will outgrow the problem.

**Take Charge** Imagine you are the parent of a six-year-old child who has episodes of wetting the bed. How would you respond if someone invited your child to sleep over?

---

## Parenting Skills

### What Is the Best Way to Handle Bedwetting?

Ask students: How do you think a child would feel if a parent ridiculed her for wetting her bed? Do you think this would help her to stop? Why or why not? (She would probably be embarrassed and possibly angry. Because she probably had no control over the bedwetting, ridicule or criticism would not help her to stop.)

**Take Charge**
Answers will vary but may include that it is best to postpone overnights until the child has better bladder control. The age of six is young to be sleeping overnight with a friend and a bedwetting accident could be distressing for everyone. Underwear specially designed for overnight accidents is also an option.

## Reteach cont.

**R Reading Strategy**
**Summarize** Remind students that when summarizing to stick to the facts. Have students work individually to write a single-sentence summary of the first paragraph under Sleeping. Ask for volunteers to read their summaries aloud. (Summaries should be similar to: Because many children no longer take naps by the time they are four, it is more important than ever that they get ten to twelve hours of sleep at night.)

**C₂ Critical Thinking**
**Generalize** Tell students that children mature at different rates and, if given time, some behaviors that create difficulties will go away on their own. Bedwetting is just one example. Have students create a list of other habits or behaviors that children typically outgrow over time. (Habits or behaviors might include a fear of the dark, nightmares, having imaginary friends, or sucking a thumb.)

**Professional Development**

**Mini Clip Reading: Obstacles to Achievement**
Teachers work together to determine why their students are struggling with a particular standard.

## Reteach cont.

### W Writing Support

**Question and Answer**

**Protect Children** As a class, come up with a typical question that a parent might ask about how to teach a six-year-old to behave around strangers. Then tell students to imagine they are pediatricians who write an advice column on parenting. Students should work individually to write an answer to the question. (Refer to p. 380 for tips on writing a question and answer. Student responses may include that children should avoid contact with people they do not know and that it is not their job to help strangers.)

### U Universal Access

**Verbal Learners** Many communities have programs designed to teach safety to young children. Often these programs are built around make-believe "safety towns." Instruct students to research one of these programs (either a local program or one that they locate on the Internet). Students should then create a newspaper advertisement describing the program's features and encouraging parents to register their children. (Students should create a newspaper ad for a community safety program.)

### ✓ Reading Check

**Explain** Four-year-olds need ten to twelve hours of sleep each day.

---

### SAFE CHILD HEALTHY CHILD

#### Keep Children Safe from Strangers

Strangers are not always people who will harm children. Nonetheless, children should be taught to avoid contact with people they do not know unless the stranger is accompanied by an adult whom they do know. Help the child recite the names of the adults they know and can trust.

Children need to understand that it is not their job to help strangers. If a stranger asks for help, children should know to go tell an adult they can trust. Children should also be taught that if a stranger says, "Your mommy sent me to pick you up," they should not go with the person. They should tell a trusted adult right away.

☀ **Be Prepared** Some children, because of age or disability, cannot be taught to follow the guidelines above. Research ways to keep these children safe from strangers that might want to harm them. Create a detailed list of your findings.

---

A child who has been dry at night may wet the bed again in response to stress or changes happening around him. If bedwetting recurs, put the child back in training pants at bedtime for a while. In some cases, a toileting accident is an indication that the child has an illness or infection. If problems with toileting persist, consult a physician.

In most cases, the following steps can help minimize accidents:

- Make sure the child uses the bathroom before leaving home.
- When arriving at a public place, point out where the bathroom is and remind the child to ask to use it.
- Keep an extra outfit available in the event of an accident. Handle the situation quietly, without calling unnecessary attention to it.

When they begin school, some children may suffer from constipation. Other children sometimes wet their pants. The stress children sometimes feel in their new school and with their routine can cause these problems. Most children adjust to the school routine within a few weeks. The adjustment period depends on the individual child though. For some children, the problem may recur at the beginning of school for several years. Children should not be punished when this occurs. Rather, they need to be reassured that they are still loved. Parents and teachers should work together to help relieve the stress the child is feeling. The child will probably overcome the toileting problems once he or she is more comfortable with the new routine.

✓ **Reading Check** **Explain** How many hours of sleep do four-year-olds need each day?

## Outdoor Safety

Children ages four to six spend much of their time playing outside. For this reason, it is very important to teach children about outdoor safety. Here are some safety guidelines for outdoor play.

### Bicycles

Bicycles can be fun for five- and six-year-olds, but can also pose dangers to the rider. A safety helmet should always be worn to protect the head from injury. Children should be taught the rules of the road when riding a bike. For more information on bicycle safety, see the Learning Through Play feature on page 560.

### Traffic

Traffic is one of the most dangerous situations children can encounter when playing outside. Children must be taught to look both ways before crossing the street. Children should never play near parked cars.

### Playgrounds

Public playgrounds are a great place for children this age to play outside. Children can socialize with other children. Playgrounds also offer a variety of equipment to help develop motor skills. There are safety precautions to take when using this equipment though.

---

### SAFE CHILD HEALTHY CHILD

#### Keep Children Safe from Strangers

**Analyze** Ask students: How can parents protect children and yet keep them from thinking of the world as a scary place? (Responses will vary. Parents can emphasize that while most people are honest and caring, children must be on the alert for those who are not.)

☀ **Be Prepared** Lists will vary. Possible answers include: Parents and caregivers must increase supervision and physically restrain the children with devices such as keyed locks that the children cannot open to go outdoors. Assign a responsible buddy to the child at school.

## Swings

Swings are the most common cause of injury from moving equipment on a playground. To reduce the risk of injuries on swings, children should always sit in the swing, not stand or kneel. Only one child at a time should sit in a swing. Children need to stay a safe distance away from other children who are swinging. Children should not be allowed to jump out of a moving swing.

## Slides

Slides are safe if children are careful when using them. Children should always hold onto the handrails when climbing ladders to the top. They should also slide down feet-first and one at a time, not in groups. Be aware that slides may get too hot in the sun.

## Climbing Equipment

Climbing equipment poses the greatest risk of any stationary, or non-moving, equipment on public playgrounds. Falling is the most common cause of injury for children of all ages.

Equipment must be properly anchored to the ground. Wood-framed structures should be inspected to ensure that they have been properly treated and have not splintered. There should be adequate cushioning material under playground equipment. This could include grass, mulch, or shredded tires.

Make sure there are not too many children on the equipment at once. Adult supervision is especially important for younger children, who might not have the arm strength necessary to play on climbing equipment. Make sure any equipment is age-appropriate for the child.

---

## Section 13.2 — After You Read

### Review Key Concepts

1. **List** the factors that influence the amount of food a child needs.
2. **Describe** two things parents and caregivers can do to encourage children who do not like to bathe.
3. **Explain** three reasons why toileting accidents might occur.
4. **Recall** the most common cause of injury from moving equipment on a playground.

### Practice Academic Skills

 **English Language Arts**

5. Review the MyPyramid Web site to determine which foods are nutritious. Talk to a child who is between the ages of four and six about foods. Does the child know which foods are nutritious and which are not? What nutritious foods does he or she like to eat? Summarize your interview in a report.

> **NCTE 7** Conduct research and gather, evaluate, and synthesize data to communicate discoveries.

 **Science**

6. Use your knowledge of the personal hygiene needs of four- to six-year-olds to develop a checklist of hygiene routines. Put the checklist on a poster and illustrate. If possible, give the poster to a four- to six-year-old to use.

> **NSES F** Develop understanding of personal and community health.

**Check Your Answers** Check your answers at this book's Online Learning Center at **glencoe.com**.

Section 13.2    Caring for Children from Four to Six    **397**

---

## Section 13.2 — After You Read

### Review Key Concepts

1. Weight, temperament, and level of physical activity influence the amount of food a child needs.
2. Parents and caregivers can praise children for taking a bath or shower and they can set up and maintain hygiene routines to help the children accept these tasks as expected behavior.

3. Answers may vary but should include three of the following: The child does not know where the bathroom is in a strange place. The child forgets to use the toilet. The child may wet the bed in response to stress or changes. The child may have an illness or infection.
4. Swings are the most common cause of injury from moving equipment on a playground.

### Practice Academic Skills

5. Answers will vary depending on the child interviewed and the child's knowledge of nutritious foods. Reports should use clear language and be free of grammatical errors.
6. Checklists will vary but may include: washing and bathing, brushing teeth, combing hair, or dressing.

**397**

---

## Section 13.2

### Assess

**Study Tools**

Have students go to the Online Learning Center at **glencoe.com**:

- Take the **Practice Test**.
- Download **Study-to-Go** content.

Use the **Student Activity Workbook** for additional practice.

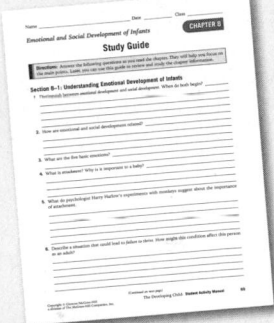

### Close

**Culminating Activity**

**Summarize** Draw a Web diagram on the board. In the center, write Parental Responsibilities. Ask students for examples of these responsibilities and place each around the central oval. (Responsibilities may include teaching good food habits, seeing that children are physically active, teaching children to wash and dress themselves, modeling good habits, and teaching safety.)

**NCLB** connects academic correlations to book content.

### Careers
#### With Children

## Children's Activity Director

**Discussion Starter**

**Children's Activity Director** Ask students if they have ever been to a place that had a children's activity director. Perhaps they have visited a city recreation center or their local science museum. While these professionals' responsibilities can vary tremendously, they all involve planning activities that young people will enjoy.

### C Critical Thinking

**Compare** As a class, create a list of facilities where children's activity directors might work. Then have students create a list of the goals they think each director might have. Ask: How are these goals similar? How are they different? (While all want children to have fun, other goals may vary. A zoo's activity director might be concerned with education whereas a recreation center's director might want to encourage children to be physically active.)

**Make Connections**

Ask students to list specific correlations between academic subjects and the kinds of skills a good children's activity director needs. (Answers will vary. Students should show an understanding of how academic skills relate to the job of being a children's activity director. For example, many activity directors need a background in child development.)

 **NCLB** This relates academic skills to specific tasks that are performed for this job.

**S**ome cities, counties, states, and organizations such as churches have public facilities. These may include beaches, picnic grounds, gardens, or swimming pools. Children's activity directors plan and coordinate events for the different facilities. These events include concerts, sports, and educational programs for children.

### ⚙ What Does a Children's Activity Director Do?

**C**    Activity directors must begin planning events months in advance. They contact and make arrangements with performers. They decide how long the event should last, and whether food or seats need to be ordered. Children's activity directors make sure that events are appealing to children and safe for all involved.

### ⚙ Where Do Children's Activity Directors Work?

Children's activity directors for cities, counties, and states typically work in offices, but they often visit the parks and other facilities. Sometimes the activity directors are directly involved in the programs and work with the children.

### Preparation and Skills

**Education and Training**
Many children's activity directors study management of nonprofit organizations. They usually have a background in recreation. Some learn a second language. An understanding of child development and age-appropriate activities is also helpful.

**Aptitudes, Abilities, and Skills**
Successful children's activity directors have energy, good organizational skills, resourcefulness, and an ability to make budgets. They also need imagination and a sense of fun to think of events and programs to sponsor.

**Academic Skills**
English language arts are used to communicate with others. Those who work in areas with large immigrant populations may need to know a second language.

NCLB

**Explore Careers** Work with your teacher to arrange to shadow a children's activity director. Ask the director if you may help teach a group of children a song or finger play. Write a one-page report of your experience and include whether you think you would enjoy this career.

 **Careers Online** For more information on careers, visit the Occupational Outlook Handbook Web site through the link on this book's Online Learning Center at **glencoe.com**.

**Culminating Activity**

**Plan an Activity** Instruct students to choose a facility where they might like to work as a children's activity directory and write a paragraph describing an appropriate activity. (Activities will vary, but should be appropriate for the chosen facility. For example, if students worked at a recreation center, they might develop team games for the pool.)

**Explore Careers** Reports will vary but should include a description of the time they spent shadowing the director, and the activity they helped plan or conduct. Students should also discuss whether they feel they would like to pursue this career.

## Chapter Summary

Children between the ages of four and six grow steadily, and their body shape changes. Permanent teeth begin replacing the primary teeth. From ages four to six, children refine their motor skills. The eating habits children learn will influence their adult eating habits and health. Physical inactivity is a major cause of overweight in children. Four- to six-year-olds can wash and dress themselves and can help care for their own clothes. They may still have toileting accidents.

## Vocabulary Review

**1.** Create a fill-in-the-blank sentence for each of these vocabulary terms. The sentence should contain enough information to help determine the missing word.

### Content Vocabulary

◇ permanent teeth (p. 384)
◇ ambidextrous (p. 387)
◇ group identification (p. 394)
◇ fluoride (p. 394)
◇ enamel (p. 394)

### Academic Vocabulary

■ erect (p. 384)
■ dexterity (p. 386)
■ persuade (p. 390)
■ undermine (p. 392)

## Review Key Concepts

**2. Summarize** how an average child's posture and body shape change from ages four to six.

**3. Compare and contrast** average motor skills development for four-, five-, and six-year-olds.

**4. Explain** why good nutrition is essential for children ages four to six.

**5. Identify** three ways that four- to six-year-olds are able to care for themselves.

**6. Describe** three steps that can help minimize toileting accidents.

**7. List** three areas of outdoor safety to discuss with four- to six-year-old children.

## Critical Thinking

**8. Develop** Imagine that you are the parent of a five-year-old. Plan three nutritious meals or snacks that you feel would appeal to your child.

**9. Demonstrate** Show the steps you would use to teach a five-year-old how to tie shoelaces. Use words that a child can understand.

**10. Apply** Suppose you are an advice columnist. A parent writes in to say that her six-year-old is having bedwetting accidents. Write a response in which you provide advice. Use what you have learned about child development to offer tips for helping her child.

Chapter 13   Physical Development from Four to Six   **399**

## Content and Academic Vocabulary Review

**1.** Students should write fill-in-the-blank sentences for each term.

## Review Key Concepts

**2.** Children's bodies become straighter and slimmer, and the protruding tummy from babyhood flattens. Children this age hold their shoulders back and their upper bodies more erect. The chest broadens and flattens with improved abdominal strength. The legs lengthen rapidly.

**3.** After age four, children are learning how to throw and catch both large and small balls. Five-year-olds show improved speed and coordination. Six-year-olds enjoy balancing activities. Most four-year-olds can learn to lace their shoes, but cannot tie them until they are five. Five-year-olds can pour liquids from a pitcher into a glass. They enjoy cutting, pasting, and using glue. Five-year-olds can print some letters. Most six-year-olds draw detailed pictures, use scissors, and write their own names.

**4.** Nutritious food is the best fuel for children's physical and intellectual development.

**5.** bathe themselves, brush their own teeth, and dress and help care for clothes

**6.** Before leaving home, make sure the child uses the bathroom; when arriving at a public place, point out where the bathroom is and remind the child to ask to use it.

**7.** bicycles, traffic, and playgrounds

## Critical Thinking

**8.** Answers will vary but should show an understanding of nutritious foods children this age like to eat such as apple slices, grapes, cheese, yogurt, and raisins. Students should also focus on balance, texture, and color.

**9.** Demonstrations will vary. Students should use words that a five-year-old will understand.

**10.** Advice columns will vary but should include the following tips: Treat bedwetting accidents casually, shaming or scolding a child does not help. Make sure the child understands that the wetting is not his or her fault and will eventually stop. Reduce fluid intake before bed.

### Family & Community Connections

**11.** Reports will vary depending on the book chosen. Students should explain why they believe the book would appeal to four- to six-year-old children.

### Health Skills

**12.** Essays will vary depending on the disease or cause students research. Students should report the cause (if known), the symptoms, and any treatments.

### Observation Skills

**13.** Charts will vary depending on the commercials watched. Charts should include the types of foods advertised, the number of times that type of food was shown, and whether the students think the food is nutritious for young children.

### Real-World Skills

**14.** Posters will vary. Staff poster might include: "Remind children to wash hands," "Thoroughly clean toys every night," "Change crib sheets." Poster for children might include: "Wash your hands," "Do you need to potty?"

**15.** Types of graphs will vary but should contain the information provided in Figure 13.1.

**16.** Answers will vary depending on the fast-food and frozen meals surveyed. Students should recognize that price should not be the only determinant for purchasing a meal. Nutrition should also be considered.

 **NCLB** Activity correlated to Science standards.

---

 **Family & Community Connection**

**11. Consult a Librarian** Ask a librarian to recommend a book that would be suitable as a bedtime story for a four- to six-year-old. Read the book and write a one-page report that describes the book and tells what aspects you feel would make it appealing to children.

### Health Skills

**12. Research Childhood Disabilities** In this chapter you learned that cerebral palsy is a disease that can cause physical disabilities or impairments in young children. This is only one of many causes though. Research a different disease or cause of physical disabilities in young children. Look for the cause of the disease, symptoms, and treatments. Write an essay that summarizes your findings.

### Observation Skills

**13. Observe Children's Television** Watch children's television programs for at least one hour. Saturday morning or early evening are usually good times to do this.

**Procedure** As you watch the programs, pay attention to the commercials. Keep track of the commercials for food items. Note whether they are snack foods, breakfast foods, and so on.

**Analysis** Create a chart of your observations. The chart should indicate the type of food, such as snack or breakfast, the number of commercials for that type of food, and whether you think the food advertised is nutritious for young children.

**NSES 1** Develop an understanding of science unifying concepts and processes: systems, order, and organization; evidence, models, and explanation.

**N C L B**

---

## Real-World Skills

| Interpersonal and Collaborative Skills | **14. PlanAction** Follow your teacher's instructions to form groups. Brainstorm with your group to come up with hygiene practices to follow for infants, toddlers, and staff in a child care center. Create two posters to remind children and staff members of these practices. |
|---|---|
| Technology Skills | **15. Make a Graph** Use the information in Figure 13.1 on page 384 to create a bar or line graph comparing the average height and weight for boys and girls at ages four, five, and six. Use word processing or spreadsheet software to create your graph. |
| Financial Literacy | **16. Comparison Shop** Research the cost of fast-food meals and frozen dinners created especially for children. Compare these costs against the cost to prepare a home-made nutritious meal. Which is the better buy? Should cost determine which meal to purchase? Why or why not? |

**Additional Activities** For additional activities, go to this book's Online Learning Center at **glencoe.com**.

## Academic Skills

**17.** Essays will vary. Students should provide information about average weight and height gain (see Figure 13.1 on page 384) and average motor skill development (see Figure 13.2 on page 386).

**18.** 48 blocks, 64 crayons, 80 pieces of paper, 8 balloons, 8 pairs of scissors, and 16 foam balls.

The *Early Childhood Observations CD* offers additional lessons with videos to build students' observation skills.

**Part 1:** Learning to Observe
**Part 2:** How Children Develop
**Part 3:** Working With Young Children
**Part 4:** Extended Observations
**Part 5:** Resources and Answer File

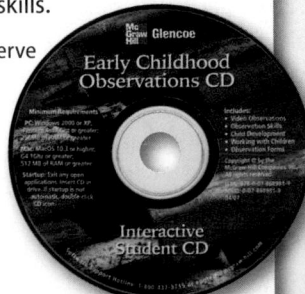

## Academic Skills

 **English Language Arts**

**17. Determine Necessary Knowledge** Care-givers of young children need to know the average rate of development to provide appropriate care and to assess whether there might be a developmental prob-lem. List and describe the knowledge that caregivers should know about the rate of development of four- to six-year-olds. Summarize your ideas in a one-page essay.

> **NCTE 4** Use written language to communicate effectively.

 **Mathematics**

**18. Party Preparation** When a toddler wants something, she typically wants it imme-diately. To reduce the amount of conflict at an upcoming party for eight children, a mother plans ahead to make sure there are enough materials for everyone. Each child needs 6 blocks, 8 crayons, 10 pieces of paper, 1 balloon, 1 pair of safety scissors, and 2 foam balls. How many of each item is needed for the party of eight?

**Math Concept** **Multiples** Multiples are the products of a given number and various integers.

**Starting Hint** Multiply each integer (the number of each item needed) by the given number of children. For example, the number of blocks needed is six and $6 \times 8 = 48$.

 For math help, go to the Math Appendix at the back of the book.

> **NCTM Number and Operations** Compute fluently and make reasonable estimates.

**Science**

**19. Conduct a Survey** Research has linked television viewing to an increased intake of calories, especially from snack foods. Children who eat while watching televi-sion tend to eat more snacks and many of the snacks are fatty foods.

**Procedure** Survey parents or caregivers of four- to six-year-olds. Ask them what snack foods their children eat while watch-ing television or videos. How much do they eat?

**Analysis** Create a list of the snacks from your survey and report whether the snacks are high in fat. Do your findings agree with the research results? Write a paragraph to summarize your findings.

> **NSES A** Develop understandings about scientific inquiry.

## Standardized Test Practice

**MULTIPLE CHOICE**

Read the paragraph, then the question that follows. Read the answer choices and choose the best answer to fill in the blank. Write your answer on a separate sheet of paper.

> As children start school, two factors become important in choosing clothing for children. First, children this age have definite likes and dislikes. Second, group identification becomes important and may bring with it a desire to wear clothes like those of classmates.

**20.** In this passage, group identification means ___.
  **a.** recognizing others in a group
  **b.** participating in group activities
  **c.** a feeling of belonging
  **d.** losing your identity in a group

> **Test-Taking Tip** In a multiple-choice test, the answers should be specific and precise. Read the question first, then read all the answer choices. Eliminate answers that you know are incorrect.

**19.** Students' lists and analyses will vary. Summaries should indicate whether students' findings agree with the research.

 **Professional Development**

**Mini Clip**
**Reading: Standards-Based Instruction**
Emily M. Schell, EdD, educator and author, discusses standards-based instruction.

**NCLB** connects academic correlations to book content.

## Standardized Test Practice

**20.** c. a feeling of belonging

**Test-Taking Tips** Explain to students that double-negative options can be very confusing. They may want to rewrite these choices using positive wording.

**Multiple Choice Tests** Tell students that if two options in a multiple choice test both appear to be true, carefully examine the differences between them. This will help them make the best choice they can.

# TECHNOLOGY Solutions

**Use these technology solutions to streamline chapter assessment!**

 ***ExamView Assessment Suite*** CD allows you to create and print out customized tests or ready-made unit and chapter tests, complete with answer keys.

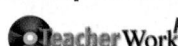 **TeacherWorks Plus** is an electronic lesson planner that provides instant access to complete teacher resources in one convenient package.

 **Online Learning Center** includes resources and activities for students and teachers.

**STANDARDS BASED LESSON PLANNING** *The Developing Child* provides students with instruction and assessment in the following fundamental content areas:

## National Standards Correlations

| Standards | Pages |
|---|---|
| **12.1.1** Analyze physical, emotional, social, spiritual, and intellectual development. | 405–412, 414–420 |
| **12.1.3** Analyze current and emerging research about human growth and development, including research on brain development. | 409 |
| **12.2.1** Analyze the effect of heredity and environment on human growth and development. | 418–419 |
| **12.2.3** Analyze the effects of gender, ethnicity, and culture on individual development. | 411 |
| **12.3.1** Analyze the role of nurturance on human growth and development. | 410–411 |
| **15.1.2** Analyze expectations and responsibilities of parenting. | 416–418 |
| **15.2.1** Choose nurturing practices that support human growth and development. | 409, 410–411, 412 |
| **15.2.2** Apply communication strategies that promote positive self-esteem in family members. | 411–412 |
| **15.2.3** Assess common practices and emerging research about discipline on human growth and development. | 416–418, 419, 423 |

**NO CHILD LEFT BEHIND** NCLB activities, information, and skills practice will help your students attain NCLB proficiency. Students will improve their abilities in the following academic standards areas:

## Academic Standards Correlations

| Discipline | Standard | Feature/Activity |
|---|---|---|
| **English Language Arts** | **NCTE 1** Read texts to acquire new information. | **Reading Guide (pp. 404, 413)** |
| | **NCTE 2** Read literature to build an understanding of the human experience. | **After You Read (p. 412)** |
| | **NCTE 4** Use written language to communicate effectively. | **Writing Activity (p. 402)** <br> **Academic Skills (p. 423)** |
| | **NCTE 11** Participate as members of literacy communities. | **After You Read (p. 420)** |
| **Mathematics** | **NCTM Number and Operations** Compute fluently and make reasonable estimates. | **Academic Skills (p. 423)** |
| **Science** | **NSES A** Develop abilities necessary to do scientific inquiry, understandings about scientific inquiry. | **Science in Action (p. 410)** <br> **Observation Skills (p. 422)** <br> **Academic Skills (p. 423)** |
| **Social Studies** | **NCSS I C Culture** Apply an understanding of culture as an integrated whole that explains the functions and interactions of traditions, beliefs and values, and behavior patterns. | **Culture Matters (p. 411)** |
| | **NCSS V B Individuals, Groups, and Institutions** Analyze group and institutional influences on people, events, and elements of culture. | **After You Read (p. 420)** |
| | **NCSS V D Individuals, Groups, and Institutions** Apply concepts such as role, status, and social class in describing the connections and interactions of individuals and groups in society. | **After You Read (p. 412)** |

## McGraw Hill Professional Development

### MINI CLIP VIDEO LIBRARY

Targeted professional development is correlated throughout *The Developing Child*. **The McGraw-Hill Professional Development Mini Clip Video Library** provides teaching strategies to strengthen academic and learning skills. Log on to **glencoe.com**.

In this chapter, you will find these Mini Clips:
- **ELL** Building the Context, p. 403
- **ELL** Providing Clear Directions, p. 405
- **Reading** Extending the Big Idea, p. 410
- **ELL** Vocabulary Activities, p. 413
- **Reading** Student Involvement, p. 418

## Reading and Writing Strategies

**Writing Activity: Character Analysis** (p. 402)
Students use writing tips to describe themselves when they were five years old.

**Before You Read** (pp. 404, 413)
A pre-reading question or statement will help students make a personal connection to content.

**Graphic Organizer** (pp. 404, 413)
A visual tool will help students organize and remember new content.

**Reading Check** (pp. 407, 411, 416, 419)
A question allows students to make a quick comprehension self-check.

**After You Read** (pp. 412, 420)
Organize and process students' understanding of what they have read.

## Chapter Features

**ADHD** (p. 407)
ADHD becomes apparent in some children in preschool.

**Understanding Success** (p. 408)
Many children become frustrated when they cannot do something.

**Fear of the Dark** (p. 409)
Fear of the dark may be "hard-wired" in the brain.

**Worry and Your Health** (p. 410)
Worry can affect children's health as well as adults' health.

**Raising a Child in Austria** (p. 411)
In Austria, parents are encouraged to stay home and raise their children.

**Handling Family Conflict** (p. 415)
Children learn self-control by accepting the consequences of their actions.

**Play by the Rules** (p. 416)
Playing games helps teach a child to follow rules.

**Guide Children's Behavior** (p. 417)
There are several ways to guide children effectively.

## Chapter Overview

### Introduce the Chapter

In this chapter, students learn how four- to six-year-olds develop both emotionally and socially. They learn about the emotional and social behaviors that four- to six-year-olds exhibit, and about the requirements for healthy emotional and social growth.

### Build Background

Discuss with students that as four- to six-year-olds develop, they express different emotions. Divide students into groups of three or four. Instruct each group to create a list of the different ways in which they have seen four- to six-year-olds displaying emotion. Then ask for volunteers from each group to share their lists with the class.

### Writing Activity
#### Character Analysis

This active learning activity prompts students to write a character analysis about themselves when they were five years old. After students have completed the writing activity, ask for volunteers to share their writing with the class. Student responses can be used as a basis for classroom discussion. (Students' character analyses will vary, but should be 60–80 words in length and discuss physical, emotional, and social characteristics of themselves as five-year-olds. Students may focus on one specific event or occasion, or they may be more general in their character analysis. Use these criteria when evaluating your students' writing: Did the student describe his or her appearance? Did the student analyze his or her emotional and social characteristics?)

---

Chapter

**14**

# Emotional and Social Development from Four to Six

## Chapter Objectives

After completing this chapter, you will be able to:

- **Identify** a single characteristic that marks the emotional development of four- to six-year-olds.
- **List** five ways to help children reduce worry and tension.
- **Describe** how to help children develop self-confidence.
- **List** three social skills children must learn as they begin school.
- **Identify** seven guidelines for encouraging moral development in children.
- **Describe** three ways to encourage conflict resolution and cooperation in children.

### Writing Activity 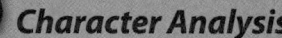 Character Analysis

**Looking Back**  One way to describe a person is by writing a character analysis. A character analysis is a look at a person's traits, feelings, and behaviors. Write a 60- to 80-word character analysis of yourself when you were five years old. It might help to remember a specific event or occasion from your youth.

**Writing Tips**  Begin by spending a few minutes thinking about what you were like when you were five. Then use these tips to write your character analysis:
1. Be specific in describing physical characteristics such as curly hair or big feet.
2. Describe emotional and social characteristics. Did you feel you were not good at soccer? Were you shy or outgoing?
3. Try to make the character analysis interesting. List facts that the reader might not expect.

---

## CLASSROOM Solutions

### Print Resources

 **Student Edition**

 **Teacher Wraparound Edition**

 **Student Activity Workbook**

 **Student Activity Workbook Teacher Annotated Edition**

### Technology Resources

 **Online Learning Center** has resources and activities for students and teachers. Includes an Online Student Edition.

 **Interactive Student Edition** allows students to instantly access review materials, examples, and exercises.

## Section **14.1** Emotional Development from Four to Six

## Section **14.2** Social and Moral Development from Four to Six

**Explore the Photo**
Family members have a great impact on a child's emotional and social development. *How do you think this parent is aiding in the emotional development of his children?*

403

### Review the Sections
Introduce the chapter by reviewing the sections:

**Section 14.1**
Children develop increased independence, curiosity, and boldness as they mature from ages four to six. They show emotions such as anger, jealousy, and worry. The rich imagination and fantasy life of preschoolers can lead to fears of ghosts and monsters.

**Section 14.2**
As they mature, children learn to express anger with words rather than physical attacks. Children ages four to six begin to develop an internal sense of right and wrong. They also learn to play both competitive and cooperative games.

 **Explore the Photo**

**Caption Answer** Answers will vary. The parent is promoting feelings of happiness and security, as well as positive self-esteem in the children.

**Discussion** Ask students why it is important for parents and caregivers to spend time interacting with children. (Answers will vary. Point out that children learn just by being around adults. Parents can use time with children to teach social values and appropriate emotional responses.)

 **Professional Development**

**Mini Clip ELL: Building the Context**

A teacher models an activity that will provide students with background information they may need to understand the text they are about to read.

 **TeacherWorks Plus** is an electronic lesson planner that provides instant access to complete teacher resources in one convenient package.

**Presentation Plus!** provides visual teaching aids for every section.

**The Early Childhood Observations CD** presents video observations and lessons on observation skills and child development.

**The Developing Brain eTransparencies and Guide** include information and activities to offer insights into brain development and diseases of the brain.

### Bell Ringer Activity

**Stress Support**

Ask students to identify a recent time when having friends around helped them during a stressful event. Ask: In addition to drawing on support from friends, what other ways do you think children learn confidence in new situations? (Answers will vary. Students may suggest that young children especially rely on parents and siblings for support.)

## Preteaching
### Vocabulary

Call students' attention to the two terms that end with the suffix *-ive.* Tell students that this suffix means "performs an action." Based on this definition, ask students to define initiative (possible answer: acts initially) and impulsive (possible answer: acts on an impulse).

### Graphic Organizer

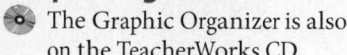 The Graphic Organizer is also on the TeacherWorks CD.

(Graphic organizers should include: accept their fear, let the child express the fear without ridicule, and help the child feel able to face the fear.)

**NCLB** connects academic correlations to book content.

## Reading Guide

### Before You Read

**Identifying Main Points** Identifying an author's main points keeps your thinking on-track. As you read, write down the main points for each head or subhead.

### Read to Learn
#### Key Concepts

- **Identify** a single characteristic that marks the emotional development of four- to six-year-olds.
- **List** five ways to help children reduce worry and tension.
- **Describe** how to help children develop self-confidence.

**D** ⎰ ### Main Idea

Between the ages of four and six, children grow more independent and express a wide range of emotions. These children become more self-confident as they learn new skills and learn how to make decisions.

#### Content Vocabulary
◇ tension
◇ self-confidence
◇ initiative

### Academic Vocabulary

You will find these words in your reading and on your tests. Use the glossary to look up their definitions if necessary.
- impulsive
- turmoil

### Graphic Organizer

As you read, look for ways that parents can help children handle fears. Use a chart like the one shown to help organize your information.

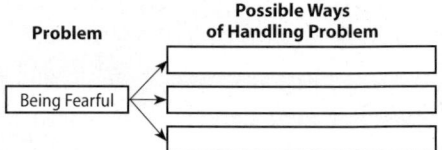

| Problem | Possible Ways of Handling Problem |
|---|---|
| Being Fearful | |
| | |
| | |

 **Graphic Organizer** Go to this book's Online Learning Center at **glencoe.com** to print out this graphic organizer.

---

**NCLB** ⎱

### Academic Standards · · · · · · · · · · · · · · · ·

 **English Language Arts**

**NCTE 2** Read literature to build an understanding of the human experience.

 **Science**

**NSES A** Develop abilities necessary to do scientific inquiry, understanding about scientific inquiry.

 **Social Studies**

**NCSS I C Culture** Apply an understanding of culture as an integrated whole that explains the functions and interactions of traditions, beliefs and values, and behavior patterns.

**NCSS V D Individuals, Groups, and Institutions** Apply concepts such as role, status, and social class in describing the connections and interactions of individuals and groups in society.

**NCTE** *National Council of Teachers of English*
**NCTM** *National Council of Teachers of Mathematics*

**NSES** *National Science Education Standards*
**NCSS** *National Council for the Social Studies*

---

 **404** Chapter 14 Emotional and Social Development from Four to Six

---

## Reading Guide

### Before You Read

Ask students: Have you ever heard a four- or five-year-old use inappropriate language? If so, how was the situation handled? (Students' answers will vary. Most parents and caregivers are quick to let a child know what is inappropriate and why it is inappropriate.)

### **D** Develop Concepts

**Main Idea** Discuss the main idea with the students. Ask: Why do you think four- to six-year-olds gain confidence as they learn new skills and learn how to make decisions? (Answers may include that children feel more in control of their lives when they know how to do more things.)

## Emotional Patterns

Justin was unusually quiet as he walked to school with his mother. It was his first day. He was both excited and fearful. His new teacher was there to greet them. As his mother talked with the teacher, Justin peered into the classroom and saw two of his friends from preschool. "Can I go and play with Scott and Dakota?" he asked. When the teacher said yes, he walked off. Justin was proud to be old enough for school. He was also glad to share the experience with familiar freinds.

Justin's behavior shows the increase in independence that is common for four- to six-year-olds. This independence is one characteristic that marks most clearly the emotional development for this age group. It is at this age that many children venture out of the home environment to attend preschool, daycare, or kindergarten. Perhaps for the first time, they find themselves with unfamiliar adults and large groups of other children. Each child responds to these challenges differently. There are, however, certain milestones that children in this age group generally attain.

## Four Years

Most four-year-olds are still very self-centered. They can be defiant, impatient, loud, and boastful. They might argue and be bossy with other children and even with adults. At other times, four-year-olds may be very loving and affectionate. This is because they still need and seek the approval of parents and other caregivers.

Four-year-olds want to see themselves as separate from their parents or other main caregivers. They want to do things for themselves, such as washing and dressing. They enjoy the feeling of independence that they get from doing these tasks.

The vocabulary and language skills of four-year-olds show clear improvements from the skills of toddlers. At this age, children enjoy testing out the sounds of language and making up nonsense words. Four-year-old Martin, for example, goes around chanting phrases like "Antsy, wantsy, pantsy," and then breaks into hysterical laughter. Children of this age might also try using rude words, just to see how adults will react.

**↑ Young Children at Play**
Children are hurt easily and often disagree with other children. *What can caregivers do to help children manage these feelings?*

Section 14.1    Emotional Development from Four to Six    **405**

---

**◆••• ▶ Explore the Photo**

**Caption Answer** Caregivers can discuss with children how their behavior affects other children's feelings and encourage them to treat others the way they would like to be treated.

**Discussion** Young children often think they are the center of their world. What are some activities parents and caregivers can do to help young children learn to live in a world with others? (Responses will vary; students may suggest working on activities that involve sharing or waiting one's turn.)

---

## Teach

### Discussion Starter

**First Day of School** Tell students that one of the milestones four- to six-year-olds attain is beginning school. This can be a challenging and, in some cases, terrifying, experience. Ask students to recall their first day of preschool or kindergarten. What was it like? How did they feel? Did they have confidence or were they afraid? (Answers will vary but may include: they felt confident, scared, or a little of both.)

###  Writing Support
**Poetry**

**Emotions** Tell students to write a poem about the different emotions typical four-year-olds exhibit. Remind students that a stanza in poetry is similar to a paragraph in a prose piece. Encourage students to write five stanzas. You might suggest that students use poetic devices such as sensory details, similes, and metaphors. Students must decide whether rhyme or free verse will be more effective. Ask volunteers to read their poems to the class. (Students' poems will vary but should focus on the varied emotions of four-year-olds. The poems should have a pattern. If it is traditional verse, it should adhere to the appropriate rhyme or rhythm structure.)

**Professional Development**

**Mini Clip**
ELL: Providing Clear Directions

A teacher provides clear written and oral directions for a classroom assignment and checks for student understanding.

**U Universal Access**

**Interpersonal Learners** Divide the class into groups. Have each group imagine that they are a group of kindergarten teachers, meeting together to brainstorm activities for their classes. Remind students that kindergartners usually cannot focus their attention on one task for long. Ask each group to write a lesson plan for one or two activities that would be suitable for kindergartners. (Lesson plans will vary. Groups should recognize the need to develop short activities and to vary the activities from very active to very quiet. If time allows, have groups choose a "teacher" who will guide the rest of the group through the activities as a "class.") **ELL**

**C Critical Thinking**

**Problem Solve** Read this scenario to students: Whenever six-year-old Mark comes home from school, his father, Adam, tells him to change out of his school uniform and into play clothes. However, Mark will sit around in his uniform for at least a half hour before Adam has to remind him again. Then Mark becomes quarrelsome and storms into his room and slams the door. Have students brainstorm what Adam can do to solve this problem. (Student answers will vary. They may suggest that Adam not allow Mark to sit down before changing into play clothes, or that Adam take privileges away from Mark until he learns to change his clothes on his own.)

---

Four-year-olds have an active imagination. This allows them to enjoy a rich fantasy life. A four-year-old mind often cannot separate fantasy from reality. For example, Owen's teacher read the class a story about a superhero that could fly. Owen was very excited when he went home to tell his dad about it. Owen saw no reason why he would not be able to learn how to fly, too. This lack of separation, combined with an active imagination, can lead to fears. Shadows in a dark bedroom, for example, can become a monster in the child's mind. Parents can help a child get over these fears by acknowledging them and talking about them.

### Five Years

By the age of five, children have begun to view themselves as whole persons, with a body, mind, and feelings. They are eager to explore the larger world, but at the same time they may be fearful of unfamiliar people, places, and experiences.

Five is the age at which a child typically begins kindergarten. Not all children welcome that first day of school. When Katrina's mother brought her to the kindergarten classroom, Katrina clung to her mother's legs and begged not to be left there. Katrina, like many five-year-olds, was afraid of being left alone in an unfamiliar situation. Chelsea, though, was excited about her first day of school. She could barely sit still long enough to eat her breakfast. When they got to the school, she was jumping up and down to try and find her friends to play with and to see who her new friends would be.

Children this age may experience anxiety, or stress, about the strangeness of the school setting and about unfamiliar routines. It is important to help children cope with their anxieties by listening to their concerns and offering love and support. Children who have already attended a child care center or preschool may adapt more easily.

Five-year-olds are still emotionally impulsive. **Impulsive** means to act spontaneously, without considering the consequences. They try to wander around, talk, and play whenever they want. In school, though, they must sit still,

**New Situations**
Beginning school and separating from parents or caregivers can be difficult for some children. *How can a teacher help put a child at ease?*

listen, and focus on a task. This is when they start learning to control their impulses.

At this age, children also begin to feel more empathy for others. Recall that empathy is the ability to understand how someone else feels. This empathy makes them better able to play together and cooperate. They are able to see another person's point of view.

### Six Years

As children turn six, they are likely to go through a period of emotional turmoil. **Turmoil** is a state of extreme confusion or agitation. Some children are in school all day for the first time. They face the task of finding their role outside of the home. At times they long to feel grown-up, but often they feel small and dependent. Six-year-olds crave praise and approval, and are easily hurt and discouraged.

Six-year-olds are often stubborn and quarrelsome. They are the center of their own universe. They try to please others only to win praise for themselves. Six-year-olds are often at their worst with their own parents. They may resent being given direction, and their first response is likely to be "No!"

---

**▶ Explore the Photo**

**Caption Answer** Answers may vary. The teacher can introduce the child to other children, show the child around the classroom, and explain the routine so that the child understands what will be happening.

**Discussion** Ask students how parents and caregivers can help prepare a child for the first day of kindergarten. (Responses will vary. Students may suggest that parents put the child in preschool prior to kindergarten so the child becomes used to being away from parents and with other adults and children.)

At six, children experience rapid mood changes. They love and hate, accept and reject, smile and rage, sometimes for no apparent reason. At the same time, a six-year-old is beginning to experience stronger feelings of happiness and joy. This leads to an appreciation of more activities. A six-year-old can enjoy music or dance lessons and organized sports. This is a good time to start a child on such activities. Learning new skills builds a child's sense of competence.

✓ **Reading Check** **Analyze** Why is six such a difficult age emotionally?

## Specific Emotions

As children grow older they become better able to recognize and express a variety of emotions, including anger, jealousy, and worry. At the same time, their growing feeling of competence as they master various tasks helps them to control their emotions. They also continue to experience fears during the ages of four through six. The nature of those fears, though, changes over time.

## Anger

The expression of anger changes more during early childhood than the expression of any other emotion. Toddlers show anger freely and without restraint, sometimes biting, kicking, and hitting. Preschoolers are less likely than toddlers to express their anger with physical violence. A four-year-old who is upset because her mother will not let her play outside is more likely to scream, "I hate you, Mommy!" than to try and hit her mother.

As children grow from four to six years old, they use increasingly subtle ways to express their anger:

- **Four Years** An angry episode lasts longer in a four-year-old than in a younger child. Four-year-olds may still use physical violence, or they may threaten and attempt to get even.
- **Five Years** Five-year-olds are more likely to try to hurt other children's feelings than to hurt them physically.
- **Six Years** Six-year-olds are even more hurtful with words. They tease, insult, nag, and make fun of others.

### RESPOND TO SPECIAL NEEDS — ADHD

Attention deficit hyperactivity disorder (ADHD) is a condition that becomes apparent in some children in the preschool and early school years. It is estimated that between 3 and 5 percent of children have ADHD. This is about 2 million children in the United States. The most common characteristics are the inability to pay attention, hyperactivity, and acting on impulses. Because many children may have these symptoms, but at a low level, or the symptoms may be caused by another disorder, it is important that the child receive a thorough examination and appropriate diagnosis by a well-qualified professional. Parents can ask their pediatrician to refer them to a child psychiatrist who can diagnose

and treat this condition. Although medication is often used as treatment, there has been recent concern about over-diagnosis and over-medication. Children with ADHD need guidance and understanding from parents, therapists, and school in order to achieve their full potential.

**Critical Thinking** Conduct research to learn about two different methods of treating ADHD. Write a report summarizing each method. Be sure to discuss the advantages and disadvantages of each method.

### RESPOND TO SPECIAL NEEDS — ADHD

**Discussion** Ask the class if they know of any children who take medication for attention deficit hyperactivity disorder. If so, ask how the child's behavior changes when he or she is on medication. Ask if the changes are all positive. (Answers will vary but might include: the child is calmer and can focus on tasks more easily. Negative changes might include loss of appetite or insomnia.)

**Critical Thinking** Student reports will vary, but the reports should summarize two treatments and discuss the advantages and disadvantages of each one. Treatments may include medication management or behavioral treatment.

### Teach *cont.*

**S** **Skill Practice**
**Guided Practice** *ask...*

**Recall** Have students think back to when they were young children. Discuss how they showed anger at this time. Ask how their angry behavior today compares to their angry behavior then. (Students may mention that when younger they screamed and hit when angry. Hopefully, they handle things in much calmer, controlled ways today.) **L1** **ELL**

**Act** Have groups of students write and perform skits that deal with one of the emotions associated with four- to six-year-olds. The skits may take any form—from a realistic portrayal of caregivers dealing with the emotions exhibited by a child, to a talk-show discussing the development of the emotion in children. (Skits will vary but should deal with one of the emotions associated with four- to six-year-olds.) **L2** **ELL**

**Analyze** Discuss with students how caregivers who show their anger inappropriately can affect children between the ages of four and six. What behaviors do *ask* they think these children might exhibit after watching angry outbursts? How is this harmful to them? (Students should recognize that if a child sees angry outbursts from caregivers, he or she is likely to show anger in the same ways. This can be harmful to the child if the parent is modeling one thing and telling the child to act in a different way.) **L3**

✓ **Reading Check**

**Analyze** Six-year-olds are beginning to find their status outside the home and want independence, but are still dependent on others. They are the center of their universe and experience rapid mood changes.

## Teach cont.

### R Reading Strategy

**Reading Comprehension** Tell students that to enhance their comprehension as they read, they should keep in mind these questions: Can I state the ideas in my own words? Do I need to look up any words? Do I understand how the new information fits in with information I have learned before? Do I need to read a section again? Ask students to read the three paragraphs on this page and write answers to these questions. (Answers will vary. However, students should be able to restate the main ideas in their own words and understand how the information fits with what they have already learned.)

### C₁ Critical Thinking

**Apply** Tell students that self-confidence can help eliminate some childhood frustrations. Caregivers should be aware that they can promote healthy self-confidence with these tips: Compliment specific skills and efforts and try not to be too general with praise or overuse it. Provide children with safe and appropriate ways to express themselves. Challenge children by giving them responsibilities suitable for their age. Ask students how these tips can help lessen a child's frustrations. (Answers will vary. A child with self-confidence can make mistakes without becoming angry. He will be less likely to take frustrations out on others.)

**Write About It** Scenarios will vary. Perhaps Lori could be shown how to make snakes and coil them into small bowls.

### Understanding Success

Danielle and her five-year-old daughter Lori are enrolled in a parent-child art class at the park district. Each week, the teacher introduces them to new materials and techniques to use in their artwork. The first week focused on drawing. Lori likes to draw and works very hard to stay within the lines when coloring her drawings. This is something she has observed her mother do. The next week they began to make little clay pots. Lori had trouble with the process. She could not smooth out the walls of her pot the same way the teacher did. She pushed it away and said she did not like art anymore. Danielle knew that Lori was just frustrated. Danielle wanted to help Lori enjoy the class again.

**Write About It** Many children Lori's age feel that there is a right and a wrong way to perform tasks. They are afraid to continue if they think they are doing a task wrong. Write a scenario explaining how you might help Lori feel she is succeeding in her art class.

There are many reasons for these changes in the expression of anger. Frustration is a major cause of anger, and a child's tolerance for frustration generally increases with age. Also, some sources of earlier frustration are eliminated as the child's skills improve. Finally, by age six, children have better social skills, which can help them deal with situations that lead to anger. They can usually work in groups, for example, and recognize that some things belong to other people.

Disagreements with other children are the most common cause of anger. Although quarrels are still loud and verbal, five- and six-year-old children begin to conceal and disguise their feelings. Sometimes their methods of revenge are indirect. They may pretend indifference, sneer, or make sly remarks. Often they make exaggerated threats. Occasionally, they take their anger out on a scapegoat, such as a younger sibling, a pet, or even a toy. A *scapegoat* is one that takes the blame for others.

Criticism can also be a cause of anger. Six-year-olds do not like to be criticized. Children who are scolded for doing something wrong may try to punish a parent by breaking yet another rule.

**Childhood Fears**
Fear of the dark can be common at this age. *What can parents do to help a child with this fear?*

**408** Chapter 14 Emotional and Social Development from Four to Six

### ➤ Explore the Photo

**Caption Answer** Parents can listen and say they understand without ridiculing the child. They can also use talking and acting out to help the child face the fearful situation.

**Discussion** Ask students to discuss how parents and other caregivers might talk with a child about safety issues without scaring them or passing along their own fears. (Answers will vary, but students may suggest that they will need to exercise self-control so the child does not pick up on any fear the adult may have.)

Children vary greatly in how much anger they show and how they show it. Variations depend on a child's temperament and the child's environment. Children tend to imitate the behavior of adults. Parents and other caregivers can teach children self-control by expressing their own anger in appropriate ways.

## Fear

Imagination is a major emotional force in children from four to six, and many of their fears center on imaginary dangers. They may be afraid of ghosts or monsters. Many children of this age are afraid of the dark. Some may worry about being left alone or abandoned. Fear of thunder and lightning is also common at this age. Many children fear situations related to school. They may be afraid of being criticized by a teacher or teased by other children. They may even fear that they will not perform as well as the other children.

Here are some ways that caregivers can help children deal with fears:

- **Accept the fear.** Just listening and saying you understand can greatly help a fearful child. Never say that what the child fears does not exist. It is very real to the child.
- **Let the child express the fear without ridicule.** Children this age fear being made fun of. If they worry that they might be ridiculed, they may not be open about their fears.
- **Help the child feel able to face the fear.** Use talking and acting out to help the child learn to face the fearful situation. Reading a book together about another child who dealt with a similar fear might also help.

Sometimes, of course, a child's fear about a certain situation is justified. A bully at school, for example, could be a cause for real concern. In such cases, parents need to take action to deal with the source of the fear and give support and reassurance.

## Jealousy

Sibling rivalry is jealousy of brothers and sisters. It is common during this period. Some parents unintentionally make the problem

---

worse. They may try to improve behavior by comparing one child to another. One father, for example, asked his daughter, "Why can't you be neat like your sister Selena? I never have to tell her to put her toys away." Comparisons such as this are rarely effective. They can actually damage a child's self-esteem and undermine family relationships.

Children at this age sometimes express their feelings of jealousy by tattling, criticizing, or lying. Some may feel jealous and react by boasting.

Parents and other caregivers can help children work through jealous feelings by encouraging cooperation and empathy. It is best to avoid taking sides and to give children a chance to practice working out their own problems. Sibling rivalry tends to fade as children mature and find interests outside the home.

## Worry

Children, like people of all ages, experience tension. **Tension** is another word for emotional stress. Children may worry about everything from a fire in their home, to a stranger taking them, to a bully in the neighborhood. Their active imagination contributes to the stress that they experience.

---

### Assess

**Quiz**
Ask students to answer the following questions:

1. **What makes five-year-olds anxious?** (Separation from parents, unfamiliar routines, and strange new settings can make five-year-olds anxious.)
2. **How does the expression of anger change between the ages of four and six?** (It changes from physical violence to hurting others' feelings, teasing, insulting, and making fun of others.)
3. **What are some ways that caregivers can help children deal with their fears?** (Listen and say you understand; do not ridicule the child about their fears; talk or act out the fear; read a book about another child with the same fear.)

### Reteach

**C₂ Critical Thinking**

**Making Predictions** Have students make predictions about how Pedro will be affected by his mother's reaction in this scenario: Pedro avoids walking on the grass whenever possible. He thinks the worms in the grass will crawl in his shoes and into his feet. When Pedro expressed this fear to his mother, she told Pedro to stop being silly. Whenever Pedro and his mother take a walk, she tickles him and says, "Beware of the worms!" (Answers will vary. However, students may predict that the mother's behaviors will not help to lessen Pedro's fears. Instead, they may make the fears worse.)

---

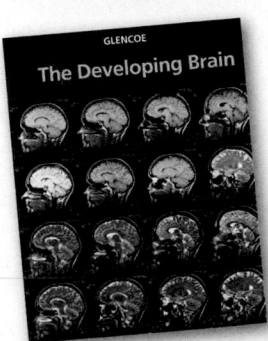

## Reteach *cont.*

### C₁ Critical Thinking

**Recognize Symptoms of Stress**

Have pairs of students take turns measuring each other's resting pulse rate by counting the pulse beats for ten seconds, then multiplying that number by six. Then ask students to take turns thinking of issues or situations that are currently causing them stress. After the first student has thought about stressful topics for a couple of minutes, ask the other student to measure the pulse rate again. Repeat with the second student. Are there differences between the resting and stressed pulse rates? Did students notice any other physical reactions while thinking about stressful subjects? Discuss why the body might react this way. (The stressed pulse rate should be higher. Students might also notice tense muscles in the jaw or a headache after thinking about stressful topics. The body might react this way because of the buildup of adrenaline in readiness for flight from a potentially harmful situation.)

**Professional Development**

**Mini Clip**
**Reading: Extending the Big Idea**

A teacher assigns group collaborations to promote student discussions about a reading selection.

---

## Science in Action

### Worry and Your Health

Larisa was concerned about her six-year-old son, Aaron. Several times a week he had such bad headaches that he was sent home from school early. Aaron finally admitted to his mother that he was worried because he was in the lowest reading group in his class. This worry was causing his headaches. He had literally worried himself sick.

### Procedure

Worry can affect our health in many ways. Conduct research using print or online resources to find out how worry can make people sick and the physical symptoms it causes.

### Analysis

Create a presentation explaining how worry can make people sick. In your presentation, mention specific health problems that can be caused by worrying.

> **NSES A** Develop abilities necessary to do scientific inquiry, understanding about scientific inquiry.

---

In addition to the emotional strain of tension, children may also develop physical symptoms, such as stomachaches, headaches, and sleeping difficulties. Children may cry, scream, or throw temper tantrums. Many preschoolers express tension by biting their nails, swinging their legs, or grinding their teeth. Here are some ways to help preschoolers and kindergarteners reduce worry and tension:

- **Look for the cause.** Ask children showing signs of stress to draw pictures of themselves. One preschooler whose parents had just divorced drew a picture of herself split in two. Another option is to use a puppet or stuffed animal. Explain that the toy is not feeling happy, and then ask the child what the problem is. The child may describe his or her own problems.
- **Give children time to calm down.** If tension turns into a tantrum or uncontrollable crying, call for time out. Send the child to a quiet room for a brief time to be alone and calm down. This is not for punishment.
- **Provide chances to get rid of tension.** Give children a physical way of releasing stress. Have them jump up and down or

**Children and Worry**
Habits such as biting nails or grinding teeth may be signs of stress and tension. *What kinds of things might this child be worrying about?*

---

## Science in Action

### Worry and Your Health

Worrying can cause us to be in a fight-or-flight state, which takes energy from our brains. Other effects of this constant stress include headaches, digestive tract problems, high blood pressure, and chest pains.

---

### ➤ Explore the Photo

**Caption Answer** Possible answers might include schoolwork, a sense of disorder at home, or being bullied by other children.

**Discussion** Ask the class: What should a caregiver do if they notice signs of stress and tension in their child? (Answers may vary but should include the tips listed on pp. 410–411.)

take them to a park or playground where they can run around. Teaching appropriate ways to reduce stress now will be helpful throughout life.

- **Read a book about the issue causing stress.** There are children's books that deal with stressful issues, from moving to a new home to facing someone's death. Reading a book together can help the child learn ways to handle the situation.
- **Maintain normal limits on behavior.** Some parents ease up on rules because they want to make life easier for a child. This approach can actually confuse the child and cause added stress and tension.

✓ **Reading Check** **List** What are some ways that children this age might express jealousy?

## Self-Confidence

As children become preschoolers, they learn new skills and deal with unfamiliar situations. This learning increases their self-confidence. **Self-confidence** is belief in one's own abilities. Preschoolers also start taking initiative and making decisions on their own. **Initiative** is the motivation to accomplish more. According to psychologist Erik Erikson, those who are encouraged in these efforts gain self-confidence. Repeated discouragement or punishment, on the other hand, can lead to feelings of inferiority or inadequacy. Children who feel self-confident will develop initiative.

The best way to help preschoolers develop self-confidence is to give them opportunities to perform well. Children need to feel good about what they do. Internal satisfaction will go farther than praise from others in helping them develop self-esteem. Self-esteem will help them develop self-control.

One complicating factor at this age is the tendency of children ages five and six to see their world in terms of all or nothing. If a project does not go the way a six-year-old intends, the child may think, "I can't do anything right." The child's self-esteem and self-confidence are lowered. It is important to help children this age experience more successes than failures. The saying "success breeds success" is especially true when applied to six-year-olds.

### CULTURE MATTERS

## Raising a Child in Austria

In Austria, the government encourages parents to stay home to raise their children. By law, women cannot work eight weeks before or after giving birth. This leave from work is fully paid. Families receive financial support that allows one parent to stay home, often for years. Weekends are reserved for family time. During this time, adults relax and play, showing children how to relieve the stress of the work week.

Until they are in the sixth grade, Austrian children come home from school, eat lunch, and then may spend the rest of the afternoon playing with friends, practicing sports, or learning an instrument.

★ **Build Connections** *Do you think people in the United States would enjoy the Austrian way of life? Why or why not?*

**NCSS I C Culture** Apply an understanding of culture as an integrated whole that explains the functions and interactions of traditions, beliefs and values, and behavior patterns.

### Reteach *cont.*

**C₂ Critical Thinking**

**Recognize Stressors** Work with students to brainstorm a list of issues and situations that might cause stress in children between the ages of four and six. Have students visit a local library and locate picture books for this age group that deal with the issues on your list. Have students write recommendations of these books indicating their strengths in dealing with particular issues and situations. (Recommendations will vary but should show an understanding of the issues and situations that cause stress, and appropriate books that deal with it. If time allows, you might have volunteers bring books to class and read them to the class.)

**W Writing Support**

**Dialogue**

**Encouragement** Have students write a dialogue between a parent and child in which the parent is encouraging the child. Tell students that to write an effective dialogue, they should let the people speak for themselves; use dialogue for a purpose; use language that sounds real and appropriate to the people talking; and use quotation marks appropriately. Ask volunteers to share their dialogues with the rest of the class. (Students' dialogues will vary. Use the following criteria to evaluate the dialogues: Do the details reflect the age, personality, and background of each person? Did the student use quotation marks correctly?)

✓ **Reading Check**

**List** Children might express their feelings by tattling, criticizing, lying, or boasting.

### CULTURE MATTERS

## Raising a Child in Austria

**Discussion** Ask students to identify the differences between the Austrian way of raising children and the United States way. (Answers will vary but may include: In the United States, maternity and paternity leave typically last no longer than three months—unpaid. Men and women in the United States must return to work while the baby is very young, which often means the baby is placed in a child care facility.)

**Building Connections** *Student answers will vary. People in the United States might enjoy having more free time with their families, but might not be willing to reduce the cost of their lifestyle to achieve it.*

### Assess

#### Study Tools

Have students go to the Online Learning Center at **glencoe.com**:

- Take the **Practice Test**.
- Download **Study-to-Go** content.

Use the **Student Activity Workbook** for additional practice.

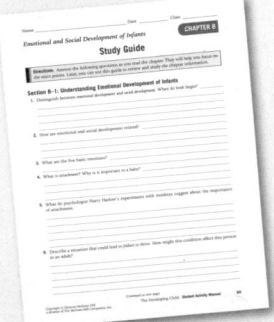

### Close

#### Culminating Activity

**Understanding Fears** Have students interview three children about their fears. What is each child afraid of the most? What reason(s) are given for the fears? How do they cope with the fears? (Answers will vary. Students should write a paragraph summarizing their interview.)

 **NCLB** connects academic correlations to book content.

Parents and other caregivers can help preschoolers and kindergartners develop self-confidence in many ways. Four of the best ways to help build self-confidence are showing respect, offering praise, planning activities, and encouraging individuality.

### Show Respect

Express confidence in the child's abilities. Offer the child choices whenever possible. Then show respect by going along with the child's decisions. When you make a decision, show respect by explaining your reasons rather than saying, "Because I said so."

### Give Praise and Encouragement

Try to catch the child doing something right, and then praise the action or accomplishment.

Be specific, such as "I really appreciate it when you help clear the table after dinner." Children might not know what you are referring to when you use general comments such as, "Good job."

### Plan Activities

Select activities that are challenging, but not overwhelming. Be sure the child has the ability to perform a given task to help avoid frustration and failure. Then give the child plenty of time and opportunity to practice. Be sure not to plan too many activities though. Children need downtime to relax and play.

### Encourage Individuality

Give boys and girls opportunities to develop a wide range of skills. This can include skills such as making breakfast or learning how to drive screws or pound nails.

---

## Section 14.1 After You Read

### Review Key Concepts

1. **Identify** three main emotional differences in children ages four, five, and six.
2. **Explain** the relationship between imagination and fear in the mind of a preschooler.
3. **Describe** how initiative and self-confidence are related.

### Practice Academic Skills

**English Language Arts**

4.  Carefully read the classic children's book *Where the Wild Things Are* by Maurice Sendak. Write an essay discussing how the book deals with common childhood emotions such as anger and fear. Also discuss how the book might build a child's self-confidence.

**Social Studies**

5.  Follow your teacher's instructions to form into groups. Work with your group to create a skit that shows the emotional behavior of four-, five-, or six-year-old children. As you develop your skit, keep in mind the emotional characteristics of children in your chosen age group. Be sure to use appropriate language in your skit.

**Check Your Answers** Check your answers at this book's Online Learning Center at **glencoe.com**.

> **NCTE 2** Read literature to build an understanding of the human experience.

> **NCSS V D** Apply concepts such as role, status, and social class in describing the connections and interactions of individuals and groups in society.

---

## Section 14.1 After You Read

### Review Key Concepts

1. Any three: **Four-year-olds** are self-centered, can be argumentative, seek approval and want to do things for themselves, have active imaginations and may have fears. **Five-year-olds** view themselves as whole persons, are eager to explore but may have difficulty in unfamiliar situations, are emotionally impulsive but feel more empathy than younger children. **Six-year-olds** are in emotional turmoil, may be stubborn, have rapid mood swings, and have deeper feelings of joy than younger children.

2. Preschoolers' fears typically center on imaginary dangers.

3. A child who is self-confident will develop initiative, or the motivation to try new things and achieve more.

### Practice Academic Skills

4. Essays will vary but might include that Max shows his power over fear by conquering scary monsters, demonstrating self-confidence.

5. Students should choose one of the three age groups and then create a skit showing how these children play with one another.

# Section 14.2 Social and Moral Development from Four to Six

## Reading Guide

### Before You Read

**Helpful Memory Tools** Successful readers use tricks to help them remember. For example, the acronym HOMES is a memory aid where each letter stands for one of the five Great Lakes. As you read the section, look for opportunities to make up your own memory aids.

### Read to Learn
**Key Concepts**
- **List** three social skills children must learn as they begin school.
- **Identify** seven guidelines for encouraging moral development in children.
- **Describe** three ways to encourage conflict resolution and cooperation in children.

### Main Idea
From four to six, children become increasingly involved in the outside world. Friends become important and moral values begin to develop. Children learn about teamwork and competition.

### Content Vocabulary
- ◇ peer
- ◇ moral development
- ◇ aggressive behavior
- ◇ competition

 **Graphic Organizer** Go to this book's Online Learning Center at **glencoe.com** to print out this graphic organizer.

### Academic Vocabulary
You will find these words in your reading and on your tests. Use the glossary to look up their definitions if necessary.
- ■ refine
- ■ resort

### Graphic Organizer
As you read, look for reasons to encourage and discourage competition. Use a chart like the one shown to organize your information.

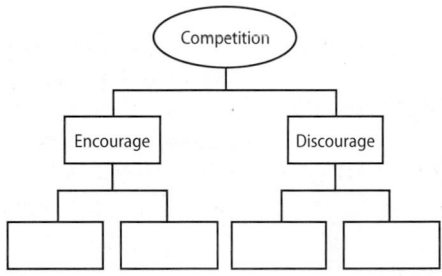

### Academic Standards · · · · · · · · · · · · · · · · · · · ·

 **English Language Arts**
**NCTE 11** Participate as members of literacy communities.

 **Social Studies**
**NCSS V B Individuals, Groups, and Institutions** Analyze group and institutional influences on people, events, and elements of culture.

**NCTE** National Council of Teachers of English
**NCTM** National Council of Teachers of Mathematics

**NSES** National Science Education Standards
**NCSS** National Council for the Social Studies

---

## Reading Guide

### Before You Read

Ask students to read the headings in red in this section. (General Social Patterns, Moral Development, Resolving Conflicts) For each head, ask students to write down one question that they think will be answered in that part of the section. Discuss the questions. (Questions will vary but should relate to the headings.)

### D Develop Concepts

**Main Idea** Discuss the main idea with students. Ask if they think caregivers should be aware that children in this age group are developing moral values. If so, why? (Students should recognize that everyone who comes in contact with children are teachers of moral values.)

---

## Focus

### Bell Ringer Activity

#### Who's in Charge?
Ask: Why it might be difficult for four- to six-year-olds to distinguish whose authority to accept? (Answers will vary. Children may think everyone older is an authority. Or, they may not recognize anyone from outside their home as an authority.)

## Preteaching

### Vocabulary
Remind students that a synonym is a word that has the same or a similar meaning as another word. Ask students to provide synonyms for the word, *moral*. (Answers will vary but may include: righteous, ethical, virtuous, noble.)

**Professional Development**

**Mini Clip**
**ELL: Vocabulary Activities**

Students practice vocabulary using synonyms.

### Graphic Organizer
 The Graphic Organizer is also on the TeacherWorks CD.

(Graphic organizers should include: Encourage—stimulates efforts, promotes higher standards, helps children gain a realistic view of abilities; Discourage—may instill idea that success depends on ability to outdo others, can lead to hostile relationships, lowers self-esteem of those who rarely win.)

 **NCLB** connects academic correlations to book content.

### Discussion Starter

Ask students to recall when they were four-, five-, or six-years-old. Did they play on an organized sports team? If so, what kinds of things did they learn? Ask students if they would recommend that parents have their young children play organized sports. (Answers will vary. Students may have had very good or not-so-good experiences playing organized sports as a young child. They may have learned skills that helped them play well with others such as sharing, or taking turns. Whether students would recommend organized sports for young children might depend on their own experiences.)

### R Reading Strategy

**Prior Knowledge** Based on what students know about the stages of emotional development in four- to six-year-olds, ask students to discuss what problems might occur when children in this age group play together. (Answers will vary but may include that children this age are often self-centered and want to have things their own way so they might not be willing to share. They may become upset when another child has the ball, for example. With four-year-olds especially, there may be fights when one does not get his or her own way. They may have trouble sharing and be inconsiderate of others' feelings. They also may become frustrated if they are not able to perform as well as their peers.)

## General Social Patterns

**R** Children four through six years of age find themselves in an expanding world. As they begin preschool, kindergarten, and elementary school, they must learn three important social skills: how to interact with new people, how to make friends, and how to work and play in organized groups. Children must also learn how to take direction and accept authority from adults outside the home. Increasingly, young children must determine right and wrong and act accordingly.

A major task of the preschool, kindergarten, and early elementary school years is to develop social skills. As children spend more time outside the home, they need to **refine**, or improve, their skills at getting along with their peers. A **peer** is someone close to one's own age.

Adult authority figures other than parents and main caregivers also gain more importance. Although the rate at which individual children learn social skills varies, there are general patterns common at each age.

### Four Years

Four-year-olds form friendships with their playmates. Unlike toddlers, who tend to engage in parallel play, four-year-olds spend more time in cooperative play. They can play in groups of three or four, sharing toys and taking turns. Four-year-olds are often bossy and inconsiderate, however, so fighting may occur.

Although friends are important to four-year-olds, the family is still more important. Children this age actively seek approval by making such remarks as "I'm good at drawing pictures, aren't I?" or "Look how high I can climb!" If things go wrong, they look to parents and other caregivers for comfort.

### Five Years

Five-year-olds tend to be more outgoing and talkative than four-year-olds. They can play in groups of five or six, and their play is more complicated. Fights break out less frequently. When they do quarrel, five-year-olds typically resort to name-calling and wild threats.

**➡ Cooperation**
Four-year-olds often engage in cooperative play. *What skills do you think these children are learning while playing together?*

### ➤ Explore the Photo

**Caption Answer** Answers will vary. They could be learning empathy, to take turns, and to share. They might also be learning about friendly competition.

**Discussion** Ask students to define poor sportsmanship. What does it say about a child's self-concept? How can parents and caregivers help encourage good sportsmanship? (Answers will vary, but students should recognize that good sportsmanship means being able to play well with others. Parents can encourage sportsmanship by teaching the child to treat others with kindness.)

C By age five, children have developed more respect for others' belongings. A five-year-old may still try to grab another child's toy, but such behavior is less common.

U When children begin school, social acceptance by peers becomes more important. Five-year-olds are concerned about what their friends say and do. They do not want to be thought of as different, and they fear ridicule.

At about this age, some children begin to gossip about other children. Typically they talk about which children they consider to be friends or who has what toys. Gossip indicates what behaviors the children as a group value, and what actions they consider undesirable.

## Six Years

The social relations of six-year-olds are often characterized by friction, threats, and stubbornness. Children this age want everything, and they want to do things their own way. They may not want to share their toys. They may be jealous of other children's toys.

Best friends at this age are usually children of the same sex, though six-year-olds play readily in mixed groups. They enjoy group play and organized teams for games. If they tire of playing, however, they will simply drop out of a game. They have no regard for team effort.

## What Would You Do?

### Handling Family Conflict

The relationship between six-year-old Pam and her family was strained. Nothing seemed to please her. When she screamed and protested after her parents took her television privileges away, they relented. After her parents gave in to her demands, her behavior grew worse. At their wits' end, Pam's parents went to see the school counselor.

"Pam is acting out all the time. How can we get her to change?" they asked. "Perhaps you need to ask what you can do to change the situation," the counselor advised. "Let's begin by looking at your expectations. It is reasonable to expect a six-year-old to follow the family rules or face the consequences. It is not realistic to expect her to be happy about the consequences. You want Pam to learn self-control by accepting the consequences of her actions."

🖊 **Write About It** Imagine that you are one of Pam's parents the day after this meeting. Pam is throwing a temper tantrum because you will not let her go to a friend's house until she has cleaned her room. Write a dialog between you and Pam showing how you would respond to this situation.

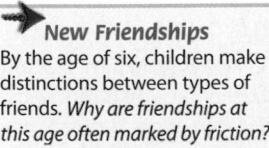

> **New Friendships**
> By the age of six, children make distinctions between types of friends. *Why are friendships at this age often marked by friction?*

Section 14.2    Social and Moral Development from Four to Six    **415**

## Section 14.2

## Teach cont.

### C Critical Thinking

**Problem Solving** Read this scenario to students: You are a caregiver playing a game with a five-year-old boy and his eight-year-old sister. The boy is obviously cheating, and his sister begins to complain about it. What should you do? (Students should focus on multiple aspects of the situation, including considering their own possible feelings of anger, the child's reasons for cheating, and whether to talk to the boy about the issue in front of his sister. You might ask students whether they would continue playing the game, and to explain their answers.)

### U Universal Access

**Gifted Learners** Ask gifted learners to conduct library or Internet research to find answers to these questions: What can preschool and elementary school teachers do to teach four-, five-, and six-year-olds how to resolve conflicts without violence? Is it possible or advisable to teach conflict resolution to children this young? (Students should find that even preschool and elementary school teachers can teach simplified conflict resolution techniques to young children. One technique is to teach children to tell the person with whom you have the conflict what you didn't like, then tell him or her how it made you feel, tell him or her what you want in the future, and then the other child responds with what they can do to change their behavior in the future.)

## What Would You Do?

**Write About It** Dialogues will vary but should demonstrate what the student has learned by stating that Pam will not be allowed to go to her friend's house until her room is cleaned.

## ➤ Explore the Photo

**Caption Answer** Answers may vary. Children in this age group want to do things their own way and have no regard for team effort. Also, children may not want to share their toys.

**Discussion** Ask students what issues and situations might cause conflicts for four-, five-, and six-year-old children. (Answers may include: four-year-olds tend to be bossy, may lead to conflicts; five-year-olds may still have trouble sharing and taking turns; six-year-olds can be stubborn.)

## Teach cont.

## S Skill Practice

### Guided Practice

**Describe a Personal Experience**
Have students describe a time when they told a lie when they were younger. They should also share the consequences of their lie. (Students' personal accounts will vary. They should share any consequences they might have faced because of the lie. Ask if they felt the situation was handled in a positive way.) **L1**

**Drawing Conclusions** Ask students to discuss the following question: Why do you think it is emotionally difficult for some parents to enforce the standards of behavior they have set for their children? (Answers will vary but may include: Parents are tired at the end of the day and do not want to spend time arguing with their children. Some parents feel guilty for working long hours and want to make it up to children by being lenient.) **L2**

**Analyze Gender Differences**
Ask students if they think boys and girls develop a sense of right and wrong at the same time and at the same rate. Have them support their answers with specific examples. (Students' specific examples will vary. Studies done based on Kohlberg's stages of moral development do not suggest gender differences regarding when children learn and develop a sense of right and wrong.) **L3**

### ✓ Reading Check

**Compare** Six-year-olds tend to be more self-centered and often fight more with their families than five-year-olds. Five-year-olds typically enjoy being part of the family.

**416**

---

# Learning Through PLAY

## Play by the Rules

Playing a board game with a four-year-old can be fun, but at the same time very frustrating. Children delight in playing games, though they often create their own set of rules as they go along. Most preschoolers think the world revolves around them. As a child matures, the world seems to get bigger and include more people. Social rules become more important. Playing games allows a child to follow rules. The child learns to take turns and learns that he or she cannot always be the winner. The child is able to see the world from another person's perspective and is able to understand why rules are needed for things to be fair.

**Think About It** Work with a partner to create a skit in which you are playing a board game. One of you should be a four-year-old and the other the parent. The child keeps trying to change the rules so that she can win. Act out how the parent might respond appropriately.

---

## Family Relationships

Relationships within a family change as a child advances from age four to age six. Four-year-olds feel close ties to home and want to feel important in the family. They are proud that they can help with chores. However, they often quarrel and bicker with their siblings.

Five-year-olds also delight in helping out at home. They now play much better with their brothers and sisters. They are usually protective and kind toward younger siblings.

Six-year-olds do not get along as well with other family members. This is in part because they are more self-centered. Their own feelings and needs come first. Six-year-olds commonly argue with adult family members. They can be rough and impatient with younger brothers and sisters, and may fight with older siblings.

### ✓ Reading Check **Compare** How are six-year-olds' relationships with their families different from those of five-year-olds?

## Moral Development

The process of learning to base one's behavior on beliefs about what is right and wrong is called **moral development**. Moral development begins early in life. Toddlers learn the rules their parents and other caregivers set. At that stage, however, they do not understand the reasons for the rules. They just learn that some actions, such as hitting another person, make their caregivers unhappy with them. They do not want to lose love and approval, so they learn to avoid those behaviors.

Preschoolers, on the other hand, are beginning to understand the reasons behind such rules. They are beginning to develop a conscience. A *conscience* is an inner sense of right and wrong that guides people's behavior and helps them make judgments about what is good and bad behavior. The rules that they learn in early childhood form the basis of their developing conscience.

## Guidelines for Moral Development

Parents and other caregivers have a responsibility to help children develop a moral sense that will guide their behavior. Here are some suggestions:

- **Set clear standards of behavior.** Tell children, for example, "We do not hit other people. Hitting will hurt them and make them sad." Teaching children the reasons for rules helps them understand why the rules are important.

---

# Learning Through PLAY

## Play by the Rules

**Discussion** Ask students if they have ever played a game with a young child. Did the child try to change the rules to his or her advantage? If so, how did the students handle the situation? (Responses will vary. Some students might just ignore the cheating. Others might discuss it with the child.)

**Think About It** Students create a skit in which a child refuses to obey the rules of a board game. The parent then should respond appropriately. The parent may explain that following rules is an important part of games.

- **Respond to inappropriate behavior.** When rules are broken, deal with the problem immediately and appropriately. Repeat the rule and the reason for the rule.
- **Talk about mistakes in private.** Six-year-olds, especially, do not like to be criticized. Correcting their behavior in front of others may make them feel humiliated.
- **Understand that children will test the limits.** As children develop a moral awareness, they might try disobeying or refusing to cooperate. This is a sign that they are beginning to understand what is acceptable and what is forbidden behavior.
- **Consider the child's age and abilities.** For example, at preschool, Beth was playing at a shallow table filled with rice and containers. She started tossing the rice into the air and watching it land on the floor. The teacher reminded Beth that she must keep the rice in the table, then handed her a broom and a dustpan to sweep up the mess. Beth's teacher knows that children this age cannot always remember the rules but will learn from the consequences of their actions.
- **It is a lifelong task to learn self-discipline.** It is unfair to expect perfection from children. Instead, help children learn from their mistakes. Always recognize and praise their steps in the right direction.
- **Continue to show love despite misbehavior.** Children need to know that, although you do not like what they did, you continue to love them. Separate the deed from the doer.

## Handling Lying

Many children tell tall tales and exaggerate. Young children often confuse stories with reality. These are not deliberate deceptions. Adults can show the child that they know the difference by saying, "I will listen to your story, and then I need to know what really happened."

## Parenting Skills

### Guide Children's Behavior

Parental guidance makes a major difference in whether children grow up to be happy, well-adjusted adults. Here are some ways to guide children effectively:

- **Build trust.** Respond to their needs lovingly so that they know they can count on you, no matter what.
- **Accentuate the positive.** When you *accentuate* something, you place more emphasis on it. Comment when children show positive behaviors such as kindness and cheerfulness.
- **Build empathy.** Remind children that others have feelings, too.
- **Respect fears and feelings.** Guide children's behavior by offering respect and reassurance.
- **Teach actions and consequences.** Explain that if children angrily throw a toy, and it breaks, it will not be replaced. They will soon avoid actions that have negative consequences.
- **Encourage responsibility.** Assign a daily job. Doing a chore well helps children develop pride in themselves.
- **Guide by example.** Model ways to treat siblings, friends, neighbors, and relatives with kindness and respect.

**Take Charge** Your child gets angry at the family dog for knocking over his block tower. He kicks the dog, who yelps. What would you say to the child?

Section 14.2 Social and Moral Development from Four to Six **417**

## Parenting Skills

### Guide Children's Behavior

Ask students what they think the word *trust* means. Why is it important to build trust in children? How does having a sense of trust help society as a whole? (People who trust others are more likely to be kind to them and to think of the good of society as a whole, rather than only being concerned with meeting their own personal needs.)

**Take Charge**
Explain to the child that he hurt the dog when he kicked it. Remind the child that he would not like to be kicked and that the dog did not know it was doing anything wrong.

### Assess

**Quiz** ask
Ask students to answer the following questions:

1. What are the social patterns of five-year-olds? (They play in groups of five or six, play is more complicated than that of four-year-olds, fights are less frequent.)
2. Why are the relations of six-year-olds characterized by friction, threats, and stubbornness? (because they want everything, want to do things their own way, and may not want to share)
3. How can parents and caregivers guide children to express their anger in nonaggressive ways? (encourage them to talk about feelings; praise and encourage them when they try to resolve conflicts; model appropriate ways to deal with anger)

### Reteach

**U Universal Access**

**Visual Learners** Have students create flowcharts directing parents how to respond to inappropriate behavior in either a four-year-old, a five-year-old, or a six-year-old. Charts should start and stop, using circle shapes. Directions for the parent should appear in rectangles. Questions should appear in diamond shapes. Encourage students to use the charts to explore the processes of cause and effect, action and consequence, and cycles of repetition by which children learn about right and wrong. (Flowcharts will vary but should show that students have a good understanding of appropriate ways to respond to inappropriate behaviors in four-, five-, and six-year-olds.)

### Reteach *cont.*

**Writing Support**

**Character Analysis**

**Guiding Behavior** Have students speak with their own parents or other parents they know about techniques they used for guiding young children's behavior. Students should ask for a specific example of one of these guidelines: build trust; accentuate the positive; build empathy; respect fears and feelings; teach actions and consequences; encourage responsibility; or guide by example. Have students write a character analysis of either the parent or the child described in the example. (Refer to p. 402 for tips on writing a character analysis. Students' writing will vary, but should vividly describe one of the people in the scenario.)

---

**Professional Development**

**Mini Clip**
**Reading: Student Involvement**

Students work in small groups to choose objects that represent them first as individuals and then as part of a group.

---

**Universal Access**

**Interpersonal Learners** Divide the class into small teams. Have each team create a video that teaches children about manners. Students will need to define what manners are, and also remember the needs and attention span of their audience. When finished, show the videos to the class. (Team's videos will vary but should show an understanding of the age level for which the video is being prepared.)

---

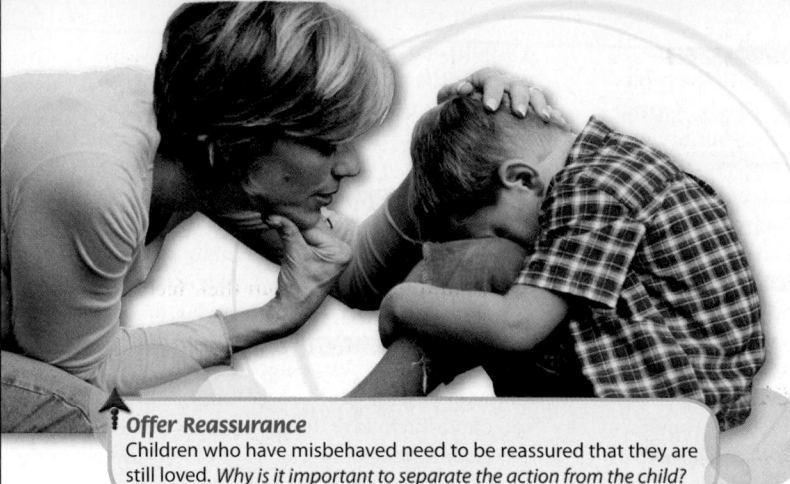

**Offer Reassurance**
Children who have misbehaved need to be reassured that they are still loved. *Why is it important to separate the action from the child?*

Sometimes a statement that sounds like a lie is really a misunderstanding. The child who says, "I did what you told me," may believe that a task is done, even though a parent may not agree. Be sure the child understood the instructions. However, sometimes children do tell deliberate lies. Here are a few reasons why:

- To get attention from adults
- To avoid punishment
- To please others and not risk losing love

When dealing with a child who is lying, consider these points:

- Does the child know that what he said is not true?
- Why might the child be lying?
- Do you need more information about the situation?
- Is the child asking for more attention?

Help children separate fact from fiction. Do not punish children when they are being imaginative. Do, however, teach them that there is a difference between reality and fantasy. Children need to know that telling the truth is important because people rely on what others say in deciding how to act.

### Model Moral Behavior

One of the best ways to teach children moral behavior is to model it in everyday actions. Children learn by following an example. If they are told that lying is wrong, but then hear their parents telling lies, they will be confused by the mixed message.

Josh's dad, for example, was eating his dinner when the telephone rang. Josh's mother got up to answer the phone. "If that's for me," said his dad, "tell them I'm not at home."

"Dad, didn't you tell me that it's wrong to tell a lie?" asked Josh.

"That's right," said Josh's dad as he returned to his dinner.

"But didn't you just tell a lie?"

"Do as I say, not as I do," came the response.

The next time Josh's parents talked to him about what is right and wrong, he did not take the message very seriously.

Moral behavior is learned behavior, but parents are not their child's only teachers. The influence of peers increases as children spend more time away from home. They pick up language and speech patterns from their friends. They also notice that other families live by different rules.

Television, movies, and other media also influence what children learn. As children gain independence, they may watch more television. Some of the shows they see may reflect different values than those of their family. Parents should be aware of what their children are seeing. Parents can talk to their children about why their family has the values it does, and why some things they see in movies or television shows are wrong.

**418** Chapter 14 Emotional and Social Development from Four to Six

---

### Explore the Photo

**Caption Answer** Children need to know that parents and caregivers love and accept them and will always be there for them, even when they have misbehaved.

**Discussion** Ask students: How might a child be affected if they felt a parent no longer loved them? (Answers will vary. The child would likely be devastated. He or she might become depressed and begin to act out in abnormal ways.)

Parents and caregivers are responsible for what children watch and for how much they watch. One way to prevent television from having a negative effect is to limit television viewing. If children develop other ways of learning and playing, watching television is less likely to become a habit.

**✓ Reading Check** **Identify** What are some of the reasons that children tell lies?

## Resolving Conflicts

Children ages four through six spend a lot of time with other children. They may have to compete for toys, attention, or a turn on playground equipment. Such circumstances can lead to conflict.

Preschoolers might **resort** to, or choose, aggressive behavior. **Aggressive behavior** is hostile, and at times destructive, behavior that people display when faced with conflict. Such behavior usually erupts when they are angry or frustrated, and often results from conflicts over objects or control of space. Hitting, biting, pushing, and forcibly taking objects away from others are some examples of aggressive behavior.

Children need to learn that aggressive behavior is unacceptable. Through their own example and through their teaching, parents and other caregivers can guide children in non-aggressive ways to express anger and resolve conflicts with their peers. Here are some suggestions for encouraging conflict resolution and cooperation:

- **Urge children to talk about their feelings.** When Carla's father heard her lash out at her friend Erin, "You're ugly, and I hate you!" he had the girls sit down and tell what they were feeling. Carla admitted she was angry because Erin had used up all of her red markers. Erin told Carla how much the angry words had hurt her feelings.
- **Acknowledge the efforts of children to resolve conflicts.** Offer specific praise and encouragement, such as "You and Jeremy did the right thing in deciding to take turns playing on the swing."
- **Model appropriate behavior.** In your daily life, show appropriate ways to deal with anger and conflict. Studies show that many children who engage in acts of aggression were exposed to adults who used or allowed aggressive behavior.

**↑ Handle Conflicts**
Caregivers need to encourage angry preschoolers to talk about their feelings as a start toward resolving conflicts. *What is this adult teaching these children about dealing with conflicts?*

Section 14.2   Social and Moral Development from Four to Six   **419**

**Section 14.2**

### Reteach *cont.*

**R Reading Strategy**

**Outlining** Ask students to read the section Resolving Conflicts and create an outline of the content. You might take time to review outlining with students and to determine the style you would prefer they use. (Students' outlines will vary. A typical outline will use Resolving Conflicts as the main head and Competition and Teamwork and Cooperation as minor heads. Each minor head should have at least two factual points to support it.)

**C Critical Thinking**

**Problem Solving** Parents, caregivers, and teachers are often anxious for a conflict between children to be over, but forcing children to say they are sorry to each other only sends the conflict underground for a time where it waits to resurface. Have groups of three students take turns playing the role of a parent mediating peace between two siblings, five and six years old, who are engaged in a conflict over which movie the family should watch. Encourage students acting as mediators to find a solution that is acceptable to all parties. Ask teams to share their best solution with the rest of the class. (Solutions will vary but should show students understand the content about conflict resolution.)

**✓ Reading Check**

**Identify** Reasons for lying include to get attention from adults, to avoid punishment, to please others, and to not risk losing love.

**419**

## ➤ Explore the Photo

**Caption Answer** Possible answers include that settling conflicts by behaving aggressively is not acceptable and that they can resolve conflicts by talking and sharing their feelings with one another.

**Discussion** Ask students to describe what they would do if a five-year-old lied about taking a cookie. (Answers will vary. Students might suggest emphasizing the importance of telling the truth or exhibiting a willingness to hear the truth without blaming or shaming.)

## Assess

### Study Tools

Have students go to the Online Learning Center at **glencoe.com**:

- Take the **Practice Test**.
- Download **Study-to-Go** content.
- Use the **Student Activity Workbook** for additional practice.

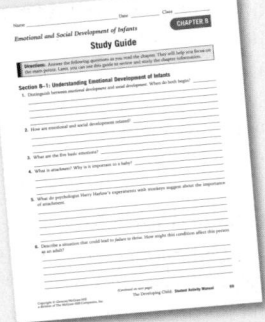

## Close

### Culminating Activity

**Understanding Children** Ask students to define the word *friend*. Now ask them how they think a four-, five-, or six-year-old would define friend. (Definitions will vary. Students should recognize that young children will have a much simpler definition; they may simply supply someone's name.)

 **NCLB** connects academic correlations to book content.

## Competition

**Competition** is rivalry with the goal of winning or outperforming others. Not everyone has the same views about the role that competition should play in children's lives. Some say that children benefit from competition because it stimulates individual efforts and promotes higher standards. Competition helps children gain a realistic view of their own abilities in relation to others. It helps children excel and prepares them for the adult world.

Others feel that competition is harmful to children because it instills the idea that success depends on the ability to outdo others. This mindset, they say, can lead to hostile relationships. In addition, they feel competition can discourage initiative in those who rarely win because it points out their inadequacies and lowers their status and self-esteem.

## Teamwork and Cooperation

Most preschoolers and kindergartners prefer cooperative play to competitive games. Children can actually engage in both kinds of play. They can play cooperatively in competitive games by working together with their teammates.

Children not playing at a particular time can cheer for their teammates. When they are playing, children can share in the game. For example, in a ball game, each child can have a turn.

Whatever the game, caregivers need to teach children not to compare themselves with others. Show them, instead, how to compare their skills today with their skills in the past. Is Carlos running faster than last month? Children can get a feeling of satisfaction from seeing improvement in their own performance.

## Section 14.2 After You Read

### Review Key Concepts

1. **Describe** how the nature of play changes between the ages of two and four.
2. **Explain** how parents should respond to a child who is lying.
3. **Identify** ways that competitive games can build cooperation among children.

### Practice Academic Skills

 **English Language Arts**

4. A fable is not just a story. It is a story with a purpose. Fables are short stories designed to teach moral lessons. Write a fable that a four- to six-year-old could understand. Create simple illustrations for your fable. Read your story to a young child. Ask the child: What lesson did you learn?

> **NCTE 11** Participate as members of literacy communities.

 **Social Studies**

5. Suppose you are part of a group of adults setting up a T-ball league for six-year-olds. Prepare a list of six rules of behavior that the children are to follow. All of the rules must concern appropriate behavior, rather than athletic concerns.

> **NCSS V B** Analyze group and institutional influences on people, events, and elements of culture.

 **Check Your Answers** Check your answers at this book's Online Learning Center at **glencoe.com**.

---

### Section 14.2 After You Read

### Review Key Concepts

1. Children begin to interact with one another more during play and to develop friendships.
2. They should let the child know that they realize the child is lying and help the child to distinguish fact from fiction. They should explain that it is important to tell the truth because people rely on what others say in deciding how to act.
3. They can build cooperation by encouraging children to work together as a team.

### Practice Academic Skills

4. Students should have written a fable at a level appropriate for a four- to six-year-old child that teaches a moral lesson. Students should also read their fable to a child to ensure the moral is clear.

5. Rules will vary but might include: Play fair; Be kind to others; Treat everyone, including opponents, with respect; Praise others' efforts; Be respectful of the rulings of the officials; Be a good loser and a good winner.

## Chapter Summary

Children develop increased independence, curiosity, and boldness as they mature from ages four to six. They show emotions such as anger, jealousy, and worry. The rich imagination and fantasy life of preschoolers can lead to fears of ghosts and monsters. As they mature, children learn to express anger with words rather than physical attacks. Children develop an internal sense of right and wrong. They also learn to play both competitive and cooperative games.

## Vocabulary Review

1. Write a sentence using two or more of these content and vocabulary terms. The sentence should clearly show how the terms are related.

**Content Vocabulary**
◇ tension (p. 409)
◇ self-confidence (p. 411)
◇ initiative (p. 411)
◇ peer (p. 414)
◇ moral development (p. 416)
◇ aggressive behavior (p. 419)
◇ competition (p. 420)

**Academic Vocabulary**
■ impulsive (p. 406)
■ turmoil (p. 406)
■ refine (p. 414)
■ resort (p. 419)

## Review Key Concepts

2. **Identify** a single characteristic that marks the emotional development of four- to six-year-olds.
3. **List** five ways to help children reduce worry and tension.
4. **Describe** how to help children develop self-confidence.
5. **List** three social skills children must learn as they begin school.
6. **Identify** seven guidelines for encouraging moral development in children.
7. **Describe** three ways to encourage conflict resolution and cooperation in children.

## Critical Thinking

8. **Analyze** Why might family members experience more friction with a six-year-old than with a younger child?
9. **Hypothesize** Is it possible for parents to treat all of their children equally at all times? Can they always prevent sibling rivalry? Can they reduce it?
10. **Judge** Some adults who think competition should be encouraged in children say that it prepares them for the adult world. Do you agree with this point of view? Explain your answer.

Chapter 14   Emotional and Social Development from Four to Six   **421**

## Content and Academic Vocabulary Review

1. Students should write a sentence that clearly shows the relation between two of the terms.

## Review Key Concepts

2. The most important characteristic of this group is an increasing desire for independence.
3. Answers should include: look for the cause, give the child time to calm down, provide opportunities to get rid of tension, read a book about the issue causing stress, and maintain normal limits on behavior.
4. Ways to encourage self-confidence include showing respect, and offering praise and encouragement.
5. They must learn how to interact with new people, make friends, and work and play in organized groups.
6. Answers should include: set clear standards of behavior, respond to inappropriate behavior, talk about mistakes in private, understand that children will test the limits, consider the child's age and abilities, realize that it is a lifelong task to learn self-discipline, and continue to show love despite misbehavior.
7. Encourage children to talk about their feelings, acknowledge the efforts of children to resolve conflicts, and model appropriate behavior.

## Critical Thinking

8. Six-year-olds often go through a period of emotional turmoil, and want to be grown-up, but may often feel dependent. They may resent being given directions, especially by their parents.
9. No, because children are different and different situations arise with each one. However, they can reduce sibling rivalry by encouraging cooperation and empathy, making it clear that they love all their children, avoiding taking sides, and letting children work out their problems.
10. Students' responses will vary, but they should provide specific reasons for their responses.

**Family & Community Connections**

**11.** Students should write a paragraph comparing their definition of the word friend with that of at least two four- or five-year-olds.

### Health Skills

**12.** Reports will vary. Laughter has been shown to reduce the levels of stress hormones like cortisol and adrenaline. It can increase people's pain threshold, strengthen the immune system, and help injured people to heal more quickly.

### Observation Skills

**13.** Students' reports will vary, but the student should describe how the child displayed either anger, fear, or worry. The student should explain how the parent responded to the child's behavior.

### Real-World Skills

**14.** Students should create an original board game, demonstrate the game to the class, and explain the social skill the game is designed to teach.

**15.** Web pages should list five reasons preschoolers often have difficulty with anger. Reasons might include a sense of frustration, inability to explain feelings, lack of social skills, disagreements with other children, and criticism or punishment from an adult.

**16.** The student should create a chart showing the costs of their chosen activity for one year for a family of four.

**N C L B**   **NCLB** Activity correlated to Science standards.

**422**

---

**Family & Community Connection**

**11. Friendship** Write a definition in your own words of the word *friend*. Then talk with at least two children between the ages of four and five. Ask each child what he or she thinks it means to be a friend. Write a paragraph comparing your definition of the word friend with the children's definitions. Why do you think they are different?

### Health Skills

**12. Laughter** Perhaps you have heard the saying, "Laughter is the best medicine." Laughing can help us relax and get rid of daily tensions. Science has shown that laughter can even improve our health. Conduct research using print or online resources to learn about the health effects of laughter. Then write a one-page report to share what you learn.

**Observation Skills**

**13. Preschoolers and Emotions** Preschoolers quickly shift from one emotion to another, often with little or no apparent reason. Some emotions, such as anger, fear, and worry, are typically seen by adults as undesirable.

**Procedure** Observe two preschoolers with their parents. Watch for the preschoolers to display anger, fear, or worry. Note how the child expressed the emotion and the parent's response.

**Analysis** Prepare a written report in which you describe the emotion the child displayed and the parent's response. Analyze whether the response appeared to have the desired effect.

**NSES A** Develop abilities necessary to do scientific inquiry, understandings about scientific inquiry.

**N C L B**

## Real-World Skills

| | |
|---|---|
| **Problem-Solving** | **14. Teach Skills** You want to design a board game to help your younger nieces and nephews learn social skills. Create an original game out of common materials, such as cardboard and clay. Demonstrate your game to the class and explain the skill it is designed to teach. |
| **Technology Skills** | **15. Design a Web Page** A parents' group is developing a Web site to help parents cope with common problems associated with four- to five-year-olds. Create a Web page listing at least five reasons that children in this age group often have difficulties with anger. |
| **Financial Literacy** | **16. Playing Together** One way to reduce stress is by being physically active. Pick an activity that a family of four might enjoy, such as bicycling or joining a recreation center. Research the cost of this activity. Include, if necessary, membership fees, and buying or renting equipment. Create a chart showing your chosen activity's cost for one year. |

**Additional Activities** For additional activities, go to this book's Online Learning Center at **glencoe.com**.

## Academic Skills

**17.** Lists will vary. Rules might include: Say "please" and "thank you;" do not interrupt others when they are talking, take turns, use silverware appropriately, chew with mouth closed, sit appropriately during meals, obey adults, try to avoid becoming angry, do not tease or bully others, and be kind to people and animals.

**18.** Groups of 2, 3, 4 or 6 are possible. ($12 \div 2 = 6$; $12 \div 3 = 4$; $12 \div 4 = 3$; $12 \div 6 = 2$. $12 \div 5 = 2$, with a remainder of 2, so 5 is not a possible group size.)

The *Early Childhood Observations CD* offers additional lessons with videos to build students' observation skills.

**Part 1:** Learning to Observe
**Part 2:** How Children Develop
**Part 3:** Working With Young Children
**Part 4:** Extended Observations
**Part 5:** Resources and Answer File

## Academic Skills

 **English Language Arts**

**17.** Research what various child development experts think constitutes *etiquette*, or good manners, in young children. Use this information to create a list of ten etiquette rules that parents can use to guide their preschoolers. Be aware of differences that may occur across different cultures.

> **NCTE 4** Use written language to communicate effectively.

 **Mathematics**

**18. Social Development** Child psychologist Erik Erikson believes that four- to six-year-olds learn to cooperate with others, and to lead as well as to follow. A mother is planning a party and wants to encourage all the kids to get to know each other during a variety of games. If there will be 12 children at the party, what are all the sizes of groups possible if each group is the same size?

**Math Concept** **Common Multiples** Multiples are the products of a given number and various integers.

**Starting Hint** Divide 12 by 1, 2, 3, 4, 5, and 6. Any dividend without a remainder is a possible group size.

 **Math** For math help, go to the Math Appendix at the back of the book.

> **NCTM Number and Operations** Compute fluently and make reasonable estimates.

 **Science**

**19. Children and Media** Many parents restrict their children's exposure to television and movies. For example, parents may limit their children to watching only one hour of television a day, or only allow them to watch movies that are rated G for General Audience.

**Procedure** Ask 10 parents if they limit their young children's exposure to television or movies. If so, ask them how. Keep track of the types of restrictions.

**Analysis** Write a report on what you learned. Include a chart summarizing the kinds of restrictions parents placed.

> **NSES A** Develop abilities necessary to do scientific inquiry, understandings about scientific inquiry.

### Standardized Test Practice

**TIMED WRITING**
Because many standardized tests are timed, it is important to develop a good strategy for taking them. Imagine that you have 10 minutes to write an answer to the following question. Read the Test-Taking Tip, and then write your answer.

**20.** What are some ways in which parents and caregivers can help children deal with sibling rivalry?

> **Test-Taking Tip** Avoid the temptation to immediately begin writing. Start by thinking through your answer and creating an ordered list of your major points. Then begin writing.

**NCLB**

**19.** Students conduct research on how 10 parents restrict their children's viewing of television and movies. They should write a report describing what they learned and include a chart summarizing the types of restrictions.

> **NCLB** NCLB connects academic correlations to book content.

### Standardized Test Practice

**20.** Answers will vary. Parents and caregivers can help children deal with sibling rivalry by encouraging cooperation and empathy. They should avoid taking sides and give children a chance to work out their own problems.

**Test-Taking Tips** Explain that students should carefully read essay questions to make sure they understand exactly what is expected of their answer.

**Timed Writing** Essay and short-answer test questions are usually timed. Have your students take one or more timed essay tests or free writing exercises so that they become comfortable with writing for a fixed length of time.

---

## TECHNOLOGY **Solutions**

**Use these technology solutions to streamline chapter assessment!**

 *ExamView Assessment Suite* CD allows you to create and print out customized tests or ready-made unit and chapter tests, complete with answer keys.

 **TeacherWorks Plus** is an electronic lesson planner that provides instant access to complete teacher resources in one convenient package.

 **Online Learning Center** includes resources and activities for students and teachers.

**STANDARDS BASED LESSON PLANNING** *The Developing Child* provides students with instruction and assessment in the following fundamental content areas:

## National Standards Correlations

| Standards | Pages |
|---|---|
| **12.1.1** Analyze physical, emotional, social, spiritual, and intellectual development. | **429, 430–432, 434–441** |
| **12.1.3** Analyze current and emerging research about human growth and development, including research on brain development. | **428–429, 435, 436, 444, 445** |
| **12.2.1** Analyze the effect of heredity and environment on human growth and development. | **434–437** |
| **12.2.3** Analyze the effects of gender, ethnicity, and culture on individual development. | **441** |
| **12.2.4** Analyze the effects of life events on individuals' physical, intellectual, social, moral, and emotional development. | **434–437, 439–441** |
| **15.2.1** Choose nurturing practices that support human growth and development. | **435–437, 439–441, 443** |
| **15.2.2** Apply communication strategies that promote positive self-esteem in family members. | **445** |

**NO CHILD LEFT BEHIND** NCLB activities, information, and skills practice will help your students attain NCLB proficiency. Students will improve their abilities in the following academic standards areas:

## Academic Standards Correlations

| Discipline | Standard | Feature/Activity |
|---|---|---|
| **English Language Arts** | **NCTE 1** Read texts to acquire new information. | **Reading Guide (pp. 426, 433)** |
| | **NCTE 4** Use written language to communicate effectively. | **Writing Activity (p. 424)** **After You Read (p. 432)** **Academic Skills (p. 445)** |
| | **NCTE 8** Use information resources to gather information and create and communicate knowledge. | **Observation Skills (p. 444)** |
| | **NCTE 9** Develop an understanding of diversity in language use across cultures. | **After You Read (p. 441)** |
| **Mathematics** | **NCTM Number and Operations** Compute fluently and make reasonable estimates. | **Academic Skills (p. 445)** |
| | **NCTM Geometry** Use visualization, spatial reasoning, and geometric modeling to solve problems. | **After You Read (p. 432)** |
| **Science** | **NSES C** Develop understanding of the cell; biological evolution; matter, energy, and organization in living systems; and behavior or organisms. | **Academic Skills (p. 445)** |
| **Social Studies** | **NCSS IV D Individual Development and Identity** Apply concepts, methods, and theories about the study of human growth and development, such as learning, motivation, and behavior. | **After You Read (p. 441)** |

## Professional Development

**MINI CLIP VIDEO LIBRARY**

Targeted professional development is correlated throughout *The Developing Child*. **The McGraw-Hill Professional Development Mini Clip Video Library** provides teaching strategies to strengthen academic and learning skills. Log on to **glencoe.com**.

In this chapter, you will find these Mini Clips:
- **ELL** Words in Action, p. 428
- **Reading** Strategies for Student Achievement, p. 431
- **Reading** Another Point of View, p. 435
- **Reading** Strategic Readers, p. 436
- **ELL** Group Discussions, p. 439
- **Math** Introducing Multi-Step Equations, p. 445

## Reading and Writing Strategies

**Writing Activity: Humor** (p. 424)
Students use writing tips in employing humor to see the lighter side of a situation.

**Before You Read** (pp. 426, 433)
A pre-reading question or statement will help students make a personal connection to content.

**Graphic Organizer** (pp. 426, 433)
A visual tool will help students organize and remember new content.

**Reading Check** (pp. 429, 437, 439)
A question allows students to make a quick comprehension self-check.

**After You Read** (pp. 432, 441)
Organize and process students' understanding of what they have read.

## Chapter Features

**Learning by Doing** (p. 430)
Children can learn about nature through observation and activities.

**How Much Television Is Too Much?** (p. 435)
Watching television causes children to miss out on other experiences and is associated with poorer academic performance.

**Language Builds the Brain** (p. 436)
Learning more than one language between ages four and six can increase a child's overall language abilities.

**Playing Grown-Up** (p. 439)
Imaginative play aids in children's intellectual development.

**Kindergarten Teacher** (p. 442)
Learn the skills needed to succeed as a Kindergarten Teacher.

## Chapter Overview

### Introduce the Chapter

In this chapter, students learn about the eight basic types of intelligence identified by Howard Gardner. The theories of Piaget, Vygotsky, and Montessori are also presented. Students examine the ways that parents and caregivers can encourage learning and prepare children to start school.

### Build Background

Remind students of what they have learned about how a stimulating environment promotes learning. Sensory input is so vital to human development that Piaget named the period from birth to 2 years the sensorimotor period. Discuss that 4- to 6-year-olds can learn from a wide variety of experiences including being read to, playing make-believe, and making music.

## Writing Activity

### Humor

This active learning activity prompts students to write a humorous story involving a learning experience. After students have completed the writing activity, ask for volunteers to share their story with the class. Student responses can be used as a basis for classroom discussion. (Students' stories will vary but should show an attempt at humor. Humor is difficult to grade because it is subjective. Check stories for proper grammar and good writing skills. Make sure humor is appropriate and not offensive.)

# Intellectual Development from Four to Six

## Chapter Objectives

After completing this chapter, you will be able to:

- **List** eight types of intelligences.
- **Identify** the common element of all theories of intellectual development.
- **Identify** three ways to encourage children's interest in learning.
- **Describe** the link between speech development and physical development.
- **Explain** how parents can help their children adjust to kindergarten.

## Writing Activity

### Humor

**Learning to Learn** The learning process varies from child to child. Sometimes a learning experience can be humorous. Humor is the ability to see the lighter side of a situation. You can show a sense of humor by laughing during experiences such as:

- Getting caught in the rain without an umbrella on your way to school.
- Shrinking your favorite shirt by washing it in the wrong temperature.
- Misreading a recipe and adding too much pepper.

Mistakes are part of learning. But being able to laugh at your mistakes makes the learning experience fun. Write a story about a time you or someone else had a humorous learning experience.

**Writing Tips** To write an effective story with humor, follow these steps.

1. If you have trouble thinking of something, try freewriting or brainstorming with a friend to think of a humorous experience.
2. Let your natural humor come through in your writing. Do not try to force the humor.
3. Be sure to explain what you learned from the experience and how humor helped you get through it.

424

## CLASSROOM Solutions

### Print Resources

 **Student Edition**

 **Teacher Wraparound Edition**

 **Student Activity Workbook**

 **Student Activity Workbook Teacher Annotated Edition**

### Technology Resources

 **Online Learning Center** has resources and activities for students and teachers. Includes an Online Student Edition.

 **Interactive Student Edition** allows students to instantly access review materials, examples, and exercises.

**Section 15.1** Brain Development from Four to Six

**Section 15.2** Learning from Four to Six

## Review the Sections
Introduce the chapter by reviewing the sections:

### Section 15.1
Over the years, educators and psychologists have come up with a variety of learning theories. Psychologist Howard Gardner determined that there are eight types of intelligence. Piaget divided learning into four categories and stated that children from ages two to seven were in the preoperational period during which they learn from concrete evidence. Other important learning theories include those of Lev Vygotsky and Maria Montessori.

### Section 15.2
In this age group, children learn primarily from everyday experiences. Parents and caregivers play a major role in this learning process. Reading, creating artwork, and composing music are all important learning experiences. Children's speech and vocabularies develop dramatically as they make the transition to kindergarten.

### ▶ Explore the Photo

**Caption Answer** Answers will vary but may include that play exercises a child's creativity as well as gross and fine motor skills.

**Discussion** Ask students how playing with blocks might help children develop three-dimensional thinking skills. (Possible answers: It teaches them that a flat surface provides the most solid base and that if a tower begins to tilt in one direction, you can counterbalance by placing weight in the opposite direction.)

🔺 **Explore the Photo**
As children's brains develop, they are able to create more complex structures with blocks. *Why is play an important part of a child's learning?*

425

 **TeacherWorks Plus** is an electronic lesson planner that provides instant access to complete teacher resources in one convenient package.

**Presentation Plus!** provides visual teaching aids for every section.

**The Early Childhood Observations CD** presents video observations and lessons on observation skills and child development.

**The Developing Brain eTransparencies and Guide** include information and activities to offer insights into brain development and diseases of the brain.

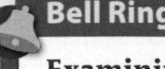 

## Focus

### Bell Ringer Activity

#### Examining Intelligence

Show students a picture of Albert Einstein. Ask: Do you think Einstein was intelligent? What makes one person more intelligent than another? Explain that these are questions developmental scientists and educators study. They also study why some people appear to be intelligent in some ways, but not other ways.

## Preteaching

### Vocabulary

Note that sometimes abbreviations become so common in our language that periods are no longer placed after the individual letters. Explain that this is true of IQ. Ask students to think of other abbreviations that commonly do not include periods. (Answers may include UN, NFL, or YMCA.)

### Graphic Organizer

 The Graphic Organizer is also on the TeacherWorks CD.

(Graphic organizers should include: Piaget—Children are oriented inward and learn from concrete evidence, and cannot think in abstract terms. Vygotsky—Learning is dependent on the social environment; parents, teachers, and peers promote learning. Montessori—Children will learn naturally if placed in a prepared learning environment containing the appropriate materials or learning games.)

 **NCLB** connects academic correlations to book content.

## Reading Guide

### Before You Read

**Predict with Photos** Look at the photos in this section and read their captions. Write one or two sentences predicting what you think the section will be about.

### Read to Learn
#### Key Concepts
- **List** eight types of intelligences.
- **Identify** the common element of all theories of intellectual development.

 **D**

### Main Idea
There are eight basic types of intelligence. Piaget, Vygotsky, and Montessori developed three of the many theories about intelligence and how people learn.

### Content Vocabulary
◇ intelligence quotient (IQ)
◇ cultural bias
◇ multiple intelligences

 **Graphic Organizer** Go to this book's Online Learning Center at **glencoe.com** to print out this graphic organizer.

### Academic Vocabulary
You will find these words in your reading and on your tests. Use the glossary to look up their definitions if necessary.
■ regulate
■ oriented

### Graphic Organizer
As you read, note three theories of intellectual development. Use a chart like the one shown to help organize your information.

| Theorist | Theory |
|----------|--------|
| 1.       |        |
| 2.       |        |
| 3.       |        |

 **Academic Standards** · · · · · · · · · · · · · · · · · · · · · · · · · ·

**English Language Arts**
**NCTE 4** Use written language to communicate effectively.

**Mathematics**
**NCTM Geometry** Use visualization, spatial reasoning, and geometric modeling to solve problems.

**NCTE** *National Council of Teachers of English*
**NCTM** *National Council of Teachers of Mathematics*

**NSES** *National Science Education Standards*
**NCSS** *National Council for the Social Studies*

## Reading Guide

 ### Before You Read

Ask students: Do you think you would learn more about the history of Thailand from reading a book or watching a television series? Why? Discuss that researchers and educators have learned that different people learn in different ways. This chapter will introduce students to some of the theories concerning how people learn.

### **D** Develop Concepts

**Main Idea** Discuss the main idea with the students. Ask: Do you think it is important for parents and teachers to understand the different ways in which children learn? (Yes, because then they can adjust their teaching methods accordingly.)

# What Is Intelligence?

Many parents wonder how intelligent their children are. Will they do well in school? Will they quickly learn to read and count? These skills build the basis for later work in school. How will their school experiences shape their lives?

## Intelligence Tests

Educators use formal intelligence tests to try to assess children's thinking skills. The test results can help teachers, principals, and learning specialists understand and meet students' educational needs.

The first usable intelligence test was developed by a psychologist named Alfred Binet in 1905. The main goal of this test was to identify students who needed help with schoolwork. In 1916, Lewis M. Terman of Stanford University made a major revision of Binet's test. The revised test is commonly called the Stanford-Binet. This test was the standard instrument of intelligence measurement for many years. Today, it is just one of many tests used to measure intelligence in children.

Using results from the Stanford-Binet test, Terman developed a mathematical formula that could be used to give a child's intelligence a number value. The **intelligence quotient (IQ)** is a number obtained by comparing a child's test results to those of other children the same age. The average child of any age has an IQ between 80 and 119. Those who score higher or lower than this average are said to be of above- or below-average intelligence.

Intelligence tests are composed of tasks and questions that correspond to what is expected of children of various ages. For example, two-year-olds cannot read. An intelligence test for that age group might include building a tower of blocks, identifying parts of the body, and fitting simple geometric shapes into corresponding holes.

Over the years, critics have pointed out that relying on intelligence tests to rank children's mental abilities has several drawbacks:

- No single test can give an accurate measure of a child's mental abilities. Some tests give greater weight to certain abilities and less weight to others.

**↑ A Preschooler's Intelligence**
Intelligence tests for young children cannot rely on written questions and answers. *What forms of questions might be included on a test for young children?*

---

## ▶ Explore the Photo

**Caption Answer** Answers will vary. Teachers might read questions aloud to students. Children might use blocks to create shapes, analyze pictures, or draw simple pictures and shapes.

**Discussion** Tell students that this woman has asked the child to describe the picture she is holding. Ask students what they think can be learned from the child's response. (Possible answers: the child's language skills and vocabulary and the level and the complexity of the child's imagination and thinking skills.)

---

## Teach

### Discussion Starter

**Can Intelligence Be Measured?**
Ask students whether they think intelligence tests actually measure a person's innate intelligence. Encourage them to discuss the topic with one another and to provide reasons for their responses. (Students should discuss whether they think intelligence tests are capable of measuring the intelligence of an individual and provide reasons for their opinions.)

### R Reading Strategy

**Visualize** Explain to students that visualizing material can sometimes help you remember it. Have students read the first paragraph at the top of the right column. Then draw a graph illustrating the concept of IQ. Create a bell-shaped curve and label the section from 80 to 119 "Average." Then label the left section "Below Average" and the right section "Above Average."

### C Critical Thinking

**Analyze** Explain that intelligence tests for children commonly have a pattern recognition component in which a child is shown a colorful pattern. The pattern is then hidden from sight. The child is then asked to replicate the pattern with blocks. Ask: Do you think this activity is "culture free"? Do you think children from some backgrounds might do better on this activity than others? Why or why not? (Possible answer: children from cultures in which they are taught to recognize and replicate patterns in artwork such as weaving might do better.)

**427**

### S Skill Practice

**Guided Practice**

**Make a Table** Instruct students to create a table. In the left column, they should list the eight intelligences. In the right column, they should list abilities that require the corresponding type of intelligence. (Students should create a table that lists the eight intelligences and abilities requiring each type of intelligence.) **L1 ELL**

**Create a Game** Instruct students to work in pairs to create a game in which the player must match a list of abilities with the type of intelligence each ability requires. Have students play one another's games. Encourage students to suggest ways in which one another's games can be improved. (Students should create games that require the player to match abilities with the type of intelligence required for each ability.) **L2 ELL**

**Teach a Lesson** Have students work in pairs to choose a historical event, such as the beginning of the Revolutionary War. Instruct each pair to create a role play in which the material is being taught to a student with a high degree of linguistic intelligence. Then have them switch roles to show how it would be taught to students with a different type of intelligence. (Students should create role plays explaining how they would teach specific historical information to students with linguistic intelligence and another type of intelligence.) **L3**

**Mc Graw Hill Professional Development**

**Mini Clip ELL: Words in Action**

Students act our or mime the words they are trying to learn.

↑ **English Language Learners**
Intelligence tests must be valid for children whose first language is not English. *Why might a child whose first language is not English have a difficult time with an intelligence test written in English?*

- Factors that have nothing to do with intelligence can influence results. These factors can include whether a child feels ill or stressed on the day of testing. A child's previous experience with the kinds of tasks included in the test also can affect test scores.

- Overall scores, such as IQ scores, do not tell us much about individual strengths and weaknesses. Two people with the same IQ may have very different abilities. It is important for the person giving the test to explain how the child scored on all measures. Some tests are composed of many subtests, each measuring different abilities.

Educators must use intelligence tests with caution. The National Association for the Education of Young Children (NAEYC) is an association dedicated to improving the well-being of children from birth through age eight. NAEYC warns that no decision about a child's placement in school should be based on a single test. Today, schools are more likely to use several techniques to gain an overview of a child's level of development in all areas, not just thinking skills. If the child falls outside the norms of development for his or her age, then an in-depth assessment of skills may be necessary. This will help educators identify problem areas and plan appropriate activities.

Some intelligence tests have been criticized for cultural bias. **Cultural bias** means that many of the test questions favored or gave an advantage to people from one culture over other cultures. Language differences can also affect test results. A child whose first language is not English may not earn as high a score as an equally intelligent child who has learned English from birth. New tests have been designed in response to these criticisms. They have been screened for cultural bias. Children may take them in their native language. The goal is for all children to be assessed fairly.

## Multiple Intelligences

In recent years, psychologist Howard Gardner has presented a different way of looking at intelligence. He argues that humans have multiple intelligences. **Multiple intelligences** are abilities in problem solving or creating materials that have value. Gardner has identified eight such intelligences:

- **Linguistic intelligence** involves sensitivity to language, the ability to learn languages, and the ability to use language to accomplish goals. Writers, poets, and lawyers have high linguistic intelligence, according to Gardner.

- **Logical-mathematical intelligence** consists of the ability to analyze problems using logic, perform mathematical operations, and explore issues scientifically. This intelligence is associated with scientific and mathematical thinking and research.

- **Spatial intelligence** involves an understanding of the potential use of space, thinking in three-dimensional terms, and imagining things in clear visual images. Architects and landscape designers are among the careers that rely on this type of intelligence.

- **Musical intelligence** involves skill in performing, composing, and appreciating musical patterns.

- **Bodily-kinesthetic intelligence** has to do with the potential to use one's body to solve problems, and using the mind to coordinate body movements.

**S**

---

▶ **Explore the Photo**

**Caption Answer** Answers may vary but should indicate that children whose first language is not English may not have the language background necessary to understand the directions and questions.

**Discussion** Ask students: What kinds of test items do you think would cause the most difficulties for an English language learner? What kinds of items might be easier? Why? (Items that require understanding complex written words would probably cause the most difficulties whereas those that depend more on abilities in math and problem solving would probably cause the fewest difficulties.)

- **Interpersonal intelligence** involves the potential to understand the intentions, desires, and motivations of others. This type of intelligence helps teachers, counselors, and religious and political leaders work better with other people.
- **Intrapersonal intelligence** implies the capacity to understand oneself, including fears, hopes, and motivations. According to Gardner, it means having a good working model of ourselves and using it to **regulate**, or control, our actions.
- **Naturalist intelligence** involves recognizing, categorizing, and drawing upon the features of the environment.

Gardner believes that the intelligences usually operate at the same time and balance each other as people develop skills and solve problems. Each person has a blend of intelligences. Gardner believed that deciding how best to take advantage of each person's unique blend is a major challenge.

If caregivers recognize that a child is particularly high in one type of intelligence, they can provide the child with learning opportunities that will build those strengths as well as challenge the child and encourage an interest in learning.

**✓ Reading Check** **Apply** What intelligence is associated with people who know their own strengths and weaknesses?

## Figure 15.1 Intellectual Developmental Milestones—Ages 4–6

There are many skills commonly seen in children in this age group. *At what age do children understand about 13,000 words?*

| Age | Developmental Milestone |
|---|---|
| **4 Years**  | ❖ Speaks in complete sentences of five to six words<br>❖ Makes up stories<br>❖ Asks many *when, where, how,* and *why* questions<br>❖ Understands three-step directions<br>❖ Knows colors and shapes<br>❖ Understands *same* and *different, top* and *bottom* |
| **5 Years** | ❖ Uses six- to eight-word sentences with correct grammar<br>❖ Understands about 13,000 words<br>❖ Learns alphabet and many letter sounds<br>❖ Recalls part of a story<br>❖ Counts up to ten objects and can sort by size<br>❖ Understands *above* and *below, before* and *after* |
| **6 Years** | ❖ Reads words and simple sentences<br>❖ Writes simple words<br>❖ Solves problems more effectively<br>❖ Plays pretend games<br>❖ Has longer attention span<br>❖ Understands *right* and *left* and other time concepts |

## Figure 15.1 Intellectual Developmental Milestones—Ages 4–6

**Caption Answer** Children understand about 13,000 words when they are five years old.

**Discussion** At what age does a child typically begin asking questions such as, "Why does snow only fall in winter?" What does this type of question tell you about the child's development? (These kinds of questions typically begin at age 4. They tell you that the child is becoming observant and is learning to use words to express questions about the world.)

## Assess

### Quiz
Ask students to answer the following questions:

1. What are two criticisms of intelligence tests? (Criticisms include that no single test can accurately measure a child's mental abilities, factors that have nothing to do with intelligence can influence the results, and the overall scores do not tell us much about individual strengths and weaknesses.)
2. What are the characteristics of individuals with bodily-kinesthetic intelligence? (They have the potential to use their bodies to solve problems and to use their minds to coordinate body movements.)
3. At what age have children typically developed an understanding of terms such as *before* and *after*? (They typically understand these concepts at five.)

## Reteach

### C Critical Thinking
**Contrast** Ask students: How is interpersonal intelligence different from intrapersonal intelligence? Why is it important to have both? (Interpersonal intelligence involves having an understanding of the intentions and motivations of others. Intrapersonal intelligence involves having an understanding of the intentions and motivations of oneself. In order to accomplish goals and work with others, it is important to have an understanding of both your own motivations and those around you.)

**✓ Reading Check**

**Apply** intrapersonal intelligence

### Reteach cont.

**U₁ Universal Access**

**Intrapersonal Learners** Have students think of an event that happened to them when they were preschoolers. Perhaps they were in a minor car accident or got lost in a department store. Instruct students to write a paragraph describing the incident as they viewed it at that time. (Remind students that preschoolers are very egocentric.) Then have them rewrite the event as they would view it today. Ask for volunteers to share their writings with the class. Encourage students to discuss the differences between the two descriptions. (Students should choose an incident from when they were a preschooler and write about the event as they viewed it at the time and also write about the event as they view it today.)

**W Writing Support**

**Humor**

**Let's Pretend** Have students think of a funny experience they had when they played make-believe as a child. Perhaps they were playing school and the students kept causing trouble. (If they cannot think of any real-life experiences, encourage them to make up one.) Have students then write a humorous story about this experience. (Refer to p. 424 to review tips on writing humorous stories. Students' stories should take a light-hearted look at playing make-believe.)

**What Would You Do?**

**Write About It** Articles will vary depending on what is offered by your local recreation and parks department. Articles should contain answers to the questions posed.

**430**

---

**→ Pretend Play for Real Skills** Children learn through fantasy and dramatic play. *What skills might dress-up and make-believe play help children develop?*

**What Would You Do?**

**Learning by Doing**

Four-year-old Haley had always loved to take walks in the nearby forest with her father. Her dad noticed that she spent lots of time looking around her as she walked, and asked questions about the things she saw. "Why do the leaves change color in the fall?" "Where does dirt come from?" "How do trees, grass, and flowers grow?" "Why does a heavy rain made big puddles?"

Haley's father gave her a small shovel and rake for her birthday, and he took her to see the butterflies at the local zoo. Haley and her dad planted a small garden in their yard. Haley learned to distinguish weeds from other plants in the garden. She watered the plants and pulled the weeds. Haley's father would like to enroll her in nature and gardening classes appropriate for her age.

✏ **Write About It** Write an article for a preschool's newsletter in which you share with parents how to get their children involved in outdoor nature activities. Contact your local recreation and parks department for answers to these questions: When is a class held? Where is the class held? Who can attend the class?

---

# Intellectual Development

Researchers have identified intellectual skills commonly seen in children ages four to six. Some of these are included in the Intellectual Developmental Milestones chart seen in **Figure 15.1** on page 429. As you learn about different theories of intellectual development, check this chart to see if children's skills match each theory. Though the theories vary greatly, all researchers agree that a child's brain is able to handle increasingly complex skills over this time span.

## Piaget's Theory

As seen in **Figure 15.2,** Jean Piaget described the time between ages two and seven as the preoperational period. Piaget believed that in this period, children are **oriented**, or directed, inward and learn from concrete evidence. Children this age can only view the world from their own perspective, and cannot think in abstract terms.

**U₁**

Four-, five-, and six-year-olds show the following signs of preoperational thinking:

- **Make-Believe Play** Children continue to learn through imaginative play, which is fantasy or dramatic play in which they may imitate real-life situations, as when they play house or school.

**W**

---

**⟶ Explore the Photo**

**Caption Answer** Answers will vary, but might include that children can develop real-life skills such as how to set the table or fold laundry, as well as social skills and interpersonal skills.

**Discussion** Ask students why they think children in this age group enjoy dramatic play so much. (Possible answer: It provides them with a chance to explore their world in a non-threatening way and to re-enact events so that they can better understand them.)

## Figure 15.2 Piaget's Four Periods of Learning

Children in the preoperational period of learning tend to focus on themselves. *At what age do children typically begin to think logically?*

| Period | Characteristics |
|---|---|
| **Sensorimotor** *Birth–2 years* | Children learn through their senses and own actions. |
| **Preoperational** *2–7 years* | Children think in terms of their own activities and what they perceive at the moment. |
| **Concrete Operations** *7–11 years* | Children can think logically but still learn best through experience. |
| **Formal Operations** *11–adult* | People are capable of abstract thinking. |

- **Use of Symbols** Children learn that objects and words can be symbols. This means they can represent something else. A child this age can recognize that a stop sign means stop.
- **Egocentric Viewpoint** Children continue to view the world in terms of their own thoughts and feelings. One five-year-old explained that grass grew so that she would not hurt herself if she fell.
- **Limited Focus** The preoperational child makes decisions based on his perceptions, which are often limited. For example, pour the same quantity of water in a tall, thin container and a short, wide one. A child in this stage would say that the taller one contains more water. The child in this stage might also say that all apples are red, so green fruits cannot be apples.

### Vygotsky's Theory

Lev Vygotsky was an influential psychologist whose work differed somewhat from Piaget's. Piaget maintained that the learning stages children go through are a natural part of the human maturation process, just like gains in height and weight. Vygotsky, however, believed that development is too complex to be divided into neat stages. He stressed that each child is an individual who learns distinctively.

Vygotsky believed that learning is based on language and social interaction. According to him, parents, teachers, and peers promote learning. Children play key roles in their own education and that of their peers. Learning takes place in, and is dependent upon, the social environment.

Vygotsky believed that teachers should collaborate with students rather than lecturing, and that students should collaborate with each other. A classroom based on Vygotsky's theories would provide clustered tables for teamwork and small group learning. Children of different ages would learn from each other. Teachers and students might take turns leading small group discussions on a particular topic, for example.

Vygotsky stressed the importance of past experiences and prior knowledge. He felt these were necessary to understand new experiences. Anyone could be a teacher so long as he or she possessed more knowledge about a topic than the child being taught.

---

### U₂ Universal Access

**Logical Learners** Have students think of simple tests they could administer to a child in each of Piaget's four age groups to determine the child's learning period. For example, to find out if an 11-year-old is in the formal operations period, they might determine whether she understands a joke that requires abstract thinking, such as "Algebraic symbols are used when you don't know what you are talking about." (Students should develop four tests to determine the current learning period of a child.)

### C Critical Thinking

**Categorize** Ask students which signs of preoperational thinking these children demonstrate:

- Emily says that it is a cloudy day because she is unhappy. (has egocentric viewpoint)
- Jamal likes to wear his superman costume and rescue his pets. (enjoys make-believe play)
- Marta learns that a dot on a map stands for a place. (understands symbols)
- Kevin laughs when he is told trees can grow from acorns. (has limited focus, or difficulty understanding what is not happening at the moment)

**Professional Development**

**Mini Clip Reading: Strategies for Student Achievement**

Teachers discuss strategies for helping all learners meet curriculum standards.

---

## Figure 15.2 Piaget's Four Periods of Learning

**Caption Answer** Children begin to think logically around age seven.

**Discussion** Ask students how each of Piaget's four periods of learning differ. Discuss what abilities are developing as children go through these stages, and what the difference is between concrete thinking and abstract thinking.

## Assess

### Study Tools

Have students go to the Online Learning Center at **glencoe.com**:

- Take the **Practice Test**.
- Download **Study-to-Go** content.

Use the **Student Activity Workbook** for additional practice.

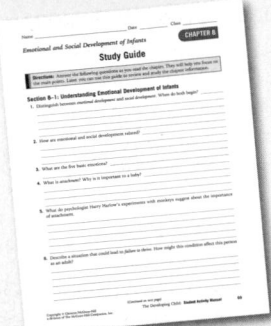

## Close

### Culminating Activity

**Posters on Learning Theories**
Organize students into four groups. Assign Gardner, Piaget, Vygotsky, or Montessori to each group. Have each group create an illustrated poster summarizing that person's learning theories. (Posters should illustrate the assigned person's learning theories.)

 **NCLB** connects academic correlations to book content.

## Montessori's Theory

Dr. Maria Montessori (1870–1952), studied children and developed her own theories about childhood learning. Today, Montessori's methods are used at approximately 4,000 Montessori schools in North America and thousands more around the world. In addition, many public and private schools use Montessori's ideas in some way, as do many parents.

Montessori believed that children would learn naturally if placed in a prepared learning environment containing the appropriate materials or learning games. For example, before they learn to write, children play games and engage in activities designed to strengthen the muscles of the hand and fingers. The Montessori method focuses on the development of the senses, language, and motor skills. This focus will prepare a child's mind and body for further learning.

A Montessori classroom is designed to be an environment in which children can learn by themselves and from each other. It commonly has several learning stations arranged by subject area. The materials are all within the children's reach. Pictures on the walls are at children's eye level. Everything in the room has a place on a shelf or in a container.

Teachers allow students a great deal of independence. Teachers never interrupt a student engaged in a task. Great respect is shown for a student's instinctive pursuit of individual learning. A four-year-old pouring water from a pitcher into cups is not playing with a toy pitcher. The pitcher is real and breakable, only child-size. If the child drops it, it breaks. This teaches the child that actions have consequences, and that it is important to be careful. By using arm muscles and fingers, gross and fine motor skills develop. The child is also learning about the properties of water.

Montessori teachers receive special training in the Montessori method. These schools are increasing in popularity throughout the world. This method also has been shown to work with children with special needs. Since there are no text books, this environment can be used successfully with English language learners.

## Section **15.1**     After You Read

### Review Key Concepts

1. **Explain** what an *IQ* score of 105 indicates about a child. What information does it not give?
2. **Discuss** what *cultural bias* in intelligence testing means.

### Practice Academic Skills

 **English Language Arts**

3. Choose one of the multiple intelligences identified by Howard Gardner and write a half-page essay in which you explain how you see this intelligence at work in your life.

> **NCTE 4** Use written language to communicate effectively.

 **Mathematics**

4. Think of a design for two classrooms for first-graders. One should reflect Vygotsky's theories of social learning and the other Montessori's theories. Create a diagram of each classroom. Each diagram should show where desks and learning materials would go.

> **NCTM Geometry** Use visualization, spatial reasoning, and geometric modeling to solve problems.

 **Check Your Answers** Check your answers at this book's Online Learning Center at **glencoe.com**.

**432**     **Chapter 15**   Intellectual Development from Four to Six

---

## Section **15.1**     After You Read

### Review Key Concepts

1. The child has an average IQ. The score does not give details about the individual's strengths or weaknesses.
2. Cultural bias occurs when questions on an assessment test tend to favor one culture over another in the language or examples used.

### Practice Academic Skills

3. Students' essays will vary but should include a detailed explanation of how one type of intelligence is at work in his or her life.
4. Diagrams will vary. The Vygotsky classroom should provide clustered tables for teamwork and small group learning. The Montessori classroom should have learning stations arranged by subject area; materials will be at eye level for the students and within their reach; and there will be a place for everything.

## Reading Guide

### Before You Read

**Prepare with a Partner** Work with a partner to ask each other and answer questions about the topics that will be discussed in this section.

### Read to Learn
#### Key Concepts
- **Identify** three ways to encourage children's interest in learning.
- **Describe** the link between speech development and physical development.
- **Explain** how parents can help their children adjust to kindergarten.

### Main Idea
Parents and caregivers find ways to assist their children in learning, to promote interest in the arts, and to help them with speech development. Parents also prepare children for the transition to school.

### Content Vocabulary

◇ phoneme
◇ alliteration
◇ bilingual
◇ finger play

**Graphic Organizer** Go to this book's Online Learning Center at **glencoe.com** to print out this graphic organizer.

### Academic Vocabulary
You will find these words in your reading and on your tests. Use the glossary to look up their definitions if necessary.
■ foster
■ articulation

### Graphic Organizer
As you read, look for ways in which art helps children and for art materials children enjoy. Use a chart like the one shown to help organize your information.

| Art and Four- to Six-Year-Olds | |
|---|---|
| Art helps children . . . | Art materials children enjoy include . . . |
| | |

**Academic Standards** · · · · · · · · · · · · · · · · · · · · · · · · · · · · · · · ·

**English Language Arts**

**NCTE 9** Develop an understanding of diversity in language use across cultures.

**Social Studies**

**NCSS IV D Individual Development and Identity** Apply concepts, methods, and theories about the study of human growth and development, such as learning, motivation, and behavior.

| | |
|---|---|
| **NCTE** National Council of Teachers of English | **NSES** National Science Education Standards |
| **NCTM** National Council of Teachers of Mathematics | **NCSS** National Council for the Social Studies |

---

## Reading Guide

### Before You Read

Ask students: What did your parents do to help you learn when you were a preschooler? Do you think they adjusted your learning experiences to your individual abilities? If so, how? (Answers to the first part might include that their parents read and played games with them. Answers to the last two questions will vary based on experiences and perceptions.)

### **D** Develop Concepts

**Main Idea** Discuss the main idea with the students. Ask students: Why is the parents' role in preparing a child for school so important? (Parents are the people who know their children the best and therefore can provide the most appropriate guidance.)

---

### Bell Ringer Activity

#### Encourage Learning
Display groups of objects that can promote learning in young children. For example, one group might include household cleaning equipment and a second might include rhythm instruments. Ask students: How do you think each of these groups could be used to encourage learning in young children? (Responses will vary. For example, rhythm instruments can teach children to keep time to music.)

## Preteaching

### Vocabulary
Discuss that prefixes can be used to modify the meaning of a word. Write *bilingual* on the board. Separately underline *bi* and *lingual*. Explain that *bi* is Latin for "two" and *lingual* means "tongue." Ask for examples of other words having the prefix *bi-*.

### Graphic Organizer
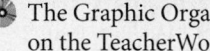 The Graphic Organizer is also on the TeacherWorks CD.

(Graphic organizers should include: Art helps children express their feelings, develop fine motor skills, and express creativity. Art materials children enjoy include modeling clay, crayons, paint, and scissors.)

 **NCLB** connects academic correlations to book content.

### Discussion Starter

**Everyday Learning** Discuss with students that one of the best ways for children to learn is by participating in everyday activities. Have the class choose a chore a family might perform together, such as raking leaves. Ask: If you were a parent, how might you encourage learning in a five-year-old while doing this chore? (Possible answers: The parent might teach the child how to use a small rake and to identify the different types of leaves.)

### C Critical Thinking

**Analyze** Read aloud the first paragraph on this page. Ask: How might having a rabbit in the classroom help a child develop intellectually? (He can learn about rabbits and their needs.) How might the rabbit help with emotional and social development? (Emotional: The child develops empathy for the rabbit and realizes it is dependent on the students for its care. Social development: The child learns to take turns playing with and caring for the rabbit.)

### U₁ Universal Access

**Interpersonal Learners** Have students work in groups to investigate places in the community that offer interesting learning experiences for children ages four to six. Have students compile their information into a helpful directory for parents and caregivers. (Students should create a directory of local places that provide appropriate learning experiences for four- to six-year-olds.) **ELL**

## Help Children Learn

Jorge came home from kindergarten, bursting with excitement about his day. "We have a real bunny at school now," he said. "And Miss Jackson said I can help take care of him! Today I cleaned his cage, and then I filled his water bottle, and then I got to feed him. He has special food to eat, and I gave him some." Jorge thrust a note into his mother's hand. "Look! Mary and I get to feed him every Wednesday! Can I bring some lettuce on those days?"

Four- to six-year-olds are often excited about learning. Parents and caregivers can encourage this enthusiasm in many ways.

## Experiences in Everyday Life

Experiences, especially those shared with adults, form the basis for children's learning. Talking with children about their world and what they are doing encourages interests. Positive comments teach vocabulary and encourage feelings of self-worth. These can be as simple as "Wow, the building you are making is so tall. And it has so many windows!"

You can also ask children questions that help them think about their experiences in new ways and focus on the process of their play. Encourage them to organize their thoughts by asking questions like, "How did you do that?" and "What are you going to do next?"

Explanations and suggestions can also be helpful. They must use age-appropriate language, though. You might explain in simple terms why water from a faucet can come out cold or hot. If a child grows frustrated trying to find room to put together a train set, you could suggest removing other toys from the floor to make the job easier.

Asking a child's advice is another effective technique for promoting learning. For example, ask how to fold napkins for a meal and then fold them the way the child suggests.

Trips and activities are important to learning. A ride on a bus, train, or plane can be an adventure that leads a child to discuss what is seen and to ask questions. Nature walks are also fun. Nature walks are free and everyone in the family can learn about the natural world by taking a close look at plants and animals.

**Good Helper**
Children can learn many skills by helping out around the house. *What can a child learn by washing the car?*

## ▶ Explore the Photo

**Caption Answer** Answers will vary but may include teamwork, how to follow steps, or motor skills.

**Discussion** Ask students how parents can help children learn to properly perform chores.

(Answers will vary. Parents should make certain that they assign chores that the child is capable of performing successfully. Parents should clearly explain and demonstrate the steps in completing the chore.)

Helping around the house provides great learning opportunities. Four- to six-year-olds can help sort laundry to be washed into lights and darks. They can also set the table and put their toys away. Helping around the house gives children a sense that they are part of the family and play an important role in it.

## Reading

Developing an interest in reading is important because books provide an opportunity to learn about and understand the world. Children who enjoy reading will find learning easier and more fun. Reading to young children regularly helps them associate books with enjoyment at an early age. Reading together can remain part of a daily routine even as children start school and begin learning to read on their own.

An important factor in learning to read is the ability to hear phonemes. A **phoneme** ('fō-,nēm) is the smallest individual sound in a word, such as the *ou* in *house*. Rhyming words help develop phoneme awareness, so reading rhyming books to children is a good learning activity. When a book becomes familiar, stop from time to time and let the child fill in the sounds and words. When Jessica's mom reads, "Hey diddle, diddle, the cat and the…" Jessica shouts, "Fiddle!"

Another way to develop phoneme awareness is through alliteration. **Alliteration** is the repetition of certain sounds. Many alphabet books provide opportunities to use alliteration because they collect words that begin with the same letter. After children have learned the sound, they can begin to associate the letter with the sound, which is an important step in learning to read. You can also help the child by making associations beyond the book.

## ♡ Parenting Skills

### How Much Television Is Too Much?

From ages four to six, children's brains are rapidly developing. Watching television may affect their brain development. When children watch television, they are missing out on other experiences, like forming relationships, getting exercise, and using their imagination. Children who spend a lot of time watching television are less active. This can lead to weight problems and other health problems.

Researchers suspect that attention deficit disorders and weak problem-solving skills among children are related to watching too much television. Watching more television is associated with poorer academic performance, especially in reading.

While watching television is no substitute for reading or other challenging activities, some programs for children are educational and interactive. For example, many public television programs encourage imaginative play and pose questions for children to answer. There are also educational videos available to help reinforce language or math skills. Parents should restrict children's viewing of programs that depict violence or that contain material that is not appropriate to a child's level of development.

**Take Charge** What activities would you suggest to a six-year-old instead of watching television? Create a poster titled "Ten Things to Do Instead of Watching Television."

### Teach *cont.*

**R** **Reading Strategy**

**Connect** Remind students that the study of child development frequently uses terms that students may recognize from other classes. Discuss that the terms *rhyming* and *alliteration* are used in English language and literature classes. Ask for examples of how these terms are used in nursery rhymes, tongue-twisters, and so forth.

**McGraw Hill** **Professional Development**

**Mini Clip Reading: Another Point of View**

Lois Moseley, author and educator, discusses the benefits of teacher collaboration with regard to assessment.

**U₂** **Universal Access**

**Visual Learners** Have students watch four television shows designed for four- to six-year-old children. Instruct students to choose two shows from public television and two shows from commercial television. Students should then rank the shows according to how educational they are. (Students should view four television shows aimed at four- to six-year-olds and rate them according to their educational value.)

## ♡ Parenting Skills

### How Much Television Is Too Much?

Have students imagine that they are parents of a five-year-old. Ask: What rules would you establish for watching television or DVDs of children's movies? Why? (Responses will vary, but students should provide specific reasons for their rules, such as children need to develop social and language skills by interacting with others.)

**Take Charge**
Students' posters will vary but may include read, play board games, take a walk, draw, play dress up, color, ride a bike, play tag, sing, play with others, or help around the house.

**Teach** *cont.*

**S Skill Practice**

### Independent Practice

**Create a Flyer** Have students imagine that they are kindergarten teachers. Several parents have asked for help in selecting appropriate books for their children. Have students create a flyer to send home to these parents. The flyer should contain all the points for selecting appropriate books that are mentioned in this section. (Flyers should list appropriate criteria similar to the bulleted items listed on page 436.) **L1 ELL**

**Review a Book** Have students select and read a book that is appropriate for kindergarteners. Students should write a review in which they discuss which of the seven criteria the book meets and which it does not, and why. (Students should write a brief review of a kindergarten-level book discussing whether the book meets each of the seven criteria. If the book does not meet a specific criterion, students should explain why.) **L2**

**Choose Books** Tell students that they are kindergarten teachers who must select five new books for their classroom library. The students should examine a selection of young children's books and create a list of five books that they think meet the seven criteria listed here. (Students should come up with a list of five kindergarten-level books that they think meet the seven criteria.) **L3**

---

**McGraw Hill Professional Development**

**Mini Clip Reading: Strategic Readers**

Author Scott Paris discusses the characteristics of strategic readers.

**436**

---

For example, Hayden's mother read "A is for apple and alligator." She then paused and asked "What else starts with A?" Hayden was able to answer "Ants!"

Watching television is not a substitute for reading. Studies have shown that children whose caregivers read to them have an easier time learning to read.

Some research suggests that children who are bilingual find it easier to learn to read. **Bilingual** means being able to speak two languages. Children who are bilingual seem to understand that printed words convey a specific meaning sooner than children who speak only one language. This may give them an edge when learning to read.

### Choosing Books

Young children love books and stories. When caregivers encourage this interest, children are more likely to read for pleasure as they grow older. Books are still a fairly inexpensive form of entertainment. There are many different types of books to choose from. This means there is generally something that will appeal to any child.

Most communities have public libraries that lend children's books. In some cases, children can get their own library cards. This symbol of being grown up helps children look forward to going to the library and choosing their own books. Many libraries also offer story time or other programs to help foster a child's interest in reading.

---

**THE DEVELOPING BRAIN**

**Language Builds the Brain**

Children between birth and six-years-old are at the ideal age to learn their own first language as well as other languages. Exposure to more than one language rewires the neurons in the still developing brain in such a way that a child's overall language abilities increase greatly.

■ **Science Inquiry** Adults typically do not learn new languages as easily as children. What might explain this?

---

How can you tell which books will appeal to children? The following questions will help you make appropriate choices:

- Are the pictures colorful, interesting, and easy to understand?
- Will the story appeal to the child's interests?
- Does the story include action that will hold the child's attention?
- Will the child understand most of the words?
- Does the book use descriptive language that brings the story to life?
- For younger children, is the story short enough to read in one sitting?
- If you are considering buying the book, is it sturdy enough to stand up to hard use?

**S**

What kind of books do four- to six-year-olds like? Many like stories about experiences that are different from their own. Through books, children who live in cities can learn about farm life. Children who live in rural areas can experience subways, apartments, and other aspects of city life.

Children this age also enjoy humor, including funny rhymes and unusual situations. When they giggle over a picture of a horse in a bathtub, they show that they are beginning to separate reality from fantasy.

### Art and Music

Art and music help children express their feelings, develop fine motor skills, and express their creativity. Music often provides an emotional outlet for children who do not yet have the words to express what they are feeling.

### Creating Artwork

Four- to six-year-olds benefit from working with many different art materials, such as modeling clay, crayons, paper, paste, paint, and scissors. Even buttons or dried macaroni can be strung into a necklace or painted and pasted onto a sheet of construction paper to make a design.

Children should be encouraged to experiment with art materials without being corrected or criticized. What matters to the child is the creative process. You can help children feel proud of their artwork by displaying it and sharing it with others.

---

**THE DEVELOPING BRAIN**

**Language Builds the Brain**

**Science Inquiry** Students' answers may vary but should indicate that adults' brains are generally not still developing as are children's brains. The neurons in an adult's brain have already developed and cannot be rewired as readily as neurons in a child's brain.

For more information and activities, see **The Developing Brain** guide and eTransparencies.

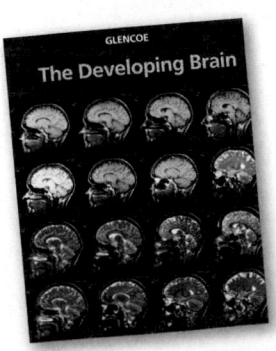

GLENCOE
The Developing Brain

**Learn Through Books**
Children love to go to the library and choose their own books. *Why should parents help children make their choices?*

When you talk to children about their artwork, you **foster**, or encourage, a sense of accomplishment. You also help develop their verbal skills. By asking, "How did you make that?" you can help the child find the words to explain it to you. Rather than guessing what a picture represents, ask the child to tell you. Then find specific aspects of the work that you can praise. For example, you might say, "I really like the bright colors you used for the flowers." Or, "That was very creative to use buttons for the wheels."

### Composing Music

The rhythm of music intrigues children. Rhythm can be the thud of a ball bouncing on the sidewalk or the sound of footsteps. Children this age become more aware of rhythms and enjoy singing simple, repetitive songs.

Many children are introduced to singing by a finger play. A **finger play** is a song or chant with accompanying hand motions. *The Itsy, Bitsy Spider* and *I'm a Little Teapot* are examples of popular finger plays. Finger play helps children improve their motor skills.

Music is also a great teaching tool. For example, most children learn the alphabet by singing their ABCs. Many children will set other facts to music to help remember them, such as "one plus one is two."

The opportunity to play simple instruments helps develop children's interest in music. Children enjoy using bells, drums, tambourines, or almost anything that makes a noise. There is no need to buy instruments. Old pans, bowls, and mixing spoons work just as well.

✓ **Reading Check** **Explain** Why is it important to talk to children about their art?

## Speech Development

By the time they start school, children have gained an extensive knowledge of language just by listening and talking at home. They probably do not know what an adjective is, but they can use adjectives confidently and correctly. As children grow older, their vocabularies increase and the sentences they use become more complex. However, children learn all the basic forms of language almost effortlessly in the preschool years.

Children ages four, five, and six typically show a rapid increase in their vocabulary. A normally developing six-year-old can understand and use approximately 2,500 words. **Articulation**, or distinct speech, improves dramatically in this period as well. By age six, children can correctly say 90 percent of the words they know.

Section 15.2    Learning from Four to Six    **437**

### Explore the Photo

**Caption Answer** Parents need to help children choose books that are appropriate for their age and reading level and be sure that the book does not teach anything contrary to their own beliefs or standards.

**Discussion** What kinds of services might a public library offer to help young children enjoy books more? (The library staff might be available to help children select appropriate books. The library might have a story hour in which books are read and possibly acted out.)

### Assess

**Quiz**
Ask students to answer the following questions:

1. Why is asking a child's advice an effective way to promote learning? (It encourages the child to think of different approaches to a problem or situation and lets the child know that you value his or her opinion.)
2. What are phonemes? How many phonemes are in the word *cat*? (Phonemes are the smallest individual sounds in words. The word *cat* has three phonemes.)
3. How do researchers think that being bilingual helps children learn to read? (Researchers think that being bilingual helps children understand that printed words convey a specific meaning at an earlier age than children who speak only one language.)

### Reteach

**U Universal Access**
**Kinesthetic Learners** Organize students into groups of four. Instruct each group to prepare a standard finger play to present to the class. Make certain that the groups do not duplicate one another. (If necessary, they may want to conduct research on the Internet to locate an appropriate finger play.) Have each group teach its finger play to the rest of the class. (Each group should learn and teach a finger play to the class.) **ELL**

✓ **Reading Check**

**Explain** Talking with children about their art fosters a sense of accomplishment and helps develop their verbal skills.

**U₁ Universal Access**

**Verbal Learners** Organize students into groups of three. Each student in the group should be assigned to interview children who are either four, five, or six years old. Students should keep a written record of the speech development of each child they interview. For example, they should write down any pronunciation difficulties the child has. The group should then write a summary of their findings on the speech development of these three age groups. (Based on their interviews, students should write a summary on the speech development of children in each of the three age groups. Students may note that six-year-olds speak very clearly while four-year-olds have trouble with certain sounds, such as *pl* or *th*.)

**C Critical Thinking**

**Draw Conclusions** Explain to students that recent research shows people who learn a second language early in life have more gray matter in their parietal cortex than people who speak only one language or people who learn a second language after the age of ten. Ask students: What implication does this finding have for schools and the teaching of young children? (Answers may vary but students should say that schools should be encouraged to teach foreign languages to young children.)

**U₁**

Much of this improvement in speech depends on physical development. Some sounds are more difficult to make than others. The sounds represented by *b, m,* and *p* are produced simply by moving the lips. By three, most children can make these sounds. The *f* and *v* sounds, among others, involve both the lips and the teeth. Children may not master these sounds until age five. The most difficult sounds are those represented by *j, ch, st, pl, th,* and *sl.* They require the smooth coordination of lip, tongue, and throat muscles. Some children may reach six or seven before *pwease* becomes *please.*

## Speech Difficulties

Although most children develop good language skills at home, some have problems with spoken language. They may have plenty of opportunities to listen and speak at home, but they may hear and use only a limited number of simple words. Children need to hear language that is specific and rich in detail. They also need to be encouraged to use this language. For example, rather than using the very general verb *go,* encourage children to use a variety of descriptive verbs. The boys *race* across the field. Mom *jogs* every morning. The bugs *creep* down the tree.

Some children have a head start. When parents and other caregivers begin talking to children from the time they are very young, it helps speech development. Describing what a child is seeing and doing builds vocabulary.

Children who do not speak English at home often face challenges when they begin school. They must learn English language skills and, at the same time, keep up with the class. Some schools have classes with bilingual teachers or aides for English language learners.

Children who move from one part of the country to another may also have difficulty because of differences in pronunciation. Some

**C**

▶ **Learn with Laughter**
By the age of six, children's language skills have reached the point where they can understand and enjoy a simple joke. *How can telling jokes enhance a child's language skills?*

## ⟩ Explore the Photo

**Caption Answer** Possible answers: Telling jokes can help increase a child's vocabulary and can teach them to tell stories in a sequential manner.

**Discussion** Why do you think young children have so much fun trading jokes? (Answers will vary. It allows them to laugh with their friends and develop social skills.)

# Learning Through PLAY

## Playing Grown-Up

Between the ages of two and nine, children often engage in imaginative play, or make believe. This kind of play aids intellectual development in many ways. In imaginative play, children act out imaginary situations. They often imitate what they see in the adult world. After watching an adult bake a cake, a child may pretend to bake a cake for a favorite stuffed animal. After visiting a parent's workplace, a child may play in a pretend office or store.

Children might also use fantasy play by drawing images from stories or films, perhaps acting out an explorer's voyage across the Atlantic Ocean. Most children show an interest in imaginative play at some time. Adults who provide opportunities for imaginative play do children a great favor.

**Think About It** Imagine that you are caring for your five-year-old niece and six-year-old nephew who want to play detectives. What materials could you provide for children who want to pretend to be detectives?

---

children have physical problems that prevent normal speech. Others may be intellectually or emotionally delayed.

All these situations may cause children to have difficulties at school. They may not be able to understand the teacher or to make themselves understood. As a result, learning becomes harder.

This situation may cause emotional problems as well. Classmates may be mean to a child whose speech is different, even if the difference is just an accent. Teasing and jokes can add to a child's sense of isolation. Whatever the cause, children with speech problems need special help. They should get this help before they begin school.

**✓ Reading Check** **Recall** About how many words can a normally developing six-year-old use and understand?

## The School Experience

Because children attend school for many years, it is vital that they develop a positive attitude from the start. Parents and caregivers should plan carefully to make the transition, or change, from home to school as smooth as possible.

## Preparing for School

Many parents place their children in a preschool so that they can become used to a school setting. In preschool, children learn to pay attention, take turns, sit quietly for a time, and interact with other children. **W**

At age five or six, most children enter kindergarten. The standard for entering the public school system is usually when the child reaches his or her fifth birthday. Most systems have a cutoff date, such as September 1. If a child is five by that date, the child may enter kindergarten.

Many states require that a child have a physical exam before starting school. Parents also have to show that their children have had the immunizations the school requires. For more information on immunizations, see Chapter 20.

In the past, kindergarten was usually only a half-day long. Today, however, full-day kindergarten programs are common. Research has shown that children in full-day kindergarten programs perform better in elementary school. Why do you think this is true?

### Readiness

The question of when a child is ready to start school is a difficult one. Should a child of school age who would be among the youngest

---

## Learning Through PLAY

### Playing Grown-Up

**Discussion** Tell students that some schools have either eliminated recess or are considering eliminating it. Ask students: What kind of effect might this have on children? How do you think this might affect children's imaginative play? (Answers may vary. It would reduce the amount of time children have to engage in physical activity and imaginative play.)

**Think About It** Answers will vary but might include that you could provide a magnifying glass, hat, pad of paper, pencil, or toy telephone.

---

## U₂ Universal Access

**Logical Learners** Discuss with the class that more and more teens are engaging in imaginative play through the use of video games and online gaming. Organize students into small groups. Instruct each group to discuss how they think teens' enjoyment of imaginative play is similar to and different from that of a young child. Each group should present a brief summary of their discussion to the class. (Each group should present a summary comparing the typical teen's imaginative play to the imaginary play of a young child.)

 **Professional Development**

 **Mini Clip ELL: Group Discussions**

Students work together to decide where to place illustrations on a chart.

## W Writing Support

### Humor

**Off to School** Tell students to write a humorous story about a child's first day in kindergarten. They can base their stories on real life, or they can make up the story. Encourage students to be creative. For example, a child might have to wear someone else's boots home because they are the only pair left. (Refer to p. 424 to review tips on writing humorous stories. Students' stories should take a humorous look at a child's first day in kindergarten.)

**✓ Reading Check**

**Recall** A normally developing six-year-old can use and understand approximately 2,500 words.

## Reteach *cont.*

## C Critical Thinking

**Solve Problems** Megan does not want to go to kindergarten on the first day, and she clings to her mother at the schoolhouse door, crying. The next morning she refuses to go to school. Ask students: If you were Megan's mother, what would you do? (Answers will vary. Possible suggestions might include talk with Megan to determine if she has a specific fear that could be dealt with and asking classmates to come over to play so that Megan will feel more comfortable with the other children.)

## U Universal Access

**Interpersonal Learners** Organize students into pairs. Each pair should create a brochure or a Web page that helps parents determine whether their children are ready for school. Students should create a bulleted list of the six signs of readiness. Then they should obtain illustrations to accompany each of the signs. Students can create original illustrations, use clip art, or a combination of the two. (Students should create an illustrated brochure or Web page listing the six signs that indicate a child is ready for school.)

↑ **Starting School**
The first day of school can be exciting, scary, or a mixture of both for a young child. *How would you prepare a child for the first day of school?*

in the class wait another year before starting school? What about a child who does not seem emotionally ready?

**C** One study showed that even children with high intelligence had emotional problems if they began school before they were ready. Another study, however, suggests that the opposite is true. In this research, children who started later had problems with behavior later in their school careers.

{ **Expert Advice...** }

*"School readiness involves a child's social/emotional and physical development as well as his cognitive development."*

— Ann Barbour, child development expert

What, then, should a parent do? Many school systems offer screenings to help assess a child's readiness. Parents whose child is enrolled in preschool can talk to the child's preschool teachers. They can judge the child's readiness based on what they have observed.

Parents can also talk with the pediatrician and look for certain signs. A child is ready for school if he or she can do the following.

- **Communicate with Adults** A child must be able to talk to adults other than his or her parents and be understood.
- **Manage Personal Needs** A child should be able to put on and take off his or her coat and shoes, and use the bathroom without help.
- **Complete a Task** A child should be able to complete a task such as finishing a drawing or putting away supplies.
- **Listen Attentively** A child should be able to listen attentively to a story and answer questions about it.

**U**

····◆ ▶ **Explore the Photo**

**Caption Answer** Answers will vary but may include to be sure the child knows his or her full name, address, and telephone number; explain what to expect; be sure that the child has plenty of rest; let the child pick out the clothes to wear; or arrange to meet some of the child's classmates.

**Discussion** Ask students why kindergarteners are often happy and excited to be going to school. (Possible answers: They look forward to new experiences and to playing with other children. They are proud to be old enough to go to school on their own.)

- **Follow Directions and Take Turns** A child must be able to participate in activities and cooperate with classmates.
- **Be Patient** A child should be willing to wait for a request to be met or to have a question answered.

## Making the Transition

Starting kindergarten can be a major adjustment for a child. This is true even if the child has gone to preschool. The school is generally bigger than the preschool, and it includes children several years older. A child switching from a half-day preschool to a full-day kindergarten must adjust to the longer hours away from home. Many children entering kindergarten also begin riding a school bus for the first time. Parents can help their children adjust to this new experience in several ways:

- Be sure the child knows his or her full name, address, and telephone number.

- Explain what to expect at school. If possible, visit the school together before the child's first day and meet the teachers. Some schools offer open house or orientation days for new students and their parents.
- Be sure that the child has plenty of rest. It can help to start an earlier bedtime a few weeks before school begins.
- Let the child choose a lunch box or backpack, and pick out the clothes to wear on the first day of school. This will help the child link the new school to feelings of increased independence.
- If possible, arrange to have the child play with future classmates before the first day of school. Seeing people they know helps reassure children in new situations.
- Above all, share positive feelings about school with the child. Tell the child how much fun you had at school as a child.

### Section 15.2

## Assess

### Study Tools

Have students go to the Online Learning Center at **glencoe.com**:

- Take the **Practice Test**.
- Download **Study-to-Go** content.

Use the **Student Activity Workbook** for additional practice.

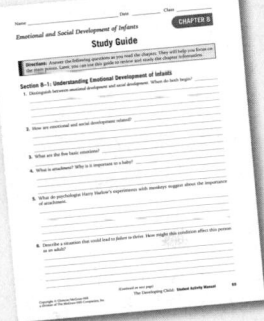

---

### Section 15.2 — After You Read

#### Review Key Concepts

1. **Give examples** of how parents can encourage a child's interest in reading, art, and music.
2. **Describe** types of school activities that might be challenging for a student with a speech difficulty.
3. **Explain** two steps parents can take to prepare children for kindergarten.

#### Practice Academic Skills

**English Language Arts**

4. What challenges might young children whose first language is not English face at school? How can teachers help the child overcome these challenges? Record your ideas in a half-page essay.

> **NCTE 9** Develop an understanding of diversity in language use across cultures.

**Social Studies**

5. Think of an experience or activity not mentioned in the chapter that a caregiver could use to teach new skills to a child. Perhaps you remember how you learned a new skill as a child. Describe the activity and explain why you feel it is well-suited to a four- to six-year-old.

> **NCSS IV D** Apply concepts, methods, and theories about the study of human growth and development, such as learning, motivation, and behavior.

 **Check Your Answers** Check your answers at this book's Online Learning Center at **glencoe.com**.

Section 15.2 Learning from Four to Six **441**

## Close

### Culminating Activity

**Write a Persuasive Essay** Have students write persuasive essays on the importance of providing preschoolers with a wide variety of experiences. (Essays will vary but might include that creating artwork can encourage children's enthusiasm for learning and expand their minds.)

**NCLB** connects academic correlations to book content.

---

### Section 15.2 — After You Read

#### Review Key Concepts

1. Possible answers: going to the library, finger painting, singing songs.
2. singing songs with difficult pronunciations, responding out loud to questions, show-and-tell in front of the class
3. Possible answers: visiting the school so the child knows what to expect, and allowing the child to choose clothes or a lunchbox.

#### Practice Academic Skills

4. Essays will vary but may include that children will have to learn English while developing their skills in their home language. Teachers can help these students by setting up a bilingual environment that uses elements of both languages.
5. Answers will vary but may include activities such as making musical instruments out of pots, pans, and other household objects or letting children help read recipes, nutrition labels, and other incidental text.

**Careers With Children**

## Focus

### Discussion Starter

**Kindergarten Teacher** Encourage students to discuss the kinds of things their kindergarten teachers did with them, such as telling stories and helping them learn letters and sounds. Ask: Why is having a skilled, enthusiastic kindergarten teacher important? (Possible answer: Having a positive kindergarten year often sets the tone for students' later academic experiences.)

## Teach

### C Critical Thinking

**Predict** Do you think a sixth-grade teacher would have difficulty becoming a kindergarten teacher? What kinds of challenges do you think the teacher might face? (Possible answer: Yes, because five-year-olds have lower-level language skills, so everything must be explained simply and completely. They also do best in learning environments that are much more interactive and physical.)

## Assess

### Make Connections

Ask students to list specific correlations between academic subjects and the kinds of skills a good kindergarten teacher needs. (Answers will vary. Students should show an understanding of how academic skills relate directly to the job of kindergarten teacher. Teaching kindergarten requires a wide range of academic skills, including English language, math, science, and social studies.)

**NCLB** This relates academic skills to specific tasks that are performed for this job.

**442**

---

# Kindergarten Teacher

**K**indergarten teachers introduce students to concepts they will build on throughout their lives. They teach children how to take turns, share, and treat others with respect. They also build an enthusiasm for learning.

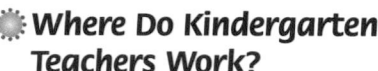

### ⚙ What Does a Kindergarten Teacher Do?

Kindergarten teachers are responsible for planning lessons and activities. They often use hands-on activities, such as making letters out of clay to teach the alphabet. They read books aloud, make learning tools, and even dance, sing, and do artwork. Kindergarteners have a short attention span, so lessons must be interesting and interactive.

### ⚙ Where Do Kindergarten Teachers Work?

Kindergarten teachers work in classrooms in public or private schools. A kindergarten classroom is a bright, colorful place with students' work decorating the walls. Kindergarten teachers work with children individually, in small groups, and as a class.

## Preparation and Skills

### Education and Training

Kindergarten teachers need to complete a bachelor's degree and an approved teacher-training program. Public school teachers must be licensed to teach.

### Aptitudes, Abilities, and Skills

Kindergarten teachers must have patience, creativity, and the ability to motivate children. The ability to recognize children's academic and emotional needs is also important. Teachers should have organizational skills.

### Academic Skills

English language arts and math skills are used by kindergarten teachers. They also use science and social studies to teach various lessons.

**NCLB**

**Explore Careers**

Research a teaching career for any grade level. As part of your research, create a list of resources teachers use for curriculum development. Write a paragraph in which you tell whether you think you would like a career in teaching.

 **Careers Online** For more information on careers, visit the Occupational Outlook Handbook Web site through the link on this book's Online Learning Center at **glencoe.com**.

---

## Close

### Culminating Activity

**Ranking Skills and Abilities** Organize students into small groups. Have each group create a list of abilities and skills, including academic skills, that are required of a kindergarten teacher. As a group, they should rank these items in order of importance. (Students should rank the required abilities and skills of a kindergarten teacher in what they think is their order of importance.)

**Explore Careers**

Answers will vary but should include a list of resources teachers use to develop curriculum, and a paragraph stating whether the students would enjoy a career in teaching.

## Chapter Summary

Intelligence tests vary for children of different ages. Gardner identified eight types of intelligence. Piaget's theory says children ages two to seven are in the preoperational period of thinking. Vygotsky and Montessori introduced influential theories of learning. Making reading a regular part of children's lives will encourage them to enjoy books in the future and promote learning. Between ages four and six, children's language skills usually improve rapidly, but some children need help. Children starting school can be helped to prepare for new situations.

## Vocabulary Review

1. Create a fill-in-the-blank sentence for each vocabulary term. The sentence should have enough information to determine the missing word.

**Content Vocabulary**
◇ intelligence quotient (IQ) (p. 427)
◇ cultural bias (p. 428)
◇ multiple intelligences (p. 428)
◇ phoneme (p. 435)
◇ alliteration (p. 435)
◇ bilingual (p. 436)
◇ finger play (p. 437)

**Academic Vocabulary**
■ regulate (p. 429)
■ oriented (p. 430)
■ foster (p. 437)
■ articulation (p. 437)

## Review Key Concepts

2. **List** eight types of intelligences.
3. **Identify** the common element of all theories of intellectual development.
4. **Identify** three ways to encourage children's interest in learning.
5. **Describe** the link between speech development and physical development.
6. **Explain** how parents can help their children adjust to kindergarten.

## Critical Thinking

7. **Predict** Choose two types of intelligences. Predict three professions not mentioned that someone high in each intelligence might choose.
8. **Apply** What are five ways that the parent of an only child could help the child develop his or her interpersonal intelligence?
9. **Infer** Five-year-olds Sue and Jennifer use make-believe play to have a tea party for their dolls. Give examples of how they might show the other characteristics of preoperational thinking at their tea party.
10. **Analyze** Determine what intelligences are needed for the following tasks: writing an autobiography, making and selling crafts, writing songs to be used in television commercials, and painting landscapes.

**Chapter 15** Intellectual Development from Four to Six **443**

## Content and Academic Vocabulary Review

1. Students should write fill-in-the-blank sentences that have context clues for the missing terms.

## Review Key Concepts

2. linguistic, logical-mathematical, spatial, musical, bodily-kinesthetic, interpersonal, intrapersonal, and naturalistic

3. All theories of intellectual development agree that a child's brain is able to handle increasingly complex skills over the time span of four to six years of age.

4. experiences in everyday life, reading, and art and music

5. The ability to make many of the sounds necessary for speech depends on physical development. Some sounds are more difficult to make than others and require the smooth coordination of lip, tongue, and throat muscles.

6. Parents can help their children adjust to kndergarten in several ways. Be sure the child knows his or her full name, address, and telephone number. Explain what to expect at school. Be sure that the child has plenty of rest. Let the child choose a lunch box or backpack, etc. If possible, arrange to have the child play with future classmates before the first day of school. Share positive feelings about school with the child.

## Critical Thinking

7. Any two: linguistic, logical-mathematical, spatial, musical, bodily-kinesthetic, interpersonal, intrapersonal, naturalist. Examples of professions may include: spatial—architect; interpersonal—social worker.

8. Answers may include encouraging the child to talk about himself or herself, having the child tell stories about someone his or her own age, or having the child draw pictures of self and family.

9. Examples will vary but may include the use of symbols—they use the dolls as symbols for real people such as Mommy or Daddy; egocentric viewpoint—their conversation with the dolls may be about their own points of view.

10. Answers may vary. Writing an autobiography uses linguistic and intrapersonal intelligences. Making and selling crafts requires spatial and naturalist intelligence. Writing songs needs musical and linguistic intelligences. Painting landscapes uses spatial and naturalist intelligences.

# Chapter **15** Review and Applications

## Family & Community Connections

**11.** Brochures will vary but should include information about what the program does, how a person can become involved in the program, and who is helped by the program.

## Health Skills

**12.** Answers will vary depending on the theory researched. Reports should show thorough research and offer specific details about the theory, as well as how it can promote learning.

## Observation Skills

**13.** Students charts or graphs will vary depending on the television programs watched. Recommendations may include that parents should limit their children's television viewing time and should monitor what their children watch.

## Real-World Skills

**14.** Students' advice will vary but may include encouraging the parent to sit with the child and for them to read a book together. The parent should also model reading by reading books when the child is present.

**15.** Presentations will vary but should include one of Piaget's experiments and an explanation that relates what the experiment means about preoperational thinking.

**16.** Lists will vary but should include age-appropriate activities and equipment that will promote bodily-kinesthetic intelligence in young children. The items on the list should not cost more than $150.

## Family & Community Connection

**11. Interview a Literacy Worker** Work with your teacher to arrange an interview with someone who works in a literacy program. During the interview find out what the program does, how someone gets involved in the program, and who is helped by the program. Create a brochure to promote the program using the information learned during your interview.

## Health Skills

**12. Research Intellectual Development** Use print and online resources to conduct research about intellectual development in children four to six years of age. Research a theory that is not discussed in this chapter. Write a one-page report to share the results of your research. Include a summary of how the theory could be used to help promote learning.

## Observation Skills

**13. Television and Behavior** Scientists have established a link between exposure to visual electronic media (VEM) and violent behavior, even in young children. One source recommends limiting television viewing to one or two hours a day. Another source recommends no more than four hours of television viewing per week.

**Procedure** Watch two hours of children's television programming. As you watch, keep track of the number of violent incidents you see in the program.

**Analysis** Use the information you gather to create a graph or chart. Provide recommendations for parents of young children who view television based on your findings.

**NCTE 8** Use information resources to gather information and create and communicate knowledge.

## Real-World Skills

| | |
|---|---|
| **Problem-Solving Skills** | **14. Generate Solutions** Imagine you are a parenting expert with a magazine column. A parent writes in saying he wants to get his five-year-old son interested in reading, but has trouble getting him to sit still with a book. Write your advice to the parent to be printed in your magazine column. |
| **Technology Skills** | **15. Create a Presentation** Research the experiments that Piaget used to understand preoperational thinking. Choose one experiment to present to the class and explain how it shows preoperational thinking. Use presentation software to present your findings to the class. |
| **Financial Literacy** | **16. Intelligent Spending** Imagine that you have $150 to spend on activities for use at the day care center where you volunteer. You will focus on activities that promote bodily-kinesthetic intelligence for four- to six-year-olds. Go online or to a local educational supply store and create a list of activities and equipment you can purchase. |

 **Additional Activities** For additional activities, go to this book's Online Learning Center at **glencoe.com**.

## Academic Skills

**17.** Essays will vary but should include at least five comments or questions directed to the child about the drawing and an explanation of why the student feels these would encourage the child.

**NCLB** Activity correlated to English Language Arts standards.

The *Early Childhood Observations CD* offers additional lessons with videos to build students' observation skills.

**Part 1:** Learning to Observe

**Part 2:** How Children Develop

**Part 3:** Working With Young Children

**Part 4:** Extended Observations

**Part 5:** Resources and Answer File

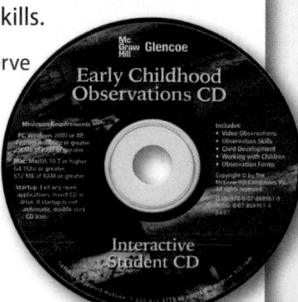

## Academic Skills

###  English Language Arts

**17. Encourage Learning** Imagine that a five-year-old is drawing a picture of her family and where they live. Write a list of five comments you could make or questions you could ask to encourage the child's learning and to promote positive feelings about herself. Write a brief essay in which you explain why you feel these comments or questions would be encouraging.

> **NCTE 4** Use written language to communicate effectively.

###  Mathematics

**18. Intellectual Development** Psychologist Jean Piaget describes this age as intuitive. Children have the ability to perform multiple classification tasks or order objects in a logical sequence. Such an order exists in mathematics and is called the order of operations. Use the order of operations to evaluate this expression:

$$55 - 2 \times (3 + 4) + 15 \times 2 - 4$$

**Math Concept** **Order of Operations** The order of operations is parentheses, exponents, multiplication and division from left to right, and then addition and subtraction from left to right.

**Starting Hint** Following the order of operations, complete one step of the problem at a time, starting with the operation in parentheses.

 For math help, go to the Math Appendix at the back of the book.

> **NCTM Number and Operations** Compute fluently and make reasonable estimates.

###  Science

**19. Research Behavior** The developing brain needs stimulation of all five senses: taste, smell, sight, touch, and hearing. Research shows that experiences that stimulate more than one sense at a time are more easily retained in the long-term memory.

**Procedure** Research why children remember multi-sensory experiences better. Give examples of multi-sensory experiences.

**Analysis** Create a list of multi-sensory experiences and write a one-page summary of your research findings.

> **NSES C** Develop understanding of the cell; biological evolution; matter, energy, and organization in living systems; and behavior of organisms.

### Standardized Test Practice

**TRUE/FALSE**
Read the following passage, then answer the question.

> Do you enjoy art, reading, or music? It is quite possible that your interest in these subjects first started when you were between the ages of four and six. At this time, children are exposed to new ideas and activities. These experiences have a significant impact on their growing minds.

**20.** According to this passage, children between the ages of four and six love music.
  **a.** True
  **b.** False

> **Test-Taking Tip** With true/false questions that rely on information given, read the paragraph carefully to make sure you understand it. Read the answer choices. Read the paragraph again before choosing the answer.

**18.** $7 [55 - 2 \times (3 + 4) + 15 \times 2$
$- 4 = 55 - 2 \times 7 + 15 \times 2 - 4$
$= 55 - 14 + 30 - 4$
$= 55 - 44 - 4 = 7$

 **Professional Development**

**Mini Clip**
**Math: Introducing Multi-Step Equations**
A teacher walks his students through the process of solving multi-step equations.

**19.** Answers will vary but should include research results and a list of multi-sensory experiences such as television or video, which include visual and auditory stimulation, or dance, which includes auditory and kinesthetic stimulation.

 **NCLB** connects academic correlations to book content.

### Standardized Test Practice

**20.** b. False

**Test-Taking Tips** Tell students to judge the amount of time they have for each question and attempt to allot their time accordingly.

**True/False Test** Tell students that true/false tests tend to have more true questions than false questions. Also, questions containing specific details are more likely to be true.

## TECHNOLOGY Solutions

**Use these technology solutions to streamline chapter assessment!**

 ***ExamView Assessment Suite*** CD allows you to create and print out customized tests or ready-made unit and chapter tests, complete with answer keys.

 **TeacherWorks Plus** is an electronic lesson planner that provides instant access to complete teacher resources in one convenient package.

 **Online Learning Center** includes resources and activities for students and teachers.

## Unit Thematic Project

# Teach New Skills

## Discussion Starter

**Learning and Growing** Ask students to list things they remember learning when they were four- to six-years-old. (Examples may include riding a bike, jumping rope, tying shoes, learning the alphabet, or learning to count to one hundred.)

 Project correlated to English Language Arts standards.

### Step 1

## Choose a Professional to Interview

Students can select a child care expert in your community. If students can think of another professional not listed, they are welcome to interview him or her. Students might also consider interviewing a parent or foster parent who has raised multiple children.

**Teach**

### Step 2

## Write Your Interview Questions

Interview questions should include specific questions about age-appropriate activities for children ages four to six years. Students should tailor the questions to the professional being interviewed and should organize the questions into the four areas of child development. Questions should be free of spelling and grammatical errors.

In this unit you have learned that there are many things parents and caregivers can do to help four- to six-year-olds grow and develop physically, emotionally, socially, and intellectually. In this project, you will interview a child care professional. You will use what you learn to create a brochure that will list activities for caregivers to use to promote growth and development in four- to six-year-olds.

 **My Journal**

If you completed the journal entry from page 379, refer to it to see if your thoughts have changed after reading the unit.

## Project Assignment

In this project, you will:
- Choose a person in your community who knows about the growth and development of four- to six-year-olds.
- Write a list of interview questions to ask about activities that will help four- to

six-year-olds develop physically, socially, emotionally, and intellectually.
- Arrange and conduct an interview.
- Use what you learned in the interview to create a brochure. The brochure should list activities that will help children develop physically, emotionally, socially, and intellectually.

### Step 1 Choose a Professional to Interview

Listed below are child growth and development experts you may have in your community. Select one of these professionals to contact and interview.
- Preschool teacher
- Kindergarten teacher
- Day care worker
- Pediatrician
- Child psychologist
- Pediatric nurse
- College or high school child development instructor

### Step 2 Write Your Interview Questions

Make a list of interview questions to ask the child development professional. Use information from this text and from your own knowledge to write questions about the physical, emotional, social, and intellectual development of four- to six-year-olds.

---

### Child Development Skills Behind the Project

- Identify physical activities appropriate for four- to six-year-olds.
- List activities that will promote emotional and social growth in four- to six-year-olds.
- Describe intellectual activities that will stimulate four- to six-year-olds.

### Academic Skills

 **English Language Arts**

> **NCTE 4** Use written language to communicate effectively.
>
> **NCTE 7** Conduct research and gather, evaluate, and synthesize data to communicate discoveries.

### Step 3

## Connect to Your Community

Ask students to explain who they think might benefit from the information they gain through their interview. (Answers may include parents of young children, babysitters, or people who may consider becoming a child care professional or child development expert.) Ask how this information might benefit these people. (Answers will vary but may include that it can help people understand what activities are age-appropriate for the children they care for.)

### Step 4

## Create and Present Your Brochure

Give students these tips on creating and presenting their brochures:
- Make sure your brochure is visible to the entire audience.
- Know your audience.
- Speak concisely (briefly but completely).
- Use simple language.

### Writing Skills
★ Use complete sentences.
★ Organize your questions into the four areas of development: physical, emotional, social, and intellectual.
★ Use correct spelling and grammar.

### Step 3 Connect to Your Community
Arrange to speak to the professional you chose in Step 1. Use the interview questions you prepared to find out about age-appropriate activities for four- to six-year-olds. Take notes during the interview.

### Nonverbal Communication Skills
★ Dress neatly for the interview.
★ Listen attentively.
★ Make eye contact and smile when it is appropriate.

### Step 4 Create and Present Your Brochure
Use the Unit Thematic Project Checklist on the right to create your brochure and share it with the other members of your class.

### Presentation Skills
★ Organize your presentation by developing an outline.
★ Present your ideas clearly.
★ Be sensitive to the needs of your audience.

### Step 5 Evaluate Your Child Development Skills and Academic Skills
Your project will be evaluated based on:
- Content and organization of your information.
- Mechanics—presentation and neatness.
- Speaking and listening skills.

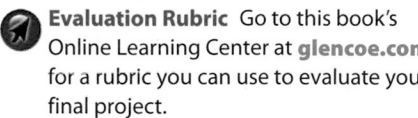 **Evaluation Rubric** Go to this book's Online Learning Center at **glencoe.com** for a rubric you can use to evaluate your final project.

## Unit Thematic Project Checklist

| | |
|---|---|
| **Brochure** | ✓ Use word processing software to create and illustrate your brochure. <br> ✓ In your brochure, list activities that will help four- to six-year-olds develop physically, emotionally, socially, and intellectually. <br> ✓ Organize the brochure so that activities are easy to locate. <br> ✓ Include the heads: Physical, Emotional, Social, and Intellectual. <br> ✓ Include a title on the front of your brochure. <br> ✓ Add illustrations to your brochure. |
| **Presentation** | ✓ Make a presentation to your class to share your brochure and discuss what you learned. <br> ✓ Invite the students in your class to ask you any questions they may have. Answer three questions. <br> ✓ When students ask you questions, demonstrate in your answers that you respect their perspectives. <br> ✓ Turn in the notes from your interview and your brochure to your teacher. |
| **Academic Skills** | ✓ Organize your brochure and presentation so the audience can follow along easily. <br> ✓ Speak clearly and concisely. <br> ✓ Thoughtfully express your ideas. |

## Assess

### Step 5
**Evaluate Your Child Development Skills and Academic Skills**

**Rubric** Encourage students to go to this book's Online Learning Center at **glencoe.com** for a rubric they can use to evaluate their brochure and presentation. Students can use the rubric as a content checklist when forming their interview questions, creating their brochure, and giving their presentation.

## Close

### Culminating Activity

**Project Assessment** In this project, students identified activities appropriate for helping four- to six-year-olds grow and develop physically, emotionally, socially, and intellectually. Have students work in pairs to constructively critique their partner's activities. Partners should offer helpful suggestions for improving the activities based on their knowledge of children of this age group. Students may want to make the changes to the activities in their brochures.

## Developing Community Involvement

### Helping Caregivers
In this unit students have learned information that will be useful for them if they become parents, babysitters, child care workers, or if they are involved in other areas of child development. Students have put together valuable information that can be used by caregivers of four- to six-year-olds. Suggest that students make copies of their brochures and

distribute them to preschools, kindergarten classes, and babysitters they might know in your community.

A **Family & Community Involvement** worksheet about this topic is available:

- At this book's Online Learning Center at **glencoe.com**
- On the TeacherWorks CD

# Unit 6   The Child from Seven to Twelve

| Title | Objectives |
|---|---|
| **CHAPTER 16** Physical Development from Seven to Twelve | • **Describe** the two significant stages that occur between ages seven and twelve.<br>• **Explain** why children's motor skills improve between the ages of seven and twelve.<br>• **List** the nine topics in the Dietary Guidelines for Americans.<br>• **Identify** five areas that contribute to overall physical health and wellness. |
| **CHAPTER 17** Emotional and Social Development from Seven to Twelve | • **Identify** four ways to help ease emotional upsets.<br>• **Explain** how to help children control and express their anger in socially acceptable ways.<br>• **List** six ways to help a child develop a sense of competence.<br>• **Summarize** the four main qualities children look for in friendships.<br>• **Identify** typical changes that occur in children's attitudes toward their parents.<br>• **Describe** five ways to help prepare children to make good moral choices. |
| **CHAPTER 18** Intellectual Development from Seven to Twelve | • **Identify** four signs of intellectual development in children ages seven to twelve.<br>• **Explain** four thinking skills that build a foundation for mastering school work.<br>• **Describe** three learning methods that are effective for children ages seven to twelve.<br>• **Identify** characteristics of the middle school experience that make it well suited to preteen learning.<br>• **Compare and contrast** three types of standardized tests. |
| Unit **Thematic Project** Develop an Exercise Program | • **Write** a My Journal entry on Exercise and Development.<br>• **Choose** an exercise program appropriate for seven- to twelve-year-olds.<br>• **Interview** a professional about the fitness needs of this age group.<br>• **Create and demonstrate** an exercise program for seven- to twelve-year-olds. |

## Understanding Brackets, Letters, and Ability Levels in the Teacher Wraparound Edition

**Brackets** Brackets on the reduced student edition page correspond to teaching strategies and activities in the Teacher Wraparound Edition. As you teach the lesson, the brackets show you exactly where to use the teaching strategies and activities.

**Letters** The letters on the reduced student edition page identify the type of strategy or activity. See the key below to learn about the different types of strategies and activities.

**Ability Levels** Teaching Strategies that appear throughout the chapters have been identified by one of three codes to give you an idea of their suitability for students of varying learning styles and abilities.

**Resources** Key program resources are listed in each chapter. Icons indicate the format of resources.

### KEY TO LETTERS

**D** **Develop Concepts** activities help teachers gauge and plan for students' concept development.

**R** **Reading Strategy** activities help you teach reading skills and vocabulary.

**S** **Skill Practice** provides leveled instruction for meeting individual needs and learning styles.

**W** **Writing Support** activities provide writing opportunities to help students comprehend the text.

**C** **Critical Thinking** strategies help students apply and extend what they have learned.

**U** **Universal Access** activities provide differentiated instruction for English language learners, and suggestions for teaching various types of learners.

**NCLB** **No Child Left Behind** activities help students practice and improve their abilities in academic subjects.

### KEY TO ABILITY LEVELS

**L1** Strategies should be within the ability range of all students. Often full class participation is required.

**L2** Strategies are for average to above-average students or for small groups. Some teacher direction is necessary.

**L3** Strategies are designed for students able and willing to work independently. Minimal teacher direction is necessary.

**ELL** Strategies are especially accessible to English Language Learners.

### KEY TO RESOURCE ICONS

📁 Print Material

💿 CD or DVD Resources

🖱 Online Learning Center (OLC)

## TeacherWorks™
### All-In-One Planner and Resource Center

**Teacher Wraparound Edition**

**Unit Resources:**
Unit Thematic Project Student Rubrics
Unit Family and Community Involvement Activities

**Chapter Resources:**
Lesson Plans
Chapter Summaries, Content and Academic Vocabulary
Graphic Organizers

**Textbook Resources:**
Student Activity Workbook with Academic Integration
Additional Activities
Enrichment Activities

 Link to the *The Developing Child* **Online Learning Center** at **glencoe.com**.

## Unit Overview

### Introduce the Unit

Introduce the unit by describing the main concepts of each chapter in the unit.

### Unit 6

This unit discusses the physical, emotional, social, and intellectual growth and development of seven- to twelve-year-olds.

**Chapter 16** This chapter focuses on children from ages seven to twelve in terms of their physical growth and development, as well as nutrition and self-care. Students will learn that most children grow steadily during middle childhood, but have occasional growth spurts. Also, there is often an increased interest in personal hygiene during this time.

**Chapter 17** Chapter 17 looks at the emotional and social development of children ages seven to twelve. Students will discover that during this time, children develop a sense of self; children with a sense of competence are likely to have high self-esteem; and peers become more important.

**Chapter 18** Students are introduced to the developing brain's distinct intellectual and emotional needs, as well as the characteristics of learning that become evident during the ages of seven to twelve. The benefits of middle school and the characteristics of standardized tests are also discussed.

# Unit **6**

# The Child from Seven to Twelve

**Explore the Photo**
Independence usually increases as a child gets older. *How can seven- to twelve-year-olds show independence?*

448

▶ **Explore the Photo**

**Caption Answer** Answers will vary but may include: They can show independence by doing chores or schoolwork without being reminded; they might spend time with friends without adult supervision; they might select their own clothing; or they can be responsible for taking care of a pet.

**Discussion** Ask students how the seven- to twelve-year-olds in the photo differ from four- to six-year-olds. (The most obvious difference is size; seven- to twelve-year-olds typically are taller and heavier than four- to six-year-olds. Students might also mention that older children are often more into fashion and wanting to dress like young adults.)

Chapter **16** Physical Development from Seven to Twelve

Chapter **17** Emotional and Social Development from Seven to Twelve

Chapter **18** Intellectual Development from Seven to Twelve

## Unit Thematic Project Preview

### Develop an Exercise Program

By completing this unit, you will learn that children ages seven to twelve experience significant changes in their physical, emotional, social, and intellectual growth and development. In your unit thematic project, you can show how getting plenty of exercise plays an important role in these changes.

 **My Journal**

**Exercise and Development** Write a journal entry about one of the topics below. This will help you prepare for the unit project at the end of the unit.

- Explain why getting regular exercise is important to growth and development.
- Identify exercises that are appropriate for growing children.
- Discuss how lack of physical exercise might affect a growing child physically, emotionally, socially, and intellectually.

**449**

**STANDARDS BASED LESSON PLANNING** *The Developing Child* provides students with instruction and assessment in the following fundamental content areas:

## National Standards Correlations

| Standards | Pages |
|---|---|
| **12.1.1** Analyze physical, emotional, social, spiritual, and intellectual development. | **453–454, 456–457** |
| **12.1.2** Analyze interrelationships among physical, emotional, social, and intellectual aspects of human growth and development. | **454, 455** |
| **12.1.3** Analyze current and emerging research about human growth and development, including research on brain development. | **456** |
| **12.2.1** Analyze the effect of heredity and environment on human growth and development. | **456** |
| **12.2.2** Analyze the impact of social, economic, and technological forces on individual growth and development. | **456** |
| **12.2.3** Analyze the effects of gender, ethnicity, and culture on individual development. | **456** |
| **12.3.1** Analyze the role of nurturance on human growth and development. | **462** |
| **15.1.2** Analyze expectations and responsibilities of parenting. | **463** |
| **15.1.4** Analyze societal conditions that influence parenting across the life span. | **463** |
| **15.2.1** Choose nurturing practices that support human growth and development. | **462, 466** |

**NO CHILD LEFT BEHIND** NCLB activities, information, and skills practice will help your students attain NCLB proficiency. Students will improve their abilities in the following academic standards areas:

## Academic Standards Correlations

| Discipline | Standard | Feature/Activity |
|---|---|---|
| **English Language Arts** | **NCTE 1** Read texts to acquire new information. | **Reading Guide (pp. 452, 458)** |
| | **NCTE 5** Use different writing process elements to communicate effectively. | **Writing Activity (p. 450)** **After You Read (p. 457)** |
| | **NCTE 7** Conduct research and gather, evaluate, and synthesize data to communicate discoveries. | **After You Read (p. 466)** **Observation Skills (p. 468)** **Academic Skills (p. 469)** |
| **Mathematics** | **NCTM Algebra** Use mathematical models to represent and understand quantitative relationships. | **Academic Skills (p. 469)** |
| | **NCTM Number and Operations** Understand numbers, ways of representing numbers, relationships among numbers, and number systems. | **After You Read (p. 457)** |
| **Science** | **NSES A** Develop abilities necessary to do scientific inquiry, understanding about scientific inquiry. | **After You Read (p. 466)** |
| | **NSES C** Develop understanding of the behavior of organisms. | **Science in Action (p. 456)** |
| | **NSES F** Students should develop understanding of personal and community health. | **Academic Skills (p. 469)** |
| **Social Studies** | **NCSS V F Individuals, Groups, and Institutions** Evaluate the role of institutions in furthering both continuity and change. | **Culture Matters (p. 461)** |

 **Professional Development**

## MINI CLIP VIDEO LIBRARY

Targeted professional development is correlated throughout *The Developing Child*. **The McGraw-Hill Professional Development Mini Clip Video Library** provides teaching strategies to strengthen academic and learning skills. Log on to **glencoe.com**.

In this chapter, you will find these Mini Clips:
- **Reading** Standards-Based Instruction, p. 452
- **Math** Medians and Quartiles, p. 453
- **ELL** Vocabulary Activities, p. 458
- **ELL** Previewing a Text, p. 459
- **Reading** Fluency Development, p. 463
- **Math** Rates and Ratios, p. 469

## Reading and Writing Strategies

**Writing Activity: Advertising** (p. 450)
Students use writing tips to write an attention-getting advertisement that is directed at a specific audience.

**Before You Read** (pp. 452, 458)
A pre-reading question or statement will help students make a personal connection to content.

**Graphic Organizer** (pp. 452, 458)
A visual tool will help students organize and remember new content.

**Reading Check** (pp. 456, 462)
A question allows students to make a quick comprehension self-check.

**After You Read** (pp. 457, 466)
Organize and process students' understanding of what they have read.

## Chapter Features

**Puberty and Television** (p. 456)
Researchers believe that the less television a child watches, the more melatonin the child's body produces.

**Fine Motor Skills** (p. 456)
Learning activities that teach the brain to control finger and hand movement can improve fine motor skills.

**Lessons You Can Eat** (p. 461)
At Martin Luther King Jr. Middle School, students grow and cook their own food.

**How Can Parents Help an Overweight Child?** (p. 462)
Learn some useful tips for parents to help an overweight child.

**Dealing with Acne** (p. 465)
Parents can provide support and guidance for children with acne.

## Chapter Overview

### Introduce the Chapter

In this chapter, students learn how children from ages seven through twelve grow and develop. Between nine and sixteen, children typically enter puberty. During this time, children require guidance in nutritious eating and in being physically fit. They also need guidance in caring for their bodies and getting adequate sleep.

### Build Background

Remind students that so far they have studied the extremely rapid growth of infants and babies, followed by a somewhat slower growth period in young children. In this chapter, they once again will see dramatic changes as children begin to take on adult characteristics. Encourage students to discuss changes that a typical twelve-year-old might be going through that make him or her more adult-like.

### Writing Activity

#### Advertisement

This is an active learning activity that prompts the student to identify a class that could improve motor skills and teach new skills. Then, they need to create an advertisement to encourage participation in that class. After students have completed their writing activity, encourage them to share their advertisements in class. Student ads can be used to prompt classroom discussions. (The student should have written an advertisement for a class that will improve young people's motor skills, such as ballet or karate. The ad should contain a title and introduction that attract the reader's attention, focus on the class's benefits, and use short and simple sentences.)

# Physical Development from Seven to Twelve

## Chapter Objectives

After completing this chapter, you will be able to:

- **Describe** the two significant stages that occur between ages seven and twelve.
- **Explain** why children's motor skills improve between the ages of seven and twelve.
- **List** the nine topics in the Dietary Guidelines for Americans.
- **Identify** five areas that contribute to overall physical health and wellness.

### Writing Activity    Advertisement

**Improving Motor Skills** To improve their motor skills and learn new skills, many young people take classes. Examples might include ballet, tap dancing, or karate. Choose one type of class that interests you. Use the tips listed below to write an advertisement for the class.

**Writing Tips** When writing an advertisement, always keep your audience in mind. Otherwise, you will not be able to attract and hold their attention. Here are some tips for writing an advertisement:

1. Write a title and introduction that will grab the reader's attention.
2. Focus on the benefits of your class.
3. Keep your sentences short and simple; avoid using jargon, or terms specific to your activity. People might not know what those words mean.

## CLASSROOM    Solutions

### Print Resources

 **Student Edition**

 **Teacher Wraparound Edition**

 **Student Activity Workbook**

 **Student Activity Workbook Teacher Annotated Edition**

### Technology Resources

 **Online Learning Center** has resources and activities for students and teachers. Includes an Online Student Edition.

 **Interactive Student Edition** allows students to instantly access review materials, examples, and exercises.

Section **16.1** **Growth and Development from Seven to Twelve**

Section **16.2** **Caring for Children from Seven to Twelve**

↑ **Explore the Photo**
Children from seven to twelve vary greatly in weight and height. *Why might a ten-year-old be worried if he is shorter than his friends?*

451

**Review the Sections**
Introduce the chapter by reviewing the sections:

**Section 16.1**
Children's bodies develop rapidly as they travel down the road to puberty. Sex-specific characteristics also begin to develop. Because of these rapid changes, some children are sensitive about their body image. Organized sports can be helpful in encouraging physical activity, cooperation, and in teaching skills such as good sportsmanship.

**Section 16.2**
Children need to be taught appropriate dietary guidelines, including appropriate food choices and the importance of maintaining a healthy weight. Parents can set a good example by eating meals as a family and offering healthy food choices. Parents also should teach and model healthy habits such as being physically active and practicing good hygiene.

▶ **Explore the Photo**

**Caption Answer** Answers will vary. Children at this age want to look similar to their peers and to not stand out in the group. In addition, the child may think he will always be short, and see this as undesirable.

**Discussion** Ask students what difficulties might occur in physical education classes if children of the same age vary greatly in size and weight. What might a teacher do to handle these differences? (Answers will vary. In games where size and weight provide an advantage, smaller students might not do well and could be more likely to be injured. Teachers could select activities that depend more on skill, rather than size.)

 **TeacherWorks Plus** is an electronic lesson planner that provides instant access to complete teacher resources in one convenient package.

**Presentation Plus!** provides visual teaching aids for every section.

 **The Early Childhood Observations CD** presents video observations and lessons on observation skills and child development.

**The Developing Brain eTransparencies and Guide** include information and activities to offer insights into brain development and diseases of the brain.

## Focus

### Bell Ringer Activity

**Lots of Variety**

Hold up a photo of a group of young people ages ten through twelve. Make certain that they vary noticeably in height and maturity. Talk with the class about the considerable variation in height and weight. Some preteens look much younger than they are, while others look much older.

## Preteaching

### Vocabulary

Write the word *scoliosis* on the board and explain that it is an abnormal curvature of the spine. *Scolio* comes from the Greek *skolios*, and means "crooked." *-osis* is a suffix meaning "condition." Discuss other medical terms that use the *-osis* suffix, such as tuberculosis and neurosis.

### Graphic Organizer

 The Graphic Organizer is also on the TeacherWorks CD.

(Graphic organizers should include: significant growth spurts, hair appearing under arms and in pubic area, and sweat and oil glands becoming more active.)

**NCLB** connects academic correlations to book content.

 **Professional Development**

**Mini Clip**
Reading: Standards-Based Instruction

Emily M. Schell, EdD, educator and author, discusses standards-based instruction.

---

### Reading Guide

**Before You Read**

**Two-Column Note-Taking** Fold a sheet of paper in half lengthwise. Label the left side "Main Ideas," and the right side "Details." As you read, fill in each side.

**Read to Learn**
**Key Concepts**
- **Describe** the two significant stages that occur between ages seven and twelve.
- **Explain** why children's motor skills improve between the ages of seven and twelve.

**Main Idea**
Children ages seven through twelve go through many changes, ending with puberty. Because of these extensive changes, they often become sensitive about the appearance of their bodies.

**Content Vocabulary**
◇ growth spurt
◇ puberty
◇ scoliosis
◇ body image
◇ eating disorder
◇ menstruation

**Academic Vocabulary**
You will find these words in your reading and on your tests. Use the glossary to look up their definitions if necessary.
■ profound
■ ultimate

**Graphic Organizer**
As you read, look for three changes that occur in both boys and girls during puberty. Use a diagram like the one shown to help organize your information.

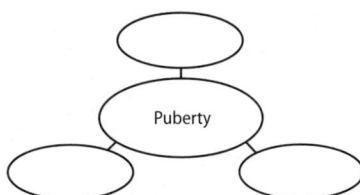

Puberty

 **Graphic Organizer** Go to this book's Online Learning Center at **glencoe.com** to print out this graphic organizer.

**Academic Standards** . . . . . . . . . . . . . . . . . . . . . . . . .

 **English Language Arts**
**NCTE 5** Use different writing process elements to communicate effectively.

 **Mathematics**
**NCTM Number and Operations** Understand numbers, ways of representing numbers, relationships among numbers, and number systems.

**Science**
**NSES C** Develop an understanding of the behavior of organisms.

**NCTE** *National Council of Teachers of English*
**NCTM** *National Council of Teachers of Mathematics*

**NSES** *National Science Education Standards*
**NCSS** *National Council for the Social Studies*

---

### Reading Guide

**Before You Read**

Ask students: Have you ever gone through a growth spurt? When was it? Did it have any effect on how you thought about yourself? How might a growth spurt affect a child's self-image?

### D Develop Concepts

**Main Idea** Discuss the main idea with the students. Have students list some of the physical changes that lead up to puberty. (Lists might include that children grow taller and become heavier, they begin to develop body hair, and their body shape changes depending on their sex.)

## Growth from Seven to Twelve

From the ages of seven to twelve, children go through a period of **profound**, or overwhelming, physical changes. A sudden spurt of growth adds to their height. Their bodies begin to take on the physical characteristics of adulthood. There are two significant stages during these years: middle childhood and the preteen years. Middle childhood runs from ages seven through ten. During this period, children build on the growth and skills that began in early childhood. Eleven- and twelve-year-olds are in the preteen years. They are just beginning the path to being an adult.

### Height and Weight

From the ages of seven to ten, boys and girls grow in height an average of just over two inches (5.1 cm) per year. This is a slower rate of growth than they experienced as preschoolers, toddlers, or infants. The gain in height is usually at a regular pace, but a child can have a growth spurt. A **growth spurt** occurs when a child grows very rapidly in a short period of time. For nine-year-old Ahmad, that meant the pants he bought at the start of the school year were too small by November.

The average rate of growth increases during the preteen years. It is during this time that many children go through puberty. **Puberty** is the set of changes that result in a physically mature body that is able to reproduce. Girls tend to go through puberty a bit earlier than boys.

This means the girls are often taller than the boys in their class at this time. Boys have larger average gains in height between the ages of 12 and 14, when they typically go through puberty. **Figure 16.1** on page 454 shows the average heights of boys and girls from seven- to twelve-years-old.

During this period, growth takes place in different parts of the body at different times. Typically, the hands and the feet are the first to grow, followed by the arms and legs, and then finally the torso. Sometimes one part of the body grows faster than other parts. This can cause embarrassment.

In terms of weight, boys and girls gain an average of about 6½ pounds (2.9 kg) each year during middle childhood. During the preteen years, this increases to about 10½ pounds (4.7 kg) for girls and 9½ pounds (4.3 kg) for boys. Because puberty typically occurs in boys about two years later than girls, boys have a greater annual weight gain than girls after about age twelve.

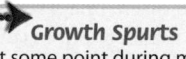

> **Growth Spurts**
> At some point during middle childhood, boys often experience growth spurts. *What other changes do they experience?*

Section 16.1   Growth and Development from Seven to Twelve   **453**

---

### Explore the Photo

**Caption Answer**  They gain weight, begin to grow body hair, and become stronger.

**Discussion**  Ask students: How do you think a boy who experiences a growth spurt might feel when adults such as his grandparents say to him, "You sure have grown." Do you think it is a good idea for adults to make these kinds of comments? Why or why not? (Responses will vary; many preteens are sensitive about any discussion of changes in their bodies while others are proud to be growing up.)

---

## Teach

### Discussion Starter

**The 'Tween Years**  Ask students: What do you think is meant by "the 'tween years"? How are these years different from the times before and after them? (The 'tween [short for between] years typically refer to the time after childhood but before the teen years. It is the time when young people feel they are no longer children but are not yet teens.)

### R Reading Strategy

**Ask Questions**  Instruct students to read the text under Height and Weight. Then organize students into pairs. Students should take turns asking one another comprehension questions based on this text. Instruct students to each ask one question concerning each of the paragraphs. **ELL**

### C Critical Thinking

**Analyze**  Review the mathematical concept of median (the middle number in a value set.) In a value set with an odd total of values, the median has as many values below it as above it. In a value set with an even total of values, calculate the median by averaging the two middle values. Write the following heights for eight-year-old boys on the board: 50, 41, 66, 53, 58, 48, 45, 55, 52, and 49. Instruct students to calculate the median. (It is 51.)

**Professional Development**

**Mini Clip**
Math:
**Medians and Quartiles**

Algebra teacher Brad Fulton suggests a strategy for helping students understand the meaning of median and quartile.

## S Skill Practice

### Guided Practice

**Create a Mural** Organize students into small groups. Each group should create a mural that shows children from seven to twelve exhibiting good sportsmanship. Students may wish to use a collection of original drawings or paintings along with images they have taken from magazines, or newspapers. (Murals should show images of children and preteens exhibiting good sportsmanship.) **L1 ELL**

**Observe Sportsmanship** Instruct students to watch a game played by children ages seven to twelve. Students should keep track of instances in which children and coaches exhibit either good sportsmanship or poor sportsmanship. They then should write a summary of what they observed. (Students should write a summary of any behavior they witnessed that showed players or coaches exhibiting either good sportsmanship or poor sportsmanship.) **L2**

**Prepare a Pep Talk** Have students imagine they are coaches of a coed soccer team of nine- and ten-year-olds. Ask students to write a pep talk they might give the team before a game. Emphasize the importance of being positive and supportive and exhibiting good sportsmanship. Invite volunteers to deliver their pep talks to the class. (Students should write a coach's pep talk that emphasizes positive and supportive behavior.) **L3**

**Figure 16.1 Average Heights and Weights—Ages 7–12**

Children in middle childhood and the preteen years vary greatly in height. *At what ages are the average heights for boys and girls the same?*

| Age | BOYS | | GIRLS | |
| | Height / Inches | Weight / Pounds | Height / Inches | Weight / Pounds |
|---|---|---|---|---|
| **7 years** | 48 | 51 | 47¾ | 50 |
| **8 years** | 50 | 56 | 50½ | 56 |
| **9 years** | 52½ | 63 | 52½ | 64 |
| **10 years** | 54½ | 70 | 54½ | 72 |
| **11 years** | 56½ | 79 | 57½ | 82 |
| **12 years** | 58¾ | 89 | 59½ | 92 |

Experts believe that heredity is the most influential factor in determining a child's **ultimate**, or final, height. When parents are considered to be below average in height, it is likely that their children will be short.

Nutrition is an important influence on a child's weight during these years. A child who eats foods low in fat and high in nutrients is less likely to have a weight problem than one who eats fatty foods that are low in nutrients. Physically active children are also less likely to be overweight. **Figure 16.2** offers tips on how to help children enjoy organized sports.

### Proportion and Posture

A tall and lean five-year-old typically remains tall and slim through middle childhood. However, as seven- to twelve-year-olds grow, their proportions change. Their legs lengthen, adding height and bringing the head more in proportion to their body. Children also become stronger and develop greater muscle tone in their legs, arms, and torso. Balance and coordination continue to improve.

Some older children and preteens develop a curve of the spine called scoliosis. **Scoliosis** is a sideways curvature of the spine, affecting posture. Scoliosis may be treated with exercise, a brace, or surgery.

### Body Image

Some children become sensitive about their body image. **Body image** refers to how a person thinks his or her body looks. Children may become self-conscious about the changing shape of their bodies. Too often, images of thin celebrities and models make children think that they must be thin to be beautiful.

Preteens may experience an unhealthy preoccupation with food and thinness. They see themselves as overweight when they really are not. This, along with other factors, can put preteens at risk for developing an eating disorder. An **eating disorder** is a serious pattern of overeating or restrictive eating. Eating disorders can have a devastating effect on the body and can even lead to death. For more information about eating disorders, see page 462.

**Figure 16.1 Average Heights and Weights—Ages 7–12**

**Caption Answer** The average heights are the same at ages nine and ten.

**Discussion** As a class, calculate the ratio of a 7-year-old boy's height to his weight. (about 0.94) Then calculate a 12-year-old boy's height-to-weight ratio. (about 0.66) Ask students: What generalization can you make based on the changes in this ratio? What does this tell you about boys' bodies? (The ratio becomes smaller as they get older. It tells you that their bodies are filling out, and, if the boy is in good shape, the body is becoming more muscular.)

## Figure 16.2 Organized Sports

Children typically learn team sports in groups and often compete against others. *Why is it more important for children to play for fun than to play to simply win?*

*Team sports give children the opportunity to have fun, be physically active, and learn teamwork and other skills. Individual sports, such as swimming, provide some of the same benefits.*

**Appropriate Sports** Children should only play sports for which they have the physical maturity.

**Play for Fun** Children benefit more when they are encouraged to play for fun and for individual skill development, rather than playing just to win. Look for a coach with this attitude.

**Good Sportsmanship** Respect for other players and the game should be one of the most important lessons a child learns.

**Good Days and Bad Days** Prepare children for both failure and success in sports.

Section 16.1   Growth and Development from Seven to Twelve   **455**

## Figure 16.2 Organized Sports

**Caption Answer** They are more likely to enjoy physical activity, and to keep it up throughout their lives. It also promotes good sportsmanship and makes it easier to deal with losses.

**Discussion** Have students look at the last photo in this figure. Then ask: Have you ever heard the expression "Life isn't fair." Do you agree or disagree with this statement? How is preparing a child for both wins and losses related to this expression? (Children need to learn that they will have both wins and losses in life and that these are not an indication of their self-worth.)

## Section 16.1

### Assess

**Quiz**

Ask students to answer the following questions:

1. Describe two factors that might influence an eleven-year-old's body image. (Possible answers: Sudden changes in the child's body, such as a growth spurt or the development of body hair, and unrealistic images of celebrities or models that they think they must emulate.)

2. What factor determines a child's ultimate height more—nutrition or heredity? (Heredity is a more important factor than nutrition.)

3. Why is it important that children see physical activity as fun? (They are more likely to be physically active throughout their lives if they enjoy it.)

### Reteach

**W Writing Support**
**Advertisement**

**Learn to Be Part of a Team** Have students write an advertisement for a workshop that teaches preteens how to become team players. Tell students to list specific skills the workshop will teach and also emphasize the importance of being a productive member of a team. (Refer to p. 450 to review the tips on writing advertisements. Students' advertisements will vary, but should focus on the skills that will be taught at the workshop and the value in learning to be a team player. Skills might include sportsmanship or cooperation.)

**455**

### Reteach *cont.*

### U Universal Access

**Gifted Learners** Discuss that precocious puberty occurs when a girl experiences the onset of puberty before eight years or a boy experiences it before nine years. Instruct students to research the effect early menarche (first menstrual period) in girls has on their lifetime risk of developing breast cancer and other possible health problems. Have students write a report presenting their findings. (Students should write a report discussing how the earlier a girl begins menstruating, the greater her chances of developing certain types of cancer, including breast and ovarian cancer.)

**N C L B** **NCLB** Activity correlated to Science standards.

### Science in Action

**Puberty and Television**

Students' reports will vary, but students should conclude their reports with their opinions on whether or not melatonin production can be increased by television watching. Research has shown that children who did not watch television for just one week had a 30 percent increase in their melatonin levels. Lower melatonin levels delay the onset of puberty. Some researchers think that light and radiation from television screens may disturb the production of melatonin.

---

**N C L B**

### Science in Action

**Puberty and Television**

Melatonin is a hormone that causes drowsiness. Researchers have found that when children do not watch television, their bodies produce more melatonin. This is linked to puberty starting earlier.

**Procedure**

Conduct research to learn more about the link between a child's melatonin levels and the amount of time spent watching television.

**Analysis**

Prepare an oral report explaining what you have learned from your research. End your report with your opinion as to whether watching television can cause children to enter puberty earlier.

**NSES C** Develop understanding of the behavior of organisms.

## Permanent Teeth

Primary teeth are the first set of teeth formed. Most children lose all of their primary teeth between the ages of five and thirteen, and most of the permanent teeth appear at this time, too. Permanent teeth are the second set of teeth formed. There are 32 permanent teeth. As mentioned in Chapter 13, the first permanent teeth to emerge are the set of molars that appear around the age of six. Around age twelve, a second set of molars emerges behind the first set. A third set of molars, called the wisdom teeth, appears later. The last four teeth appear between the ages of 17 and 21.

## Puberty

Puberty usually occurs between the ages of nine and sixteen. Researchers believe that the start of puberty is related to heredity as well as nutritional and environmental factors. On average, however, puberty starts at about the age of ten for girls and about one to two years later for boys. Significant physical changes trigger

---

the onset of puberty. The pituitary gland, found in the brain, begins sending out hormones that cause a number of profound physical changes in the body.

In both boys and girls, a significant growth spurt occurs during puberty. Children gain 25 percent of their total adult height through this growth spurt. Hair appears under the arms and in the pubic area for males and females. Sweat and oil glands become more active, and a child can begin to experience body odor and acne.

### Boys

In boys, facial hair begins to appear, and the voice deepens during puberty. Sometimes the deepening does not take place smoothly, and a boy's voice may occasionally crack, or change tones. This is due to the growth of the larynx and vocal cords. A boy's shoulders broaden, and his muscles grow larger.

### Girls

Girls typically experience more profound changes at puberty. Their breasts begin to enlarge, their waist narrows, and their hips widen. The sexual organs develop and become capable of releasing mature eggs. Most girls begin to have menstrual periods about two years after puberty begins. **Menstruation** is the monthly cycle in which an egg is released and the uterus prepares for a

**U**

### THE DEVELOPING BRAIN

**Fine Motor Skills**

Fine motor skills are skills that involve the refined use of small muscles. It is possible to work on one's fine motor skills with activities that teach the brain to control hand and finger movements to a high degree. One such activity is typing. The more a person practices typing, the better his or her fine motor skills will become. This is why learning to type often involves performing routine drills over and over again.

**Science Inquiry** Typing can help develop fine motor skills. What other activities do you think could help in this development?

---

### THE DEVELOPING BRAIN

**Fine Motor Skills**
**Science Inquiry** Answers will vary, but might include playing video games and musical instruments, and manipulating small objects, such as putting together jigsaw puzzles.

For more information and activities, see *The Developing Brain* guide and eTransparencies.

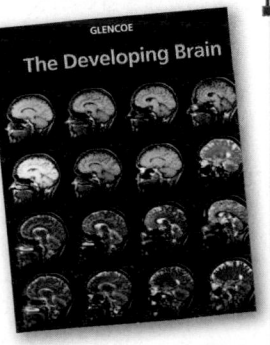
GLENCOE
The Developing Brain

possible pregnancy. Girls' menstrual periods may be irregular at first, and not occur every month. Some girls experience discomfort and cramping with menstrual periods.

✓ **Reading Check** **Explain** Why are preteen girls often taller than the boys in their class?

## Motor Skills

In the years from seven to twelve, a child's motor skills improve greatly. As the body matures, most children experience the following:

- Greater muscle strength
- Faster reaction time for responding to a stimulus, such as catching a ball
- Improved precision in activities such as balancing and aiming
- Greater speed
- Increased flexibility for bending and stretching easily

Thanks to all these more developed skills, children at these ages enjoy active play. Some take lessons to learn to swim and dance, and participate in gymnastics. Team sports are popular. Many children this age will prefer sports that use their improved motor skills, such as skating or bicycling, over simpler activities such as running or jumping.

With the increase in muscular strength comes more muscle control. Hand-eye coordination improves and both gross and fine motor skills become easier and smoother. More complex tasks become possible. For example, catching a baseball is a challenge for a seven-year-old, but a ten-year-old can manage it quite easily. Playing computer games can help children improve their fine motor skills. However, parents should still limit a child's time with computer games due to the impact on brain development.

Fine motor skills development is also evident in children's abilities to play musical instruments, do arts and crafts, and even writing. There is an obvious improvement in handwriting between five and seven years. And by eight, children start writing in script. As with any skill, motor skills improve with practice.

---

## Section 16.1 — After You Read

### Review Key Concepts

1. **Explain** how a growth spurt affects a child's body during puberty. Why do children sometimes feel awkward at this stage?
2. **Describe** the benefits a child can gain from participating in sports.

### Practice Academic Skills

 **English Language Skills**

3. Pretend you write an advice column for children and teens. Write an encouraging response to a letter from an eleven-year-old boy who is bothered by being the shortest student in his class.

**Mathematics**

4. Use the information found in Figure 16.1 to create a line graph showing the average height of boys and girls from ages seven to twelve. Your chart should contain two lines, one for boys and one for girls.

> **NCTE 5** Use different writing process elements to communicate effectively.

> **NCTM Number and Operations** Understand numbers, ways of representing numbers, relationships among numbers, and number systems.

**Check Your Answers** Check your answers at this book's Online Learning Center at **glencoe.com**.

---

## Section 16.1 — After You Read

**Review Key Concepts**

1. A growth spurt means that certain parts of the body grow rapidly in a short period of time. Children may feel awkward because one part of the body has grown faster than other parts.
2. Participating in sports helps children develop muscles, motor skills, and hand-eye coordination. It also helps them learn to be part of a team.

**Practice Academic Skills**

3. Students should write an encouraging letter explaining that eleven-year-olds vary greatly in height mainly because they enter puberty at different ages. Many experience growth spurts during which they quickly catch up.
4. Line graphs should accurately reflect the data found in Figure 16.1.

---

## Section 16.1

✓ **Reading Check**

**Explain** Preteen girls are often taller than boys because they typically go through puberty earlier.

## Assess

### Study Tools

Have students go to the Online Learning Center at **glencoe.com**:

- Take the **Practice Test**.
- Download **Study-to-Go** content.

Use the **Student Activity Workbook** for additional practice.

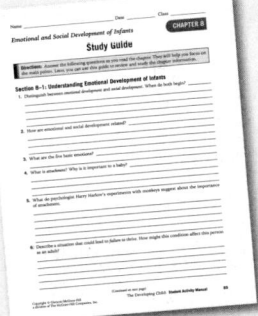

## Close

### Culminating Activity

**Displaying Different Emotions** Have students create a list of similarities and differences in the ways in which boys and girls mature between seven and twelve. (Similarities: Both increase in height and weight and their sweat and oil glands become more active. Differences: Boys develop facial hair and deeper voices; girls develop breasts, narrower waists and broader hips, and may begin menstruating.)

 **NCLB** connects academic correlations to book content.

## Section 16.2

# Caring for Children from Seven to Twelve

## FOCUS

### Bell Ringer Activity

**Changing Needs**
Have students imagine that they are 11 years old. Remind students of what they have learned about the physical changes a pre-teen is going through. As a class, create a list of ways in which the preteen's needs are changing. Encourage the class to discuss ways in which parents and teachers might be able to meet these needs.

## Preteaching
### Vocabulary

Write the term *sedentary activity* on the board. Ask the students for synonyms for sedentary. (Examples might include inactive, deskbound, sitting, or stationary.) Then ask for antonyms. (Examples might include active, vigorous, vivacious, or energetic.)

**Professional Development**

**Mini Clip**
**ELL: Vocabulary Activities**

Students practice vocabulary using synonyms, antonyms.

## Graphic Organizer

The Graphic Organizer is also on the TeacherWorks CD.

(Graphic Organizers should list grains, vegetables, fruits, milk, and meat and beans.)

**NCLB** connects academic correlations to book content.

## Reading Guide

### Before You Read

**Take Breaks** It is important to take frequent study breaks. They allow your brain time to process what you have already covered and get ready to remember new information.

### Read to Learn
**Key Concepts**
- **List** the nine topics in the Dietary Guidelines for Americans.
- **Identify** five areas that contribute to overall physical health and wellness.

### Main Idea

The Dietary Guidelines for Americans and the USDA's MyPyramid Plan are helpful in meeting nutritional needs. Children need to stay active and learn to take care of their bodies.

### Content Vocabulary
◇ fiber
◇ MyPyramid
◇ sedentary activity
◇ sealant
◇ orthodontist

**Graphic Organizer** Go to this book's Online Learning Center at **glencoe.com** to print out this graphic organizer.

### Academic Vocabulary
You will find these words in your reading and on your tests. Use the glossary to look up their definitions if necessary.
- capacity
- suppress

### Graphic Organizer
As you read, look for the five food groups included in MyPyramid. Use a chart like the one shown to help organize your information.

| MyPyramid |
| --- |
| 1. |
| 2. |
| 3. |
| 4. |
| 5. |

### Academic Standards • • • • • • • • • • • • • • • • • • •

**English Language Arts**
**NCTE 7** Conduct research and gather, evaluate, and synthesize data to communicate discoveries.

**Science**
**NSES A** Develop abilities necessary to do scientific inquiry, understanding about scientific inquiry.

**Social Studies**
**NCSS V F Individuals, Groups, and Institutions**
Evaluate the role of institutions in furthering both continuity and change.

**NCTE** *National Council of Teachers of English*
**NCTM** *National Council of Teachers of Mathematics*

**NSES** *National Science Education Standards*
**NCSS** *National Council for the Social Studies*

**458** Chapter 16 Physical Development from Seven to Twelve

## Reading Guide

### Before You Read

Ask students: Are there specific foods that do not agree with you? Do you ever feel sluggish if you eat foods with too much sugar or fat? If so, why do you think this is? Discuss that our bodies require healthy foods to run efficiently.

### D Develop Concepts

**Main Idea** Discuss the main idea with the students. Ask students why it is important that children understand their nutritional needs at a young age. (The earlier children understand what is needed to meet their nutritional needs, the more likely they are to make healthy eating a permanent lifestyle.)

## Nutrition

During middle childhood and the pre-teen years, children experience tremendous physical and emotional growth. Good nutrition from a well-balanced diet is essential for growth, development, learning, and health. Children in this age group require good nutrition to grow, develop, learn in school, and feel their best. Such diets contain essential nutrients and a good balance of carbohydrates, fat, and protein. The Dietary Guidelines for Americans and the U.S. Department of Agriculture's MyPyramid Plan can help ensure that meals and snacks have the variety and amount of food that children need for a healthful diet.

### Dietary Guidelines

The Dietary Guidelines for Americans is a useful tool for children and adults. The guidelines present a comprehensive plan for incorporating nutritious foods and physical activity into daily life. They include 41 recommendations, grouped into the following nine topics:

- **Get enough nutrients within your calorie needs.** Everyone needs a certain amount of calories in a day. The amount each child needs will vary based on age, activity level, and current weight.
- **Maintain a healthy weight.** Parents should ask their doctor what a healthy weight range is for their child. Being overweight can cause many health problems both in childhood and later in life.
- **Be physically active every day.** Children and teens need at least one hour of physical activity most or all days of the week. Physical activity has both short-term and long-term health benefits for children.
- **Choose whole grains, fruits, vegetables, and milk.** Foods made from whole grains help form the foundation of a healthy diet. They provide fiber plus many nutrients. **Fiber** is an indigestible plant material that helps the digestive system work properly. Many children fail to get the recommended servings of fruits and vegetables. These foods contain essential vitamins and minerals, fiber, and other substances important for good health. It is important for young children to drink milk every day. It provides vitamins and minerals necessary for the developing bones and body systems.

**Nutrition at School**
School-age children have greater independence in choosing the foods they wish to eat during the day. *How can parents teach children to make healthy food choices?*

Section 16.2 Caring for Children from Seven to Twelve **459**

---

### ► Explore the Photo

**Caption Answer** Parents can teach them about balanced diets, fix meals that meet the Dietary Guidelines for Americans, and set an example by eating healthfully.

**Discussion** Discuss that no matter how nutritious a lunch is, it does no good if children will not eat it. Have students discuss ideas concerning how a school lunch program could encourage students to eat their lunches. (Answers will vary. Possible answer: the school might have students vote on a list of nutritious lunches and prepare those with the most votes. The school also should make certain the food is fresh and attractive looking.)

---

### Teach

**Discussion Starter**

**Energy Drinks and Nutrition**
Hold up several energy drinks that are currently on the market. Encourage students to discuss these drinks. Ask: Do you think it is healthier to drink one of these or to eat a well-balanced meal of vegetables, fruits, lean meat, and milk? Why or why not? (No drink can provide all the benefits of eating a well-balanced diet. For example, a drink cannot provide fiber or the sense of fullness one gets from eating foods such as grains, vegetables, and fruits. In addition, many energy drinks contain caffeine, which can lead to behavioral problems in children.)

**Professional Development**

**Mini Clip ELL: Previewing a Text**

A teacher previews a text with students.

### U Universal Access

**Verbal Learners** Tell students that some foods have been shown to have specific healing properties. Blueberries and fennel seeds, for instance, help end diarrhea, and garlic can lower blood pressure. Instruct students to work in groups to research more healing foods. They should then prepare an oral presentation on what they learn. (Groups should prepare an oral presentation in which they discuss the healing powers of specific foods. For example, black cherries have been shown to reduce inflammation and nuts such as walnuts have been shown to improve heart health.) **ELL**

### S Skill Practice

**Guided Practice**

**List Favorite Foods** Have students make a table that lists the five food groups in the left column. In the right column, students should list at least three foods that they like for each group. (Tables should list the five food groups along with examples of at least three foods in each group that the student likes.) **L1 ELL**

**Make a Matching Game** Instruct students to work in pairs to create a game that a child between ages seven and ten might enjoy playing. The game should have a board which contains squares representing each of the five food groups. In addition, there should be a stack of 20 to 30 cards. Each card contains a picture of a particular food, such as peanuts or squash. The player must place each card on the correct square on the board. (Students create a board games which requires the player to match 20 to 30 foods to their correct categories. Cards can be made using cut-out photos from magazines, hand-drawn pictures, or photos printed from a computer.) **L2 ELL**

**Create a Menu** Instruct students to interview a child age 7 through 12 to determine his or her food likes and dislikes. Students then should go to the MyPyramid Plan Web site to find out the quantity of food from each group the child should be eating. Students should then create a day's menu for the child, keeping likes and dislikes in mind. The menu should include three meals and at least two snacks. (Students should create a one-day menu for a 7- to 12-year-old that meets the MyPyramid guidelines and is appealing to the child.) **L3**

- **Limit fats and cholesterol.** You need to eat fats, but only in small amounts. No one needs a diet high in fatty or fried foods and snacks. Most fats that are eaten should come from fish, nuts, and vegetable oils, rather than from red meat sources.
- **Be choosy about carbohydrate foods.** Sugars and starches are carbohydrates. Children should get carbohydrates from sugar that is naturally present in fruit and milk. Foods with added sugar such as candy can lead to tooth decay.
- **Reduce sodium and increase potassium.** Sodium helps control body fluids. However, too much sodium is linked to high blood pressure, heart attack, and stroke. Choose and prepare foods and beverages with little added salt. Potassium is found in many fruits and vegetables.
- **Avoid alcoholic beverages.** Just as the mother should avoid alcohol when pregnant, a child should never be given alcohol. Even a taste can be harmful to a child's developing body.
- **Keep food safe.** Food needs to be properly stored and prepared to help avoid food-borne illness.

## MyPyramid

**MyPyramid** is a guide for healthful eating and active living that was developed by the U.S. Department of Agriculture (USDA). By entering information such as your age, weight, and activity level, the MyPyramid Web site will create a customized plan just for you! It shows how much and what kinds of foods you need each day. It also offers physical activity advice.

MyPyramid is divided into five food groups, plus an oils category. The five food groups include grains, vegetables, fruits, milk, and meat and beans. The meat and beans group is where you get your protein. Eating from all five food groups each day will ensure you get all the nutrients your body needs. This is especially important for children since their bodies are still developing.

### Making Food Choices

As children become more independent, they begin to make more of their own food choices. They may make or buy some of their own snacks and meals. Peers or the media may influence these choices, which often take place away from home. For example, Leah can choose from various foods offered at her

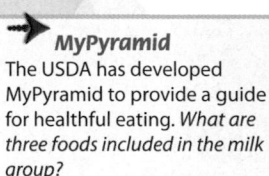

**MyPyramid**
The USDA has developed MyPyramid to provide a guide for healthful eating. *What are three foods included in the milk group?*

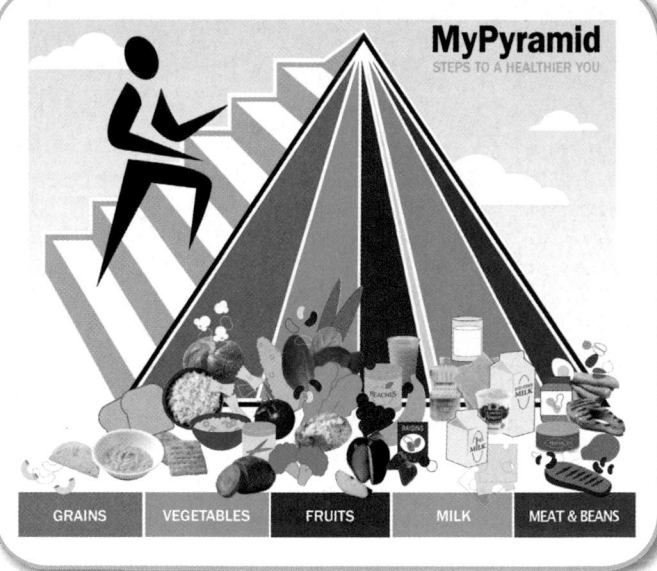

GRAINS   VEGETABLES   FRUITS   MILK   MEAT & BEANS

---

➥ **Explore the Photo**

**Caption Answer** Answers will vary but may include whole milk, yogurt, cheese, or ice cream.

**Discussion** Ask students: Why are fats not listed as a separate food group? (Because fats are contained in other foods, such as fish, nuts, meats, and some vegetables.) Why should fried foods be kept to a minimum? (They are high in calories with little nutritional value.)

## CULTURE MATTERS

### Lessons You Can Eat

Martin Luther King Jr. Middle School in Berkeley, California, is home to a program called the Edible Schoolyard. Alice Waters, a chef, had the idea of creating a garden so that students could learn to take care of plants and cook foods they helped grow. Today, students learn how to plant seedlings, identify ripe vegetables, and gather eggs from hens. Establishing a sense of competence is important for students this age. Assigning each student a daily job in the garden enables them to reach goals. Jobs can include activities such as chopping apples to be pressed for their juice. Students learn to take responsibility for their actions.

⭐ **Build Connections** *Do you think these children will be more likely to eat vegetables they have grown rather than ones bought in a store? Explain your answer.*

**NCSS V F Individuals, Groups, and Institutions** Evaluate the role of institutions in furthering both continuity and change.

school for lunch. When she brings a lunch from home, Leah sometimes trades the fruit from her packed lunch for cookies or chips.

Despite outside influences, family remains the primary influence on a child. Modeling good eating behavior is one of the best ways to teach a child good eating habits. Here are a few specific things that families can do:

- **Eat meals together.** Show by example that healthful eating habits include eating both the right foods and the right amounts.
- **Offer healthy choices.** Serve varied, well-balanced meals that are low in fat, sugar, and salt. Offer appealing choices from all the food groups.
- **Be prepared.** Stock the kitchen with a variety of nutritious foods for snacks.
- **Make treats special.** Limit sweets and deep-fried foods to special occasions.
- **Control portions.** Offer children smaller portions than an adult would eat. Allow and encourage children to stop eating when they feel full.
- **Serve dairy daily.** Make calcium-rich foods and beverages a part of a child's diet to help ensure strong bones.

### Starting the Day Right

Breakfast is an important meal for both children and adults. It provides the vital fuel that people need to begin the day. Researchers have found that children who eat breakfast have a greater **capacity**, or ability, for learning and participation. They also have a greater ability to concentrate, especially on tasks that require problem solving and creativity. Skipping breakfast can result in headaches, fatigue, and restless behavior, which interfere with classroom learning.

A healthy breakfast includes two servings from the grain group, one from the dairy group, and one from the fruit group. An example of a nutritious breakfast might include a bowl of cereal and a piece of fruit. National school breakfast programs help provide this nutrition and ensure that all children can begin the school day the right way.

### Eating Disorders

Most children go through periods when they rebel against what is served at mealtime. Many children sneak sugary treats from time to time. This is normal behavior. However, a

### U Universal Access

**Interpersonal Learners** Organize students into small groups. Each group should design a vegetable garden and then create a poster illustrating their design. The garden should contain the group members' favorite vegetables. Discuss that different colored vegetables often contain different types of nutrients, so students should design a colorful garden. Encourage students to look at seed catalogs to get ideas for additional vegetables. When students are done, place their designs where the entire class can view them. (Each group should design a garden that includes the group members' favorite vegetables. It also should contain other vegetables and have a wide range of colors.)

### C Critical Thinking

**Apply** Tell students to imagine they have just gotten their first summer job, which involves preparing meals for a family of five. The parents both work full-time and are concerned their three children, ages 4, 6, and 10, are not eating healthfully. The children are allowed to eat whatever they want and the family rarely eats together. Encourage students to discuss what they might do to improve the family's eating habits. (Suggestions might include: Discuss with the children what nutritious snacks they like and then buy those items instead of snacks high in fat and sugar, discuss with parents the importance of eating as a family, and make certain the children are not served portions larger than they require.)

## CULTURE MATTERS

### Lessons You Can Eat

**Discussion** Discuss with students that not all families can grow their own vegetables. Have students divide into small groups and discuss ways in which parents might be able to help their children become more involved in obtaining the family's food. Have each group report its ideas to the class. (Possible answers might include: They could visit a local farmer's market or go to an orchard to pick apples.)

**Building Connections** *Answers will vary. Students may say yes, because they will feel a connection to the vegetables that they have grown themselves.*

**Quiz**

Ask students to answer the following questions:

1. Why is it important to eat an adequate amount of fiber? (Fiber helps the digestive system work properly.)

2. Why should sodium be limited in the diet? (Excess sodium has been linked to high blood pressure, heart attack, and stroke.)

3. List three ways that families can teach children good eating habits. (Any three of the following: eat meals together, offer healthy choices, be prepared, make treats special, control portions, and serve dairy daily.)

### Reteach

**C₁ Critical Thinking**

**Compare and Contrast** How are anorexia nervosa, bulimia, and binge eating similar? How are they different? (Similarities: All are eating disorders in which the individual has difficulties handling food appropriately. Differences: In anorexia nervosa the person does not eat an adequate amount of food and becomes excessively thin whereas in bulimia the individual overeats but purges, and therefore remains thin. In binge eating the individual also overeats, but does not purge and therefore gains weight.)

✓ **Reading Check**

**Analyze** Research has shown that children who eat breakfast have a greater capacity for learning and participation, and a greater ability to concentrate.

**462**

---

small percentage of children begin to develop eating disorders. There are several types of eating disorders. The three main types include:

**C₁**
- **Anorexia Nervosa** This is an intense fear of weight gain distinguished by starvation techniques and severe weight loss. Symptoms can include fatigue, dizziness, refusal to eat, or excessive exercise.
- **Bulimia** Bulimia involves periods of out-of-control eating followed by purging the body of food, often through vomiting. Symptoms can include fatigue, scars on the hands, laxative use, and going to the bathroom after or during meals.
- **Binge Eating** This disorder includes periods of highly excessive eating, followed by weight gain. Symptoms can include eating to the point of pain, frequent dieting without weight loss, or hiding food.

Researchers believe that some children with eating disorders may be preoccupied with being thin due to a poor body image. Others might see people they admire display eating disorders and want to be like them. Some might have psychological problems, such as depression or low self-esteem. Many strive to please others and feel that food is the only thing they can control in their lives. Children with eating disorders need counseling from a trained professional. Parents should not hesitate to consult a professional if they notice unusual eating patterns or sudden weight gain or loss in their daughter or son. Also encourage children to tell a teacher or school counselor if they notice or suspect a problem in their friends.

✓ **Reading Check** **Analyze** Why is eating breakfast important for children?

## ♡ Parenting Skills

### How Can Parents Help an Overweight Child?

Parents of an overweight child are often concerned about the health and emotional issues their child may face. They may be unsure of how to help. Here are some ways parents can offer support and guidance.

- ☞ **Consult with the child's doctor.** Ask for guidance on providing a healthy diet.
- ☞ **Focus on health rather than weight.** Do not make losing weight the main issue. Involve the whole family in a healthy eating plan.
- ☞ **Make a variety of healthy foods available.** Giving children choices makes them more willing to try new things.
- ☞ **Encourage regular physical activity and limit television viewing.** Encourage the child to participate in physical activities he or she enjoys. Be active daily and plan activities the whole family can participate in.
- ☞ **Offer unconditional love and support.** Caregivers should make it clear that the child is loved and accepted at any weight.

**Take Charge** Imagine you are the parent of an overweight child. Write a list of five steps you plan to take to encourage your family to eat a healthier diet.

---

## ♡ Parenting Skills

### How Can Parents Help an Overweight Child?

Tell students that 11-year-old Emily's parents are concerned that she is overweight. They are considering sending her to a camp that helps children with weight difficulties. Discuss whether this is a good idea. (Students' responses will vary. Possible response: It may show Emily that her parents care about her health.)

**Take Charge**

Lists will vary. Possible steps: reduce the amount of junk food in the house; eat out less; encourage everyone to help in preparing meals; and begin growing some of your own food.

**Sedentary Activities**
Television and video games have significantly reduced the amount of physical activity among children. *How can parents encourage children to be more physically active?*

# Physical Health and Wellness

Everyone wants to help children be as physically healthy as possible. Being physically active can greatly increase overall health. Establishing healthy habits now will help children be healthier adults. Getting enough sleep, taking care of your body and teeth, and following safety rules are also important.

## Physical Fitness

Children today are less likely to walk or ride their bikes to school than were their parents. Many children are less fit than they should be. They run the risk of becoming set in a pattern of inactivity that could result in health problems, especially when they are older.

One reason for the decline in fitness levels is that children spend hours every day in sedentary activities. A **sedentary activity** is an activity that involves little exercise, such as watching television or playing computer and electronic games. The hours children spend in front of a screen take time away from physical activity. Parents and other caregivers make the best role models for healthy living by limiting their own television viewing and their children's time in front of screens, and by joining children in physical activities.

To promote physical fitness, parents should look for a variety of developmentally appropriate activities that their children might enjoy. It is good to include activities that can be continued later in life, such as hiking, biking, swimming, dancing, skating, basketball, or tennis. Children need at least an hour of physical activity each day. Parents who remain physically active are role models for their children.

> ### { Expert Advice... }
>
> *"Physical growth that occurs during this time is more rapid than at any time since infancy. Besides growing bigger and taller, the maturing child begins to develop bodily characteristics that distinguish the male and female adult."*
>
> — Virginia K. Molgaard, family life specialist, Iowa State University

Section 16.2 Caring for Children from Seven to Twelve **463**

### C₂ Critical Thinking

**Evaluate** Remind students that playing video games has been linked to childhood obesity. Ask students: How many of you have played video games which require you to be physically active, such as playing virtual tennis or bowling? Encourage students to discuss whether they think these games can reduce obesity. What advantages might these games have over playing traditional team sports? What disadvantages? (Answers will vary. Advantages might include that they can play the game whenever they want and are not dependent on the weather. Disadvantages might include they do not get the social interaction of playing with others and do not learn about sportsmanship.)

### R Reading Strategy

**Use Context to Determine Meaning** Read aloud the first sentence in the first full paragraph of the right column. Ask students: Based on its context, what do you think the term *developmentally appropriate* means? (It refers to activities that the child is capable of performing based on his or her age and physical and intellectual abilities.)

**Professional Development**

**Mini Clip Reading: Fluency Development**

A teacher uses instructional strategies to help develop her students' reading fluency.

---

**Explore the Photo**

**Caption Answer** Answers will vary. Parents can participate in activities, such as bike-riding or hiking with their children. They can also continue to be physically active themselves.

**Discussion** Ask students: If you were a parent, would you restrict the amount of time your children could spend playing video games? Why or why not? (Responses will vary, but students should give specific reasons for their responses. Possible response: Yes, I would restrict the time because I would want my children to be physically active.)

**Reteach** cont.

**C₁ Critical Thinking**

**Analyze** Organize students into small groups. Have each group's members share a time when they were between seven and twelve years old and felt their personal safety was endangered. Also have students explain how the situation was resolved. Then instruct them to discuss whether they would respond differently to the situation if it were to happen today. (Students should discuss a situation when they were between seven and twelve and felt their personal safety was endangered. They then should discuss whether they would respond differently to the situation today.)

**U Universal Access**

**Musical Learners** Have students write a song that teaches children ages seven to nine about personal safety. For example, the song may discuss the importance of wearing a bike helmet or walking to and from school in groups. Students may want to set their lyrics to the tune of a familiar children's song. Encourage volunteers to present their songs to the class (either individually or with a group of classmates.) (Students should write a song that teaches personal safety to seven- to nine-year-olds.)

## Figure 16.3 Personal Safety from Ages 7–12

As children spend more time away from home and family, they are exposed to more dangers. *How would you reassure a child who is constantly concerned about personal safety?*

| Safe Practice | Examples |
|---|---|
| **Keep doors locked when home alone.** | ✤ Never open the door to a stranger when home alone, even to someone who is wearing a uniform. |
| **Wear protective gear.** | ✤ Never engage in sports without the proper protective gear, such as a bike helmet or shin guards.  |
| **Know how to get help in an emergency.** | ✤ Know what constitutes an emergency. <br> ✤ Know how to dial 911 in an emergency. <br> ✤ Practice by playing the "What If?" game. For example: "What if you woke up at night and smelled smoke?" |
| **Pay attention to traffic.**  | ✤ Cross streets at crosswalks only after checking for oncoming cars. <br> ✤ Obey any restrictions concerning which streets may be crossed. |
| **Stay away from strangers.** | ✤ Never get into a stranger's car or go near a stranger. <br> ✤ Run and scream if you feel threatened. |
| **Walk in groups.**  | ✤ Older children can accompany younger children when they walk to school. |
| **Trust your feelings.** | ✤ If someone, including an adult, makes you feel afraid or uncomfortable, get away and tell a trusted adult. |

## Figure 16.3 Personal Safety from Ages 7–12

**Caption Answer** Answers may vary. You can explain to students that they can go a long way toward protecting themselves by following the safety rules you have taught them.

**Discussion** Ask students: Have you ever been in a situation in which you felt uncomfortable when you were around a specific person? Did you listen to those feelings? What should a child do if he or she feels uncomfortable when around a specific person? (Answers to the first two questions will vary. Answer to last question: The child should avoid the person and immediately tell a trusted adult about his or her concerns.)

## Sleep

Most children get busier as they get older. During the evening, school-age children have homework to complete, and perhaps a karate class or a music lesson. Getting to bed on time can be a challenge, but experts recommend enforcing a bedtime for school-age children. The National Sleep Foundation recommends that children this age get from ten to eleven hours of sleep each night. It helps their performance in school, as well as their mood.

## Caring for Teeth

By age seven, children may need reminders, but they can brush their own teeth at least twice a day and floss daily. Additional brushings may be needed if very sugary or gummy food is eaten. A dental checkup and cleaning at least once a year is recommended to help prevent tooth decay. Sometimes fluoride treatments are given. Pediatric dentists can help ease fears about visiting the dentist.

Tooth decay occurs when bacteria in the mouth produce acids that break down tooth enamel and expose the softer parts of the tooth. Bacteria produce acids from sugars that a person eats or drinks. As children get older, they have more access to sugary foods and drinks. These have negative health effects and are linked to tooth decay. For these reasons, sugary foods and sweet drinks should always be limited in a child's diet.

To prevent tooth decay, some dentists place a sealant on children's teeth. A **sealant** is a thick plastic coating. Dentists usually place these sealants on permanent molars. Molars are teeth that are especially adapted to grinding food. Sealants have proven to be an effective way to help prevent decay.

Sometimes permanent teeth do not come in straight. This can sometimes cause problems with the way teeth fit together. If so, a dentist may refer the child to an orthodontist. An **orthodontist** is a dental specialist who concentrates on fixing irregularities of the teeth. The orthodontist can determine whether the child would benefit by having braces, separators, or retainers to straighten the teeth.

**Dealing with Acne**

Jerome started going through puberty before his friends. He began feeling self-conscious about his acne. He scrubbed his face every day, but the acne persisted. Finally he decided to ask his parents for help. His father revealed that he, too, had acne as a teen and he knew how it felt to be self-conscious about it. Jerome's dad suggested cleaning his face gently, then using a drying lotion at night. Jerome's mom suggested visiting his doctor to ask about treatments that could help prevent acne from forming. Jerome felt relieved that there might be a way to minimize the problem.

 *Write About It* Write a script of a parent talking with his or her child who has acne. In addition to providing help, be sure the parent explains why the child is having acne at this time of life.

## Personal Hygiene

Seven- to ten-year-olds are often unconcerned about good hygiene. This is not because they want to be dirty. They just cannot be bothered to take the time to bathe or shower. They would rather spend their time playing games or reading books. To prevent battles over bathing, there are several things parents or caregivers can do:

- **Focus on the essentials.** Make sure that the child washes hands before eating and after using the bathroom. Brushing teeth should be done daily.
- **Give choices when possible.** Let the child choose between showering and taking a bath. Give a choice of shampoo. Let the child choose the day's outfit. Children, like adults, respond well to having control over decisions that affect them.
- **Send positive messages.** Comment on how refreshing a shower is, or how relaxing and warm a bath feels. This signals to children that bathing and showering bring benefits besides simply getting clean.

## Reteach *cont.*

### C₂ Critical Thinking
**Understand Cause and Effect**
Ask students to brainstorm reasons a child age seven to twelve might have difficulty getting to sleep at night. Also ask them to propose ways in which parents might be able to help the child deal with these difficulties. (Possible answers: fear of nightmares, or worry about school. Ways to cope with problems will vary. For example, the parent might help the child with homework for classes that are causing concern.)

### W Writing Support
**Advertisement**
**Hygiene Products** Tell students to imagine that they are the director of marketing for a new line of hygiene products aimed at 7- to 10-year-olds. Have students create an attractive, persuasive advertisement for their product line. The ad should be designed to be placed in a preteen magazine. Encourage students to use both text and graphics in their ads and to make them colorful. Ask for volunteers to share their finished ads with the class. (Refer to p. 450 to review the tips on writing advertisements. Students' ads will vary, but should be colorful, include both text and graphics, and explain how their products can be helpful to children.)

**Write About It** Scripts will vary but should discuss accepted methods of dealing with acne, such as gentle cleansing or using a drying lotion. In addition, they should explain that the child is experiencing acne because when he or she enters puberty, the oil glands become more active. Acne is a sign of maturing.

**Study Tools**

Have students go to the Online Learning Center at **glencoe.com**:

- Take the **Practice Test**.
- Download **Study-to-Go** content.

Use the **Student Activity Workbook** for additional practice.

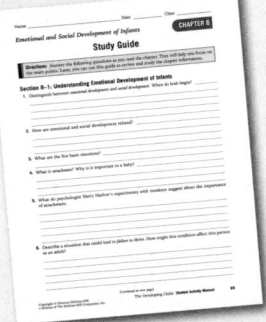

### Close

**Culminating Activity**

**Plan** Have students list two ways they can share what they have learned about healthful eating with their families. Ask for volunteers to share their lists. (Lists will vary but may include limiting the amounts of oils eaten or eating more whole grains.)

 **NCLB** connects academic correlations to book content.

---

The lack of interest in hygiene often changes around age ten. At about this time, the physical changes of puberty increase the need for cleanliness. With puberty, the body produces more sweat, so preteens may develop body odor. In addition to a daily bath or shower, they may need to start using deodorant or antiperspirant. Preteens often need to change into fresh clothes after physical activity. Parents should help preteens make this transition, or change. Sometimes children are unaware of body odor. Parents can help by offering a change of clothes, rather than pointing out the child's smell. Often, preteens will become more interested in choosing their own soap or shampoo, based on the scent.

During puberty, the oil glands in the pores of the skin produce more oil. At times the production can be excessive, resulting in acne and a greasy appearance to the hair. These problems usually go away over time, as the body's production of skin oil goes down. Encourage preteens to remedy the problem. Acne-prone skin should be washed twice a day with warm water and mild soap to help **suppress**, or control, outbreaks. Excessive scrubbing can make acne worse. For extreme cases, there are prescription medications that can be used. Also, shampoo and conditioner are available that are formulated for oily hair.

## Checkups and Vaccines

Annual checkups can help prevent illnesses. Before starting fifth grade children typically receive a tetanus and diphtheria booster, and sometimes an MMR booster. MMR stands for measles, mumps, and rubella. A booster is a shot that increases the effectiveness of a previous immunization. Chicken pox and hepatitis B vaccinations are also strongly recommended before the age of thirteen. Children should also receive annual flu shots. This is especially true for children with weak immune systems or chronic lung conditions, such as asthma.

---

## Section 16.2 After You Read

### Review Key Concepts

1. **Describe** three eating disorders.
2. **Explain** why plenty of physical activity is vital for seven- to twelve-year-olds. What is the minimum length of time that should be spent on daily exercise?

### Practice Academic Skills

 **English Language Arts**

3. Talk to five adults about what they did between the ages of seven and twelve to stay physically active. Write a paragraph summarizing what you learn. Also discuss which of those activities children still enjoy today and why you think they are still popular.

> **NCTE 7** Conduct research and gather, evaluate, and synthesize data to communicate discoveries.

 **Science**

4. Conduct research to learn about medical treatments for acne that does not respond to over-the-counter medications. Write a report discussing at least three of the most common treatments. Also discuss any advantages or disadvantages of each type of treatment.

> **NSES A** Develop abilities necessary to do scientific inquiry, understanding about scientific inquiry.

**Check Your Answers** Check your answers at this book's Online Learning Center at **glencoe.com**.

---

### Review Key Concepts

1. Anorexia nervosa is an intense fear of weight gain characterized by starvation techniques and severe weight loss. Bulimia involves periods of out-of-control eating followed by purging the body of food. Binge eating means periods of highly excessive eating, followed by weight gain.

2. Children need physical activity to stay healthy, and need to be taught to continue exercising when they are older to avoid health problems. At least one hour of physical activity daily is recommended.

### Practice Academic Skills

3. Students should write a paragraph summarizing what they learn from five adults about the physical activities they engaged in from ages seven to twelve. In their paragraphs, students should also list those activities that are still popular and explain why they think these activities have remained popular.

4. Students reports will vary, but should explain at least three common treatments, along with each one's success rate.

## Chapter Summary

Most children grow steadily during middle childhood. Some may become sensitive about their body image, which can put them at risk for eating disorders. Good dental hygiene practices are important. The Dietary Guidelines for Americans and the USDA's MyPyramid Plan can be helpful in developing good eating habits and are essential for good health. Increased interest in personal hygiene often begins during the preteen years. Annual checkups and vaccinations help to prevent illnesses.

## Vocabulary Review

1. Create multiple-choice test questions for each content and academic vocabulary term.

### Content Vocabulary
◇ growth spurt (p. 453)
◇ puberty (p. 453)
◇ scoliosis (p. 454)
◇ body image (p. 454)
◇ eating disorder (p. 454)
◇ menstruation (p. 456)
◇ fiber (p. 459)
◇ MyPyramid (p. 460)
◇ sedentary activity (p. 463)
◇ sealant (p. 465)
◇ orthodontist (p. 465)

### Academic Vocabulary
■ profound (p. 453)
■ ultimate (p. 454)
■ capacity (p. 461)
■ suppress (p. 465)

## Review Key Concepts

2. **Describe** the two significant stages that occur between ages seven and twelve.
3. **Explain** why children's motor skills improve between the ages of seven and twelve.
4. **List** the nine topics in the Dietary Guidelines for Americans.
5. **Identify** five areas that contribute to overall physical health and wellness.

## Critical Thinking

6. **Predict** What might happen to a child who is not taught the importance of a balanced diet?
7. **Make Inferences** Why do you think eating disorders are developing at a younger age?
8. **Contrast** How are personal hygiene needs different for a preteen and a seven- to ten-year-old?
9. **Analyze** Why do you think preteens may not get enough sleep?
10. **Apply** Suppose that you help coach a team of young athletes. How might you educate parents about the importance of being a positive influence at sporting events?

Chapter 16   Physical Development from Seven to Twelve   **467**

## Content and Academic Vocabulary Review

1. Students should write multiple-choice questions with possible answers for each vocabulary term.

## Review Key Concepts

2. Middle childhood is from ages seven through ten. This is when children build on the growth and skills that began in early childhood. The preteen years are ages eleven and twelve. This is the period when children enter puberty.

3. During this time, children's muscular strength increases, leading to greater muscle control and improved motor skills.

4. The nine topics are: get enough nutrients within your calorie needs; maintain a healthy weight; be physically active every day; choose whole grains, fruits, vegetables, and milk; limit fats and cholesterol; be choosy about carbohydrate foods; reduce sodium and increase potassium; avoid alcoholic beverages; and keep food safe.

5. Five areas that contribute to overall physical health and wellness are physical fitness, sleep, caring for teeth, personal hygiene, and checkups and vaccines.

## Critical Thinking

6. Answers will vary. They may lack energy for physical activity. They might not be healthy because their bodies are lacking necessary nutrients.

7. Answers will vary. Children are exposed to the media more and at earlier ages.

8. Seven- to ten-year-olds typically do not experience the increased activity of sweat and oil glands that occurs at puberty. Younger children need to take regular baths or showers and wash their hands. Preteens need to wash regularly as well as wear deodorant and wash their faces twice a day.

9. Possible answers might include that they are busy with activities such as sports and homework, they prefer to watch television or play video games rather than sleep, or that their parents do not enforce bedtime rules.

10. Answers will vary. You might tell parents that having a positive attitude about sports, whether children win or lose, will help children learn that being physically active is fun.

## Family & Community Connections

**11.** Students should learn about a physical activity enjoyed by children from a specific culture and than demonstrate it for the class.

## Health Skills

**12.** Reports will vary but should explain that people with celiac disease cannot tolerate gluten. Foods with gluten include wheat, barley, and rye. Possible substitutes are rice, corn, millet, buckwheat, and quinoa.

## Observation Skills

**13.** Answers will vary. The teacher might find out what kinds of activities interest the children and obtain the needed equipment for them.

## Real-World Skills

**14.** Checklists will vary but should include items such as brush teeth at least twice a day, bathe, wash hair, and use antiperspirant. Dialogue should use realistic language and explain the importance of each item on the list.

**15.** Slide shows will vary but should explain how to properly brush and floss teeth.

**16.** Charts will vary. Possible snacks include five crackers with cheese (50 cents), four fruit slices (50 cents), or popcorn (30 cents).

**NCLB** Activity correlated to English Language Arts standards.

---

## Family & Community Connection

**11.** **Children's Games** Choose a cultural group, such as Hispanic or Chinese, to which some people in your community belong. Interview a member of this group or conduct research to learn about games the children in this culture play. Focus on games that involve physical activity. Demonstrate one of the games to your class.

## Health Skills

**12.** **Food Intolerances** Many people have problems tolerating certain foods. Imagine that you have just learned you have celiac disease. Conduct research to learn about celiac disease and write a report explaining it. Include in the report a list of the foods you cannot eat and a list of foods you can use as substitutes.

## Observation Skills

**13.** **Encourage Physical Activity** Physical activity can help children remain strong and healthy. It can also help improve their self-image. Parents and teachers can be central in helping children achieve an active lifestyle.

**Procedure** Observe preteens at a playground. Note how many are engaged in active play or sports. Also note how many are just sitting and talking.

**Analysis** Write a report in which you discuss the percentage of preteens that were inactive. Then present ideas on how a teacher might encourage these less active children to engage in more physical activity.

> **NCTE 7** Conduct research and gather, evaluate, and synthesize data to communicate discoveries.

## Real-World Skills

**Problem-Solving**

**14.** **Encourage Good Hygiene** Imagine you are the parent of a 12-year-old boy. You think your son should pay more attention to his personal hygiene. Create a checklist of items to help him remember all the tasks he needs to complete each day. Then write a dialogue in which you present the checklist and explain why his hygiene is important.

**Technology Skills**

**15.** **Create a Slide Show** Suppose you need to teach seven-year-olds how to care for their teeth. Use application software to create a slide show that explains how to brush and floss teeth. The slide show should include art and language appropriate for seven-year-olds.

**Financial Literacy**

**16.** **Plan Snacks** Imagine that you work at an after-school program for seven- to ten-year-olds. Plan five nutritious snacks for the children. Research the cost of each planned snack. Each snack should cost no more than 50 cents per child. Create a chart listing the snacks and the cost of each.

**Additional Activities** For additional activities, go to this book's Online Learning Center at **glencoe.com**.

## Academic Skills

**17.** Letters will vary. Vaccines have proven to be one of the greatest victories in public health and must be licensed by the U.S. Food and Drug Administration, which extensively tests them for safety.

The *Early Childhood Observations CD* offers additional lessons with videos to build students' observation skills.

**Part 1:** Learning to Observe
**Part 2:** How Children Develop
**Part 3:** Working With Young Children
**Part 4:** Extended Observations
**Part 5:** Resources and Answer File

## Academic Skills

 **English Language Arts**

**17. Write a Letter** Imagine that you are a school nurse. A group of parents is stating that childhood vaccines can cause health problems. Write a letter to the editor of your local newspaper in which you explain why vaccines are safe and vital to the health of children. Conduct research to learn facts to include in your letter.

> **NCTE 7** Conduct research and gather, evaluate, and synthesize data to communicate discoveries.

 **Mathematics**

**18. Take a Hike** It is often difficult to fit family time into busy lifestyles. A family walk is a great way for parents and children to interact and talk. Suppose a family goes for a 1½ hour hike. According to the trail map, the hike was 2.3 miles round trip. How fast was the family walking?

> **Math Concept** **Rate** A rate is a ratio of two measurements having different kinds of units, such as miles per hour.

**Starting Hint** Divide the total distance (2.3 miles) by the total time (1½ hours). To convert the fraction to a decimal, first write it as an improper fraction (³⁄₂), then divide the numerator (3) by the denominator (2).

 For math help, go to the Math Appendix at the back of the book.

> **NCTM Algebra** Use mathematical models to represent and understand quantitative relationships.

 **Science**

**19. Evaluate a Child's Diet** The U.S. Department of Agriculture (USDA) has established guidelines for healthy eating for children. The MyPyramid Web site can provide guidelines based on a person's age, height, weight, and activity level.

**Procedure** Ask a preteen to keep track of all the food he or she eats for one day.

**Analysis** Go to the MyPyramid Web site to determine the dietary guidelines for the child. Create a chart that compares the child's diet to these guidelines.

> **NSES F** Students should develop understanding of personal and community health.

### Standardized Test Practice

**MULTIPLE CHOICE**
Carefully read the passage and then answer the question.

> Research has determined that eating trans fat raises low-density lipoprotein (LDL) levels in the blood. This increases the chances of getting coronary heart disease. Manufacturers make trans fat by adding hydrogen to vegetable oil. This increases the shelf life of the oil and stabilizes its flavor.

**20.** According to this passage, ingesting trans fats can _____.
 **a.** increase your chances of having diabetes
 **b.** make you obese
 **c.** increase your chances of having a heart attack
 **d.** lead to a vitamin deficiency

> **Test-Taking Tip** If you do not know the answer to a question, first cross off any choices you know are wrong. This will make it easier to evaluate the remaining ones.

### TECHNOLOGY Solutions

**Use these technology solutions to streamline chapter assessment!**

 **ExamView Assessment Suite** CD allows you to create and print out customized tests or ready-made unit and chapter tests, complete with answer keys.

 **TeacherWorks Plus** is an electronic lesson planner that provides instant access to complete teacher resources in one convenient package.

 **Online Learning Center** includes resources and activities for students and teachers.

---

**18.** 1.53 miles per hour (1½ = 3/2 = 1.5; 2.3 ÷ 1.5 = 1.53)

 **Professional Development**

**Mini Clip Math: Rates and Ratios**

Students collect and record sports statistics and manipulate them using ratios.

**19.** The student should create a chart listing the foods eaten by an eleven- or twelve-year-old over the period of one day and comparing this intake with the recommended daily guidelines on MyPyramid.

 **NCLB** connects academic correlations to book content.

### Standardized Test Practice

**20.** c. increase your chances of having a heart attack

**Test-Taking Tips** Tell students: If you are taking a test for a specific class, review any tests you have previously taken for that class. This will remind you of the types of questions the teacher asks.

**Multiple Choice Tests** Tell students to begin by reading the question. Then try to come up with the answer before reading the options. This way they are less likely to become confused by the incorrect options.

**STANDARDS BASED LESSON PLANNING** *The Developing Child* provides students with instruction and assessment in the following fundamental content areas:

## National Standards Correlations

| Standards | Pages |
|---|---|
| **12.1.1** Analyze physical, emotional, social, spiritual, and intellectual development. | 473–480, 482–489 |
| **12.1.3** Analyze current and emerging research about human growth and development, including research on brain development. | 478 |
| **12.2.1** Analyze the effect of heredity and environment on human growth and development. | 478 |
| **12.2.3** Analyze the effects of gender, ethnicity, and culture on individual development. | 480 |
| **12.3.2** Analyze the role of communication on human growth and development. | 484 |
| **12.3.3** Analyze the role of family and social services support systems in meeting human growth and development needs. | 490 |
| **15.2.1** Choose nurturing practices that support human growth and development. | 474, 478–479, 487 |
| **15.2.2** Apply communication strategies that promote positive self-esteem in family members. | 477, 484 |
| **15.2.3** Assess common practices and emerging research about discipline on human growth and development. | 488 |
| **15.3.1** Assess community resources and services available to families. | 490 |

**NO CHILD LEFT BEHIND** NCLB activities, information, and skills practice will help your students attain NCLB proficiency. Students will improve their abilities in the following academic standards areas:

## Academic Standards Correlations

| Discipline | Standard | Feature/Activity |
|---|---|---|
| **English Language Arts** | **NCTE 1** Read texts to acquire new information. | **Reading Guide (pp. 472, 481)** |
| | **NCTE 5** Use different writing process elements to communicate effectively. | **Writing Activity (p. 470)** **Academic Skills (p. 493)** |
| | **NCTE 12** Use language to accomplish individual purposes. | **After You Read (pp. 480, 489)** |
| **Mathematics** | **NCTM Measurement** Apply appropriate techniques, tools, and formulas to determine measurements. | **Academic Skills (p. 493)** |
| | **NCTM Number and Operations** Understand numbers, ways of representing numbers, relationships among numbers, and number systems. | **Math in Action (p. 485)** |
| **Science** | **NSES A** Develop abilities necessary to do scientific inquiry, understandings about scientific inquiry. | **Academic Skills (p. 493)** |
| **Social Studies** | **NCSS IV C Individual Development and Identity** Describe the ways family and other group and cultural influences contribute to the development of a sense of self. | **After You Read (p. 489)** |
| | **NCSS IV D Individual Development and Identity** Apply concepts, methods, and theories about the study of human growth and development, such as behavior, perception, and personality. | **After You Read (p. 480)** **Observation Skills (p. 492)** |

## Professional Development

**MINI CLIP VIDEO LIBRARY**
Targeted professional development is correlated throughout *The Developing Child*. **The McGraw-Hill Professional Development Mini Clip Video Library** provides teaching strategies to strengthen academic and learning skills. Log on to **glencoe.com**.

In this chapter, you will find these Mini Clips:
- **Reading** Vocabulary, p. 472
- **ELL** Reading Aloud, p. 479
- **ELL** Strategies for English Learners, p. 484
- **Reading** Modeling Reading Strategies, p. 487
- **Reading** Assessment in Standards-Based Instruction, p. 493

## Reading and Writing Strategies

**Writing Activity: Personal Narrative** (p. 470)
Students use writing tips to write about a specific time when they had to make new friends.

**Before You Read** (pp. 472, 481)
A pre-reading question or statement will help students make a personal connection to content.

**Graphic Organizer** (pp. 472, 481)
A visual tool will help students organize and remember new content.

**Reading Check** (pp. 474, 477, 485, 487)
A question allows students to make a quick comprehension self-check.

**After You Read** (pp. 480, 489)
Organize and process students' understanding of what they have read.

## Chapter Features

**Generalized Anxiety Disorder** (p. 475) Children with generalized anxiety disorder engage in extreme worry.

**Help a Child Work Through a Difficult Situation** (p. 477) Caring adults can help a child deal with difficulties in many ways.

**Stimulation Builds Competence** (p. 478) A stimulating environment helps children with mental tasks.

**Learning to Build Confidence** (p. 479) The messages a parent sends to a child can affect the child's level of confidence.

**Problem Solving** (p. 483) Good problem-solving skills helps children throughout their lives.

**The Cost of Child Delinquency** (p. 485) The most common offense in children younger than 13 is arson.

**Negative Peer Pressure** (p. 486) Problems can occur if friends try to get someone to go against his values.

**Teach a Child Tolerance** (p. 487) It is a parent's responsibility to teach children to be respectful.

**Internet Safety** (p. 488) Children must be taught the potential dangers of the Internet.

**Child Life Specialist** (p. 490) Learn the skills needed to succeed as a Child Life Specialist.

## Chapter Overview

### Introduce the Chapter

In this chapter, students learn about the emotional and social development of older children and preteens. They learn about the different stages children go through as they become increasingly independent from their parents and more involved with their peers. They learn how parents can aid children in moral development and help them handle negative peer pressure.

### Build Background

Organize students into small groups. Encourage group members to share the different types of emotional changes they experienced as preteens. In addition, the students should discuss how they dealt with these changes. Ask each group to summarize what types of emotional changes seemed the most common.

## Writing Activity

### *Personal Narrative*

This is an active learning activity that prompts the student to write a personal narrative on making new friends. After students have completed their writing activity, encourage them to share some of their responses in class. Responses can be used to prompt classroom discussions. (Use these criteria when evaluating your students' writing: students used freewriting or other techniques to generate ideas, events are organized chronologically, all basic elements are included, the story builds on ideas listed in the prewriting.)

---

# Emotional and Social Development from Seven to Twelve

## Chapter Objectives

After completing this chapter, you will be able to:

- **Identify** four ways to help ease emotional upsets.
- **Explain** how to help children control and express their anger in socially acceptable ways.
- **List** six ways to help a child develop a sense of competence.
- **Summarize** the four main qualities children look for in friendships.
- **Identify** typical changes that occur in children's attitudes toward their parents.
- **Describe** five ways to help prepare children to make good moral choices.

## Writing Activity 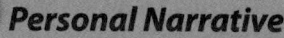 *Personal Narrative*

**Making Friends** Developing new friendships is easy for some people and difficult for others. Some people are naturally shy. Others are outgoing. Some people belong to many clubs and groups. This lets them meet and interact with many people. Other people prefer to spend more time alone. Write a personal narrative about a specific time when you had to make new friends.

**Writing Tips** To write an effective personal narrative, follow these steps:
1. Test your ideas by talking them through with a friend or by freewriting.
2. Ask yourself questions to fill out details of the narrative.
3. Construct a time line or other graphic organizer for your narrative.

---

## CLASSROOM Solutions

### Print Resources

 **Student Edition**

 **Teacher Wraparound Edition**

 **Student Activity Workbook**

**Student Activity Workbook Teacher Annotated Edition**

### Technology Resources

 **Online Learning Center** has resources and activities for students and teachers. Includes an Online Student Edition.

 **Interactive Student Edition** allows students to instantly access review materials, examples, and exercises.

| Section | 17.1 | **Emotional Development from Seven to Twelve** |

| Section | 17.2 | **Social and Moral Development from Seven to Twelve** |

**Explore the Photo**
Interacting with peers can be a positive or negative experience. *What kind of peer interactions have you experienced?*

471

**Review the Sections**
Introduce the chapter by reviewing the sections:

**Section 17.1**
From ages seven to twelve, children go through extensive emotional changes. Puberty can bring broad mood swings. Parents must remember to be objective about the child's erratic behavior, but must help the child learn to control socially unacceptable feelings. Parents also must help the child develop a sense of competence.

**Section 17.2**
Peer groups become increasingly important as children develop more independence. Characteristics that children look for in friends include loyalty and trustworthiness. Children must understand that bullying is never allowed. Parents must continue to provide moral guidance, for example, by setting a good example and appealing to the child's sense of fairness.

 **Explore the Photo**

**Caption Answer**
Students' answers will vary but should be honest and express feelings about peer interactions they have experienced.

**Discussion** Have students list several words to describe how they think the children in this photo are feeling. Ask students: What do these children's expressions tell you? What does their body language tell you? (Students might list words such as happy, interested, and friendly when describing the children. Their expressions and body language indicate that they like one another and are enjoying each other's company.)

 **TeacherWorks Plus** is an electronic lesson planner that provides instant access to complete teacher resources in one convenient package.

**Presentation Plus!** provides visual teaching aids for every section.

**The Early Childhood Observations CD** presents video observations and lessons on observation skills and child development.

**The Developing Brain eTransparencies and Guide** include information and activities to offer insights into brain development and diseases of the brain.

## Focus

### Bell Ringer Activity

**Appealing to Emotional Needs**

Bring in three or four advertisements from pre-teen magazines. These ads should appeal to the reader's emotional needs, such as their need to be accepted by a peer group. Share the ads with the class. Encourage them to analyze each ad's appeal.

## Preteaching

### Vocabulary

Many words have multiple meanings. Ask students: What is the definition of shift? Point out that some definitions are nouns (a change, or a period of work) and some are verbs (to change gears or to move).

**McGraw Hill Professional Development**

**Mini Clip Reading: Vocabulary**

Author Josefina Tinajero describes the critical importance of academic language.

## Graphic Organizer

 The Graphic Organizer is also on the TeacherWorks CD.

(Graphic organizers should list anger, fear, anxiety, and jealousy.)

 **NCLB** connects academic correlations to book content.

### Reading Guide

**Before You Read**

**Guilt-Free Rest** If you feel guilty about resting, you create more stress. Your reading skills are more effective if you are relaxed and ready to learn.

**Read to Learn**
**Key Concepts**
- **Identify** four ways to help ease emotional upsets.
- **Explain** how to help children control and express their anger in socially acceptable ways.
- **List** six ways to help a child develop a sense of competence.

**D** **Main Idea**
Children from seven to twelve experience emotional changes. They learn to better control and express emotions. They also develop a sense of self.

**Content Vocabulary**
◇ anxiety
◇ sense of self
◇ sense of competence
◇ gender identity

 **Graphic Organizer** Go to this book's Online Learning Center at **glencoe.com** to print out this graphic organizer.

**Academic Vocabulary**
You will find these words in your reading and on your tests. Use the glossary to look up their definitions if necessary.
■ shift
■ persevere

**Graphic Organizer**
As you read, look for four emotions that seven- to twelve-year-olds need help learning to control. Use a web diagram like the one shown to help organize your information.

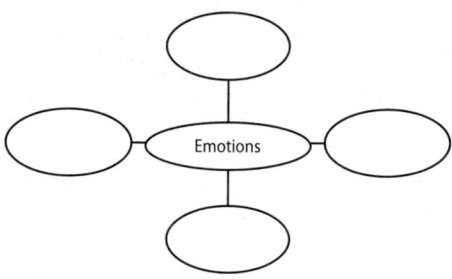

**NCLB**

 **English Language Arts**
**NCTE 12** Use language to accomplish individual purposes.

 **Social Studies**
**NCSS IV D Individual Development and Identity** Apply concepts, methods, and theories about the study of human growth and development, such as behavior and personality.

**NCTE** *National Council of Teachers of English*
**NCTM** *National Council of Teachers of Mathematics*

**NSES** *National Science Education Standards*
**NCSS** *National Council for the Social Studies*

### Reading Guide

**Before You Read**

Have students write down one way in which parents, or other adults, guided their emotional development when they were seven to twelve years old. You may wish to provide several examples; for instance, perhaps a parent always listened respectfully when the child was having difficulties with friends. Encourage students to share their writing with the class.

**D** **Develop Concepts**

**Main Idea** Discuss the main idea with the students. Ask: Why do you think children become better at controlling their emotions as they get older? (Answers may include that they develop a better sense of self and they learn others will not tolerate inappropriate behavior.)

## Emotional Changes

Andrea's parents had a hard time describing her to others. When she was seven, Andrea often stayed in her room. By age ten, she had become more outgoing. Her parents were relieved that she was more cheerful and showed more affection. A year later, she became moody and did not want to spend time with her parents at all.

There is nothing unusual about going through an emotional **shift**, or change. Even the multiple shifts that Andrea experienced are normal. They are typical of the changes children go through at this age. Children ages seven to twelve may sometimes feel that they are on an emotional roller coaster. One year they are withdrawn; the next year they are outgoing. One year they feel anxious; the next year they are relaxed. These changes are a normal part of the emotional development that occurs along with physical, social, and intellectual development.

## Middle Childhood

Between the ages of seven and ten, children generally progress from negative to positive, or from unhappiness to happiness. Children in this age span are gaining independence and self-confidence.

### Age Seven

Seven-year-olds are typically withdrawn and quiet. They tend to stay close to home. Many children this age worry a great deal about all kinds of issues. They may not want to talk about their feelings. Some are particularly sensitive to what others say about them.

### Age Eight

Eight-year-olds generally have a more positive attitude than at age seven. They are willing to explore and become curious about new things. They enjoy spending time with friends. They are lively and active. They also are often very dramatic. They might, for example, exaggerate when telling stories or describing their feelings. Parents might need to ask many questions to determine what really happened when an eight-year-old describes it.

### Age Nine

Nine-year-olds tend to be absorbed in their thoughts. They can be very harsh about their own failings and even embarrassed by them. Some nine-year-olds keep their feelings hidden and show signs of anxiety and tension. At times, they may become completely absorbed in their own concerns.

➤ **Growing and Changing**
Preteens change physically and emotionally. *How did you feel about yourself as a preteen?*

Section 17.1   Emotional Development from Seven to Twelve   **473**

**Overreacting**
Angry outbursts over seemingly minor events are common for preteens. *Why do you think preteens sometimes find it hard to control their anger?*

### Age Ten

By age ten, children are usually once again more positive and happy. They have a growing sense of self and increasing feelings of competence. They start to spend more time with their friends. They might make new friends by joining clubs or sports teams. This helps them focus on their strengths rather than their failings.

### The Preteen Years

Puberty usually begins around ages eleven or twelve. These are known as the preteen years. The physical changes of puberty, caused by the release of hormones, bring emotional changes as well. Preteens often feel and act awkward. Mood swings can carry them from happiness to sadness—and back again—in just minutes.

Preteens tend to be very absorbed in their own thoughts and concerns. They may pay little attention to people other than their peers. Their peers are extremely important to them. They usually crave group acceptance and become worried if they stand out in any way from their peers. They hate the thought of being different. It is not unusual for preteens to hide their true feelings behind a mask of not caring. This behavior is a sign of growing emotional control.

### Living with Children Seven to Twelve

Children ages seven to twelve can be easily upset. The hormones released into the body during puberty can cause emotional changes. Preteens may start feeling the mood swings that are associated with teenagers. A quiet, withdrawn seven-year-old might not be willing to talk about his feelings. An eight-year-old girl, though cheerful, might cling to her mother. An eleven-year-old boy might be experiencing secret fears. Here are some tips to keep minor emotional upsets from becoming major problems:

- **Be patient.** Remember that school-age children still do not have full self-control. When preteens show anger, it is often due to the difficulty they are having adjusting to the changes in their bodies.

- **Avoid taking it personally.** A child who is angry or upset may say nasty things to a parent or caregiver. Remember that children do not usually mean what they say in angry moments.

- **Help the child maintain self-control.** Make sure children understand that their behavior must stay within acceptable limits. Actions that break the rules need to be dealt with. If misbehavior is not serious, talking it through may be enough.

- **Listen attentively.** Ask the child to explain what happened and why. There may have been a valid problem. Help the child express his emotions. Even if there is a valid problem, this does not excuse inappropriately expressed anger. Let the child know that you do not approve of the behavior, and discuss more appropriate options.

**✓ Reading Check** **Recall** At what age do children generally have a sense of self and increased feelings of competence?

### Specific Emotions

The emotional life of young children centers on the family. In older children and preteens, the focus shifts to the wider world. People and events outside the family have more impact on children's emotions than before.

**➤ Explore the Photo**

Children gradually gain better control of their emotions. They begin expressing emotions in more socially acceptable ways. Socially acceptable ways of expressing emotions do not conflict with society's morals and are approved by most people.

## Anger

Children at any age can feel angry and let others know it. Even ten-year-olds, who are typically quite happy, show anger. When they do, though, it usually passes quickly. Depending on temperament and environment, some children become angry more often than others.

Preteens tend to be moody. Anger can erupt at any time. Often the outbursts of anger are eruptions that boil over and pass quickly. A preteen may storm out of a room and slam a door but then return a little while later as if nothing had happened.

Many times, these outbursts have little to do with the event that seemed to trigger them. Courtney, for example, became very angry when her mother asked her to hang up her coat after school. Within minutes, though, she was cheerful. Courtney was really angry because her friends went shopping without her.

By age seven, children generally know that they should express their anger in socially acceptable ways. For example, they should use words to talk about their anger. They should not lash out with violence or words that can hurt others' feelings. They know that they should seek a compromise to settle their differences or turn away from the situation.

On occasion, however, an older child may show aggression. It is important to avoid responding in the same way. Setting a good example is the best method of teaching a child. Here are some additional approaches that may work:

- **Teach the child how to gain self-control.** Counting to ten and taking deep breaths are two ways of helping an angry child learn to calm down.
- **Help the child learn nonaggressive ways to resolve conflicts.** Children who learn how to express their anger appropriately at home will be better equipped to settle conflicts at school. They might have learned this when angry with their siblings.
- **Reward the child for controlling anger.** Saying something like "I'm proud of the way you responded to the teasing," reinforces self-control.

**S**

## RESPOND TO SPECIAL NEEDS

### Generalized Anxiety Disorder

Children and adolescents with generalized anxiety disorder engage in extreme, unrealistic worry about everyday life activities. They worry too much about their academic performance, sporting activities, or even about being on time. These young people are generally very self-conscious, feel tense, and have a strong need for reassurance. They may complain about stomachaches or other discomforts that do not appear to have any physical cause.

Parents or other caregivers who notice repeated symptoms of an anxiety disorder in their child should talk with the child's doctor.

Doctors can help determine whether the symptoms are caused by an anxiety disorder or by some other condition. They can also provide a referral to a mental health professional, if needed.

> **Critical Thinking** There are many anxiety disorders such as separation anxiety and panic disorders. Research one anxiety disorder to learn how it affects children and how it can be treated. Share your findings in a one-page essay.

## RESPOND TO SPECIAL NEEDS

### Generalized Anxiety Disorder

**Discussion** Discuss with the class that everyone feels anxious on occasion. For example, starting a new school year might make students feel uncomfortable. Ask: How do you think these feelings are different from having an anxiety disorder? (The primary difference is that an anxiety disorder is an ongoing condition and people with this disorder worry about everyday events.)

> **Critical Thinking** Essays will vary depending on the anxiety disorder students choose to research. Essays should include how the disorder affects children and how it is treated.

## Teach cont.

### S Skill Practice
#### Guided Practice

**Provide Examples** Review with students the ways of appropriately dealing with anger listed here. Assign each student one of the four bulleted items. Instruct students to think of a specific example of how a parent could use this method. Have the students share their examples with the group. (Students should present specific examples of how parents can teach children to deal with anger. For example, for the first bulleted item, an example might be to go elsewhere until they have calmed down.) **L1 ELL**

**Evaluate a Situation** Instruct students to think of a television show in which one person became angry with another. Have students write a summary explaining how the person handled his or her anger. Students should state whether they think the person handled the situation in a positive way. If not, students should offer a more appropriate response. (Students should describe a situation in a television show in which someone became angry. They should explain whether the individual handled the anger appropriately and, if not, offer an alternative resolution.) **L2**

**Prepare a Presentation** Tell students to imagine that they have been assigned to teach an anger management class. Have them prepare a presentation in which they present at least three ways of handling anger and provide specific examples of how each method might be used. (Students should prepare a presentation explaining three appropriate ways of handling anger, such as reaching a resolution by talking.) **L3 ELL**

▶ **Envy and Jealousy**
Preteens often experience feelings of envy and jealousy. *How can parents help preteens deal with these emotions?*

- **Help the child learn to use unrelated physical activity to work off anger.** Exercise can help relieve stress and make a person feel calmer. Throwing a basketball, running, or walking the family dog are all harmless ways to blow off steam.

### Fear and Worry

All children have fears, but the nature of their fears changes. Seven-year-olds may still have some of their earlier fears, such as a fear of the dark. Look for easy solutions such as leaving a light on at night.

By age ten, the fears of earlier years have largely disappeared. However, as childhood fears disappear, new worries may take their place. News reports of terrorism, fatal car accidents, or natural disasters can set off worries in some older children and preteens. They may worry that such events will strike their families. They need to be reassured that adults will take all the steps necessary to protect them.

Other worries that occupy this age group have to do with how others see them. Until the age of ten, most children are concerned mainly with how adults see them. During the preteen years, however, the focus of these fears shifts toward the attitudes of their peers. Parents can help children by teaching self-confidence early on. Remind school-age children of their strengths.

### Anxiety

**Anxiety** is a state of uncertainty and fear, often about an unspecified but seemingly immediate threat. A certain amount of anxiety, especially about specific problems or events, is normal. For example, anxiety about passing a major test or a parent's serious illness is understandable. In these instances, offer the child support and reassurance.

Excessive anxiety, though, can be a sign of an anxiety disorder. People who have an anxiety disorder often worry that something terrible is about to happen. Preteens or teens with an anxiety disorder can develop constant physical symptoms such as tension headaches, nausea, or rapid heartbeat. Parents who suspect an anxiety problem in their child should talk to the child's doctor.

### Envy and Jealousy

As older children become more aware of the world around them, they are apt to develop feelings of envy and jealousy. Envy is the feeling of wanting something another person has. It can often lead to a feeling of intense dislike for that person.

"I hate Erica," Kayla told another friend. "She gets everything she wants. Now that her parents bought her a new TV for her bedroom, I'm not going to talk to her anymore."

**476** Chapter 17 Emotional and Social Development from Seven to Twelve

---

Jealousy is a complex emotion involving the fear that a loved one might prefer someone else. A seven-year-old might be jealous of a parent's attention to a sibling. A ten-year-old might feel jealous when a best friend spends time with another friend. A preteen, learning to feel comfortable with the opposite sex, might feel jealous of a peer who seems to be at ease and to get all the attention.

At the middle school dance, for example, Nicholas was happy that he found the courage to ask Yasmine to dance, and that she accepted. They had a great time dancing together. His happiness turned to painful jealousy, however, when another boy asked Yasmine to dance and they danced several songs together.

Children between the ages of seven and twelve are often very aware of their changing bodies, absorbed with their feelings, and anxious to fit in with their peers. For these reasons, jealousy is especially common.

✓ **Reading Check**  **Define** What is anxiety?

## A Sense of Self

One of the most important changes that occurs between the ages of seven and twelve is the development of a sense of self. Your **sense of self** is your idea of who you are, based on your emotions, personality, and the ways you perceive the world. As children grow, they develop the ability to think in more abstract terms. This affects the way they see themselves.

## Parenting Skills

### Help a Child Work Through a Difficult Situation

All children and adolescents need help sometimes. Children ages seven to twelve become less likely to confide in their parents. They can develop secret fears or worries. Relationships with others become more complex than they were before. More than ever, they need guidance from caring adults to help them figure out how to deal with difficult situations.

❥ **Establish genuine communication.** Accept each child as a unique individual. The child will sense your genuine interest and may become more willing to confide about issues.

❥ **Take their concerns seriously.** Do not belittle or dismiss any fears or worries that cause children emotional distress. Let children know that you are available to talk about anything that is troubling them.

❥ **Put any worries into perspective.** Brandon worried constantly that his mother might die and that he would be left alone. When his mother had to take a plane trip for business, Brandon begged her not to go. His mother reminded him that plane crashes were much less likely than car accidents.

❥ **Try to determine how serious the problem might be.** Be aware of such danger signs as depression, feelings of hopelessness, or increased self-centeredness and lack of concern for others. Consult a professional for help in dealing with the situation.

**Take Charge** If you were a caregiver of a child who was struggling with working through a difficult situation, do you think the child would benefit from seeing a counselor? Write a letter explaining why or why not.

## Reteach *cont.*

### R Reading Strategy

**Compare and Contrast** Draw on the board an empty Venn diagram labeled Jealousy and Envy. Have the class complete it by identifying similarities and differences between these two terms. (Similarities: Both involve feelings that can create difficulties and conflicts between individuals. Differences: Envy involves wanting something another person has, such as a particular friend; jealousy involves fear that a loved one might prefer someone else and is a common cause of sibling rivalry.)

### U₂ Universal Access

**Gifted Learners** Introduce students to the concept of emotional intelligence based on the brain and behavioral research of Daniel Goleman. Goleman states that emotional intelligence is related to self-awareness, responsibility, motivation, empathy, and the ability to love and be loved. Have students read and prepare a report on Goleman's book *Emotional Intelligence: Why It Can Matter More Than IQ*. (Reports will vary but should show an understanding of Goleman's research.)

✓ **Reading Check**

**Define** Anxiety is a state of uncertainty and fear, often about an unspecified yet seemingly immediate threat.

## Parenting Skills

### Help a Child Work Through a Difficult Situation

Encourage volunteers to discuss worries they had when they were younger. Ask how parents might help place these fears into perspective. (Students should discuss fears they had and how a parent might help place each in perspective. For example, if a preteen is afraid of getting behind in school because she is sick, the parent might discuss similar fears he had as a child and how his teacher helped him catch up.)

**Take Charge**
Letters will vary but students should support their opinions with logical reasoning. Students may write that a counselor could help the child work through the situation based on fact or logic instead of emotion.

## Reteach *cont.*

### W Writing Support
**Personal Narrative**
**A Growing Sense of Competence**
Have students think of one skill they learned between ages seven and twelve that gave them a sense of competence. Instruct students to write a personal narrative describing how this skill made them feel successful and proud of themselves. (Refer to p. 470 to review the characteristics of personal narratives. Students' narratives will vary, but should describe a specific skill they learned which gave them a sense of competence.)

---

**THE DEVELOPING BRAIN**

**Stimulation Builds Competence**
**Science Inquiry** Stimulation allows the child more opportunities to try, fail, and learn new things. The more things a child tries and learns, the more competent the child becomes.

For more information and activities, see *The Developing Brain* guide and eTransparencies.

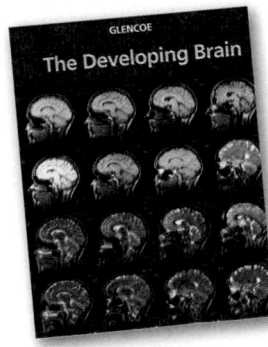

---

**↑ Sense of Competence**
Most children gain a sense of competence during their early school years. *What impact does that have on later success in school?*

Compare the following answers that were given by a five-year-old and a nine-year-old to a researcher's questions. The researcher asked a five-year-old girl whether she could become the family dog. The girl said no, but based her

**THE DEVELOPING BRAIN**

**Stimulation Builds Competence**
Why do some children become more competent at mental tasks than other children the same age? Are those individuals simply smarter than others? Some children do have a genetic inheritance that makes them better equipped to learn than some of their peers. But most people have far more intellectual capacity than they use. Growing up in a stimulating environment and having determination to succeed are two other factors that can lead to success and feelings of competence.

**■ Science Inquiry** A stimulating environment can help a child gain competence. What might explain this?

reasoning on physical traits. "The dog," she said, "has brown eyes and walks like a dog." When a nine-year-old was asked whether she could become her brother, she also answered no but for a different reason. "I'm me and he's him. I can't change in any way because I've got to stay like myself."

Children between the ages of seven and twelve recognize that they have a personality that is uniquely theirs. They see themselves as a mixture of many qualities. Some of those qualities are based on physical appearance, others on talents or abilities. By age ten, children are able to see themselves as being highly skilled in one area and less so in another. By ages eleven and twelve, children also use personal qualities to define themselves. For example, "I'm honest," or "I'm a good friend," or "I can be counted on."

They also see that they behave differently in different situations. Dionte always thought of himself as being friendly and outgoing until he went to a party at his cousin's house. The only person he knew there was his cousin, and he found it hard to talk to anyone else. "How can I be both friendly and shy?" he wondered. As he thought about it, Dionte realized that he is shy around strangers. He also realized that his behavior is influenced by the situation he is in.

Dionte recognized that different people might perceive him in different ways. To people he knows, he seems friendly and outgoing. However, strangers might think of him as quiet or even stuck-up, or conceited. Dionte's ability to understand how others might see him is a good example of his growing thinking skills.

### Sense of Competence
According to theorist Erik Erikson, the early school years mark the stage when children strive to develop a sense of competence. A **sense of competence** is the feeling that one can be successful and meet most challenges. Children gain this feeling by acquiring and improving a wide range of skills. In the classroom, these skills include reading, math, and writing. Outside the classroom, children may develop skills in sports, music, art, or crafts. Erikson believed that as children refine these

---

**▶ Explore the Photo**

**Caption Answer** A sense of competence greatly increases the probability of later success in school.

**Discussion** Describe to students a sixth-grade classroom in which several children never raise their hands. However, if called upon, they generally give correct answers. Ask: Why do you think these children are reluctant to raise their hands? What might a teacher do to encourage these students to raise their hands? (Possible answer: They may be shy or fearful of giving the wrong answer and appearing stupid. The teacher may be able to encourage them by providing positive feedback when they do answer questions.)

skills, they see themselves as competent and increase their self-esteem.

A child's feelings about his or her competence can have a real effect on the choices he or she makes and on satisfaction later in life. Children with high self-esteem are more willing to try new things and to **persevere**, or persist, at difficult tasks. In contrast, Erikson believed that those who experience repeated failures and disappointments begin to see themselves as inferior and incompetent. Children's beliefs about their competence can greatly affect their choices and their satisfaction in later life. For these reasons, Erikson said it is essential that children ages seven to twelve experience more successes than failures.

Eleven-year-old Andrew went home to an empty house every day after school. His parents would not let him have friends over. He did not mind this much because he did not have many friends. Unsupervised and with time on his hands, he often got into trouble. One day he was caught shooting a BB gun at cars in a nearby office parking lot and was given a stern warning. About a month later, Andrew scratched, "A loser was here" into the front door of the office building. His way of identifying himself revealed much about his self-esteem.

Sound relationships with peers are an important part of developing a sense of competence. As children grow from seven to twelve, their peers become much more important to them. They begin to let go of their total reliance on parents and start to depend on friends for help and reassurance.

Children ages seven to twelve are going through other changes that prepare them for the learning and mastery that lead to competence. Their brains develop connections that allow their memory to expand. Increased memory allows children to learn and understand more.

There are a variety of ways to help seven- to twelve-year-olds develop a sense of competence:

## What Would You Do?

### Learning to Build Confidence

Margaret, the mother of eleven-year-old Hannah, was surprised at what she was hearing from her daughter's teacher. Mrs. Schwartz said that whenever she asked Hannah to do something, her response was, "I can't."

"I don't understand Hannah," said Margaret. "She seems confident. I know I have high expectations, but she's a bright child. If she gets Bs, I ask why she didn't get As. If she gets an A, I ask why it wasn't an A+, because I know that she could get those grades if she applied herself."

Mrs. Schwartz thought for a moment and said, "Maybe Hannah says she can't because she is becoming afraid of failing to meet others' expectations." She suggested that Margaret rethink the messages she was sending. Hannah might be feeling that nothing she did would ever be good enough to please her mother.

 **Write About It** Think about the questions Margaret asks Hannah when she sees her grades. What do you think Hannah would prefer to hear? Rewrite the statements to help build Hannah's self-confidence.

- **Help children focus on their strengths.** Ask them to make a list of the things that they are good at. Encourage them to develop special skills and talents.
- **Provide opportunities.** Include children in the work of the family. Doing chores can help them learn practical skills and contribute to the family.
- **Encourage learning.** Recognize the importance of learning. Make sure children have a quiet time and place to do homework and practice skills.
- **Establish reachable goals.** Help children break large tasks down into smaller parts. They can focus on accomplishing one part at a time. Eventually, they will see that they have completed the larger goal.
- **Recognize successes.** Look for things children do well, and be specific in praise. "You did a great job of explaining the book's plot in your book report."

Section 17.1 Emotional Development from Seven to Twelve **479**

## Reteach *cont.*

### U Universal Access

**Auditory Learners** Read aloud the list of ways to help seven- to twelve-year-olds develop a sense of competence. Ask for volunteers to restate each of the six bulleted items in their own words. (Students should restate each bulleted item in their own words; for example, the first one might be stated as, "Remind children that there are many things they can do well.") **ELL**

 Professional Development

**Mini Clip**
**ELL: Reading Aloud**

A teacher reads aloud, modeling fluency, pronunciation, expression, and comprehension strategies.

### R Reading Strategy

**Use Prior Knowledge** Read aloud the third bulleted point in the right column. Ask students: Have you ever heard the expression "Divide and conquer"? How might this expression be applied to the point the author is making here? (A task may feel overwhelming if you try to tackle it all at once. However, if you first divide it into manageable parts and then complete each part in turn, you are more likely to be successful.)

## What Would You Do?

**Write About It** Students' answers will vary but may include: This is a good grade, Hannah, I'm proud of you. Do you feel like you did your very best?

### Study Tools

Have students go to the Online Learning Center at **glencoe.com**:

- Take the **Practice Test**.
- Download **Study-to-Go** content.

Use the **Student Activity Workbook** for additional practice.

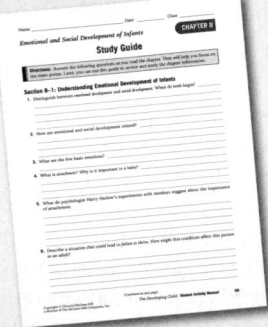

### Culminating Activity

**Handling Emotions** Have students write words of advice for children ages seven to twelve who are experiencing changes in their emotions. (*Advice will vary but should be constructive rather than condescending or patronizing.*)

 **NCLB** connects academic correlations to book content.

---

- **Focus on the positive.** "You got twelve out of fourteen right on that math test! That's much better than you did on the last test."

### Sense of Gender

An important part of a child's growing sense of self is gender identity. **Gender identity** is the awareness of being male or female. It is a complex process that begins in early childhood and is usually firmly fixed by about age four. In middle childhood and early adolescence that identity becomes stronger as children become more aware of their bodies and of gender differences. Between the ages of seven and twelve, children generally:

- Choose to spend more time with others of the same sex. Close friendships at this stage are almost always with children of the same sex.
- Show an increased desire to act and talk like others of the same sex.

- Choose adults of the same sex as their role models. Role models are the people whom children admire and try to pattern their behavior after.
- Begin to explore relationships with the opposite sex late in this stage.

There are many influences on gender identity such as family, other adults, peers, and media. Children begin taking in information about gender identity from birth. You are a role model to any child you meet or interact with. Children observe the behavior of people around them. This lets them learn which feelings and responses are appropriate for their gender. It is important to be aware of this so you can be a better role model for children. No single gender identity fits everyone. You can help children appreciate and develop their positive traits, talents, and qualities. Encourage them to pursue their unique interests.

---

# Section 17.1 — After You Read

### Review Key Concepts

1. **Describe** the typical emotional state of a seven-, eight-, nine-, and ten-year-old child.
2. **List** the kinds of fears a ten-year-old might have.
3. **Summarize** two signs of a child's growing sense of self.

### Practice Academic Skills

 **English Language Arts**

4. Children who have a high sense of competence are generally more successful in school than children who do not. Write a one-page essay in which you explain why a sense of competence in school-age children is important to future success in life.

> **NCTE 12** Use language to accomplish individual purposes.

 **Social Studies**

5. Observe older children and preteens. Look for typical behaviors that you read about in this chapter. Record the behaviors you observe. Then try to estimate the ages of those you observed. Turn in your notes and estimates.

> **NCSS IV D** Apply concepts, methods, and theories about the study of human growth and development, such as behavior and personality.

 **Check Your Answers** Check your answers at this book's Online Learning Center at **glencoe.com**.

---

### Review Key Concepts

1. Children tend to have the following emotional states: age seven—withdrawn and quiet; age eight—positive attitude and willing to explore new things; age nine—absorbed in own thoughts and self-conscious; age ten—starting to focus on strengths instead of failings.

2. Ten-year-olds might be afraid of terrorism or natural disasters, as well as how peers view them.

3. Children use personal qualities when defining themselves and they recognize that they have unique personalities.

### Practice Academic Skills

4. Essays will vary but should state that children with a high sense of competence will take the initiative to learn new things and have a better chance at success and satisfaction in their later lives.

5. Students' answers will vary but should show an understanding of what behaviors are typical at what age.

# Section 17.2 Social and Moral Development from Seven to Twelve

## Reading Guide

### Before You Read

**Predict** Look at the photos in this section and read their captions. Write one or two sentences predicting what the section will be about.

### Read to Learn
#### Key Concepts
- **Summarize** the four main qualities children look for in friendships.
- **Identify** typical changes that occur in children's attitudes toward their parents.
- **Describe** five ways to help prepare children to make good moral choices.

**D**

### Main Idea
Relationships become stronger and more complex as children grow. Older children and preteens must learn to deal with peer pressure and accept responsibility for decisions and actions taken.

### Content Vocabulary
 bullying
 peer pressure
 conformity

### Academic Vocabulary
You will find these words in your reading and on your tests. Use the glossary to look up their definitions if necessary.
- paramount
- counterproductive

### Graphic Organizer
As you read, list guidelines for helping people resolve their differences. Use a chart like the one below to organize your information.

| Guidelines for Resolving Conflicts |
|---|
| 1. |
| 2. |
| 3. |
| 4. |

 **Graphic Organizer** Go to this book's Online Learning Center at **glencoe.com** to print out this graphic organizer.

**N C L B**

### Academic Standards . . . . . . . . . . . . . . . . . . . . . . . . . . . . . . .

 **English Language Arts**
**NCTE 12** Use language to accomplish individual purposes.

 **Social Studies**
**NCSS IV C Individual Development and Identity** Describe the ways family and other group and cultural influences contribute to the development of a sense of self.

**NCTE** *National Council of Teachers of English*
**NCTM** *National Council of Teachers of Mathematics*

**NSES** *National Science Education Standards*
**NCSS** *National Council for the Social Studies*

---

## Reading Guide

### Before You Read

Ask students if they noticed any differences in their relationships between themselves and their friends from seven to twelve. Did they look for different traits in friends as they became old? If so, what were the changes?

### D Develop Concepts

**Main Idea** Discuss the main idea with the students. Ask students what they think might happen to a preteen who is not made to take responsibility for inappropriate decisions that he or she makes. (The child may go on making inappropriate decisions and therefore not grow up to be a happy, productive adult.)

---

## Focus

### Bell Ringer Activity

#### Friendship Qualities
Fill a paper bag with pieces of paper each containing one of the following qualities: loyalty, trustworthiness, kindness, understanding, empathy, and fun. Have individual students pull out the slips one-at-a-time, read them aloud to the class, and give an example of the quality. Discuss that these are qualities that people look for in friends. Ask students if there are any other qualities they would add to this list. Discuss that developing friendships is an important part of the social development of children from seven to twelve.

## Preteaching

### Vocabulary
Tell students that as they learn new terms, they will often discover that the terms are related to one another. Discuss that peer pressure and conformity are related because young people often exert peer pressure on individuals to conform to the standards of the group.

### Graphic Organizer
The Graphic Organizer is also on the TeacherWorks CD.

(Graphic organizers should include: set some ground rules, listen to both sides, find common ground, and reach a solution that is acceptable to both sides.)

**N C L B** **NCLB** connects academic correlations to book content.

### Discussion Starter

**What Is Moral Behavior?** Discuss that ages seven to twelve is the time period during which children develop their sense of morals. Ask students: What is moral behavior? What are some morals that you have? (Answers will vary. Possible answer: Morals involve having a sense of right and wrong. For the last question, students might answer that it is wrong to steal, cheat on tests, or treat people differently because of their race or culture.)

### R Reading Strategy

**Contrast** Have students discuss how loyalty is different from trustworthiness and provide examples of each. (Examples will vary. Loyalty refers to standing by someone you care about, no matter what the situation, whereas trustworthiness refers to the ability to keep confidences.)

### U₁ Universal Access

**Verbal Learners** Provide students with a list of popular preteen fiction titles. Choose titles in which friendships play a major role. Have each student read a different book from the list. Have students write a description of the friendships of the main character or characters. If any conflicts occur, students should state whether they were resolved, and, if so, how. (Students should write a description of the friendships in their chosen book, including any conflicts that may have occurred among characters.)

## Relationships with Peers

As children grow, their friendships get stronger. Because seven- to twelve-year-olds have a sense of self and are better able to communicate their thoughts and feelings, their friendships become more personal. Beginning around age seven or eight, children look for the following qualities in their friendships:

- **Loyalty** Older children value friends who will stand by them when they are in a difficult situation or feeling low.
- **Trustworthiness** Older children need to feel comfortable talking about their inner feelings. They look for friends they can trust. They want friends who will not pass on personal secrets.
- **Kindness and Understanding** Children this age seek friends who will listen and be sympathetic to their feelings, which are often tumultuous.
- **Fun** Most people look for friends whose company they enjoy and with whom they can have a good time.

Children this age still enjoy active, physical play with their friends, but they spend increasing amounts of time simply talking. Preteens who are close friends might spend an afternoon together. Then they go home and call each other and spend an hour or more talking in the evening as well. They might talk about anything from school to peers, or movie stars to personal feelings.

It is development in many areas that brings about these changes. Intellectual growth makes deeper friendships possible. Because they can now think abstractly, older children and preteens can better understand how others see them. At the same time, they can more easily see another person's point of view and feel empathy for him or her. These new skills make it easier to relate to friends in a deeper way.

The physical and emotional changes of puberty also play a role in friendships. Preteens are curious about the changes they are going through. They are trying to figure out the new aspects of their relationships with people of the opposite gender. Talking to their friends helps them explore and think through these issues.

## Peer Groups

For older children and preteens, acceptance by peers is closely related to high self-esteem. Children who feel that they fit in are more confident, more likely to make and keep friends, and more likely to succeed at school. Feelings of rejection by peers may negatively affect performance at school and family relationships.

 **Best Friends**
At this stage, close friendships are almost always with people of the same sex. *Who were your closest friends at this stage?*

### ➤ Explore the Photo

**Caption Answer** Students' answers will vary but should be honest. Most of their answers will probably reflect people of the same gender.

**Discussion** Ask students: Why do you think these girls are more likely to have other girls as their friends, rather than boys? (Answers will vary but may include that they have more in common with those of the same gender.)

## Learning Through PLAY

### Problem Solving

Refer to p. 470

Older children and preteens are learning more about themselves as individuals, as well as about their classmates. During this time, some children experience pressures and problems such as lying, cheating, or bullying. One way to help children work through these problems is to act out typical situations, focusing on ways to prevent and deal with them. Involving children in the problem-solving process helps them develop the skills they will need throughout their lives. Acting out situations and modeling their resolution can give children ideas about how to handle situations if they arise again.

> **Think About It** Imagine that your best friend since childhood has told another friend something personal about you. Now this personal information is being spread around the school. You are very angry. How would you resolve this problem with your friend who betrayed your trust?

---

Children at this age generally have many peer groups. Peer groups may include classmates, sports teammates, or children who live in the same neighborhood. Adults can help children gain peer acceptance by teaching social skills and encouraging participation in group activities. Children who experience rejection by their peers may need professional counseling to prevent lifelong difficulties.

### Making Friends

Tara and Nate were neighbors. They began playing together when they were two years old. When they were six, they played on the same soccer team. At age eight, however, their friendship began to change. Tara began spending more time with her new best friend, Kari, and other girls from school. Nate would pal around with the boys.

The experiences of Tara and Nate show how gender differences become more important as children grow older. Young children play with children of either gender. As children grow older they are more likely to become friends only with children of the same gender. This is true even though puberty makes them more interested in preteens of the opposite gender.

By age twelve, Tara began to see Nate in a whole new way. "I think he's really cute," Tara confided to Kari. "Why don't you tell him?" teased Kari. "Or maybe I will." "Don't you dare," squealed Tara, "I would just die!"

One reason preteens avoid opposite-gender friendships is that such relationships raise questions of being romantically involved. Most eleven- and twelve-year-olds are not ready to take that step. They want to avoid the teasing they may encounter if they have a friend of the opposite gender.

The number of friends children have at this stage varies. Some children have many friends. Some have several friends. And some have just one or two friends. The number of friendships may depend on the child's temperament. Some children enjoy being part of a large group. Others are more private and quiet. These children do not want or need many friends.

Another influence is the child's social environment. Children who are in after-school programs, clubs, or teams have more opportunities to make friends. Therefore, they may naturally have more friends.

There is no set number of friends that children should have. Still, some older children and preteens may "collect" friends. They use the number of friends they have as a way to measure their popularity. Those with fewer friends may feel that they are not liked as well.

---

### Teach *cont.*

### W Writing Support

**Personal Narrative**

**Difficult Choices** Have students think back to a time when they were preteens and faced a difficult situation. Perhaps someone was bullying them or a friend wanted their help in cheating on an assignment. Instruct students to write a personal narrative about this situation and how they dealt with it. (Refer to p. 470 to review the characteristics of personal narratives. Students' narratives will vary, but students should write about an appropriate situation and also describe how they responded to it.)

### U₂ Universal Access

**Visual Learners** Have students go to a public place where preteens hang out together in groups, such as a park or mall. Instruct students to observe how the preteens treat one another. In class, invite students to share their findings and compare and contrast the behaviors they observed. Did students see any similarities between groups of girls, groups of boys, and mixed-gender groups? (Findings will vary. Students should observe preteens in a public place and discuss what they observed, including any differences in behavior based on the gender of the group.) **ELL**

---

## Learning Through PLAY

### Problem Solving

**Discussion** Ask students: Do you think role-playing difficult situations before they happen can help children handle the actual situations better? Why or why not? (Possible answer: Yes, because when they find themselves in the actual situation, they have some idea of how to handle it.)

> **Think About It** Students' answers will vary but should include confronting the friend, trying to talk things out without violence, and possibly getting someone to help mediate the conflict.

## Teach *cont.*

### S Skill Practice

**Guided Practice**

**Create a Poster** Have students create posters listing the guidelines for resolving conflicts. Encourage them to add interest to their posters by illustrating them. (Posters will vary but should list conflict resolution guidelines.) **L1 ELL**

**Practice Conflict Resolution** As a class, discuss how students would help older children and preteens deal with these peer conflicts: (1) Rosa gets angry with her cousin for taking her CD; (2) Traci is offended when she learns Shing-Ling is spreading rumors about her; (3) Steve is upset when his friends do not ask him to be on their team. (Students should present appropriate conflict resolution strategies for each conflict. For example, for the first conflict, students might suggest Rosa talk with her cousin about how hurt she was that the cousin took her CD without asking.) **L2 ELL**

**Act Out a Conflict** Organize students into pairs. Instruct each pair to create a skit based on a conflict between two twelve-year-olds. Each pair should present their skits to the class. The class should then brainstorm how the two preteens could work together to resolve their conflicts. (Each pair should present a skit based on a specific conflict; the class should then brainstorm possible resolutions.) **L3 ELL**

**McGraw Hill Professional Development**

**Mini Clip**
**ELL: Strategies for English Learners**
Author Jana Echevarria discusses strategies for teaching English learners.

---

→ **Make New Friends**
Participating in a variety of activities presents more opportunities to meet people and make friends. *What other factors contribute to a healthy social life?*

In reality, the key to a healthy social life is not how many friends a child has. Whether the child has the social skills for forming and maintaining friendships is what counts. It is important to help and encourage children to build social skills and get involved in activities that interest them.

## Resolving Conflicts

The nature of friendship changes as children grow. So too does the nature of conflicts they face. Young children may have conflicts over toys. Older children and preteens have conflicts over more complex issues.

Many conflicts among children arise from envy, jealousy, or gossip. Whitney, for example, heard a rumor that Caitlin had been spreading gossip about her. She confronted Caitlin and accused her of telling lies. Caitlin heatedly denied this, and a shouting match ensued. A crowd of girls soon gathered around them to watch.

Other conflicts may be based on emotional needs. Older children and preteens have a need to belong. Conflicts may arise if they feel excluded from a group or if they think someone is showing them disrespect.

### Avoiding Violence

In general, children at this stage should be able to use words to express their anger. Those who received guidance at an earlier age on how to deal with anger are more likely to have self-control. Occasionally, however, anger can lead to aggressive behavior. Preteen boys are more likely than girls to use aggressive behavior to express anger.

If a conflict looks as if it might escalate into violence, others should intervene. Here are some guidelines for helping people in conflict resolve their differences:

- **Set some ground rules.** Establish an agreement to work peacefully toward resolution. Letitia and Emily stepped out of the group around Whitney and Caitlin and tried to calm them down. "Let's get to the bottom of this, but no more yelling or name-calling, okay?"
- **Listen to both sides.** Ask both people to give their side of the story, and listen carefully to what they say. Whitney was less concerned about the silly gossip than about the idea that Caitlin did not respect her. Caitlin was hurt that Whitney did not trust her. "I never said those things. How could you even think I would?" asked Caitlin.
- **Find common ground.** Find something that both people can agree on so that they can move forward. Sometimes this is as simple as deciding to end the disagreement.
- **Reach a solution that is acceptable to both sides.** Win-win solutions, in which both parties gain something they want, are best because both people can feel good about the resolution. At first, Whitney wanted Caitlin to apologize. Caitlin refused, saying

**S**

---

▶ **Explore the Photo**

**Caption Answer** Answers will vary but may include how one feels about oneself and whether one has the social skills for forming and maintaining relationships.

**Discussion** Discuss that the children in this picture are acting in a play. Ask: What are some of the ways that being in a play might help a ten-year-old develop her social skills? (Possible answer: It might encourage her to interact with children and adults whom she may not know, and it teaches cooperation and working together to achieve a goal.)

there was nothing to apologize for. Finally, they agreed to apologize to each other for the situation and how it made them feel. "I'm sorry that the rumor made you think I didn't respect you," said Caitlin. "I'm sorry that my reaction made you feel that I don't trust you," said Whitney.

## Dealing with Bullies

**Bullying** means directing aggression or abuse toward another person, usually someone weaker. It can take many forms, including pushing, shoving, or other physical abuse; teasing; spreading rumors; or making offensive comments. Boys are more likely than girls to be bullies and to be the victims of bullies. However, some girls are bullies too.

Bullying can cause both physical and emotional pain for victims. Unfortunately, children who are being bullied often do not tell their parents or other adults. They may fear that telling on a bully will only make the bullying worse. This is often a threat made by the bully.

Parents, teachers, and other caregivers need to be on the lookout for signs of bullying. They should suspect bullying if a child:

- Comes home with cuts, bruises, or torn clothing.
- Frequently loses lunch money or other valuable items.
- Does not want to go to school.
- Becomes unusually moody, withdrawn, and bad tempered.
- Is always anxious and has trouble sleeping.

An adult who suspects that a child is being bullied should question the child in a supportive way. The adult could ask how the child's day went and follow up with questions such as, "What was your favorite activity at school today?" "What was your least favorite thing?"

A child who is being bullied needs to be reassured that it is not his or her fault. Emphasize that no one has the right to bully anyone else. Report the situation to a teacher, principal, or school counselor. Schools usually take the problem of bullying very seriously.

**C**

✓ **Reading Check** **Explain** What are some typical conflicts among preteens?

---

### Math in Action

**The Cost of Child Delinquency**

Data collected by the Federal Bureau of Investigation's Uniform Crime Reporting Program show that law enforcement agencies made approximately 253,000 arrests of children younger than 13 in 1997. The highest offense in those arrests was arson, at an alarming rate of 35 percent. How many children younger than 13 were arrested for arson in 1997?

**Math Concept** **Multiply by Percents** To multiply by percents, change the percent to a fraction with 100 in the denominator. Then change the fraction to a decimal.

**Starting Hint** Convert 35 percent to a decimal by dividing 35 by 100. Then multiply the result by the total number of arrests.

**Math** For math help, go to the Math Appendix at the back of the book.

**NCTM Number and Operations** Understand numbers, ways of representing numbers, relationships among numbers, and number systems.

**NCLB**

---

## Family Relationships

There are many changes occurring between the ages of seven and twelve. Therefore, it is no surprise that family relationships change too. Children move from dependence to greater independence. The complex relationships between children and their parents and siblings reflect that transition.

Family situations vary greatly. Some families have two parents in the home. Others have only one. Some children live with a guardian or in a foster home. The main caregiver may be a person other than a parent. It might be a grandparent or other relative. Extended family members, such as a grandparent or aunt, may live with the family.

In many families, both parents work outside the home. This affects how much family time is available. The number and ages of siblings also affect family relationships.

---

## Assess

### Quiz
Ask students to answer the following questions:

1. Why is talking with friends important for preteens? (Talking helps them to explore and think through issues related to physical, sexual, and emotional changes that are occurring.)
2. List three peer groups that a typical ten-year-old might have. (Possible answers: classmates, sports teammates, and children in the neighborhood.)
3. How can parents and caregivers encourage children to develop a healthy social life? (They can encourage them to build their social skills by frequently interacting with others of their age and by being involved in activities that interest them.)

## Reteach

**C** **Critical Thinking**

**Apply** Organize students into small groups. Tell students to imagine that they are sixth-graders whose middle school is having an anti-bullying campaign. Their job is to come up with an appropriate slogan for the campaign. Have each group share its slogan with the class. (Slogans will vary but should be brief and catchy and should convey an anti-bullying message.) **ELL**

✓ **Reading Check**

**Explain** Typical conflicts include those arising out of envy or jealousy, conflicts based on emotional needs, or unresolved angry feelings that can lead to aggressive behaviors.

---

**NCLB** **NCLB** Activity correlated to Math standards.

### Math in Action

**The Cost of Child Delinquency**

88,550 children under 13 years of age were arrested for arson. (35% = 0.35; 0.35 × 253,000 = 88,550)

**Reteach** *cont.*

**U** **Universal Access**

**Learners Having Difficulties and English Language Learners** Ask for volunteers to read aloud the list of ways in which children's attitudes toward their parents typically change between ages seven and twelve. Then have students work individually to create time lines summarizing the changes that occur during this time. (Time lines may vary but should accurately show how children's attitudes toward their parents change during the later childhood and preteen periods.) **ELL**

**Write About It** Answers will vary. Samantha's options are to go along with the stealing, urge her friends to stop stealing, or find new friends. If she goes along with it, she will suffer from doing what she knows is wrong and may be caught. If she stands up to her friends, they may reject her. If she finds new friends, she may be happier in the long run.

↑ *Spend Time Together*
Parents often have to work hard to maintain positive relationships with their preteen children. *Why do preteens tend to be critical of their parents' values?*

**What Would** *You* **Do?**

**Negative Peer Pressure**
Nine-year-old Samantha moved to a new neighborhood. When she first started at her new school, she was concerned about making new friends. Then the group of girls who sat under the trees at recess invited her over to join them. They wanted to be friends with her! At first, being included felt great. After a while, though, the girls started daring each other to steal things. First it was a book from the school library. Then it was lipstick from the drugstore. When Samantha would not steal the lipstick, the girls stopped talking to her. Samantha tried to make new friends but the group of girls spread rumors about Samantha. Soon almost no one in Samantha's class was talking to her.

✎ *Write About It* Samantha does not know what to do. What options does she have for dealing with the situation? What are the possible outcomes of each? Write a report with your answers to these questions.

### Parents

As children grow older, their attitudes toward their parents typically change in the following ways:

- Seven-year-olds depend on their parents, but often challenge parental authority. Tommie is mad that his parents will not let him go out to play until his room is clean. However, he still expects them to feed him dinner an hour later.
- At eight, children tend to cling to their parents. Natalie wants to go shopping with her mother on Saturday instead of playing at her friend Nicole's house.
- By nine, children become wrapped up in their own thoughts and sometimes ignore their parents. Drew's father reminded him three times on Thursday night to take out the trash. Drew was not disobeying; he was preoccupied thinking about his math test and forgot.
- Ten is generally a smooth year. Children are happier and more communicative. Walt and his mother enjoy the drive to and from school everyday. They talk about what Walt is doing at school and with his friends.

**U**

 **Explore the Photo**

**Caption Answer** Answers will vary but may include that preteens are trying to develop their independence and often see their parents' values as a hindrance to their independence. Also, preteens may be influenced by peers.

**Discussion** Tell students to imagine that they are the parent of an eleven-year-old who has indicated he has no interest in participating in the family's traditional Sunday board-game night. Ask: How would you respond? (Answers will vary. Possible answer: Sometimes it is best to not make an issue of these changes as the child is struggling to gain some independence.)

- At eleven and twelve, children begin to move away from the direct control and influence of parents. Preteens may become quite critical of their parents' values. The preteen years are often challenging for parents, no matter how healthy the family relationship. Patricia and her parents had a good family relationship. They enjoyed spending Fridays together as a designated "family night." Sometimes they would play games, other times they would watch movies together. However, after Patricia turned eleven, this relationship began to change. Patricia no longer wanted to hang out with her parents. She begged out of family night to go to the movies with her friends instead. She wanted to spend less time at home and more time with her friends. Her parents were disappointed but tried to understand that she needed to build her independence.

## Siblings

Starting at age seven, children generally get along well with siblings who are much younger or much older. They are helpful and protective of children under two. They tend to respect and admire siblings in their late teens.

Seven- to twelve-year-olds often have difficult relationships with siblings who are closer to their own age. They tend to judge each other harshly and conflicts are common. Parents and other adults need to help close-in-age siblings develop empathy and a sense of cooperation.

✓ **Reading Check** **Recall** Describe a typical nine-year-old's relationship with his or her parents.

## Moral Development

As they spend more time outside the home, children face more decisions about right and wrong. They must make these decisions alone,

# Parenting Skills

## Teach a Child Tolerance

Prejudice and intolerance are learned from others. Young children are ready to be tolerant of anyone. Parents need to make sure that they stay that way. Tolerance is a moral issue that deals with fairness. Here are some strategies to help parents teach tolerance.

- As with any moral behavior, teach by example. Avoid any behavior that signals prejudice.
- At work, home, or in public, show that you are willing to get along with anyone who behaves appropriately.
- Help children understand and respect the traditions of other cultures or religions. Different does not mean wrong. Teach children that all human beings deserve fair treatment.
- Encourage tolerance as a continuous process. Children hear intolerant messages from many outside sources, including the media and peers.
- Raise the subject of prejudice anytime the opportunity presents itself. Children are more likely to retain messages about accepting differences if they are repeated.

**Take Charge** What would you do if your child told a joke that makes fun of a group of people? Write your answer in a half-page essay.

# Parenting Skills

## Teach a Child Tolerance

Describe for students a scenario in which they are parents of a nine-year-old. Twice a year, the family visits the child's great aunt. Unfortunately, the great aunt frequently makes negative remarks about people of different races. You do not want to be disrespectful, but you also want your child to know that you do not agree with these views. What would you do? (Possible answer: On the way home, you could emphasize the importance of accepting all people as individuals.)

**Take Charge**
Answers will vary but students may say that they would explain to the child that the joke was hurtful to others.

## Reteach cont.

**R** **Reading Strategy**
**The Importance of Examples**
Tell students that authors often use examples to drive home their main points. Have a volunteer read aloud the text in the left column of this page. Then encourage students to discuss how the author uses Patricia's behavior as an example of how peer relationships become increasingly important to preteens.

**Professional Development**

**Mini Clip Reading: Modeling Reading Strategies**
A teacher uses a read-aloud to model fluent reading strategies.

**W** **Writing Support**
**Personal Narrative**
**Being a Victim** Have students write a personal narrative describing a time when they, or someone they care about, was a victim of prejudice or intolerance. In their writing, they should provide a detailed description of their feelings about the event. (Refer to p. 470 to review the characteristics of personal narratives. Students' narratives will vary, but should convey the student's feelings concerning the event. For example, maybe a friend was criticized for attending synagogue because she was Jewish.)

✓ **Reading Check**

**Recall** Nine-year-olds are often wrapped up in their own thoughts so they may ignore their parents.

**487**

## Reteach cont.

### C Critical Thinking

**Make Judgments** Describe a scenario to the class in which a group of classmates teases someone for not being a good athlete. Ask: Is this an example of teasing or is it bullying? How can you tell the difference? (Answers will vary. Students should realize that true teasing does not make the person feel bad or excluded from the group; in fact, teasing can strengthen the ties among individuals. Bullying, however, causes a feeling of exclusion.)

### W Writing Support

#### Journal Entry

**Volunteering** Ask students to think about a volunteer experience that they were involved in as a preteen. Maybe they picked up trash in a park or helped teach young children sports. Have students write a journal entry describing this experience. (Refer to p. 54 to review the characteristics of journal entries. Journal entries will vary, but students should write about a volunteer experience they had as a preteen. Encourage students to describe the action as well as how they felt during and after the experience.)

---

### SAFE CHILD HEALTHY CHILD

#### Internet Safety

Internet safety is a concern for parents and children alike. Parents must be aware of what their children are viewing on the Internet. Children must be aware of potential dangers of the Internet. Parents can use software to limit use to appropriate sites. Chat rooms are another concern. Children in this age group may not realize possible dangers and might give out personal information. Keeping the computer in a family area, rather than in a child's room, helps parents monitor use.

☀ **Be Prepared** There are a number of things parents and their children can do to stay safe while surfing the Internet. Research guidelines for Internet safety for children and teens. Create a poster with the guidelines.

---

 without an adult to guide them. What will they do if a group of classmates teases someone for not being a good athlete? What will they say if a peer dares them to smoke a cigarette or to try drugs? What will they do when a friend asks to cheat off of their homework?

### Guidance

Parents, other adults, and older siblings can help prepare children to make the right moral choices in a number of ways. Here are some ways to offer moral guidance.

- **Set a good example.** Modeling moral behavior is the best method of teaching a child to act in a moral way.
- **Support the child's growing conscience.** Sometimes going along with the group may seem like a means to feeling accepted, even if the group is doing something wrong. Children need to be reminded that they will regret doing the wrong thing.
- **Talk about how to handle situations that might occur.** Discussing "what-ifs" ahead

---

of time can help a child develop coping strategies for difficult situations.

- **Reinforce empathy.** Ask children to put themselves in another person's place. How would they feel if they were the object of their group's teasing? Being able to feel empathy can deter a child from teasing or otherwise harassing someone just to go along with the group.
- **Use the child's sense of fairness.** Children in this age group value fairness. Encourage them to use that sense of fairness to lead them to the right decisions.

### Peer Pressure

Children ages eleven and twelve generally become less dependent on their parents. They identify more and more with their peer groups. Being accepted by peers is of **paramount**, or extreme, importance.

Because of this, peer pressure becomes very strong. **Peer pressure** is a social group's influence on the way individuals behave. The desire to be accepted leads preteens to adopt the words, behaviors, habits, and ideas of others in their social group. In their drive for conformity they may dress alike, adopt similar hairstyles, and find other ways to show that they belong. **Conformity** means being like one another.

A child who is different from others in some way can have a hard time during this period. A preteen who likes music that differs from what is currently popular or who dresses differently may be teased by others.

Peer pressure can be a powerful influence on a young person's life. It can be an influence for good or for bad. Those whose friends have positive values are more likely to avoid drugs, alcohol, and other risky behaviors. The urge to go along with dishonest or unethical actions can be equally strong. Older children and preteens are more likely to avoid or resist negative peer pressure if they:

- Join a peer group that shows positive moral values.
- Find others with similar hobbies and interests to spend time with.
- Rely upon their conscience to help make decisions about what is right and wrong.

---

### SAFE CHILD HEALTHY CHILD

#### Internet Safety

**Identify** Ask students: Why do you think a preteen might give out personal information to someone they met on a social networking site? (Answers will vary. Possibly the preteen wants to be seen as being friendly.)

☀ **Be Prepared** Posters will vary but may include: Never give out your social security number, your birth date, or your mother's maiden name without adult consent. Never give personal information of any sort to someone you meet in a chat room. Check with an adult if you are unsure about giving out information.

- Try not to appear upset when teased by peers. People who tease are looking for a reaction. If there is none, they may stop.
- Talk about the problem with a parent or other trusted adult.

Parents and others who work with children can help them avoid the influence of negative peer pressure by giving their love and support.

## Taking Responsibility

Children in this age group need to learn that with independence comes responsibility. They need safe opportunities to explore, test, and learn about their new responsibilities. Parents can help in many ways:

- Treat eleven- and twelve-year-olds less like children. Spend time talking and having fun.
- Allow preteens to make low-risk decisions when possible. Preteens need to rebel and test limits. Choosing how to decorate their room is a harmless way to do so.

- Encourage preteens to think through the consequences of their decisions. If they do not do their homework, what will happen to their grades?
- Within reason, let preteens experience the consequences of making bad decisions. Going to bed late means being tired all day. Spending their entire allowance early in the week means having no money at the end of the week.
- Negotiate family rules. Listen to any objections or special needs that a preteen might have. Compromise whenever practical.
- Stick to the family rules. Breaking these rules calls for clear, effective consequences. Physical punishment is counterproductive. **Counterproductive** means something hinders the original goal. Time-out usually does not work with this age group. Grounding and taking away privileges are more effective ways to teach preteens that their behavior has consequences.

### Assess

**Study Tools**

Have students go to the Online Learning Center at **glencoe.com**:

- Take the **Practice Test**.
- Download **Study-to-Go** content.

Use the **Student Activity Workbook** for additional practice.

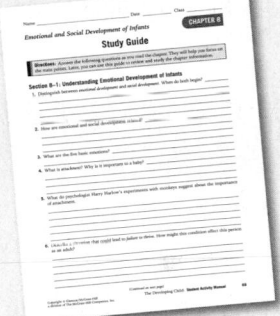

---

## Section 17.2 — After You Read

### Review Key Concepts

1. **List** the ways in which friendships change for seven- and eight-year-olds.
2. **Describe** the factors that contribute to changes in family relationships during this period.
3. **Discuss** the relationship between independence and responsibility.

### Practice Academic Skills

 **English Language Arts**

4. Imagine that you are the parent of a preteen who is having a conflict with his or her best friend. Write a conversation you could have with your child and his or her friend to help them resolve their conflict.

> **NCTE 12** Use language to accomplish individual purposes.

 **Social Studies**

5. Imagine that the preteen you mentor has asked for your help. He wants to know how he can use positive peer pressure to his advantage and resist negative peer pressure. Write a letter to him with your answer.

> **NCSS IV C** Describe the ways family and other group and cultural influences contribute to the development of a sense of self.

 **Check Your Answers** Check your answers at this book's Online Learning Center at **glencoe.com**.

### Close

## Culminating Activity

**Explain** Discuss how developing conflict resolution skills can help older children and preteens maintain friendships. Then discuss how these skills can help in relationships with parents. *(Possible response: listening to both sides and finding common ground can help in working through misunderstandings with friends and parents.)*

**NCLB** connects academic correlations to book content.

---

## Section 17.2 — After You Read

### Review Key Concepts

1. Friendships become more personal during this time due to children's ability to communicate their feelings and their growing sense of themselves.
2. Factors that contribute to changes in family relationships during this time include children growing more independent, changing family structures, and sibling conflicts.
3. More independence brings with it more responsibility.

### Practice Academic Skills

4. Answers will vary but should include information that reflects setting ground rules for both friends, listening to both sides of the argument, finding common ground between both sides, and helping both sides reach a solution that they accept.
5. Letters will vary but may include that he can associate himself with peers who have positive moral values and similar interests, which will help him make good decisions and avoid being tempted by bad ones.

### Careers
### With Children
### Child Life Specialist

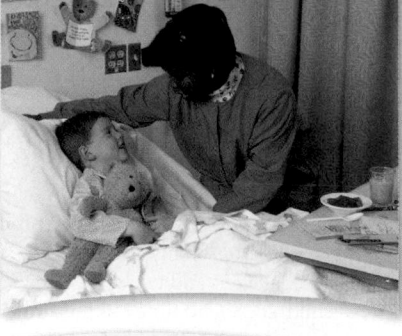

## Focus

### Discussion Starter

**Child Life Specialist** Ask students if they have ever been in the hospital. If any students have, encourage them to share their concerns or fears. Discuss that these fears are common among children and often increase with children who have illnesses that require long hospital stays. Child life specialists help children deal with these fears.

## Teach

### C Critical Thinking

**Analyze** Ask: Why do you think a child life specialist must have excellent communication skills? (A child life specialist must deal with an enormous variety of people and be able to use appropriate language depending on the situation. The child life specialist must be able to talk with children so that the child's needs can be met. He or she also must be able to talk with parents or other caregivers and with health care professionals.)

## Assess

### Make Connections

Ask students to list specific correlations between academic subjects and the kinds of skills a child life specialist needs. (Answers will vary. Students should show an understanding of how academic skills relate directly to the profession of child life specialist. For example, the ability to understand the psychological needs of both patients and families is vital.)

**NCLB** This relates academic skills to specific tasks that are performed for this job.

**C**hild life specialists are members of pediatric health care teams who focus on the emotional and social aspects of children who are sick. They help children understand what is happening in the hospital and provide emotional support.

### ☀ What Does a Child Life Specialist Do?

Child life specialists explain medical procedures in ways that make children feel safe. They offer children age-appropriate toys and teach them how to relax. Child life specialists also provide information to parents and siblings. They plan and host visits from musicians, clowns, and animals while children recuperate.

### ☀ Where Do Child Life Specialists Work?

Most child life specialists work in hospitals. They might work in emergency rooms or surgical departments. They also sometimes work in neonatal or pediatric intensive care units in children's hospitals.

### Preparation and Skills

**Education and Training**
Child life specialists earn bachelor's degrees, usually in psychology or education. They must also complete an internship, gain work experience, and pass an exam to become certified.

**Aptitudes, Abilities, and Skills**
A child life specialist must have energy and stamina. They also need the ability to communicate clearly and relate to children. Resourcefulness, emotional stability, and an understanding of family dynamics are helpful.

**Academic Skills**
English language arts are used to communicate to patients, families, and team members. Social studies skills, such as psychology, are used to better understand patients and families.

**C**

**NCLB**

**Explore Careers** Research other careers that provide aid to children and their families. Choose one career and write a paragraph describing it. Tell whether the career interests you and why.

**Careers Online** For more information on careers, visit the Occupational Outlook Handbook Web site through the link on this book's Online Learning Center at **glencoe.com**.

## Close

### Culminating Activity

**Interview a Child Life Specialist** Contact a local hospital to see if there is a child life specialist. See if the individual is willing to conduct an interview with a group of students. If so, have students prepare a list of questions. When the group is done, have them present to the class what they learned. (A group of students should conduct an interview with a child life specialist and report what they learn to the class.)

**Explore Careers** Students' answers will vary but should include a career that helps children and their families, and tell whether the student is interested in the career.

## Chapter Summary

Emotions play a major role in the development of children. The focus of the child shifts from the home to the larger world. Children must learn to control emotions in socially acceptable ways. Between the ages of seven and twelve, children develop a sense of self. Children with a sense of competence are likely to have high self-esteem and be willing to try new things. Older children's friendships become more personal. Peers become more important, but conflicts are common. As children gain more independence, they need help making moral choices.

## Vocabulary Review

1. Use at least six of these content and academic vocabulary terms in a short essay about yourself as a preteen.

### Content Vocabulary
◇ anxiety (p. 476)
◇ sense of self (p. 477)
◇ sense of competence (p. 478)
◇ gender identity (p. 480)
◇ bullying (p. 485)
◇ peer pressure (p. 488)
◇ conformity (p. 488)

### Academic Vocabulary
■ shift (p. 473)
■ persevere (p. 478)
■ paramount (p. 488)
■ counterproductive (p. 489)

## Review Key Concepts

2. **Identify** four ways to help ease emotional upsets.
3. **Explain** how to help children control and express their anger in socially acceptable ways.
4. **List** six ways to help a child develop a sense of competence.
5. **Summarize** the four main qualities children look for in friendships.
6. **Identify** typical changes that occur in children's attitudes toward their parents.
7. **Describe** five ways to help prepare children to make good moral choices.

## Critical Thinking

8. **Predict** How might a child with a good sense of competence be likely to deal with failure?
9. **Analyze** What social skills do you think a person needs to have in order to make friends?
10. **Apply** Why might a child be afraid to tell an adult that he or she is being bullied? How can an adult deal with the situation?

## Content and Academic Vocabulary Review

1. Essays will vary but should include at least six vocabulary terms.

## Review Key Concepts

2. be patient, avoid taking it personally, help the child maintain self-control, and listen attentively
3. model socially acceptable behavior, teach the child how to gain self-control, and help the child learn nonaggressive ways to resolve conflicts
4. help children focus on their strengths, provide opportunities, encourage learning, establish reachable goals, recognize successes, and focus on the positive
5. loyalty, trustworthiness, kindness and understanding, and fun
6. Seven-year-olds depend on their parents but often challenge parental authority. At eight, children tend to cling to their parents. By nine, children become wrapped up in their own thoughts and sometimes ignore their parents. Ten is generally a smooth year, children are happier and more communicative. At eleven and twelve, as they begin to move away from the direct control and influence of parents, preteens may become quite critical of their parents' values.
7. set a good example, support the child's growing conscience, talk about how to handle specific situations, reinforce empathy, and use the child's sense of fairness

## Critical Thinking

8. Answers will vary but may include that a child with a sense of competence would probably think that he or she is good at other things and try to focus on those.
9. Answers will vary but may include empathy, kindness, loyalty, or a sense of fun.
10. Answers will vary but may include: A child may fear that telling may make the situation worse, may fear embarrassment, or may want to try to handle the situation on his or her own. An adult can ask questions, give reassurance, and report the problem.

### Family & Community Connections

**11.** Answers will vary but should include a ranking of the most common issues the school counselor deals with.

## Health Skills

**12.** Reports will vary. Not all states have laws against bullying. Those that do vary in the way they define bullying and in the way it is dealt with. Several states encourage or require employee training on bullying and bullying prevention. Some states require individuals to report school bullying incidents to authorities.

## Observation Skills

**13.** Tables will vary but should include data collected. Students should also summarize their findings in a paragraph.

## Real-World Skills

**14.** Letters will vary but should include that the friend and her parents can model socially acceptable behavior, teach the child how to gain self-control, help the child learn nonaggressive ways to resolve conflicts, reward the child for controlling anger, and help the child learn to use unrelated physical activity to work off anger.

**15.** Posters will vary but should include examples of physical and emotional bullying and ways children can protect themselves from bullies.

**16.** Sam lost $80. ($4 × 5 days = $20 per week; $20 × 4 weeks = $80)

### Family & Community Connection

**11. Interview a School Counselor** Many of the issues discussed in this chapter continue to be challenges for teenagers. Arrange to talk with one of your school counselors about the issues he or she typically deals with. Create a list of issues such as bullying, anger, or anxiety. Ask the counselor to rank the items in order of occurrence in the student population. Write a paragraph to summarize the results of your interview.

### Health Skills

**12. Research Bullying** Bullying is a form of harassment that can affect mental, emotional, or physical health. Many preteens are affected by bullying. Adults are also common victims of bullying. Research the laws that govern bullying. This might include bullying at school, in the workplace, or on the Internet. Pay special attention to the rights of the victims. Write a one-page report with your findings.

### Observation Skills

**13. Observe Children at Play** Work with your teacher to arrange to observe children ages seven to twelve playing at a school or park.

**Procedure** During your observation, keep track of the emotions, such as joy, anger, or anxiety, expressed by individual children.

**Analysis** Create a table to present the information you collect. Across the top of the table, put fictitious names or numbers for the children observed to maintain confidentiality. Down the side, list the emotions observed. Fill in the corresponding cell of the table with the number of times you observed the emotion in each child. Write a paragraph summarizing your findings.

**NCSS IV D Individual Development and Identity** Apply concepts and methods about the study of human growth and development, such as behavior, perception, and personality.

**N C L B**

## Real-World Skills

| | |
|---|---|
| **Problem-Solving Skills** | **14. Offer Advice** Suppose a friend confides that her twelve-year-old brother is angry all the time and is upsetting the family. The brother seems to have no limits and even throws and breaks things. Write a letter advising your friend how to handle the situation. |
| **Technology Skills** | **15. Create a Poster** Use word processing or graphics software to make a poster for a campaign aimed at stopping bullying in schools. Include examples of physical and emotional bullying. Illustrate ways that children can protect themselves from bullies. |
| **Financial Literacy** | **16. The Cost of Bullying** Sam was allowed $4.00 each day for lunch at school. Before Sam reported it, bullies took his lunch money every school day for four weeks. How much money did Sam lose to the bullies? |

 **Additional Activities** For additional activities, go to this book's Online Learning Center at **glencoe.com**.

## Academic Skills

**17.** Skits will vary but should reflect what students have learned in this chapter.

**18.** The 8-inch line is longer so Purcell is correct (8 × 2.5 = 20 centimeters; 20 is longer than 19).

The *Early Childhood Observations CD* offers additional lessons with videos to build students' observation skills.

**Part 1:** Learning to Observe
**Part 2:** How Children Develop
**Part 3:** Working With Young Children
**Part 4:** Extended Observations
**Part 5:** Resources and Answer File

## Academic Skills

 **English Language Arts**

**17. Write a Skit** A preteen boy believes a friend has betrayed him by telling a secret. The friend is actually innocent. Write a skit that shows the interaction between the two boys. The behavior of the characters should not be aggressive but should reflect what you have learned about preteens.

> **NCTE 5** Use different writing process elements to communicate effectively.

 **Mathematics**

**18. Peer Pressure Decisions** Purcell, age 8, and Bethany, age 12, are each asked to compare the lengths of two lines. One line is 8 inches, and the other line is 19 centimeters. Kay, a 13-year-old, tells them that the line measuring 19 centimeters is longer. Bethany agrees with Kay, showing peer conformity. Purcell gives the matter some thought and says he thinks the 8-inch line is longer. Who is correct?

**Math Concept** **Unit Conversions** Centimeters are a measurement of the metric system, while inches are a measurement in the customary system. To compare measurements, you should convert both numbers to the same system.

**Starting Hint** 1 inch = 2.5 centimeters. Mulitply 8 inches by 2.5 to convert it to centimeters.

 For math help, go to the Math Appendix at the back of the book.

> **NCTM Measurement** Apply appropriate techniques, tools, and formulas to determine measurements.

 **Science**

**19. Design a Survey** A survey can be a very straightforward way to get information. A survey also can be used to test a hypothesis. An example of a hypothesis is: Children who are in after-school programs, clubs, or teams have more friends than children who do not participate in these activities.

**Procedure** Design a survey that will test this hypothesis.

**Analysis** Create a presentation to explain how your survey would test whether the hypothesis is valid or invalid.

> **NSES A** Develop abilities necessary to do scientific inquiry, understandings about scientific inquiry.

### Standardized Test Practice

**ESSAY**

Read the scenario, then write your answer on a separate sheet of paper.

> Researchers have found that teens who witness bullying may feel helpless and guilty for not reporting the incident or standing up to a bully. They have also found that witnessing bullying may influence students to model their own behavior after that of bullies.

**20.** Do you agree with this research finding? Why or why not? Write your thoughts in a one-page essay.

> **Test-Taking Tip** Before answering an essay question, write down a few notes to help you organize your thoughts. Number your thoughts in the order you will write about them.

---

 **NCLB**

**19.** Presentations will vary but should explain how to conduct a survey to attain the required information.

 **NCLB** connects academic correlations to book content.

**McGraw Hill** **Professional Development**

**Mini Clip Reading: Assessment in Standards-Based Instruction**
Lois Moseley, author and educator, discusses the role of assessment in standards-based instruction.

### Standardized Test Practice

**20.** Students' essays will vary but should show organized thoughts, good grammar, and correct punctuation.

**Test-Taking Tips** If a test includes a variety of question types, many test-takers prefer to complete the essay questions first. This is because they are freshest at this point and see the essay questions as requiring the most energy and detailed thought.

**Essay Tests** Discuss with students that essay tests will often give you a choice of questions to answer. Students should resist the urge to decide too quickly on which question to answer. The one that looks easiest at first glance may be more difficult to satisfactorily complete.

---

## TECHNOLOGY Solutions

### Use these technology solutions to streamline chapter assessment!

 **ExamView Assessment Suite** CD allows you to create and print out customized tests or ready-made unit and chapter tests, complete with answer keys.

 **TeacherWorks Plus** is an electronic lesson planner that provides instant access to complete teacher resources in one convenient package.

**Online Learning Center** includes resources and activities for students and teachers.

**STANDARDS BASED LESSON PLANNING** *The Developing Child* provides students with instruction and assessment in the following fundamental content areas:

## National Standards Correlations

| Standards | Pages |
|---|---|
| **12.1.1** Analyze physical, emotional, social, spiritual, and intellectual development. | 497–498, 508–510 |
| **12.1.2** Analyze interrelationships among physical, emotional, social, and intellectual aspects of human growth and development. | 506–507 |
| **12.1.3** Analyze current and emerging research about human growth and development, including research on brain development. | 499–503, 505–506 |
| **12.2.3** Analyze the effects of gender, ethnicity, and culture on individual development. | 498, 510, 513 |
| **12.3.3** Analyze the role of family and social services support systems in meeting human growth and development needs. | 512 |
| **15.1.2** Analyze expectations and responsibilities of parenting. | 507–508 |
| **15.2.1** Choose nurturing practices that support human growth and development. | 508 |
| **15.3.1** Assess community resources and services available to families. | 512 |

**NO CHILD LEFT BEHIND** NCLB activities, information, and skills practice will help your students attain NCLB proficiency. Students will improve their abilities in the following academic standards areas:

## Academic Standards Correlations

| Discipline | Standard | Feature/Activity |
|---|---|---|
| **English Language Arts** | **NCTE 1** Read texts to acquire new information. | **Reading Guide (pp. 496, 504)** |
| | **NCTE 3** Apply strategies to interpret texts. | **After You Read (p. 503)** |
| | **NCTE 4** Use written language to communicate effectively. | **Academic Skills (p. 513)** |
| | **NCTE 5** Use different writing process elements to communicate effectively. | **Writing Activity (p. 494)** **After You Read (p. 510)** |
| **Mathematics** | **NCTM Geometry** Use visualization, spatial reasoning, and geometric modeling to solve problems. | **Academic Skills (p. 513)** |
| | **NCTM Data Analysis and Probability** Select and use appropriate statistical methods to analyze data. | **After You Read (p. 503)** |
| **Science** | **NSES A** Develop abilities necessary to do scientific inquiry, understandings about scientific inquiry. | **Academic Skills (p. 513)** |
| **Social Studies** | **NCSS IV D Individual Development and Identity** Apply concepts, methods, and theories about the study of human growth and development. | **Observation Skills (p. 512)** |
| | **NCSS IV E Individual Development and Identity** Examine the interaction of ethnic, national, or cultural influences in specific situations or events. | **After You Read (p. 510)** |
| | **NCSS IX A Global Connections** Explain how language, art, music, belief systems, and other cultural elements can facilitate global understanding or cause misunderstanding. | **Culture Matters (p. 498)** |

## McGraw Hill Professional Development

### MINI CLIP VIDEO LIBRARY

Targeted professional development is correlated throughout *The Developing Child*. **The McGraw-Hill Professional Development Mini Clip Video Library** provides teaching strategies to strengthen academic and learning skills. Log on to **glencoe.com**.

In this chapter, you will find these Mini Clips:
- **ELL** Accessing Prior Knowledge, p. 494
- **Reading** Flexible Groupings, p. 499
- **Math** Real-Life Ratios, p. 502
- **ELL** Academic Language, p. 504
- **ELL** Group Discussions, p. 509
- **Reading** Lesson Reflections, p. 513

## Reading and Writing Strategies

**Writing Activity: Editing** (p. 494)
Students use writing tips to edit a paragraph.

**Before You Read** (pp. 496, 504)
A pre-reading question or statement will help students make a personal connection to content.

**Graphic Organizer** (pp. 496, 504)
A visual tool will help students organize and remember new content.

**Reading Check** (pp. 498, 506, 508)
A question allows students to make a quick comprehension self-check.

**After You Read** (pp. 503, 510)
Organize and process students' understanding of what they have read.

## Chapter Features

**Analyzing Media Messages** (p. 498)
Look at the picture the media paints of our society and the world.

**Dyslexia** (p. 500)
Dyslexia makes it difficult for children to learn to read and spell.

**Children's Museums** (p. 501)
In these museums, learning takes place through actual experience.

**Peer Pressure** (p. 506)
Parents can help preteens deal with negative peer pressure.

**A Group Project** (p. 507)
Help students understand the dynamics of working in groups.

**Helping with Homework** (p. 508)
When children start to have homework, caregivers must make almost as many adjustments as the child.

# Chapter

## 18

## Chapter Overview

### Introduce the Chapter

In this chapter, students learn how thinking skills develop, theories of intellectual development, and understanding intelligence. They also learn about modes of learning, the school experience, and standardized tests.

### Build Background

Tell students that between the ages of seven and twelve, children increase their intellectual growth. Ask students to recall when they were seven to twelve years old. Ask if they can remember whether they experienced a change in their memory, awareness and curiosity, abstract thinking skills, or attention span. Allow volunteers to share their experiences.

**Professional Development**

**Mini Clip**
ELL: Accessing Prior Knowlege

A teacher helps students make connections between what they know and the upcoming reading selection.

## Writing Activity

### Editing

Tell students that most of the time, the material they edit will be their own work. Provide them with these guidelines: Be objective when editing your own work. Proofread closely to find errors. (Corrections for paragraph: When editing, you probably will need **to** read through the document several times. For example, you may read through once to check for grammar error**s** and a second time to determine whether the text makes ~~cents~~sense.)

---

# Chapter

## 18 Intellectual Development from Seven to Twelve

## Chapter Objectives

After completing this chapter, you will be able to:

- **Identify** four signs of intellectual development in children ages seven to twelve.
- **Explain** four thinking skills that build a foundation for mastering school work.
- **Describe** three learning methods that are effective for children ages seven to twelve.
- **Identify** characteristics of the middle school experience that make it well suited to preteen learning.
- **Compare and contrast** three types of standardized tests.

## Writing Activity

### Editing

**Improving Your Writing** Read the Writing Tips below. Then edit the following paragraph.

When editing, you probably will need read through the document several times. For example, you may read through once to check for grammar error and a second time to determine whether the text makes cents.

**Writing Tips** Good editing can improve almost anyone's writing. Here are some tips that should prove helpful:

1. Read slowly and carefully. Some editors think reading aloud makes it easier to spot problems.
2. Delete any unnecessary words. Extra words can hide the main idea.
3. Make certain the text is well organized. The text should flow naturally from one idea to the next.

---

## CLASSROOM Solutions

### Print Resources

 **Student Edition**

 **Teacher Wraparound Edition**

 **Student Activity Workbook**

 **Student Activity Workbook Teacher Annotated Edition**

### Technology Resources

 **Online Learning Center** has resources and activities for students and teachers. Includes an Online Student Edition.

 **Interactive Student Edition** allows students to instantly access review materials, examples, and exercises.

Section **18.1** The Developing Brain from Seven to Twelve

Section **18.2** Learning from Seven to Twelve

## Review the Sections
Introduce the chapter by reviewing the sections:

### Section 18.1
In middle childhood and the preteen years, children make many advances in their intellectual abilities. Children move from the concrete operations stage to the formal operations stage at about age twelve, when they become capable of abstract thinking. Piaget, Vygotsky, Montessori, and Gardner developed important theories about intellectual development.

### Section 18.2
Direct learning, peer learning, and independent learning are different modes of learning that are appropriate to children ages seven to twelve. Middle school programs are specially designed to meet the educational and emotional needs of preteens. Between the ages of seven and twelve, students begin to take specially designed standardized tests.

↑ **Explore the Photo**
Strategy games such as checkers and chess can help improve thinking skills. *What kinds of skills do you think these young people are learning?*

495

➤ **Explore the Photo**

**Caption Answer** Answers may vary. Possible answers include that they are learning to plan ahead, to concentrate, to anticipate their opponent's responses, and to think spatially.

**Discussion** Ask students to share what kinds of games they like to play. (Some may mention athletic games, video games, card games, or board games.) Ask what thinking skills they think they develop by playing games. (Answers will vary; students may mention memory, concentration, or thinking ahead.)

**☉TeacherWorks™** *Plus* **TeacherWorks Plus** is an electronic lesson planner that provides instant access to complete teacher resources in one convenient package.

**PRESENTATION** *Plus!* **Presentation Plus!** provides visual teaching aids for every section.

 **The Early Childhood Observations CD** presents video observations and lessons on observation skills and child development.

**The Developing Brain eTransparencies and Guide** include information and activities to offer insights into brain development and diseases of the brain.

# Focus

## Bell Ringer Activity

### Growing Minds

Instruct students to individually write down a definition for the word *intelligence*. Ask for volunteers to share their definitions with the class. Then ask: What are some factors that play a role in how much children grow intellectually? (Answers will vary but may include: opportunities children have and things they are exposed to.)

## Preteaching

### Vocabulary

Knowing the meanings of Greek roots can help you make an educated guess about the meaning of a new word. Explain that *hypothetical* comes from Greek *hupothetikos*, meaning "to suppose." Read a sentence with the word *hypothetical* and ask students to guess the meaning.

### Graphic Organizer

 The Graphic Organizer is also on the TeacherWorks CD.

(Graphic organizers will include 3 columns. "What I Know" and "What I Want to Know" columns will vary. "What I Learned" column will vary, but may include any of the concepts learned in the section.)

**NCLB** connects academic correlations to book content.

---

## Reading Guide

### Before You Read

**Create a Table** Spend a minute skimming this section. Note that the second part discusses the learning theories of five individuals. As you read, create a table to keep track of these theories.

### Read to Learn
#### Key Concepts
- **Identify** four signs of intellectual development in children ages seven to twelve.
- **Explain** four thinking skills that build a foundation for mastering school work.

### Main Idea
From seven to twelve, children's memory improves, they become more curious and idealistic, and they begin thinking abstractly. There are different theories about how children learn.

### Content Vocabulary
 transitivity
◇ conservation
◇ hypothetical

 **Graphic Organizer** Go to this book's Online Learning Center at **glencoe.com** to print out this graphic organizer.

### Academic Vocabulary
You will find these words in your reading and on your tests. Use the glossary to look up their definitions if necessary.
- concrete
- multifaceted

### Graphic Organizer
Create a KWL chart like the one shown. Before you begin reading, fill in the first two columns. As you read, fill in the third.

| Brain Development in 7- to 12-Year-Olds | | |
|---|---|---|
| What I Know | What I Want to Know | What I Learned |
| | | |

**Academic Standards** . . . . . . . . . . . . . . . . . . . . . . . . .

 **English Language Arts**
**NCTE 3** Apply strategies to interpret texts.

**Mathematics**
**NCTM Data Analysis and Probability** Select and use appropriate statistical methods to analyze data.

**Social Studies**
**NCSS IX A Global Connections** Explain how language, art, music, belief systems, and other cultural elements can facilitate global understanding or cause misunderstanding.

---

**NCTE** National Council of Teachers of English
**NCTM** National Council of Teachers of Mathematics

**NSES** National Science Education Standards
**NCSS** National Council for the Social Studies

---

## Reading Guide

### Before You Read

Ask students if they have ever played a game with a seven- to twelve-year-old. Ask how it is different playing with a seven-year-old and a twelve-year-old. (Answers may include: the twelve-year-old has better thinking skills.) Tell students that in this section they will learn how intelligence increases in seven- to twelve-year-olds.

### D Develop Concepts

**Main Idea** Discuss the main idea with the students. Ask: What is idealism? (Answers will vary but may include: the belief that perfection can be attained in the physical world.)

# Signs of Increased Intellectual Growth

The brain is the center of learning. As children grow from ages seven to twelve, brain development continues to increase their ability to learn. Their intellectual development improves steadily, becoming capable of new ways of thinking. The emotional and intellectual needs of preteens differ from those of younger and older children. Educators created middle schools, or junior highs, in an effort to address these special needs.

Advances in intellectual growth between the ages of seven and twelve are exciting to witness. Learned routines become automatic, so children are able to use their brain power for higher-level learning. Four signs of intellectual development for this age occur in memory, awareness, idealism, and attention span.

## Memory

Memory is central to all learning. It is critical to success in school. People use both short-term memory and long-term memory to learn. For example, if you have studied for a test, you have memorized the necessary information. To do so, you brought information into your short-term memory to concentrate on it. You then stored it in your long-term memory. You may forget all about that information until you get to the test. Once there, you recall the information by bringing it back into your short-term memory and answering the question. Then you let it go so that you can recall the answer to the next question.

Improvements in the way the brain functions allow older children and preteens to learn more and to use their knowledge more efficiently. For example, children in this age group generally do not count on their fingers. They can recall and apply basic math operations, such as adding and subtracting, almost automatically. This is because they have done them so many times.

## Awareness and Curiosity

Children from age seven to twelve develop a more intense awareness of themselves and those around them. They become better at planning their own behavior. They also get better at understanding their abilities and the abilities of others. Children eight and older begin to recognize another person's point of view and to figure out what that person is thinking. They show more concern about what people think of them.

**An Interest in Learning**
Many preteens become more involved in learning as they study topics that spark their curiosity. *What kinds of topics do you think preteens are particularly interested in?*

## Teach

### Discussion Starter

**Intellectual Growth** Ask students: What do you think intellectual growth includes? How can you tell when intellectual growth takes place? How are schools set up to enhance intellectual growth? (Answers may include: intellectual growth is an increase in brain power that allows for higher-level learning and thinking. It affects memory, awareness and curiosity, idealism, and abstract thinking. Growth is evident when people think and operate at a higher-level—they remember things because of repetition, they no longer count on their fingers, and so on. Schools and teachers are specially prepared to help students attain higher-level thinking. Activities and instruction are planned to achieve this.)

### R Reading Strategy

**Activating Prior Knowledge** Ask a volunteer to read the two paragraphs under the head Memory. Ask students to recall a point in their lives when they moved from one level of learning to another. (Answers will vary. Students might recall when they had memorized the addition facts so they no longer had to think about adding single digit numbers. They might recall when they had memorized all of the steps to do a load of laundry and was able to do it automatically.)

## ➤ Explore the Photo

**Caption Answer** Student answers will vary. Answers might include photography, nature, languages, history, biology, mathematics, or computers.

**Discussion** Have students think about a project or class assignment that helped them realize what subject areas they enjoyed. Ask volunteers to share their experiences. (Responses will vary; students may be interested in many different subject areas.)

## C Critical Thinking

**Problem Solving** Have students attempt to think like a preteen and come up with idealistic solutions to some complex problems. Have students choose from this list and create idealistic and imaginative solutions to the problems: landfills, homelessness, water pollution, hunger, war. After students have created their solutions, discuss the practicality of the solutions. (Students' solutions will vary but should be imaginative and idealistic. Possible solutions include: make people recycle more or allow the homeless to live in empty buildings.)

## U Universal Access

**Gifted Learners** Have gifted learners research theories about why attention span becomes shorter toward the end of the preteen period. Instruct students to choose the theory that seems most plausible to them and to write a one-page report in which they describe its ideas and strengths. After students have completed their reports, divide them into groups (be sure a variety of theories are represented in each group). Have each student describe and defend the theory he or she chose. (Students' reports will vary but should discuss the theory they choose and describe its ideas and strengths. Reports should be written in paragraph format and be free of grammar and spelling errors.)

### ✓ Reading Check

**Recall** Children become more aware of themselves and others around them and develop an understanding of their abilities in relationship to the abilities of others. They become more concerned about what others think of them and begin to recognize that others may have different points of view than they do.

**498**

In this stage, children begin to think of themselves according to their unique qualities, such as their feelings and beliefs, instead of just their physical features. They are able to strive to achieve a goal because they are learning to control their behavior. At school, they become increasingly independent in their learning. They can determine which learning strategies work best for them. They practice organizing their work so that they can complete long-term projects. Preteens often develop interests that can last a lifetime, such as playing sports, acting in plays, or loving to read.

## Idealism and Abstract Thinking

Young children judge whether something is right or wrong by how much pleasure or pain it involves. For example, will they be punished for a particular behavior? Three-year-old Jack knew hitting was wrong only because he was put in time-out for it. Older children and teens adopt moral standards that authority figures, such as parents, will approve of.

By the preteen years, children can recognize complex social problems such as prejudice or crime. However, they do not understand why the problems are difficult to solve. For example, these idealistic children tend to believe that to prevent theft, thieves just need to stop stealing. They cannot yet analyze their ideas to see if they are realistic. Even so, their idealism can help them become involved in improving their world. Parents can encourage preteens to be involved in the community through volunteer work.

## Attention Span

For reasons that are not yet understood, at around age twelve, preteens' attention span actually grows shorter. They tend to learn less because they cannot concentrate as long. Their grades may drop at school, and test scores may decline.

### ✓ Reading Check
**Recall** How does children's awareness and curiosity change from ages seven to twelve?

## CULTURE MATTERS

### Analyzing Media Messages

What kind of picture does the media paint of our society and our world? Is it an accurate picture? These questions are the foundation of many media education courses. Some countries, such as Canada and Hungary, require students to take media education courses. Teachers present material from newspapers, magazines, the Internet, films, and television. Teachers show students how to look critically at the media and make comparisons between media outlets. Students then provide real-world examples. Our world is growing more complex. Many people feel that students need to learn how to analyze the media and its messages now more than ever.

**Build Connections** What kind of a picture do you think students in a country such as Egypt or China might get of the United States from viewing American movies? Give an example to support your beliefs.

**NCSS IX A Global Connections** Explain how language, art, music, belief systems, and other cultural elements can facilitate global understanding or cause misunderstanding.

## CULTURE MATTERS

### Analyzing Media Messages

**Discussion** Bring in various examples of news media such as newspapers (well-respected as well as questionable), magazines, and video clips. As students look through the news articles, ask what kinds of criteria they use to determine whether the information is reliable. (Students' answers will vary but may include that if two or more media provide the same information, it is true.)

**Building Connections** Student answers will vary, but they should provide concrete examples to back up their beliefs. Students in other countries might think Americans are very violent because of the large amounts of fighting and violence in many U.S. movies.

## Figure 18.1 Piaget's Four Periods of Learning

Each of Piaget's four periods of learning build on the previous one. *How are concrete operations different from formal operations?*

| Period | Characteristics |
|---|---|
| **Sensorimotor** Birth–2 years | Children learn through their senses and own actions. |
| **Preoperational** 2–7 years | Children think in terms of their own activities and what they perceive at the moment. |
| **Concrete operations** 7–11 years | Children can think logically but still learn best through experience. |
| **Formal operations** 11–Adult | People are capable of abstract thinking. |

## Theories About How Children Learn

Questions about how and why thinking skills expand continue to interest child development professionals. Jean Piaget was the earliest researcher to study children scientifically. Piaget's work was followed by some studies that built on his theories, as well as some studies that contradicted his ideas. Some of the best known theories were developed by Lev Vygotsky, Maria Montessori, Howard Gardner, and Robert Sternberg.

### Piaget's Theory

As you learned earlier, Jean Piaget proposed a theory to explain how children's thinking skills develop. He divided childhood intellectual development into four stages. Children from ages seven to twelve fall into the last two periods, as shown in **Figure 18.1**.

### Concrete Operations Stage

Most children begin to move into Piaget's concrete operations stage at about age seven. Their thinking works effectively on **concrete**, or actual, objects and tasks. They can generalize from their own experiences, but they cannot yet understand abstract ideas. For example, a five-year-old probably could not draw a map of the route from home to a nearby playground visited regularly. An eight-year-old might be able to visualize the neighborhood and draw a rough map. However, a child this age would likely have difficulty imagining what route to take if the usual one was blocked and another had to be found.

During the concrete operations stage, children develop several important thinking skills. These skills include classifying objects, placing objects in a series, extending relationships, and conservation.

**Classifying Objects** In Piaget's preoperational stage, children as young as three can classify objects, or group them, according to one similar characteristic, such as shape or color. For example, they can find all of the red blocks or all of the square blocks in a set. However, they cannot distinguish the blocks that are both red and square. By age seven, children can usually sort items by two or more different characteristics at the same time.

Section 18.1    The Developing Brain from Seven to Twelve    **499**

## Teach cont.

### S Skill Practice
#### Guided Practice

**Identify** Have students look up time frames for the five theorists discussed in the text and create a time line of the dates they find. (Time lines should include the following dates: Piaget (1896–1980); Vygotsky (1896–1934); Montessori (1870–1952); Gardner (1943– ); Sternberg (1949– .) **L1 ELL**

**Report** Have students survey child care professionals to determine on which researcher's theories (Piaget, Vygotsky, Montessori, Gardner, or Sternberg) they base their learning activities for children. Students should present an oral report with the information they gather. (Reports will vary. Students will likely find that child care professionals typically use theories from most, if not all, of the theorists listed.) **L2**

**Instruct** Divide the class into five groups. Assign each group one of the theorists from the text. Each group should compile the basic theories of their assigned theorist. Students may use information from the text or from other sources. Then redistribute the groups so that each group now has a member from each of the five original groups. Students should take turns teaching their new group the basic theories of the theorist they studied. (Basic theories may vary but should closely follow the information presented in the text on pages 499–503.) **L3**

## Figure 18.1 Piaget's Four Periods of Learning

**Caption Answer** Concrete operations can require logical thinking, but do not require the high degree of abstract thinking required of formal operations.

**Discussion** Have students categorize the children described below according to Piaget's stages: a child who assembles a model according to a diagram (preoperational); a child who sorts into yellow triangles, red rectangles, and blue circles (concrete operations); a child who walks to a new friend's house after getting directions over the phone (formal operations).

**Professional Development**

**Mini Clip Reading: Flexible Groupings**

Teachers use flexible groupings to promote student discussions.

### Quiz

Ask students to answer the following questions:

1. At what age do children start to realize that they can know someone else's point of view and figure out what that person is thinking? (at about age eight)
2. How does idealism develop in the preteen years? (Preteens can recognize complex social problems, but they don't understand how underlying causes can make problems difficult to solve.)
3. What term refers to the understanding that an object has the same characteristics even if there is a change in the way it is presented? (conservation)

## Reteach

### C₁ Critical Thinking

**Problem Solving** Read the following scenario to students: Twelve-year-old Trey has been treating his nine-year-old brother, Shane, badly. When he is not mocking something Shane has said, he is ignoring him. Shane admires his older brother, and this treatment hurts his feelings. How might Trey's parents use their older son's newly developing abilities to imagine hypothetical situations and use "if . . . then" reasoning to help solve this problem? (Answers will vary but may include: telling Trey that *if* he continues tormenting his brother, *then* he will be grounded.)

---

## RESPOND TO SPECIAL NEEDS — Dyslexia

Can you imagine what it would be like to see the word "learn" as "nrael"? Or, no matter how hard you tried, not to be able to remember how to spell "thought"? Children who have dyslexia must deal with these kinds of problems every day. Dyslexia is a learning disability that makes it hard for children to read and spell. An estimated 3 to 6 percent of school-age children have dyslexia. Researchers believe that dyslexia is a type of brain disorder. People with dyslexia have problems learning to decode written language. Because reading is central to much of learning, these children often do poorly in other subjects, such as social studies and science. Dyslexia is not related to intelligence. People with dyslexia can score high on learning ability tests, as long as the tests do not require them to read.

**Critical Thinking** Conduct research to learn about one or two of the teaching methods that have been developed to help children with dyslexia. Analyze why you think these methods work. Prepare a presentation to share what you learned and your analysis.

**Placing Objects in a Series** In the concrete operations stage, children can arrange objects in ascending or descending order, such as from largest to smallest. This requires the ability to compare objects mentally and to make logical connections between what they know and what they are learning.

**Extending Relationships** Piaget believed that children in this period learn transitivity. **Transitivity** is the concept that a relative relationship between two objects can extend to a third object. For example, if three is greater than two, and two is greater than one, then three must also be greater than one.

**Conservation** Piaget showed that during the concrete operations stage, children learn the principle of conservation. **Conservation** means that an object has the same characteristics even if there is a change in the way it looks. To test this ability, Piaget showed children of different ages two balls of clay. The balls were of equal size. He then rolled one ball into a long cylinder and asked the children whether one was larger now or if the two pieces of clay were the same size. Younger children thought that the longer piece of clay was larger because it appeared to take up more space. Children age seven and older could see that the amount of clay had not changed just because the shape had changed.

### Formal Operations Stage

At about age eleven, children begin to move into Piaget's formal operations stage. They develop the ability to think abstractly and to see different sides of an issue. Abstract thinking shows in a variety of ways, such as:

- Imagining hypothetical situations. **Hypothetical** means involving something that could possibly happen.
- Solving problems by anticipating and preparing for different situations.
- Debating issues.
- Using "if . . . then" formulas to consider what they might decide to do under changing sets of circumstances.
- Recognizing societal problems and understanding the complex reasons for them.

Preteens who begin to show these types of thinking are likely to use them only selectively at first. They will not use them in all situations or at all times. As they gain experience, they will use them more often and with more success.

**C₁**

---

## RESPOND TO SPECIAL NEEDS — Dyslexia

**Discussion** Ask the class: If a teacher knows one of his students has dyslexia, what are some practical ways he might help the student learn? (Answers will vary but might include having the textbooks recorded so the student could listen to them and read along; or giving the student oral tests in which the student listens and responds orally to the questions.)

**Critical Thinking** Presentations will vary. A possible answer is to use multisensory teaching methods, which use other senses, such as hearing and touch to teach instead of relying solely on sight or reading.

Piaget felt that the complex, multilevel framework of stages which he proposed was biologically based and universal. Each child experiences the stages in the same order. His ideas deeply influenced several generations of parents and educators. However, other theories arose that offered different views on the way children develop. These theories included children from ages seven to twelve.

## Vygotsky's Theory

Vygotsky's theory was that biological development and cultural experience both influenced children's ability to learn. He believed that children learned most, and best, from one another and from adults. Children ages seven to twelve are learning to evaluate themselves and others. This means that the more they interact with other people, the more they will learn. Working together with adults and teachers and receiving their guidance are important. Peer and small-group learning in the classroom are also vital. Social activities such as clubs, team sports, and other events where children can interact and learn from watching and communicating with one another are essential.

## Montessori's Theory

In contrast to Vygotsky, Montessori stressed the importance of self-directed learning. She believed that teachers should provide the needed tools for children to learn independently. Teachers should then intrude on the learning experience as little as possible. For seven- to twelve-year-olds, the Montessori classroom might offer a combination of language, history, geography, the sciences, and the arts. However, group lessons are kept to a minimum as teachers allow children to exercise their growing independence by exploring their interests in their own way. Real-life experiences are stressed.

## Gardner's Theory

Howard Gardner, who proposed the theory of multiple intelligences, theorized that knowledge is **multifaceted**, or many-sided. For example, a seven-year-old who is at a certain stage in understanding numbers may be at a different stage in visual-spatial development. Educators have supported Gardner's theories because they see their students learning and thinking in different ways every day.

## Learning Through PLAY

### Children's Museums

Traditional museums are typically filled with historical objects, paintings, and other treasures. Touching these items is usually not allowed. That is one reason children are sometimes less than enthusiastic about visiting museums. Looking at seashells in a case behind glass does not give children the chance to experience them. In special museums designed for children, learning takes place through actual experience. Children might be able to touch a variety of real seashells and feel the differences in texture and size. They might experience how aspects of science work. They can learn through interactive displays. For example, they might learn about gravity and momentum by performing simple experiments with golf balls. Children's museums are based on the belief that children learn best through actual experience.

> **Think About It** Imagine that you work at a children's museum designed to teach young people about the ocean. Think of an exhibit you might create. Describe the exhibit. Then list three things that children could learn from this exhibit.

## Learning Through PLAY

### Children's Museums

**Discussion** Think of something that might be featured at a children's museum. Think of ways children could learn more information about it. (Responses might include a tornado chamber or electricity. Students might do research, talk to an expert, observe natural phenomena, do science experiments, or take other field trips to learn more.)

> **Think About It** Answers will vary. The museum might contain a coral reef through which children could walk and learn about the different types of coral, plants, and fish and learn the way in which human behavior affects reefs.

### C₂ Critical Thinking

**Determine** Read students the following scenario: Eight-year-old Tim's parents are worried because Tim has been bringing home reports from his teacher that he is talking at inappropriate times during class. Discuss the following questions with students: How does Tim's behavior fit into Vygotsky's theory about how children learn? (Vygotsky believed that the more children interact with others, the more they will learn. Tim is interacting and (hopefully) learning.) What options do Tim's parents have for managing his behavior in school? (Answers may include: The parents could remind Tim that he needs to respect the teacher and class rules, including talking only when it is appropriate. They might get him involved in other activities where he is able to interact with others.)

### W Writing Support
**Paragraph**

**School Environment** Read the following to students: Summerhill School in England bases its programs on the theory that children will be compelled from within to learn and only need to be provided a rich environment, the freedom to follow their own interests, and access to the guidance of knowledgeable adults. Ask students to write a paragraph in which they determine which of the educational theorists might approve of this school. Would students send their children to such a school? Explain. (Refer to p. 192 for tips on writing a good paragraph. Students should recognize that Montessori's theory is very similar to that of Summerhill School. Whether students would send their children to such a school will vary.)

## Reteach *cont.*

### C Critical Thinking

**Making Predictions** Ask students to predict which of Gardner's intelligences might be evident in the children listed below. Encourage students to choose more than one type of intelligence for each child. (Possible answers are listed.)

- Loves making things out of clay (visual-spatial, bodily-kinesthetic)
- Enjoys playing the cello (musical, bodily-kinesthetic)
- Likes being captain of the soccer team (bodily-kinesthetic, interpersonal)
- Loves to garden (naturalist, intrapersonal)
- Loves numbers (logical-mathematical)
- Likes to bake (logical-mathematical, visual-spatial)

### U Universal Access

**Mathematical Learners** Make a chart with a heading for each of Gardner's multiple intelligences and another chart with a heading for each of Sternberg's three types of intelligence. Ask students to classify themselves according to their primary intelligence in each system. Have mathematical students tally the results and figure what percentage of the class identifies with each type of intelligence. (Answers will vary. Ask students if they are surprised at the results. Why or why not?)

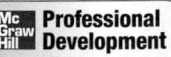
**Professional Development**

**Mini Clip**
**Math: Real-Life Ratios**

A teacher discusses real-life applications of ratios.

➤ **Multiple Intelligences**
Gardner's theory of multiple intelligences says that children have different ways of learning. A child might be strong in visual-spatial intelligence but not as advanced in the verbal-linguistic intelligence. *Which kinds of learning do you think you are best at?*

The more students develop their different intelligences, the greater their skills and knowledge will become, according to Gardner. For children ages seven to twelve, this could mean offering school activities each day that support as many of their growing interests and abilities as possible. Here are examples of activities that can encourage children this age to develop their different intelligences:

- **Verbal-Linguistic** Write a story, act in a play, speak to the class about an issue important to students
- **Logical-Mathematical** Create a weekly budget, learn to play chess, conduct a science experiment
- **Visual-Spatial** Create a design, paint a neighborhood scene, diagram the school grounds
- **Musical** Talk about how a piece of music "feels," practice playing an instrument
- **Bodily-Kinesthetic** Dance, practice sports, learn new crafts
- **Interpersonal** Identify and help solve a class problem, lead a class project
- **Intrapersonal** Create a comic book, start an online blog or journal, create a class photo album
- **Naturalist** Visit a nature museum, report on how to save an endangered species, participate in a nature walk

{ **Expert Advice...** }

*"During the latency years, American children need experiences that promote academic talents, a sense of responsibility, and most important, a belief that they can attain the goals valued by self and community. They need reassurance that these goals are attainable."*

— Jerome Kagan, professor of developmental psychology and author, *In Support of Families*

### Sternberg's Theory

Sternberg's research suggests an answer to why some students who did well in school do not excel in the working world. It also explains why others who experience success at working did not excel in school. His theory proposes that people have varying degrees of analytical, creative, and practical intelligence. Whether people are successful in a particular environment can depend on how strong or weak these intelligences are. When parents, caregivers, and educators encourage all three kinds of intelligence, then all children can show their talents. Schools can find ways to reward and encourage each student.

**502** Chapter 18 Intellectual Development from Seven to Twelve

➤ **Explore the Photo**

**Caption Answer** Student answers will vary. Students should offer reasons or examples to support their answers.

**Discussion** Ask students to think of examples in their own lives in which they have exhibited each of Gardner's eight intelligences. Ask volunteers to share their examples with the class. (Answers will vary, but students should give specific examples of when they have exhibited each of the eight intelligences.)

### Analytical Intelligence

This involves the abilities to recall, recognize, analyze, compare and contrast, evaluate, and explain problem-solving strategies. Children with high analytical intelligence are often considered to be smart because they are good at the types of activities and tests given in schools, including intelligence tests.

### Creative Intelligence

Sternberg believes that school programs are often so focused on improving student knowledge that they can hinder creativity. Creative intelligence is required whenever children imagine, pretend, invent, and design. Children high in creative intelligence might not follow directions well. They also might score lower on tests. Caregivers and educators can encourage this type of intelligence by allowing children plenty of free time for play. Children should be given access to tools for participating in imaginative play. These tools can include clothes for dress up, paper and markers or pencils for drawing, or string, beads, glue, and scissors for creating craft projects.

### Practical Intelligence

Children's practical intelligence helps them to apply experience or knowledge to solve a real-world problem. These "street smart" children can quickly assess a problem and the resources available. They can then figure out the fastest and most practical way to solve the problem. These children might not be the top performers at school, but they have the potential to become tomorrow's leading managers, politicians, and businesspeople. Parents and educators can encourage children to use practical intelligence by helping them volunteer in the community. Educators can encourage students to lead a class project, such as a book drive, or lead a group science project.

---

## Section 18.1 — After You Read

### Review Key Concepts

1. **Explain** what happens to preteens' attention span at about age twelve. What problems can this cause?
2. **List** eight different types of intelligence proposed by Gardner.

### Practice Academic Skills

**English Language Arts**

3. Locate an article that discusses a theory about how children learn by Piaget, Montessori, or Gardner. Write a review of the article. Answer these questions in your review: What do you think was the main point of the article? Do you think the article was clearly written? What did you learn from the article?

> **NCTE 3** Apply strategies to interpret texts.

**Mathematics**

4. Research and choose one of Piaget's conservation tasks to duplicate. Give the test to ten children. Five should be between the ages of four and six, and five between ages eight and ten. Calculate the percentage in each group that understood the principle.

> **NCTM Data Analysis and Probability** Select and use appropriate statistical methods to analyze data.

 **Check Your Answers** Check your answers at this book's Online Learning Center at **glencoe.com**.

---

**Study Tools**

Have students go to the Online Learning Center at **glencoe.com**:

- Take the **Practice Test**.
- Download **Study-to-Go** content.

Use the **Student Activity Workbook** for additional practice.

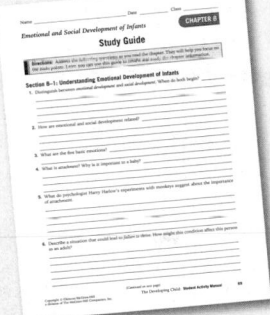

### Close

**Culminating Activity**

**Give Examples** Have students give an example of each type of intelligence or intellectual development proposed by the theorists discussed in this section. (Students' examples will vary but should accurately depict the theories of Piaget, Vygotsky, Montessori, Gardner, and Sternberg.)

**NCLB** connects academic correlations to book content.

---

## Section 18.1 — After You Read

### Review Key Concepts

1. Their attention span grows shorter, which can cause grades and test scores to drop.
2. Types of intelligence include verbal-linguistic, logical-mathematical, visual-spatial, musical, bodily-kinesthetic, interpersonal, intrapersonal, and naturalist.

### Practice Academic Skills

3. Reviews will vary based on the theory and article selected. Students should review an article that discusses the learning theories of Piaget, Montessori, or Gardner. In their review, they should discuss the article's main idea, whether they think the article was clearly written, and what they learned from the article.

4. Tests and percentages will vary. Students should develop a test that shows comprehension of the principle of conservation. The older group of children should have a much higher percentage who understood the principle.

## Focus

### Bell Ringer Activity

**Time of Transition**
Ask students to think back on their middle school experience. Ask how it was transitional. (Students may mention that they had more independence at school, or they changed classes instead of being in the same room all day.)

## Preteaching

### Vocabulary

Suffixes have their own meaning and can be added to word roots to create words with meanings. The suffix *-ate* means "to act on" or "cause to be modified." Have students look up the word roots in integrate and mandate.

**Professional Development**

**Mini Clip**
**ELL: Academic Language**

Discuss the importance of academic language for English language learners.

### Graphic Organizer

 The Graphic Organizer is also on the TeacherWorks CD.

(Graphic organizers should include: Advantages (any two): sense of students' progress; assess needs; determine how to help children; Disadvantages (any two): measure a small sample of students' abilities; scores can vary; may not accurately assess intellectual development.)

 **NCLB** connects academic correlations to book content.

**504**

## Reading Guide

### Before You Read

**Explaining What You Read** As you read, pause each time you come to a new heading. Explain what you have just read to an imaginary person who is unfamiliar with the information. This will help you monitor your comprehension.

### Read to Learn
**Key Concepts**
- **Describe** three learning methods that are effective for children ages seven to twelve.
- **Identify** characteristics of the middle school experience that make it well suited to preteen learning.
- **Compare and contrast** three types of standardized tests.

### Main Idea
Methods of learning for children in this group include direct learning, peer learning, and independent learning. Middle school provides a needed bridge between elementary and high school. Standardized tests are used to evaluate students' learning abilities, achievements, and aptitudes.

### Content Vocabulary
◇ learning method
◇ peer learning
◇ standardized test

### Academic Vocabulary
You will find these words in your reading and on your tests. Use the glossary to look up their definitions if necessary.
■ integrate
■ mandate

### Graphic Organizer
As you read, note two advantages and two disadvantages to standardized testing. Use a tree diagram like the one shown to help organize your information.

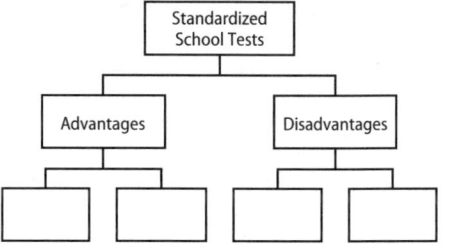

 **Graphic Organizer** Go to this book's Online Learning Center at **glencoe.com** to print out this graphic organizer.

---

**Academic Standards** . . . . . . . . . . . . . . . . . . . . . . . . . . . . . . . . .

 **English Language Arts**
**NCTE 5** Use different writing process elements to communicate effectively.

 **Social Studies**
**NCSS IV E Individual Development and Identity** Examine the interaction of ethnic, national, or cultural influences in specific situations or events.

**NCTE** *National Council of Teachers of English*
**NCTM** *National Council of Teachers of Mathematics*

**NSES** *National Science Education Standards*
**NCSS** *National Council for the Social Studies*

---

**504** Chapter 18 Intellectual Development from Seven to Twelve

## Reading Guide

### Before You Read

Ask students to discuss whether they feel that taking standardized tests during their school career has been a positive or negative experience. Ask volunteers to explain their answers. (Students' answers will vary but may include: "They help me know which subject areas to focus on," or "I freeze during tests so I don't do well.")

### D Develop Concepts

**Main Idea** Discuss the main idea with the students. Ask students if they view middle school as a bridge between elementary school and high school. Ask volunteers to explain. (Students' answers will vary but may focus on having more independence during middle school.)

## R Learning Methods

Young children learn skills mainly through imitating older children and adults. Seven- to twelve-year-olds become more capable of abstract thought and of more demanding work. A **learning method** is a way to learn. In order to meet the needs of different children, teachers use a variety of learning methods. Three of the most common methods are direct, peer, and independent learning.

### Direct Learning

In their first years in school, children's learning is more activity based. It uses sensory aids such as finger paints, posters, play money, and games. In contrast, language-based, direct learning becomes the more common form of instruction for older children.

Children capable of direct learning can get facts and ideas by listening and reading. For example, the teacher might talk to the class about the Civil War and assign reading in the textbook. The children must pay close attention to the teacher. They also must learn to take notes and read their textbooks on their own. Their progress in mastering these skills is gradual. How well they learn the material can be measured with tests, quizzes, and essays.

### Peer Learning

**Peer learning** is a learning method in which students interact with one another. In peer learning, students work together in pairs, small groups, or as a class on a project or task. One advantage of peer learning is that it provides an environment in which students may feel less awkward about asking questions or expressing confusion. Working on group projects helps students learn to work together cooperatively, to communicate, and to build time- and resource-management skills.

### Independent Learning

Teachers should help students build the skills needed for independent learning. Independent learning allows students to work on their own. It also lets them use the information they gather in a variety of challenging ways. It prepares them for long-term assignments common in high school, college, and the working world.

A teacher may, for example, suggest an area of study, such as farming in North America. Students choose a specific topic, perhaps crops of the American desert. Then they will get a week or more to complete the assignment. Students will research and select topics, collect materials, and continue their research, finally preparing a finished assignment.

**Direct Learning**
Much of what children learn in school is through direct learning. *Do you think an eight-year-old would enjoy activity-based learning or direct learning more? Why?*

---

## ►► Explore the Photo

**Caption Answer** Students' answers will vary. Possible answer is activity-based learning, because the student has more hands-on involvement in the learning process.

**Discussion** Ask students if they are kinesthetic learners. (Learn best by actually carrying out a physical activity.) If so, ask how they cope in a direct learning situation. (Answers will vary. Students might say they ask questions, take notes, and include illustrations in their notes to stay active during lectures.)

---

## Section 18.2

## Teach

### Discussion Starter

**Methods of Learning** Ask students to consider the blue heads on this page. Ask them to explain which they believe is their favored method of learning and why. (Answers will vary. Interpersonal learners may consider peer learning their favored method; intrapersonal learners may consider independent learning their favored method. Students should offer reasons for their choices.)

### R Reading Strategy

**Pre-reading** Give students approximately two minutes to pre-read this section. Instruct them to pay particular attention to the headings, photographs, and figures. Then have them create a list of information they think they will learn while reading. As they read, students should check off items on their list when they encounter them. (Lists will vary, but should be based on what students learned as they pre-read the section.)

### W Writing Support
#### Essay

**Learning Methods** Have students write short essays explaining the advantages and disadvantages of direct and independent learning methods. Is one method more appropriate for seven- to nine-year-olds than it is for ten- to twelve-year-olds? (Answers will vary but students may suggest that direct learning might be more appropriate for seven- to nine-year-olds and independent learning might be more appropriate for ten- to twelve-year-olds because of the increased maturity and intellectual levels of ten- to twelve-year-olds.)

## Teach cont.

### S Skill Practice

**Guided Practice**

**List Signs** Middle school students strive for independence and yet can be overwhelmed by new responsibilities. Have the class brainstorm a list of signs that parents, caregivers, and teachers might look for to gauge whether a middle school student needs adult help or guidance. (Lists will vary but may include: stress, depression, or unusual behavior.) **L1 ELL**

**Create a Time Line** Have students create a time line labeled with the school years from fourth grade through middle school. Next to each grade on the time line, have students list concerns and needs that might be experienced at that age. (Time lines will vary but should show an understanding of the changes that occur in children.) **L2 ELL**

**Analyze Responsibilities** Have students write a half-page essay to answer these questions: What responsibilities should parents expect from a child who gets an allowance? What are the consequences if those responsibilities are not met? Are there circumstances under which children should not get an allowance? What methods should parents use to determine when to increase a child's allowance? (Essays will vary. Possible answers include: children who receive an allowance should have chores to do and would forfeit their allowance if the chores were not done; children who are too young to do chores should not get an allowance; parents might increase an allowance when they see that the child can do more around the house.) **L3**

### ✓ Reading Check

**Recall** working in pairs or groups to observe, interact, and learn from one another

### SAFE CHILD HEALTHY CHILD

**Peer Pressure**

Middle school is a period of major changes for preteens. They often begin spending more time with their friends with less supervision. To prepare preteens for this freedom, parents should discuss the importance of not going along with friends if their behavior appears to be wrong. Even if the other person is a long-time friend, preteens can stop a friendship that makes them uncomfortable. If necessary, let children know they can make the parent a scapegoat. They might say something like, "My mom won't let me do that," or "My dad always finds out everything I do."

☀ **Be Prepared** Act out a situation with a partner in which one of you is a preteen and the other is the parent. Have a discussion about what to do if a friend tries to get the preteen involved in an activity that makes him or her feel uncomfortable.

A sixth-grade teacher might give specific directions for each step of the process. Students would complete each step by a designated time to meet the final deadline. Teachers may need to help students allocate their time between steps. Preteens may be given more responsibility in planning their work and meeting their deadlines.

✓ **Reading Check** **Recall** What is peer learning?

## Middle School—A Time of Transition

The typical school day of a fourth grader and a high school freshman are not at all alike. Fourth graders still perform best in the type of classroom setting used with younger children, with one teacher who is almost like a parent.

This teacher leads them through most of their coursework and gives them personal, individual care and guidance. The children know all their classmates and spend most of their time in their familiar classroom surroundings.

On the other hand, high school students rotate from class to class all day with changing teachers and classmates. Their learning environment is more impersonal than elementary school. They are expected to do much of their work independently.

## New Independence and Social Skills

The period of time between fourth grade and high school can be very stressful for students as they begin to have new concerns and needs. They become increasingly aware of their changing bodies. At the same time, they are becoming more and more focused on what people think about them. Most are looking for peer acceptance.

**S**

They also are more independent. This independence may have led to greater responsibilities at home, though. That may limit personal activities. They are developing social skills, but they are not yet ready for the less personal high school setting.

## Effective Middle Schools

Educators often disagree on what is the best education setting for preteens. The main challenge is that preteens want and need more freedom than younger children. However, educators do agree on some approaches to what can be a very stressful age.

Middle school homeroom teachers offer the personal contact that a preteen still needs. They provide someone familiar the students can go to with problems. The best middle schools have a low number of students per teacher or advisor. This might be 10 students to 1 teacher. These schools involve parents and community leaders in their classroom activities. In addition, they **integrate**, or combine, coursework from several classes rather than offering disconnected classes in rigid time frames.

### SAFE CHILD HEALTHY CHILD

**Peer Pressure**

**Discussion** Ask students if they have been in a situation in which they were uncomfortable with what their friends were doing. Ask how they handled the situation. If they had it to do over again, would they handle it the same way? (Answers will vary but should show an understanding of how to handle an uncomfortable situation.)

☀ **Be Prepared** Skits will vary. Partners should act out a scene that includes a parent and a preteen. They should discuss how the preteen might respond when he or she does not want to go along with a proposed activity, such as smoking or pulling a prank on someone.

Middle school educators try to personalize the school setting. They also try to provide an environment where students can enjoy being more grown up. Students may be able to choose some of their subjects. They can choose new friends. More challenging academic work can increase their confidence in their ability to learn. All these positive aspects of the middle school can create a comfortable bridge to high school.

## The Importance of Parent Involvement

 Parents who get involved in their child's education send the message that school counts. Here are some ways parents can be involved:

- **Meet the staff.** Many schools have a back-to-school night for visiting children's classes and meeting the teachers. Teachers describe the curriculum, as well as their expectations and rules.
- **Talk to the teachers personally.** Many schools schedule one-on-one parent-teacher conferences. If the teacher does not request a meeting, the parent can ask for one.
- **Read messages sent by the school.** Teachers and principals often send home important information about the school and activities. They may mail or e-mail the information, or send a note home with the students.

 **What Would You Do?**

### A Group Project

Vince, Kirsten, and several of their seventh-grade classmates were working on a project for the science fair. Kirsten and Vince's group was having trouble agreeing on how the project should go. Although Vince and Kirsten were supposed to be working together on a drawing of a single-celled amoeba, Vince was hoarding the markers. Philip, another group member, was trying to slack off and let the others take over. Jared was not letting him get away with it. "Get the scissors and start cutting out the game pieces," he said. Sydney, a bright, hardworking girl who wanted to impress her teacher and classmates, had taken charge of writing an essay for the group. She was worried that Philip's lack of motivation would hurt the group's grade.

**Write About It** When working in groups, a few members often do most of the work, while others do little. Why do you think this is? Write a paragraph describing what you would do if you were Sydney in the situation that was just described.

▶ **Parent Involvement**
Involved parents send a message to their children and their children's teachers. *If you were a middle school teacher, what would you think about parents who did not respond to your messages concerning their child?*

## Teach cont.

### U Universal Access

**Verbal Learners** Discuss the following with students: Many children answer "Nothing" or something vague such as "Just stuff" when asked what they did in school. If you were a parent, how would you ask about your child's day in school to be sure to get an answer that has real information? (Answers will vary. Encourage students to think of specific questions, such as "What did you learn about in math today?" Parents can use information gleaned one day to follow up the next day, as in, "Are you still working on adding fractions?")

### C Critical Thinking

**Predict Your Actions** Ask students to imagine that they are working on a group project with three other students. Ask: If someone in your group wasn't making much of a contribution, how would you handle the situation? (Students' answers will vary. Students who are the enforcer type might say they would continue to confront the person not working; those who are hard workers might go to the teacher with their concerns.)

 **What Would You Do?**

**Write About It** Answers will vary. Some students are more concerned about doing well and pleasing their teachers while others are happy to sit back and let others do the work.

▶ **Explore the Photo**

**Caption Answer** Answers will vary. The teacher might think the parents did not have the time or interest to be concerned about their child's schooling.

**Discussion** Ask students why it is important for parents to be involved in their children's education. (Answers will vary but may include: parents who become involved in their children's schooling send the message that school is important.)

### Quiz

Ask students to answer the following questions:

1. Why is it advantageous to provide opportunities for peer learning in middle school classrooms? (Students may feel less awkward about asking questions or expressing confusion.)

2. Which learning method prepares students for activities in high school, college, and the working world? (independent learning)

3. What is the purpose of standardized testing? (to measure the learning achievement of students; to see how well schools are meeting students' learning needs)

## Reteach

### W Writing Support

**Write a Dialogue** Have students write a dialogue between a parent and his or her child's teacher during back to school night. The parent should ask some questions and the teacher should provide some information. Students should: let the people speak for themselves; use language that sounds real and appropriate to the people talking; and use quotation marks appropriately. (Answers will vary. Use these criteria when evaluating your students' writing: Do the details reflect the age, personality, and background of each person? Did the student use quotation marks correctly?)

### ✓ Reading Check

**List** any four: meet the staff, talk to teachers personally, read messages sent by the school, review the child's homework, help out with school activities, join the parents' group, or talk with the child about school

- **Review the child's homework.** Parents can judge a child's performance by reviewing homework. Looking at assignments that have been graded helps to identify areas that need improvement.
- **Help out with school activities.** Parents can volunteer to help in the class or for field trips and special activities.
- **Join the parents' group.** Parents can learn about the school and offer constructive suggestions.
- **Talk to the child.** Parents can stay involved simply by talking to their child about school. Encourage students to describe the work they did that day and any important events that took place.

**✓ Reading Check** **List** What are four ways in which parents can be involved in their child's education?

## Intellectual Development

Schools often rely on tests to evaluate how well students are developing intellectually and how much knowledge they are gaining. Schools periodically may give standardized tests. A **standardized test** is a test that lets educators see how students are performing intellectually when compared to the thousands of other students who have taken the same test. Many states now **mandate**, or require, that standardized tests be given to students to measure their learning achievement. These tests are also used as an indicator of how well the schools are meeting the learning needs of their students.

## Creating Standardized Tests

Standardized tests have a special usefulness in assessing how well children are able to learn, and how much they have learned. Most seven- to twelve-year-olds take standardized tests in one or more grades.

## Parenting Skills

### Helping with Homework

When children start to have homework, parents and caregivers need to make almost as many adjustments as the child does. They also need to decide just how much help to give. Here are some tips to find the right balance:

- **Avoid doing too much.** Try helping the child think through the assignment and decide how to tackle it.
- **Offer help when it is really needed.** If a child cannot figure out how to do a problem, you may be able to help by showing how to solve a similar one.
- **Supply materials and help with organization.** For example, color-coded folders can help a middle school child organize work by class.
- **Allow time for a break after school.** This gives children a mental break before focusing on studying again.
- **Above all, be there.** It is wonderfully reassuring for a child to have a trusted adult available while doing homework.

**Take Charge** Imagine you are the parent of a preteen who has asked for help writing a report about Alaska. Write a paragraph describing how you would respond.

## Parenting Skills

### Helping with Homework

Ask students if they can think of any disadvantages to having an adult help with homework. (Possible answer: Children learning subjects like math and reading often use different methods than those used when their parents or caregivers were in school.)

### Take Charge

Paragraphs will vary but should explain how they would respond to the child's request. They might help the child organize the project, give tips on where to go for research, and possibly help with proofreading. They should encourage the child to write the actual report on his or her own.

Teams of scientists and educators design standardized tests for schools. Along with the tests come exact instructions for giving and scoring them. Before standardized tests are ready for use, they are repeatedly tested with students and revised. This effort guarantees that the tests have three properties that are necessary to make them good tests.

- **Validity** A standardized test is valid when it measures what it is supposed to measure. For example, if a test is supposed to measure reading comprehension, enough time must be given for the students to complete reading the selections and answer the questions.
- **Reliability** Standardized tests must be consistent. The test is reliable if it can be given to the same age group, again and again, with similar results.
- **Practicality** Standardized tests must be practical for schools to be able to use them. They cannot be difficult to give, and they must be quick and relatively easy to score. They must also be affordable.

### Kinds of Standardized School Tests

There are many kinds of standardized tests. Three kinds that are given to children ages seven to twelve include tests that measure how well they can learn, how much they have already learned, and what they might have a special ability or interest in learning.

**Learning Ability Tests** Learning ability tests are designed to help educators predict how well a student might do in a particular learning situation. All the students taking the test answer the same set of questions. Their scores are then compared. Learning ability tests go by several names. They are also called intelligence tests, mental ability tests, scholastic aptitude tests, and academic aptitude tests.

Most tests require students to read questions and write answers. A student with highly developed language skills may earn a higher score than a student with highly developed musical skills. Having a higher IQ on this one test does not mean that the top scoring student is smarter. The second student's learning ability is just different.

**Achievement Tests** Achievement tests are used to help measure what students have actually learned about a particular topic or subject. Standardized achievement tests are the most prevalent standardized test used in schools. These tests are generally given to students once per school year. Many teachers will give their students practice tests throughout the year. This helps lessen student anxiety when taking the test. These tests give educators a sense of the progress students are making in gaining knowledge. A certain score on these types of tests may be required for graduation.

**Standardized Testing**
Schools use standardized tests to determine what knowledge a child has gained. *What are three things that standardized tests can measure for seven- to twelve-year-olds?*

---

### Explore the Photo

**Caption Answer** Standardized tests can measure how well a student might do in a particular learning situation, what students have actually learned about a particular topic, and people's talents and preferences.

**Discussion** Ask students to share their feelings about standardized tests. (Answers will vary. Some students might find them helpful in pointing out areas that need work; others may think they are a waste of time.)

---

## Reteach *cont.*

### U Universal Access

**Interpersonal Learners** Have students work in small groups to interview friends and family members about standardized testing. Students should learn how many kinds of tests the interviewees know about and how important they think the tests are. Have students draw conclusions about how complete and accurate the interviewees' understandings are about the tests and the scores. Then have students combine and share their findings with the rest of the class. (Interview results will vary. Students may find some people who are knowledgeable about standardized tests and others who are not. Students should present their findings in a logical format.)

**Professional Development**

**Mini Clip**
**ELL: Group Discussions**

Students work together to decide where to place illustrations on a chart.

### C Critical Thinking

**Analyze** Read the following scenario to students: Over dinner one night, seven-year-old Adam tells his parent how nervous the teachers and students at the elementary school are about the upcoming achievement tests. The whole school will be taking tests all week. Adam asks if he is going to be in trouble if he does not do well on the tests. What should his parents tell him? (Answers will vary but may include: Adam's parents should encourage Adam to relax and do his best. He should not be in trouble if does not do well; not all children are good test takers even if they know the material.)

**509**

## Assess

### Study Tools

Have students go to the Online Learning Center at **glencoe.com**:

- Take the **Practice Test**.
- Download **Study-to-Go**  content.

Use the **Student Activity Workbook** for additional practice.

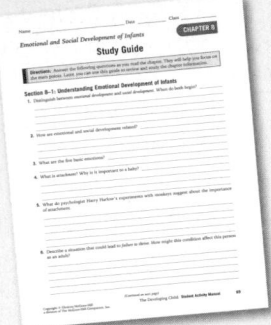

## Close

### Culminating Activity

**Create** Have students create a manual that describes the learning methods discussed in this section. Manuals should be created for middle school students. (Students' manuals will vary but should accurately describe direct learning, peer learning, and independent learning.)

 **NCLB** connects academic correlations to book content.

---

**Aptitude and Interest Tests** Aptitude and interest tests offer important measures of people's talents and preferences. A student who scores high in mathematical aptitude might strive to become an engineer or a scientist. Another name for interest tests is interest inventories. Students select what they like best from different groups of ideas, activities, or situations. Patterns in their answers are analyzed to see where their interests are strongest.

## Criticism of Standardized Tests

While standardized tests provide useful indicators of how students are developing intellectually, they have important limitations. These tests are estimates that measure only a small sample of a student's abilities or achievements. Even with tests of considerable reliability, scores can vary due to factors such as the age of the test taker and conditions at the test's location. Many critics argue that standardized tests do not accurately assess the intellectual development of minority and disadvantaged students, or English language learners. They feel this is true no matter how culture fair and culture free the test makers claim them to be.

Teachers feel pressured to have their students get high test scores. They are sometimes criticized for teaching only what is going to be on achievement tests, ignoring opportunities to share other important information with students that could enliven their studies.

In spite of the criticism, most educators still feel that standardized testing is needed. Along with teacher tests, it remains the best way to keep informed about what students need and how to best help them develop intellectually.

---

## Section **18.2**    After You Read

### Review Key Concepts

1. **Describe** how a teacher might use direct learning to teach fourth-graders that water boils at 212 degrees Fahrenheit. How might the teacher use peer learning to help students learn the same fact?
2. **Explain** why middle school is considered a time of transition.
3. **Define** what it means for a standardized test to be valid, reliable, and practical.

### Practice Academic Skills

#### English Language Arts

4. Write a quiz containing five questions. Each question should give an example of one type of learning. The person taking the test must identify each example as direct learning, peer learning, or independent learning. Trade quizzes with your classmates and practice identifying the learning styles.

> **NCTE 5** Use different writing process elements to communicate effectively.

#### Social Studies

5. Imagine you are a second grader whose family does not speak English at home. You started learning English in kindergarten, but are still working to catch up to your peers. Write a paragraph describing how this might affect your scores on standardized tests.

> **NCSS IV E** Examine the interaction of ethnic, national, or cultural influences in specific situations or events.

**Check Your Answers** Check your answers at this book's Online Learning Center at **glencoe.com**.

---

## Section **18.2**    After You Read

### Review Key Concepts

1. In direct learning, the teacher might tell the students that water boils at 212 degrees. In peer learning, the students could divide into small groups and conduct a hands-on experiment to determine the boiling point of water.

2. It has some of the characteristics of elementary school, along with some of the freedoms of high school.

3. Standardized tests must be valid to measure what they are supposed to measure. They must be reliable so the results are consistent. They also must be practical, or relatively easy to give and score.

### Practice Academic Skills

4. Quizzes will vary, but should have questions describing a learning activity that uses direct learning, peer learning, or independent learning.

5. Paragraphs will vary. The second grader would not have as fluent an understanding of English as most classmates, which could cause the child to misinterpret directions or questions.

## Chapter Summary

Children make many advances in their intellectual abilities between the ages of seven and twelve. Children move from the concrete operations stage to the formal operations stage at about age eleven. Piaget, Vygotsky, Montessori, Gardner, and Sternberg developed theories about intellectual development. Direct learning, peer learning, and independent learning are all modes of learning. Middle school programs are specially designed to meet the educational and emotional needs of preteens. Between the ages of seven and twelve, students take standardized tests that are designed to measure intellectual performance and aptitudes.

## Vocabulary Review

1. Create multiple-choice test questions for each vocabulary term.

### Content Vocabulary
◇ transitivity (p. 500)
◇ conservation (p. 500)
◇ hypothetical (p. 500)
◇ learning method (p. 505)
◇ peer learning (p. 505)
◇ standardized test (p. 508)

### Academic Vocabulary
■ concrete (p. 499)
■ multifaceted (p. 501)
■ integrate (p. 506)
■ mandate (p. 508)

## Review Key Concepts

2. **Identify** four signs of intellectual development in children ages seven to twelve.
3. **Explain** four thinking skills that build a foundation for mastering school work.
4. **Describe** three learning methods that are effective for children ages seven to twelve.
5. **Identify** characteristics of the middle school experience that make it well suited to preteen learning.
6. **Compare and contrast** three types of standardized tests.

## Critical Thinking

7. **Draw Conclusions** Why do you think that children from seven to twelve have a stronger sense of awareness and curiosity?
8. **Apply** What could a middle school teacher say to help parents become more involved in their child's learning?
9. **Analyze** What might be some of the causes of math anxiety?
10. **Decide** Would you rather score high on an achievement test or on an aptitude test in a subject you like? Explain your answer.

## Content and Academic Vocabulary Review

1. Students should write multiple-choice questions with possible answers for each vocabulary term.

## Review Key Concepts

2. Four signs of intellectual development are improved memory, awareness and curiosity, idealism and abstract thinking, and changes in attention span.

3. Four thinking skills: classifying objects, placing objects in a series, extending relationships, and understanding the principle of conservation.

4. Three learning methods are direct learning, independent learning, and peer learning.

5. Middle school typically provides the stability of a homeroom teacher but provides more freedom than elementary school.

6. Learning ability tests help predict how well a student might do in a particular learning situation. Achievement tests are used to measure what students have actually learned about a particular subject. Aptitude and interest tests measure a person's talents and preferences. All three depend somewhat on the student's language skills, but students with poor language skills or English language learners are most likely to be penalized in learning ability tests. Results of aptitude tests are the least dependent on academic skills.

## Critical Thinking

7. Answers will vary. These children are beginning to understand themselves better and to compare their abilities to those around them.

8. Possible answer: Children at this age want to be independent, and yet they still need guidance.

9. Possible answers might include parents' attitudes and behaviors, past experiences with teachers, poor self-concept and feelings of incompetence, timed tests, and gender bias (teachers typically having lower expectations of girls).

10. Students' responses will vary, but they should provide a reason for their choice. Possible answer: Achievement tests, so that I can prove I have learned the concepts presented.

## Chapter 18 Review and Applications

### Family & Community Connections

**11.** Brochures will vary but should summarize what students learn about the kinds of tutoring offered locally.

### Health Skills

**12.** Presentations will vary but should be based on research. Student presentations should discuss how adequate sleep helps people learn. One important way is that sleep helps us to store new information permanently in our memories.

### Observation Skills

**13.** Students should create a table listing Sternberg's three types of intelligence: analytical, creative, and practical. They should then describe the examples of each type that they observed.

### Real-World Skills

**14.** Students' debates will vary, but each side should present specific ideas about why their side's theory is more accurate. For example, the Sternberg side might state that Gardner's theory of multiple intelligences is too specific and that there is too much overlap between the different types of intelligence, making them difficult to differentiate.

**15.** Students' reports will vary, but they should state their opinions concerning these tests and provide specific reasons to back up their opinions.

**NCLB** Activity correlated to Social Studies standards.

---

## Chapter 18 Review and Applications

### Family & Community Connection

**11. Tutoring** Find out what kinds of tutoring are offered by a local middle school for students having difficulties in a particular subject. Alternatively, find out what kinds of professional tutoring services are available in your community. Summarize what you learn and create a brochure to share the information with other students.

### Health Skills

**12. Importance of Sleep** Not getting adequate sleep can greatly affect students' ability to learn. It also can cause them to do poorly on standardized tests. Conduct research to learn more about the effects of a lack of sleep on learning. Prepare a short presentation to share what you learn. Conclude your presentation with suggestions on how students could get more sleep.

### Observation Skills

**13. Sternberg's Theory** Sternberg divided intelligence into three categories: analytical, creative, and practical.

**Procedure** Observe seven- to ten-year-olds in at least two different settings. For example, you might observe them in a classroom and on the playground. Keep track of instances in which the children exhibited each of Sternberg's three types of intelligence. Write down a description of exactly how they exhibit a particular type of intelligence.

**Analysis** Create a table listing Sternberg's three types of intelligence. Under each type, describe the examples you observed. Be specific in your descriptions.

**NCSS IV D Individual Development and Identity** Apply concepts, methods, and theories about the study of human growth and development, such as learning, motivation, and behavior.

### Real-World Skills

| | |
|---|---|
| **Interpersonal and Collaborative Skills** | **14. Work in Teams** Follow your teacher's instructions to form into groups of four. Each group should divide into pairs. With your partner, prepare a debate about learning. One pair will argue that Gardner's multiple intelligences theory is more accurate, and the other will argue for Sternberg's intelligence theory. Each group should present their debate to the class. |
| **Technology Skills** | **15. Analyze Online Practice Tests** Some Web sites offer practice tests that claim to help students prepare for standardized tests. Research some of these sites. Then use word processing software to write a report discussing whether you think this is a good use of instructional technology. |
| **Financial Literacy** | **16. Raising Money** Think of a local financial need. Maybe a family has had a house fire or a school needs new playground equipment. Think of an activity that preteens could do to help raise money for this cause. Write a summary of the activity and estimate how much money it might raise. |

 **Additional Activities** For additional activities, go to this book's Online Learning Center at **glencoe.com**.

**16.** Student responses will vary, but students should offer specific details about the proposed activity and be reasonably realistic about the amount of money they estimate could be raised.

The *Early Childhood Observations CD* offers additional lessons with videos to build students' observation skills.

**Part 1:** Learning to Observe
**Part 2:** How Children Develop
**Part 3:** Working With Young Children
**Part 4:** Extended Observations
**Part 5:** Resources and Answer File

# Academic Skills

### English Language Arts

**17. Standardized Testing** Imagine education without standardized testing. Think about specific parts of education that might change. Write a paragraph describing what your education would be like. Be sure to emphasize the areas that are different from your current education.

> **NCTE 4** Use written language to communicate effectively.

### Mathematics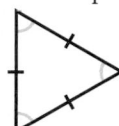

**18. Logical Grouping** At this age, children develop class logic. This means they can classify unlike objects into logical groups. Previously sorting was based on a perceived attribute such as color. Classify the triangle below in the most detailed and specific classification possible.

**Math Concept** **Triangle Classification** Different types of triangles include acute, isosceles, equiangular, right, equilateral, scalene, and obtuse.

**Starting Hint** The tic marks on each side of the triangle mean they are equal in length. The arcs on all three angles mean the angles are equal. Use the classifications to describe the triangle. Look up definitions for the triangle types if needed.

 **Math** For math help, go to the Math Appendix at the back of the book.

> **NCTM Geometry** Use visualization, spatial reasoning, and geometric modeling to solve problems.

### Science

**19. Math Anxiety** Researchers have found that males and females show similar levels of math anxiety in elementary school. However, females show more math anxiety than males in high school and college. Females typically begin to doubt their math abilities around seventh grade.

**Procedure** Ask 20 people, "Do you think you are good at math?" Half of your respondents should be male and half female. All should be between the ages of 8 and 20.

**Analysis** Total the number of yes and no responses by age and sex. Write a short analysis of your results.

> **NSES A** Students should develop abilities necessary to do scientific inquiry, understandings about scientific inquiry.

## Standardized Test Practice

**TRUE/FALSE QUESTIONS**
True/false questions have both advantages and disadvantages. One advantage is there are only two possible solutions. A disadvantage is that it is vital to read the question very carefully. The way in which the question is worded is all-important. Read the Test-Taking Tip and then answer the question.

**20.** Taking a Karate class would help a preteen with bodily-kinesthetic learning
   **a.** True
   **b.** False

> **Test-Taking Tip** When answering true/false questions, find out if there is a penalty for guessing. If not, make a guess. You have a 50 percent chance of getting it right.

# Academic Skills

**17.** Paragraphs will vary but students should offer specific details on how education would be different without standardized testing. Teachers might teach different subjects or use different teaching methods.

**18.** The triangle is equilateral and equiangular.

**19.** Results will vary. Generally, older girls tend to have less confidence in their math skills than younger girls and boys of all ages.

 **NCLB** connects academic correlations to book content.

 **Professional Development**

**Mini Clip Reading: Lesson Reflections**

A narrator discusses various instructional strategies suitable for use with English learners.

## Standardized Test Practice

**20.** a. True

**Test-Taking Tips** Help your students become familiar with the format of the specific test they are going to take by practicing with test items that imitate the actual test items as closely as possible.

**Fill in the Bubble** Tell students that neatness counts on automated tests. Tell them to fill in answers carefully.

## TECHNOLOGY Solutions

### Use these technology solutions to streamline chapter assessment!

 **ExamView Assessment Suite** CD allows you to create and print out customized tests or ready-made unit and chapter tests, complete with answer keys.

 **TeacherWorks Plus** is an electronic lesson planner that provides instant access to complete teacher resources in one convenient package.

 **Online Learning Center** includes resources and activities for students and teachers.

# Thematic Unit Project

## Develop an Exercise Program

In this unit, you have learned about the dramatic physical, emotional, social, and intellectual changes experienced by seven- to twelve-year-olds. You have also learned about the important role exercise plays in their growth and development. In this project, you will research exercises appropriate for seven- to twelve-year-olds. You will use what you learn to create an exercise program that will meet the needs of children in this age group.

### My Journal

If you completed the journal entry from page 449, refer to it to see if your thoughts have changed after reading the unit.

## Focus

### Discussion Starter

**Exercise for Healthy Living** Ask students to think about how they feel physically, emotionally, socially, and intellectually based on the amount of time they spend sedentary. For example if they have been sitting for a long period of time, does it affect their concentration? (Answers will vary but should indicate that exercise affects all areas of life.)

Project correlated to English Language Arts standards.

### Step 1

### Choose an Exercise Program to Develop

Students can select one exercise option that interests them. Be sure students understand that the exercise programs must include a variety of exercises. If students can think of another exercise option not listed, they are welcome to use it.

## Teach

### Step 2

### Research Appropriate Exercises

Research should focus on the physical exercise needs of seven- to twelve-year-olds. Students should cite their research sources and avoid plagiarism. You might take time to explain what constitutes plagiarism and how to avoid it. Students should deliver a two-page report based on the results of their research. The report should include resources used.

## Project Assignment

In this project, you will:
- Choose exercises appropriate for seven- to twelve-year-olds.
- Research the fitness needs of children in this age group.

### Child Development Skills Behind the Project

- Determine the exercises appropriate for seven- to twelve-year-olds.
- Identify ways to meet the fitness needs of seven- to twelve-year-olds.
- Develop an exercise program to meet the needs of this age group.

### Academic Skills

 **English Language Arts**

> **NCTE 4** Use written language to communicate effectively.
>
> **NCTE 8** Use information resources to gather information and create and communicate knowledge.

514 **Unit 6** The Child from Seven to Twelve

- Write a list of interview questions that focus on the kinds of exercises appropriate for this age group.
- Identify and interview a professional in the community who is knowledgeable about the fitness needs of children.
- Arrange, take notes, and type the interview.
- Use what you learned in the interview to create an exercise program that will meet the needs of seven- to twelve-year-olds.

### Step 1 Choose an Exercise Program to Develop

Fitness affects the growth and development of all areas of life—physical, emotional, social, and intellectual. Choose an exercise program to develop that provides for the needs of seven- to twelve-year-olds. The program should provide both aerobic and strength exercises. Choose one of the following to develop:
- Three one-hour exercise programs.
- Five 30-minute exercise programs.
- Five physically active games that can be played for at least 30 minutes.

### Step 3

### Connect to Your Community

Ask students how the community member they talk with might encourage them to critique and modify their own exercise program. (Students should realize that getting enough exercise is important for all age groups.) Ask students to think of ways they might help others in their community improve their exercise habits. (Students may suggest a poster campaign or speaking to younger children.)

### Step 4

### Develop and Present Your Exercise Program

Give students these tips on presenting their demonstrations and speaking:
- Organize your presentation by developing an outline. Focus on the most important points.
- Present your ideas clearly.
- Ensure that your visuals can be seen by the entire audience.

### Step 2 Research Appropriate Exercises

Fitness needs vary among different groups. Conduct research to learn the fitness needs for seven- to twelve-year-old children. Write a summary of your research.

**Research Skills**

★ Use information that is corroborated in more than one source.

★ Cite the sources you use; give credit to the author of the information.

### Step 3 Connect to Your Community

Identify and arrange to talk with a member of your community who is knowledgeable about the fitness needs of seven- to twelve-year-olds. The community member might be an exercise specialist, medical doctor, nurse, or physical education teacher.

**Interviewing Skills**

★ Take notes during your talk.

★ Use the knowledge you gained from your research to ask questions so there is a give and take of ideas and information.

★ Listen attentively and use appropriate body language.

### Step 4 Develop and Present Your Exercise Program

Use the Unit Thematic Project Checklist on the right to plan and develop your exercise program and make your presentation.

**Speaking Skills**

★ Speak clearly and concisely.

★ Be sensitive to the needs of your audience.

★ Use standard English to communicate.

### Step 5 Evaluate Your Child Development Skills and Academic Skills

Your project will be evaluated based on:

• Content and organization of your information.

• Mechanics—presentation and neatness.

• Speaking and listening skills.

 **Evaluation Rubric** Go to this book's Online Learning Center at **glencoe.com** for a rubric you can use to evaluate your final project.

## Unit Thematic Project Checklist

| | |
|---|---|
| **Exercise Program** | ✓ Use the information from your research and interview to develop an exercise program that fits the category chosen in Step 1. <br> ✓ Take photos or a video of someone doing your exercise program, or ask volunteers from your class to help you demonstrate some of the exercises in the classroom. <br> ✓ Show the correct way to perform the exercises for maximum physical benefit and to avoid injury. <br> ✓ Create an outline to follow when giving your demonstration. |
| **Presentation** | ✓ Make a presentation to your class to share your demonstration and discuss what you learned. <br> ✓ Invite the students to ask you questions. <br> ✓ When students ask you questions, demonstrate in your answers that you respect their perspectives. <br> ✓ Turn in your research summary, the notes from your interview, and your presentation outline. |
| **Academic Skills** | ✓ Synthesize data from different resources concisely. <br> ✓ Organize your presentation so the audience can follow along easily. <br> ✓ Adapt and modify language to suit different purposes. <br> ✓ Thoughtfully express your ideas. |

# Thematic Unit Project

## Assess

### Step 5

**Evaluate Your Child Development Skills and Academic Skills**

**Rubric** Encourage students to go to this book's Online Learning Center at **glencoe.com** for a rubric they can use to evaluate their exercise program and presentation. Students can use the rubric as a content checklist when forming their interview questions, developing their program, and giving their presentation.

## Close

### Culminating Activity

**Project Assessment** In this activity, students identified exercises appropriate for seven- to twelve-year-olds to help maintain optimum health. Students then developed an exercise program for that age group. Assist students in contacting a teacher of seven- to twelve-year-olds in your community. Have the student ask about sharing his or her demonstration with the teacher's class. (Students should prepare a pep talk to encourage the younger students to include an exercise program in their lives.)

---

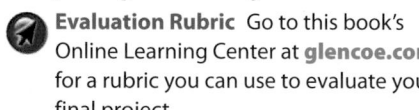

## Developing Community Involvement

### Meeting Nutritional Needs

Proper nutrition plays a key role in the physical, emotional, social, and intellectual growth and development of seven- to twelve-year-olds. Have students create a list of agencies in your community that help provide for the nutritional needs of those who are financially unable to do so on their own. Suggest that students provide copies of the list to social agencies, homeless centers, religious centers, and schools in your community.

A **Family & Community Involvement** worksheet about this topic is available:

● At this book's Online Learning Center at **glencoe.com**

● On the TeacherWorks CD

| Title | Objectives |
|---|---|
| **CHAPTER 19**<br>**Adolescence** | • **List** three main areas of change for adolescents.<br>• **Identify** three ways parents can help adolescents make good nutrition choices.<br>• **Describe** the four main influences on personal identity development.<br>• **Identify** the three roles of peers on a teen's social development.<br>• **List** the major influences on a teen's moral development.<br>• **Identify** three factors that influence how a student learns in school.<br>• **Compare and contrast** Piaget and Vygotsky's theories of intellectual development in adolescence. |
| **CHAPTER 20**<br>**Children's Health and Safety** | • **Explain** how regular checkups and immunizations can help prevent illness.<br>• **Summarize** effective ways to care for a sick child.<br>• **Outline** the steps to follow in an emergency situation.<br>• **Describe** appropriate first-aid procedures for three types of bleeding.<br>• **Compare and contrast** rescue breathing and CPR. |
| **CHAPTER 21**<br>**Family Challenges** | • **Describe** how parents can help children cope with stress.<br>• **List** eight possible causes of stress in children.<br>• **Identify** nine categories of disabilities.<br>• **Describe** some of the traits exhibited by gifted children.<br>• **Identify** four major types of maltreatment.<br>• **Summarize** common reasons behind abuse and maltreatment.<br>• **Explain** what can be done to prevent child abuse. |
| **CHAPTER 22**<br>**Child Care and Early Education** | • **Describe** two types of substitute care for younger children.<br>• **List** questions a parent should ask when choosing home-based care.<br>• **Describe** the benefits of having learning centers in early childhood classrooms.<br>• **Explain** the factors to consider when planning activities.<br>• **Identify** methods for promoting positive behavior in the classroom. |
| **CHAPTER 23**<br>**Careers Working with Children** | • **Describe** three different ways to gain work experience.<br>• **Identify** factors to consider when evaluating careers.<br>• **Explain** the relationship between a career goal and a career path.<br>• **List** six steps involved in a job search.<br>• **Compare and contrast** job-specific skills and transferable skills.<br>• **Summarize** an employee's responsibilities when leaving a job. |
| **Unit Thematic Project**<br>**Explore Careers in Child Care** | • **Write** a My Journal entry about Thoughts on Child Care.<br>• **Choose** a child care career.<br>• **Interview** or shadow a worker in the career chosen.<br>• **Create** a skit to share what they learned. |

## Understanding Brackets, Letters, and Ability Levels in the Teacher Wraparound Edition

**Brackets** Brackets on the reduced student edition page correspond to teaching strategies and activities in the Teacher Wraparound Edition. As you teach the lesson, the brackets show you exactly where to use the teaching strategies and activities.

**Letters** The letters on the reduced student edition page identify the type of strategy or activity. See the key below to learn about the different types of strategies and activities.

**Ability Levels** Teaching Strategies that appear throughout the chapters have been identified by one of three codes to give you an idea of their suitability for students of varying learning styles and abilities.

**Resources** Key program resources are listed in each chapter. Icons indicate the format of resources.

### KEY TO LETTERS

**D** **Develop Concepts** activities help teachers gauge and plan for students' concept development.

**R** **Reading Strategy** activities help you teach reading skills and vocabulary.

**S** **Skill Practice** provides leveled instruction for meeting individual needs and learning styles.

**W** **Writing Support** activities provide writing opportunities to help students comprehend the text.

**C** **Critical Thinking** strategies help students apply and extend what they have learned.

**U** **Universal Access** activities provide differentiated instruction for English language learners, and suggestions for teaching various types of learners.

**NCLB** **No Child Left Behind** activities help students practice and improve their abilities in academic subjects.

### KEY TO ABILITY LEVELS

**L1** Strategies should be within the ability range of all students. Often full class participation is required.

**L2** Strategies are for average to above-average students or for small groups. Some teacher direction is necessary.

**L3** Strategies are designed for students able and willing to work independently. Minimal teacher direction is necessary.

**ELL** Strategies are especially accessible to English Language Learners.

### KEY TO RESOURCE ICONS

📁 Print Material

💿 CD or DVD Resources

🧭 Online Learning Center (OLC)

### TeacherWorks™
**All-In-One Planner and Resource Center**

**Teacher Wraparound Edition**

**Unit Resources:**
Unit Thematic Project Student Rubrics
Unit Family and Community Involvement Activities

**Chapter Resources:**
Lesson Plans
Chapter Summaries, Content and Academic Vocabulary
Graphic Organizers

**Textbook Resources:**
Student Activity Workbook with Academic Integration
Additional Activities
Enrichment Activities

 Link to the ***The Developing Child* Online Learning Center** at **glencoe.com**.

# Additional Topics of Study

## Unit Overview

**Introduce the Unit**
Introduce the unit by describing the main concepts of each chapter in the unit.

**Unit 7**
This unit contains a variety of information. Discussions include adolescence, health and safety for children, challenges faced by families, issues related to child care and early education, and careers working with children.

**Chapter 19** Students will learn about the many aspects of physical, emotional, social, and intellectual development during adolescence in this chapter.

**Chapter 20** Chapter 20 introduces students to health and safety issues related to young children. Defenses against illnesses, guidelines for quick response to safety issues, and rescue techniques are discussed.

**Chapter 21** Challenges faced by families are covered in this chapter. Students will learn how children with special needs, emotional disabilities, developmental disorders, or special abilities affect families.

**Chapter 22** Information on why people must rely on child care, options they have, how to make a choice, and the early childhood classroom is presented in this chapter.

**Chapter 23** This final chapter looks at careers working with children. Students will learn about options and how to find, analyze, and prepare for a career working with children.

**Explore the Photo**
The teen years can be both fun and challenging. *How would you describe your teen years?*

516

▸ **Explore the Photo**

**Caption Answer** Students' answers will vary. Some students will have very positive things to say about their teen experience. Others might be extremely negative. Suggest to those who are negative that there is help available for teens with problems to solve. Encourage them to seek out help.

**Discussion** Have students brainstorm activities teens can participate in that will help them develop physically, emotionally, socially, and intellectually. You might create a class list that contains detailed descriptions and contact information for use by those students who are looking for activities in which to participate.

## Unit Thematic Project Preview

### Explore Careers in Child Care

After completing this unit, you will learn that there are many career choices for those who wish to work in child care or early childhood learning. In your unit thematic project you can look at some of the options available.

### My Journal

**Thoughts on Child Care** Write a journal entry about one of the topics below. This will help you prepare for the unit project at the end of the unit.

- Discuss reasons you may or may not be interested in a career in child care or early childhood learning.
- Describe experiences you have had with child care either as a baby-sitter, or as a child when someone cared for you.

517

### Discussion Starter

**Table of Predictions**
A variety of information is presented in this unit. To help students identify the broad concepts covered, have them make a five-column table. They should use the chapter titles for this unit as the column heads. Students should list three items they predict they will learn under each chapter title. After completing the unit, have students look at this table again and determine whether their predictions were correct.

**FCCLA** Teaching Healthy Eating Habits

Using the *Student Body* program, have students prepare and taste nutritious, healthy snacks. Ask students to create games and activities using the Dietary Guidelines for Americans. Make arrangements for students to give presentations about good nutrition to elementary school students.

### OUT OF TIME?

If class time is too short to cover all of the chapters in this unit, have students:

- Write down the vocabulary terms and their definitions.
- Read the chapter summaries at the beginning of each chapter review.
- Go to *The Developing Child* Online Learning Center at **glencoe.com** to download Study-to-Go content.

## Unit Thematic Project Preview

### Explore Careers in Child Care
Tell students that as part of this unit, they will learn about different careers available in the area of child care and early childhood learning. Students will consider how they might gain valuable information about careers in this area through interviewing and shadowing a professional child care worker or early childhood educator.

### My Journal

**Thoughts on Child Care** Students should select one topic to write a journal entry about. The journal entry will relate to the subject of the thematic project: Explore Careers in Child Care. The purpose of the journal entry is to prepare students for the project at the end of the unit. (Journal entries will vary depending on the topic selected and students' personal opinions.)

**STANDARDS BASED LESSON PLANNING** *The Developing Child* provides students with instruction and assessment in the following fundamental content areas:

## National Standards Correlations

| Standards | Pages |
|---|---|
| **12.1.1** Analyze physical, emotional, social, spiritual, and intellectual development. | 521–523, 528–533, 533–538, 542–543 |
| **12.1.2** Analyze interrelationships among physical, emotional, social, and intellectual aspects of human growth and development. | 537 |
| **12.1.3** Analyze current and emerging research about human growth and development, including research on brain development. | 525, 529–530, 535–536, 540–541, 542–543 |
| **12.2.1** Analyze the effect of heredity and environment on human growth and development. | 536–537 |
| **12.2.2** Analyze the impact of social, economic, and technological forces on individual growth and development. | 534–535 |
| **12.2.3** Analyze the effects of gender, ethnicity, and culture on individual development. | 522–523, 526, 528–529 |
| **12.2.4** Analyze the effects of life events on individuals' physical, intellectual, social, moral, and emotional development. | 522–523 |
| **12.3.3** Analyze the role of family and social services support systems in meeting human growth and development needs. | 524 |
| **15.1.1** Analyze parenting roles across the life span. | 542, 543 |
| **15.1.2** Analyze expectations and responsibilities of parenting. | 521, 532 |
| **15.2.2** Apply communication strategies that promote positive self-esteem in family members. | 532 |
| **15.2.3** Assess common practices and emerging research about discipline on human growth and development. | 541–542 |

**NO CHILD LEFT BEHIND** NCLB activities, information, and skills practice will help your students attain NCLB proficiency. Students will improve their abilities in the following academic standards areas:

## Academic Standards Correlations

| Discipline | Standard | Feature/Activity |
|---|---|---|
| English Language Arts | **NCTE 1** Read texts to acquire new information. | **Reading Guide (pp. 520, 527, 539)** |
| | **NCTE 4** Use written language to communicate effectively. | **After You Read (p. 543)** |
| | **NCTE 5** Use different writing process elements to communicate effectively. | **Academic Skills (p. 547)** |
| | **NCTE 12** Use language to accomplish individual purposes. | **Writing Activity (p. 518) After You Read (pp. 526, 538)** |
| Mathematics | **NCTM Number and Operations** Compute fluently and make reasonable estimates. | **After You Read (p. 526)** |
| | **NCTM Number and Operations** Understand numbers, ways of representing numbers, relationships among numbers, and number systems. | **Academic Skills (p. 547)** |
| Science | **NSES A** Students should develop abilities necessary to do scientific inquiry, understandings about scientific inquiry. | **Academic Skills (p. 547)** |
| Social Studies | **NCSS IV C Individual Development and Identity** Describe the ways group and cultural influences contribute to the development of a sense of self. | **After You Read (p. 538)** |
| | **NCSS IV D Individual Development and Identity** Apply concepts, methods, and theories about the study of human growth and development. | **After You Read (p. 543) Observation Skills (p. 546)** |

## McGraw Hill Professional Development

### MINI CLIP VIDEO LIBRARY

Targeted professional development is correlated throughout *The Developing Child*. **The McGraw-Hill Professional Development Mini Clip Video Library** provides teaching strategies to strengthen academic and learning skills. Log on to **glencoe.com**.

In this chapter, you will find these Mini Clips:
- **ELL** Previewing a Text, p. 520
- **ELL** Graphic Organizers, p. 522
- **Reading** Understanding English Language Learners, p. 529
- **Reading** Attentive Reading, p. 534
- **ELL** Level 3 Proficiency, p. 539
- **Math** Simple Events—Probability, p. 547

## Reading and Writing Strategies

**Writing Activity: Journal Entry** (p. 518)
Students use writing tips to create a journal entry discussing changes they have experienced since becoming teens.

**Before You Read** (pp. 520, 527, 539)
A pre-reading question or statement will help students make a personal connection to content.

**Graphic Organizer** (pp. 520, 527, 539)
A visual tool will help students organize and remember new content.

**Reading Check** (pp. 523, 533, 535, 542)
A question allows students to make a quick comprehension self-check.

**After You Read** (pp. 526, 538, 543)
Organize and process students' understanding of what they have read.

## Chapter Features

 **Discussing Problems** (p. 522)
Talking about problems can be helpful to many young people.

 **Sleep and the Brain** (p. 525)
Lack of sleep can keep the brain from functioning properly.

 **Dealing with Feelings** (p. 530)
Adolescents often have difficulties with their parents.

 **Provide Guidance for Teens** (p. 532)
Parents can guide teens to becoming successful adults.

 **Eating Disorders** (p. 534)
Adolescents with eating disorders tend to have lower self-esteem.

 **Dealing with Mood Swings** (p. 537)
Parents need to be flexible when dealing with teens' mood swings.

 **Self-Destructive Behaviors** (p. 541)
Experimenting with drugs and alcohol can be dangerous.

**Coach** (p. 544)
Learn skills to succeed as a Coach.

## Chapter Overview

### Introduce the Chapter

In this chapter, students learn about the importance of good personal hygiene, diet, and exercise as adolescents continue to develop physically. They also learn more about gender differences and how on-going brain development allows teens to reason better and control impulses.

### Build Background

Discuss the meaning of the term *wellness* (the state of being in good health). Tell students to write down three choices they have made recently that promote wellness. Ask for volunteers to share their lists and discuss how the different choices promoted wellness.

### Writing Activity

#### Journal Entry

This active learning activity prompts students to write a journal entry describing changes that occurred when they became teens. After students complete the activity, encourage them to share their writing with their classmates, if they are comfortable doing so. Student responses can be used as a basis for classroom discussion. (Use the following criteria to evaluate your students' journal entries:

- Does one idea lead to another?
- Does it convey personal reactions and feelings?
- Does it contain possible writing ideas?)

## Chapter Objectives

After completing this chapter, you will be able to:

- **List** three main areas of change for adolescents.
- **Identify** three ways parents can help adolescents make good nutrition choices.
- **Describe** the four main influences on personal identity development.
- **Identify** the three roles of peers on a teen's social development.
- **List** the major influences on a teen's moral development.
- **Identify** three factors that influence how a student learns in school.
- **Compare and contrast** Piaget and Vygotsky's theories of intellectual development in adolescence.

### Writing Activity

#### Journal Entry

**Growing and Changing** Many changes occur during the teen years. You change physically, emotionally, socially, morally, and intellectually. Write a journal entry describing some of the changes you have experienced since becoming a teen.

**Writing Tips** Use these tips to write an effective journal entry:

1. Use freewriting to write whatever comes to mind.
2. Use details to make images clear.
3. Tell how you feel now and how you felt before.

## CLASSROOM Solutions

### Print Resources

 **Student Edition**

 **Teacher Wraparound Edition**

 **Student Activity Workbook**

 **Student Activity Workbook Teacher Annotated Edition**

### Technology Resources

 **Online Learning Center** has resources and activities for students and teachers. Includes an Online Student Edition.

 **Interactive Student Edition** allows students to instantly access review materials, examples, and exercises.

## Review the Sections

Introduce the chapter by reviewing the sections:

### Section 19.1

Teens continue to mature physically. Boys begin producing more testosterone and girls more estrogen, leading to them becoming capable of sexual reproduction. Teens need to learn to eat healthful foods, practice good hygiene, get adequate rest, and exercise regularly.

### Section 19.2

As teens mature emotionally, they become less dependent on their families and closer to their peers. They also learn to control their emotions. Influences that affect their personal identity include family, peers, media, and the future. Some teens experience emotional difficulties such as anxiety and depression.

### Section 19.3

Major changes in the brain occur during adolescence, including the growth and maturation of the prefrontal cortex, which is responsible for reasoning. Factors that influence learning include the classroom environment, the degree of discipline and guidance at school, and parental involvement. Two leaders in the study of adolescent intellectual growth are Piaget and Vygotsky.

**↑ Explore the Photo**
During adolescence, teens continue to develop socially. *What kinds of social activities do you enjoy with your friends?*

**▶ Explore the Photo**

**Caption Answer** Answers will vary but may include going out to eat, going to the movies, skating, or biking.

**Discussion** Ask students why they think social activities, such as hanging out together or talking on the phone, are so important to adolescents. (Possible answer: They give teens a sense of belonging and help them develop their social skills.)

 **TeacherWorks Plus** is an electronic lesson planner that provides instant access to complete teacher resources in one convenient package.

**Presentation Plus!** provides visual teaching aids for every section.

**The Early Childhood Observations CD** presents video observations and lessons on observation skills and child development.

**The Developing Brain eTransparencies and Guide** include information and activities to offer insights into brain development and diseases of the brain.

# Section **19.1**

# Physical Development of Adolescents

### Bell Ringer Activity

**Developing Healthy Habits**

Hold up several objects, such as a soccer ball, to represent exercise; several food items, such as bananas and a milk carton, to represent adequate nutrition; a tooth brush, to represent good hygiene; and pajamas to represent adequate rest. Discuss that as adolescents mature, it is important that they develop healthy habits in all of these areas.

**Professional Development**

**Mini Clip**
**ELL: Previewing a Text**

A teacher previews a text with students, pointing out strategies to promote student comprehension.

## Preteaching

### Vocabulary

Sometimes medical terms can be difficult to pronounce. Read aloud the two terms *testosterone* and *estrogen*. Have the class repeat the words after you.

### Graphic Organizer

The Graphic Organizer is also on the TeacherWorks CD.

(Graphic organizers should list avoiding foods high in fat, avoiding foods high in sugar, avoiding foods high in salt, and taking sensible portions.)

**NCLB** connects academic correlations to book content.

---

## Reading Guide

### Before You Read

**Adjust Reading Speed** Improve your comprehension by adjusting reading speed to match the difficulty of the text. Reading slower may take longer, but you will understand and remember more.

### Read to Learn
**Key Concepts**
- **List** three main areas of change for adolescents.
- **Identify** three ways parents can help adolescents make good nutrition choices.

### Main Idea
During puberty, many physical changes occur. These changes make good hygiene, eating well, exercising, and getting enough sleep especially important.

### Content Vocabulary
◇ testosterone
◇ estrogen

### Academic Vocabulary
You will find these words in your reading and on your tests. Use the glossary to look up their definitions if necessary.
- adolescent
- extracurricular

### Graphic Organizer
As you read, list what it means to eat right. Use a diagram similar to the one shown to organize your information.

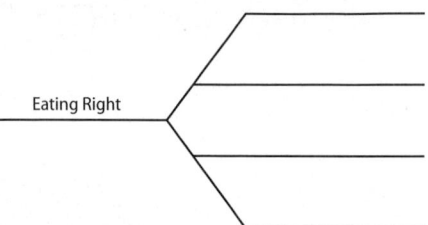
Eating Right

**Graphic Organizer** Go to this book's Online Learning Center at **glencoe.com** to print out this graphic organizer.

### Academic Standards ● ● ● ● ● ● ● ● ● ● ● ● ● ● ● ● ● ● ● ● ● ●

**English Language Arts**
**NCTE 12** Use language to accomplish individual purposes.

**Mathematics**
**NCTM Number and Operations** Compute fluently and make reasonable estimates.

**NCTE** *National Council of Teachers of English*
**NCTM** *National Council of Teachers of Mathematics*

**NSES** *National Science Education Standards*
**NCSS** *National Council for the Social Studies*

---

## Reading Guide

### Before You Read

Ask: Do you think your size and weight are different from your great-grandparents? How about the foods you eat or the types of exercise you get? (Answers may vary. Generally, teens are somewhat taller and weigh more than two or three generations ago. They get less exercise and eat more processed foods, fats, and sugars.)

### **D** Develop Concepts

**Main Idea** Discuss the main idea with the students. Ask: Why do you think that going through puberty makes it especially important that teens practice good nutrition? (Teens' bodies are growing and changing rapidly, and therefore require a well-balanced diet. In addition, the eating habits they develop may follow them throughout their lives.)

## Physical Development During Adolescence

The term adolescence has a number of meanings. Generally, it refers to the complex time of life when a child begins to mature into an adult. In that sense, the ages of adolescence vary from person to person. It may begin at age 11 or 12. In this chapter, adolescence refers to the teen years, ages 13 to 19.

The teen years are among the most challenging for both the teens and their families. An **adolescent**, or teen, experiences many changes. Three main areas of change include coping with changing emotions, handling new social situations and influences, and using new intellectual abilities. However, the physical changes associated with adolescence are the most obvious signs that a teen is moving toward adulthood.

Adolescence is a time of rapid growth in height and weight. It is also a time of physical changes throughout the body. Both males and females grow taller and become stronger. At the same time, they mature sexually, going through the changes brought on by puberty. While this phase marks the development of sexual characteristics, puberty also includes other kinds of physical changes. Powerful hormones in the body bring on the physical changes of adolescence.

Once the changes of puberty begin, they continue with a rush that can be confusing and even a bit scary. This is especially true when teens or preteens are not prepared. Their only information may come from their friends, who may not be reliable sources. Parents need to prepare their children before puberty begins. Parents should reassure their children that this type of physical growth is normal. A delay in puberty is also usually normal.

### Height and Weight

Charts showing average heights are less helpful during this stage because individual growth patterns are so inconsistent. During puberty, it is not unusual for a teen to grow three to five inches (7.6 to 12.7 cm) in height each year for several years. By about age 16, males are often bigger and stronger than most females of the same age. Many teens reach their full adult height by age 16.

To image-conscious teens, size matters. Those who go through puberty early may feel uneasy while at the same time being the object of their peers' envy. Others who mature later may feel that there is something wrong with their bodies. In many sports, players who are larger tend to have an advantage. Cultural expectations also shape teens' feelings about size. In the United States, for example, it is more acceptable to be a small adult female than a small male.

**Adolescent Changes**
Many physical changes take place during adolescence. *How have your height and weight changed during your teen years?*

## Teach

### Discussion Starter

**Maturation Rates** Ask students: How do you think maturing early or late might affect teens emotionally? How do you think it could affect them socially? (Answers will vary. Both groups may feel that they are outside of the mainstream. Maturing early can lead to being interested in the opposite sex at an earlier age. Maturing late can cause teens to not be as active in sports because they may be smaller or not as strong as other teens.)

### U Universal Access

**Verbal Learners** Discuss that many cultures have specific customs for celebrating young people becoming adults. Examples include the bar mitzvah in Jewish culture and the *quinceañera* in Hispanic culture. Assign students to research the customs of a culture other than their own that occur around the time of puberty. Students should create a poster that explains the customs for their chosen culture. (Posters will vary based on the culture chosen. Students should choose a culture and create a poster explaining a tradition from that culture that occurs around the time of puberty.)

### ►►►► Explore the Photo

**Caption Answer** Answers will vary. Young teens may not see any change. Older teens will likely see an increase in both height and weight.

**Discussion** How can parents help children deal with the rapid changes their bodies are experiencing? (Answers will vary. Possible answer: A parent can emphasize that these changes are entirely normal and share that the parent went through them at this age.)

## U Universal Access

**Visual Learners** Have students conduct research to determine the average height of both males and females for each year between the ages of 11 and 18. Students should then create a line graph showing the average heights of males and the average heights of females for each of these eight years. (Students should create a line graph showing the average height of males for each year from 11 through 18 and the average height of females for each year from 11 through 18.)

## R Reading Strategy

**Make a Chart** As they read the material under Sexual Development, have students create a hierarchical chart. The top box should be labeled Sexual Differences. The box below that on the left should be labeled Males and the one on the right Females. Under each of these boxes, they should place additional boxes containing sexual changes that occur during this time. (Charts may vary but should include: males—genitals become larger, testes produce sperm, testosterone increases; females—menstruation begins, estrogen increases, ovaries release eggs.)

**Professional Development**

**Mini Clip**
ELL:
Graphic
Organizers

Students use graphic organizers to distinguish between major and minor details.

### Males

Between the ages of 11 and 18, a typical male will double his weight from about 75 pounds to 150 pounds (34 kg to 68 kg). In the same time span, he will grow about 14 inches (36 cm) taller.

Eighteen-year-old Mario is average for his age. At nearly 70 inches (178 cm) tall, Mario weighs 150 pounds (68 kg). His shoulders are wider than they were a few years earlier, and he has become noticeably more muscular.

### U Females

Gina's growth has been typical for an adolescent girl. As an 11-year-old, she was 57 inches (145 cm) tall and weighed 80 pounds (36 kg). By the age of 14, she was slightly smaller than average at 62 inches (157 cm) tall and 105 pounds (48 kg). Now at age 15, she has grown about another 2 inches (5 cm) and has gained 9 more pounds (4 kg).

Girls usually do not grow much taller after about age 15. The average height for females in late adolescence remains just slightly over

## What Would *You* Do?

### Discussing Problems

As they were walking home from school, TJ noticed his brother Jack was angry. When TJ asked him what was wrong, Jack yelled, "Forget it! I don't want to talk about it!" So TJ left him alone for a while. Later that evening, TJ tried to talk to him again. Jack said, "I hate school. I'm never going back. I'm the shortest kid in the class, and I always get picked last for sports. On the field, the other boys yell, 'Hey, Jack, short-stack!' The older boys are always saying they're going to beat me up."

*Write About It* Write a conversation between TJ and Jack. How can TJ help Jack with his problem? What can TJ say or do to help Jack feel better about himself? With a partner, role-play the conversation for the class.

5 feet 4 inches. Many girls do, however, gain some additional weight. The average female weighs 125 pounds (57 kg) at age 18. Of course, few teens are exactly average. **U**

## Sexual Development

Some of the most significant changes in adolescence are those of sexual development. As teens experience rapid growth spurts, girls develop physically into women and boys grow into men. During this time, teens become capable of sexual reproduction. Girls' bodies release eggs, and boys' begin to produce sperm.

### Males

Males, on average, mature sexually about two years later than females. Between the ages of 13 and 15, boys' genitals become larger, and their testes, or testicles, begin to produce sperm. Sperm are the male reproductive cells.

Additional changes are caused by testosterone (tes-ˈtäs-tə-ˌrōn). **Testosterone** is a hormone produced by the testicles. Testosterone levels in a boy's body begin to rise rapidly at the beginning of puberty. A boy has reached puberty when he experiences ejaculation, the ejecting of semen. Semen is fluid that contains sperm. The first ejaculation often occurs during sleep. **R**

### Females

As you learned in Chapter 16, girls generally begin to mature sexually by the age of 11 or 12. As teens, they experience rapid growth. They also go through the outward changes associated with sexual development.

Menstruation begins about two years after breasts begin to develop. The beginning of menstrual periods indicates that a girl's body has increased its production of estrogen. **Estrogen** is a hormone produced by the ovaries. Ovaries are two small glands located next to the uterus, the organ in which a baby develops in a pregnant female. The ovaries also produce eggs, the female reproductive cells.

Usually, an ovary releases one ovum, or egg, every 28 to 32 days. If the ovum is not fertilized

## What Would *You* Do?

**Write About It** Conversations will vary. TJ might remind his brother that he had been the shortest boy in his class just a few years earlier. TJ might tell Jack that there is more to him than his height. Perhaps Jack tells funny jokes and has a lot of friends.

**Talk Honestly**
During puberty, parents can help to reassure teens about the changes that are happening in their bodies. *How much do parents need to tell young adolescents about their sexuality?*

by male sperm, it dissolves and drains out of the body along with a bloody discharge. This is the menstrual flow. Thus the menstrual cycle is the way the female body discards an unfertilized egg each month and then replaces it with a new one. An average menstrual period lasts from three to seven days.

Some girls experience irregular periods when they first start to menstruate. An erratic menstrual cycle is usually nothing to worry about. In the great majority of cases, a girl's cycle evens out within a year or so. However, if menstrual periods are extremely irregular, or if they are painful or prolonged, she should see a doctor.

Girls entering puberty may experience weight gain. This is normal. The addition of body fat is one of the effects of estrogen. The young teen is becoming a woman, and her body is beginning to round out.

✓ **Reading Check** **Explain** By what age do many teens reach their full adult height?

## Health and Wellness

Health and hygiene needs change during adolescence. However, making wise food choices, keeping clean, exercising, and getting enough sleep are still the keys to good health.

With their busy schedules, teens often do not take good care of themselves. It often seems easier to grab a snack than to sit down for a well-balanced meal. Adequate sleep and exercise may also be neglected. Thus, it is not surprising that low self-esteem is common among teens. There is a relationship among these factors. See **Figure 19.1** for tips on improving your self-image while staying healthy.

## Nutrition

Puberty and related growth spurts have an impact on nutritional needs. A balanced diet of nutritious foods is needed to fuel growth, as well as normal body processes. Teens typically consume more calories than usual during growth spurts.

Certain vitamins, such as zinc and iron, are especially important during the teen years. Use the MyPyramid Plan to help ensure your body is getting the nutrients it needs to help it stay strong and active during your teen years.

Eating right means avoiding foods high in fat, sugar, and salt, as well as taking sensible portions. Overeating, especially of high-calorie foods, can lead to obesity. Parents can help by making nutritious food choices available, setting a good example, and paying attention to portion sizes.

In the Hasegawa household, for example, bowls of food are not set on the table for family members to help themselves. Instead, Mrs. Hasegawa serves each person a plate of food with reasonable portions. If her children are still hungry, they can ask for seconds.

Section 19.1   Physical Development of Adolescents   **523**

**S** **Skill Practice**
**Guided Practice**
**Create a Presentation** Students should create oral presentations on teen health and wellness issues, including the importance of good nutrition, good hygiene, and getting adequate exercise and sleep. Encourage students to use visual aids during their presentations. (Students should prepare oral presentations that discuss the importance of good hygiene, nutrition, and adequate exercise and sleep.) **L1** **ELL**

**Conduct an Interview** Organize students into pairs. One person will role play an expert on adolescent health and wellness and the other will play an interviewer. They should conduct an interview on a television show aimed at adolescents. The interviewer should ask the expert questions about teen health and wellness. (Students should present a mock-television interview in which they discuss teen health and wellness.) **L2** **ELL**

**Write a Letter** Tell students that they live in a small town that has no teen center. The town is thinking of opening a teen center to provide recreational facilities for teens. In addition, it will offer classes on exercise and nutrition. Have students write a letter to the local newspaper explaining the kinds of activities and classes the proposed center could have and why it is important to the community. (Students should write a letter discussing that encouraging exercise and good nutritional habits in teens will improve their overall health and therefore help the entire community.) **L3**

✓ **Reading Check**

**Explain** Many teens reach their full adult height by age 16.

## ➤ Explore the Photo

**Caption Answer** Answers will vary. Some students will say that parents need to tell adolescents everything about sexuality. Some may say it should be on a need-to-know basis, or only answering questions posed by the adolescent.

**Discussion** Some parents provide their teens with books on their sexuality rather than speaking directly with their children. Encourage students to discuss the advantages and disadvantages of this method. (Possible answer: Many available books are well-written and may be able to do a more thorough job than a parent, but many teens want the comfort and reassurance of being able to talk with a parent.)

## Assess

### Quiz

Ask students to answer the following questions:

1. How does a boy's weight typically change between ages 11 and 18? (*It typically doubles.*)
2. What is the function of the ovaries? (*They produce estrogen and each month release an egg, the female reproductive cell.*)
3. Levels of what hormone begin to rise rapidly in a boy's body at the start of puberty? (*Testosterone levels rise rapidly during this time.*)

## Reteach

### W Writing Support
### Journal Entry

**Making Better Choices** Have students write a journal entry about one of these areas in which they believe they need improvement: improving their eating habits, getting more exercise, or thinking more positively. Encourage students to write about their specific challenges in this area and how they plan to make changes. (*Refer to p. 518 to review the characteristics of writing an effective journal entry. Students should write about a specific area that they believe they need to improve and how they plan to make these improvements. Students may consider bringing fruit for a snack each day, or going for a jog with friends after school.*)

---

**Figure 19.1 Improving Self-Image**

Most people would like to have confidence. *What advice would you give to a friend who wanted to become more confident?*

| W | | |
|---|---|---|
| **Choose good nutrition.** | The body needs breakfast to get the body and mind going, but it is the most skipped meal. Starting the day with a nutritious breakfast can boost achievement. | |
| **Exercise regularly.** | Any type of exercise can improve fitness and give a feeling of well being when done regularly. | |
| **Think positively.** | Everyone has some good features. They might include an interesting face, a strong body, or a great personality. Those who concentrate on their good features instead of real or imagined imperfections stand out for their positive attitude. | |
| **Look inside.** | It is common to worry about what others think, but the solution is not to just follow the crowd. Having the courage to be an individual makes it easier to see and appreciate the best qualities in others. | |
| **Be strong.** | Make decisions independently. Teens who have a good self-concept can withstand peer pressure because they believe in themselves. Their strength comes from within, not from what others say about them. | |

Teens are often "on the go" and find it hard to eat right. But even teens can practice good nutrition. They should make an effort to carry healthful snacks, such as fruit or granola bars, to maintain energy through the day. They should also be sure to drink plenty of water. Some other tips for teens to follow are:

- **Eat slower.** It takes time for your body to feel full. Eating slower can help you eat the right portions of food.
- **Eat breakfast.** It is important for teens to eat a healthy breakfast to get the energy to start their day.
- **Make better choices.** You can still eat out with your friends, but order juice instead of soda. Ask for vegetable toppings on your pizza instead of meat. Order smaller portions instead of upsizing.

### Sleep

Everyone needs adequate sleep. The body, especially the brain and nervous system, restores itself during sleep. Teens need at least eight and one-half hours of sleep every night. Unfortunately, most only sleep about seven hours. They tend to go to bed late. Then they find it difficult to get up in the morning. Negative effects of too little sleep can include:

- Difficulty concentrating in school. This can lead to lower grades.
- Becoming irritated more easily and losing emotional control.
- Impaired coordination and slower reaction time. This can affect performance in activities such as sports or driving.
- Decreased resistance to illness.

**524** Chapter 19 Adolescence

---

**Figure 19.1 Improving Self-Image**

**Caption Answer** Advice will vary but might include to master new skills, participate in positive self-talk, visualize success, improve grooming, focus on others, or talk with a trusted adult.

**Discussion** Ask students: If you are having a difficult time, what might you do to encourage yourself to think positively? Why is it important to think positively? (Answers will vary. Possible answer: Remember how you have helped someone who was down, or how someone has helped you. Being optimistic and upbeat helps people project a positive image that attracts others to them.)

Many teens enjoy **extracurricular**, or optional, activities such as athletics or clubs that are outside the regular curriculum. Some teens take on too many of these activities though. Some teens have part-time jobs during the school week. Others spend late nights on the computer or watching television. Good choices, time-management skills, and a regular sleep schedule can help teens get the rest they need.

## Physical Fitness

A moderate amount of daily exercise is important for everyone, including teens. It builds strong bones and muscles and benefits the heart and blood vessels. Unfortunately, nearly half of Americans between the ages of 12 and 21 do not exercise on a regular basis. Physical inactivity sets the stage for possible obesity and the development of other health problems later in life.

There are many ways teens can add physical activity to their daily routine. Doing so helps the body cope with stress and strengthens muscles, including heart muscles. Physical activity is any activity that gets your body moving. It can be as simple as walking the dog before school or playing ball in the afternoon with friends.

Teens should try and get at least 60 minutes a day of moderate to vigorous physical activity. This can help maintain a healthy weight, increase your flexibility and endurance, and improve your health. Try joining a sport team after school. Or get a friend to join you for regular walks or bike rides. Even helping out with household chores like mowing the lawn can count towards your daily physical activity.

↑ **Get Fit**
Getting 60 minutes of exercise each day is important for staying healthy and preventing obesity. *What physical activities do you participate in on a regular basis?*

Section 19.1 Physical Development of Adolescents **525**

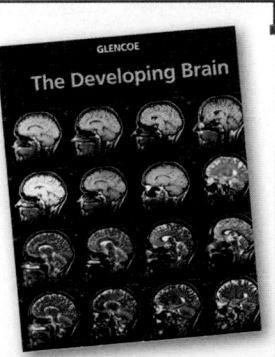

## Assess

### Study Tools

Have students go to the Online Learning Center at **glencoe.com**:

- Take the **Practice Test**.
- Download **Study-to-Go** content.

Use the **Student Activity Workbook** for additional practice.

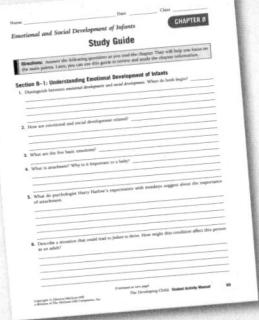

## Close

### Culminating Activity

**A Healthy Adolescence** Have students review this section by listing ways in which teens can maintain wellness. Encourage students to discuss why wellness is important not only to the teen, but also to the teen's future. (Students should state that teens can improve their wellness by eating a healthy diet, getting adequate sleep and exercise, and practicing good hygiene. Wellness is important to insure that the teen stays healthy and keeps good habits throughout adulthood.)

**NCLB** connects academic correlations to book content.

It is often helpful for teens to set a fitness goal. Keeping a fitness log of your daily activity can help to reach your goal. Note the intensity and duration of each activity. Perhaps your goal would be to jog in a 5K charity run. You could begin by running just 15 minutes a day. Gradually increase your time and distance. Be sure to keep track of what you do each day. Use your log to check your progress toward your goal. Once you reach your goal, set a new goal. Reward yourself with something other than food.

## Hygiene

Personal cleanliness routines become more important in adolescence. Perspiration odor and oily skin and hair are common problems. Fortunately, most teens care about their appearance and how they are perceived by others. Regular baths or showers remove dirt, sweat, and dead skin cells. Deodorant or antiperspirant helps control body odor. Clean clothes also help present a fresh image. Make sure to wear clean socks every day so that your feet stay healthy.

Teens should use water and a mild soap to wash their face each morning and at night. In addition, you should try to avoid touching your face with your hands throughout the day. Brushing your hair each day and regular shampooing will help keep dirt from building up. Brushing or combing will also help distribute the natural oils in your hair.

Fingernails and toenails should be kept clean and trimmed. Your nails help protect and support the tissues of your fingers and toes. They also add to your overall appearance and image. Just as important to your health and appearance are your teeth. You should brush and floss your teeth every day. Brushing your teeth after eating can help prevent tooth decay and other diseases. Nothing helps make a better first impression than a good-looking smile.

## Section **19.1** After You Read

### Review Key Concepts

1. **Describe** the roles of estrogen and testosterone.
2. **Explain** why teens need to pay more attention to hygiene than younger children.

### Practice Academic Skills

**NCLB**

 **English Language Arts**

3. Follow your teacher's instructions to form into groups. Work with your group to brainstorm answers to the following questions. Write a list of your answers. Between adolescent girls and adolescent boys, who do you think has a more difficult experience in terms of physical changes and development? Why? Compare your group's list of answers with the other groups' lists.

> **NCTE 12** Use language to accomplish individual purposes.

 **Mathematics**

4. John's weight increased from 75 pounds at age 11 to 150 pounds at age 18. This is an increase of 100 percent. Angie's weight increased from 80 pounds to 125 pounds in the same time. By what percentage did Angie's weight increase? Show how you arrive at your answer.

> **NCTM Number and Operations** Compute fluently and make reasonable estimates.

**Check Your Answers** Check your answers at this book's Online Learning Center at **glencoe.com**.

## Section **19.1** After You Read

### Review Key Concepts

1. Estrogen production in females signals the beginning of menstruation. The rising level of testosterone signals the beginning of puberty in males.
2. The development of oil and odor glands leads to the increased need for hygiene at this age.

### Practice Academic Skills

3. Groups should include both male and female students. Lists will vary. Males may think that males have a more difficult experience. Females may think that females have a more difficult experience. Reasons should be logical.
4. Angie's weight increase by approximately 56 percent. (125 − 80 = 45; 45 ÷ 80 = 56.25%)

# Section 19.2 — Emotional, Social, and Moral Development of Adolescents

## Reading Guide

### Before You Read
**Be Organized** A messy environment can be distracting. To lessen distractions, organize an area where you can read this section comfortably.

### Read to Learn
**Key Concepts**
- **Describe** the four main influences on personal identity development.
- **Identify** the three roles of peers on a teen's social development.
- **List** the major influences on a teen's moral development.

### Main Idea
Adolescents must form a personal identity and handle emotional difficulties. They also develop social relationships and a personal value system.

### Content Vocabulary
◇ personal identity
◇ identity crisis
◇ depression
◇ bipolar disorder
◇ morality
◇ moral maturity
◇ popular culture

### Academic Vocabulary
You will find these words in your reading and on your tests. Use the glossary to look up their definitions if necessary.
■ stifle
■ conviction

### Graphic Organizer
As you read, list and describe three emotional difficulties that many teens experience. Use a chart like the one shown to help organize your information.

| Emotional Difficulties of Teens | |
|---|---|
| Difficulty | Description |
|  |  |
|  |  |
|  |  |

 **Graphic Organizer** Go to this book's Online Learning Center at **glencoe.com** to print out this graphic organizer.

### Academic Standards . . . . . . . . . . . . . . . . . . . .

 **English Language Arts**
**NCTE 12** Use language to accomplish individual purposes.

 **Social Studies**
**NCSS IV C Individual Development and Identity** Describe the ways group and cultural influences contribute to the development of a sense of self.

**NCTE** *National Council of Teachers of English*
**NCTM** *National Council of Teachers of Mathematics*

**NSES** *National Science Education Standards*
**NCSS** *National Council for the Social Studies*

---

## Section 19.2

## Focus

### Bell Ringer Activity
Write on the board the world's shortest poem: "I, Why?"
Ask students: How would you respond to this poem? How does the poem tie into an adolescent's need to establish a personal identity? Explain that this section discusses the various factors that affect how young people create their personal images.

## Preteaching

### Vocabulary
Point out to students that terms are often formed by placing an adjective before a noun. Ask for a volunteer to read the content vocabulary terms for this section that consist of both an adjective and a noun and discuss how adding an adjective affects each term's meaning.

### Graphic Organizer
 The Graphic Organizer is also on the TeacherWorks CD.

(Graphic organizers should include: depression—feelings of intense sadness last for long periods of time and prevent a person from leading a normal life; anxiety—heightened feeling of uneasiness, fear, or uncertainty; and bipolar disorder—extreme changes in mood from manic to depression.)

 **NCLB** connects academic correlations to book content.

---

## Reading Guide

### Before You Read
Ask students: How is your view of yourself affected by your family? Your peers? Encourage students to provide specific examples. Tell students to keep these influences in mind as they read this section.

### D Develop Concepts

**Main Idea** Discuss the main idea with the students. Ask students how they think a teen's social relationships might relate to the teen's value system. (Possible answer: The opinions and beliefs of the people a teen interacts with can cause the teen to re-evaluate his or her values.)

## Discussion Starter

**Changing Relationship** Ask students how they think relationships change during adolescence. What do teens look for in friends? How would they like their parents to treat them? (Answers will vary. Possible answers: They want friends who are trustworthy and on whom they can depend. They want their parents to give them more independence and to respect their judgment.)

## W₁ Writing Support

### Poem

**Personal Identity** Instruct students to write a poem titled "Who Am I?" The poem should explain how the student sees him- or herself. Encourage students to describe their personal identity and how they feel they fit into the world. Ask for volunteers to read their poems to the class. (Refer to p. 318 for tips on writing a poem. Students' poems will vary but should describe how they see themselves. Poems may be rhyming or non-rhyming, but should use descriptive terms.)

## U₁ Universal Access

**Visual Learners** Have students make a list of ten ideas, attitudes, or opinions that they feel contribute strongly to their unique personality. Then have students use their list to create a personal identity collage. Pictures may be hand-drawn, printed from the computer, or torn from magazines. (Collages should show the ten items from the list, and should accurately represent how each student views himself or herself.) **ELL**

# Emotional Development of Adolescents

As teens move toward adulthood, they work to establish their individuality. They typically become more attached to their friends and less dependent on their families. These and related changes can cause tension between teens and their parents.

Adolescence is the time of life when a person asks, "Who am I?" and tries to answer that question. While it is often a period of confusion, it can also lead to a strong sense of self.

Teens find that their emotions become more powerful and more difficult to control. Emotions can even be frightening. Teens must learn to control their emotions. Sometimes they struggle to do so. When teens' emotions become too overwhelming, they may need the help of friends and family to cope.

## Personal Identity

During early adolescence, young teens begin to develop the mental capacity to form ideas and opinions that are theirs alone. They see that these ideas and opinions may differ from those of their family and friends. In this way, they begin to experience a strong personal identity. **Personal identity** is a sense of oneself as a unique individual. Teens begin to understand that their ideas, attitudes, and opinions are what form their personality. At this stage, adolescents are forming the personality that they will present to the world as adults.

As they develop a personal identity, teens grow more concerned with what their peers think of them. Some become self-conscious or self-absorbed. Young teens, in particular, tend to worry about their physical appearance.

Later in adolescence, a teen's sense of personal identity strengthens. Teens become better at understanding others' feelings. Their personalities often show more compassion and responsibility.

### Influences on Identity Development

Social and cultural influences strongly affect the formation of a personal identity. These influences include family, peers, media, and the future.

**Helping Others**
Many teens are willing to volunteer their time for community and charitable projects. *What volunteer opportunities are available in your community?*

## ► Explore the Photo

**Caption Answer** Answers will vary depending on your community. Students should list opportunities in which they could participate, such as a soup kitchen or a mentoring program.

**Discussion** Encourage students to discuss charitable projects that they have been involved with. Ask: Did helping with this project change how you thought about yourself? If so, how? (Possible answer: It made me feel that I could have a positive effect on people's lives and that made me feel good about myself.)

**Family** Even though teens sometimes rebel against parental authority, family continues to be an important influence. Some teens and their parents maintain close emotional ties through this period. Other teens become especially close to another family member, such as a sibling or grandparent.

To parents it may sometimes seem that their teen is rejecting the family's values and beliefs. This may be true in the short term. However, an adult's personal identity usually incorporates much of what he or she learned while growing up.

**Peers** A teen's classmates and friends are forming their own personal identities. Peer pressure is an especially strong influence for teens. Those in a peer group often adopt the tastes and beliefs of more popular members. More confident teens evaluate those ideas and beliefs, accepting some and rejecting others. In this way, they can form a strong identity that is their own.

**Media** Popular media can also influence your personal identity. Television, movies, books, advertisements, and music all portray different values and beliefs. It is important to remember that much of what you see in the media is not realistic. The actions of characters in books, movies, and television shows are often exaggerated. These are all created to be entertaining. Advertisements are designed to try and influence you. Be sure to evaluate what the ads are saying and decide for yourself if it is true.

**The Future** By mid to late adolescence, teens have to start thinking about their lives as adults. By planning for a career or further education, they can start to see themselves as unique and independent individuals in the adult world. Deciding what they want to do or be in the future can affect the choices they make today. A teen who decides he or she wants to be an engineer in the future might join the science club today.

**W₂**

### Theories of Identity Development

Many researchers have studied how adolescents form their sense of self. Two leaders in this field of study are Erik Erikson (1902–1994) and James Marcia (b. 1937).

**Erikson's Identity vs. Confusion** Erik Erikson noted that even the most well-adjusted adolescent may experience some confusion about identity or sense of self. He and other psychologists considered this normal because adolescence is the time of life when teens strive to discover who they are. Erikson recognized that this confusion can become a serious problem for some teens.

Erikson believed that social and cultural influences have a strong effect on how teens develop a sense of self. He believed that one of the most significant influences is peer pressure. Peer pressure is the influence of friends in the same age group. Erikson held that conforming too rigidly to the attitudes and opinions of one's peers could result in an identity crisis. An **identity crisis** is a confusion about one's personal identity that results from failing to find a strong identity, or sense of self, through personal exploration.

**C**

**Marcia's Identity Processes** James Marcia elaborated on Erikson's theory by offering ways for teens to solve their identity crisis. Marcia believes that there are four paths to a sense of personal identity. Most teens explore more than one of these paths.

**U₂**

On the first path, teens accept the values of their parents and other respected adults without questioning those values. On the second

**Teach** *cont.*

### W₂ Writing Support
**Journal Entry**

**Looking Ahead** Have students write a journal entry in which they discuss how their hopes for the future affect their personal identity. Encourage them to include specific examples; for instance, they may see themselves as being good with young children if they want to be preschool teachers. (Refer to p. 518 to review the characteristics of writing an effective journal entry. Students should write about their hopes for the future and how they have affected their personal identity.)

### C Critical Thinking

**Analyze** Remind students of the discussion of Erikson's views in Chapter 17; Erikson stated that the degree to which children develop a sense of competence in their early school years has a major effect on their later decisions. Encourage students to discuss how this relates to how people develop a sense of identity in their teen years. (Answers will vary. Possible answer: To a large degree, people establish their personal identities based on their sense of competence and incompetence in various areas.)

### U₂ Universal Access

**Visual Learners** Have students create a graphic organizer that illustrates Marcia's four paths to a sense of personal identity. (Graphic organizers may vary but should illustrate the four paths: [1] Teen accepts values of parents and other respected adults; [2] Teen is uncertain of identity, but is searching; [3] Teen has no clear identity and is not searching; [4] Teen has solidified values and developed a sense of identity.) **ELL**

**Mc Graw Hill Professional Development**

**Mini Clip**
**Reading: Understanding English Language Learners**

Ruben Zepeda, EdD, discusses the issues teachers must address when they have English learners in their classrooms.

### C Critical Thinking

**Draw Conclusions** Have students think of a way in which their own parents have adjusted to the students' growing independence. Perhaps the parents have extended their curfew. Ask for volunteers to share these changes with the class. Ask students: Do you think making these changes is easy for parents? Why or why not? (Answers will vary. Each student should think of one adjustment his or her parent has made, such as letting the student borrow the car. Possible answer to questions: No, because it may be hard to accept that their children are growing up and will soon be gone from home. Parents also may worry about the teen's safety.)

### U Universal Access

**Logical Learners** Organize students into pairs and have them create a skit in which a teen is asking a parent for more freedom. Have one student role play the parent, and the other the teen. The parent should go through the bulleted items listed here to try to logically determine whether to grant the request. Have each pair perform their skit for the class. (Skits will vary but should portray a teen asking for more freedom. The parent should use the bulleted items listed here to reach a decision. Possible requests might include later curfew, taking a part-time job, or going on a trip with friends.) **ELL**

## What Would You Do?

**Dealing with Feelings**

Cameron grinned and waved his new driver's license as he walked in the house. He had been confident he would pass the test and had planned to drive his friends to a game on the weekend. But when he asked to use the car, his parents said no. They told him he was still too inexperienced to drive the family car without an adult along. Cameron was angry and humiliated. He had bragged to his friends that he would be driving them. He had to call and tell them that his parents would not let him drive. Cameron refused to speak to his parents for two days. He felt they treated him like a child, and he was determined to make sure they understood how upset he was.

**✎ Write About It** Put yourself in Cameron's parents' place. Why might they have made the decision they did? Write a paragraph in which you explain to Cameron why his parents made their decision.

path, teens are unsure of their values. They are determined to find an identity, but they are still in the process of developing it. On the third path, adolescents have no clear sense of identity and they are not attempting to find one. On the fourth path, adolescents have solidified their values and have developed a sense of identity. These individuals may redefine this identity in adulthood, but they have made choices they are comfortable with for now.

## The Push for Independence

Teens naturally want more freedom. Many parents are often reluctant to grant that freedom. Parents want to protect their children from the dangers and disappointments that more freedom brings. As one mother put it, "Aiden can't remember to pick up his dirty socks or take his homework to school. The idea of his roaming around on that motorcycle he wants to buy is very scary. My goal is to keep

him alive and well, even if he hates me for it." Parents want teens to prove they are ready for more independence. Teens do not always see the need to do so.

Teens want to spend more time with friends and less time with family. Parents often want more time with their teens because they know the teens are getting ready to leave home. These opposing positions can lead to friction and arguments at home. Teens' tendency to begin questioning adult wisdom and authority also causes tension. All of these changes in attitudes and actions can cause tension between teens and adults.

The need to move toward independence is a major concern of teens. Understanding the importance of this need can help parents better respond to teens' concerns. Teens typically want to spend more time with their friends without adult supervision. They enjoy practicing adult skills, such as driving, and want to explore the world on their own.

Parents sometimes worry that lack of supervision can lead to reckless or even illegal behavior, sexual activity, and possibly pregnancy. They may also worry about a teen's safety while driving alone. They may worry that a teen with too much freedom will neglect schoolwork. Teens need to experience a reasonable amount of independence. That is how they learn the consequences of their decisions as they transition to young adulthood. When a teen asks for more freedom, parents should consider:

- Has the teen usually been responsible, well behaved, and truthful?
- Do I know and trust the teen's friends and their families?
- Does the teen drive safely and understand all traffic laws?
- Is he or she doing well in school?

If parents answer yes to all of these questions, they should consider increasing a teen's privileges. However, it should be clear that these privileges will be taken away if any serious trouble results. This understanding will be a strong incentive to use the newly won independence in a responsible way. Often, parents and teens can come to agreeable rules by talking about them together.

## What Would You Do?

**Write About It** Paragraphs will vary. Cameron's parents would likely tell him that he has not had enough practice driving yet. They want to keep him from getting into an accident because he is inexperienced. They want to let him know there are limits to using the car.

## Handling Emotional Difficulties

Adolescence is a very emotional time of life. Ideally, its pleasures include making new friends, learning new skills, and becoming active at school and possibly in the community. However, life does not always go smoothly. Sometimes the pressures of school, family, social life, and physical changes can be difficult to handle.

Everyone goes through difficult times. For teens, emotional ups and downs are normal. But sometimes significant emotional problems do occur. Recognizing the symptoms of emotional problems in a teen is an important step in preventing those problems from leading to serious consequences.

### Depression

Feeling disappointed or sad from time to time is common, but there is an important difference between temporary sadness and true depression. With **depression**, feelings of intense sadness last for long periods of time and prevent a person from leading a normal life. Depression can result from the loss of a loved one, family problems, the break-up of a close friendship, or failure in school. It can also be linked to the accumulation of smaller problems. A teen's feelings of being unable to cope with stressful situations can be unbearable.

Females have a higher risk of depression because of hormonal changes. However, they also are more likely to seek help for depression than males. Some of the warning signs for depression include:

- Feelings of sadness most or all of the time.
- Feelings of emptiness.
- Lack of energy.
- Difficulty concentrating.
- Loss of interest in social activities, school, or activities that were formerly pleasurable.
- Unexpectedly poor grades.
- A change in eating or sleeping habits.

If these warning signs are ignored, there are risks for further consequences. Anyone who sees signs of depression in a teen should act. Friends can tell the teen's parents, school counselor, or other responsible adult. Consulting a family physician or school counselor is a good first step. If the depression persists, the parents should consult a mental health professional.

**Feelings of Depression**
Teens sometimes sink into depression if their lives are not going the way they want them to. *How can you help a friend who is suffering from depression?*

---

 **Explore the Photo**

**Caption Answer** Answers may vary. You can tell the teen's parents, school counselor, or other responsible adult that you suspect the teen is struggling with depression.

**Discussion** Ask students how they might be able to tell the difference between a friend who has normal feelings of sadness and a friend who is truly depressed. (Everyone has times when they feel down, but depression involves long periods of intense sadness that make it impossible for the person to lead a normal life.)

---

**Teach** *cont.*

### S Skill Practice

**Guided Practice**

**List Emotional Difficulties** Have students create a chart that lists significant emotional difficulties that teens may face. Charts should also include a list of symptoms for each problem. (Charts should include depression, anxiety, and bipolar disorder. Students should list symptoms for each difficulty. For example, anxiety symptoms might include constant worrying and a heightened feeling of uneasiness, fear, or uncertainty.) **L1** **ELL**

**Describe Alternatives** As a class, create a list of emotional difficulties teens may face and describe possible positive ways of dealing with these difficulties. Encourage students to suggest ways that they may have used themselves. (Lists will vary, but problems might include feelings of depression or anxiety. Ways of dealing with depression might include exercising, spending time with friends, or volunteering time to a worthwhile cause.) **L2**

**Identify Types of Emotional Difficulty** Describe a scenario in which a teen is experiencing severe emotional difficulties. The students should identify questions they might ask this person to determine the type of emotional difficulty. For example, to determine whether the teen is depressed, they might ask: How do you feel when you first wake up in the morning? Encourage students to conduct research to determine appropriate questions to ask. (Questions will vary. Students should write a series of questions to ask a teen to determine the type of emotional difficulty he or she is experiencing.) **L3**

## Teach cont.

### R Reading Strategy

**Analyze Terms** Write *bipolar disorder* on the board. Discuss that *bi-* is a prefix meaning "two." Polar is from the Latin *Polaris* meaning "pole." Ask students: Based on this information, what do you think bipolar disorder means? (Explain that bipolar disorder is a condition in which the individual fluctuates between two extreme moods—very energetic and very depressed.)

### U Universal Access

**Gifted Learners** Explain to students that each of the following famous people had bipolar disorder: Sir Isaac Newton; Abraham Lincoln; and Ludwig Van Beethoven. Have students conduct research to identify a famous person with this disorder and then write an essay about how it affected the individual's life. (Essays will vary depending on the person chosen. Beethoven, for example, experienced periods of intense depression, one of which he stated lasted two years. On the other hand, his periods of mania led to great joy and a strong sense of self-confidence, resulting in his composing pieces such as the Choral Symphony.)

### C Critical Thinking

**Evaluate** Discuss that most experts recommend the parenting approach called *assertive-democratic* (discussed in Chapter 3) as a way of dealing with friction between teens and parents. Ask students: Do you think this is the best approach for parents of teens? Why or why not? (Possible answer: Probably; while the parent clearly exerts his or her authority, the parent also allows the teen to have input in decision-making.)

### Anxiety

Many people who suffer from depression also show signs of anxiety. A large number of people, including teens, experience this heightened feeling of uneasiness, fear, or uncertainty. Although there are different types of anxiety, all involve some degree of worry.

Some possible traits of anxiety include fear of social situations, shortness of breath or racing heart, sadness, difficulty sleeping, and panic attacks. Heather, who suffers from anxiety, avoids elevators, crowded areas such as movie theaters, and parties where there will be strangers. She knows being in such places makes her feel faint.

Teens who experience excessive worry should talk to a guidance counselor or doctor about the problem. If anxiety sufferers turn to alcohol or drugs to help cope, they can easily develop substance abuse problems. For information on anxiety disorders, see the Respond to Special Needs feature on page 475.

### Bipolar Disorder

Mood swings and other emotional changes are a normal part of growing up. Sometimes, though, mood swings go beyond what is normal for most teens. Some teens exhibit signs of bipolar disorder. A **bipolar disorder** is a psychiatric disorder characterized by extreme changes in mood, from highly energetic to depressed and withdrawn, sometimes fluctuating rapidly. One week they may be manic. Manic means intense experiences of heightened mood. The next week, they are depressed and withdrawn again, causing others to wonder what is going on. These changes could occur over the course of days, weeks, or months.

Bipolar disorder was formerly called manic depression. It can affect people of nearly all ages. It affects males and females about equally. Scientists are not sure what causes the condition, but they think it results mostly from chemical imbalances in the brain.

During the manic phase of bipolar disorder, the individual may experience exaggerated happiness and optimism, racing thoughts and speech, and reckless behavior. When in the

## ♡ Parenting Skills

### Provide Guidance for Teens

There is a hymn titled "Keep Your Eyes on the Prize." The prize in the hymn is equal rights for all. For parents of teens, the prize is a young adult who can successfully live on his or her own. Many teens often struggle for independence. Here are some tips for providing stability and guidance:

- **Talk regularly.** No matter how stubborn teens may appear, most listen to their parents.
- **Discuss specifics.** Try sharing appropriate personal experiences. For example, you may have been required to make a difficult ethical decision at work.
- **Set limits.** Enforce rules about things that are important, such as personal safety. If a teen asks for more freedom, listen carefully and explain your answer.
- **Hold on.** Keep focused on what really matters, such as getting a good education and treating others with respect.

**Take Charge** Write a paragraph describing what it means to "Keep Your Eyes on the Prize" when helping a teen develop emotionally.

## ♡ Parenting Skills

### Provide Guidance for Teens

Describe for students the following scenario: A friend is having serious difficulties with her 15-year-old daughter. The daughter has skipped school several times and is failing one of her classes. What might you say to your friend? (Possible answer: You might remind her that many people who had difficult teen years later went on to lead happy, productive lives. You also might suggest practical solutions, such as family counseling.)

### Take Charge

It means to remember your final goal of raising an emotionally mature individual and not get bogged down in all the day-to-day challenges of raising a teen.

**Changing Relationships**
Teens often spend more time with friends than with family. *Who do you like to spend time with?*

depressive phase, the individual may have feelings of guilt or worthlessness, a loss of energy, and an inability to take joy in anything.

The cycles of manic behavior and depression can each last for weeks or months, but sometimes they are much shorter in length. The periods of abnormal behavior may be separated by a time when the person acts more normally. Although there is no cure for bipolar disorder, it can be managed with medication and supportive treatment.

✓ **Reading Check** **Explain** What may happen if someone who suffers from anxiety does not seek help?

## Social Relationships in Adolescence

During adolescence, teens explore their independence and self-expression through their social relationships with friends. Teens may hang out with their friends, talk to them on the phone, and communicate online. They may do all of these in the same day. Parents may wonder how they find so much to talk about.

At the same time, teens may begin to rebel against the authority of their parents and other adults. Teens may feel that the adults are trying to **stifle**, or discourage, their self-expression.

## Peer Influences on Social Development

Peers play an important role in teens' social development. Adolescents become less dependent on parents and other adults. Most teens become more involved with peers.

### Peer Groups

There may never be a time in life when the need for acceptance is greater than during adolescence. Not making the volleyball team or not being invited to a classmate's party can be devastating. As teens form their identity, they may place great importance on the acceptance and admiration of their peer group. **W**

During this time, there is a tendency for teens to conform to the ideas and behavior of the group. They may listen to the same music and watch the same television shows. Most teens do not want to stand out as being different. This is especially true in the early teen years. Charlie would go see the latest horror movie with his friends so he would fit in. But at home, he liked to watch romantic comedies.

An adolescent's conformist behavior can upset parents. The parents worry that teens will forget their many years of careful guidance. Such worries are often unfounded. Often, a teen seeks out a peer group that shares some of the same values.

Section 19.2 Emotional, Social, and Moral Development of Adolescents **533**

---

**▶ Explore the Photo**

**Caption Answer** Answers will vary but may include school mates, team members, friends from a religious organization, or family members.

**Discussion** Describe a scenario in which a teen begins spending less and less time with his twelve-year-old sister. The sister complains that she misses the fun they used to have together. If you were the teen, how would you respond? (Possible answer: The teen might explain that he is busier with his friends and high school activities than in the past. He might suggest that they set aside a specific time each week to spend together.)

---

### Reteach cont.

## R₁ Reading Strategy

**Read to Answer Questions** Read aloud, or have a student volunteer read aloud, the text under Close Friends. Then ask students to answer this question: Why do teens need close friends? (Answers should be similar to the following: Teens need close friends so that they can freely share their thoughts with someone without fear of rejection.) **ELL**

**Professional Development**

**Mini Clip Reading: Attentive Reading**

A teacher uses read aloud and direct questioning to help her students identify elements of a persuasive essay.

## U₁ Universal Access

**Interpersonal Learners** Challenge students to plan a project to benefit a charity of their choice. As a class, brainstorm ideas, such as a clothing drive for a local shelter or a volunteer day where the whole class could work at a local soup kitchen or animal shelter. Once ideas are listed, take a vote to choose one. If needed, separate the class into groups to be sure all aspects of the project are handled. Once the project is complete, encourage students to discuss what they learned from doing the project. (Projects will vary. Students may say they learned something about themselves by helping others, or they may say they learned more about an area of community need.)

---

## RESPOND TO SPECIAL NEEDS — Eating Disorders

Eating disorders such as anorexia nervosa (anorexia) and bulimia nervosa (bulimia) are psychological disorders. Anorexia is characterized by a refusal to maintain a minimally normal body weight. Bulimia is repeated episodes of binge eating followed by behaviors such as self-induced vomiting.

Eating disorders often start in adolescence. More than 90 percent of cases occur among females. Anorexia and bulimia affect as many as 3 percent of adolescent and young adult females. The incidence of anorexia appears to have increased in recent decades. Compared with adolescents who have normal eating patterns, those who have eating disorders tend to have lower self-esteem and a negative body image. They also have feelings of inadequacy, anxiety, social dysfunction, depression, and moodiness. Eating disorders can cause many severe complications. People who have eating disorders should receive immediate medical and psychological treatment.

**Critical Thinking** Conduct research to learn more about the medical and psychological treatments available for eating disorders. Compile your findings in a one-page report.

### Romantic Involvement

During adolescence, most teens gain experience being part of a couple through dating relationships. Young teens may spend more time thinking about their appearance and how to be noticed than actually dating. The rise and fall of romantic relationships can bring emotions that are difficult to control. However, such experiences give teens a better idea of what to look for in someone to marry.

### Close Friends

**R₁** The most important peers in a teen's life are the close friends with whom teens share their secret dreams and fears. A teen may tell things to a best friend that he or she would never confide to a parent or other adult.

Having at least one close friend helps a teen navigate the trials of adolescence. Because friends are free to speak their minds with one another, adolescents can learn from a close friend how to alter their behavior or ideas. This lets them do so without the fear of rejection present in a larger group. Having a best friend also gives teens someone to talk to when things are worrying or angering them.

## Opportunities for Social Interaction

As adolescents move into their middle and late teens, they typically become involved in more social activities. These activities can be both for pleasure and in service of the community.

### Having a Good Time

There are many ways teens can have fun. These range from parties and time with friends, to sports and after-school activities. School and community organizations such as student government or the Boys and Girls Clubs provide opportunities for new friendships.

Taking part in such activities is not just enjoyable. It is also a vital part of becoming a well-adjusted person. It may also help discover what career one might pursue. An adult who did not participate in a variety of activities as a teen may have more trouble developing social skills.

### Making a Social Contribution

It is also valuable for teens to become involved in activities that aid their communities. Some teens volunteer in hospitals, with charity events, or on environmental projects. **U₁**

---

## RESPOND TO SPECIAL NEEDS — Eating Disorders

**Discussion** Ask students why they think eating disorders often first show up during adolescence. (Possible answer: This is the time when young people are most likely to be influenced by others' opinions of them and by the media, which often portrays extremely thin people as attractive.)

**Critical Thinking** Reports will vary but may include that psychological and medical treatments are effective for many eating disorders. However, in more chronic cases, specific treatments have not yet been identified.

There are always organizations and programs seeking volunteer workers. Groups such as the Family, Career and Community Leaders of America (FCCLA) can give teens opportunities to design and carry out community projects.

**✓ Reading Check** **Explain** What are two sources of tension between teens and their families?

# Moral Development of Adolescents

Peers, family, community, and the media all play a role as teens develop their own ideas about right and wrong. Moral development guides teens' behavior as it gives them a greater awareness of the rules of society. Some teens test the limits and make unwise choices.

As they leave childhood behind, teens look forward to taking their places in the adult world. Part of the quest for adulthood involves developing morality. **Morality** is a sense of right and wrong that guides decisions and actions.

Morality is based on values. A person's set of values may be referred to as a moral compass. Like the tools that help hikers find their way and avoid getting lost, values give direction to life. They help people make decisions that are right

for them and help people avoid losing their way. During adolescence, teens must develop a moral compass to guide them through life.

Moral development is an important part of the maturing process. Teens who develop a reliable moral compass are more likely to make positive decisions. They are less likely to be lured into negative behaviors. Those who do not have a good moral compass are more likely to make poor choices. They may find themselves at odds with society's rules and laws.

## Kohlberg's Levels of Moral Development

One of the most prominent theorists on the subject of moral development was psychologist Lawrence Kohlberg (1927–1987). Kohlberg believed that moral development takes place in six stages and that awareness of other people increases at each stage.

At the first stage, the notion of what is right and wrong is quite simple. It is based on the idea of law and order. The individual obeys rules to avoid being punished. He or she does not hit for fear of being hit in return. At Kohlberg's second stage, the level of morality is egocentric. What is right is what benefits the self. In the third stage, the individual seeks to do what is right in order to gain the approval of others.

**→ Moral Compass**
As teens develop a strong set of values to guide them, they often join people who share the same values. *Do your friends tend to have the same or different values than you?*

**Section 19.2** Emotional, Social, and Moral Development of Adolescents **535**

---

**→→→ Explore the Photo**

**Caption Answer** Answers may vary. However most students will likely say their friends share the same values.

**Discussion** Ask students: What is the most important value that you look for in a friend? (Answers will vary. Possible answers might include a sense of honesty and trustworthiness, treating all people equally, or showing respect for others and their beliefs.)

## Section 19.2

**Reteach** *cont.*

**C Critical Thinking**
**Solve Problems** Present this scenario to the class: Eva's friend is experimenting with drugs that Eva knows are harmful, but she does not want to tattle on her friend. What do you think is the most moral response to this situation? (Student responses will vary. Some may think her top considerations should be for her friend's health and safety, and Eva should therefore do what is necessary to obtain help.)

**U₂ Universal Access**
**Auditory Learners** Discuss that there are numerous newspaper, magazine, and Internet advice columns. Read aloud a letter to an advice columnist that describes a moral dilemma. Also read the columnist's response. Students should discuss whether they believe that the advice was the best option in terms of their own moral standards. (Answers will vary. Students should discuss whether they think the columnist gave advice that was consistent with the students' moral standards.) **ELL**

**R₂ Reading Strategy**
**Illustrate Concepts** Have students create a diagram of a ladder that explains Kohlberg's six stages of moral development. Stage one should be at the bottom of the ladder and stage six at the top. Students should use their own words to explain each stage. (Ladders may vary but should explain Kohlberg's six stages of moral development.) **ELL**

**✓ Reading Check**

**Explain** Answers should include that teens want more freedom than parents want to give and teens question parental wisdom and authority.

### C₁ Critical Thinking

**Contrast** Have students review the text about Kohlberg's six stages of moral development. Ask students: How is Kohlberg's sixth stage different from the earlier stages? (The sixth stage is different because in this stage people gain moral maturity. They are able to recognize and respect others' points of views and make decisions based on this respect. In previous stages, individuals' decisions are primarily based either on their own points of view or on the recognition that people must obey and uphold the law for the good of all society.)

### W Writing Support
**Freewriting**

**Positive Feedback** Tell students that they constantly give and receive feedback from their peers. This feedback can be either positive or negative. Unfortunately, it is often much easier to give negative feedback than it is positive. Tell students to spend a few minutes freewriting to generate ideas on how they can offer positive feedback to their peers. Encourage volunteers to share some of their ideas. (Refer to p. 4 for tips on effective freewriting. Answers will vary. Ideas may include complimenting an outfit or offering support at a sporting event. Encourage students to keep the ideas in mind and to try them out during the next few days.)

The individual in the fourth stage of moral development seeks to obey the law and fulfill his or her duty. This person recognizes that a safe society must have rules of behavior. The person accepts and agrees to the rules that have been decided by others.

Kohlberg did not believe that all adults reach the fifth stage of moral development. At this stage, the individual better understands the feelings of others. He or she develops a genuine interest in others' welfare. The person becomes more aware of belonging to a family and community, and having social responsibilities. He or she recognizes that moral principles are based on individual values. Moral principles are tied to the need to uphold a system of moral laws for the good of society.

Kohlberg's sixth and highest stage of moral development, in which people are able to recognize and respect other people's points of view, is called **moral maturity**. The individual is concerned about whether the rules of society are just and fair. People at this stage make decisions based on equal respect for all people.

According to Kohlberg, each stage represents a milestone in moral development. Most people who reach the higher stages do so during adolescence and adulthood.

## Influences on Moral Development

Moral development is an ongoing process that occurs within the context of a person's family, community, and society as a whole. As teens decide what is important to them and strive to establish their own value system, the positive and negative influence of others grows more important.

### Peer Pressure

Peer groups can have a big influence on teens' moral development. Because teens are still discovering who they are and what is important to them, they look to their peers for approval and guidance. Peers also help teens clarify their values by discussing what is important and providing feedback. Positive influence from peers helps teens build stronger **convictions**, or beliefs, and behave according to their values.

Teens who are desperate to become more popular or to gain acceptance can be more open to negative peer pressure. They may look up to peers who break the rules and show little regard for their own well-being or that of others. Instead of condemning immoral or

**Media Messages**
A popular movie can send messages. *Do you think today's movies are more likely to influence teens positively or negatively? Why?*

---

### ➤ Explore the Photo

**Caption Answer** Answers will vary. Some will say movies have a positive influence. They show that people can achieve great things with hard work. Others will say they have a negative influence because many show that violence and drugs are okay.

**Discussion** Ask students: If you were a parent, would you let your teen attend movies that disagreed with your moral values? Why or why not? (Answers will vary. Possible answer: I would let the teen attend movies that disagreed with my moral values, as long as they were appropriately rated, but I would then explain to my teen why I disagreed with some of the moral values expressed in the movie.)

illegal conduct, these teens imitate it in the hope of gaining praise and acceptance. This is how many teens get involved in drugs, drinking, sexual activity, shoplifting, and other negative behaviors that they later regret.

### Popular Culture

Teens' moral development is also influenced by the popular culture. **Popular culture** is the culture that prevails in modern society. Today, the media tend to dominate popular culture. Television, movies, music, magazines, and advertising all show behaviors and can influence perceptions of right and wrong.

The media sometimes present negative behaviors in ways that may seem glamorous to adolescents. A rock star uses vulgar language. A movie shows violence as an acceptable way to resolve differences. Advertisements for alcohol suggest that people have more fun when they drink. Television programs show rude, immoral, and selfish behavior as amusing and harmless. Teens who are trying to establish their own identities need critical thinking skills to interpret all these messages.

### Family and Community

Parents have a responsibility to teach their children moral values and help them develop an accurate moral compass. Schools reinforce the basic values a society needs to function, such as honesty and cooperation. Many families and individuals also draw on their religious faith for moral guidance. Some teens seem to reject the values of their parents, but with time most come to recognize the importance of a system of morality that all can live by. Parents who practice what they preach and live according to their stated values are more likely to have a positive influence.

Open and honest communication within the family helps teens learn values. Parents should discuss core values such as honesty and responsibility within the context of daily life. This can help teens see the role these values play in keeping families and societies functioning. Teens also learn more about values by having more responsibility within the family. As they make their own choices and mistakes, they can learn from each experience.

## What Would You Do?

**Dealing with Mood Swings**

"I never know what to expect from my fourteen-year-old son," said Yolanda. "One minute, Tyrell is hugging me before he leaves for school and telling me he loves me. The next minute, he's making fun of his sister's singing and telling me I need clothes that don't make me look so much like an old lady. When I confront him about it, he always shrugs and says, 'Mama, you know I was just joking.' He spends a lot of time in the basement alone instead of being with his family."

*Write About It* How could Tyrell help his family understand and deal with his mood swings? Write a script of a possible conversation between Tyrell and his mother and sister in which Tyrell explains his feelings.

Of course, some teens do break the rules and get into trouble. Parents who know or suspect that a teen is engaging in morally unacceptable behavior need to confront the teen. Even though teens may be reluctant to talk to their parents about such problems, it is their parents' duty to help them change their wrong behavior.

Teens learn moral responsibility within the community too. Every community has expectations and rules to follow. Teens discover that they must follow the rules or suffer the consequences. Gradually, they also recognize the reasons behind rules and laws. As they learn to respect the rules of society, teens become better prepared to live successfully in that society.

Sometimes, despite a family's best efforts, a teen seems determined to pursue immoral and harmful behaviors. In such cases, the family may need to seek outside help. The teen might be more willing to listen to a favorite teacher than to a family member. Some families choose to get assistance from a member of the clergy or a school counselor. Teens with serious behavioral problems may need help from professional counselors. Counseling may include the family as well as the teen.

### Reteach *cont.*

### U Universal Access

**Kinesthetic Learners** Organize students into small groups. Have each group create and present a skit in which they discuss how the media, including magazines, music, television, and movies might influence teens' perceptions of right and wrong. Encourage the group to focus on a specific topic, such as use of alcohol or illegal drugs, or violence as a solution to problems. (Skits will vary but should discuss how the media might influence teens' views on right and wrong moral behavior. For example, if young people repeatedly see adults trying to solve problems by using violence, they might be led to believe that this behavior is moral.) **ELL**

### C₂ Critical Thinking

**Apply** Discuss that conflicts often arise when adolescents challenge a family's moral values. Ask students for examples of situations in which this might happen. Brainstorm ways that parents can maintain communication and at the same time set limits. (Responses will vary. For example, a family value might state that no member should work on Sundays, which are set aside for family time. However, the teen might want to get a part-time job working Sundays. Both sides might reach a compromise in which the teen only works every other Sunday.) **ELL**

## What Would You Do?

**Write About It** Scripts will vary but may include such suggestions as Tyrell should talk to his family when he is calm and in a good mood. The script might have Tyrell explaining that he does not understand his mood swings and does not know how to deal with them. His mother and sister should offer support.

### Study Tools

Have students go to the Online Learning Center at **glencoe.com**:

- Take the **Practice Test**.
- Download **Study-to-Go** content.

Use the **Student Activity Workbook** for additional practice.

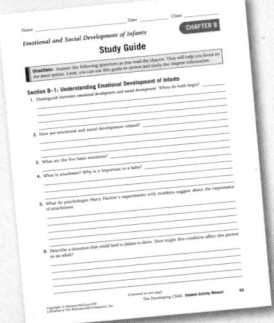

## Close

### Culminating Activity

**Relate** Have students discuss how emotional, social, and moral development are related to one another. (Possible answer: As a person matures emotionally and establishes his personal identity, he becomes better able to relate to others and develop and stand up for independent values and moral beliefs.)

 **NCLB** connects academic correlations to book content.

## Linking Behavior to Personal Values

A teen's personal values will guide his or her behavior. Teens who develop strong values are most likely to avoid negative behaviors. Those who give little thought to morals are more likely to have problems. Teens who mature early are most at risk for engaging in negative behavior. They look older than other teens their age, and are often pulled into older peer groups. Unfortunately, their mental and emotional maturity lags behind their physical maturity.

Sexual activity carries many risks for teens, including pregnancy and sexually transmitted infections (STIs). Some STIs can be cured if they are caught early. Others are incurable. Teens who engage in sexual behavior run the risk of serious long-term consequences. Teens who choose abstinence from sexual behavior avoid the risk of STIs.

Other risky behaviors that can have consequences include drug use and crime. Teens who use drugs risk serious damage to their health. Death rates are significantly higher for teens who use drugs than for those who do not. Teen drug users also run the risk of contracting HIV/AIDS because the disease can be transmitted by sharing needles. People who become addicted to drugs also may resort to crime to support their drug habit. By abstaining from premature sexual activity, drugs, and other self-destructive behaviors, teens show they value and respect themselves.

Consider the risks, negative influences, and potential problems teens encounter. It is hardly surprising that parents are concerned about helping teens develop a good moral compass to guide their behavior. Teens who receive careful and caring guidance as they build their value system are most likely to stand up to negative peer pressure and media influences.

## Section 19.2 — After You Read

### Review Key Concepts

1. **Define** the term *personal identity*. How does it develop during adolescence?
2. **Explain** why teens are likely to conform to the behavior of others in their peer group.
3. **Identify** the risks teens face if they do not have moral values to guide them.

### Practice Academic Skills

 **English Language Arts**

4. Give an example of a teen in the media who presents a positive message about moral values. Was it difficult to find a positive example? If so, why? Organize your thoughts in a half-page essay.

> **NCTE 12** Use language to accomplish individual purposes.

 **Social Studies**

5. Observe a group of peers at school. Note how certain group members influence others in the group. In what ways are the teens similar? In what ways are they different? Record your findings in a one-page report.

> **NCSS IV C** Describe the ways group and cultural influences contribute to the development of a sense of self.

 **Check Your Answers** Check your answers at this book's Online Learning Center at **glencoe.com**.

---

## Section 19.2 — After You Read

### Review Key Concepts

1. Personal identity is knowing you are a unique individual with a unique personality. It develops as teens form their own opinions and thoughts that may differ from other people's.
2. Teens become more involved with peers and less dependent on parents, so they find it important to be accepted by peer groups at this time. This often leads to conformity in order to fit in.
3. Teens may get involved in drugs, crime, and sexual relationships, which carry the risk of pregnancy and STIs.

### Practice Academic Skills

4. Students' answers will vary but should describe a specific teen in the media with good moral values. Essays might say that images portrayed in the media often do not present positive messages about moral values.
5. Answers will vary but should show an understanding that the stronger personalities in the group will influence other group members, often to the point that their behavior, whether positive or negative, will be copied.

# Section 19.3 Intellectual Development of Adolescents

## Reading Guide

### Before You Read

**Use Color** As you read this section, try using different color pens to take notes. This can help you learn new material and study for tests. You could use red for main ideas, blue for details, and green for examples.

### Read to Learn
**Key Concepts**
- **Identify** three factors that influence how a student learns in school.
- **Compare and contrast** Piaget and Vygotsky's theories of intellectual development in adolescence.

**D**

### Main Idea
Teens experience great intellectual growth due in part to educational experiences. There are different theories about teen intellectual development.

### Content Vocabulary
◇ prefrontal cortex
◇ amygdala
◇ abstract thought

 **Graphic Organizer** Go to this book's Online Learning Center at **glencoe.com** to print out this graphic organizer.

### Academic Vocabulary
You will find these words in your reading and on your tests. Use the glossary to look up their definitions if necessary.
- sophisticated
- profound

### Graphic Organizer
As you read, list the reasons adolescents experience significant intellectual growth. Use a web diagram like the one shown to organize your information.

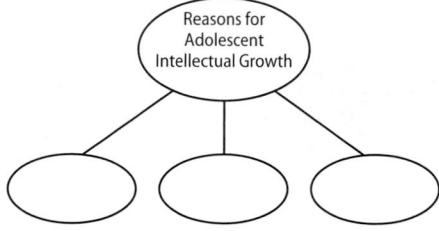

**NCLB**

### Academic Standards . . . . . . . . . . . . . . . . . . . . . . . .

 **English Language Arts**

**NCTE 4** Use written language to communicate effectively.

 **Social Studies**

**NCSS IV D Individual Development and Identity** Apply concepts, methods, and theories about the study of human growth and development, such as learning, motivation, and behavior.

**NCTE** *National Council of Teachers of English*
**NCTM** *National Council of Teachers of Mathematics*

**NSES** *National Science Education Standards*
**NCSS** *National Council for the Social Studies*

## Reading Guide

### Before You Read

Ask students to list some of the ways in which school is important to them. Discuss that school plays an important role in the intellectual development of teens. Explain that this section presents theories developed by Piaget and Vygotsky to explain teen intellectual development.

### **D** Develop Concepts

**Main Idea** Discuss the main idea with the students. Ask: Why do you think it is important to understand how teens develop intellectually? (Possible answer: Understanding how teens develop intellectually can help explain how teens' thought processes are different from those of children and adults. It can help in developing appropriate teaching techniques.)

 **Bell Ringer Activity**

### The Fourth Period of Learning
Display for students a chart showing Piaget's periods of learning. Briefly review the first three. Then tell students that in this section they will learn about the last period, formal operations, in which teens become capable of the abstract thinking that Is associated with being a mature individual.

## Preteaching

### Vocabulary
Tell students that various prefixes indicate position, such as *pre-*, *post-*, and *sub-*. Discuss that the prefix *pre-* is a sign that the prefrontal cortex is the anterior (or front) part of the frontal lobe.

### Graphic Organizer
 The Graphic Organizer is also on the TeacherWorks CD.

(Graphic organizers should include changes in the brain, gains in education, and gains in life experience.)

 **NCLB** connects academic correlations to book content.

 **Professional Development**

**Mini Clip**
ELL:
Level 3
Proficiency

Jana Echevarria discusses the characteristics of Level 3 proficiency English learners.

**539**

## Discussion Starter

**Enjoying Learning** Ask students: Why is learning sometimes exciting and sometimes a chore? Can adults make a difference in whether teens enjoy learning? If so, how? (Possible answer: Learning is more fun if both you and the person who is teaching you are interested in what you are learning. It also can be more fun if you can see how the material can be applied to your life.)

## S Skill Practice

### Guided Practice

**Define Terms** Display a diagram of the human brain. Point to the prefrontal cortex, the frontal lobes, and the amygdala. Then have students write down the terms *prefrontal cortex* and *amygdala* and write a definition of each. (Students should write a definition of prefrontal cortex and amygdala. The prefrontal cortex sits just behind the forehead and controls complex thought processes such as organizing. The amygdala controls emotional reactions.) **L1** **ELL**

**Draw and Label a Diagram** Have students draw a diagram (or make a clay model) of the brain and label the prefrontal cortex and amygdala. Next to each label, students should write a description of that brain part (Students should create a diagram of the brain and label and describe both the prefrontal cortex and the amygdala.) **L2**

**Learn More About a Brain Component** Have students conduct research on either the prefrontal cortex or the amygdala. Students should then create a poster illustrating this brain component and discussing its purpose in more detail. (Posters will vary but should describe in detail either the prefrontal cortex or the amygdala.) **L3**

**540**

# Brain Development in Adolescents

Dramatic advances in brain development come with the physical and emotional changes of the adolescent years. Teens start to think less like children and more like adults as their brains mature. They gain the ability to think in more complex and **sophisticated**, or refined, ways. This ability lets teens do increasingly difficult mental tasks and use better judgment.

In the early teen years, adolescents experience major intellectual growth. One reason for this growth is the physical changes in the brain. Other reasons include gains in education and life experience.

## Changes in the Brain

There are brain imaging techniques that allow scientists to observe the changes that occur in brain functioning during adolescence. It is now known that the brain starts to grow again just before puberty. The brain then continues to mature for several years.

The part of the brain that undergoes the most dramatic changes is the prefrontal cortex. The **prefrontal cortex** is the part of the brain that sits just behind the forehead and controls planning, organization, prioritizing, and other complex thought processes. The growth and maturing of the prefrontal cortex makes it possible for teens to reason better and to control their impulses. As teens mature they rely more on the prefrontal cortex and less on impulses.

Until the prefrontal cortex is fully developed, teens tend to rely more on the amygdala (ə-ˈmig-də-lə). The **amygdala** is the part of the brain that controls fear, joy, and other emotional reactions. Teens have a tendency to use the emotional part of their brain more than the thinking part. This can lead to impulsive actions based primarily on instinct.

Just as in earlier stages of development, the teen brain makes many more new connections than it actually needs. It then goes through a period of consolidation, in which unused connections cease functioning.

**S**

**Increase Brain Power**
The "use it or lose it" principle suggests that teens can increase their intellectual powers. *How can teens take advantage of this opportunity?*

**540** Chapter 19 Adolescence

---

## ▶ Explore the Photo

**Caption Answer** Answers will vary but may include that teens can challenge themselves to develop their intellectual powers by consciously learning new things.

**Discussion** Remind students that if a neural connection is not used, it will stop functioning. Ask: What is this process called? (pruning) Ask students how this is similar to the pruning of a tree. (We trim a tree to get it to grow the way we want, and the brain is pruned in order to maintain those connections that are needed.)

Brain researchers say this process indicates that the adolescent brain is a work in progress. They suggest that what teens do during this period of development can affect their thinking skills for the rest of their lives. Those who challenge themselves to develop their intellectual powers are more likely to develop strong brain connections and more advanced thinking skills.

## Educational Experiences

Even though there are different theories about intellectual development, there can be no doubt that education has a **profound**, or deep, impact on learning. This is true for students of all ages. The school experience is especially important for teens, though. This is because of the changes that take place in the brain at this stage.

Research has identified factors that influence how a student learns in school. Three main factors are the classroom environment, the degree of discipline and guidance at the school, and the involvement of parents.

### Classroom Environment

How would you describe the environment in your favorite class? It is not surprising that when the learning environment is positive and stimulating, more learning takes place. Those who know that they will not be criticized for giving a wrong answer in class feel more comfortable participating.

---

{ **Expert Advice...** }

*"Critical thinking skills begin to develop during puberty, and no one is quite sure when these skills stop developing. Children entering the teen life stage are now able to think in gray areas. No longer is everything black and white."*

— Denise Witmer, teen development expert and author, *The Everything Parent's Guide to Raising a Successful Child*

---

When students feel at ease in the classroom, they generally have a more positive attitude about school. This usually translates into more learning when compared with similar students who have negative feelings about school.

### School Discipline and Guidance

The degree of discipline and guidance in a school also add to the atmosphere of the classroom and the success of the students. Students who respect their teachers are more willing to learn. Less discipline can mean more disorder. This makes it harder for students to focus and learn. A low level of discipline can also lead to misbehavior which disrupts class activities and interferes with learning. Studies have shown that the level of discipline in a school is not related to its size, financial status, or location.

A school with strong discipline generally has close ties to the community. This means more parental involvement. These schools also have high behavioral expectations. With this comes a commitment by all of the school staff to maintain appropriate behavior. In addition, these schools usually have a strong guidance

---

## Section 19.3

### Assess

**Quiz**
Ask students to answer the following questions:

1. What part of the brain undergoes the most dramatic changes during puberty? (The prefrontal cortex undergoes the most dramatic changes.)
2. In what kind of classroom environment does the most learning take place? (The most learning takes place in an environment that is positive and stimulating.)
3. What typically happens to students' ability to learn when there is disorder and confusion in the classroom? (Disorder makes it harder for students to focus and learn.)

### Reteach

**U** **Universal Access**

**Interpersonal Learners** Organize students into groups of three. Have each group predict the level of alcohol, tobacco, and drug use among teens. Then the group should locate current statistics about actual usage and compare them to their predictions. Each group should present an oral summary on how their predictions compared to actual usage. (Presentations will vary but should summarize how their predictions of alcohol, tobacco, and drug usage among teens compared to actual figures. Students may find that the actual numbers were higher or lower than their predictions. Encourage students to discuss why they think this is.)

---

## Reteach cont.

### C Critical Thinking

**Categorize** Pose questions to the class that require either abstract or concrete thinking skills. For example, for concrete thinking you might state, "Determine the shortest route between school and your home." For abstract thinking, you might ask, "Why is it important to our society that citizens obey the law?" Ask students to categorize each question as requiring either abstract or concrete thinking skills. (Students should categorize items as requiring either concrete or abstract thinking skills. If students disagree about a classification, discuss it as a class to reach a consensus.) **ELL**

### W Writing Support

**Journal Entry**

**Educational Guidance** Have students write a journal entry about a time when they had to make a decision about their education and a parent or caregiver provided them with guidance. For example, a parent might have encouraged them to take a more difficult math class than they otherwise would have. Encourage students to write about what this guidance meant to them. (Refer to p. 518 to review the characteristics of writing an effective journal entry. Students should write about a time when a parent or caregiver provided specific educational guidance and what this meant to the student.)

### ✓ Reading Check

**Recall** The prefrontal cortex controls planning, organization, prioritizing, and other complex thought processes.

**542**

---

### Figure 19.2 Piaget's Four Periods of Learning

Piaget believed the teen years are part of the formal operations period. *Why is the formal operations period important?*

| Period | Characteristics |
|---|---|
| **Sensorimotor** *Birth–2 years* | Children learn through their senses and own actions. |
| **Preoperational** *2–7 years* | Children think in terms of their own activities and what they perceive at the moment. |
| **Concrete Operations** *7–11 years* | Children can think logically but still learn best through experience. |
| **Formal Operations** *11–adult* | People are capable of abstract thinking. |

**C**

program. Guidance counselors should be able to identify and address any problems that would interfere with a student's ability to learn, succeed, or participate in school.

#### The Role of Parents

**W** Although teens often seem embarrassed by their parents, they generally still want their parents' support. Caring parents do more than simply make sure that their teen goes to school every day and does the required homework. They might ask questions about schoolwork, offer suggestions for completing assignments, assist their children as needed, or attend school functions.

Parents also need to emphasize the importance they place on education. If teens skip school or fail to complete homework, parents need to get to the root of the problem. They can then help the teen find ways to resolve it. Regular attendance and homework are essential parts of a good education. A good education is a key to a fulfilling life.

### ✓ Reading Check **Recall** What does the prefrontal cortex control?

## Teen Intellectual Development

Many people have studied the intellectual growth of adolescents. Two leaders in this field of research were Jean Piaget and Lev Vygotsky.

### Piaget's Theory

Adolescents have reached the fourth and final stage of Piaget's four main stages of intellectual development. Piaget called this stage the period of formal operations.

As shown in **Figure 19.2**, Piaget said this stage of intellectual growth begins at about age 11 and continues into adulthood. During this period, young people become capable of abstract thought. **Abstract thought** is the capacity to consider "what if" situations, to create sophisticated arguments, and to reason from different points of view.

With their expanding intellectual abilities, young people can organize their thoughts and find solutions to everyday problems. They can also absorb information and apply it to their own lives. Thus they can start making intelligent decisions about their future.

---

### Figure 19.2 Piaget's Four Periods of Learning

**Caption Answer** The formal operations period is when adolescents become capable of abstract thinking and being able to make decisions about their future.

**Discussion** Ask students: Based on what you know about Piaget's periods of learning, at what age do you think young people should be allowed to choose the classes they take in school? Why? (Possible answer: When they are old enough to be capable of abstract thinking and can begin planning for their future, which is about age 11. However, they can still benefit from the input of adults in these decisions.)

Piaget has had a very strong influence on the field of child psychology. However, some people have criticized his theories. They argue that his four stages present too rigid a picture of intellectual development. Many believe that there are more than four stages throughout a person's life span. Some of Piaget's critics also believe that he underestimated the influence of culture and social interaction on learning. One theorist that felt this was Lev Vygotsky.

## Vygotsky's Theory

Vygotsky differed from Piaget in that he placed a stronger emphasis on social interactions. In fact, he saw a clear connection between intellectual development and social interaction. Vygotsky believed that children develop the ability to think by interacting with parents, teachers, and peers. In this way, they learn to think, gain mastery over their environment, and use language.

Vygotsky believed that language is the most important tool for influencing intellectual development. Younger children use it simply to communicate. Adolescents use it as a kind of inner speech to guide what they think and do.

Vygotsky used the term *zone of proximal development* to explain his theory about the role of instruction in a child's learning. The zone of proximal development is the difference between what a child is capable of learning unaided and what the child could learn with the help of a parent or teacher or by working with peers. It is a measure of learning potential. Vygotsky emphasized that only through teamwork with teachers and other students could students meet their potential.

This is put into practice in the classroom when the teacher assigns projects to a group instead of an individual. Also, some teachers offer additional help with assignments outside of the normal classroom hours. In this way, the student can learn from the teacher's expertise.

## Section 19.3 After You Read

### Review Key Concepts

1. **Explain** why the brain of an adolescent is said to be a work in progress.
2. **Define** Vygotsky's term *zone of proximal development*.

### Practice Academic Skills

**English Language Arts**

3. Consider your classes. Do you feel that you learn better in a small-group setting in which you work with peers? Or do you work better on your own? Write a letter to one of your teachers explaining why you do or do not learn better in small-group settings.

> **NCTE 4** Use written language to communicate effectively.

**Social Studies**

4. Parents generally have a desire to participate in their child's growth and development. This includes their intellectual development. Conduct research to create a list of actions parents can take to enhance intellectual development in their teen children. Your research might include reading articles on brain development or an interview with a parent educator.

> **NCSS IV D** Apply concepts, methods, and theories about the study of human growth and development, such as learning, motivation, and behavior.

  **Check Your Answers** Check your answers at this book's Online Learning Center at **glencoe.com**.

**N C L B**

Section 19.3   Intellectual Development of Adolescents   **543**

## Section 19.3 After You Read

### Review Key Concepts

1. The teen brain is in a stage of making new connections while pruning, or eliminating unused ones.
2. The zone of proximal development is the difference between what an individual can learn on his or her own and what the individual can learn from working with parents, teachers, or peers.

### Practice Academic Skills

3. Letters will vary. Some students may feel they learn better in small groups where they can help one another. Others may prefer to work on their own so they do not have to depend on others. Letters should contain explanations of why students feel the way they do.

4. Lists will vary but may include that parents can ask children about assignments, offer suggestions concerning homework, attend school functions, show support for their intellectual progress and development, and express the importance of attending school and learning.

---

## Assess

### Study Tools

Have students go to the Online Learning Center at **glencoe.com**:

- Take the **Practice Test**.
- Download **Study-to-Go** content.

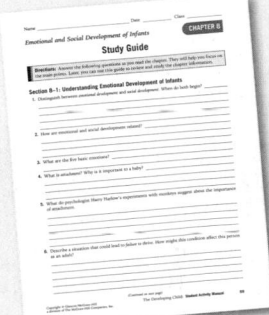

Use the **Student Activity Workbook** for additional practice.

## Close

### Culminating Activity

**Examine Interaction of Factors** Have students discuss how the three main factors in how students learn in school (see page 541) interact with one another (Answers will vary. Possible answer: When a child receives adequate guidance from teachers and parents, the classroom environment becomes more positive.)

  **NCLB** connects academic correlations to book content.

## Focus

### Discussion Starter

**Coaching** Ask: How many of you have ever had a coach who had an influence on your life? Ask for volunteers to discuss what kind of influence their coaches had and what this meant to them. Discuss that coaches do much more than teach athletic skills. They also teach how to get along with others and work as a team. Good coaches encourage their athletes to set goals and strive toward them.

## Teach

### C Critical Thinking

**Make Judgments** Ask students: What kinds of values do you think a coach who works with teens should have? How important are these values? (Answers will vary. Possible answer: Coaches should have enthusiasm and an innate sense of fairness. While they should enjoy competition, they also should understand the importance of teamwork and respect for all individuals.)

## Assess

### Make Connections

Ask students to list specific correlations between academic subjects and the kinds of skills a good coach needs. (Answers will vary. Students should show an understanding of how academic skills relate directly to the job of a coach. Coaches need good English language skills to communicate effectively and inspire their athletes. A knowledge of human anatomy and physiology are useful.)

**NCLB** This relates academic skills to specific tasks that are performed for this job.

---

Careers
With Children    **Coach**

**C**oaches train athletes to improve their skills. America is a nation of sports fans and sports players. Some who participate in amateur sports dream of becoming paid professional coaches. Coaches can work with teams, such as a football or baseball team, or with individual athletes, such as a gymnast or swimmer.

### ✺ What Does a Coach Do?

Coaches organize athletes and teach them the fundamentals of individual and team sports. They train athletes for competition by holding practice sessions to perform drills that improve the athletes' form, technique, skills, and stamina. Along with refining athletes' individual skills, coaches are responsible for teaching good sportsmanship, a competitive spirit, and teamwork.

### ✺ Where Do Coaches Work?

Some coaches form businesses to train athletes. Others work for schools, recreation centers, or universities. Some coaches work with individual athletes, while others coach teams in competition.

### Preparation and Skills

**Education and Training**
Education and training requirements for coaches vary greatly by the level and type of sport. Coaching jobs require immense overall knowledge of the sport, usually acquired through years of experience at lower levels.

**Aptitudes, Abilities, and Skills**
Coaches must have the ability to teach. Energy, physical endurance and strength, and an interest in working with young people are also needed.

**Academic Skills**
English language arts are used by coaches to communicate with athletes, their families, and other staff. Science skills are used to develop fitness and training routines. Psychology skills can help with motivating the athletes.

**NCLB**

**Explore Careers**

Research related careers such as sports instructors, umpires, trainers, or sports officials. Choose one career and write a paragraph to describe it. Explain whether this career interests you, and why.

**Careers Online** For more information on careers, visit the Occupational Outlook Handbook Web site through the link on this book's Online Learning Center at **glencoe.com**.

**544** **Chapter 19** Adolescence

---

## Close

### Culminating Activity

**Interviewing a Coach** Organize students into small groups. Each group should interview a coach who works with teens. The group should ask questions such as: What do you see as your most important goals when working with young people? How do you try to accomplish these goals? The group should present a brief summary of their interview.

**Explore Careers**

Students should research careers such as sports instructors, umpires, referees, and sports officials. Paragraphs should describe a chosen career and tell whether it interests the students.

## Chapter Summary

During adolescence, the physical changes that occur due to puberty are completed. It is important for teens to practice good personal hygiene, eat well, exercise, and get enough sleep. An important part of adolescence is establishing a strong personal identity. During the teen years, peers become more important. Social and cultural influences affect moral development. Changes in the brain during adolescence enable teens to reason better and control impulses. In Piaget's stage of formal operations, teens become capable of abstract thought. Vygotsky believed that social interactions are essential for learning. Positive educational experiences contribute to intellectual growth.

## Vocabulary Review

1. Use at least six of these content and academic vocabulary terms in a short essay about peer pressure.

### Content Vocabulary
◇ testosterone (p. 522)
◇ estrogen (p. 522)
◇ personal identity (p. 528)
◇ identity crisis (p. 529)
◇ depression (p. 531)
◇ bipolar disorder (p. 532)
◇ morality (p. 535)
◇ moral maturity (p. 536)
◇ popular culture (p. 537)
◇ prefrontal cortex (p. 540)
◇ amygdala (p. 540)
◇ abstract thought (p. 542)

### Academic Vocabulary
■ adolescent (p. 521)
■ extracurricular (p. 525)
■ stifle (p. 533)
■ conviction (p. 536)
■ sophisticated (p. 540)
■ profound (p. 541)

## Review Key Concepts

2. **List** three main areas of change for adolescents.
3. **Identify** three ways parents can help adolescents make good nutrition choices.
4. **Describe** the four main influences on personal identity development.
5. **Identify** the three roles of peers on a teen's social development.
6. **List** the major influences on a teen's moral development.
7. **Identify** three factors that influence how a student learns in school.
8. **Compare and contrast** Piaget and Vygotsky's theories of intellectual development in adolescence.

## Critical Thinking

9. **Draw Conclusions** Why can the teen years be both the most difficult and the most rewarding period of life for many people?
10. **Infer** What qualities or characteristics do you think allow some teens to get along well with others while remaining true to their own opinions and beliefs?

## Content and Academic Vocabulary Review

1. Essays will vary but should relate to peer pressure and include at least six vocabulary terms.

## Review Key Concepts

2. coping with changing emotions, handling new social situations and influences, and using new intellectual abilities
3. making nutritious food choices available, setting a good example, and paying attention to portion sizes
4. family, peers, media, and the future
5. peer groups, romantic involvement, and close friends
6. peer pressure, popular culture, and family and community
7. the classroom environment, the degree of discipline and guidance at the school, and the involvement of parents
8. Piaget's formal operations stage focused on the expanding intellectual abilities of adolescents. He believed that with these expanding abilities, young people can organize their thoughts and find solutions to everyday problems. Vygotsky placed a stronger emphasis on social interactions. He believed that children develop the ability to think by interacting with parents, teachers, and peers. In this way, they also gain mastery over their environment and use language.

## Critical Thinking

9. Answers will vary. Possible answers include that the teen years can be difficult because of the physical, emotional, social, and intellectual changes occurring at that time. It can be rewarding because teens are better able to think abstractly and can take advantage of their intellectual potential.

10. Answers will vary. Possible answers include that teens who have high levels of self-confidence and a supportive family are better able to get along with others and remain true to their own beliefs.

## Family & Community Connections

**11.** Answers will vary depending on the known incidences of eating disorders at your school. Students' charts should show a break-down by gender and age. The paragraph should include any help that is available to students with eating disorders.

## Health Skills

**12.** Answers will vary. Suggestions for getting more sleep might include watching less television or playing fewer video games and going to bed earlier.

## Observation Skills

**13.** Students' answers will vary. Students may note that classes such as history typically include more lectures, while math and science classes include more demonstrations.

## Real-World Skills

**14.** Dialogues will vary depending on the possible reasons listed and the reason used to write the dialogue.

**15.** Answers will vary. Advantages may include that they can share their worries, fears, and anger without fear of rejection. They can give and receive advice. Any disadvantages listed should be minimal and should be outweighed by advantages.

**16.** Answers will vary depending on the fitness programs students choose to research. Students should consider clothes, exercise equipment, rental fees, and membership fees, as appropriate.

**NCLB** Activity correlated to Social Studies standards.

**546**

---

## Family & Community Connection

**11. Interview a School Counselor** Interview a school counselor about the frequency of eating disorders among students. Ask for the rate of incidences among males and females, and by age level. Also ask about local resources to help with eating disorders. Compile your information in a chart. Include a paragraph about help that is available to students with eating disorders.

## Health Skills

**12. Research Sleep Habits** Keep track of the number of hours of sleep you get during the next seven days. Are you getting the recommended eight and one-half hours of sleep each night? If not, what changes could you make in your habits? Write a realistic plan of action that would give yourself enough sleep time.

## Observation Skills

**13. Observe Teaching Styles** There are many different teaching methods. A teaching method that works for you may not work for your friend.

**Procedure** During each of your classes, note how the teacher teaches. Is the class mostly lecture or demonstration? Is there interaction between students and teacher? Are assignments given to groups or individuals?

**Analysis** Use your notes to create a table that shows the teaching methods used, the subjects of the classes, and the number of teachers who use them. Write a summary of your findings.

**NCSS IV D Individual Development and Identity** Apply concepts, methods, and theories about the study of human growth and development, such as learning, motivation, and behavior.

**NCLB**

## Real-World Skills

| Interpersonal and Collaborative Skills | **14. Work in Teams** Follow your teachers instructions to form into groups. Brainstorm a list of possible reasons why teens may engage in negative behaviors. Based on one of the reasons, work together to write a dialogue in which you persuade a peer to change her negative actions. |
|---|---|
| Technology Skills | **15. Information Literacy** List the advantages and disadvantages of having a close friend. Do the advantages outweigh the disadvantages? Use word processing software to create a report of your findings. |
| Financial Literacy | **16. The Cost of Fitness** Choose three types of fitness programs you might enjoy and research the cost of each. For example, you might choose taking classes at a gym or hiking with friends. Be sure to consider the cost of any equipment needed, as well as any membership fees. Create a table to compare the costs and write a paragraph telling which activity you would like to try and why. Is cost the most important factor in your decision? |

 **Additional Activities** For additional activities, go to this book's Online Learning Center at **glencoe.com**.

---

## Academic Skills

**17.** Essays will vary but should show a well-thought-out plan to persuade teens that blindly following the crowd is potentially dangerous and will jeopardize one's own beliefs and ideas.

**18.** $19.32 ($2.99 + 3.95 + 4.49 + 1.49 + .75 + 4.39 = 18.06; 18.06 × .07 = 1.26; 18.06 + 1.26 = $19.32)

The *Early Childhood Observations CD* offers additional lessons with videos to build students' observation skills.

**Part 1:** Learning to Observe
**Part 2:** How Children Develop
**Part 3:** Working With Young Children
**Part 4:** Extended Observations
**Part 5:** Resources and Answer File

# Academic Skills

 **English Language Arts**

**17. Persuade Your Audience** Teens in a peer group often adopt the tastes and beliefs of more popular members. Write a persuasive essay to convince other teens about the potential dangers of blindly following the crowd.

> **NCTE 5** Use different writing process elements to communicate effectively.

 **Mathematics**

**18. Meal Planning** To practice budgeting, a mother assigns one day of the week to her teenaged son Bryce to plan and prepare dinner. Bryce is given $20 to spend. He decides to make cheeseburgers and fries. At the store, he finds buns for $2.99, a package of cheese for $3.95, one pound of lean meat for $4.49, lettuce for $1.49, a tomato for $0.75, and a bag of frozen fries for $4.39. Bryce is worried that he will not have enough money. If the tax rate is 7%, how much money will he need total?

**Math Concept** **Multiplying by Percents** To multiply by percents, change the percent to a fraction with 100 in the denominator. Then change the fraction to a decimal.

**Starting Hint** Add up the cost of all the items. Then multiply your answer by 7 percent to get the amount of tax. Add the tax to the cost of the items for a total cost.

**Math** For math help, go to the Math Appendix at the back of the book.

> **NCTM Number and Operations** Understand numbers, ways of representing numbers, relationships among numbers, and number systems.

## Science

**19. Create a Hypothesis** Follow your teachers instructions to form teams of two. Think about this question: Do you think that thin, average, and overweight people eat different portion sizes when compared to one another?

**Procedure** Work with your partner to create a hypothesis of the eating habits of people for each weight category. At a food court or cafeteria, discreetly observe and take notes on the eating habits of four anonymous people in each weight group.

**Analysis** Report your findings in a chart. Does your hypothesis seem true? What other possible factors are involved in weight besides portion sizes?

> **NSES A** Students should develop abilities necessary to do scientific inquiry, understandings about scientific inquiry.

## Standardized Test Practice

**ESSAY**

Read the prompt. Then answer the question by writing an essay. Use details and examples to illustrate your points.

> According to sleep experts, sometime in late puberty, the teen body secretes the sleep-related hormone melatonin later than before. This means that teens may feel fully alert later into the evening, making it physically more difficult for them to get up in the morning.

**20.** How might teens best deal with this hormonal change?

> **Test-Taking Tip** Plan your essay before you begin writing. Jot down the main points you want to focus on. Refer to these points as you write.

**19.** Students' analyses and reports will vary. However, they will likely observe that portion size often increases along with weight. Stress that students be discreet in their observations and maintain the anonymity of the people observed.

 **Professional Development**

**Mini Clip**
**Math: Simple Events— Probability**

Small groups of students conduct probability experiments and later discuss results as a whole class.

 **NCLB** connects academic correlations to book content.

## Standardized Test Practice

**20.** Essays will vary but should include details and examples that illustrate the points students make.

**Test-Taking Tips** Explain to students that feeling an adrenaline rush when taking an important test is normal. Students need to use this feeling to help them focus on the task at hand. Taking a deep breath and relaxing for a moment can help organize their thoughts.

**Essay Tests** When responding to essay questions, students should remember that the teacher has to read their answer. Writing clearly can have a positive impact on the final score they receive.

## TECHNOLOGY Solutions

### Use these technology solutions to streamline chapter assessment!

 **ExamView Assessment Suite** CD allows you to create and print out customized tests or ready-made unit and chapter tests, complete with answer keys.

**TeacherWorks Plus** is an electronic lesson planner that provides instant access to complete teacher resources in one convenient package.

 **Online Learning Center** includes resources and activities for students and teachers.

**STANDARDS BASED LESSON PLANNING** *The Developing Child* provides students with instruction and assessment in the following fundamental content areas:

## National Standards Correlations

| Standards | Pages |
|---|---|
| **12.2.1** Analyze the effect of heredity and environment on human growth and development. | 552 |
| **12.2.2** Analyze the impact of social, economic, and technological forces on individual growth and development. | 551, 559 |
| **12.3.1** Analyze the role of nurturance on human growth and development. | 554–556 |
| **15.1.2** Analyze expectations and responsibilities of parenting. | 551 |
| **15.2.1** Choose nurturing practices that support human growth and development. | 551, 554–556 |
| **15.3.3** Summarize current laws and policies related to parenting. | 551 |

**NO CHILD LEFT BEHIND** NCLB activities, information, and skills practice will help your students attain NCLB proficiency. Students will improve their abilities in the following academic standards areas:

## Academic Standards Correlations

| Discipline | Standard | Feature/Activity |
|---|---|---|
| **English Language Arts** | **NCTE 1** Read texts to acquire new information. | **Reading Guide (pp. 550, 557)** |
| | **NCTE 3** Apply strategies to interpret texts. | **After You Read (pp. 556, 566)** |
| | **NCTE 4** Use written language to communicate effectively. | **Writing Activity (p. 548)** |
| | **NCTE 5** Use different writing process elements to communicate effectively. | **Academic Skills (p. 569)** |
| **Mathematics** | **NCTM Number and Operations** Understand numbers, ways of representing numbers, relationships among numbers, and number systems. | **Academic Skills (p. 569)** |
| **Science** | **NSES A** Develop abilities necessary to do scientific inquiry, understandings about scientific inquiry. | **Academic Skills (p. 569)** |
| | **NSES C** Develop understanding of the cell; biological evolution; matter, energy, and organization in living systems; and behavior of organisms. | **Science in Action (p. 561)** |
| | **NSES F** Develop understanding of personal and community health; science in local, national, and global challenges. | **After You Read (p. 556)** **Observation Skills (p. 568)** |
| **Social Studies** | **NCSS V F Individuals, Groups, and Institutions** Evaluate the role of institutions in furthering both continuity and change. | **Culture Matters (p. 559)** |
| | **NCSS V G Individuals, Groups, and Institutions** Analyze the extent to which groups and institutions meet individual needs and promote the common good in contemporary and historical settings. | **After You Read (p. 566)** |

## Professional Development

**MINI CLIP VIDEO LIBRARY**

Targeted professional development is correlated throughout *The Developing Child*. **The McGraw-Hill Professional Development Mini Clip Video Library** provides teaching strategies to strengthen academic and learning skills. Log on to **glencoe.com**.

In this chapter, you will find these Mini Clips:
- **ELL** Words and Pictures, p. 550
- **Reading** Modeling Reading Strategies, p. 551
- **ELL** Words in Action, p. 555
- **Reading** Options for Learning, p. 560
- **Reading** Planning and Management, p. 561
- **ELL** Elaborating on Student Responses, p. 564
- **Reading** Building Vocabulary, p. 565

## Reading and Writing Strategies

**Writing Activity: Descriptive Paragraph** (p. 548)
Students use writing tips to write a descriptive paragraph about a time when they were sick.

**Before You Read** (pp. 550, 557)
A pre-reading question or statement will help students make a personal connection to content.

**Graphic Organizer** (pp. 550, 557)
A visual tool will help students organize and remember new content.

**Reading Check** (pp. 554, 558, 565)
A question allows students to make a quick comprehension self-check.

**After You Read** (pp. 556, 566)
Organize and process students' understanding of what they have read.

## Chapter Features

**Asthma and Sports** (p. 553)
Children with asthma should be encouraged to play sports, but always have an inhaler handy.

**Provide Good Nutrition During an Illness** (p. 554)
Sick children must receive adequate liquids to prevent dehydration; they also should be encouraged to eat.

**Preventing Infant Death in Australia** (p. 559)
Australia has reduced infant deaths through improved medical technology and campaigns to prevent SIDS.

**Bicycle Safety Classes** (p. 560)
Children must be taught safe bike-riding techniques and the importance of wearing protective gear.

**Science in Action**

**Resistance to Antibiotics** (p. 561)
Germs have become increasingly resistant to antibiotics.

## Chapter Overview

### Introduce the Chapter

In this chapter, students learn about children's health and safety issues. They learn about the importance of regular checkups and vaccinations. The chapter discusses the symptoms and treatments of common childhood diseases, basic first aid techniques, and emergency treatments such as rescue breathing and poison treatment.

### Build Background

Ask students: What do you think poses the greatest single threat to the health and safety of children? Do you think it is a specific illness? Or maybe it is accidents such as automobile crashes or accidental poisonings? Encourage students to provide reasons for their choices.

## Writing Activity

### Descriptive Paragraph

This active learning activity prompts students to write a descriptive paragraph about a time when they were sick. After students complete the activity, encourage them to share their writing with their classmates, if they are comfortable doing so. Student responses can be used as a basis for classroom discussion. (Students' answers will vary, but the student should have written a descriptive paragraph about how he or she felt when sick. The paragraph should use interesting adjectives and adverbs and paint a picture in the reader's head.)

## Chapter Objectives

After completing this chapter, you will be able to:

- **Explain** how regular checkups and immunizations can help prevent illness.
- **Summarize** effective ways to care for a sick child.
- **Outline** the steps to follow in an emergency situation.
- **Describe** appropriate first-aid procedures for three types of bleeding.
- **Compare and contrast** rescue breathing and CPR.

## Writing Activity — Descriptive Paragraph

**Being Sick** Spend a few minutes thinking back to a time when you were sick. Were you miserable? Scared? Lonely? Bored? Use these memories to write a descriptive paragraph about yourself during that time.

**Writing Tips** Descriptive writing is attention-getting. It draws in the reader with details. Use these tips to help you write your descriptive paragraph:

1. Focus on using interesting adjectives and adverbs.
2. Work at painting a picture in the reader's mind.
3. Keep your words varied. Use a thesaurus to come up with appealing synonyms.

548

## CLASSROOM Solutions

### Print Resources

 **Student Edition**

 **Teacher Wraparound Edition**

 **Student Activity Workbook**

 **Student Activity Workbook Teacher Annotated Edition**

### Technology Resources

 **Online Learning Center** has resources and activities for students and teachers. Includes an Online Student Edition.

 **Interactive Student Edition** allows students to instantly access review materials, examples, and exercises.

**Section 20.1** Childhood Illnesses

**Section 20.2** Accidents and Emergencies

**Review the Sections**
Introduce the chapter by reviewing the sections:

**Section 20.1**
Regular checkups and immunizations are important to maintaining children's health. Common childhood diseases include the common cold, influenza, and ear infections. Parents should comfort sick children, encourage them to eat, and make certain that they do not become dehydrated. Properly preparing children for a hospital stay can decrease their fears.

**Section 20.2**
General first aid techniques can be used to care for everyday injuries such as minor cuts, bruises, and splinters. Major injuries, such as fractures, require treatment by a qualified medical professional. Choking requires an immediate response. While anyone can perform rescue breathing, CPR requires a trained individual.

▶ **Explore the Photo**

**Caption Answer** Parents are telling children that their health and well-being are important and should be protected at all times.

**Discussion** Ask students for examples of sports in which they participate or that they enjoy watching. For each sport, have students list the necessary safety gear. Ask for volunteers to explain the purpose of each piece of safety gear. (Students should list safety gear associated with various sports. For example, baseball would include catcher's mitts to protect the hand, batting helmets to protect the head from balls, and catcher's pads to protect the catcher from balls and bats.)

**Explore the Photo**
Appropriate safety gear is important at any age. *What messages are parents sending to children when they insist the children wear safety gear?*

549

**TeacherWorks Plus** is an electronic lesson planner that provides instant access to complete teacher resources in one convenient package.

**Presentation Plus!** provides visual teaching aids for every section.

**The Early Childhood Observations CD** presents video observations and lessons on observation skills and child development.

**The Developing Brain eTransparencies and Guide** include information and activities to offer insights into brain development and diseases of the brain.

## Focus

### Bell Ringer Activity

#### Getting Checked

Hold up a picture of a doctor examining a toddler. Ask: Why do you think periodic checkups are often referred to as well-baby exams? (because the child is not brought to the doctor because of an illness, but to make certain the child is developing properly and that there are no problems)

**McGraw Hill Professional Development**

**Mini Clip**
ELL: Words and Pictures

A teacher uses words and media examples to teach new vocabulary.

## Preteaching

### Vocabulary

Remind students that sometimes they can use a word they already know to determine the meaning of a new word. For example, knowing the meaning of *communicate* can help in understanding *communicable*. Both words involve transmitting something from one individual to another.

### Graphic Organizer

 The Graphic Organizer is also on the TeacherWorks CD.

(Graphic organizers should list chicken pox, the common cold, ear infection, influenza, strep throat, and scarlet fever.)

 **NCLB** connects academic correlations to book content.

---

### Reading Guide

#### Before You Read

**Use a Dictionary** Many of the names of diseases are difficult to pronounce. When you encounter a word you cannot pronounce, look it up in a dictionary or other appropriate resource.

#### Read to Learn
**Key Concepts**
- **Explain** how regular checkups and immunizations can help prevent illness.
- **Summarize** effective ways to care for a sick child.

#### Main Idea
Regular checkups and immunizations can help prevent many health problems and diseases. Common childhood illnesses include allergies, asthma, ear infections, colds, and diseases such as chicken pox.

#### Content Vocabulary
◇ communicable disease
◇ pollen
◇ asthma
◇ contagious

 **Graphic Organizer** Go to this book's Online Learning Center at **glencoe.com** to print out this graphic organizer.

#### Academic Vocabulary
You will find these words in your reading and on your tests. Use the glossary to look up their definitions if necessary.
- detection
- sensitivity

#### Graphic Organizer
As you read, list common childhood illnesses. Use a diagram like the one shown to help organize your information. Add additional lines as needed.

**Childhood Illnesses**

**Academic Standards** . . . . . . . . . . . . . . . . . . .

 **English Language Arts**
**NCTE 3** Apply strategies to interpret texts.

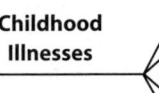 **Science**
**NSES F** Develop understanding of personal and community health; science in local, national, and global challenges.

**NCTE** *National Council of Teachers of English*
**NCTM** *National Council of Teachers of Mathematics*

**NSES** *National Science Education Standards*
**NCSS** *National Council for the Social Studies*

---

### Reading Guide

#### Before You Read

Ask students: What kinds of vaccinations do you remember receiving? Why do you think your parents or guardians made certain you received these vaccinations? (Answers to the first question will vary. Possible answer to the second question: They wanted to help me stay healthy.)

#### D Develop Concepts

**Main Idea** Discuss the main idea with the students. Ask: How are regular checkups and immunizations related to one another? (Pediatricians administer vaccines during regular checkups. By having the child come in regularly, the doctor can make certain the child maintains an apprpriate immunization schedule.)

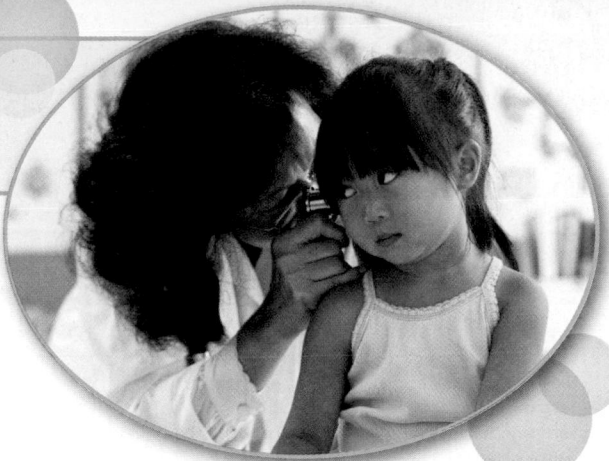

## Regular Checkups

Children, like adults, should have regular medical checkups. Early **detection**, or discovery, followed by early treatment may keep a minor condition from becoming serious. Checkups also let parents know that their children are developing normally. Regular checkups and immunizations can help prevent many illnesses.

During their first year, babies should be examined regularly. After the first year, healthy children need checkups less frequently. However, they still need one at least once a year. Because these checkups are so important, many local health departments have free or inexpensive clinics that provide examinations and medical care for children who do not have their own pediatrician.

When a child becomes sick, parents and other caregivers need to know what to do. They need to be able to recognize common childhood illnesses. They also need to distinguish between minor conditions and those that need medical attention.

If a child shows symptoms that cause concern, caregivers should call the child's doctor. In younger children, fever, lack of energy, prolonged diarrhea, constipation, vomiting, or difficulty breathing all warrant a call to the doctor. In older children, symptoms to bring to a doctor's attention include fever, persistent cough, vomiting, severe headache, or dizziness.

## Immunizations

To immunize is to protect a person against a particular disease. People can be protected from communicable diseases by being immunized. A **communicable disease** is a disease that is passed from one person to another.

The most common way to immunize people is to administer a vaccine. A vaccine is a small amount of a disease-causing agent that is introduced into the body so that a person can build resistance to it. After getting a vaccine, a person's body produces antibodies. These are substances capable of fighting off germs for the disease. For example, if Monica gets the vaccine for chicken pox at twelve months of age, she will have the antibodies to fight it if she is later exposed to the disease.

**Figure 20.1** shows what immunizations a child should receive and when. Parents are responsible for making sure their children get the immunizations they need at the right times. Parents should keep a record of each child's immunizations.

Many states require all children to be immunized for certain diseases before they enter school. Many also require that children in child care centers be immunized. Children under the age of five are the most likely to develop complications from the diseases. Therefore, parents should not wait until their children start elementary school to have them immunized.

Section 20.1 Childhood Illnesses **551**

## Section 20.1

### Teach

**Discussion Starter**

**Childhood Illness** Have students think about a time when they were sick as a child. Did they have a contagious illness? Did they have to see a doctor or stay at a hospital? How many days were they home from school? Do they think the illness could have been prevented? Why or why not? (Answers to the first two questions will vary. For the last two questions, students should state whether they think the illness could have been prevented, and if so, how; for example by a vaccination.)

**R Reading Strategy**

**Identify** Read aloud the first paragraph under Regular Checkups. Ask: What are the two main points the author is making about regular checkups? (They allow for the early detection and treatment of conditions in the hopes they will not become serious, and they provide a time for immunizations.)

**Professional Development**

**Mini Clip**
Reading: Modeling Reading Strategies
A teacher uses a read-aloud to model fluent reading strategies.

---

 **Explore the Photo**

**Caption Answer** Checkups should be the most frequent during the first year.

**Discussion** Why do you think a doctor examines a child's weight and height during a checkup? (The doctor wants to make certain that the weight and height have increased since the last checkup and are within healthy ranges.)

## Teach cont.

### U Universal Access

**Logical Learners** Have students create a vaccination schedule for a two-year-old child who has not been immunized for Hepatitis B. Instruct students to space the vaccinations as equally as possible across the recommended period. The child should receive the final vaccination no later than eighteen years of age. (Schedules may vary but should specify that the series of three vaccinations will be equally spaced between ages two and eighteen. Possible schedule: ages two, seven, and twelve.)

### C Critical Thinking

**Infer** Discuss that some of the diseases in this chart are rarely deadly. For example, mumps mainly causes the parotid glands to swell. Despite the high fever, mumps is rarely life threatening. Ask students why they think health professionals work to develop vaccines for illness like mumps and chicken pox that are usually not deadly. (Answers may vary. Even if the diseases are rarely deadly, they can still have significant health effects. For example, chicken pox can lead to pneumonia. In addition, parents who must stay home to care for a child can lose significant income.)

**Figure 20.1 Schedule of Immunizations**

The Centers for Disease Control and Prevention (CDC) establishes schedules for children's immunizations. *How many polio vaccines should a child have received by age 12?*

| Vaccine | Birth | 1 mo | 2 mo | 4 mo | 6 mo | 12 mo | 15 mo | 18 mo | 24 mo | 4–6 yrs | 11–12 yrs | 13–18 yrs |
|---|---|---|---|---|---|---|---|---|---|---|---|---|
| Hepatitis B | HepB #1 | HepB #2[b] | | | | HepB #3[b] | | | | HepB[a b] | | |
| Diphtheria, Tetanus, Pertussis (DPT) 4-dose series with boosters | | | DPT #1 | DPT #2 | DPT #3 | DPT #4 | | | | DPT #5 | Booster | Booster[c] |
| H. Influenza type B | | | HiB #1 | HiB #2 | HiB #3 | HiB #4[b f] | | | | | | |
| Polio | | | Polio #1 | Polio #2 | Polio #3[b] | | | | | Polio #4 | | |
| Measles, Mumps, Rubella | | | | | | MMR #1[b] | | | | MMR #2 | MMR #2[b] | |
| Varicella (chicken pox) | | | | | | Varicella[b] | | | Varicella[b g] | | | |
| Pneumococcal | | | PCV #1 | PCV #2 | PCV #3 | PCV #4[b] | | | PCV[b] | | | |
| Influenza | | | | | | Influenza (yearly)[d] | | | | | | |
| Hepatitis A | | | | | | | | | Hepatitis A[e] | | | |

**Notes:**

○ Green shading indicates that if child did not receive a dose of vaccine earlier, she or he can receive it during the period in green.

○ Yellow shading indicates a range of recommended ages.

a If the child did not receive the Hepatitis B vaccine earlier, the three-dose series should be given in this period.

b Can be given any time during this period.

c Tetanus and diphtheria boosters should be repeated every 10 years after this.

d Influenza vaccine is recommended yearly for children older than 6 months who have certain risk factors, including asthma, HIV, and other diseases. The vaccine is also recommended for healthy children between 6 and 23 months of age.

e Hepatitis A vaccine is recommended for children and adolescents who live in high-risk areas or belong to high-risk groups.

f May not be necessary if a certain brand of vaccine was given in the first two doses.

g Second dose should be given before the age of 12.

**Note: This information is periodically reviewed and updated. Check the Web site of the Centers for Disease Control and Prevention for the most current information.**

**Figure 20.1 Schedule of Immunizations**

**Caption Answer** A child should have received four polio vaccines by age 12.

**Discussion** Ask students: Why do you think the Centers for Disease Control and Prevention periodically changes the information in this schedule? (New vaccines are constantly being developed and new information is being learned about existing ones, such as how they can be more effectively administered.)

Some parents worry that a vaccine could harm their child. In extremely rare cases, a child does have a bad reaction to a vaccine. Parents should discuss these concerns with their child's doctor. In most cases, the chances of getting the disease are much greater than the chances of having a bad reaction to a vaccine.

## Common Childhood Conditions

Allergies and asthma are becoming more and more common among children. Most children can live normal lives with these conditions as long as they receive proper medical care.

### Allergies

An allergy is an extreme **sensitivity**, or reaction, to one or more common substances. Children may have allergic reactions when they eat or drink certain foods or inhale certain airborne particles. Foods that commonly cause allergic reactions in babies and children include milk, grains, eggs, shellfish, nuts, fruit juices, chocolate, and food additives. Airborne substances that can cause reactions include pollens, dust mites, molds, air pollution, and tobacco smoke. **Pollen** is a powder-like grain that comes from seed plants. Symptoms of an allergic reaction may be mild, such as a rash, a runny nose with clear drainage, or itchy eyes. Some allergic reactions, however, may be serious or even life-threatening. Sometimes, for instance, the air sacs in the lungs may become constricted, cutting the flow of oxygen in the body.

More than one-third of the children in the United States develop some type of allergy. Specific allergies are not inherited, but the tendency to be allergic seems to be. If both parents have allergies, their child has a 70 percent chance of having at least one.

Allergies cannot be cured, but their effects can often be prevented. For example, a child who is allergic to a specific food can avoid that food. One who is allergic to pollens can be encouraged to play indoors during peak pollen periods. A series of allergy tests can determine which specific substances are causing problems so that they can be avoided in the future. Medication or injections are used to control allergies.

### Asthma and Sports

Playing sports helps children keep physically fit and teaches them to be part of a team. However, some parents are tempted to pull their child from a sport when they see that it induces asthma attacks. It is important to know that recent government guidelines indicate keeping fit through exercise and maintaining a healthy weight can help control asthma. While exercise can strengthen the lungs, it also can cause airways to become irritated, leading to constriction and an asthma attack. Fortunately, inhalers can be used to expand the airways. A child with asthma should always have an inhaler available when participating in sports.

☀ **Be Prepared** Conduct research to learn which sports are less likely to induce asthma attacks. Write a report discussing why some sports are more likely to cause asthma attacks than others. Which sports may be more appropriate for children with asthma?

### Asthma

A growing health problem among children in this country is asthma. **Asthma** is a condition that causes the lungs to contract more than they should, narrowing the air passages and making it difficult to breathe. When this contraction of the lungs occurs, it is called an asthma attack.

Asthma attacks can be brought on by an allergic reaction. They may also be caused by a cold or the flu, physical activity, or exposure to cold air, smoke, or other irritants. Signs that a child may be having an asthma attack include coughing, wheezing, rapid breathing, and shortness of breath.

Children with asthma can take medication to open their airways and breathe more easily. A doctor must prescribe the medicine. Some medicines are taken every day to prevent asthma attacks.

**S**

## Teach cont.

### S Skill Practice
#### Guided Practice
**Illustrate How Asthma Attacks Occur** Have students conduct research to learn more about what happens to air passages during an asthma attack. They then should draw a poster showing the respiratory system during an attack. Instruct students to clearly label each part of the respiratory system. (Posters should illustrate what happens during an asthma attack. The parts of the respiratory system should be clearly labeled.) **L1 ELL**

**Explain How Inhalers Work** Have students conduct research to learn how inhalers and the medication they contain work. They then should draw a poster or create a slide presentation showing how an inhaler works to stop an asthma attack. (Posters or slide shows should explain how an inhaler can stop an asthma attack.) **L2**

**Prepare a Presentation** Tell students to imagine that they have been assigned to create a presentation for seven- to ten-year-olds who have asthma. The presentation should show what happens during an asthma attack and how an inhaler can stop it. Students should prepare visual aids such as slide presentations or Web pages to accompany their presentations. If possible, students might want to consider having a child demonstrate the proper use of an inhaler. (Presentations will vary but should explain what happens during an asthma attack and how an inhaler can stop an attack.) **L3**

### Asthma and Sports

**Identify** Ask students: According to recent government guidelines, what two things can help control asthma? (Keeping fit and controlling weight can help prevent asthma.)

☀ **Be Prepared** Students' reports will vary, but should list sports that are less likely to induce asthma attacks than others and explain why this is the case. Swimming, because of the high level of humidity in the air, is a good choice. Stop-and-go sports, such as karate, baseball, and sprinting also are less likely to cause problems than those sports that require a high level of activity over an extended time, such as soccer and long-distance running.

## Assess

### Quiz

Ask students to answer the following questions:

1. **What are three symptoms a young child might exhibit that would warrant calling a doctor?** (Answers may include any three: fever, lack of energy, prolonged diarrhea, constipation, vomiting, or difficulty breathing.)

2. **What three diseases does the DPT vaccine protect against?** (It protects against diphtheria, tetanus, and pertussis.)

3. **If a child is allergic to a particular plant, what part of the plant is typically causing the allergic reaction?** (Pollen, or the powder-like grain from a seed plant, is typically what causes the allergic reaction.)

## Reteach

### C₁ Critical Thinking

**Solve Problems** Describe the following scenario: Rhonda's nine-month-old daughter has a slight fever, a runny nose, and a dry cough. She has hardly eaten anything for two days, and she woke Rhonda several times last night with her cries. Have students brainstorm what Rhonda should do in this situation. (Possible answer: She could give the baby rehydrating liquids and call the doctor's office for additional advice.)

### ✓ Reading Check

**Recall** Signs of an asthma attack include coughing, wheezing, rapid breathing, and shortness of breath.

Other medications are taken only to relieve an attack when it happens. Older children can be taught to give themselves their medication when they need it.

**✓ Reading Check** **Recall** What signs indicate a possible asthma attack?

## Caring for a Sick Child

All children get sick. Caregivers need to recognize the symptoms of common illnesses. Parents should feel free to call the doctor's office. Often, a nurse assesses the symptoms, consults with the doctor, and decides if the child should be seen. **Figure 20.2** provides detailed information about some childhood diseases.

Caring for a sick child may involve little more than keeping the child inside and comfortable for a while. Recovery from many childhood illnesses takes only a few days. It may also be important to keep the child away from other children during the contagious period of an illness. When a child is **contagious**, the child can pass the illness on to someone else. In general, children with a fever should not go to school or to a child care setting.

Children may need medicine to relieve pain or to reduce fever. However, some children who take aspirin develop a serious illness called Reye syndrome. Be sure to use only children's medicines recommended by the doctor, not those meant for adults. Parents should always check with their pediatrician before giving a child any over-the-counter medicine.

### Comforting a Sick Child

It is important to maintain a calm and cheerful manner around a child who is sick. Treat the illness matter-of-factly while remembering that the child may need some extra love and attention.

Children who are very ill do not have much energy and may spend a lot of time sleeping. However, children who have only a mild illness and those who are recovering after a serious illness may get restless or easily bored. Quiet play or reading, especially with a caregiver, helps pass the time.

## ♡ Parenting Skills

### Provide Good Nutrition During an Illness

Poor appetite during an illness is normal. If you have had the flu, you probably remember that eating was the last thing on your mind. The same response occurs in babies and children, but their smaller bodies cannot go as long without food and liquids. If illness and poor appetite persist for more than a few days, consult your doctor. Here are some ways to provide the nutrition sick children need:

- **Give the child more liquids.** Children need liquids to avoid dehydration. This is the depletion of needed body fluids. One good liquid is a sugar and mineral (glucose-electrolyte) solution, which can be found in most drugstores.
- **Encourage the child to eat.** Keep offering foods the child likes, a little at a time and as often as possible.
- **Do not force the child to eat.** One or two days of low food intake will not be harmful, as long as the child gets enough liquids.

**Take Charge** Write a paragraph describing ways to make food and liquids more appealing to a sick child who is not interested in either.

## ♡ Parenting Skills

### Provide Good Nutrition During an Illness

Ask students: Why is a six-month-old more likely to suffer from dehydration than a six-year-old? (The baby's body is smaller. In addition, the baby cannot ask for a drink or get the drink on its own.)

**Take Charge**
Answers will vary, but might include offering foods in appealing or unusual ways. For example, the parent might cut gelatin into decorative squares or freeze juice into ice cubes.

**Figure 20.2** Identifying and Treating Diseases

Children often get illnesses such as the common cold. *Which illnesses in this chart require a doctor's attention?*

C₂

U

| Disease | Signs | Treatment |
|---------|-------|-----------|
| **Chicken Pox** | A red, itchy rash appears first, usually on the head and back. It may spread to cover the entire body. The rash begins as small bumps that look like pimples. These develop into fluid-filled blisters, which break open, leaving sores that become dry, brown scabs. Fever usually rises no higher than 102°F (39°C). | Rest in bed during initial stage. Give acetaminophen to relieve fever. Keep the child cool in loose clothing. Apply calamine lotion to relieve itching, or give cool baths with baking soda or oatmeal added. Usually lasts 7 to 10 days. Marks left on the skin may take 6 to 12 months to fade. |
| **Common Cold** | Stuffy or runny nose, sneezing or coughing, mild fever, sore throat, diminished appetite. | Encourage rest and plenty of liquids. Give acetaminophen to reduce fever. Recovery takes 7 to 10 days. |
| **Ear Infection** | An infant may pull at the ear and cry. An older child is likely to say that the ear hurts. During the infection, there may be some temporary hearing loss. There is usually a fever. | See a doctor, who may prescribe an antibiotic. For a fever, use cool baths and acetaminophen. |
| **Influenza (Flu)** | Sudden onset of fever, chills, shakes, nausea, tiredness, and aching muscles. After a few days, a sore throat and stuffy nose may occur. The disease may last as long as a week. | Encourage rest and plenty of liquids. Doctors may prescribe antiviral medications for certain strains of flu. They may reduce the severity of the symptoms and shorten their duration. |
| **Strep Throat and Scarlet Fever** | Sudden onset, with headache, fever, sore throat not accompanied by runny nose or congestion, painful swallowing, white patches on the tonsils, loss of appetite, and fatigue. In scarlet fever, a rash of fine red dots usually appears within 24 hours. The rash is seen first on the neck and upper part of the chest before spreading. When it fades, the skin peels. | See a doctor, who will prescribe antibiotics for a positive throat culture. The child should rest in a warm, well-ventilated room. Throat lozenges and iced drinks can help reduce pain. Patients usually recover in a week. (The rash is the only sign that differentiates scarlet fever from strep throat.) |

**C₂ Critical Thinking**

**Apply** Have students imagine that they are parents of an eight-year-old home with the chicken pox. Ask them what kinds of food, beverages, and medications they might purchase at the store to help the child through the illness. (Possible answer: Foods and liquids, such as soups and fruit juices, that the child likes, acetaminophen to reduce the fever, and calamine lotion and baking soda to help with itching.)

**U Universal Access**

**Interpersonal Learners** Write the five diseases listed in Figure 20.2 on slips of paper. Organize students into teams of three. One member will role play a doctor and the other two will play a parent and sick child. Give one of the slips of paper to the parent and child. The team then presents a skit in which the doctor asks the parent and child questions to determine the child's illness. (Skits will vary. Students present skits in which a doctor asks appropriate questions of a parent and sick child to determine the child's illness.)

**Professional Development**

**Mini Clip**
ELL: Words in Action

Students act out or mime the words they are trying to learn.

---

**Figure 20.2** Identifying and Treating Diseases

**Caption Answer** Illnesses requiring a doctor's attention include ear infections, strep throat, scarlet fever, and possibly influenza.

**Discussion** Ask: How are the symptoms of the flu different from those of a common cold? How are they similar? (Children with the flu are more likely to experience chills, shakes, nausea, and extremely sore muscles. However, after a few days of the flu, a child may experience a sore throat and stuffy nose, which are also symptoms of a cold.)

## Assess

### Study Tools

Have students go to the Online Learning Center at **glencoe.com**:

- Take the **Practice Test**.
- Download **Study-to-Go** content.

Use the **Student Activity Workbook** for additional practice.

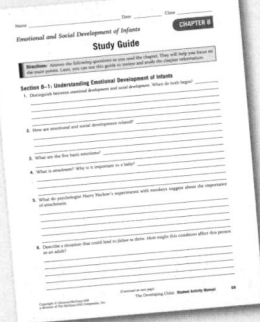

## Close

### Culminating Activity

**Reviewing Childhood Illnesses**
As a class, review the common childhood illnesses that are listed in Figure 20.2, including their symptoms and treatments. Then discuss those diseases, such as diphtheria, polio, and influenza, for which there are vaccinations.

**NCLB** connects academic correlations to book content.

---

Children's behavior and needs during illness depend on their age. Infants may sleep much more than usual and tend to want lots of physical comforting. Children between one and three are usually very active and may have trouble staying in bed. Doctors might allow them to play quietly in the house. Older children can often help take care of themselves. They usually enjoy reading books, doing puzzles, or playing games while recovering.

## Going to the Hospital

A hospital stay can be a difficult experience for a child. Children may fear that they will never go home, that they will be hurt, or that they will die. They may be frightened by unfamiliar doctors and nurses.

Parents can prepare their child for a hospital stay, unless it is an emergency. They can explain in simple terms what to expect. If possible, parents should take the child to tour the hospital. They may be able to see patient rooms, operating rooms, and recovery rooms. When the child is admitted, these things are already familiar and therefore less frightening.

### The Hospital Stay

Hospital staff recognize that children are more at ease and may recover more quickly if a parent stays with them. Some hospitals provide a cot in the child's room so that a parent can sleep nearby. Other hospitals have rooms with space for both the child and a parent. Even when there are no such arrangements, parents can often visit their child any time.

A child may need many tests and forms of treatment. If the child asks, "Will this hurt?" the parent should answer truthfully. Parents may not want to upset the child, but it is more helpful to say something like, "It will hurt for a while, but then you will feel much better. It's all right to cry, if you want."

---

## Section 20.1 — After You Read

### Review Key Concepts

1. **Identify** what antibodies are and what the purpose is behind producing them by vaccination.
2. **Explain** why a sick child should be kept away from other children during the contagious period of a disease.

### Practice Academic Skills

**English Language Arts**

3. Go to a library and locate a book designed to help children prepare for a hospital stay. Read the book. Write a review discussing how the book attempts to help children and whether you think it is successful.

> **NCTE 3** Apply strategies to interpret texts.

**Science**

4. Conduct research to learn more about polio and the development of the first polio vaccine. Write a report discussing the effects of polio in the years immediately prior to the vaccine. Also discuss the scientists who developed the first vaccine.

> **NSES F** Develop understanding of personal and community health; science in local, national, and global challenges.

**Check Your Answers** Check your answers at this book's Online Learning Center at **glencoe.com**.

---

## Section 20.1 After You Read

### Review Key Concepts

1. Antibodies are substances that can fight off the germs of a particular disease. A vaccine contains a disease-causing agent to which the body responds by producing antibodies for that disease.
2. The contagious period is the time during when they can pass on the illness.

### Practice Academic Skills

3. Reviews will vary based on the book read. The student should choose an appropriate book and write a review discussing how the book attempts to help children who must go to the hospital and whether the student thinks the book would help.
4. Students' reports will vary. In the mid-1900s, hundreds of thousands of children contracted polio each year. Many were permanently crippled or even died. The inactivated poliovirus vaccine (IPV) was developed by Dr. Jonas Salk and released for use in the United States in 1955. Dr. Albert Sabin developed an oral poliovirus vaccine that was released a little later. As a result, polio has been largely eliminated.

## Reading Guide

### Before You Read

**Visualizing** As you read this section, visualize yourself actually performing the first-aid instructions on a child. This will help you remember the necessary steps.

### Read to Learn
#### Key Concepts
- **Outline** the steps to follow in an emergency situation.
- **Describe** appropriate first-aid procedures for three types of bleeding.
- **Compare and contrast** rescue breathing and CPR.

### Main Idea
**D** The steps to take in an emergency depend on several factors. If a child is choking or stops breathing, immediate action is essential.

### Content Vocabulary
◇ antiseptic    ◇ hives
◇ fracture    ◇ shock
◇ sprain    ◇ rescue breathing
◇ abdominal thrust    ◇ cardiopulmonary
◇ convulsion     resuscitation (CPR)

**Graphic Organizer** Go to this book's Online Learning Center at **glencoe.com** to print out this graphic organizer.

### Academic Vocabulary
You will find these words in your reading and on your tests. Use the glossary to look up their definitions if necessary.
- elevate
- expel

### Graphic Organizer
As you read, list the four steps of rescue breathing for small children. Use a chart like the one shown to organize your information.

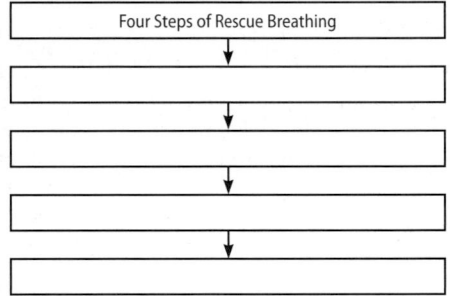

Four Steps of Rescue Breathing

### Academic Standards ...........................

 **English Language Arts**
**NCTE 3** Apply strategies to interpret texts.

 **Science**
**NSES C** Develop understanding of the cell; biological evolution; matter, energy, and organization in living systems; and behavior of organisms.

 **Social Studies**
**NCSS V F Individuals, Groups, and Institutions** Evaluate the role of institutions in furthering both continuity and change.

**NCSS V G Individuals, Groups, and Institutions** Analyze the extent to which groups and institutions meet individual needs and promote the common good in contemporary and historical settings.

**NCTE** *National Council of Teachers of English*
**NCTM** *National Council of Teachers of Mathematics*
**NSES** *National Science Education Standards*
**NCSS** *National Council for the Social Studies*

---

## Focus

### Bell Ringer Activity

#### An Accident
Engage several students to act out an emergency situation, such as a child injuring her arm in a fall off a bike. Ask the class: What would you do in this situation? Discuss that in this section students will learn more about what to do when these types of accidents happen.

## Preteaching

### Vocabulary
Remind students that, like many medical terms, the meaning of *cardiopulmonary* can be determined by breaking it into parts. Ask students what the terms *cardio* and *pulmonary* mean. If necessary, have someone look them up in a dictionary.

### Graphic Organizer
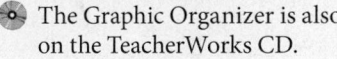 The Graphic Organizer is also on the TeacherWorks CD.

(Graphic organizers should list: (1) Place child face up on firm surface; (2) Lift chin with one hand and push down on forehead with other; (3) Take a breath, pinch child's nose, cover child's mouth with your mouth, and give one slow breath; repeat if necessary; (4) If there are no signs of life, start CPR immediately.)

 **NCLB** connects academic correlations to book content.

---

## Reading Guide

### Before You Read
Ask students whether they have ever been in a situation where they helped an injured child. Ask for volunteers to discuss what happened and how they responded. Did they administer first aid? Did they have to get help from an adult?

### **D** Develop Concepts

**Main Idea** Discuss the main idea with the students. Explain that there are many situations which they can treat, such as minor bleeding and bruises. However, others require fast action by professionals. The ability to recognize the difference between the two types of situations is vital.

## Discussion Starter

**Responding to an Emergency**
Invite students to describe how they usually respond in emergency situations. What happens to them mentally? Physically? Do they think being prepared in the event of an emergency will help them to respond more appropriately? Why or why not? (Answers will vary. Some students will probably state that if they know how to respond to an emergency, they will be calmer.)

## C Critical Thinking

**Solve Problems** Discuss that using backpacks has caused numerous problems for school-age children, including back pain and muscle strains. Have students discuss ways these problems might be prevented. Assign one or two students to conduct research to learn about additional solutions and report to the class. (Suggested solutions might include carrying fewer books or using a rolling backpack. Children should not carry more than 10 to 15 percent of their body weight in a backpack.)

## U₁ Universal Access

**Visual Learners** Learning the five steps listed in the text can help a person respond without hesitation in an emergency. Have students create a poster to illustrate the guidelines in a way that will help them remember each step. (Posters will vary but should show each of the five steps. Illustrations may be hand-drawn or be cut from magazines.)

✓ **Reading Check**

**Analyze** Unlike younger children, they are very mobile. However, they have not yet learned to avoid dangerous situations.

# Safety

A caregiver's most important responsibility is to keep children safe. Young children do not know what can harm them. To keep children safe, caregivers should know what to expect. Each age has different hazards because of different interests and abilities.

The Safe Child, Healthy Child features throughout this textbook highlight some of the dangers. Infants, for example, will chew on almost anything and run the risk of choking. Toddlers are so mobile that they can quickly get into dangerous situations. Safety in and around vehicles is essential for all children.

If you care for children in their own home, you need to plan for the possibility of a fire. Locate all outside doors. Note escape routes from the home. Find out whether the home has smoke detectors and a fire extinguisher. Ask parents to go over their escape plan.

If a fire does occur, the children are your first responsibility. Lead or carry them to safety. Then call the fire department.

## Guidelines for Fast Action

Even if you do not spend a great deal of time with children, you should be prepared to act quickly in an emergency. Fast action can make the difference between minor harm and more serious injury. Memorizing the following five steps will help you if an accident occurs:

1. **Stay calm.** A soothing approach helps reassure the child and keeps your thoughts clear.
2. **Evaluate the situation.** Is the injury minor or serious? Can you handle it on your own, or do you need someone else to help?
3. **Provide comfort.** Offer words of comfort, along with treatment, if the injury is minor. If the injury is serious, keep the child warm until help arrives. Do not move the child.
4. **Call for help if necessary.** If you do not know what to do or if the child is seriously injured, call for help. Keep a list of emergency numbers on hand. In many communities, you can get help by calling 911. Know how to contact an ambulance service, the child's doctor, and nearby hospitals. When you call for help, give the child's age, your name, and your relationship to the child, as well as your location's address. Describe the problem clearly and follow instructions.
5. **Give basic first aid.** If you know what to do, provide the necessary treatment. If you are not sure how to handle the injury, keep the child comfortable and wait until help arrives.

✓ **Reading Check** **Analyze** Why do you think toddlers are especially likely to be involved in accidents?

**A House Fire**
In case of a house fire, your first responsibility is to get everyone to safety. *What are two ways that you can prepare for a fire?*

## Explore the Photo

**Caption Answer** You can determine where all outside doors and escape routes are and know where fire extinguishers are kept.

**Discussion** Ask students: Imagine a fire starts in your home's kitchen. What factors might determine whether your mother should try to put out it out with a fire extinguisher or immediately get everyone out of the house? (She should consider the size of the fire and whether it is contained in a small place. For example, a grease fire on the stove can typically be extinguished with a home fire extinguisher. If small children are present, their safety must come first.)

## CULTURE MATTERS

### Preventing Infant Death in Australia

Infant mortality refers to the death of children under age one. These deaths are usually caused by genetic diseases, birth defects, or diseases that can be transmitted to others. Infant mortality rates are thought to indicate the overall health of a population. Australian rates of infant death declined sharply in the 20th century. Why?

In the first part of the century, the decline was linked to improvements in sanitation and health education, as well as the use of antibiotics. In the second half of the 20th century, declines were attributed to improved medical technology and campaigns to prevent sudden infant death syndrome (SIDS).

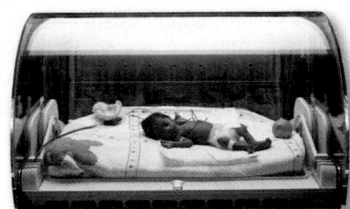

★ **Build Connections** *What did Australians do in the second half of the 20th century to reduce infant mortality?*

**NCSS V F Individuals, Groups, and Institutions** Evaluate the role of institutions in furthering both continuity and change.

## First Aid

Following are some general first aid guidelines. Reading about first aid is no substitute, though, for getting hands-on training. If you plan to take care of children, contact the American Red Cross for information about first aid training classes.

## Bleeding

Many common injuries involve bleeding. To prevent the spread of disease, child care workers are advised to wear disposable gloves when giving first aid to a bleeding child.

### Minor Cuts or Scrapes

Place a clean cloth or gauze pad on the cut and apply firm pressure until the bleeding stops. Then clean the area with mild soap and warm water. Dry the wound, and apply an antiseptic. An **antiseptic** is a substance that prevents or stops the growth of germs. Cover the wound with an adhesive bandage or sterile gauze.

### Deep Cuts or Wounds

If a cut or wound seems very deep, or if the bleeding does not stop, seek medical attention immediately. Continue to try to stop the bleeding until help arrives. Do not try to use a tourniquet. This is a bandage that cuts off the blood supply to a part of the body. This could seriously harm the victim.

### Nosebleeds

Have the child sit or stand and lean slightly forward over a sink or bowl. Squeeze the lower half of the child's nose with a tissue for about ten minutes. Then release your hold and check to see if a clot has formed and the bleeding has stopped. If not, apply pressure again for ten minutes. If you cannot stop the bleeding, get medical help.

## Bumps and Bruises

Minor bruises should be treated for ten minutes with a cold pack or a bag of frozen vegetables. Place a towel between the cold pack and the child's skin. You should **elevate**, or raise, a bruised arm or leg for a while.

A fall resulting in a hard blow to the head can be serious. Seek medical help right away if a child loses consciousness, becomes drowsy or irritable, complains of a headache, or vomits after receiving a blow to the head.

Section 20.2 Accidents and Emergencies  **559**

## CULTURE MATTERS

### Preventing Infant Death in Australia

**Discussion** Why do you think improved health education was an important reason for the decline in infant deaths in the first half of the 20th century? (Possible answer: Until the beginning of the 20th century, most people did not know that germs could cause illness and that many germs could be eliminated with basic sanitation.)

**Build Connections** *Australians improved medical technology and conducted educational campaigns to prevent SIDS.*

## Teach *cont.*

### U₂ Universal Access

**Gifted Learners** Have students conduct research to learn how a major reduction in all deaths, including those of infants, occurred as a result of the introduction of antibiotics. This antibiotic revolution began with the discovery of penicillin in 1928. Have students write a report covering what they learned. (Reports will vary but should explain how the introduction of antibiotics reduced deaths. Infant mortality rates dropped by 52 percent between 1930 and 1949, due in large part to the discovery and use of penicillin and other antibiotics.)

### R Reading Strategy

**Contrast** Ask students: What are some ways that caring for a cut is different from caring for a bruise? (With cuts, pressure is used to stop bleeding whereas with a bruise, a cold pack is applied to stop bleeding under the skin. A cut is cleaned with soap and water and an antiseptic and a bandage or gauze are applied to it, whereas these steps are not necessary with bruises because the skin has not been broken.)

### Cooperative Learning

**First Aid Brochure** Invite a Red Cross health trainer or nurse to speak to the class about first aid. Then divide the class into small groups. Using information from the lecture as well as the textbook, have each group create a brochure with proper first-aid guidelines for bleeding, bumps and bruises, and splinters and thorns. Encourage students to illustrate their brochures. If possible, make copies for each member of the group. (Brochures will vary but should follow the basic information found in the text and should include when to call for professional help.)

## Teach *cont.*

### C Critical Thinking

**Apply** Organize students into groups of three or four. Tell them to imagine that they have been assigned to present a three-hour workshop on bicycle safety to a group of seven- and eight-year-olds. The group should work together to determine what topics should be covered. Based on these decisions, they should create an outline for the workshop. (Students should work in groups to develop an outline for a three-hour bicycle safety course that covers appropriate topics for seven- and eight-year-olds.)

### U Universal Access

**Interpersonal Learners** Organize students into teams of three and have each team come up with a workable plan for the following scenario: A group of friends is hiking when one falls and strikes his head. He also seems to have sprained an ankle. The group does not have a cell phone. Have students create and present a skit showing what they would do. (Skits will vary. Students should not move the victim, but keep him calm, try to make him comfortable, and cover him with whatever they have. They should elevate the ankle. One person should go for help while the other remains with the victim.)

**Professional Development**

**Mini Clip**
Reading: Options for Learning

Two teachers explain to their students multiple ways to read and respond to the assigned text.

## Learning Through  PLAY

### Bicycle Safety Classes

While bike riding is fun, it also raises serious safety concerns. Each year, about 500,000 bicycle accidents require emergency room visits. Children fourteen and under are five times more likely to have injuries than older cyclists. Every child who rides a bike should know and practice safe bike-riding techniques. Some park districts, schools, and bicycle shops offer bicycle safety classes for children of various ages. Learning the rules of the road is very important. Knowing which side of the street to ride on and how to signal to make a turn are just two of these rules. In addition, the bike should be the correct size for the child and the rider should always wear a protective helmet. This helps shield the brain if an accident occurs.

> **Think About It** You often see an eleven-year-old child in your neighborhood riding her bike unsafely. She never wears a helmet and frequently darts into traffic without looking. Write a paragraph describing what you might do to improve this situation.

### Fractures and Sprains

A **fracture** is a break or crack in a bone. A **sprain** is an injury caused by sudden, violent stretching of a joint or muscle. Both types of injury may cause pain, swelling, and bruising. It is often difficult to tell a fracture from a sprain without an X-ray.

If you suspect that a child has a fracture or a sprain, do not move the child until you know how serious the injury is. This is especially important if the injury is to the head, neck, or back. Movement can cause further damage. Call for qualified medical help.

> { **Expert Advice...** }
>
> *"With a toddler on the loose, accidents are bound to happen once in a while. One study showed that the typical toddler has three minor bumps or boo-boos a day."*
>
> — Heidi Murkoff, Arlene Eisenberg, and Sandee Hathaway, coauthors, *What to Expect: The Toddler Years*

For a mild sprain, elevate the injured area and apply cold packs to help reduce swelling. If the pain persists, check with a doctor about further treatment.

### Splinters and Thorns

A splinter is a tiny piece of wood, metal, glass, or plastic that becomes embedded in the skin. Thorns are treated like splinters. Although splinters are usually not dangerous, they do hurt and can cause an infection.

If the splinter is sticking out of the skin and is small, you can use tweezers to remove it. Sterilize the tweezers in boiling water or in the flame of a candle or match. Pull evenly on the exposed part of the splinter to remove it. Then put antiseptic and a bandage on the wound.

If a splinter is just under the surface of the skin and is not glass, you can remove it with a sterilized needle and tweezers. Use the needle to break the skin and expose the end of the splinter. Grasp the end of the splinter with the tweezers, and gently pull it out. Clean and cover the wound.

Large, deeply embedded splinters, glass splinters, or those in the eye can be more serious. These should be removed by a medical professional.

**560** **Chapter 20** Children's Health and Safety

## Learning Through PLAY

### Bicycle Safety Classes

**Discussion** Tell students that many bike riders do not think they need to follow traffic rules, such as making a complete stop at a stop sign. Ask: Do you agree with this attitude? Why or why not? (Answers will vary. Bike riders can get fined if they disobey traffic laws. Car drivers can become confused when bike riders do not obey the law.)

> **Think About It** Answers will vary. The student might suggest that his or her parents speak to the child's parents. Perhaps the student could research local safety classes and give the information to the parents. The student could discuss bike safety with the child.

## Burns

First aid for burns depends on the cause and how serious the burn is. Most burns are serious because they may cause shock, infection, or scarring. Burns are classified by degrees.

### First-Degree Burns

First-degree burns are mild and may turn the skin pink or red. There are no blisters or peeling. First-degree burns may be caused by too much sun, hot objects, hot water, or steam. Put the burned area under cold water or a cold, wet cloth. Then keep it dry and clean. Do not put ointment on the burn.

### Second-Degree Burns

Second-degree burns are red and form blisters. They can be caused by too much sun or by hot liquids and flames. If the burned area is small, cover it with a clean, wet cloth and take the child to a doctor. If the burned area is large, cover the child with a blanket or clean sheet and call for emergency help.

### Third-Degree Burns

Third-degree burns leave the skin blackened or white. These burns do not always cause pain because nerve endings may have been destroyed. They can be caused by flames, very hot objects, or electricity. Immediate medical care is essential.

### Chemical Burns

Some products, such as disinfectants, can burn the skin. These products should always be kept away from children. Always read the directions and cautions on product labels. Should a burn occur, use protective gloves to thoroughly wash off the affected area with cool water. Remove any clothing with the chemical on it, unless the clothing has stuck to the skin. Seek immediate medical attention.

### Electrical Burns

These burns may be deep, but appear to be minor. They may leave only a small black dot on the skin. Cool the burn with water. Cover it with a clean, smooth cloth. Lay the child down with legs elevated and head turned to one side to prevent shock. Call emergency services.

### Resistance to Antibiotics

Germs are natural-born survivors. When scientists develop antibiotics to kill specific germs, the germs often mutate so that they are immune to the drugs. This mutation has caused many diseases to become more resistant to antibiotics. Conditions such as ear infections and tuberculosis are becoming harder to treat.

### Procedure

Conduct research to find out what scientists think is causing this growing resistance. What can be done to reduce it?

### Analysis

Analyze what scientists and doctors say can be done to reduce antibiotic resistance. Choose two of these ideas and prepare a presentation to explain the ideas to your class.

**NSES C** Develop understanding of the cell; biological evolution; matter, energy, and organization in living systems; and behavior of organisms.

## Choking

Choking occurs when a person's airway becomes blocked by a piece of food or some other object. Young children are especially prone to choking because they tend to put all kinds of objects, including small toys, into their mouths. If the object is not removed, air will not reach the lungs and the person could die.

A choking child may wheeze or make high-pitched noises or gurgling sounds. An inability to speak, breathe, or cry and a bluish tint to the face are other signs of choking.

If a child is choking, you must act quickly. For a choking infant, follow the steps shown in **Figure 20.3** on page 562. For children older than one and adults, use abdominal thrusts. An **abdominal thrust** is a quick upward thrust with the heel of the hand into the abdomen that forces the air in the lungs to **expel**, or force out, an object caught in the throat. **Figure 20.4** on page 563 illustrates this technique.

### S Skill Practice
**Guided Practice**

**Make a Quick-Reference Card** Have students create a quick-reference card to include in first aid kits. The card should contain a chart explaining how to identify and respond to first-, second-, and third-degree burns. Because the card will be small (about three inches by six inches), the students should use as few words as possible. (Students should create a quick-reference card that allows people to identify types of burns and explains each type's treatment.) **L1** **ELL**

**Create Illustrations** Instruct students to conduct research on how each type of burn affects the skin. Students should then create illustrations showing how the skin's layers are affected by each type. The layers of the skin and other related structures should be thoroughly labeled. (Illustrations will vary but should show how the skin and related structures are affected by each type of burn. For example, first degree burns affect only the outer layer, or epidermis.) **L2**

**Research a Burn Unit** Discuss that third-degree burns require highly specialized medical care. Have students conduct research on the ways in which hospital burn units aid in the healing of these victims. Students should prepare a slide show, Web page, or similar presentation to share what they learn. (Student should prepare a slide show, Web page, etc., explaining how burn units aid severely burned patients. For example, they take extensive precautions to prevent infections.) **L3**

**NCLB** Activity correlated to Science standards.

## Professional Development
### Mini Clip
**Reading: Planning and Management**

Emily M. Schell, EdD, educator and author, discusses the role of the teacher in presenting standards to students.

# Science in Action

### Resistance to Antibiotics

Students should research what can be done to reduce antibiotic resistance and prepare a presentation explaining two options. Options include reducing the prescribing of antibiotics unless absolutely necessary, educating the public that antibiotics do not work against many ailments, and making sure physicians stay within recommended dosages.

**Quiz**

Ask students to answer the following questions:

1. In what cases should you seek medical attention for a cut? (Seek medical attention if the bleeding does not stop or seems very deep.)

2. Why do some people with third-degree burns not feel any pain? (The skin's nerve endings may have been destroyed.)

3. What steps should you take if a child has a convulsion? (Do not move the child; move hard objects out of the way; loosen tight clothing; if the child vomits, turn the head to the side; apply cool washcloths to the forehead and neck; If the child remains confused or groggy, call emergency services.)

## Reteach

**W Writing Support**

**Descriptive Paragraph**

**Rescuing a Choking Child** Have students imagine that they are at a park when an infant begins choking. An adult then administers the rescue technique shown in Figure 20.3. Have students write a descriptive paragraph about the event. (Refer to p. 548 to review the characteristics of descriptive paragraphs. Students' writings will vary, but should describe how the adult responded to the infant's choking.)

The amount of pressure to use depends on the age and size of the choking person. Too much pressure can harm a child. Get training before you use abdominal thrusts.

### Convulsions

A **convulsion**, or seizure, is a brief period during which muscles suddenly contract, causing the person to fall and twitch or jerk. Most convulsions last less than five minutes. There are many causes of convulsions. In infants and toddlers, the most common cause is a high fever.

During a convulsion, do not move the child. Move any hard objects out of the way. Do not try to restrain the child or stop the movements. Loosen any tight clothing, especially around the neck. If the child vomits, or if saliva builds up in the mouth, turn the child onto his or her side or stomach to help drain the fluids. Do not attempt to put anything into the child's mouth.

Bring the fever down by applying cool washcloths to the forehead and neck. Once the convulsion is over, give the child acetaminophen. If the seizure lasts more than five minutes, or if the child remains confused or groggy, call emergency services.

### Bites and Stings

Many young children suffer bites, mostly from household pets or from other children. It also is common for a child to be stung by an insect such as a bee. The type of treatment depends on the seriousness of the injury and the child's response to the injury.

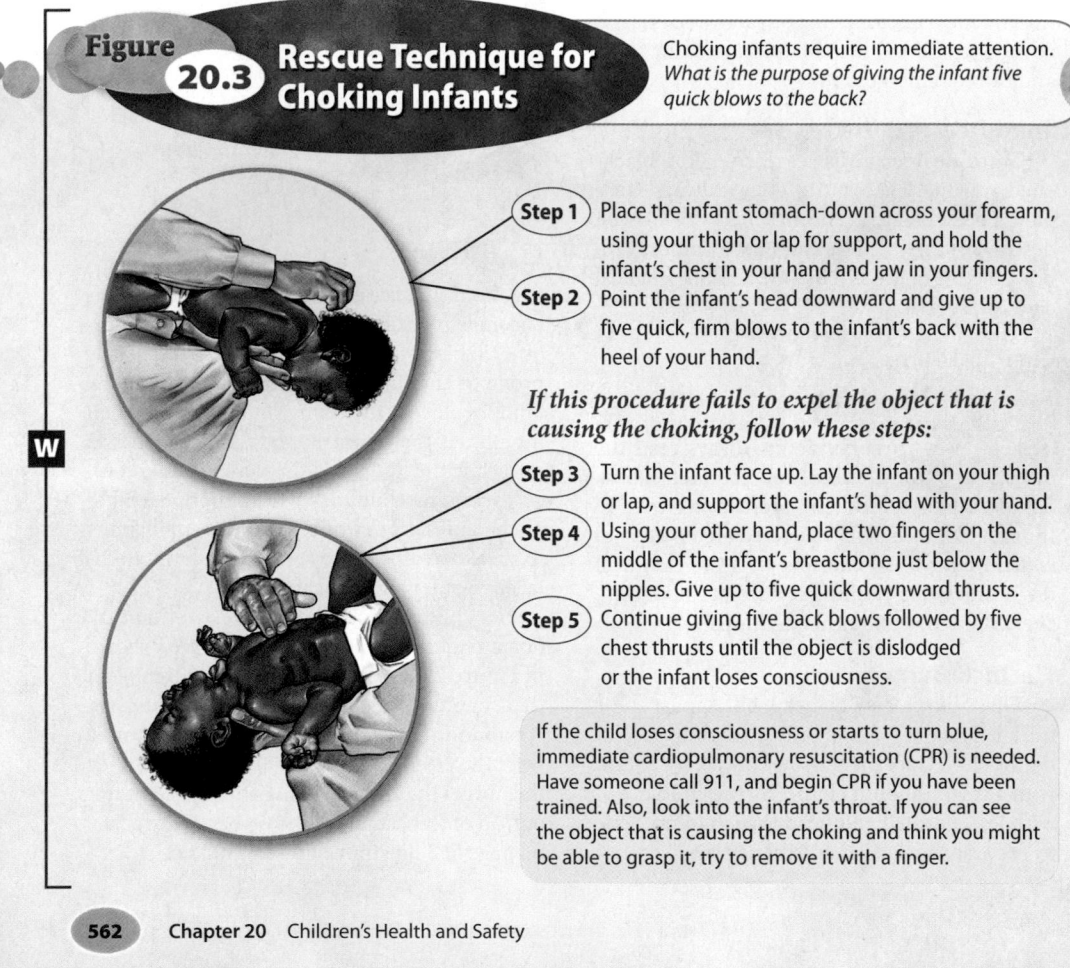

**Figure 20.3 Rescue Technique for Choking Infants**

Choking infants require immediate attention. *What is the purpose of giving the infant five quick blows to the back?*

**Step 1** Place the infant stomach-down across your forearm, using your thigh or lap for support, and hold the infant's chest in your hand and jaw in your fingers.

**Step 2** Point the infant's head downward and give up to five quick, firm blows to the infant's back with the heel of your hand.

*If this procedure fails to expel the object that is causing the choking, follow these steps:*

**Step 3** Turn the infant face up. Lay the infant on your thigh or lap, and support the infant's head with your hand.

**Step 4** Using your other hand, place two fingers on the middle of the infant's breastbone just below the nipples. Give up to five quick downward thrusts.

**Step 5** Continue giving five back blows followed by five chest thrusts until the object is dislodged or the infant loses consciousness.

If the child loses consciousness or starts to turn blue, immediate cardiopulmonary resuscitation (CPR) is needed. Have someone call 911, and begin CPR if you have been trained. Also, look into the infant's throat. If you can see the object that is causing the choking and think you might be able to grasp it, try to remove it with a finger.

562 Chapter 20 Children's Health and Safety

**Figure 20.3 Rescue Technique for Choking Infants**

**Caption Answer** The purpose of the blows to the back is to try to dislodge any foreign object.

**Discussion** Ask students: Why do you think you should only try to grasp an object in an infant's throat if you can see the object? (If you blindly reach into the infant's throat in an attempt to locate an object, you could accidently push the object further in, or cause it to become more firmly lodged in the throat.)

### Animal or Human Bites

For a bite that does not break the skin or has a small puncture wound, wash the area with soap and water. Flush with water for several minutes. Apply antibiotic ointment and give acetaminophen for pain relief if necessary.

If the wound is more serious and is actively bleeding, apply pressure to stop the bleeding. Then elevate the area of the bite. If the wound is bleeding heavily and the child cannot move or is too weak to stand, apply pressure to the wound and call emergency services. If the animal that bit the child was a bat, fox, coyote, skunk, or raccoon, call the local health department so that the animal can be caught and tested for rabies. The child must be given shots to prevent the disease after being bitten by an infected animal.

Any bite that punctures the skin carries a risk of infection. Cat bites, in particular, tend to cause infection. The site of a bite should be checked for several days. If the bite becomes infected, medical help is needed.

### Insect Stings and Bites

The greatest risks from stings and bites are allergic reactions and infections. Any child known to be allergic to bee stings should be taken to a doctor immediately after being stung. Other symptoms after a sting that require immediate medical attention include wheezing, tightness in the chest, vomiting or dizziness, and heavy perspiration. A severe allergic reaction called *anaphylactic shock* can cause the airway to swell shut and a person to die.

---

**Figure 20.4** **Rescue Technique for Choking Children and Adults**

Rescue techniques are different depending on whether or not the victim is conscious. *If a victim is unconscious, what should you do first?*

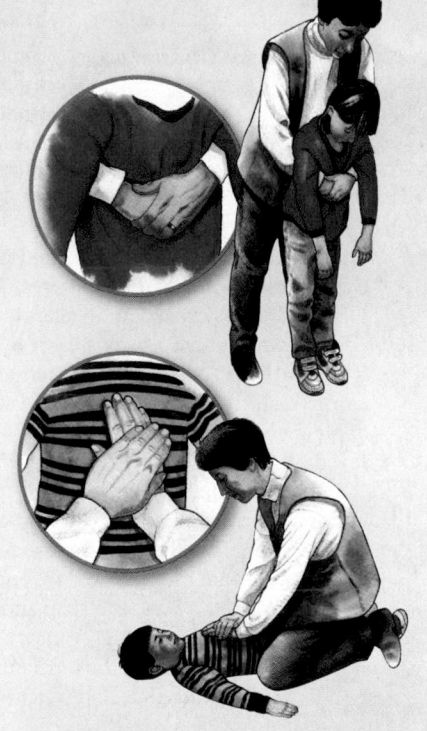

*If the victim is standing or sitting:*

**Step 1** Stand behind the victim and wrap your arms around his or her waist.

**Step 2** Make a fist with one hand and place it, with the thumb toward the victim, just above the child's navel. Grasp the fist with your other hand.

**Step 3** Thrust your fist upward and inward quickly. Repeat the technique until you dislodge the object.

*If the victim is unconscious:*

**Step 1** Position the victim on his or her back, and look inside the mouth. If you can see the object, use a sweeping motion with your index finger to remove it.

**Step 2** If not, kneel over the victim, place the heel of one hand in the middle of the abdomen just above the navel, and place your other hand on top of the first hand.

**Step 3** Give five quick thrusts, pressing your hands in and up.

**Step 4** Open the victim's mouth again, and sweep the area again to try to remove the blockage.

**Step 5** Repeat these steps until the object is expelled or help arrives.

**Step 6** If the victim stops breathing, begin CPR if you have been trained in this technique.

Section 20.2   Accidents and Emergencies   **563**

---

**Figure 20.4** **Rescue Technique for Choking Children and Adults**

**Caption Answer** Place the victim on his or her back and check to see if anything is in the mouth; remove any visible foreign object with a sweeping motion of your index finger.

**Discussion** Discuss that if someone is choking, he or she may be unable to explain the situation to others. Ask: What are some signs that a person may be choking? (Signs include wheezing, making high-pitched noises or gurgling sounds, inability to speak or breathe, and a bluish tint to the face.)

### Reteach *cont.*

**C Critical Thinking**

**Make Decisions** Share the following scenario with the class: Damian's seven-year-old daughter comes running into the house one afternoon. There is a strange dog in the yard. Ask students to discuss what Damian should do about the dog, and make a list of student suggestions. Then poll the class on which suggestion should be followed first. (Students should make suggestions and vote on which should be followed first. Possible answer: Make certain the child stays inside and call animal control officials or police.)

**U Universal Access**

**Learners Having Difficulties** Have students divide a piece of paper in half. One side should be labeled "Standing or Sitting Victim," and the other side should be labeled "Unconscious Victim." Instruct students to create a flowchart that shows the steps involved in using rescue techniques on victims in both situations. If necessary, look up the proper format for a flowchart online. (Students should create two flowcharts, each listing the appropriate steps from Figure 20.4.)

**R Reading Strategy**

**Draw Conclusions** Have students read the steps for helping a choking child if the victim is unconscious (Figure 20.4). Then have them study the corresponding illustrations. Ask: Would these instructions be as useful if there were no illustrations? Why or why not? (Possible answer: No, the instructions probably would not be as useful because the illustrations show exactly how the victim and rescuer should be positioned.)

## Reteach cont.

### U Universal Access

**Logical Learners** Have students locate a specific toxic product, such as a household cleaner or an insect spray. The students should then conduct research to determine whether there are any non-toxic alternatives to the product. Students should write a paragraph explaining any alternatives they locate. (Students should write a paragraph discussing any possible non-toxic alternatives to a toxic product of their choosing. For example, there are some non-toxic products, such as baking soda, that can be used in place of commercial oven cleaners.)

### C₁ Critical Thinking

**Explain** Ask students: What kinds of diseases can be caused by ticks? What are their symptoms? Have students research this topic. Encourage volunteers to share their findings with the class. Did any of the findings disagree? If so, why? (Research may vary. Lyme disease symptoms include rash, fever, and fatigue, and, if untreated, can lead to infection of the joints and even the heart and nervous system. Rocky Mountain spotted fever symptoms initially include fever and muscle pain, leading to a rash. It can be fatal if left untreated. Findings may differ due to the level of information available from varying sources, or because different studies often find slightly different results.)

**Mc Graw Hill Professional Development**

**Mini Clip**
**ELL: Elaborating on Student Responses**

A teacher elaborates on a student response using explanatory language.

## Figure 20.5 Common Household Poisons

Most poisonings occur when children eat or drink a substance they have found. *What plants should you keep away from children?*

| Type of Poison | Examples | Type of Contact |
|---|---|---|
| Medicines | Painkillers, stimulants, sleeping pills, aspirin, vitamins, cold medicines | Swallowing |
| Cleaning Products | Ammonia, automatic dishwashing detergent, laundry detergent, bleach, drain and toilet-bowl cleaner, disinfectant, furniture polish | Swallowing, contact with skin or eyes, inhaling |
| Personal Care Products | Shampoo, conditioner, soap, nail polish remover, perfume, aftershave lotions, mouthwash, rubbing alcohol | Swallowing, contact with skin or eyes, inhaling |
| Gardening and Garage Products | Insecticides, fertilizers, rat and mouse poisons, acids, gasoline, paint thinner, charcoal, lighter fluid, antifreeze | Swallowing, contact with skin or eyes, inhaling |
| Plants | Some wild mushrooms, English ivy, daffodil bulbs, rhubarb leaves, holly berries, poinsettias, poison ivy, poison oak | Swallowing, contact with skin or eyes |

You should also seek help if a child is stung in the mouth or breaks out in hives. **Hives** are blisterlike sores caused by an allergic reaction.

You can remove a bee's stinger by scraping it with a blunt-edged object, such as a credit card. Wash the area with soap and water, and apply a cold pack. Watch the site for the next few days for signs of infection.

Ticks are small insects that cling to the skin and may carry diseases. If you find a tick, use tweezers to grasp the tick as close to the skin as possible. Pull the tick off in one smooth motion. Wash the area with soap and water.

Mosquito, ant, and chigger bites are annoying but not usually dangerous. Calamine lotion or a paste of baking soda and water will generally relieve itching. Using witch hazel or rubbing alcohol on the spot may also provide relief.

### Poisoning

Children are curious and do not always comprehend danger. Young children tend to put things in their mouth. These factors can lead to poisoning. It is not always easy to tell that a child has been poisoned. The following symptoms may indicate poisoning:
- Inability to track movement with the eyes
- Burns or stains around the mouth
- Strange-smelling breath
- Difficulty breathing
- Unconsciousness
- Fever

**564** Chapter 20 Children's Health and Safety

## Figure 20.5 Common Household Poisons

**Caption Answer** Some wild mushrooms, English ivy, daffodil bulbs, rhubarb leaves, holly berries, poinsettias, poison ivy, and poison oak.

**Discussion** Ask for a volunteer to read aloud the examples in the Plants row. Emphasize to students not to worry if they are unfamiliar with many of these plants. The important information is that some plants are poisonous; if they believe a child has eaten a poisonous plant, they should call a poison control center to find out how to proceed.

- Rash
- Burning or irritation of the eyes or blindness
- Choking, coughing, nausea, dizziness

If you believe a child has swallowed, breathed, or touched poison, call the hospital or a poison control center. Describe the poison, how it was taken, and if the child has vomited. You will also be asked the child's age, weight, and height, and any health problems the child has. Keep the poison's container with you when you call so that you can answer any questions. Follow the directions you receive. Take the container with you if you take the child to the emergency room. **Figure 20.5** gives examples of poisons and lists the ways children usually come into contact with them.

## Shock

When a person suffers a severe injury, loses a great deal of blood, or is poisoned, the body may go into shock. **Shock** is a serious medical condition in which important body functions, including breathing and heartbeat, are impaired. Symptoms of shock can include cool, clammy skin; a rapid and weak pulse; shallow breathing; enlarged pupils; or loss of consciousness. Shock must be treated quickly. If you suspect shock, seek medical help. Lay the child down and elevate the feet. Loosen tight clothing, and keep the child warm until help arrives.

**C₂**

✓ **Reading Check** **Recall** What should you do if a child appears to be in shock?

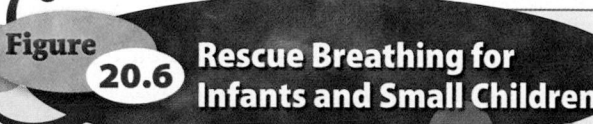

**Figure 20.6** **Rescue Breathing for Infants and Small Children**

If an infant or small child has stopped breathing, it is vital to get air into his or her lungs as quickly as possible. *What steps should you take to open the airway?*

*If you determine that a child is not breathing, send someone to call 911 and follow the steps below. If you are alone and no one hears your call for help, continue the following steps for one minute. Then make the 911 call yourself.*

**Step 1**

Place the child face up on a firm surface. Turn the child's head to one side and clear the mouth of any fluid or foreign matter. If there is an object caught in the child's throat, use the procedure for choking described on pages 561–563. You should remove the object only if it is visible and loose.

**Step 2**

To open the child's airway, lift the child's chin with one hand and push down on the forehead with the other.

**Step 3**

Take a breath, cover the child's mouth with your mouth, and pinch the nose closed. Keeping the child's chin lifted, give one slow breath. If you see the child's chest rise, remove your mouth and let the child's lungs expel the air. Then repeat the breathing. If the chest does not rise, position the head, as in Step 2, and attempt another breath. If the second breath does not make the chest rise, use the procedure for choking described on pages 561–563.

**Step 4**

If the child is still not breathing and there are no signs of life, CPR, which combines chest compressions with rescue breathing, should be started immediately.

Section 20.2   Accidents and Emergencies   **565**

**Figure** **20.6** **Rescue Breathing for Infants and Small Children**

**Caption Answer** Remove any loose and visible objects and lift the child's chin with one hand while pressing down on the forehead with the other.

**Discussion** Ask students: What might happen if a person started rescue breathing without checking the child's throat for foreign matter? (The air might not be able to reach the lungs because of blockage; in addition, foreign objects might be forced further into the airway.)

## Reteach cont.

## Cooperative Learning

**Review Key Terms** Have students work in small groups to create a game that tests players' knowledge of terms used in this section. Game types might include concentration-style games, tic-tac-toe, or board games in which the player moves from one location to another. Have students play each others' games to review the vocabulary terms. (Students should create games that test players' knowledge of terms from this section. Terms may include content and academic vocabulary, as well as any other unfamiliar terms.) **ELL**

**Mc Graw Hill** **Professional Development**

**Mini Clip** **Reading: Building Vocabulary**

A teacher introduces and plays two vocabulary building games with her students.

**C₂ Critical Thinking**

**Analyze** Ask students: How do you think the widespread use of cell phones has helped in the event of emergencies such as an injured person going into shock? (Cell phones make it quick and easy to call 911, allowing emergency help to be quickly dispatched.)

✓ **Reading Check**

**Recall** Seek medical help immediately, lay the child on a soft surface and raise the feet higher than the head, loosen tight clothing, and keep the child warm until help arrives.

## Assess

### Study Tools

Have students go to the Online Learning Center at **glencoe.com**:

- Take the **Practice Test**.
- Download **Study-to-Go** content.

Use the **Student Activity Workbook** for additional practice.

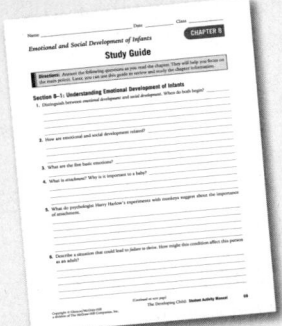

## Close

### Culminating Activity

**Create Lists** Have students create a list of situations in which they believe they could aid an injured person themselves and a list of situations in which they should get help. (The first list might include minor cuts, bruises, or removal of splinters. The second list might include major bleeding or fractures.)

 **NCLB** connects academic correlations to book content.

## Rescue Techniques

When a child stops breathing, or when a child's heart stops beating, immediate and correct action is vital. Learning rescue techniques will allow you to respond quickly and possibly save a life.

### Rescue Breathing

**Rescue breathing** is a procedure for forcing air into the lungs of a person who is not breathing. In children, breathing may stop as a result of drowning, choking, serious head injury, poisoning, or other emergency situations. If the brain is deprived of oxygen for five minutes, brain damage may result. Longer periods without oxygen usually result in death.

The technique to use with infants and small children is shown in **Figure 20.6** on page 565. Child care workers should wear gloves and use a protective face mask when using this technique. You can learn more about rescue breathing in a rescue training class.

### Cardiopulmonary Resuscitation (CPR)

**Cardiopulmonary resuscitation (CPR)** combines rescue breathing with chest compressions to restore breathing and circulation. CPR can save the life of a person who has stopped breathing and whose heart has stopped beating. The technique used for infants and children is different from that used for adults. Only people who have received training from a certified instructor can perform CPR. Many communities offer training programs. For information, call your local chapter of the American Red Cross or the American Heart Association.

### Review Key Concepts

1. **Identify** the steps you would take to be prepared in case a fire broke out where you were caring for children.
2. **Explain** what you should do if you think a child has been poisoned.
3. **Define** rescue breathing. Under what circumstances would rescue breathing be needed?

### Practice Academic Skills

 **English Language Arts**

4. Locate three different articles containing instructions on how to care for burns. Carefully read each article. Write an analysis in which you choose the article that you think gives the best instructions. Explain why you chose this article as the best.

> **NCTE 3** Apply strategies to interpret texts.

 **Social Studies**

5. Lead poisoning is a serious problem that can lead to brain damage in children. Conduct research to determine what federal and state governments are doing to reduce lead poisoning in children. Prepare a presentation to share the information you learn with your class.

> **NCSS V G** Analyze the extent to which groups and institutions meet individual needs and promote the common good in contemporary and historical settings.

 **Check Your Answers** Check your answers at this book's Online Learning Center at **glencoe.com**.

---

## Section 20.2 After You Read

### Review Key Concepts

1. Locate all outside doors. Note escape routes from various parts of the home. Find out whether the home has smoke detectors and a fire extinguisher. Ask whether the parents have an escape plan for a fire, and, if so, ask them to review it with you.
2. You should call the nearest hospital or a poison control center and be prepared to describe the poison; how it was taken; if the child has vomited; the child's age, weight, and height; and any health problems.
3. Rescue breathing is forcing air into the lungs of someone who is not breathing. It may be used in case of drowning, poisoning, choking, head injury, or other emergency situations.

### Practice Academic Skills

4. Analyses will vary. The student should explain which article he or she thinks gives the best instructions.
5. Students' presentations will vary. The U.S. Environmental Protection Agency's Web site provides guidelines on how parents can determine if their children have lead poisoning and lists steps that can be taken to reduce their exposure.

## Chapter Summary

Regular checkups allow health problems to be detected early. Immunizations help prevent certain diseases. Children who have allergies and asthma can take steps to avoid the causes and treat the symptoms. Caregivers should know what steps to follow when a child gets sick or injured. The rescue technique to use with a choking victim depends on the person's age. Rescue breathing is needed for someone who stops breathing. If the person does not respond to rescue breathing, CPR should be used.

## Vocabulary Review

**1.** Arrange the vocabulary terms below into groups of related words. Explain why you put the words together.

### Content Vocabulary

◇ communicable disease (p. 551)
◇ pollen (p. 553)
◇ asthma (p. 553)
◇ contagious (p. 554)
◇ antiseptic (p. 559)
◇ fracture (p. 560)
◇ sprain (p. 560)

◇ abdominal thrust (p. 561)
◇ convulsion (p. 562)
◇ hives (p. 564)
◇ shock (p. 565)
◇ rescue breathing (p. 566)
◇ cardiopulmonary resuscitation (CPR) (p. 566)

### Academic Vocabulary

■ detection (p. 551)
■ sensitivity (p. 553)
■ elevate (p. 559)
■ expel (p. 561)

## Review Key Concepts

**2. Explain** how regular checkups and immunizations can help prevent illness.
**3. Summarize** effective ways to care for a sick child.
**4. Outline** the steps to follow in an emergency situation.
**5. Describe** appropriate first-aid procedures for three types of bleeding.
**6. Compare and contrast** rescue breathing and CPR.

## Critical Thinking

**7. Analyze** Why do you think infants need more frequent checkups than older children?
**8. Draw Conclusions** Suppose you are taking a group of children on a campout. As a leader, what safety skills should you have?
**9. Predict** Imagine you are going to care for two small children. Do you think you would prepare differently now than you would have before reading this chapter? Explain your answer.
**10. Apply** You have a neighbor who has not been taking her eight-month-old to the doctor for routine checkups. She says it costs too much. What might you say to her to encourage her to take the child?

Chapter 20   Children's Health and Safety   **567**

## Content and Academic Vocabulary Review

**1.** Students should provide logical reasons for how they grouped the vocabulary terms.

## Review Key Concepts

**2.** Prompt treatment may prevent minor conditions from becoming major problems. Immunizations provide children with antibodies to prevent diseases.

**3.** Parents may contact a doctor. Sick children should be kept indoors, comfortable, and away from other children. Medicine may be given to reduce pain or fever. The child should rest, eat a nutritious diet, and drink plenty of liquids.

**4.** Stay calm, evaluate the situation, provide comfort, call for help if necessary, and give basic first aid.

**5.** For minor cuts or scrapes, place a clean cloth or gauze pad on the cut and apply firm pressure. When bleeding has stopped, clean and dry the wound, apply antiseptic ointment, and cover. For deep cuts or wounds, seek medical attention immediately. Try to stop bleeding, but do not use a tourniquet. For nosebleeds, squeeze the lower half of the nose for about ten minutes.

**6.** In rescue breathing, one's own breath is forced into the other person's mouth to supply oxygen and restart breathing. CPR is used when both a person's breathing and heart have stopped. It includes both rescue breathing and chest compressions.

## Critical Thinking

**7.** Infants must complete a series of immunizations, they are developing very quickly, they are less able to express problems, and they may still have undiagnosed birth defects.

**8.** You should have basic first-aid training from a respected resource, know how to react if a child is choking, and know how to perform CPR.

**9.** Answers will vary. The student should state whether or not he or she would prepare differently and provide an explanation for the answer.

**10.** You might emphasize that routine checkups can prevent future problems and possibly save money. Staying up-to-date on immunizations is vital to the child's well-being. You also might locate any local free clinics and tell your neighbor about them.

### Family & Community Connections

11. Students' reports will vary, but should discuss what they learned about improvements in children's health and safety over the years. The reports should also discuss why the interviewee thinks these improvements have occurred.

### Health Skills

12. Posters will vary but should explain the five steps in PRICE (protect, rest, ice, compression, and elevation).

### Observation Skills

13. Lists will vary. Student should note all potential hazards they see, explain why it is a hazard, and suggest solutions for each hazard.

### Real-World Skills

14. Students' forms will vary, but should include space for information such as how to reach the parents, all the children's full names and ages, the home's address, the phone number of the poison control hotline, and so forth.

15. E-mails will vary, but should explain how tragedy can be avoided when CPR is administered to a child. The e-mail should then explain where the recipient can go to learn CPR.

16. Student should have conducted research to determine what should be contained in a home first-aid kit and then created a table listing each item and its cost. The student then should have totaled the items, added 25 percent, and calculated the profit on each kit.

**NCLB** Activity correlated to Science standards.

**568**

---

### Family & Community Connection

11. **Health and Safety Improvements** Interview an adult over age fifty. Ask the person to discuss how concerns about children's health and safety have changed over the years. For example, they might discuss improvements in automobile safety or in immunizations. Also ask them to discuss why they think these changes have occurred. Write a report discussing what you learn.

### Health Skills

12. **PRICE** A series of steps commonly called PRICE (for *protect, rest, ice, compression,* and *elevation*) is commonly used for minor injuries, such as a bruise. Research the steps in PRICE. Then create a poster containing both text and illustrations that explains the procedure.

### Real-World Skills

| | |
|---|---|
| **Problem-Solving Skills** | 14. **Organize Information** Many babysitters may not have the needed information in case of an emergency. Create a form babysitters can take with them and complete when caring for children. Be sure to include space for all the needed information, such as the children's names and ages, and any needed phone numbers. |
| **Technology Skills** | 15. **Write an E-mail** When a child stops breathing, immediate action can help save his or her life. Write an e-mail to a friend who babysits explaining how tragedy can be avoided when caregivers know CPR. Explain in your e-mail the options for learning CPR in your community. |
| **Financial Literacy Skills** | 16. **First-Aid Kits** Imagine that you have decided to sell home first aid kits. Research what each kit should contain and each item's cost. Create a table listing each item and its cost. Calculate the total. Add 25 percent to this total to obtain a selling price. Then calculate how much you will make on each kit. |

 **Additional Activities** For additional activities, go to this book's Online Learning Center at **glencoe.com**.

**568** Chapter 20 Children's Health and Safety

---

### Observation Skills

13. **Hazards in the Home** Many parents and grandparents are unaware of the hazards present in their homes. As a child grows from a baby to a toddler, they may not realize how much more mobile the child has become.

    **Procedure** Ask a parent or grandparent of a child from one to three if you may evaluate their home for safety hazards. When you visit, tour the home and identify any potential hazards.

    **Analysis** Write a list of the items you notice along with an explanation of why each is a hazard. Also offer potential solutions.

    **NSES F** Develop understanding of personal and community health; natural and human-induced hazards.

**N C L B**

---

### Academic Skills

17. Poems will vary but should contain at least four bicycle safety rules. The poem should be written at a third- to fourth-grade level.

18. On average, there are 556 injuries per day (1 year = 365 days; 203,000 ÷ 365 = 556.16; rounded to 556).

19. Paragraphs will vary. Students should have interviewed at least eight people who have faced emergencies. Paragraphs should summarize what they learned and what people can do to be better prepared for an emergency.

---

The *Early Childhood Observations CD* offers additional lessons with videos to build students' observation skills.

**Part 1:** Learning to Observe
**Part 2:** How Children Develop
**Part 3:** Working With Young Children
**Part 4:** Extended Observations
**Part 5:** Resources and Answer File

## Academic Skills

### English Language Arts

**17. Bike Safety Poem** Write a poem about bicycle safety. Your poem should contain at least four bicycle safety rules. Use words that can be understood by third- and fourth-graders. If possible, make arrangements to read your poem aloud to a group of elementary school children.

> **NCTE 5** Use different writing process elements to communicate effectively.

### Mathematics

**18. Automobile Safety** The Centers for Disease Control and Prevention reported that in the United States during 2005, 1,451 children ages 16 years and younger died as occupants in motor vehicle crashes, and approximately 203,000 were injured. How many injuries, on average, is that each day?

**Math Concept** **Mean or Average** The mean is one type of average. The mean is calculated by dividing the sum of a set of terms by the number of terms.

**Starting Hint** Convert years to days (1 year = 365 days). Then divide the number of days by the total number of injuries. Round your answer to the nearest whole number.

 For math help, go to the Math Appendix at the back of the book.

> **NCTM Number and Operations** Understand numbers, ways of representing numbers, relationships among numbers, and number systems.

### Science

**19. Emergency Preparedness** When people confront an emergency, they often realize they do not have the information they need. Perhaps the information is as simple as "Where is the fire extinguisher?" or "What is the house's address?"

**Procedure** Locate at least eight people who have dealt with emergencies. Find out whether or not they have an emergency plan. Ask each, "Was there any needed information that you did not have? What was it?"

**Analysis** Write a paragraph summarizing the survey's results. Based on this information, how do you think people can better prepare for emergencies?

> **NSES A** Develop abilities necessary to do scientific inquiry, understandings about scientific inquiry.

## Standardized Test Practice

**ESSAY**

Read the essay question. Then write a one-half page answer on a separate sheet of paper.

**20.** Describe the three degrees of burns. Explain how you would treat each type of burn.

> **Test-Taking Tip** When writing an answer to an essay question, imagine you are traveling down a narrow country road. Beware of any detours or side paths. Stay focused on the question!

**NCLB** NCLB connects academic correlations to book content.

## Standardized Test Practice

**20.** Answers will vary. Students should accurately describe first-, second-, and third-degree burns and explain treatments for each. Essays should contain proper grammar and be free of spelling mistakes.

**Test-Taking Tips** Remind students to look for key words in the instructions. Examples might include identify, compare, describe, differences, or explain. Discuss the importance of keeping these words in mind when writing answers.

**Essay Tests** Essay questions will often ask students to discuss several related items. In this question, they are asked to describe the three degrees of burns. The students' response should build on previous descriptions, for example, by explaining how a second-degree burn is worse than a first-degree burn.

## TECHNOLOGY Solutions

**Use these technology solutions to streamline chapter assessment!**

 *ExamView Assessment Suite* CD allows you to create and print out customized tests or ready-made unit and chapter tests, complete with answer keys.

 **Online Learning Center** includes resources and activities for students and teachers.

 **TeacherWorks Plus** is an electronic lesson planner that provides instant access to complete teacher resources in one convenient package.

**STANDARDS BASED LESSON PLANNING** *The Developing Child* provides students with instruction and assessment in the following fundamental content areas:

## National Standards Correlations

| Standards | Pages |
|---|---|
| **12.1.3** Analyze current and emerging research about human growth and development, including research on brain development. | 584 |
| **12.3.3** Analyze the role of family and social services support systems in meeting human growth and development needs. | 579–580, 587–588, 589, 595, 598 |
| **15.1.2** Analyze expectations and responsibilities of parenting. | 573, 582 |
| **15.2.1** Choose nurturing practices that support human growth and development. | 577, 579 |
| **15.2.2** Apply communication strategies that promote positive self-esteem in family members. | 588 |
| **15.2.4** Assess the effects of abuse and neglect on children and families and determine methods for prevention. | 591–592, 593 |
| **15.3.1** Assess community resources and services available to families. | 579–580, 587–588, 589, 594–595, 598 |
| **15.3.3** Summarize current laws and policies related to parenting. | 586–587, 591, 593–594 |

**NO CHILD LEFT BEHIND** NCLB activities, information, and skills practice will help your students attain NCLB proficiency. Students will improve their abilities in the following academic standards areas:

## Academic Standards Correlations

| Discipline | Standard | Feature/Activity |
|---|---|---|
| **English Language Arts** | **NCTE 1** Read texts to acquire new information. | **Reading Guide (pp. 572, 581, 590)** |
| | **NCTE 2** Read literature to build an understanding of the human experience. | **After You Read (p. 589)** **Academic Skills (p. 599)** |
| | **NCTE 4** Use written language to communicate effectively. | **Writing Activity (p. 570)** |
| | **NCTE 5** Use different writing process elements to communicate effectively. | **After You Read (pp. 580, 595)** |
| **Mathematics** | **NCTM Number and Operations** Understand numbers, ways of representing numbers, relationships among numbers, and number systems. | **Academic Skills (p. 599)** |
| **Science** | **NSES A** Develop understandings about scientific inquiry. | **Academic Skills (p. 599)** |
| **Social Studies** | **NCSS IV D Individual Development and Identity** Apply concepts, methods, and theories about the study of human growth and development. | **Observation Skills (p. 598)** |
| | **NCSS IV H Individual Development and Identity** Work independently and cooperatively to accomplish goals. | **After You Read (p. 589)** |
| | **NCSS IV I Individual Development and Identity** Examine factors that contribute to and damage one's mental health and analyze issues related to mental health and behavioral disorders in contemporary society. | **After You Read (p. 595)** |
| | **NCSS V G Individuals, Groups, and Institutions** Analyze the extent to which groups stand institutions meet individual needs and promote the common good. | **After You Read (p. 580)** |

## Professional Development

**MINI CLIP VIDEO LIBRARY**

Targeted professional development is correlated throughout *The Developing Child*. **The McGraw-Hill Professional Development Mini Clip Video Library** provides teaching strategies to strengthen academic and learning skills. Log on to **glencoe.com**.

In this chapter, you will find these Mini Clips:
- **Reading** Differentiated Activities, p. 572
- **Reading** Connecting the Pieces, p. 574
- **ELL** Accessing Prior Knowledge, p. 581
- **Reading** Attentive Reading, p. 585
- **Reading** Extending the Big Idea, p. 587
- **ELL** Group Discussions, p. 591

## Reading and Writing Strategies

**Writing Activity: Persuasive Essay** (p. 570)
Students use writing tips to encourage readers to support a local crisis nursery.

**Before You Read** (pp. 572, 581, 590)
A pre-reading question or statement will help students make a personal connection to content.

**Graphic Organizer** (pp. 572, 581, 590)
A visual tool will help students organize and remember new content.

**Reading Check** (pp. 573, 588, 592, 593)
A question allows students to make a quick comprehension self-check.

**After You Read** (pp. 580, 589, 595)
Organize and process students' understanding of what they have read.

## Chapter Features

**Depression in Children and Teens** (p. 575)
At any given time, about 5 percent of adolescents will have symptoms of depression.

**Type 1 Diabetes** (p. 583)
People with type 1 diabetes face many challenges.

**Autistic Savants** (p. 584)
Autistic savants often have astonishing skills in music, art, or mathematics.

**Family Dilemma** (p. 587)
Adolescents may find it difficult to discuss dilemmas with parents.

**Guiding Gifted Children** (p. 588)
Gifted children often need additional challenges to overcome boredom.

**Healing Past Abuse** (p. 593)
Adults, not children, are responsible for healthy parent-child interactions.

**Camp Counselor** (p. 596)
Learn the skills needed to succeed as a Camp Counselor.

## Chapter Overview

### Introduce the Chapter

In this chapter, students learn about children and stress. They will learn about children with special needs such as developmental disorders and giftedness. They will also learn types of maltreatment and why abuse occurs.

### Build Background

Discuss with students that like adults, children also suffer from stress. Ask students if they ever suffered from stress as a child. Ask volunteers to share reasons for their stress. (Answers will vary but may include an ill parent, death of a grandparent, or parents divorcing caused them to feel stress.)

### Writing Activity
#### Persuasive Essay

This active learning activity prompts students to write a persuasive essay to support a local crisis nursery. After students complete the activity, encourage them to share their writing with their classmates. Student responses can be used as a basis for classroom discussion. (Essays will vary. The student should explain the importance of providing a safe place for children to stay if their parents are unable to cope with the children or the circumstances. The essay should have an interesting opening, clearly state the writer's views, and provide specific reasons as to why a crisis nursery is important to families and to the community at large. Essays should not contain any grammatical or spelling errors.)

## Chapter Objectives

After completing this chapter, you will be able to:
- **Describe** how parents can help children cope with stress.
- **List** eight possible causes of stress in children.
- **Identify** nine categories of disabilities.
- **Describe** some of the traits exhibited by gifted children.
- **Identify** four major types of maltreatment.
- **Summarize** common reasons behind abuse and maltreatment.
- **Explain** what can be done to prevent child abuse.

### Writing Activity  Persuasive Essay

**Crisis Nursery**  A crisis nursery is a safe place where parents can temporarily leave their children if they are unable to cope with them. Suppose that you feel your neighborhood needs a crisis nursery. Write a persuasive essay to encourage readers to support a local crisis nursery.

**Writing Tips**  When writing a persuasive essay, you are trying to convince the reader to agree with your point of view. Here are some tips to get you started:
1. Write an opening that will capture the reader's attention.
2. Express your view on the topic clearly.
3. Provide specific reasons why the reader should agree with your view.

570

### CLASSROOM Solutions

**Print Resources**

 **Student Edition**

 **Teacher Wraparound Edition**

 **Student Activity Workbook**

 **Student Activity Workbook Teacher Annotated Edition**

**Technology Resources**

 **Online Learning Center** has resources and activities for students and teachers. Includes an Online Student Edition.

 **Interactive Student Edition** allows students to instantly access review materials, examples, and exercises.

Section **21.1** Family Stresses

Section **21.2** Children with Special Needs

Section **21.3** Child Abuse and Neglect

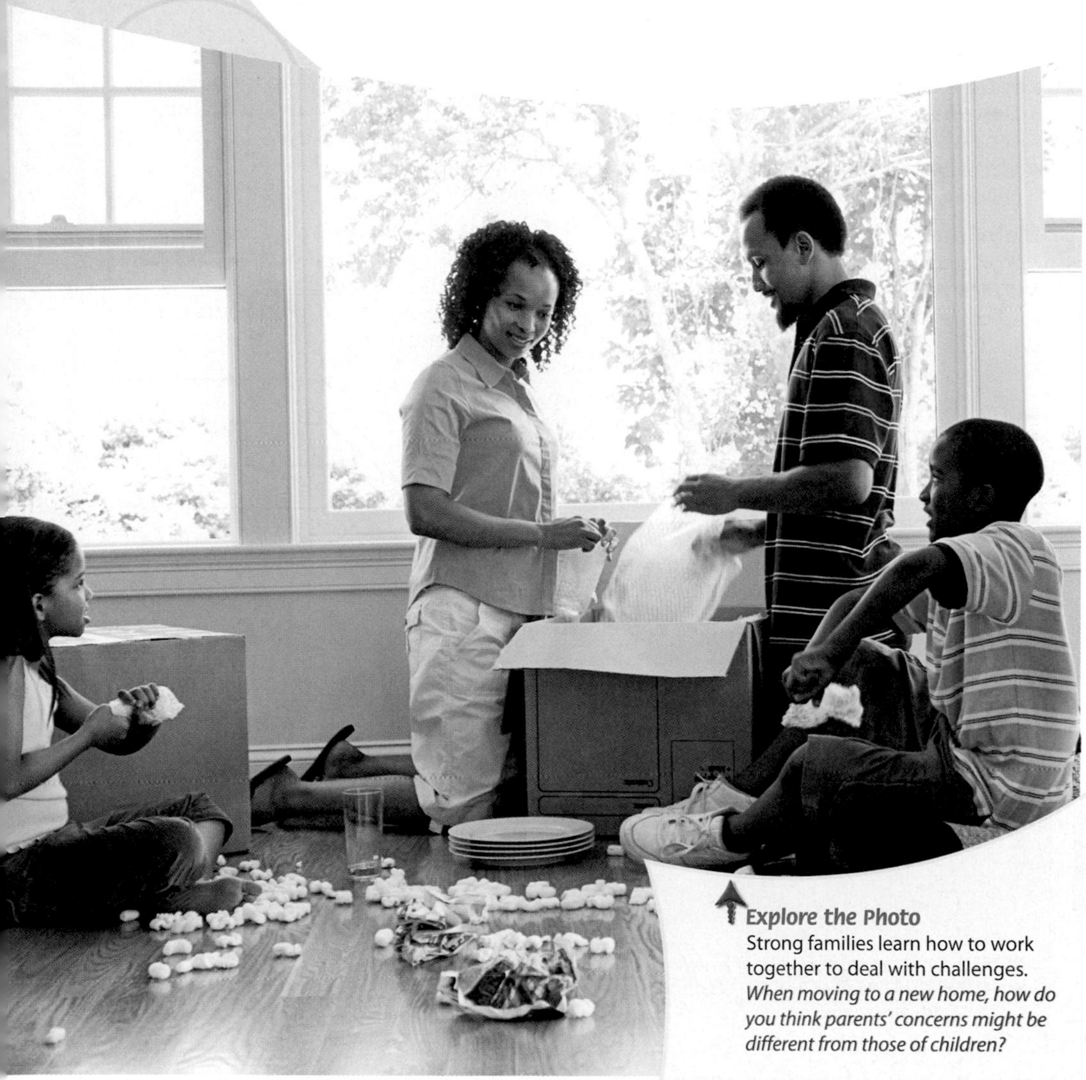

**▲ Explore the Photo**
Strong families learn how to work together to deal with challenges. *When moving to a new home, how do you think parents' concerns might be different from those of children?*

571

**►► Explore the Photo**

**Caption Answer** Parents may be concerned about new jobs, paying bills, and getting children enrolled in school. Children may be concerned about making new friends and feeling uncomfortable in a new school.

**Discussion** Ask students if they ever moved and had to attend a new school. Ask if they started at the beginning of the school year or after school had already started. Which is more difficult, to begin with a new school year or in the middle of the school year?

 **TeacherWorks Plus** is an electronic lesson planner that provides instant access to complete teacher resources in one convenient package.

**Presentation Plus!** provides visual teaching aids for every section.

 **The Early Childhood Observations CD** presents video observations and lessons on observation skills and child development.

**The Developing Brain eTransparencies and Guide** include information and activities to offer insights into brain development and diseases of the brain.

## Focus

### Bell Ringer Activity

**Responding to Difficult Times**

Ask students whether they think children are more vulnerable than adults during difficult times. Why might some children be more resilient than others? (Some children might be more resilient because of the way they were raised.)

## Preteaching

### Vocabulary

Have students create vocabulary cards to help learn the vocabulary terms. Tell students to write the term on one side of the card and encourage them to draw or paste pictures of what the term means on the back of the card.

**Mini Clip Reading: Differentiated Activities**

A teacher models for students how to create vocabulary cards that will support different learning styles.

### Graphic Organizer

The Graphic Organizer is also on the TeacherWorks CD.

(Graphic organizers should include: keeping things as normal as possible, maintaining ties, creating a special place, developing new traditions, watching for changes, and working with the school.)

 NCLB connects academic correlations to book

### Reading Guide

### Before You Read

**Preview** Preview this section by reading the headings and subheadings. Write one sentence summarizing what you think this section covers. When you are done with the section, reread your sentence and modify it if necessary.

### Read to Learn
**Key Concepts**
- **Describe** how parents can help children cope with stress.
- **List** eight possible causes of stress in children.

**D**

### Main Idea
Many situations, such as moving, divorce, and difficulties at school, can cause children to become stressed. Adults must watch for signs of stress, including regression, disturbed sleep, and unusual aggression.

### Content Vocabulary
◇ regression
◇ situational stress
◇ addiction
◇ support group

 **Graphic Organizer** Go to this book's Online Learning Center at **glencoe.com** to print out this graphic organizer.

### Academic Vocabulary
You will find these words in your reading and on your tests. Use the glossary to look up their definitions if necessary.
- vulnerable
- irrational

### Graphic Organizer
As you read, note six ways parents can help their children cope with divorce. Use a diagram like the one shown to help organize your information.

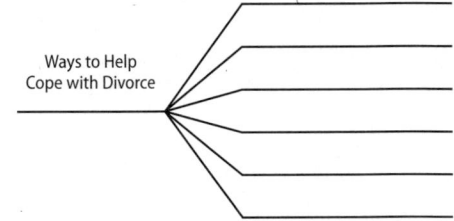

Ways to Help Cope with Divorce

**N C L B**

### Academic Standards ......................

 **English Language Arts**
**NCTE 5** Use different writing process elements to communicate effectively.

 **Social Studies**
**NCSS V G Individuals, Groups, and Institutions** Analyze the extent to which groups and institutions meet individual needs and promote the common good in contemporary and historical settings.

**NCTE** *National Council of Teachers of English*
**NCTM** *National Council of Teachers of Mathematics*

**NSES** *National Science Education Standards*
**NCSS** *National Council for the Social Studies*

**572** Chapter 21 Family Challenges

### Reading Guide

### Before You Read

Ask students to brainstorm stressful events that affect families. Have a volunteer list items on the board. (Answers will vary but may include: hurricanes, earthquakes, death of a member, divorce, moving, loss of job, homelessness, alcoholism, or abuse.) Tell students that in this section, they will learn about families and their stresses.

### D Develop Concepts

**Main Idea** Discuss the main idea with the students. Ask: Why should parents and caregivers be aware of and watch for signs of stress in children? (Answers may include that if the adults are aware of the child's stress, help can be obtained.)

## Children and Stress

Children often can be more **vulnerable**, or helpless, than adults. They may lack an understanding of events, as well as effective coping skills. Parents can help children cope with stress by listening patiently and accepting their feelings of anger, grief, and sadness. Children are often much more aware of parents' worries than their parents realize. It helps when parents are able to admit their own emotions and provide an example of how to cope.

### Possible Responses

Children react to stress in a variety of ways, but age is a factor. **Figure 21.1** on page 574 shows typical ways that children of various ages may show stress.

When times are tough, adults should observe children closely for any signs of stress. It is important to be alert for changes in behavior or regression. **Regression** is the temporary backward movement to an earlier stage of development. If a toilet-trained child begins having accidents, for example, it may be a sign of stress.

> ✓ **Reading Check** **Explain** Why is it important to watch for signs of regression?

## Causes of Stress

**Situational stress** is stress that comes from the environment a child lives in or from certain circumstances and changes. Certain stress factors are a part of every child's life. For example, every child may feel stress when a parent leaves a room. Some of the stress factors that have the greatest impact on a child's daily life include parents' divorce, moving, family financial problems, substance abuse by a family member, illness, or the death of a loved one. The way the parents handle the situation has a huge impact on the child's stress level. One of the worst things a parent or caregiver can do is to say "You shouldn't feel that way." Instead, they should accept the child's feelings. They can then use those feelings as a starting point for trying to offer help.

### School

A common cause of situational stress is school. Students can feel the stress of needing to get good grades, peer pressure and fitting in with friends and classmates, and stress from being the target of bullies.

Many children feel they cannot do as well in school as parents and teachers expect. This can lead to feelings of stress. Children may give up

**Children and Stress**
Children respond to stress in a variety of ways. *What are some signs that a child might be under stress?*

Section 21.1   Family Stresses   **573**

### Teach

**Discussion Starter**

**Two Kinds of Stress** Ask students if they are aware that there is good stress as well as bad stress. Stress that motivates people to positive action is beneficial stress. Ask students to think about times when stress might be good. (Answers will vary but may include: mom's urging student to get out of bed and get ready for school or studying every night for a big exam.) Bad stress can be harmful and can cause illness. Ask students for examples of when stress might be bad. (Answers may include: being yelled at on a continual basis or family having no source of income.)

**C Critical Thinking**

**Inferring** Ask students: What does the word *infer* mean? (To derive a conclusion based on other facts or events.) Ask students to infer why they might be less happy at school on the days when they have an argument with their mom at breakfast than when they had a pleasant morning at home. (Students should realize that the argument with their mom will cause them to feel sadness, stress, and possibly other emotions. Help students understand the connection between things that happen and the way it makes them feel.)

> ✓ **Reading Check**

**Explain** Regression can be a sign that the child is suffering from stress.

---

### ►►► Explore the Photo

**Caption Answer** Answers will vary. Signs of stress might include regression or changes in behavior, excessive attachment to parents or caregivers, fear of being left alone, or sleeping problems.

**Discussion** Ask students if they think that a parent or caregiver should assume a child is experiencing stress if the child does not sleep well one night. Why or why not? (Students should realize that parents and caregivers should look for patterns such as a child not sleeping for several nights before assuming the child is stressed.)

**573**

## Teach cont.

**R Reading Strategy**

**Pre-Question** Write this question on the board: Why do you think Quinn has a stomachache before a final examination? Then read aloud to students the second paragraph under School, which begins on page 573. After you have finished reading the paragraph, ask students to suggest answers to the question. (Quinn may have test anxiety or extreme nervousness and tension about being tested. He may perform poorly on tests, which would increase his stress level.)

**C Critical Thinking**

**Problem Solving** Read the following scenario to students: Lynn has been part of the popular girls' group since middle school. The group always dresses in the latest fashions and sometimes ridicules those whose clothes are out of date. Lynn's father has been laid off at work and money is tight at home. She can no longer buy the latest fashions. Lynn's friends are beginning to make remarks about Lynn's clothing. Ask students to write a paragraph explaining what they would recommend that Lynn do. (Students' answers will vary. They may mention that if Lynn's friends only focus on clothing, they're not really friends at all. She might look for people who accept her for who she is rather than for her clothing.)

**Mc Graw Hill Professional Development**

**Mini Clip**

**Reading: Connecting the Pieces**

A teacher helps students develop predictions and inferences about characters.

---

**Figure 21.1 Signs of Stress in Children and Teens**

Signs of stress vary depending on the age of the child. *How are signs of stress in a small child different from signs of stress in a teen?*

| Age | Signs of Stress |
|---|---|
| **Under age 5** | ❖ Excessive attachment to parents<br>❖ Fear of being left alone<br>❖ Increased sensitivity to loud noises<br>❖ Eating problems<br>❖ Uncontrollable crying |
| **Ages 5–11** | ❖ Disturbed sleep<br>❖ Headache, nausea, or other physical problems<br>❖ Pretending to be ill to avoid going to school<br>❖ Fighting<br>❖ Poor school performance |
| **Ages 11–14** | ❖ Withdrawing from others<br>❖ Depression<br>❖ Aggression<br>❖ Confusion<br>❖ Acting out, such as stealing or fighting<br>❖ Excessive sleeping |
| **Ages 15 and older** | ❖ Anxiety or panic attacks<br>❖ Irritability and moodiness<br>❖ Physical symptoms such as stomach problems, headaches, or chest pain<br>❖ Sleeping problems<br>❖ Sadness or depression<br>❖ Overeating<br>❖ Drinking alcohol, smoking, or taking drugs |

**R** trying. This makes the situation worse. Many young people have test anxiety, or extreme nervousness and tension about being tested. This causes them to perform poorly on tests, increasing the pressure they feel. It is important that children know parents accept them as they are.

**C** Children and teens who see themselves as outsiders often suffer from stress. They may feel worthless if certain groups do not accept them. Even those who are part of a group may feel pressure to dress and act in certain ways. It is the duty of both adults and children to work toward accepting others. When you interact with classmates and friends, focus on their strong points. This will strengthen both you and others. **C**

In many places, bullying has become a major issue. Bullying involves any written, verbal, or physical harassment or intimidation of another

**574** Chapter 21 Family Challenges

---

**Figure 21.1 Signs of Stress in Children and Teens**

**Caption Answer** Young children tend to become overly attached to their parents, whereas teens typically withdraw from others or become aggressive.

**Discussion** Review the signs of stress with students and discuss the different kinds of stress reactions that students have experienced. Ask students why they think different age groups react differently to stress. (Possible answers: young children become more dependent, teens push away those they think are responsible for the stress.)

person. Schools should not tolerate bullying. Children who are being bullied should report it to a teacher or other adult right away.

## Crime

News reports are filled with examples of people hurting others. Most adults would like to keep young people from being exposed to violence. But the reality is that in today's world, this is not possible. Children need to be told that adults are doing everything possible to keep them safe. They also should be taught ways of protecting themselves, such as walking in groups and reporting anything unusual to an adult. Knowing the steps to help keep themselves safe encourages children to feel less stressed and more secure.

## Moving

Moving to a new community or a different neighborhood interrupts friendships, affects school performance, and disrupts activities. Moving can be especially difficult for older children because of the importance they place on peer relationships.

Adults can help children by explaining why a move is necessary. Helping in the move can give children a sense of control over the event. For example, children can pack toys and arrange items in a new room. After the move, parents should help their children get involved in activities that allow them to meet others their age. They might sign up for swimming or art lessons, and check out other group opportunities, such as story hour at the library. Gavin's parents signed him up for T-ball and a summer day camp. By the time school started, Gavin already knew several children who would also be in first grade at his new school.

## Money

Family money problems can stem from many factors. Unemployment, gambling, shopping addiction, illness and medical bills, and poor money management are just a few. As leaders of the family, parents often set the tone

for their children's comfort and stress levels. When families are struggling with finances, parents should make a special effort not to argue about money in front of children or take out their worries on them.

Now a young adult, Jane recalls the summer her family spent camping. A few years later she learned that the family's fun adventure had occurred because they were homeless. Because she and her siblings were young and their mother's attitude was positive, the children were spared the stress that might have been expected.

Section 21.1 Family Stresses **575**

---

### SAFE CHILD HEALTHY CHILD

### Depression in Children and Teens

Depression is a brain disorder that leads to intense feelings of sadness and worthlessness. It is not just a temporary feeling of being down that everyone experiences occasionally. At any given time, about 5 percent of adolescents will have symptoms of depression. Here are some signs to watch for:

- Extreme sadness
- Unusual irritability
- Loss of interest in previously enjoyed activities
- Appetite and weight changes
- Fatigue and difficulty sleeping
- Feelings of worthlessness, hopelessness, or self-hatred
- Talk of suicide or a preoccupation with death

If children or teenagers exhibit any of these symptoms, they should be evaluated by a doctor.

**Be Prepared** Conduct research to learn about the ways in which depression in children and teens is treated. Find out which treatments, or combinations of treatments, appear to be the most effective. Prepare a speech on what you learn. If possible, use presentation software to create a slide show to go with your speech.

---

### SAFE CHILD HEALTHY CHILD

### Depression in Children and Teens

**Discussion** Ask the class: If you know of a child or teen that exhibits one or more of the signs of depression, what would you do? (Students' answers will vary but may include talk to the person or discuss it with a caring adult. Stress that if a friend talks about suicide, they should seek help immediately.)

**Be Prepared** Reports will vary but may include: Treatments include psychotherapy (cognitive-behavioral therapy) and antidepressant medications. This study by the National Institute of Mental Health showed that the best results are obtained by using a combination.

---

## Teach cont.

### S Skill Practice
#### Guided Practice

**List** Have students create and illustrate a brochure that lists suggestions for how to help children with a move. Brochures should contain these suggestions: Explain the move and reasons for the move ahead of time; Encourage children to express their feelings about the move; Keep routines as regular as possible; For school-age children, visit the school ahead of time with the child. (Brochures will vary. Students may include other suggestions that may have helped them cope with a move.) **L1**

**Draw Conclusions** Poll the class to find out how many students have moved. Then have students create line graphs showing how many class members have never moved, have moved once, twice, or three or more times. Ask students what conclusions they can draw from the graphs. (Conclusions will vary. Depending on the area in which you live, few or no moves may be normal or many moves may be the norm.) **L2**

**Interview and Report** Have students talk with an elementary school teacher about the activities he or she does when a new child enters the class after the school year has already started. Students should write a one-page report of their interview and be prepared to share it with the rest of the class. (Students' reports will vary but may contain such activities as assigning a buddy to the new student to show him or her where all of the school facilities are, to help learn the daily routines, and to just be a friend.) **L3**

## C₁ Critical Thinking

**Discuss** Tell students that when a family is going through a stressful period, it is especially important to talk about the situation and resulting feelings. Despite difficulties, parents can communicate optimism and resilience. Families who support each other during tough times can become closer than ever. Divide the class into groups and have groups discuss what parents could tell children about the following: loss of a job; financial problems, divorce, and remarriage. Each group should create a list for each of the four stressful events. When groups are finished, you might compile a class list from the group lists. (Lists will vary but may contain suggestions such as: talk to the children, be honest with them; or don't ignore the children's feelings.)

## U Universal Access

**Kinesthetic Learners** Have students brainstorm a list of feelings that children might have when their parents divorce. (Answers may include: "It's my fault." "I'm scared." "Maybe they'll get back together." "Why me?" "How will it affect my life?") Children need repeated reassurance that the divorce is not related to anything they did or did not do. Have kinesthetic learners role-play situations in which children express their feelings about divorce to friends or parents. Role-plays should include appropriate responses and reassurances from the friend or parent.

---

When money is scarce, older children may worry about what will happen to them. Without spending money, adolescents may be concerned about loss of status in their peer group. However, it is important that parents not hide money problems from older children. Parents need to be clear about possible consequences of the problems and the need to budget money.

### Divorce

Research has shown that children experience the effects of divorce at the time of the breakup and for decades afterward. Many children of divorced parents face greater fears that their own relationships will fail as they grow up. A child will suffer much less when parents make a joint effort to help him or her adjust to the new family situation. See **Figure 21.2**.

Parents should tell their children together about the divorce and discuss where the children will live. Children often blame themselves for the failure of their parents' marriage. Parents must emphasize that the children did nothing wrong. Parents should remind children of their love for them often.

Some children ask questions. Some cry. Some appear not to react at all when they learn their parents are divorcing. Parents should accept any reaction, including none at all.

Most children want to know how the divorce will affect them. "Where will I live?" "Can I still go to summer camp?" "Will I go to a new school?" Parents must be honest with children about possible outcomes and involve children in decision making. Parents should never give children false hope that parents might get back together.

Parents should resist the urge to spoil children who are feeling sad. It is also important not to confide in children or place them in the middle of arguments. This unfairly makes them feel that they have to take sides. Children need love from both parents to cope.

Many children show behavior problems after their parents' breakup. Even children who appear happy on the surface may be hiding their pain to keep parents from worrying.

### Substance Abuse

Some people develop an addiction to a substance, such as alcohol, cocaine, crack, or prescription drugs. An **addiction** is a dependence on a substance, such as alcohol or drugs. People often feel that they cannot live without the substance. Substance abuse causes serious problems for families.

Some adults who abuse substances hurt their families with words or physical violence. Often they are emotionally unavailable. Some parents lose their jobs because of their addiction, or turn to crime to support their addiction.

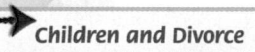
**Children and Divorce**
Children should be able to talk about their feelings, even if they are negative. *What should parents never do to children when the parents are getting divorced?*

---

### ▶ Explore the Photo

**Caption Answer** Parents should never confide in children or place them in the middle of an argument. They should also resist the urge to spoil children who are feeling sad.

**Discussion** Ask the class: Do you believe that the parents' behavior during a divorce can help the children better deal with the stressful situation? Why or why not? (Answers will vary. Some students may say yes because if the parents are civil to one another, there will be less stress overall.)

## Figure **21.2** Helping Children Cope with Divorce

Both parents need to help minimize the impact of divorce and help children adjust to changes. *Why is it important that parents work with the school during a divorce?*

| Tip | Examples |
| --- | --- |
| **Keep things as normal as possible.** | Maintain routines, including family mealtimes and rules of behavior. |
| **Maintain ties.** | Help children stay in touch with their friends and members of both sides of the family. Encourage visits, calls, and e-mails to help maintain these important relationships. |
| **Create a special place.** | If the child must move, help the child personalize his or her space in the new home. Have children keep personal belongings in each parent's home if they go back and forth frequently. |
| **Develop new traditions.** | Holiday activities may change. Children may spend holidays with only one parent or with a newly blended family. Invite children to invent new holiday traditions while maintaining some old favorites. |
| **Watch for changes.** | Observe changes in the child's behavior, school performance, and temperament. If a child withdraws or shows a major shift in behavior, talk to the pediatrician or a counselor. |
| **Work with the school.** | Make the child's teacher aware of the situation. Many schools offer professional resources, referrals, and even lunch groups to help children cope. |

C₂

Even though family members are aware of a substance abuse problem, they do not always want to admit it. They sometimes help the addict hide the problem or they take on the person's responsibilities. Sometimes they try to rescue the addict, or react so strongly that the focus turns from the addict's behavior to the family member's reaction.

Most addicts become skilled at hiding the evidence of their problem from others. However, they and their families must deal with the problem to get better. Nagging or threatening a substance abuser will not help. Substance abusers will not seek help until they are ready. Usually, this happens when the consequences of the behavior become especially painful, as when they lose their jobs or their families.

In the meantime, family members should take steps to protect themselves. A **support group** is a collection of individuals who work together to explore and accept their feelings. They come to realize that they are not alone with their problems. There are several well-known groups, such as Al-Anon (for the families and friends of alcoholics) and Nar-Anon (for the families and friends of narcotics abusers) available for help.

Anyone who has a friend or family member who is abusing alcohol or drugs can join these groups at no cost. Families can draw on the strength and experience of other people in similar situations. Adolescents might also talk to a school counselor, trusted teacher, or religious leader.

C₂

**Section 21.1** Family Stresses **577**

## Figure **21.2** Helping Children Cope with Divorce

**Caption Answer** Schools often can offer support and a variety of services to parents. They may have professional resources or lunch groups to help the children cope.

**Discussion** Holiday activities may change with a divorce. Have students discuss how a divorce may change a family's traditions. Ask students to brainstorm ways parents can maintain family traditions, holidays, and celebrations after a divorce. (Answers will vary. Students may suggest asking the children to invent new traditions or spending two holidays—one with each parent.)

## Assess

**Quiz**
Ask students to answer the following questions:

1. **What are three signs of stress in teens?** (any three: anxiety or panic attacks; irritability and moodiness; physical symptoms; sleeping problems; sadness or depression; overeating; drinking alcohol; smoking; or taking drugs)
2. **What are some factors that can cause money problems in families?** (unemployment, gambling, shopping addiction, illness and medical bills, poor money management)
3. **Why is it important that parents who are divorcing emphasize that the children did nothing wrong?** (Children often blame themselves for the failure of their parents' marriage.)

## Reteach

**C₂ Critical Thinking**
**Problem Solving** Read these scenarios to students: Kelley's dad frequently gets aggressive. Lisa's dad recently was expelled from the police force because of his addiction to illegal drugs. Jeremy's mom sometimes cannot go to work because she has been drinking; Jeremy calls her boss to say she is sick so she won't lose her job. Have students discuss the impact of these addictions on families, what the children are feeling, and how the families or children can get help. (Students' answers will vary. They should discuss the impact on the children such as loss of finances because a parent lost his job or having to lie for one's parent. Families can seek help from counselors or support groups. The children can talk to another trusted adult, such as a teacher, counselor, or religious leader.)

**577**

### Reteach cont.

**W** **Writing Support**

**Descriptive Paragraph**

**Death and Grieving** Ask students to read a book about coping with death and grieving. The book can be written for any age group. Have students write a review of the book. Reviews should consist of at least two paragraphs. Students should decide what mood they want to create in the paragraph, write a strong topic sentence, orient the reader by presenting details in a logical order, and use precise transition words. (Book summaries will vary. Refer to p. 548 for tips on writing a descriptive paragraph. Use the following criteria to evaluate students' summaries: Does the paragraph include a strong topic sentence? Does the paragraph convey a mood that is supported by all of the details? Does the paragraph present details in a logical order? Does the paragraph include precise transition words?)

**C** **Critical Thinking**

**Give Examples** Review the reactions children have to death at different stages in their lives. Have students discuss and give examples of how parents and caregivers can help children at each of the stages. (Answers may include: For children under age three, nurturing care and consistent routines are most important, while children three- to five-years-old need explanations of death. Children six to nine may need reassurances, play opportunities, and opportunities for discussion. Preteens and teens may need to know they are not at fault, and teens need to be kept from taking on too many responsibilities.)

**Support Groups**
Support groups help friends and family members cope with addictions as well as death of a loved one. *How might you find a group in your community?*

## Illness

When a family member is ill, the routines of family life are upset. Children need an honest explanation of what is happening. Of course, it should be geared to their ability to understand. When the illness is minor, children can be reassured that the person should soon be well again. If the illness is serious or the person is dying, adults should tell children the truth in a calm, reassuring way. They might be told, "The doctors are doing everything they can to help Aunt Debbie feel better."

Children sometimes have irrational fears or false beliefs about illness. **Irrational** means lacking reason. Children may worry that they are somehow at fault. They might think that a disease like cancer is contagious. Adults should reassure them that nothing they did caused the illness. Unless the disease is contagious, the child should be assured that no one else in the family will come down with it. A child may also misunderstand what is said. One four-year-old overheard that someone had died in bed. It took her parents days to figure out why she cried wildly at bedtime.

## Death

Children's grief, like that of adults, is a complex set of emotions that may include fear, anger, despair, agitation, and guilt. While each child grieves differently, the age of the child influences his or her reaction. Researchers have found that two factors influence their views of death. These two factors are the children's level of development and religious or cultural background. Here are some common reactions by age:

- **Children under three** cannot understand more than a brief separation. They may react to a death in the same way they react to a parent's weeklong vacation.
- **Children ages three to five** think that death is like sleep: you are dead, and then you wake up and are alive again. As a result, they may seem unfeeling when a person dies. They do not understand that death is permanent.
- **Children ages six to nine** may believe that angry words or thoughts caused death. They may fear that other family members will abandon them. Most children this age recognize that death is final, but they may not understand that everyone dies.
- **Preteens** may still feel that the person died because of some bad deed. They may feel angry toward the person who died or toward other family members.

{ **Expert Advice...** }

*"Dealing with stressful situations in the family ultimately becomes the responsibility of the family members. If a family is to remain 'strong,' each member needs to recognize stress within the family, its causes, and how to effectively handle it."*

— Bryan Adcock, child and family development specialist, University of Missouri

**W**

**C**

▶ **Explore the Photo**

**Caption Answer** Answers will vary. Students might check with their school counselors, look in a phone book, or contact a local social service agency.

**Discussion** Invite students or community members who are in support groups to come to class as guest speakers to discuss the value of support groups, how someone gets into a group, the purpose of the group, and so on. Support groups are often listed in the phone book under headings like Self-Help or Support Groups.

- **Teens** may assume too much responsibility for financial or other family concerns. They understand the finality of death and its impact on the family.

### Help Children Cope

By age five, many children have had some contact with death. They may have seen a dead bird or lost a beloved pet, for example. They may not fully understand what has happened, but they will have reactions to the loss. There are a number of ways that parents can help children cope with the loss of a loved one.

- Funerals and memorial services are rituals that allow people to vent feelings and to honor the deceased person. When children want to go, experts believe they should be allowed to attend these services.
- Very young children need simple explanations about death. These might include the loss of functions like eating, sleeping, thinking, or feeling.
- Religion and spiritual beliefs are a source of comfort to many people who have suffered a loss. Beliefs offer explanations and give meaning to life and death. Letting children know that things are the way they are supposed to be, according to the family's faith, can help them feel secure. Parents should let children know that pain is a part of living and that it will lessen in time.

### Death of a Parent

The death of a parent is probably the most tragic thing that can happen to a child. A child whose parent dies needs support for an extended period. Many children react with guilt. The child may think, "I wasn't always good when he wanted me to be," or "I wasn't quiet enough when she was sick." Even infants go through a period of excessive crying and searching for a parent who has died.

Parents should reassure children that, no matter what happens, they will always receive loving care. If asked, parents should talk to their children about who would take care of them in the unlikely event of their death. Experts say that children whose parents have died or are dying need three things:

- Someone to meet their emotional and physical needs
- Reassurance that they will always be loved and cared for, no matter what happens
- Explanations that are age-appropriate

Child therapists recommend telling children the truth when death is near. This lets them say goodbye. Children should be allowed to visit the dying parent.

Some people mistakenly believe that it is best to avoid talking about the deceased person. Actually, the opposite is true. When a parent dies, children should be encouraged to express their grief by drawing pictures or talking.

**Remembering Loved Ones**
A healthy response to a family member's death is to keep memories alive through photos and stories. *What other ideas do you have for keeping memories alive?*

**U Universal Access**

**Intrapersonal Learners** Divide the class into small groups. Tell students they will discover the range of funeral customs in different cultures. Assign each group a country to research and have them create a presentation to share their information with the class. Encourage students to be creative with their presentations. All presentations should include visual aids. (Students' presentation and information will vary depending on the country researched. For example, Ireland tradition was to hold wakes instead of funerals. During a wake, the body is cleaned and laid out in the deceased person's home, then specific visiting and crying rituals are observed. The wake also included eating, drinking, and celebrating of the person's life, rather than mourning his death. Presentations may include power point presentations, skits, or oral reports with photographs.) **ELL**

**R Reading Strategy**

**Religious Beliefs** Have students research different religions and their beliefs about death and dying. Students should list the religion, state the belief about dying, and indicate whether the religion believes in life after death and if so, in what form. When students have finished their research, have them share their findings with the rest of the class. You may compile the students' research findings into a comprehensive class list of all the religions studied. (Students' research results will vary depending on the religions studied. For example, Hinduism believes death is a natural process that leads to reincarnation of a person's soul.)

### Explore the Photo

**Caption Answer** Ideas might include remembering people on special occasions such as their birthdays and engaging in activities they enjoyed, such as specific sports.

**Discussion** Remind students that children need to know that their feelings regarding a death are normal. The surviving parent or other family members could say something like, "I thought about your mom today" to let the child know that it is all right to think about the deceased.

## Study Tools

Have students go to the Online Learning Center at **glencoe.com**:

- Take the **Practice Test**.
- Download **Study-to-Go** content.

Use the **Student Activity Workbook** for additional practice.

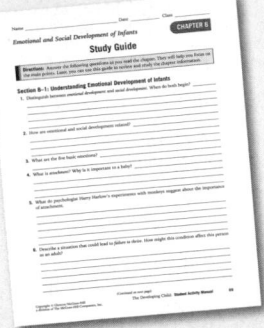

## Culminating Activity

**The Grief Process** Discuss with students the different stages of the grief process. Tell them that Elizabeth Kubler-Ross listed these typical responses: denial, anger, bargaining, depression, and acceptance. Ask volunteers to share their responses to grief.

 **NCLB** connects academic correlations to book content.

---

If the child has fears, adults should deal with them. Older children and teens should not be placed in a role with adult responsibilities.

Healthy children sometimes ask, "When will I die?" Often, they simply want to know if they will die. Parents can say that while every living thing dies, most people live a long time. They can also be told that eating healthy foods and wearing seat belts help people live longer.

### Suicide

Some people feel overwhelmed by their problems, overcome by depression. They may be irrationally angry at others, and decide that taking their own lives is the solution. Sadly, some of the people who attempt suicide are children and teenagers.

When an adult commits suicide, children who are old enough to understand should be told. Adults can stress that there are many ways of getting help and dealing with problems that are not harmful to anyone.

Anyone who is thinking about suicide should seek help from a parent, friend, doctor, or counselor. Many survivors of a suicide attempt say that they later realized their problems had other solutions. Warning signs of suicide include talking about suicide or giving away possessions. If you know anyone who is doing these things, talk to a school counselor or another adult. Most people who commit suicide are depressed. With modern treatment options, they can find hope again.

Older children and teens who know someone who committed suicide may wonder if they could have done something to prevent it. They may feel betrayed or abandoned. These feelings are a normal part of the grieving process.

Grieving takes time. Talking to a professional counselor can help. Finding a way to accept and express intense feelings is also important. Survivors can do something positive that they believe the person would have wanted them to do.

---

## Section 21.1 — After You Read

### Review Key Concepts

1. **Explain** why children may be more vulnerable to stress than adults.
2. **Describe** how joining a support group can help a child deal with a stressful situation, such as when a parent abuses alcohol.

### Practice Academic Skills

 **English Language Arts**

3. Imagine you are a 10-year-old child who has just moved to a new town. You do not know anyone and school starts next week. Create a journal entry expressing any fears you might be feeling about the new school and the stress you are feeling.

> **NCTE 5** Use different writing process elements to communicate effectively.

 **Social Science**

4. Many children face the stress of being bullied at school. Conduct research to determine what schools include in anti-bullying policies. Then work with a partner to create an illustrated poster that explains why bullying is wrong and how to deal with it. Be sure your poster defines the different types of bullying.

> **NCSS V G** Analyze the extent to which groups and institutions meet individual needs and promote the common good in contemporary and historical settings.

 **Check Your Answers** Check your answers at this book's Online Learning Center at **glencoe.com**.

**580** Chapter 21 Family Challenges

---

### Section 21.1 After You Read

### Review Key Concepts

1. Children may be more vulnerable to stress because they may not understand why events occur and they usually lack effective coping skills.
2. A child can draw on the strength and experience of other people in similar situations and have a group with whom they can freely share feelings.

### Practice Academic Skills

3. Journal entries will vary, but the student should state any fears concerning going to a new school and any feelings of stress this situation might cause.

4. Posters will vary but should explain that bullying can include written, verbal, or physical harassment or intimidation in any form and causes harm to both the recipient and the person doing the bullying. It should also offer suggestions for dealing with bullying.

### Reading Guide

#### Before You Read

**Pace Yourself** Short blocks of concentrated reading, repeated frequently, are more effective than one long session. Focus on reading for 10 minutes. Take a short break. Then read for another 10 minutes.

#### Read to Learn
**Key Concepts**
- **Identify** nine categories of disabilities.
- **Describe** some of the traits exhibited by gifted children.

**D**

#### Main Idea
Children with special needs include those with disabilities and those with special abilities. Parents and teachers must work to meet the educational needs of both groups.

#### Content Vocabulary
◇ learning disability      ◇ asthma
◇ dyslexia                 ◇ autism
◇ ADHD                     ◇ autism spectrum
◇ ADD                         disorders (ASD)
◇ mental retardation       ◇ inclusion
◇ type 1 diabetes          ◇ gifted

 **Graphic Organizer** Go to this book's Online Learning Center at **glencoe.com** to print out this graphic organizer.

#### Academic Vocabulary
You will find these words in your reading and on your tests. Use the glossary to look up their definitions if necessary.
■ profound
■ adaptation

#### Graphic Organizer
As you read, look for eight common traits of autism or ASD. Use a chart like the one shown to help organize your information.

| Traits of Autism and ASD |
|---|
| 1. |
| 2. |
| 3. |
| 4. |
| 5. |
| 6. |
| 7. |
| 8. |

---

**NCLB**

#### Academic Standards · · · · · · · · · · · · · · · · · · · · ·

 **English Language Arts**
**NCTE 2** Read literature to build an understanding of the human experience.

**Social Studies**
**NCSS IV H Individual Development and Identity** Work independently and cooperatively within groups and institutions to accomplish goals.

---

**NCTE** *National Council of Teachers of English*
**NCTM** *National Council of Teachers of Mathematics*

**NSES** *National Science Education Standards*
**NCSS** *National Council for the Social Studies*

 **Bell Ringer Activity**

#### Special Children
Ask students if they know a child with special needs. What are the child's needs? What accommodations does the child's school make for the child's education? What modifications has the child's family made?

 **Professional Development**

#### Mini Clip
**ELL: Accessing Prior Knowledge**

A teacher helps students make connections between what they know and the upcoming reading selection.

### Preteaching

#### Vocabulary
Tell students that letters that stand for words are called acronyms. ADHD stands for attention deficit hyperactive disorder. ADD stands for attention deficit disorder. Ask students to name other acronyms with which they are familiar.

#### Graphic Organizer
 The Graphic Organizer is also on the TeacherWorks CD.

(Graphic organizers should include: resistance to change, absence of empathy, little or no eye contact, repetition of words, repetitive movements, difficulty focusing and inability to remain attentive, distress without cause, loss of skills learned.)

**NCLB** connects academic correlations to book content.

---

### Reading Guide

#### Before You Read

Ask students if they have ever needed extra help learning something that was particularly difficult. Tell them that children with learning disabilities constantly face this challenge. These children must work extra hard to achieve what comes easily for many people.

#### D Develop Concepts

**Main Idea** Discuss the main idea with students. Ask: Why must parents and teachers work together to meet the educational needs of children with special needs? (Answers may include: Parents can help the teacher better understand the child. Teachers know techniques for helping the child learn.)

## Discussion Starter

**Parents and Children with Disabilities** Parenting is challenging even when the child does not have special needs. Ask students to imagine being a parent of a child with a disability. How would this change your family? (Answers will vary. Students should realize that a child with disabilities will take more of the parents' time and attention and may also take more of the family's financial resources for special care.)

## C Critical Thinking

**Problem Solving** Read the following scenario to students: Twelve-year-old Kari has just been diagnosed with juvenile diabetes, a disease in which the body does not produce enough insulin to control sugars in the blood. What kinds of accommodations do you think she will need at home and at school? Discuss how to talk with Kari about her condition and how to understand the problems of children with invisible disabilities and how to help them get the accommodations they need. (Answers will vary. Possible answers might include: Kari might need to eat extra meals throughout the day to help keep her blood sugar regulated. She might need to have a place where she can test her blood sugar and give herself insulin injections. Kari is a regular child and should be treated as such. She should receive the same considerations from others and should receive extra accommodations when needed.)

# Children with Disabilities

Some children have different needs from the average child. They are said to have special needs. These children fall into two categories: children with disabilities and children with special abilities. Children with special abilities are also referred to as gifted children.

Parenting, family life, education, and interaction with the world must undergo adjustment. Both children with disabilities and those who are gifted are sometimes called exceptional children. Most children with physical, mental, or emotional disabilities need special adaptations in some aspect of their lives. Gifted children need additional stimulation.

The attitude of parents and other caregivers has a deep impact on children's futures. Like all children, children with disabilities want to have success and feel good about what they do. The goal is to help children with special needs become as independent as possible by involving them in family and school life.

## Types of Disabilities

Disabilities may result from difficulties with mobility, vision, or hearing. Some disabilities affect a child's ability to learn, speak, or express emotions. Some problems are apparent at birth. Others may not be discovered for months or years. Some children have a disability that is clearly apparent. Many have so-called invisible disabilities. These are disabilities that people might not notice right away. Children with a learning disorder, for example, or those with diabetes, have invisible disabilities. Some of the most common types of disabilities, visible and invisible, are described here.

### Learning Disabilities

A **learning disability** interferes with a child's ability to learn, listen, think, speak, read, write, spell, or do math. Children with a learning disability often have average or above-average intelligence, but they achieve below their potential because of the difficulties they experience with learning. Learning disabilities result from disorders in the brain and central nervous system. Most learning disabilities are detected in children when standardized testing begins, between the ages of seven and twelve. Early diagnostic testing, followed by intervention is critical to their educational success. Intervention means involvement by professionals using special teaching methods.

A common learning disability is dyslexia. **Dyslexia** is a learning disorder that prevents a child from understanding printed symbols in a normal way. A child with dyslexia may be very intelligent but have trouble processing visual information. Letters and numbers may be reversed or absent, so children with dyslexia may have difficulty with reading, writing, spelling, and math. They may find it hard to understand directions and to **distinguish**, or see a difference in, left from right.

C

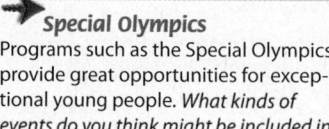
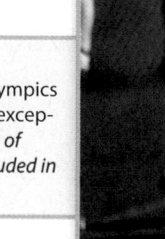

**Special Olympics**
Programs such as the Special Olympics provide great opportunities for exceptional young people. *What kinds of events do you think might be included in the Special Olympics?*

---

▶ **Explore the Photo**

**Caption Answer** Student answers will vary, but summer games might include gymnastics, judo, badminton, basketball, and cycling. Winter games might include snowboarding, alpine skiing, snowshoeing, and cross country skiing.

**Discussion** Ask students if they have ever watched any Special Olympics events, either in person or on television. Ask what they thought about the athletes and coaches. Is this something students would like to become involved with? (Answers will vary. Some students may recognize the support given and have an interest in the Special Olympics.)

## RESPOND TO SPECIAL NEEDS — Type 1 Diabetes

Mason was thirteen when he started being tired much of the time. He discovered he had type 1 diabetes. Because of his diabetes, Mason faces a number of challenges. The main one is to keep his blood sugar level as even as possible. He pricks his finger several times a day to check his blood sugar level. When Mason's body does not have enough insulin, his blood sugar level is too high. If there is too much insulin, it is too low. Either way, he must adjust the food he eats and the amount of insulin he takes. At first, Mason injected insulin into his body. Now he uses an insulin pump.

The pump places insulin into his blood stream more regularly than injections. Mason also monitors what he eats and exercises regularly. He knows all these activities are necessary to control his diabetes and live an active life.

**Critical Thinking** Conduct online research to find out at least one way in which scientists are working to find a cure for diabetes. Write a report summarizing what you learn.

### Attention Deficit Hyperactive Disorder

**ADHD**, attention deficit hyperactive disorder, is a behavioral disorder in which children often fail to finish what they start, do not seem to listen, and are easily distracted. These children may always be active and may have trouble staying in their seats. Some have a lack of emotional control. ADHD may be accompanied by learning disabilities. Parents and teachers can learn special teaching methods that may be useful for students with ADHD. Medication is often prescribed for children with ADHD. This practice, though, remains controversial. **ADD**, attention deficit disorder, is similar to ADHD, but does not involve hyperactivity.

### Speech and Language Impairments

Speech and language impairments interfere with a child's ability to communicate. A child with a speech disorder may have trouble making certain speech sounds or modulating the volume or quality of the voice. A child with a language disorder may find it difficult to understand and use words correctly. This makes it difficult for the child to express ideas or follow directions.

Some speech and language disorders are associated with hearing impairment, mental retardation, and brain injury. In many cases, though, the cause is not known. Because speech and language are so important to learning in general, it is important that children with these impairments receive help at an early age. Speech-language pathologists can work with teachers and parents to help individual children get effective therapy.

### Mental Retardation

Children with **mental retardation** have below-average intelligence and skills. This condition is also known as cognitive impairment or developmental disability. Besides problems with thinking and learning, children with mental retardation may have difficulty paying attention, remembering, communicating, and interacting with others. Levels of mental retardation range from mild to profound, or extreme. There is no cure. Mental retardation may result from a genetic disorder, brain damage, poor prenatal care, or a variety of factors. In many cases, the cause is unknown.

Down syndrome is an example of a genetic disorder resulting in varying degrees of mental retardation. Children with this condition also have distinctive physical features. Fetal alcohol syndrome is a condition that affects children born to some mothers who drank alcohol

**S** **Skill Practice**

**Guided Practice**

**Describe Difficulties** Ask students to read the paragraph under Attention Deficit Hyperactive Disorder. While they are reading, create distractions in the classroom—drop a book, drag a chair across the floor, and so on. After students have finished reading, have them write a paragraph in which they describe any difficulties they had concentrating while trying to read the paragraph. Ask students if they were able to completely tune out the noises and distractions. Were any unable to concentrate at all? Discuss with students the fact that people with ADHD tend to lack the ability to tune out distractions that other people might be able to ignore. (Paragraphs will vary but should honestly describe their feelings and level of concentration.) **L1**

**Comprehension Check** Have students skim the first paragraph on the page and write down ADHD and ADD, what the acronyms stand for, and their definitions. (ADHD, attention deficit hyperactive disorder, is a behavioral disorder in which children often fail to finish what they start, do not seem to listen, and are easily distracted. ADD, attention deficit disorder, is similar to ADHD but does not involve hyperactivity.) **L2**

**Analyze Medication** Have students research the medication Ritalin, which is commonly prescribed for children with ADHD. Ask students to analyze why a stimulant would be prescribed for someone who already appears to be over stimulated. (Ritalin "wakes up" areas of the brain that screen out distractions, which allows a child to concentrate without distractions.) **L3**

## RESPOND TO SPECIAL NEEDS — Type 1 Diabetes

**Discussion** Ask students if they know anyone with diabetes. What must they do to control the disease? Do students see this as interfering with life? (Answers will vary. Some students may know someone with diabetes and may know that they must control their eating, exercise, and blood sugar. Some students might see this as interfering with life; others might see it as making life possible.)

**Critical Thinking** Student reports will vary. Scientists are currently transplanting insulin-producing cells into living organisms in an effort to get the organisms to produce their own insulin.

### Teach *cont.*

### R₁ Reading Strategy

**Cooperative Learning** Organize students into pairs and ask them to read and discuss the four paragraphs under the heading Health Conditions. Ask students to write a quiz question, including the answer, for each of the paragraphs. You might have pairs exchange quiz questions and take the quiz prepared by the other pair. (Quiz questions will vary but should relate to the content.)

### W Writing Support

**Persuasive Essay**

**Finding Help** Tell students that there are different resources available for children with serious emotional problems. Have students gather information about one of the following resources: counselor, psychiatrist, psychoanalyst, psychologist, or social worker. Encourage students to set up a face-to-face or telephone interview to ask about the nature of the job and the help they can offer. Using the information they gather, have students write a persuasive essay to encourage the parents of a child with serious emotional problems to seek help from the resource they investigated. (Refer to p. 570 for tips on writing a persuasive essay. Students' essays will vary. Include the following criteria when evaluating students' work: Has the student made arrangements to interview sources? Has the student included enough information in his or her essay to persuade someone to use the resource?)

---

## THE DEVELOPING BRAIN

### Autistic Savants

About 10 percent of people with autism are called autistic savants. Some of these people have a compulsive, or uncontrollable, interest in some narrow activity such as the memorization of sports trivia. Others develop an amazing ability in a certain area, such as music or mathematics. One common mathematical skill among savants is known as calendar calculation. Savants with this ability can mentally calculate the day of the week that any given date fell on, or will fall on, over a span of tens of thousands of years. Scientists do not understand how the brains of autistic savants can do such things.

■ **Science Inquiry** Autistic savants often have astonishing skills in music, art, or performing mathematical calculations. However, they are not good at language skills. Why do you think this is?

---

during pregnancy. It is another disorder characterized by developmental delays, mental retardation, and physical abnormalities.

Children with mental retardation have lifelong limitations. However, with effective parenting and the right approach to their education, they can experience success. The goal is to help them become as independent as possible. Many are able to learn skills that enable them to live alone or in a group home and to earn a living.

### Health Conditions

All children get sick at times. It is often just with a cold or the flu. However, there are some children who have ongoing health conditions. These include conditions such as diabetes and asthma. These can affect their lives in major ways. Parents of children with ongoing conditions should point out that many well-known people with these challenges have led active, productive lives.

**Type 1 diabetes** is a lifelong condition caused by the body's inability to produce

---

enough insulin. Insulin is a hormone produced by the pancreas. Type 1 diabetes is also called juvenile diabetes. The lack of insulin means that the body cannot control the amount of sugar in the blood. If untreated, type 1 diabetes can result in major damage to body organs, and even death. There is no cure for diabetes. People with type 1 diabetes must take insulin for their entire lives to make up for the body's lack of the hormone. Young people with diabetes often join support groups so that they can talk with others who are managing this disease.

Asthma is a condition that results in sporadic difficulty in breathing and shortness of breath. The airways in the lungs become sore and swollen. More than 50 percent of asthma cases in the United States are caused by allergies. Other causes include irritants such as cigarette smoke, and changes in the weather. The severity of asthma varies greatly from one person to another.

Most people with asthma use a special device called an inhaler to deliver medicine directly to their lungs. This medicine helps open the airways. Some people believe that children with asthma should not participate in sports and other activities. However, with proper control, most children can fully participate in sports. Being in good physical shape also helps keep asthma under control.

### Serious Emotional Disturbances

Children with serious emotional disturbances generally have one or more of the following characteristics:
- Inability to learn that cannot be explained by other factors
- Inability to build or maintain satisfactory relationships with others
- Inappropriate behavior or feelings
- General unhappiness or depression
- Irrational fears

Troublesome emotions and behavior may have to do with a child's stage of development. In some cases, though, a child's behavior indicates a more serious problem. Some parents may deny there is a problem and hope the child outgrows it. However, if a serious problem is suspected, the child should be evaluated promptly.

---

## THE DEVELOPING BRAIN

### Autistic Savants

**Science Inquiry** Responses will vary. People with autism are not good at communicating and interacting with others, acts that typically help build language skills. Students may be interested to know that the musical and artistic skills of savants are controlled in the right hemisphere of the brain while communication skills are controlled in the left hemisphere.

For more information and activities, see *The Developing Brain* guide and eTransparencies.

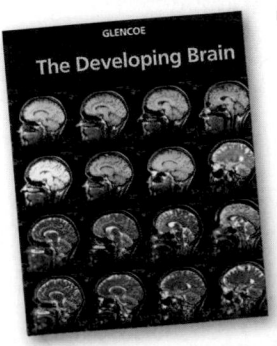

GLENCOE
The Developing Brain

Treatment options include counseling for the child, the parents, or the entire family. Psychiatrists, psychologists, family therapists, and some social workers are trained to help children with emotional difficulties and their families.

### Autism and Autism Spectrum Disorders

**Autism** is a disorder that affects a child's ability to communicate and interact with others. It is one of the most common developmental disorders. Autism affects about four times more boys than girls. It usually appears during the first three years of life.

Autism is one of a group of disorders collectively known as **autism spectrum disorders (ASD)**. Children who have one of these conditions may exhibit many of these symptoms or very few:

- Resistance to change
- Absence of empathy
- Little or no eye contact
- Repetition of words or phrases
- Repetitive movements and play
- Difficulty focusing and inability to remain attentive
- Distress without apparent cause
- Loss of skills already learned

While symptoms of autism and ASD vary widely, parents should seek help if their child does not babble or coo by 12 months, is overly attached to a single toy or object, or becomes withdrawn and unresponsive. Children who are diagnosed early and who receive appropriate therapy do better in the long run.

### Hearing and Visual Impairments

Some children with hearing impairments are totally deaf. Others are hard of hearing. This means they can hear some speech with the help of a hearing aid. Communication skills vary. Some children with hearing impairments can speak, but others cannot.

Children with visual impairments may be totally blind or may have very low vision. It can be hard for them to follow traditional classroom instruction since so much teaching is visual.

### Physical Disabilities

Physical disabilities take a wide range of forms. They may range from mild to severe involvement. Some may be present at birth. Others may develop over time or result from an injury.

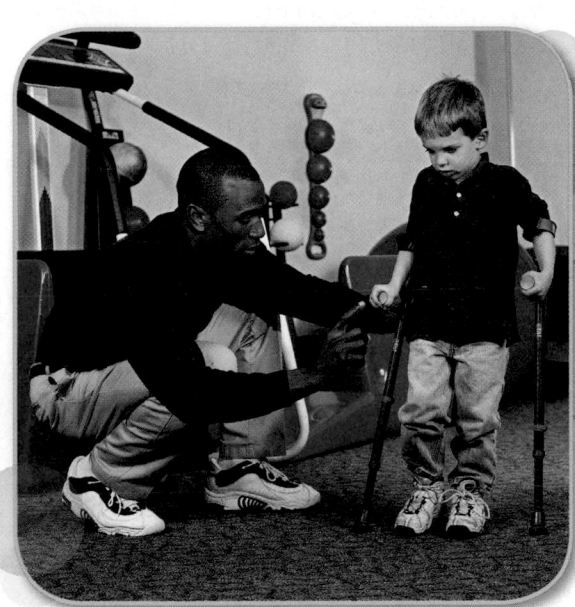

**Coping with Physical Disabilities** Children with physical disabilities often must work hard to be able to perform everyday tasks. *How might having a physical disability affect a child's social life at school?*

 **Explore the Photo**

**Caption Answer** Having a physical disability might make it difficult for the child to communicate with classmates or to engage in sports and play.

**Discussion** Ask students if they have ever been injured. Ask how it affected their daily routine. Encourage students to share their experiences with the class. (Students' experiences will vary—some may have broken bones and been unable to play sports, others may have injured their dominant hand and struggled to do simple tasks.)

## Teach *cont.*

###  Reading Strategy

**Question and Answer** Read aloud the section under the head Autism and Autism Spectrum Disorders. Ask students basic comprehension questions about what you have read. Tell students that symptoms of autism usually show up between 18 and 36 months of age. Caregivers should be aware of the symptoms so that children may be diagnosed as soon as possible. Tell students about Asperger syndrome, which is an autism spectrum disorder that severely interferes with social interactions. Many of the symptoms of Asperger syndrome are similar to the symptoms of autism but children with Asperger syndrome retain their early language skills.

 **Professional Development**

**Mini Clip Reading: Attentive Reading**

A teacher uses read aloud and direct questioning to help students identify elements of a persuasive essay.

### U Universal Access

**Kinesthetic Learners** Bring in ear plugs, ear muffs, goggles, blindfolds, very dark sunglasses, and glasses with scratched lenses. Distribute the implements at the beginning of class and have students wear them during class. At the end of class, ask students to share their feelings and frustrations at having to perform with their "impairment." Ask how this can help them understand people with hearing or visual impairments. (Answers will vary. They should be better able to appreciate what people with visual and hearing impairments face every day.)

**Quiz**

Ask students to answer the following questions:

1. What is the difference between ADHD and ADD? (ADD does not involve hyperactivity.)

2. Why should children with speech and language disorders get help at an early age? (Because speech and language are foundations to learning in general.)

3. What disorder affects a child's ability to communicate and interact with people? (autism and autism spectrum disorders)

**C₁ Critical Thinking**

**Compare** Invite a special education teacher to talk to the class about common disabilities that children experience. Suggest that the teacher talk about any special challenges that each disability brings and ways that people can support the learning and development of children with disabilities. In the follow-up discussion, have students compare and list the commonalities of people rather than the differences. You might also make arrangements for your students to visit an elementary school to read or play games with children in special education classes. (Commonalities will vary. Students may suggest that all people want to be liked and cared for or all people need others.)

---

Normal daily routines that others take for granted can be difficult or impossible for people with disabilities. Children with coordination problems may need assistance with bathing, eating, and getting ready for school. Some children with disabilities need regular physical therapy or specialized equipment. All children with physical disabilities need patient and understanding caregivers who can help them learn how to perform basic activities and enjoy greater independence.

## Education of Children with Special Needs

**C₁** The educational needs of children with disabilities vary. Some can function in a regular classroom and need no special **adaptation**, or adjustment. Others need extra attention but can be placed in a regular classroom. Those with certain disabilities require specialized education in programs designed to meet their specific needs.

Many children receive help from teachers who are specially trained to work with students with learning disabilities. A teacher might give both spoken and written directions, for example, to help children who have trouble with reading. Some students with disabilities have teacher assistants who attend class with them.

### Rights of Children with Disabilities

The Individuals with Disabilities Education Act (IDEA) is a federal law. It ensures that children with disabilities receive a free public education that meets their needs. IDEA emphasizes the need for higher academic standards. It also specifies the rights of these children and their parents. These rights include:

- Children have a right to a free public education that meets their needs.
- Parents or caregivers must be notified if a school system plans to evaluate a child or change the child's school arrangement.
- Parents have the right to request that the school evaluate a child.
- Children must be retested at least every three years and their school situation must be reviewed at least every year.
- Children can be tested in the language they know best. Parents must be spoken to in the language they know best.
- Parents can request to see the child's school records.
- The school must draw up an educational program specifically for the child. The plan is called an Individualized Education Plan, or IEP. The child and his or her parents can take part in the process of developing that plan.

**Inclusion in the Classroom**
Many children with special needs are educated in a regular classroom. *What law ensures that these children receive the education they deserve?*

---

## ►►► Explore the Photo

**Caption Answer** The Individuals with Disabilities Education Act (IDEA), which is a federal law, ensures that children with disabilities receive the education they deserve.

**Discussion** Ask the class: How does IDEA guarantee parents an active role in their child's education? (IDEA—Individuals with Disabilities Education Act—allows parents to disagree with the educational program and to have their children reevaluated.)

The law also requires schools to make every effort to practice inclusion. **Inclusion** means placing children with disabilities in regular classrooms while they also receive special education services. This is also referred to as mainstreaming. Education experts believe that inclusion benefits both children with special needs and children without those challenges. It allows them to learn together, develop empathy, and improve communication and social skills.

## Classifications of Children Served by IDEA

About 50 percent of American students served by IDEA have been classified as having a specific learning disability, such as dyslexia. Almost 20 percent have a speech or language impairment. Slightly more than 10 percent receive special education services because of mental retardation. About 8 percent have emotional disturbances.

There are also thousands of children who have autism, orthopedic impairments, and hearing and visual impairments. They represent a relatively small percentage of the students receiving special education services. Some children have multiple disabilities.

## Raising Children with Disabilities

The responsibilities and demands of raising a child with disabilities or serious health conditions can seem overwhelming. Many parents have difficulty accepting that their child has a disability. They may regret that their child will not be able to do some of the things they imagined. They may feel guilty about devoting more time and energy to the child with special needs. They might fear that they are not giving other family members the time they deserve.

## Support for Families

Support groups for parents of children with disabilities can help. Members of these groups share advice and solutions to everyday problems. Members keep each other up to date on research and treatments. They can also help parents meet their children's emotional needs.

### What Would You Do?

**Family Dilemma**

Brooke could hardly wait to tell her family that she had made the volleyball team at her middle school. Then she saw the schedule of games. At least half were on Tuesday nights, the night that her family went to diabetes support group meetings. They had been going for about five years, ever since her sister Melissa was diagnosed with diabetes at age two. Brooke did not mind the meetings. The parents and the kids were broken into separate groups and it was usually fun to go. Their family also worked to raise money for diabetes research. Their group had been the top fundraiser at the annual walk last fall. Brooke was proud of their success, but sometimes it seemed that everything revolved around Melissa's diabetes, including their mealtimes and the foods they ate. "Volleyball isn't going to be much fun if nobody can be there to watch my games," Brooke thought.

**Write About It** Imagine that you are one of Brooke's parents and she discusses this dilemma with you. How would you respond? Write a paragraph describing your response.

Children who get emotional support from their caregivers are more likely to view themselves in a positive light.

In addition to support groups, hundreds of organizations exist to help children with special needs and their families. The child's doctor can often help you find resources. Some financial aid is available for parents who meet certain income guidelines. State funds may offer money for testing and treatment for children with disabilities. Community agencies may also make funds available.

No two children, including children with the same disability, are exactly alike. Some will find it easier to learn self-care skills, such as dressing, bathing, and using toilet facilities, than others. Some may need help with just a few tasks, while others need greater assistance.

## Reteach *cont.*

### C₂ Critical Thinking

**Drawing Conclusions** Ask students the following questions: How can inclusion prepare students for the real world? (Answers will vary but may include: Inclusion will give both the students with disabilities and children without these challenges a better idea of what the real world is like. It provides both parties opportunities to interact with one another.) What do you think can make inclusion most effective? (Answers will vary. Students may suggest that cooperation from all involved will help make inclusion most effective.)

### U Universal Access

**Interpersonal Learners** Divide the class into groups. Have group members work together to brainstorm strategies that parents and caregivers might use to help children with learning disabilities learn better. Then have groups discuss the value of the techniques listed. (Techniques will vary but may include: eliminating distractions to help a child focus on a task; using time organizers, such as planners, to-do lists, schedules, and timers; using visual organizers such as a card to track reading; keeping regular, predictable routines; having a place for everything; writing everything down to help stay organized and focused.)

### What Would You Do?

**Write About It** Student responses will vary. The parent could reassure Brooke that it will be fine to miss the support group. The parents might plan to take turns going to the volleyball games and the diabetes support group meetings, so one parent is always there for both girls.

**Professional Development**

**Mini Clip Reading: Extending the Big Idea**

A teacher assigns group collaborations and consensus building to promote student discussions about a reading selection.

## Reteach cont.

## C Critical Thinking

**Problem Solving** Present this case study to students: Christine just found out that her two-year-old son Gabriel is autistic. She worries that she won't be able to help him enough and that his caregivers will ignore him because of the difficulty in communicating with him. Ask students what they would suggest to Christine about coping with her worries and ensuring that Gabriel gets adequate help. (Suggestions may include: Christine should seek out support groups in her area for help and advice on raising Gabriel.)

## W Writing Support

### Reporting Information

**Identifying Gifted Children**
Discuss with students the value of identifying gifted children early. Have students find out how local schools identify gifted children and what programs the schools in your district offer. In addition, have students investigate other available programs and resources for gifted children, especially through schools, universities, national organizations, and private institutions. Have students write a one-page report to present their findings. (Information in students' reports will vary but should cover the items listed above. Reports should be one page in length and contain paragraphs that include topic sentences and supporting details. Reports should be free of grammar and spelling errors.)

✓ **Reading Check**

**Explain** IDEA provides parents with a number of guarantees including the right to have their child evaluated, to see their child's school records, and to take part in developing the child's educational program.

---

C Parenting a child with disabilities is just as rewarding and important as parenting any other child. A child with special needs still wants and needs love and support from his parents. Many children with special needs will grow up to be successful, independent adults. These children often just need extra patience. Parents and caregivers who know what they can reasonably expect of a child with disabilities at different ages and stages are more likely to see the child reach his or her full potential.

✓ **Reading Check** **Explain** How does IDEA guarantee parents an active role in their child's education?

## Gifted Children

**Gifted** children show, or have the potential to show, special abilities in one or more areas. Gifted children may present challenges for parents, teachers, and other caregivers. Sometimes it can be difficult to keep them motivated and help them reach their potential. They may find school boring or their talents may be in areas not taught in the classroom.

They might, for example, have a special talent for music, art, mathematics, or language. For a child gifted in mathematics, English or social studies may not be very interesting. Some gifted children are highly creative. They may have the potential to invent new technologies or develop new ways of solving problems.

W

## Parenting Skills

### Guiding Gifted Children

Gifted children sometimes become bored with schoolwork. Some gifted children will lose their motivation and stop trying to excel. Here are some tips that parents and caregivers can use to help gifted children reach their potential and still have a happy childhood.

- **Provide learning opportunities in and out of school.** If the school has a program for gifted children, find out how to enroll your child. Expose your child to opportunities outside of school as well. If he or she is interested in history, plan trips to museums. Look for classes or camps that might interest your child.

- **Do not overload the child.** When planning extracurricular activities, make sure you still allow for downtime. Children need free time to play, read, relieve stress, and to process what they have learned.

- **Teach the child social skills.** Gifted children often dislike being labeled. They will sometimes "play dumb" to fit in better with their peers. Teaching them social skills can help them to have more positive experiences and still be themselves.

- **Love the child unconditionally.** All children need to know that they are loved and accepted for who they are rather than what they accomplish. Encourage the child to pursue his or her interests but do not force your desires on the child.

**Take Charge** Suppose a friend told you that their gifted child had become withdrawn and was suddenly getting poor grades in school. Write a letter to your friend with suggestions on how to help motivate her child.

---

## Parenting Skills

### Guiding Gifted Children

Share with students these additional tips for parenting gifted students: make sure they get the educational challenge they need; don't coddle them or let them be lazy; be sure they have an opportunity to be with other gifted students; make sure they have social experiences to use their social skills.

**Take Charge**
Students' answers will vary, but letters should discuss some or all of the following: provide learning opportunities in and out of school, do not overload the child, teach the child social skills, love the child unconditionally.

## Identify Gifted Children

It is not always easy to identify gifted children. Children who talk and read early, have large vocabularies, and retain information about what they read or observe may be classified as gifted. Such traits do not always show up in gifted individuals, however. Many gifted people even develop language abilities fairly late.

On the other hand, some gifted children can be identified very early in life. They may learn to walk and talk early. Some display advanced skills in writing, coloring, or building. As they grow older, they often have wide-ranging interests and prefer to interact with adults rather than with other children. They might show awareness of serious issues such as world hunger.

Despite their special ability, not all gifted children are high achievers. Some do not have the patience to complete tasks that seem unimportant to them. They may be bored in the classroom, in part because they may be able to perform two or three grades above their actual grade level. They may question classroom procedures or give unexpected answers to questions.

## Special Programs

In school districts that offer programs for gifted children, students may be tested to determine if they qualify. These tests sometimes fail to identify all gifted children, however. This is especially true of those who do not perform well in class or who have limited language abilities.

Some gifted students feel isolated and misunderstood. While they benefit from playing with a variety of children, they also need time with other gifted learners. They need stimulation and challenges so that they can make the most of their abilities. They also need to be accepted and to feel good about what makes them different. They need to be valued for themselves, not just for their special abilities.

## Section 21.2 After You Read

### Review Key Concepts

1. **Describe** how the policy of inclusion benefits both children with disabilities and children without them.

2. **Compare** how the challenges faced by gifted children are similar to those faced by children with disabilities.

### Practice Academic Skills

 **English Language Arts**

3. Many books and magazine articles have been written about individual autistic savants. Locate one and read it. Write a short essay describing this person's unusual ability to someone who has never heard of the term *autistic savant*.

> **NCTE 2** Read literature to build an understanding of the human experience.

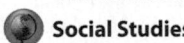 **Social Studies**

4. Follow your teacher's instructions to form into groups. Imagine you are in the fifth grade and have a new classmate who is either blind or deaf. Write and prepare a skit demonstrating what you could do to make the new classmate feel welcome in your class.

> **NCSS IV H** Work independently and cooperatively within groups and institutions to accomplish goals.

 **Check Your Answers** Check your answers at this book's Online Learning Center at **glencoe.com**.

**NCLB**

Section 21.2 Children with Special Needs **589**

## Assess

### Study Tools

Have students go to the Online Learning Center at **glencoe.com**:

- Take the **Practice Test**.
- Download **Study-to-Go** content.

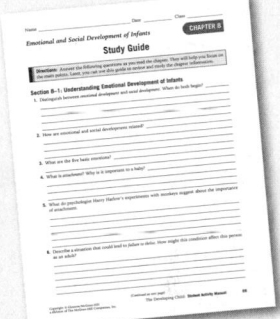

Use the **Student Activity Workbook** for additional practice.

## Close

### Culminating Activity

**Summarize** Have students create a chart that lists special needs and how parents, caregivers, and teachers can meet those needs. (Charts will vary but should show that students have an understanding of special needs and how those needs can be met.)

**NCLB** connects academic correlations to book content.

---

## Section 21.2 After You Read

### Review Key Concepts

1. It allows children with disabilities to learn in a more normal setting than if they are separated from other children and helps them improve their communication and social skills. It helps children without disabilities to develop empathy for others.

2. Both may face difficulties in traditional classrooms, feel isolated and misunderstood, and may require special programs to reach their fullest potential.

### Practice Academic Skills

3. Students should have written a short essay based on a book or article about an autistic savant. The report should discuss the unusual ability the person possesses.

4. Skits will vary but should demonstrate how to help a new student who was either blind or deaf feel included in the class.

**589**

# Focus

## Bell Ringer Activity

### Understanding Abuse

Ask students what they think child abuse includes. (physical abuse, neglect, sexual abuse, and emotional and verbal abuse) Ask students why they think child abuse occurs. (Answers may include: immature parents who do not understand child development, substance abuse, mental illness, or unemployment.)

## Preteaching

### Vocabulary

Have students note the two different suffixes on the terms *addiction counselor* and *mandated reporter*. One ends with the suffix *-or* and the other ends with the suffix *-er*. Tell students that both suffixes mean the same thing—one who does something.

### Graphic Organizer

 The Graphic Organizer is also on the TeacherWorks CD.

(Graphic organizers should include: sees child as bad or worthless, makes frequent demands child cannot achieve, asks teachers to use physical discipline, denies child has problems, sees child as burden, and rarely looks at child.)

 **NCLB** connects academic correlations to book content.

## Reading Guide

### Before You Read

**Prepare with a Partner** Work with a partner to ask each other questions and then answer them about the topics that will be discussed in this section.

### Read to Learn
**Key Concepts**
- **Identify** four major types of maltreatment.
- **Summarize** common reasons behind abuse and maltreatment.
- **Explain** what can be done to prevent child abuse.

**D**

### Main Idea
Adults must watch for children who are suffering from maltreatment, such as neglect or physical abuse. Abused children can be helped by improving family communication and providing a safe place to express feelings.

### Content Vocabulary
◇ addiction counselor
◇ mandated reporter
◇ crisis nursery

 **Graphic Organizer** Go to this book's Online Learning Center at **glencoe.com** to print out this graphic organizer.

### Academic Vocabulary
You will find these words in your reading and on your tests. Use the glossary to look up their definitions if necessary.
- constructive
- terminate

### Graphic Organizer
As you read this section, look for six behaviors that may be seen in adults who are mistreating children. Use a tree diagram like the one shown to help organize your information.

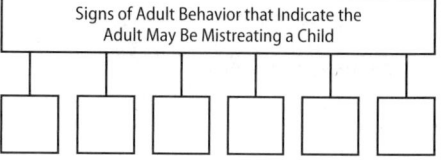

### Academic Standards . . . . . . . . . . . . . . . . .

**NCLB**

**English Language Arts**
**NCTE 5** Use different writing process elements to communicate effectively.

**Social Studies**
**NCSS IV I Individual Development and Identity.** Examine factors that contribute to and damage one's mental health and analyze issues related to mental health and behavioral disorders in contemporary society.

**NCTE** National Council of Teachers of English
**NCTM** National Council of Teachers of Mathematics
**NSES** National Science Education Standards
**NCSS** National Council for the Social Studies

## Reading Guide

### Before You Read

Ask students to give examples of cause and effect in child abuse. For example, if a child is physically abused, he or she may grow up to physically abuse his or her children. Or if a child is neglected, he or she may be sick frequently.

### **D** Develop Concepts

**Main Idea** Discuss the main idea with the students. Ask students how they think adults can tell a child is being abused. (Answers may include: absence from school, steal food or money, many bruises or broken bones, or lack of appropriate clothing for the weather.)

# Maltreatment

Hundreds of thousands of children become the victims of child abuse and neglect each year, often at the hands of their parents. Most victims, however, never come to the attention of authorities. Their abusers may have threatened them with harm if they tell anyone. Victims also may feel intense guilt for things that are not their fault. Emotional and physical scars can last well into adulthood. These scars can affect the overall health of former victims, as well as their future relationships with others.

## Forms of Maltreatment

The federal Child Abuse Prevention and Treatment Act (CAPTA) defines maltreatment, and so does each state. Generally speaking, the government recognizes four major types of maltreatment:

**R**

- **Physical Abuse** This means intentionally causing an injury to a child. This includes hitting, burning, shaking, or otherwise harming a child.
- **Neglect** Both physical and emotional neglect are possible. Neglect means failing to provide for a child's basic needs, including food, water, a place to live, love, and attention.

- **Sexual Abuse** This category includes any inappropriate sexual behavior with a child, including touching or taking photographs.
- **Emotional and Verbal Abuse** This means rejecting children, blaming them, or constantly scolding them, particularly for problems beyond their control.

Death is the most tragic consequence of maltreatment. More than 1,000 children die in the United States each year because of abuse or neglect. More than half of all victims of child maltreatment are victims of neglect. Neglected children may fail to develop mentally and physically at the same rate as their peers.

**R**

Physically abused children may bear physical scars or become permanently disabled. All abused children suffer emotionally. They often feel lonely, unloved, guilty, and unworthy of care and attention. These feelings may last and cause problems in adult relationships.

## Signs and Symptoms

When abuse or neglect occurs, there are usually signs in both children and adults. Neglected children are often absent from school, steal food or money, have poor personal hygiene, and lack protective clothing for wet or cold weather.

**Risk of Abuse**
Children who are abused often feel unloved and lonely. *Why might some children be more at risk for abuse than others?*

Section 21.3　Child Abuse and Neglect　**591**

## Explore the Photo

**Caption Answer** Children with physical or mental disabilities are more likely to be abused. Younger children are more often neglected. Girls are more often the victims of sexual abuse.

**Discussion** Stress with students that it is *never* the victim's fault that abuse occurs. Ask volunteers to explain why abuse is not the victim's fault. (Answers may include that the parents or caregivers are responsible for the child's well-being. Also, a child has little control over what an adult might do.)

## Teach

### Discussion Starter

**Children and Maltreatment** Ask students to consider how maltreatment of children can go unreported or unnoticed. Focus students' attention on the sentence "Their abusers may have threatened them with harm if they tell anyone." Have students imagine that they are a seven-year-old child who is being maltreated and threatened. Ask volunteers to describe what the child might be feeling. (Answers will vary. Students may suggest hopelessness, fear, anger, or frustration.)

### **R** Reading Strategy

**Critical Reading** Have students read the passage under Types of Maltreatment. Tell students that parents can help children understand the difference between keeping secrets and helping a friend. Have students determine which of the following secrets should be shared with an adult: Vicki is afraid her father will get mad because she failed a test; James does not want to go home because he will be alone all night without parental supervision; Alejandro was angry with his mother, who often calls him names and hits him; Lila does not want her uncle to stay at her house because he touches her inappropriately. (Students should realize that all of the instances, with the exception of Vicki, should be reported because the safety and welfare of the child may be at stake.)

**Professional Development**

**Mini Clip**
ELL: Group Discussions

Students discuss academic content they have just read.

## Teach cont.

### S Skill Practice

**Guided Practice**

**List Suggestions** Have students work in pairs to create lists of suggestions of ways families can redirect anger before it becomes abusive. Suggestions might include exercising or taking some alone time. Pairs of students should create a poster with suggestions and illustrations. (Posters will vary but should illustrate suggestions for redirecting anger.) **L1** **ELL**

**Recognize Assumptions** Tell students that adults can have unrealistic expectations for children, such as acting older than their age. Sometimes these expectations can lead to maltreatment. Have students write a short essay in which they discuss how unreasonable expectations may lead to maltreatment. (Essays will vary. Students may mention that parents often expect babies not to cry, which is an unrealistic expectation. However, a parent who is stressed and cannot make the baby stop crying may harm the child in an attempt to make it be quiet.) **L2**

**Compile Data** Have students contact workers at elementary schools such as principals, teachers, office personnel, or grounds-keepers—and ask how they are trained to spot possible maltreatment among the children. Students should prepare questions in advance and write complete answers. As a class, compile the information students accumulate. (Information may vary but should include signs and symptoms of maltreatment.) **L3**

### ✓ Reading Check

**Recall** failing to provide for a child's basic needs, either emotionally or physically

---

### Figure 21.3 Signs of Maltreatment

Adults such as caregivers and teachers must watch children for these signs of mistreatment. *Can you think of any other signs that a child may be mistreated?*

| Signs that children may be receiving mistreatment: | Signs that adults may be mistreating children: |
| --- | --- |
| ❖ Learning problems that cannot be explained<br>❖ No adult supervision<br>❖ Withdrawal from others<br>❖ No desire to go home after school or other activities<br>❖ Fearfulness, as though waiting for something bad to happen<br>❖ Changes in school performance or behavior<br>❖ Untreated medical conditions | ❖ Sees the child as bad or worthless<br>❖ Makes frequent demands that the child cannot achieve<br>❖ Asks teachers to use physical discipline if the child misbehaves<br>❖ Denies child's problems in school or at home<br>❖ Sees the child as a burden<br>❖ Rarely looks at the child<br>❖ Over-protective and demands secrecy (in cases of sexual abuse) |

Physically abused children may have bruises, broken bones, or burn marks that cannot be explained. This is not always the case, though. Not all physical abuse leaves marks on visible parts of the child's body, such as the face or arms. Some abusers intentionally leave no marks when they hurt children. **Figure 21.3** lists more signs of mistreatment in children and adults.

### Consequences

Regardless of the type of abuse a child suffers, there are always consequences to these actions. Children who are sexually abused sometimes run away from home, refuse to participate in physical activities, and exhibit sexual knowledge beyond their normal level of development.

Emotionally abused children often show aggression. They may act inappropriately like an adult (bossing other children), or like a very young child (rocking back and forth).

### ✓ Reading Check · Recall What is meant by the term *neglect*?

### Why Does Abuse Occur?

Children are never responsible for the abuse or harm that others inflict on them. Some children, however, are more at risk of maltreatment than others. Children with physical and mental disabilities are more likely to be abused. Younger children are neglected more often, and they are more likely to die of maltreatment. When children are sexually abused, the abuse most often begins before age seven. Girls are more often the victims of sexual abuse than boys.

Immature mothers who have children at a young age are more likely to abuse children. So are people who live in poverty and have fewer resources to help with child care or other responsibilities. Child abusers may be socially isolated or stressed due to unemployment. However, abuse can occur in households of any income or education level, ethnicity, or religious background. In families with domestic violence, where one parent abuses the other, children are more likely to be hurt as well.

Abusive parents often do not know enough about child development to have reasonable

**S**

---

### Figure 21.3 Signs of Maltreatment

**Caption Answer** Answers will vary. They might expand on signs given, such as noting specific mood or behavior changes. A calm child may become aggressive or an aggressive child may become subdued.

**Discussion** Have students use information from Figure 21.3 to create a pamphlet for caregivers. In addition to signs that children are being mistreated and signs that adults may be mistreating children, pamphlets should include a true/false quiz about signs of maltreatment. Students might distribute the pamphlets to preschools and child care centers in your area.

## What Would You Do?

### Healing Past Abuse

Miranda is eleven years old. She was nine when she started going to counseling with Dr. Mitchell, a psychologist. She had been abused by her mother from ages six to eight, at which time she went to live with her aunt. She was suffering from anxiety, feelings of guilt, and sleeping problems. Dr. Mitchell helped Miranda recognize that adults, not children, are responsible for healthy parent-child interactions. This helped ease Miranda's feelings of guilt about the abuse. Dr. Mitchell taught Miranda some ways to cope with her sad feelings and established a plan to help her deal with her feelings of anxiety. This plan includes having supportive people to whom she can turn when she feels insecure.

✎ **Write About It** Imagine that you are Miranda's aunt, with whom she is now living. What would you do to help Miranda cope with her past abuse? Write a list of at least five steps you would take.

**S**

expectations. Some expect even very young children to obey them promptly or remember rules given earlier. If abusers get help, they can learn what to expect from children of various ages and how to nurture them.

**C**

Studies have shown that a large percentage of child maltreatment cases involve substance abuse. When parents become dependent on alcohol and other drugs, they neglect their children's needs. Substance abusers are often emotionally unavailable and can be violent due to the effects of drugs. They might buy drugs with money that should have been spent on food and other basics for their children.

Many problems, such as mental illness, depression, unemployment, and high stress levels, can go along with substance abuse. So many maltreatment cases involve substance abuse that social service agencies are working hard to manage these cases better. A therapist trained to help substance abusers is called an

---

**addiction counselor**. Addiction counselors are trained to help abusive parents who are also addicted to drugs or alcohol.

*those who were abused themselves as children*

### Who Abuses Children?

An adult in the home is most often to blame for physical abuse. Statistics indicate that mothers abuse children more often than fathers do. In sexual abuse cases, however, it is most often not a parent, but a relative or a family friend who harms the child, .

People who abuse children often have difficulty controlling their impulses. While many parents feel frustrated when a child is crying or whining, people who abuse children often act without thinking. Abusers often feel depressed, extremely anxious, or overwhelmed. In many cases, they were abused themselves as children and they do not know how to discipline children in a **constructive**, or positive, way. Abuse may come from only one parent. The other parent may deny that it is happening. Sometimes, only one child in a family is targeted for abuse.

✓ **Reading Check** **Describe** What are possible emotional traits of people who abuse children?

### Stop Maltreatment

Abuse happens for many reasons. Preventing abuse requires changing the situations in which abuse occurs. Sometimes a parent is too young or immature to handle the challenges of parenthood. Encouraging young people to wait until they are older and more financially stable is important. Parenting classes can help people learn skills for raising children. This helps them avoid feeling overwhelmed. Support groups help stressed parents discuss their emotions and share solutions.

Abusing or neglecting children in any way is illegal. People who work with children, including teachers, doctors, nurses, and counselors, are required by law to report maltreatment if they see evidence of it. A person who is required by law to report maltreatment is called a **mandated reporter**. While others may not have a legal obligation to report abuse, they

Section 21.3  Child Abuse and Neglect  **593**

---

✓ **Reading Check**

**Describe** Emotional traits include people who have difficulty controlling their impulses and who are depressed, extremely anxious, or feeling overwhelmed.

## What Would You Do?

**Write About It** Lists will vary but might include reminding Miranda that she is now safe, continuing to tell her that only her mother was responsible for her abuse, and so on.

---

## Section 21.3

### Assess

**Quiz**

Ask students to answer the following questions:

1. **What are some signs that children are being neglected?** (They may be absent from school often, steal food or money, have poor personal hygiene, or lack protective clothing for wet or cold weather.)
2. **What are some possible causes for abuse?** (Abusers may feel depressed, anxious, or overwhelmed; may have been abused themselves as children; may not know how to discipline children constructively.)
3. **How can learning about child development help abusive parents?** (They can learn realistic expectations for each stage of development.)

### Reteach

**C** **Critical Thinking**

**Plan a Strategy** Present this scenario to the class: A mother drinks too much several times a week. On those nights, she yells at her children more than she would like. How might the family confront her about her problem? What issues should be discussed? What might the outcomes be? Have students work in small groups to write skits that answer these questions. Have volunteers from each group act out the skits in as realistic fashion as possible. (Skits will vary but should show realistic conversations between concerned family members and the mother. Suggestions for getting help should be included as well as possible outcomes.)

**593**

## Reteach *cont.*

### W Writing Support

**Persuasive Essay**

**Getting Help** Tell students to imagine that a friend who has an 11-month-old son tells you that sometimes she cannot take his crying and is worried she will do something she regrets. What would students say and do to prevent child abuse? Students should write a brief persuasive essay in which they discuss the importance of being informed about crisis intervention services. Essays should clearly state the writer's position and use facts to back up the position. (Refer to p. 570 for tips on writing a persuasive essay. Essays will vary but should contain suggestions for knowing when and where to find help so that abuse can be avoided. To evaluate essays, consider these questions: Is the writer's position stated clearly? Does the writing include benefits or reasons to back up the position?)

### R Reading Strategy

**Supporting Details** Tell students that in the United States each year three million children are reported abused—one report every ten seconds—and more than three children a day die because of child abuse. Ask students to locate and read a news article about a program to combat child abuse such as the establishment of crisis nurseries. Have students summarize the article in a paragraph in which they include details that support their main theme. (Paragraphs will vary but should discuss a program to combat child abuse and contain details that support the main theme.)

should contact child protective services agencies as soon as they suspect it.

Every state has a child welfare agency. When an agency hears a report of possible child abuse, it sends someone to investigate. If the child is thought to be in danger, the court may place the child in a foster home. If there is a history of abuse, or if the child has severe injuries, parents may be arrested and charged with crimes. Ultimately, the court may **terminate**, or end, their parental rights and their children may never live with them again.

Putting abusers in prison gives children temporary protection but does not solve the problem. In most cases, abusers receive treatment and counseling to understand the reasons for the abuse and to end it.

Most abusive parents must learn how to care for their children and treat them in loving ways. Several programs are available to help. Members of Parents Anonymous, one of the best-known groups, support each other as they work to change their behavior.

A community may have a crisis nursery. A **crisis nursery** is a child care facility where troubled parents can go to receive short-term, free child care. Many crisis nurseries are open 24 hours a day and provide children with a safe environment. Using a crisis nursery gives parents a chance to cool off and cope with their frustrations, anger, and problems without hurting their children. These facilities often also provide parenting classes, counseling, and job training.

## Treatment for Abused Children

Children who have been abused are usually treated through counseling sessions with mental health professionals who have experience with victimized children. Counseling involves helping people make sense of their feelings and behavior, and improving interactions with others. Counselors who work with abused children have many goals, including:

- Protecting children from further harm.
- Improving family communication.
- Encouraging healthy friendships between children and their peers.

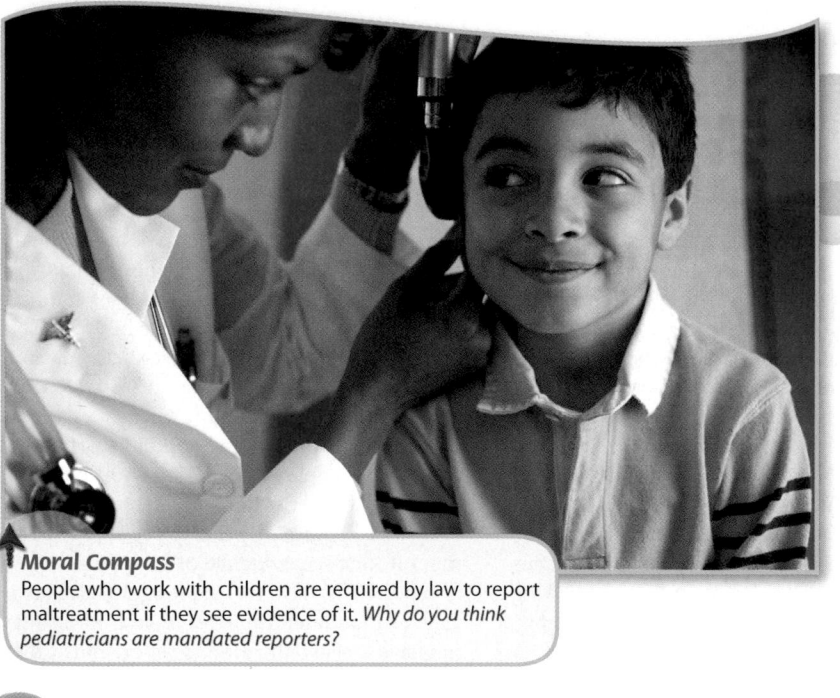

**Moral Compass**

People who work with children are required by law to report maltreatment if they see evidence of it. *Why do you think pediatricians are mandated reporters?*

### ▶ Explore the Photo

**Caption Answer** Answers will vary. Pediatricians see children regularly and are responsible for the well-being of children.

**Discussion** Ask the class: Do you think teachers should be held accountable if they do not notice and report suspected child abuse? Why or why not? (Answers will vary, but students should provide reasons and examples for why they think they way they do.)

- Teaching mistreated children to take care of themselves and to make choices that help keep them safe.
- Helping children have realistic expectations of parents who have problems.
- Providing a safe place to express anger, disappointment, and sadness.

Counseling may take many forms. It should always be appropriate for the child's age. Many counselors use techniques that let young children express their feelings about abuse through play.

Each affected person, including the victimized child, the abusers, and other family members, may be involved in individual counseling. Treatment may involve just the child and the nonabusive parent. It also may involve the whole family, with the goal of bringing everyone back together. The abuser must acknowledge responsibility for the abuse and make a commitment to change before the family can be reunited.

Counselors often agree not to tell parents anything without telling the child first. This allows children to feel free to talk to their counselors about anything that worries them. Counselors cannot, however, keep secrets regarding the child's safety from the parents. Counselors will not tell anyone outside the family about what happens in sessions unless the child is in danger or the family requests a release of information.

Many family problems are related to poor parenting skills and lack of knowledge about child development. Classes like the one you are taking give parents and future parents more realistic expectations about children and what it takes to care for them properly. With education, as well as more knowledge about support resources, maltreatment can be prevented. Remember that all parents have to learn parenting skills. A little education and a lot of love can lead to a happy family.

### Study Tools

Have students go to the Online Learning Center at **glencoe.com**:
- Take the **Practice Test**.
- Download **Study-to-Go** content.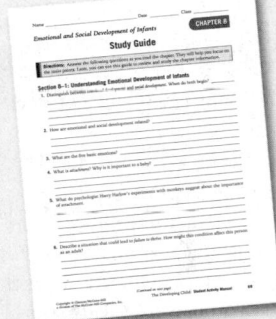

Use the **Student Activity Workbook** for additional practice.

---

## Section 21.3   After You Read

### Review Key Concepts

1. **List** five possible signs of abuse in children.
2. **Explain** how substance abuse and child abuse are linked.
3. **Identify** the responsibilities of mandated reporters.

### Practice Academic Skills

 **English Language Skills**

4. Communities have different resources to assist children who are being maltreated. Research local organizations in your area, how to contact them, and what services they offer. Create a brochure that shows the options available to victims of maltreatment and their families.

> **NCTE 5** Use different writing process elements to communicate effectively.

 **Social Studies**

5. A National Institute of Justice study showed that maltreated children are more likely to commit violent crimes as adults. Identify one research study supporting this link and one countering it. Write a report analyzing the studies. Explain which one you think is more persuasive.

> **NCSS IV I** Examine factors that contribute to and damage one's mental health and analyze issue related to mental health and behavioral disorders in contemporary society.

 **Check Your Answers** Check your answers at this book's Online Learning Center at **glencoe.com**.

**NCLB**

Section 21.3   Child Abuse and Neglect   **595**

## Close

### Culminating Activity

**List** Have students make a poster that informs abused children of where they can go for help. The contact information should be for your local area. (Posters and information will vary depending on the area in which you live.)

 **NCLB** connects academic correlations to book content.

---

**Section 21.3** After You Read

**Review Key Concepts**

1. Answers may include any five: frequent absences from school, stealing food or money, poor personal hygiene, lack of proper clothing, learning problems that cannot be explained, lack of adult supervision, withdrawal from others, no desire to go home after school, fearfulness, and changes in school performance or behavior.

2. When parents abuse drugs or alcohol, they typically neglect their children's needs, are emotionally unavailable, and may use money for drugs rather than food and other basic items.

3. Mandated reporters are required by law to report evidence of maltreatment of children.

**Practice Academic Skills**

4. Brochures will vary based on community resources. Students should have researched how to contact the organizations and what services they offer.

5. Reports will vary but should offer details as to why they think one report is more persuasive than the other.

## Focus

### Discussion Starter

**Experiencing Camp** Ask students if they ever went to camp as a child—either a day camp at a local park or a week-long camp away from home. Ask if they felt it was a positive experience. Why? (Answers will vary. Students should share their feelings about their camp experiences.)

## Teach

### **C** Critical Thinking

**Compare and Contrast** Have students create a Venn diagram to compare the responsibilities of a day camp counselor and a week-long camp counselor. Students should write the duties exclusive to the day camp counselor in one oval and the duties exclusive to the week-long camp counselor in the other oval. Where the ovals overlap, they should list duties that are common to both. (There will be more similarities than differences; week-long camp counselors would have to spend the night at camp.)

## Assess

### Make Connections

Ask students to list specific correlations between academic subjects and the kinds of skills a camp counselor needs. (Answers will vary. Students should show an understanding of how academic skills relate directly to the job of camp counselor. For example, being skilled in math would be necessary to be a counselor at a math camp.)

**NCLB** This relates academic skills to specific tasks that are performed for this job.

---

Careers
With Children     **Camp Counselor**

**C**amps provide experiences that children may not be able to have in their hometowns. There are many different types of camps. There are day camps, week-long camps, and summer camps. Camp counselors are responsible for the health, safety, and well-being of these campers. They help with home-sickness as well as minor injuries.

### ☼ What Does a Camp Counselor Do?

Camp counselors make sure that campers are safe and have a successful camp experience. A camp counselor may teach horseback riding, lead singing sessions, and toast marshmallows by a fire. They are expected to set a good example, deal with any difficulties that arise, and enforce camp rules.

### ☼ Where Do Camp Counselors Work?

Some of the different kinds of camps include day camps, overnight camps, religious camps, and camps that serve children with special needs. Many camps are geared toward learning specific sports skills, such as soccer. Some are even aimed at academic skills, such as space camp or computer camp.

### Preparation and Skills

**Education and Training**
Being a camp counselor generally requires someone who is enthusiastic, relates well to children, and understands nature. Some camps may require specific training, licenses, affiliations, or accreditations.

**Aptitudes, Abilities, and Skills**
Good camp counselors should model good behavior. They need patience and humor, as well as knowledge of the principles of health, safety, and nutrition. Counselors should be able to react to unexpected situations.

**Academic Skills**
Camp counselors will use English language arts skills to communicate with and teach children. Specialized camps may require counselors to have specific academic skills.

**N C L B**

**Explore Careers**

Think of a skill you have, such as playing baseball or making pottery. Conduct research to learn about a camp where your skill would be useful. Write a paragraph discussing whether you think you would enjoy being a counselor there.

 **Careers Online** For more information on careers, visit the Occupational Outlook Handbook Web site through the link on this book's Online Learning Center at **glencoe.com**.

---

## Close

### Culminating Activity

**Becoming a Camp Counselor** Have students create a cover letter and résumé for a job as a camp counselor. In the letter, they should describe the kind of camp they would like to work at (day camp, soccer camp, week-long camp, religious camp, and so on) and their specific skills that would make them a good counselor. Résumés should include their strengths and experiences that will help them be good counselors.

**Explore Careers**

Answers will vary. Students should have conducted research to learn about a camp that could make use of one of the student's skills. Students should discuss whether they think they would enjoy being a counselor at the camp.

## Chapter Summary

Most families face difficult situations at times. Children should be told about problems honestly and in a way suited to their age. Some children respond to difficulties by showing signs of stress. When this occurs, children need extra support. Physical, learning, and emotional disabilities can affect children. Early diagnosis and treatment help children with disabilities reach their potential. Federal law requires that public schools meet the needs of children with disabilities. There are four major types of maltreatment. Treatment and counseling can help abusive parents learn to stop patterns of abuse.

## Vocabulary Review

**1.** Write your own definition for each content and academic vocabulary term.

### Content Vocabulary
◇ regression (p. 573)
◇ situational stress (p. 573)
◇ addiction (p. 576)
◇ support group (p. 577)
◇ learning disability (p. 582)
◇ dyslexia (p. 582)
◇ ADHD (p. 583)
◇ ADD (p. 583)
◇ mental retardation (p. 583)
◇ type 1 diabetes (p. 584)
◇ autism (p. 585)
◇ autism spectrum disorder (ASD) (p. 585)
◇ inclusion (p. 587)
◇ gifted (p. 588)
◇ addiction counselor (p. 593)
◇ mandated reporter (p. 593)
◇ crisis nursery (p. 594)

### Academic Vocabulary
■ vulnerable (p. 573)
■ irrational (p. 578)
■ distinguish (p. 582)
■ adaptation (p. 586)
■ constructive (p. 593)
■ terminate (p. 594)

## Review Key Concepts

**2. Describe** how parents can help children cope with stress.
**3. List** eight possible causes of stress in children.
**4. Identify** nine categories of disabilities.
**5. Describe** some of the traits exhibited by gifted children.
**6. Identify** four major types of maltreatment.
**7. Summarize** common reasons behind abuse and maltreatment.
**8. Explain** what can be done to prevent child abuse.

## Critical Thinking

**9. Apply** Imagine that a family moved in next door to you. If you learned the parents were newly divorced, what could you do to help the children, ages seven and ten, adjust to their new situation?
**10. Infer** Why do you think many families do not consider seeking outside help when they are dealing with a problem?

### Content and Academic Vocabulary Review

**1.** Students should write an accurate definition for each term in their own words.

### Review Key Concepts

**2.** Parents should listen and accept the child's feelings of anger, grief, and sadness.

**3.** school, crime, moving, money, divorce, substance abuse, illness, and death

**4.** Categories include learning disabilities, attention deficit hyperactive disorder, speech and language impairments, mental retardation, health conditions, serious emotional disturbances, autism and autism spectrum disorders, hearing and visual impairments, and physical disabilities.

**5.** Traits include talking and walking early, a large vocabulary for their age, and advanced skills in areas such as writing, coloring, or building.

**6.** physical abuse, neglect, sexual abuse, and emotional and verbal abuse

**7.** Reasons include immature parents, living in poverty with few resources for child care, social isolation, and stress due to unemployment.

**8.** Report suspected abuse to the appropriate agency, have child welfare agencies promptly investigate all reports, have abusive parents involved in programs such as Parent Anonymous, and have a crisis nursery to give parents a break.

## Critical Thinking

**9.** Answers will vary. Students might offer to play with the children or invite them to a game or other activity. Giving the children attention and a friendly ear might help ease their stress.

**10.** Student responses will vary. Many families may feel that the problems are personal. Some people think admitting the need for help shows weakness.

## Family & Community Connections

**11.** Students should have interviewed someone from a community organization that provides services for families and prepared a speech summarizing the organization's services.

## Health Skills

**12.** Posters should explain that the person is required by law to report any suspected abuse and should watch for signs such as withdrawal, bruises, fearfulness, and changes in behavior.

## Observation Skills

**13.** Students should spend time observing a teen with a physical disability and write one or two paragraphs summarizing how the teen deals with any challenges caused by the disability.

## Real-Word Skills

**14.** Students scenarios will vary, but should discuss their concerns with the child's parent. An appropriate approach would be to present the facts, such as "Yesterday, when I spoke to Jeremy, he did not even turn his head, even though he was only ten feet away."

**15.** Newsletters will vary. Students should have developed a creative list of activities appropriate for gifted students.

**16.** Costs of camps will vary, but generally a specialized camp will provide more services, and therefore cost more.

 **NCLB** Activity correlated to Social Studies standards.

## Family & Community Connection

**11. Supporting Families** Find out about an organization in your community that provides support for families having difficulties. It may be a crisis nursery, a faith-based organization that provides temporary housing, or something similar. Interview someone from the organization on the services provided. Prepare a speech to share the information you learn about the organization's services.

## Health Skills

**12. Mandated Reporters** Talk with an individual, such as a teacher or counselor, who is a mandated reporter. Ask them to explain the duties of a mandated reporter. Also ask what they watch for when trying to spot abuse. Use what you learn to create a poster describing the duties of mandated reporters.

## Observation Skills

**13. Dealing with Disabilities** Having a physical disability teaches resourcefulness. Disabled people must come up with solutions to performing tasks that others take for granted. For example, a deaf student may need to sit in the front of a classroom.

**Procedure** Ask a teen with a physical disability if you could spend several hours with him or her. Observe how this person adapts everyday activities to cope with the disability.

**Analysis** Write one or two paragraphs summarizing any modifications in daily routine this person makes to deal with his or her disability.

> **NCSS IV D Individual Development and Identity** Apply concepts, methods, and theories about the study of human growth and development, such as physical endowment, learning, motivation, behavior, perception, and personality.

**N C L B**

## Real-World Skills

| | |
|---|---|
| **Problem-Solving** | **14. Share Concerns** Suppose that you babysit a 4-year-old. You are concerned because the child rarely talks and does not seem to understand what you are saying. Write a scenario in which you present your concerns to the child's parent. |
| **Technology Skills** | **15. Create a Newsletter** Imagine that you are in charge of a special Saturday program for gifted students. Use word processing or desktop publishing software to create a monthly newsletter listing upcoming activities for the program. Be creative in your selection of activities. |
| **Financial Literacy** | **16. Summer Camp** Choose one type of disability discussed in this chapter, such as blindness or diabetes. Find a camp designed for children with this disability. Research how much the camp costs and compare it to the cost of a similar camp for children without disabilities. |

 **Additional Activities** For additional activities, go to this book's Online Learning Center at **glencoe.com**.

## Academic Skills

**17.** Students' reports will vary depending on the person chosen. Reports should describe why the person had a difficult childhood and how that impacted the person's adult life.

**18.** 1.84 million to 2.07 million (80% = .8, 90% = .9; 2,300,000 × .8 = 1,840,000 or 1.84 million; 2,300,000 × .9 = 2,070,000 or 2.07 million)

The *Early Childhood Observations CD* offers additional lessons with videos to build students' observation skills.

**Part 1:** Learning to Observe
**Part 2:** How Children Develop
**Part 3:** Working With Young Children
**Part 4:** Extended Observations
**Part 5:** Resources and Answer File

## Academic Skills

###  English Language Arts

**17. A Difficult Beginning** Many well-known people grew up in difficult circumstances such as abuse. Research books or magazine articles to learn about one of these individuals. Write an essay discussing what impact you think the person's childhood had on the adult he or she became.

> **NCTE 2** Read literature to build an understanding of the human experience.

###  Mathematics

**18. Family Challenges** Reports show that between 80 and 90 percent of children in homes affected by domestic violence are aware of the abuse and can provide detailed accounts of it. Studies also show that there are about 2.3 million incidents of domestic violence each year. What is the range of the number of children that witnessed those incidents?

> **Math Concept** **Range** A range is a sequence, series, or scale between limits.

**Starting Hint:** Convert the percentages to decimals by dividing by 100. Then multiply each decimal by 2.3 million. Order those numbers from least to greatest for your range.

 For math help, go to the Math Appendix at the back of the book.

> **NCTM Number and Operations** Understand numbers, ways of representing numbers, relationships among numbers, and number systems.

###  Science

**19. Situational Stress** As you have learned, situational stress in children is usually caused by events that have a major impact on their lives, such as moving, parents divorcing, a serious illness in the family, or financial difficulties.

**Procedure** Ask ten children between ages 12 and 15 to state the most stressful event in their lives. Record their responses.

**Analysis** Combine your results with those of four classmates. Look for any patterns in the responses. Write a summary of your findings.

> **NSES A** Develop understandings about scientific inquiry.

## Standardized Test Practice

**MULTIPLE CHOICE**

Read the passage and then answer the question.

Rett syndrome is a developmental disorder in which children appear to be growing normally and then suddenly quit developing, and even lose skills. Scientists think it is caused by a defective chromosome. Rett syndrome is considered to be one of the autism spectrum disorders.

**20.** According to this passage, what is the probable cause of Rett syndrome?
a. genetic abnormality
b. poor development skills
c. neglect
d. autism

> **Test-Taking Tip** In multiple choice questions, do not go back and change an answer unless you made an obvious mistake the first time, such as misreading the question.

**NCLB**

**19.** Students should write a summary of the entire group's results in which they note any common patterns among the responses, such as several students mentioning going through a divorce or a time of financial stress.

> **NCLB** NCLB connects academic correlations to book content.

## Standardized Test Practice

**20.** a. genetic abnormality

**Test-Taking Tips** Help students prepare for standardized tests by planning review sessions two or three times a week so they continually review class material. Remind them that cramming the night before will not help them do well on standardized tests, and they will be better served by getting a good night's sleep.

**Multiple-Choice Tests** Answer choices on multiple-choice test items are called distracters because they do just that. Incorrect answer choices, especially those that look similar, can distract the test-taker's attention from the best answer. A strategy that many students find effective is to cover the answer choices before reading the question, answering the question, and then reading the answer choices. Tell students to look for the answer choice that most closely matches the answer they came up with on their own.

---

## TECHNOLOGY Solutions

**Use these technology solutions to streamline chapter assessment!**

 **ExamView Assessment Suite** CD allows you to create and print out customized tests or ready-made unit and chapter tests, complete with answer keys.

 **TeacherWorks Plus** is an electronic lesson planner that provides instant access to complete teacher resources in one convenient package.

 **Online Learning Center** includes resources and activities for students and teachers.

**STANDARDS BASED LESSON PLANNING** *The Developing Child* provides students with instruction and assessment in the following fundamental content areas:

## National Standards Correlations

| Standards | Pages |
|---|---|
| **12.1.3** Analyze current and emerging research about human growth and development, including research on brain development. | 604 |
| **12.2.1** Analyze the effect of heredity and environment on human growth and development. | 627 |
| **12.2.2** Analyze the impact of social, economic, and technological forces on individual growth and development. | 627 |
| **12.3.1** Analyze the role of nurturance on human growth and development. | 622 |
| **15.1.5** Explain cultural differences in roles and responsibilities of parenting. | 618 |
| **15.2.3** Assess common practices and emerging research about discipline on human growth and development. | 622–624 |
| **15.2.5** Apply criteria for selecting care and services for children. | 603–608, 609–612, 625 |
| **15.3.1** Assess community resources and services available to families. | 612 |

**NO CHILD LEFT BEHIND** NCLB activities, information, and skills practice will help your students attain NCLB proficiency. Students will improve their abilities in the following academic standards areas:

## Academic Standards Correlations

| Discipline | Standard | Feature/Activity |
|---|---|---|
| **English Language Arts** | **NCTE 1** Read texts to acquire new information. | **Reading Guide (pp. 602, 613)** |
| | **NCTE 4** Use written language to communicate effectively. | **After You Read (p. 612)** |
| | **NCTE 7** Conduct research and gather, evaluate, and synthesize data to communicate discoveries. | **Academic Skills (p. 627)** |
| | **NCTE 12** Use language to accomplish individual purposes. | **Writing Activity (p. 600)** **After You Read (p. 624)** |
| **Mathematics** | **NCTM Number and Operations** Understand numbers, ways of representing numbers, relationships among numbers, and number systems. | **After You Read (p. 612)** |
| | **NCTM Number and Operations** Compute fluently and make reasonable estimates. | **Academic Skills (p. 627)** |
| | **NCTM Data Analysis and Probability** Select and use appropriate statistical methods to analyze data. | **Math in Action (p. 608)** |
| **Science** | **NSES C** Develop understanding of matter, energy, and organization in living systems; and behavior of organisms. | **Academic Skills (p. 627)** |
| | **NSES F** Develop understanding of personal and community health. | **After You Read (p. 624)** |
| **Social Studies** | **NCSS I A Culture** Analyze and explain the ways groups, societies, and cultures address human needs and concerns. | **Culture Matters (p. 618)** |
| | **NCSS IV D Individual Development and Identity** Apply concepts, methods, and theories about the study of human growth and development, such as learning. | **Observation Skills (p. 626)** |

## McGraw Hill Professional Development

**MINI CLIP VIDEO LIBRARY**

Targeted professional development is correlated throughout *The Developing Child*. **The McGraw-Hill Professional Development Mini Clip Video Library** provides teaching strategies to strengthen academic and learning skills. Log on to **glencoe.com**.

In this chapter, you will find these Mini Clips:
- **Reading** Prereading Strategies, p. 603
- **Reading** Modeling Reading Strategies, p. 609
- **ELL** Language Practice, p. 611
- **ELL** Scaffolding Questions, p. 614
- **Reading** Strategies for Student Achievement, p. 617
- **Reading** Assessment Planning and Management, p. 627

## Reading and Writing Strategies

**Writing Activity: Compare and Contrast** (p. 600)
Students use writing tips to compare and contrast in-home child care with child care centers.

**Before You Read** (pp. 602, 613)
A pre-reading question or statement will help students make a personal connection to content.

**Graphic Organizer** (pp. 602, 613)
A visual tool will help students organize and remember new content.

**Reading Check** (pp. 608, 618, 622)
A question allows students to make a quick comprehension self-check.

**After You Read** (pp. 612, 624)
Organize and process students' understanding of what they have read.

## Chapter Features

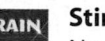 
**Stimulating the Brain** (p. 604)
Nurturing and supportive child care can promote brain development.

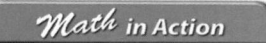
**Starting Salaries** (p. 608)
Learn to calculate an average salary.

**Choosing Child Care** (p. 609)
Parents should examine several child care centers before choosing one.

**Food Safety Routines** (p. 615)
Keeping food safe involves clean eating areas and proper storage.

**Child Care in Denmark** (p. 618)
Denmark provides free child care for all children.

**Play in a Montessori School** (p. 620)
In Montessori schools, children play purposefully.

**Choosing Early Childhood Materials** (p. 621)
Materials in an early childhood classroom must meet specific requirements.

**Time-Outs** (p. 623)
Time-outs are useful in teaching children acceptable behavior.

## Chapter Overview

### Introduce the Chapter

In this chapter, students learn about the different types of substitute care available for young children, including the types of home-based care and center-based care. They also learn about the structure of the early childhood classroom and the various learning activities it provides.

### Build Background

Remind students that preschool children are in Piaget's preoperational learning period. This means that they learn best from activities in which they are directly engaged. As students will see in this chapter, the early childhood classroom is centered around these kinds of hands-on experiences.

### Writing Activity

### Compare and Contrast

This active learning activity prompts students to write a compare-and-contrast report about different types of in-home child care. After students have completed the writing activity, ask for volunteers to share their reports with the class. Encourage the class to discuss the advantages and disadvantages to each and to explain which they think they might prefer to use. (Use these criteria when evaluating your students' writing: Are two items compared and contrasted? Does the paper employ subject-by-subject or feature-by-feature analysis? Does the paper include enough specific details to see similarities and differences?)

---

**Chapter**

**22** Child Care and Early Education

## Chapter Objectives

After completing this chapter, you will be able to:

- **Describe** two types of substitute care for younger children.
- **List** questions a parent should ask when choosing home-based care.
- **Describe** the benefits of having learning centers in early childhood classrooms.
- **Explain** the factors to consider when planning activities.
- **Identify** methods for promoting positive behavior in the classroom.

### Writing Activity  Compare and Contrast

**Understanding Child Care** Many parents, at some point in time, will need to rely on substitute care for their children. Write a report in which you compare and contrast what you know about in-home child care, such as babysitting, and day-care centers.

**Writing Tips** Use these tips to write an effective compare-and-contrast report:
1. Choose related items.
2. Organize your paper by comparing subjects or by comparing features.
3. Use appropriate transitions between comparisons and contrasts.

600

---

## CLASSROOM Solutions

### Print Resources
 Student Edition
 Teacher Wraparound Edition
 Student Activity Workbook
Student Activity Workbook Teacher Annotated Edition

### Technology Resources
 **Online Learning Center** has resources and activities for students and teachers. Includes an Online Student Edition.

 **Interactive Student Edition** allows students to instantly access review materials, examples, and exercises.

## Section **22.1**  Child Care Options

## Section **22.2**  Participating in Early Childhood Education

**Review the Sections**

Introduce the chapter by reviewing the sections:

**Section 22.1**
There are a variety of substitute child care options available to parents. Home-based care includes in-home care and family child care. Center-based care includes profit and non-profit centers and parent cooperatives. When evaluating child care, parents should consider the caregivers, the programs provided, and the facility itself, including any licensing or accreditation it may have.

**Section 22.2**
Early childhood classrooms are typically divided into learning centers. Examples include the art center, dramatic play center, and music center. Early childhood centers must ensure children's health and safety by having rules against sick children attending and encouraging good hygiene. Teachers typically develop overall daily schedules plus more specific activity plans.

► **Explore the Photo**

**Caption Answer** Students' answers will vary but may include: the child may have more varied opportunities and activities in which to participate or children are able to practice social skills.

**Discussion** Describe a family in which one parent works and the other stays home with their child. Ask: Do you think this family should send the child to a child care program even though one parent is at home? How about a preschool? At what age? (Possible answer: The parents might want to keep the child home until about age four and then send the child to a preschool in preparation for kindergarten.)

↑ Explore the Photo
Many children attend child care programs. *How might being in a child care program benefit a child?*

601

**TeacherWorks Plus** is an electronic lesson planner that provides instant access to complete teacher resources in one convenient package.

**Presentation Plus!** provides visual teaching aids for every section.

 **The Early Childhood Observations CD** presents video observations and lessons on observation skills and child development.

**The Developing Brain eTransparencies and Guide** include information and activities to offer insights into brain development and diseases of the brain.

## Focus

### Bell Ringer Activity

#### Child Care Advertisements

Display advertisements for two child care centers. Encourage students to discuss what each ad emphasizes. For example, do they emphasize convenience and long hours, caring workers, or educational opportunities for the children? Ask students: Which ad do you find more appealing? Why?

## Preteaching

### Vocabulary

Discuss that some words retain their Latin or Greek plural forms. For example, *criteria* is the plural form of *criterion*.

### Graphic Organizer

The Graphic Organizer is also on the TeacherWorks CD.

(Graphic organizers should include: Care in the child's own home—convenient, costly. Family child care—small group, individual attention. Play groups—different homes, different caregivers, is usually free.)

**NCLB** connects academic correlations to book content.

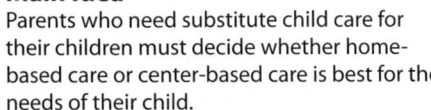

### Reading Guide

#### Before You Read

**Predict** Look at the photos in this section and read their captions. Write one or two sentences predicting what the section will be about.

#### Read to Learn
**Key Concepts**
- **Describe** two types of substitute care for younger children.
- **List** questions a parent should ask when choosing home-based care.

**D**

#### Main Idea
Parents who need substitute child care for their children must decide whether home-based care or center-based care is best for the needs of their child.

#### Content Vocabulary
- ◇ child care center
- ◇ in-home care
- ◇ family child care
- ◇ nanny
- ◇ license
- ◇ accreditation
- ◇ play group
- ◇ parent cooperative
- ◇ Head Start

 **Graphic Organizer** Go to this book's Online Learning Center at **glencoe.com** to print out this graphic organizer.

#### Academic Vocabulary
You will find these words in your reading and on your tests. Use the glossary to look up their definitions if necessary.
- ■ socialize
- ■ criteria

#### Graphic Organizer
As you read, look for three types of home-based care. Note characteristics of each one. Use a chart like the one shown to help organize your information. Add additional squares as needed.

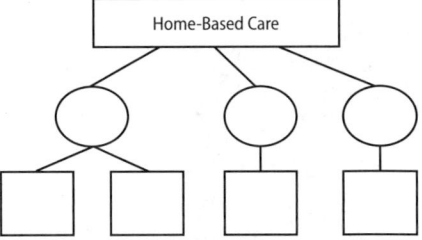

Home-Based Care

**NCLB**

#### Academic Standards · · · · · · · · · · · · · · · · · · · · ·

 **English Language Arts**

**NCTE 4** Use written language to communicate effectively.

**Mathematics**

**NCTM Data Analysis and Probability** Select and use appropriate statistical methods to analyze data.

**NCTM Number and Operations** Understand numbers, ways of representing numbers, relationships among numbers, and number systems.

**NCTE** *National Council of Teachers of English*
**NCTM** *National Council of Teachers of Mathematics*

**NSES** *National Science Education Standards*
**NCSS** *National Council for the Social Studies*

### Reading Guide

#### Before You Read

Invite those students who went to a child care center or preschool when they were young to share what they liked most and least about this experience. (Answers will vary. Possible answer: I liked playing with the other children the most and clean-up time the least.)

#### D Develop Concepts

**Main Idea** Discuss the main idea with the students. Ask: Do you think most parents realize the importance of the quality of substitute child care they choose for their child? (Possible answer: Some do, because they spend time considering various alternatives; however, others choose child care based only on factors such as convenience or cost.)

# Substitute Care

On his way to work each day, Luis takes his son, Alberto, to the Sunny Day Child Care Center. At the end of her workday, Alberto's mother, Elena, comes to get him and brings him home. Luis and Elena, just like millions of other parents, rely on substitute child care.

More and more parents have come to rely on other people to care for their children at least some of the time. Why is there such a demand for substitute care? There are many reasons, including:

- In many two-parent families, both parents work outside the home. When both parents have jobs, their children usually need substitute care.
- Many children live with a single parent who has a full-time job. Parents in this situation need full- or part-time care for their children.
- Some parents who care for a child at home feel that the child could benefit from spending time with a group of other children. They place their child in a child care setting for some time each week.

## Types of Substitute Care

Parents who need substitute care have a variety of options. All these options provide the child with physical care and a place to play. Some place greater emphasis than others on education. Substitute care is provided in two general settings. Some services are offered in a home. Others are provided in a child care center. A **child care center** is a facility in which a staff of adults provides care for children.

### Home-Based Care

**In-home care** is provided to many young children from a caregiver who comes to their home. **Family child care** takes place in the caregiver's home. Parents may choose home-based care because they feel a home setting may be easier for their children to adjust to. Home-based care may also be convenient for parents. It may be located close to home and the hours may be more flexible. Some parents like this arrangement because the child care provider is a relative, friend, or neighbor—someone they know and trust.

↑ **Providing Child Care**
People who run home-based child care programs may be required to get a license from their state. *Why do you think some states insist on licensing for child care providers?*

Section 22.1 Child Care Options **603**

## Explore the Photo

**Caption Answer** Answers will vary but might include that states must make sure that child care providers meet health and safety standards; a license also allows the state to know who is providing in-home care so they can be monitored.

**Discussion** Ask students: If you were choosing home-based care for a child, how important would it be to you that the care provider was licensed? (Responses will vary. Possible answer: I would want the person to be licensed so that I would know that they had met certain standards.)

## Teach

### Discussion Starter
**Considerations in Child Care**
Ask students: What characteristics are common to high-quality child care centers? Write students' responses on the board and encourage them to discuss which of these characteristics they think are the most important. (Possible answers: They encourage children to learn, build motor skills, be creative, explore their imaginations, develop social skills, and prepare for kindergarten.)

**Mc Graw Hill Professional Development**

**Mini Clip**
**Reading: Prereading Strategies**

A teacher assesses students' prior knowledge about a text selection.

### U Universal Access
**Interpersonal Learners** Organize students into two teams. Tell the teams they will debate whether home-based care or a child care center is a better option for the typical three-year-old. Encourage students to conduct research to obtain additional information to support their points of view and remind them to back up their viewpoints with facts. Have students conduct the debate. (Students should debate whether home-based care or a child care center is preferable for a typical three-year-old. Debates will vary. There is no one choice that is better for all children. Students should recognize that all children and families are unique and therefore have different child care needs.)

## Teach cont.

### C1 Critical Thinking

**Propose** Discuss that many people think the term *nanny* implies a female, but some males also work at this job. Organize students into small groups. Have each group come up with a word or term to replace *nanny*. The name should not indicate the person's gender. Encourage them to make the terms descriptive and fun. Each group should then present its word or term to the class. The class should vote on a favorite term. (Answers will vary. Students should work in groups to come up with a gender-neutral term to replace *nanny*. Each group should present its name and the class should vote on a favorite.)

### W Writing Support
**Research**

**Child Care Providers** Instruct students to conduct research to learn when a child care provider must be licensed in your state. If your state does not require child care providers to have a license, have the students find out if there are other state standards or requirements the providers must follow. Have students write a paragraph summarizing their findings. (Paragraphs will vary but should summarize if and when a child care provider must be licensed in your state. For example, in California, child care providers must be licensed if they care for children from more than one family who are not related to the provider. Paragraphs should demonstrate that adequate research was conducted to thoroughly answer the question.)

## THE DEVELOPING BRAIN

### Stimulating the Brain

Studies show that nurturing and supportive child care outside the home can promote a child's brain development. For optimal brain development, children need a stimulating environment, individualized attention, and exposure to language.

■ **Science Inquiry** Children up to three years old learn primarily through their senses. How might a child care provider stimulate a child's senses?

Home-based care usually involves a smaller group of children than a child care center. For this reason, many parents prefer home-based care for infants or other children who need a lot of individual attention. There are three main types of home-based care.

**Care in the Child's Own Home** Many parents have their child cared for by someone who comes to their home. In-home care is convenient, but it can be costly. Also, the child may not have a chance to play with other children. Some families hire a nanny. A **nanny** is a person trained to provide child care. The nanny may live with the family or come to the home daily. Although this arrangement is fairly expensive, a nanny can offer reliable and stable care at almost any time of day.

**Family Child Care** Another option for parents is family child care. In this situation, a child care provider cares for a small group of children in his or her own home. The group often includes the provider's own children. Family child care offers children the comfort of a home setting with opportunities for social interaction. Also, because the group size is small, the child care provider can give the children more individual attention. Family child care usually costs less than in-home care.

Some states require child care providers to have a license. A **license** is a registration with the state that indicates child care providers meet health and safety standards. A license

does not indicate the quality of the care provided, however. Some family child care providers go a step further and earn accreditation from a recognized organization such as the National Association for Family Child Care (NAFCC). **Accreditation** means that the child care provider has met strict official standards for quality child care.

**Play Groups** Some parents and children take part in a play group. A **play group** is an arrangement in which parents take turns caring for one another's children in their own homes. A play group is similar to family child care, but it involves a number of different homes and different caregivers. Most play groups involve no fees because the work is shared. This type of care is best suited for parents who do not work full time but who want their children to have the opportunity to **socialize**, or participate, with other children.

### Center-Based Care

In child care centers, several adults care for one or more groups of children. Centers vary widely in their hours, their fees, and the ages of children they accept. They also differ in the activities, equipment, and play areas provided, and in the training and experience of the staff.

Some child care centers are businesses run for profit. Others are called non-profit organizations. This means that they charge only enough fees to cover expenses. Still others are funded by the city, state, or federal government. Finally, some centers are run by businesses that offer child care as a benefit to their employees or customers.

Each state has an agency that licenses child care centers. A center must meet minimum health and safety requirements to receive a license. The license also limits the number of children a center may accept, depending on space, facilities, and number of people on the staff.

Professionals in the child care field have created a system to recognize centers that meet high standards. Child care centers can choose to join the National Association for the Education of Young Children (NAEYC). This association is dedicated to improving the

## THE DEVELOPING BRAIN

**Stimulating the Brain**
**Science Inquiry** Answers will vary but may include: child care providers might provide items with different textures to stimulate touch; play music to stimulate hearing; provide different foods to stimulate taste; provide a colorful environment to stimulate sight.

For more information and activities, see *The Developing Brain* guide and eTransparencies.

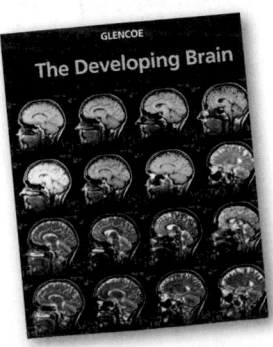

GLENCOE
The Developing Brain

professional care and education of children from birth through age eight. Members must apply to the association. Accreditation involves a review of the facility's staff, programs, and environment to see if they meet the association's strict **criteria**, or standards. These include strict staff-to-children ratios, as seen in **Figure 22.1**. You will note in this chart that some of the ages overlap. These are general guidelines, but the NAEYC will also take into account the total number of children in a facility to decide the final allowed ratio. A low staff-to-child ratio allows children to get the attention needed to enhance their learning experiences.

Parents can choose from several center-based child care options. These include child care centers, parent cooperatives, preschools, and Head Start centers. Different center-based child care options will meet the needs of different families. See **Figure 22.2** on page 607 for tips on how to make sure your child is doing well in whichever child care you choose.

**Child Care Centers** Child care centers primarily serve children whose parents work outside the home. The typical center offers children a variety of activities. Some centers emphasize specific learning activities, while others allow more time for informal play. Usually there is a daily routine with time set aside for meals, naps, and indoor and outdoor play. Child care centers may offer half-day or full-day programs. Some child care centers are designed for children two years old and older. Some provide care for infants and young toddlers as well.

**Parent Cooperatives** A **parent cooperative**, or co-op, is child care that is provided by the parents of the children in the co-op. The parents take turns staffing the co-op, which is usually in a facility other than a home. A preschool teacher or another qualified child care provider may organize the program and guide the parents. A co-op program costs considerably less than a child care center. It may not be an option, however, for families in which both parents work full time.

## Figure 22.1 NAEYC Staff-to-Children Guidelines

A low staff-to-child ratio allows children to receive more individualized attention. *How many 13-month-old toddlers could be in a group with two staff persons?*

| Ages | Number of Staff | Number of Children |
| --- | --- | --- |
| Infants (birth–15 months) | 1 | 4 |
| Toddlers (12–28 months) | 1 | 4 |
| Toddlers (21–36 months) | 1 | 4 |
| Preschoolers (2.5–3 years) | 1 | 9 |
| Preschoolers (4 years) | 1 | 10 |
| Kindergarteners (5 years) | 1 | 12 |

## Figure 22.1 NAEYC Staff-to-Children Guidelines

**Caption Answer** A group with two staff persons could have as many as eight 13-month-old toddlers.

**Discussion** Point out that three times as many staff members are needed to care for infants as to care for kindergarteners. Ask students if they think this difference is appropriate. (Reponses will vary, but should focus on the extensive individual care and attention infants require, such as diaper changes and the need to be held and comforted.)

**C₂ Critical Thinking**

**Analyze** Tell students that the parents of five children have decided to start a parent cooperative for their children. Ask students: Why do you think these parents decided to start a parent cooperative rather than sending their children to a commercial child care center? What advantages do you think these parents see to the arrangement? (Possible advantages: They would have more control over the school's curriculum, hours, rules, and so forth. In addition, the co-op might be less expensive than a commercial child care center.)

**U Universal Access**

**Gifted Learners** Have students conduct research to learn more about the National Association for the Education of Young Children (NAEYC). Instruct students to create a flier for parents that explains the purpose of the NAEYC. The flier should discuss topics such as the NAEYC's goals and the types of issues the organization addresses. (Fliers will vary but should accurately explain NAEYC to parents. Its primary goal is the improvement of the well-being of young children, especially in educational and developmental areas. It deals with a wide variety of issues, such as early childhood literacy and difficulties associated with getting and retaining child care workers.)

## C Critical Thinking

**Evaluate** Discuss that many parents send their four-year-olds to centers which provide preschool half of the day and general child care the other half. Ask students: Why do you think parents might choose this option over a full-day preschool or a full-day of general child care? How might it meet the child's needs? (Student responses will vary. They might say this option provides children with a more structured learning experience for part of the day in preparation for kindergarten. In addition, it provides them with more freedom during the remainder of the day.)

## R Reading Strategy

**Cause and Effect** Discuss that understanding cause and effect can help the reader see the big picture. Instruct students to read these paragraphs. Then ask: What is the cause of this situation? What is the effect? (Answers may vary. The cause is that many working parents do not want their school-age children left alone after school, during school holidays, and during summer vacation. The effect is that a variety of programs have been developed to meet these children's needs.)

**Preschools** Preschools provide educational programs for children ages three to five. They typically offer activities that help children develop in all areas. The staff usually includes one or more teachers as well as a number of assistant teachers. Preschools usually offer half-day sessions from two to five days a week. Some centers offer both child care for younger children and preschool programs for three- to five-year-olds. A growing trend is for children to attend a pre-kindergarten program the year before kindergarten.

Some preschools provide specialized programs that differ from the traditional approach. Montessori preschools, for example, use special learning materials and follow the ideas of Maria Montessori, an Italian educator. See Chapter 15 to learn more about Montessori's theory of learning. Children are encouraged to learn by exploring and experimenting. They are given the freedom to move from one activity to another as they wish. Another example is called High/Scope. This program encourages children to learn through active experiences with people, material, and events rather than through direct teaching.

**Head Start Centers** Head Start is a program that provides locally run child care facilities designed to help lower-income and disadvantaged children from birth to five years of age become ready for school. It is funded by the federal government. Most Head Start centers have half-day sessions. Head Start programs offer a variety of activities. They also provide children with meals, health care, and social services. Parents are expected to be actively involved in the Head Start program.

### Care for Older Children

Many parents wonder at what age their children can be left unsupervised. Child care experts advise against leaving children ages twelve and under home alone. This means that many parents and other caregivers need substitute care for their school-age children before and after school and during school holidays, breaks, and summers.

Some children go to the home of a neighbor or relative. Others depend on before- and after-school programs. These may be run by schools or religious or community groups. Such programs offer a safe place where children can have a snack, do their homework, and enjoy supervised activities.

Finding child care for school holidays and summer vacation can be more difficult. Fortunately, parents and other caregivers know in advance when school holidays will occur, so they can make plans well in advance. Often parents take their own vacations from work during the school holidays.

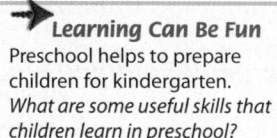

**Learning Can Be Fun**
Preschool helps to prepare children for kindergarten. *What are some useful skills that children learn in preschool?*

## ▶ Explore the Photo

**Caption Answer** Answers will vary, but may include: preschoolers learn colors, shapes, numbers, the alphabet, how to get along with others, sharing, or following directions.

**Discussion** Tell students that some social critics believe that preschool should be freely available to all children. They state that families who are well-off can afford high-quality preschools and those with lower incomes can send their children to Head Start, but many in-between families cannot afford this expense. Encourage students to discuss this topic. (Student's opinions will vary. Possible answer: Preschool should be freely available to all because it provides children with a strong educational foundation.)

## Figure 22.2 Is Your Child Doing Well in Child Care?

Parents want to know if their child is happy and doing well in child care. *What kinds of questions should a parent ask a child care provider?*

| Action | Description |
| --- | --- |
| **Look for bonding.** | Children need time to adapt and warm up gradually. After an adjustment period, look for a bond to develop between the child and staff. The child might also develop friendships with the other children depending on his or her age. |
| **Ask for updates.** | Sometimes caregivers will answer questions or give feedback at the end of the day or by appointment. Find out how the provider thinks the child is doing. Child care professionals often can give insight about a child's development. |
| **Talk to the child.** | Of course, the child is the best source of information if he or she is old enough to talk. Ask questions about activities, meals, and playtime. What is the child learning? Does she or he have fun? With younger children, a reluctance to stay with the caregiver, especially if it lasts beyond the first few minutes, could indicate a problem. |
| **Take time to observe.** | Visit the child care center or home. Many allow parents to just drop in. Some centers have a one-way mirror for observation. Some may offer password-protected videos via the Internet. Parents can see how their child acts on a typical day. |
| **Get involved.** | If possible, volunteer for special parties or help with field trips. Young children especially are happy to share these occasions with a parent. |
| **Be aware.** | Although most child care experiences are positive, be aware of possible warning signs. Listen if a child complains about being bullied, mistreated, or ignored by the staff. Check it out and take any appropriate action. Also be aware of sudden mood changes in the child. If an outgoing toddler suddenly becomes withdrawn or quiet, it could indicate a problem. |

**S**

## S Skill Practice

### Guided Practice

**Create a Skit** Organize students into pairs. Instruct each pair to present a brief skit showing a child who has adjusted well to a child care center. They then should present a skit of a child who is having problems. Encourage the entire group to discuss signs parents can look for. (Skits will vary but should show a child who has adjusted to a child care center and a child having difficulties.) **L1** **ELL**

**Make a Checklist** Have students create checklists that parents can use to determine how well their child is doing in child care. For example, for the first item, "Look for bonding," one item might be: "The staff talks to my child in a friendly way." The parent would then check one of these boxes: "Definitely," "Probably," "Not Sure," or "No." (Students should create checklists for parents to evaluate how well their child is doing in child care.) **L2**

**Interview a Parent** Have students interview a parent of a child who goes to a child care center. They should ask: How do you determine whether your child is doing well at the center? What do you watch for? What questions do you ask? Have students present oral summaries of their interviews. (Summaries will vary but should discuss how parents determine whether the child is doing well in child care, based on the interview answers.) **L3**

## Figure 22.2 Is Your Child Doing Well in Child Care?

**Caption Answer** Possible answers include: "How many children are in the program?" "What is the staff-to-child ratio?" "Do you have references I can contact?"

**Discussion** Ask students: What kinds of updates do you think caregivers should give parents? Should they tell parents if the child never eats his peas? Or if she frequently hits other children? Should the situation be mentioned when the child is picked up or should a formal appointment be scheduled? (Answers will vary; minor issues, such as not eating certain foods, might be discussed in passing. Major difficulties might require an appointment.)

## Assess

### Quiz

Ask students to answer the following questions:

1. **Why do some parents prefer home-based care for their children?** (It may be easier for the child to adjust to, closer to home, have more flexible hours, the provider may be a relative, and there are usually fewer children.)

2. **What is Head Start?** (It is a program that provides locally run child care facilities to help lower-income and disadvantaged children become ready for school.)

3. **In which type of child care do parents work at the center?** (Parents take turns working at parent cooperatives.)

### Math in Action

**Starting Salaries**

The average starting salary for child care workers in Tran's area is $31,550. ($32,000 + $31,800 + $30,850 = $94,650; $94,650 ÷ 3 = $31,550)

### ✓ Reading Check

**Explain** A preschool provides educational programs; they offer activities that help a child develop in all areas; the staff usually includes one or more teachers. Child care centers generally offer a variety of activities but have children of varying ages.

**NCLB** Activity correlated to Mathematics standards.

---

### Math in Action

**Starting Salaries**

Tran did an analysis of starting salaries for child care workers in his area. He called three child care centers and was quoted the following salaries: $32,000, $31,800, and $30,850. What is the average salary in his area?

**Math Concept** **Measures of Central Tendency** The mean, median, and mode are all measures of central tendency because they provide a summary of numerical data in one number. The mean is the same as the average.

**Starting Hint** To find the mean, add all of the values ($32,000, $31,800, and $30,850) together. Then divide the total by the number of values in the set of data (3).

**Math** For math help, go to the Math Appendix at the back of the book.

**NCTM Data Analysis and Probability** Select and use appropriate statistical methods to analyze data.

---

Few parents can take all of the school holidays off, though. And even fewer can take the whole summer off. They need to find ways to fill the gaps. Here are some suggestions.

- Some parents arrange to share child care with several other families.
- High school and college students on similar school schedules are often available to provide in-home care.
- Some of the programs that offer before- and after-school care also offer care for school holidays. Some also offer some summer programs.
- Museums, zoos, parks and recreation departments, and other community organizations may offer day camps or other programs for longer breaks and summer vacation.

Parents looking for holiday child care should ask the same questions they would ask when looking for any other kind of substitute care. Safety, provider training, and child-to-adult ratios are still very important.

### ✓ Reading Check

**Explain** How do preschools differ from child care centers?

**▲ After-school Care**
Many organizations offer after-school care for school-age children. *In what ways would this care differ from that provided for younger children?*

---

### ➤ Explore the Photo

**Caption Answer** Possible answers include: there will likely be larger groups with fewer staff, or activities will be geared for students who are more independent and can do more on their own.

**Discussion** Ask for volunteers to discuss any after-school programs at the schools they attended when younger. Were children encouraged to do homework? What kinds of activities did they provide? (Responses will vary. Many after-school programs have a set time for participants to do homework. Activities might include sports, board games, or art projects.)

## Choosing Substitute Child Care

There are many factors to consider when choosing substitute care for a child. Foremost is the quality of care. In addition, the cost, convenience, qualifications of the caregivers, and the facilities and activities provided are all considerations.

### What to Look For

When parents start searching for care, it is helpful to use an organized approach. **Figure 22.3** on page 610 provides a list of important considerations when evaluating child care options. The questions are tailored to a child care center, but they could be adapted to other situations as well. Parents should ask some of the questions directly. Other questions require parents to observe the facility and the providers. Because the quality of care has such an impact on a child's well-being and development, it is important to put in the time and effort to find the best choice. Parents will generally visit several child care providers before selecting the best one for their child.

Parents should remember that each child is unique. Therefore, the needs of their child may be different from the needs of another child. A child care center may be perfect for one family but not be right for another. Parents must consider the child's temperament along with that of the caregiver. Does the caregiver's values match the family's values? If a child is not allowed to watch television at home, a child care center with scheduled television time may not be the right choice.

As a child grows, parents may need to make new child care arrangements. Connie put two-year-old Todd in family child care because she liked the idea of a home setting. When Todd turned four, however, she moved him to a preschool program so that he could start to prepare for kindergarten.

A child's behavior also could signal a need to change. If a child suddenly begins to cause trouble at child care, it may be because he or she is bored. Perhaps the activities are no longer interesting or challenging. If a child begins

---

### Choosing Child Care

Charlotte and her husband have toured a few child care centers, and she does not feel that any are right for their 18-month-old son, Noah. Charlotte still has doubts about putting Noah in child care. She worries that he will find it hard to make friends or that he will get sick more often if he is with other children. At the same time, she feels that because he is an only child, he needs contact with other children.

Charlotte and her husband arrange to visit another child care center. This experience is more positive. Noah seems to like it there and soon starts playing while the director of the center talks with his parents. The director is able to ease some of Charlotte's fears. Charlotte learns, for example, that the center has a policy that children must stay home when they are sick. Most of all, she notices that the children seem happy.

**✎ Write About It** Even though the visit to the last child care center was positive, Charlotte and her husband are still not completely comfortable with putting Noah in child care. Write a letter to Charlotte and her husband with suggestions for further steps they might take to help them make their decision.

---

to cry regularly when being dropped off at child care, this could be a sign that a child no longer feels comfortable in that setting.

### Issues Specific to Home-Based Care

Home-based care generally operates on a smaller scale than center-based care and involves fewer caregivers. For these reasons, parents considering home-based care for their children need to ask some additional questions.

- **How many children does the provider care for?** Most experts recommend that a family child care home have no more than six children per adult, including the child care provider's own children. This number should be even lower if infants and

---

**C Critical Thinking**

**Make Decisions** Three-and-one-half-year-old Quinn has attended Montessori school since he was two. Because there is no Montessori program for children over five in the area, Quinn's father will send him to a traditional kindergarten when he is five. Quinn's father is also considering sending him to a traditional preschool next year to help him transition to kindergarten. Have students discuss what they think is the father's best option. (Possible answer: Leave Quinn in the Montessori school until kindergarten because children are amazingly flexible and he will probably adapt without any difficulty.)

**R Reading Strategy**

**Using Examples** Read aloud the third paragraph under What to Look For. Ask: How does this example help you understand the author's point? Can you think of other examples? (Answers will vary but might include: It provides a specific example of when a parent decided to change care arrangements because a child's needs were changing. Other examples might include when a child has developed special interests. For example, if a child is especially interested in musical instruments, parents might want to move her to a preschool that places special emphasis on this area.)

---

---

**Write About It** Student's answers should be written in correct letter format with no spelling or grammar errors. Suggestions will vary but may include: Charlotte and her husband might ask for the names and phone numbers of parents who have children at the center and talk to them about their child's experience.

**Reteach** cont.

**C Critical Thinking**

**Make Judgments** Discuss that some child care centers restrict access to the building. For example, some require parents to enter a code before the door will open. Ask students: If you were director of a child care center, would you want to have these kinds of security measures? Do you think it is possible for a center to be overly restrictive? Encourage students to explain their responses. (Responses will vary, but should be thought out. Some may say you cannot be overly restrictive when the safety of children is a concern.)

**U₁ Universal Access**

**Visual Learners** Have students visit a child care center and evaluate the physical facility. They should answer at least six of the questions listed under the Facility heading in Figure 22.3. Students should report their findings to the class. (Findings will vary based on the facility visited. For example, they might determine that each child has a place to store belongings.)

**R Reading Strategy**

**KWL Chart** Have students create a KWL chart on evaluating programs at child care centers. In the first column, they should fill in what they already know. In the middle column, they should enter what they would like to learn. Students should then read the Program row of Figure 22.3 and fill in the last column of their KWL charts with what they learned. (Students should create KWL charts on evaluating child care center programs.) **ELL**

---

**Figure 22.3 Evaluating Child Care**

There are many questions parents or other caregivers might ask when evaluating substitute care options. *How could this list be adapted to provide a record of a visit to each facility?*

| Aspect of Care | Questions to Consider |
|---|---|
| **Caregiver** | ❖ Does the number of children per adult meet NAEYC criteria?<br>❖ What education, training, and experience do providers have?<br>❖ How long have providers worked at this facility? How often are new providers hired?<br>❖ What safety and first-aid training do providers have?<br>❖ How do providers ensure that children are released only to authorized persons?<br>❖ What arrangements are made if a provider is ill?<br>❖ Do the providers seem to enjoy caring for the children? Are there joyful interactions between the children and the providers? |
| **Facility** | ❖ Does the physical space in the facility match NAEYC criteria?<br>❖ Is the facility licensed or accredited?<br>❖ Are both indoor and outdoor areas safe, comfortable, and clean?<br>❖ If meals or snacks are provided, are they nutritious? Are they served in a clean area?<br>❖ Are sleeping areas separate from noisy areas?<br>❖ What happens if a parent must pick a child up late?<br>❖ Does each child have a place for his or her belongings?<br>❖ Is there a clean diaper-changing area for infants and toddlers?<br>❖ Are the toilets and sinks clean and easy to reach? Can children reach clean towels, liquid soap, and toilet paper? |
| **Program** | ❖ Do providers guide children's behavior in appropriate ways?<br>❖ Are the policies in writing? If so, ask for a copy.<br>❖ Are rules reasonable for the children's ages?<br>❖ Are the toys suitable for the children's ages?<br>❖ Are activities varied and matched to the children's levels?<br>❖ Do children have time for self-directed free play?<br>❖ Is there a regular method for the provider to report to parents?<br>❖ Do the children seem involved and happy?<br>❖ If you were a child, would you like to spend time here?<br>❖ What is the policy for sick children? |

C

U₁

R

**Figure 22.3 Evaluating Child Care**

**Caption Answer** Answers will vary but may include: Questions could be asked and answers written next to the question. Name of child care center and date of visit could be added to the page.

**Discussion** Why do you think it is important that a child care center's policies are in writing? (Having policies in writing can help avoid misunderstandings between parents and the staff and allow parents to double-check policies if necessary.)

toddlers are part of the mix. When there are fewer children, each child gets more individual attention. A child care provider working alone should handle no more than two children younger than age two.

- **Is there a back-up plan for illness or vacations?** What happens when the family child care provider must be gone? Are there arrangements for someone to fill in? If not, parents will need to consider a back-up care plan.

U₂

- **Who else will be in the home?** Parents need to know who else will be around their children. They should ask about other children, teens, or adults who live in the home. Who are they, what are their backgrounds, and how might they interact with the children?

W

- **Are there both quiet and active times for children?** Children need a good mix of planned activities and informal play. Children should not simply sit in front of the television much of the day or be left without supervision. Most young children also need scheduled nap times. Often, if a

child will not sleep, he or she is allowed to rest quietly with a book.

- **What if there is an emergency?** In most home-based care settings, there is only one adult child care provider. To deal with emergencies—such as an injured child who needs medical attention—the provider should have someone on call who can fill in at short notice.

U₂

## Consider the Cost

While quality of care is the primary consideration in choosing child care, cost is also an important factor. The cost of child care varies significantly depending on the type of care and where it is located. In some cities, for example, families may pay more than $1,000 per month for a single toddler at a child care center. In general, the least expensive child care option is care provided by family or friends. Nannies are usually the most costly choice. Center-based care is usually more expensive than home-based care, but the cost varies widely from place to place. The age of the child needing care is also a factor. Care of

**Home-Based Child Care**
Parents need to find out how many children are in a home-based child care. *What would be some advantages and disadvantages to a child being the only one in a home-based child care program?*

Section 22.1 Child Care Options **611**

---

▶ **Explore the Photo**

**Caption Answer** Answers will vary. Advantages might include that the child would get all of the caregiver's attention and would be less likely to catch illnesses. Disadvantages might include that the child would not have an opportunity to socialize with other children or could become bored.

**Discussion** In home-based care, children are more likely to interact with others of various ages than at a child care center. Ask students: If you were a parent, would you prefer to have your child with others of a similar age or a more mixed group? Why? (Answers will vary. If ages are similar, children can engage in the same activities.)

## Section **22.1**

## Reteach *cont.*

**U₂ Universal Access**

**English Language Learners** Pair English language learners with students who are fluent in English. Have each pair create a list of ten questions parents should ask when considering home-based care. Because these questions will be used by parents who are not fluent in English, they should be written in simple language. Students should use these bulleted items as a guideline. (Students should write a list of ten questions for parents to ask home-based care providers. The questions should use simple language.) **ELL**

**Professional Development**

**Mini Clip ELL: Language Practice**

Students of varying language proficiencies work together to review content they have read.

**W Writing Support**

**Compare and Contrast**

**Planned Activities Versus Informal Play** Have students write a comparison of planned activities and informal play. Students should discuss how they are similar and how they are different. (Refer to p. 600 to review how to effectively compare and contrast two items. Students might state both can provide socialization and learning experiences. However, planned activities are more likely to control learning whereas informal play provides a greater outlet for physical energy.)

**611**

## Study Tools

Have students go to the Online Learning Center at **glencoe.com**:

- Take the **Practice Test**.
- Download **Study-to-Go** content.

Use the **Student Activity Workbook** for additional practice.

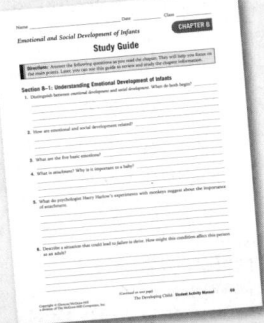

### Close

## Culminating Activity

**Choosing a Child Care Option** Organize students into pairs. Each pair should create a skit in which they are parents deciding the type of child care they want for their three-year-old. They should discuss the pros and cons of each child care option.

 **NCLB** connects academic correlations to book content.

---

infants is typically more costly than for preschoolers.

No matter what the cost, however, it adds up. Depending on the parents' working hours, children may need substitute care for up to ten hours a day, five days a week.

In two-parent families, when earnings are compared to child care and other job-related costs such as transportation and clothing, it is sometimes less expensive for one parent to stay at home and provide care.

### Sources of Information

How can parents locate potential sources of substitute care? Community groups, libraries, and local government agencies can supply listings. Groups such as Child Care Aware, NAEYC, and Nation's Network of Child Care Resource and Referral offer listings for many areas. All three groups have Web sites that provide easy access to their referral services and other information, including helpful information for parents and caregivers and links to other reputable Web sites. Many parents find substitute care by asking friends for referrals.

It is essential that parents visit each home or child care center they are considering before choosing one. This takes time, but it allows them to see the facility and the child care providers firsthand. In fact, taking the child to visit can help a parent see how the child responds to the place and the people, and how the child care providers respond to the child.

Anyone considering a substitute care option should ask for references. Any child care provider should be willing to give the names and phone numbers of parents whose children attend. This is true for a center or a home-based provider.

Children are a precious resource and a responsibility. Parents must do everything possible to ensure their children are receiving quality care.

---

## Section 22.1 — After You Read

### Review Key Concepts

1. **List** three reasons parents might need substitute care for their children.
2. **Explain** why it is so important for parents to ask questions of possible substitute child care providers.

### Practice Academic Skills

 **English Language Arts**

3. Work with a partner to write an interview between a parent and a director of a child care center. Using the questions in Figure 22.3, decide twelve of the most important questions for the parent to ask. Act out the interview for the class.

> **NCTE 4** Use written language to communicate effectively.

 **Mathematics**

4. Research the cost of some in-home child care providers and child care centers in your area. Find out their costs to provide care for one two-year-old child. List the names of the providers and their costs in order from least expensive to most expensive.

> **NCTM Number and Operations** Understand numbers, ways of representing numbers, relationships among numbers, and number systems.

 **Check Your Answers** Check your answers at this book's Online Learning Center at **glencoe.com**.

**612** Chapter 22 Child Care and Early Education

---

## Section 22.1 — After You Read

### Review Key Concepts

1. Answers may include: Both parents work outside the home; children live with one parent who works full time; and the child could benefit from social interaction.
2. Parents need to ask questions so they can trust the care provider will give their child the best possible care and support the family's values.

### Practice Academic Skills

3. The 12 questions to ask may vary but should be taken from Figure 22.3. Students should use a question/answer format for conducting the interview.

4. Students' answers will vary depending on the in-home child care providers and child care centers contacted. Lists should be in order from least expensive to most expensive.

# Section **22.2** Participating in Early Childhood Education

## Reading Guide

### Before You Read

**Prior Knowledge** Look over the Key Concepts for this section. Write down what you already know about each concept and what you want to find out by reading the section.

### Read to Learn
#### Key Concepts
- **Describe** the benefits of having learning centers in early childhood classrooms.
- **Explain** the factors to consider when planning activities.
- **Identify** methods for promoting positive behavior in the classroom.

**D**

### Main Idea
Early childhood classrooms should provide a safe and healthy environment for children. Classrooms should promote positive behavior and plan lessons and activities.

### Content Vocabulary
◇ learning center
◇ circle time
◇ free play
◇ transition

 **Graphic Organizer** Go to this book's Online Learning Center at **glencoe.com** to print out this graphic organizer.

### Academic Vocabulary
You will find these words in your reading and on your tests. Use the glossary to look up their definitions if necessary.
- self-sufficiency
- expectation

### Graphic Organizer
As you read, list three precautions child care providers must take to provide a safe environment. Use a fishbone diagram like the one shown to help organize your information.

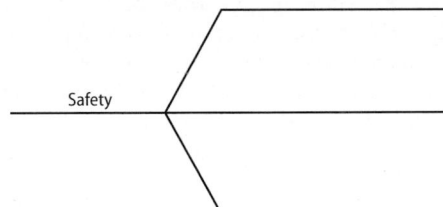
Safety

**NCLB**

### Academic Standards . . . . . . . . . . . . . . . . . .

 **English Language Arts**

**NCTE 12** Use language to accomplish individual purposes.

 **Science**

**NSES F** Develop understanding of personal and community health.

 **Social Studies**

**NCSS I A Culture** Analyze and explain the ways groups, societies, and cultures address human needs and concerns.

**NCTE** *National Council of Teachers of English*
**NCTM** *National Council of Teachers of Mathematics*

**NSES** *National Science Education Standards*
**NCSS** *National Council for the Social Studies*

Section 22.2 Participating in Early Childhood Education · **613**

---

## Reading Guide

### Before You Read

Ask those students who attended preschool whether they think it helped them prepare for kindergarten. If so, how? Encourage them to discuss not just how it prepared them intellectually, but also socially and emotionally.

### **D** Develop Concepts

**Main Idea** Discuss the main idea with the students. Ask students what they think early childhood classrooms can do to promote a safe and healthy environment. (Possible answers: They can routinely check all classroom equipment and supplies to make certain they are safe, and not allow sick children to attend school.)

---

## Focus

### Bell Ringer Activity

#### Examining an Early Childhood Classroom

Play a video showing an early childhood classroom. The video should show individual learning centers. Pause the video at each center and encourage students to discuss the kinds of activities children might engage in there. If possible, the video should also show drinking fountains, restrooms, etc. Encourage students to discuss how these features have been modified for children's use.

## Preteaching

### Vocabulary
Tell students that words that have similar meaning are called synonyms. Knowing synonyms can improve your vocabulary and help you learn the meaning of unfamiliar terms. A synonym for the word *transition* is "change." Brainstorm other synonyms for transition. If necessary, refer to a dictionary or thesaurus for ideas.

### Graphic Organizer
 The Graphic Organizer is also on the TeacherWorks CD.

(Graphic organizers should include: create a safe environment, practice and teach safe behaviors, and know what to do in an emergency.)

**NCLB** connects academic correlations to book content.

**613**

# The Early Childhood Classroom

While you are studying child development, you may have an opportunity to visit an early childhood classroom. Perhaps you will observe the children to better understand their development and behavior. You might be a volunteer helping the child care staff. You might also work with children as part of your course work. No matter what your role, you should understand how such programs are organized and the roles, responsibilities, and concerns of the staff. This will help make your experience more rewarding.

If you visit an early childhood classroom, you will notice that it is carefully designed to meet children's varied needs. It takes a special kind of environment to promote the physical, social, emotional, and intellectual development of young children.

**C₁** First, the classroom environment needs to be child-size. Chairs should allow children to sit with their feet touching the floor. Having shelves within reach allows children to reach and return materials on their own. Posters and other wall decorations should be at the children's eye level. Drinking fountains, sinks, and other facilities should also be accessible.

A child-size environment promotes independence. The children are able to use materials without having to ask adults for help. This helps promote feelings of success and **self-sufficiency**, which is the ability to take care of oneself.

## Learning Centers

Early childhood classrooms are often divided into learning centers. A **learning center** is an area designed for certain types of play and learning. Learning centers allow children to make choices. They can explore different areas of knowledge and develop skills through hands-on experiences. **Figure 22.4** on pages 616–617 shows an ideal arrangement of learning centers in an early childhood classroom.

Early childhood educators use guidelines such as these when designing a classroom and setting up learning centers:

- Use low shelves, colored floor coverings, wall decorations, or storage containers to separate learning centers.
- Separate noisy centers from quiet centers.
- Place the art center near a source of water for clean up. The floor should be easy to clean if it gets wet.
- Leave a large, open area for large-group activities, such as dancing or story time.

➤ **Early Childhood Learning** Learning centers are developed with young children in mind. *How can you tell that this learning center is for young children?*

---

➤ **Explore the Photo**

**Caption Answer** Answers may vary but could include that the shelving is low and books are face out so that the covers are visible.

**Discussion** Ask students if they think it is possible for a learning center to be overly stimulating to a child. For example, can it have too many colors or contain too many items? (Possible answer: Yes; while children enjoy color and interesting activities, too much clutter and color can be agitating and make it difficult to focus on the activity at hand.)

**Health Care Routines**
Frequent hand washing helps prevent the spread of illness. *How can young children be encouraged to wash their hands regularly?*

## Health and Safety

Ensuring the health and safety of the children in the classroom is the most important responsibility of teachers and other child care providers. They must follow health care routines to prevent illness, make sure the environment is safe, and supervise play.

### Health Care Routines

Health care routines prevent the spread of illness. Early childhood classrooms usually have strict policies regarding illness and attendance. For example, many early childhood programs do not allow sick children to stay in the classroom. They also ask that sick children be free of fever for at least 24 hours before returning to the classroom.

As children enter the classroom, staff members look for obvious signs of illness, such as a runny nose or fever. Children who are sick or become sick in the classroom will not be allowed to stay with the group. The child's parent or another caregiver will be called to pick the child up. If a major illness, such as chicken pox, occurs, all parents should be notified.

### SAFE CHILD HEALTHY CHILD

**Food Safety Routines**

To prevent cases of food-related illness, child care workers need to follow careful routines when handling food. Their main concerns are to keep eating areas clean and to store foods at safe temperatures.

Eating areas should be thoroughly washed with warm water and food-safe disinfectant both before and after the children eat. The sponges or cloths used to clean these surfaces need to be cleaned and disinfected regularly.

A child care center that serves meals and snacks must follow strict standards when preparing and serving food. Centers that serve food must be licensed and are subject to regular safety and sanitation inspections.

**Be Prepared** Observe the cafeteria in your own school. Look for things such as cleanliness of the equipment, freshness of the food, and food handling procedures. Write an evaluation of the attention paid to food safety routines.

## Teach *cont.*

### C₂ Critical Thinking

**Apply** Describe a scenario in which a parent brings a child to a child care center with a cold. Discuss how a staff member might explain why the child cannot remain at the center. Ask students: Do you think the way in which this is explained will affect the parent's reaction? What problems might this cause for the parent? (Answers will vary. Possible answer: If the staff member clearly explains the results of having a sick child present, the parent may be more receptive than if the parent is simply told the child cannot stay. The parent may have to stay home from work or make other arrangements for child care.)

### U Universal Access

**Gifted Learners** Tell students that the Centers for Disease Control and Prevention estimates that there are 76 million cases of illness per year in the United States caused by eating food contaminated with bacteria. Have students investigate a specific bacterial organism that causes foodborne illness. Instruct students to write a report answering the following questions: Where is this organism found? What are some symptoms of infection by this organism? (Reports will vary depending on the organism chosen. *E. coli*, for example, is found in the intestinal tract of some mammals, as well as contaminated water. Symptoms of infection include diarrhea, cramping, nausea, and exhaustion.)

 **Explore the Photo**

**Caption Answer** Students' answers will vary but may include: they can be praised for washing their hands or the adults can teach by example.

**Discussion** Ask students what other behaviors children can be taught to prevent the spread of illness. (They can be taught to cover their mouths when they cough or sneeze, to use and dispose of tissues properly, and to only use their own combs and brushes.)

### SAFE CHILD HEALTHY CHILD

**Food Safety Routines**

**Identify** Ask students to identify the requirements for centers that serve food. (They must be licensed and are subject to regular safety and sanitation inspections.)

**Be Prepared** Answers will vary but should include an evaluation of the school's cafeteria based on cleanliness, freshness of food, and food handling procedures.

## Teach cont.

### R Reading Strategy

**Classify** Ask students: Which of these centers are designed primarily for quiet activities and which for noisier activities? Which centers primarily emphasize fine motor skills and which gross motor skills? (Answers may vary but students should classify learning centers as specified. For example, the art center would emphasize fine motor skills and the active play area would emphasize gross motor skills. The language arts center would be classified for quiet activities.)

### W Writing Support

**Compare and Contrast**
**Dramatic Play Versus Active Play Areas** Have students write a paragraph in which they compare and contrast the dramatic play center with the active play area. (Refer to p. 600 to review how to effectively compare and contrast two items. Students might state that both allow the child to play freely, but dramatic play is more likely to encourage the use of imagination whereas the active play area provides more large-muscle exercise.)

**Figure 22.4 Learning Centers in the Early Childhood Classroom**

Early childhood classrooms may have some or all of the learning centers shown here. *What might a child find in the music center?*

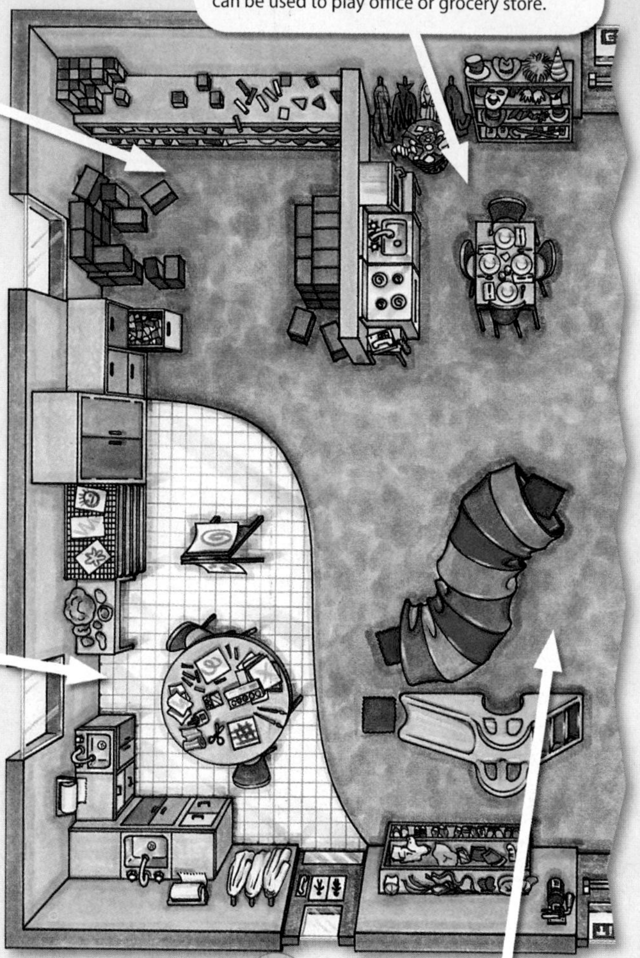

**1 Block Center**
This area may include small and large blocks, building logs, trucks and cars, and people and animal figures. Placing a rug or carpeting on the floor in the block center cuts down on noise.

**2 Dramatic Play Center**
This area provides children with opportunities for make-believe play. It can include clothes for dressing up, a play kitchen, and materials that can be used to play office or grocery store.

**9 Art Center**
The art center allows children to be creative and exercise their imaginations through drawing, painting, and working with clay and fabric. It should include paper, scissors, glue, crayons, paints, chalk, clay, and fabric. There should be smocks for children to wear when they work with these materials.

**8 Active Play Area**
Children exercise their large muscles in the active play area. It can include streamers for tossing; bean bags; areas for climbing, tumbling, and sliding; and a work bench for hammering.

**Figure 22.4 Learning Centers in the Early Childhood Classroom**

**Caption Answer** The music center might include musical instruments such as finger cymbals, tambourines, drums, triangles, keyboard, or piano.

**Discussion** Ask students: Why are activity centers, such as the ones shown here, appropriate for children who are in Piaget's preoperational learning period? (Learning centers are appropriate because they allow these children to learn by seeing and doing. For example, a child who is working with clay gets direct tactile and visual feedback.)

**3 Music Center**

The music center can include musical instruments such as tambourines, finger cymbals, triangles, and drums. It can also include a piano or keyboard and CDs.

**4 Math and Science Center**

In this area, children can learn math concepts such as matching, sorting, classifying, and counting. They can also learn about colors, sizes, and shapes. Children can explore their world using science tools such as magnifying glasses, scales, and magnets. Specimens of natural objects, such as rocks, leaves, or a hamster, help children experience the world around them.

**5 Computer Center**

Children can learn basic computer skills. A wide variety of educational software programs can help children practice specific skills.

**6 Language Arts Center**

This area includes materials related to speaking, listening, reading, and writing. It should be a quiet area with good lighting and comfortable chairs or pillows.

**7 Director's Office**

Large, one-way observation windows allow the program director to handle paperwork and meet with parents while viewing the children. Parents might use this observation area to check on their child's progress.

**S**

Section 22.2    Participating in Early Childhood Education    **617**

---

## Teach *cont.*

### **S** Skill Practice
### Guided Practice

**Create a Collage** Tell students to select one learning center described in the figure. Then have students find pictures in magazines to create a collage of items that they might choose to put in the learning center. (Collages will vary. A language arts learning center might include photos of some appropriate children's books, as well as comfortable child-sized chairs. You might want to provide some magazines for the students to cut up.)

**Make a Brochure** Divide students into pairs. Tell them to imagine that they are in charge of marketing for a local child care center. Their job is to create a brochure that explains to parents the different learning centers in the center's early childhood classroom. The brochure should include photos or illustrations and emphasize the types of learning that occur at each center. (Brochures will vary but should explain the purpose of each learning center in an early childhood classroom.) **L2** **ELL**

**Visit an Early Childhood Classroom** Instruct students to visit an early childhood classroom and create a drawing showing its floor plan. Students should then write a report analyzing the layout of the classroom and the kinds of learning centers it contains. Based on what they have learned in this chapter, students should make suggestions for improvements. (Students should write a report analyzing the layout of an early childhood classroom along with its learning centers. Students should make appropriate suggestions for improvements. For example, perhaps there is not adequate separation between active and quiet areas.) **L3**

---

**Professional Development**

**Mini Clip**
**Reading: Strategies for Student Achievement**

Teachers discuss strategies for helping all learners meet curriculum standards.

# Section 22.2

## Teach cont.

### U₁ Universal Access

**Visual Learners** Instruct students to create a poster designed for an early childhood classroom. The poster should teach the importance of careful hand washing and contain only illustrations. Students may want to make the poster child-friendly by using cartoon-style drawings to get the point across. (Students should create an illustrated poster that explains the importance of hand washing to young children.) **ELL**

### C Critical Thinking

**Make Judgments** Ask students: Why might playground equipment that is suitable for preschoolers not be suitable for toddlers? Ask for specific examples of such equipment. (Answers may vary. Preschoolers are more physically advanced and have better motor skills than toddlers. For example, a preschooler may be able to safely hang onto hand rails while climbing a slide's ladder while a toddler cannot.)

### ✓ Reading Check

**Explain** Child care environments can be kept safe through regular inspection of equipment and play areas, regular cleaning of equipment and toys, close supervision of children at all times, and having an adequate number of adults present to watch each area.

---

## CULTURE MATTERS

### Child Care in Denmark

In Denmark the government provides funding for child care for all children beginning at birth. The care is free for parents who cannot afford to pay. Child care for very young children does not include specific learning goals, but rather emphasizes play and the development of social skills. There are usually three child care workers for every ten children, and at least one of the workers must have a teaching degree. Danish employers accommodate parents' schedules. It is acceptable, for example, for parents to leave work so that they can pick their children up from child care on time.

⭐ **Build Connections** *What do you think providing child care beginning at birth indicates about a country's culture?*

**NCSS I A Culture** Analyze and explain the ways groups, societies, and cultures address human needs and concerns.

---

Parents or other caregivers should receive a written copy of the center's health policies. Having the rules in writing helps to prevent misunderstandings about when children should stay home and how illnesses will be handled if they occur when the child is in the classroom.

Careful hand washing is one of the best ways to prevent the spread of illness. Hands need to be washed after using the toilet; after blowing the nose; and before cooking, eating, or playing with materials such as clay. Children should be taught to wash their own hands thoroughly with warm water and soap and to dry them with a clean paper towel.

Child care providers also must wash their own hands often, especially after helping children in the bathroom and before preparing food. This helps protect everyone's health and sets a good example for the children.

Other good health habits that caregivers can teach children include:

- Blowing and wiping their noses and disposing of the tissue.
- Covering their mouths when they cough.
- Using only their own comb, brush, or headwear. They should never use those of another child.
- Avoiding sharing of food and eating utensils.

### Safety

To keep children safe, caregivers must create a safe environment, practice and teach safe behaviors, and know what to do in an emergency. A safe environment takes into account the age and developmental levels of the children using it. Playground equipment suitable for preschoolers, for example, could be hazardous for younger children. Older children also should have equipment suitable for their age group.

The classroom and outdoor play areas, and all equipment, should be inspected regularly for possible safety hazards such as uncovered electrical outlets or cords, and broken toys. Toys and equipment should be cleaned regularly to help prevent the spreading of germs and illnesses.

An important part of keeping children safe is to provide close supervision at all times. There should always be an adequate number of adults present to watch the children in each area. If there is an emergency, an adult should stay with the children in the classroom while another adult goes for help.

### ✓ Reading Check **Explain** What can caregivers do to keep the child care environment safe?

**618** Chapter 22 Child Care and Early Education

---

## CULTURE MATTERS

### Child Care in Denmark

**Discussion** Ask students if they think the United States could provide the type of child care offered in Denmark. Encourage them to offer reasons for their responses. (Responses will vary. Possible response: Probably not because it would cost the government a great deal of money.)

**Build Connections** *Possible answer: Providing child care beginning at birth indicates that a country places great importance on early childhood and social skills.*

# Planning Appropriate Activities

Planning plays an important role in providing appropriate learning experiences for young children. The daily schedule should provide a variety of types of activities. There are several factors to consider when planning the activities. Activities need to provide opportunities in each area of development. Of course, activities also must be appropriate to the age and skill levels of the children, too.

## Learning Through Play

Young children learn primarily through play. When planning activities for them, it is important to remember that the more involved the children are and the more realistic their experiences are, the more they learn. For example, reading children a story about a fire truck can help them learn about fire safety and community helpers. However, reading the book becomes a much more powerful learning tool when followed by a trip to the fire station and a chance to climb aboard a real fire truck.

Of course, children cannot go on field trips every day, so care providers need to find other ways to help them experience what they are learning. Children need play experiences that focus on these areas of development:

**R**
- Thinking and problem solving
- Movement of large and small muscles
- Creativity, including music, dance, art, and dramatic play
- Relationships with others

Children need a variety of activities that involve different experiences. When several children sit at a table and work on separate puzzles, they are playing individually alongside one another. If they work on the same puzzle, they practice teamwork and getting along with others. Sometimes children play alone, such as when they look at a book by themselves. When the teacher reads the book to the group and they talk about it, they experience the same book in a different way. Children also play in small groups, perhaps dressing up and pretending to be a family. A teacher can guide group music or movement activities. The entire class may also come together at circle time. **Circle time** is when the children share their experiences in show-and-tell or listen to a story together. **U₂**

 **Learn Together**
Circle time is a time for learning together. *What are some activities that might take place during circle time?*

## Teach *cont.*

### **R** Reading Strategy
**Think of Examples** Ask for volunteers to suggest examples of play experiences that focus on each of the areas of development listed here. Have students create a table listing these examples. (Examples will vary. Students should come up with play experiences for each developmental area. For example, for movement of small muscles, children could sing songs that include finger movements. For relationships with others, children could be placed in pairs or groups to play games or complete a project. Students should create a table to list the examples discussed.)

### **U₂** Universal Access
**Musical Learners** Have students write a song that tells preschoolers to put away what they are doing and come together for circle time. Songs should describe the kinds of activities children will do during circle time. Students can use a melody from a known children's song or they can create an original melody. Ask for volunteers to present their songs to the class, either alone or with other students. (Songs will vary but should tell preschoolers that it is circle time. Songs should describe circle time activities and the fun the children will have. Encourage students to be creative with the activities described and the lyrics created.)

## ➤ Explore the Photo

**Caption Answer** Answers will vary but may include children sharing their experiences in show-and-tell or listening to stories together.

**Discussion** Ask students: What skills might children learn during circle time? (Possible answers: To sit quietly in a group, to follow directions, or to take turns.)

### Quiz

Ask students to answer the following questions:

1. What are some advantages of having learning centers in early childhood classrooms? (They allow children to make choices, explore different areas of knowledge, and obtain hands-on experiences.)

2. What are some guidelines used in setting up learning centers? (Answers might include: Use different-colored furniture and flooring to separate the centers, separate noisy centers from quieter ones, place the art center near a water source, leave a large open area for large-group activities.)

3. What are some typical policies regarding illness in early childhood classrooms? (Sick children are not allowed in the classroom and must be free of fever for 24 hours before returning to school.)

## Reteach

### C Critical Thinking

**Solve Problems** Tell students to imagine that they are teachers in a preschool. One child, Jin, refuses to put away items at the end of free play. Each day, several other children step in to clean up after Jin. Ask: What might you do about this situation? (Student responses will vary. Perhaps they can talk with the entire group about the importance of being responsible for any items they take out. They might also increase the transition time at the end of free play. Another option might be to assign other tasks to those who are picking up after Jin.)

# Learning Through PLAY

## Play in a Montessori School

What is a morning like in a typical child care facility? A child might spend 15 minutes at the science center and then 15 minutes at the language arts center. Then the child might be able to play for 15 minutes in the center of the room. However, all early childhood centers are not structured this way. In a Montessori early childhood room, you would also find learning centers, but they would be called work areas. And children are free to move from area to area at their own will. That is, they do not wait for a caregiver to tell them to move to a different area. The Montessori method of teaching is named after Italian educator Maria Montessori. Her philosophy of education was that when children play purposefully, such as when they play with math manipulatives, they are learning.

**Think About It** Imagine that you want to put your young son in a child care facility. Would you choose a Montessori school? What questions would you consider to help you make your decision? Write a half-page essay that includes your answer and the reasons behind your decision.

## Daily Schedule

The daily schedule is the plan for how children will spend their time in the early childhood classroom. A good schedule for young children features a balance of active and quiet activities and small- and large-group activities. It should also have both teacher-directed and child-selected activities. **Free play** is a time when children can choose any activity they want. Here is a sample schedule for a three-hour session for four-year-olds:

8:30–8:45 Arrival and free play
8:45–9:15 Circle time
9:15–9:45 Learning centers
9:45–10:00 Toilet and hand washing
10:00–10:15 Snack
10:15–10:45 Outdoor play
10:45–11:15 Learning centers
11:15–11:30 Group time and goodbyes

A good daily schedule allows time for transitions. A **transition** is a period during which children move from one activity to the next. During a transition, the children need to finish one activity, put their materials away, and get ready for the next activity. Children should always be warned a few minutes ahead of time that they will soon have to make a change. This helps them mentally prepare for the change and encourages cooperation.

Lucas was happily playing with the blocks. When the teacher said it was time to go wash for snack time, Lucas got upset. He was not finished building his tower and he did not want to leave the blocks. Later, when Lucas was drawing in the art center, the teacher told him he had five minutes to finish his drawing and put the crayons away. Lucas then knew he was almost out of time and happily put the finishing touches on his drawing before cleaning up to leave. The advance warning that it was almost time to go gave Lucas the transition he needed.

**C**

## Activity Plans

A daily schedule outlines the children's day in general. The lead teacher then plans the specific activities that children will do in the learning centers and during circle time or other group times. There are at least two types of forms that many teachers use to write these plans.

The first form is called the planning chart. This is based on the daily schedule. This form lists the activities that will take place in each learning center during the day. Roger teaches in a preschool and he is preparing a weeklong

**U**

# Learning Through PLAY

## Play in a Montessori School

**Discussion** Do you think a child who has gone to a Montessori early childhood classroom is likely to be more or less independent than a child who has gone to a traditional early childhood classroom? (Answers will vary. Possible answer: They may be more independent because they are used to directing their own learning.)

**Think About It** Essays will vary but should include reasons for the students' decision. One item to consider is that in Montessori schools, learning is primarily child-directed rather than teacher-directed.

planning chart based on the daily schedule shown for a three-hour session. His students are currently learning about communities, so he is planning activities for each learning center that relate to this topic in some way. For example, he will have vehicles used by various community workers added to the block center. He will have dress-up clothes for different community members in the dramatic play center. Roger plans to read stories about communities during circle time.

The second form is called an activity plan. This form allows teachers to record detailed information about each planned activity. On this form, teachers include specific information under the following headings:

- Title of the activity
- Objective, or purpose, of the activity
- Type of activity—for a learning center, small group, or large group
- Materials needed
- Procedures
- Evaluation—a recap of the success and challenges with the activity

When Rajee created her activity plan for the following day, it included much more detail than Roger's planning chart. Rajee noted that the children would be making finger puppets to work on their fine motor skills. She noted that the activity would be done with a small group. Rajee also listed that she would need several colors of construction paper, scissors, tape, markers, glitter, glue, and fabric for creating the puppets. She typed up and neatly printed step-by-step instructions for making

## ♥ Parenting Skills

### Choosing Early Childhood Materials

At some point, you may want to donate materials to your child's early childhood classroom. Here are some questions to ask when choosing those materials:

➤ **Are they safe?** Edges should be rounded rather than sharp. Art materials must be non-toxic.

➤ **Are they durable?** Materials and equipment should be able to withstand rough use by a group of children.

➤ **Are they easy to clean?** This is important in the classroom because materials are used by many children.

➤ **Are they appropriate?** Materials should be appropriate for both boys and girls and for different ages. They should also be free of stereotypes.

➤ **Are they effective?** Children should be able to learn basic concepts while using the materials.

➤ **Are they versatile?** Items that have more than one use are usually good choices.

➤ **Will they hold a child's interest?** Materials should encourage children's active play.

➤ **Are they enjoyable?** Children should have fun using the materials.

> **Take Charge** You are buying art materials for a preschool. Identify two items to buy. How well do they meet the guidelines for selection?

Section 22.2  Participating in Early Childhood Education  **621**

## ♥ Parenting Skills

### Choosing Early Childhood Materials

Discuss that some families like to donate books as gifts to the classroom, for example, for their child's birthday. What might staff members do to make certain appropriate books are donated? (The school might provide a list of appropriate titles from which families can choose to donate.)

**Take Charge**
Answers will vary depending on the items students choose. Students should explain how the items meet the criteria suggested in the feature. For example, if an art easel is donated, it should be sturdy and safe.

### Reteach cont.

### U Universal Access

**Logical Learners** Instruct students to create a planning chart for a day's activities in an early childhood classroom. Students should begin by thinking of an overall theme for the day. For example, the theme might be cars or the ocean. Then the plan should describe a related activity for each learning center. (Students should create a planning chart that includes an overall theme and related activities for each learning center. For example, if the theme is the ocean, children might try to make wave-like sounds in the music center.)

### R Reading Strategy

**Using Realia** Bring in several items that might be used in an early childhood classroom, such as crayons, books, blocks, safety scissors, or bubbles. Divide the class into small groups and have each group evaluate the materials based on the questions in the Parenting Skills feature. Allow students to try out the materials as needed to make an evaluation. Each group should then prepare a brief presentation with their findings. If any of the groups disagree on a specific item, discuss it as a class until a consensus is reached. (Groups should work together to agree on whether each item is appropriate for an early childhood classroom. They should take notes and offer reasons for why each item would or would not meet the criteria. For example, wooden blocks would be good because they are easy to clean and can be used to build things or to practice letters, making them versatile. Students may say that bubbles are good because they are fun, but they may also feel that they are messy or that the children cannot use them on their own.) **ELL**

### U₁ Universal Access

**Musical Learners** Instruct students to choose a specific holiday, such as Thanksgiving or Valentine's Day. Then have them create an activity plan centered on this holiday that makes use of the music center. Students may wish to use the Internet to get ideas for songs or finger plays that they can incorporate into their plan. (Plans will vary. Students should create an activity plan for the music center that is centered on a specific holiday. For example, students might make up a song to the tune of B-I-N-G-O using the word heart for Valentine's Day.)

### W Writing Support

**Persuasive Essay**

**Positive Reinforcement** Have students write a persuasive essay to encourage child care providers to use positive reinforcement techniques to encourage appropriate behavior. Essays should include specific examples of positive reinforcement techniques and how they can be used. Students should refer back to Chapter 3 if needed to review positive reinforcement guidelines. (Essays will vary but should offer specific examples of how to use positive reinforcement as well as why it should be encouraged. For example, when a child picks up all his blocks at the end of free time, the teacher might reward the child by allowing him to choose the book for circle time. Positive reinforcement should be encouraged to achieve desired behavior.)

### ✓ Reading Check

**Explain** Transitions allow the children to conclude one activity, put materials away, and get ready for the next activity.

---

the puppets that she could read to the children. She then left space on her form to complete an evaluation after the project was complete.

The forms teachers use to plan activities are less important than the fact that they make careful plans. Writing plans ahead of time helps teachers think through the appropriateness of each activity. It also provides a list of materials needed so that the activities can be set up before children arrive. Written plans can be filed for future reference and reuse. They are also an excellent way to show parents what their children do each day.

**✓ Reading Check** **Explain** Why does a good daily schedule allow time for transitions?

## Promoting Positive Behavior

For a classroom to function smoothly, teachers need to promote positive behavior. They must let children know what is expected of them. They must also model good behavior and use positive reinforcement when children behave appropriately. At the same time, they need strategies for dealing with unacceptable behavior in a safe and nurturing manner. As with other caregivers, teachers must be consistent in maintaining rules.

### Setting Classroom Expectations

Teachers should describe **expectations**, or expected behaviors, in positive terms. That is, they should tell the children what they should do instead of what they should not do. Each expectation should also have a clear purpose and be appropriate for the age of the children involved. The younger the child, the shorter the list of expectations should be. Younger children will also not understand all of the reasons for the expectations.

When children are old enough, it is a good idea to involve them in establishing classroom expectations. You might open the discussion by asking what they already know about appropriate behavior at home or in their community. Then they can come up with some of their own ideas for classroom expectations and the reasons why each is necessary. When children are

**Positive Behavior**
When positive behavior is stressed, children are more likely to be cooperative. *How should teachers describe expected behaviors?*

---

#### ➤ Explore the Photo

**Caption Answer** Teachers should describe expected behaviors in positive terms—telling the students what they should do rather than what they should not do.

**Discussion** Ask students: Should parents use the same techniques to encourage appropriate behavior as those used by preschool teachers? Why or why not? (Yes, both parents and teachers should use positive, rather than negative reinforcement, to teach children what behavior is expected.)

involved in this process, they feel more ownership in the classroom and they are more likely to meet expectations.

Some classrooms will have expectations that are specific to their facility. For example, "We do not use the back door." But there are many general expectations used by most classrooms. Here are some examples of reasonable expectations for an early childhood classroom:

- **Keep your hands to yourself.** This discourages hitting or pushing.
- **Always walk when you are inside the building.** This helps keep children calmer and prevents accidents and falls.
- **Put things away when you are finished.** This keeps the room well organized. Children are able to find materials when they want them. It also helps prevent tripping over unused toys.
- **Use your inside voice in the classroom.** This helps keep the classroom from being too noisy.
- **Be a friend to others.** This promotes cooperation and builds a pleasant atmosphere.

## Using Positive Reinforcement

Children enjoy being recognized and rewarded with attention. They tend to repeat behaviors that are rewarded. To make this technique effective, however, teachers must be sincere in their response to a child's behavior. If they give only automatic or inattentive comments and praise, the children will not see them as rewards. Teachers must also be consistent. If Clay is praised for cleaning up after himself, then Nina and Alexandra should be praised for the same action.

## Being a Good Role Model

In the classroom, the teacher's own behavior has a powerful influence on children. Children are more likely to do what their caregivers do. If teachers want the children to use inside voices, then they, too, must use a quiet voice indoors. If teachers want children to treat each other with kindness, they should show kindness to the children and to their coworkers. The teacher told Tyler to put away his materials. The teacher left her

papers spread out on the table though. Tyler saw that the teacher did not clean up so he felt he did not really need to either. Remember that actions speak louder than words.

## Dealing with Misbehavior

Of course, children will behave in unacceptable ways from time to time. All adults in the classroom need to know in advance how they will handle such situations. The children should also understand what will happen if they misbehave. Cases of misbehavior must be handled consistently in each situation and with each child.

In most cases, a simple statement of what the child should do is an effective way of dealing with misbehavior. If Jesse is using his voice too loudly, for example, he should be reminded

### What Would You Do?

**Time-Outs**

As a child care provider, Paige knows that one of her tasks is to help children learn what is expected of them. Paige makes sure that the children follow her directions and those of the other adults in charge. "Sometimes," she says, "I have to remind the kids to return from the playground equipment when the five-minute whistle blows. Some of them don't want to come back inside." Paige uses time-outs when children misbehave. She says, "Today one of the children kept poking another child with her paintbrushes. I had to ask her to leave the activity and take a time-out. After a few minutes, I asked her what she needed to do in order to come back. She said that she needed to say 'sorry' to the classmate she poked. She did that, and she was allowed to paint again."

✏️ **Write About It** Not all misbehaviors qualify for a time-out. Think of at least two misbehaviors that you feel do not qualify for a time-out. Write a half-page essay describing the misbehavior and explaining how you would handle it.

### Reteach cont.

**R** **Reading Strategy**

**Identify Main Points** Tell students to identify three main points the author is making in the section titled Using Positive Reinforcement. Read the section aloud as students write down the three main points. Ask for volunteers to read aloud their lists and encourage the class to discuss them. (Main points should include: children repeat behaviors that are rewarded; teachers must be sincere in praising behavior; and teachers must be consistent in praising behavior.)

**U₂** **Universal Access**

**Verbal Learners** Have students imagine that they work at a new child care center. They have been assigned the task of setting up the rules for time-outs. Instruct them to conduct research to learn about the rules for time-outs at other child care centers. Then, based on these findings and their own personal experience, have students write the rules for their center. (Rules will vary but should be based on the rules of other child care centers and their own personal experience. Rules should include guidelines for what behaviors would elicit a time-out, as well as how long the time-outs should last.)

### What Would You Do?

**Write About It** Students' answers will vary. Some students might believe that hurting another child calls for sterner punishment than time-out. They might restrict the child's play time and talk to the parents. Students should identify at least two misbehaviors and explain how they would handle them.

## Assess

### Study Tools

Have students go to the Online Learning Center at **glencoe.com**:

- Take the **Practice Test**.
- Download **Study-to-Go** content.

Use the **Student Activity Workbook** for additional practice.

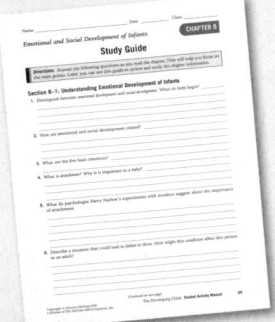

## Close

### Culminating Activity

**Identify Learning Center** Organize students into pairs. One student should describe a specific classroom activity. The other student should then identify which learning center would be most appropriate for this activity. (Possible answer: creating placemats for a Mexican meal would probably take place in the art center.)

 **NCLB** connects academic correlations to book content.

of the expectation regarding noise level in the classroom: "Jesse, please use your inside voice. Others can't hear well when you are shouting."

In other situations, a child may be offered a choice of more acceptable activities. If Jackie is not playing well in the block center, she might be told, "Jackie, you may choose to go to the dramatic play center or the art center. You can't stay in the block center because you keep taking Emilio's blocks." Notice that each example includes an explanation of why the child's behavior was unacceptable.

For some types of unacceptable behavior, a stronger response is necessary. Behavior that could hurt other people or damage property must not be permitted at any time. Children who exhibit this type of behavior should receive an immediate and consistent response. One effective approach is to give the child a time-out. This is a set time away from the activity or other children. When a time-out is used, the caregiver should continue to show the child that he or she is cared for but that the actions are not acceptable. For more information about time-outs, see page 79.

---

{ **Expert Advice...** }

*"No school can work well for children if parents and teachers do not act in partnership on behalf of the children's best interests."*

— Dorothy H. Cohen, educator and child development specialist

---

# Section 22.2 After You Read

## Review Key Concepts

1. **Explain** why child care centers need written policies concerning sick children.
2. **Describe** how writing activity plans can help teachers educate young children.
3. **List** three examples of clearly stated behavior expectations for an early childhood classroom.

## Practice Academic Skills

 **English Language Arts**

4. Think about methods that you might use to teach a group of young children about fire safety. Separate the methods into two groups—active and passive. Create a list for each method to share with the rest of the class.

**NCTE 12** Use language to accomplish individual purposes.

 **Science**

5. Imagine that a third grade student visits the child care center where you work. The young student does not understand why everyone washes their hands so often. Write a dialogue between you and the child in which you explain why regular hand washing is important in a child care setting.

**NSES F** Develop understanding of personal and community health.

**Check Your Answers** Check your answers at this book's Online Learning Center at **glencoe.com**.

---

### Review Key Concepts

1. Written policies help to prevent any miscommunication or misunderstanding. Child care providers need to keep children away from illness as much as possible, so they must have this policy in place.
2. Writing out plans allows the teacher to think about the appropriateness of the activities beforehand, ensures smooth transitions in the classroom, and helps the teacher gather materials needed for activities beforehand.
3. Answers may vary but could include: Keep your hands to yourself; always walk when you are inside a building; put things away when you are finished with them; use your inside voice in the classroom; be a friend to others.

### Practice Academic Skills

4. Lists will vary but may include: Active—play firefighter, take a trip to a fire station; Passive—read a story about a fire truck.
5. Dialogues will vary but should focus on the fact that illnesses can spread rapidly in a setting with many children. Washing hands helps to prevent the spread of illness and teaches children good habits.

## Chapter Summary

Substitute care for children may be provided in a home- or center-based setting. Home-based care options include in-home care, family child care, and play groups. Center-based care options include child care centers, parent cooperatives, preschools, and Head Start centers. When choosing substitute care, it is important to carefully evaluate choices.

A typical early childhood classroom includes different learning centers. Caregivers' primary duty is for the health and safety of the children in their care. A daily schedule and written plans help ensure good learning experiences. Rules and positive reinforcement help promote appropriate behavior.

## Vocabulary Review

1. Write a sentence using two or more of these vocabulary terms. The sentence should clearly show how the terms are related.

**Content Vocabulary**
- ◇ child care center (p. 603)
- ◇ in-home care (p. 603)
- ◇ family child care (p. 603)
- ◇ nanny (p. 604)
- ◇ license (p. 604)
- ◇ accreditation (p. 604)
- ◇ play group (p. 604)
- ◇ parent cooperative (p. 605)
- ◇ Head Start (p. 606)
- ◇ learning center (p. 614)
- ◇ circle time (p. 619)
- ◇ free play (p. 620)
- ◇ transition (p. 620)

**Academic Vocabulary**
- ■ socialize (p. 604)
- ■ criteria (p. 605)
- ■ self-sufficiency (p. 614)
- ■ expectation (p. 622)

## Review Key Concepts

2. **Describe** two types of substitute care for younger children.
3. **List** questions a parent should ask when choosing home-based care.
4. **Describe** the benefits of having learning centers in early childhood classrooms.
5. **Explain** the factors to consider when planning activities.
6. **Identify** methods for promoting positive behavior in the classroom.

## Critical Thinking

7. **Analyze** Which five questions would you rank as most important when evaluating substitute child care? Explain your answers.
8. **Infer** Why do you think it is more effective to tell children what they should do, rather than what they should not do?
9. **Examine** For young children, play is a learning experience. Provide examples of how children learn through play.
10. **Differentiate** What is the difference between a child care center that is licensed and one that is accredited?

**Chapter 22** Child Care and Early Education **625**

## Content and Academic Vocabulary Review

1. Sentences should correctly use and show the relationship between two vocabulary terms.

## Review Key Concepts

2. Two types of substitute care for younger children are home-based care and center-based care.

3. Questions include: How many children does the provider care for? Is there a back-up plan for illness or vacations? Who else will be in the home? Are there both quiet and active times for the children? What if there is an emergency?

4. Benefits include: learning centers allow children to make choices; children can explore different areas of knowledge and develop skills through hands-on experience; learning centers provide a structure for the way children move through their day.

5. The daily schedule should provide a variety of types of activities. Activities need to provide opportunities in each area of development. Activities also must be appropriate to the age and skill levels of the children.

6. The teachers must let children know what is expected of them. They must also model good behavior and use positive reinforcement when children behave appropriately. They also need strategies for dealing with unacceptable behavior in a safe and nurturing manner.

## Critical Thinking

7. Students' answers will vary but should include five questions from Figure 22.3 and an explanation for why they chose the questions they did.

8. Answers will vary. Possible answers include: young children might become confused if told what they should not do—they may misunderstand and think that is what they should do; and teachers and other adults can model what the children should do.

9. Answers will vary but may include: When children are playing make-believe, they are using their imaginations and developing their creativity. When they play with blocks, they are learning about the properties of objects and how they can be manipulated.

10. A licensed child care center is registered with the state and meets health and safety standards. An accredited child care center meets strict standards for quality.

**Family & Community Connections**

**11.** Papers will vary but should include the students' questions and the answers elicited from the child care worker.

## Health Skills

**12.** Answers will vary. They might include the common cold, conjunctivitis, or head lice. These health issues are typically spread by close contact with the infected person or by touching something the infected person has touched. They can be prevented by frequent hand washing.

## Observation Skills

**13.** Tables will vary but should list the learning centers, the learning opportunities offered, and the children's responses to the learning opportunities.

## Real-World Skills

**14.** Floor plans will vary but should include the names of centers and area for each center, space for group activities, and office space for staff.

**15.** Brochures will vary but should be creative, eye-catching, and contain information that allows parents to make a choice about your services.

**16.** Income for a year is $26,365. [($30 × 5 days a week) × 4 children = $600 per week; $600 × 52 weeks in a year = $31,200; $80 × 52 weeks = $4,160; $31,200 − $4,160 − $675 = $26,365]

**NCLB** NCLB Activity correlated to Social Studies standards.

---

 **Family & Community Connection**

**11. Interview a Child Care Worker** Interview a home-based or center-based child care worker. Prepare questions ahead of time. Questions should ask for information about how the children interact with one another and with the care providers. Use your notes to create a paper in question and answer format to share with classmates. Be sure to include the ages of the children in your answers.

### Health Skills

**12. Research Health Issues** Use print or online resources to research common health issues that must be dealt with by child care workers. Create a chart in which you list the health issue, how it is spread, and prevention techniques.

### Observation Skills

**13. Observe a Child Care Center** Work with your teacher to arrange a visit to a child care center. You might want to observe at either a Montessori child care center or a traditional child care center.

**Procedure** During your visit, observe the learning opportunities offered to children in the learning centers or the work areas. Note how the children respond to the learning opportunities offered.

**Analysis** Organize your notes in a three-column table in which you list the learning center, the learning opportunities offered, and the children's responses to the learning opportunities.

**NCSS IV D Individual Development and Identity** Apply concepts, methods, and theories about the study of human growth and development, such as learning, motivation, behavior, and personality.

**NCLB**

---

## Real-World Skills

| | |
|---|---|
| **Interpersonal and Collaborative Skills** | **14. Work Together** Work with a partner to develop a floor plan for a child care center. Your space is 50 feet wide and 100 feet long. Decide what centers to include and how much space to use for each center. Include space for group activities and office space. |
| **Technology Skills** | **15. Create a Brochure** Imagine that you are starting your own home-based child care service. Use word-processing software to create a brochure advertising your service. Be sure to provide information parents will want to know such as the child-to-caregiver provider ratio and learning opportunities. |
| **Financial Literacy** | **16. Calculate Income** Imagine that you care for four children in a home-based child care service and charge $30 a day per child. You pay $80 a week for meals and spend $675 a year on equipment. How much money will you make in a year, if all four children come five days a week? |

**Additional Activities** For additional activities, go to this book's Online Learning Center at **glencoe.com**.

---

## Academic Skills

**17.** Answers will vary but may include: adult-to-child ratio—the fewer the children for each adult, the better for children; group size—the smaller the group, the better; caregiver qualifications—caregivers with degrees and/or special training in working with children will be better able to help children learn.

**18.** $111.35 per week (1 year = 52 weeks; $5,790 ÷ 52 = $111.35)

The *Early Childhood Observations CD* offers additional lessons with videos to build students' observation skills.

**Part 1:** Learning to Observe
**Part 2:** How Children Develop
**Part 3:** Working With Young Children
**Part 4:** Extended Observations
**Part 5:** Resources and Answer File

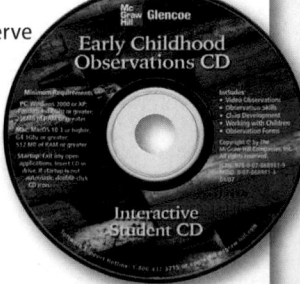

## Academic Skills

 **English Language Arts**

**17. Determine Quality Care** Several studies have found that the quality of care a child receives plays a major role in his or her development. Conduct research to find the characteristics of quality care provided in early childhood classrooms and to evaluate its effects on child development. Present your findings in a one-page essay.

> **NCTE 7** Conduct research and gather, evaluate, and synthesize data to communicate discoveries.

 **Mathematics**

**18. Child Care Costs** Early care and education for a four-year-old in a child care center in an urban area averages $5,790 per year. How much would a family have to save weekly to pay for child care?

**Math Concept** **Multistep Problems** When solving problems with more than one step, think through each step first.

**Starting Hint** First, convert one year into weeks (52). Then divide the total cost by the number of weeks. Be sure the decimal point is in the correct place in your answer.

 For math help, go to the Math Appendix at the back of the book.

> **NCTM Number and Operations** Compute fluently and make reasonable estimates.

 **Science**

**19. Research Computer Use** Children are learning to use computers much earlier than in previous years. Many child care centers for young children have computers and encourage the children to use them as part of their daily activities.

**Procedure** Research the various ways computers are used in early childhood classrooms.

**Analysis** Write a one-page report that discusses the impact computer use might have on small and large motor skill development.

> **NSES C** Students should develop understanding of the cell; biological evolution; matter, energy, and organization in living systems; and behavior of organisms.

## Standardized Test Practice

**MULTIPLE CHOICE**

Read the passage, then answer the question.

Children enjoy being recognized and rewarded with attention. They tend to repeat behaviors that are rewarded. To make this technique effective, however, teachers must be sincere in their response to a child's behavior. If they give only automatic or inattentive comments and praise, the children will not see them as rewards. Teachers must also be consistent.

**20.** According to the passage, teachers
  **a.** must be sincere when rewarding behavior.
  **b.** should respond to a child's behavior.
  **c.** must be sincere and consistent when rewarding behavior.
  **d.** should give automatic praise to children.

> **Test-Taking Tip** Be sure to read the directions carefully. If you are asked to choose the best answer, there may be more than one *correct* answer from which to choose.

**19.** Reports will vary. Computers may help students develop small motor skills, but they may hinder large motor skill development if children spend more time at computers than they do in active play.

>  **NCLB** connects academic correlations to book content.

## Standardized Test Practice

**20.** c. must be sincere and consistent when rewarding behavior.

**Test-Taking Tips**
Remind students not to panic if they are still in the middle of a test and others are already done. The secret is to take a deep breath, focus, and try to block out other things going on in the room.

**Multiple Choice Tests**
Emphasize the importance of not spending too much time on a single question. If students do not know the answer, they should mark off any answers they know are wrong and continue on to the next question.

 **Professional Development**

**Mini Clip**
**Reading: Assessment Planning and Management**
Lois Moseley, author and educator, discusses planning for, and evaluation of, an assessment.

## TECHNOLOGY Solutions

**Use these technology solutions to streamline chapter assessment!**

 **ExamView Assessment Suite** CD allows you to create and print out customized tests or ready-made unit and chapter tests, complete with answer keys.

 **Online Learning Center** includes resources and activities for students and teachers.

 **TeacherWorks Plus** is an electronic lesson planner that provides instant access to complete teacher resources in one convenient package.

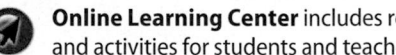

**STANDARDS BASED LESSON PLANNING** *The Developing Child* provides students with instruction and assessment in the following fundamental content areas:

## National Standards Correlations

| Standards | Pages |
|---|---|
| **12.2.3** Analyze the effects of gender, ethnicity, and culture on individual development. | 632 |
| **15.2.1** Choose nurturing practices that support human growth and development. | 652 |
| **15.2.5** Apply criteria for selecting care and services for children. | 652 |

**NO CHILD LEFT BEHIND** NCLB activities, information, and skills practice will help your students attain NCLB proficiency. Students will improve their abilities in the following academic standards areas:

## Academic Standards Correlations

| Discipline | Standard | Feature/Activity |
|---|---|---|
| **English Language Arts** | **NCTE 1** Read texts to acquire new information. | **Reading Guide (pp. 630, 638)** |
| | **NCTE 3** Apply strategies to interpret texts. | **After You Read (p. 637)** |
| | **NCTE 4** Use written language to communicate effectively. | **Writing Activity (p. 628)** |
| | **NCTE 5** Use different writing process elements to communicate effectively. | **Academic Skills (p. 653)** |
| | **NCTE 12** Use language to accomplish individual purposes. | **After You Read (p. 649)** |
| **Mathematics** | **NCTM Number and Operations** Understand numbers, ways of representing numbers, relationships among numbers, and number systems. | **After You Read (p. 649)** **Academic Skills (p. 653)** |
| **Science** | **NSES A** Develop understandings about scientific inquiry. | **Academic Skills (p. 653)** |
| **Social Studies** | **NCSS I A Culture** Analyze and explain the ways groups, societies, and cultures address human needs and concerns. | **Culture Matters (p. 632)** |
| | **NCSS I D Culture** Compare and analyze societal patterns for preserving and transmitting culture while adapting to environmental or societal change. | **After You Read (p. 637)** |
| | **NCSS IV D Individual Development and Identity** Apply concepts, methods, and theories about the study of human growth and development, such as physical endowment, learning, motivation, behavior, perception, and personality. | **Observation Skills (p. 652)** |

## Mc Graw Hill Professional Development

**MINI CLIP VIDEO LIBRARY**
Targeted professional development is correlated throughout *The Developing Child*. **The McGraw-Hill Professional Development Mini Clip Video Library** provides teaching strategies to strengthen academic and learning skills. Log on to **glencoe.com**.

In this chapter, you will find these Mini Clips:
- **Reading** Vocabulary, p. 631
- **Reading** Flexible Groupings, p. 640
- **ELL** Level 4 Proficiency, p. 641
- **ELL** Graphic Organizers, p. 643
- **Reading** During and After Reading, p. 645
- **Reading** Another Point of View, p. 648

## Reading and Writing Strategies

**Writing Activity: Business Letter** (p. 628)
Students use writing tips to create a business letter explaining why they are a good choice to fill a volunteer position.

**Before You Read** (pp. 630, 638)
A pre-reading question or statement will help students make a personal connection to content.

**Graphic Organizer** (pp. 630, 638)
A visual tool will help students organize and remember new content.

**Reading Check** (pp. 634, 636, 646, 648)
A question allows students to make a quick comprehension self-check.

**After You Read** (pp. 637, 649)
Organize and process students' understanding of what they have read.

## Chapter Features

**A School Where Teachers Fly to Work** (p. 632)
The Shetland Islands are so remote that in 2004 the school had only two students and three of the six teachers had to be flown to school.

**Work or College** (p. 635)
Young people must sometimes decide whether to continue work that they enjoy or obtain more schooling.

**Job Interview** (p. 643)
While going for job interviews may be difficult, it is a vital part of getting a position you want.

**Actor in Children's Theatre** (p. 650)
Learn the skills needed to succeed as an actor in children's theatre.

## Chapter Overview

### Introduce the Chapter

In this chapter, students learn about different career options. They also learn the importance of obtaining a job that matches their interests, aptitudes, and abilities. Writing an appropriate résumé and cover letter is also discussed, along with how to properly present yourself at a job interview.

### Build Background

Ask students to raise their hands if they are currently considering careers that involve children. Because there are so many careers in this area, they also may be thinking about how they can tie in their other talents. Encourage students to share their thoughts about those careers that might tie together two or more of their interests and abilities.

## Writing Activity
### Business Letter

This active learning activity prompts students to write a business letter to apply for a volunteer position. After students complete the activity, encourage them to share their letters with the class, if they are comfortable doing so. Student responses can be used as a basis for classroom discussion. (Students should write a brief business letter stating the volunteer position for which they are applying and the qualifications that make them well-suited to this position.)

## Chapter Objectives

After completing this chapter, you will be able to:

- **Describe** three different ways to gain work experience.
- **Identify** factors to consider when evaluating careers.
- **Explain** the relationship between a career goal and a career path.
- **List** six steps involved in a job search.
- **Compare and contrast** job-specific skills and transferable skills.
- **Summarize** an employee's responsibilities when leaving a job.

## Writing Activity
### Business Letter

**Volunteering** Think of a volunteer position that might interest you, such as being an assistant soccer coach or working in a day care. Write a business letter to the individual in charge of this position explaining why you feel you would be a good choice for this position.

**Writing Tips** If you are going to succeed in your career, you must be able to create a well-written business letter. Here are some tips to keep in mind:
1. Address the letter to a specific person, if possible.
2. Explain the purpose of the letter clearly.
3. Be brief and to-the-point.

628

## CLASSROOM Solutions

### Print Resources

 **Student Edition**

 **Teacher Wraparound Edition**

 **Student Activity Workbook**

 **Student Activity Workbook Teacher Annotated Edition**

### Technology Resources

 **Online Learning Center** has resources and activities for students and teachers. Includes an Online Student Edition.

 **Interactive Student Edition** allows students to instantly access review materials, examples, and exercises.

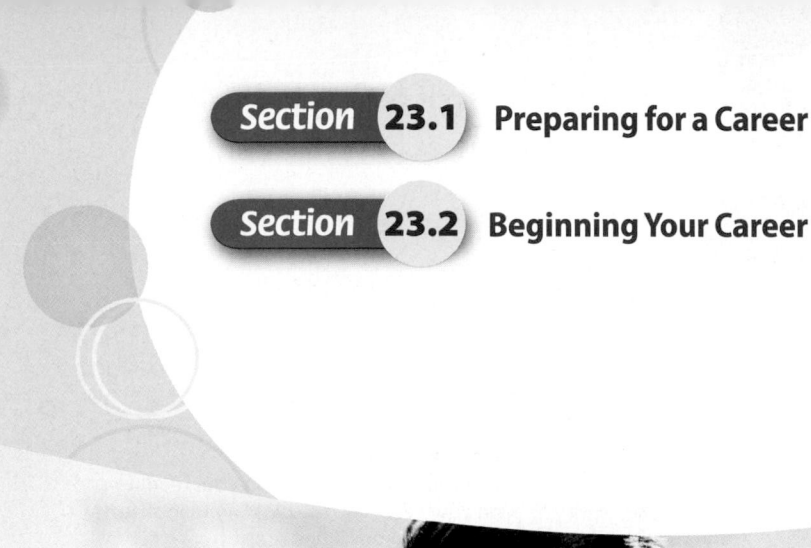

## Section **23.1** Preparing for a Career

## Section **23.2** Beginning Your Career

### Review the Sections

Introduce the chapter by reviewing the sections:

**Section 23.1**
A wide variety of careers involve working with children. Levels of available jobs include entry-level, paraprofessional, and professional. When choosing a career, students should make that it matches their interests, aptitudes, and abilities. Once a career goal is determined, a career path, which includes all the steps to reach the goal, can be established.

**Section 23.2**
Common ways of finding jobs include the Internet, classified ads, friends, relatives, and acquaintances. A résumé is a concise document that summarizes the job-seeker's career objectives, education, work experience, and accomplishments. When going to a job interview, it is important to conduct research on the company ahead of time, dress suitably, and ask appropriate questions.

 **Explore the Photo**

**Caption Answer** Student answers will vary; many adults enjoy interacting with children and are pleased at being able to have a positive effect on their futures.

**Discussion** Have students work individually to write a sentence describing what they think is the greatest reward for working with children. Ask for volunteers to read their sentences to the class. Encourage class members to discuss the sentences.

⬆ **Explore the Photo**
Large numbers of adults have jobs that involve working directly with children. *Why do you think people might choose these careers?*

629

 **TeacherWorks Plus** is an electronic lesson planner that provides instant access to complete teacher resources in one convenient package.

 **Presentation Plus!** provides visual teaching aids for every section.

 **The Early Childhood Observations CD** presents video observations and lessons on observation skills and child development.

**The Developing Brain eTransparencies and Guide** include information and activities to offer insights into brain development and diseases of the brain.

### Bell Ringer Activity

**Looking for Work**
Gather together a collection of advertisements for jobs that involve working with young children. Allow the students to read the ads or read the ads aloud to the class. As a class, make a list of the kinds of skills the jobs require.

## Preteaching

### Vocabulary
Ask the class: In words such as *paraprofessional* what do you think the prefix *para-* means? (beside or alongside) Based on this definition, ask students to define *paraprofessional*.

### Graphic Organizer
The Graphic Organizer is also on the TeacherWorks CD.

(Graphic organizers should include: (1) Evaluate interests, aptitudes, and abilities; (2) Gather information; (3) Gain work experience; and (4) Evaluate careers)

**NCLB** connects academic correlations to book content.

## Reading Guide

### Before You Read

**Study New Terms** This section contains a variety of terms. Spend a minute skimming the section and reading the definition of each term. As you thoroughly read the section, you will better understand its main points.

### Read to Learn
**Key Concepts**
- **Describe** three different ways to gain work experience.
- **Identify** factors to consider when evaluating careers.
- **Explain** the relationship between a career goal and a career path.

**D**

### Main Idea
You are most likely to thrive in a career that matches your interests, aptitudes, and abilities. When choosing a career, you should consider factors such as work environment and the required education.

### Content Vocabulary
 entry-level job
◇ paraprofessional
◇ professional
◇ entrepreneur
◇ aptitude
◇ internship
◇ job shadowing
◇ service learning
◇ work-based learning
◇ career path
◇ career ladder

### Academic Vocabulary
You will find these words in your reading and on your tests. Use the glossary to look up their definitions if necessary.
- ability
- visualization

### Graphic Organizer
As you read, note the four steps in choosing a career. Use a chart like the one shown to help organize your information.

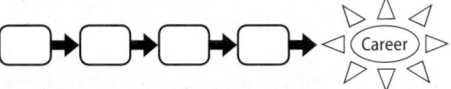

 **Graphic Organizer** Go to this book's Online Learning Center at **glencoe.com** to print out this graphic organizer.

---

**Academic Standards** . . . . . . . . . . . . . . . . . . . . . . . . . . .

**N C L B**

🌐 **English Language Arts**
**NCTE 1** Read texts to acquire new information.

🌐 **Social Studies**
**NCSS I A Culture** Analyze and explain the ways groups, societies, and cultures address human needs and concerns.

**NCSS I D Culture** Compare and analyze societal patterns for preserving and transmitting culture while adapting to environmental or societal change.

**NCTE** *National Council of Teachers of English*
**NCTM** *National Council of Teachers of Mathematics*
**NSES** *National Science Education Standards*
**NCSS** *National Council for the Social Studies*

---

### Before You Read

Ask students to raise their hands if they have part-time jobs or do volunteer work. Ask for volunteers to discuss how they obtained these positions. Discuss what they looked for in their jobs. For example, did they do it mainly for the money, for experience, or for the social benefits?

### D Develop Concepts

**Main Idea** Discuss the main idea with the students. Ask: What do you think might happen if you went into a career that did not match your interests or abilities? (Possible answer: You might be bored or feel like a failure.)

## Career Options

Choosing a career may seem like a hard decision. There are many jobs to choose from. Where do you begin? Most people start by choosing a career area or career field. This is a group of similar careers. Once they have learned more about the career field, they can choose a specific career to prepare for.

Taking a class in an area of interest is a good way to explore career options. Perhaps you are taking this class because you are interested in working with children. The knowledge and skills gained in this class will help prepare you to make a choice that is right for you.

## Working with Children

Those interested in working directly with children often choose careers related to child development or child care. A pediatrician, for example, specializes in medical care for children. In-depth knowledge of child development and medicine are required. A lead teacher in a child care center needs to know about child development to plan appropriate activities and care.

Many careers may not immediately come to mind when you think of working with children. Here are some specialized careers that may interest you:

- Wildlife educator
- Emergency medical technician
- Adoption consultant
- Child development researcher

- Puppeteer
- Occupational therapist
- Play therapist

Look for the Careers with Children features throughout this book for profiles of additional careers that involve working with children.

## Levels of Jobs

Within a career area, there are usually jobs available at several levels. These levels depend on the amount of education and training required and the degree of responsibility the job carries.

### Entry-Level

An **entry-level job** is the kind of job many people take when they first enter a career area. Most people, however, do not stay at this level. With more experience or education, many move up to jobs with more responsibility. After he received his high school diploma, Russell took an entry-level job at a child care center to explore his interest in helping children. Within a few years, and after earning a degree from a four-year college program, he had moved into a lead teacher position at the center.

### Paraprofessional

A **paraprofessional** is someone with some education beyond high school that trains him or her for a certain field. Many paraprofessional jobs require a related degree from a two-year college. An assistant teacher in a preschool, for instance, is a paraprofessional.

 **Working with Children**
People who work with children need to understand child development. *How can an understanding of child development help this teacher do her job?*

Section 23.1   Preparing for a Career   **631**

**► Explore the Photo**

**Caption Answer** Understanding the way that children develop motor skills could help this teacher modify her methods based on a child's age and abilities.

**Discussion** Tell students to imagine they are in charge of the music center at a child care center for three- to five-year-olds. Ask: How might the activities you plan for three-year-olds be different than those for five-year-olds? (Responses will vary. The lyrics and finger plays for the three-year-olds' songs would need to be simpler. Three-year-olds could play simple rhythm instruments whereas five-year-olds might be ready for more complex instruments.)

## Teach

### Discussion Starter

**Career Decisions** Ask students: What factors influence career decisions? What personal qualities are essential for professional success? As students list qualities, write them on the board and encourage the class to discuss each one's importance. (Responses will vary. Career decisions are based on factors such as the individual's interests, aptitudes, and willingness to obtain additional education. Qualities might include the desire to complete a job, to do the best possible job, or to be able to communicate well with others.)

### R Reading Strategy

**Vocabulary Chart** Have each student create a vocabulary chart. The first column should contain a list of the vocabulary words in this section. The second column should state whether the student already knows each word's definition. As students read, they should fill in the third column with the word's definition. When they later study these words, they should pay special attention to those they did not previously know. (Students should create a chart of vocabulary words along with their definitions. They also should indicate whether the words were new to them.)

**Professional Development**

**Mini Clip**
**Reading: Vocabulary**

Author Josefina Tinajero describes the critical importance of academic language.

## Teach *cont.*

### S Skill Practice

**Guided Practice**

**Create a Chart** Instruct students to create a chart listing the characteristics of each of these job levels: entry-level, paraprofessional, and professional. (Charts should list characteristics of each of the three job levels. For example, paraprofessional characteristics might include having some education beyond high school that provides training in a specific field.) **L1 ELL**

**Identify** Bring in several photos from magazines or print some out from the Internet that show people in a variety of careers related to children. Ask students to identify which job level is probably portrayed by the person in the photo. Students should be prepared to offer reasons for their classification if another student disagrees. (Answers may vary. If students disagree about any of the professions, encourage discussions on why. Students should use the descriptions of the different levels from the text to support their positions. Note that some professions may have more than one correct possibility.) **L2 ELL**

**Summarize** Have students choose a career involving young children in which they are interested. Instruct them to read about jobs in that field at these three levels: entry-level, paraprofessional, and professional. Students should write a summary paragraph describing jobs at each level. (Paragraphs will vary but should describe entry-level, paraprofessional, and professional jobs in a specific career involving young children. Encourage students to use the *Occupational Outlook Handbook* on the Internet if they need help choosing a career.) **L3**

---

## CULTURE MATTERS

### A School Where Teachers Fly to Work

The school on Out Skerries Island, in the Shetland Islands off the coast of Scotland, had only two students, who are brothers, and six teachers in 2004. It cost the government over $100,000 a year to teach the two boys, because three of their teachers are flown in every week from another island. The boys' lives are a mix of new and old. In keeping with traditional practices on the islands, the boys have learned to catch lobsters, mend nets, and repair boats. However, they also keep in touch with friends on other islands through e-mail and text messaging.

**Build Connections** *Write a paragraph contrasting a day in the life of these two boys with a day in your life.*

**NCSS I A Culture** Analyze and explain the ways groups, societies, and cultures address human needs and concerns.

### Professional

A **professional** has a position that requires at least a degree from a four-year college or technical school in a specific area of study. Many professionals have a more advanced degree, such as a master's degree, and years of experience. Professionals may be in charge of programs or supervise entry-level workers and paraprofessionals. Kindergarten teachers are professionals.

### Entrepreneurs

Most people work for someone else. For example, an elementary teacher works for a school district, a toy designer works for a manufacturer. Someone who chooses to be self-employed or to own his or her own business is an **entrepreneur** (ˌän-trə-p(r)ə-ˈnər). An entrepreneur's life can be both exciting and challenging.

Because entrepreneurs have no boss, they get to make the rules, set their own schedules, and make the decisions. However, they also assume all the risks of the business and often end up working very long hours. People who are self-employed must be self-motivated, self-disciplined, good problem solvers, and willing to work hard.

There are many entrepreneurial opportunities related to children. Examples include owning a daycare, writing children's books, or providing entertainment for children's parties. The best entrepreneurs develop businesses around their own personal interests and skills. For example, a children's book author must truly enjoy writing and be able to look at the world from a child's point of view.

Many entrepreneurs start out working for others, and gradually establish their own businesses. After finishing college, a music teacher may work for a public school and then start teaching private lessons. Finally, she might be established enough to open her own studio. Entrepreneurs have the reward of knowing they have succeeded on their own.

### Evaluate Interests, Aptitudes, and Abilities

When choosing a career, make sure the job will be a good fit for you. Some careers may sound exciting, but when you look at them more closely, you might realize that they would not be right for you. As you explore various career choices, you need to consider them in light of your own interests and values, aptitudes, and abilities.

---

## CULTURE MATTERS

### A School Where Teachers Fly to Work

**Discussion** Ask students: What might be some advantages of the type of education these boys receive? Some disadvantages? (Advantages might include they get more attention from teachers and the curriculum can be tailored to them. Disadvantages might include that they do not get to socialize with classmates or take part in typical extra-curricular activities.)

**Build Connections** *Student answers will vary. They might describe how they typically interact with many friends during the day, but the boys only have one another and their teachers. They also might compare their daily chores with those of the boys.*

## Interests and Values

If you work toward a career that does not match your interests, it could set you up for years of unfulfilling work. Your interests might include areas of study that you enjoy, such as psychology or science, or activities that you enjoy, such as photography or music. You also need to consider your values. What is important to you? Do you want a career that pays a high salary? Are you concerned about gaining satisfaction from your work? Are you willing to work weekends or long hours, or is time with family and friends more important?

## Aptitudes

An **aptitude** is a natural talent or potential for learning a skill. What kinds of learning come most easily to you? Perhaps you have an aptitude for communicating with young children or learning new computer programs. High school counselors have tests that can help you decide what your aptitudes are. You should consider careers that match your strengths.

## Abilities

An **ability** is a skill you have already developed. Identifying what your skills are can help you make career decisions. As you begin to take on more responsibilities, you can expand and improve your abilities. This includes skills specific to career areas that interest you and general skills, such as teamwork or reliability.

## Find Career Information

Another important part of career decision making is research. Learning more about areas that interest you will help you narrow your choices. The Career Skills Handbook in the back of this textbook offers valuable tips on career research.

## Gather Information

You can gather information from a variety of sources. Online sources, libraries, and people can all be helpful. The Internet can put you in touch with trade and professional organizations, government resources, job listings, and people working in various careers. Most libraries have excellent career information resources. These two government publications are available in print and online:

- *The Occupational Outlook Handbook* gives detailed information on hundreds of jobs.
- *The Occupational Outlook Quarterly* updates information on career trends every three months.

Probably the best way to find out what a career is really like is to talk to people who are in that career. After all, who knows better than a teacher what the day-to-day life of a teacher is like? You can ask school counselors, teachers, relatives, and friends about possible contacts in specific career areas. Most people are happy to share information about their careers.

**➤ Career Fair**
There are many opportunities for learning more about career areas. *What kinds of questions might these teens ask a potential employer?*

## Teach *cont.*

### U Universal Access

**Intrapersonal Learners** Emphasize that the first step in career exploration is for students to know themselves and understand their interests. Have students think of a career that involves working with children that closely matches their interests. Students should then create multimedia artwork that shows them working in this career. Ask volunteers to discuss their artwork. (Students should create multimedia artwork showing them working in a career that involves children and that closely matches their areas of interest. For example, a student interested in the outdoors might create artwork that shows him or her giving a nature tour to children in a national park.)

### C Critical Thinking

**Solve Problems** Carlos is graduating from high school and needs to find a job. His family is trying to help him with a career search, but he says he does not have any skills and rules out all jobs they suggest. Ask students how teens like Carlos can come to understand their own abilities and aptitudes. (Student responses will vary. Perhaps Carlos can talk with a guidance counselor at school or with some friends that are a few years older than him to get ideas. Most people have skills even if they are not aware of them as being skills. Carlos should also clarify what he expects to get out of a job at this time of his life.)

## ➤ Explore the Photo

**Caption Answer** Student answers will vary; they might ask the exact skills a particular job requires, the hours, the advancement opportunities, or the salary and benefits offered.

**Discussion** Employers come to career fairs because they need good workers. Ask students what they think employers might do to attract visitors to their booths. (Responses will vary. They might make their booths attractive and colorful. They also might show interesting videos that explain their business or hand out small gifts, such as tote bags and candy.)

### Quiz

Ask students to answer the following questions:

1. **What is an entry-level job?** (It is a job that people get when they first enter a particular career area.)
2. **What personal characteristics do entrepreneurs need?** (They need to be self-motivated, self-disciplined, good problem solvers, and willing to work hard.)
3. **Name two resources that can provide information about careers.** (Possible responses: *The Occupational Outlook Handbook, The Occupational Outlook Quarterly,* people who are in a career, or job-related Web sites.)

###  Writing Support

**Business Letter**

**Job Shadowing Request** Have students think of a person in their community whom they would like to job shadow in order to learn more about their work. Students then should write this individual a business letter requesting to spend a day shadowing, or observing, him or her on the job. In the letter, they should state specific reasons for their request. (Refer to p. 628 to review tips on creating a well-written business letter. Students should write a letter requesting to job shadow a specific person in their community. They should state specific reasons for their request.)

### ✓ Reading Check

**Define** An ability is a skill that you have already developed.

---

### Gain Work Experience

You can learn a lot about a career, and about yourself, by working. Summer work and part-time jobs are good ways to get started. Another way to learn about a job is through an internship. An **internship** is a job in which a person works for little or no pay while gaining experience and receiving supervision. For example, you might get an internship with a coach at a recreational facility such as a YMCA.

You might also be able to arrange to do job shadowing. **Job shadowing** means to observe someone performing his or her job. You would need to contact someone whose career interests you and arrange to spend time at work with that person, following the person around like a shadow. Your guidance counselor may be able to help you make arrangements for job-shadowing experiences. Job shadowing is especially helpful in specialized fields, such as pediatrics, because it allows you to see the variety of skills the professional must have.

Another way to learn about a career is by volunteering. Many organizations, especially those that operate on limited funds, welcome volunteers. The opportunities may be temporary or longer term. Arielle volunteers as a children's storyteller at her local library once a month, while Isaac volunteers as an assistant for children's activities at a city park each weekend. Guidance counselors often have a list of organizations looking for volunteers. Community centers are also a good resource for volunteering opportunities.

Although volunteers are not paid for their work, volunteering offers a great experience. It may even lead to a paying job. One added benefit of volunteering is the satisfaction of helping others in the community. In addition, colleges and employers are impressed by people who make the effort to help out in their community through volunteer work.

Some school programs offer direct work experience. **Service learning** is a school program in which students volunteer in their community as a graduation requirement. **Work-based learning** is a school program that offers students the opportunity to combine in-school and on-the-job learning.

Work experience offers another benefit besides a feel for what it is like to have a job. You may meet people who know someone in the career area that interests you. Supervisors and coworkers may also be willing to serve as references whom a prospective employer can contact for information about your skills and character.

**✓ Reading Check** **Define** What is an ability?

**➡ Volunteer Work**
You can gain valuable work experience by volunteering. *What are some benefits of getting work experience while you are still in school?*

---

### ▶ Explore the Photo

**Caption Answer** Student answers will vary; the experience gives you a chance to learn the exact requirements for a particular job and whether you are suited to that type of work.

**Discussion** Encourage students who have performed volunteer work to list some of the skills they learned from their experiences. (Skills might include actual abilities. For example, a student who volunteered at a library might have learned how to shelve books. Other skills might include learning to communicate with people of all ages and the importance of being dependable.)

## Evaluate Careers

Knowing where to look for career information is one thing, but then what? There are many factors to consider when choosing a career. Following is a list of some of the most important factors to consider. Can you think of others?

- **Tasks and Responsibilities** What does a worker in this career do? Is the work the same every day or is it varied? Is the pace fast or slow? How much control does an employee have over the work? Is the work mostly physical or mental? Child care workers have a very active work environment. They spend the day playing, leading activities, cleaning spills, and running after children. A child development researcher may spend time observing children but will probably not interact with them. A researcher's job generally involves very little physical activity.

- **Work with People, Information, or Technology** Each career tends to emphasize one area over another. Which do you prefer? A reading teacher works mainly with people. An editor of children's books works mainly with information. A designer of children's clothing works mainly with technology.

- **Work Environment** The work environment is the physical and social surroundings at the workplace. Camp counselors and coaches work outdoors. Nurses and teachers work indoors. Social workers spend a majority of their day in their cars driving to meet different clients in their homes. Some people work alone. Others work in teams. Workers in runaway youth shelters must often deal with children who have psychological or behavioral problems. Child care workers can work in small day care centers; in a private home; or in spacious, well-funded, private nursery schools. Which kind of environment is most appealing to you?

- **Working Hours** Many people work from 9:00 in the morning to 5:00 at night. Many others work different hours. Many social service workers or suicide-prevention

### Work or College?

Twenty-year-old Patrick has worked in a drop-in center for runaway and homeless teens for four years. He loves the job. When new clients come in, he makes sure they have a meal, learn their way around the center, and get counseling if needed. Patrick knows that he wants a career that involves helping people, so three years ago he enrolled part-time at a nearby community college and studied for an associate's degree in human services. He will finish his degree in a few months and is considering whether to continue his studies. With a bachelor's degree in social work, he could get a higher-paying job with more responsibility. He could even work as a school social worker or probation officer. On the other hand, it would mean going to college full time and giving up his current job that he enjoys.

✏ **Write About It** Put yourself in Patrick's position. You must decide whether to keep your job at the drop-in center, which you really enjoy, or continue on in school to get a bachelor's degree in social work. Write a paragraph explaining which decision you would make and why.

hotline workers need to work through the night. Some jobs, like storyteller or magician, require weekend and holiday work. Many jobs require overtime or travel. What is acceptable to you?

- **Aptitudes** Compare the aptitudes needed for a career with your own aptitudes. How well do they match?

- **Education and Training** Although many people gain experience on the job, they need the right education to land that job in the first place. What education and training are required for the careers that interest you? School counselors, libraries, and the Internet offer information about education and training opportunities beyond high school, as well as ways to pay for them.

### Reteach *cont.*

### U Universal Access

**Verbal Learners** Instruct students to choose a career in which they are interested that involves working with young children. They should then go *to The Occupational Outlook Handbook* to answer these questions about the career:

- What are its tasks and responsibilities?
- What is the work environment typically like?
- What education and training are required?

Students should prepare an oral presentation in which they discuss the answers to these questions. (Oral presentations will vary but should answer the specified questions concerning a specific career of their choosing. You might also encourage students to explain why this career interests them.)

### C Critical Thinking

**Hypothesize** Discuss that some jobs require long hours. For example, a doctor's office does not close until all patients have been seen. Ask students: Why might some of the staff have problems with this type of schedule? (Answers will vary. A possible answer includes: Some of the staff may need to pick their children up from child care or after-school programs by a specific time.)

**Write About It** Students should write a paragraph explaining their decision. The student might decide to quit the job at the drop-in center and go to college full time in order to have more career options in the future.

**U** **Universal Access**

**Logical Learners** Organize students into two teams. The teams will debate one another. One side will argue that students should only consider careers for which the demand is growing. The other side will argue that the most important consideration is choosing a career for which they are well-suited and will enjoy. Remind students to make their points as concise as possible. Conduct the debate. (Debates will vary. One side should argue that people should choose careers for which the demand is growing and the other side that careers should be chosen based on individuals' interests and abilities. Some students may feel it is more important to have job security to be able to support a family while others may argue that you cannot be happy if you don't enjoy your job.) **ELL**

**C** **Critical Thinking**

**Extrapolate** Ask for a volunteer to share his or her long-term goals with the class. Then, as a class, work on some of the short-term goals that might lead to this long-term goal. Encourage students to be creative in their ideas. (Students should develop short-term goals designed to reach a specific long-term goal. For example, if a student wanted to be a children's librarian, one short-term goal might be to become a volunteer in the children's section of the local public library.)

### ✓ Reading Check

**Recall** Benefits might include paid holidays, sick days, retirement plans, or health insurance.

• **Salary and Benefits** Income generally increases with training and education. Income also tends to rise as workers gain experience. A first-year paraprofessional can expect to earn less than a coworker with five years in the same job. Many employers offer benefits such as paid holidays, health insurance, retirement plans, and paid vacation time. These benefits are in addition to the regular salary.

• **Career Outlook** What do experts think will happen to this career in the future? Will the demand for the career grow or shrink? Answers to these questions affect how easy it will be to find a job in certain career areas. Many sources estimate future trends for various jobs.

### ✓ Reading Check **Recall** Give examples of three kinds of benefits.

## Setting and Achieving Goals

Some people simply take whatever job comes their way. While this approach sometimes works out, it is much smarter to think carefully about the career you would like and then work to achieve it. After all, you will spend most of your waking hours at work. Would it be better if that work were satisfying, challenging, and worthwhile? Establishing career goals can help you achieve this.

Career goals are like a road map to your future. As with other goals, you need both long-term and short-term career goals. If you decide that you want a career as a kindergarten teacher, that is your long-term goal. Getting there will take years and require many smaller achievements. To reach your long-term goal, you will need short-term goals. These are specific actions to achieve in the next few days, months, or year. Without short-term goals, it is less likely that you will achieve your long-term goal.

Lynette's goal was to become a physical therapist. To help achieve that long-term goal, she set a short-term goal of working with children on a daily basis to make certain she would

like that aspect of the career. Through her job as a camp counselor, she met that goal.

There are two basic types of career goals: general and specific. General career goals are goals for the type of work you want to do. Some examples of general career goals are "I want to work with children," or "I want to work outdoors." Specific career goals are goals for the specific job you want. For example, "I want to be a preschool teacher," or "I want to write children's books." If your career goal is too general, you will not know where to start. Make your goal more specific. The more specific and realistic your goals are, the more likely you will be to achieve them.

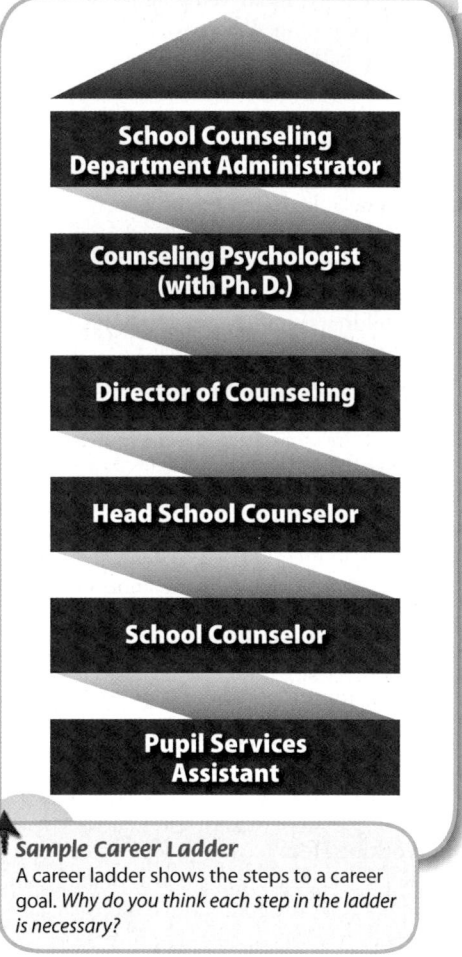

**Sample Career Ladder**
A career ladder shows the steps to a career goal. *Why do you think each step in the ladder is necessary?*

School Counseling Department Administrator

Counseling Psychologist (with Ph. D.)

Director of Counseling

Head School Counselor

School Counselor

Pupil Services Assistant

### ➤ Explore the Photo

**Caption Answer** Answers will vary. Students might say that important skills are learned at each step that will prepare you for the next one.

**Discussion** Ask students what they think might happen to someone who skipped over one or more of these steps. For example, what difficulties might occur if someone went

directly from being a school counselor to director of counseling? (Possible answer: going through the steps allows the person to see how the different components of the system work together. Skipping steps might make it more difficult to make good decisions.)

## Setting a Career Path

Once you have chosen a specific career goal, you must look ahead and consider your career path. A **career path** is all of the career moves and job experience that a person gains as he or she works toward a career goal. There are usually many steps to reaching your final career goal.

For a career in social work, for example, you might begin as a caseworker. Caseworkers help clients get the assistance they need. As you gain experience in this position, you might take on more clients and begin to supervise other caseworkers. With more experience and education, such as a master's degree in social work, you could begin supervising other caseworkers. As you learn more on the job and gain more experience, you might be promoted to executive director of your agency.

A **career ladder** is a visualization of your chosen career path. A **visualization** is a mental image. This helps you see where you currently are in reaching your goals. It also helps you decide what your next career step might be.

## Modifying Goals

Your career plan is not set in stone. Your goals and the time you spend on them may change over time. You must face your future with an open mind. The motivation to achieve your goals comes from within. If you are not reaching your goals, do not lose motivation. Figure out why you are stuck. You might need to revise your goals to renew your motivation.

The most important thing is to have a plan. Without a plan, you just have an idea or a dream. With a plan, you are moving toward your ultimate career goal, step by step. You will find the career that is right for you.

**Study Tools**

Have students go to the Online Learning Center at **glencoe.com**:

- Take the **Practice Test**.
- Download **Study-to-Go** content.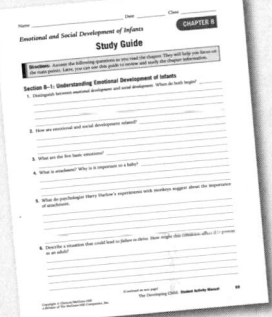

Use the **Student Activity Workbook** for additional practice.

### Close

**Culminating Activity**

**Creating a Checklist** Have students work individually to create checklists that they can use to evaluate careers they may be considering. (Checklists will vary but should cover the information in the text.)

 **NCLB** connects academic correlations to book content.

---

## Section 23.1    After You Read

### Review Key Concepts

1. **Explain** why you should evaluate your interests, aptitudes, and abilities when researching careers.
2. **Describe** some of the benefits of gaining work experience through part-time and volunteer work.
3. **Identify** why it is important to have short-term goals.

### Practice Academic Skills

 **English Language Arts**

4. Locate and read at least three different articles on service learning programs and the types of volunteer projects students have worked on. Use what you learn from the articles to write a persuasive essay in support of service learning.

> **NCTE 3** Apply strategies to interpret texts.

**Social Studies**

5. Some organizations are devoted to teaching cultural heritages to young people. For example, a summer camp might teach Native American traditions. Research such an organization. Write a brief summary of the skills an individual would need to work for this organization.

> **NCSS I D** Compare and analyze societal patterns for preserving and transmitting culture while adapting to environmental or societal change.

**Check Your Answers** Check your answers at this book's Online Learning Center at **glencoe.com**.

**NCLB**

Section 23.1   Preparing for a Career    **637**

---

## Section 23.1   After You Read

### Review Key Concepts

1. You will probably have more success and find more enjoyment in a job for which you are well-suited in an area that you find interesting.
2. Both of these experiences let you see how well you like a particular kind of work without committing to it full-time. They also let you learn about the job benefits and responsibilities. Part-time work also provides some income.
3. Short-term goals keep you on the path to achieving your long-term goals.

### Practice Academic Skills

4. Essays will vary but should persuade readers of the value of service learning.
5. Summaries will vary but should describe the kinds of skills an individual would need to work for an organization that teaches cultural heritage.

## Focus

### 🔔 Bell Ringer Activity

#### Compare Two Résumés

Show students two résumés—one that is neat and well-written and one that has errors, is cluttered with graphics, or contains irrelevant information. Based on these résumés, ask students which applicant they would interview and why.

## Preteaching

### Vocabulary

Write the words *resume* and *résumé* on the board. Pronounce each and explain that the difference in pronunciation is due to the accents in *résumé*, which is from the French. If time allows, you may want to show how to use word processing software to insert the accents.

### Graphic Organizer

 The Graphic Organizer is also on the TeacherWorks CD.

(Graphic organizers should include: basic skills, communication skills, relationship skills, leadership skills, managing multiple roles, learning from performance evaluations, and behaving ethically.)

**NCLB** connects academic correlations to book content.

---

## Section 23.2 Beginning Your Career

### Reading Guide

#### 📖 Before You Read

**Find Answers** Before reading this section, write down what you would like to learn about looking for a job. When you are done, determine whether your questions were answered.

#### Read to Learn
##### Key Concepts
- **List** six steps involved in a job search.
- **Compare and contrast** job-specific skills and transferable skills.
- **Summarize** an employee's responsibilities when leaving a job.

#### D Main Idea
When looking for a job, it is important to be resourceful. A well-written résumé and cover letter show your professionalism and abilities. Always be prepared when going for a job interview.

#### Content Vocabulary
◇ networking
◇ job fair
◇ résumé
◇ cover letter
◇ job-specific skills
◇ transferable skills
◇ ethical
◇ lifelong learner
◇ unemployment benefits
◇ COBRA

 **Graphic Organizer** Go to this book's Online Learning Center at **glencoe.com** to print out this graphic organizer.

#### Academic Vocabulary
You will find these words in your reading and on your tests. Use the glossary to look up their definitions if necessary.
- convey
- legible

#### Graphic Organizer
As you read this section, look for seven transferable skills, or skills that are useful in any job. Use a web diagram like the one shown to help organize your information.

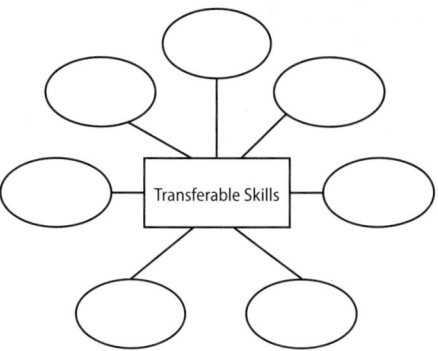

Transferable Skills

---

#### Academic Standards · · · · · · · · · · · · · · · · · · · · ·

##### 🌐 English
NCTE 12 Use language to accomplish individual purposes.

##### 🧮 Mathematics
**NCTM Number and Operations** Understand numbers, ways of representing numbers, relationships among numbers, and number systems.

**NCTE** *National Council of Teachers of English*
**NCTM** *National Council of Teachers of Mathematics*

**NSES** *National Science Education Standards*
**NCSS** *National Council for the Social Studies*

---

### Reading Guide

#### 📖 Before You Read

Ask students to raise their hands if they have ever interviewed for a job. Encourage them to discuss how the situation made them feel. Do they think they could have been better prepared? If so, how?

#### D Develop Concepts

**Main Idea** Discuss the main idea with the students. Ask students why they think it is vital that résumés and cover letters use good grammar and be free of spelling errors. (It shows that they have good communication skills and take the job-hunting process seriously.)

## Look for a Job

A few people find themselves in the right place at the right time and are hired for their dream job. Others are fortunate to have an internship or a part-time job turn into a full-time position. Most people, however, must devote a lot of time and effort to their job search. You should plan to invest time and energy in your own job search. After all, you will be spending many hours at work each week. It is worth the effort to find the right job.

As with all major goals, it is best to break down job hunting into a series of smaller steps. The six steps to secure employment are finding an opening, preparing a résumé, filling out an application, interviewing, following up, and evaluating a job offer. These steps can be accomplished one at a time.

The key to a successful job search is organization. A notebook or computer file used to record names, addresses, and dates is one way many people keep track of their job search. For instance, Will uses his computer to record the dates he responds to newspaper ads, the dates employers contact him, the times and locations of his interviews, and the dates he sends follow-up letters. See the Career Skills handbook at the back of this textbook for more great tips on every step of your job search.

## Find Job Openings

The Internet and classified ads from the newspaper are great ways to find job openings, but they are not your only resources. Finding a job often begins with a tip from a friend, relative, or acquaintance. That is why it is a good idea to let people know that you are job hunting. The more people who know that you are looking for a job, the better the chances are that you will find one that is right for you.

For example, Tristan's neighbor has a sister who is a Girl Scout leader. She knows that the organization will be looking for a new staff member soon. Logan's roommate knows of an opening for a teacher at the preschool where his girlfriend works. The practice of using personal and professional contacts to further your career goals is called **networking**. Many people find that networking is the best way to find a job.

Another way to find out about job openings is to attend a job fair. A **job fair** is an event where employers with current or future job openings meet with potential employees. Sometimes community colleges or universities sponsor such events. You may not land the perfect job by attending a job fair, but you will be able to make valuable contacts by meeting some employers.

**Computer Resources**
A computer can be used to find job openings, locate information about employers, and develop a résumé. *How might you locate information about a potential employer?*

---

**Explore the Photo**

**Caption Answer** Student answers will vary; if the company has a Web site, you could go to it to learn about the company in general and the specific jobs available.

**Discussion** Ask students: How might employers use computers and the Internet to locate and screen potential employees? (Possible answer: They could post jobs on job-related Web sites. They also can use e-mail to communicate with potential employees, asking them specific questions about their job experience or availability.)

### Teach

**Discussion Starter**

**The Employer's Point of View**
Have students imagine that they are in charge of hiring for a local child care center. Ask: How would you advertise any available jobs? What kind of person would you hire to work in the center? (Answers will vary. Students might choose to advertise in the local paper, online, or in trade magazines. They would probably choose workers who enjoyed being around children, behaved ethically, and possessed the needed skills.)

**U Universal Access**

**Gifted Students** Have students conduct research on a Web site that helps individuals find jobs. Students should then create a presentation on the services provided by the Web site. Encourage students to create a slide show to accompany their presentations. (Presentations will vary but should explain the kinds of services provided by a particular Web site. For example, it may allow individuals to post their résumés and search for specific jobs in their region. These Web sites often provide additional information such as local job fairs and tips on writing résumés. People can generally apply for jobs through these Web sites as well.)

**R Reading Strategy**

**Infer** Ask students if they have ever heard of the concept "six degrees of separation." Explain that it is based on the idea that everyone is connected to everyone else through an average of only six other people. Ask: How might this concept emphasize the importance of networking? (Possible answer: Establishing a career network ties you to more people than you realize. Often you will develop contacts because someone you have met knows someone who may be able to give you an important lead.)

## C₁ Critical Thinking

**Judge** Some applicants believe that the only way to get an interview is by making themselves sound better than they are on their résumés. Ask students why misrepresenting one's education or skills, even a small amount, is unfair and unethical. (Answers may vary. Students should realize that misrepresenting themselves on a résumé is lying. If someone gets a job by lying about their skills, they might soon be asked to perform tasks that they cannot and they will probably lose the job. This would also probably prevent the employer from trusting them or considering them for future job positions.)

## W Writing Support

### Revising and Editing

**Résumés** Have students write their own résumés. Then assign each student a partner. Partners should trade résumés and provide feedback regarding the content as well as any punctuation, formatting, grammar, or spelling errors. Students should then revise and edit their résumés based on the feedback they received. (Résumés will vary but should be accurate and follow the guidelines in the text. Emphasize to students the importance of revising and editing a résumé to ensure that it is as accurate as possible.)

**McGraw Hill Professional Development**

**Mini Clip Reading: Flexible Groupings**

Teachers use flexible groupings and partner sharing to promote student discussions.

**↑ Job Fairs**
Job fairs are a good way to talk to professionals from different careers. *What sort of questions might you ask of employers at a job fair?*

## Prepare a Résumé

A **résumé** is a concise document that summarizes your career objectives, education, work experience, and accomplishments. It is like a personal advertisement to show prospective employers.

You should create your résumé on a computer. Many word processing programs provide sample résumés with different layouts, typefaces, and designs. Find a sample that fits your needs and customize it with your own information. The résumé in **Figure 23.1** shows the sections that are usually included.

### Sections of a Résumé

The first section of the résumé is the objective. It is made up of one or two sentences that state the type of position you are seeking. It should **convey**, or express, a sense of purpose and direction. You should customize the objective for each potential employer or job listing.

In the section on education, list the schools you attended starting with the most recent, along with any degrees, honors, or awards you have received. If you have received several honors or awards, you could list them separately under Honors.

If you do not have much work experience, focus on your skills. If you have done volunteer work, include it. Volunteering shows that you are a responsible and active community member. Also include information about any committees or projects you have worked on. Here are some additional tips for preparing an effective résumé.

- Be concise, keeping the résumé to one page if possible. Two pages is the maximum length.
- Be truthful. Do not misrepresent your work history, accomplishments, or education.
- Use action verbs to describe accomplishments. Words such as achieved, developed, coordinated, produced, led, and conducted are good choices.
- Proofread the document carefully. Have someone else proofread it, too. Poor grammar or misspelled words could cause employers to remove you from consideration.
- Keep it simple. Do not clutter your résumé with pictures, graphics, or a fancy format.
- Ask any references for permission before including their names and contact information. References may be listed on your résumé or on a separate page.
- If an employer requests that your résumé be sent by e-mail, ask for formatting guidelines.

 **Explore the Photo**

**Caption Answer** Questions will vary but might be related to hours of work, skills or education needed, salary and benefits, or advancement opportunities.

**Discussion** Tell students that while job fairs are helpful for people looking for employment, they are also useful for employers. Ask students how job fairs might benefit employers. (Answers will vary but might include that they help employers prescreen applicants and reach a wider market than job advertisements.)

**Desiray T. Minter**
6412 Elmhurst Drive
Asheville, NC 28810
828.555.1234
DTM@anymail.com

| | |
|---|---|
| **Objective:** | To work with children as a teacher's assistant in a bilingual education program. |
| **Education:** | Ashton Community College, Asheville, North Carolina
Associate in Applied Science, Child Development, 2009

Whittier High School, Asheville, North Carolina
High School Diploma, 2006 |
| **Skills:** | Excellent organizational skills
Fluent in Spanish and French
Able to work independently or on a team |
| **Experience:** | |
| 2006-Present | Photography Assistant
Angelface Photography Studio, Asheville, North Carolina
Assist children's photographer with studio sittings;
schedule appointments. |
| 2004–2006 | Foreign Language Tutor in Spanish and French
Tutored four to five high school students each semester. |
| 2001–2003 | Counselor
Far Hills Equestrian Camp, Greenville, North Carolina
Supervised eight campers each session. |
| **Honors:** | FCCLA State Vice President of STAR Events, 2008
American Legion Award, 2008
National French Honor Society |
| **Membership:** | Family, Career and Community Leaders of America (FCCLA)
4-H (Chairperson of Horse Leader's Conference) |

References available upon request.

**U**

**C₂**

---

**Figure 23.1 Sample Résumé**

**Caption Answer** The most recent job is photography assistant.

**Discussion** Organize students into pairs. Have each pair go over the résumé in this figure to look for ways in which it might be improved.

Perhaps they think the wording should be changed or more emphasis should be placed on a particular skill. When done, have students share their ideas with the class.

---

**U Universal Access**

**English Language Learners**

Create a résumé similar to the one shown on this page, but with minor changes. In addition, introduce six to eight spelling, punctuation, or grammar errors. Give each student a copy of the résumé, and ask them to work individually to correct any errors. When they are done, discuss the errors as a group. Alternatively, you might have the students work together, pairing an English language learner with a more proficient speaker. Be sure that the pairs work together to find the errors and that the more proficient speaker helps the English learner rather than doing the entire assignment. (Students should locate any spelling, punctuation, and grammar errors in the supplied résumé.) **ELL**

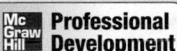 **Professional Development**

**Mini Clip**
**ELL: Level 4 Proficiency**

Author Jana Echevarria discusses the characteristics of Level 4 proficiency English learners.

**C₂ Critical Thinking**

**Predict** The owner of a preschool receives two résumés for a teaching assistant position. Both individuals have similar objectives, skills, and educations. The first résumé also lists two jobs at fast-food restaurants. The second one mentions several volunteer positions working with young children at local community centers and camps. Which person do you think the owner will interview? Why? (Possible answer: The second one because that person has more experience working with young children.)

## Teach cont.

### S Skill Practice

### Guided Practice

**Make a Poster** Instruct students to create a poster that explains the purpose of a cover letter, along with at least six tips for writing a cover letter. Encourage students to include graphics in their posters. (Posters will vary but should explain the purpose of a cover letter and at least six tips on writing good cover letters.) **L1** **ELL**

**Analyze a Cover Letter** Have students examine this cover letter and determine how well it matches the key points for cover letters discussed on page 643. Students should write a paragraph analyzing the cover letter and making any appropriate suggestions for improvements. (Students' paragraphs should analyze the cover letter. The cover letter is appropriately addressed to a specific person and signed by the author. It clearly states the position being applied for. It requests an interview and provides contact information. The letter does a good job of expanding on the applicable skills listed in the résumé.) **L2**

**Write a Cover Letter** Provide students with a résumé along with an advertisement for a job requiring many of the skills listed in the résumé. Instruct students to use both the résumé and the ad to write an appropriate cover letter. (Cover letters will vary but should be well-designed and based on the supplied résumé and job advertisement. Students should have followed the key points on page 643 in writing their cover letters.) **L3**

**Figure 23.2 Sample Cover Letter** Cover letters should be short and clearly explain why you think you are well-qualified for the job. *What are the two ways that Desiray suggests Ms. Hansen can reach her?*

6412 Elmhurst Drive
Asheville, North Carolina 28810

June 15, 2009

Ms. Michelle Hansen
Director, Human Resources
School District 184
Asheville, North Carolina 28810

Dear Ms. Hansen:

I am replying to the ad on the Asheville Citizen-Times Web site seeking a teacher's assistant for the Bilingual Education program at the Early Childhood Education Center. I believe that my skills are an excellent match for this position.

As a high school and college student, I enjoyed courses in child development. I have successfully worked with children of all ages—as a camp counselor, tutor, and active member of FCCLA and 4-H. Currently, my job as a photography assistant involves working with preschool and elementary school children.

My other main interest is foreign languages. In 2008, I had the opportunity to participate in a month-long exchange program in Mexico. I speak fluent Spanish and have four years of credit in French. As a language student at Whittier High School, I frequently assisted with special events in an elementary school program for English-language learners.

I am available for an interview any morning of the week. The best time to reach me at home is before noon. My telephone number is 828.555.1234. My e-mail address is DTM@anymail.com. Thank you for your consideration.

Sincerely,

Desiray T. Minter

Desiray T. Minter

**S**

**Figure 23.2 Sample Cover Letter**

**Caption Answer** Desiray suggests that Ms. Hansen can reach her by phone and by e-mail.

**Discussion** Ask students: What are two ways that Desiray emphasizes her suitability for this position? (She is fluent in Spanish, has four years of French, and has had a variety of jobs working with children of various ages.)

### Write a Cover Letter

An employer may receive dozens, or even hundreds, of résumés in response to a posted advertisement. A **cover letter** is an introductory letter sent with a résumé. The cover letter is the first thing a potential employer sees, and it can make a powerful impression. An interesting cover letter can set your résumé apart from the rest and result in a request for an interview. **Figure 23.2** shows a sample cover letter.

A cover letter provides an opportunity for you to make a good impression. Your cover letter should highlight your relevant talents and skills, prompt the employer to read the résumé, and ultimately result in an interview. Your cover letter introduces you to the employer and lets you sell yourself. Tell the employer what you can do for the company.

Here are some key points to remember when writing a cover letter:

- Highlight your skills and background but do not repeat everything in the résumé.
- Limit the letter to one page.
- Be sure the letter fits the particular situation. If you are answering an ad, for example, be sure to address the requirements cited in the ad. Always begin the letter with a sentence stating where you heard of the job opening.
- Try to address the letter to an individual rather than "To Whom It May Concern." It is often possible to call the employer to obtain the name of a contact person or the person's title. This information may also be on an employer's Web site.
- End your letter with a request for an interview.
- As with the résumé, make sure your spelling and grammar are flawless.
- Use high-quality white or cream paper. When you sign your name, make certain that it is **legible**, or readable, and signed in black ink.
- Include a cover letter when sending a résumé by e-mail.
- Read and re-read your letter to make sure each sentence is correctly worded and there are no errors in spelling, punctuation, or grammar.

## What Would You Do?

### Job Interview

Greg was nervous about going on an interview. Although he had just received a four-year degree in physical education, he still was not sure at what level he wanted to teach. His career counselor at college suggested that he apply for a variety of jobs. That day, Greg was on his way to an interview for an elementary physical education teacher position. He arrived a bit early and went to the school office to check in. The secretary told him to take a seat. The principal called Greg into his office and asked him about his education, his experience, and his desire to teach physical education. Then he took Greg on a tour of the school. Greg told the principal that he hoped to hear from him soon.

✎ **Write About It** Imagine that you are this school's principal. Write a list of eight specific questions you would ask Greg to determine whether he was a good candidate for this job.

## Fill Out an Application

Most employers ask applicants to fill out a job application. An application is a tool that helps employers decide who deserves further consideration. Follow these tips for filling out an application:

- If you have an appointment, arrive on time or a few minutes early.
- Be well groomed and neatly dressed when you go to fill out an application, or to pick up or deliver an application.
- Read and follow the directions on the application carefully. If it is an electronic application, make sure you know how to use the computer before you start.
- Print neatly or type carefully, and answer questions truthfully and as positively as possible. If a question does not apply, write NA, for not applicable, in the space.
- Some applications ask for salary requirements. "Negotiable" is a good response.

### Teach cont.

**R** **Reading Strategy**

**Graphic Organizer** Draw a Venn diagram on the board. One circle should be labeled Résumé and the other Cover Letter. As a class, fill in the diagram with the similarities and differences between the two items. (Similarities include that both emphasize abilities and strengths and are intended to convince a prospective employer to hire the applicant. A résumé is a formal presentation of objectives, education, skills, and experience. A cover letter introduces the job-seeker, and tells why the person is particularly well-suited for a specific job.)

**U** **Universal Access**

**Gifted Learners** Show students some other types of applications they will likely fill out in their lifetime, such as college applications, credit card applications, or rental applications. Have students compare these applications with the ones used for jobs. Discuss the following questions: What information is required on all applications? What information is specific to the purpose of the application? Why is it important to take filling out any application seriously? Ask students to write a one-page report summarizing their analysis and offering answers to the posed questions. (Reports will vary. Students may note that all applications ask for name and address. Information specific to applications might include household income. It is important to take applications seriously because it is the only way to get what you want.)

### Professional Development

**Mini Clip**
**ELL: Graphic Organizers**

Students use graphic organizers to distinguish between major and minor details.

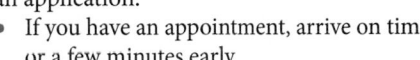

## What Would You Do?

**Write About It** Questions will vary but might include: Why did you get a degree in physical education? What do you think should be the major goals of a physical education teacher? What kind of experience do you have working with elementary school children? What are your specific interests in physical education and sports?

### Quiz

Ask students to answer the following questions:

1. Why do job-seekers find attending job fairs helpful? (They let job-seekers talk with many different employers in a single location and are helpful in developing new contacts.)
2. What is the first section of a résumé and what is its purpose? (It is the Objective section and it should state the type of position desired and convey a sense of purpose and direction.)
3. What key points should be considered when writing a cover letter? (Cover letters should highlight the applicant's skills, but not repeat the résumé. They should be limited to one page, error-free, designed to fit the particular situation, printed on high-quality paper, and signed in blank ink. If possible, they should be addressed to a specific person.)

## Reteach

### C Critical Thinking

**Make Decisions** Explain that sometimes interviews do not happen as planned. Ask students how they might handle these situations gracefully in a job interview:

- Because of unexpected problems at work, the interviewer asks you to come back later.
- The interviewer asks if you have any questions.
- You realize that you are not qualified for the job.
- The interviewer offers you the job, but you now realize that you do not want it.

**A Job Interview**
Your appearance counts at a job interview, so be sure to dress appropriately. *What are some other ways you can prepare for an interview?*

- Bring your job search notebook or printouts from your computer file, and a copy of your résumé. You will need specific information about your educational background and work history. Make sure you bring the name, address, and phone number of your current supervisor to the interview. You will also need to bring personal information such as a driver's license number, your social security number, and former addresses.
- Most applications ask for an availability date. If you are not currently working, write "Immediately". If you have a job and must give notice, write "Upon two weeks' notice".

### Interviews

The thought of a job interview makes some people nervous. You are more likely to feel confident if you prepare well for each interview. The interview is your chance to show that you are more than a name on a piece of paper.

If a company is interested in hiring you, it may require you to undergo a drug test or submit to a background check. Many jobs today require this. In many states, people who have drug problems or who have been convicted of a crime against a child will be rejected.

### Be Prepared

There are many ways to prepare for an interview. Here are some suggestions to help you:

- **Dress appropriately.** Try to match your outfit to the job. Being well dressed will help you feel confident. Avoid very baggy or tight clothing and keep jewelry to a minimum.
- **Research.** Learn about the company before the interview. Study the employer's Web site. Talk to people who are familiar with the employer.
- **Rehearse.** Practice for the interview with a friend or relative. Remember to keep a positive attitude. You might want to videotape the process and then look for ways you could improve your performance.
- **Arrive early.** Allow for possible traffic delays and arrive a few minutes early. If possible, drive to the location the day before the interview to make sure you know where to go. You can also see how long the journey takes.
- **Greet the interviewer.** Shake the person's hand firmly and make eye contact. Try not to appear anxious or overly eager.
- **Listen carefully.** Pay attention to the questions you are asked. Do not try to change the subject or interrupt the interviewer.

**644** Chapter 23 Careers Working with Children

### ➤ Explore the Photo

**Caption Answer** Answers will vary. You could learn general information about the company and specific information about the available job; you could think of questions you might be asked and practice your answers; you could prepare several questions to ask the interviewer.

**Discussion** Ask students: Would you prefer to be dressed more formally or less formally than the person conducting a job interview? Why? (Possible answer: More formally, because it would show that you took the interview seriously.)

- **Ask appropriate questions.** When the employer asks if you have any questions, focus on the nature of the job, its responsibilities, and the work environment. Try to fill in any gaps in your knowledge about the position. Do not discuss salary and benefits at a first interview unless the interviewer brings it up first.
- **Leave gracefully.** Thank the interviewer and voice your interest in the job as you shake hands to leave.

### Common Questions

Knowing the kinds of questions likely to be asked can help you feel more comfortable when preparing for a job interview. Think of replies to these common questions:

- What are your strengths? What are your weaknesses?
- What are your qualifications for this position?
- Why would you like to work for this company or school?
- What do you want to be doing in five years?
- How would a past teacher or employer describe you?
- Why did you leave your last job?
- What rewards are the most important in your career?
- Why did you choose this career?
- How do you work under pressure?
- What two or three accomplishments have given you the most satisfaction?
- What is a major problem you have encountered at school or on the job? How did you deal with it?
- What are some examples of your creativity?
- Have you worked as part of a team? What were the pluses and minuses of the experience?
- Why should we hire you?
- What is the hardest job you have ever done?
- What questions do you have about the job or this company?

### Interview Follow-Up

After an interview, it can be hard waiting to find out whether you got the job. Remember that the interviewer might have additional candidates to see before a decision can be made. As you wait, there are tasks you can do to remind the employer of your interest.

**Practice Patience**
One must practice patience when waiting to find out about a job. *What might you put in a follow-up letter to help sell yourself?*

### Send a Letter

Within 24 hours after an interview, it is appropriate to write a follow-up letter. You can mail your letter or use e-mail. In either case, keep your language formal and businesslike. If more than one person interviewed you, send a separate letter to each. Make sure the letters are different for each person. Here are some points to cover in the letter:

- Refer to information you gathered in the interview. This builds a personal bridge back to the person receiving the letter. It also serves as a reminder and clarification of that information.
- Thank the person for his or her courtesy and time. This shows good manners.
- Turn any concerns or objections that came up during the interview to your advantage.
- Add additional information regarding your qualifications. It is important to sell yourself as the right person for the job.
- If you promised to send any other information, include it with your letter. Prospective employers may request letters of reference, transcripts, or other additional information. Say that you will call to check about the job.

Section 23.2  Beginning Your Career  **645**

## Reteach *cont.*

### U Universal Access

**Logical Learners** Have students conduct research on a particular business or nonprofit agency that they might like to work for. Students then should write a paragraph on what they learned from their research and how this information might help them answer questions in a job interview. (Paragraphs will vary but should contain information on a specific company that might be useful in a job interview. For example, a knowledge of company goals might be helpful in explaining to the interviewer how your particular skills would aid the company.)

### R Reading Strategy

**Make Judgments** Organize students into small groups. Tell students that their team has been assigned the task of interviewing potential employees. Because time is limited, they can only ask five questions. Have them evaluate each of the questions in this bulleted list and create a list of the five they think are most important. (Lists will vary but contain only five questions. Students should be able to explain why they felt those five were the most important.)

**Professional Development**

**Mini Clip Reading: During and After Reading**
A teacher models for her students and then has them practice what a good reader thinks about.

### ▶ Explore the Photo

**Caption Answer** Answers will vary. You can appropriately address any concerns or objections that came up during the interview or supply any additional information that may have been requested.

**Discussion** Ask students if they think it is a good idea to ask an interviewer why they were not chosen for a job. Encourage students to explain their responses. (Possible answer: Unless there is a specific reason, it is usually best to just graciously accept the news and continue to look for other positions.)

**Reteach** *cont.*

**U₁ Universal Access**

**Learners Having Difficulties**
Have students create a checklist of questions to ask themselves when evaluating a job offer. They should refer to the ideas under the heading Evaluate a Job Offer while creating their checklists. Their checklists should include at least six items. (Checklists will vary but should contain at least six items to consider when evaluating a job offer. Lists might include: Does the company seem to have a bright future? Is there potential for advancement? Is the salary acceptable? Are the benefits good? Will the job give me experience that I want? Are the hours acceptable? Is the job close to home?) **ELL**

**C Critical Thinking**

**Evaluate** Read aloud this sentence from the text: Changing jobs frequently does not look good on your résumé. Ask students why they think this statement is true. (Answers will vary. Students should recognize that frequently changing jobs indicates a lack of responsibility, commitment, and dependability. Also, employers generally spend time and money hiring and training a new employee. They need to feel that the employee will work there long enough to give something back to the company. )

**✓ Reading Check**

**Analyze** The purpose of a cover letter is to highlight your talents and skills that would be particularly useful in the available position and to encourage the employer to read your résumé and ultimately give you an interview.

➤ **Entry-Level Jobs**
An entry-level job provides an opportunity to gain valuable experience and skills. *How might this worker obtain a higher-level position?*

**Be Patient**

Many job seekers become frustrated with the waiting game they must play after an interview. If the interviewer says that he or she will be in touch within two weeks, you should wait at least that length of time. After that, it is okay to call and politely ask about the status of the application. A good way to approach this situation would be to say, "Could you please tell me what the next step is in the hiring process?" The employer might want you to come in for a second interview, or you might be told that someone else has been hired.

While you might be tempted to ask why you did not get the job, it is better to be gracious in accepting the news. The employer does not have to explain his or her decision. Try to learn from the experience and move on. Reflect on your interview skills so that you learn from this experience. If you felt that some aspects of the interview did not go well, practice improving them for next time.

**U₁ Evaluate a Job Offer**

You might think that the most important factor in deciding whether to accept or reject a job offer is the salary. Compensation is important, but there are other factors to consider.

Perhaps the company is one that could provide a bright future. Many employees have started at entry-level positions simply to "get their foot in the door" at a desirable company or school. If there is potential for advancement, avoid thinking that the job is not good enough. Remember that in the early years of your career, you are building experience and a work history.

When an employer makes a job offer, you do not have to give an answer right away. It is okay to ask for a day to think about the offer. Do not put off the decision for too long. If it is a tough decision, make a list of the pros and cons. The pros are the benefits that go along with the paycheck, such as health insurance and the chance to gain experience. The cons are the disadvantages of the job, such as a long drive or weekend hours. **U₁**

If you are offered a job but feel that you would want to move on as quickly as possible, it may be best not to take it. Changing jobs frequently does not look good on your résumé. Always be polite when turning down a job offer. You might want to apply for another position with the same employer at another time. **C**

**✓ Reading Check** **Analyze** What is the purpose of a cover letter?

➤➤ **Explore the Photo**

**Caption Answer** Student answers may include: show competence at the current job, be responsible and resourceful, take additional coursework and possibly get a college degree, and indicate a desire to get a higher-level job.

**Discussion** Ask students: Why might some individuals not want to begin their careers at entry-level positions? (Possible answer: Some people are anxious to have more authority and make more money than is possible at entry-level positions. However, this step is usually necessary.)

## Build Career Skills

Beginning a new job is an exciting time. You will learn new skills and practice those you already have. Whether you are working at a private school or at a children's museum, many of the needed skills will be similar.

Employers expect workers to have two basic types of skills. **Job-specific skills** are the skills or abilities needed to do a specific job. For example, programming a computer is a job-specific skill. **Transferable skills** are general skills used in school and in various types of jobs. Being honest and friendly are examples of transferable skills.

## Transferable Skills

Transferable skills are needed for any career you choose. Here are some transferable skills that will help ensure success at any job:

- **Basic skills.** Employees need to have basic skills such as the ability to understand instructions and solve math problems. For many jobs, technology skills, such as using word processing and spreadsheet software, are classified as basic skills.

- **Communication skills.** The way you speak, listen, and write will have an impact on your success in the workplace. Make an effort to speak clearly, listen carefully, and write clearly and concisely.

- **Relationship skills.** Whenever a group of people must work together, there is potential for conflict. Learn to respect differences, work as part of a team, and resolve conflicts before they get out of hand. Good team players are dependable, responsible, and honest.

- **Leadership skills.** Leadership involves making decisions, acting fairly, and supervising and inspiring others. Leaders must be able to set goals and use available resources to get the work done efficiently. Leadership skills are needed for many of the careers that relate to children. After all, children look to the adults in their lives for guidance and leadership.

- **Managing multiple roles.** Throughout your career, you will have many roles. It will be necessary to juggle work, family, social, and community obligations, so learn to prioritize and manage your time.

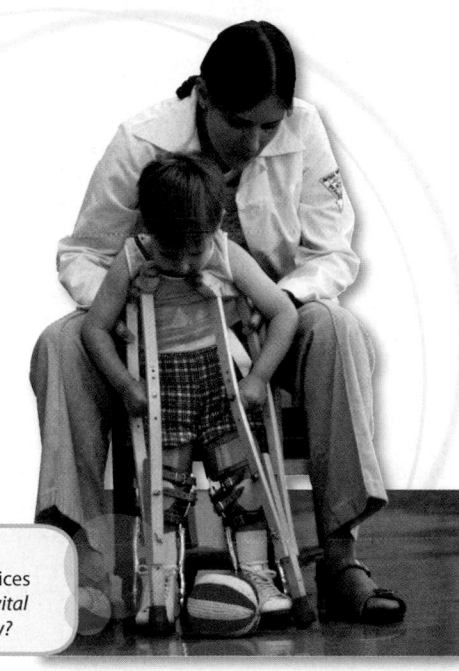

**Ethical Behavior**
People who work with children must follow ethical practices and strictly obey any rules governing behavior. *Why is it vital that people who work with children always behave ethically?*

## Reteach *cont.*

### R Reading Strategy

**Apply** Tell students that as they read, it is helpful to determine how information applies directly to their lives. As students read the text under Transferable Skills, have them create a list of their own transferable skills. (Students should create lists of their transferable skills. Examples might include technology, communication, or leadership skills.)

### U₂ Universal Access

**Interpersonal Learners** Have students interview a person who hires staff for a child care center or preschool. Students should ask the individual what kinds of background checks are conducted before a job is offered to a potential employee. Students also should ask what legal requirements they must follow regarding background checks. Students should give an oral presentation to the class covering what they learned. (Presentations will vary. Students should interview a person in charge of hiring employees at a child care center or preschool. They should ask what kinds of background checks they conduct on potential employees. Legal requirements for background checks vary by state.)

---

### Explore the Photo

**Caption Answer** Children's parents and other caregivers must know that their children will be safe and properly cared for when they are with others.

**Discussion** Discuss that one of the more difficult tasks teachers and child care workers face is treating children as equally as possible.

Each child is different and some may be more amenable to following rules or accepting guidance. Encourage students to discuss ways in which they can work to treat students equally. (Ideas will vary. Having guidelines in writing can be helpful in treating all students fairly.)

### Reteach *cont.*

## W Writing Support
### Freewriting

**Lifelong Learners** Ask students how they might continue learning after high school to help make themselves a more valuable employee or prospective employee. Have students use freewriting to help generate and document ideas. When students are done, ask for volunteers to share their ideas with the class. (Refer to p. 4 for tips on successful freewriting. Ideas may vary. Students may include going to college or a trade school to learn new skills. They may also suggest learning skills on-the-job from coworkers; self-learning new software programs by trial-and-error; doing private research; or even taking private lessons for skills such as playing a musical instrument or speaking another language.)

## C Critical Thinking

**Analyze** Ask students what they think the expression "Don't burn your bridges behind you" means. Encourage them to discuss whether they think this saying applies to leaving a job. Ask: Why might you not want to burn any bridges when leaving a job? (Responses will vary. Students may say the expression means to maintain relationships with people. They should recognize that you may need the help of your previous boss or coworkers in the future, for example as references.)

### ✓ Reading Check

**Explain** Lifelong learners enjoy improving their skills and are not afraid of change. Because they are flexible and willing to try new ways of performing tasks, they make effective and valuable employees.

---

{ **Expert Advice...** }

*"Besides formal training you must have energy and enthusiasm to work successfully with children."*

— Marjorie Eberts and Margaret Gisler, coauthors, *Careers for Kids at Heart and Others Who Adore Children*

---

- **Learning from performance evaluations.** Wherever you work, you will have periodic performance evaluations. Your supervisor will comment on what you have been doing well and point out areas that need improvement. You may be given, or asked to develop, goals for the following year. Working to improve in these areas should help you advance in your career.
- **Behaving ethically.** Being **ethical** means doing the right thing. In the workplace, it means being honest, following the rules, and reporting violations of the rules. Following ethical practices is particularly important in child care settings. It is essential that parents can trust and rely on the people who care for their children.

## Lifelong Learning

To succeed in today's work environment, you must be flexible and willing to change. You should commit to being a lifelong learner. A **lifelong learner** is someone who is willing to learn new information and acquire skills throughout his or her working life. This will help you maintain employment by making you a better worker and a valued employee.

One way to continue learning is with continuing education. Some employers are willing to pay for all or part of the costs. Continuing education can mean attending conferences or workshops, earning credentials through a professional organization, or taking college classes.

### ✓ Reading Check

**Explain** Why would an employer want to hire employees committed to lifelong learning?

---

## Leaving a Job

Most people today do not stay in the same job until retirement. In fact, it is highly likely that you will change jobs and perhaps careers a number of times during your working life. You need to know how to make the transition from one job to another as smooth as possible.

It is usually not a good idea to quit one job before you have another one lined up. After all, you do not know how long it will take to find another job and you probably need to keep earning money. As you seek new employment, you should do it on your own time, though. It is unethical to use work time to interview for another job. It is also wrong to use company time to write or print résumés and cover letters, or to contact prospective employers.

## Employee's Obligations

When you leave a job, you should make every effort to leave under the best possible circumstances. Follow any established procedures for notifying your employer of your intent to resign. Give as much notice as possible so your employer can find a replacement. A two-week notice is typical. Make sure you express your appreciation for the job opportunity. You may need a reference from your current employer.

Continue to do your job well up to the time you leave. If you are asked to train a replacement, strive to give that person the best possible start. After all, you might work with some of your coworkers in the future. You might even want to return to the same employer later in your career.

## Employer's Obligations

Employees do not always leave their jobs because they want to. Employers can terminate employment as well. Some people lose their jobs because they do not perform well. In other cases, such as when business is slow, jobs may be cut through no fault of the employees.

---

**McGraw Hill** Professional Development

### Mini Clip
**Reading: Another Point of View**
Emily M. Schell, Ed.D., educator and author, discusses standards-based instruction.

If you lose your job, you may be entitled to claim unemployment benefits. **Unemployment benefits** are funds paid by individual states to unemployed people who are actively seeking employment. Employers are also responsible for paying into the fund that provides for unemployment benefits. Make sure that you clearly understand what benefits you can receive and how long you can receive them. You may not be eligible for unemployment benefits if you simply quit a job.

You may also be able to keep any health insurance that you received through your employer. **COBRA** (Consolidated Omnibus Budget Reconciliation Act) is a law ensuring that former employees can keep the health insurance plan they received through their former employer for up to 18 months. The former employee must pay the entire cost of the premiums.

## Ongoing Employability

If you are being laid off or face downsizing, it can make you feel angry or depressed. Try to view it as a career-change opportunity. The company might offer job-search services or help in finding new employment. Go back to the networking and contact lists you created when you searched for this job. Reach out for support from friends, family, and other acquaintances. Consider joining a job-search club. Assess your skills. Upgrade them if needed. Decide the direction you wish to take and move on!

As you move along your career path, be sure to remember the keys to employment success. Commit yourself to excellence. Continue learning. Do all that you can to show that you are reliable, flexible, honest, and responsible. Show that you have what it takes to succeed in the world of work!

**Study Tools**

Have students go to the Online Learning Center at **glencoe.com**:

- Take the **Practice Test**.
- Download **Study-to-Go** content.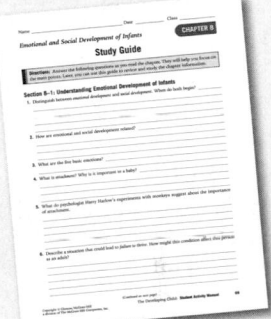

Use the **Student Activity Workbook** for additional practice.

### Close

**Culminating Activity**

**List Job-Hunting Steps** As a class, create a ladder that lists the typical steps in finding a job. The first step on the ladder should be "Locate appropriate job openings" and the last step should be "Accept a job offer." (Steps are located on pages 639–647.)

**NCLB** connects academic correlations to book content.

---

## Section 23.2    After You Read

### Review Key Concepts

1. **Identify** what a job seeker with little work experience could emphasize on his or her résumé.
2. **Describe** how you can be a lifelong learner.
3. **Explain** why you should continue to do your best after you have resigned.

### Practice Academic Skills

 **English**

4. Follow your teacher's instructions to form into groups of four. Each person in the group writes a description of a job he or she would like to interview for. A second team member conducts a mock interview with this individual. The remaining team members offer suggestions for improving the interview.

> **NCTE 12** Use language to accomplish individual purposes.

 **Mathematics**

5. Interview at least ten working adults. Ask, "How did you get your current job?" Categorize the responses into five or six groups. Use these categories in creating a bar graph illustrating the different ways these people got their current jobs.

> **NCTM Number and Operations**
> Understand numbers, ways of representing numbers, relationships among numbers, and number systems.

 **Check Your Answers** Check your answers at this book's Online Learning Center at **glencoe.com**.

---

### Review Key Concepts

1. The job seeker could emphasize any courses that would provide preparation for this kind of work. Any volunteer work should also be listed.
2. By continuing education through conferences, workshops, certification, or college classes.
3. You might work with some of your coworkers in the future, or you might want to return to the employer later in your career.

### Practice Academic Skills

4. Each student in the group should be interviewed for a job of his or her choosing. Based on what they have learned in this class and in other life situations, the remaining team members should offer constructive suggestions for improving the interview process.
5. Students should interview at least ten working adults and determine how each got their current job. They should divide these responses into categories and use the results to create a bar graph.

Careers With Children

## Actor in Children's Theatre

### Discussion Starter

**Actor in Children's Theatre**
Ask students if they have ever seen a play at a children's theatre. Encourage them to discuss how it was different from theatre that is aimed primarily at adults. Ask questions such as: What was the play? Was there any interaction between the actors and the audience? (Responses will vary. There is more likely to be interaction between actors and the audience in children's theatre than in adult theatre.)

### C Critical Thinking

**Infer** Ask: Why do you think actors often interact with the audience in children's theatre? (Answers will vary. Interacting can help children stay focused on the story and may also help them understand the story being told.)

### Make Connections

Ask students to list specific correlations between academic subjects and the kinds of skills a good children's theatre actor needs. (Answers will vary. Students should show an understanding of how academic skills relate directly to being an actor in children's theatre. For example, a good understanding of English is useful in presenting dialogue in a meaningful way.)

**NCLB** This relates academic skills to specific tasks that are performed for this job.

---

**A**ctors in children's theatres present plays that children will enjoy and find meaningful. These actors are artists, and their task is to bring characters to life. Children's theatres are sometimes performed in the round. The actors often interact with the audience.

C

### ☀ What Does an Actor in Children's Theatre Do?

Many actors love performing for children because children often respond more candidly to theatre than adults. If children love a play, the performers will know it! Because many children's theatres have small staffs, actors must be resourceful and be able to perform a variety of roles.

### ☀ Where Do Actors Work?

Many large cities have children's theatres. There are also theatre companies that will travel to different theatres or cities. Because it can be hard to find steady work, many of these actors hold other jobs as well.

### Preparation and Skills

**Education and Training**
Aspiring actors can take small roles in community theatre productions. They can also take acting classes, or pursue a performing arts degree at a college or university. Public speaking is good preparation as well.

**Aptitudes, Abilities, and Skills**
Actors need to memorize lines and have stamina for rehearsals and performances. They must love to entertain and perform. It is also helpful to have skills such as singing and dancing.

**Academic Skills**
English language arts are used to memorize lines and speak them well, as well as to take direction. Social studies skills can be helpful in portraying other cultures.

NCLB

**Explore Careers**
Conduct research to learn about a children's theatre. Write an advertisement for an actor to perform in a play being performed by this theatre. In the ad, list the specific aptitudes and abilities the actor must have.

 **Careers Online** For more information on careers, visit the Occupational Outlook Handbook Web site through the link on this book's Online Learning Center at **glencoe.com**.

### Culminating Activity

**Present a Play** Organize students into groups. Have each group develop a short play for preschoolers. For example, they might base their play on a traditional folk tale. Remind students to gear their play toward holding the children's interest. (Students should create a short play that is interesting enough to hold the attention of a group of preschoolers.)

**Explore Careers**
Student should have researched a particular children's theatre, chosen a play being performed by that theatre, and then written an advertisement for an actor to perform in that play. The ad should specify the aptitudes and abilities required of the actor.

## Chapter Summary

Within career areas, there are various levels of jobs. When choosing a career, consider your interests, aptitudes, and abilities. You can gain work experience through part-time work, internships, volunteering, service learning, and work-based learning. When evaluating careers, there are many factors to consider. Sources of job openings include the Internet, newspapers, other people, and job fairs. Prepare for an interview. Always write a follow-up letter afterward. Transferable skills are needed for success in any workplace.

## Vocabulary Review

1. Use these content and academic vocabulary terms to create a crossword puzzle on graph paper. Use the definitions as clues.

### Content Vocabulary

◇ entry-level job (p. 631)
◇ paraprofessional (p. 631)
◇ professional (p. 632)
◇ entrepreneur (p. 632)
◇ aptitude (p. 633)
◇ internship (p. 634)
◇ job shadowing (p. 634)
◇ service learning (p. 634)
◇ work-based learning (p. 634)

◇ career path (p. 637)
◇ career ladder (p. 637)
◇ networking (p. 639)
◇ job fair (p. 639)
◇ résumé (p. 640)
◇ cover letter (p. 643)
◇ job-specific skills (p. 647)
◇ transferable skills (p. 647)
◇ ethical (p. 648)
◇ lifelong learner (p. 648)

◇ unemployment benefits (p. 649)
◇ COBRA (p. 649)

### Academic Vocabulary

■ ability (p. 633)
■ visualization (p. 637)
■ convey (p. 640)
■ legible (p. 643)

## Review Key Concepts

2. **Describe** three different ways to gain work experience.
3. **Identify** factors to consider when evaluating careers.
4. **Explain** the relationship between a career goal and a career path.
5. **List** six steps involved in a job search.
6. **Compare and contrast** job-specific skills and transferable skills.
7. **Summarize** an employee's responsibilities when leaving a job.

## Critical Thinking

8. **Infer** Why do you think many employers prefer to interview potential employees who are currently working?
9. **Predict** On her résumé, Zoe falsely stated she was a supervisor at her last job. What do you think might happen as a result of this inaccuracy?
10. **Analyze** In your career, do you think you would prefer to work primarily with people, information, or technology? Explain your choice.

## Content and Academic Vocabulary Review

1. Students should use graph paper to create a crossword puzzle with all of the vocabulary terms.

## Review Key Concepts

2. Any three of the following: internships, job shadowing, volunteering, service learning, or work-based learning.

3. Factors to consider include tasks and responsibilities; whether it involves working with people, information, or technology; work environment; hours; required aptitudes; required education and training; salary and benefits; and career outlook.

4. A career goal is something you want to achieve. A career path is the career moves and job experiences you use to reach your goals.

5. Steps are: find job openings, prepare résumé, fill out application, interview, send follow-up letter, evaluate job offer.

6. Job-specific skills are abilities that apply to a particular job whereas transferable skills are general skills that are useful in a variety of jobs.

7. An employee's responsibilities when leaving a job include trying to leave under the best possible circumstances, following any establish procedures, giving as much notice as possible, continuing to do your job well until you leave, and, if asked, training your replacement.

## Critical Thinking

8. Student answers will vary. If a person is already working, this indicates to the employer that the individual can hold down a job. Someone who is working may be seen as having more desirable and up-to-date skills.

9. Student answers will vary. When prospective employers check with her previous employer, they might find out that she was not a supervisor and would then question her honesty and wonder if she lied about other items on her résumé.

10. Students should specify whether they would prefer to work primarily with people, information, or technology and provide reasons.

**Family & Community Connections**

11. Student presentations will vary. The student should discuss how the people interviewed thought their jobs might change in the future and use this information to predict future job markets.

## Health Skills

12. Students' posters will vary, but should contain text and illustrations explaining needed skills, such as the ability to treat minor cuts and abrasions and to perform CPR.

## Observation Skills

13. Paragraphs will vary but should explain any techniques the teacher used to motivate the students and also include any additional motivational ideas the students have.

## Real-World Skills

14. Responses will vary, but students should give specific reasons for their responses. They have committed to the after-school program and the children are in the elementary age group, so it would probably provide better preparation for teaching.

15. Brochures will vary but should contain tips on preparing for a job interview. Appropriate tips may include dressing appropriately, rehearsing, arriving early, listening carefully, or asking appropriate questions.

---

**Family & Community Connection**

11. **Future Job Markets** Interview several people who have worked at least ten years in a field you are interested in. Ask them how they think their field will change in the future. Prepare a brief presentation in which you predict the future of this job market based on the information gained in your interviews.

**Health Skills**

12. **Emergency Skills** A preschool teacher needs to be prepared for many different emergencies. Use print or online resources to research the kinds of emergency skills a preschool teacher should have. Also find out how they might best obtain the training needed to get these skills. Create an illustrated poster explaining the skills and training needed.

**Observation Skills**

13. **Motivate Children** Being a good teacher means more than just knowing the material you are presenting. Good teachers have the ability to motivate children. They make each child want to learn.

    **Procedure** Observe a coach, music instructor, or other adult working with a group of children between the ages of 9 and 12. What does the teacher do to motivate the children?

    **Analysis** Write a paragraph analyzing how the teacher motivated the students. Discuss any additional ways you can think of that the children could have been motivated.

    **NCSS IV D Individual Development and Identity**
    Apply concepts, methods, and theories about the study of human growth and development, such as physical endowment, learning, motivation, behavior, perception, and personality.

**NCLB**

## Real-World Skills

| Problem Solving | 14. **Make Decisions** Suppose you want to become an elementary school teacher. You have just promised to volunteer at an after-school program for children ages 8 to 10. Unexpectedly, a neighbor offers you a part-time job in her infant daycare. What would you do? Why? |
| --- | --- |
| Technology Skills | 15. **Design a Brochure** A counselor at a community college who works with students looking for their first professional jobs has asked for your help. Use word processing or desktop publishing software to create an illustrated brochure with tips on preparing for a job interview. |
| Financial Literacy | 16. **A Business Wardrobe** Conduct research to determine what is generally meant by the term *business casual*. Then determine how much five outfits would cost. Create a table showing the cost and where the outfits would be purchased. |

**Additional Activities** For additional activities, go to this book's Online Learning Center at **glencoe.com**.

---

16. Students' tables will vary, but should list the clothing needed to create five business casual outfits along with their cost and where they could be purchased.

**NCLB** Activity correlated to Social Studies standards.

The *Early Childhood Observations CD* offers additional lessons with videos to build students' observation skills.

**Part 1:** Learning to Observe
**Part 2:** How Children Develop
**Part 3:** Working With Young Children
**Part 4:** Extended Observations
**Part 5:** Resources and Answer File

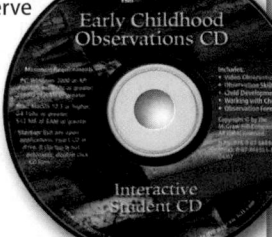

## Academic Skills

###  English Language Arts

**17. Using Transferable Skills** Choose two transferable skills, such as communication skills or ethical behavior. Write a scenario showing how you might use these skills in a job in which you are interested. Be specific about how you would apply the skills.

> **NCTE 5** Use different writing process elements to communicate effectively.

###  Mathematics

**18. How Many Teachers?** Out of the 3,954,000 teachers employed in 2006, median annual earnings of kindergarten, elementary, middle, and secondary school teachers ranged from $43,580 to $48,690 in May 2006. The lowest 10 percent earned $28,590 to $33,070. The top 10 percent earned $67,490 to $76,100. How many teachers are in the lowest 10 percent?

**Math Concept** **Multiplying by Percents**
To multiply by percents, change the percent to a fraction with 100 in the denominator. Then change the fraction to a decimal. For example, $5\% = \frac{5}{100} = 0.05$.

**Starting Hint** To compute how many teachers made up the lowest 10 percent, multiply the total number of teachers by the percentage.

**Math** For math help, go to the Math Appendix at the back of the book.

> **NCTM Number and Operations** Understand numbers, ways of representing numbers, relationships among numbers, and number systems.

###  Science

**19.** Imagine that you are a preschool teacher who wants to teach simple scientific concepts to your class. Examples might include that warm air rises, or that some objects float in water while others sink.

**Procedure** Choose a concept you want to teach. Present it to a group of at least three preschoolers in a fun way that they can understand.

**Analysis** Ask the preschoolers to state what they have learned in their own words. Calculate the percentage who were able to do so.

> **NSES A** Develop understandings about scientific inquiry.

**NCLB**

## Standardized Test Practice

**MATHEMATICS**

Many students find test questions involving mathematics intimidating, often because they require a number of steps. Read the test-taking tip and then determine the answer to this question.

**20.** You teach piano lessons to 12 students each week. Beginning lessons are $20.00 while advanced lessons are $28.00. You have twice as many beginning students as advanced. How much do you make each week?

> **Test-Taking Tip** When answering a math question, it is a good idea to estimate the answer before performing the actual calculations. If your answer is considerably different than your estimate, carefully check it.

## Academic Skills

**17.** Scenarios will vary, but students should write about how two of the transferable skills discussed in this chapter could be applied in a specific job situation.

**18.** 395,400 (10% = 0.10; 3,954,000 × 0.10 = 395,400)

**19.** Student should have presented a simple scientific concept to a group of at least three preschoolers and then determined the percentage of children who were able to state the concept in their own words.

**NCLB** **NCLB** connects academic correlations to book content.

## Standardized Test Practice

**20.** $272 per week ((8 × 20.00) + (4 × 28.00) = $272.00)

**Test-Taking Tips** Remind students that test taking is a skill, just like any of the other skills discussed in this book. They more they practice it, the better they will become.

**Mathematics** Discuss that a high percentage of errors made on math tests are caused by carelessness. Breaking the problem down into small steps can reduce these kinds of errors. And, of course, students should try to allow time to double-check their answers.

## TECHNOLOGY *Solutions*

**Use these technology solutions to streamline chapter assessment!**

 ***ExamView Assessment Suite*** CD allows you to create and print out customized tests or ready-made unit and chapter tests, complete with answer keys.

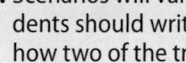 **TeacherWorks Plus** is an electronic lesson planner that provides instant access to complete teacher resources in one convenient package.

 **Online Learning Center** includes resources and activities for students and teachers.

## Unit | Thematic Project

# Focus

## Discussion Starter

**Interacting with Children** Ask students to list times they have spent interacting with younger children. (Examples may include babysitting, living with younger siblings, acting as camp counselor, or working at an after-school child care center.)

 Project correlated to English Language Arts standards.

## Step 1

### Choose a Child Care Career that Interests You

Students can select a career that interests them. Students may want to look for additional jobs or do some preliminary research in this area by using the *Occupational Outlook Handbook,* which is available online. If students can think of another career not listed, they are welcome to use it.

# Teach

## Step 2

### Write Your Interview Questions

Interview questions should focus on the qualifications, prerequisites, and education necessary for the career of interest. Students can also ask about pay and what a typical day on the job is like. (Be sure students do not ask about the professional's salary.) Students might also ask what the professional likes and dislikes about the job.

# Explore Careers in Child Care

In this unit, you have learned about adolescence, childhood illnesses, challenges that families face, and child care options. You have also learned that there are many different careers within the child care industry. In this project, you will interview and shadow a professional child care worker. You will use what you learn to create a skit that shows a child care worker interacting with children.

 **My Journal**

If you completed the journal entry from page 517, refer to it to see if your thoughts have changed after reading the unit.

## Project Assignment

In this project, you will:
- Choose a type of child care worker that you would like to know more about.
- Write a list of interview questions. Ask about qualifications needed for the job.

---

### Child Development Skills Behind the Project

- Evaluate careers available in the area of child care and early learning.
- Identify the qualifications needed for a particular career in child care.
- Describe the ways child care workers interact with children.

### Academic Skills

 **English Language Arts**

> **NCTE 4** Use written language to communicate effectively.
>
> **NCTE 12** Use language to accomplish individual purposes.

- Identify and interview a professional in the community who works in the child care industry.
- Arrange, take notes, and key the interview with your candidate.
- Use what you learned in the interview to create a skit. It should show a child care worker interacting with children.

## Step 1 Choose a Child Care Career that Interests You

The careers below are representative of those typically found in the child care industry. Choose a child care job that you would like to learn more about.
- Center-based child care worker
- Home-based child care worker
- Camp counselor
- After school day care worker
- Preschool teacher
- Pediatrician
- Pediatric nurse

## Step 2 Write Your Interview Questions

Make a list of questions you would like to ask about the child care career that interests you. Be sure to ask about the qualifications and education needed for the job and about starting pay for an entry level job.

## Step 3

### Connect to Your Community

Ask students what they expect to learn from interviewing and observing the child care professional they have chosen. (Students' answers will vary. They may say that they hope to learn whether they would be interested in this career for themselves.) Ask students if they might consider volunteering in a child care situation to gain experience. (Answers will vary. Some may be interested in volunteer work; others may not.)

## Step 4

### Write and Present Your Skit

Students may perform the skit in front of the class or film their skit outside of the class and play the recording. Give students these tips on writing and performing a skit:

- Write the dialogue as an actual conversation.
- Use terminology that will be understood by the audience.
- Write suggestions for actions for each character in the skit.

## Writing Skills

★ Use complete sentences.
★ Use correct spelling and grammar.
★ Organize your questions in the order you want to ask them.
★ Write concisely (briefly but completely).

### Step 3 Connect to Your Community

Arrange to interview or shadow a member of the community who works in the child care profession you selected in Step 1. Ask the interview questions you wrote in Step 2.

**Interview Skills**

★ Listen carefully.
★ During the interview, record responses and take notes.
★ If you shadow a professional, take good notes of their interactions but be sure to maintain confidentiality.
★ When you transcribe your notes, write in complete sentences and use correct spelling and grammar.

### Step 4 Write and Present Your Skit

Use the Unit Thematic Project Checklist on the right to plan, write, and present a skit sharing what you have learned.

**Presentation Skills**

★ Act naturally.
★ Use gestures when appropriate.
★ Speak loudly and clearly so the entire audience can hear and understand you.

### Step 5 Evaluate Your Child Development Skills and Academic Skills

Your project will be evaluated based on:
● Content and organization of your information.
● Mechanics—presentation and neatness.
● Speaking and listening skills.

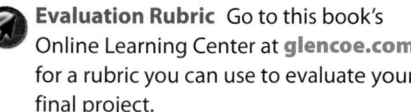 **Evaluation Rubric** Go to this book's Online Learning Center at **glencoe.com** for a rubric you can use to evaluate your final project.

### Unit Thematic Project Checklist

| | |
|---|---|
| **Skit** | ✓ Consider who will play the different roles. You should play the caregiver; ask for one or two volunteers to play the children.<br>✓ Re-create one of the activities you observed during your shadowing or interview experience in a skit.<br>✓ Use props to represent the child care setting.<br>✓ Write a summary at the end of the skit. What did you hope to teach the children? How did you hope to help the children? |
| **Presentation** | ✓ Make a presentation for the students in your class to share your skit and discuss what you learned.<br>✓ Invite the students to ask you any questions. Answer three questions.<br>✓ Demonstrate in your answers that you respect their perspectives.<br>✓ Turn in the notes from your interview and your skit script. |
| **Academic Skills** | ✓ Write dialogue between two or more people.<br>✓ Express your ideas clearly.<br>✓ Speak clearly and concisely. |

### Assess

### Step 5

**Evaluate Your Child Development Skills and Academic Skills**

**Rubric** Encourage students to go to this book's Online Learning Center at **glencoe.com** for a rubric they can use to evaluate their skit and presentation. Students can use the rubric as a content checklist when forming their interview questions, writing their skit, and giving their presentation.

### Close

### Culminating Activity

**Project Assessment** In this activity, students identified a career in the child care industry that interested them. Have students work with a partner to evaluate their experiences. Partners should interview one another, asking such questions as: Did you feel you had a positive experience? Explain your answer. Would you consider this career for yourself? Why or why not? (Partners should write down answers to the interview questions and allow the interviewee to check them for accuracy before turning them in.)

 ## Developing Community Involvement

### Comparing Child Care

There are many career opportunities in the field of child care. Students can work as a babysitter now or as a pediatrician after many years in school to receive the required education and training. Have students speak with an older adult with children about the child care services that were available when his or her children were young. Students should compare the list to what is available today and write a paragraph explaining how the world of child care has changed.

**A Family & Community Involvement** worksheet about this topic is available:

🖊 At this book's Online Learning Center at **glencoe.com**

💿 On the TeacherWorks CD

## Math Appendix

# Number and Operations

▶ **Understand numbers, ways of representing numbers, relationships among numbers, and number systems**

### Fraction, Decimal, and Percent

A percent is a ratio that compares a number to 100. To write a percent as a fraction, drop the percent sign, and use the number as the numerator in a fraction with a denominator of 100. Simplify, if possible. For example, 76% = $\frac{76}{100}$, or $\frac{19}{25}$. To write a fraction as a percent, convert it to an equivalent fraction with a denominator of 100. For example, $\frac{3}{4} = \frac{75}{100}$, or 75%. A fraction can be expressed as a percent by first converting the fraction to a decimal (divide the numerator by the denominator) and then converting the decimal to a percent by moving the decimal point two places to the right.

### Comparing Numbers on a Number Line

In order to compare and understand the relationship between real numbers in various forms, it is helpful to use a number line. The zero point on a number line is called the origin; the points to the left of the origin are negative, and those to the right are positive. The number line below shows how numbers in fraction, decimal, percent, and integer form can be compared.

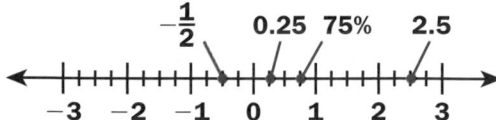

### Percents Greater Than 100 and Less Than 1

Percents greater than 100% represent values greater than 1. For example, if the weight of an object is 250% of another, it is 2.5, or $2\frac{1}{2}$, times the weight.

Percents less than 1 represent values less than $\frac{1}{100}$. In other words, 0.1% is one tenth of one percent, which can also be represented in decimal form as 0.001, or in fraction form as $\frac{1}{1,000}$. Similarly, 0.01% is one hundredth of one percent or 0.0001 or $\frac{1}{10,000}$.

### Ratio, Rate, and Proportion

A ratio is a comparison of two numbers using division. If a basketball player makes 8 out of 10 free throws, the ratio is written as 8 to 10, 8:10, or $\frac{8}{10}$. Ratios are usually written in simplest form. In simplest form, the ratio "8 out of 10" is 4 to 5, 4:5, or $\frac{4}{5}$. A rate is a ratio of two measurements having different kinds of units—cups per gallon, or miles per hour, for example. When a rate is simplified so that it has a denominator of 1, it is called a unit rate. An example of a unit rate is 9 miles per hour. A proportion is an equation stating that two ratios are equal. $\frac{3}{18} = \frac{13}{78}$ is an example of a proportion. The cross products of a proportion are also equal. $\frac{3}{18} = \frac{13}{78}$ and $3 \times 78 = 18 \times 13$.

### Representing Large and Small Numbers

In order to represent large and small numbers, it is important to understand the number system. Our number system is based on 10, and the value of each place is 10 times the value of the place to its right.

The value of a digit is the product of a digit and its place value. For instance, in the number 6,400, the 6 has a value of six thousands and the 4 has a value of four hundreds. A place value chart can help you read numbers. In the chart, each group of three digits is called a period. Commas separate the periods: the ones period, the thousands period, the millions period, and so on. Values to the right of the ones period are decimals. By understanding place value you can write very large numbers like 5 billion and more, and very small numbers that are less than 1, like one-tenth.

## Scientific Notation

When dealing with very large numbers like 1,500,000, or very small numbers like 0.000015, it is helpful to keep track of their value by writing the numbers in scientific notation. Powers of 10 with positive exponents are used with a decimal between 1 and 10 to express large numbers. The exponent represents the number of places the decimal point is moved to the right. So, 528,000 is written in scientific notation as $5.28 \times 10^5$. Powers of 10 with negative exponents are used with a decimal between 1 and 10 to express small numbers. The exponent represents the number of places the decimal point is moved to the left. The number 0.00047 is expressed as $4.7 \times 10^{-4}$.

## Factor, Multiple, and Prime Factorization

Two or more numbers that are multiplied to form a product are called factors. Divisibility rules can be used to determine whether 2, 3, 4, 5, 6, 8, 9, or 10 are factors of a given number. Multiples are the products of a given number and various integers. For example, 8 is a multiple of 4 because $4 \times 2 = 8$. A prime number is a whole number that has exactly two factors: 1 and itself. A composite number is a whole number that has more than two factors. Zero and 1 are neither prime nor composite. A composite number can be expressed as the product of its prime factors. The prime factorization of 40 is $2 \times 2 \times 2 \times 5$, or $2^3 \times 5$. The numbers 2 and 5 are prime numbers.

## Integers

A negative number is a number less than zero. Negative numbers like −8, positive numbers like +6, and zero are members of the set of integers. Integers can be represented as points on a number line. A set of integers can be written {…, −3, −2, −1, 0, 1, 2, 3, …} where … means "continues indefinitely."

## Real, Rational, and Irrational Numbers

The real number system is made up of the sets of rational and irrational numbers. Rational numbers are numbers that can be written in the form $a/b$ where $a$ and $b$ are integers and $b \neq 0$. Examples are 0.45, $\frac{1}{2}$, and $\sqrt{36}$. Irrational numbers are non-repeating, non-terminating decimals. Examples are $\sqrt{71}$, $\pi$, and 0.020020002….

## Complex and Imaginary Numbers

A complex number is a mathematical expression with a real number element and an imaginary number element. Imaginary numbers are multiples of $i$, the "imaginary" square root of −1. Complex numbers are represented by $a + bi$, where $a$ and $b$ are real numbers and $i$ represents the imaginary element. When a quadratic equation does not have a real number solution, the solution can be represented by a complex number. Like real numbers, complex numbers can be added, subtracted, multiplied, and divided.

## Vectors and Matrices

A matrix is a set of numbers or elements arranged in rows and columns to form a rectangle. The number of rows is represented by $m$ and the number of columns is represented by $n$. To describe the number of rows and columns in a matrix, list the number of rows first using the format $m \times n$. Matrix A below is a $3 \times 3$ matrix because it has 3 rows and 3 columns. To name an element of a matrix, the letter $i$ is used to denote the row and $j$ is used to denote the column, and the element is labeled in the form $a_{i,j}$. In matrix A below, $a_{3,2}$ is 4.

$$\text{Matrix A} = \begin{pmatrix} 1 & 3 & 5 \\ 0 & 6 & 8 \\ 3 & 4 & 5 \end{pmatrix}$$

A vector is a matrix with only one column or row of elements. A transposed column vector, or a column vector turned on its side, is a row vector. In the example below, row vector $b'$ is the transpose of column vector $b$.

$$b = \begin{pmatrix} 1 \\ 2 \\ 3 \\ 4 \end{pmatrix}$$

$$b' = \begin{pmatrix} 1 & 2 & 3 & 4 \end{pmatrix}$$

## ▶ Understand meanings of operations and how they relate to one another

### Properties of Addition and Multiplication

Properties are statements that are true for any numbers. For example, $3 + 8$ is the same as $8 + 3$ because each expression equals 11. This illustrates the Commutative Property of Addition. Likewise, $3 \times 8 = 8 \times 3$ illustrates the Commutative Property of Multiplication.

When evaluating expressions, it is often helpful to group or associate the numbers. The Associative Property says that the way in which numbers are grouped when added or multiplied does not change the sum or product. The following properties are also true:

- **Additive Identity Property:** When 0 is added to any number, the sum is the number.

- **Multiplicative Identity Property:** When any number is multiplied by 1, the product is the number.

- **Multiplicative Property of Zero:** When any number is multiplied by 0, the product is 0.

### Rational Numbers

A number that can be written as a fraction is called a rational number. Terminating and repeating decimals are rational numbers because both can be written as fractions.

Decimals that are neither terminating nor repeating are called irrational numbers because they cannot be written as fractions. Terminating decimals can be converted to fractions by placing the number (without the decimal point) in the numerator. Count the number of places to the right of the decimal point, and in the denominator, place a 1 followed by a number of zeros equal to the number of places that you counted. The fraction can then be reduced to its simplest form.

### Writing a Fraction as a Decimal

Any fraction $\frac{a}{b}$, where $b \neq 0$, can be written as a decimal by dividing the numerator by the denominator. So, $\frac{a}{b} = a \div b$. If the division ends, or terminates, when the remainder is zero, the decimal is a terminating decimal. Not all fractions can be written as terminating decimals. Some have a repeating decimal. A bar indicates that the decimal repeats forever. For example, the fraction $\frac{4}{9}$ can be converted to a repeating decimal, $0.\overline{4}$.

### Adding and Subtracting Like Fractions

Fractions with the same denominator are called like fractions. To add like fractions, add the numerators and write the sum over the denominator. To add mixed numbers with like fractions, add the whole numbers and fractions separately, adding the numerators of the fractions, then simplifying if necessary. The rule for subtracting fractions with like denominators is similar to the rule for adding. The numerators can be subtracted and the difference written over the denominator. Mixed numbers are written as improper fractions before subtracting. These same rules apply to adding or subtracting like algebraic fractions. An algebraic fraction is a fraction that contains one or more variables in the numerator or denominator.

### Adding and Subtracting Unlike Fractions

Fractions with different denominators are called unlike fractions. The least common multiple of the denominators is used to rename the fractions with a common denominator. After a common denominator is found, the numerators can then be added or subtracted. To add mixed numbers with unlike fractions, rename the mixed numbers as improper fractions. Then find a common denominator, add the numerators, and simplify the answer.

### Multiplying Rational Numbers

To multiply fractions, multiply the numerators and multiply the denominators. If the numerators and denominators have common factors, they can be simplified before multiplication. If the fractions have different signs, then the product will be negative. Mixed numbers can be multiplied in the same manner, after first renaming them as improper fractions. Algebraic fractions may be multiplied using the same method described above.

## Dividing Rational Numbers

To divide a number by a rational number (a fraction, for example), multiply the first number by the multiplicative inverse of the second. Two numbers whose product is 1 are called multiplicative inverses, or reciprocals. $\frac{7}{4} \times \frac{4}{7} = 1$. When dividing by a mixed number, first rename it as an improper fraction, and then multiply by its multiplicative inverse. This process of multiplying by a number's reciprocal can also be used when dividing algebraic fractions.

## Adding Integers

To add integers with the same sign, add their absolute values. The sum takes the same sign as the addends. An addend is a number that is added to another number (the augend). The equation $-5 + (-2) = -7$ is an example of adding two integers with the same sign. To add integers with different signs, subtract their absolute values. The sum takes the same sign as the addend with the greater absolute value.

## Subtracting Integers

The rules for adding integers are extended to the subtraction of integers. To subtract an integer, add its additive inverse. For example, to find the difference $2 - 5$, add the additive inverse of 5 to 2: $2 + (-5) = -3$. The rule for subtracting integers can be used to solve real-world problems and to evaluate algebraic expressions.

## Additive Inverse Property

Two numbers with the same absolute value but different signs are called opposites. For example, $-4$ and $4$ are opposites. An integer and its opposite are also called additive inverses. The Additive Inverse Property says that the sum of any number and its additive inverse is zero. The Commutative, Associative, and Identity Properties also apply to integers. These properties help when adding more than two integers.

## Absolute Value

In mathematics, when two integers on a number line are on opposite sides of zero, and they are the same distance from zero, they have the same absolute value. The symbol for absolute value is two vertical bars on either side of the number. For example, $|-5| = 5$.

## Multiplying Integers

Since multiplication is repeated addition, $3(-7)$ means that $-7$ is used as an addend 3 times. By the Commutative Property of Multiplication, $3(-7) = -7(3)$. The product of two integers with different signs is always negative. The product of two integers with the same sign is always positive.

## Dividing Integers

The quotient of two integers can be found by dividing the numbers using their absolute values. The quotient of two integers with the same sign is positive, and the quotient of two integers with a different sign is negative. $-12 \div (-4) = 3$ and $12 \div (-4) = -3$. The division of integers is used in statistics to find the average, or mean, of a set of data. When finding the mean of a set of numbers, find the sum of the numbers, and then divide by the number in the set.

## Adding and Multiplying Vectors and Matrices

In order to add two matrices together, they must have the same number of rows and columns. In matrix addition, the corresponding elements are added to each other. In other words $(a + b)_{ij} = a_{ij} + b_{ij}$. For example,

$$\begin{pmatrix} 1 & 2 \\ 2 & 1 \end{pmatrix} + \begin{pmatrix} 3 & 6 \\ 0 & 1 \end{pmatrix} = \begin{pmatrix} 1+3 & 2+6 \\ 2+0 & 1+1 \end{pmatrix} = \begin{pmatrix} 4 & 8 \\ 2 & 2 \end{pmatrix}$$

Matrix multiplication requires that the number of elements in each row in the first matrix is equal to the number of elements in each column in the second. The elements of the first row of the first matrix are multiplied by the corresponding elements of the first column of the second matrix and then added together to get the first element of the product matrix. To get the second element, the elements in the first row of the first matrix are multiplied by the corresponding elements in the second column of the second matrix then added, and so on, until every row of the first matrix is multiplied by every column of the second. See the example below.

$$\begin{pmatrix} 1 & 2 \\ 3 & 4 \end{pmatrix} \times \begin{pmatrix} 3 & 6 \\ 0 & 1 \end{pmatrix} = \begin{pmatrix} (1\times3)+(2\times0) & (1\times6)+(2\times1) \\ (3\times3)+(4\times0) & (3\times6)+(4\times1) \end{pmatrix} = \begin{pmatrix} 3 & 8 \\ 9 & 22 \end{pmatrix}$$

Vector addition and multiplication are performed in the same way, but there is only one column and one row.

## Permutations and Combinations

Permutations and combinations are used to determine the number of possible outcomes in different situations. An arrangement, listing, or pattern in which order is important is called a permutation. The symbol P(6, 3) represents the number of permutations of 6 things taken 3 at a time. For P(6, 3), there are $6 \times 5 \times 4$ or 120 possible outcomes. An arrangement or listing where order is not important is called a combination. The symbol C(10, 5) represents the number of combinations of 10 things taken 5 at a time. For C(10, 5), there are $(10 \times 9 \times 8 \times 7 \times 6) \div (5 \times 4 \times 3 \times 2 \times 1)$ or 252 possible outcomes.

## Powers and Exponents

An expression such as $3 \times 3 \times 3 \times 3$ can be written as a power. A power has two parts, a base and an exponent. $3 \times 3 \times 3 \times 3 = 3^4$. The base is the number that is multiplied (3). The exponent tells how many times the base is used as a factor (4 times). Numbers and variables can be written using exponents. For example, $8 \times 8 \times 8 \times m \times m \times m \times m \times m$ can be expressed $8^3 m^5$. Exponents also can be used with place value to express numbers in expanded form. Using this method, 1,462 can be written as $(1 \times 10^3) + (4 \times 10^2) + (6 \times 10^1) + (2 \times 10^0)$.

## Squares and Square Roots

The square root of a number is one of two equal factors of a number. Every positive number has both a positive and a negative square root. For example, since $8 \times 8 = 64$, 8 is a square root of 64. Since $(-8) \times (-8) = 64$, $-8$ is also a square root of 64. The notation $\sqrt{\phantom{x}}$ indicates the positive square root, $-\sqrt{\phantom{x}}$ indicates the negative square root, and $\pm\sqrt{\phantom{x}}$ indicates both square roots. For example, $\sqrt{81} = 9$, $-\sqrt{49} = -7$, and $\pm\sqrt{4} = \pm2$. The square root of a negative number is an imaginary number because any two factors of a negative number must have different signs, and are therefore not equivalent.

## Logarithm

A logarithm is the inverse of exponentiation. The logarithm of a number $x$ in base $b$ is equal to the number $n$. Therefore, $b^n = x$ and $\log_b x = n$. For example, $\log_4(64) = 3$ because $4^3 = 64$. The most commonly used bases for logarithms are 10, the common logarithm; 2, the binary logarithm; and the constant $e$, the natural logarithm (also called $ln(x)$ instead of $\log_e(x)$). Below is a list of some of the rules of logarithms that are important to understand if you are going to use them.

$$\log_b(xy) = \log_b(x) + \log_b(y)$$
$$\log_b(x/y) = \log_b(x) - \log_b(y)$$
$$\log_b(1/x) = -\log_b(x)$$
$$\log_b(x)y = y\log_b(x)$$

## ▶ Compute fluently and make reasonable estimates

### Estimation by Rounding

When rounding numbers, look at the digit to the right of the place to which you are rounding. If the digit is 5 or greater, round up. If it is less than 5, round down. For example, to round 65,137 to the nearest hundred, look at the number in the tens place. Since 3 is less than 5, round down to 65,100. To round the same number to the nearest ten thousandth, look at the number in the thousandths place. Since it is 5, round up to 70,000.

### Finding Equivalent Ratios

Equivalent ratios have the same meaning. Just like finding equivalent fractions, to find an equivalent ratio, multiply or divide both sides by the same number. For example, you can multiply 7 by both sides of the ratio 6:8 to get 42:56. Instead, you can also divide both sides of the same ratio by 2 to get 3:4. Find the simplest form of a ratio by dividing to find equivalent ratios until you can't go any further without going into decimals. So, 160:240 in simplest form is 2:3. To write a ratio in the form *1:n*, divide both sides by the left-hand number. In other words, to change 8:20 to *1:n*, divide both sides by 8 to get 1:2.5.

### Front-End Estimation

Front-end estimation can be used to quickly estimate sums and differences before adding or subtracting. To use this technique, add or subtract just the digits of the two highest place values, and replace the other place values with zero. This will give you an estimation of the solution of a problem. For example, 93,471 − 22,825 can be changed to 93,000 − 22,000 or 71,000. This estimate can be compared to your final answer to judge its correctness.

### Judging Reasonableness

When solving an equation, it is important to check your work by considering how reasonable your answer is. For example, consider the equation $9\frac{3}{4} \times 4\frac{1}{3}$. Since $9\frac{3}{4}$ is between 9 and 10 and $4\frac{1}{3}$ is between 4 and 5, only values that are between $9 \times 4$ or 36 and $10 \times 5$ or 50 will be reasonable. You can also use front-end estimation, or you can round and estimate a reasonable answer. In the equation $73 \times 25$, you can round and solve to estimate a reasonable answer to be near $70 \times 30$ or 2,100.

# Algebra

## ▶ Understand patterns, relations, and functions

### Relation

A relation is a generalization comparing sets of ordered pairs for an equation or inequality such as $x = y + 1$ or $x > y$. The first element in each pair, the $x$ values, forms the domain. The second element in each pair, the $y$ values, forms the range.

### Function

A function is a special relation in which each member of the domain is paired with exactly one member in the range. Functions may be represented using ordered pairs, tables, or graphs. One way to determine whether a relation is a function is to use the vertical line test. Using an object to represent a vertical line, move the object from left to right across the graph. If, for each value of $x$ in the domain, the object passes through no more than one point on the graph, then the graph represents a function.

### Linear and Nonlinear Functions

Linear functions have graphs that are straight lines. These graphs represent constant rates of change. In other words, the slope between any two pairs of points on the graph is the same. Nonlinear functions do not have constant rates of change. The slope changes along these graphs. Therefore, the graphs of nonlinear functions are *not* straight lines. Graphs of curves represent nonlinear functions. The equation for a linear function can be written in the form $y = mx + b$, where $m$ represents the constant rate of change, or the slope. Therefore, you can determine whether a function is linear by looking at the equation. For example, the equation $y = \frac{3}{x}$ is nonlinear because $x$ is in the denominator and the equation cannot be written in the form $y = mx + b$. A nonlinear function does not increase or decrease at a constant rate. You can check this by using a table and finding the increase or decrease in $y$ for each regular increase in $x$. For example, if for each increase in $x$ by 2, $y$ does not increase or decrease the same amount each time, the function is nonlinear.

### Linear Equations in Two Variables

In a linear equation with two variables, such as $y = x - 3$, the variables appear in separate terms and neither variable contains an exponent other than 1. The graphs of all linear equations are straight lines. All points on a line are solutions of the equation that is graphed.

### Quadratic and Cubic Functions

A quadratic function is a polynomial equation of the second degree, generally expressed as $ax^2 + bx + c = 0$, where $a$, $b$, and $c$ are real numbers and $a$ is not equal to zero. Similarly, a cubic function is a polynomial equation of the third degree, usually expressed as $ax^3 + bx^2 + cx + d = 0$. Quadratic functions can be graphed using an equation or a table of values. For example, to graph $y = 3x^2 + 1$, substitute the values −1, −0.5, 0, 0.5, and 1 for $x$ to yield the point coordinates (−1, 4), (−0.5, 1.75), (0, 1), (0.5, 1.75), and (1, 4).

Plot these points on a coordinate grid and connect the points in the form of a parabola. Cubic functions also can be graphed by making a table of values. The points of a cubic function form a curve. There is one point at which the curve changes from opening upward to opening downward, or vice versa, called the point of inflection.

## Slope

Slope is the ratio of the rise, or vertical change, to the run, or horizontal change of a line: slope = rise/run. Slope ($m$) is the same for any two points on a straight line and can be found by using the coordinates of any two points on the line:

$$m = \frac{y_2 - y_1}{x_2 - x_1}, \text{ where } x_2 \neq x_1$$

## Asymptotes

An asymptote is a straight line that a curve approaches but never actually meets or crosses. Theoretically, the asymptote meets the curve at infinity. For example, in the function $f(x) = \frac{1}{x}$, two asymptotes are being approached: the line $y = 0$ and $x = 0$. See the graph of the function below.

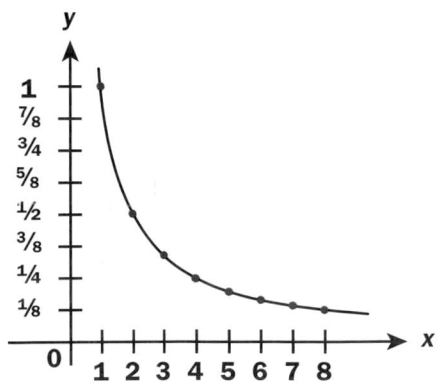

## Represent and analyze mathematical situations and structures using algebraic symbols

### Variables and Expressions

Algebra is a language of symbols. A variable is a placeholder for a changing value. Any letter, such as $x$, can be used as a variable. Expressions such as $x + 2$ and $4x$ are algebraic expressions because they represent sums and/or products of variables and numbers. Usually, mathematicians avoid the use of $i$ and $e$ for variables because they have other mathematical meanings ($i = \sqrt{-1}$ and $e$ is used with natural logarithms). To evaluate an algebraic expression, replace the variable or variables with known values, and then solve using order of operations. Translate verbal phrases into algebraic expressions by first defining a variable: Choose a variable and a quantity for the variable to represent. In this way, algebraic expressions can be used to represent real-world situations.

### Constant and Coefficient

A constant is a fixed value unlike a variable, which can change. Constants are usually represented by numbers, but they can also be represented by symbols. For example, $\pi$ is a symbolic representation of the value 3.1415.... A coefficient is a constant by which a variable or other object is multiplied. For example, in the expression $7x^2 + 5x + 9$, the coefficient of $x^2$ is 7 and the coefficient of $x$ is 5. The number 9 is a constant and not a coefficient.

### Monomial and Polynomial

A monomial is a number, a variable, or a product of numbers and/or variables such as $3 \times 4$. An algebraic expression that contains one or more monomials is called a polynomial. In a polynomial, there are no terms with variables in the denominator and no terms with variables under a radical sign. Polynomials can be classified by the number of terms contained in the expression. Therefore, a polynomial with two terms is called a binomial ($z^2 - 1$), and a polynomial with three terms is called a trinomial ($2y^3 + 4y^2 - y$). Polynomials also can be classified by their degrees. The degree of a monomial is the sum of the exponents of its variables. The degree of a nonzero constant such as 6 or 10 is 0. The constant 0 has no degree. For example, the monomial $4b^5c^2$ had a degree of 7. The degree of a polynomial is the same as that of the term with the greatest degree. For example, the polynomial $3x^4 - 2y^3 + 4y^2 - y$ has a degree of 4.

## Equation

An equation is a mathematical sentence that states that two expressions are equal. The two expressions in an equation are always separated by an equal sign. When solving for a variable in an equation, you must perform the same operations on both sides of the equation in order for the mathematical sentence to remain true.

## Solving Equations with Variables

To solve equations with variables on both sides, use the Addition or Subtraction Property of Equality to write an equivalent equation with the variables on the same side. For example, to solve $5x - 8 = 3x$, subtract $3x$ from each side to get $2x - 8 = 0$. Then add 8 to each side to get $2x = 8$. Finally, divide each side by 2 to find that $x = 4$.

## Solving Equations with Grouping Symbols

Equations often contain grouping symbols such as parentheses or brackets. The first step in solving these equations is to use the Distributive Property to remove the grouping symbols. For example $5(x + 2) = 25$ can be changed to $5x + 10 = 25$, and then solved to find that $x = 3$.

Some equations have no solution. That is, there is no value of the variable that results in a true sentence. For such an equation, the solution set is called the null or empty set, and is represented by the symbol $\varnothing$ or {}. Other equations may have every number as the solution. An equation that is true for every value of the variable is called the identity.

## Inequality

A mathematical sentence that contains the symbols < (less than), > (greater than), ≤ (less than or equal to), or ≥ (greater than or equal to) is called an inequality. For example, the statement that it is legal to drive 55 miles per hour or slower on a stretch of the highway can be shown by the sentence $s \leq 55$. Inequalities with variables are called open sentences. When a variable is replaced with a number, the inequality may be true or false.

## Solving Inequalities

Solving an inequality means finding values for the variable that make the inequality true. Just as with equations, when you add or subtract the same number from each side of an inequality, the inequality remains true. For example, if you add 5 to each side of the inequality $3x < 6$, the resulting inequality $3x + 5 < 11$ is also true. Adding or subtracting the same number from each side of an inequality does not affect the inequality sign. When multiplying or dividing each side of an inequality by the same positive number, the inequality remains true. In such cases, the inequality symbol does not change. When multiplying or dividing each side of an inequality by a negative number, the inequality symbol must be reversed. For example, when dividing each side of the inequality $-4x \geq -8$ by $-2$, the inequality sign must be changed to $\leq$ for the resulting inequality, $2x \leq 4$, to be true. Since the solutions to an inequality include all rational numbers satisfying it, inequalities have an infinite number of solutions.

### Representing Inequalities on a Number Line

The solutions of inequalities can be graphed on a number line. For example, if the solution of an inequality is $x < 5$, start an arrow at 5 on the number line, and continue the arrow to the left to show all values less than 5 as the solution. Put an open circle at 5 to show that the point 5 is *not* included in the graph. Use a closed circle when graphing solutions that are greater than or equal to, or less than or equal to, a number.

### Order of Operations

Solving a problem may involve using more than one operation. The answer can depend on the order in which you do the operations. To make sure that there is just one answer to a series of computations, mathematicians have agreed upon an order in which to do the operations. First simplify within the parentheses, often called grouping symbols, and then evaluate any exponents. Then multiply and divide from left to right, and finally add and subtract from left to right.

### Parametric Equations

Given an equation with more than one unknown, a statistician can draw conclusions about those unknown quantities through the use of parameters, independent variables that the statistician already knows something about. For example, you can find the velocity of an object if you make some assumptions about distance and time parameters.

### Recursive Equations

In recursive equations, every value is determined by the previous value. You must first plug an initial value into the equation to get the first value, and then you can use the first value to determine the next one, and so on. For example, in order to determine what the population of pigeons will be in New York City in three years, you can use an equation with the birth, death, immigration, and emigration rates of the birds. Input the current population size into the equation to determine next year's population size, then repeat until you have calculated the value for which you are looking.

▶ *Use mathematical models to represent and understand quantitative relationships*

### Solving Systems of Equations

Two or more equations together are called a system of equations. A system of equations can have one solution, no solution, or infinitely many solutions. One method for solving a system of equations is to graph the equations on the same coordinate plane. The coordinates of the point where the graphs intersect is the solution. In other words, the solution of a system is the ordered pair that is a solution of all equations. A more accurate way to solve a system of two equations is by using a method called substitution. Write both equations in terms of $y$. Replace $y$ in the first equation with the right side of the second equation. Check the solution by graphing. You can solve a system of three equations using matrix algebra.

## Graphing Inequalities

To graph an inequality, first graph the related equation, which is the boundary. All points in the shaded region are solutions of the inequality. If an inequality contains the symbol $\leq$ or $\geq$, then use a solid line to indicate that the boundary is included in the graph. If an inequality contains the symbol $<$ or $>$, then use a dashed line to indicate that the boundary is not included in the graph.

## ▶ Analyze change in various contexts

## Rate of Change

A change in one quantity with respect to another quantity is called the rate of change. Rates of change can be described using slope:

$$\text{slope} = \frac{\text{change in } y}{\text{change in } x}$$

You can find rates of change from an equation, a table, or a graph. A special type of linear equation that describes rate of change is called a direct variation. The graph of a direct variation always passes through the origin and represents a proportional situation. In the equation $y = kx$, $k$ is called the constant of variation. It is the slope, or rate of change. As $x$ increases in value, $y$ increases or decreases at a constant rate $k$, or $y$ varies directly with $x$. Another way to say this is that $y$ is directly proportional to $x$. The direct variation $y = kx$ also can be written as $k = \frac{y}{x}$. In this form, you can see that the ratio of $y$ to $x$ is the same for any corresponding values of $y$ and $x$.

## Slope-Intercept Form

Equations written as $y = mx + b$, where $m$ is the slope and $b$ is the $y$-intercept, are linear equations in slope-intercept form. For example, the graph of $y = 5x - 6$ is a line that has a slope of 5 and crosses the $y$-axis at $(0, -6)$. Sometimes you must first write an equation in slope-intercept form before finding the slope and $y$-intercept. For example, the equation $2x + 3y = 15$ can be expressed in slope-intercept form by subtracting $2x$ from each side and then dividing by 3: $y = -\frac{2}{3}x + 5$, revealing a slope of $-\frac{2}{3}$ and a $y$-intercept of 5. You can use the slope-intercept form of an equation to graph a line easily. Graph the $y$-intercept and use the slope to find another point on the line, then connect the two points with a line.

# Geometry

▶ *Analyze characteristics and properties of two- and three-dimensional geometric shapes and develop mathematical arguments about geometric relationships*

## Angles

Two rays that have the same endpoint form an angle. The common endpoint is called the vertex, and the two rays that make up the angle are called the sides of the angle. The most common unit of measure for angles is the degree. Protractors can be used to measure angles or to draw an angle of a given measure. Angles can be classified by their degree measure. Acute angles have measures less than 90° but greater than 0°. Obtuse angles have measures greater than 90° but less than 180°. Right angles have measures of 90°.

## Triangles

A triangle is a figure formed by three line segments that intersect only at their endpoints. The sum of the measures of the angles of a triangle is 180°. Triangles can be classified by their angles. An acute triangle contains all acute angles. An obtuse triangle has one obtuse angle. A right triangle has one right angle. Triangles can also be classified by their sides. A scalene triangle has no congruent sides. An isosceles triangle has at least two congruent sides. In an equilateral triangle all sides are congruent.

## Quadrilaterals

A quadrilateral is a closed figure with four sides and four vertices. The segments of a quadrilateral intersect only at their endpoints. Quadrilaterals can be separated into two triangles. Since the sum of the interior angles of all triangles totals 180°, the measures of the interior angles of a quadrilateral equal 360°. Quadrilaterals are classified according to their characteristics, and include trapezoids, parallelograms, rectangles, squares, and rhombuses.

## Two-Dimensional Figures

A two-dimensional figure exists within a plane and has only the dimensions of length and width. Examples of two-dimensional figures include circles and polygons. Polygons are figures that have three or more angles, including triangles, quadrilaterals, pentagons, hexagons, and many more. The sum of the angles of any polygon totals at least 180° (triangle), and each additional side adds 180° to the measure of the first three angles. The sum of the angles of a quadrilateral, for example, is 360°. The sum of the angles of a pentagon is 540°.

## Three-Dimensional Figures

A plane is a two-dimensional flat surface that extends in all directions. Intersecting planes can form the edges and vertices of three-dimensional figures or solids. A polyhedron is a solid with flat surfaces that are polygons. Polyhedrons are composed of faces, edges, and vertices and are differentiated by their shape and by their number of bases. Skew lines are lines that lie in different planes. They are neither intersecting nor parallel.

## Congruence
Figures that have the same size and shape are congruent. The parts of congruent triangles that match are called corresponding parts. Congruence statements are used to identify corresponding parts of congruent triangles. When writing a congruence statement, the letters must be written so that corresponding vertices appear in the same order. Corresponding parts can be used to find the measures of angles and sides in a figure that is congruent to a figure with known measures.

## Similarity
If two figures have the same shape but not the same size they are called similar figures. For example, the triangles below are similar, so angles $A$, $B$, and $C$ have the same measurements as angles $D$, $E$, and $F$, respectively. However, segments $AB$, $BC$, and $CA$ do not have the same measurements as segments $DE$, $EF$, and $FD$, but the measures of the sides are proportional.

For example, $\dfrac{\overline{AB}}{\overline{DE}} = \dfrac{\overline{BC}}{\overline{EF}} = \dfrac{\overline{CA}}{\overline{FD}}$.

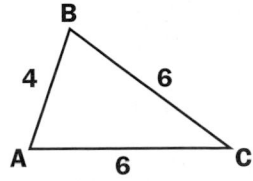
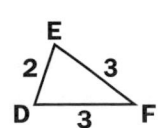

Solid figures are considered to be similar if they have the same shape and their corresponding linear measures are proportional. As with two-dimensional figures, they can be tested for similarity by comparing corresponding measures. If the compared ratios are proportional, then the figures are similar solids. Missing measures of similar solids can also be determined by using proportions.

## The Pythagorean Theorem
The sides that are adjacent to a right angle are called legs. The side opposite the right angle is the hypotenuse.

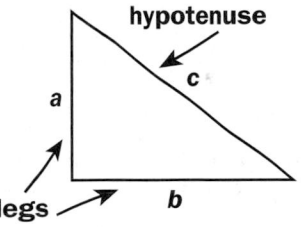

The Pythagorean Theorem describes the relationship between the lengths of the legs $a$ and $b$ and the hypotenuse $c$. It states that if a triangle is a right triangle, then the square of the length of the hypotenuse is equal to the sum of the squares of the lengths of the legs. In symbols, $c^2 = a^2 + b^2$.

## Sine, Cosine, and Tangent Ratios
Trigonometry is the study of the properties of triangles. A trigonometric ratio is a ratio of the lengths of two sides of a right triangle. The most common trigonometric ratios are the sine, cosine, and

tangent ratios. These ratios are abbreviated as *sin*, *cos*, and *tan*, respectively.

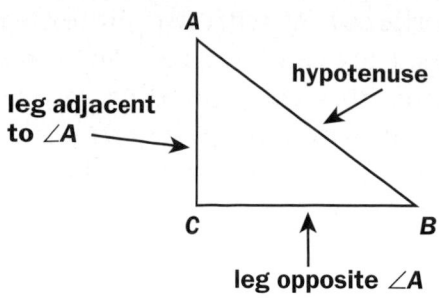

If ∠*A* is an acute angle of a right triangle, then

$$sin\ \angle A = \frac{\text{measure of leg opposite } \angle A}{\text{measure of hypotenuse}},$$

$$cos\ \angle A = \frac{\text{measure of leg adjacent to } \angle A}{\text{measure of hypotenuse}},\text{ and}$$

$$tan\ \angle A = \frac{\text{measure of leg opposite } \angle A}{\text{measure of leg adjacent to } \angle A}.$$

## ▶ Specify locations and describe spatial relationships using coordinate geometry and other representational systems

### Polygons
A polygon is a simple, closed figure formed by three or more line segments. The line segments meet only at their endpoints. The points of intersection are called vertices, and the line segments are called sides. Polygons are classified by the number of sides they have. The diagonals of a polygon divide the polygon into triangles. The number of triangles formed is two less than the number of sides. To find the sum of the measures of the interior angles of any polygon, multiply the number of triangles within the polygon by 180. That is, if *n* equals the number of sides, then (*n* − 2) 180 gives the sum of the measures of the polygon's interior angles.

### Cartesian Coordinates
In the Cartesian coordinate system, the *y*-axis extends above and below the origin and the *x*-axis extends to the right and left of the origin, which is the point at which the *x*- and *y*-axes intersect. Numbers below and to the left of the origin are negative. A point graphed on the coordinate grid is said to have an *x*-coordinate and a *y*-coordinate. For example, the point (1,−2) has as its *x*-coordinate the number 1, and has as its *y*-coordinate the number −2. This point is graphed by locating the position on the grid that is 1 unit to the right of the origin and 2 units below the origin.

The *x*-axis and the *y*-axis separate the coordinate plane into four regions, called quadrants. The axes and points located on the axes themselves are not located in any of the quadrants. The quadrants are labeled I to IV, starting in the upper right and proceeding counterclockwise. In quadrant I, both coordinates are positive. In quadrant II, the *x*-coordinate is negative and the *y*-coordinate is positive. In quadrant III, both coordinates are negative. In quadrant IV, the *x*-coordinate is positive and the *y*-coordinate is negative. A coordinate graph can be used to show algebraic relationships among numbers.

## ▶ Apply transformations and use symmetry to analyze mathematical situations

### Similar Triangles and Indirect Measurement
Triangles that have the same shape but not necessarily the same dimensions are called similar triangles. Similar

triangles have corresponding angles and corresponding sides. Arcs are used to show congruent angles. If two triangles are similar, then the corresponding angles have the same measure, and the corresponding sides are proportional. Therefore, to determine the measures of the sides of similar triangles when some measures are known, proportions can be used.

### Transformations

A transformation is a movement of a geometric figure. There are several types of transformations. In a translation, also called a slide, a figure is slid from one position to another without turning it. Every point of the original figure is moved the same distance and in the same direction. In a reflection, also called a flip, a figure is flipped over a line to form a mirror image. Every point of the original figure has a corresponding point on the other side of the line of symmetry. In a rotation, also called a turn, a figure is turned around a fixed point. A figure can be rotated 0°–360° clockwise or counterclockwise. A dilation transforms each line to a parallel line whose length is a fixed multiple of the length of the original line to create a similar figure that will be either larger or smaller.

### ▶ Use visualizations, spatial reasoning, and geometric modeling to solve problems

### Two-Dimensional Representations of Three-Dimensional Objects

Three-dimensional objects can be represented in a two-dimensional drawing in order to more easily determine properties such as surface area and volume. When you look at the triangular prism,

you can see the orientation of its three dimensions, length, width, and height. Using the drawing and the formulas for surface area and volume, you can easily calculate these properties.

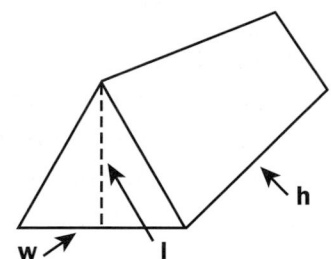

Another way to represent a three-dimensional object in a two-dimensional plane is by using a net, which is the unfolded representation. Imagine cutting the vertices of a box until it is flat then drawing an outline of it. That's a net. Most objects have more than one net, but any one can be measured to determine surface area. Below is a cube and one of its nets.

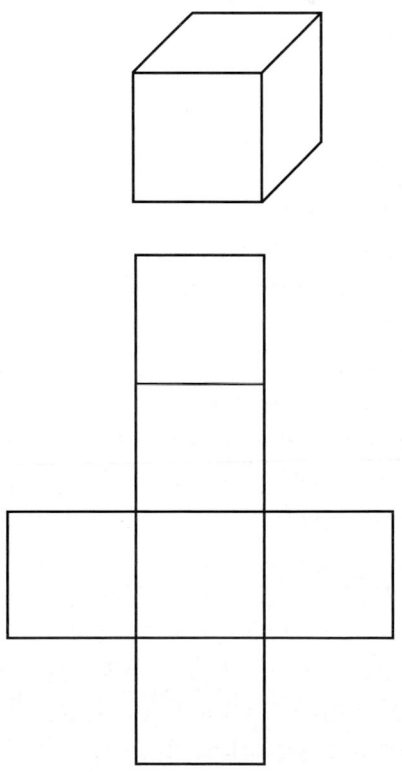

# Measurement

▶ *Understand measurable attributes of objects and the units, systems, and processes of measurement*

### Customary System
The customary system is the system of weights and measures used in the United States. The main units of weight are ounces, pounds (1 equal to 16 ounces), and tons (1 equal to 2,000 pounds). Length is typically measured in inches, feet (1 equal to 12 inches), yards (1 equal to 3 feet), and miles (1 equal to 5,280 feet), while area is measured in square feet and acres (1 equal to 43,560 square feet). Liquid is measured in cups, pints (1 equal to 2 cups), quarts (1 equal to 2 pints), and gallons (1 equal to 4 quarts). Finally, temperature is measured in degrees Fahrenheit.

### Metric System
The metric system is a decimal system of weights and measurements in which the prefixes of the words for the units of measure indicate the relationships between the different measurements. In this system, the main units of weight, or mass, are grams and kilograms. Length is measured in millimeters, centimeters, meters, and kilometers, and the units of area are square millimeters, centimeters, meters, and kilometers. Liquid is typically measured in milliliters and liters, while temperature is in degrees Celsius.

### Selecting Units of Measure
When measuring something, it is important to select the appropriate type and size of unit. For example, in the United States it would be appropriate when describing someone's height to use feet and inches. These units of height or length are good to use because they are in the customary system, and they are of appropriate size. In the customary system, use inches, feet, and miles for lengths and perimeters; square inches, feet, and miles for area and surface area; and cups, pints, quarts, gallons or cubic inches and feet (and less commonly miles) for volume. In the metric system use millimeters, centimeters, meters, and kilometers for lengths and perimeters; square units millimeters, centimeters, meters, and kilometers for area and surface area; and milliliters and liters for volume. Finally, always use degrees to measure angles.

▶ *Apply appropriate techniques, tools, and formulas to determine measurements*

### Precision and Significant Digits
The precision of measurement is the exactness to which a measurement is made. Precision depends on the smallest unit of measure being used, or the precision unit. One way to record a measure is to estimate to the nearest precision unit. A more precise method is to include all of the digits that are actually measured, plus one estimated digit. The digits recorded, called significant digits, indicate the precision of the measurement. There are special rules for determining significant digits. If a number contains a decimal point, the number of significant digits is found by counting from left to right, starting with the first nonzero digit. If the

number does not contain a decimal point, the number of significant digits is found by counting the digits from left to right, starting with the first digit and ending with the last nonzero digit.

### Surface Area

The amount of material needed to cover the surface of a figure is called the surface area. It can be calculated by finding the area of each face and adding them together. To find the surface area of a rectangular prism, for example, the formula $S = 2lw + 2lh + 2wh$ applies. A cylinder, on the other hand, may be unrolled to reveal two circles and a rectangle. Its surface area can be determined by finding the area of the two circles, $2\pi r^2$, and adding it to the area of the rectangle, $2\pi rh$ (the length of the rectangle is the circumference of one of the circles), or $S = 2\pi r^2 + 2\pi rh$. The surface area of a pyramid is measured in a slightly different way because the sides of a pyramid are triangles that intersect at the vertex. These sides are called lateral faces and the height of each is called the slant height. The sum of their areas is the lateral area of a pyramid. The surface area of a square pyramid is the lateral area $\frac{1}{2}bh$ (area of a lateral face) times 4 (number of lateral faces), plus the area of the base. The surface area of a cone is the area of its circular base ($\pi r^2$) plus its lateral area ($\pi rl$, where $l$ is the slant height).

### Volume

Volume is the measure of space occupied by a solid region. To find the volume of a prism, the area of the base is multiplied by the measure of the height, $V = Bh$. A solid containing several prisms can be broken down into its component prisms. Then the volume of each component can be found and the volumes added. The volume of a cylinder can be determined by finding the area of its circular base, $\pi r^2$, and then multiplying by the height of the cylinder. A pyramid has one-third the volume of a prism with the same base and height. To find the volume of a pyramid, multiply the area of the base by the pyramid's height, and then divide by 3. Simply stated, the formula for the volume of a pyramid is $V = \frac{1}{3}bh$. A cone is a three-dimensional figure with one circular base and a curved surface connecting the base and the vertex. The volume of a cone is one-third the volume of a cylinder with the same base area and height. Like a pyramid, the formula for the volume of a cone is $V = \frac{1}{3}bh$. More specifically, the formula is $V = \frac{1}{3}\pi r^2 h$.

### Upper and Lower Bounds

Upper and lower bounds have to do with the accuracy of a measurement. When a measurement is given, the degree of accuracy is also stated to tell you what the upper and lower bounds of the measurement are. The upper bound is the largest possible value that a measurement could have had before being rounded down, and the lower bound is the lowest possible value it could have had before being rounded up.

# Data Analysis and Probability

► *Formulate questions that can be addressed with data and collect, organize, and display relevant data to answer them*

## Histograms

A histogram displays numerical data that have been organized into equal intervals using bars that have the same width and no space between them. While a histogram does not give exact data points, its shape shows the distribution of the data. Histograms also can be used to compare data.

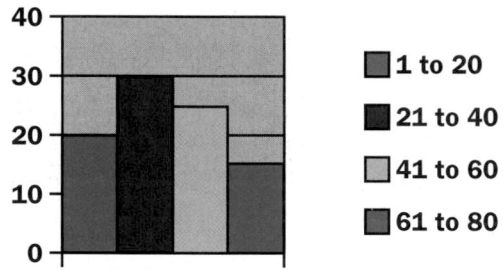

## Box-and-Whisker Plot

A box-and-whisker plot displays the measures of central tendency and variation. A box is drawn around the quartile values, and whiskers extend from each quartile to the extreme data points. To make a box plot for a set of data, draw a number line that covers the range of data. Find the median, the extremes, and the upper and lower quartiles. Mark these points on the number line with bullets, then draw a box and the whiskers. The length of a whisker or box shows whether the values of the data in that part are concentrated or spread out.

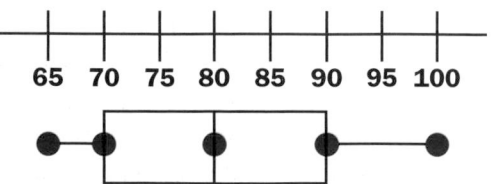

## Scatter Plots

A scatter plot is a graph that shows the relationship between two sets of data. In a scatter plot, two sets of data are graphed as ordered pairs on a coordinate system. Two sets of data can have a positive correlation (as *x* increases, *y* increases), a negative correlation (as *x* increases, *y* decreases), or no correlation (no obvious pattern is shown). Scatter plots can be used to spot trends, draw conclusions, and make predictions about data.

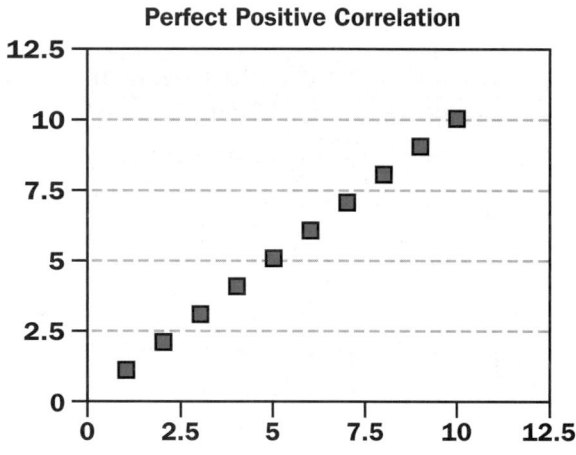

## Randomization

The idea of randomization is a very important principle of statistics and the design of experiments. Data must be selected randomly to prevent bias from influencing the results. For example, you want to know the average income of people in your town but you can only use a sample of 100 individuals to make determinations about everyone. If you select 100 individuals who are all doctors, you will have a biased sample. However, if you chose a random sample of 100 people out of the phone book, you are much more likely to accurately represent average income in the town.

## Statistics and Parameters

Statistics is a science that involves collecting, analyzing, and presenting data. The data can be collected in various ways—for example through a census or by making physical measurements. The data can then be analyzed by creating summary statistics, which have to do with the distribution of the data sample, including the mean, range, and standard error. They can also be illustrated in tables and graphs, like boxplots, scatter plots, and histograms. The presentation of the data typically involves describing the strength or validity of the data and what they show. For example, an analysis of ancestry of people in a city might tell you something about immigration patterns, unless the data set is very small or biased in some way, in which case it is not likely to be very accurate or useful.

## Categorical and Measurement Data

When analyzing data, it is important to understand if the data is qualitative or quantitative. Categorical data is qualitative and measurement, or numerical, data is quantitative. Categorical data describes a quality of something and can be placed into different categories. For example, if you are analyzing the number of students in different grades in a school, each grade is a category. On the other hand, measurement data is continuous, like height, weight, or any other measurable variable. Measurement data can be converted into categorical data if you decide to group the data. Using height as an example, you can group the continuous data set into categories like under 5 feet, 5 feet to 5 feet 5 inches, over 5 feet five inches to 6 feet, and so on.

## Univariate and Bivariate Data

In data analysis, a researcher can analyze one variable at a time or look at how multiple variables behave together. Univariate data involves only one variable, for example height in humans. You can measure the height in a population of people then plot the results in a histogram to look at how height is distributed in humans. To summarize univariate data, you can use statistics like the mean, mode, median, range, and standard deviation, which is a measure of variation. When looking at more than one variable at once, you use multivariate data. Bivariate data involves two variables. For example, you can look at height and age in humans together by gathering information on both variables from individuals in a population. You can then plot both variables in a scatter plot, look at how the variables behave in relation to each other, and create an equation that represents the relationship, also called a regression. These equations could help answer questions such as, for example, does height increase with age in humans?

## ▶ Select and use appropriate statistical methods to analyze data

### Measures of Central Tendency

When you have a list of numerical data, it is often helpful to use one or more numbers to represent the whole set. These numbers are called measures of central tendency. Three measures of central tendency are mean, median, and mode. The mean is the sum of the data divided by the number of items in the data set. The median is the middle number of the ordered data (or the mean of the two middle numbers). The mode is the number or numbers that occur most often. These measures of central tendency allow data to be analyzed and better understood.

## Measures of Spread

In statistics, measures of spread or variation are used to describe how data are distributed. The range of a set of data is the difference between the greatest and the least values of the data set. The quartiles are the values that divide the data into four equal parts. The median of data separates the set in half. Similarly, the median of the lower half of a set of data is the lower quartile. The median of the upper half of a set of data is the upper quartile. The interquartile range is the difference between the upper quartile and the lower quartile.

## Line of Best Fit

When real-life data are collected, the points graphed usually do not form a straight line, but they may approximate a linear relationship. A line of best fit is a line that lies very close to most of the data points. It can be used to predict data. You also can use the equation of the best-fit line to make predictions.

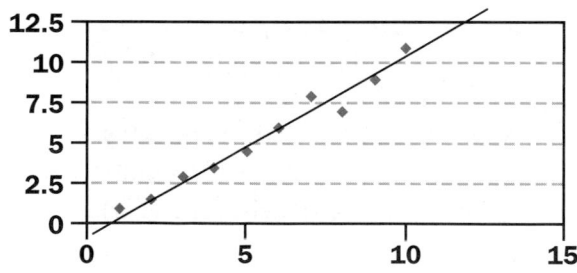

## Stem and Leaf Plots

In a stem and leaf plot, numerical data are listed in ascending or descending order. The greatest place value of the data is used for the stems. The next greatest place value forms the leaves. For example, if the least number in a set of data is 8 and the greatest number is 95, draw a vertical line and write the stems from 0 to 9 to the left of the line. Write the leaves to the right of the line, with the corresponding stem. Next, rearrange the leaves so they are ordered from least to greatest. Then include a key or explanation, such as 1|3 = 13. Notice that the stem-and-leaf plot below is like a histogram turned on its side.

```
0|8
1|3 6
2|5 6 9
3|0 2 7 8
4|0 1 4 7 9
5|1 4 5 8
6|1 3 7
7|5 8
8|2 6
9|5
```
Key: **1|3 = 13**

▶ *Develop and evaluate inferences and predictions that are based on data*

## Sampling Distribution

The sampling distribution of a population is the distribution that would result if you could take an infinite number of samples from the population, average each, and then average the averages. The more normal the distribution of the population, that is, how closely the distribution follows a bell curve, the more likely the sampling distribution will also follow a normal distribution. Furthermore, the larger the sample, the more likely it will accurately represent the entire population. For instance, you are more likely to gain more representative results from a population of 1,000 with a sample of 100 than with a sample of 2.

## Validity

In statistics, validity refers to acquiring results that accurately reflect that which is being measured. In other words, it is important when performing statistical analyses, to ensure that the data are valid in that the sample being analyzed represents the population to the best extent possible. Randomization of data and using appropriate sample sizes are two important aspects of making valid inferences about a population.

## ▶ Understand and apply basic concepts of probability

### Complementary, Mutually Exclusive Events

To understand probability theory, it is important to know if two events are mutually exclusive, or complementary: the occurrence of one event automatically implies the non-occurrence of the other. That is, two complementary events cannot both occur. If you roll a pair of dice, the event of rolling 6 and rolling doubles have an outcome in common (3, 3), so they are not mutually exclusive. If you roll (3, 3), you also roll doubles. However, the events of rolling a 9 and rolling doubles are mutually exclusive because they have no outcomes in common. If you roll a 9, you will not also roll doubles.

### Independent and Dependent Events

Determining the probability of a series of events requires that you know whether the events are independent or dependent. An independent event has no influence on the occurrence of subsequent events, whereas, a dependent event does influence subsequent events. The chances that a woman's first child will be a girl are $\frac{1}{2}$, and the chances that her second child will be a girl are also $\frac{1}{2}$ because the two events are independent of each other. However, if there are 7 red marbles in a bag of 15 marbles, the chances that the first marble you pick will be red are $\frac{7}{15}$ and if you indeed pick a red marble and remove it, you have reduced the chances of picking another red marble to $\frac{6}{14}$.

### Sample Space

The sample space is the group of all possible outcomes for an event. For example, if you are tossing a single six-sided die, the sample space is {1, 2, 3, 4, 5, 6}. Similarly, you can determine the sample space for the possible outcomes of two events. If you are going to toss a coin twice, the sample space is {(heads, heads), (heads, tails), (tails, heads), (tails, tails)}.

### Computing the Probability of a Compound Event

If two events are independent, the outcome of one event does not influence the outcome of the second. For example, if a bag contains 2 blue and 3 red marbles, then the probability of selecting a blue marble, replacing it, and then selecting a red marble is $P(A) \times P(B) = \frac{2}{5} \times \frac{3}{5}$ or $\frac{6}{25}$.

If two events are dependent, the outcome of one event affects the outcome of the second. For example, if a bag contains 2 blue and 3 red marbles, then the probability of selecting a blue and then a red marble without replacing the first marble is $P(A) \times P(B$ following $A) = \frac{2}{5} \times \frac{3}{4}$ or $\frac{3}{10}$. Two events that cannot happen at the same time are mutually exclusive. For example, when you roll two number cubes, you cannot roll a sum that is both 5 and even. So, $P(A$ or $B) = \frac{4}{36} + \frac{18}{36}$ or $\frac{11}{18}$.

##  MAKING CAREER CHOICES

A career differs from a job in that it is a series of progressively more responsible jobs in one field or a related field. You will need to learn some special skills to choose a career and to help you in your job search. Choosing a career and identifying career opportunities require careful thought and preparation. To aid you in making important career choices, follow these steps:

### STEPS TO MAKING A CAREER DECISION

1. Conduct a self-assessment to determine your:
   - values
   - lifestyle goals
   - interests
   - skills and aptitudes
   - personality
   - work environment preferences
   - relationship preferences

2. Identify possible career choices based on your self-assessment.

3. Gather information on each choice, including future trends.

4. Evaluate your choices based on your self-assessment.

5. Make your decision.

After you make your decision, plan how you will reach your goal. It is best to have short-term, medium-term, and long-term goals. In making your choices, explore the future opportunities in this field or fields over the next several years. What impact will new technology and automation have on job opportunities in the next few years? Remember, if you plan, you make your own career opportunities.

##  PERSONAL CAREER PORTFOLIO

You will want to create and maintain a personal career portfolio. In it you will keep all the documents you create and receive in your job search:

- Contact list
- Résumé
- Letters of recommendation
- Employer evaluations
- Awards
- Evidence of participation in school, community, and volunteer activities
- Notes about your job search
- Notes made after your interviews

##  CAREER RESEARCH RESOURCES

In order to gather information on various career opportunities, there are a variety of sources to research:

- **Libraries.** Your school or public library offers good career information resources. Here you will find books, magazines, pamphlets, films, videos, and special reference materials on careers. In particular, the U.S. Department of Labor publishes three reference books that are especially helpful: the *Dictionary of Occupational Titles (DOT)*, which describes about 20,000 jobs and their relationships with data, people, and things; the *Occupational Outlook Handbook (OOH)*, with information on more than 200 occupations; and the *Guide for Occupational Exploration (GOE)*, a reference that organizes the world of work into 12 interest areas that are subdivided into work groups and subgroups.

- **The Internet.** The Internet is becoming a primary source of research on any topic. It is especially helpful in researching careers.

- **Career Consultations.** Career consultation, an informational interview with a professional who works in a career that interests you, provides an opportunity to learn about the day-to-day realities of a career.

- **On-the-Job Experience.** On-the-job experience can be valuable in learning firsthand about a job or career. You can find out if your school has a work-experience program, or look into a company or organization's internship opportunities. Interning gives you direct work experience and often allows you to make valuable contacts for future full-time employment.

##  THE JOB SEARCH

To aid you in your actual job search, there are various sources to explore. You should contact and research all the sources that might produce a job lead, or information about a job. Keep a contact list as you proceed with your search. Some of these resources include:

- **Networking with family, friends, and acquaintances.** This means contacting people you know personally, including school counselors, former employers, and professional people.

- **Cooperative education and work-experience programs.** Many schools have such programs in which students work part-time on a job related to one of their classes. Many also offer work-experience programs that are not limited to just one career area, such as marketing.

- **Newspaper ads.** Reading the Help Wanted advertisements in your local papers will provide a source of job leads, as well as teach you about the local job market.

- **Employment agencies.** Most cities have two types of employment agencies, public and private. These employment agencies match workers with jobs. Some private agencies may charge a fee, so be sure to know who is expected to pay the fee and what the fee is.

- **Company personnel offices.** Large and medium-sized companies have personnel offices to handle employment matters, including the hiring of new workers. You can check on job openings by contacting the office by telephone or by scheduling a personal visit.

- **Searching the Internet.** Cyberspace offers multiple opportunities for your job search. Web sites, such as Hotjobs.com or Monster.com, provide lists of companies offering employment. There are tens of thousands of career-related Web sites, so the challenge is finding those that have jobs that interest you and that are up-to-date in their listings. Companies that interest you may have a Web site, which will provide valuable information on their benefits and opportunities for employment.

# APPLYING FOR A JOB

When you have contacted the sources of job leads and found some jobs that interest you, the next step is to apply for them. You will need to complete application forms, write letters of application, and prepare your own résumé. Before you apply for a job, you will need to have a work permit if you are under the age of 18 in most states. Some state and federal labor laws designate certain jobs as too dangerous for young workers. Laws also limit the number of hours of work allowed during a day, a week, or the school year. You will also need to have proper documentation, such as a green card if you are not a U.S. citizen.

## JOB APPLICATION

You can obtain the job application form directly at the place of business, by requesting it in writing, or over the Internet. It is best if you can fill the form out at home, but some businesses require that you fill it out at the place of work.

Fill out the job application forms neatly and accurately, using standard English, the formal style of speaking and writing you learned in school. You must be truthful and pay attention to detail in filling out the form.

## PERSONAL FACT SHEET

To be sure that the answers you write on a job application form are accurate, make a personal fact sheet before filling out the application:

- Your name, home address, and phone number
- Your Social Security number
- The job you are applying for
- The date you can begin work
- The days and hours you can work
- The pay you want
- Whether or not you have been convicted of a crime
- Your education
- Your previous work experience
- Your birth date
- Your driver's license number if you have one
- Your interests and hobbies, and awards you have won
- Your previous work experience, including dates
- Schools you have attended
- Places you have lived
- Accommodations you may need from the employer
- A list of references—people who will tell an employer that you will do a good job, such as relatives, students, former employers, and the like

## LETTERS OF RECOMMENDATION

Letters of recommendation are helpful. You can request teachers, counselors, relatives, and other acquaintances who know you well to write these letters. They should be short, to the point, and give a brief overview of your assets. A brief description of any of your important accomplishments or projects should follow. The letter should end with a brief description of your character and work ethic.

## LETTER OF APPLICATION

Some employees prefer a letter of application, rather than an application form. This letter is like writing a sales pitch about yourself. You need to tell why you are the best person for the job, what special qualifications you have, and include all the information usually found on an application form. Write the letter in standard English, making certain that it is neat, accurate, and correct.

## RÉSUMÉ

The purpose of a résumé is to make an employer want to interview you. A résumé tells prospective employers what you are like and what you can do for them. A good résumé summarizes you at your best in a one- or two-page outline. It should include the following information:

1. **Identification.** Include your name, address, telephone number, and e-mail address.

2. **Objective.** Indicate the type of job you are looking for.

3. **Experience.** List experience related to the specific job for which you are applying. List other work if you have not worked in a related field.

4. **Education.** Include schools attended from high school on, the dates of attendance, and diplomas or degrees earned. You may also include courses related to the job you are applying for.

5. **References.** Include up to three references or indicate that they are available. Always ask people ahead of time if they are willing to be listed as references for you.

A résumé that you put online or send by e-mail is called an *electronic résumé*. Some Web sites allow you to post them on their sites without charge. Employers access these sites to find new employees. Your electronic résumé should follow the guidelines for a regular one. It needs to be accurate. Stress your skills and sell yourself to prospective employers.

## COVER LETTER

If you are going to get the job you want, you need to write a great cover letter to accompany your résumé. Think of a cover letter as an introduction: a piece of paper that conveys a smile, a confident hello, and a nice, firm handshake. The cover letter is the first thing a potential employer sees, and it can make a powerful impression. The following are some tips for creating a cover letter that is professional and gets the attention you want:

- **Keep it short.** Your cover letter should be one page, no more.
- **Make it look professional.** These days, you need to type your letter on a computer and print it on a laser printer. Do not use an inkjet printer unless it produces extremely crisp type. Use white or buff-colored paper; anything else will draw the wrong kind of attention. Type your name, address, phone number, and e-mail address at the top of the page.
- **Explain why you are writing.** Start your letter with one sentence describing where you heard of the opening. "Joan Wright suggested I contact you regarding a position in your marketing department," or "I am writing to apply for the position you advertised in the Sun City Journal."
- **Introduce yourself.** Give a short description of your professional abilities and background. Refer to your attached résumé: "As you will see in the attached résumé, I am an experienced editor with a background in newspapers, magazines, and textbooks." Then highlight one or two specific accomplishments.

- **Sell yourself.** Your cover letter should leave the reader thinking, "This person is exactly what we are looking for." Focus on what you can do for the company. Relate your skills to the skills and responsibilities mentioned in the job listing. If the ad mentions solving problems, relate a problem you solved at school or work. If the ad mentions specific skills or knowledge required, mention your mastery of these in your letter. (Also be sure these skills are included on your résumé.)

- **Provide all requested information.** If the Help Wanted ad asked for "salary requirements" or "salary history," include this information in your cover letter. However, you do not have to give specific numbers. It is okay to say, "My wage is in the range of $10 to $15 per hour." If the employer does not ask for salary information, do not offer any.

- **Ask for an interview.** You have sold yourself, now wrap it up. Be confident, but not pushy. "If you agree that I would be an asset to your company, please call me at [insert your phone number]. I am available for an interview at your convenience." Finally, thank the person. "Thank you for your consideration. I look forward to hearing from you soon." Always close with a "Sincerely," followed by your full name and signature.

- **Check for errors.** Read and re-read your letter to make sure each sentence is correctly worded and there are no errors in spelling, punctuation, or grammar. Do not rely on your computer's spell checker or grammar checker. A spell check will not detect if you typed "tot he" instead of "to the." It is a good idea to have someone else read your letter, too. He or she might notice an error you overlooked.

## INTERVIEW

Understanding how to best prepare for and follow up on interviews is critical to your career success. At different times in your life, you may interview with a teacher or professor, a prospective employer, a supervisor, or a promotion or tenure committee. Just as having an excellent résumé is vital for opening the door, interview skills are critical for putting your best foot forward and seizing the opportunity to clearly articulate why you are the best person for the job.

### RESEARCH THE COMPANY

Your ability to convince an employer that you understand and are interested in the field you are interviewing to enter is important. Show that you have knowledge about the company and the industry. What products or services does the company offer? How is it doing? What is the competition? Use your research to demonstrate your understanding of the company.

### PREPARE QUESTIONS FOR THE INTERVIEWER

Prepare interview questions to ask the interviewer. Some examples include:

- "What would my responsibilities be?"
- "Could you describe my work environment?"
- "What are the chances to move up in the company?"
- "Do you offer training?"
- "What can you tell me about the people who work here?"

### DRESS APPROPRIATELY

You will never get a second chance to make a good first impression. Nonverbal communication is 90 percent of communication, so dressing appropriately is of the utmost importance. Every job is different, and you should wear clothing that is appropriate for the job for which you are applying. In most situations, you will be safe if you wear clean, pressed, conservative business clothes in neutral colors. Pay special attention to grooming. Keep makeup light and wear very little jewelry. Make certain your nails and hair are clean, trimmed, and neat. Do not carry a large purse, backpack, books, or coat. Simply carry a pad of paper, a pen, and extra copies of your résumé and letters of reference in a small folder.

## EXHIBIT GOOD BEHAVIOR

Conduct yourself properly during an interview. Go alone; be courteous and polite to everyone you meet. Relax and focus on your purpose: to make the best possible impression.

- Be on time.
- Be poised and relaxed.
- Avoid nervous habits.
- Avoid littering your speech with verbal clutter such as "you know," "um," and "like."
- Look your interviewer in the eye and speak with confidence.
- Use nonverbal techniques to reinforce your confidence, such as a firm handshake and poised demeanor.
- Convey maturity by exhibiting the ability to tolerate differences of opinion.
- Never call anyone by a first name unless you are asked to do so.
- Know the name, title, and the pronunciation of the interviewer's name.
- Do not sit down until the interviewer does.
- Do not talk too much about your personal life.
- Never bad-mouth your former employers.

## BE PREPARED FOR COMMON INTERVIEW QUESTIONS

You can never be sure exactly what will happen at an interview, but you can be prepared for common interview questions. There are some interview questions that are illegal. Interviewers should not ask you about your age, gender, color, race, or religion. Employers should not ask whether you are married or pregnant, or question your health or disabilities.

Take time to think about your answers now. You might even write them down to clarify your thinking. The key to all interview questions is to be honest, and to be positive. Focus your answers on skills and abilities that apply to the job you are seeking. Practice answering the following questions with a friend:

- "Tell me about yourself."
- "Why do you want to work at this company?"
- "What did you like/dislike about your last job?"
- "What is your biggest accomplishment?"
- "What is your greatest strength?"
- "What is your greatest weakness?"
- "Do you prefer to work with others or on your own?"
- "What are your career goals?" or "Where do you see yourself in five years?"
- "Tell me about a time that you had a lot of work to do in a short time. How did you manage the situation?"
- "Have you ever had to work closely with a person you didn't get along with? How did you handle the situation?"

## AFTER THE INTERVIEW

Be sure to thank the interviewer after the interview for his or her time and effort. Do not forget to follow up after the interview. Ask, "What is the next step?" If you are told to call in a few days, wait two or three days before calling back.

If the interview went well, the employer may call you to offer you the job. Find out the terms of the job offer, including job title and pay. Decide whether you want the job. If you decide not to accept the job, write a letter of rejection. Be courteous and thank the person for the opportunity and the offer. You may wish to give a brief general reason for not accepting the job. Leave the door open for possible employment in the future.

### FOLLOW UP WITH A LETTER

Write a thank-you letter as soon as the interview is over. This shows your good manners, interest, and enthusiasm for the job. It also shows that you are organized. Make the letter neat and courteous. Thank the interviewer. Sell yourself again.

### ACCEPTING A NEW JOB

If you decide to take the job, write a letter of acceptance. The letter should include some words of appreciation for the opportunity, written acceptance of the job offer, the terms of employment (salary, hours, benefits), and the starting date. Make sure the letter is neat and correct.

 ## STARTING A NEW JOB

Your first day of work will be busy. Determine what the dress code is and dress appropriately. Learn to do each task assigned properly. Ask for help when you need it. Learn the rules and regulations of the workplace.

You will do some paperwork on your first day. Bring your personal fact sheet with you. You will need to fill out some forms. Form W-4 tells your employer how much money to withhold for taxes. You may also need to fill out Form I-9. This shows that you are allowed to work in the United States. You will need your Social Security number and proof that you are allowed to work in the United States. You can bring your U.S. passport, your Certificate of Naturalization, or your Certificate of U.S. Citizenship. If you are not a permanent resident of the United States, bring your green card. If you are a resident of the United States, you will need to bring your work permit on your first day. If you are under the age of 16 in some states, you need a different kind of work permit.

You might be requested to take a drug test as a requirement for employment in some states. This could be for the safety of you and your coworkers, especially when working with machinery or other equipment.

### IMPORTANT SKILLS AND QUALITIES

You will not work alone on a job. You will need to learn skills for getting along and being a team player. There are many good qualities necessary to get along in the workplace. They include being positive, showing sympathy, taking an interest in others, tolerating differences, laughing a little, and showing respect. Your employer may promote you or give you a raise if you show good employability skills.

Career Skills

There are several qualities necessary to be a good employee and get ahead in your job:

- be cooperative
- possess good character
- be responsible
- finish what you start
- work fast but do a good job
- have a strong work ethic
- work well without supervision
- work well with others
- possess initiative
- show enthusiasm for what you do
- be on time
- make the best of your time
- obey company laws and rules
- be honest
- be loyal
- exhibit good health habits

### LEAVING A JOB

If you are considering leaving your job or are being laid off, you are facing one of the most difficult aspects in your career. The first step in resigning is to prepare a short resignation letter to offer your supervisor at the conclusion of the meeting you set up with him or her. Keep the letter short and to the point. Express your appreciation for the opportunity you had with the company. Do not try to list all that was wrong with the job.

You want to leave on good terms. Do not forget to ask for a reference. Do not talk about your employer or any of your coworkers. Do not talk negatively about your employer when you apply for a new job.

If you are being laid off or face downsizing, it can make you feel angry or depressed. Try to view it as a career-change opportunity. If possible, negotiate a good severance package. Find out about any benefits you may be entitled to. Perhaps the company will offer job-search services or consultation for finding new employment.

### ⬤ TAKE ACTION!

It is time for action. Remember the networking and contact lists you created when you searched for this job. Reach out for support from friends, family, and other acquaintances. Consider joining a job-search club. Assess your skills. Upgrade them if necessary. Examine your attitude and your vocational choices. Decide the direction you wish to take and move on!

# Glossary

## How to Use This Glossary

- Content vocabulary terms in this glossary are words that relate to this book's content. They are **highlighted yellow** in your text.

- Words in this glossary that have an asterisk (*) are academic vocabulary terms. They help you understand your school subjects and are used on tests. They are **boldfaced blue** in your text.

- Some of the vocabulary words in this book include pronunciation symbols to help you sound out the words. Use the pronunciation key to help you pronounce the words.

| Pronunciation Key | | |
|---|---|---|
| **a** . . . . **a**t | **ô** . . . . f**or**k, **a**ll | **th** . . . **th**in |
| **ā** . . . . **a**pe | **oo** . . . w**oo**d, p**u**t | **th** . . . **th**is |
| **ä** . . . . f**a**ther | **ōō** . . . f**oo**l | **zh** . . . trea**s**ure |
| **e** . . . . **e**nd | **oi** . . . **oi**l | **ə** . . . . **a**go, tak**e**n, penc**i**l, lem**o**n, circ**u**s |
| **ē** . . . . m**e** | **ou** . . . **ou**t | |
| **i** . . . . **i**t | **u** . . . . **u**p | **'** . . . . indicates primary stress (symbol in front of and *above* letter) |
| **ī** . . . . **i**ce | **ū** . . . . **u**se | |
| **o** . . . . h**o**t | **ü** . . . . r**u**le | **,** . . . . indicates secondary stress (symbol in front of and *below* letter) |
| **ō** . . . . h**o**pe | **u** . . . . p**u**ll | |
| **ȯ** . . . . s**a**w | **ŋ** . . . . si**ng** | |

**abdominal thrust • adequate**

**A**

**abdominal thrust** A quick upward thrust with the heel of the hand into the abdomen that forces the air in the lungs to force out an object caught in the throat. (p. 561)

* **ability** A skill you have already developed. (p. 633)

**abstinence** A deliberate decision to avoid high-risk behaviors, including sexual activity and the use of tobacco, alcohol, and other drugs. (p. 44)

**abstract thought** The capacity to consider "what if " situations, to create sophisticated arguments, and to reason from different points of view. (p. 542)

* **accommodate** To make room for. (p. 200)

**accreditation** Official recognition as having met a standard, such as child care provider for quality child care. (p. 604)

* **adaptation** Adjustment; the process of changing to fit new circumstances. (p. 586)

**ADD** Attention deficit disorder; similar to ADHD, but does not involve hyperactivity. (p. 583)

**addiction** A dependence on a substance, such as alcohol or drugs. (p. 576)

**addiction counselor** A therapist trained to help substance abusers. (p. 593)

* **adequate** Sufficient in quantity or quality to meet a need. (p. 332)

**ADHD** Attention deficit hyperactive disorder; a behavioral disorder in which children often fail to finish what they start, do not seem to listen, and are easily distracted. (p. 583)

\* **adolescent** Teen; someone who has reached puberty but is not yet an adult. (p. 521)

**age appropriate** Something is suitable for the age and individual needs of a child. (p. 274)

\* **aggravate** To anger or irritate. (p. 212)

**aggressive behavior** Hostile, and at times destructive, behavior that people display when faced with conflict. (p. 419)

\* **alleviate** Ease, make less severe. (p. 133)

**alliteration** The repetition of beginning sounds. (p. 435)

**alternative birth center** A facility that provides a more homelike environment for labor and delivery. (p. 157)

**ambidextrous** The ability to use both hands with equal skill. (p. 387)

**amniocentesis** (ˌam-nē-ō-(ˌ)sen-ˈtē-səs) The process of withdrawing a sample of the amniotic fluid surrounding the unborn baby. (p. 113)

**amniotic fluid** (ˌam-nē-ˈä-tik) The liquid that surrounds and protects the developing baby in the uterus. (p. 100)

**amygdala** (ə-ˈmig-də-lə) The part of the brain that controls fear, joy, and other emotional reactions. (p. 540)

**anecdotal record** A report of a child's actions that concentrates on a specific behavior or area of development. (p. 22)

**anemia** A condition that results from not having enough red blood cells. (p. 130)

\* **anesthesia** Drugs that cause a loss of feeling, used for pain relief. (p. 171)

**antibody** A substance produced by the body to fight off germs. (p. 213)

**antiseptic** A substance that prevents or stops the growth of germs. (p. 559)

**anxiety** A state of uncertainty and fear, often about an unspecified but seemingly immediate threat. (p. 476)

**Apgar scale** A system of rating the physical condition of a newborn baby. (p. 177)

**aptitude** A natural talent or potential for learning a skill. (p. 633)

**articulation** The ability to use clear, distinct speech. (pp. 369, 437)

\* **assumption** A fact that is taken for granted. (p. 21)

**asthma** A condition that causes the lungs to contract more than they should, narrowing the air passages and making it difficult to breathe. (p. 553)

**attachment** A baby's bond to his or her main caregiver. (p. 239)

**attention span** The length of time a person can concentrate on a task without getting bored. (p. 268)

**autism** A disorder that affects a child's ability to communicate and interact with others. (p. 585)

**autism spectrum disorders (ASD)** A group of disorders that includes autism. (p. 585)

**autonomy** Personal independence and the capacity to make decisions and act on them. (p. 342)

**axon** The connection between neurons that transmits instructions from the cell body to another neuron. (p. 259)

---

**B**

**baseline** A count made before any steps are taken to try to change a behavior. (p. 22)

**bilingual** Able to speak two languages. (p. 436)

**bilirubin** A substance produced by the breakdown of red blood cells. (p. 180)

**bipolar disorder** A psychiatric disorder characterized by extreme changes in mood, from highly energetic to depressed and withdrawn, sometimes fluctuating rapidly. (p. 532)

**blended family** A family that is formed when a single parent marries another person, who may or may not have children. (p. 63)

**body image** How a person thinks his or her body looks. (p. 454)

**bonding** The act of forming emotional ties between parents and child. (p. 180)

**bullying** Directing aggression or abuse toward another person, usually someone weaker. (p. 485)

**C**

* **capacity** The ability to do or experience something. (p. 461)

**cardiopulmonary resuscitation (CPR)** A technique that combines rescue breathing with chest compressions to restore breathing and circulation. (p. 566)

**career ladder** A visualization of your chosen career path. (p. 637)

**career path** All of the career moves and job experience that a person gains as he or she works toward a career goal. (p. 637)

**caregiver** A person who takes care of a child. (p. 8)

**cause and effect** A relationship between events in which one event, the effect, is caused by another event. (p. 245)

**cervix** The lower part of the uterus. (p. 165)

**cesarean birth** (si-ˈzer-ē-ən) Also known as a cesarean section or c-section, it is the delivery of a baby through a surgical incision in the mother's abdomen. (p. 172)

**child care center** A facility in which a staff of adults provides care for children. (p. 603)

**childproof** To take steps to protect the child from possible dangers. (p. 275)

**chromosome** A tiny threadlike structure in the nucleus of every cell. (p. 95)

**circle time** When the children share their experiences in show-and-tell or listen to a story together. (p. 619)

**COBRA** (Consolidated Omnibus Budget Reconciliation Act) A law ensuring that former employees can keep the health insurance plan they received through their former employer for up to 18 months. (p. 649)

**colic** Uncontrollable crying by an otherwise healthy baby. (p. 238)

**colostrum** (kə-ˈläs-trəm) A high-calorie, high-protein early breast milk. (p. 181)

**communicable disease** A disease that is passed from one person to another. (p. 551)

**competition** Rivalry with the goal of winning or outperforming others. (p. 420)

* **complication** A problem; something that makes something else more difficult. (p. 155)

* **compressed** Flattened; pressed together. (p. 156)

**concept** A general category of objects and information that can also include abstract ideas. (p. 269)

**conception** The process of the sperm fertilizing the ovum. (p. 95)

* **concrete** Actual; certain; specific. (p. 499)

**confidential adoption** An adoption in which the birth parents do not know the names of the adoptive parents. (p. 49)

**confidentiality** (ˌkän-fə-ˌden(t)shē-ˈa-lə-tē) The protection of another person's privacy by limiting access to personal information. (p. 25)

**conformity** Choosing to be like one another. (p. 488)

* **congenital** Present at birth. (p. 120)

**conscience** An inner sense of what is right. (p. 74)

**conservation** When an object has the same characteristics even if there is a change in the way it looks. (p. 500)

**consistent** Continually the same. (p. 81)

* **constructive** Positive; carefully considered and meant to be helpful. (p. 593)

**contagious** Transmitted from one person to another, such as touching an infected person. (p. 554)

**contraction** The tightening and releasing of the muscles of the uterus. This is also a sign of labor. (p. 166)

* **controversial** Causing extremely opposing views. (p. 99)

* **convey** To express or communicate something and make it known. (p. 640)

* **convictions** Firmly held beliefs or opinions. (p. 536)

**convulsion** A seizure; a brief period during which muscles suddenly contract, causing the person to fall and twitch or jerk. (p. 562)

**cooperative play** A type of play in which children play and interact with one another. (p. 336)

**cord blood** The blood left behind in the umbilical cord and placenta following birth. (p. 171)

**cortex** Part of the brain's cerebrum; its growth permits more complex learning. (p. 259)

* **counterproductive** Producing difficulties or problems instead of helping achieve a goal. (p. 489)

**cover letter** An introductory letter sent with a résumé. (p. 643)

**cradle cap** A skin condition known for yellowish, crusty patches on the scalp. (p. 223)

**creativity** A mental ability that involves using the imagination to produce original ideas. (p. 361)

**crisis nursery** A child care facility where troubled parents can go to receive short-term, free child care. (p. 594)

* **criteria** Accepted standards. (p. 605)

* **crucial** Essential; very important. (p. 239)

**cultural bias** An advantage to people from one culture over other cultures. (p. 428)

* **curb** To limit or control something. (p. 213)

**custodial parent** The parent with whom the child resides. (p. 62)

---

**D**

* **decipher** To interpret; to study something until it can be understood. (p. 368)

* **deformity** A defect in normal body structure. (p. 116)

**delivery** The birth of the baby. (p. 154)

**dendrite** A branchlike feature at the end of each axon that receives the messages from other neurons. (p. 259)

**depression** Feelings of intense sadness that last for long periods of time and prevent a person from leading a normal life. (p. 531)

**deprivation** A lack of the critical needs and encouraging environment that are essential for physical, emotional, and intellectual well-being. (p. 70)

**depth perception** The ability to perceive objects that are three-dimensional. (p. 201)

* **designate** To specify or choose. (p. 224)

* **detection** Discovery; the act of noticing the existence of something. (p. 551)

* **determined** Reasoned; to bring to light or disclose. (p. 270)

**developmental checklist** A list of skills children should master, or behaviors they should exhibit at a certain age. (p. 23)

**developmental milestone** A key skill used to check a child's progress. (p. 195)

**developmental task** The challenge to be met or skill to be acquired in each stage of the human life cycle. (p. 18)

**developmentally appropriate** Toys, activities, and tasks that are suitable for a child at a specific age. (p. 297)

**dexterity** The skillful use of the hands and fingers. (p. 299)

\* **dexterity** Ease and skill in physical activity. (p. 386)

**diaper rash** A condition that includes patches of rough, red, irritated skin in the diaper area. (p. 223)

**dilate** To widen or open. (p. 170)

**directed learning** Learning that results from being taught, often by parents, other caregivers, teachers, or older siblings. (p. 356)

**dispute** Quarrel. (p. 73)

\* **distinguish** See or perceive a difference in. (p. 582)

\* **distraction** A diversion; something that interferes with concentration. (p. 341)

**DNA** (deoxyribonucleic acid) The complex molecules that make up genes. (p. 95)

**dyslexia** A learning disorder that prevents a child from understanding printed symbols in a normal way. (p. 582)

— E —

**eating disorder** A serious pattern of overeating or restrictive eating. (p. 454)

\* **elevate** To raise up. (p. 559)

\* **elicit** To bring forth; to produce some sort of reaction or response. (pp. 269, 360)

**embryo** The developing baby from about the third week of pregnancy through the eighth week. (p. 100)

\* **emerge** To appear out of or from behind something. (p. 225)

**emotion** A feeling response to the world around us. (p. 235)

**emotional development** The process of learning to recognize and express feelings and to establish a personal identity. (p. 235)

**emotional maturity** Being responsible enough to consistently put someone else's needs before your own needs. (p. 35)

**empathy** The ability to understand how another person feels. (p. 330)

**enamel** The hard, outer coating of teeth. (p. 394)

**entrepreneur** (ˌäⁿn-trə-p(r)ə-ˈnər) Someone who chooses to be self-employed or to own his or her own business. (p. 632)

**entry-level job** The kind of job many people take when they first enter a career area. (p. 631)

**environment** The people, places, and things that surround and influence a person, including family, home, school, and community. (p. 14)

\* **erect** Straight; in an upright position. (p. 384)

\* **essential** Necessary; of the highest importance. (p. 48)

**estrogen** A hormone produced by the ovaries. (p. 522)

**ethical** Doing the right thing. (p. 648)

\* **expectations** Expected behaviors; a standard expected by or of someone. (p. 622)

\* **expel** To force out. (p. 561)

**extended family** A family that includes a parent or parents, at least one child, and other relatives who live with them. (p. 63)

\* **extracurricular** Optional; not part of the normal courses of a school or college. (p. 525)

Glossary

**failure to thrive** A condition in which babies do not grow and develop properly. (p. 240)

**fallopian tube** A tube that connects the ovary to the uterus. (p. 93)

**family child care** Care that takes place in the caregiver's home. (p. 603)

**fetal alcohol effects** Abnormalities caused by the mother consuming alcohol during pregnancy. (p. 116)

**fetal alcohol syndrome (FAS)** An incurable condition found in some children of mothers who consumed alcohol during pregnancy. (p. 116)

**fetal monitoring** The watching of an unborn baby's heart rate for indications of stress. (p. 166)

**fetus** (ˈfē-təs) The developing baby from around the eighth or ninth week of pregnancy until birth. (p. 101)

**fiber** An indigestible plant material that helps the digestive system work properly. (p. 459)

**fidelity** Faithfulness to an obligation, duty, or trust. (p. 50)

**fine motor skill** A skill that involves the smaller muscles of the body such as those in the fingers. (p. 206)

**finger play** A song or chant with accompanying hand motions. (p. 437)

**fixed expense** A payment that generally cannot be changed, such as bills, housing payment, and taxes. (p. 150)

**flame-resistant** Something that is treated to not burn as quickly as other materials. (p. 314)

**flexible expense** An expense that can be changed, such as food costs, household items, clothes, and entertainment. (p. 150)

**fluoride** A substance that strengthens the enamel of teeth to help prevent decay. (p. 394)

**fontanel** An open space found on the baby's head where the bones are not yet joined. (p. 176)

**formula** A mixture of milk or milk substitutes, water, and essential nutrients fed to babies. (p. 149)

* **foster** To encourage the development of something. (p. 437)

**foster child** A child that comes from a troubled family or difficult circumstances and is placed in the temporary care of another person or family. (p. 64)

**fracture** A break or crack in a bone. (p. 560)

**free play** A time when children can choose any activity they want. (p. 620)

**frequency count** A tally of how often a certain behavior occurs. (p. 22)

* **function** A job or action for which something is suited or designed. (p. 259)

* **fuse** To combine; to unite or blend. (p. 176)

* **gauge** To form a judgment of something uncertain or variable. (p. 336)

**gender identity** The awareness of being male or female. (p. 480)

**gene** A unit that determines a human's inherited characteristics. (p. 95)

**genome** The complete blueprint for the creation of a person. (p. 95)

**gestational diabetes** A form of diabetes that occurs only during pregnancy. If left untreated, gestational diabetes can cause the baby to be heavier than is normal or healthy. (p. 131)

**Glossary**

**gifted** Showing, or having the potential to show, special abilities in one or more areas. (p. 588)

**gross motor skill** A skill that involves the large muscles of the body such as those of the legs and shoulders. (p. 206)

**group identification** A feeling of belonging with others. (p. 394)

**growth chart** A chart that shows the average weight and height of girls and boys at various ages. (p. 198)

**growth spurt** When a child grows very rapidly in a short period of time. (p. 453)

**guidance** Using firmness and understanding to help children learn how to behave. (p. 73)

**hand-eye coordination** The ability to move the hands and fingers precisely in relation to what is seen. (p. 207)

* **hazard** Something that is potentially dangerous. (p. 281)

**Head Start** A program that provides locally run child care facilities designed to help lower-income and disadvantaged children from birth to five years of age become ready for school. (p. 606)

**heredity** The biological transfer of certain characteristics from earlier generations. (p. 14)

* **hinder** To delay or obstruct the development of someone or something. (p. 243)

**hives** Blisterlike sores caused by an allergic reaction. (p. 564)

**hormone** A chemical in the body that controls the changes that occur as teens become sexually mature. (p. 43)

**human life cycle** A set of stages of human development that each present different challenges to be met or skills to be acquired. (p. 18)

**hygiene** Personal care and cleanliness. (p. 310)

**hypothetical** Involving something that could possibly happen. (p. 500)

**identity crisis** A confusion about one's personal identity that results from failing to find a strong identity, or sense of self, through personal exploration. (p. 529)

**imaginative play** Pretending; seeing or hearing things that might happen but have not happened yet. (p. 272)

**imitation** Learning by watching and copying others. (p. 356)

**immunization** A shot of a small amount of a dead or weak disease-carrying germ given so that the body can build up resistance to the disease. (p. 227)

* **impact** A significant effect. (p. 7)

* **impulsive** Having a tendency to act spontaneously without considering the consequences. (p. 406)

* **incident** An action, occurrence, or event. (p. 303)

**incidental learning** Unplanned learning. (p. 355)

**inclusion** Placing children with disabilities in regular classrooms while they also receive special education services. (p. 587)

**incubator** A special enclosed crib where the oxygen supply, temperature, and humidity can be closely controlled. (p. 173)

* **induce** To start; to make the process of labor or a birth begin by a medical intervention. (p. 166)

**infertility** The inability of a man or woman to contribute to conception. (p. 97)

**in-home care** Care that is provided to many young children from a caregiver who comes to their home. (p. 603)

**initiative** The motivation to accomplish more. (p. 411)

* **integrate** To combine; to join together to make something part of a larger whole. (p. 506)

**intelligence** The ability to interpret and understand everyday situations and to use prior experiences when faced with new situations or problems. (p. 354)

**intelligence quotient (IQ)** A number obtained by comparing a child's test results to those of other children the same age. (p. 427)

**intergenerational** Occurring between older and younger age groups. (p. 65)

**internship** A job in which a person works for little or no pay while gaining experience and receiving supervision. (p. 634)

**interpretation** The analysis an observer forms and expresses about what was observed. (p. 25)

* **intimacy** A closeness between two people. (p. 43)

* **irrational** Lacking reason. (p. 578)

---

**jaundice** (ˈjȯn-dəs) A condition that causes the baby's skin and eyes to look slightly yellow. (p. 180)

**job fair** An event where employers with current or future job openings meet with potential employees. (p. 639)

**job shadowing** To observe someone performing his or her job. (p. 634)

**job-specific skills** The skills or abilities needed to do a specific job. (p. 647)

* **judgment** An opinion. (p. 22)

---

**labor** The process in which the baby gradually moves out of the uterus and into the vagina to be born. (p. 154)

**lactase** An enzyme that helps digest lactose. (p. 142)

**lactation consultant** A professional breast-feeding specialist who shows mothers how to encourage adequate milk production and how to position babies properly so that they can nurse. (p. 181)

**lactose intolerant** Having a condition in which milk products cause symptoms such as abdominal pain and gas. (p. 142)

**lanugo** Fine, downy hair growing on newborns' foreheads, backs, and shoulders. (p. 177)

* **lead** An example or precedent. (p. 248)

**learning center** An area designed for certain types of play and learning. (p. 614)

**learning disability** A condition that interferes with a child's ability to learn, listen, think, speak, read, write, spell, or do math. (p. 582)

**learning method** A way to learn. (p. 505)

**legal guardian** A person who is designated by a legal process to assume responsibility for raising a child. (p. 64)

* **legible** Clear enough to be read. (p. 643)

**license** An official printed document that gives permission, such as one from the state that indicates child care providers meet health and safety standards. (p. 604)

**lifelong learner** Someone who is willing to learn new information and acquire skills throughout his or her working life. (p. 648)

---

* **major** Significant; of considerable importance. (p. 180)

* **makeup** Structure or arrangement. (p. 195)

**malnutrition** Inadequate nutrition. (p. 218)

* **mandate** To require or order. (p. 508)

**Glossary**

**mandated reporter** A person who is required by law to report maltreatment. (p. 594)

**manipulate** To work with the hands. (p. 280)

**maternity leave** Time taken off work by a mother after the birth of a baby. (p. 151)

**math readiness** The level of knowledge of basic math concepts, such as number recognition, needed for learning math. (p. 366)

**menstruation** The monthly cycle in which an egg is released and the uterus prepares for a possible pregnancy. (p. 456)

**mental retardation** Having below-average intelligence and skills. This condition is also known as cognitive impairment or developmental disability. (p. 583)

**midwife** A professional trained to assist women in childbirth. (p. 155)

**miscarriage** When the developing baby dies prior to the twentieth week of pregnancy. (p. 106)

**model** To base a behavior on somebody else; to teach it through example. (p. 245)

\* **moral** Ethical; relating to issues of right and wrong. (p. 10)

**moral development** The process of learning to base one's behavior on beliefs about what is right and wrong. (p. 416)

**moral maturity** When people are able to recognize and respect other people's points of view. (p. 536)

**morality** A sense of right and wrong that guides decisions and actions. (p. 535)

\* **motivate** To provide a reason to do something. (p. 250)

\* **multifaceted** Many-sided; with many qualities or features. (p. 501)

**multiple intelligences** Abilities in problem solving or creating materials that have value. (p. 428)

**myelin** (ˈmī-ə-lən) A waxy, protein-based substance that coats axons and helps transmit information from one nerve cell to another. (p. 259)

**MyPyramid** A guide for healthful eating and active living that was developed by the U.S. Department of Agriculture (USDA). (p. 460)

**nanny** A person trained to provide child care. (p. 604)

**negative reinforcement** A response aimed at strengthening desired behavior by removing an unpleasant trigger. (p. 79)

**negativism** Doing the opposite of what others want. (p. 323)

**neonatal period** The first month after the baby is born. (p. 180)

**networking** The practice of using personal and professional contacts to further your career goals. (p. 640)

**neural pathway** The link between neurons. (p. 257)

**neuron** A nerve cell. (p. 257)

**neuroscience** The modern study of the brain. (p. 353)

**neurotransmitter** (ˌnu̇r-ō-tran(t)s-ˈmi-tər) is a chemical released by the axon. The neurotransmitter acts as a messenger between the neurons. (p. 260)

**night terrors** A type of sleep disturbance that occurs during the first few hours of sleep, when children are sleeping deeply. (p. 303)

**NREM sleep** A cycle of sleep in which rapid eye movement does not occur. (p. 333)

**nuclear family** A family that includes a mother and father and at least one child. (p. 62)

**O**

**object permanence** The concept that objects will continue to exist, even when they are out of sight. (p. 271)

**objective** Something is factual, and leaves aside personal feelings and prejudices. (p. 21)

**obstetrician** (ˌäb-stə-ˈtri-shən) A doctor who specializes in pregnancy and childbirth. (p. 129)

**open adoption** An adoption in which the birth parents and adoptive parents know something about each other. (p. 50)

* **oriented** Directed or positioned in a particular way. (p. 430)

**orthodontist** A dental specialist who concentrates on fixing irregularities of the teeth. (p. 465)

**osteoporosis** A condition in which bones become fragile and break easily. (p. 139)

**ovum** An egg cell. (p. 93)

**P**

**parallel play** When children play near, but not actually with, other children. (p. 335)

* **paramount** Of extreme importance or significance. (p. 488)

**paraprofessional** Someone with some education beyond high school that trains him or her for a certain field. (p. 631)

**parent cooperative** Also called co-op, it is child care that is provided by the parents of the children in the co-op. (p. 605)

**parenting** The process of caring for children and helping them grow and develop. (p. 33)

**parenting style** The way parents and other caregivers care for and discipline children. (p. 72)

**paternity** The legal identification of a man as the biological father of a child. (p. 48)

**paternity leave** Time taken off work by the father after a baby's birth. (p. 151)

**pediatrician** A doctor who specializes in treating children. (p. 149)

**peer** Someone close to one's own age. (p. 414)

**peer learning** A learning method in which students observe and interact with one another by working together in pairs, small groups, or as a class on a project or task. (p. 505)

**peer pressure** A social group's influence on the way individuals behave. (p. 488)

**perception** The ability to learn from sensory information. (p. 266)

* **perceptive** Observant; quick to understand things. (p. 321)

**permanent teeth** Teeth that will not be naturally replaced by another set. (p. 384)

* **persevere** To persist steadily in an action or belief. (p. 479)

**personal identity** A sense of oneself as a unique individual. (p. 528)

* **persuade** To convince; to make somebody believe something. (p. 390)

**phobia** An unexplainable and illogical fear. (p. 327)

**phoneme** (ˈfō-ˌnēm) The smallest individual sound in a word, such as the *ou* in house. (p. 435)

**placenta** (plə-ˈsen-tə) A tissue that connects the developing baby to the uterus. (p. 100)

**play environment** A comfortable space free of dangers and with toys that are safe and interesting. (p. 249)

**play group** An arrangement in which parents take turns caring for one another's children in their own homes. (p. 604)

**pollen** Powder-like grains that come from seed plants. (p. 553)

* **pollutant** Something that makes the environment dirty. (p. 308)

Glossary

**popular culture** The culture that prevails in modern society. (p. 537)

**positive reinforcement** A response that encourages a particular behavior. (p. 76)

**postnatal period** The time following the baby's birth. (p. 183)

**postpartum depression** A condition in which new mothers may feel very sad, cry a lot, have little energy, feel overly anxious about the baby or have little interest in the baby, and, in extreme cases, think of harming the baby. (p. 184)

**preeclampsia** (ˌprē-i-ˈklam(p)-sē-ə) A condition characterized by high blood pressure and the presence of protein in the mother's urine. (p. 132)

\* **predisposition** A tendency to do something or behave in a certain way. (p. 111)

**prefrontal cortex** The part of the brain that sits just behind the forehead and controls planning, organization, prioritizing, and other complex thought processes. (p. 540)

**prenatal development** The baby's development during a pregnancy (p. 99)

**prepared childbirth** A plan for reducing pain and fear during the birth process through education, and the use of breathing and conditioning exercises. (p. 154)

**preschooler** A child from age three to about age five. (p. 293)

\* **pride** Pleasure; a happy satisfied feeling with oneself. (p. 33)

**professional** Someone with a position that requires at least a degree from a four-year college or technical school in a specific area of study. (p. 632)

\* **profound** Overwhelming, very strong, intense; extreme. (pp. 453, 541)

**proportion** The size relationship between different parts of the body. (p. 200)

\* **proportion** Size. (p. 294)

\* **prospective** Likely, or expected to happen. (p. 35)

**puberty** The set of changes that result in a physically mature body that is able to reproduce. (p. 453)

**reading readiness** Learning the skills necessary for reading, including letter recognition and the understanding that letters of the alphabet combine to form words on a page. (p. 365)

\* **receptor** A receiver; a nerve ending that is sensitive to stimuli. (p. 260)

\* **refine** To improve something through small changes. (p. 414)

**reflex** An instinctive, automatic response, such as grasping or sucking. (p. 206)

**reflux** A condition in which partially digested food rises in the throat. (p. 238)

**regression** The temporary backward movement to an earlier stage of development. (p. 573)

\* **regulate** To control and bring to a desired level. (p. 429)

\* **reimbursement** Repayment. (p. 151)

**REM sleep** A sleep cycle characterized by rapid eye movement. (p. 333)

**rescue breathing** A procedure for forcing air into the lungs of a person who is not breathing. (p. 566)

\* **responsiveness** Reactions, usually strong or favorable, to something. (p. 274)

**Rh factor** A protein present in most people's red blood cells. A mother's blood is tested for this protein to determine if it is positive or negative in order to protect the fetus. (p. 131)

\* **resort** To choose; to turn to something for help, often extreme, in dealing with a problem. (p. 419)

**résumé** A concise document that summarizes your career objectives, education, work experience, and accomplishments. (p. 640)

* **robust** Thriving, strong, healthy. (p. 132)

**rooming-in** When the baby remains with the mother in her room during the hospital stay; it can be a full-time or part-time arrangement. (p. 181)

**running record** A record of everything observed for a set period, such as 15 minutes. (p. 22)

── **S** ──

**scoliosis** A sideways curvature of the spine affecting posture. (p. 454)

**sealant** A thick plastic coating, often used by dentists on teeth. (p. 465)

* **secure** Safe; untroubled by feelings of fear. (p. 177)

**sedentary activity** An activity that involves little exercise, such as watching television. (p. 463)

**self-centered** Thinking about one's own needs and wants and not those of others. (p. 322)

**self-concept** How people see themselves. (p. 331)

**self-confidence** Belief in one's own abilities. (p. 411)

**self-discipline** The ability of children to control their own behavior. (pp. 73, 340)

**self-esteem** Self-worth; the value people place on themselves. (p. 17)

* **self-sufficiency** The ability to take care of oneself. (p. 614)

**sense of competence** The feeling that one can be successful and meet most challenges. (p. 478)

**sense of self** Your idea of who you are, based on your emotions, personality, and the ways you perceive the world. (p. 477)

* **sensitivity** A reaction; ability to be easily damaged or physically irritated. (p. 553)

**sensorimotor period** Piaget's first stage of learning that lasts from birth to about age two. (p. 270)

**sensory integration** The process by which the brain combines information taken in through the senses to make a whole. (p. 296)

**separation anxiety** The fear of being away from parents, familiar caregivers, or the normal environment. (p. 327)

* **sequence** An order of steps. (p. 14)

* **serious** Severe; important enough to require attention. (p. 111)

**service learning** A school program in which students volunteer in their community as a graduation requirement. (p. 634)

**sexuality** Your beliefs and values about sexual behavior. (p. 43)

**sexually transmitted infection (STI)** A disease that is spread from one person to another by sexual contact. (p. 45)

**shaken baby syndrome** A condition that occurs when someone severely shakes a baby, usually in an effort to make him or her stop crying. (p. 211)

* **shift** To change; to move to a different position. (p. 473)

**shock** A serious medical condition in which important body functions, including breathing and heartbeat, are impaired. (p. 565)

**sibling rivalry** The competition between brothers or sisters for parents' affection and attention. (p. 328)

**SIDS** Sudden infant death syndrome; the sudden, unexpected death of a baby under one year of age with no clear cause. (p. 118)

**single-parent family** A family that includes either a mother or a father and at least one child. (p. 62)

**Glossary**

**Glossary**

**situational stress** Stress that comes from the environment a child lives in or from certain circumstances and changes. (p. 573)

*** slat** A flat, narrow strip of wood, such as on the sides of a crib. (p. 147)

**sleep-deprived** Lacking adequate sleep. (p. 332)

**social development** The process of learning how to interact and express oneself with others. (p. 245)

**socialization** The process of learning to get along with others. (p. 335)

*** socialize** To participate; to behave in a friendly way to others. (p. 604)

*** sophisticated** Refined; self-confident; complex; advanced. (p. 540)

**sperm** The male reproductive cell. (p. 93)

**sphincter** (ˈsfiŋ(k)-tər) **muscles** The muscles that help regulate elimination from the bowels. (p. 311)

*** spontaneous** Unplanned, without external influence. (p. 101)

**sprain** An injury caused by sudden, violent stretching of a joint or muscle. (p. 560)

*** stable** Unchanging; steady and firm. (p. 183)

**standardized test** A test that lets educators see how students are performing intellectually when compared to the thousands of other students who have taken the same test. (p. 508)

**stem cells** Cells capable of producing all types of blood cells. (p. 171)

*** stifle** To suppress, or prevent the development of something. (pp. 362, 533)

**stillbirth** When the fetus dies after the twentieth week of pregnancy. (p. 106)

**stimulating environment** An environment in which one has a wide variety of things to see, taste, smell, hear, and touch. (p. 197)

**stimulation** Any activity that arouses a baby's sense of sight, sound, touch, taste, and smell. (p. 13)

**stranger anxiety** A fear of unfamiliar people, usually expressed by crying. (p. 247)

**stuttering** When a person speaks with sporadic repetition or prolonged sounds. (p. 370)

**subjective** To rely on personal opinions and feelings, rather than facts, to judge an event. (p. 21)

**support group** A collection of individuals who work together to explore and accept their feelings. (p. 577)

*** suppress** To control; to prevent from happening. (p. 466)

**surrogate** (ˈsər-ə-ˌgāt) A substitute. A surrogate mother is a woman who becomes pregnant to have a baby for another woman. (p. 98)

**symbolic thinking** The use of words and numbers to stand for ideas. (p. 272)

**synapse** (ˈsi-ˌnaps) The tiny gap between the dendrites where messages are transmitted from one neuron to another. (p. 260)

**synthetic fibers** Fabrics made from chemicals, rather than natural sources. (p. 314)

---

**teething** The process of the teeth pushing their way through the gums. (p. 225)

**temper tantrum** When children release anger or frustration by screaming, crying, kicking, pounding, and sometimes holding their breath. (p. 324)

**temperament** A person's unique emotional makeup. (p. 240)

*** terminate** To end. (p. 594)

**tension** Emotional stress. (p. 409)

**testosterone** (tes-ˈtäs-tə-ˌrōn) A hormone produced by the testicles. (p. 522)

**time-out** When a child is removed from the group, perhaps by being required to sit in a special chair for a short period of time. (pp. 79, 345)

**toddler** A term that refers to one- and two-year-olds. (p. 293)

**toxoplasmosis** (ˌtäk-sə-ˌplaz-ˈmō-səs) An infection caused by a parasite. (p. 120)

**transferable skills** General skills used in school and in various types of jobs. (p. 647)

**transition** A period during which children move from one activity to the next. (p. 620)

**transitivity** The concept that a relative relationship between two objects can extend to a third object. (p. 500)

**trial-and-error learning** Learning that takes place when a child tries several solutions to find one that works. (p. 355)

* **turmoil** A state of extreme confusion or agitation. (p. 406)

**type 1 diabetes** A lifelong condition caused by the body's inability to produce enough insulin. (p. 584)

**typical behavior** A way of acting or responding that is common at each stage of childhood. (p. 7)

* **ultimate** Final; coming at the very last. (p. 454)

**ultrasound** A test that uses sound waves to make a video image of an unborn baby. (p. 112)

**umbilical cord** A long tube that connects the baby to the placenta. (p. 100)

* **undermine** To weaken or diminish. (p. 392)

**unemployment benefits** Funds paid by individual states to unemployed people who are actively seeking employment. (p. 649)

* **unstructured** Lacking formal organization. (p. 367)

**uterus** The organ in a woman's body in which a baby develops during pregnancy. (p. 93)

**vaccine** A disease-carrying germ that usually is injected in the body to build resistance to a disease. (p. 227)

* **variation** The state of differing from a former state or value. (p. 294)

* **venture** To proceed; to presume or dare to do something. (p. 61)

**vernix** A thick, white, pasty substance made up of the fetus's old skin cells and the secretions of skin glands. (p. 177)

* **visualization** A mental image; a clear picture of something in the mind. (p. 637)

* **vital** Necessary; extremely important and necessary. (p. 57)

* **vulnerable** Helpless, exposed to harm or damage. (p. 573)

**weaning** Changing from drinking from the bottle or breast to a cup. (p. 217)

**work-based learning** A school program that offers students the opportunity to combine in-school and on-the-job learning. (p. 634)

**Z**

**zygote** (ˈzī-ˌgōt) The fertilized egg. (p. 99)

*Glossary*

# Index

Index

Index

Index

Index

*Family, Career and Community Leaders of America (FCCLA) is a dynamic and effective national student organization that helps young men and women become leaders and address important personal, family, work, and societal issues through Family and Consumer Sciences education.*

FCCLA has more than 220,000 members and nearly 7,000 chapters from 50 state associations and the District of Columbia, Puerto Rico, and the Virgin Islands. The organization has involved more than ten million youth since its founding in 1945. *FCCLA: The Ultimate Leadership Experience* is unique among youth organizations because its programs are planned and run by members. It is the only career and technical in-school student organization with the family as its central focus. Participation in national programs and chapter activities helps members become strong leaders in their families, careers, and communities.

## Who Is Eligible to Be Part of It?

Any student who has taken a course in Family and Consumer Sciences as determined by the state department of education through grade 12 is eligible for active membership in an organized chapter within their school. Once the state and national dues are paid, the student will be an official affiliated member. Affiliated members are eligible to hold office, make motions, and vote. Affiliated members can expect to receive *Teen Times* magazine, a membership card, and all the privileges that come with being a member of the only Career and Technical Student Organization with family as its central focus. Teachers can be a part of it, too! Teachers certified to teach Family and Consumer Sciences education or courses as determined by the state department of education can serve as the FCCLA chapter adviser. Once the chapter is affiliated with its respective state as well as the national organization, teachers/advisers will reap the rewards of integrating FCCLA into their course curriculum. FCCLA offers co-curricular programs that address a variety of learning styles from individual projects that introduce and strengthen critical thinking and decision making skills, to team projects and cooperative learning activities. The national Family and Consumer Sciences standards are incorporated into all FCCLA programs.

> **"What is the common bond in our society? Family! Through the ultimate leadership experience of Family, Career and Community Leaders of America, members learn to better every aspect of their lives. By participating in thrilling meetings, national programs and opportunities in leadership training, members are becoming leaders today for a better world tomorrow. Since 1945, FCCLA has impacted over 10 million youth. Members become leaders inside and outside their families. We have something for everybody!"**
>
> **—The FCCLA National Executive Council**

# FCCLA Creed

We are the Family, Career and Community Leaders of America.

We face the future with warm courage and high hope.

For we have the clear consciousness of seeking old and precious values.

For we are the builders of homes, Homes for America's future,

Homes where living will be the expression of everything that is good and fair,

Homes where truth and love and security and faith will be realities, not dreams.

We are the Family, Career and Community Leaders of America.

We face the future with warm courage and high hope.

# FCCLA Mission Statement

To promote personal growth and leadership development through Family and Consumer Sciences education. Focusing on the multiple roles of family member, wage earner, and community leader, members develop skills for life through character development, creative and critical thinking, interpersonal communications, practical knowledge, and career preparation.

# Purposes

1. To provide opportunities for personal development and preparation for adult life.
2. To strengthen the function of the family as a basic unit of society.
3. To encourage democracy through cooperative action in the home and community.
4. To encourage individual and group involvement in helping achieve global cooperation and harmony.
5. To promote greater understanding between youth and adults.
6. To provide opportunities for making decisions and for assuming responsibilities.
7. To prepare for the multiple roles of men and women in today's society.
8. To promote Family and Consumer Sciences education and related occupations.

# Tagline

The Ultimate Leadership Experience

# Motto

Toward New Horizons

# FCCLA National Programs

FCCLA provides a menu of programs with ready-to-use materials to guide students through creating and carrying out projects. National programs encourage members to enhance their personal growth and build leadership skills. As students plan projects and execute their ideas, they experience the satisfaction of making a difference in their own lives, their families, their schools, and their communities.

**Dynamic Leadership**—Dynamic Leadership helps young people learn about leadership; recognize the lifelong benefits of leadership skills; practice leadership skills through FCCLA involvement; and become strong leaders for families, careers, and communities. Dynamic Leadership interacts with other national programs.

**Career Connection**—A national program that guides young people to link their options and skills for success in careers, families, and communities.

**Leaders at Work**—A unit of Career Connection that motivates students to prepare for career success and recognizes FCCLA members who create projects to strengthen leadership skills on the job.

**Community Service**—A national program that guides students to develop, plan, carry out, and evaluate projects that improve the quality of life in their communities.

**Families Acting for Community Traffic Safety**—A national peer education program through which young people strive to save lives through sober driving, seat belt use, and safe driving habits.

**Families First**—A national peer education program through which young people gain a better understanding of how families work and learn skills to become strong family members.

**Japanese Exchange**—FCCLA members are selected for scholarship opportunities to travel to Japan for four to six weeks and live with a Japanese host family. The opportunity to experience the day-to-day life of another country and its people enhances students' awareness of cultural issues.

**Financial Fitness**—A national peer education program that involves youth teaching other young people how to make, save, and spend money wisely.

**Power of One**—A national program that helps students find and use their personal power. Members set their own goals, work to achieve them, and enjoy the results.

**STOP the Violence**—Students Taking On Prevention—A national peer education program that empowers youth with attitudes, skills, and resources to recognize, report, and reduce youth violence.

**Student Body**—A national peer education program that helps young people learn to eat right, be fit, and make healthy choices.

# STAR Events

**STAR Events**—Students Taking Action With Recognition

National competitive events in which members are recognized for proficiency and achievement in chapter and individual projects, leadership skills, and career preparation.

| | | |
|---|---|---|
| **Applied Technology** | **Life Event Planning** | **National Programs in Action** |
| **Career Investigations** | **Focus on Children** | **Parliamentary Procedure** |
| **Chapter Service Project** | **Hospitality** | **Promote and Publicize FCCLA** |
| **Chapter Showcase** | **Illustrated Talk** | |
| **Culinary Arts** | **Interior Design** | **Recycle and Redesign** |
| **Early Childhood** | **Interpersonal Communications** | **Teach and Train** |
| **Entrepreneurship** | | |
| **Fashion Construction** | **Job Interview** | |

# FCCLA STAR Events

STAR Events offer individual skill development and application of learning through the following activities:

- cooperative—teams work to accomplish specific goals
- individualized—an individual member works alone to accomplish specific goals
- competitive—individual or team performance measured by an established set of criteria.

 **STAR Events include:**

**Applied Technology**   An individual or team event—recognizes participants who develop a project using technology that addresses a concern related to Family and Consumer Sciences and/or related occupations. The project integrates and applies content from academic subjects.

**Career Investigation**   An individual event—recognizes participants for their ability to perform self-assessments, research and explore a career, set career goals, create a plan for achieving goals, and describe the relationship of Family and Consumer Sciences coursework to the selected career.

**Chapter Service Project (Display and Manual)**   A team event—recognizes chapters that develop and implement an in-depth service project that makes a worthwhile contribution to families, schools, and communities. Students must use Family and Consumer Sciences content and skills to address and take action on a community need.

**Chapter Showcase (Display and Manual)**   A team event—recognizes chapters that develop and implement a well-balanced program of work and promote FCCLA and Family and Consumer Sciences and/or related occupations and skills to the community.

**Culinary Arts**   A team event—recognizes participants enrolled in occupational culinary arts/food service training programs for their ability to work as members of a team to produce a quality meal using industrial culinary arts/food service techniques and equipment.

**Early Childhood**   An individual event—recognizes participants who demonstrate their ability to use knowledge and skills gained from their enrollment in an occupational early childhood program.

**Entrepreneurship**   An individual or team event—recognizes participants who develop a plan for a small business using Family and Consumer Sciences skills and sound business practices. The business must relate to an area of Family and Consumer Sciences education or related occupations.

**Fashion Construction**   An individual event—recognizes participants who apply fashion construction skills learned in Family and Consumer Sciences courses to create a display using samples of their skills.

**Focus on Children**   An individual or team event—recognizes participants who use Family and Consumer Sciences skills to plan and conduct a child development project that has a positive impact on children and the community.

**Hospitality**   An individual or team event—recognizes participants who demonstrate their ability to use knowledge and skills gained from their enrollment in a hospitality program.

**Illustrated Talk**   An individual or team event—recognizes participants who make an oral presentation about issues concerning Family and Consumer Sciences and/or related occupations. Participants use visuals to illustrate content of the presentation.

**Interior Design**   An individual or team event—recognizes participants who apply interior design skills learned in Family and Consumer Sciences courses to design interiors that meet the living space needs of clients.

**Interpersonal Communications**   An individual event—recognizes participants who use Family and Consumer Sciences and/or related occupations skills and apply communication techniques to develop a project designed to strengthen communication.

**Job Interview**   An individual event—recognizes participants who use Family and Consumer Sciences and/or related occupations skills to develop a portfolio, participate in an interview, and communicate a personal understanding of job requirements.

**Life Event Planning**   An individual or team event—recognizes participants who apply skills learned in Family and Consumer Sciences courses to manage the costs of an event.

**National Programs in Action**   An individual or team event—recognizes participants who explain how the FCCLA planning process was used to implement a national program project.

**Parliamentary Procedure**   A team event—recognizes chapters that develop a working knowledge of parliamentary law and the ability to conduct an FCCLA business meeting.

**Promote and Publicize FCCLA!**   An individual or team event—recognizes participants who use communications skills and techniques to educate their schools and communities about FCCLA with the intention of growing chapters and strengthening Family and Consumer Sciences education and FCCLA programs.

**Recycle and Redesign**   An individual event—recognizes participants who select a used fashion or home apparel item to recycle into a new product.

**Teach and Train**   An individual event—recognizes participants for their exploration of the education and training fields through research and hands-on experience.

# How To Integrate FCCLA in the Classroom

Integrated FCCLA activities are initiated during class time and complement classroom learning. They use FCCLA resources but are initiated, developed, and evaluated by students. Projects can be planned and completed by individuals, small groups, or as a class or chapter. These activities relate to the FCCLA Purposes and therefore provide incentives and recognition that are not part of class requirements. Because the projects are related to the FACS course of study, they enhance Family and Consumer Sciences education.

Most of the work occurs in class. As needed, outside resources are brought into the classroom setting, or the class may visit other settings. Although much of the work is done in class, many activities involve out-of-class assignments. They often involve school and community action on weekends, before or after school, or during activity periods.

## Examples of FCCLA in the Classroom

The following are sample projects. For more information or project ideas, please visit the FCCLA website at fcclainc.org.

---

### Family Challenges Resource Directory

**High School**

**FACS topics:** family challenges; community resources and systems of support for families

**FCCLA National Program:** Families First ("Meet the Challenge" unit)

♦ While studying the challenges faced by families, the in-class chapter decides to launch a project to provide information to help families cope with challenges.

♦ By organizing themselves in committees, students collect information on local agencies and organizations that help families deal with challenges and crises.

♦ They invite representatives of selected agencies to speak in class.

♦ They compile a list of local agencies, their services, and contact information. Members post the list on the school Web site and also publish it in a flyer that they distribute to local schools, libraries, grocery stores, and places of worship.

♦ The chapter applies for Families First recognition, and a three-student team prepares a related Chapter Service Project STAR Events entry.

# Conflict Management for Kids

Middle Level or High School

**FACS topic:** impact of environment on human growth and development

**FCCLA National Program:** STOP the Violence—Students Taking on Prevention

♦ Students decide to teach elementary students ways to settle conflicts without violence.

♦ Working in teams, students develop age-appropriate learning activities in conflict management.

♦ They arrange to present related lessons in an elementary classroom and summarize the information in a flyer for children to take home to their families.

♦ To share the project with peers, students display anti-violence posters created by the elementary class.

♦ They also report the project on the STOP the Violence home page and apply for the National FCCLA STOP the Violence Awards

# Focus on Children

High School

**FACS topic:** Analyze factors that impact child growth and development.

**FCCLA National Program:** Focus on Children STAR Event

Note: Excellent mid-term, final, culminating, or graduation project.

♦ Students in child development classes plan and conduct a child development project that has a positive impact on children and the community (individual or group projects created by one to three students).

♦ Students follow guidelines from the STAR Events Manual to create a display board and presentation.

♦ Teacher, students, parents, and/or advisory committee members evaluate projects, using rating sheet for Focus on Children STAR Event.

♦ Well-rated students who are interested continue to develop and practice their presentations, then participate in district-region or state STAR Events.